PRESCHOOL PERIOD
(3 to 6 years)

MIDDLE CHILDHOOD
(6 to 12 years)

- Height and weight continue to increase rapidly.
- The body becomes less rounded, more muscular.
- The brain grows larger, neural interconnections continue to develop, and lateralization emerges.
- Gross and fine motor skills advance quickly. Children can throw and catch balls, run, use forks and spoons, and tie shoelaces.
- Children begin to develop handedness.

- Growth becomes slow and steady. Muscles develop, and "baby fat" is lost.
- Gross motor skills (biking, swimming, skating, ball handling) and fine motor skills (writing, typing, fastening buttons) continue to improve.

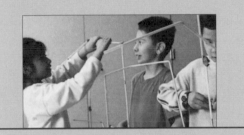

- Children show egocentric thinking (viewing world from their own perspective) and "centration," a focus on only one aspect of a stimulus.
- Memory, attention span, and symbolic thinking improve, and intuitive thought begins.
- Language (sentence length, vocabulary, syntax, and grammar) improves rapidly.

- Children apply logical operations to problems.
- Understanding of conservation (that changes in shape do not necessarily affect quantity) and transformation (that objects can go through many states without changing) emerge.
- Children can "decenter"—take multiple perspectives into account.
- Memory encoding, storage, and retrieval improve, and control strategies (meta-memory) develop.
- Language pragmatics (social conventions) and metalinguistic awareness (self-monitoring) improve.

- Children develop self concepts, which may be exaggerated.
- A sense of gender and racial identity emerges.
- Children begin to see peers as individuals and form friendships based on trust and shared interests.
- Morality is rule-based and focused on rewards and punishments.
- Play becomes more constructive and cooperative, and social skills become important.

- Children refer to psychological traits to define themselves. Sense of self becomes differentiated.
- Social comparison is used to understand one's standing and identity.
- Self-esteem grows differentiated, and a sense of self-efficacy (an appraisal of what one can and cannot do) develops.
- Children approach moral problems intent on maintaining social respect and accepting what society defines as right.
- Friendship patterns of boys and girls differ. Boys mostly interact with boys in groups, and girls tend to interact singly or in pairs with other girls.

Preoperational stage	Concrete operational stage
Initiative-versus-guilt stage	Industry-versus-inferiority stage
Phallic stage	Latency period
Preconventional morality level	Conventional morality level

Development Across the Life Span

THIRD EDITION

Robert S. Feldman

University of Massachusetts at Amherst

Prentice
Hall

Upper Saddle River, New Jersey 07458

Library of Congress Cataloging-in-Publication Data

Feldman, Robert S. (Robert Stephen)
    Development across the life span / Robert S. Feldman.—3rd ed.
        p.   cm.
    Includes bibliographical references and indexes.
    ISBN 0–13–098281–4
    1. Developmental psychology.   I. Title

    BF713.F45 2003
    155—dc21

                                    2001052383

Senior Acquisitions Editor: Jennifer Gilliland
VP, Director of Production and Manufacturing: Barbara Kittle
Director of Marketing: Beth Gillett Mejia
Executive Marketing Manager: Sheryl Adams
Marketing Assistant: Ron Fox
Senior Managing Editor: Mary Rottino
Production Liaison: Fran Russello
Editorial/Production Supervision: Bruce Hobart (Pine Tree Composition)
Associate Editor in Chief/Development Editor: Rochelle Diogenes
Development Editor: Sheralee Connors
Manufacturing Manager: Nick Sklitsis
Prepress and Manufacturing Buyer: Tricia Kenny
Creative Design Director: Leslie Osher
Line Art Coordinator: Guy Ruggiero
Art Director/Interior and Cover Design: Maria Lange
Electronic Illustrations: Mirella Signoretto
Director, Image Resource Center: Lori Morris-Nantz
Photo Research Supervisor: Melinda Reo
Manager Rights and Permissions: Kay Dellosa
Photo Researcher: Francelle Carapetyan
Editorial Assistant: Nicole Girrbach

Acknowledgments for copyrighted material may be found beginning
on p. 729, which constitutes an extension of this copyright page.

This book was set in 10/13 Minion by Pine Tree Composition
and was printed by RR Donnelley & Sons Company.
The cover was printed by Phoenix Color Corp.

ISBN 0-13-098281-4

Pearson Education Ltd., *London*
Pearson Education Australia Pte. Ltd., *Sydney*
Pearson Education Singapore, Pte. Ltd.
Pearson Education North Asia Ltd., *Hong Kong*
Pearson Education Canada, Ltd., *Toronto*
Pearson Educación de Mexico, S.A. de C.V.
Pearson Education—Japan, *Tokyo*
Pearson Education Malaysia, Pte. Ltd.
Pearson Educaiotn, *Upper Saddle River, New Jersey*

to my family

Brief Contents

Contents

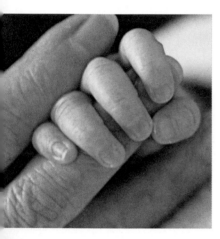

iv

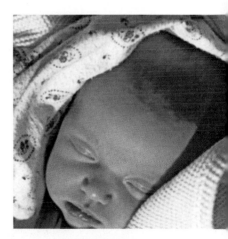

BRIDGES 115

PART 2 INFANCY FORMING THE FOUNDATIONS OF LIFE

CHAPTER 4 Physical Development in Infancy 116

CHAPTER **5** Cognitive Development in Infancy 150

CHAPTER **6** Social and Personality Development in Infancy 184

BRIDGES 213

PART 3 THE PRESCHOOL YEARS

**CHAPTER 8 Social and Personality Development
in the Preschool Years 256**

PART 4 THE MIDDLE CHILDHOOD YEARS

**CHAPTER 9 Physical and Cognitive Development
in Middle Childhood 292**

B R I D G E S 381

PART 5 ADOLESCENCE

CHAPTER 11 Physical and Cognitive Development in Adolescence 382

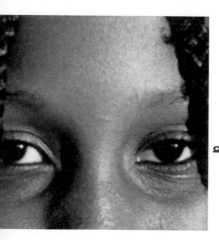

CHAPTER 12 Social and Personality Development in Adolescence 414

BRIDGES 447

PART 6 EARLY ADULTHOOD

CHAPTER 13 Physical and Cognitive Development in Early Adulthood 448

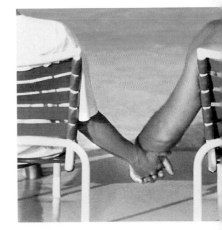

PART 9 **ENDINGS**

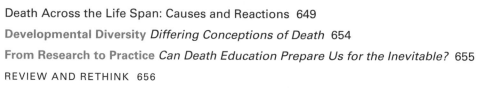

BRIDGES 671

P r e f a c e

his book tells a story: the story of our lives, and our parents' lives, and the lives of our children. It is the story of human beings and how they get to be the way they are.

Unlike any other area of study, lifespan development speaks to us in a very personal sense. It encompasses the range of human existence from its beginnings at conception to its inevitable ending at death. It is a discipline that deals with ideas and concepts and theories, but one that above all has at its heart people—our fathers and mothers, our friends and acquaintances, our very selves.

Development Across the Life Span seeks to capture the discipline in a way that sparks and nurtures and shapes readers' interest. It is meant to excite students about the field, to draw them into its way of looking at the world, and to build their understanding of developmental issues. By exposing readers to both the current content and the promise inherent in lifespan development, the text is designed to keep interest in the discipline alive long after students' formal study of the field has ended.

Overview of the Third Edition

Development Across the Life Span, third edition—like its predecessors—provides a broad overview of the field of human development. It covers the entire range of the human life, from the moment of conception through death. The text furnishes a broad, comprehensive introduction to the field, covering basic theories and research findings, as well as highlighting current applications outside the laboratory. It covers the life span chronologically, encompassing the prenatal period, infancy and toddlerhood, the preschool years, middle childhood, adolescence, early and middle adulthood, and late adulthood. Within these periods, it focuses on physical, cognitive, and social and personality development.

The book seeks to accomplish the following four major goals:

▶ First and foremost, the book is designed to provide a broad, balanced overview of the field of lifespan development. It introduces readers to the theories, research, and applications that constitute the discipline, examining both the traditional areas of the field as well as more recent innovations. It pays particular attention to the applications developed by lifespan development specialists, demonstrating how lifespan developmentalists use theory, research, and applications to help solve significant social problems.

▶ The second goal of the text is to explicitly tie development to students' lives. Findings from the study of lifespan development have a significant degree of relevance to students, and this text illustrates how these findings can be applied in a meaningful, practical sense. Applications are presented in a contemporaneous framework, including current news items, timely world events, and contemporary uses of lifespan development that draw readers into the field. Numerous descriptive scenarios and vignettes reflect everyday situations in people's lives, explaining how they relate to the field.

▶ The third goal is to highlight both the commonalities and diversity of today's multicultural society. Consequently, the book incorporates material relevant to diversity in all its forms—racial, ethnic, gender, sexual orientation, religion, and cultural diversity—throughout every chapter. In addition, every chapter has at least one "De-

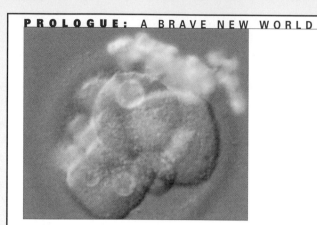

PROLOGUE: A BRAVE NEW WORLD

It was not much to look at: a blob-like mass of six cells, visible only through a microscope. But what these cells represented was nothing short of revolutionary: the first cloned human embryo (Cibelli, Lanza, & West, 2002).

CHAPTER-OPENING PROLOGUES

Each chapter begins with a short vignette, describing an individual or situation that is relevant to the basic developmental issues being addressed in the chapter. For instance, the chapter on birth describes several actual births; one of the chapters on adolescence provides an account of Cedric Jennings' life as a student in an inner-city school; and a chapter on late adulthood discusses the lives of Eva and Joseph Solymosi, married for more than seven decades.

LOOKING AHEAD SECTIONS

These opening sections orient readers to the topics to be covered, bridging the opening prologue with the remainder of the chapter and providing orienting questions.

Looking Ahead Even infants know the pleasures that the senses offer. In a remarkable way, they engage the world on a variety of levels, responding to the stimulation of taste, sound, touch, sight, and several other modalities.

The ability of infants to take in and respond to the world around them is among a variety of dramatic physical attainments that characterize infancy. In this chapter we consider the nature of physical development during the period of infancy, which starts at birth and continues until the second birthday. We begin by discussing the pace of growth during infancy, noting obvious changes in height and weight as well as less apparent changes in the nervous system. We also consider how infants quickly develop stable patterns in which their basic activities, such as sleeping, eating, and attending to the world, take on some degree of order.

From Research to Practice
Homework in Middle Childhood: Forget It?

Adam's homework began in the first grade . . . . It was just a little in the beginning—maybe 15 minutes a night, plus reading. Now, in fourth grade, it has soared to three hours a night, and Adam, identified as a gifted student, "is completely frustrated," says his mother. "Last night he was up until 10:15 finishing a project, and he is crying more and more

the worst. The reason? Students for whom homework takes the greatest amount of time are frequently taking so long because they are struggling with the material. If school is already difficult for them, piling on more of the same unpleasant experience at home is demoralizing and can reinforce negative attitudes about schooling (Cooper, 1989; Begley, 1998b).

Research into homework during middle childhood also

FROM RESEARCH TO PRACTICE

Each chapter includes a section that describes current developmental research or research issues, applied to everyday problems. For instance, these sections include discussions of ways of dealing with violence, training parents, and reversing intellectual declines in the elderly.

DEVELOPMENTAL DIVERSITY

Every chapter has at least one "Developmental Diversity" section incorporated into the text. These sections highlight issues relevant to today's multicultural society. Examples of these sections include discussions of cross-cultural differences in relationships, developing racial and ethnic awareness in childhood, adolescent race segregation, and racial differences in IQ and The Bell Curve controversy.

Developmental Diversity
Cultural Differences in Attributions for Academic Performance: Explaining Asian Academic Success

Consider two students, Ben and Hannah, each performing poorly in school. Suppose you thought that Ben's poor performance was due to unalterable, stable causes, such as a lack of intelligence, while Hannah's was produced by temporary causes, such as a lack of hard work. Who would you think would ultimately do better in school?

The Informed Consumer of Development

Keeping Children Fit

Here is a brief portrait of a contemporary American: Sam works all week at a desk and gets no regular physical exercise. On weekends he spends many hours sitting in front of the TV, often snacking on sodas and sweets. Both at home and at restaurants, his meals feature high-calorie, fat-saturated foods. (Segal & Segal, 1992, p. 235)

Although this sketch could apply to many adult men and women, Sam is actually a 6-year-old. He is one of many

▶ Encourage the child to find a partner. It could be a friend, a sibling, or a parent. Exercising can involve a variety of activities, such as roller skating or hiking, but almost all activities are carried out more readily if someone else is doing them too.

▶ Start slowly. Sedentary children—those who haven't habitually engaged in physical activity—should start off gradually. For instance, they could start with 5 minutes of exercise a day, 7 days a week. Over ten weeks, they could move toward a

SPEAKING OF DEVELOPMENT

Helen Shwe, Toy Designer Consultant

EDUCATION: BA, Cognitive Science, University of Rochester, New York; MA & PhD, Developmental Psychology, Stanford University, California.

HOME: Redwood City, California

Toys have traditionally been provided to children for entertainment, but over the years it has become apparent that what were once considered mere playthings have become important components of a child's development. As a result, toy researchers and designers, like Helen Shwe, are designing

For children around age 3, Shwe explained, you try to have a toy that will "allow multiple children to play with it: a toy that will encourage social interaction and cooperation. Fantasy and pretend play is popular, and you would want to bring some of that into the design.

"For example, a social action toy will allow children to compose a song together. One would push a button to add one phrase, and the other child would add another musical phrase," she said.

One area of toy design that has grown quickly over the past 5 years has been that of incorporating technology into toys.

Review and Rethink

REVIEW

- Information-processing approaches consider quantitative changes in children's abilities to organize and use information. Cognitive growth is regarded as the increasing sophistication of encoding, storage, and retrieval.

RETHINK

- What information from this chapter could you use to refute the claims of books or educational programs that promise to help parents multiply their babies' intelligence or instill advanced intellectual skills in infants?

case studies studies that involve extensive, in-depth interviews with a particular individual or small group of individuals

survey research a type of study where a group of people chosen to represent some larger population are asked questions about their attitudes, behavior, or thinking on a given topic

Case studies involve extensive, in-depth interviews with a particular individual or small group of individuals. They often are used not just to learn about the individual being interviewed, but to derive broader principles or draw tentative conclusions that might apply to others. For example, case studies have been conducted on children who display unusual genius and on children who have spent their early years in the wild, apparently without human contact. These case studies have provided important information to researchers, and have suggested hypotheses for future investigation (Lane, 1976; Feldman & Goldsmith, 1991; Hebert, 1998; Goldsmith, 2000).

Surveys represent another sort of correlational research. In **survey research,** a group

EPILOGUE

This chapter has introduced us to the growing field of life span development. We have reviewed the broad scope of the field, touching on the wide range of topics that life span developmentalists may address, and have discussed the key issues and questions that have shaped the field since its inception. We have also looked at the means by which developmentalists answer questions of interest.

Key Terms and Concepts

lifespan development (p. 5)
physical development (p. 6)
cognitive development (p. 6)

discontinuous change (p. 13)
critical period (p. 13)
sensitive period (p. 13)

behavioral perspective (p. 18)
classical conditioning (p. 19)
operant conditioning (p. 19)

velopmental Diversity" section. These features explicitly consider how cultural factors relevant to development both unite and diversify our contemporary, global society.

▶ Finally, the fourth goal is one that is implicit in the other three: making the field of lifespan development engaging, accessible, and interesting to students. Lifespan development is a joy both to study and teach, because so much of it has direct, immediate meaning to our lives. Because all of us are involved in our own developmental paths, we are tied in very personal ways to the content areas covered by the book. **Development Across the Life Span,** then, is meant to engage and nurture this interest, planting a seed that will develop and flourish throughout readers' lifetimes.

In accomplishing these goals, the book strives to be user-friendly. Written in a direct, conversational voice, it replicates as much as possible a dialogue between author and student. The text is meant to be understood and mastered on its own by students of every level of interest and motivation. To that end, it includes a variety of pedagogical features that promote mastery of the material and encourage critical thinking.

In short, the book blends and integrates theory, research, and applications, focusing on the breadth of human development. Furthermore, rather than attempting to provide a detailed historical record of the field, it focuses on the here-and-now, drawing on the past where appropriate, but with a view toward delineating the field as it now stands and the directions toward which it is evolving. Similarly, while providing descriptions of classic studies, the emphasis is more on current research findings and trends.

Development Across the Life Span is meant to be a book that readers will want to keep in their own personal libraries, one that they will take off the shelf when considering problems related to that most intriguing of questions: How do people come to be the way they are?

What's New in the Third Edition?

The third edition of **Development Across the Life Span** has been extensively revised in response to the comments of dozens of reviewers. Among the major changes are the following:

Additions of New and Updated Material

The revision incorporates a significant amount of new and updated information. For instance, advances in such areas as brain development, mapping the human genome, cognitive development, and cultural approaches to development receive expanded and new coverage. Overall, hundreds of new citations have been added, with most of those from articles and books published in the last three years.

Several areas received special attention in this revision, particularly in terms of coverage of middle and late adulthood. In addition, new material on genetics and brain development was added, fueled by the rapid changes in our understanding of these areas.

New topics were added to every chapter. The following sample of new and revised topics featured in this edition provides a good indication of the currency of the revision:

human genome	brain development
number of human genes	corticotropin-releasing hormone (CRH)
nonorganic failure to thrive	virginity pledges
affordances	benevolent sexism

referential and expressive language styles	emotional intelligence
interactional synchrony	psychoneuroimmunology
epigenetic theory	expertise
use of antidepressants in children	regret
fast mapping	estrogen loss
emotion regulation	age stratification
early puberty onset	passive and active euthanasia

Revisions to Foster Student Critical Thinking and Mastery of the Material

One thread that ran through the reviews of the previous edition was instructors' concerns regarding their students' thorough mastery of the material, permitting them to think critically about the material. In order to foster student mastery, a number of subtle changes were made to this edition to reinforce the existing features:

▶ **Critical thinking questions added to captions.** Many critical thinking questions were added to photo and figure captions, helping students to think more deeply about the material and to help students make connections between text concepts and the photo illustrations.

▶ **End-of-part Bridges.** Each major part of the book ends with a "Bridges" section. "Bridges" help students understand the relationship between the developmental achievements of the previous period and the upcoming one.

Ancillaries

Development Across the Life Span, Third Edition is accompanied by a superb set of teaching and learning materials.

For the Instructor:

NEW **Prentice Hall's Observations in Child Development, Volume I by David Daniel.** *FREE* when packaged with the text, this CD-ROM brings to life more than 30 key concepts discussed in the narrative of the text. Students get to view each video twice: once with an introduction to the concept being illustrated and again with commentary describing what is taking place at crucial points in the video. Students are then quizzed to test their understanding of what they just watched. Whether your course has an observation component or not, this CD-ROM provides your students the opportunity to see children in action.

Instructor's Resource Manual. Written by Susan Horton, Mesa Community College, this Instructor's Resource Manual contains a wealth of material for new and experienced instructors alike. Each chapter includes Objectives, Key Terms and Concepts, a Chapter Outline, Lecture Suggestions, Demonstrations and Classroom Activities, Group Activities, Critical Thinking Exercises, Assignment Ideas, Journal Exercises, Suggested Films and Videos, and Classroom Handouts.

NEW **Instructor's Resource CD-ROM.** This valuable, time-saving supplement brings together all of the Third Edition's instructor's resources in one convenient place. The CD-

ROM offers presentation resources, including video clips from Prentice Hall's Observations in Child Development CD-ROM, chapter specific PowerPoint presentations, electronic versions of the overhead transparencies and text graphics. It also includes the electronic files for the Instructor's Resource Manual and the Test Item File.

Prentice Hall's Color Transparencies for Developmental Psychology. Designed in a large-type format for lecture settings, these full color overhead transparencies add visual appeal to your lectures by augmenting the visuals in the text with a variety of new illustrations.

Test Item File. Written by Carolyn Meyer, Lake-Sumter Community College, this test bank contains over 3000 multiple choice, true/false, short answer, and essay questions that test for factual, applied, and conceptual knowledge.

Prentice Hall Test Manager. One of the best-selling test-generating software programs on the market, Test Manager is available in Windows and Macintosh formats. Both formats contain a Grade Book, Online Network Testing, and many tools to help you edit and create tests. The program comes with full Technical Support and telephone "Request a Test" service.

NEW PsychologyCentral **Website** at *www.prenhall.com/psychology.* Password protected for instructor's use only, this site allows you instant online access to Prentice Hall Psychology supplements. You'll find a multitude of resources for teaching developmental psychology—and many other psychology courses, too. From this site, you can download the following key supplements for *Development Across the Life Span, Third Edition:* Instructor's Resource Manual, Overhead Transparencies, Chapter Art and Chapter Specific PowerPoint presentations. Contact your Prentice Hall representative for the User ID and Password to access this site.

Films for the Humanities and Sciences. A wealth of full-length videos from the extensive library of Films for the Humanities and Sciences, on a variety of topics in developmental psychology, are available to qualified adopters. Contact your Prentice Hall representative for a list of videos.

ABC News/Prentice Hall Video Library Consisting of brief segments from award-winning news programs such as *Good Morning America, Nightline, 20/20 and World News Tonight,* these videos discuss current issues and are a great way to launch your lectures.

> *NEW* **Issues in Child and Adolescent Development, 2002**
> **Human Development, Series IV 1999**

Online Course Management. For professors interested in using the Internet and online course management in their courses, Prentice Hall offers fully customizable online courses in BlackBoard and Pearson's Course Compass powered by BlackBoard. Contact your Prentice Hall Representative or visit *www.prenhall.com/demo* for more information.

For the Student:

NEW **Prentice Hall's Observations in Child Development, Volume I by David Daniel.** *FREE* when packaged with the text, this CD-ROM brings to life more than 30 key concepts discussed in the narrative of the text. Students get to view each video twice: once with an introduction to the concept being illustrated and again with commentary describing what is taking place at crucial points in the video. Students are then quizzed to test their understanding of what they just watched. Whether your course has an observation component or not, this CD-ROM provides your students the opportunity to see children in action.

Study Guide. Written by Carolyn Meyer, Lake-Sumter Community College, this study guide is designed to help students get the most out of the textbook. Each chapter of the Study Guide includes Learning Objectives, Key Names and Terms, a Pre-Test and Post-Test, Programmed Review, Critical Thinking Questions and Answers.

www.prenhall.com/feldman **Companion Website.** This free online Study Guide allows students to review each chapter's material, take practice tests, research topics for course projects and more.

NEW **Prentice Hall Guide to Evaluating Online Resources: Psychology, 2003.** This guide provides students with a hands-on introduction to the Internet, features numerous websites related to Psychology and gives students guidelines on how to evaluate online resources. Now with **FREE** access to *ContentSelect*, a customized research database for students of psychology. Created by Prentice Hall and EBSCO, the world leader in online journal subscription management, this site provides students access to the text of many peer-reviewed publications and popular periodicals in Psychology.

Acknowledgments

I am grateful to the following reviewers who provided a wealth of comments, criticism, and encouragement:

Nancy L. Ashton, R. Stockton College; Libby Balter Blume, University of Detroit Mercy; Bobby Carlsen, Averett College; Ingrid Cominsky, Onondaga Community College; Amanda Cunningham, Emporia State University; Felice J. Green, University of North Alabama; Mark Hartlaub, Texas A&M University—Corpus Christi; Kathleen Hulbert, University of Massachusetts—Lowell; Susan Jacob, Central Michigan University; Laura Levine, Central Connecticut State University; Pamelyn M. MacDonald, Washburn University; Jessica Miller, Mesa State College; Shirley Albertson Owens, Vanguard University of Southern California; Stephanie Weyers, Emporia State University; Karen L. Yanowitz, Arkansas State University.

Many others deserve a great deal of thanks. I am indebted to the many people who provided me with a superb education, first at Wesleyan University and later at the University of Wisconsin. Specifically, Karl Scheibe played a pivotal role in my undergraduate education, and the late Vernon Allen acted as mentor and guide through my graduate years. It was in graduate school that I learned about development, being exposed to such experts as Ross Parke, John Balling, Joel Levin, Herb Klausmeier, and many others.

My education continued when I became a professor. I am especially grateful to my colleagues at the University of Massachusetts, who make the university such a wonderful place in which to teach and do research.

Several people played central roles in the development of this book. Edward Murphy brought a keen intelligence and editorial eye to the process. Christopher Poirier provided research assistance, and I am thankful for his help. Most of all, John Graiff was essential in juggling and coordinating the multiple aspects of writing a book, and I am very grateful for the substantial role he played.

I am also grateful to the superb Prentice Hall team that was instrumental in the inception and development of this book. Jennifer Gilliland, Senior Editor, vigilently watched over the project, constantly demonstrating a rare level of insight and creativity. Laura Pearson and Phil Miller stood behind the project, and I am grateful for their continuing support. Sheralee Connors, development editor, provided a wealth of valuable input, and the book is much improved by her thoughtful contributions. On the production end of things, Bruce Hobart, the production supervisor, and Francelle Carapetyan, photo editor, helped in giving the book its distinctive look. Finally, I'd like to thank (in advance) marketing manager Sheryl Adams, on whose skills I'm counting.

I also wish to acknowledge the members of my family, who play such a pivotal role in my life. My brother, Michael, my sisters-in-law and brother-in-law, my nieces and nephews, all make up an important part of my life. In addition, I am always indebted to the older generation of my family, who led the way in a manner I can only hope to emulate. I will always be obligated to Ethel Radler, Harry Brochstein, and the late Mary Vorwerk. Most of all, the list is headed by my father, the late Saul Feldman, and my mother, Leah Brochstein.

In the end, it is my immediate family who deserve the greatest thanks. My terrific kids, Jonathan (and his wife, Leigh), Joshua, and Sarah, not only are nice, smart, and good-looking, but my pride and joy. And ultimately my wife, Katherine Vorwerk, provides the love and grounding that makes everything worthwhile. I thank them, with all my love.

Robert S. Feldman
University of Massachusetts at Amherst

About the Author

Robert S. Feldman is professor of psychology at the University of Massachusetts in Amherst, where he is Director of Undergraduate Studies and recipient of the College Distinguished Teacher Award. He is both a Hewlett Teaching Fellow and a Senior On-line Teaching Fellow at UMass.

Professor Feldman was educated as an undergraduate at Wesleyan University, from which he graduated with High Honors, and received a M.S. and Ph.D. from the University of Wisconsin in Madison, where he specialized in social and developmental psychology.

Among his more than 100 books, chapters, and articles, he has edited *Development of Nonverbal Behavior in Children* (Springer-Verlag), *Applications of Nonverbal Behavioral Theory and Research* (Erlbaum), and co-edited *Fundamentals of Nonverbal Behavior* (Cambridge University Press). He is the recipient of grants from the National Institute of Mental Health and the National Institute of the Disabilities and Rehabilitation Research, which have supported his research on the development of nonverbal behavior in children. A past Fulbright lecturer and research scholar, he is a Fellow of the American Psychological Association and American Psychological Society.

During the course of nearly two decades as a college instructor, he has taught both undergraduate and graduate courses at Mount Holyoke College, Wesleyan University, Virginia Commonwealth University, in addition to the University of Massachusetts.

Professor Feldman loves music, is an enthusiastic, if not particularly accomplished, pianist, and is an excellent cook. He has three children, and he and his wife, a psychologist, live in Amherst, Massachusetts, in a home overlooking the Holyoke mountain range.

BEGINNINGS

An Introduction to Lifespan Development

PROLOGUE: A BRAVE NEW WORLD

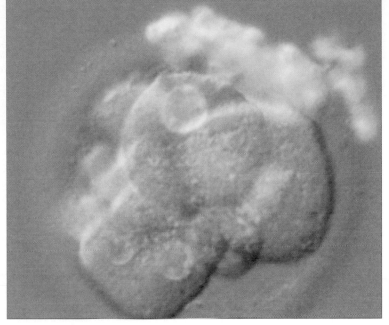

These six microscopic cells hold immense promise as the first cloned human embryo.

It was not much to look at: a blob-like mass of six cells, visible only through a microscope. But what these cells represented was nothing short of revolutionary: the first cloned human embryo (Cibelli, Lanza, & West, 2002).

To Dr. Judson Somerville, who donated the cells that formed the embryo, those six cells represented the dream that someday he might walk again. Injured in a cycling accident while training for a triathlon, Somerville, a 40-year-old anesthesiologist from Laredo, Texas, has been in a wheelchair for a decade. Not that Somerville feels sorry for himself. "Before, I could do 10,000 things," he says. "Now I can do 9,000" (Smolowe, 2001, p. 69.)

But this father of two has many reasons for participating in the controversial research that produced the embryo. His daughter, Madison, hopes he will walk with her down the wedding aisle when she marries. His wife of 19 years, Melanie, says, "I'd love for him to take a run with me." And ultimately, Somerville says, "Something like this could help a billion people" (Smolowe, 2001, p. 69).

Looking Ahead   Welcome to the brave new world of the 21st century, where human cloning is becoming more of a reality with each passing day. Or rather, welcome to just one of the brave new worlds. Issues ranging from cloning to the consequences of poverty on development to the prevention of AIDS raise significant developmental concerns. Underlying these are even more fundamental issues: How do we develop physically? How does our understanding of the world grow and change throughout our lives? And how do our personalities and our social world develop as we move from birth through the entire span of our lives?

Each of these questions, and many others we'll encounter throughout this book, are central to the field of lifespan development, and they underlie the lives of each of us. Consider, for example, the range of approaches that different specialists in lifespan development might take when considering the cloning of genetic material from Judson Somerville:

- Lifespan development researchers who investigate behavior at the level of biological processes might focus on how cloned genetic material could be used to treat and ultimately prevent inherited diseases.

- Specialists in lifespan development who study the ways thinking changes over the course of life might consider how our understanding of the ethics of cloning is altered with age.

- Lifespan development experts who specialize in the social world might examine how controversies regarding cloning might be expected to affect Somerville's social relationships.

Although their interests take many forms, these specialists in lifespan development share one concern: understanding the growth and change that occur during the course of life. Taking many differing approaches, developmentalists study how both our biological inheritance from our parents and the environment in which we live jointly affect our behavior.

Some developmentalists focus on explaining how our genetic background can determine not only how we look but also how we behave and relate to others in a consistent manner—that is, matters of personality. They explore ways to identify how much of our potential as human beings is provided—or limited—by heredity. Other lifespan development specialists look to the environment, exploring ways in which our lives are shaped by the world that we encounter. They investigate the extent to which we are shaped by our early environments, and how our current circumstances influence our behavior in both subtle and evident ways.

Whether they focus on heredity or environment, all developmental specialists acknowledge that neither heredity nor environment alone can account for the full range of human development and change. Instead, our understanding of people's development requires that we look at the joint effects of the interaction of heredity and environment, attempting to grasp how both, in the end, underlie human behavior.

In this chapter, we orient ourselves to the field of lifespan development. We begin with a discussion of the scope of the discipline, illustrating the wide array of topics it covers and the full range of ages it examines. We also survey the key issues and controversies of the field and consider the broad perspectives that developmentalists take. Finally, we discuss the ways developmentalists use research to ask and answer questions.

After reading this chapter, you will be able to answer these questions:

▶ **What is lifespan development, and what are some of the basic influences on human development?**

▶ **What are the key issues in the field of development?**

▶ **Which theoretical perspectives have guided lifespan development?**

❭ **What role do theories and hypotheses play in the study of development?**

❭ **How are developmental research studies conducted?**

An Orientation to Lifespan Development

Have you ever marveled at the way an infant tightly grips your finger with tiny, perfectly formed hands? Or at how a preschooler methodically draws a picture? Or at the way an adolescent can make involved decisions about whom to invite to a party? Or the way a middle-aged politician can deliver a long, flawless speech from memory? Or how an 80-year-old grandfather is able to roughhouse with his grandchild?

If you've ever wondered about such things, you are asking the kinds of questions that scientists in the field of lifespan development pose. **Lifespan development** is the field of study that examines patterns of growth, change, and stability in behavior that occur throughout the entire lifespan.

Although the definition of the field seems straightforward, the simplicity is somewhat misleading. In order to understand what development is actually about, we need to look underneath the various parts of the definition.

In its study of growth, change, and stability, lifespan development takes a *scientific* approach. Like members of other scientific disciplines, researchers in lifespan development test their assumptions about the nature and course of human development by applying scientific methods. As we'll see later in the chapter, they develop theories about development, and they use methodical, scientific techniques to validate the accuracy of their assumptions systematically.

Lifespan development focuses on *human* development. Although there are developmentalists who study the course of development in nonhuman species, the vast majority examine growth and change in people. Some seek to understand universal principles of development, while others focus on how cultural, racial, and ethnic differences affect the course of development. Still others aim to understand the unique aspects of individuals, looking at the traits and characteristics that differentiate one person from another. Regardless of approach, however, all developmentalists view development as a continuing process throughout the lifespan.

As developmental specialists focus on the ways people change and grow during their lives, they also consider stability in people's lives. They ask in which areas, and in what periods, people show change and growth, and when and how their behavior reveals consistency and continuity with prior behavior.

Finally, developmentalists assume that the process of development persists throughout every part of people's lives, beginning with the moment of conception and continuing until death. Developmental specialists assume that in some ways people continue to grow and change right up to the end of their lives, while in other respects their behavior remains stable. At the same time, developmentalists believe that no particular, single period of life governs all development. Instead, they believe that every period of life contains the potential for both growth and decline in abilities, and that individuals maintain the capacity for substantial growth and change throughout their lives.

lifespan development the field of study that examines patterns of growth, change, and stability in behavior that occur throughout the entire life span.

cw

Characterizing Lifespan Development: The Scope of the Field

Clearly, the definition of lifespan development is broad and the scope of the field is extensive. Consequently, lifespan development specialists cover several quite diverse areas, and a typical developmentalist specializes in two ways: topical area and age range.

physical development development involving the body's physical makeup, including the brain, nervous system, muscles, and senses, and the need for food, drink, and sleep

cognitive development development involving the ways that growth and change in intellectual capabilities influence a person's behavior

personality development development involving the ways that the enduring characteristics that differentiate one person from another change over the life span

social development the way in which individuals' interactions with others and their social relationships grow, change, and remain stable over the course of life

Topical Areas in Lifespan Development. Some developmentalists focus on **physical development,** examining the ways in which the body's makeup—the brain, nervous system, muscles, and senses, and the need for food, drink, and sleep—helps determine behavior. For example, one specialist in physical development might examine the effects of malnutrition on the pace of growth in children, while another might look at how reaction time changes during adulthood.

Other developmental specialists examine **cognitive development,** seeking to understand how growth and change in intellectual capabilities influence a person's behavior. Cognitive developmentalists examine learning, memory, problem-solving, and intelligence. For example, specialists in cognitive development might want to see how intellectual abilities change over the course of life, or if cultural differences exist in the factors to which people attribute their academic successes and failures. They would also be interested in how a person who experiences significant events early in life would be remembered later in life.

Finally, some developmental specialists focus on personality and social development. **Personality development** is the study of stability and change in the enduring characteristics that differentiate one person from another over the lifespan. **Social development** is the way in which individuals' interactions with others and their social relationships grow, change, and remain stable over the course of life. A developmentalist interested in personality development might ask whether there are stable, enduring personality traits throughout the lifespan, while a specialist in social development might examine marriage and divorce during adulthood. (The major approaches are summarized in Table 1-1.)

Age Ranges and Individual Differences. As they specialize in chosen topical areas, developmentalists typically look at particular age ranges. The lifespan is usually divided into broad age ranges: the prenatal period (the period from conception to birth); infancy and toddlerhood (birth to age 3); the preschool period (ages 3 to 6); middle childhood (ages 6 to 12); adolescence (ages 12 to 20); young adulthood (ages 20 to 40); middle adulthood (ages 40 to 60); and late adulthood (age 60 to death).

Although most lifespan developmentalists accept these broad periods, the age ranges themselves are in many ways arbitrary. While some periods have one clear-cut boundary (infancy begins with birth, the preschool period ends with entry into public school, and adolescence starts with sexual maturity), others don't.

For instance, consider the period of young adulthood, which is typically assumed to begin at age 20. That age, however, is notable only because it marks the end of the teenage period. In fact, for many people, such as those enrolled in higher education, the age change from 19 to 20 has little special significance, coming as it does in the middle of the college years. For them, more substantial changes may occur when they leave college and enter the workforce, which is more likely to happen around age 22.

In short, there are substantial individual differences in the timing of events in people's lives. In part, this is a biological fact of life: People mature at different rates and reach developmental milestones at different points. However, environmental factors also play a significant role in determining the age at which a particular event is likely to occur. For example, the typical age of marriage varies substantially from one culture to another, depending in part on the functions that marriage plays in a given culture.

It is important to keep in mind, then, that when developmental specialists discuss age ranges, they are talking about averages—the times when people, on average, reach particular milestones. Some people will reach the milestone earlier, some later, and many will reach it around the time of the average. Such variation becomes noteworthy only when children show substantial deviation from the average. For example, parents whose child begins to speak at a much later age than average might decide to have their son or daughter evaluated by a speech therapist.

This wedding of two children in India is an example of how environmental factors can play a significant role in determining the age when a particular event is likely to occur.

Table 1-1

APPROACHES TO LIFESPAN DEVELOPMENT

Orientation	Defining Characteristics	Examples of Questions Asked*
Physical development	Examines how brain, nervous system, muscles, sensory capabilities, needs for food, drink, and sleep affect behavior	What determines the sex of a child? (2) What are the long-term results of premature birth? (3) What are the benefits of breast-feeding? (4) What are the consequences of early or late sexual maturation? (11) What leads to obesity in adulthood? (13) How do adults cope with stress? (15) What are the outward and internal signs of aging? (17) How do we define death? (19)
Cognitive development	Examines intellectual abilities, including learning, memory, problem solving, and intelligence	What are the earliest memories that can be recalled from infancy? (5) What are the consequences of watching television? (7) Do spatial reasoning skills relate to music practice? (7) Are there benefits to bilingualism? (9) How does an adolescent's egocentrism affect his or her view of the world? (11) Are there ethnic and racial differences in intelligence? (9) How does creativity relate to intelligence? (13) Does intelligence decline in late adulthood? (17)
Personality and social development	Examines enduring characteristics that differentiate one person from another, and how interactions with others and social relationships grow and change over the lifetime	Do newborns respond differently to their mothers than to others? (3) What is the best procedure for disciplining children? (8) When does a sense of gender develop? (8) How can we promote cross-race friendships? (10) What are the causes of adolescent suicide? (12) How do we choose a romantic partner? (14) Do the effects of parental divorce last into old age? (18) Do people withdraw from others in late adulthood? (18) What are the stages of confronting death? (19)

*Numbers in parentheses indicate in which chapter the question is addressed.

The Links Between Topics and Ages. Each of the broad topical areas of lifespan development—physical, cognitive, and social and personality development—plays a role throughout the lifespan. Consequently, some developmental experts focus on physical development during the prenatal period, and others during adolescence. Some might specialize in social development during the preschool years, while others look at social relationships in late adulthood. And still others might take a broader approach, looking at cognitive development through every period of life. In this book, we'll take a comprehensive approach, proceeding chronologically from the prenatal period through late adulthood and death. Within each period, we'll look at different topical areas: physical, cognitive, and social.

The Context of Development: Taking a Broad Perspective

Considering the course of development in terms of physical, cognitive, and personality and social factors has advantages and disadvantages. It allows us to divide developmental influences into reasonably neat and compact packages. But such a categorization has one serious drawback: In the real world, none of these broad influences occurs in isolation from any other. Instead, there is a constant, ongoing interaction between the different types of influence. Consequently, what occurs on a cognitive level has repercussions for personality, social, and physical development, while what is happening on a physical level has an impact on cognitive, personality, and social development. For example, a middle-aged person might learn about the importance of exercise (a cognitive change), and then start a fitness program, leading to physical, and perhaps social, changes.

The Ecological Approach to Development. In acknowledging the problem with traditional approaches to lifespan development, psychologist Urie Bronfenbrenner (1979, 1989) has proposed an alternative perspective, called the ecological approach. The **ecological approach** suggests there are four levels of the environment that simultaneously influence individuals. Bronfenbrenner suggests that we cannot fully understand development without considering how a person fits into each of these levels (illustrated in Figure 1-1).

The *microsystem* is the everyday, immediate environment in which people lead their daily lives. Homes, caregivers, friends, and teachers all are examples of the influences that are part of the microsystem.

The *mesosystem* provides connections between the various aspects of the microsystem. Like links in a chain, the mesosystem binds children to parents, students to teachers, employees to bosses, friends to friends. It acknowledges the direct and indirect influences that bind us to one another, such as those that affect a mother who has a bad day at the office and then is short-tempered with her daughter at home.

The *exosystem* represents broader influences, encompassing societal institutions such as local government, the community, schools, places of worship, and the local media. Each of these larger institutions of society can have an immediate, and major, impact on personal development, and each affects how the microsystem and mesosystem operate.

Finally, the *macrosystem* represents the larger cultural influences on an individual. Society in general, types of governments, religious systems, political thought, and other broad, encompassing factors are parts of the macrosystem.

The ecological approach provides several advantages. For one thing, it emphasizes the interconnectedness of the influences on development. Because the various levels are related to one another, a change in one part of the system affects other parts of the system.

ecological approach the perspective suggesting that different levels of the environment simultaneously influence individuals

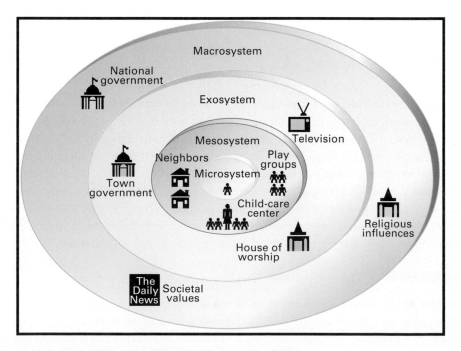

Figure 1-1 **Bronfenbrenner's Approach to Development**

Urie Bronfenbrenner's ecological approach to development offers four levels of the environment that simultaneously influence individuals: the macrosystem, exosystem, mesosystem, and microsystem. (Source: Koop & Krakow, 1982)

For instance, a parent's loss of a job (involving the mesosystem) has an impact upon a child's microsystem.

Conversely, changes on one environmental level may make little difference if other levels are not also changed. For instance, improving the school environment may have a negligible effect on academic performance if children receive little support for academic success in their home environment. Similarly, the ecological approach illustrates that the influences among different family members are multidirectional. Parents don't just influence their child's behavior—the child also influences the parents' behavior.

Finally, the ecological approach stresses the importance of broad cultural factors that affect development. Researchers in development increasingly look at how membership in cultural and subcultural groups influences behavior.

Consider, for instance, whether you agree that children should be taught that their classmates' assistance is indispensable to getting good grades in school, or that they should definitely plan to continue their fathers' businesses, or that children should follow their parents' advice in determining their career plans. If you have been raised in the most widespread North American culture, you would likely disagree with all three statements, since they violate the premises of *individualism*, the dominant Western philosophy that emphasizes personal identity, uniqueness, freedom, and the worth of the individual.

On the other hand, if you were raised in a traditional Asian culture, your agreement with the three statements is considerably more likely. The reason? The statements reflect the value orientation known as collectivism. *Collectivism* is the notion that the well-being of the group is more important than that of the individual. People raised in collectivistic cultures tend to emphasize the welfare of the groups to which they belong, sometimes even at the expense of their own personal well-being.

The individualism–collectivism spectrum is one of several dimensions along which cultures differ, and it illustrates differences in the cultural contexts in which people operate. As we'll see in Chapter 12, such broad cultural values play an important role in shaping the ways people view the world and behave (Kim et al., 1994; Dent-Read & Zukow-Goldring, 1997; de Mooij, 1998).

Development, according to Bronfenbrenner's ecological approach, is also influenced by the social institutions that form the exosystem. In this case teachers and parents demonstrate for better schools. Can you think of other examples of the influence of the exosystem?

Developmental Diversity

How Culture, Ethnicity, and Race Influence Development

South American Mayan mothers are certain that almost constant contact between themselves and their infant children is necessary for good parenting, and they are physically upset if contact is not possible. They are shocked when they see a North American mother lay her infant down, and they attribute the baby's crying to the poor parenting of the North American (Morelli et al., 1992).

Two views of parenting are at odds in this passage. Is one right and the other wrong? Probably not, if we take into consideration the cultural context in which the mothers are operating. In fact, different cultures and subcultures have their own views of appropriate and inappropriate childrearing, just as they have different developmental goals for children (Greenfield, 1995, 1997; Francasso et al., 1997).

We've seen that developmentalists must take into consideration broad cultural factors, such as an orientation toward individualism or collectivism. They must also take into account finer ethnic, racial, socioeconomic, and gender differences if they are to achieve an understanding of how people change and grow throughout the lifespan. If developmentalists succeed in doing so, not only can they achieve a better understanding of human development, but they may be able to derive more precise applications for improving the human social condition.

Although the field of lifespan development is increasingly concerned with issues of human diversity, its actual progress in this domain has been slow, and in some ways it has actually regressed. For instance, between 1970 and 1989, only 4.6 percent of the articles published in *Developmental Psychology*, the premier journal of the discipline, focused on African American participants. Moreover, the number of published studies involving African American participants actually declined over that 20-year period (Graham, 1992; MacPhee, Kreutzer, & Fritz, 1994).

Furthermore, members of the research community—as well as society at large— have sometimes used terms such as *race* and *ethnic group* in inappropriate ways. *Race* is a biological concept, which should be employed to refer to classifications based on physical and structural characteristics of species. In contrast, *ethnic group* and *ethnicity* are broader terms, referring to cultural background, nationality, religion, and language.

The concept of race has proven particularly problematic. Although it formally refers to biological factors, race has taken on substantially more meanings—many of them inappropriate—that range from skin color to religion to culture. Moreover, the concept of race is exceedingly imprecise; depending on how it is defined, there are between 3 and 300 races, and no race is biologically pure. Furthermore, the fact that 99.9 percent of humans' genetic makeup is identical in all humans makes the question of race seem comparatively insignificant (Betancourt & Lopez, 1993; Angier, 2000; Carpenter, 2000).

In addition, there is little agreement about which names best reflect different races and ethnic groups. Should the term *African American*—which has geographical and cultural implications—be preferred over *black,* which focuses primarily on race and skin color? Is *Native American* preferable to *Indian?* Is *Hispanic* more appropriate than *Latino?* And how can researchers accurately categorize people with multiracial backgrounds?

The choice of category has important implications for the validity (and usefulness) of research. The choice even has political implications. For example, the decision to permit people to identify themselves as "multiracial" on U.S. government forms and in the U.S. Census was highly controversial (Evinger, 1996).

Finally, it is important to keep in mind that race—a biological factor—is not independent of environmental and cultural contexts. Consequently, it is impossible to attribute a particular behavior or set of behaviors to race *per se*, without considering the environments in which people are developing.

In short, as the proportion of minorities in U.S. society continues to increase, it becomes crucial to take the complex issues associated with human diversity into account in order to fully understand development (Fowers & Richardson, 1996). In fact, it is only by looking for similarities and differences among various ethnic, cultural, and racial groups that developmental researchers can distinguish principles of development that are universal from ones that are culturally determined. In the years ahead, then, it is likely that lifespan development will move from a discipline that primarily focuses on North American and European development to one that encompasses development around the globe. ☐

Cohort and Normative Influences on Development: Developing with Others in a Social World. Bob, born in 1947, is a baby boomer; he was born soon after the end of World War II, when an enormous bulge in the birth rate occurred as soldiers returned to the United States from overseas. He was an adolescent at the height of the Civil Rights movement and the beginning of protests against the Vietnam War. His mother, Leah, was born in 1922; she is part of the generation that passed its childhood and teenage years in the shadow of the depression. Bob's son, Jon, was born in 1975. Now starting a career after graduating from college and newly married, he is a member of what has been called Generation X.

These people are in part products of the social times in which they live. Each belongs to a particular **cohort,** a group of people born at around the same time in the same place. Such major social events as wars, economic upturns and depressions, famines, and epidemics (like the one due to the AIDS virus) work similar influences on members of a particular cohort.

Cohort effects provide an example of **normative history-graded influences,** which are biological and environmental influences associated with a particular historical moment. For instance, people who lived in Seattle, Washington, in February 2001 shared both biological and environmental challenges due to a major earthquake that rocked the city.

Normative history-graded influences contrast with **normative age-graded influences,** biological and environmental influences that are similar for individuals in a particular age group, regardless of when or where they are raised. For example, biological events such as puberty and menopause are universal events that occur at relatively the same time throughout all societies. Similarly, a sociocultural event such as entry into formal education can be considered a normative age-graded influence because it occurs in most cultures around age six.

Development is also affected by normative sociocultural-graded influences. **Normative sociocultural-graded influences** represent the impact of social and cultural factors present at a particular time for a particular individual, depending on such variables as ethnicity, social class, and subcultural membership. For example, sociocultural-graded influences will be considerably different for children who are white and affluent than for children who are members of a minority group and living in poverty.

Finally, nonnormative life events also influence development. **Nonnormative life events** are specific, atypical events that occur in a particular person's life at a time when such events do not happen to most people. For example, children who lost a parent in the terrorist attacks on the World Trade Center and Pentagon experienced a significant nonnormative life event.

cohort a group of people born at around the same time in the same place

normative history-graded influences biological and environmental influences associated with a particular historical moment

normative age-graded influences biological and environmental influences that are similar for individuals in a particular age group, regardless of when or where they are raised

normative sociocultural-graded influences the impact of social and cultural factors present at a particular time for a particular individual, depending on such variables as ethnicity, social class, and subcultural membership

nonnormative life events specific, atypical events that occur in a particular person's life at a time when they do not happen to most people

Key Issues and Questions: Determining the Nature—and Nurture —of Lifespan Development

Compared to other sciences, lifespan development is one of the new kids on the block. Although its roots can be traced back to the ancient Egyptians and Greeks, it became established as a separate field only in the late nineteenth and early twentieth centuries.

From the time of its establishment, several key issues and questions have dominated the field. Among the major issues (summarized in Table 1-2) are the nature of developmental change, the importance of critical periods, lifespan approaches versus more focused approaches, and the nature–nurture issue (Kagan et al., 1994; Parke et al., 1994).

Continuous Change Versus Discontinuous Change. One of the primary issues challenging developmentalists is whether development proceeds in a continuous or discontinuous fashion. In **continuous change,** development is gradual, with achievements at one level building on those of previous levels. Continuous change is quantitative in nature; the basic underlying developmental processes that drive change remain the same over the course of the life span. Continuous change, then, produces changes that are a matter of degree, not of kind. Changes in height prior to adulthood, for example, are continuous. Similarly, as we'll see later in the chapter, some theorists suggest that changes in people's thinking capabilities are also continuous, showing gradual quantitative improvements rather than developing entirely new ways of cognitive processing capabilities.

continuous change gradual development in which achievements at one level build on those of previous levels

Table 1-2

MAJOR ISSUES IN LIFESPAN DEVELOPMENT

Continuous Change	Discontinuous Change
• Change is gradual. • Achievements at one level build on previous level. • Underlying developmental processes remain the same over the life span.	• Change occurs in distinct steps or stages. • Behavior and processes are qualitatively different at different stages.
Critical Periods	**Sensitive Periods**
• Certain environmental stimuli are necessary for normal development. • Emphasized by early developmentalists.	• People are susceptible to certain environmental stimuli, but consequences of absent stimuli are reversible. • Current emphasis in lifespan development.
Life Span Approach	**Focus on Particular Periods**
• Current theories emphasize growth and change throughout life, relatedness of different periods.	• Infancy and adolescence emphasized by early developmentalists as most important periods.
Nature (Genetic Factors)	**Nurture (Environmental Factors)**
• Emphasis is on discovering inherited genetic traits and abilities.	• Emphasis is on environmental influences that affect a person's development.

In contrast, **discontinuous change** occurs in distinct stages. Each stage brings about behavior that is assumed to be qualitatively different from behavior at earlier stages. Consider the example of cognitive development again. We'll see later in the chapter that some cognitive developmentalists suggest that our thinking changes in fundamental ways as we develop, and that such development is not just a matter of quantitive change but of qualititative change.

Most developmentalists agree that taking an either/or position on the continuous–discontinuous issue is inappropriate. While many types of developmental change are continuous, others are clearly discontinuous (Rutter, 1987; Flavell, 1994).

Critical Periods: Gauging the Impact of Environmental Events. If a woman comes down with a case of rubella (German measles) in the eleventh week of pregnancy, the consequences for the child she is carrying are likely to be devastating: They include the potential for blindness, deafness, and heart defects. However, if she comes down with the exact same strain of rubella in the thirtieth week of pregnancy, damage to the child is unlikely.

The differing outcomes of the disease in the two periods demonstrate the concept of critical periods. A **critical period** is a specific time during development when a particular event has its greatest consequences. Critical periods occur when the presence of certain kinds of environmental stimuli are necessary for development to proceed normally.

Although early specialists in lifespan development placed great emphasis on the importance of critical periods, more recent thinking suggests that in many realms individuals may be more malleable than was first thought, particularly in the domain of personality and social development. For instance, rather than suffering permanent damage from a lack of certain kinds of early social experiences, there is increasing evidence that people can use later experiences to their benefit, to help them overcome earlier deficits. Consequently, developmentalists are now more likely to speak of **sensitive periods** rather than critical periods. In a sensitive period, organisms are particularly susceptible to certain kinds of stimuli in their environments. In contrast to a critical period, however, the absence of those stimuli during a sensitive period does not always produce irreversible consequences (Bornstein, 1989a; Barinaga, 2000; Thompson & Nelson, 2001).

Lifespan Approaches Versus a Focus on Particular Periods. On which part of the life span should developmentalists focus their attention? For early developmentalists, the answers tended to be infancy and adolescence. Most attention was clearly concentrated on those two periods, largely to the exclusion of other parts of the life span.

Today, however, the story is different. Developmentalists now believe the entire life span is important, for several reasons. One is the discovery that developmental growth and change continue during every part of life—as we'll discuss throughout this book.

Furthermore, an important part of every person's environment is the other people around him or her, the person's social environment. To fully understand the social influences on people of a given age, we need to understand the people who are in large measure providing those influences. For instance, to understand development in infants, we need to unravel the effects of their parents' ages on their social environments. It is likely that a 15-year-old mother will present parental influences of a very different sort from those presented by a 37-year-old mother. Consequently, infant development is in part an outgrowth consequence of adult development (Parke, 1989).

The Relative Influence of Nature and Nurture on Development. One of the enduring questions of development involves how much of people's behavior is due to their genetically determined nature and how much is due to nurture, the physical and social environment in which a child is raised. This issue, which has deep philosophical and historical roots, has dominated much work in lifespan development.

In this context, *nature* refers to traits, abilities, and capacities that are inherited from one's parents. It encompasses any factor that is produced by the predetermined unfolding of genetic information—a process known as **maturation.** These genetic, inherited influ-

discontinuous change development that occurs in distinct steps or stages, with each stage bringing about behavior that is assumed to be qualitatively different from behavior at earlier stages

critical period a specific time during development when a particular event has its greatest consequences and the presence of certain kinds of environmental stimuli are necessary for development to proceed normally

sensitive period a point in development when organisms are particularly susceptible to certain kinds of stimuli in their environments, but the absence of those stimuli does not always produce irreversible consequences

maturation the predetermined unfolding of genetic information

ences are at work as we move from the one-cell organism that is created at the moment of conception to the billions of cells that make up a fully formed human. Nature influences whether our eyes are blue or brown, whether we have thick hair throughout life or eventually go bald, and how good we are at athletics. Nature allows our brains to develop in such a way that we can read the words on this page.

In contrast, *nurture* refers to the environmental influences that shape behavior. Some of these influences may be biological, such as the impact of a pregnant mother's use of cocaine on her unborn child or the amount and kind of food available to children. Other environmental influences are more social, such as the ways parents discipline their children and the effects of peer pressure on an adolescent. Finally, some influences are a result of larger, societal-level factors, such as the socioeconomic circumstances in which people find themselves.

If our traits and behavior were determined solely by either nature or nurture, there would probably be little debate regarding the issue. However, for most critical behaviors this is hardly the case. Take, for instance, one of the most controversial arenas: intelligence. As we'll consider in detail in Chapter 9, the question of whether intelligence is determined primarily by inherited, genetic factors—nature—or is shaped by environmental factors—nurture—has caused lively and often bitter arguments that have spilled out of the scientific arena and into the realm of politics and social policy.

Consider the implications of the issue: If the extent of one's intelligence is primarily determined by heredity and consequently is largely fixed at birth, then efforts to improve intellectual performance later in life may be doomed to failure. In contrast, if intelligence is primarily a result of environmental factors, such as the amount and quality of schooling and stimulation to which one is exposed, then we would expect that an improvement in social conditions could bring about an increase in intelligence.

The extent of social policy affected by ideas about the origins of intelligence illustrates the significance of issues that involve the nature–nurture question. As we address it in relation to several topical areas throughout this book, we should keep in mind that developmentalists reject the notion that behavior is the result solely of either nature *or* nurture. Instead, the question is one of degree. Furthermore, the interaction of genetic and environmental factors is complex, in part because certain genetically determined traits have not only a direct influence on children's behavior, but an indirect influence in shaping children's *environments* as well. For example, a child who is consistently cranky and who cries a great deal—a trait that may be produced by genetic factors—may influence his or her environment by making his or her parents so highly responsive to the insistent crying that they rush to comfort the child whenever he or she cries. Their responsivity to the child's genetically determined behavior consequently becomes an environmental influence on his or her subsequent development.

In sum, the question of how much of a given behavior is due to nature, and how much to nurture, is a challenging one. Ultimately, we should consider the two sides of the nature–nurture issue as opposite ends of a continuum, with particular behaviors falling somewhere between the two ends. We can say something similar about the other controversies that we have considered. For instance, continuous versus discontinuous development is not an either/or proposition; some forms of development fall toward the continuous end of the continuum, while others lie closer to the discontinuous end. In short, few statements about development involve either/or absolutes.

Review and Rethink

REVIEW

■ Lifespan development, a scientific approach to understanding human growth and change throughout life, encompasses physical, cognitive, and social and personality development.

■ The ecological approach considers interrelationships among aspects of human development, and relationships between the individual and four levels of the environment.

- Culture and ethnicity also play an important role in development, both broad culture and aspects of culture, such as race, ethnicity, and socioeconomic status.
- Membership in a cohort, based on age and place of birth, subjects people to influences based on historical events (normative history-graded influences). People are also subject to normative age-graded influences, normative sociocultural-graded influences, and nonnormative life events.
- Four important issues in lifespan development are continuity versus discontinuity in development, the importance of critical periods, whether to focus on certain periods or on the entire life span, and the nature–nurture controversy.

RETHINK

- What are some examples of the ways culture (either broad culture or aspects of culture) affects human development?
- What are some events that might have a shared significance for members of your age cohort as normative history-graded influences? How might they produce different effects from events shared by members of different age cohorts?

Theoretical Perspectives

Until the seventeenth century in Europe, there was no concept of "childhood." Instead, children were simply thought of as miniature adults. They were assumed to be subject to the same needs and desires as adults, to have the same vices and virtues as adults, and to warrant no more privileges than adults. They were dressed the same as adults, and their work hours were the same as adults'. Children also received the same punishments for misdeeds. If they stole, they were hanged; if they did well, they could achieve prosperity.

This view of childhood seems wrong-headed now, but at the time it is what passed for lifespan development. From this perspective, there were no differences due to age; except for size, people were assumed to be virtually unchanging, at least on a psychological level, throughout most of the life span (Aries, 1962; Hwang, Lamb, & Sigel, 1996).

Although, looking back over several centuries, it is easy to reject the medieval view of childhood, it is less clear how to formulate a contemporary substitute. Should our view of development focus on the biological aspects of change, growth, and stability over the life span? The cognitive or social aspects? Or some other factors?

Society's view of childhood, and what is appropriate to ask of children, has changed through the ages. These children worked full-time in mines in the early 1900s.

theories explanations and predictions concerning phenomena of interest, providing a framework for understanding the relationships among an organized set of facts or principles

psychodynamic perspective the approach that states behavior is motivated by inner forces, memories, and conflicts that are generally beyond people's awareness and control

psychoanalytic theory the theory proposed by Freud that suggests that unconscious forces act to determine personality and behavior

id according to Freud, the raw, unorganized, inborn part of personality, present at birth, that represents primitive drives related to hunger, sex, aggression, and irrational impulses

ego according to Freud, the part of personality that is rational and reasonable

superego according to Freud, the aspect of personality that represents a person's conscience, incorporating distinctions between right and wrong

In fact, people who study lifespan development approach the field from a number of different perspectives. Each broad perspective encompasses one or more **theories,** explanations and predictions concerning phenomena of interest. A theory provides a framework for understanding the relationships among a seemingly unorganized set of facts or principles.

We all develop theories about development, based on our experience, folklore, and articles in magazines and newspapers. However, theories in lifespan development are different. Whereas our own personal theories are built on unverified observations that are developed haphazardly, developmentalists' theories are more formal, based on a systematic integration of prior findings and theorizing. These theories allow developmentalists to summarize and organize prior observations, and they allow them to move beyond existing observations to draw deductions that may not be immediately apparent (Thomas, 2001).

We will consider five major theoretical perspectives used in lifespan development: the psychodynamic, behavioral, cognitive, humanistic, and evolutionary perspectives. Each emphasizes somewhat different aspects of development and steers developmentalists in particular directions. Furthermore, each perspective continues to evolve and change, as befits a growing and dynamic discipline.

The Psychodynamic Perspective: Focusing on the Inner Person

When Janet was six months old, she was involved in a bloody automobile accident—or so her parents tell her, since she has no conscious recollection of it. Now, however, at age 24, she is having difficulty maintaining relationships, and her therapist is seeking to determine whether her current problems are a result of the earlier accident.

Looking for such a link might seem a bit far-fetched, but to proponents of the **psychodynamic perspective,** it is not so improbable. Advocates of the psychodynamic perspective believe that behavior is motivated by inner forces, memories, and conflicts of which a person has little awareness or control. The inner forces, which may stem from one's childhood, continually influence behavior throughout the life span.

Freud's Psychoanalytic Theory. The psychodynamic perspective is most closely associated with a single person and theory: Sigmund Freud and his psychoanalytic theory. Freud, who lived from 1856 to 1939, was a Viennese physician whose revolutionary ideas ultimately had a profound effect not only on the fields of psychology and psychiatry, but on Western thought in general (Masling & Bornstein, 1996).

Freud's **psychoanalytic theory** suggests that unconscious forces act to determine personality and behavior. To Freud, the *unconscious* is a part of the personality about which a person is unaware. It contains infantile wishes, desires, demands, and needs that are hidden, because of their disturbing nature, from conscious awareness. Freud suggested that the unconscious is responsible for a good part of our everyday behavior.

According to Freud, everyone's personality has three aspects: id, ego, and superego. The **id** is the raw, unorganized, inborn part of personality that is present at birth. It represents primitive drives related to hunger, sex, aggression, and irrational impulses. The id operates according to the *pleasure principle*, in which the goal is to maximize satisfaction and reduce tension.

The **ego** is the part of personality that is rational and reasonable. The ego acts as a buffer between the real world outside of us and the primitive id. The ego operates on the *reality principle*, in which instinctual energy is restrained in order to maintain the safety of the individual and help integrate the person into society.

Finally, Freud proposed that the **superego** represents a person's conscience, incorporating distinctions between right and wrong. It develops around age 5 or 6 and is learned from an individual's parents, teachers, and other significant figures.

In addition to providing an account of the various parts of the personality, Freud also suggested the ways in which personality developed during childhood. He argued that

Sigmund Freud

psychosexual development occurs as children pass through a series of stages in which pleasure, or gratification, is focused on a particular biological function and body part. As illustrated in Table 1-3, he suggested that pleasure shifts from the mouth (the *oral stage*) to the anus (the *anal stage*) and eventually to the genitals (the *phallic stage* and the *genital stage*).

According to Freud, if children are unable to gratify themselves sufficiently during a particular stage, or conversely, if they receive too much gratification, fixation may occur. **Fixation** is behavior reflecting an earlier stage of development due to an unresolved conflict. For instance, fixation at the oral stage might produce an adult unusually absorbed in oral activities—eating, talking, or chewing gum. Freud also argued that fixation is represented through symbolic sorts of oral activities, such as the use of "biting" sarcasm.

Erikson's Psychosocial Theory. Psychoanalyst Erik Erikson, who lived from 1902 to 1994, provided an alternative psychodynamic view in his theory of psychosocial development, which emphasizes our social interaction with other people. In Erikson's view, society and culture both challenge and shape us. **Psychosocial development** encompasses changes in our interactions with and understandings of one another as well as in our knowledge and understanding of ourselves as members of society (Erikson, 1963).

Erikson's theory suggests that developmental change occurs throughout our lives in eight distinct stages (see Table 1-3). The stages emerge in a fixed pattern and are similar for all people. Erikson argued that each stage presents a crisis or conflict that the individual must resolve. Although no crisis is ever fully resolved, making life increasingly complicated, the individual must at least address the crisis of each stage sufficiently to deal with demands made during the next stage of development.

Unlike Freud, who regarded development as relatively complete by adolescence, Erikson suggested that growth and change continue throughout the life span. For instance, as we'll discuss further in Chapter 16, he suggested that during middle adulthood, people pass through the *generativity versus stagnation stage*, in which their contributions to family, community, and society can produce either positive feelings about the continuity of life or a sense of stagnation and disappointment about what they are passing on to future generations.

Assessing the Psychodynamic Perspective. It is hard for us to grasp the full significance of psychodynamic theories represented by Freud's psychoanalytic theory and Erikson's theory of psychosocial development. Freud's introduction of the notion that unconscious influences affect behavior was a monumental accomplishment, and that it seems at all reasonable to us shows how extensively the idea of the unconscious has pervaded thinking in Western cultures. In fact, work by contemporary researchers studying memory and learning suggests that we carry with us memories—of which we are not consciously aware—that have a significant impact on our behavior. The example of Janet, who was in a car accident when she was a baby, shows one application of psychodynamically based thinking and research.

Some of the most basic principles of Freud's psychoanalytic theory have been called into question, however, because they have not been validated by subsequent research. In particular, the notion that people pass through stages in childhood that determine their adult personalities has little definitive research support. In addition, because much of Freud's theory was based on a limited population of upper-middle-class Austrians living during a strict, puritanical era, its application to broad, multicultural populations is questionable. Finally, because Freud's theory focuses primarily on male development, it has been criticized as sexist and may be interpreted as devaluing women. For such reasons, many developmentalists question Freud's theory (Guthrie & Lonner, 1986; Brislin, 1993; Crews, 1993).

Erikson's view that development continues throughout the lifespan is highly important—and has received considerable support (Whitbourne, et al., 1992; Hetherington & Weinberger, 1993; Zauszniewski & Martin, 1999).

psychosexual development according to Freud, a series of stages that children pass through in which pleasure, or gratification, is focused on a particular biological function and body part

fixation behavior reflecting an earlier stage of development due to an unresolved conflict

psychosocial development the approach that encompasses changes in our interactions with and understandings of one another, as well as in our knowledge and understanding of ourselves as members of society

Erik Erikson

Table 1-3

FREUD'S AND ERIKSON'S THEORIES

Approximate Age	Freud's Stages of Psychosexual Development	Major Characteristics of Freud's Stages	Erikson's Stages of Psychosocial Development	Positive and Negative Outcomes of Erikson's Stages
Birth to 12–18 months	Oral	Interest in oral gratification from sucking, eating, mouthing, biting	Trust vs. mistrust	*Positive:* Feelings of trust from environmental support *Negative:* Fear and concern regarding others
12–18 months to 3 years	Anal	Gratification from expelling and withholding feces; coming to terms with society's controls relating to toilet training	Autonomy vs. shame and doubt	*Positive:* Self-sufficiency if exploration is encouraged *Negative:* Doubts about self, lack of independence
3 to 5–6 years	Phallic	Interest in the genitals; coming to terms with Oedipal conflict, leading to identification with same-sex parent	Initiative vs. guilt	*Positive:* Discovery of ways to initiate actions *Negative:* Guilt from actions and thoughts
5–6 years to adolescence	Latency	Sexual concerns largely unimportant	Industry vs. inferiority	*Positive:* Development of sense of competence *Negative:* Feelings of inferiority, no sense of mastery
Adolescence to adulthood (Freud) Adolescence (Erikson)	Genital	Reemergence of sexual interests and establishment of mature sexual relationships	Identity vs. role diffusion	*Positive:* Awareness of uniqueness of self, knowledge of role to be followed *Negative:* Inability to identify appropriate roles in life
Early adult-hood (Erikson)			Intimacy vs. isolation	*Positive:* Development of loving, sexual relationships and close friendships *Negative:* Fear of relationships with others
Middle adult-hood (Erikson)			Generativity vs. stagnation	*Positive:* Sense of contribution to continuity of life *Negative:* Trivialization of one's activities
Late adult-hood (Erikson)			Ego-integrity vs. despair	*Positive:* Sense of unity in life's accomplishments *Negative:* Regret over lost opportunities of life

However, the theory also has its drawbacks. Like Freud's theory, it focuses more on men's than women's development. It is also vague in some respects, making it difficult for researchers to test rigorously. And, as is the case with psychodynamic theories in general, it is difficult to make definitive predictions about a given individual's behavior using the theory. In sum, then, the psychodynamic perspective provides good descriptions of past behavior, but imprecise predictions of future behavior.

The Behavioral Perspective: Considering the Outer Person

When Elissa Sheehan was three, a large brown dog bit her, and she needed dozens of stitches and several operations. From the time she was bitten, she broke into a sweat whenever she saw a dog, and in fact never enjoyed being around any pet.

To a lifespan development specialist using the behavioral perspective, the explanation for Elissa's behavior is straightforward: She has a learned fear of dogs. Rather than looking inside the organism at unconscious processes, the **behavioral perspective** suggests

behavioral perspective the approach that suggests that the keys to understanding development are observable behavior and outside stimuli in the environment

that the keys to understanding development are observable behavior and outside stimuli in the environment. If we know the stimuli, we can predict the behavior.

Behavioral theories reject the notion that people universally pass through a series of stages. Instead, people are assumed to be affected by the environmental stimuli to which they happen to be exposed. Developmental patterns, then, are personal, reflecting a particular set of environmental stimuli, and behavior is the result of continuing exposure to specific factors in the environment. Furthermore, developmental change is viewed in quantitative, rather than qualitative, terms. For instance, behavioral theories hold that advances in problem-solving capabilities as children age are largely a result of greater mental *capacities*, rather than changes in the *kind* of thinking that children are able to bring to bear on a problem.

Classical Conditioning: Stimulus Substitution

John B. Watson

> Give me a dozen healthy infants, well-formed, and my own specified world to bring them up in and I'll guarantee to take any one at random and train him to become any type of specialist I might select—doctor, lawyer, artist, merchant-chief, and yes, even beggar-man and thief, regardless of his talents, penchants, tendencies, abilities. . . . (Watson, 1925)

With these words, John B. Watson, one of the first American psychologists to advocate a behavioral approach, summed up the behavioral perspective. Watson, who lived from 1878 to 1958, believed strongly that we could gain a full understanding of development by carefully studying the stimuli that compose the environment. In fact, he argued that by effectively controlling a person's environment, it was possible to produce virtually any behavior.

As we'll consider further in Chapter 5, **classical conditioning** occurs when an organism learns to respond in a particular way to a neutral stimulus that normally does not evoke that type of response. For instance, if a dog is repeatedly exposed to the pairing of two stimuli, such as the sound of a bell and the presentation of meat, it may learn to react to the bell alone in the same way it reacts to the meat—by salivating and wagging its tail with excitement. Dogs don't typically respond to bells in this way; the behavior is a result of stimulus substitution.

The same process of classical conditioning explains how we learn emotional responses. In the case of dog-bite victim Elissa Sheehan, for instance, one stimulus has been substituted for another: Elissa's unpleasant experience with a particular dog (the initial stimulus) has been transferred to other dogs and to pets in general.

classical conditioning a type of learning in which an organism responds in a particular way to a neutral stimulus that normally does not bring about that type of response

operant conditioning a form of learning in which a voluntary response is strengthened or weakened by its association with positive or negative consequences

Operant Conditioning. In addition to classical conditioning, other types of learning derive from the behavioral perspective. In fact, the learning approach that probably has had the greatest influence is operant conditioning. **Operant conditioning** is a form of learning in which a voluntary response is strengthened or weakened by its association with positive or negative consequences.

In operant conditioning, formulated and championed by psychologist B. F. Skinner (1904–1990), individuals learn to act deliberately on their environments in order to bring about desired consequences (Skinner, 1975). In a sense, then, people *operate* on their environments to bring about a desired state of affairs.

Whether or not children and adults will seek to repeat a behavior depends on whether it is followed by reinforcement. *Reinforcement* is the process by which a stimulus is provided that increases the probability that a preceding behavior will be repeated. Hence, a student is apt to work harder in school if he or she receives good grades; workers are likely to labor harder at their jobs if their efforts are tied to pay increases; and people are more apt to buy lottery tickets if they are reinforced by winning occasionally. In addition, *punishment*, the introduction of an unpleasant or painful stimulus or the removal of a desirable stimulus, will decrease the probability that a preceding behavior will occur in the future.

Behavior that is reinforced, then, is more likely to be repeated in the future, while behavior that receives no reinforcement or is punished is likely to be discontinued, or in the language of operant conditioning, *extinguished*. Principles of operant conditioning are used in **behavior modification,** a formal technique for promoting the frequency of desirable behaviors and decreasing the incidence of unwanted ones. Behavior modification has been used in a variety of situations, ranging from teaching severely retarded people the rudiments of language to helping people stick to diets (Sulzer-Azaroff & Mayer, 1991; Berigan & Deagle, 1999; Katz, 2001).

Social-Cognitive Learning Theory: Learning through Imitation. Beavis and Butt-head, cartoon characters on MTV, discuss how enjoyable it is to set fires. On at least one occasion, one of them lights the other's hair on fire using matches and an aerosol spray can. Not long after seeing the show, 5-year-old Austin Messner sets his bed on fire with a cigarette lighter, starting a blaze that kills his younger sister.

Cause and effect? We can't know for sure, but it certainly seems possible, especially looking at the situation from the perspective of social-cognitive learning theory. According to developmental psychologist Albert Bandura and colleagues, a significant amount of learning is explained by **social-cognitve learning theory,** an approach that emphasizes learning by observing the behavior of another person, called a *model* (Bandura, 1977, 1994).

Rather than learning being a matter of trial and error, as it is with operant conditioning, in social-cognitive learning theory behavior is learned through observation. We don't need to experience the consequences of a behavior ourselves to learn it. Social-cognitive learning theory holds that when we see the behavior of a model being rewarded, we are likely to imitate that behavior. For instance, in one classic experiment, children who were afraid of dogs were exposed to a model, nicknamed the "Fearless Peer," who was seen playing happily with a dog (Bandura, Grusec, & Menlove, 1967). After exposure, the children who previously had been afraid were more likely to approach a strange dog than children who had not seen the model.

Bandura suggests that social-cognitive learning proceeds in four steps (Bandura, 1986). First, an observer must pay attention and perceive the most critical features of a model's behavior. Second, the observer must successfully recall the behavior. Third, the observer must reproduce the behavior accurately. Finally, the observer must be motivated to learn and carry out the behavior.

Assessing the Behavioral Perspective. The behavioral perspective has had an important influence within the field of lifespan development. Work using the behavioral perspective has made significant contributions, ranging from techniques for educating children with severe mental retardation to identifying procedures for curbing aggression.

At the same time, there are controversies regarding the behavioral perspective. For example, although they are part of the same general behavioral perspective, classical and operant conditioning and social learning theory disagree in some basic ways. Both classical and operant conditioning consider learning in terms of external stimuli and responses, in which the only important factors are the observable features of the environment. In such an analysis, people and other organisms are "black boxes"; nothing that occurs inside the box is understood—nor much cared about, for that matter.

To social learning theorists, such an analysis is an oversimplification. They argue that what makes people different from rats and pigeons is mental activity, in the form of thoughts and expectations. A full understanding of people's development, they maintain, cannot occur without moving beyond external stimuli and responses.

behavior modification a formal technique for promoting the frequency of desirable behaviors and decreasing the incidence of unwanted ones

social-cognitive learning theory learning by observing the behavior of another person, called a model

According to social-cognitive learning theory, observation of shows such as Beavis and Butthead can produce significant amounts of learning—not all of it positive.

In many ways, social learning theory has come to predominate in recent decades over classical and operant conditioning theories. In fact, another perspective that focuses explicitly on internal mental activity has become enormously influential. This is the cognitive approach, which we consider next.

The Cognitive Perspective: Examining the Roots of Understanding

When 3-year-old Jake is asked why it sometimes rains, he answers "so the flowers can grow." When his 11-year-old sister Lila is asked the same question, she responds "because of evaporation from the surface of the Earth." And when their cousin Ajima, who is studying meteorology in graduate school, considers the same question, her extended answer includes a discussion of cumulonimbus clouds, the Coriolis effect, and synoptic charts.

To a developmental theorist using the cognitive perspective, the difference in the sophistication of the answers is evidence of a different degree of knowledge and understanding, or cognition. The **cognitive perspective** focuses on the processes that allow people to know, understand, and think about the world.

The cognitive perspective emphasizes how people internally represent and think about the world. By using this perspective, developmental researchers hope to understand how children and adults process information and how their ways of thinking and understanding affect their behavior. They also seek to learn how cognitive abilities change as people develop, the degree to which cognitive development represents quantitative and qualitative growth in intellectual abilities, and how different cognitive abilities are related to one another (Salthouse, 1989).

Piaget's Theory of Cognitive Development. No single person has had a greater impact on the study of cognitive development than Jean Piaget. A Swiss psychologist who lived from 1896 to 1980, Piaget proposed that all people pass in a fixed sequence through a series of universal stages of cognitive development. He suggested that not only does the quantity of information increase in each stage, but the quality of knowledge and understanding changes as well. His focus was on the change in cognition that occurs as children move from one stage to the next (Piaget, 1952, 1962, 1983).

Although we'll consider Piaget's theory in detail beginning in Chapter 5, we can get a broad sense of it now by looking at some of its main features. Piaget suggested that human thinking is arranged into *schemes*, organized mental patterns that represent behaviors and actions. In infants, such schemes represent concrete behavior—a scheme for sucking, for reaching, and for each separate behavior. In older children, the schemes become more sophisticated and abstract. Schemes are like intellectual computer software that directs and determines how data from the world are looked at and dealt with (Achenbach, 1992).

Piaget suggests that the growth in children's understanding of the world can be explained by two basic principles. **Assimilation** is the process in which people understand an experience in terms of their current stage of cognitive development and way of thinking. In contrast, **accommodation** refers to changes in existing ways of thinking in response to encounters with new stimuli or events.

Assimilation occurs when people use their current ways of thinking about and understanding the world to perceive and understand a new experience. For example, a young child who has not yet learned to count will look at two rows of buttons, each containing the same number of buttons, and say that a row in which the buttons are closely spaced together has fewer buttons than a row in which the buttons are more spread out. The experience of counting buttons, then, is *assimilated* to already existing schemes that contain the principle "bigger is more."

Later, however, when the child is older and has had sufficient exposure to new experiences, the content of the scheme will undergo change. In understanding that the quan-

cognitive perspective the approach that focuses on the processes that allow people to know, understand, and think about the world

assimilation the process in which people understand an experience in terms of their current stage of cognitive development and way of thinking

accommodation the process that changes existing ways of thinking in response to encounters with new stimuli or events

tity of buttons is identical whether they are spread out or closely spaced, the child has *accommodated* to the experience. Assimilation and accommodation work in tandem to bring about cognitive development.

Assessing Piaget's Theory. Piaget was without peer in influencing our understanding of cognitive development, and he is one of the towering figures in lifespan development. He provided masterful descriptions of how intellectual growth proceeds during childhood—descriptions which have stood the test of literally thousands of investigations. By and large, then, Piaget's broad view of the sequence of cognitive development is accurate.

However, the specifics of the theory, particularly in terms of change in cognitive capabilities over time, have been called into question. For instance, some cognitive skills clearly emerge earlier than Piaget suggested. Furthermore, the universality of Piaget's stages has been disputed. A growing amount of evidence suggests that the emergence of particular cognitive skills occurs according to a different timetable in non-Western cultures. And in every culture, some people never seem to reach Piaget's highest level of cognitive sophistication: formal, logical thought (Rogoff & Chavajay, 1995).

Ultimately, the greatest criticism leveled at the Piagetian perspective is that cognitive development is not necessarily as discontinuous as Piaget's stage theory suggests. Remember that Piaget argued that growth proceeds in four distinct stages in which the quality of cognition differs from one stage to the next. However, many developmental researchers argue that growth is considerably more continuous. These critics have suggested an alternative perspective, known as the information processing approach, that focuses on the processes that underlie learning, memory, and thinking throughout the life span.

Information Processing Approaches. Information processing approaches have become an important alternative to Piagetian approaches. **Information processing approaches** to cognitive development seek to identify the ways individuals take in, use, and store information.

Information processing approaches grew out of developments in the electronic processing of information, particularly as carried out by computers. They assume that even complex behavior such as learning, remembering, categorizing, and thinking can be broken down into a series of individual, specific steps.

In stark contrast to Piaget's view that thinking undergoes qualitative advances as children age, information-processing approaches assume that development is marked more by quantitative advances. Our capacity to handle information changes with age, as does our processing speed and efficiency. Furthermore, information processing approaches suggest that as people age, we are better able to control the nature of processing and that we can change in the strategies we choose to process information.

Assessing Information Processing Approaches. As we'll see in future chapters, information-processing approaches have become a central part of our understanding of development. At the same time, they do not offer a complete explanation for behavior. For example, information-processing approaches have paid little attention to behavior such as creativity, in which the most profound ideas often are developed in a seemingly nonlogical, nonlinear manner. In addition, they do not take into account the social context in which development takes place. That's one of the reasons that theories that emphasize the social and cultural aspects of development have become increasingly popular—as we'll discuss next.

Vygotsky's Sociocultural Theory. To Russian child developmentalist Lev Semenovich Vygotsky, a full understanding of development was impossible without taking into account the culture in which children develop. Vygotsky's **sociocultural theory** emphasizes how cognitive development proceeds as a result of social interactions between members of a culture. (Vygotsky, 1979, 1926/1997; Wertsch & Tulviste, 1992; Beilin, 1996; Daniels, 1996).

information processing approaches the model that seeks to identify the ways individuals take in, use, and store information

sociocultural theory the approach that emphasizes how cognitive development proceeds as a result of social interactions between members of a culture

Vygotsky, who lived from 1896 to 1934, argued that children's understanding of the world is acquired through their problem-solving interactions with adults and other children. As children play and cooperate with others, they learn what is important in their society and, at the same time, advance cognitively in their understanding of the world. Consequently, to understand the course of development, we must consider what is meaningful to members of a given culture.

Assessing Vygotsky's Theory. Sociocultural theory has become increasingly influential, despite Vygotsky's death almost 70 years ago. The reason is the growing acknowledgment of the central importance of cultural factors in development. Children do not develop in a cultural vacuum. Instead, their attention is directed by society to certain areas, and as a consequence, they develop particular kinds of skills that are an outcome of their cultural environment. Vygotsky was one of the first developmentalists to recognize and acknowledge the importance of culture, and—as today's society becomes increasingly multicultural—sociocultural theory is helping us to understand the rich and varied influences that shape development (Reis, Collins, & Berscheid, 2000; Matusov & Hayes, 2000).

Sociocultural theory is not without its critics, however. Some suggest that Vygotsky's strong emphasis on the role of culture and social experience led him to ignore the effects of biological factors on development. In addition, his perspective seems to minimize the role that individuals can play in shaping their own environment. In fact, as we can see from the emphasis of the humanistic perspective—described next—each individual can play a central role in determining the course of his or her own development.

The Humanistic Perspective:
Concentrating on the Unique Qualities of Human Beings

The special qualities of humans provide the centerpiece of the humanistic perspective, the fourth of the major theories used by lifespan developmentalists. Rejecting the notion that our behavior is largely determined by unconscious processes, by learning from our environment, or by rational cognitive processing, the **humanistic perspective** contends that people

humanistic perspective the theory that contends that people have a natural capacity to make decisions about their lives and control their behavior

According to Vygotsky, children can develop cognitively in their understanding of the world, and learn what is important in society, through play and cooperation with others.

have a natural capacity to make decisions about their lives and to control their behavior. According to this approach, each individual has the ability and motivation to reach more advanced levels of maturity, and people naturally seek to reach their full potential.

The humanistic perspective emphasizes *free will*, the ability of humans to make choices and come to decisions about their lives. Instead of relying on societal standards, then, people are assumed to be motivated to make their own decisions about what they do with their lives.

Carl Rogers (1971), one of the major proponents of the humanistic perspective, suggests that all people have a need for positive regard that results from an underlying wish to be loved and respected. Because it is other people who provide this positive regard, we become dependent upon them. Consequently, our view of ourselves and our self-worth is a reflection of how we think others view us.

Rogers, along with another key figure in the humanistic perspective, Abraham Maslow, suggests that self-actualization is a primary goal in life. *Self-actualization* is a state of self-fulfillment in which people achieve their highest potential in their own unique way. Although the concept initially was deemed to apply to only a few select, famous people, such as Eleanor Roosevelt, Abraham Lincoln, and Albert Einstein, later theorists expanded the concept to apply to any person who realizes his or her own potential and possibilities (Maslow, 1970; Jones & Crandall, 1991).

Assessing the Humanistic Perspective. Despite its emphasis on important and unique human qualities, the humanistic perspective has not had a major impact upon the field of lifespan development. Its lack of influence is primarily due to its inability to identify any sort of broad developmental change that is the result of increasing age or experience. Still, some of the concepts drawn from the humanistic perspective, such as self-actualization, have helped describe important aspects of human behavior and are widely discussed in areas ranging from health care to business (Haymes, Green, & Quinto, 1984; Weiss, 1991; Neher, 1991).

Evolutionary Perspectives: Our Ancestors' Contributions to Behavior

One increasingly influential approach is the evolutionary perspective, the fifth and final developmental perspective that we will consider. The **evolutionary perspective** seeks to identify behavior that is the result of our genetic inheritance from our ancestors (Bjorklund & Pellegrini, 2000; Geary & Bjorklund, 2000).

Evolutionary approaches grow out of the groundbreaking work of Charles Darwin. In 1859, Darwin argued in his book *On the Origin of Species* that a process of natural selection creates traits in a species that are adaptive to its environment. Using Darwin's arguments, evolutionary approaches contend that our genetic inheritance not only determines such physical traits as skin and eye color, but certain personality traits and social behaviors as well. For instance, as we'll discuss further in future chapters, some evolutionary developmentalists suggest that people's levels of shyness or sociability are influenced by genetic factors (Plomin & McClearn, 1993).

The evolutionary perspective draws heavily on the field of *ethology*, which examines the ways in which our biological makeup influences our behavior. A primary proponent of ethology was Konrad Lorenz (1903–1989), who discovered that newborn geese are genetically preprogrammed to become attached to the first moving object they see after birth. His work, which demonstrated the importance of biological determinants in influencing behavior patterns, ultimately led developmentalists to consider the ways in which human behavior might reflect inborn genetic patterns.

As we'll consider further in Chapter 2, the evolutionary perspective encompasses one of the fastest growing areas within the field of lifespan development: behavioral genetics. *Behavioral genetics* studies the effects of heredity on behavior. Behavioral geneticists seek to un-

evolutionary perspective the theory that seeks to identify behavior that is a result of our genetic inheritance from our ancestors

Konrad Lorenz, seen here with geese imprinted to him, considered the ways in which behavior reflects inborn genetic patterns.

derstand how we might inherit certain behavioral traits and how the environment influences whether we actually display such traits. It also considers how genetic factors may produce psychological disorders such as schizophrenia (Bouchard, 1994; Lander & Schork, 1994; Mowry, Nancarrow, & Levinson, 1997; Freedman, Adler, & Leonard, 1999).

Assessing the Evolutionary Perspective. Although the evolutionary perspective is increasingly visible in the field of lifespan development, it has been subjected to considerable criticism. Some developmentalists are concerned that because of its focus on genetic and biological aspects of behavior, the evolutionary perspective pays insufficient attention to the environmental and social factors involved in producing children's and adults' behavior. Other critics argue that there is no good way to experimentally test theories derived from the evolutionary approach. Still, the evolutionary approach has stimulated a significant amount of research on how our biological inheritance influences at least partially our traits and behaviors (Baltes, 1997; Dent-Read & Zukow-Goldring, 1997; Bjorklund, 1997a; Leonard,1998).

Which Approach Is Right? The Wrong Question

We have considered the five major perspectives on development: psychodynamic, behavioral, cognitive, humanistic, and evolutionary—summarized in Table 1-4. It would be natural to wonder which of the five provides the most accurate account of human development.

For several reasons, this is not an entirely appropriate question. For one thing, each perspective emphasizes somewhat different aspects of development. For instance, the psychodynamic approach emphasizes emotions, motivational conflicts, and unconscious determinants of behavior. In contrast, behavioral perspectives emphasize overt behavior, paying far more attention to what people *do* than to what goes on inside their heads, which is deemed largely irrelevant. The cognitive and humanistic perspectives take quite the opposite tack, looking more at what people *think* than at what they do. Finally, the evolutionary perspective focuses on how inherited biological factors underlie development.

Table 1-4

MAJOR PERSPECTIVES ON LIFE SPAN DEVELOPMENT

Perspective	Key Ideas about Human Behavior and Development	Major Proponents	Example
Psychodynamic	Behavior throughout life is motivated by inner, unconscious forces, stemming from childhood, over which we have little control.	Sigmund Freud, Erik Erikson	This view might suggest that a young adult who is overweight has a fixation in the oral stage of development.
Behavioral	Development can be understood through studying observable behavior and environmental stimuli.	John B. Watson, B.F. Skinner, Albert Bandura	In this perspective, a young adult who is overweight might be seen as not being rewarded for good nutritional and exercise habits.
Cognitive	Emphasis is on how changes or growth in the ways people know, understand, and think about the world affect behavior.	Jean Piaget, Lev Vygotsky	This view might suggest that a young adult who is overweight hasn't learned effective ways to stay at a healthy weight and doesn't value good nutrition.
Humanistic	Behavior is chosen through *free will* and motivated by our natural capacity to strive to reach our full potential.	Carl Rogers, Abraham Maslow	In this view, a young adult who is overweight may eventually choose to seek an optimal weight as part of an overall pattern of individual growth.
Evolutionary	Behavior is the result of genetic inheritance from our ancestors; traits and behavior that are adaptive for promoting the survival of our species have been inherited through natural selection.	Influenced by early work of Charles Darwin, Konrad Lorenz	This view might suggest that a young adult might have a genetic tendency towards obesity because extra fat helped his or her ancestors to survive in times of famine.

For example, a developmentalist using the psychodynamic approach might consider how the terrorist attacks on the World Trade Center and Pentagon might affect children, unconsciously, for their entire life span. A cognitive approach might focus on how children perceived and came to interpret and understand the terrorism, while a humanistic approach might focus on how children's aspirations and ability to reach their potential were affected.

Clearly, each perspective is based on its own premises and focuses on different aspects of development. Furthermore, the same developmental phenomenon can be looked at from a number of perspectives simultaneously. In fact, some lifespan developmentalists use an *eclectic* approach, drawing on several perspectives simultaneously.

We can think of the different perspectives as analogous to a set of maps of the same general geographic area. One map may contain detailed depictions of roads; another map may show geographical features; another may show political subdivisions, such as cities, towns, and counties; and still another may highlight particular points of interest, such as scenic areas and historical landmarks. Each of the maps is accurate, but each provides a different point of view and way of thinking. No one map is "complete," but by considering them together, we can come to a fuller understanding of the area.

In the same way, the various theoretical perspectives provide different ways of looking at development. Considering them together paints a full portrait of the myriad ways human beings change and grow over the course of their lives. However, not all theories and claims derived from the various perspectives are accurate. How do we choose among competing explanations? The answer is *research,* which we consider in the final part of this chapter.

The diversity of America is reflected in these children's faces.

Review and Rethink

REVIEW

■ The psychodynamic perspective looks primarily at the influence of internal, unconscious forces on development.

■ The behavioral perspective focuses on external, observable behaviors as the key to development.

■ The cognitive perspective focuses on mental activity.

■ The humanistic perspective concentrates on the theory that each individual has the ability and motivation to reach more advanced levels of maturity and that people naturally seek to reach their full potential.

■ Finally, the evolutionary perspective seeks to identify behavior that is a result of our genetic inheritance from our ancestors.

RETHINK

■ How do the concepts of social learning and modeling relate to the mass media?

■ What examples of human behavior have you seen that seem as though they may have been inherited from our ancestors? Why do you think they are inherited?

Research Methods

The Egyptians had long believed that they were the most ancient race on earth, and Psamtik [King of Egypt in the 7th century, B.C.], driven by intellectual curiosity, wanted to prove that flattering belief. Like a good researcher, he began with a hypothesis: If children had no opportunity to learn a language from older people around them, they would spontaneously speak the primal, inborn language of humankind—the natural language of its most ancient people—which, he expected to show, was Egyptian.

To test his hypothesis, Psamtik commandeered two infants of a lower-class mother and turned them over to a herdsman to bring up in a remote area. They were to be kept in a sequestered cottage, properly fed and cared for, but were never to hear anyone speak so much as a word. The Greek historian Herodotus, who tracked the story down and learned what he calls "the real facts" from priests of Hephaestus in Memphis, says that Psamtik's goal "was to know, after the indistinct babblings of infancy were over, what word they would first articulate."

The experiment, he tells us, worked. One day, when the children were two years old, they ran up to the herdsman as he opened the door of their cottage and cried out "Becos!" Since this meant nothing to him, he paid no attention, but when it happened repeatedly, he sent word to Psamtik, who at once ordered the children brought to him. When he too heard them say it, Psamtik made inquiries and learned that becos *was the Phrygian word for bread. He concluded that, disappointingly, the Phrygians were an older race than the Egyptians. (Hunt, 1993, pp. 1–2)*

With the perspective of several thousand years, we can easily see the shortcomings—both scientific and ethical—in Psamtik's approach. Yet his procedure represents an improvement over mere speculation, and as such is sometimes looked upon as the first developmental experiment in recorded history (Hunt, 1993).

Theories and Hypotheses: Posing Developmental Questions

Questions such as those raised by Psamtik lie at the heart of the study of development. Is language innate? What are the effects of malnutrition on later intellectual performance? How do infants form relationships with their parents, and does participation in day care disrupt such relationships? Why are adolescents susceptible to peer pressure? Are there declines in intellectual abilities related to aging?

To resolve such questions, developmentalists rely on the scientific method. The **scientific method** is the process of posing and answering questions using careful, controlled techniques that include systematic, orderly observation and the collection of data.

scientific method the process of posing and answering questions using careful, controlled techniques that include systematic, orderly observation and the collection of data

The scientific method involves the formulation of theories, broad explanations, and predictions about phenomena of interest. We've just reviewed the five major theoretical perspectives that most strongly influence researchers in lifespan development. Researchers also develop more specific theories. In fact, all of us develop theories about development. For instance, many people theorize that there is a crucial bonding period between parent and child immediately after birth, which is a necessary ingredient in forming a lasting parent–child relationship. Without such a bonding period, they assume, the parent–child relationship will be forever compromised (Furnham & Weir, 1996).

hypothesis a prediction stated in a way that permits it to be tested

Developmental researchers use theories to form hypotheses. A **hypothesis** is a prediction stated in a way that permits it to be tested. For instance, someone who subscribes to the general theory that bonding is a crucial ingredient in the parent–child relationship might derive the more specific hypothesis that adopted children whose adoptive parents never had the chance to bond with them immediately after birth may ultimately have less secure relationships with their adoptive parents. Others might derive other hypotheses, such as that effective bonding occurs only if it lasts for a certain length of time, or that bonding affects the mother–child relationship, but not the father–child relationship. (In case you're wondering: As we'll discuss in Chapter 3, these particular hypotheses have *not* been upheld; there are no long-term reactions to the separation of parent and child immediately after birth, even if the separation lasts several days.)

Choosing a Research Strategy: Answering Questions

Once researchers have formed a hypothesis, they must develop a research strategy for testing its validity. There are two major categories of research: correlational research and experimental research. **Correlational research** seeks to identify whether an association or relationship between two factors exists. As we'll see, correlational research cannot be used to determine whether one factor causes changes in the other. For instance, correlational research could tell us if there is an association between the number of minutes a mother and her newborn child are together immediately after birth and the quality of the mother–child relationship when the child reaches 2 years of age. Such correlational research indicates whether the two factors are *associated* or *related* to one another, but not whether the initial contact caused the relationship to develop in a particular way (Schutt, 2001).

In contrast, **experimental research** is designed to discover *causal* relationships between various factors. In experimental research, researchers deliberately introduce a change in a situation in order to see the consequences of that change. For instance, a researcher conducting an experiment might vary the number of minutes that mothers and children interact immediately following birth, in an attempt to see whether the amount of bonding time affects the mother–child relationship.

Because experimental research is able to answer questions of causality, it represents the heart of developmental research. However, some research questions cannot be answered through experiments, for either technical or ethical reasons. In fact, a great deal of pioneering developmental research—such as that conducted by Piaget and Vygotsky—employed correlational techniques. Consequently, correlational research remains an important tool in the developmental researcher's toolbox.

Correlational Studies

As we've noted, correlational research examines the relationship between two variables to determine whether they are associated, or *correlated*. For instance, researchers interested in the relationship between televised aggression and subsequent behavior have found that children who watch a good deal of aggression on television—murders, crime shows, shootings, and the like—tend to be more aggressive than those who watch only a little. In other words, as we'll discuss in greater detail in Chapter 15, viewing of aggression and actual aggression are strongly associated, or correlated, with one another (Center for Communication & Social Policy, 1998).

But does this mean we can conclude that the viewing of televised aggression *causes* the more aggressive behavior of the viewers? Not at all. Consider some of the other possibilities: It might be that being aggressive in the first place makes children more likely to choose to watch violent programs. In such a case, then, it is the aggressive tendency that causes the viewing behavior, and not the other way around.

Or consider another possibility. Suppose that children who are raised in poverty are more likely to behave aggressively *and* to watch higher levels of aggressive television than those raised in more affluent settings. In this case, it is socioeconomic status that causes *both* the aggressive behavior and the television viewing. (The various possibilities are illustrated in Figure 1-2).

In short, finding that two variables are correlated proves nothing about causality. Although it is possible that the variables are linked causally, this is not necessarily the case.

correlational research research that seeks to identify whether an association or relationship between two factors exists

experimental research research designed to discover causal relationships between various factors

In experimental research, one uses controlled conditions to attempt to discover causal relationships between various factors.

On the other hand, correlational studies can provide important information. For instance, as we'll see in later chapters, we know from correlational studies that the closer the genetic link between two people, the more highly associated is their intelligence. We have learned that the more parents speak to their young children, the more extensive are the children's vocabularies. And we know from correlational studies that the better the nutri-

Figure 1-2 **Finding a Correlation**

Finding a correlation between two factors does not imply that one factor *causes* the other factor to vary. For instance, suppose a study found that viewing television shows with high levels of aggression is correlated with actual aggression in children. The correlation may reflect at least three possibilities: (a) watching television programs containing high levels of aggression causes aggression in viewers; (b) children who behave aggressively choose to watch TV programs with high levels of aggression; or (c) some third factor, such as a child's socioeconomic status, leads both to high viewer aggression and to choosing to watch television programs with high viewer aggression. What other factors, besides socioeconomic status, might be plausible third factors?

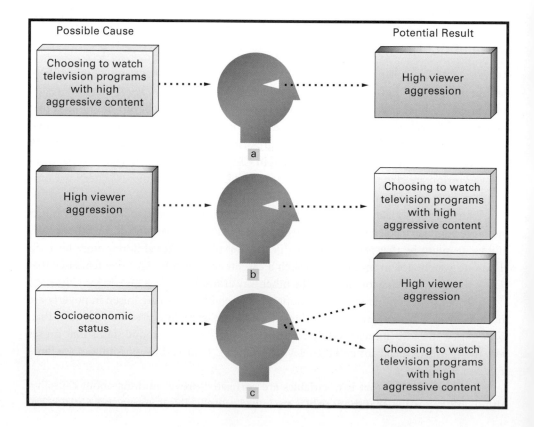

tion that infants receive, the fewer the cognitive and social problems they experience later (Pollitt et al., 1993; Hart & Risley, 1995).

The Correlation Coefficient. The strength and direction of a relationship between two factors is represented by a mathematical score, called a *correlation coefficient*, that ranges from +1.0 to −1.0. A positive correlation indicates that as the value of one factor increases, it can be predicted that the value of the other will also increase. For instance, if we find that the more money people make in their first job after college, the higher their scores on a survey of job satisfaction, and that people who make less money have lower scores when surveyed about their job satisfaction, we have found a positive correlation. (Higher values of the factor "salary" are associated with higher values of the factor "job satisfaction," and lower values of "salary" are associated with lower values of "job satisfaction.") The correlation coefficient, then, would be indicated by a positive number, and the stronger the association between salary and job satisfaction, the closer the number would be to +1.0.

In contrast, a correlation coefficient with a negative value informs us that as the value of one factor increases, the value of the other factor declines. For example, suppose we found that the greater the number of hours adolescents spend using instant messaging on their computers, the worse their academic performance is. Such a finding would result in a negative correlation, ranging between 0 and −1. More instant messaging is associated with lower performance, and less instant messaging is associated with better performance. The stronger the association between instant messaging and school performance, the closer the correlation coefficient will be to −1.0.

Finally, it is possible that two factors are unrelated to one another. For example, it is unlikely that we would find a correlation between school performance and shoe size. In this case, the lack of a relationship would be indicated by a correlation coefficient close to 0.

It is important to reiterate what we noted earlier: Even if the correlation coefficient involving two variables is very strong, there is no way we can know whether one factor *causes* another factor to vary. It simply means that the two factors are associated with one another in a predictable way.

Types of Correlational Studies. There are several types of correlational studies. **Naturalistic observation** is the observation of a naturally occurring behavior without intervention in the situation. For instance, an investigator who wishes to learn how often preschool children share toys with one another might observe a classroom over a 3-week period, recording how often the preschoolers spontaneously share with one another. The key point about naturalistic observation is that the investigator simply observes the children, without interfering with the situation whatsoever (Erlandson et al., 1993; Adler & Adler, 1994; Blasko, et al., 1998).

> **naturalistic observation** a type of correlational study in which some naturally occurring behavior is observed without intervention in the situation

While naturalistic observation has the advantage of identifying what children do in their "natural habitat," there is an important drawback to the method: Researchers are unable to exert control over factors of interest. For instance, in some cases researchers might find so few naturally occurring instances of the behavior of interest that they are unable to draw any conclusions at all. In addition, children who know they are being watched may modify their behavior as a result of the observation. Consequently, their behavior may not be representative of how they would behave if they were not being watched.

Increasingly, naturalistic observation employs *ethnography*, a method borrowed from the field of anthropology and used to investigate cultural questions. In ethnography, a researcher's goal is to understand a culture's values and attitudes through careful, extended examination. Typically, researchers using ethnography act as participant observers, living for a period of weeks, months, or even years in another culture. By carefully observing everyday life and conducting in-depth interviews, researchers are able to obtain a deep understanding of the nature of life within another culture (Fetterman, 1998).

Although ethnographic studies provide a fine-grained view of everyday behavior in another culture, they suffer from several drawbacks. As mentioned, the presence of a participant observer may influence the behavior of the individuals being studied. Furthermore, because only a small number of individuals are studied, it may be hard to generalize the findings to people in other cultures. Finally, ethnographers may misinterpret and misconceive what they are observing, particularly in cultures that are very different from their own (Hammersley, 1992).

Case studies involve extensive, in-depth interviews with a particular individual or small group of individuals. They often are used not just to learn about the individual being interviewed, but to derive broader principles or draw tentative conclusions that might apply to others. For example, case studies have been conducted on children who display unusual genius and on children who have spent their early years in the wild, apparently without human contact. These case studies have provided important information to researchers, and have suggested hypotheses for future investigation (Lane, 1976; Feldman & Goldsmith, 1991; Hebert, 1998; Goldsmith, 2000).

Surveys represent another sort of correlational research. In **survey research,** a group of people chosen to represent some larger population are asked questions about their attitudes, behavior, or thinking on a given topic. For instance, surveys have been conducted about parents' use of punishment on their children and on attitudes toward breastfeeding. From the responses, inferences are drawn regarding the larger population represented by the individuals being surveyed. (An example of the kind of developmental information about children and families that can be obtained from surveys is provided in the *Speaking of Development* box.)

Experiments: Determining Cause and Effect

In an **experiment**, an investigator, called an *experimenter*, typically devises two different experiences for *participants*, or *subjects*. These two different experiences are called treatments. A **treatment** is a procedure applied by an investigator. One group of participants receives one of the treatments, while another group of participants receives either no treatment or an alternative treatment. The group receiving the treatment is known as the **treatment group** (sometimes called the *experimental group*), while the no-treatment or alternative-treatment group is called the **control group.**

Although the terminology may seem daunting at first, there is an underlying logic to it that helps sort it out. Think in terms of a medical experiment in which the aim is to test the effectiveness of a new drug. In testing the drug, we wish to see if the drug successfully *treats* the disease. Consequently, the group that receives the drug would be called the *treatment* group. In comparison, another group of participants would not receive the drug treatment. Instead, they would be part of the no-treatment *control* group.

Similarly, suppose we wish to explore the consequences of exposure to movie violence on viewers' subsequent aggression. We might take a group of adolescents and show them a series of movies that contain a great deal of violent imagery. We would then measure their subsequent aggression. This group would constitute the treatment group. But we would also need another group—a control group. To fulfill this need, we might take a second group of adolescents, show them movies that contain no aggressive imagery, and then measure their subsequent aggression. This would be the control group.

By comparing the amount of aggression displayed by members of the treatment and control groups, we would be able to determine if exposure to violent imagery produces aggression in viewers. And this is just what a group of researchers found: Running an experi-

case studies studies that involve extensive, in-depth interviews with a particular individual or small group of individuals

survey research a type of study where a group of people chosen to represent some larger population are asked questions about their attitudes, behavior, or thinking on a given topic

experiment a process in which an investigator, called an experimenter, devises two different experiences for subjects or participants

treatment a procedure applied by an investigator based on two different experiences devised for participants (See **Experiment**)

treatment group the group in an experiment that receives the treatment

control group the group in an experiment that receives either no treatment or alternative treatment

SPEAKING OF DEVELOPMENT

Donald J. Hernandez

EDUCATION: University of Illinois at Urbana, B.A. in sociology University of California at Berkeley, M.A. and Ph.D. in sociology

POSITION: Chief of the Marriage and Family Statistics branch of the U.S. Bureau of the Census

HOME: Silver Spring, Maryland

According to Donald J. Hernandez, when it comes to family life, there wasn't just one American Revolution; there have been five—and counting.

Hernandez, who conducts research on the evolution of the family, has uncovered statistics that put into clear perspective where the American family came from and where it is today. Hernandez is the chief of the Marriage and Family Statistics branch of the U.S. Bureau of the Census, and he has published his research findings in a book entitled *America's Children: Resources from Family, Government and the Economy.*

Hernandez's findings indicate that over the past 150 years, the family in America has been completely transformed by a series of revolutions. "Three of these revolutions started in the 1800s," he explains. "The first was caused by the rise in non-farm work by the father of the family. In the mid-1800s most families were farm families. Fathers, mothers, and children worked together on the farm, day-in and day-out, to support themselves. But by the mid-1900s most fathers worked outside the home much of the day, earning income to support the family, while the mother's role became that of homemaker.

"During the same period," Hernandez continues, "a second revolution occurred—this one in family size. While most families in the mid-1800s had eight or more children, the figure dropped to two or three children in the 1930s. There was enormous pressure at the time to move off farms and to have fewer children."

The third major change, according to Hernandez, was a marked increase in schooling for America's children. "About half of children aged 5 to 19 were enrolled in school in 1870, but by the 1930s 95 percent of children 7 to 13, and 79 percent of children 14 to 17, were enrolled."

The next two revolutions uncovered by Hernandez involve women's entry into the workforce and, since 1960, the rise of the one-parent, mother-only family.

"In 1940, one in 10 children had a working mother. Today about 60 percent of children have mothers who work for pay," he explains. "Similarly, from 1940 to 1960 only 6 to 8 percent of children lived in a mother-only family. As of 1993 the figure was close to 23 percent."

A number of factors have contributed to the changes in the American family, says Hernandez, including the shift of the country's focus from agriculture to industry, new government policies, and the economy.

"There has been an increase of children born into poverty since the late 1970s. This is widely attributed to the rise in one-parent families, but the fact is that the economy and unemployment continue to be major contributors," he explains. "Parents face many obstacles. They don't have much money and they have to deal constantly with economic insecurity. This can lead to divorce. Economic factors have been very important influences on family changes, and on the poverty that results."

One statistic that amazed Hernandez clearly demonstrates that the so-called "Ozzie and Harriet family" is a myth. Hernandez defines such a family as one in which the father works full-time, the mother is not in the paid labor force, and all the children are born after the parents' only marriage.

"Not once in the last 50 years have the majority of children lived in Ozzie and Harriet families," he says. "In 1940, 41 percent of children under one year of age lived in such families. The figure jumped a bit—to 43 percent—in 1960. Estimates today indicate that less than one-fourth of children under one year of age live in families that meet the definition."

---

ment of this very sort, psychologist Jacques-Philippe Leyens and colleagues at the University of Louvain in Belgium found that the level of aggression rose significantly for the adolescents who had seen the movies containing violence (Leyens et al., 1975).

The central feature of this experiment—and all experiments—is the comparison of the consequences of different treatments. The use of both treatment and control groups allows researchers to rule out the possibility that something other than the experimental manipulation produced the results found in the experiment. For instance, if a control

independent variable the variable that researchers manipulate in an experiment

dependent variable the variable that researchers measure in an experiment and expect to change as a result of the experimental manipulation

sample the group of participants chosen for the experiment

field study a research investigation carried out in a naturally occurring setting

group was not used, experimenters could not be certain that some other factor, such as the time of day the movies were shown, the need to sit still during the movie, or even the mere passage of time, produced the changes that were observed. By employing a control group, then, experimenters can draw accurate conclusions about causes and effects.

The formation of treatment and control groups represents the independent variable in an experiment. The **independent variable** is the variable that researchers manipulate in the experiment. In contrast, the **dependent variable** is the variable that researchers measure in an experiment and expect to change as a result of the experimental manipulation. (One way to remember the difference: A hypothesis predicts how a dependent variable *depends* on the manipulation of the independent variable.) In an experiment studying the effects of taking a drug, for instance, manipulating whether participants receive or don't receive a drug is the independent variable. Measurement of the effectiveness of the drug or no-drug treatment is the dependent variable.

To consider another example, let's take the Belgian study of the consequences of observing filmed aggression on future aggression. In this experiment, the independent variable is the *level of aggressive imagery* viewed by participants—determined by whether they viewed films containing aggressive imagery (the treatment group) or devoid of aggressive imagery (the control group). The dependent variable in the study? It was what the experimenters expected to vary as a consequence of viewing a film: the *aggressive behavior* shown by participants after they had viewed the films, as measured by the experimenters. Every experiment has an independent and dependent variable.

One critical step in the design of experiments is to assign participants to different treatment groups. The procedure that is used is known as random assignment. In *random assignment*, participants are assigned to different experimental groups or "conditions" on the basis of chance and chance alone. By using this technique, the laws of statistics ensure that personal characteristics that might affect the outcome of the experiment are divided proportionally among the participants in the different groups, making groups equivalent. Equivalent groups achieved by random assignment allow an experimenter to draw conclusions with confidence (Boruch, 1998).

Given the advantage of experimental research—that it provides a means of determining causality—why aren't experiments always used? The answer is that there are some situations that a researcher, no matter how ingenious, simply cannot control. And there are some situations in which control would be unethical, even if it were possible. For instance, no researcher would be able to assign different groups of infants to parents of high and low socioeconomic status in order to learn the effects of such status on subsequent development. Similarly, we cannot control what a group of children watch on television throughout their childhood years in order to learn if childhood exposure to televised aggression leads to aggressive behavior later in life. Consequently, in situations in which experiments are logistically or ethically impossible, developmentalists employ correlational research.

Choosing a Research Setting. Deciding *where* to conduct a study may be as important as determining *what* to do. In the Belgian experiment on the influence of exposure to media aggression, the researchers used a real-world setting—a group home for boys who had been convicted of juvenile delinquency. They chose this **sample,** the group of participants chosen for the experiment, because it was useful to have adolescents whose normal level of aggression was relatively high, and because they could incorporate showing the films into the everyday life of the home with minimal disruption.

Using a real-world setting like the one in the aggression experiment is the hallmark of a field study. A **field study** is a research investigation carried out in a naturally occurring setting. Field studies may be carried out in preschool classrooms, at community play-

Naturalistic observation is utilized to examine a situation in its natural habitat without interference of any sort. What are some disadvantages of naturalistic observation?

grounds, on school buses, or on street corners. Field studies capture behavior in real-life settings, and research participants may behave more naturally than they would if they were brought into a laboratory.

Field studies may be used in both correlational studies and experiments. Field studies typically employ naturalistic observation, the technique we discussed above in which researchers observe some naturally occurring behavior without intervening or making changes in the situation. For instance, a researcher might examine behavior in a child-care center, view the groupings of adolescents in high school corridors, or observe elderly adults in a senior center.

However, it often is difficult to run an experiment in real-world settings, where it is hard to exert control over the situation and environment. Consequently, field studies are more typical of correlational designs than experimental designs, and most developmental research experiments are conducted in laboratory settings. A **laboratory study** is a research investigation conducted in a controlled setting explicitly designed to hold events constant. The laboratory may be a room or building designed for research, as in a university's psychology department. Their ability to control the settings in laboratory studies enables researchers to learn more clearly how their treatments affect participants.

Theoretical and Applied Research: Complementary Approaches

Developmental researchers typically focus on one of two approaches to research, carrying out either theoretical research or applied research. **Theoretical research** is designed specifically to test some developmental explanation and expand scientific knowledge, while **applied research** is meant to provide practical solutions to immediate problems. For instance, if we were interested in the processes of cognitive change during childhood, we might carry out a study of how many digits children of various ages can remember after one exposure to multidigit numbers—a theoretical approach. Alternatively, we might focus on how children learn by examining ways in which elementary school instructors can teach children to remember information more easily. Such a study would represent applied research, because the findings are applied to a particular setting and problem.

Often, the distinctions between theoretical and applied research are blurred. For instance, is a study that examines the consequences of ear infections in infancy on later hearing loss theoretical or applied research? Because such a study may help illuminate the basic processes involved in hearing, it can be considered theoretical. But to the extent that the study helps us to understand how to prevent hearing loss in children and how various medicines may ease the consequences of the infection, it may be considered applied research (Lerner, Fisher, & Weinberg, 2000).

In short, even the most applied research can help advance our theoretical understanding of a particular topical area, and theoretical research can provide concrete solutions to a range of practical problems. In fact, as we discuss in the accompanying *From Research to Practice* box, research of both a theoretical and applied nature has played a significant role in shaping and resolving a variety of public policy questions.

Measuring Developmental Change

For developmental researchers, an interest in how people grow and change through the life span is central to their discipline. Consequently, one of the thorniest research issues they face concerns the measurement of change and differences over age and time. To solve this problem, researchers have developed three major strategies: longitudinal research, cross-sectional research, and cross-sequential research.

laboratory study a research investigation conducted in a controlled setting explicitly designed to hold events constant

theoretical research research designed specifically to test some developmental explanation and expand scientific knowledge

applied research research meant to provide practical solutions to immediate problems

From Research to Practice
Using Research to Improve Public Policy

Do children benefit from preschool?

What is the best approach to reducing the number of unwed teenage mothers?

Does research support the legalization of marijuana?

Should preschoolers diagnosed with attention deficit hyperactivity disorder receive drugs to treat their condition?

Will a series of national educational achievement tests improve scholastic performance?

Each of these questions represents a major national policy issue that can be answered appropriately in only one way: by considering the results of relevant research studies. By conducting controlled studies, developmental researchers have made a number of important contributions in a variety of areas. Consider, for instance, the variety of ways that public policy issues have been informed by various types of research findings (Lorion et al., 1996; Susman-Stillman et al., 1996; Marshall, 2000):

▶ **Asking the right questions.** Research findings can provide a means of determining what questions to ask in the first place. For example, studies of children's caregivers (some of which we'll consider in Chapter 10) have led policymakers to question whether the benefits of infant day care are outweighed by possible deterioration in parent–child bonds.

▶ **Writing legislation and laws that improve the lives of children**. A good deal of legislation has been passed based on findings from developmental researchers. For example, research revealed that children with developmental disabilities benefit from exposure to children without special needs, ultimately leading to passage of national legislation mandating that children with disabilities be placed in regular school classes as much as possible.

▶ **Developing effective intervention programs.** Research has often helped policymakers and other professionals determine how to implement programs designed to improve the lives of children, adolescents, and adults. Research has shaped programs designed to reduce the incidence of unsafe sex among teenagers, to increase the level of prenatal care for pregnant mothers, to raise class attendance rates in school-age children, and to promote flu shots for older adults. The common thread among such programs is that many of the details of the programs are built upon basic research findings.

▶ **Program evaluation.** Once a public policy has been implemented, it is necessary to determine whether it has been effective and successful in accomplishing its goals. To do this, researchers employ formal evaluation techniques, developed from basic research procedures. For instance, researchers have continually scrutinized the Head Start preschool program, which has received massive federal funding, to ensure that it is effective in improving children's academic performance.

By building upon research findings, developmentalists have worked hand-in-hand with policymakers, and research has a substantial impact on public policies that can benefit us all.

---

cw

longitudinal research research in which the behavior of one or more participants in a study is measured as they age

Longitudinal Studies: Measuring Individual Change. If you were interested in learning how a child's moral development changes between the ages of 3 and 5, the most direct approach would be to take a group of 3-year-olds and follow them until they were 5, testing them periodically.

Such a strategy illustrates longitudinal research. In **longitudinal research**, the behavior of one or more study participants is measured as they age. Longitudinal research measures change over time. By following many individuals over time, researchers can understand the general course of change across some period of life.

The granddaddy of longitudinal studies, which has become a classic, is a study of gifted children begun by Lewis Terman more than 75 years ago. In the study—which has yet to be concluded—a group of 1,500 children with high IQs were tested about every 5 years. Now in their 80s, the participants—who call themselves "Termites"—have provided information on everything from intellectual accomplishment to personality and longevity (Terman & Oden, 1959; Friedman et al., 1995b; Lippa, Martin, & Friedman, 2000).

Longitudinal research has also provided great insight into language development. For instance, by tracing how children's vocabularies increase on a day-by-day basis, researchers have been able to understand the processes that underlie the human ability to become competent in using language.

Longitudinal studies can provide a wealth of information about change over time (Bullock, 1995; Elder, 1998). However, they have several drawbacks. For one thing, they require a tremendous investment of time, because researchers must wait for participants to become older. Furthermore, there is a significant possibility of participant *attrition*, or loss, over the course of the research. Participants may drop out of a study, move away, or become ill or even die as the research proceeds.

Finally, participants who are observed or tested may become "test-wise" and perform better each time they are assessed as they become more familiar with the procedure. Even if the observations of participants in a study are not terribly intrusive (such as simply recording, over a lengthy period of time, vocabulary increases in infants and preschoolers), experimental participants may be affected by the repeated presence of an experimenter or observer.

Consequently, despite the benefits of longitudinal research, particularly its ability to look at change within individuals, developmental researchers often turn to other methods in conducting research. The alternative they choose most often is the cross-sectional study.

Cross-sectional research allows researchers to compare representatives of different age groups at the same time.

Cross-Sectional Studies. Let's return to the issue of moral development in children 3 to 5 years of age. Instead of using a longitudinal approach and following the same children over several years, we might conduct the study by simultaneously looking at three groups of children: 3-year-olds, 4-year-olds, and 5-year-olds.

Such an approach typifies cross-sectional research. In **cross-sectional research,** people of different ages are compared at the same point in time. Cross-sectional studies provide information about differences in development between different age groups.

cross-sectional research research in which people of different ages are compared at the same point in time

Cross-sectional research is considerably more economical in terms of time than longitudinal research: Participants are tested at just one point in time. For instance, Terman's study conceivably might have been completed 75 years ago if Terman had simply looked at a group of gifted 15-year-olds, 20-year-olds, 25-year-olds, and so forth, all the way through a group of 80-year-olds. Because the participants would not be periodically tested, there would be no chance that they would become test-wise, and problems of participant attrition would not occur. Why, then, would anyone choose to use a procedure other than cross-sectional research?

The answer is that cross-sectional research brings its own set of difficulties. We can start with cohort effects. Recall that every person belongs to a particular *cohort*, the group of people born at around the same time in the same place. If we find that people of different ages vary along some dimension, it may be due to differences in cohort membership, not age *per se*.

Consider a concrete example: If we find in a correlational study that people who are 25 years old perform better on a test of intelligence than those who are 75 years old, there are several explanations. Although the finding may be due to decreased intelligence in older people, it may also be attributable to cohort differences. The group of 75-year-olds may have had less formal education than the 15-year-olds, because members of the older cohort were less likely to finish high school and attend college than members of the younger one. Or perhaps the older group performed less well because as infants they received less adequate nutrition than members of the younger group. In short, we cannot fully rule out the possibility that differences we find between people of different age groups in cross-sectional studies are due to cohort differences.

Cross-sectional studies also may suffer from *selective dropout*, in which participants in some age groups are more likely to quit participating in a study than others. For

cross-sequential studies research in which researchers examine a number of different age groups over several points in time

example, suppose a study of cognitive development in preschoolers includes a lengthy assessment of cognitive abilities. It is possible that young preschoolers would find the task more difficult and demanding than older preschoolers. As a result, the younger preschoolers would be more likely to discontinue participation in the study than the older preschoolers. If the least competent young preschoolers are the ones who drop out, then the remaining sample of participants in the study will consist of the more competent young preschoolers—together with a broader and more representative sample of older preschoolers. Clearly, the results of such a study would be questionable (Miller, 1998).

Finally, cross-sectional studies have an additional, and more basic, disadvantage: They are unable to inform us about changes in individuals or groups. Although we can establish differences related to age, we cannot fully determine if such differences are related to change over time.

Cross-Sequential Studies. Because both longitudinal and cross-sectional studies have drawbacks, researchers have turned to some compromise techniques. Among the most frequently employed are cross-sequential studies, which are essentially a combination of longitudinal and cross-sectional studies.

In **cross-sequential studies,** researchers examine a number of different age groups at several points in time. For instance, an investigator interested in children's moral behavior might begin a cross-sequential study by examining the behavior of three groups of children, who are either 3 years old, 4 years old, or 5 years old at the time the study begins. (This is no different from the way a cross-sectional study would be done.)

However, the study wouldn't stop there, but would continue for the next several years. During this period, each of the research participants would be tested annually. Thus, the 3-year-olds would be tested at ages 3, 4, and 5; the 4-year-olds at ages 4, 5, and 6; and the 5-year-olds at ages 5, 6, and 7. Such an approach combines the advantages of longitudinal and cross-sectional research, and it permits developmental researchers to tease out the consequences of age *change* versus age *difference*. (The major research techniques for studying development are summarized in Figure 1-3).

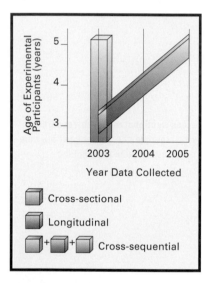

***Figure 1-3* Research Techniques for Studying Development**

In a *cross-sectional study*, 3-, 4-, and 5-year-olds are compared at a similar point in time (in 2003). In *longitudinal research*, a set of participants who are 3 years old in 2003 are studied when they are 4 years old (in 2004) and when they are 5 years old (in 2005). Finally, a *cross-sequential study* combines cross-sectional and longitudinal techniques; here, a group of 3-year-olds would be compared initially in 2003 with 4- and 5-year-olds, but would also be studied 1 and 2 years later, when they themselves were 4 and 5 years old. Although the graph does not illustrate this, researchers carrying out this cross-sequential study might also choose to retest the children who were 4 and 5 in 2003 for the next 2 years. What advantages do the three kinds of studies offer?

Ethics and Research: The Morality of Research

Return, for a moment, to the "study" conducted by Egyptian King Psamtik, in which two children were removed from their mothers and held in isolation in an effort to learn about the roots of language. Clearly, such an experiment raises blatant ethical concerns, and nothing like it would ever be done today.

But sometimes ethical issues are more subtle. For instance, in seeking to understand the roots of aggressive behavior, U.S. government researchers proposed holding a conference to examine possible genetic roots of aggression. Based on work conducted by biopsychologists and geneticists, some researchers had begun to raise the possibility that genetic markers might be found that would allow the identification of children as being particularly violence-prone. In such cases, it might be possible to track these violence-prone children and provide interventions that might reduce the likelihood of later violence.

Critics objected strenuously, however. They argued that such identification might lead to a self-fulfilling prophecy. Children labeled as violence-prone might be treated in a way that would actually *cause* them to be more aggressive than if they hadn't been so labeled. Ultimately, under intense political pressure, the conference was canceled (Wright, 1995).

In order to help researchers deal with such ethical problems, the major organizations of developmentalists, including the Society for Research in Child Development and the American Psychological Association, have developed comprehensive ethical guidelines for researchers. Among the basic principles that must be followed are those involving freedom from harm, informed consent, the use of deception, and maintenance of subjects' privacy (American Psychological Association, 1992; Sales & Folkman, 2000).

Becoming an Informed Consumer of Development

Assessing Information on Development

If you immediately comfort crying babies, you'll spoil them.

If you let babies cry without comforting them, they'll be untrusting and clingy as adults.

***

Spanking is one of the best ways to discipline your child.

Never hit your child.

***

If a marriage is unhappy, children are better off if their parents divorce than if they stay together.
No matter how difficult a marriage is, parents should avoid divorce for the sake of their children.

There is no lack of advice on the best way to raise a child or, more generally, to lead one's life. From bestsellers with incomprehensible titles such as *Men Are From Mars, Women Are From Venus* to magazine and newspaper columns that provide advice on every imaginable topic, each of us is exposed to tremendous amounts of information.

Yet not all advice is equally valid. The mere fact that something is in print or on television does not automatically make it legitimate or accurate. Fortunately, some guidelines can help distinguish when recommendations and suggestions are reasonable and when they are not:

▶ Consider the source of the advice. Information from established, respected organizations such as the American Medical Association, the American Psychological Association, and the American Academy of Pediatrics are likely to be the result of years of study, and their accuracy is probably high.

▶ Evaluate the credentials of the person providing advice. Information coming from established, acknowledged researchers and experts in a field is likely to be more accurate

than that coming from a person whose credentials are obscure.

▶ Understand the difference between anecdotal evidence and scientific evidence. Anecdotal evidence is based on one or two instances of a phenomenon, haphazardly discovered or encountered; scientific evidence is based on careful, systematic procedures.

▶ Keep cultural context in mind. Although an assertion may be valid in some contexts, it may not be true in all. For example, it is typically assumed that providing infants the freedom to move about and exercise their limbs facilitates their muscular development and mobility. Yet in some cultures, infants spend most of their time closely bound to their mothers—with no apparent long-term damage (Kaplan & Dove, 1987; Tronick, 1995).

▶ Don't assume that because many people believe something, it is necessarily true. Scientific evaluation has often proved that some of the most basic presumptions about the effectiveness of various techniques are invalid. For instance, consider *DARE*, the Drug Abuse Resistance Education anti-drug program that is used in about half the school systems in the United States. DARE is designed to prevent the spread of drugs through lectures and question-and-answer sessions run by police officers. One problem, though: Careful evaluation finds no evidence that the program is effective in reducing drug use (Lyman et al., 1999).

In short, the key to evaluating information relating to human development is to maintain a healthy dose of skepticism. No source of information is invariably, unfailingly accurate. By keeping a critical eye on the statements you encounter, you'll be in a better position to determine the very real contributions made by developmentalists to understanding how humans develop over the course of the life span.

Freedom from Harm. Researchers must protect participants from physical and psychological harm. Their welfare, interests, and rights come before those of researchers. In research, subjects' rights always come first (Sieber, 1998).

Informed Consent. Researchers must obtain consent from subjects before their participation in a study. If they are above the age of 7, participants must voluntarily agree to be in a study. For those under 18, their parents or guardians must also provide consent.

The requirement for informed consent raises some difficult issues. Suppose, for instance, researchers wish to learn the psychological consequences of abortion on adolescents. Although they may be able to obtain the consent of an adolescent who has had an abortion, the researchers may need to get her parents' permission as well, because she is a minor. But suppose the adolescent hasn't told her parents that she has had an abortion. In such a case, the mere request for permission from the parents would violate the privacy of the adolescent—leading to a breach of ethics.

Use of Deception. Although deception to disguise the true purpose of an experiment is permissible, any experiment that uses deception must undergo careful scrutiny by an independent panel before it is conducted. Suppose, for example, we want to know the reaction of subjects to success and failure. It is ethical to tell subjects that they will be playing a game when the true purpose is actually to observe how they respond to doing well or poorly on the task. However, such a procedure is ethical only if it causes no harm to participants, has been approved by a review panel, and ultimately includes a full debriefing, or explanation, for participants when the study is over.

Maintenance of Privacy. Subjects' privacy must be maintained. If they are videotaped during the course of a study, for example, they must give their permission for the videotapes to be viewed. Furthermore, access to the tapes must be carefully restricted.

Review and Rethink

REVIEW

- Theories in development are systematically derived explanations of facts or phenomena. Theories suggest hypotheses, which are predictions that can be tested.
- Correlational studies examine relationships between factors without demonstrating causality. Naturalistic observation, case studies, and survey research are types of correlational studies.
- Experimental research seeks to discover cause-and-effect relationships by the use of a treatment group and a control group. By manipulating the independent variable and observing changes in the dependent variable, researchers find evidence of causal links between variables.

- Research studies may be conducted in field settings, where participants are subject to natural conditions, or in laboratories, where conditions can be controlled.
- Researchers measure age-related change by longitudinal studies, cross-sectional studies, and cross-sequential studies.

RETHINK

- Formulate a theory about one aspect of human development and a hypothesis that relates to it.
- Would a laboratory or a field setting be most appropriate for each research strategy you identified?

Looking Back

▶ *What is lifespan development, and what are some of the basic influences on human development?*

- Lifespan development is a scientific approach to questions about growth, change, and stability in the physical, cognitive, and social and personality characteristics at all ages from conception to death.

- The ecological approach to development suggests that four levels of the environment simultaneously affect the individual: the microsystem, the mesosystem, the exosystem, and the macrosystem. The ecological approach stresses the interrelatedness of developmental areas and the importance of broad cultural factors in human development.

■ Culture—both broad and narrow—is an important issue in lifespan development. Many aspects of development are influenced not only by broad cultural differences, but by ethnic, racial, and socioeconomic differences within a particular culture.

■ Each individual is subject to normative history-graded influences, normative age-graded influences, normative sociocultural-graded influences, and nonnormative life events.

▶ *What are the key issues in the field of development?*

■ Four key issues in lifespan development are (1) whether developmental change is continuous or discontinuous; (2) whether development is largely governed by critical periods during which certain influences or experiences must occur for development to be normal; (3) whether to focus on certain particularly important periods in human development or on the entire life span; and (4) the nature–nurture controversy, which focuses on the relative importance of genetic versus environmental influences.

▶ *Which theoretical perspectives have guided lifespan development?*

■ Five major theoretical perspectives currently dominate lifespan development: the psychodynamic perspective (which focuses on inner, largely unconscious forces), the behavioral perspective (which focuses on external, observable actions), the cognitive perspective (which focuses on intellectual, cognitive processes), the humanistic perspective (which focuses on the unique qualities of human beings), and the evolutionary perspective (which focuses on our genetic inheritance).

■ The psychodynamic perspective is exemplified by the psychoanalytic theory of Freud and the psychosocial theory of Erikson. Freud focused attention on the unconscious and on stages through which children must pass successfully to avoid harmful fixations. Erikson identified eight distinct stages of development, each characterized by a conflict, or crisis, to work out.

■ The behavioral perspective typically concerns stimulus–response learning, exemplified by classical conditioning, the operant conditioning of Skinner, and Bandura's social-cognitive learning theory.

■ Within the cognitive perspective, the most notable theorist is Piaget, who identified developmental stages through which all children are assumed to pass. Each stage involves qualitative differences in thinking.

■ In contrast, information-processing approaches attribute cognitive growth to quantitative changes in mental processes and capacities. Vygotsky's sociocultural theory emphasizes the central influence on cognitive development exerted by social interactions between members of a culture.

■ The humanistic perspective contends that people have a natural capacity to make decisions about their lives and control their behavior. The humanistic perspective emphasizes free will and the natural desire of humans to reach their full potential.

■ The evolutionary perspective attributes behavior to genetic inheritance from our ancestors, contending that genes determine not only traits such as skin and eye color, but certain personality traits and social behaviors as well.

▶ *What role do theories and hypotheses play in the study of development?*

■ Theories are broad explanations of facts or phenomena of interest, based on a systematic integration of prior findings and theories. Hypotheses are theory-based predictions that can be tested. The process of posing and answering questions systematically is called the scientific method.

■ Researchers test hypotheses by correlational research (to determine if two factors are associated) and experimental research (to discover cause-and-effect relationships).

▶ *How are developmental research studies conducted?*

■ Correlational studies use naturalistic observation, case studies, and survey research to investigate whether certain characteristics of interest are associated with other characteristics. Correlational studies lead to no direct conclusions about cause and effect.

■ Typically, experimental research studies are conducted on participants in a treatment group who receive the experimental treatment and participants in a control group who do not. Following the treatment, differences between the two groups can help the experimenter to determine the effects of the treatment. Experiments may be conducted in a laboratory or in a real-world setting.

■ To measure change across human ages, researchers use longitudinal studies of the same participants over time, cross-sectional studies of different-age participants conducted at one time, and cross-sequential studies of different-age participants at several points in time.

■ Ethical guidelines for research include the protection of participants from harm, informed consent of participants, limits on the use of deception, and the maintenance of privacy.

EPILOGUE

This chapter has introduced us to the growing field of lifespan development. We have reviewed the broad scope of the field, touching on the wide range of topics that lifespan developmentalists may address, and have discussed the key issues and questions that have shaped the field since its inception. We have also looked at the means by which developmentalists answer questions of interest.

Before we proceed to the next chapter, take a few minutes to reconsider the prologue of this chapter—about the cloning of cells from Dr. Judson Somerville. Based on what you now know about developmental research, answer the following questions.

1. What are some of the potential benefits, and the costs, of the type of cloning that was carried out from the cells that Dr. Somerville provided?

2. What are some questions that developmentalists who study either physical, cognitive, or personality and social development might ask about the effects on Dr. Somerville of the accident that left him in a wheelchair, unable to walk?

3. Although we are far from the time when complete clones could be created, the theoretical possibility does raise some important questions. For example, what do you think the psychological consequences of being cloned would be? What would be the consequences of *being* a clone?

4. If clones could actually be produced, how might it help scientists understand the relative impact of heredity and environment on devleopment?

Key Terms and Concepts

lifespan development (p. 5)
physical development (p. 6)
cognitive development (p. 6)
personality development (p. 6)
social development (p. 6)
ecological approach (p. 8)
cohort (p. 11)
normative history-graded influences (p. 11)
normative age-graded influences (p. 11)
normative sociocultural-graded influences (p. 11)
nonnormative life events (p. 11)
continuous change (p. 12)

discontinuous change (p. 13)
critical period (p. 13)
sensitive period (p. 13)
maturation (p. 13)
theories (p. 16)
psychodynamic perspective (p. 16)
psychoanalytic theory (p. 16)
id (p. 16)
ego (p. 16)
superego (p. 16)
psychosexual development (p. 17)
fixation (p. 17)
psychosocial development (p. 17)

behavioral perspective (p. 18)
classical conditioning (p. 19)
operant conditioning (p. 19)
behavior modification (p. 20)
social-cognitive learning theory (p. 20)
cognitive perspective (p. 21)
assimilation (p. 21)
accommodation (p. 21)
information processing approaches (p. 22)
sociocultural theory (p. 22)
humanistic perspective (p. 23)
evolutionary perspective (p. 24)

scientific method (p. 28)

hypothesis (p. 28)

correlational research (p. 29)

experimental research (p. 29)

naturalistic observation (p. 31)

case studies (p. 32)

survey research (p. 32)

experiment (p. 32)

treatment (p. 32)

treatment group (p. 32)

control group (p. 32)

independent variable (p. 34)

dependent variable (p. 34)

sample (p. 34)

field study (p. 34)

laboratory study (p. 35)

theoretical research (p. 35)

applied research (p. 35)

longitudinal research (p. 36)

cross-sectional research (p. 37)

cross-sequential studies (p. 38)

The Start of Life: Genetics and Prenatal Development

PROLOGUE: GIANT STEPS

Ethan Buchkovich and family

A routine prenatal test brought Jennifer and Brian Buchkovich horrifying news: Their unborn baby, Ethan, was afflicted with spina bifida, a failure of the spine to close over the spinal cord. The birth defect, which affects 2,000 children a year, usually leads to paralysis and cognitive delays. But doctors offered the Windber, Pennsylvania, couple a glimmer of hope—an experimental operation designed to reduce the damage and to eliminate or delay the need for a surgically implanted shunt to drain excess fluid from the brain. The hitch: The surgery would have to be performed while Ethan was still inside Jennifer's womb (*People Weekly*, 2000, p. 117).

Looking Ahead   The Buchkoviches took the risk, and it appears to have paid off: Although Ethan has shown some developmental delays, he's just a bit behind schedule.

Operations on unborn children are becoming nearly routine as scientists learn more about the course of development prior to birth. In this chapter, we'll examine what developmental researchers and other scientists have learned about ways that heredity and the environment work in tandem to create and shape human beings. We begin with the basics of heredity, examining how we receive our genetic endowment. We'll consider a burgeoning area of study, behavioral genetics, that specializes in the consequences of heredity on behavior. We'll also discuss what happens when genetic factors cause development to go awry, and how such problems are dealt with through genetic counseling and the brave new world of cloning and genetic engineering.

Next, we'll turn to a discussion of the interaction of heredity and environment. We'll consider the relative influence of genes and environment on a variety of characteristics, including physical traits, intelligence, and even personality.

Finally, we'll focus on the very first stage of development, tracing prenatal growth and change. We'll see that prenatal growth begins at the moment of conception, and we'll review some of the alternatives available to couples who find it difficult to conceive. We'll also talk about the stages of the prenatal period and how the prenatal environment offers both threats to—and the promise of—future growth.

After reading this chapter, you will be able to answer these questions:

▶ **What is our basic genetic endowment, and how can human development go awry?**

▶ **How do the environment and genetics work together to determine human characteristics?**

▶ **Which human characteristics are significantly influenced by heredity?**

▶ **What happens during the prenatal stages of development?**

▶ **What are the threats to the fetal environment, and what can be done about them?**

Heredity

We humans begin the course of our lives simply.

Like individuals from tens of thousands of other species, we start as a single cell, a tiny speck probably weighing no more than one twenty-millionth of an ounce. But from this humble beginning, human development follows its own unique path, accomplishing a journey that leads to the flowering of humankind's vast potential.

What determines the process that transforms the single cell into something that we can more easily identify as a person? The answer is the human genetic code, transmitted at the moment of conception from the mother and father, and embedded in that single, first cell.

Genes and Chromosomes: The Code of Life

Our genetic code is stored and communicated in our **genes,** the basic units of genetic information. Genes are the biological equivalent of "software" that programs the future development of all parts of the body's "hardware."

Humans have some 30,000 genes. All genes are composed of specific sequences of **DNA (deoxyribonucleic acid)** molecules. They are arranged in specific locations and in a specific order along 46 **chromosomes**, rod-shaped portions of DNA that are organized in 23 pairs. A child's mother and father each provide one of the two chromosomes in each of the 23 pairs. At the moment of conception, or fertilization, the 23 maternal and 23 paternal chromosomes unite within a single new cell, called a **zygote.** The 46 chromosomes in the new zygote contain the genetic blueprint that will guide cell activity for the rest of the individual's life (Pennisi, 2000; International Human Genome Sequencing Consortium, 2001; see Figure 2-1). Through a cell replication process called *mitosis*, nearly all the cells of the body will contain the same 46 chromosomes as the zygote.

Specific genes in precise locations on the chain of chromosomes determine the nature and function of every cell in the body. For instance, genes determine which cells will ultimately become part of the heart and which will become part of the muscles of the leg. Genes also establish how different parts of the body will function: how rapidly the heart will beat, or how much strength a muscle will have.

If each parent provides just 23 chromosomes, where does the potential for the vast diversity of human beings come from? The answer resides primarily in the nature of the processes that underlie the cell division of the gametes. When **gametes**—the sex cells, sperm and ova—are formed in the adult human body in a process called *meiosis*, each gamete receives one of the (male or female) body's two pairs of 23 chromosomes. Because for each of the 23 pairs it is largely a matter of chance which member of the pair is contributed, there are 2^{23}, or some eight million, different combinations possible. Furthermore, other processes, such as random transformations of particular genes, add to the variability of the genetic brew. The ultimate outcome: tens of *trillions* of possible genetic combinations.

genes the basic unit of genetic information

DNA (deoxyribonucleic acid) the substance that genes are composed of that determines the nature of every cell in the body and how it will function

chromosomes rod-shaped portions of DNA that are organized in 23 pairs

zygote the new cell formed by the process of fertilization

gametes the sex cells from the mother and father that form a new cell at conception

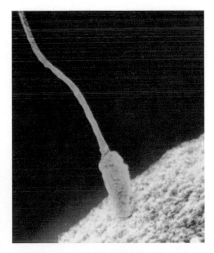
(a) conception

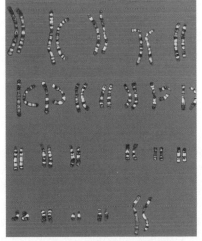
(b) 23 pairs of chromosomes

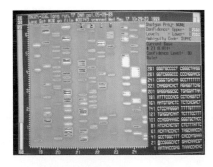
(c) a map of gene sequences

Figure 2-1 **Genes and Chromosomes**

At the moment of conception (a), humans receive 23 pairs of chromosomes (b), half from the mother and half from the father. These chromosomes contain thousands of genes, shown in the computer-generated map in (c).

With so many possible genetic mixtures provided by heredity, there is no likelihood that someday you'll bump into a genetic duplicate of yourself—with one exception: an identical twin.

Multiple Births: Two—or More—for the Genetic Price of One. Although it doesn't seem surprising when dogs and cats give birth to several offspring at one time, in humans multiple births are cause for comment. They should be: Less than two percent of all pregnancies produce twins, and the odds are even slimmer for three or more children.

Why do multiple births occur? Some occur when a cluster of cells in the ovum splits off within the first two weeks after fertilization. The result is two genetically identical zygotes, which, because they come from the same original zygote, are called monozygotic. **Monozygotic twins** are twins who are genetically identical. Any differences in their future development can be attributed only to environmental factors, since genetically they are exactly the same.

There is a second, and actually more common, mechanism that produces multiple births. In these cases, two separate ova are fertilized by two separate sperm at roughly the same time. Twins produced in this fashion are known as **dizygotic twins**. Because they are the result of two separate ovum-sperm combinations, they are no more genetically similar than two siblings born at different times.

Of course, not all multiple births produce only two babies. Triplets, quadruplets, and even more births are produced by either (or both) of the mechanisms that yield twins. Thus, triplets may be some combination of monozygotic, dizygotic, or trizygotic.

Although the chances of having a multiple birth are typically slim, the odds rise considerably when couples use fertility drugs to improve the probability they will conceive a child. For example, 1 in 10 couples using fertility drugs have dizygotic twins, compared to an overall figure of 1 in 86 for Caucasian couples in the United States. Older women, too, are more likely to have multiple births, and multiple births are also more common in some families than in others. The increased use of fertility drugs and rising average age of mothers giving birth has meant that multiple births have increased in the last 25 years (see Figure 2-2; Lang, 1999).

There are also racial, ethnic, and national differences in the rate of multiple births, probably due to inherited differences in the likelihood that more than one ovum will be released at a time. One out of 70 African-American couples have dizygotic births, compared with the 1 out of 86 figure for white American couples (Vaughan, McKay, & Behrman, 1979; Wood, 1997).

Mothers carrying multiple children run a higher-than-average risk of premature delivery and birth complications. Consequently, these mothers must be particularly concerned about their prenatal care.

Boy or Girl?: Establishing the Sex of the Child. Recall that there are 23 matched pairs of chromosomes. In 22 of these pairs, each chromosome is similar to the other member of its pair. The one exception is the 23rd pair, which is the one that determines the sex of the child. In females, the 23rd pair consists of two matching, relatively large X-shaped chromosomes, appropriately identified as XX. In males, on the other hand, the members of the pair are dissimilar. One consists of an X-shaped chromosome, but the other is a smaller Y-shaped chromosome. This pair is identified as XY.

As we discussed earlier, each gamete carries one chromosome from each of the parent's 23 pairs of chromosomes. Since a female's 23rd pair of chromosomes are both Xs, an ovum will always carry an X chromosome, no matter which chromosome of the 23rd pair it gets. A male's 23rd pair is XY, so each sperm could carry either an X or a Y chromosome.

If the sperm contributes an X chromosome when it meets an ovum (which, remember, will always contribute an X chromosome), the child will have an XX pairing on the

monozygotic twins twins who are genetically identical

dizygotic twins twins who are produced when two separate ova are fertilized by two separate sperm at roughly the same time

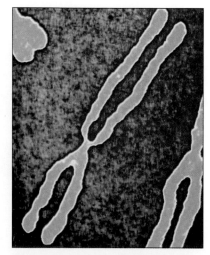

The X chromosome is not only important in determining gender but is also the site of genes controlling other aspects of development.

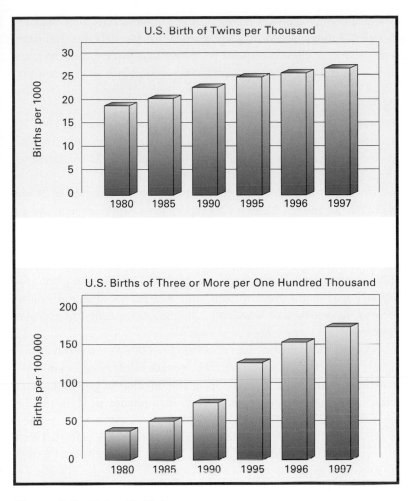

Figure 2-2 **Rising Multiples**

Multiple births have increased significantly over the last 25 years. What are some of the reasons for this phenomenon?

(Source: Martin & Park, 1999).

23rd chromosome—and will be a female. If the sperm contributes a Y chromosome, the result will be an XY pairing—a male (see Figure 2-3).

It is clear from this process that the father's sperm determines the gender of the child. This fact is leading to the development of techniques that will allow parents to increase the chances of specifying the gender of their child. In one new technique, lasers measure the DNA in sperm. By discarding sperm that harbor the unwanted sex chromosome, the chances of having a child of the desired sex increase dramatically (Hayden, 1998; Belkin, 1999).

Of course, procedures for choosing a child's sex raise ethical and practical issues. For example, in cultures that value one gender over the other, might there be a kind of gender discrimination prior to birth? Furthermore, a shortage of children of the less-preferred sex might ultimately emerge. Many questions remain, then, before sex selection becomes routine.

The Basics of Genetics: The Mixing and Matching of Heredity

What determined the color of your hair? Why are you tall or short? What made you susceptible to hay fever? And why do you have so many freckles? To answer these questions, we need to consider the basic mechanisms involved in the way that the genes we inherit from our parents transmit information.

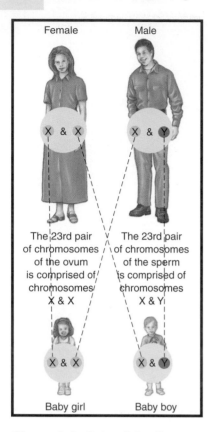

Female   Male

X & X   X & Y

The 23rd pair   The 23rd pair
of chromosomes   of chromosomes
of the ovum   of the sperm
is comprised of   is comprised of
chromosomes   chromosomes
X & X   X & Y

X & X   X & Y

Baby girl   Baby boy

Figure 2-3 **Determining Sex**

When an ovum and sperm meet at the moment of fertilization, the ovum is certain to provide an X chromosome, while the sperm will provide either an X or a Y chromosome. If the sperm contributes its X chromosome, the child will have an XX pairing on the 23rd chromosome and will be a girl. If the sperm contributes a Y chromosome, the result will be an XY pairing—a boy. Does this mean that girls are more likely to be conceived than boys?

dominant trait the one trait that is expressed when two competing traits are present

recessive trait a trait within an organism that is present, but is not expressed

genotype the underlying combination of genetic material present (but not outwardly visible) in an organism

phenotype an observable trait; the trait that actually is seen

homozygous inheriting from parents similar genes for a given trait

heterozygous inheriting from parents different forms of a gene for a given trait

We can start by examining the discoveries of an Austrian monk, Gregor Mendel, in the mid-1800s. In a series of simple yet convincing experiments, Mendel cross-pollinated pea plants that always produced yellow seeds with pea plants that always produced green seeds. The result was not, as one might guess, a plant with a combination of yellow and green seeds. Instead, all of the resulting plants had yellow seeds. At first it appeared that the green-seeded plants had had no influence.

However, additional research on Mendel's part proved that this was not true. He bred together plants from the new, yellow-seeded generation that had resulted from his original cross—breeding of the green-seeded and yellow-seeded plants. The consistent result was a ratio of three-quarters yellow seeds to one-quarter green seeds.

Why did this 3-to-1 ratio of yellow to green seeds appear so consistently? It was Mendel's genius to provide an answer. Based on his experiments with pea plants, he argued that when two competing traits, such as a green or yellow coloring of seeds, were both present, only one could be expressed. The one that was expressed was called a **dominant trait.** Meanwhile, the other trait remained present in the organism, although not expressed. This was called a **recessive trait.** In the case of Mendel's original pea plants, the offspring plants received genetic information from both the green-seeded and yellow-seeded parents. However, the yellow trait was dominant, and consequently the recessive green trait did not assert itself.

Keep in mind, however, that genetic material relating to both parent plants is present in the offspring, even though it cannot be seen. The genetic information is known as the organism's genotype. A **genotype** is the underlying combination of genetic material present (but outwardly invisible) in an organism. In contrast, a **phenotype** is the observable trait, the trait that actually is seen.

Although the offspring of the yellow-seeded and green-seeded pea plants all have yellow seeds (i.e., they have a yellow-seeded phenotype), the genotype consists of genetic information relating to both parents.

And what is the nature of the information in the genotype? To answer that question, let's turn from peas to people. In fact, the principles are the same not just for plants and humans, but for the majority of species.

Recall that parents transmit genetic information to their offspring via the chromosomes they contribute through the gamete they provide during fertilization. Some of the genes form pairs called *alleles*, genes governing traits that may take alternate forms, such as hair or eye color. A child's allele may contain similar or dissimilar genes from each parent. If the child receives similar genes, he or she is said to be **homozygous** for the trait. On the other hand, if the child receives different forms of the gene from its parents, he or she is said to be **heterozygous.** In the case of heterozygous alleles, the dominant characteristic is expressed. However, if the child happens to receive a recessive allele from each of its parents, and therefore lacks a dominant characteristic, it will display the recessive characteristic.

Transmission of Genetic Information in Humans. We can see this process at work in humans by considering the transmission of *phenylketonuria (PKU)*, an inherited disorder in which a child is unable to make use of phenylalanine, an essential amino acid present in proteins found in milk and other foods. If left untreated, PKU allows phenylalanine to build up to toxic levels, causing brain damage and mental retardation.

PKU is produced by a single allele, or pair of genes. As shown in Figure 2-4, we can label each gene of the pair with a *P* if it carries a dominant gene, which causes the normal production of phenylalanine, or a *p* if it carries the recessive gene that produces PKU. In cases in which neither parent is a PKU carrier, both the mother's and the father's pairs of genes are the dominant form, symbolized as *PP*. Consequently, no matter which member of the pair is contributed by the mother and father, the resulting pair of genes in the child will be *PP*, and the child will not have PKU.

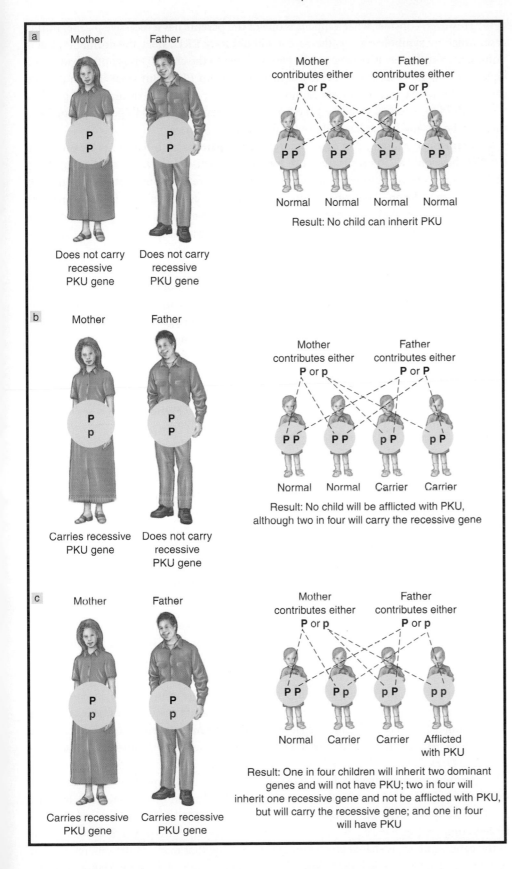

Figure 2-4 PKU Probabilities

PKU, a disease that causes brain damage and mental retardation, is produced by a single pair of genes inherited from one's mother and father. If neither parent carries a gene for the disease (a), a child cannot develop PKU. Even if one parent carries the recessive gene, but the other doesn't (b), the child cannot inherit the disease. However, if both parents carry the recessive gene (c), there is a one in four chance that the child will have PKU.

However, consider what happens if one of the parents has a recessive *p* gene. In this case, which we symbolize as *Pp*, the parent will not have PKU, since the normal *P* gene is dominant. But the recessive gene can be passed down to the child. This is not so bad: If the child has only one recessive gene, it will not suffer from PKU. But what if both parents carry a recessive *p* gene? In this case, although neither parent has the disorder, it is possible for the child to receive a recessive gene from both parents. The child's genotype for PKU then will be *pp*, and he or she will have the disorder.

Remember, though, that even children whose parents both have the recessive gene for PKU have only a 25 percent chance of inheriting the disorder. Due to the laws of probability, 25 percent of children with *Pp* parents will receive the dominant gene from each parent (these children's genotype would be *PP*), and 50 percent will receive the dominant gene from one parent and the recessive gene from the other (their genotypes would be either *Pp* or *pP*). Only the unlucky 25 percent who receive the recessive gene from each parent and end up with the genotype *pp* will suffer from PKU.

The transmission of PKU illustrates the basic principles of how genetic information passes from parent to child. However, in some respects, the case of PKU is simpler than most cases of genetic transmission. Relatively few traits are governed by a single pair of genes. Instead, most traits are the result of polygenic inheritance. In **polygenic inheritance**, a combination of multiple gene pairs is responsible for the production of a particular trait.

> **polygenic inheritance** inheritance in which a combination of multiple gene pairs is responsible for the production of a particular trait
>
> **X-linked genes** genes that are considered recessive and located only on the X chromosome

Furthermore, some genes come in several alternate forms, and still others act to modify the way that particular genetic traits (produced by other alleles) are displayed. And some traits, such as blood type, are produced by genes in which neither member of a pair of genes can be classified as purely dominant or recessive. Instead, the trait is expressed in terms of a combination of the two genes—such as type AB blood.

A number of recessive genes, called **X-linked genes**, are located only on the X chromosome. Recall that in females, the 23rd pair of chromosomes is an XX pair, while in males it is an XY pair. One result is that males have a higher risk for a variety of X-linked disorders, since males lack a second X chromosome that can counteract the genetic information that produces the disorder. For example, males are significantly more apt to have red-green color blindness, a disorder produced by a set of genes on the X chromosome.

Similarly, *hemophilia*, a blood disorder, is produced by X-linked genes. Hemophilia has been a recurrent problem in the royal families of Europe, as illustrated in Figure 2-5, which shows the inheritance of hemophilia in many of the descendants of Queen Victoria of Great Britain.

The Human Genome and Behavioral Genetics: Cracking the Genetic Code. Mendel's achievements in recognizing the basics of genetic transmission of traits were trailblazing. However, they mark only the beginning of our understanding of the ways that particular sorts of characteristics are passed on from one generation to the next.

The most recent milestone in understanding genetics was reached in early 2001, when molecular biologists succeeded in mapping the specific sequence of genes on each chromosome. This accomplishment stands as one of the most important moments in the history of genetics, and, for that matter, all of biology (International Human Genome Sequencing Consortium, 2001).

Already, the mapping of the gene sequence has provided important advances in our understanding of genetics. For instance, the number of human genes, long thought to be 100,000, has been revised downward to 30,000—not many more than organisms that are far less complex (see Figure 2-6). Furthermore, scientists have discovered that 99.9 percent of the gene sequence is shared by all humans, indicating that many of the differences that seemingly separate people—such as race—are, literally, only skin-deep. Mapping of the human genome will also help in the identification of particular disorders to which a given individual is susceptible (Carpenter, 2000; Levy, 2000; International Human Genome Sequencing Consortium, 2001).

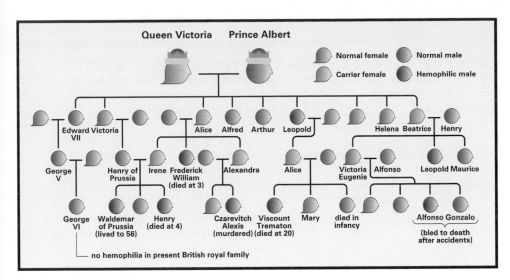

Figure 2-5 **Inheriting Hemophilia**

Hemophilia, a blood-clotting disorder, has been an inherited problem throughout the royal families of Europe, as illustrated by the descendants of Queen Victoria of Britain.

(Adapted from Kimball, 1983.)

The mapping of the human gene sequence is supporting the rapidly burgeoning field of behavioral genetics. As the name implies, **behavioral genetics** studies the effects of heredity on behavior. Rather than simply examining stable, unchanging characteristics such as hair or eye color, behavioral genetics takes a broader approach, considering how our personality and behavioral habits are affected by genetic factors. Behavioral genetics merges the interests of psychologists, who focus on the causes of behavior, with those of geneticists, who focus on the processes that permit the transmission of characteristics through heredity (McGuffin, Riley, & Plomin, 2001).

The promise of behavioral genetics is substantial. For one thing, researchers working within the field have gained a better understanding of the specifics of the genetic code that underlie human behavior and development. Such advances have provided knowledge of the workings of genetics at a molecular and chemical level. Furthermore, scientists are learning how various behavioral difficulties, including psychological disorders such as schizophrenia, may have a genetic basis (see Table 2-1).

Even more important, researchers are seeking to identify how genetic defects may be remedied (Peltonen & McKusick, 2001). To understand how that possibility might come about, we need to consider the ways in which genetic factors, which normally cause development to proceed so smoothly, may falter.

behavioral genetics the study of the effects of heredity on behavior

Inherited and Genetic Disorders: When Development Goes Awry

PKU is just one of several disorders that may be inherited. Like a bomb that is harmless until its fuse is lit, a recessive gene responsible for a disorder may be passed on unknowingly from one generation to the next, revealing itself only when, by chance, it is paired with another recessive gene. It is only when two recessive genes come together like a match and a fuse that the gene will express itself and a child will inherit the genetic disorder.

But there is another way that genes are a source of concern: In some cases, genes become physically damaged. For instance, genes may break down due to wear-and-tear or chance events occurring during the cell division processes of meiosis and mitosis. Sometimes genes, for no known reason, spontaneously change their form, a process called *spontaneous mutation*. Alternatively, certain environmental factors, such as exposure to X-rays, may produce a malformation of genetic material. When such damaged genes are passed on to a child, the results can be disastrous in terms of future physical and cognitive development.

In addition to PKU, which occurs once in 10 thousand to 20 thousand births, other inherited and genetic disorders include:

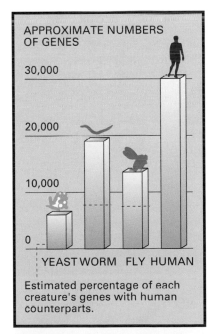

APPROXIMATE NUMBERS OF GENES

30,000

20,000

10,000

0

YEAST WORM FLY HUMAN

Estimated percentage of each creature's genes with human counterparts.

Figure 2-6 **Uniquely Human?**

Once thought to contain more than 100,000 genes, humans actually have about 30,000 genes, making them not much more genetically complex than some primitive species.

(*Source:* Celera Genomics: International Human Genome Sequencing Consortium, 2001.)

Table 2-1

CURRENT UNDERSTANDING OF THE GENETIC BASIS OF SELECTED BEHAVIORAL DISORDERS AND TRAITS

Behavioral Trait	Current Ideas of Genetic Basis
Huntington's disease	Huntington gene identified.
Early onset (familial) Alzheimer's disease	Three distinct genes have been identified.
Fragile X mental retardation	Two genes have been identified.
Late onset Alzheimer's disease	One allele has been associated with increased risk.
Attention deficit hyperactivity disorder	Three locations related to the genetics involved with the neurotransmitter dopamine may contribute.
Dyslexia	Relationships to two locations, on chromosomes 6 and 15, have been suggested.
Schizophrenia	There is no consensus, but links to numerous chromosomes, including 1, 5, 6, 10, 13, 15, and 22 have been reported.

Source: Adapted from McGuffin, P., Riley, B., & Plomin, R. (2001, Feb. 16). Toward behavioral genomics. *Science,* 291, 1232–1249.

Down syndrome a disorder produced by the presence of an extra chromosome on the 21st pair; once referred to as mongolism

fragile X syndrome a disorder produced by injury to a gene on the X chromosome, producing mild to moderate mental retardation

sickle-cell anemia a blood disorder that gets its name from the shape of the red blood cells in those who have it

Tay-Sachs disease a disorder that produces blindness and muscle degeneration prior to death; there is no treatment.

Klinefelter's syndrome a disorder resulting from the presence of an extra X chromosome that produces underdeveloped genitals, extreme height, and enlarged breasts

Sickle cell anemia, named for the presence of misshapen red blood cells, is carried in the genes of 1 in 10 African Americans.

■ *Down syndrome.* As we noted earlier, most people have 46 chromosomes, arranged in 23 pairs. One exception is individuals with **Down syndrome,** a disorder produced by the presence of an extra chromosome on the 21st pair. Once referred to as mongolism, Down syndrome is the most frequent cause of mental retardation. It occurs in about 1 out of 500 births, although the risk is much greater in mothers who are unusually young or old (Carr, 1995; Cicchetti & Beeghly, 1990).

■ *Fragile X syndrome.* **Fragile X syndrome** occurs when a particular gene is injured on the X chromosome. The result is mild to moderate mental retardation.

■ *Sickle-cell anemia.* Around one-tenth of the African American population carry genes that produce sickle-cell anemia, and one African American in 400 actually has the disease. **Sickle-cell anemia** is a blood disorder that gets its name from the shape of the red blood cells in those who have it. Symptoms include poor appetite, stunted growth, swollen stomach, and yellowish eyes. People afflicted with the most severe form of the disease rarely live beyond childhood. However, for those with less severe cases, medical advances have produced significant increases in life expectancy.

■ *Tay-Sachs disease.* Occurring mainly in Jews of eastern European ancestry and in French-Canadians, **Tay-Sachs disease** usually causes death before its victims reach school age. There is no treatment for the disorder, which produces blindness and muscle degeneration prior to death.

■ *Klinefelter's syndrome.* One male out of every 400 is born with **Klinefelter's syndrome**, the presence of an extra X chromosome. The resulting XXY complement produces underdeveloped genitals, extreme height, and enlarged breasts. Klinefelter's syndrome is one of a number of genetic abnormalities that result from receiving the improper number of sex chromosomes. For instance, there are disorders produced by an extra Y chromosome (XYY), a missing second chromosome (X0), and three X chromosomes (XXX). Such disorders are typically characterized by problems relating to sexual characteristics and by intellectual deficits (Sorenson, 1992; Sotos, 1997).

It is important to keep in mind that the mere fact that a disorder has genetic roots does not mean that environmental factors do not also play a role (Moldin & Gottesman,

1997). Consider, for instance, sickle-cell anemia, which primarily afflicts people of African descent. Because the disease can be fatal in childhood, we'd expect that those who suffer from it would be unlikely to live long enough to pass it on. And this does seem to be true, at least in the United States: Compared with parts of West Africa, the incidence in the United States is much lower.

But why shouldn't the incidence of sickle-cell anemia also be gradually reduced for people in West Africa? This question proved puzzling for many years, until scientists determined that carrying the sickle-cell gene raises immunity to malaria, which is a common disease in West Africa (Allison, 1954). This heightened immunity meant that people with the sickle-cell gene had a genetic advantage (in terms of resistance to malaria) that offset, to some degree, the disadvantage of being a carrier of the sickle-cell gene.

The lesson of sickle-cell anemia is that genetic factors are intertwined with environmental considerations and can't be looked at in isolation. Furthermore, we need to remember that although we've been focusing on inherited factors that can go awry, in the vast majority of cases the genetic mechanisms with which we are endowed work quite well. Overall, just under 95 percent of children born in the United States are healthy and normal. For the some 250,000 who are born with some sort of physical or mental disorder, appropriate intervention often can help treat and, in some cases, cure the problem.

Moreover, due to advances in behavioral genetics, genetic difficulties increasingly can be forecast, anticipated, and planned for before a child's birth. Recall, for example, Ethan Buchkovich, described in the chapter prologue, whose parents not only learned about his spina bifida before his birth, but were even able to take steps before he was born to reduce the severity of his condition. In fact, as scientists' knowledge regarding the specific location of particular genes expands, predictions of what the genetic future may hold are becoming increasingly exact, as we discuss next (Plomin & Rutter, 1998).

Genetic Counseling: Predicting the Future from the Genes of the Present

The last thing Joey Paulowsky needs is another bout with cancer. Only 7 years old, the Dallas native has already fought off leukemia, and now his family worries that Joey could be hit again. The Paulowsky family carries a genetic burden—a rare form of inherited cancer of the thyroid. Deborah, his mother, found a lump in her neck six years ago, and since then one family member has died of the cancer and 10 others have had to have their thyroids removed. "Do I have cancer?" Joey asks his mother. "Will it hurt?" The Paulowskys will know the answer next month, when the results of a genetic test will show whether their son carries the family's fateful mutation (Brownlee, Cook, & Hardigg, 1994, p. 59).

The answer will be delivered by a member of a field that, just a few decades ago, was nonexistent: genetic counseling. **Genetic counseling** focuses on helping people deal with issues relating to inherited disorders.

Genetic counselors use a variety of data in their work (Lindhout, Frets, & Niermeijer, 1991). For instance, couples contemplating having a child may seek to determine the risks involved in a future pregnancy. In such a case, a counselor will take a thorough family history, seeking any familial incidence of birth defects that might indicate a pattern of recessive or X-linked genes. In addition, the counselor will take into account factors such as the age of the mother and father and any previous abnormalities in other children they may have already had.

genetic counseling the discipline that focuses on helping people deal with issues relating to inherited disorders

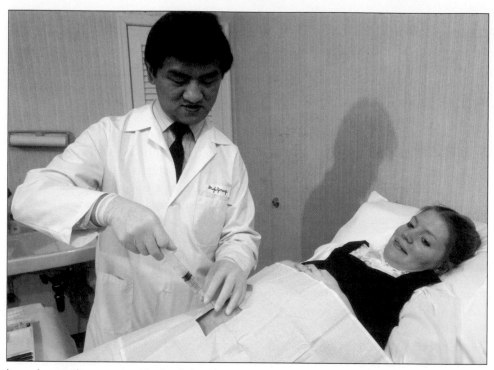

In amniocentesis, a sample of fetal cells is withdrawn from the amniotic sac and used to identify a number of genetic defects.

amniocentesis the process of identifying genetic defects by examining a small sample of fetal cells drawn by a needle inserted into the amniotic fluid surrounding the unborn fetus

chorionic villus sampling (CVS) a test used to find genetic defects that involves taking samples of hairlike material that surrounds the embryo

ultrasound sonography a process in which high-frequency sound waves scan the mother's womb to produce an image of the unborn baby, whose size and shape can then be assessed

Typically, genetic counselors suggest a thorough physical examination. Such an exam may identify physical abnormalities that potential parents may have and not be aware of. In addition, samples of blood, skin, and urine may be used to isolate and examine specific chromosomes. Possible genetic defects, such as the presence of an extra sex chromosome, can be identified by assembling a *karyotype*, a chart containing enlarged photos of each of the chromosomes.

If the woman is already pregnant, testing of the unborn child itself is possible. In **amniocentesis,** a small sample of fetal cells is drawn by a tiny needle inserted into the amniotic fluid surrounding the unborn fetus. By analyzing the fetal cells, technicians can identify a variety of genetic defects. In addition, they can determine the sex of the child. Although there is always a danger to the fetus in such an invasive procedure, amniocentesis is generally safe when carried out between the 12th and 16th weeks of pregnancy.

An additional test, **chorionic villus sampling (CVS)**, can be employed even earlier. The test involves taking small samples of hairlike material that surrounds the embryo. CVS can be done between the 8th and 11th weeks of pregnancy. However, because it is riskier than amniocentesis and can identify fewer genetic problems, its use is relatively infrequent.

Other tests that are less invasive and therefore less risky are also possible. For instance, the unborn child may be examined through **ultrasound sonography,** in which high-frequency sound waves are used to bombard the mother's womb. These waves produce a rather indistinct, but useful, image of the unborn baby, whose size and shape can then be assessed. Repeated use of ultrasound sonography can reveal developmental patterns.

After the various tests are complete and all possible information is available, the couple will meet with the genetic counselor again. Typically, counselors avoid giving specific recommendations. Instead, they lay out the facts and present various options, ranging from doing nothing to taking more drastic steps, such as terminating the pregnancy through abortion. Ultimately, it is the parents who must decide what course of action to follow.

The newest role of genetic counselors involves testing people to identify whether they themselves, rather than their children, are susceptible to future disorders because of genetic abnormalities. For instance, *Huntington's disease*, a devastating, always fatal disorder marked by tremors and intellectual deterioration, typically does not appear until people reach their 40s. However, genetic testing can identify much earlier whether a person carries the flawed gene that produces Huntington's disease. Presumably, people's knowledge that they carry the gene can help them prepare themselves for the future (van't Spijker & ten Kroode, 1997).

In addition to Huntington's disease, more than 450 disorders can be predicted on the basis of genetic testing (see Table 2-2). Although such testing may bring welcome relief from future worries—if the results are negative—positive results may produce just the opposite effect. In fact, genetic testing raises difficult practical and ethical questions (Painter, 1997; Haederle, 1999; Kenen, et al., 2000; Meiser & Dunn, 2000).

Suppose, for instance, a person who thought she was susceptible to Huntington's disease was tested in her 20s and found that she did not carry the defective gene. Obviously, she would experience tremendous relief. But suppose she found that she did carry the flawed gene and was therefore going to get the disease. She might well experience depression and remorse. In fact, some studies show that 10 percent of people who find they have the flawed gene that leads to Huntington's disease never recover fully on an emotional level (Nowak, 1994a; Groopman, 1998).

Genetic testing clearly is a complicated issue. It rarely provides a simple yes or no answer as to whether an individual will be susceptible to a disorder. Instead, typically it

Table 2-2

DNA TESTS AVAILABLE NOW

Disease	Description	Incidence	Cost
Adult polycystic kidney disease	Multiple kidney growths	1 in 1,000	$350
Alpha-1-antitrypsin deficiency	Can cause hepatitis, cirrhosis of the liver, emphysema	1 in 2,000 to 1 in 4,000	$200
Charcot-Marie-Tooth disease	Progressive degeneration of muscles	1 in 2,500	$250–$350
Familial adenomatous polyposos	Colon polyps by age 35, often leading to cancer	1 in 5,000	$1,000
Cystic fibrosis	Lungs clog with mucus; usually fatal by age 40	1 in 2,500 Caucasians	$125–$150
Duchenne/Becker muscular dystrophy	Progressive degeneration of muscles	1 in 3,000 males	$300–$900
Hemophilia	Blood fails to clot properly	1 in 10,000	$250–$350
Fragile X syndrome	Most common cause of inherited mental retardation	1 in 1,250 males; 1 in 2,500 females	$250
Gaucher's disease	Mild to deadly enzyme deficiency	1 in 400 Ashkenazi Jews	$100–$150
Huntington's disease	Lethal neurological deterioration	1 in 10,000 Caucasians	$250–$300
"Lou Gehrig's disease" (ALS)	Fatal degeneration of the nervous system	1 in 50,000, 10% familial	$150–$450
Myotonic dystrophy	Progressive degeneration of muscles	1 in 8,000	$250
Multiple endocrine neoplastia	Endocrine gland tumors	1 in 50,000	$900
Neurofibromatosis	*Café au lait* spots to large tumors	1 in 3,000	$900
Retinoblastoma	Blindness; potentially fatal eye tumors	1 in 20,000	$1,500
Spinal muscular atrophy	Progressive degeneration of muscles	7 in 100,000	$100–$900
Tay-Sachs disease	Lethal childhood neurological disorder	1 in 3,600 Ashkenazi Jews	$150
Thalassemia	Mild to fatal anemia	1 in 100,000	$300

Tests of the Future

Alzheimer's	Most likely multiple genes involved	4 million cases	Not available
Breast cancer	Five to 10% of all cases are thought to be hereditary	2.6 million cases	Not available
Diabetes	Most likely multiple genes involved	13–14 million cases	Not available
Nonpolyposis colon cancer	Several genes cause up to 20% of all cases	150,000 cases per year	Not available
Manic-depression	Most likely multiple genes involved	2 million cases	Not available

From Research to Practice

A Small Step by ANDi: Genetic Engineering, Gene Therapy, and Cloning

In all ways he looks like an ordinary rhesus monkey. But in one respect, this monkey is unique: He is the first genetically modified primate. Named ANDi (for "Inserted DNA" in reverse), the monkey was the recipient of a gene taken from jellyfish. Scientists inserted the gene into monkey eggs and fertilized the modified eggs with monkey sperm in the lab. Ultimately, three baby monkeys were born, one of which— ANDi—included the new gene in his DNA (Chan et al., 2001).

ANDi is the result of genetic engineering. He joins fruit flies, rabbits, sheep, and cows that carry genes from other species. Other genetically engineered animals have been produced that are exact genetic replicas, or *clones*, of members of the same species (Kolata, 1998; Pennisi & Vogel, 2000).

The technological advance that ANDi represents takes us one step further down the road toward genetic engineering in humans. Genetic engineering has the potential to go beyond the kind of prenatal surgery used in the case of Ethan Buchkovich, described in the chapter prologue, to allow scientists to correct genetic flaws even before an individual is born.

Genetic engineering is likely to revolutionize medicine in the 21st century. Already, some forms of gene therapy are being used to correct genetic defects in humans after they are born. In *gene therapy*, genes that are targeted to correct a particular disease are injected into a patient's bloodstream. When the genes arrive at the site of the defective genes that are causing the disease, their presence leads to the production of chemicals that can treat the problem. For instance, in the case of cancer, corrective genes might be engineered to produce proteins that could kill tumor cells. In other cases, new genes can be added to make up for missing or ineffective cells (Kmiec, 1999; Levy, 2000).

The list of diseases currently being treated through gene therapy is still relatively short, although the number is growing. For instance, experiments using gene therapy are now being employed for cystic fibrosis, hemophilia, rheumatoid arthritis, AIDS, and several other diseases. When such treatments will move from the experimental to the routine, however, remains to be seen (Begley, 1998).

Advances in genetic engineering promise to make gene therapy even more useful. In a process called *germ-line gene therapy*, genetic modifications can correct problems not only for unborn individuals, but for future generations as well. In germ-line gene therapy, scientists might "harvest" defective cells soon after conception, removing them from the fertilized egg within the mother and placing them in a test-tube culture. Gene therapy could be employed to correct the defects in the cells. Next, one of the corrected cells—a slightly altered clone of the initial cells—could be returned to the mother. In a more extreme possibility, cells from one parent might be altered genetically to remove any defects, and this clone could then be permitted to grow. The result would be a clone, genetically identical to the parent except for the lack of the genetic defect. Obviously, such possibilities raise serious ethical questions (Wilmut, 1998; Zanjani & Anderson, 1999).

Will the technology that is making gene therapy possible lead to the ultimate science fiction feat: cloning a complete human being? Some scientists are beginning to think so, for use in such cases as a husband and wife who are both infertile wishing to clone themselves in order to have genetically related children. Although important technological hurdles remain to be overcome before cloning will be routine, the confidence of researchers appears to have spurred political leaders to think about the ethical and moral consequences of cloning, and laws limiting human cloning have already been enacted (Angier, 2000; Gordon, 1999; Stolberg, 2001).

The first patient to ever receive gene therapy was Ashanti DeSilva, a 4-year-old with a rare, inherited disease called severe combined immunodeficiency (SCID), which caused her immune system to shut down. Consequently, she was continually susceptible to a huge number of infections. To remedy the situation, scientists removed some white blood cells from Ashanti's immune system and inserted nondiseased copies of the defective gene. These nondiseased copies were then injected into her body. Five years later, Ashanti was a normal 9-year-old with no immune-system problems (Anderson, 1995). Photo © 1995 Jessica Boyatt.

presents a range of probabilities. In some cases, the likelihood of actually becoming ill depends on the type of environmental stressors to which a person is exposed. Personal differences also affect a given person's susceptibility to a disorder (Brownlee, Cook, & Hardigg, 1994).

As our understanding of genetics continues to grow, researchers and medical practitioners have moved beyond testing and counseling to actively working to change flawed genes. The possibilities for genetic intervention and manipulation increasingly border on what once was science fiction—as we consider in the accompanying *From Research to Practice* box about cloning.

Review and Rethink

REVIEW

- In humans, the male sex cell (the sperm) and the female sex cell (the ovum) provide the developing baby with 23 chromosomes each.
- A genotype is the underlying combination of genetic material present in an organism, but invisible; a phenotype is the visible trait, the expression of the genotype.
- The field of behavioral genetics, a combination of psychology and genetics, studies the effects of genetics on behavior.
- Several inherited and genetic disorders are due to damaged or mutated genes.
- Genetic counselors use a variety of data and techniques to advise future parents of possible genetic risks to their unborn children.

RETHINK

- What are some ethical and philosophical questions that surround the issue of genetic counseling? Might it sometimes be unwise to know ahead of time about possible genetically linked disorders that might afflict your child or yourself?
- How can the study of identical twins who were separated at birth help researchers determine the effects of genetic and environmental factors on human development? How might you design such a study?

The Interaction of Heredity and Environment

Like many other parents, Jared's mother, Leesha, and his father, Jamal, tried to figure out which one of them their new baby most resembled. He seemed to have Leesha's big, wide eyes and Jamal's generous smile. As he grew, Jared came to resemble his mother and father even more. His hair grew in with a hairline just like Leesha's, and his teeth, when they came, made his smile resemble Jamal's even more. He also seemed to act like his parents. For example, he was a charming little baby, always ready to smile at people who visited the house—just like his friendly, jovial dad. He seemed to sleep like his mom, which was lucky, since Jamal was an extremely light sleeper who could do with as little as 4 hours a night, while Leesha liked a regular 7 or 8 hours.

Were Jared's ready smile and regular sleeping habits something he just luckily inherited from his parents? Or did Jamal and Leesha provide a happy and stable home that encouraged these welcome traits? What causes our behavior? Is it heredity or environment? Nature or nurture? This enduring question about the root causes of human behavior has intrigued and puzzled developmental researchers. Is behavior produced by inherited, genetic influences, or is it triggered by factors in the environment?

The simple answer is, there is no simple answer.

The Role of the Environment in Determining the Expression of Genes: From Genotypes to Phenotypes

As developmental research accumulates, it is becoming increasingly clear that to view behavior as due to *either* genetic *or* environmental factors is inappropriate. A given behavior is not caused just by genetic factors; nor is it caused solely by environmental forces. Instead, as we first discussed in Chapter 1, the behavior is the product of some combination of the two (Rutter et al., 1997).

For instance, consider **temperament,** patterns of arousal and emotionality that represent consistent and enduring characteristics in an individual. Suppose we found—as increasing evidence suggests is the case—that a small percentage of children are born with temperaments that produce an unusual degree of physiological reactivity. Having a tendency to shrink from anything unusual, such infants react to novel stimuli with a rapid increase in heartbeat and unusual excitability of the limbic system of the brain. Such heightened reactivity to stimuli at the start of life, which seems to be linked to inherited factors, is also likely to cause children, by the time they are four or five, to be considered shy by their parents and teachers. But not always: some of them behave indistinguishably from their peers at the same age (Kagan & Snidman, 1991; McCrae et al., 2000).

What makes the difference? The answer seems to be the environment in which the children are raised. Children whose parents encourage them to be outgoing by arranging supportive opportunities for them to engage in new activities may overcome their shyness. In contrast, children raised in a stressful environment marked by marital discord or a prolonged illness may be more likely to retain their shyness later in life (Kagan, Arcus, & Snidman, 1993; Pedlow et al., 1993; Joseph, 1999). Jared, described earlier, may have been born with an easy temperament, which was easily reinforced by his caring parents.

Such findings illustrate that many traits represent **multifactorial transmission,** meaning that they are determined by a combination of both genetic and environmental

temperament patterns of arousal and emotionality that represent consistent and enduring characteristics in an individual

multifactorial transmission the determination of traits by a combination of both genetic and environmental factors in which a genotype provides a range within which a phenotype may be expressed

"I'm their real child, and you're just a frozen embryo thingy they bought from some laboratory."

factors. In multifactorial transmission, a genotype provides a particular range within which a phenotype may achieve expression. For instance, people with a genotype that permits them to gain weight easily may never be slim, no matter how much they diet. They may be *relatively* slim, given their genetic heritage, but they may never be able to get beyond a certain degree of thinness (Faith, Johnson, & Allison, 1997). In many cases, then, it is the environment that determines the way in which a particular genotype will be expressed as a phenotype (Wachs, 1993, 1996).

On the other hand, certain genotypes are relatively unaffected by environmental factors. In such cases, development follows a preordained pattern, relatively independent of the specific environment in which a person is raised. For instance, research on pregnant women who were severely malnourished during famines caused by World War II found that their children were, on average, unaffected physically or intellectually as adults (Stein et al., 1975). Similarly, no matter how much health food people eat, they are not going to grow beyond certain genetically imposed limitations in height. Little Jared's hairline was probably very little affected by any actions on the part of his parents.

Ultimately, of course, it is the unique interaction of inherited and environmental factors that determines people's patterns of development. As Jerome Kagan writes:

> No human quality, psychological or physiological, is free of the contribution of events both within and outside the organism. . . . [E]very psychological quality is like a pale gray fabric woven from thin black threads, which represent biology, and thin white ones, which represent experience. But it is not possible to detect any quite black or white threads in the gray cloth. (Kagan, Arcus, & Snidman, 1993, p. 209)

The more appropriate question, then, is *how much* of the behavior is caused by genetic factors, and *how much* by environmental factors? (See, for example, the range of possibilities for the determinants of intelligence, illustrated in Figure 2-7.)

Answering the Nature–Nurture Riddle

Developmental researchers have used several strategies to try to resolve the question of the degree to which traits, characteristics, and behavior are produced by genetic or environmental factors. In seeking a resolution, they have turned to studies involving both nonhuman species and humans (Plomin, 1994a; Wahlsten & Gottlieb, 1997; Collins et al., 2000).

Nonhuman Studies: Controlling Both Genetics and Environment. One approach to understanding the relative contribution of heredity and environment makes use of nonhuman animals. It is relatively simple to develop breeds of animals that are genetically similar to one another in terms of specific traits. The people who raise Butterball turkeys for Thanksgiving do it all the time, producing turkeys that grow especially rapidly so that they can be brought to market inexpensively. Similarly, strains of laboratory animals can be bred to share similar genetic backgrounds.

By observing animals with similar genetic backgrounds in different environments, scientists can determine, with reasonable precision, the effects of specific kinds of environmental stimulation. Conversely, researchers can examine groups of animals that have been bred to have significantly *different* genetic backgrounds on particular traits. Then, by exposing such animals to identical environments, they can determine the role that genetic background plays.

Of course, the drawback to using nonhumans as research subjects is that we can't be sure how well the findings we obtain can be generalized to people. Still, the opportunities that animal research offers are substantial.

Nature ▶▶▶▶▶▶▶▶▶▶▶				◀◀◀◀◀◀◀◀ Nurture
Intelligence is provided entirely by genetic factors; environment plays no role. Even a highly enriched environment and excellent education make no difference.	Although largely inherited, intelligence is affected by an extremely enriched or deprived environment.	Intelligence is affected both by a person's genetic endowment and environment. A person genetically predisposed to low intelligence may perform better if raised in an enriched environment or worse in a deprived environment. Similarly, a person genetically predisposed to higher intelligence may perform worse in a deprived environment or better in an enriched environment.	Although intelligence is largely a result of environment, genetic abnormalities may produce mental retardation.	Intelligence depends entirely on the environment. Genetics plays no role in determining intellectual success.

(left vertical label: Possible Causes)

Figure 2-7 Possible Causes of Intelligence

Intelligence may be explained by a range of differing possible causes, spanning the nature–nurture continuum. Which of these explanations do you find most convincing, given the evidence discussed in the chapter?

Human Studies: Exploiting Genetic Similarities and Dissimilarities. Obviously, researchers can't control either the genetic backgrounds or the environments of humans in the way they can with nonhumans. However, nature conveniently has provided the potential to carry out various kinds of "natural experiments"—in the form of twins.

Recall that identical, monozygotic twins share an identical genetic code. Because their inherited backgrounds are precisely the same, any variations in their behavior must be due entirely to environmental factors.

In a world devoid of ethics, it would be rather simple for researchers to make use of identical twins to draw unequivocal conclusions about the roles of nature and nurture. For instance, by separating identical twins at birth and placing them in totally different environments, researchers could assess the impact of environment unambiguously. Obvi-

Monozygotic and dizygotic twins present opportunities to learn about the relative contributions of heredity and situational factors. What kinds of things can psychologists learn from studying twins?

ously, ethical considerations make this impossible. However, there are a fair number of cases in which identical twins are put up for adoption at birth and are raised in substantially different environments. Such instances allow us to draw fairly confident conclusions about the relative contributions of genetics and environment (Bouchard & Pederson, 1999; Bailey et al., 2000).

Still, the data from monozygotic twins raised in different environments are not always without bias. Adoption agencies typically take the characteristics (and wishes) of birth mothers into account when they place babies in adoptive homes. For instance, children tend to be placed with families of the same race and religion. Consequently, even when monozygotic twins are placed in different adoptive homes, there are often similarities in the two home environments. The consequence is that researchers can't always unambiguously attribute differences in behavior to genetics or environment.

Dizygotic twins, too, present opportunities to learn about the relative contributions of heredity and situational factors. Recall that dizygotic twins are genetically no more similar than siblings in a family born at different times. It is possible to compare behavior within pairs of dizygotic twins with that of pairs of monozygotic twins (who are genetically identical). If monozygotic twins are more similar on a particular trait, on average, than dizygotic twins, we can assume that genetics plays an important role in determining the expression of that trait (e.g., Schulman, Keith, & Seligman, 1993).

Still another approach is to study people who are totally unrelated to one another and who therefore have dissimilar genetic backgrounds, but who share an environmental background. For instance, a family that adopts, at the same time, two very young unrelated children probably will provide them with quite similar environments throughout their childhood. In this case, similarities in the children's characteristics and behavior can be attributed with some confidence to environmental influences (Segal, 1993, 2000).

Finally, developmental researchers have examined groups of people in light of their degree of genetic similarity. For instance, if we find a high association on a particular trait between biological parents and their children, but a weaker association between adoptive parents and their children, we have evidence for the importance of genetics in determining the expression of that trait. On the other hand, if there is a stronger association on a trait between adoptive parents and their children than between biological parents and their children, we have evidence for the importance of the environment in determining that trait. In general, when a particular trait tends to occur at similar levels among genetically similar individuals, but tends to vary more among genetically more distant individuals, we can assume that genetics plays an important role in the development of that trait (Rowe, 1994).

Developmental researchers have used all these approaches, and more, to study the relative impact of genetic and environmental factors. What have they found? Before turning to their specific findings, it is important to restate the general conclusion resulting from decades of research: Virtually all traits, characteristics, and behaviors are the joint result of the combination and interaction of nature and nurture. Like love and marriage and horses and carriages, genetic and environmental factors work in tandem, creating the unique individual that each of us is and will become.

Physical Traits: Family Resemblances

When patients entered the examining room of Dr. Cyril Marcus, they didn't realize that sometimes they were actually being treated by his identical twin brother, Dr. Stewart Marcus. So similar in appearance and manner were the twins that even long-time patients were fooled by this admittedly unethical behavior, which occurred in a bizarre case made famous in the film *Dead Ringers*.

Monozygotic twins are merely the most extreme example of the fact that the more genetically similar two people are, the more likely they are to share physical characteristics. Tall parents tend to have tall children, and short ones tend to have short children. Obesity, which is defined as being more than 20 percent above the average weight for a given height, also has a strong genetic component. For example, in one study, pairs of identical twins were put on diets that contained an extra 1,000 calories a day—and ordered not to exercise. Over a 3-month period, the twins gained almost identical amounts of weight. Moreover, different pairs of twins varied substantially in how much weight they gained, with some pairs gaining almost three times as much weight as other pairs (Bouchard et al., 1990).

Other, less obvious physical characteristics also show strong genetic influences. For instance, blood pressure, respiration rates, and even the age at which life ends are more similar in closely related individuals than in those who are less genetically similar (Jost & Sontag, 1944; Sorensen et al., 1988; Price & Gottesman, 1991).

Intelligence: More Research, More Controversy

No other issue involving the relative influence of heredity and environment has generated more research than the topic of intelligence. Why? The main reason is that intelligence, generally measured in terms of an IQ score, is a core human characteristic. IQ is strongly related to success in scholastic endeavors and, somewhat less strongly, to other types of achievement.

Let's first consider the degree to which intelligence is related to genetic factors. The answer is unambiguous: Genetics plays a significant role in intelligence. Both overall intelligence and specific subcomponents of intelligence (such as spatial skills, verbal skills, and memory) show strong effects for heredity (McGue et al., 1993; Cardon & Fulker, 1993; Rowe, 1999). As can be seen in Figure 2-8, the closer the genetic link between two individuals, the greater the correspondence of their overall IQ scores.

Not only is genetics an important influence on intelligence, but the impact increases with age. For instance, as fraternal (i.e., dizygotic) twins move from infancy to adolescence, their IQ scores become less similar. In contrast, the IQ scores of identical (monozygotic) twins become increasingly similar over the course of time. These opposite patterns suggest the intensifying influence of inherited factors with increasing age (Wilson, 1983; Brody, 1993; McGue et al., 1993).

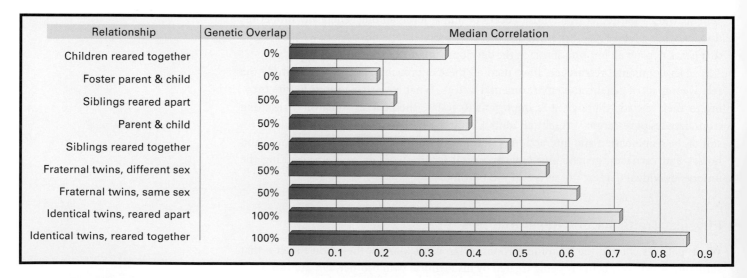

Figure 2-8   Genetics and IQ

The closer the genetic link between two individuals, the greater the correspondence between their IQ scores. Why do you think there is a sex difference in the fraternal twins figures? Might there be other sex differences in other sets of twins or siblings, not shown on this chart?

(*Source:* Bouchard & McGue, 1981.)

Although it is clear that heredity plays an important role in intelligence, investigators are much more divided on the question of how to quantify that role. Perhaps the most extreme view is held by psychologist Arthur Jensen (1969), who argues that as much as 80 percent of intelligence is a result of the influence of heredity. Others have suggested more modest figures, ranging from 50 to 70 percent. It is critical to keep in mind that such figures are averages across large groups of people, and any particular individual's degree of inheritance cannot be predicted from these averages (e.g., Herrnstein & Murray, 1994; Devlin, Daniels, & Roeder, 1997).

It is important to keep in mind that although heredity clearly plays an important role in intelligence, environmental factors are profoundly influential. Even the most extreme estimates of the role of genetics still allow for environmental factors to play a significant role. In fact, in terms of public policy for maximizing people's intellectual success, the issue is not whether primarily hereditary or environmental factors underlie intelligence. Instead, as developmental psychologist Sandra Scarr suggests, we should be asking what can be done to maximize the intellectual development of each individual (Scarr & Carter-Saltzman, 1982; Storfer, 1990; Bouchard, 1997).

Genetic and Environmental Influences on Personality: Born to Be Outgoing?

Although it seems reasonable to most people that such characteristics as race and eye color are inherited, the notion that personality characteristics are affected by genetic factors seems less credible. However, increasing evidence supports the conclusion that at least some personality traits have at least some genetic components (Rowe, 1994; Plomin & Caspi, 1998; Cohen, 1999).

For example, neuroticism and extroversion are among the personality factors that have been linked most directly to genetic factors. The term *neuroticism*, when considered in the context of personality, refers to the degree of moodiness, touchiness, or sensitivity an individual characteristically displays. In other words, neuroticism reflects

Although genetic factors clearly play a significant role in the development of intelligence, the level of environmental enrichment is also crucial.

emotional reactivity. *Extroversion* is the degree to which a person seeks to be with others, to behave in an outgoing manner, and generally to be sociable (Loehlin, 1992; Bergeman et al., 1993; Plomin, 1994b). For instance, Jared, the baby described earlier in this chapter, may have inherited a tendency to be outgoing from his extroverted father, Jamal.

How do we know which personality traits reflect genetics? Some evidence comes from examination of genes. For instance, surprising recent evidence suggests that a specific gene partially determines risk-taking behavior. According to two teams of researchers, a novelty-seeking gene affects the production of the brain chemical dopamine, making some people more prone than others to seek out novel situations and to take risks (Ebstein et al., 1996).

Other evidence for the role of genetics in the determination of personality traits comes from studies of twins. For instance, in one large-scale study, personality psychologist Auke Tellegen and colleagues studied the personality traits of hundreds of pairs of twins. Because a good number of the twins were genetically identical but had been raised apart, it was possible to determine with some confidence the influence of genetic factors (Tellegen et al., 1988).

Tellegen found that certain traits reflected the contribution of genetics considerably more than others. As you can see in Figure 2-9, social potency (the tendency to be a masterful, forceful leader who enjoys being the center of attention) and traditionalism (strict endorsement of rules and authority) are strongly associated with genetic factors.

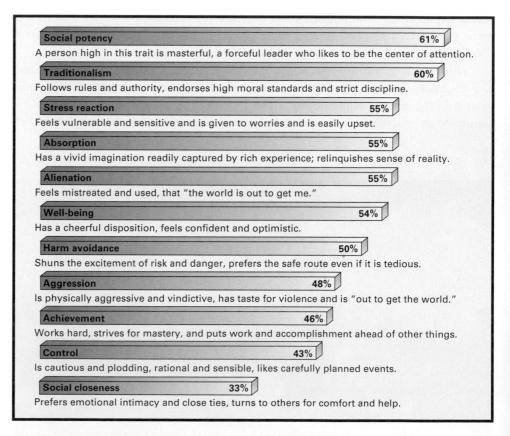

Figure 2-9 **Inheriting Traits**

These traits are among the personality factors that are related most closely to genetic factors. The higher the percentage, the greater the degree to which the trait reflects the influence of heredity. Do these figures mean that "leaders are born, not made"? Why or why not?

(Adapted from Tellegen et al., 1988.)

Other research has revealed genetic influences on other, less central personality traits. For example, a person's political attitudes, religious interests and values, and even attitudes toward human sexuality seem to have genetic components (Lykken et al., 1993a; Schulman, Keith & Seligman, 1993).

Clearly, genetic factors play a role in determining personality. At the same time, the environment in which a child is raised affects personality development. For example, some parents encourage high activity levels, seeing activity as a manifestation of independence and intelligence. Other parents may encourage lower levels of activity on the part of their children, feeling that more passive children will get along better in society. Part of these parental attitudes are culturally determined; parents in the United Sates may encourage higher activity levels, while parents in Asian cultures may encourage greater passivity. In both cases, children's personalities will be shaped in part by their parents' attitudes.

Clearly, both genetic and environmental factors have consequences for a child's personality, illustrating once again the critical interplay between nature and nurture. Furthermore, the way in which nature and nurture interact can be reflected not just in the behavior of individuals, but in the very foundations of a culture, as we see next.

"The good news is that you will have a healthy baby girl. The bad news is that she is a congenital liar."

© *The New Yorker Collection 1996. J. B. Handelsman from cartoonbank.com. All rights reserved.*

Developmental Diversity

Cultural Differences in Physical Arousal: Might a Culture's Philosophical Outlook Be Determined by Genetics?

The Buddhist philosophy, an inherent part of many Asian cultures, emphasizes harmony and peacefulness, and suggests that one should seek the eradication of human desire. In contrast, some of the traditional philosophies of Western civilization, such as those of Martin Luther and John Calvin, accentuate the importance of controlling the anxiety, fear, and guilt that are thought to be basic parts of the human condition.

Could such philosophical approaches reflect, in part, genetic factors? That is the controversial suggestion made by developmental psychologist Jerome Kagan and his colleagues. They speculate that the underlying temperament of a given society, determined genetically, may predispose people in that society toward a particular philosophy (Kagan, Arcus, & Snidman, 1993).

Kagan bases his admittedly speculative suggestion on well-confirmed findings that show clear differences in temperament between Caucasian and Asian children. For instance, one study that compared 4-month-old infants in China, Ireland, and the United States found several relevant differences. In comparison to the Caucasian-American babies and the Irish babies, the Chinese babies had significantly lower motor activity, irritability, and vocalization (see Table 2-3).

Kagan suggests that the Chinese, who enter the world temperamentally calmer, may find Buddhist philosophical notions of serenity more in tune with their natural inclinations. In contrast, Westerners, who are emotionally more volatile and tense, and who report higher levels of guilt, are more likely to be attracted to philosophies that articulate the necessity of controlling the unpleasant feelings that they are more apt to encounter in their everyday experience (Kagan et al., 1994).

It is important to note that this does not mean that one philosophical approach is necessarily better or worse than the other. Nor does it mean that either of the temperaments from which the philosophies are thought to spring is superior or inferior to the other. Similarly, we must keep in mind that any single individual within a culture can be

Table 2-3

MEAN BEHAVIORAL SCORES FOR CAUCASIAN AMERICAN, IRISH, AND CHINESE 4-MONTH-OLD INFANTS

Behavior	American	Irish	Chinese
Motor activity	48.6	36.7	11.2
Crying (in seconds)	7.0	2.9	1.1
Fretting (% trials)	10.0	6.0	1.9
Vocalizing (% trials)	31.4	31.1	8.1
Smiling (% trials)	4.1	2.6	3.6

(*Source:* Kagan, Arcus, & Snidman, 1993.)

more or less temperamentally volatile and that the range of temperaments found even within a particular culture is vast. Finally, as we noted in our initial discussion of temperament, environmental conditions can have a significant effect on the portion of a person's temperament that is not genetically determined.

Still, the notion that the very basis of culture—its philosophical traditions—may be affected by genetic factors is intriguing. More research is necessary to determine just how the unique interaction of heredity and environment within a given culture may produce a framework for viewing and understanding the world. ☐

Psychological Disorders: The Role of Genetics and Environment

> *Lori Schiller began to hear voices when she was a teenager in summer camp. Without warning, the voices screamed "You must die! Die! Die!" She ran from her bunk into the darkness, where she thought she could get away. Camp counselors found her screaming as she jumped wildly on a trampoline. "I thought I was possessed," she said later. (Bennett, 1992)*

In a sense, she was possessed: possessed with schizophrenia, one of the severest types of psychological disorder. Normal and happy through childhood, Schiller's world took a tumble during adolescence as she increasingly lost her hold on reality. For the next two decades, she would be in and out of institutions, struggling to ward off the ravages of the disorder.

What was the cause of Schiller's mental disorder? Increasing evidence suggests that schizophrenia is brought about by genetic factors. The disorder runs in families, with some families showing an unusually high incidence. Moreover, the closer the genetic links between someone with schizophrenia and another family member, the more likely it is that the other person will also develop schizophrenia. For instance, a monozygotic twin has close to a 50 percent risk of developing schizophrenia when the other twin develops the disorder (see Figure 2-10). On the other hand, a niece or nephew of a person with schizophrenia has less than a 5 percent chance of developing the disorder (Gottesman, 1991, 1993; Prescott & Gottesman, 1993).

However, these data also illustrate that genetics alone does not influence the development of the disorder. If genetics were the sole cause, the risk for an identical twin would be 100 percent. Consequently, other factors account for the disorder, ranging from structural abnormalities in the brain to a biochemical imbalance (Iacono & Grove, 1993; Wang et al., 1993; Gur & Chin, 1999).

It also seems that even if individuals harbor a genetic predisposition toward schizophrenia, they are not destined to develop the disorder. Instead, they may inherit an un-

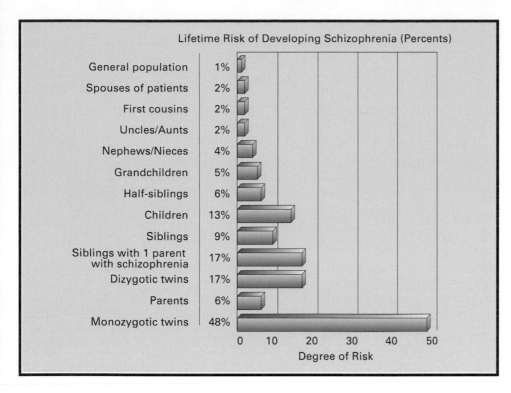

Lifetime Risk of Developing Schizophrenia (Percents)

General population	1%
Spouses of patients	2%
First cousins	2%
Uncles/Aunts	2%
Nephews/Nieces	4%
Grandchildren	5%
Half-siblings	6%
Children	13%
Siblings	9%
Siblings with 1 parent with schizophrenia	17%
Dizygotic twins	17%
Parents	6%
Monozygotic twins	48%

Degree of Risk

Figure 2-10 **The Genetics of Schizophrenia**

The psychological disorder of schizophrenia has clear genetic components. The closer the genetic links between someone with schizophrenia and another family member, the more likely it is that the other person will also develop schizophrenia.

(*Source:* Gottesman, 1991.)

usual sensitivity to stress in the environment. If stress is low, schizophrenia will not occur. But if stress is sufficiently strong, it will lead to schizophrenia. On the other hand, for someone with a strong genetic predisposition toward the disorder, even relatively weak environmental stressors may lead to schizophrenia (Gottesman, 1991; Bergen, et al., 1998; Paris, 1999; Norman & Malla, 2001).

Several other psychological disorders have been shown to be related, at least in part, to genetic factors. For instance, major depression, alcoholism, autism, and attention-deficit hyperactivity disorder have significant inherited components (Rutter et al., 1993; Roy et al., 1999).

The example of schizophrenia and other genetically related psychological disorders also illustrates a fundamental principle regarding the relationship between heredity and environment, one that underlies much of our previous discussion. Specifically, the role of genetics is often to produce preparedness for a future course of development. When and whether a certain behavioral characteristic will actually be displayed depends on the nature of the environment (Cooper, 2001). Thus, although a predisposition for schizophrenia may be present at birth, typically people do not show the disorder until adolescence—if at all.

Similarly, certain other kinds of traits are more likely to be displayed as the influence of parents and other socializing factors declines. For example, adopted children may, early in their lives, display traits that are relatively similar to their adoptive parents' traits, given the overwhelming influence of the environment on young children. In contrast, as they get older and their parents' influence declines, genetically influenced traits may begin to manifest themselves as unseen genetic factors begin to play a greater role (Loehlin, 1992; Caspi & Moffitt, 1991, 1993).

Can Genes Influence Environment?

According to developmental psychologist Sandra Scarr (1992, 1993), the genetic endowment provided to children by their parents not only determines their genetic characteristics, but also actively influences their environment. Scarr suggests three ways a child's genetic predisposition might influence his or her environment.

active genotype–environment effects
situations in which children focus on those aspects of their environment that are most congruent with their genetically determined abilities

passive genotype–environment effects
situations in which parents' genes are associated with the environment in which children are raised

evocative genotype–environment effects
situations in which a child's genes elicit a particular type of environment

Children may display **active genotype–environment effects** by focusing on those aspects of their environment that are most congruent with their genetically determined abilities. At the same time, they pay less attention to those aspects of the environment that are less compatible with their genetic endowment. For instance, two girls may be reading the same school bulletin board. One may notice the sign advertising tryouts for Little League baseball, while her less coordinated but more musically endowed friend might be more apt to spot the notice recruiting students for an after-school chorus. In each case, the child is attending to those aspects of the environment in which her genetically determined abilities can flourish.

In some cases, there are **passive genotype–environment effects,** in which *parents'* genes are associated with the environment in which children are raised. For example, a particularly sports-oriented parent, who has genes that promote good physical coordination, may provide many opportunities for a child to play sports.

There are also **evocative genotype–environment effects,** in which a child's genes elicit a particular type of environment. For instance, an infant's demanding behavior may cause parents to be more attentive to the infant's needs than they would be if the infant were less demanding. Or, for instance, a child who is genetically inclined to be well coordinated may play ball with anything in the house so often that her parents notice. They may then decide that she should have some sports equipment.

In sum, determining whether behavior is primarily attributable to nature or nurture is a bit like shooting at a moving target. Not only are behaviors and traits a joint outcome of genetic and environmental factors, but the relative influence of genes and environment for specific characteristics shifts over the course of people's lives. Although the pool of genes we inherit at birth sets the stage for our future development, the constantly shifting scenery and the other characters in our lives determine just how our development eventually plays out.

Review and Rethink

REVIEW

- Human characteristics and behavior are a joint outcome of genetic and environmental factors.
- Genetic influences have been identified in physical characteristics, intelligence, personality traits and behaviors, and psychological disorders.
- There is some speculation that entire cultures may be predisposed genetically toward certain types of philosophical viewpoints and attitudes.

RETHINK

- How might a different environment from the one you experienced have affected the development of personality characteristics that you believe you inherited from one or both of your parents?
- Some people have used the proven genetic basis of intelligence to argue against strenuous educational efforts on behalf of individuals with below-average IQs. Does this viewpoint make sense based on what you have learned about heredity and environment? Why or why not?

Prenatal Growth and Change

Robert accompanied Lisa to her first appointment with the midwife. The midwife checked the results of tests done to confirm the couple's own positive home pregnancy test. "Yep, you're going to have a baby," she confirmed, speaking to Lisa. "You'll need to set up monthly visits for the next six months, then more frequently as your due date approaches. You can get this prescription for prenatal vitamins filled at any pharmacy, and here are some guidelines about diet and exercise. You don't smoke, do you? That's good." Then she turned to Robert. "How about you? Do you smoke?" After giving lots of instructions and advice, she left the couple feeling slightly dazed, but ready to do whatever they could to have a healthy baby.

From the moment of conception, development proceeds relentlessly. As we've seen, many aspects are guided by the complex set of genetic guidelines inherited from the parents. Of course, prenatal growth, like all development, is also influenced from the start by environmental factors (Leavitt & Goldson, 1996). As we'll see, both parents, like Lisa and Robert, can take part in providing a good prenatal environment.

Fertilization: The Moment of Conception

When most of us think about the facts of life, we tend to focus on the events that cause a male's sperm cells to begin their journey toward a female's ovum. Yet the act of sex that brings about the potential for conception is both the consequence and the start of a long string of events that precede and follow **fertilization,** or conception: the joining of sperm and ovum to create the single-celled zygote from which each of us began our lives.

> **fertilization** the process by which a sperm and an ovum—the male and female gametes, respectively—join to form a single new cell

Both the male's sperm and the female's ovum come with a history of their own. Females are born with around 400,000 ova located in the two ovaries (see Figure 2-11 for the basic anatomy of the female and male sex organs). However, the ova do not mature until the female reaches puberty. From that point until she reaches menopause, the female will ovulate about every 28 days. During ovulation, an egg is released from one of the ovaries and pushed by minute hair cells through the fallopian tube toward the uterus. If the ovum meets a sperm in the fallopian tube, fertilization takes place (Aitken, 1995).

Sperm, which look a little like microscopic tadpoles, have a shorter life span. They are created by the testicles at a rapid rate: An adult male typically produces several

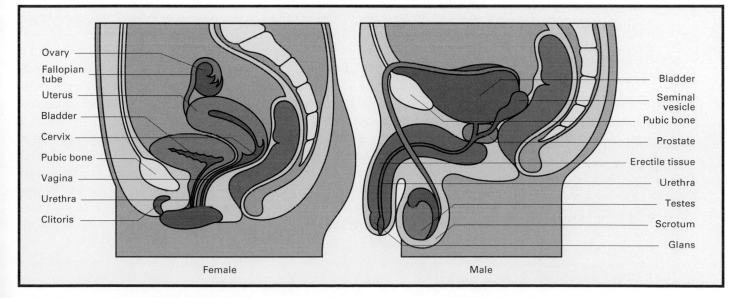

Figure 2-11 **Anatomy of the Sex Organs**

The basic anatomy of the sexual organs is illustrated in these cutaway side views.

hundred million sperm a day. Consequently, the sperm ejaculated during sexual intercourse are of considerably more recent origin than the ovum to which they are heading.

When sperm enter the vagina, they begin a winding journey that takes them through the cervix, the opening into the uterus, and into the fallopian tube, where fertilization may take place. However, only a tiny fraction of the 300 million cells that are typically ejaculated during sexual intercourse ultimately survive the arduous journey. That's usually okay, though: It takes only one sperm to fertilize an ovum, and each sperm and ovum contains all the genetic data necessary to produce a new human.

Alternative Routes to Pregnancy: Giving Nature a Boost

For some couples, conception presents a major challenge. In fact, some 15 percent of couples suffer from **infertility,** the inability to conceive after 12 to 18 months of trying to become pregnant.

Infertility is produced by several causes. In some cases, it is the age of the parents (the older the parents, the more likely infertility will occur); previous use of birth control pills; illicit drugs or cigarettes; or previous bouts of sexually transmitted diseases. In other cases, men have abnormally low sperm counts, a condition that decreases the chances that a sperm will successfully fertilize an ovum. And still other cases of infertility are a result of the woman's *mother* taking certain drugs during pregnancy.

Whatever the cause of infertility, there are several approaches that provide alternative paths to conception (Colon, 1997; Rosenthal, 1998). Some difficulties can be corrected through the use of drugs or surgery. Another option may be **artificial insemination,** a procedure in which a man's sperm is placed directly into a woman's vagina by a physician. In some situations, the woman's husband provides the sperm, while in others it is an anonymous donor from a sperm bank.

In other cases, in vitro fertilization is employed. **In vitro fertilization** (**IVF**) is a procedure in which a woman's ova are removed from her ovaries and a man's sperm are used to fertilize the ova in a laboratory. The fertilized egg is then implanted in either the woman who provided the donor eggs or in a **surrogate mother,** a woman who agrees to carry the child to term. Surrogate mothers may also be used in cases in which the mother is unable to conceive; the surrogate mother is artificially inseminated by a father and agrees to give up rights to the infant (van Balen, 1998).

The use of a surrogate mother presents a variety of ethical and legal issues, as well as many emotional concerns. In some cases, surrogate mothers have refused to give up the child after its birth, while in others the surrogate mother has sought to have a role in the child's life. In such cases, the rights of the mother, the father, the surrogate mother, and ultimately the baby are in conflict.

How do children conceived using emerging reproductive technologies such as in vitro fertilization fare? Research shows that they do quite well. In fact, one study found that the quality of parenting in families who have used such techniques may even be superior to that in families with naturally conceived children. Furthermore, the later psychological adjustment of children conceived using in vitro fertilization and artificial insemination is no different from that of children conceived using natural techniques (Hahn & DiPietro, 2001).

The Stages of the Prenatal Period: The Onset of Development

The prenatal period consists of three phases: the germinal, embryonic, and fetal stages. They are summarized in Table 2-4.

---

infertility the inability to conceive after 12 to 18 months of trying to become pregnant

artificial insemination a process of fertilization in which a man's sperm is placed directly into a woman's vagina by a physician

in vitro fertilization (IVF) a procedure in which a woman's ova are removed from her ovaries, and a man's sperm are used to fertilize the ova in a laboratory

surrogate mother a woman who agrees to carry a child to term in cases in which the mother who provides the donor eggs is unable to conceive

Table 2-4

STAGES OF THE PRENATAL PERIOD

GERMINAL	EMBRYONIC	FETAL
Fertilization to 2 Weeks	*2 Weeks to 8 Weeks*	*8 Weeks to Birth*
The germinal stage is the first and shortest, characterized by methodical cell division and the attachment of the organism to the wall of the uterus. Three days after fertilization the zygote consists of 32 cells, a number that doubles by the next day. Within a week the zygote multiplies to 100–150 cells. The cells become specialized, with some forming a protective layer around the zygote.	The zygote is now designated an embryo. The embryo develops three layers, which ultimately form a different set of structures as development proceeds. The layers are: Ectoderm: Skin, sense organs, brain, spinal cord. Endoderm: Digestive system, liver, respiratory system. Mesoderm: Muscles, blood, circulatory system. The embryo is one inch long.	The fetal stage formally starts when the differentiation of the major organs has occurred. Now called a fetus, the individual grows rapidly as length increases 20 times. At 4 months the fetus weighs an average of 4 ounces; at 7 months, 3 pounds; and at the time of birth the average child weighs just over 7 pounds.

The Germinal Stage: Fertilization to 2 Weeks. The **germinal stage,** the first—and shortest—stage of the prenatal period, takes place during the first 2 weeks following conception. During the germinal stage, the fertilized egg (now called a *blastocyst*) travels toward the *uterus,* where it becomes implanted in the uterus's wall, which is rich in nutrients. The germinal stage is characterized by methodical cell division, which gets off to a quick start: Three days after fertilization, the organism consists of some 32 cells, and by the next day the number doubles. Within a week, it is made up of 100 to 150 cells, and the number rises with increasing rapidity.

In addition to increasing in number, the cells of the organism become increasingly specialized. For instance, some cells form a protective layer around the mass of cells, while others begin to establish the rudiments of a placenta and umbilical cord. When fully developed, the **placenta** serves as a conduit between the mother and fetus, providing nourishment and oxygen via the *umbilical cord.* In addition, waste materials from the developing child are removed through the umbilical cord.

The Embryonic Stage: 2 Weeks to 8 Weeks. By the end of the germinal period—just 2 weeks after conception—the organism is firmly secured to the wall of the mother's uterus. At this point, the child is called an *embryo.* The **embryonic stage** is the period from 2 to 8 weeks following fertilization. One of the highlights of this stage is the development of the major organs and basic anatomy.

At the beginning of the embryonic stage, the developing child has three distinct layers, each of which will ultimately form a different set of structures as development proceeds. The outer layer of the embryo, the *ectoderm,* will form skin, hair, teeth, sense organs, and the brain and spinal cord. The *endoderm,* the inner layer, produces the digestive system, liver, pancreas, and respiratory system. Sandwiched between the ectoderm and endoderm is the *mesoderm,* from which the muscles, bones, blood, and circulatory system are forged. Every part of the body is formed from these three layers.

If you were looking at an embryo at the end of the embryonic stage, you might be hard-pressed to identify it as human. Only an inch long, an 8-week-old embryo has what appear to be gills and a tail-like structure. On the other hand, a closer look reveals several familiar features. Rudimentary eyes, nose, lips, and even teeth can be recognized, and the embryo has stubby bulges that will form arms and legs.

germinal stage the first—and shortest—stage of the prenatal period, which takes place during the first 2 weeks following conception

placenta a conduit between the mother and fetus, providing nourishment and oxygen via the umbilical cord

embryonic stage the period from 2 to 8 weeks following fertilization during which significant growth occurs in the major organs and body systems

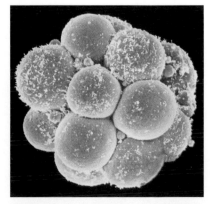

The germinal stage of the prenatal period gets off to a fast start. Here, the embryo has divided into 16 cells only days after fertilization.

fetal stage the stage that begins at about 8 weeks after conception and continues until birth

fetus a developing child, from 8 weeks after conception until birth

The Fetal Stage: 8 Weeks to Birth. It is not until the final period of prenatal development, the fetal stage, that the developing child becomes instantly recognizable. The **fetal stage** starts at about 8 weeks after conception and continues until birth. The fetal stage formally starts when the differentiation of the major organs has occurred.

Now called a **fetus**, the developing child undergoes astoundingly rapid change during the fetal stage. For instance, it increases in length some 20 times, and its proportions change dramatically. At 2 months, around half the fetus is what will ultimately be its head; by 5 months, the head accounts for just over a quarter of its total size (see Figure 2-12). The fetus also increases in weight substantially. At 4 months, the fetus weighs an average of about 4 ounces; at 7 months, it weighs about 3 pounds; and at the time of birth the average child weighs just over 7 pounds.

At the same time, the developing child is rapidly becoming more complex. Organs become more differentiated and start to work. By 3 months, for example, the fetus swallows and urinates. In addition, the interconnections between the different parts of the body become more complex and integrated. Arms develop hands; hands develop fingers; fingers develop nails.

As this is happening, the fetus makes itself known to the outside world. In the earliest stages of pregnancy, mothers may be unaware that they are, in fact, pregnant. As the fetus becomes increasingly active, however, most mothers certainly take notice. By 4 months, a mother can feel the movement of her child, and several months later others can feel the baby's kicks through the mother's skin.

During the fetal stage, the fetus develops a wide repertoire of different types of activities (Smotherman & Robinson, 1996). In addition to the kicks that alert its mother to its presence, the fetus can turn, do somersaults, cry, hiccup, clench its fist, open and close its eyes, and suck its thumb. It also is capable of hearing and can even respond to sounds that it hears repeatedly (Lecanuet, Granier-Deferre, & Busnel, 1995). For instance, researchers Anthony DeCasper and Melanie Spence (1986) asked a group of pregnant mothers to read aloud the Dr. Seuss story *The Cat in the Hat* two times a day during the latter months of pregnancy. Three days after the babies were born, they appeared to recognize the story they had heard, responding more to it than to another story that had a different rhythm.

Just as no two adults are alike, no two fetuses are the same. Although development during the prenatal period follows the broad patterns outlined here, there are significant

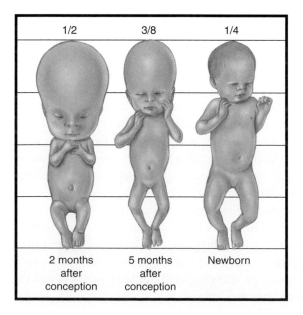

Figure 2-12 **Body Proportions**

During the fetal period, the proportions of the body change dramatically. At 2 months, the head represents about half the fetus, but by the time of birth, it is one-quarter of its total size.

differences in the specific nature of individual fetuses' behavior. Some fetuses are exceedingly active, while others are more sedentary. (The more active fetuses will probably be more active after birth.) Some have relatively quick heart rates, while others' heart rates are slower, with the typical range varying between 120 and 160 beats per minute (Lecanuet et al., 1995; Smotherman & Robinson, 1996).

Such differences in fetal behavior are due in part to genetic characteristics inherited at the moment of fertilization. Other kinds of differences, though, are brought about by the nature of the environment in which the child spends its first 9 months of life. As we will see, there are numerous ways in which the prenatal environment of infants affects their development—in good ways and bad.

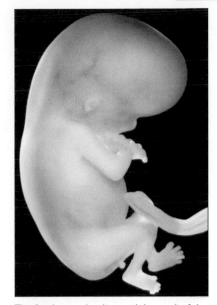

The fetal stage begins at eight weeks following conception.

Miscarriage and Abortion

A *miscarriage*—known as a spontaneous abortion—occurs when pregnancy ends before the developing child is able to survive outside the mother's womb. The embryo detaches from the wall of the uterus and is expelled.

Some 15 to 20 percent of all pregnancies end in miscarriage, usually in the first several months of pregnancy. Many occur so early that the mother is not even aware she was pregnant and may not even know she has suffered a miscarriage. Typically, miscarriages are attributable to some sort of genetic abnormality.

In *abortion*, a mother voluntarily chooses to terminate pregnancy. Involving a complex set of physical, psychological, legal, and ethical issues, abortion is a difficult choice for every woman. A task force of the American Psychological Association, which looked at the aftereffects of abortion, found that, following an abortion, most women experienced a combination of relief over terminating an unwanted pregnancy and regret and guilt. However, in most cases, the negative psychological aftereffects did not last, except for a small proportion of women who already had serious emotional problems. In all cases, abortion is a difficult choice.

The Prenatal Environment: Threats to Development

According to the Siriono people of South America, if a pregnant woman eats the meat of certain kinds of animals, she runs the risk of having a child who may act and look like those animals. According to opinions offered on daytime television talk shows such as the Oprah Winfrey show, a pregnant mother should avoid getting angry in order to spare her child from entering the world with anger (Cole, 1992).

Such views are largely the stuff of folklore, although there is some evidence that a mother's anxiety during pregnancy may affect the sleeping patterns of the fetus prior to birth. Furthermore, certain aspects of mothers' and fathers' behavior, both before and after conception, can produce lifelong consequences for the child. Some consequences show up immediately, but half the possible problems aren't apparent before birth. Other problems, more insidious, may not appear until years after birth (Jacobson et al., 1985; Groome et al., 1995).

Some of the most profound consequences are brought about by teratogenic agents. A **teratogen** is an environmental agent such as a drug, chemical, virus, or other factor that produces a birth defect. Although it is the job of the placenta to keep teratogens from reaching the fetus, the placenta is not entirely successful at this, and probably every fetus is exposed to some teratogens.

teratogen a factor that produces a birth defect

The timing and quantity of exposure to a teratogen are crucial. At some phases of prenatal development, a certain teratogen may have only a minimal impact. At other periods, however, the same teratogen may have profound consequences. Furthermore, different organ systems are vulnerable to teratogens at different times during development. For

As with adults, there are broad differences in the nature of fetuses. Some are very active while others are more reserved, characteristics that can carry over after birth.

example, the brain is most susceptible from 15 to 25 days after conception, while the heart is most vulnerable from 20 to 40 days following conception (see Figure 2-13; Needleman & Bellinger, 1994; Bookstein et al., 1996).

Mother's Diet. Most of our knowledge of the environmental factors that affect the developing fetus comes from the study of the mother. For instance, as the midwife pointed out in the example of Lisa and Robert, a mother's diet clearly plays an important role in bolstering the development of the fetus. A mother who eats a varied diet high in nutrients is apt to have fewer complications during pregnancy, an easier labor, and a generally healthier baby than a mother whose diet is restricted in nutrients (Brown, 1987; Morgane et al., 1993; Rizzo et al., 1997; Waugh & Bulik, 1999).

The problem of diet is of immense global concern. In 1992 the World Food Council estimated that there were 550 million hungry people in the world. Even worse, the number of people vulnerable to hunger was thought to be close to one *billion*. Clearly, restrictions in diet that bring about hunger on such a massive scale affect millions of children born to women living in those conditions (United Nations, 1994).

Fortunately, there are ways to counteract the types of maternal malnourishment that affect prenatal development. Dietary supplements given to mothers can reverse some of the problems produced by a poor diet (Crosby, 1991; Prentice, 1991). Furthermore, re-

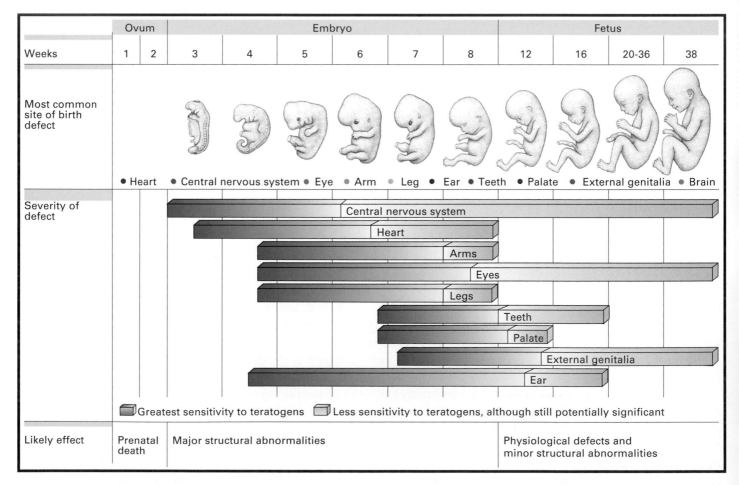

***Figure 2-13* Teratogen Sensitivity**

Depending on their state of development, various parts of the body vary in their sensitivity to teratogens.

(*Source:* Moore, 1974.)

search shows that babies who were malnourished as fetuses, but who are subsequently raised in enriched environments, can overcome some of the effects of their early malnourishment (Grantham-McGregor et al., 1994). However, the reality is that few of the world's children whose mothers were malnourished *before* their birth are apt to find themselves in enriched environments after birth (Garber, 1981; Zeskind & Ramey, 1981; Ricciuti, 1993).

Mother's Age. With a great deal of medical help from her physicians, a 63-year-old woman gave birth in 1997. At the time, she was the oldest woman ever known to have become a mother. Most of the media attention, which was substantial, focused on the medical ethics of the case and the potential psychological difficulties for a child whose mother would be so atypically old.

However, the mother's advanced age probably had physical effects on her and her child as well. Women who give birth when over the age of 30 are at greater risk for a variety of pregnancy and birth complications than younger ones. For instance, they are more apt to give birth prematurely, and their children are more likely to have low birthweights (Vercellini, et al., 1993; Cnattingius, Berendes, & Forman, 1993).

Furthermore, older mothers are considerably more likely to give birth to children with Down syndrome, a form of mental retardation. About one out of a hundred babies born to mothers over 40 has Down syndrome; for mothers over 50, the incidence increases to 25 percent, or one in four (Gaulden, 1992).

The risks involved in pregnancy are greater not only for unusually old mothers, but for atypically young women as well. Women who become pregnant during adolescence—and such pregnancies actually encompass 20 percent of all pregnancies—are more likely to have premature deliveries. Furthermore, the mortality rate of infants born to adolescent mothers is double that for mothers in their 20s.

Keep in mind, though, that the higher mortality rate for babies of adolescent mothers reflects more than just physiological problems related to the mothers' young age. Heightened mortality is also a consequence of adverse social and economic factors. Many teenage mothers do not have enough money or social support, a situation that prevents them from getting good prenatal care and parenting support after the baby is born. Poverty or social circumstances may even have set the stage for the adolescent to become pregnant in the first place. Similarly, some researchers argue that older mothers are not automatically at risk for more pregnancy problems. For instance, one study found that when women in their 40s who had not experienced health difficulties were considered, they were no more likely to have prenatal problems than those in their 20s (Ales, Druzin, & Santini, 1990; Dildy et al., 1996).

Mother's Illness. Depending on when it strikes, an illness in a pregnant woman can have devastating consequences. For instance, the onset of *rubella* (German measles) in the mother prior to the 11th week of pregnancy is likely to cause serious consequences in the baby, including blindness, deafness, heart defects, or brain damage. In later stages of a pregnancy, however, adverse consequences of rubella become increasingly less likely.

Several other diseases may affect a developing fetus, again depending on when the illness is contracted. For instance, *chicken pox* may produce birth defects, while *mumps* may increase the risk of miscarriage.

Some sexually transmitted diseases such as *syphilis* can be transmitted directly to the fetus, who will be born suffering from the disease. In some cases, sexually transmitted diseases such as *gonorrhea* are communicated to the child as it passes through the birth canal to be born.

AIDS (acquired immune deficiency syndrome) is the newest, and probably the deadliest, of the diseases to affect a newborn. Mothers who have the disease or who merely are carriers of the virus may pass it on to their fetuses through the blood that reaches the placenta. If the fetuses contract the disease—and some 30 percent of infants born to mothers with AIDS are born with the virus—they face a devastating path. Many have birth abnormalities, including small, misshapen faces, protruding lips, and brain deterioration. Ninety percent experience neurological symptoms exemplified by intellectual delays and deficits, and loss of motor coordination, facial expressions, and speech. Because AIDS causes a breakdown of the immune system, these babies are extremely susceptible to infection. The long-term prognosis for infants born with AIDS is grim: Although drugs such as AZT may stave off the symptoms of the disease, AIDS babies rarely survive beyond infancy (Chin, 1994; Frenkel & Gaur, 1994; HMHL, 1994).

Mothers' Drug Use. Mothers' use of many kinds of drugs—both legal and illegal—poses serious risks to the unborn child. Even over-the-counter remedies for common ailments can have surprisingly injurious consequences. For instance, aspirin taken for a headache can lead to bleeding in the fetus. Moreover, impairments in the physical development of 4-year-olds have been linked to the frequent use of aspirin during pregnancy (Griffith, Azuma, & Chasnoff, 1994).

Even drugs prescribed by medical professionals have sometimes had disastrous consequences. In the 1950s, many women who were told to take *thalidomide* for morning sickness during their pregnancies gave birth to children with stumps instead of arms and legs. Although the physicians who prescribed the drug did not know it, thalidomide inhibited the growth of limbs that normally would have occurred during the first 3 months of pregnancy.

Some drugs taken by mothers cause difficulties in their children literally decades after they were taken. As recently as the 1970s, the artificial hormone *DES (diethylstilbestrol)* was frequently prescribed to prevent miscarriage. Only later was it found that the daughters of mothers who took DES stood a much higher than normal chance of developing a rare form of vaginal or cervical cancer and had more difficulties during their pregnancies (Herbst, 1981). Sons of the mothers who had taken DES had their own problems, including a higher rate than average of reproductive difficulties (Herbst, 1981).

Illicit drugs may pose equally great, and sometimes even greater, risks for the environments of prenatal children. For one thing, the purity of drugs purchased illegally varies

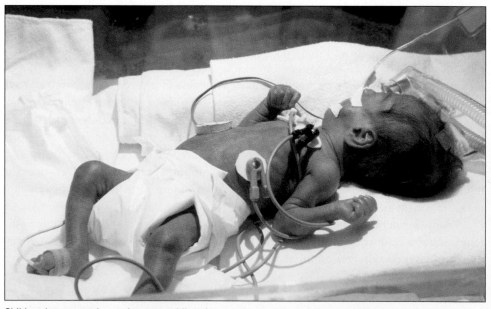

Children born to mothers who were addicted to crack cocaine, so-called crack babies, may themselves be addicted to the drug at birth.

significantly, so drug users can never be quite sure what specifically they are ingesting. Furthermore, the effects of some commonly used illicit drugs can be particularly devastating (DeCristofaro & LaGamma, 1995; Visscher, Bray, & Kroutil, 1999).

Consider, for instance, the use of *marijuana*. Certainly one of the most commonly used illegal drugs—millions of people in the United States have admitted trying it—marijuana used during pregnancy can restrict the oxygen that reaches the fetus. Its use can lead to infants who are irritable, nervous, and easily disturbed (Feng, 1993; Cornelius et al., 1999).

During the early 1990s, *cocaine* use by pregnant women led to an epidemic of thousands of so-called "crack babies." Cocaine produces an intense restriction of the arteries leading to the fetus, causing a significant reduction in the flow of blood and oxygen. This process increases the risks of fetal death.

At birth, children whose mothers were addicted to cocaine may themselves be addicted to the drug and may have to suffer through the agonies of withdrawal. Even if not addicted, they may be born with significant problems. They are often shorter and weigh less than average, and they may have serious respiratory problems, visible birth defects, or seizures. They behave quite differently from other infants: Their reactions to stimulation are muted, but once they start to cry, it may be hard to soothe them (Alessandri, Bendersky, & Lewis, 1998; Bendersky & Lewis, 1998; Andrews, Francis, & Riese, 2000; Singer et al., 2000).

It is difficult to determine the long-term effects of mothers' cocaine use in isolation, because such drug use is often accompanied by poor prenatal care and impaired nurturing following birth (Richardson & Day, 1994; Myers et al., 1996). In fact, in many cases it is the poor caregiving by mothers who use cocaine that results in children's problems, and not exposure to the drug. Treatment of children exposed to cocaine consequently requires not only that the child's mother stop using the drug, but an improvement in the level of care the mother or other caregivers provide to the infant (HMHL, 1998).

Mother's Use of Alcohol and Tobacco. A pregnant woman who reasons that having a drink every once in a while or smoking an occasional cigarette has no appreciable effect on her unborn child is, in all likelihood, kidding herself: Increasing evidence suggests that even small amounts of alcohol and nicotine can disrupt the development of the fetus.

Mothers' use of alcohol can have profound consequences for the unborn child. The children of alcoholics, who consume substantial quantities of alcohol during pregnancy, are at the greatest risk. Approximately 1 out of every 750 infants is born with **fetal alcohol syndrome (FAS)**, a disorder that may include below-average intelligence and sometimes mental retardation, delayed growth, and facial deformities. FAS is now the primary preventable cause of mental retardation (Able & Sokol, 1987; Streissguth, Randels, & Smith, 1991; Feng, 1993; Steinhausen & Spohr, 1998).

Even mothers who use smaller amounts of alcohol during pregnancy place their child at risk. **Fetal alcohol effects (FAE)** is a condition in which children display some, although not all, of the problems of FAS due to their mother's consumption of alcohol during pregnancy (Streissguth, 1997).

Children who do not have FAE may still be affected by their mothers' use of alcohol. Studies have found that maternal consumption of an average of just two alcoholic drinks a day during pregnancy is associated with lower intelligence in their offspring at age 7. Other research concurs, suggesting that relatively small quantities of alcohol taken during pregnancy can have future adverse effects on children's behavior and psychological functioning (Barr et al., 1990; Shriver & Piersel, 1994; Korkman et al., 1998; Johnson et al., 2001). Furthermore, the consequences of alcohol ingestion during pregnancy are long-lasting. For example, one study found that 14-year-olds' success on a test involving spatial

cw

fetal alcohol syndrome (FAS) a disorder caused by the pregnant mother consuming substantial quantities of alcohol during pregnancy, potentially resulting in mental retardation and delayed growth in the child

fetal alcohol effects (FAE) a condition in which children display some, although not all, of the problems of fetal alcohol syndrome due to the mother's consumption of alcohol during pregnancy

The Informed Consumer of Development

Optimizing the Prenatal Environment

If you are contemplating ever having a child, you may be overwhelmed, at this point in the chapter, by the number of things that can go wrong. Don't be. Although both genetics and the environment pose their share of risks, in the vast majority of cases, pregnancy and birth proceed without mishap. Moreover, there are several things that women can do—both before and during pregnancy—to optimize the probability that pregnancy will progress smoothly. Among them:

▶ For women who are planning to become pregnant, several precautions are in order. First, women should have nonemergency X-rays only during the first 2 weeks after their menstrual periods. Second, women should be vaccinated against rubella (German measles) at least 3, and preferably 6, months before getting pregnant. Finally, women who are planning to become pregnant should avoid the use of birth control pills at least 3 months before trying to conceive, because of disruptions to hormonal production caused by the pills.

▶ Eat well, both before and during (and after, for that matter!) pregnancy. Pregnant mothers are, as the old saying goes, eating for two. This means that it is more essential than ever to eat regular, well-balanced meals.

▶ Don't use alcohol and other drugs. The evidence is clear that many drugs pass directly to the fetus and may cause birth defects. It is also clear that the more one drinks, the greater the risk to the fetus. The best advice, whether you are already pregnant or planning to have a child: Don't use *any* drug unless directed by a physician. If you are planning to get pregnant, encourage your partner to avoid using alcohol or other drugs too.

▶ Monitor caffeine intake. Although it is still unclear whether caffeine produces birth defects, it is known that the caffeine found in coffee, tea, and chocolate can pass to the fetus, acting as a stimulant. Because of this, you probably shouldn't drink more than a few cups of coffee a day.

▶ Whether pregnant or not, don't smoke. This holds true for mothers, fathers, and anyone else in the vicinity of the pregnant mother, since research suggests that smoke in the fetal environment can affect birthweight.

▶ Exercise regularly. In most cases, women can continue to exercise, particularly exercises involving low-impact routines. On the other hand, extreme exercise should be avoided, especially on very hot or very cold days. "No pain, no gain" isn't applicable during pregnancy (Warrick, 1991; Brody, 1994a).

and visual reasoning was related to their mothers' alcohol consumption during pregnancy. The more the mothers reported drinking, the less accurately their children responded (Hunt et al., 1995).

Because of the risks associated with alcohol, physicians today counsel pregnant women (and even those who are trying to become pregnant) to avoid drinking any alcoholic beverages. In addition, they caution against another practice proven to have an adverse effect on an unborn child: smoking.

Smoking produces several consequences, none good. For starters, smoking reduces the oxygen content and increases the carbon monoxide of the mother's blood, which quickly reduces the oxygen available to the fetus. In addition, the nicotine and other toxins in cigarettes slow the respiration rate of the fetus and speed up its heart.

The ultimate result is an increased possibility of miscarriage and a higher likelihood of death during infancy. In fact, recent estimates suggest that smoking by pregnant women leads to 115,000 miscarriages and the deaths of 5,600 babies in the United States alone each year (Feng, 1993; DiFranza & Lew, 1995; Mills, 1999; Ness et al., 1999).

Smokers are two times as likely as nonsmokers to have babies with an abnormally low birthweight, and smokers' babies tend to be shorter, on average, than those of nonsmokers. Furthermore, women who smoke during pregnancy are 50 percent more likely to have mentally retarded children (Fried & Watkinson, 1990; Drews et al., 1996; Dejin-Karlsson et al., 1998).

Do Fathers Affect the Prenatal Environment? It would be easy to reason that once the father has done his part in the sequence of events leading to fertilization, he would have no role in the *prenatal* environment of the fetus. In fact, developmental researchers have in the past generally shared this view, and there is little research investigating fathers' influence on the prenatal environment.

However, it is becoming increasingly clear that fathers' behavior may well influence the prenatal environment. Consequently, as the example of Lisa and Robert's visit to the midwife, earlier in the chapter, showed, health practitioners are applying the research to suggest ways fathers can support healthy prenatal development.

For instance, fathers-to-be should avoid smoking. Secondhand smoke from a father's cigarettes may affect the mother's health, which in turn influences her unborn child. The greater the level of a father's smoking, the lower the birthweight of his children. Similarly, a father's use of alcohol and illegal drugs such as cocaine not only may lead to chromosomal damage that may affect the fetus at conception, it may also affect the prenatal environment by creating stress in the mother and generally producing an unhealthy environment (Campbell et al., 1992; Rubin et al., 1986).

Review and Rethink

REVIEW

- Fertilization joins the sperm and ovum to start the journey of prenatal development. Some couples, however, need medical help to help them conceive. Among the alternate routes to conception are artificial insemination and in vitro fertilization (IVF).

- The prenatal period consists of three stages: germinal, embryonic, and fetal.

- The prenatal environment significantly influences the development of the baby. The diet, age, and illnesses of mothers can affect their babies' health and growth.

- Mothers' use of drugs, alcohol, and tobacco can adversely affect the health and development of the unborn child. Fathers' and others' behaviors (e.g., smoking) can also affect the health of the unborn child.

RETHINK

- Studies show that "crack babies" who are now entering school have significant difficulty dealing with multiple stimuli and forming close attachments. How might both genetic and environmental influences have combined to produce these results?

- In addition to avoiding smoking, do you think there are other steps fathers might take to help their unborn children develop normally in the womb? What are they, and how might they affect the environment of the unborn child?

Looking Back

What is our basic genetic endowment, and how can human development go awry?

- A child receives 23 chromosomes from each parent. These 46 chromosomes provide the genetic blueprint that will guide cell activity for the rest of the individual's life.

- Gregor Mendel discovered an important genetic mechanism that governs the interactions of dominant and recessive genes and their expression in alleles. Traits such as hair and eye color and the presence of phenylketonuria (PKU) are alleles and follow this pattern.

- Genes may become physically damaged or may spontaneously mutate. If damaged genes are passed on to the child, the result can be a genetic disorder.

- Behavioral genetics, which studies the genetic basis of human behavior, focuses on personality characteristics and behaviors, and on psychological disorders such as schizophrenia. Researchers are now discovering how to remedy certain genetic defects through gene therapy.

■ Genetic counselors use data from tests and other sources to identify potential genetic abnormalities in women and men who plan to have children. Recently, they have begun testing individuals for genetically based disorders that may eventually appear in the individuals themselves.

▶ How do the environment and genetics work together to determine human characteristics?

■ Behavioral characteristics are often determined by a combination of genetics and environment. Genetically based traits represent a potential, called the genotype, which may be affected by the environment and is ultimately expressed in the phenotype.

■ To work out the different influences of heredity and environment, researchers use nonhuman studies and human studies, particularly of twins.

▶ Which human characteristics are significantly influenced by heredity?

■ Virtually all human traits, characteristics, and behaviors are the result of the combination and interaction of nature and nurture. Many physical characteristics show strong genetic influences. Intelligence contains a strong genetic component, but can be significantly influenced by environmental factors.

■ Some personality traits, including neuroticism and extroversion, have been linked to genetic factors, and even attitudes, values, and interests have a genetic component. Some personal behaviors may be genetically influenced through the mediation of inherited personality traits.

■ The interaction between genetic and environmental effects has been classified into three types: active genotype–environment effects, passive genotype–environment effects, and evocative genotype–environment effects.

▶ What happens during the prenatal stages of development?

■ The union of a sperm and ovum at the moment of fertilization, which begins the process of prenatal development, can be difficult for some couples. Infertility, which occurs in some 15 percent of couples, can be treated by drugs, surgery, artificial insemination, and in vitro fertilization.

■ The germinal stage (fertilization to 2 weeks) is marked by rapid cell division and specialization, and the attachment of the zygote to the wall of the uterus. During the embryonic stage (2 to 8 weeks), the ectoderm, the mesoderm, and the endoderm begin to grow and specialize. The fetal stage (8 weeks to birth) is characterized by a rapid increase in complexity and differentiation of the organs. The fetus becomes active and most of its systems operational.

▶ What are the threats to the fetal environment, and what can be done about them?

■ Factors in the mother that may affect the unborn child include diet, age, illnesses, and drug, alcohol, and tobacco use. The behaviors of fathers and others in the environment may also affect the health and development of the unborn child.

E P I L O G U E

In this chapter, we have discussed the basics of heredity and genetics, including the way in which the code of life is transmitted across generations through DNA. We have also seen how genetic transmission can go wrong, and we have discussed ways in which genetic disorders can be treated—and perhaps prevented—through new interventions such as genetic counseling and gene therapy.

One important theme in this chapter has been the interaction between hereditary and environmental factors in the determination of a number of human traits. While we have encountered a number of surprising instances in which heredity plays a part—including in the development of personality traits and even personal preferences and tastes—we have also seen that heredity alone is virtually never the sole factor in any complex trait. Environment nearly always plays an important role.

Finally, we reviewed the main stages of prenatal growth—germinal, embryonic, and fetal—and examined threats to the prenatal environment and ways to optimize that environment for the fetus.

Before moving on, return to the prologue of this chapter—about Ethan Buchkovich, who was operated on before birth—and answer the following questions.

1. In deciding whether to choose prenatal surgery for a baby, what criteria should be applied to balance the risk of surgery against the risk of a birth defect such as spina bifida?

2. A gene—or a genetic susceptibility—for spina bifida may one day be discovered. If a couple learned that a baby conceived by them would have a 20 percent chance of being born with the disorder, what issues would they have to face in deciding whether to start or continue a pregnancy? Would the issues be different if the chances were 50 percent?

3. If a genetic test exists that can reveal whether an infant is likely to be born with a genetic disorder, do parents have a responsibility to undergo that test? Why or why not?

4. How does gene therapy differ from prenatal surgery? What hopes does gene therapy hold out for couples like the Buchkoviches faced with the likclihood of a serious genetic defect in their infant?

5. Based on what you know about genetics and prenatal development, how might a disorder like spina bifida occur in an infant? If it is carried in a recessive gene, how would it express itself? Which layer of the embryo is apparently affected in the development of spina bifida: the ectoderm, mesoderm, or endoderm?

Key Terms and Concepts

genes (p. 47)
DNA (deoxyribonucleic acid) (p. 47)
chromosomes (p. 47)
zygote (p. 47)
gametes (P. 47)
monozygotic twins (p. 48)
dizygotic twins (p. 48)
dominant trait (p. 50)
recessive trait (p. 50)
genotype (p. 50)
phenotype (p. 50)
homozygous (p. 50)
heterozygous (p. 50)
polygenic inheritance (p. 52)
X-linked genes (p. 52)
behavioral genetics (p. 53)

Down syndrome (p. 54)
fragile X syndrome (p. 54)
sickle-cell anemia (p. 54)
Tay-Sachs disease (p. 54)
Klinefelter's syndrome (p. 54)
genetic counseling (p. 55)
amniocentesis (p. 56)
chorionic villus sampling (CVS) (p. 56)
ultrasound sonography (p. 56)
temperament (p. 60)
multifactorial transmission (p. 60)
active genotype-environment effects (p. 70)
passive genotype-environment effects (p. 70)

evocative genotype-environment effects (p. 70)
fertilization (p. 71)
infertility (p. 72)
artificial insemination (p. 72)
in vitro fertilization (IVF) (p. 72)
surrogate mother (p. 72)
germinal stage (p. 73)
placenta (p. 73)
embryonic stage (p. 73)
fetal stage (p. 74)
fetus (p. 74)
teratogen (p. 75)
fetal alcohol syndrome (FAS) (p. 79)
fetal alcohol effects (FAE) (p. 79)

Birth and the Newborn Infant

PROLOGUE: LABOR OF LOVE

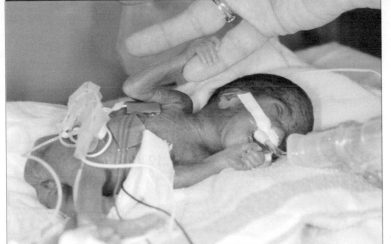

Tamara Nussbaum

Tamara Nussbaum* entered this world weighing 12.5 ounces, the weight of three sticks of butter plus a pat. She had M&M-sized kneecaps. Her thighs, the size of an adult's thumb, splayed out like frogs' legs on a platter when she was held in the palm of a hand. At 365 grams, her birth weight was 135 grams shy of what is thought to be the minimum weight necessary for a baby to have any hope at all of survival.

The first time he saw her, Mohamed Tata, a neonatologist at City Hospital, looked for some signal from the premature baby that she was ready to join the fight for life. She didn't have the lung power to cry, but she had enough muscle tone to squirm. What worked most immediately in her favor the day she was born was her skin. Plum red and dusted with downy fetal hair, it appeared tough enough to hold warmth in and keep infection out. He took her strong skin as that signal, and unleashed the arsenal of technology available in today's neonatal intensive care units, or NICUs. It was a split-second judgment call that he knew full well could result in a child who would never walk, talk, or eat by herself. Or his call could result in a child with a pretty normal life, perhaps needing only a pair of glasses or a specialized school reading program. (Brink, 1998, p. 60)

*Names have been changed to protect privacy.

Looking Ahead   So far, it appears that Dr. Tata's call was right. Tamara is developing fairly normally, although with the developmental delays that characterize many children who are born prematurely.

Every birth is tinged with a combination of excitement and some degree of anxiety. In the vast majority of cases delivery goes smoothly, and it is an amazing and joyous moment. Yet the wonder experienced at birth is far overshadowed by the extraordinary nature of newborns themselves. They enter the world with a surprising array of capabilities, ready from the first moments of life outside the womb to respond to the world and the people in it.

In this chapter we'll examine the events that lead to the delivery and birth of a child, and take an initial look at the newborn. We first consider labor and delivery, exploring how the process usually proceeds as well as several alternative approaches.

We next examine some of the possible complications of birth. Problems that can occur range from premature births to infant mortality. Finally, we consider the extraordinary range of capabilities of newborns. We'll look not only at their physical and perceptual abilities, but at the way they enter the world with the ability to learn and with skills that help form the foundations of their future relationships with others.

After reading this chapter, you will be able to answer these questions:

▶ **What is the normal process of labor?**

▶ **What complications can occur at birth, and what are their causes, effects, and treatments?**

▶ **What capabilities does the newborn have?**

Birth

Her head was cone-shaped at the top. Although I knew this was due to the normal movement of the head bones as she came through the birth canal and that this would change in a few days, I was still startled. She also had some blood on the top of her head and was damp, a result of the amniotic fluid in which she had spent the last nine months. There was some white, cheesy substance over her body, which the nurse wiped off just before she placed her in my arms. I could see a bit of downy hair on her ears, but I knew this, too, would disappear before long. Her nose looked a little as if she had been on the losing end of a fistfight: It was squashed into her face, flattened by its trip through the birth canal. But as she seemed to fix her eyes on me and grasped my finger, it was clear that she was nothing short of perfect. (Adapted from Brazelton, 1969)

neonate the term used for newborns

For those of us accustomed to thinking of newborns in the images of baby food commercials, this portrait of a typical newborn may be surprising. Yet most **neonates**—the term used for newborns—are born resembling this one. Make no mistake, however: Despite their temporary blemishes, babies are a welcome sight to their parents from the moment of their birth.

The neonate's outward appearance is caused by a variety of factors in its journey from the mother's uterus, down the birth canal, and out into the world. We can trace its passage, beginning with the release of the chemicals that initiate the process of labor.

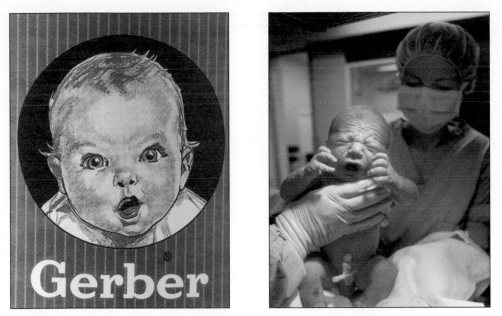

The image of newborns portrayed in commercials differs dramatically from reality.

Labor: The Process of Birth Begins

About 266 days after conception, for the average mother, a protein called *corticotropin-releasing hormone* (CRH) triggers the process that leads to birth. CRH, as its name might suggest, triggers the release of other hormones. In this case, a critical hormone is *oxytocin,* which is released by the mother's pituitary gland. When the concentration of oxytocin becomes high enough, the mother's uterus begins periodic contractions (Nathanielsz, 1996; Smith, 1999).

During the prenatal period, the uterus, which is composed of muscle tissue, slowly expands as the fetus grows. Although for most of the pregnancy it is inactive, after the fourth month it occasionally contracts in order to ready itself for the eventual delivery. These contractions, called *Braxton-Hicks contractions*, are sometimes called "false labor," because they do not necessarily signify that the baby will be born soon.

When birth is actually imminent, the uterus begins to contract intermittently. Its increasingly intense contractions act as if it were a vise, opening and closing to force the head of the fetus against the *cervix*, the neck of the uterus that separates it from the vagina. Eventually, the force of the contractions becomes strong enough to propel the fetus slowly down the birth canal until it enters the world as a newborn (Mittendorf et al., 1990).

Labor proceeds in three stages (see Figure 3-1). In the *first stage of labor,* the uterine contractions initially occur around every 8 to 10 minutes and last about 30 seconds. As labor proceeds, the contractions occur more frequently and last longer. Toward the end of labor, the contractions may occur every 2 minutes and last almost 2 minutes. During the final part of the first stage of labor, the contractions increase to their greatest intensity, a period known as *transition*. The mother's cervix fully opens, eventually expanding enough to allow the baby's head (the widest part of the body) to pass through.

This first stage of labor is the longest. Its duration varies significantly, depending on the mother's age, race, ethnicity, number of prior pregnancies, and a variety of other factors involving both the fetus and the mother. Typically, labor takes 16 to 24 hours for firstborn children, but there are wide variations. Births of subsequent children usually involve shorter periods of labor.

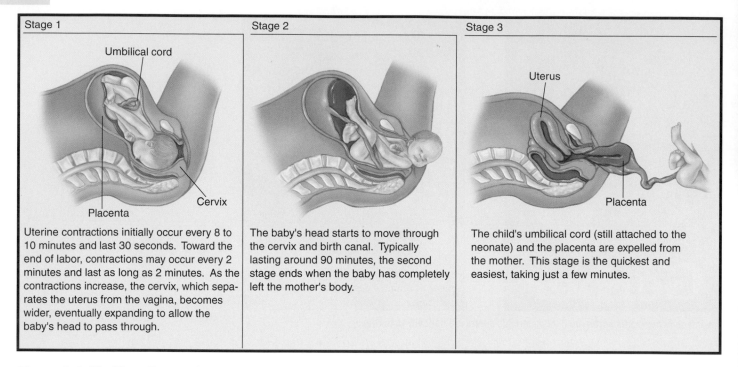

Stage 1	Stage 2	Stage 3
Uterine contractions initially occur every 8 to 10 minutes and last 30 seconds. Toward the end of labor, contractions may occur every 2 minutes and last as long as 2 minutes. As the contractions increase, the cervix, which separates the uterus from the vagina, becomes wider, eventually expanding to allow the baby's head to pass through.	The baby's head starts to move through the cervix and birth canal. Typically lasting around 90 minutes, the second stage ends when the baby has completely left the mother's body.	The child's umbilical cord (still attached to the neonate) and the placenta are expelled from the mother. This stage is the quickest and easiest, taking just a few minutes.

Figure 3-1 **The Three Stages of Labor**

episiotomy an incision sometimes made to increase the size of the opening of the vagina to allow the baby to pass

During the *second stage of labor,* which typically lasts around 90 minutes, the baby's head emerges further from the mother with each contraction, increasing the size of the vaginal opening. Because the area between the vagina and rectum must stretch a good deal, an incision called an **episiotomy** is sometimes made to increase the size of the opening of the vagina. However, this practice has been increasingly criticized in recent years as potentially causing more harm than good, and in developed areas of the world other than the United States episiotomies are uncommon (Klein et al., 1994).

The second stage of labor ends when the baby has completely left the mother's body. Finally, the *third stage of labor* occurs when the child's umbilical cord (still attached to the neonate) and the placenta are expelled from the mother. This stage is the quickest and easiest, taking just a few minutes.

The nature of a woman's reactions to labor reflect, in part, cultural factors. Although there is no evidence that the physiological aspects of labor differ among women of different cultures, expectations about labor and interpretations of its pain do vary significantly from one culture to another (Scopesi, Zanobini, & Carossino, 1997).

For instance, there is a kernel of truth to popular stories of pregnant women in certain societies putting down the tools with which they are tilling their fields, stepping aside and giving birth, and immediately returning to work with their neonates wrapped and bundled on their backs. Accounts of the !Kung people in Africa describe the woman in labor sitting calmly beside a tree and without much ado—or assistance—successfully giving birth to a child and quickly recovering. On the other hand, many societies regard childbirth as dangerous, and some even view it in terms befitting an illness. Such cultural perspectives color the way that people in a given society view the experience of childbirth (Cole, 1992; Maiden, 1997).

Birth: From Fetus to Neonate

The exact moment of birth occurs when the fetus, having left the uterus through the cervix, passes through the vagina to emerge fully from its mother's body. In most cases, babies automatically make the transition from taking in oxygen via the placenta to using their lungs to breathe air. Consequently, as soon as they are outside the mother's body, most newborns spontaneously cry. This helps them clear their lungs and breathe on their own.

What happens next varies from situation to situation and from culture to culture. In Western cultures, health care workers are almost always on hand to assist with the birth. In the United States, 99 percent of births are attended by professional health care workers, but worldwide only about 50 percent of births have professional health care workers in attendance (United Nations, 1990).

The Apgar Scale. In most cases, the newborn infant first undergoes a quick visual inspection. Parents may be counting fingers and toes, but trained health care workers look for something more. Typically, they employ the **Apgar scale,** a standard measurement system that looks for a variety of indications of good health (see Table 3-1). Developed by physician Virginia Apgar in 1953, the scale directs attention to five basic qualities, recalled most easily by using Apgar's name as a guide: *appearance* (color), *pulse* (heart rate), *grimace* (reflex irritability), *activity* (muscle tone), and *respiration* (respiratory effort).

Using the scale, health care workers assign the newborn a score ranging from 0 to 2 on each of the five qualities, producing an overall score that can range from 0 to 10. The vast majority of children score 7 or above. The 10 percent of neonates who score under 7 require help to start breathing. Newborns who score under 4, like Tamara Nussbaum, described at the beginning of the chapter, need immediate, life-saving intervention.

Although low Apgar scores may indicate problems or birth defects that were already present in the fetus, the process of birth itself may sometimes cause difficulties. Among the most profound are those relating to a temporary deprivation of oxygen.

At various junctures during labor, the fetus may not get sufficient oxygen. This can happen for any of a number of reasons. For instance, the umbilical cord may get wrapped around the neck of the fetus. The cord can also be pinched during a prolonged contraction, thereby cutting off the supply of oxygen that flows through it.

Lack of oxygen for a few seconds is not particularly harmful to the fetus, but deprivation for any longer time may cause serious harm. A restriction of oxygen, or **anoxia,** lasting a few minutes can produce brain damage as brain cells die. Furthermore, anoxia can lead to such an increase in blood pressure that bleeding occurs in the brain.

Physical Appearance and Initial Encounters. After assessing the newborn's health, health care workers next deal with the remnants of the child's passage through the birth canal. You'll recall the description of the thick, greasy substance (like cheese) that covers the newborn. This material, called *vernix,* smoothes the passage through the birth canal; it is no longer needed once the child is born and is quickly cleaned away. Newborns' bodies are also covered with a fine, dark fuzz known as *lanugo;* this soon disappears. The newborn's eyelids

Apgar scale a standard measurement system that looks for a variety of indications of good health in newborns

anoxia a restriction of oxygen to the baby, lasting a few minutes during the birth process, which can produce brain damage

Table 3-1

APGAR SCALE

Sign*	0	1	2
Appearance (color)	Blue, pale	Body pink, extremities blue	Entirely pink
Pulse (heart rate)	Absent	Slow (below 100)	Rapid (over 100)
Grimace (reflex irritability)	No response	Grimace	Coughing, sneezing, crying
Activity (muscle tone)	Limp	Weak, inactive	Strong, active
Respiration (breathing)	Absent	Irregular, slow	Good, crying

*Each sign is rated in terms of absence or presence from 0 to 2; highest overall score is 10.
(*Source:* Adapted from Apgar, 1953.)

bonding close physical and emotional contact between parent and child during the period immediately following birth, argued by some to affect later relationship strength

may be puffy due to an accumulation of fluids during labor, and the newborn may have blood or other fluids on parts of its body.

After being cleansed, the newborn is usually returned to the mother and the father, if he is present. The everyday and universal occurrence of childbirth makes it no less miraculous to parents, and most cherish this time to make their first acquaintance with their child.

However, the importance of the initial encounter between parent and child has become a matter of considerable controversy. Some psychologists and physicians argued in the 1970s and early 1980s that **bonding,** the close physical and emotional contact between parent and child during the period immediately following birth, was a crucial ingredient for forming a lasting relationship between parent and child. Their arguments were based in part on research conducted on nonhuman species such as ducklings. This work showed that there was a critical period just after birth when organisms showed a particular readiness to learn, or *imprint,* from other members of their species who happened to be present (Lorenz, 1957).

According to the concept of bonding applied to humans, a critical period begins just after birth and lasts only a few hours. During this period actual skin-to-skin contact between mother and child supposedly leads to deep, emotional bonding (Klaus & Kennell, 1976; deChateau, 1980). The corollary to this assumption is that if circumstances prevent such contact, the bond between mother and child will forever be lacking in some way. Because medical practices prevalent at the time often left little opportunity for sustained mother and child physical contact immediately after birth, the suggestion was received with alarm. The idea was taken seriously and generated a substantial amount of public attention (Eyer, 1992).

There was just one problem: Scientific evidence for the notion was lacking. When developmental researchers carefully reviewed the research literature, they found little support for the idea. Although it does appear that mothers who have early physical contact with their babies are more responsive to them than those who don't have such contact, the difference lasts only a few days. Furthermore, although parents may experience concern, anxiety, and even disappointment, there are no lingering reactions to separations immediately following birth, even for those that extend for several days. Such news is reassuring to parents whose children must receive immediate, intensive medical attention just after birth, such as the mother of Tamara Nussbaum, mentioned at the beginning of the chapter. It is also comforting to parents who adopt children and are not present at all at their births (Lamb, 1982a; Eyer, 1994; Redshaw, 1997).

Approaches to Childbirth: Where Medicine and Attitudes Meet

Ester Iverem knew herself well enough to know that she didn't like the interaction she had with medical doctors. So she opted for a nurse-midwife at Manhattan's Maternity Center where she was free to use a birthing stool and to have her husband, Nick Chiles, by her side. When contractions began, Iverem and Chiles went for a walk, stopping periodically to rock—a motion, she says, "similar to the way children dance when they first learn how, shifting from foot to foot." That helped her work through the really powerful contractions.

"I sat on the birthing chair [a Western version of the traditional African stool, which lies low to the ground and has an opening in the middle for the baby to come through] and Nick was sitting right behind me. When the midwife said 'Push!' the baby's head just went 'pop!,' and out he came." Their son, Mazi (which means "Sir" in Ibo) Iverem Chiles, was placed on Ester's breast while the midwives went to prepare for his routine examination. (Knight, 1994, p. 122)

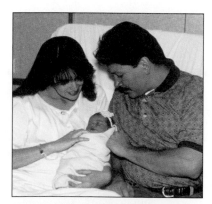

Though physical closeness with caregivers is important to newborn's well being, studies have shown that it is not true that bonding can only take place immediately following birth. Is bonding the same for fathers as it is for mothers?

For something as natural as giving birth, which occurs throughout the nonhuman animal world apparently without much thought, parents in the Western world have developed a

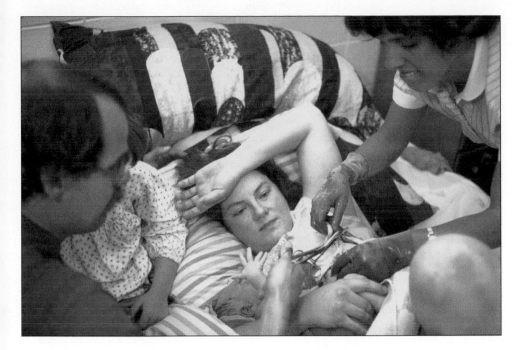

A midwife helps in this home delivery.

variety of strategies—and some very strong opinions. Should the birth take place in a hospital or in the home? Should a physician, a nurse, or a midwife assist? Is the father's presence desirable? Should siblings and other family members be on hand to participate in the birth?

Most of these questions cannot be answered definitively, primarily because the choice of childbirth techniques often comes down to a matter of values and opinions. No single procedure will be effective for all mothers and fathers, and no conclusive research evidence has proven that one procedure is significantly more effective than another. As we'll see, there is a wide variety of different issues and options involved.

The abundance of choices is largely due to a reaction to traditional medical practices that had been prevalent in the United States until the early 1970s. Before that time, the typical procedure went something like this: A woman in labor was placed in a room with many other women, all of whom were in various stages of childbirth, and some of whom were screaming in pain. Fathers and other family members were not allowed to be present. Just before delivery, the woman was rolled into a delivery room, where the birth took place. Often she was so drugged that she was not aware of the birth at all.

Physicians argued that such procedures were necessary to ensure the health of the newborn and the mother. However, critics charged that alternatives were available that not only would maximize the medical well-being of the participants in the birth, but would represent an emotional and psychological improvement as well (Pascoe, 1993).

Alternative Birthing Procedures. Not all mothers give birth in hospitals, and not all births follow a traditional course. Among the major alternatives to traditional birthing practices are the following (Smith, 1990; Mathews & Zadek, 1991):

■ *Lamaze birthing techniques.* The Lamaze method has achieved widespread popularity in the United States. Based on the writings of Dr. Fernand Lamaze, the method makes use of basic psychological techniques involving relaxation training (Lamaze, 1970). Typically, mothers-to-be participate in a series of weekly training sessions in which they learn exercises that help them relax various parts of the body on command. A "coach," most typically the father, is trained along with the future mother. The training allows women to cope with painful contractions with a relaxation response, rather than by tensing up, which may make the pain more acute. In addition, the women

In Lamaze classes, parents are taught relaxation techniques to prepare for childbirth and to reduce the need for anesthetics.

learn to focus on a relaxing stimulus, such as a tranquil scene in a picture. The goal is to learn how to deal positively with pain and to relax at the onset of a contraction.

Does the procedure work? Most mothers, as well as fathers, report that a Lamaze birth is a very positive experience. They enjoy the sense of mastery that they gain over the process of labor, a feeling of control over what can be a formidable experience (Bing, 1983; Wideman & Singer, 1984; Mackey, 1990). On the other hand, we can't be sure that parents who choose the Lamaze method aren't already more highly motivated about the experience of childbirth than parents who do not choose the technique. It is therefore possible that the accolades they express after Lamaze births are due to their initial enthusiasm, and not to the Lamaze procedures themselves.

Although it is not possible to pinpoint definitively the specific consequences of Lamaze preparation for childbirth, one thing is certain: Participation in Lamaze procedures—as well as other so-called *natural childbirth techniques* in which the emphasis is on educating the parents about the process of birth and minimizing the use of drugs—is relatively rare among members of lower income groups, including many members of ethnic minorities. Parents in these groups may not have the transportation, time, or financial resources to attend childbirth preparation classes. The result is that women in lower income groups tend to be less prepared for the events of labor and consequently may suffer more pain and anguish during childbirth (Ball, 1987).

■ *The Leboyer method.* Consider the abrupt transition faced by a neonate. Accustomed to floating in a pool of warm water (the amniotic fluid) for 9 months, hearing only muffled sounds and seeing light only dimly, the newborn is violently thrust into a very different world outside the mother. How might this transition be facilitated?

According to French physician Frederick Leboyer (pronounced "Leh-bwah-YAY"), the optimal approach is to maintain the environment of the womb as long as possible after birth (Leboyer, 1975). Under Leboyer's method, delivery rooms are kept softly lighted and a hushed atmosphere prevails. As soon as the baby is born, it is placed on the mother's stomach and then floated in a pool of warm water. The umbilical cord is not cut immediately after birth, as is traditionally done to compel the baby to breathe on its own. Instead, the cord is left intact, allowing the neonate to acclimate gradually to an air-breathing world.

Although the Leboyer technique gained some popularity in the early 1980s, today only one remnant is seen frequently: Newborns are often placed on the warmth of the mother's stomach just after birth.

■ *Family birthing centers.* When Jill Rakovich became pregnant for the third time, she and her husband, Milos, decided they wanted to find a less forbidding locale than the traditional delivery room. They had both found this setting uncomfortable and grim when their two older children were born.

After researching the possibilities, Jill discovered a family birthing center located close to a nearby hospital. The center consisted of rooms decorated like homey bedrooms. Unlike the typical forbidding hospital room, these looked warm and inviting, although they also were supplied with several pieces of medical equipment. When labor began, Jill and Milos went to the birthing center and settled into one of the rooms. Labor proceeded smoothly, and, as her husband watched, Jill gave birth to their third child.

The decision to use a birthing center is becoming increasingly common. In the majority of cases labor and delivery are uneventful, permitting births to occur in the relatively relaxed, homelike setting the birthing center provides. In the event of complications, equipment is at hand. Supporters of birthing centers suggest that they provide a more comfortable, less stressful environment than a hospital room, offering a setting that may facilitate labor and delivery (Eakins, 1986).

Because of the popularity of the philosophy behind birthing centers, many hospitals have opened birthing rooms of their own. The increasing prevalence of birthing centers reflects the view that childbirth is a natural part of life that should not be rigidly isolated from its other aspects. Rather than medical events that involve a passive patient and a dictatorial physician, labor and delivery are now typically viewed as participatory experiences involving the mother, the father, other family members, and care providers acting jointly.

This philosophy also has implications for the choice of care provider. In place of a traditional *obstetrician,* a physician who specializes in delivering babies, some parents are turning to a *midwife,* a childbirth attendant who stays with the mother throughout labor and delivery. Midwives—often nurses specializing in childbirth—are used primarily for pregnancies in which no complications are expected. Although the use of midwives is increasing in the United States, they are employed in only a minority of births (DeClercq, 1992). In contrast, midwives help deliver some 80 percent of babies in other parts of the world. Moreover, in countries at all levels of economic development many births successfully take place at home. For instance, more than a third of all births in the Netherlands occur at home (Treffers et al., 1990).

Which setting and care provider are optimal? In the majority of cases, it does not make a great deal of difference. Naturally, arrangements for care should be made thoughtfully and in advance, and backup medical help should be on call. If a birth is to occur outside a traditional hospital, such a hospital should be no more than five or ten minutes away. Furthermore, for pregnancies that stand a high risk of complications—such as those of women whose previous deliveries have been difficult—a hospital setting is preferable (Rusting, 1990). In addition to choosing the setting and who attend the birth, parents face other birthing decisions. One major area of decision-making concerns how to deal with the pain of childbirth.

Pain and Childbirth. Any woman who has delivered a baby will agree that childbirth is painful. But how painful, exactly, is it?

Such a question is largely unanswerable. One reason is that pain is a subjective, psychological phenomenon, one that cannot be easily measured. No one is able to answer the question of whether their pain is "greater" or "worse" than someone else's pain, although some studies have tried to quantify it. For instance, in one survey women were asked to rate the pain they experienced during labor on a 1- to-5 scale, with 5 being the most painful (Yarrow, 1992). Nearly half (44 percent) said "5," and an additional one-quarter said "4."

Furthermore, because pain is usually a sign that something is wrong in one's body, we have learned to react to pain with fear and concern. Yet during childbirth, pain is actually a signal that the body is working appropriately—that the contractions that are meant to propel the baby through the birth canal are doing their job. Consequently, the experience of pain during labor is difficult for women in labor to interpret, thereby potentially increasing their anxiety and making the contractions seem even more painful.

Ultimately, the nature of every woman's delivery depends on a complex series of factors. These factors encompass such variables as how much preparation and support she has before and during delivery, her culture's view of pregnancy and delivery, and the specific nature of the delivery itself (Davis-Floyd, 1994; DiMatteo & Kahn, 1997; Walker & O'Brien, 1999).

Use of Anesthesia and Pain-Reducing Drugs. Among the greatest advances of modern medicine is the ongoing discovery of drugs that reduce pain. However, the use of medication during childbirth is a practice that holds both benefits and pitfalls (Shute, 1997).

About a third of women who receive anesthesia do so in the form of *epidural anesthesia*, which produces numbness from the waist down. Traditional epidurals produce an inability to walk and in some cases prevent women from helping to push the baby out during delivery. However, a newer form of epidural, known as a *walking epidural* or *dual spinal-epidural*, uses smaller needles and a system for administering continuous doses of anesthetic. It permits women to move about more freely during labor and has fewer side effects than traditional epidural anesthesia.

It is clear that drugs hold the promise of greatly reducing, and even eliminating, pain associated with labor, which can be extreme. However, pain reduction comes at a cost: The stronger the drug, the greater its effects on the fetus and neonate. The reason is pharmacologically simple: Drugs administered during labor reach not just the mother but the fetus as well. Because of the small size of the fetus relative to the mother, drug doses that might have only a minimal effect on the mother can have a magnified effect on the fetus.

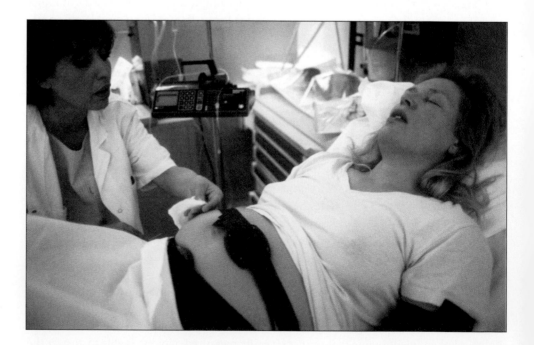

Labor can be exhausting and seem never ending, but support, communication, and a willingness to try different techniques can all be helpful.

Many studies have demonstrated the results of the use of anesthesia during delivery. Some consequences are immediate: Anesthetics may temporarily depress the flow of oxygen to the fetus and slow labor (Brackbill, 1979; Hollenbeck et al., 1984; Thorpe et al., 1993). In addition, newborns whose mothers have been anesthetized are less physiologically responsive and show poorer motor control during the first days of life after birth. And the effects may be lasting: Research shows that during the course of the first year, progress in sitting up, standing, and other physical activities is somewhat slower for children whose mothers received drugs during labor (Garbaciak, 1990; Douglas, 1991; Walker & O'Brien, 1999).

The effects of drugs show up in other, less obvious ways. For example, the use of anesthetics can produce differences in the nature of the interactions between mother and child (Scanlon & Hollenbeck, 1983; Hollenbeck et al., 1984). Even after the physical effects of the drugs have worn off and the infants are behaving in the same way as infants whose mothers did not receive drugs, mothers report feeling differently about their babies. There may be several reasons for this difference. It may be that mothers who choose to avoid medication during delivery hold more positive attitudes toward giving birth and toward their babies in the first place. More probably, the presence or absence of drugs in the infants' systems causes behavioral differences in the infants themselves, which in turn elicit differing reactions from their mothers.

Not all studies, however, find inevitable negative effects on newborns from their mothers' use of drugs during labor. In fact, some researchers argue that drugs, as they are currently employed during labor, produce only minimal risks to the fetus and neonate. For instance, one study found no differences in strength, touch sensitivity, activity level, irritability, and sleep between children whose mothers had been given drugs during labor and those whose mothers had received no drugs (Kraemer et al., 1985).

The wisdom of using drugs to control pain during labor is a difficult issue, pitting legitimate concerns regarding pain control against potential, and in many cases uncertain, concerns for the neonate. Joint guidelines issued by the American Academy of Pediatrics and the American College of Obstetricians and Gynecologists (AAP/ACOG, 1992) suggest that the proper use of minimal amounts of drugs for pain relief is reasonable and has no significant effect on a child's later well-being. Ultimately, the decision to use or not to use anesthetic drugs must be made by the mother, in conjunction with the father and medical care providers (Shute, 1997).

Postdelivery Hospital Stay: Deliver, Then Depart? When New Jersey mother Diane Mensch was sent home from the hospital just a day after the birth of her third child, she still felt exhausted. But her insurance company insisted that 24 hours was sufficient time to recover, and it refused to pay for more. Three days later, her newborn was back in the hospital, suffering from jaundice. Mensch is convinced the problem would have been discovered and treated sooner had she and her newborn been allowed to remain in the hospital longer (Begley, 1995).

Mensch's experience is not atypical. The average hospital stay following normal births decreased from 3.9 days in the 1970s to 2 days in the 1990s, prompted in large part by medical insurance companies, who advocated hospital stays of only 24 hours following birth in order to reduce costs.

However, medical care providers have fought against this trend, believing that there are definite risks involved, both for mothers and for their newborns. For instance, mothers may begin to bleed if they tear tissue injured during childbirth. It is also riskier for newborns to be discharged prematurely from the intensive medical care that hospitals can provide. Furthermore, mothers are more satisfied with their medical care when they stay longer (Finkelstein, Harper, & Rosenthal, 1998; see Figure 3-2).

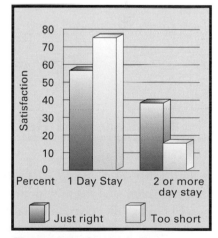

Figure 3-2 **Longer is Better**

Clearly, mothers are most satisfied with their medical care if they stay longer following a birth than if they are discharged after only one day. However, some medical insurance companies prefer for a reduction to a stay of only 24 hours following a birth. Do you think such a reduction is justified?

(*Source:* Finkelstein, Harper, & Rosenthal, 1998.)

Becoming an Informed Consumer of Development

Dealing with Labor

Every woman who is soon to give birth has some fear of labor. Most have heard gripping tales of extended, 48-hour labors or vivid descriptions of the pain that accompanies labor. Still, few mothers would dispute the notion that the rewards of giving birth are worth the effort.

There is no single right or wrong way to deal with labor. However, experts suggest several strategies that can help make the process as positive as possible (Salmon, 1993):

▶ Be flexible. Although you may have carefully worked out beforehand a scenario about what to do during labor, don't feel an obligation to follow through exactly. If a strategy is ineffective, turn to another one.

▶ Communicate with your health care providers. Let them know what you are experiencing. They may be able to suggest ways to deal with what you are encountering.

▶ Remember that labor is . . . laborious. Expect that you may become fatigued, but realize that as the final stages of labor occur, you may well get a second wind.

▶ Accept your partner's support. If a spouse or other partner is present, allow that person to make you comfortable and provide support. Research has shown that women who are supported by a spouse or partner have a more comfortable birth experience (Bader, 1995).

▶ Be realistic and honest about your reactions to pain. Even if you had planned an unmedicated delivery, realize that you may find the pain difficult to tolerate. At that point, consider the use of drugs. Above all, don't feel that asking for pain medication is a sign of failure. It isn't.

▶ Focus on the big picture. Keep in mind that labor is part of a process that ultimately leads to an event unmatched in the joy it can bring.

In accordance with these views, the American Academy of Pediatrics states that women should stay in the hospital no less than 48 hours after giving birth, and the U.S. Congress has passed legislation mandating a minimum insurance coverage of 48 hours for childbirth (American Academy of Pediatrics, 1995).

Review and Rethink

REVIEW

■ In the first stage of labor, contractions increase in frequency, duration, and intensity until the baby's head is able to pass through the cervix. In the second stage, the baby moves through the cervix and birth canal and leaves the mother's body. In the third stage, the umbilical cord and placenta emerge.

■ Immediately after birth, birthing attendants usually examine the neonate using a measurement system such as the Apgar scale.

■ Many birthing options are available to parents today. They may weigh the advantages and disadvantages of anesthetic drugs during birth, and they may choose alternatives to traditional hospital birthing, including the Lamaze method, the Leboyer method, the use of a birthing center, and the use of a midwife.

RETHINK

■ Why might cultural differences exist in expectations and interpretations of labor? Do you think such cultural differences are due primarily to physical or psychological factors?

■ While 99 percent of U.S. births are attended by professional medical workers or birthing attendants, this is the case in only about half of births worldwide. What do you think are some causal factors and implications of this statistic?

Birth Complications

In addition to the usual complimentary baby supplies that most hospitals bestow on new mothers, the maternity nurses at Greater Southeast Hospital have become practiced in handing out "grief baskets."

Inside are items memorializing one of [Washington, D.C.'s] grimmest statistics—an infant mortality rate that's more than twice the national average. The baskets contain a photograph of the dead newborn, a snip of its hair, the tiny cap it wore, and a yellow rose. (Thomas, 1994, p. A14)

The infant mortality rate in Washington, D.C., capital of the richest country in the world, is 14.9 deaths per 1,000 births, exceeding the rate of countries such as Hungary, Cuba, Kuwait, and Costa Rica. Overall, the United States ranks 26th among industrialized countries, with 7.3 deaths for every 1,000 live births (Eberstadt, 1994; Singh & Yu, 1995; National Center for Health Statistics, 2000; see Figure 3-3).

Why is infant survival less likely in the United States than in other, less developed countries? To answer this question, we need to consider the nature of the problems that can occur during labor and delivery.

Preterm Infants: Too Soon, Too Small

Like Tamara Nussbaum, whose birth was described in the chapter prologue, some 6 to 7 percent of infants are born earlier than normal. **Preterm infants,** or premature infants, are born prior to 38 weeks after conception. Because they have not had time to develop fully as fetuses, preterm infants are at high risk for illness and death (Jeng, Yau, & Teng, 1998).

The extent of danger faced by preterm babies largely depends on the child's weight at birth, which has great significance as an indicator of the extent of the baby's development. Although the average newborn weighs around 3,400 grams (about 7 1/2 pounds), **low-birthweight infants** weigh less than 2,500 grams (around 5 1/2 pounds). Although only 7 percent of all newborns in the United States fall into the low-birthweight category, they account for the majority of newborn deaths (Gross, Spiker, & Haynes, 1997).

Although most low-birthweight infants are preterm, some are small-for-gestational-age babies. **Small-for-gestational-age infants** are infants who, because of delayed fetal growth, weigh 90 percent (or less) of the average weight of infants of the same gestational age. Small-for-gestational-age infants are sometimes also preterm, but may not be (Meisels & Plunket, 1988; Shiono & Behrman, 1995).

If the degree of prematurity is not too great and weight at birth is not extremely low, the threat to the child's well-being is relatively minor. In such cases, the main treatment may be to keep the baby in the hospital to gain weight. Additional weight is critical because fat layers help prevent chilling in neonates, who are not particularly efficient at regulating body temperature.

Newborns who are born more prematurely and who have significantly below-average birthweights face a tougher road. For them, simply staying alive is a major task. For instance, low-birthweight infants are highly vulnerable to infection. Furthermore, because their lungs have not had sufficient time to develop completely, premature babies have problems taking in sufficient oxygen. As a consequence, they may experience *respiratory distress syndrome (RDS),* with potentially fatal consequences.

To deal with respiratory distress syndrome, low-birthweight infants are often placed in incubators, enclosures in which temperature and oxygen content are controlled. The exact amount of oxygen is carefully monitored. Too low a concentration of oxygen will

preterm infants infants who are born prior to 38 weeks after conception (also known as premature infants)

low-birthweight infants infants who weigh less than 2,500 grams (around 5 1/2 pounds) at birth

small-for-gestational-age infants infants who, because of delayed fetal growth, weigh 90 percent (or less) of the average weight of infants of the same gestational age

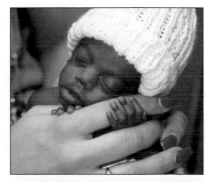

Preterm infants stand a much greater chance of survival today than they did even a decade ago.

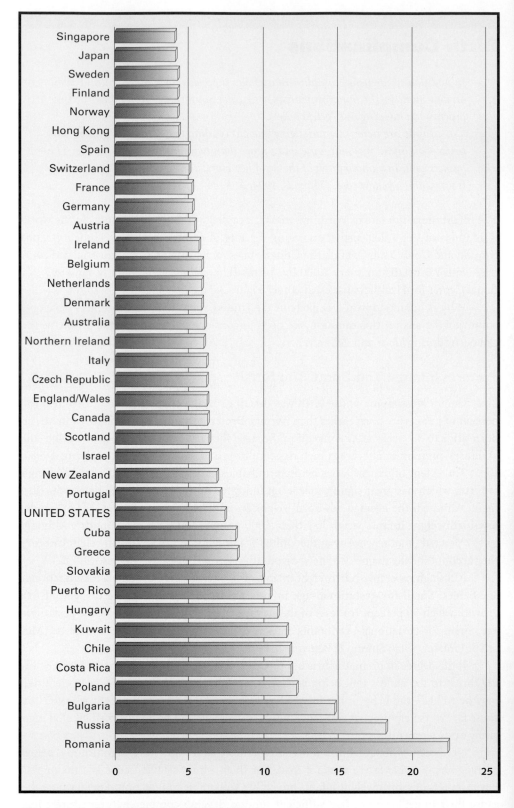

Figure 3-3 **International Infant Mortality**

While the United States has greatly reduced its infant mortality rate since 1965, it ranked 26th among industrialized countries as of 1996. What are some of the reasons for this?

(*Source:* National Center for Health Statistics, 2000.)

not provide relief, and too high a concentration can damage the delicate retinas of the eyes, leading to permanent blindness.

The immature development of preterm neonates makes them unusually sensitive to stimuli in their environment. They can easily be overwhelmed by the sights, sounds, and sensations they experience, and their breathing may be interrupted or their heart rates may slow. Furthermore, they are often unable to move smoothly; their arm and leg movements are uncoordinated, causing them to jerk about and appear startled. Such behavior is quite disconcerting to parents (Field, 1990; Doussard-Roosevelt et al., 1997).

Despite the difficulties they experience at birth, the majority of preterm infants eventually develop normally in the long run. However, the tempo of development often proceeds more slowly for preterm children compared to children born at full term, and more subtle problems sometimes emerge later. For example, by the end of their first year, only 10 percent of prematurely born infants display significant problems, and only 5 percent are seriously disabled. By the age of 6, however, approximately 38 percent have mild problems that call for special educational interventions. For instance, some preterm children show learning disabilities, behavior disorders, or lower-than-average IQ scores. Others have difficulties with physical coordination. Still, around 60 percent of preterm infants are free of even minor problems (Farel et al., 1998; Nadeau et al., 2001).

Very-Low-Birthweight Infants: The Smallest of the Small. The story is less positive for the most extreme cases of prematurity—very-low-birthweight infants. **Very-low-birthweight infants** weigh less than 1250 grams (around 2 1/4 pounds) or, regardless of weight, have been in the womb less than thirty weeks.

Very-low-birthweight infants not only are tiny, some fitting easily in the palm of the hand like little Tamara Nussbaum, they also hardly seem even to belong to the same species as full-term newborns. Their eyes may be fused shut and their earlobes may look like flaps of skin on the sides of their heads. Their skin is a darkened red color, whatever their race.

Very-low-birthweight babies are in grave danger from the moment they are born, due to the immaturity of their organ systems. Before the last two decades, these babies would not have survived outside their mothers' wombs. However, medical advances have led to a higher chance of survival, pushing the **age of viability,** the point at which an infant can survive prematurely, to about 22 weeks—some four months earlier than the term of a normal delivery. Of course, the longer the period of development beyond conception, the higher are a newborn's chances of survival. A baby born earlier than 25 weeks has less than a 50-50 chance of survival (see Figure 3-4).

The physical and cognitive problems experienced by low-birthweight and preterm babies are even more pronounced in very-low-birthweight infants, with astonishing financial consequences. A 3-month stay in an incubator in an intensive care unit can run hundreds of thousands of dollars, and about half of these newborns ultimately die, despite massive medical intervention (Taylor et al., 2000).

Even if a very-low-birthweight preterm infant survives, the medical costs can continue to mount. For instance, one estimate suggests that the average monthly cost of medical care for such infants during the first 3 years of life may be between 3 and 50 times higher than the medical costs for a full-term child. Such astronomical costs have raised ethical debates about the expenditure of substantial financial and human resources in cases in which a positive outcome may be very unlikely. As described in the chapter prologue, doctors and parents may find themselves weighing the merits of using the available medical technology for such infants (Wallace et al., 1995; Kraybill, 1998; Prince, 2000).

The difficult issues surrounding very-low-birthweight infants are not likely to diminish in the years ahead. In fact, as medical capabilities progress, the age of viability is likely to be pushed even further back. Developmental researchers, however, are formulat-

very-low-birthweight infants infants who weigh less than 1,250 grams (around 2.25 pounds) or, regardless of weight, have been in the womb less than 30 weeks

age of viability the point at which an infant can survive a premature birth

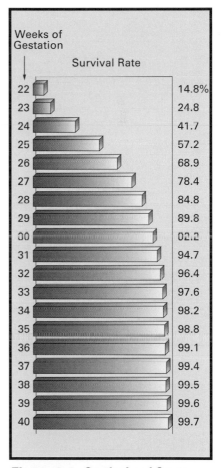

Weeks of Gestation	Survival Rate
22	14.8%
23	24.8
24	41.7
25	57.2
26	68.9
27	78.4
28	84.8
29	89.8
30	92.2
31	94.7
32	96.4
33	97.6
34	98.2
35	98.8
36	99.1
37	99.4
38	99.5
39	99.6
40	99.7

***Figure 3-4* Survival and Gestational Age**

Chances of a fetus surviving greatly improve after 28 to 32 weeks. Rates shown are the percentages of babies born in the United States after specified lengths of gestation who survive the first year of life. Rates are based on data collected from 1989 to 1991. As you can see, the odds were against little Tamara Nussbaum, who was born at only 25 weeks.

(*Source:* Stolberg, 1997.)

ing new strategies for dealing with preterm infants in the hope of improving their lives, and emerging evidence suggests that high-quality care can provide protection from some of the risks associated with prematurity (Picard, Del Dotto, & Breslau, 2000).

For instance, research shows that children who receive more responsive, stimulating, and organized care are apt to show more positive outcomes than those children whose care is not as good. Some of these interventions are quite simple. For example, "Kangaroo Care" in which infants are held skin-to-skin against their parents' chests, appears to be effective in promoting the development of preterm infants. Massaging preterm infants several times a day triggers a complex chemical reaction that assists infants in their efforts to survive (Bradley et al., 1994; Field, 1998, 2000).

Causes of Preterm and Low-Birthweight Deliveries. Although half of preterm and low-birthweight births are unexplained, several known causes account for the remainder. In some cases, difficulties relating to the mother's reproductive system cause such births. For instance, mothers carrying twins have unusual stress placed on them, which can lead to premature labor. In fact, most multiple births are preterm to some degree (Radetsky, 1994; Paneth, 1995; Cooperstock et al., 1998).

In other cases, preterm and low-birthweight babies are a result of the immaturity of the mother's reproductive system. Young mothers—under the age of 15—are more prone to deliver prematurely than older ones. In addition, a woman who has not had much time between pregnancies is more likely to deliver a preterm or low-birthweight infant than a woman whose reproductive system has had a chance to recover from a prior delivery (Du-Plessis, Bell, & Richards, 1997).

Finally, factors that affect the general health of the mother, such as nutrition, level of medical care, amount of stress in the environment, and economic support, all are related to prematurity and low birthweight. Rates of preterm births differ between racial groups, not because of race per se, but because members of racial minorities have disproportionately lower incomes. For instance, the percentage of low-birthweight infants born to African American mothers is double that for Caucasian American mothers. (A summary of the factors associated with increased risk of low birthweight is shown in Table 3-2; National Center for Health Statistics, 1993b; Radetsky, 1994; Cohen, 1995; Stein, Lu, & Gelberg, 2000).

Postmature Babies: Too Late, Too Large

One might imagine that a baby who spends extra time in the womb might have some advantages, given the opportunity to continue growth undisturbed by the outside world. Yet the reality is different. **Postmature infants**—those still unborn two weeks after the mother's due date—face several risks.

postmature infants infants still unborn 2 weeks after the mother's due date

For example, the blood supply from the placenta may become insufficient to nourish the still-growing fetus adequately. Consequently, the blood supply to the brain may be decreased, leading to the potential of brain damage. Similarly, labor becomes riskier (for both the child and the mother) as a fetus who may be equivalent in size to a one-month-old infant has to make its way through the birth canal (Boylan, 1990; Shea, Wilcox, & Little, 1998).

In some ways, difficulties involving postmature infants are more easily prevented than those involving preterm babies, since medical practitioners can induce labor artificially if the pregnancy continues too long. Not only can certain drugs bring on labor, but physicians also have the option of performing Cesarean deliveries, a form of delivery we consider in the *From Research to Practice* box.

Infant Mortality and Stillbirth: The Tragedy of Premature Death

The joy that accompanies the birth of a child is completely reversed when a newborn dies. The relative rarity of their occurrence makes infant deaths even harder for parents to bear.

Table 3-2

FACTORS ASSOCIATED WITH INCREASED RISK OF LOW BIRTHWEIGHT

I. Demographic Risks
- A. Age (less than 17; over 34)
- B. Race (minority)
- C. Low socioeconomic status
- D. Unmarried
- E. Low level of education

II. Medical Risks Predating Pregnancy
- A. Parity (0 or more than 4)
- B. Low weight for height
- C. Genitourinary anomalies/surgery
- D. Selected diseases such as diabetes, chronic hypertension
- E. Nonimmune status for selected infections such as rubella
- F. Poor obstetric history, including previous low-birthweight infant, multiple spontaneous abortions
- G. Maternal genetic factors (such as low maternal weight at own birth)

III. Medical Risks in Current Pregnancy
- A. Multiple pregnancy
- B. Poor weight gain
- C. Short interpregnancy interval
- D. Low blood pressure
- E. Hypertension/preeclampsia/toxemia
- F. Selected infections such as asymptomatic bacteriuria, rubella, and cytomegalovirus
- G. First or second trimester bleeding
- H. Placental problems such as placenta previa, abruptio placentae

    I. Severe morning sickness
- J. Anemia/abnormal hemoglobin
- K. Severe anemia in a developing baby
- L. Fetal anomalies
- M. Incompetent cervix
- N. Spontaneous premature rupture of membrane

IV. Behavioral and Environmental Risks
- A. Smoking
- B. Poor nutritional status
- C. Alcohol and other substance abuse
- D. DES exposure and other toxic exposure, including occupational hazards
- E. High altitude

V. Health Care Risks
- A. Absent or inadequate prenatal care
- B. Iatrogenic prematurity

VI. Evolving Concepts of Risks
- A. Stress, physical and psychosocial
- B. Uterine irritability
- C. Events triggering uterine contractions
- D. Cervical changes detected before onset of labor
- E. Selected infections such as mycoplasma and chlamydia trachomatis
- F. Inadequate plasma volume expansion
- G. Progesterone deficiency

(*Source:* Adapted from Committee to Study the Prevention of Low Birthweight, 1985.)

Sometimes a child does not even live beyond its passage through the birth canal. **Stillbirth,** the delivery of a child who is not alive, occurs in less than 1 delivery out of 100. Sometimes the death is detected before labor begins. In this case, labor is typically induced, or physicians may carry out a Cesarean delivery in order to remove the body from the mother as soon as possible. In other cases of stillbirth, the baby dies during its travels through the birth canal.

Infant mortality is defined as death within the first year of life. In the 1990s the overall rate in the United States was 8.5 deaths per 1,000 live births. Infant mortality has been declining since the 1960s, and U.S. government officials expect to meet their goal of lowering the overall rate to 7 deaths per 1,000 live births (Wegman, 1993; Guyer et al., 1995).

Whether the death is a stillbirth or occurs after the child is born, the loss of a baby is a tragic occurrence. The impact on parents is significant: They move through the same stages of grief and mourning (discussed in Chapter 19) as they experience when an older loved one dies. In fact, the cruel juxtaposition of the first dawning of life and an unnaturally early death may make the death particularly difficult to accept and deal with. Depression is a common aftermath (Finkbeiner, 1996; McGreal, Evans, & Burrows, 1997; Murray et al., 2000).

stillbirth the delivery of a child who is not alive, occurring in less than 1 delivery in 100

infant mortality death within the first year of life

From Research to Practice
Cesarean Delivery: Intervening in the Process of Birth

As Elena entered her 18th hour of labor, the obstetrician who was monitoring her progress began to look concerned. She told Elena and her husband, Pablo, that the fetal monitor revealed that the fetus's heart rate had begun to repeatedly fall after each contraction. After trying some simple remedies, such as repositioning Elena on her side, the obstetrician came to the conclusion that the fetus was in distress. She told them that the baby should be delivered immediately, and to accomplish that, she would have to carry out a Cesarean delivery.

Elena became one of the almost one million mothers in the United States who have a Cesarean delivery each year. In a **Cesarean delivery** (sometimes known as a *c-section*), the baby is surgically removed from the uterus, rather than traveling through the birth canal.

Cesarean deliveries occur most frequently when the fetus shows distress of some sort. For instance, if the fetus appears to be in danger, as indicated by a sudden rise in its heart rate or if blood is seen coming from the mother's vagina during labor, a Cesarean may be performed. In addition, older mothers, over the age of 40, are more likely to have Cesarean deliveries than younger ones (Dulitzki et al., 1998; Gilbert, Nesbitt, & Danielsen, 1999).

Cesarean deliveries are also used in some cases of *breech position,* in which the baby is positioned feet first in the birth canal. Breech position births, which occur in about 1 out of 25 births, place the baby at risk, because the umbilical cord is more likely to be compressed, depriving the baby of oxygen. Cesarean deliveries are also more likely in *transverse position* births, in which the baby lies crosswise in the uterus, or when the baby's head is so large it has trouble moving through the birth canal.

The routine use of **fetal monitors,** devices that measure the baby's heartbeat during labor, has contributed to a soaring rate of Cesarean deliveries. Almost 25 percent of all children in the United States are born in this way, up some 500 percent from the early 1970s (U.S. Center for Health Statistics, 1994). What benefits have resulted from this increase?

According to critics, very few. Other countries have substantially lower rates of Cesarean deliveries (see Figure 3-5), and there is no association between successful birth consequences and the rate of Cesarean deliveries. In addition, Cesarean deliveries carry dangers. Cesarean delivery represents major surgery, and recovery can be relatively lengthy, particularly when compared to a normal delivery. In addition, the risk of maternal infection is higher with Cesarean deliveries (Fisher, Astbury, & Smith, 1997; Koroukian, Trisel, & Rimm, 1998).

Finally, a Cesarean delivery presents some risks for the baby. Although Cesarean babies are spared the stresses of passing though the birth canal, their relatively easy passage into the world may deter the normal release of certain stress-related hormones, such as catecholamines, into the newborn's bloodstream. Because these hormones help prepare the neonate to deal with the stress of the world outside the womb, their absence may be detrimental to the newborn child. In fact, research indicates that babies who, due to a Cesarean delivery, have not experienced labor are more prone to initial breathing problems upon birth than those who experience at least some labor prior to being born via

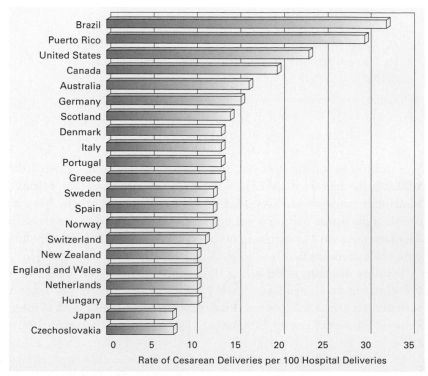

***Figure 3-5*   Cesarean Deliveries**

The rate at which Cesarean deliveries are performed varies substantially from one country to another. Why do you think the United States has one of the highest rates?

(*Source:* Notzon, 1990.)

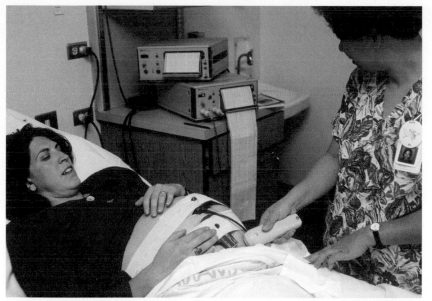

The use of fetal monitoring has contributed to a sharp increase of Cesarean deliveries in spite of evidence showing few benefits from the procedure.

a Cesarean delivery. Finally, mothers who deliver by Cesarean are less satisfied with the birth experience, although their dissatisfaction does not influence the quality of mother–child interactions (Hales, Morgan & Thurnau, 1993; Durik, Hyde, & Clark, 2000).

Due in part to the increase in Cesarean deliveries that results from their use, medical authorities currently recommend avoiding the routine use of fetal monitors. These experts cite research evidence that the outcomes are no better for newborns who have been monitored than for those who have not been monitored. Medical personnel have also noticed that monitors tend to indicate fetal distress when there is none—false alarms—with disquieting regularity (Levano et al., 1986; Albers & Krulewitch, 1993). Monitors can, however, still play a critical role in high-risk pregnancies and in cases of preterm and postmature babies.

Developmental Diversity

Overcoming Racial and Cultural Differences in Infant Mortality

Cesarean delivery a birth in which the baby is surgically removed from the uterus, rather than traveling through the birth canal

fetal monitor a device that measures the baby's heartbeat during labor

The general decline in the infant mortality rate in the United States over the past several decades masks significant racial differences. In particular, African American babies are more than twice as likely to die before the age of 1 than white babies. Such differences are largely the result of socioeconomic factors; the poverty rate among African American women is significantly greater than for Caucasian women, resulting in poorer prenatal care. As a consequence, the percentage of low-birthweight births—the factor most closely linked to infant mortality—is significantly greater among African American mothers than mothers of other racial groups (see Figure 3-6; Stolberg, 1999; Duncan & Brooks-Gunn, 2000).

But it is not just members of particular racial groups in the United States who suffer from poor mortality rates. As mentioned earlier, the overall U.S. rate of infant mortality is higher than the rate in many other countries. For example, the mortality rate in the United States is almost double that of Japan, which has the lowest mortality rate of any country in the world.

What makes the United States fare so poorly in terms of newborn survival? One answer is that the United States has a higher rate of low-birthweight and preterm deliveries than many other countries. In fact, when U.S. infants are compared to infants of the same weight who are born in other countries, the differences in mortality rates disappear (Paneth, 1995; Wilcox et al., 1995).

Another reason for the higher U.S. mortality rate relates to economic diversity. The United States has a higher proportion of people living in poverty than many other countries. Because people in lower economic categories are less likely to have adequate medical care and tend to be less healthy, the relatively high proportion of economically deprived

While infant mortality rates have declined in the United States, it still lags behind other countries in the world, including Japan whose infant mortality rate is almost half of that in the United States. What are some of the causes of high infant mortality in the United States?

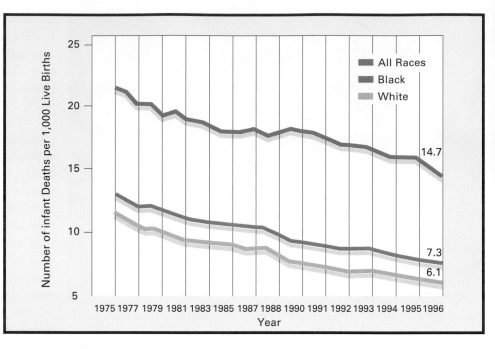

Figure 3-6 **Race and Infant Mortality**

Although infant mortality is dropping for both African American and white children, the death rate is still more than twice as high for African American children. These figures show the number of deaths in the first year of life for every 1,000 live births.

(*Source:* Child Health USA 1998.)

individuals in the United States has an impact on the overall mortality rate (Aved et al., 1993; Terry, 2000).

Furthermore, many countries do a significantly better job providing prenatal care to mothers-to-be than the United States. For instance, low-cost and even free care, both before and after delivery, is often available in other countries. Paid maternity leave is frequently provided to pregnant women, lasting in some cases as long as 51 weeks (see Table 3-3). Such opportunities for maternity leave are important: Mothers who spend more time on maternity leave may have better mental health and higher quality interactions with their infants (Hyde et al., 1995; Clark et al., 1997).

Furthermore, in certain European countries, women receive a comprehensive package of services involving general practitioner, obstetrician, and midwife. Pregnant women receive many privileges, such as transportation benefits for visits to health care providers. In Norway, pregnant women may be given living expenses for up to 10 days so they can be close to a hospital when it is time to give birth. And when their babies are born, new mothers receive, for just a small payment, the assistance of trained home helpers (Miller, 1987; Morice, 1998).

In the United States, the story is very different. The lack of national health care insurance or a national health policy means that prenatal care is often haphazardly provided to the poor. About one out of every six pregnant women has insufficient prenatal care. Some 20 percent of white women and close to 40 percent of African American women who are pregnant receive no prenatal care early in their pregnancies. Five percent of white mothers and 11 percent of African American mothers do not see a health care provider until the last three months of pregnancy; some never see a health care provider at all. In fact, the percentage of pregnant women in the United States who receive virtually no prenatal care actually increased in the 1990s (National Center for Health Statistics, 1993a; Thomas, 1994; Johnson, Primas, & Coe, 1994; Mikhail, 2000).

Table 3-3

MATERNITY LEAVE POLICIES GUARANTEED BY LAW

	Number of Weeks Allowed	Percent of Salary Replaced
Canada	17–18 weeks	55% for 15 weeks
China	13 weeks	100%
Columbia	12 weeks	100%
Egypt	7 weeks	100%
France	16–26 weeks	100%
Germany	14 weeks	100%
Iraq	9 weeks	100%
Italy	20 weeks	80%
Japan	14 weeks	60%
Mexico	12 weeks	100%
Morocco	12 weeks	100%
Netherlands	16 weeks	100%
Nigeria	12 weeks	50%
Sweden*	66 weeks	14 weeks 100%; 1 year 75%
United Kingdom	14–18 weeks	90%
United States	12 weeks	0%

*For both parents combined
(*Source:* International Labor Organization, 1998.)

The ultimate outcome of the deficiency in prenatal services to women with low incomes is the higher likelihood of death for their infants. Yet this unfortunate state of affairs can be changed if greater support is provided. A start would be to ensure that all economically disadvantaged pregnant women have access to free or inexpensive high-quality medical care from the very beginning of pregnancy. Furthermore, barriers that prevent poor women from receiving such care should be reduced. For instance, programs can be developed that help pay for transportation to a health facility or for the care of older children while the mother is making a health care visit (Aved et al., 1993).

Finally, programs that provide basic education for all mothers-to-be are of paramount importance. Increasing the level of understanding of the potential risks involved in child-bearing could prevent many problems before they actually occur (Carnegie Task Force on Meeting the Needs of Young Children, 1994; Fangman et al., 1994). ☐

Postpartum Depression: Moving from the Heights of Joy to the Depths of Despair

She had been overjoyed when she found out that she was pregnant and had spent the months of her pregnancy happily preparing for her baby's arrival. The birth was routine, the baby a healthy, pink-cheeked boy. But only a few days after her son's birth, she sank into the depths of depression. Constantly crying, confused, feeling incapable of caring for her child, she was experiencing unshakable despair.

The diagnosis: a classic case of postpartum depression. *Postpartum depression*, a period of deep depression following the birth of a child, affects some 10 percent of all new mothers. Although it takes several forms, its main symptom is an enduring, deep feeling of sadness and unhappiness, lasting in some cases for months or even years. In about 1 in 500 cases, the symptoms are even worse, evolving into a total break with reality. In extremely rare instances, postpartum depression may turn deadly. For example, a mother in Texas who was charged with drowning all five of her children in a bathtub blamed postpartum depression for her actions (Walther, 1997; Yardley, 2001).

For mothers who suffer from postpartum depression, the symptoms are often bewildering. The onset of depression usually comes as a complete surprise. Certain mothers do seem more likely to become depressed, such as those who have been clinically depressed at some point in the past or who have depressed family members. Furthermore, women who are unprepared for the range of emotions that follow the birth of a child—some positive, some negative—may be more prone to depression. Finally, postpartum depression may be triggered by the pronounced swings in hormone production that occur after birth (Murray & Cooper, 1997; Hendrick, Altshuler, & Suri, 1998; Mauthner, 1999; Swendsen & Mazure, 2000).

Whatever the cause, it is clear that maternal depression leaves its marks on the infant. As we'll see later in the chapter, babies are born with impressive social capacities, and they are highly attuned to the moods of their mothers. When depressed mothers interact with their infants, they are likely to display little emotion and to act detached and withdrawn. This lack of responsiveness leads infants to display fewer positive emotions and to withdraw from contact not only with their mothers but with other adults as well. Maternal depression also can have a negative effect on marital relations and other family members' mental health (Weinberg & Tronick, 1996a; Boath, Pryce, & Cox, 1998; Jacobsen, 1999).

Review and Rethink

REVIEW

- Largely because of low birthweight, preterm infants may have substantial difficulties after birth and later in life.
- Very-low-birthweight infants are in special danger because of the immaturity of their organ systems.
- Preterm and low-birthweight deliveries can be caused by health, age, and pregnancy-related factors in the mother. Income (and, because of its relationship with income, race) is also an important factor.
- Cesarean deliveries are performed with postmature babies or when the fetus is in distress, in the wrong position, or unable to progress through the birth canal.
- Infant mortality rates can be affected by the availability of inexpensive health care and good education programs for mothers-to-be.

- Postpartum depression affects about 10 percent of new mothers.

RETHINK

- What are some ethical considerations relating to the provision of intensive medical care to very-low-birthweight babies? Do you think such interventions should be routine practice? Why or why not?
- Why do you think the United States lacks educational and health care policies that could reduce infant mortality rates overall and among poorer people? What arguments would you make to change this situation?

The Competent Newborn

Relatives gathered around the infant car seat and its occupant, Kaita Castro. Born just two days ago, this is Kaita's first day home from the hospital with her mother. Kaita's nearest cousin, 4-year-old Tabor, seems uninterested in the new arrival. "Babies can't do anything fun. They can't even do anything at all," he says.

Kaita's cousin Tabor is partly right. There are many things babies cannot do. Neonates arrive in the world quite incapable of successfully caring for themselves, for example. Why are human infants born so dependent, while members of other species seem to arrive much better equipped for their lives?

One reason is that, in one sense, humans are born too soon. The size of the brain of the average newborn is just one-quarter what it will be at adulthood. In comparison, the brain of the macaque monkey, which is born after just 24 weeks of gestation, is 65 percent of its adult size. Because of the relative puniness of the infant human brain, some observers have suggested that we are propelled out of the womb some 6 to 12 months sooner than we ought to be.

In reality, evolution probably knew what it was doing: If we stayed inside our mothers' bodies an additional half-year to a year, our heads would be so large that we'd never manage to get through the birth canal (Schultz, 1969; Gould, 1977; Kotre & Hall, 1990).

The relatively underdeveloped brain of the human newborn helps explain the infant's apparent helplessness. Because of this, the earliest views of newborns focused on the things that they could not do, comparing them rather unfavorably to older members of the human species.

Today, however, such beliefs have taken a backseat to more favorable views of the neonate. As developmental researchers have begun to understand more about the nature of newborns, they have come to realize that infants enter this world with an astounding array of capabilities in all domains of development: physical, cognitive, and social.

Newborns enter the world pre-programmed to find, take in and digest food in the form of the rooting, sucking and swallowing reflexes.

Physical Competence: Meeting the Demands of a New Environment

The world faced by a neonate is remarkably different from the one it experienced in the womb. Consider, for instance, the significant changes in functioning that Kaita Castro encountered as she began the first moments of life in her new environment (summarized in Table 3-4).

Kaita's most immediate task was to bring sufficient air into her body. Inside her mother, air was delivered through the umbilical cord, which also provided a means for taking away carbon dioxide. The realities of the outside world are different: Once the umbilical cord was cut, Kaita's respiratory system needed to begin its lifetime's work.

For Kaita, the task was automatic. As we noted earlier, most newborn babies begin to breathe on their own as soon as they are exposed to air. The ability to breathe immediately is a good indication that the respiratory system of the normal neonate is reasonably well developed, despite its lack of rehearsal in the womb.

Neonates emerge from the uterus more practiced in other types of physical activities. For example, newborns such as Kaita show several **reflexes**—unlearned, organized

cw

reflexes unlearned, organized involuntary responses that occur automatically in the presence of certain stimuli

Table 3-4

KAITA CASTRO'S FIRST ENCOUNTERS UPON BIRTH

1. As soon as she is through the birth canal, Kaita automatically begins to breathe on her own despite no longer being attached to the umbilical cord that provided precious air in the womb.
2. Reflexes—unlearned, organized involuntary responses that occur in the presence of stimuli— begin to take over. Sucking and swallowing reflexes permit Kaita immediately to ingest food.
3. The rooting reflex, which involves turning in the direction of a source of stimulation, guides Kaita toward potential sources of food that are near her mouth, such as her mother's nipple.
4. Kaita begins to cough, sneeze, and blink—reflexes that help her avoid stimuli that are potentially bothersome or hazardous.
5. Her senses of smell and taste are highly developed. Physical activities and sucking increase when she smells peppermint. Her lips pucker when a sour taste is placed on her lips.
6. Objects with colors of blue and green seem to catch Kaita's attention more than other colors, and she reacts sharply to loud, sudden noises. She will also continue to cry if she hears other newborns cry, but will stop if she hears a recording of her own voice crying.

involuntary responses that occur automatically in the presence of certain stimuli. Some of these reflexes are well rehearsed, having been present for several months before birth. The *sucking reflex* and the *swallowing reflex* permit Kaita to begin right away to ingest food. The *rooting reflex,* which involves turning in the direction of a source of stimulation (such as a light touch) near the mouth, is also related to eating. It guides the infant toward potential sources of food that are near its mouth, such as a mother's nipple.

Not all of the reflexes that are present at birth lead the newborn to seek out desired stimuli such as food. For instance, Kaita can cough, sneeze, and blink—reflexes that help her to avoid stimuli that are potentially bothersome or hazardous.

Kaita's sucking and swallowing reflexes, which help her to consume her mother's milk, are coupled with the newfound ability to digest nutriments. The neonate's digestive system initially produces feces in the form of *meconium,* a greenish-black material that is a remnant of the neonate's days as a fetus.

Because the liver, a critical component of the digestive system, does not always work effectively at first, almost half of all newborns develop a distinctly yellowish tinge to their bodies and eyes. This change in color is a symptom of *neonatal jaundice.* It is most likely to occur in preterm and low-weight neonates, and it is typically not dangerous. Treatment most often consists of placing the baby under fluorescent lights or administering medicine.

Sensory Capabilities: Experiencing the World

Just after Kaita was born, her father was certain that she looked directly at him. Did she, in fact, see him?

This is a hard question to answer for several reasons. For one thing, when sensory experts talk of "seeing," they mean both a sensory reaction due to the stimulation of the visual sensory organs and an interpretation of that stimulation (the distinction, as you might recall from an introductory psychology class, between sensation and perception). Furthermore, as we'll discuss further when we consider sensory capabilities during infancy in Chapter 4, it is tricky, to say the least, to pinpoint the specific sensory skills of newborns who lack the ability to explain what they are experiencing.

Still, we do have some answers to the question of what newborns are capable of seeing and, for that matter, questions about their other sensory capabilities. For example, it is clear that neonates such as Kaita can see to some extent. Although their visual acuity is not fully developed, newborns actively pay attention to certain types of information in their environment (Haith, 1991).

For instance, neonates pay closest attention to portions of scenes in their field of vision that are highest in information, such as objects that sharply contrast with the rest of their environment. Furthermore, infants can discriminate different levels of brightness. There is even evidence suggesting that newborns have a sense of size constancy. They seem aware that objects stay the same size even though the size of the image on the retina varies with distance (Slater, Mattock, & Brown, 1990; Slater & Johnson, 1998).

And not only can newborn babies distinguish different colors, they seem to prefer particular ones. For example, they are able to distinguish between red, green, yellow, and blue, and they take more time staring at blue and green objects—suggesting a partiality for those colors (Adams, Mauer, & Davis, 1986).

Newborns are also clearly capable of hearing. They react to certain kinds of sounds, showing startle reactions to loud, sudden noises, for instance. The also exhibit familiarity with certain sounds. For example, a crying newborn will continue to cry when he or she hears other newborns crying. If the baby hears a recording of its own crying, on the other hand, he or she is more likely to stop crying, as if recognizing the familiar sound (Martin & Clark, 1982).

As with vision, however, the degree of auditory acuity is not as great as it will be later. The auditory system is not completely developed. Moreover, amniotic fluid, which is

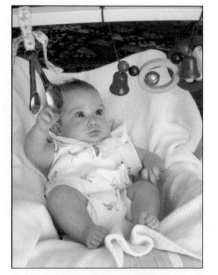

Starting at birth, infants are able to distinguish colors and even show preferences for particular ones.

initially trapped in the middle ear, must drain out before the newborn can fully hear (Reinis & Goldman, 1980).

In addition to sight and hearing, the other senses also function quite adequately in the newborn. It is obvious that newborns are sensitive to touch. For instance, they respond to stimuli such as the hairs of a brush, and they are aware of puffs of air so weak that adults cannot notice them. The senses of smell and taste are also well developed. Newborns suck and increase other physical activity when the odor of peppermint is placed near the nose. They also pucker their lips when a sour taste is placed on them, and respond with suitable facial expressions to other tastes as well. Such findings clearly indicate that the senses of touch, smell, and taste are not only present at birth, but are reasonably sophisticated (Mistretta, 1990; Marlier, Schaal, & Soussignan, 1998).

In one sense, the sophistication of the sensory systems of newborns such as Kaita is not surprising. After all, the typical neonate has had nine months to prepare for his or her encounter with the outside world. As we discussed in Chapter 2, human sensory systems begin their development well before birth. Furthermore, some researchers suggest that the passage through the birth canal places babies in a state of heightened sensory awareness, preparing them for the world that they are about to encounter for the first time (Bornstein & Lamb, 1992b).

Early Learning Capabilities

One-month-old Michael Samedi was on a car ride with his family when a thunderstorm suddenly began. The storm rapidly became violent, and flashes of lightning were quickly followed by loud thunderclaps. Michael was clearly disturbed and began to sob. With each new thunderclap, the pitch and fervor of his crying increased. Unfortunately, before very long it wasn't just the sound of the thunder that would raise Michael's anxiety; the sight of the lightning alone was enough to make him cry out in fear. In fact, even as an adult, Michael feels his chest tighten and his stomach churn at the mere sight of lightning.

Classical Conditioning. The source of Michael's fear is classical conditioning, a basic type of learning first identified by Ivan Pavlov (and first discussed in Chapter 1). In **classical conditioning** an organism learns to respond in a particular way to a neutral stimulus that normally does not bring about that type of response.

You had probably heard of the initial demonstration of classical conditioning, which involved Pavlov's research with dogs, even before we discussed it in Chapter 1. Pavlov discovered that by repeatedly pairing two stimuli, such as the sound of a bell and the arrival of meat, he could make hungry dogs learn to respond (in this case by salivating) not only when the meat was presented, but even when the bell was sounded without the presence of meat (Pavlov, 1927).

The key feature of classical conditioning is stimulus substitution, in which a stimulus that doesn't naturally bring about a particular response is paired with a stimulus that does evoke that response. Repeatedly presenting the two stimuli together results in the second stimulus taking on the properties of the first. In effect, the second stimulus is substituted for the first.

One of the earliest examples of the power of classical conditioning in shaping human emotions was demonstrated in the case of an 11-month-old infant known by researchers as "Little Albert" (Watson & Rayner, 1920). Although he initially adored furry animals and showed no fear of rats, Little Albert learned to fear them when, during a laboratory demonstration, a loud noise was sounded every time he played with a cute and harmless white rat. In fact, the fear generalized to other furry objects, including rabbits and even a Santa Claus mask. (By the way, such a demonstration would be considered unethical today, and it would never be conducted.)

Infants are capable of learning very early through classical conditioning. For instance, 1- and 2-day-old newborns who are stroked on the head just before being given a

classical conditioning a type of learning in which an organism responds in a particular way to a neutral stimulus that normally does not bring about that type of response

drop of a sweet-tasting liquid soon learn to turn their heads and suck at the head-stroking alone (Blass, Ganchrow, & Steiner, 1984). Clearly, classical conditioning is in operation from the time of birth.

Operant Conditioning. But classical conditioning is not the only mechanism through which infants learn; they also respond to operant conditioning. As we noted in Chapter 1, **operant conditioning** is a form of learning in which a voluntary response is strengthened or weakened, depending on its association with positive or negative consequences. In operant conditioning, infants learn to act deliberately on their environments in order to bring about some desired consequence. An infant who learns that crying in a certain way is apt to bring her parents' immediate attention is displaying operant conditioning.

Like classical conditioning, operant conditioning functions from the earliest days of life. For instance, researchers have found that even newborns readily learn through operant conditioning to keep sucking on a nipple when it permits them to continue hearing their mothers read a story or to listen to music (Butterfield & Siperstein, 1972; DeCasper & Fifer, 1980; Lipsitt, 1986a).

Habituation. Probably the most primitive form of learning is demonstrated by the phenomenon of habituation. **Habituation** is the decrease in the response to a stimulus that occurs after repeated presentations of the same stimulus.

Habituation in infants relies on the fact that the presentation of a novel stimulus typically produces an *orienting response*, in which the infant quiets, becomes attentive, and experiences a slowed heart rate. When the novelty wears off due to repeated exposure to the stimulus, the infant no longer reacts with an orienting response. However, when a new and different stimulus is presented, the infant once again reacts with an orienting response. When this happens, we can say that the infant has learned to recognize the original stimulus and to distinguish it from others.

Habituation occurs in every sensory system, and researchers have studied it in several ways. One is to examine changes in sucking, which stops temporarily when a new stimulus is presented. This reaction is not unlike that of an adult who temporarily puts down her knife and fork when a dinner companion makes an interesting statement to which she wishes to pay particular attention. Other measures of habituation include changes in heart rate, respiration rate, and the length of time an infant looks at a particular stimulus.

The development of habituation is linked to physical and cognitive maturation. It is present at birth and becomes more pronounced over the first 12 weeks of infancy. Difficulties involving habituation represent a signal of developmental problems (Rovee-Collier, 1987; Braddock, 1993; Tamis-Lamonda & Bornstein, 1993).

Are There Limits on Learning? Although the three basic processes of learning that we've considered—classical conditioning, operant conditioning, and habituation (summarized in Table 3-5)—are all present at birth, they initially face considerable constraints. According to researchers Marc Bornstein and Michael Lamb (1992b), three factors limit the success of learning during infancy. One is the *behavioral state* of the infant. In order for learning to occur, infants must be in a sufficiently attentive state to sense, perceive, and recognize the relationship between various stimuli and responses. Without at least a minimal level of attentiveness, learning will not be possible (Papousek & Bernstein, 1969).

Natural constraints on learning are a second limiting factor. Not all behaviors are physically possible for an infant, and infants' perceptual systems, which are not fully developed at birth, may not be sufficiently refined to respond to, or even notice, a particular stimulus. Consequently, certain types of classical and operant conditioning that are possible with older individuals are ineffective with infants.

Finally, *motivational constraints* may limit learning. In order for learning to occur, the response involved must not be so taxing on infants that they simply are unmotivated

cw

operant conditioning a form of learning in which a voluntary response is strengthened or weakened, depending on its association with positive or negative consequences

habituation the decrease in the response to a stimulus that occurs after repeated presentations of the same stimulus

Table 3-5

THREE BASIC PROCESS OF LEARNING

Type	Description	Example
Classical Conditioning	A situation in which an organism learns to respond in a particular way to a neutral stimulus that normally does not bring about that type of response.	A hungry baby stops crying when her mother picks her up because she has learned to associate being picked up with subsequent feeding.
Operant Conditioning	A form of learning in which a voluntary response is strengthened or weakened, depending on its positive or negative consequences.	An infant who learns that smiling at his or her parents brings positive attention may smile more often.
Habituation	The decrease in the response to a stimulus that occurs after repeated presentations of the same stimulus.	A baby who showed interest and surprise at first seeing a novel toy may show no interest after seeing the same toy several times.

to respond. If the response is too demanding, learning may fail to appear not because the infants haven't learned an association between a stimulus and a response, but because they just don't have the energy or skills to proceed (Rovee-Collier, 1987).

Despite these limitations, infants show great capacities to learn. But just how far do the capabilities of infants extend beyond the basic learning processes? Research on social competence in infants illustrates just how competent infants are in another important regard.

Social Competence: Responding to Others

Soon after Kaita was born, her older brother looked down at her in her crib and opened his mouth wide, pretending to be surprised. Kaita's mother, looking on, was amazed when it appeared that Kaita imitated his expression, opening her mouth as if *she* were surprised.

Researchers registered surprise of their own when they first found that newborns did indeed have the capability to imitate others' behavior. Although infants were known to have all the muscles in place to produce facial expressions related to basic emotions, the actual appearance of such expressions was assumed to be largely random.

However, research beginning in the late 1970s suggested a different conclusion. For instance, developmental researchers demonstrated that, when exposed to an adult modeling a behavior that the infant already performed spontaneously, such as opening the mouth or sticking out the tongue, the newborn was apt to imitate the behavior (Meltzoff & Moore, 1977).

Even more exciting were findings from a series of studies conducted by developmental psychologist Tiffany Field and her colleagues (Field, 1982; Field & Walden, 1982; Field et al., 1984). They initially showed that infants could discriminate between such basic facial expressions as happiness, sadness, and surprise. They then exposed newborns to an adult model with a happy, sad, or surprised facial expression. The results were clear: The newborns produced a reasonably accurate imitation of the adult's expression.

Subsequent research, conducted just minutes after birth and in a variety of cultures, has shown that all normal newborns have the ability to imitate. Imitative skills are more than a mere curiosity. Effective social interaction with others relies in part on the ability to react to other people in an appropriate manner and to understand the meaning of others' emotional states. Consequently, a newborns' ability to imitate provides him or her with an important foundation for social interaction later in life (Phillips et al., 1990; Walker-Andrews & Dickson, 1997; Meltzoff & Moore, 1999).

This infant is imitating the happy expressions of the adult. Why is this still important?

Table 3-6

FACTORS THAT ENCOURAGE SOCIAL INTERACTION BETWEEN FULL-TERM NEWBORNS AND THEIR PARENTS

Full-Term Newborn	Parent
Has organized states	Helps regulate infant's states
Attends selectively to certain stimuli	Provides these stimuli
Behaves in ways interpretable as specific communicative intent	Searches for communicative intent
Responds systematically to parent's acts	Wants to influence newborn, feel effective
Acts in temporally predictable ways	Adjusts actions to newborn's temporal rhythms
Learns from, adapts to parent's behavior	Acts repetitively and predictably

(*Source:* Eckerman & Oehler, 1992.)

Several other aspects of newborns' behavior also act as forerunners for more formal types of social interaction that they will develop as they grow. As shown in Table 3-6, certain characteristics of neonates mesh with parental behavior to help produce a social relationship between child and parent, as well as social relationships with others (Eckerman & Oehler, 1992).

For example, newborns cycle through various **states of arousal,** different degrees of sleep and wakefulness, that range from deep sleep to great agitation. Although immediately after birth these cycles are disrupted, they quickly become more regularized. Caregivers become involved when they seek to aid the infant in transitions from one state to another. For instance, a father who rhythmically rocks his crying daughter in an effort to calm her is engaged in a joint activity that is a prelude to future social interactions of different sorts. Similarly, newborns tend to pay particular attention to their mothers' voices (Hepper, Scott, & Shahidullah, 1993). In turn, parents and others modify their speech when talking to infants, using a different pitch and tempo than they use with older children and adults (DeCasper & Fifer, 1980; Fernald, 1984; Trainor, Austin, & Desjardins, 2000).

The ultimate outcome of the social interactive capabilities of the newborn infant, and the responses such behavior brings about from parents, is to pave the way for future social interactions. Just as the neonate shows remarkable skills on a physical and perceptual level, then, its social capabilities are no less sophisticated.

states of arousal different degrees of sleep and wakefulness through which newborns cycle, ranging from deep sleep to great agitation

Review and Rethink

REVIEW

- Neonates are in many ways helpless, but studies of what they *can* do, rather than what they *can't* do, have revealed some surprising capabilities.
- Newborns' respiratory and digestive systems begin to function at birth. They have an array of reflexes to help them eat, swallow, find food, and avoid unpleasant stimuli.

- Newborns' sensory competence includes the ability to distinguish objects in the visual field and to see color differences; the ability to hear and to discern familiar sounds; and sensitivity to touch, odors, and tastes.
- The processes of classical conditioning, operant conditioning, and habituation demonstrate infants' learning capabilities.
- Infants develop the foundations of social competence early.

RETHINK

■ Developmental researchers no longer view the neonate as a helpless, incompetent creature, but rather as a remarkably competent, developing human being. What do you think are some implications of this change in viewpoint for methods of child rearing and child care?

■ According to this chapter, classical conditioning relies on stimulus substitution. Can you think of examples of the use of classical conditioning on adults in everyday life, in such areas as entertainment, advertising, or politics?

Looking Back

What is the normal process of labor?

■ In the first stage of labor contractions occur about every 8 to 10 minutes, increasing in frequency, duration, and intensity until the mother's cervix expands. In the second stage of labor, which lasts about 90 minutes, the baby begins to move through the cervix and birth canal and ultimately leaves the mother's body. In the third stage of labor, which lasts only a few minutes, the umbilical cord and placenta are expelled from the mother.

■ After it emerges, the newborn, or neonate, is usually inspected for irregularities, cleaned, and returned to its mother and father.

■ Parents-to-be have a variety of choices regarding the setting for the birth, medical attendants, and whether or not to use pain-reducing medication. Sometimes, medical intervention, such as Cesarean birth, becomes necessary.

What complications can occur at birth, and what are their causes, effects, and treatments?

■ Preterm, or premature, infants, born less than 38 weeks following conception, generally have low birthweight, which can cause chilling, vulnerability to infection, respiratory distress syndrome, and hypersensitivity to environmental stimuli. They may even show adverse effects later in life, including slowed development, learning disabilities, behavior disorders, below-average IQ scores, and problems with physical coordination.

■ Very-low-birthweight infants are in special danger because of the immaturity of their organ systems. However, medical advances have pushed the age of viability of the infant back to about 24 weeks following conception.

■ Postmature babies, who spend extra time in their mothers' wombs, are also at risk. However, physicians can artificially induce labor or perform a Cesarean delivery to address this situation. Cesarean deliveries are performed when the fetus is in distress, in the wrong position, or unable to progress through the birth canal.

■ The infant mortality rate in the United States is higher than the rate in many other countries, and higher for low-income families than higher-income families.

■ Postpartum depression, an enduring, deep feeling of sadness, affects about 10 percent of new mothers. In severe cases, its effects can be harmful to the mother and the child, and aggressive treatment may be employed.

What capabilities does the newborn have?

■ Human newborns quickly master breathing through the lungs, and they are equipped with reflexes to help them eat, swallow, find food, and avoid unpleasant stimuli. Their sensory capabilities are also sophisticated.

■ From birth, infants learn through habituation, classical conditioning, and operant conditioning. Newborns are able to imitate the behavior of others, a capability that helps them form social relationships and facilitates the development of social competence.

EPILOGUE

Our discussion in this chapter focused on the processes of labor and birth. We considered the birthing options that are available to parents and the complications that can arise during the birthing process. We discussed treatments and interventions, and examined the grim topics of stillbirth and infant mortality.

We concluded with a discussion of the surprising capabilities of newborns and their early development of social competence.

Before we move on to a more detailed discussion of infants' physical development, return for a moment to the case of the very premature Tamara Nussbaum, discussed in the prologue. Using your understanding of the issues discussed in this chapter, answer the following questions.

1. Tamara Nussbaum was born at 25 weeks. Why was the fact that she was born alive so surprising? Can you discuss her birth in terms of "the age of viability"?

2. Can you apply the Apgar scale to Tamara? What procedures and activities were most likely set into motion immediately after her birth?

3. What dangers was Tamara subject to immediately after birth because of her high degree of prematurity? What dangers would be likely to continue into her childhood?

4. What ethical considerations affect the decision of whether the high costs of medical interventions for highly premature babies are justifiable? Who should pay those costs?

Key Terms and Concepts

neonate (p. 86)
episiotomy (p. 88)
Apgar scale (p. 89)
anoxia (p. 89)
bonding (p. 90)
preterm infants (p. 97)
low-birthweight infants (p. 97)

small-for-gestational-age infants (p. 97)
very-low-birthweight infants (p. 99)
age of viability (p. 99)
postmature infants (p. 100)
stillbirth (p. 101)
infant mortality (p. 101)
Cesarean delivery (p. 103)

fetal monitor (p. 103)
reflexes (p. 107)
classical conditioning (p. 109)
operant conditioning (p. 110)
habituation (p. 110)
states of arousal (p. 112)

Bridges

In Part One, we began our examination of human development, starting with conception and continuing through the process of birth. We saw how well equipped human infants are from the moment of birth—and even before—inheriting from their parents a range of instincts, traits, and capabilities. We looked at a few of the things that can go wrong during gestation and birth, but mostly we saw how, in the vast majority of instances, the complex business of forming new life proceeds flawlessly.

Our discussion featured an introduction to some of the broad themes in the field of human development, including especially the importance of critical periods and the nature—nurture controversy. We will revisit these themes frequently as we continue our consideration of human development, looking next at development during infancy.

What we encountered more than anything else as we stepped into the field of lifespan development was a sense of wonder at the way in which the process of life begins and unfolds. As we move into our consideration of infancy in Part Two, we'll continue to be awestruck with the transformations that humans undergo as they proceed through life.

INFANCY: FORMING THE FOUNDATIONS OF LIFE

Physical Development in Infancy

PROLOGUE: SENSING THE WORLD

Infancy is a time of remarkable growth, as children become increasingly engaged with the world around them.

It's Tuesday afternoon at the Epsteins' Philadelphia apartment. Seven-month-old Ana Natalia is sitting up, smiling, waiting for her favorite midafternoon activities: snack time, featuring a lovely sweet-potato purée, accompanied by a gentle back rub. When her mother, Lucia, puts some world music on the CD player, Ana Natalia arches her 15-pound body in delight. Life doesn't get any better than cool tunes, good food, and a massage (Raymond, 2000, p. 16).

Looking Ahead   Even infants know the pleasures that the senses offer. In a remarkable way, they engage the world on a variety of levels, responding to the stimulation of taste, sound, touch, sight, and several other modalities.

The ability of infants to take in and respond to the world around them is among a variety of dramatic physical attainments that characterize infancy. In this chapter we consider the nature of physical development during the period of infancy, which starts at birth and continues until the second birthday. We begin by discussing the pace of growth during infancy, noting obvious changes in height and weight as well as less apparent changes in the nervous system. We also consider how infants quickly develop stable patterns in which their basic activities, such as sleeping, eating, and attending to the world, take on some degree of order.

Our discussion then turns to motor development, the development of skills that eventually will allow an infant to roll over, take the first step, and pick up a pin from the floor—skills that ultimately form the basis of later, even more complex behaviors. We start with basic, genetically determined reflexes and consider how even these may be modified through experience. We also discuss the nature and timing of the development of particular physical skills, look at whether their emergence can be speeded up, and consider the importance of early nutrition to their development.

Finally, we explore the development of the senses during infancy. We investigate how several individual sensory systems operate, and we look at how infants sort out data from the sense organs and transform it into meaningful information.

After reading this chapter, you will be able to answer these questions:

▶ **How do the human body and nervous system develop?**

▶ **Does the environment affect the pattern of development?**

▶ **What developmental tasks must infants undertake in this period?**

▶ **What is the role of nutrition in physical development?**

▶ **What sensory capabilities do infants possess?**

Growth and Stability

The average newborn weighs just over 7 pounds, which is probably less than the weight of the average Thanksgiving turkey. Its length is a mere 20 inches, shorter than a loaf of French bread. It is helpless; if left to fend for itself, it could not survive.

Yet after just a few years, the story is very different. Babies are much larger, they are mobile, and they become increasingly independent. How does this growth happen? We can answer this question first by describing the changes in weight and height that occur over the first two years of life, and then by examining some of the principles that underlie and direct that growth.

Physical Growth: The Rapid Advances of Infancy

Over the first 2 years of a human's life, growth occurs at a rapid pace (see Figure 4-1). By the age of 5 months, the average infant's birthweight has doubled to around 15 pounds. By the first birthday, the infant's weight has tripled to about 22 pounds. Although the pace of weight gain slows during the second year, it still continues to increase. By the end of his or her second year, the average child weighs four times as much as he or she did at birth. These numbers are averages, but of course there is a good deal of variation among infants.

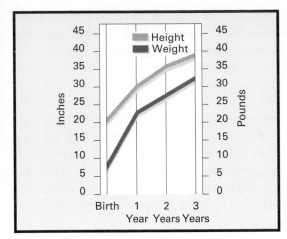

Figure 4-1 **Height and Weight Growth**

Although the greatest increase in height and weight occurs during the first year of life, children continue to grow throughout infancy and toddlerhood.

(*Source:* Cratty, 1979.)

Ana Natalia Epstein, described in the chapter prologue, for example, is within normal ranges even though her weight at 7 months is only about 15 pounds. Height and weight measurements, which are taken regularly during physician's visits during a baby's first year, provide a way to spot problems in development.

The weight gains of infancy are matched by increased length. By the end of the first year, the typical baby stands a proud 30 inches tall, an average increase from birth of almost a foot. By their second birthdays, children average a height of three feet.

Not all parts of an infant's body grow at the same rate. For instance, as we saw first in Chapter 2, at birth the head accounts for one-quarter of the newborn's entire body size. During the first 2 years of life, the rest of the body begins to catch up. By the age of 2 the baby's head is only one-fifth of body length, and by adulthood it is only one-eighth (see Figure 4-2).

The disproportionately large size of infants' heads at birth is an example of one of the major principles that govern growth: the cephalocaudal principle, which relates to the direction of growth. The **cephalocaudal principle** states that growth follows a pattern that

cephalocaudal principle the principle that growth follows a pattern that begins with the head and upper body parts and then proceeds down to the rest of the body

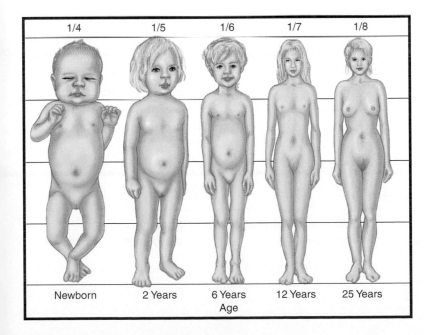

Figure 4-2 **Decreasing Proportions**

At birth, the head represents one-quarter of the neonate's body. By adulthood, the head is only one-eighth the size of the body. Why is the neonate's head so large?

proximodistal principle the principle that development proceeds from the center of the body outward

principle of hierarchical integration the principle that simple skills typically develop separately and independently but are later integrated into more complex skills

principle of the independence of systems the principle that different body systems grow at different rates

neuron the basic nerve cell of the nervous system

begins with the head and upper body parts and then proceeds to the rest of the body. The word cephalocaudal is derived Greek and Latin roots meaning "head-to-tail." The cephalocaudal growth principle means that we develop visual abilities (located in the head) well before we master the ability to walk (closer to the end of the body). The cephalocaudal principle operates both prenatally and after birth.

Three other principles (summarized in Table 4-1) help explain the patterns by which growth occurs. The **proximodistal principle** states that development proceeds from the center of the body outward. Based on the Latin words for "near" and "far," the proximodistal principle means that the trunk of the body grows before the extremities of the arms and legs. Similarly, it is only after growth has occurred in the arms and legs that the fingers and toes can grow. Furthermore, the development of the ability to use various parts of the body also follows the proximodistal principle. For instance, the effective use of the arms precedes the ability to use the hands.

Another major principle of growth concerns the way complex skills build upon simpler ones. The **principle of hierarchical integration** states that simple skills typically develop separately and independently. Later, however, these simple skills are integrated into more complex ones. Thus, the relatively complex skill of grasping something in the hand cannot be mastered until the developing infant learns how to control—and integrate—the movements of the individual fingers.

Finally, the last major principle of growth is the **principle of the independence of systems,** which suggests that different body systems grow at different rates. This principle means that growth in one system does not necessarily imply that growth is occurring in others. For instance, Figure 4-3 illustrates the patterns of growth for three very different systems: body size, which we've already discussed, the nervous system, and sexual characteristics. As you can see, both the rate and timing of these different aspects of growth are independent (Bornstein & Lamb, 1992; Bremmer, Slater, & Butterworth, 1997).

The Nervous System and Brain: The Foundations of Development

When Rina was born, she was the first baby among her parents' circle of friends. These young adults marveled at the infant, oohing and aahing at every sneeze and smile and whimper, trying to guess at their meaning. Whatever feelings, movements, and thoughts Rina was experiencing, they were all brought about by the same complex network: the infant's nervous system. The *nervous system* comprises the brain and the nerves that extend throughout the body.

Neurons are the basic cells of the nervous system. Figure 4-4 shows the structure of an adult neuron. Like all cells in the body, neurons have a cell body containing a nucleus. But unlike other cells, neurons have a distinctive ability: They can communicate with other cells,

Table 4-1

THE MAJOR PRINCIPLES GOVERNING GROWTH

Cephalocaudal Principle	Proximodistal Principle	Principle of Hierarchical Integration	Principle of the Independence of Systems
Growth follows a pattern that begins with the head and upper body parts and then proceeds to the rest of the body. Based on Greek and Latin roots meaning "head-to-tail."	Development proceeds from the center of the body outward. Based on the Latin words for "near" and "far."	Simple skills typically develop separately and independently. Later they are integrated into more complex skills.	Different body systems grow at different rates.

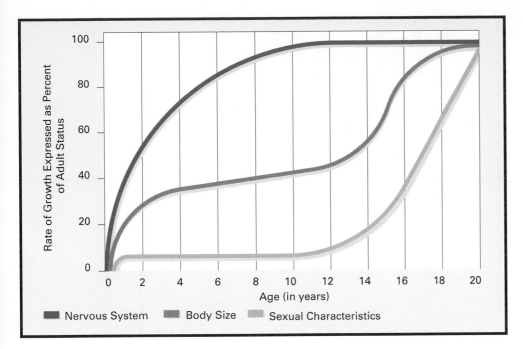

Figure 4-3 **Maturation Rates**

Different body systems mature at different rates. For instance, the nervous system is highly developed during infancy, while body size is considerably less developed. The development of sexual characteristics lags even more, maturing at adolescence. Do you think this pattern is universal among all species, or is it unique to humans?

(*Source:* Bornstein & Lamb, 1992.)

using a cluster of fibers called *dendrites* at one end. Dendrites receive messages from other cells. At their opposite end, neurons have a long extension called an *axon*, the part of the neuron that carries messages destined for other neurons. Neurons do not actually touch one another. Rather, they communicate with other neurons by means of chemical messengers, neurotransmitters, that travel across the small gaps, known as **synapses,** between neurons.

Although estimates vary, infants are born with between 100 and 200 billion neurons. In order to reach this number, neurons multiply at an amazing rate prior to birth. In fact, at some points in prenatal development, cell division creates some 250,000 additional neurons every minute.

At birth, most neurons in an infants' brain have relatively few connections to other neurons. During the first 2 years of life, however, a baby's brain will establish billions of new connections between neurons. Furthermore, the network of neurons becomes increasingly complex, as illustrated in Figure 4-5. The intricacy of neural connections continues to increase throughout life. In fact, in adulthood a single neuron is likely to have a minimum of 5,000 connections to other neurons or other body parts.

Babies are actually born with more neurons than they need. In addition, although synapses are formed throughout life, based on our changing experiences, the billions of new synapses infants form during the first 2 years are also more numerous than necessary. What happens to the extra neurons and synaptic connections?

We can liken the changes that the brain undergoes in its development after birth to the actions of a farmer who, in order to strengthen the vitality of a fruit tree, prunes away unnecessary branches. In the same way, the ultimate capabilities of the brain are brought about in part by a "pruning down" of unnecessary neurons. Neurons that do not become interconnected with other neurons as the infant's experience of the world increases become unnecessary. They eventually die out, increasing the efficiency of the nervous system.

Similarly, other connections between neurons are strengthened as a result of their use during the baby's experiences. If a baby's experiences do not stimulate certain nerve connections, these, like unused neurons, are eliminated—a process called *synaptic pruning*. The result of synaptic pruning is to allow established neurons to build more elaborate communication networks with other neurons. Unlike most other aspects of growth, then, the development of the nervous system proceeds most effectively through the loss of cells (Kolb, 1989, 1995; Johnson, 1998).

synapse the gap at the connection between neurons, through which neurons chemically communicate with one another.

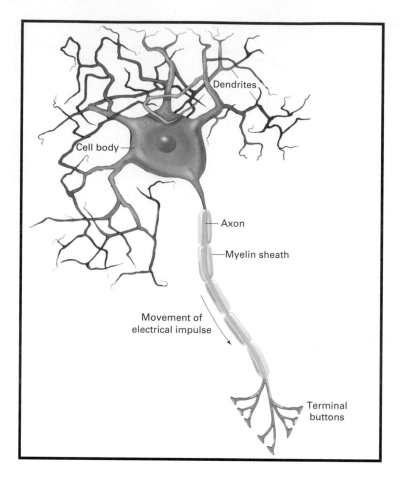

Figure 4-4 **The Neuron**

The basic element of the nervous system, the neuron is comprised of a number of components.

(*Source:* Van de Graaff, 2000.)

myelin a fatty substance that helps insulate neurons and speeds the transmission of nerve impulses

cerebral cortex the upper layer of the brain

plasticity the degree to which a developing structure or behavior is modifiable due to experience

After birth, neurons continue to increase in size. In addition to growth in dendrites, the axons of neurons become coated with **myelin,** a fatty substance that, like the insulation on an electric wire, provides protection and speeds the transmission of nerve impulses. So, even though many neurons are lost, the increasing size and complexity of the remaining ones contribute to impressive brain growth. A baby's brain triples its weight during his or her first 2 years of life, and it reaches more than three-quarters of its adult weight and size by the age of 2.

As they grow, a baby's neurons also move around, becoming arranged by function. Some move into the **cerebral cortex,** the upper layer of the brain, while others move to *subcortical levels*, which are below the cerebral cortex. The subcortical levels, which regulate such fundamental activities as breathing and heart rate, are the most fully developed at birth. As time passes, however, the cells in the cerebral cortex, which are responsible for higher-order processes such as thinking and reasoning, become more developed and interconnected.

Brain development, much of which unfolds automatically because of genetically predetermined patterns, is also strongly susceptible to environmental influences. **Plasticity,** the degree to which a developing structure or behavior is modifiable due to experience, is relatively great for the brain. For instance, as we've seen, an infant's sensory experience affects both the size of individual neurons and the structure of their interconnections. Consequently, compared with those brought up in more enriched environments, infants raised in severely restricted settings are likely to show differences in brain structure and weight (Rosenzweig & Bennett, 1976; Gottlieb, 1991; Kolb, 1995).

Work with nonhumans has been particularly illuminating in revealing the nature of the brain's plasticity. For instance, some studies have compared rats raised in an unusually

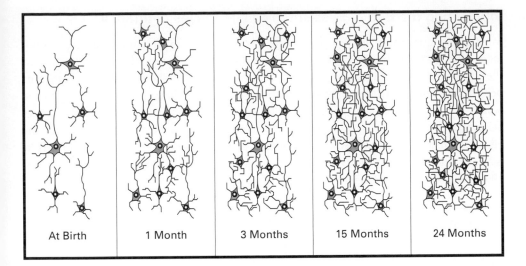

| At Birth | 1 Month | 3 Months | 15 Months | 24 Months |

Figure 4-5 Neuron Networks

Over the first 2 years of life, networks of neurons become increasingly complex and interconnected. Why are these connections important?

(*Source:* Conel, 1930/1963.)

visually stimulating environment to those raised in more typical, and less interesting, cages. Results of such research show that areas of the brain associated with vision are both thicker and heavier for the rats reared in enriched settings (Black & Greenough, 1986; Cynader, 2000).

On the other side of the coin, environments that are unusually barren or in some way restricted may impede the brain's development. Again, work with nonhumans provides some intriguing data. In one study kittens were fitted with goggles that restricted their vision so that they could view only vertical lines. When the cats grew up and had their goggles removed, they were unable to see horizontal lines, although they saw vertical lines perfectly well. Analogously, kittens whose goggles restricted their vision of vertical lines early in life were effectively blind to vertical lines during their adulthood—although their vision of horizontal lines was accurate (Hirsch & Spinelli, 1970).

On the other hand, when goggles are placed on older cats who have lived relatively normal lives as kittens, such results are not seen after the goggles are removed. The conclusion is that there is a sensitive period for the development of vision. As we noted in Chapter 1, a **sensitive period** is a specific, but limited, time, usually early in an organism's life, during which the organism is particularly susceptible to environmental influences relating to some particular facet of development. A sensitive period may be associated with a behavior—such as the development of full vision—or with the development of a structure of the body, such as the configuration of the brain.

The existence of sensitive periods raises several important issues. For one thing, it suggests that unless an infant receives a certain level of early environmental stimulation during a sensitive period, the infant may suffer damage or fail to develop capabilities that can never be fully remedied. If this is true, providing successful later intervention for such children may prove to be particularly challenging.

The opposite question also arises: Does an unusually high level of stimulation during sensitive periods produce developmental gains beyond what a more commonplace level of stimulation would provide?

Such questions have no simple answers. Determining how unusually impoverished or enriched environments affect later development is one of the central questions addressed by developmental researchers seeking to maximize opportunities for developing children. In the meantime, many developmentalists suggest that there are many simple ways parents and caregivers can provide a stimulating environment that will encourage healthy brain growth. Cuddling, talking and singing to, and playing with babies all help enrich their environment (Lamb, 1994; Lafuente et al., 1997).

sensitive period a specific, but limited, time, usually early in an organism's life, during which the organism is particularly susceptible to environmental influences relating to some particular facet of development

Integrating the Bodily Systems: The Life Cycles of Infancy

Most of the humorous "new baby" greeting cards in your local greeting card shop feature jokes about infants' bodily cycles—and the difficulty new parents have in adjusting to these irregular events. Indeed, in the first days of life, infants show a jumble of different behavioral patterns. The most basic activities—sleeping, eating, crying, attending to the world—are controlled by a variety of bodily systems. Although each of these individual behavioral patterns may be functioning effectively, it takes some time and effort for infants to integrate the separate systems. In fact, one of the neonate's major missions is to make its individual behaviors work in harmony (Thoman & Whitney, 1990; Thoman, 1990; Ingersoll & Thoman, 1999).

Rhythms and States. One of the most important ways that behavior becomes integrated is through the development of various body **rhythms,** repetitive, cyclical patterns of behavior. Some rhythms are immediately obvious, such as the change from wakefulness to sleep. Others are more subtle, but still easily noticeable, such as breathing and sucking patterns. Still other rhythms may require careful observation to be noticed. For instance, newborns may go through periods in which they jerk their legs in a regular pattern every minute or so. Although some of these rhythms are apparent just after birth, others emerge slowly over the first year as the nervous system becomes more integrated (Thelen, 1979; Robertson, 1982; Groome et al., 1997).

One of the major body rhythms is that of an infant's **state,** the degree of awareness it displays to both internal and external stimulation. As can be seen in Table 4-2, such states include various levels of wakeful behaviors, such as alertness, fussing, and crying, and different levels of sleep as well. Each change in state brings about an alteration in the amount of stimulation required to get the infant's attention (Brazelton, 1973; Thoman & Whitney, 1990; Karmel, Gardner, & Magnano, 1991; Balaban, Snidman, & Kagan, 1997).

Some of the different states that infants experience produce changes in electrical activity in the brain. These changes are reflected in different patterns of electrical *brain waves*, which can be measured by a device called an *electroencephalogram*, or *EEG*. Starting at three months before birth, these brain wave patterns are relatively irregular. However, by the time an infant reaches the age of 3 months, a more mature pattern emerges and the brain waves stabilize (Parmelee & Sigman, 1983).

rhythms repetitive, cyclical patterns of behavior

state the degree of awareness an infant displays to both internal and external stimulation

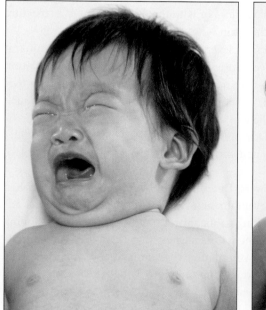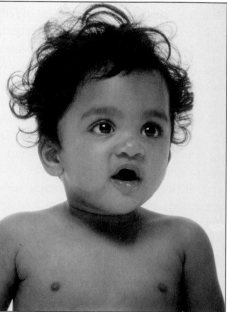

Infants cycle through various states, including crying and alertness. These states are integrated through bodily rhythms.

Table 4-2

PRIMARY BEHAVIORAL STATES

States	Characteristics	Percentage of Time When Alone in State
Awake States		
Alert	Attentive or scanning, the infant's eyes are open, bright, and shining.	6.7
Nonalert waking	Eyes are usually open, but dull and unfocused. Varied, but typically high motor activity.	2.8
Fuss	Fussing is continuous or intermittent, at low levels.	1.8
Cry	Intense vocalizations occurring singly or in succession.	1.7
Transition States Between Sleep and Waking		
Drowse	Infant's eyes are heavy-lidded, but opening and closing slowly. Low level of motor activity.	4.4
Daze	Open, but glassy and immobile eyes. State occurs between episodes of Alert and Drowse. Low level of activity.	1.0
Sleep–wake transition	Behaviors of both wakefulness and sleep are evident. Generalized motor activity; eyes may be closed, or they open and close rapidly. State occurs when baby is awakening.	1.3
Sleep States		
Active sleep	Eyes closed; uneven respiration; intermittent rapid eye movements. Other behaviors: smiles, frowns, grimaces, mouthing, sucking, sighs, and sigh-sobs.	50.3
Quiet sleep	Eyes are closed and respiration is slow and regular. Motor activity limited to occasional startles, sigh-sobs, or rhythmic mouthing.	28.1
Transitional Sleep State		
Active-quiet transition sleep	During this state, which occurs between periods of Active Sleep and Quiet Sleep, the eyes are closed and there is little motor activity. Infant shows mixed behavioral signs of Active Sleep and Quiet Sleep.	1.9

(*Source:* Adapted from Thoman & Whitney, 1990.)

Sleep: Perchance to Dream? At the beginning of infancy, the major state that occupies a baby's time is sleep—much to the relief of exhausted parents, who often regard sleep as a welcome respite from caregiving responsibilities. On average, newborn infants sleep some 16 to 17 hours a day. However, there are wide variations. Some sleep more than 20 hours, while others sleep as little as 10 hours a day (Parmalee, Wenner, & Schulz, 1964).

Even though infants sleep a lot, you probably shouldn't ever wish to "sleep like a baby," despite popular wisdom. For one thing, the sleep of infants comes in fits and starts. Rather than covering one long stretch, sleep initially comes in spurts of around 2 hours, followed by periods of wakefulness. Because of this, infants are "out of sync" with the rest of the world, for whom sleep comes at night and wakefulness during the day (Groome et al., 1997).

Luckily for their parents, infants eventually settle into a more adultlike pattern. After a week, babies sleep a bit more at night and are awake for slightly longer periods during the day. Typically, by the age of 16 weeks infants begin to sleep as much as 6 continuous hours at night, and daytime sleep falls into regular naplike patterns. Most infants sleep through the night by the end of the first year, and the total amount of sleep they need each day is down to about 15 hours (Thoman & Whitney, 1989).

Hidden beneath the supposedly tranquil sleep of infants is another cyclic pattern. During periods of sleep, infants' heart rates increase and become irregular, their blood

rapid eye movement (REM) sleep the period of sleep that is found in older children and adults and is associated with dreaming

pressure rises, and they begin to breathe more rapidly (Montgomery-Downs & Thoman, 1998). Sometimes, although not always, their closed eyes begin to move in a back-and-forth pattern, as if they were viewing an action-packed scene. This period of active sleep is similar, although not identical, to the **rapid eye movement, or REM, sleep,** that is found in older children and adults and is associated with dreaming.

At first, this active, REM-like sleep takes up around one-half of an infant's sleep, compared with just 20 percent of an adult's sleep (see Figure 4-6). However, the quantity of active sleep quickly declines, and by the age of 6 months, amounts to just one-third of total sleep time (Coons & Guilleminault, 1982; Sandyk, 1992).

The appearance of active sleep periods that are similar to REM sleep in adults raises the intriguing question of whether infants dream during those periods. No one knows the answer, although it seems unlikely. First of all, young infants do not have much to dream about, given their relatively limited experiences. Furthermore, the brain waves of sleeping infants appear to be qualitatively different from those of adults who are dreaming. It is not until the baby reaches 3 or 4 months of age that the wave patterns become similar to those of dreaming adults, suggesting that young infants are not dreaming during active sleep—or at least are not doing so in the same way as adults do (McCall, 1979; Parmelee & Sigman, 1983).

Then what is the function of REM sleep in infants? Although we don't know for certain, some researchers think it provides a means for the brain to stimulate itself—a process called *autostimulation* (Roffwarg, Muzio, & Dement, 1966). Stimulation of the nervous system would be particularly important in infants, who spend so much time sleeping and relatively little in alert states.

Although the patterns that infants show in their wakefulness–sleep cycles seem largely preprogrammed by genetic factors, environmental influences also play a part. For instance, both long- and short-term stressors in infants' environments can affect their sleep patterns. When environmental circumstances keep babies awake, sleep, when at last it comes, is apt to be less active (and quieter) than usual (Halpern, MacLean, & Baumeister, 1995; Goodlin-Jones, Burnham, & Anders, 2000).

Furthermore, cultural practices affect the sleep patterns of infants. For example, among the Kipsigis of Africa, infants sleep with their mothers at night and are allowed to nurse whenever they wake. In the daytime, they accompany their mothers during daily chores, often napping while strapped to their mothers' backs. As a result of these practices, Kipsigis infants do not sleep through the night until much later than babies in Western so-

Infants sleep in spurts, often making them out of sync with the rest of the world.

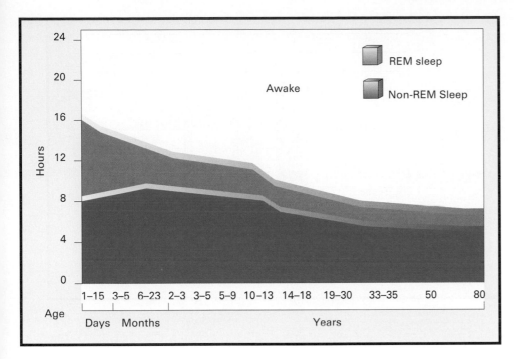

Figure 4-6 **REM Sleep through the Life Span**

As we age, the proportion of REM sleep increases as the proportion of non-REM sleep declines. In addition, the total amount of sleep falls as we get older.

(Adapted from Roffwarg, Muzio, & Dement, 1966.)

cieties, and for the first 8 months of life, they seldom sleep longer than 3 hours at a stretch. In comparison, 8-month-old infants in the United States may sleep as long as 8 hours at a time (Boismier, 1977; Super & Harkness, 1982; Cole, 1992; Anders & Taylor, 1994).

SIDS: The Unanticipated Killer. For a tiny percentage of infants, the rhythm of sleep is interrupted by a deadly affliction: sudden infant death syndrome, or SIDS. **Sudden infant death syndrome (SIDS)** is a disorder in which seemingly healthy infants die in their sleep. Put to bed for a nap or for the night, an infant simply never wakes up.

No known cause has been found to explain SIDS, which strikes about 1 in 1,000 infants in the United States each year. Although it seems to occur when the normal patterns of breathing during sleep are interrupted, scientists have been unable to discover why that might happen. It is clear that infants don't smother or choke; they die a peaceful death, simply ceasing to breathe.

No means for preventing the syndrome have been found. However, as more parents have become aware of guidelines from the American Academy of Pediatrics, which suggest that babies sleep on their backs rather than on their sides or stomachs, the number of deaths from SIDS has decreased significantly (see Figure 4-7). Still, SIDS is the leading cause of death in children under the age of 1 year (Mendelowitz, 1998).

Certain factors are associated with an increased risk of SIDS. For instance, boys and African Americans are at greater risk. In addition, low birthweight and low Apgar scores found at birth are associated with SIDS, as is having a mother who smokes during pregnancy. Some evidence also suggests that a brain defect that affects breathing may produce SIDS. In a small number of cases, child abuse may be the actual cause, although some researchers contend that abuse may actually account for a relatively high number of deaths. Still, there is no clear-cut factor that explains why some infants die from the syndrome. SIDS is found in children of every race and socioeconomic group and in children who have had no apparent health problems (Rosen, 1997; Mendelowitz, 1998; Milerad et al., 1998; Byard & Krous, 1999; Hauck & Hunt, 2000).

Because parents are unprepared for the death of an infant from SIDS, the event is particularly devastating. Parents often feel guilt, fearing that they were neglectful or somehow contributed to their child's death. Such guilt is unwarranted, since nothing has been identified so far that can prevent SIDS.

sudden infant death syndrome (SIDS) the unexplained death of a seemingly healthy baby

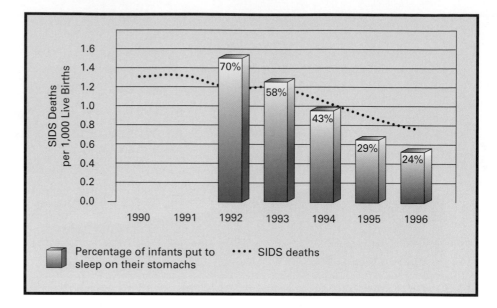

Figure 4-7 **Declining Rates of SIDS**

In the United States, SIDS rates have dropped by a dramatic 38 percent since 1992 as parents have become more informed and put babies to sleep on their backs instead of their stomachs.

(*Source:* National Institute for Child Health and Human Development, 1998.)

Review and Rethink

REVIEW

■ The major principles of growth are the cephalocaudal principle, the proximodistal principle, the principle of hierarchical integration, and the principle of the independence of systems.

■ The development of the nervous system first entails the development of billions of neurons and interconnections among them. Later, the numbers of both neurons and connections decrease as a result of the infant's experiences.

■ Brain plasticity, the susceptibility of a developing organism to environmental influences, is relatively high.

■ Researchers have identified sensitive periods during the development of body systems and behaviors—limited periods when the organism is particularly susceptible to environmental influences.

■ Babies integrate their individual behaviors by developing rhythms—repetitive, cyclical patterns of behavior. A major rhythm relates to the infant's state—the awareness it displays to internal and external stimulation.

RETHINK

■ Research indicates that there is a sensitive period during childhood for normal language acquisition. Persons deprived of normal language stimulation as babies and children may never use language with the same skill as others who were not so deprived. For babies who are born deaf, what are the implications of this research finding, particularly with regard to signed languages?

■ What are some cultural influences on infants' daily patterns of behavior that operate in the culture of which you are a part? How do they differ from the influences of other cultures (either within or outside the United States) of which you are aware?

Motor Development

Suppose you were hired by a genetic engineering firm to redesign newborns and were charged with replacing the current version with a new, more mobile one. The first change you'd probably consider in carrying out this (luckily fictitious) job would be in the conformation and composition of the baby's body.

The shape and proportions of newborn babies are simply not conducive to easy mobility. Their heads are so large and heavy that young infants lack the strength to raise them. Because their limbs are short in relation to the rest of the body, their movements are further impeded. Furthermore, their bodies are mainly fat, with a limited amount of muscle; the result is that they lack strength (Illingworth, 1973).

Fortunately, it doesn't take too long before infants begin to develop a remarkable amount of mobility. In fact, even at birth they have an extensive repertoire of behavioral possibilities brought about by innate reflexes, and their range of motor skills grows rapidly during the first 2 years of life.

Reflexes: Our Inborn Physical Skills

When her father pressed 3-day-old Christina's palm with his finger, she responded by tightly winding her small fist around his finger and grasping it. When he moved his finger upward, she held on so tightly that it seemed he might be able to lift her completely off her crib floor.

The Basic Reflexes. In fact, her father was right: Christina probably could have been lifted in this way. The reason for her resolute grip was activation of one of the dozens of reflexes with which infants are born. **Reflexes** are unlearned, organized involuntary responses that occur automatically in the presence of certain stimuli. Newborns enter the world with an expansive repertoire of behavioral patterns that, when activated, help them adapt to their new surroundings and serve to protect them.

As we can see from the list of reflexes in Table 4-3, many reflexes clearly represent behavior that has survival value, helping to ensure the well-being of the infant. For instance, the *swimming reflex* makes a baby who is lying face down in a body of water paddle and kick in a sort of swimming motion. The obvious consequence of such behavior is to help the baby move from danger and survive until a caregiver can come to its rescue. Similarly, the *eye blink reflex* seems designed to protect the eye from too much direct light, which might damage the retina.

Given the protective value of many reflexes, it might seem beneficial for them to remain with us for our entire lives. In fact, some do: The eye blink reflex remains functional throughout the full life span. On the other hand, quite a few reflexes, such as the swimming reflex, disappear after a few months. Why should this be the case?

Most researchers attribute the gradual disappearance of reflexes to the increase in voluntary control over behavior that occurs as infants become more able to control their muscles. In addition, it may be that reflexes form the foundation for future, more complex behaviors. As these more intricate behaviors become well learned, they subsume the earlier reflexes (Minkowski, 1967; Touwen, 1984; Myklebust & Gottlieb, 1993).

It may even be that the use of reflexes stimulates parts of the brain responsible for more complex behaviors. For example, some researchers argue that exercise of the stepping reflex helps the brain's cortex later develop the ability to walk. As evidence, developmental psychologist Philip R. Zelazo and his colleagues conducted a study in which they provided 2-week-old infants practice in walking for four sessions of 3 minutes each over a

cw

reflexes unlearned, organized involuntary responses that occur automatically in the presence of certain stimuli

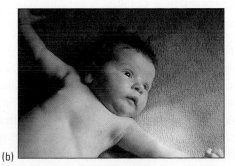

Infants showing (a) the rooting reflex, (b) the startle reflex, and (c) the Babinski reflex.

Table 4-3

SOME BASIC REFLEXES IN INFANTS

Reflex	Approximate Age of Disappearance	Description	Possible Function
Rooting reflex	3 weeks	Neonate's tendency to turn its head toward things that touch its cheek.	Food intake
Stepping reflex	2 months	Movement of legs when held upright with feet touching the floor.	Prepares infants for independent locomotion
Swimming reflex	4–6 months	Infant's tendency to paddle and kick in a sort of swimming motion when lying face down in a body of water.	Avoidance of danger
Moro reflex	6 months	Activated when support for the neck and head is suddenly removed. The arms of the infant are thrust outward and then appear to grasp onto something.	Similar to primates' protection from falling
Babinski reflex	8–12 months	An infant fans out its toes in response to a stroke on the outside of its foot.	Unknown
Startle reflex	Remains in different form	An infant, in response to a sudden noise, flings out its arms, arches its back, and spreads its fingers.	Protection
Eye-blink reflex	Remains	Rapid shutting and opening of eye on exposure to direct light.	Protection of eye from direct light
Sucking reflex	Remains	Infant's tendency to suck at things that touch its lips.	Food intake
Gag reflex	Remains	An infant's reflex to clear its throat.	Prevents choking

6-week period. The results showed that the children who had the walking practice actually began to walk unaided several months earlier than those who had had no such practice. Zelazo suggests that the training produced stimulation of the stepping reflex, which in turn led to stimulation of the brain's cortex, readying the infant earlier for independent locomotion (Zelazo et al., 1993; Zelazo, 1998).

Do these findings suggest that parents should make out-of-the-ordinary efforts to stimulate their infant's reflexes? Probably not. Although the evidence shows that intensive practice may produce an earlier appearance of certain motor activities, there is no evidence that the activities are performed qualitatively any better in practiced infants than in unpracticed infants. Furthermore, even when early gains are found, they do not seem to produce ultimately an adult who is more proficient in motor skills.

In fact, structured exercise may do more harm than good: According to the American Academy of Pediatricians, structured exercise for infants may lead to muscle strain, fractured bones, and dislocated limbs, consequences that far outweigh the unproven benefits that may come from the practice (American Academy of Pediatricians, 1988).

The Universality of Reflexes. Although reflexes are, by definition, genetically determined and universal throughout all infants, there are actually some cultural variations in the ways they are displayed. For instance, consider the *Moro reflex* (often called the *startle response*), which is activated when support for the neck and head is suddenly removed. The Moro reflex consists of the infant's arms thrusting outward and then appearing to seek to grasp onto something. Most scientists feel that the Moro reflex represents a leftover response that we humans have inherited from our nonhuman ancestors. The Moro reflex is an extremely useful behavior for monkey babies, who travel about by clinging to their mothers' backs. If they lose their grip, they fall down unless they are able to grasp quickly onto their mother's fur—in a Moro-like reflex (Prechtl, 1982).

Although the Moro reflex is found in all humans, it appears with significantly different vigor in different children. Some differences reflect cultural and ethnic variations. For instance, Caucasian infants show a pronounced response to situations that produce the Moro reflex. Not only do they fling out their arms, but they also cry and respond in a generally agitated manner. In contrast, Navajo babies react to the same situation much more calmly. Their arms do not flail out as much, and they cry only rarely (Freedman, 1979).

In some cases, reflexes can serve as helpful diagnostic tools for pediatricians. Because reflexes emerge and disappear on a regular timetable, their absence—or presence—at a given point of infancy can provide a clue that something may be amiss in an infant's development. (Even for adults, physicians include reflexes in their diagnostic bags of tricks, as anyone knows who has had his or her knee tapped with a rubber mallet to see if the lower leg jerks forward.)

Although some reflexes may be remnants from our prehuman past and seemingly have little usefulness in terms of survival today, they still may serve a very contemporary function. According to some developmental researchers, some reflexes may promote caregiving and nurturance on the part of adults in the vicinity. For instance, Christina's father, who found his daughter gripping his finger tightly when he pressed her palm, probably cares little that she is simply responding with an innate reflex. Instead, he will more likely view his daughter's action as responsiveness to him, a signal perhaps of increasing interest and affection on her part. As we will see in Chapter 6, when we discuss the social and personality development of infants, such apparent responsiveness can help cement the growing social relationship between an infant and its caregivers (Bell & Ainsworth, 1972; Belsky, Rovine, & Taylor, 1984).

Motor Development in Infancy: Landmarks of Physical Achievement

Josh's parents had intimations that his first steps would not be too far in the future. He was able to drag himself up, and by clutching the side of chairs and tables, progress slowly around the living room. But one day when Josh suddenly lunged forward toward the center of the room, taking one awkward step after another away from the safety of the furniture, his parents were still taken by surprise. Despite the appearance that he was about to keel over at any second, Josh tottered all the way across the room, finally reaching the other side. Not quite knowing how to stop, he toppled over, landing in a happy heap. It was a moment of pure glory.

Probably no physical changes are more obvious—and more eagerly anticipated—than the increasing array of motor skills that babies acquire during infancy. Most parents can remember their child's first steps with a sense of pride and awe at how quickly she or he changed from a helpless infant, unable even to roll over, into a person who could navigate quite effectively in the world.

Gross Motor Skills. Even though the motor skills of newborn infants are not terribly sophisticated, at least compared with attainments that will soon appear, infants still are able to accomplish some kinds of movement. For instance, when placed on their stomachs they wiggle their arms and legs and may try to lift their heavy heads. As their strength increases, they are able to push hard enough against the surface on which they are resting to propel their bodies in different directions. They often end up moving backwards rather than forwards, but by the age of 6 months they become rather accomplished at moving themselves in particular directions. These initial efforts are the forerunners of crawling, in which

This 5-month-old girl demonstrates her gross motor skills.

Figure 4-8 Milestones of Motor Development

Fifty percent of children are able to perform each skill at the month indicated in the figure. However, the specific timing at which each skill appears varies widely. For example, one-quarter of children are able to walk well at 11.1 months; by 14.9 months, 90 percent of children are walking well. Is knowledge of such average benchmarks helpful or harmful to parents?

(Adapted from Frankenburg et al., 1992.)

babies coordinate the motions of their arms and legs and propel themselves forward. Crawling appears typically between 8 and 10 months (Adolph, 1997). (Figure 4-8 provides a summary of some of the milestones of normal motor development.)

Walking comes later. At around the age of 9 months, most infants are able to walk by supporting themselves on furniture, and half of all infants can walk well by the end of their first year of life.

At the same time infants are learning to move around, they are perfecting the ability to remain in a stationary sitting position. At first, babies cannot remain seated upright without support. But they quickly master this ability, and most are able to sit without support by the age of 6 months.

Fine Motor Skills. As infants are perfecting their gross motor skills, such as sitting upright and walking, they are also making advances in their fine motor skills (see Table 4-4). For instance, by the age of 3 months, infants show some ability to coordinate the movements of their limbs (Thelen, 1994).

Furthermore, although infants are born with a rudimentary ability to reach toward an object, this ability is neither very sophisticated nor very accurate, and it disappears around the age of 4 weeks. A different, more precise, form of reaching reappears at 4 months. It takes some time for infants to coordinate successful grasping after they reach out, but in fairly short order they are able to reach out and hold onto an object of interest (Mathew & Cook, 1990; Rochat & Goubet, 1995; Berthier, 1996).

The sophistication of fine motor skills continues to grow. By the age of 11 months, infants are able to pick up off the ground objects as small as marbles—presenting care providers with issues of safety, since the place such objects often go next is the mouth. By

Table 4-4

MILESTONES OF FINE MOTOR DEVELOPMENT

Age (months)	Skill
3	Opens hand prominently
3.5	Grasps rattle
8.5	Grasps with thumb and finger
11	Holds crayon adaptively
14	Builds tower of two cubes
16	Places pegs in board
24	Imitates strokes on paper
33	Copies circle

(*Source:* Adapted from Frankenburg et al., 1992.)

the time they are 2 years old, children can carefully hold a cup, bring it to their lips, and take a drink without spilling a drop.

Developmental Norms: Comparing the Individual to the Group. It is important to keep in mind that the timing of the milestones that we have been discussing is based on norms. **Norms** represent the average performance of a large sample of children of a given age. They permit comparisons between a particular child's performance on a particular behavior and the average performance of the children in the norm sample.

For instance, one of the most widely used techniques to determine infants' normative standing is the **Brazelton Neonatal Behavior Assessment Scale (NBAS),** a measure designed to determine infants' neurological and behavioral responses to their environment.

The NBAS provides a supplement to the traditional Apgar test (discussed in Chapter 3) that is given immediately following birth. Taking about 30 minutes to administer, the NBAS includes 27 separate categories of responses that constitute 4 general aspects of infants' behavior: interactions with others (such as alertness and cuddliness), motor behavior, physiological control (such as the ability to be soothed after being upset), and responses to stress (Brazelton, Nugent, & Lester, 1987; Brazelton, 1973, 1990; Davis & Emory, 1995).

Although the norms provided by scales such as the NBAS are useful in making broad generalizations about the timing of various behaviors and skills, they must be interpreted with caution. Because norms are averages, they mask substantial individual differences in the times when children attain various achievements. For example, some children, like Josh, whose first steps were described earlier, may be ahead of the norm. Other perfectly normal children may be a bit behind the norm. Norms also may hide the fact that the sequence in which various behaviors are achieved may differ somewhat from one child to another.

Furthermore, norms are useful only to the extent that they are based on data from a large, heterogeneous, culturally diverse sample of children. Unfortunately, many of the norms on which developmental researchers have traditionally relied have been based on groups of infants who are predominantly Caucasian and from the middle and upper socioeconomic strata (e.g., Gesell, 1946).

This limitation would not be critical if no differences existed in the timing of development in children from different cultural, racial, and social groups. But they do. For example, as a group, African American babies show more rapid motor development than Caucasian babies throughout infancy. Moreover, there are significant variations related to

cw

norms the average performance of a large sample of children of a given age

Brazelton Neonatal Behavioral Assessment Scale (NBAS) a measure designed to determine infants' neurological and behavioral responses to their environment

cultural factors, as we discuss next (Werner, 1972; Rosser & Randolph, 1989; Brazelton, 1991; Keefer et al., 1991).

Developmental Diversity

The Cultural Dimensions of Motor Development

Among the Ache people, who live in the rain forest of South America, infants face an early life of physical restriction. Because the Ache lead a nomadic existence, living in a series of tiny camps in the rain forest, open space is at a premium. Consequently, for the first few years of life, infants spend nearly all their time in direct physical contact with their mothers. Even when they are not physically touching their mothers, they are permitted to venture no more than a few feet away.

***

Infants among the Kipsigis people, who live in a more open environment in rural Kenya, Africa, lead quite a different existence. Their lives are filled with activity and exercise. Parents seek to teach their children to sit up, stand, and walk from the earliest days of infancy. For example, very young infants are placed in shallow holes in the ground designed to keep them in an upright position. Parents begin to teach their children to walk starting at the eighth week of life. The infants are held with their feet touching the ground, and they are pushed forward.

Clearly, the infants in these two societies lead very different lives (Super, 1976; Kaplan & Dove, 1987). But do the relative lack of early motor stimulation for Ache infants and the efforts of the Kipsigis to encourage motor development really matter?

The answer is both yes and no. Yes, in that Ache infants tend to show delayed motor development, relative both to Kipsigis infants and to children raised in Western societies. Although their social abilities are no different, Ache children tend to begin walking at around 23 months, about a year later than the typical child in the United States. In contrast, Kipsigis children, who are encouraged in their motor development, learn to sit up and walk several weeks earlier, on average, than U.S. children.

In the long run, however, the differences between Ache, Kipsigis, and Western children disappear. By late childhood, there is no evidence of differences in general, overall motor skills among Ache, Kipsigis, and Western children.

Variations in the timing of motor skills seem to depend in part on parental expectations of what is the "appropriate" schedule for the emergence of specific skills. For instance, one study examined the motor skills of infants who lived in a single city in England, but whose mothers varied in ethnic origin. In the research, English, Jamaican, and Indian mothers' expectations were first assessed regarding several markers of their infants' motor skills. The Jamaican mothers expected their infants to sit and walk significantly earlier than the English and Indian mothers, and the actual emergence of these activities was in line with their expectations. The source of the Jamaican infants' earlier mastery seemed to lie in the treatment of the children by their parents. For instance, Jamaican mothers gave their children practice in stepping quite early in infancy (Hopkins & Westra, 1989, 1990).

In sum, the time at which specific motor skills appear is in part determined by cultural factors. Activities that are an intrinsic part of a culture are more apt to be purposely taught to infants in that culture, leading to the potential of their earlier emergence (Nugent, Lester, & Brazelton, 1989).

It is not all that surprising that children in a given culture who are expected by their parents to master a particular skill, and who are taught components of that skill from an early age, are more likely to be proficient in that skill earlier than children from other cultures with no such expectations and no such training. The larger question, however, is whether the earlier emergence of a basic motor behavior in a given culture has lasting consequences for specific motor skills and for achievements in other domains. On this issue, the jury is still out (Bloch, 1989).

What is clear, however, is that there are certain genetically determined constraints on how early a skill can emerge. It is physically impossible for 1-month-old infants to stand and walk, regardless of the encouragement and practice they may get within their culture. Parents who are eager to accelerate their infants' motor development, then, should be cautioned not to hold overly ambitious goals. In fact, they might well ask themselves whether it matters if an infant acquires a motor skill a few weeks earlier than his or her peers.

The most reasonable answer is "no." Although some parents may take pride in a child who walks earlier than other babies (just as some parents may be concerned over a delay of a few weeks), in the long run the timing of this activity will probably make no difference. ☐

Nutrition in Infancy: Fueling Motor Development

Rosa sighed as she sat down to nurse the baby—again. She had fed 4-week-old Juan about every hour today, and he still seemed hungry. Some days, it seemed like all she did was breast-feed her baby. "Well, he must be going through a growth spurt," she decided, as she settled into her favorite rocking chair and put the baby to her nipple.

The rapid physical growth that occurs during infancy is fueled by the nutrients that infants receive. Without proper nutrition, infants such as Juan not only cannot reach their physical potential, they may suffer cognitive and social consequences as well (Pollitt et al., 1993; Pollitt, 1994; Pollitt et al., 1996).

Malnutrition. *Malnutrition,* the condition of having an improper amount and balance of nutrients, produces several results, none good. For instance, malnutrition is more common among children living in many developing countries than among children who live in more industrialized, affluent countries. Malnourished children in these countries begin to show a slower growth rate by the age of 6 months. By the time they reach the age of 2 years, their height and weight are only 95 percent the height and weight of children in more industrialized countries.

Furthermore, children who have been chronically malnourished during infancy later score lower on IQ tests and tend to do less well in school. These effects may linger even if the children's diet has improved substantially (Barrett & Frank, 1987; Grantham-McGregor et al., 1994; Grantham-McGregor, Ani, & Fernald, 2001).

The problem of malnutrition is greatest in underdeveloped countries, where almost 10 percent of infants are severely malnourished. In the Dominican Republic, for instance, 13 percent of children under 3 years of age are underweight, and 21 percent have stunted growth. In other areas, the problem is even worse. In South Asia, for example, almost 60 percent of all children are underweight (World Food Council, 1992; see Figure 4-9).

Problems of malnourishment are not restricted to developing countries, however. In the United States, the richest country in the world, some 14 million children live in poverty, which puts them at risk for malnutrition. In fact, although overall poverty rates are no worse than they were 20 years ago, the poverty rate for children under the age of 3 has increased. Some one-quarter of families who have children 2 years old and younger live in poverty. And, as we can see in Figure 4-10, the rates are even higher for African American and Hispanic families as well as for single-parent families (Einbinder, 1992; Carnegie Task Force on Meeting the Needs of Young Children, 1994; Duncan & Brooks-Gunn, 2000).

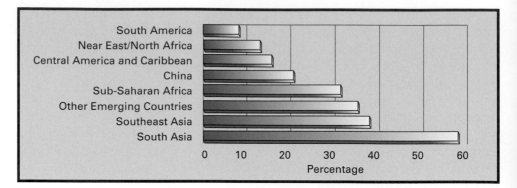

Figure 4-9 **Underweight Children**

In developing countries the number of underweight children under the age of 5 years is substantial.

(*Source:* World Food Council, 1992.)

marasmus a disease characterized by the cessation of growth

kwashiorkor a disease in which a child's stomach, limbs, and face swell with water

Although these children rarely become severely malnourished, due to adequate social safety nets, they remain susceptible to *undernutrition*, in which there is some deficiency in diet. In fact, some surveys find that as many as a quarter of 1- to 5-year-old children in the United States have diets that fall below the minimum caloric intake recommended by nutritional experts. Although the consequences are not as severe as those of malnutrition, undernutrition also has long-term costs. For instance, cognitive development later in childhood is affected by even mild to moderate undernutrition (U.S. Bureau of the Census, 1992; Pollitt et al., 1996; Sigman, 1995).

Severe malnutrition during infancy may lead to several disorders. Malnutrition during the first year can produce **marasmus,** a disease in which infants stop growing. Marasmus, attributable to a severe deficiency in proteins and calories, causes the body to waste away and ultimately results in death. Older children are susceptible to **kwashiorkor,** a disease in which a child's stomach, limbs, and face swell with water. To a casual observer, it

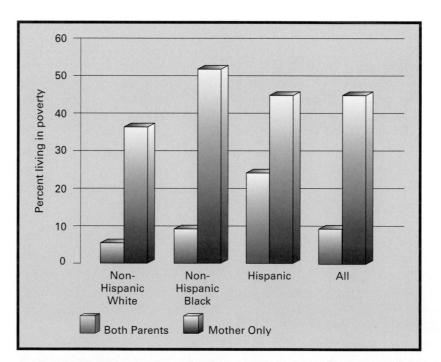

Figure 4-10   **Children Living in Poverty**

The incidence of poverty among children under the age of 3 is particularly high in minority and single-parent households. (Figures are shown only for single mothers, and not fathers, because 97 percent of all children under 3 who live with a single parent live with their mothers; only 3 percent live with their fathers.)

(*Source:* National Center for Children in Poverty at the Joseph L. Mailman School of Public Health of Columbia University. Analysis based on U.S. Bureau of the Census, 2000 Current Population Survey.)

appears that a child with kwashiorkor is actually chubby. However, this is an illusion: The child's body is in fact struggling to make use of the few nutrients that are available.

In some cases, infants who receive sufficient nutrition act as though they have been deprived of food. Looking as though they suffer from marasmus, they are underdeveloped, listless, and apathetic. The real cause, though, is emotional: They lack sufficient love and emotional support. In such cases, known as **nonorganic failure to thrive,** children stop growing not for biological reasons but due to a lack of stimulation and attention from their parents. Usually occurring by the age of 18 months, nonorganic failure to thrive can be reversed through intensive parent training or by placing children in a foster home where they can receive emotional support.

nonorganic failure to thrive a disorder in which infants stop growing due to a lack of stimulation and attention as the result of inadequate parenting

Obesity. It is clear that malnourishment during infancy has potentially disastrous consequences for an infant. Less clear, however, are the effects of *obesity*, defined as weight greater than 20 percent above the average for a given height. For one thing, there appears to be no correlation between obesity during infancy and obesity at the age of 16 years. (There is an association between obesity after the age of 6 and adult weight, however.)

Furthermore, although some research suggests that overfeeding during infancy may lead to the creation of unnecessary fat cells, which remain in the body throughout life, it is not clear that an abundance of fat cells necessarily leads to adult obesity. In fact, genetic factors are an important determinant of obesity (Knittle, 1975; Bouchard et al., 1990; Fabsitz, Carmelli, & Hewitt, 1992).

In sum, obesity during infancy is not a major concern. However, the societal view that "a fat baby is a healthy baby" is not necessarily correct, either. Rather than focusing on their infant's weight, parents should concentrate on providing appropriate nutrition. At least during the period of infancy, concerns about weight need not be central, as long as infants are provided with an appropriate diet.

Although everyone agrees on the importance of receiving proper nutrition during infancy, just how to reach that goal is a source of controversy. Because infants are not born with the ability to eat or digest solid food, at first they exist solely on a liquid diet. But just what should that liquid be—a mother's breast milk or a formula of commercially processed cow's milk with vitamin additives? The answer has changed, more than once, during the past century.

Breast or Bottle?

Some 40 years ago, if a mother asked her pediatrician whether breast-feeding or bottle-feeding was better, she would have received a simple and clear-cut answer: Bottle-feeding was the preferred method. Starting around the 1940s, the general belief among child care experts was that breast-feeding was an obsolete method that put children unnecessarily at risk.

With bottle-feeding, the argument went, parents could keep track of the amount of milk their baby was receiving and could thereby ensure that the child was taking in sufficient nutrients. In contrast, mothers who breast-fed their babies could never be certain just how much milk their infants were getting. Furthermore, use of the bottle was said to help mothers keep their feedings to a rigid schedule of one bottle every 4 hours, at that time the recommended procedure.

Today, however, a mother would get a very different answer to the same question. Child care authorities agree: For the first 12 months of life, there is no better food for an infant than breast milk (American Academy of Pediatrics, 1997). Breast milk not only contains all the nutrients necessary for growth, but it also seems to offer some degree of immunity to a variety of childhood diseases, such as respiratory and ear infections and diarrhea (see Figure 4-11). Breast milk is more easily digested than cow's milk or formula, and it is sterile, warm, and convenient for the mother to dispense. There is even some evidence that breast milk may enhance cognitive growth (Howie et al., 1990; Rogan & Gladen, 1993).

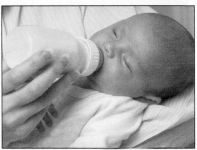

Breast or bottle? Although infants receive adequate nourishment from breast- or bottle-feeding, most authorities agree "breast is best."

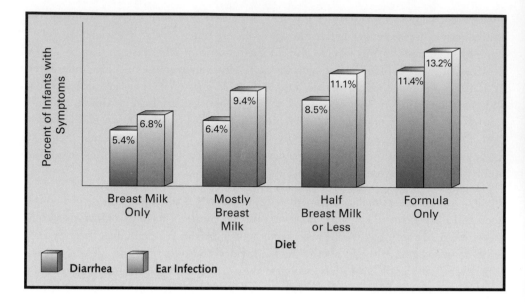

Figure 4-11 **Breast Milk Advantages**

One of the advantages to breast milk is that it contains all the nutrients necessary for growth; it also appears to offer some degree of immunity to a variety of childhood diseases. What social changes in the U.S. might encourage more mothers to breastfeed?

(*Source:* Pediatrics Electronic Pages, June 1997.)

Breast-feeding also offers significant emotional advantages for both mother and child. Most mothers report that the experience of breast-feeding brings about feelings of well-being and intimacy with their infants, perhaps because of the production of endorphins in mothers' brains. Breast-fed infants are also more responsive to their mothers' touch and their mother's gaze during feeding, and they are calmed and soothed by the experience. As we'll see in Chapter 6, this mutual responsiveness may lead to healthy social development (Epstein, 1993; Gerrish & Mennella, 2000).

Breast-feeding may even hold health-related advantages for mothers. For instance, research suggests that women who breast-feed may have lower rates of ovarian cancer and breast cancer prior to menopause. Furthermore, the hormones produced during breast-feeding help shrink the uteruses of women following birth, enabling their bodies to return more quickly to a prepregnancy state. These hormones also may inhibit ovulation, reducing (but not eliminating!) the chance of becoming pregnant, and thereby helping to space the birth of additional children. (Ross & Yu, 1994; Herbst, 1994; Altemus et al., 1995).

Obviously, breast-feeding is not the solution to every problem faced by infants, and the millions of individuals who have been raised on formula should not be concerned that they have suffered irreparable harm. In fact, recent research suggests that infants fed enriched formula show better cognitive development than those using traditional formula. But it does continue to be clear that the popular slogan used by groups advocating the use of breast-feeding is right on target: "Breast is Best" (Birch et al., 2000).

Social Patterns in Breast-Feeding. Although it has several advantages, only about half of all new mothers in the United States employ breast-feeding. This is actually a decline from the peak that was reached in 1982, when almost two-thirds of all new mothers breast-fed their babies. Although recent figures suggest that breast-feeding may once again be on the rise, the decline that occurred in the 1980s was significant (Ross Laboratories, 1993; Ryan, 1997).

Issues of age, social status, and race influence the decision whether to breast-feed. The rates of breast-feeding are highest among women who are older, have better education, are of higher socioeconomic status, and have social or cultural support. Moreover, there are ethnic and racial group differences. For instance, breast-feeding among Caucasian mothers in the United States occurs at a rate almost double that for African American mothers (Maternal and Child Health Bureau, 1993; Richardson & Champion, 1992; Mahoney & James, 2000).

If authorities are in agreement about the benefits of breast-feeding, why in so many cases do women not breast-feed? In some cases, they can't. Some women have difficulties

"I forgot to say I was breast-fed."

producing milk, while others are taking some type of medicine or have an infectious disease such as AIDS that could be passed on to their infants through breast milk. Sometimes infants are too ill to nurse successfully. And in many cases of adoption, where the birth mother is unavailable after giving birth, the adoptive mother has no choice but to bottle-feed.

In other cases, the decision not to breast-feed is based on practical considerations. Women who hold jobs outside the home may not have sufficiently flexible schedules to breast-feed their infants. This problem is particularly true with less affluent women who may have less control over their schedules. Such problems also may account for the lower rate of breast-feeding among mothers of lower socioeconomic status, who may lack social support for breast-feeding (Arlotti et al., 1998).

Education is also an issue: Some women simply do not receive adequate information and advice regarding the advantages of breast-feeding, and choose to use formula because it seems an appropriate choice. Indeed, some hospitals may inadvertently encourage the use of formula by including it in the gift packets new mothers receive as they leave the hospital.

In developing countries, the use of formula is particularly problematic. Because formula often comes in powdered form that must be mixed with water, local pollution of the water supply can make formula particularly dangerous. In poverty-stricken areas, parents may dilute formula too much because they can't afford to buy the proper amounts, leading to problems with infant malnutrition or undernutrition.

Educational, social, and cultural support for breast-feeding is particularly important. For instance, physicians need to educate their patients about the importance of the practice and to provide specific information on just how to breast-feed. Although breast-feeding is a natural act, mothers require a bit of practice to learn how to hold the baby properly, position the nipple correctly, and deal with such potential problems as sore nipples.

Introducing Solid Foods: When and What?

Although pediatricians agree that breast milk is the ideal initial food, at some point infants require more nutriments than breast milk alone can provide. The American Academy of Pediatrics and the American Academy of Family Physicians suggest that babies can start

Infants generally start solid foods at around 4 to 6 months, gradually working their way up to a variety of different foods.

solids at around 6 months, although they aren't needed until 9 to 12 months of age (American Academy of Pediatrics, 1997; American Academy of Family Physicians, 1997).

Solid foods are introduced into an infant's diet gradually, one at a time. Most often cereal comes first, followed by strained fruits. Vegetables and other foods typically are introduced next, although the order varies significantly from one infant to another.

The timing of *weaning*, the cessation of breast-feeding or bottle-feeding, varies greatly. In developed countries such as the United States, weaning from breast-feeding frequently occurs as early as 3 or 4 months. On the other hand, in certain subcultures within the United States, breast-feeding may continue for 2 or 3 years. The American Academy of Pediatrics recommends that infants be fed breast milk for the first 12 months (American Academy of Pediatrics, 1997).

Review and Rethink

REVIEW

- Reflexes are universal, genetically acquired physical behaviors.

- During infancy children achieve a series of landmarks in their physical development on a generally consistent schedule, with some individual and cultural variations.

- Training and cultural expectations affect the timing of the development of motor skills.

- Nutrition strongly affects physical development. Malnutrition can slow growth, affect intellectual performance, and cause diseases such as marasmus and kwashiorkor. The victims of undernutrition also suffer negative effects.

- The advantages of breast-feeding are numerous, including nutritional, immunological, emotional, and physical benefits for the infant, and physical and emotional benefits for the mother as well.

RETHINK

- What advice might you give a friend who is concerned about the fact that her infant is still not walking at 14 months, when every other baby she knows started walking by the first birthday?

- Given that malnourishment negatively affects physical growth, how can it also adversely affect IQ scores and school performance?

The Development of the Senses

According to William James, one of the founding fathers of psychology, the world of the infant is a "blooming, buzzing confusion" (James, 1890/1950). Was he right? In this case, James's wisdom failed him. The newborn's world does lack the clarity and stability that we can distinguish as adults, but day by day the world grows increasingly comprehensible as the infant's ability to sense and perceive the environment develops. As we saw in the case of Ana Natalia Epstein, described at the start of the chapter, babies appear to thrive in an environment enriched by pleasing sensations.

The processes that underlie infants' understanding of the world around them are sensation and perception. **Sensation** is the stimulation of the sense organs, and **perception** is the sorting out, interpretation, analysis, and integration of stimuli involving the sense organs and brain. Sensation is the responsiveness of the sense organs to stimulation, while perception is the interpretation of that stimulation. Sorting out infants' capabilities in the realm of sensation and perception presents a challenge to the ingenuity of investigators (Nelson et al., 1995).

sensation the stimulation of the sense organs

perception the sorting out, interpretation, analysis, and integration of stimuli involving the sense organs and brain

Visual Perception: Seeing the World

From the time of Lee Eng's birth, everyone who met him felt that he gazed at them intently. His eyes seemed to meet those of visitors. They seemed to bore deeply and knowingly into the faces of people who looked at him.

How good in fact was Lee's vision, and what, precisely, could he make out of his environment? Quite a bit. According to some estimates, a newborn's distance vision ranges from 20/200 to 20/600, which means that an infant cannot discern visual material beyond 20 feet that an adult with normal vision is able to see from a distance of between 200 and 600 feet (Haith, 1991).

These figures indicate that infants' distance vision is some 10 to 30 times poorer than the average adult's, perhaps suggesting that the vision of infants is inadequate. However, looking at the figures from a different perspective suggests a revised interpretation: The vision of newborns provides the same degree of distance acuity as the uncorrected vision of many adults who wear eyeglasses or contact lenses. (If you wear glasses or contact lenses, remove them to get a sense of what an infant can see of the world; see the accompanying set of photos.) Furthermore, infants' distance vision grows increasingly acute. By 6 months of age, the average infant's vision is already 20/20—in other words, identical to that of adults (Aslin, 1987; Simons, 1993).

Other visual abilities grow rapidly. For instance, *binocular vision*, the ability to combine the images coming to each eye to see depth and motion, is achieved at around 14 weeks. Before then, infants do not integrate the information from each eye.

Depth perception is a particularly useful ability, as illustrated in a classic study by developmental psychologists Eleanor Gibson and Richard Walk (1960) in which infants were placed on a sheet of heavy glass. A checkered pattern appeared under one-half of the glass sheet, making it seem that the infant was on a stable floor. However, in the middle of the glass sheet, the pattern dropped down several feet, forming an apparent "visual cliff." The question Gibson and Walk asked was whether infants would willingly crawl across the cliff when called by their mothers (see Figure 4-12).

The results were unambiguous. Most of the infants in the study, who ranged in age from 6 to 14 months, could not be coaxed over the apparent cliff. Clearly the ability to perceive depth had already developed in most of them by that age. On the other hand, the experiment did not pinpoint when depth perception emerged, since only infants who had already learned to crawl could be tested. But other experiments, in which infants of 2 and 3 months were placed on their stomachs above the apparent floor and above the visual cliff, revealed differences in heart rate between the two positions (Campos, Langer, & Krowitz, 1970).

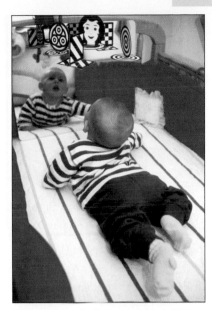

While an infant's distance vision is 10 to 30 times poorer than the average adult's, the vision of newborns provides the same degree of distance acuity as the uncorrected vision of many adults who wear eyeglasses or contact lenses.

Figure 4-12 **Visual Cliff**

The "visual cliff" experiment examines the depth perception of infants. Most infants in the age range of 6 to 14 months cannot be coaxed to cross the cliff, apparently responding to the fact that the patterned area drops several feet.

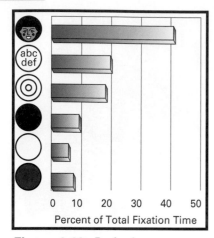

Figure 4-13 **Preferring Complexity**

In a classic experiment, researcher Robert Fantz found that 2- and 3-month-old infants preferred to look at more complex stimuli than simple ones.

(Adapted from Fantz, 1961.)

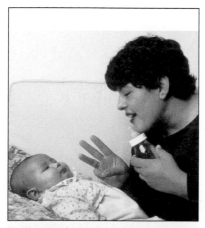

By the age of 4 months infants are able to discriminate their own names from other, similar sounding, words. What are some ways an infant is able to discriminate his or her name from other words?

Still, such findings do not permit us to know whether infants are responding to depth itself or merely to the *change* in visual stimuli that occurs when they are moved from a lack of depth to depth.

Infants also show clear visual preferences, preferences that are present from birth. For example, when given a choice, infants reliably prefer to look at stimuli that include patterns than to look at simpler stimuli (see Figure 4-13). How do we know? Developmental psychologist Robert Fantz (1963) created a classic test. He built a chamber in which babies could lie on their backs and see pairs of visual stimuli above them. Fantz could determine which of the stimuli the infants were looking at by observing the reflections of the stimuli in their eyes.

Fantz's work was the impetus for a great deal of research on the preferences of infants, most of which points to a critical conclusion: Infants are genetically preprogrammed to prefer particular kinds of stimuli. For instance, just minutes after birth they show preferences for certain colors, shapes, and configurations of various stimuli. They prefer curved over straight lines, three-dimensional figures to two-dimensional ones, and human faces to nonfaces. Such capabilities may be a reflection of the existence of highly specialized cells in the brain that react to stimuli of a particular pattern, orientation, shape, and direction of movement (Hubel & Wiesel, 1979; Rubenstein, Kalakanis, & Langlois, 1999; Csibra et al., 2000).

However, genetics is not the sole determinant of infant visual preferences. Just a few hours after birth, infants have already learned to prefer their own mother's face to other faces. Such findings provide another clear piece of evidence of how heredity and environmental experiences are woven together to determine an infant's capabilities (Bushnell, 1998; Hood, Willen, & Driver, 1998; Mondloch et al., 1999).

Auditory Perception: The World of Sound

What is it about a mother's lullaby that helps soothe a crying, fussy baby? Some clues emerge when we look at the capabilities of infants in the realm of auditory sensation and perception.

It is clear that infants hear from the time of birth—and even before. As we noted in Chapter 2, the ability to hear begins prenatally. Even in the womb, the fetus responds to sounds outside of its mother. Furthermore, infants are born with preferences for particular sound combinations. For example, an infant can more easily discern a blend of musical tones if the underlying frequencies of the tones are related as simple mathematical proportions than if the relationship between tones is a more complex combination (Schellenberg & Trehub, 1996).

Because they have had some practice in hearing before birth, it is not surprising that infants have reasonably good auditory perception after they are born. In fact, for certain very high and very low frequencies, infants actually are more sensitive to sound than adults—a sensitivity that seems to increase during the first 2 years of life. On the other hand, infants are initially less sensitive than adults to middle-range frequencies. Eventually, however, their capabilities within the middle range improve (Fenwick & Morongiello, 1991; Werner & Marean, 1996).

It is not fully clear what leads to the improvement during infancy in sensitivity to sounds, although it may be related to the maturation of the nervous system. More puzzling is why, after infancy, children's ability to hear very high and low frequencies gradually declines. One explanation may be that exposure to high levels of noise may diminish capacities at the extreme ranges (Schneider, Trehub, & Bull, 1980; Kryter, 1983; Trehub et al., 1988, 1989).

In addition to the ability to detect sound, infants need several other abilities in order to hear effectively. For instance, *sound localization* permits infants to pinpoint the direction from which a sound is emanating. Compared to adults, infants have a slight handicap in this task because effective sound localization requires the use of the slight difference in the times at which a sound reaches our two ears. Because infants' heads are smaller than those of adults, the difference in timing of the arrival of sound at the two ears is less than it is in adults.

However, despite the potential limitation brought about by their smaller heads, infants' sound localization abilities are actually fairly good even at birth, and they reach adult levels of success by the age of 1 year (Clifton, 1992; Litovsky & Ashmead, 1997). Interestingly, their improvement is not steady: Although we don't know why, the accuracy of sound localization actually declines between birth and 2 months of age, but then begins to increase (Aslin, 1987; Schneider, Bull, & Trehub, 1988; Trehub et al., 1989).

Infant discrimination of groups of different sounds, in terms of their patterns and other acoustical characteristics, is also quite good. For instance, the change of a single note in a six-tone melody can be detected by infants as young as 6 months old. They also react to changes in musical key (Trehub, Thorpe, & Morrongiello, 1985). In sum, they listen with a keen ear to the melodies of lullabies sung to them by their mothers and fathers!

Even more important to their ultimate success in the world, young infants are capable of making the fine discriminations that their future understanding of language will require (Bijeljac-Babic, Bertoncini, & Mehler, 1993). For instance, in one classic study, a group of 1- to 4-month-old infants sucked on nipples that activated a recording of a person saying "ba" every time they sucked (Eimas et al., 1971). At first, their interest in the sound made them suck vigorously. Soon, though, they became acclimated to the sound (through a process called *habituation,* discussed in Chapter 3) and sucked with less energy. On the other hand, when the experimenters changed the sound to "pa," the infants immediately showed new interest and sucked with greater vigor once again. The clear conclusion: Infants as young as 1 month old could make the distinction between the two similar sounds (Eimas et al., 1971; Goodman & Nusbaum, 1994; Miller & Eimas, 1995).

Even more intriguingly, young infants are able to discriminate certain characteristics that differentiate one language from another. By the age of 4 1/2 months, infants are able to discriminate their own names from other, similar-sounding words. By the age of 5 months, they can distinguish the difference between English and Spanish passages, even when the two are similar in meter, number of syllables, and speed of recitation. In fact, some evidence suggests that even 2-day-olds show preferences for the language spoken by those around them over other languages (Bahrick & Pickens, 1988; Moon, Cooper, & Fifer, 1993; Best, 1994; Mandel, Jusczyk, & Pisoni, 1995).

Given their ability to discriminate a difference in speech as slight as the difference between two consonants, it is not surprising that infants can distinguish different people on the basis of voice. In fact, from an early age they show clear preferences for some voices over others. For instance, in one experiment newborns were allowed to suck a nipple that turned on a recording of a human voice reading a story. The infants sucked significantly longer when the voice was that of their mother than when the voice was that of a stranger (DeCasper & Fifer, 1980; Fifer, 1987).

How do such preferences arise? One hypothesis is that prenatal exposure to the mother's voice is the key. As support for this conjecture, researchers point to the fact that newborns do not show a preference for their fathers' voices over other male voices. Furthermore, newborns prefer listening to melodies sung by their mothers before they were born to melodies that were not sung before birth. It seems, then, that the prenatal exposure to their mothers' voices—although muffled by the liquid environment of the womb—helps shape infants' listening preferences (DeCasper & Prescott, 1984; Panneton, 1985).

Smell and Taste

What do infants do when they smell a rotten egg? Pretty much what adults do—crinkle their noses and generally look unhappy. On the other hand, the scent of bananas and butter produces a pleasant reaction on the part of infants (Steiner, 1979).

The sense of smell is so well developed, even among very young infants, that at least some 12- to 18-day-old babies can distinguish their mothers on the basis of smell alone. For instance, in one experiment infants were exposed to the smell of gauze pads worn under the arms of adults the previous evening. Infants who were being breast-fed were

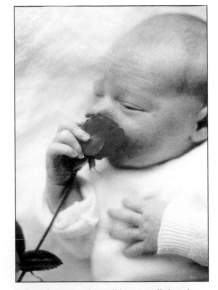

Infants' sense of smell is so well developed they can distinguish their mothers on the basis of smell alone.

able to distinguish their mothers' scent from those of other adults. However, not all infants could do this: Those who were being bottle-fed were unable to make the distinction. Moreover, both breast-fed and bottle-fed infants were unable to distinguish their fathers on the basis of odor (Porter, Bologh, & Malkin, 1988; Soussignan et al., 1997).

Taste, like smell, shows surprising sophistication during infancy. Some taste preferences are well developed at birth, such as disgust over bitter tastes. At the same time, infants seem to have an innate sweet tooth—even before they have teeth: Very young infants smile when a sweet-tasting liquid is placed on their tongues. They also suck harder at a bottle if it is sweetened. Since breast milk has a sweet taste, it is possible that this preference may be part of our evolutionary heritage, retained because it offered a survival advantage. Infants who preferred sweet tastes may have been more likely to ingest sufficient nutrients and to survive than those who did not (Steiner, 1979; Rosenstein & Oster, 1988; Porges, Lipsitt, & Lewis 1993).

Infants also develop taste preferences based on what their mothers drank while they were in the womb. For instance, one study found that women who drank carrot juice while pregnant had children who had a preference for the taste of carrots during infancy (Mennella, 2000).

Sensitivity to Pain and Touch

When Eli Rosenblatt was 8 days old, he participated in the ancient Jewish ritual of circumcision. As he lay nestled in his father's arms, the foreskin of his penis was removed. Although Eli shrieked in what seemed to his anxious parents as pain, he soon settled down and went back to sleep. Others who had watched the ceremony assured his parents, with great authority, that at Eli's age babies don't really experience pain, at least not in the same way that adults do.

Were Eli's relatives accurate in saying that young infants don't experience pain? In the past, many medical practitioners would have agreed. In fact, because they assumed that infants didn't experience pain in truly bothersome ways, many physicians routinely carried out medical procedures, and even some forms of surgery, without the use of painkillers or anesthesia. Their argument was that the risks from the use of anesthesia outweighed the potential pain that the young infants experienced.

Contemporary Views on Infant Pain. Today, however, it is widely acknowledged that infants are born with the capacity to experience pain. Obviously, no one can be sure if the experience of pain in children is identical to that in adults, any more than we can tell if an adult friend who complains of a headache is experiencing pain that is more or less severe than our own pain when we have a headache.

What we do know is that pain produces signs of distress in infants, such as a rise in heartbeat, sweating, facial expressions indicative of discomfort, and changes in the intensity and tone of crying (Johnston, 1989). Such evidence indicates that infants do, in fact, experience pain.

There also seems to be a developmental progression in reactions to pain. For example, a newborn infant who has her heel pricked for a blood test responds with signs of distress, but it takes her several seconds to show the response. In contrast, only a few months later, the same procedure brings a much more immediate response. It is possible that the delayed reaction in infants is produced by the relatively slower transmission of information within the newborn's nervous system. (Porter, Porges, & Marshall, 1988; Anand & Hickey, 1987, 1992; Axia, Bonichini, & Benini, 1995).

In addition, research with rats suggests that exposure to pain in infancy may lead to a permanent rewiring of the nervous system that results in greater sensitivity to pain during adulthood. Such findings indicate that infants who must undergo extensive, painful medical treatments and tests may be unusually sensitive to pain when older (Ruda et al., 2000).

From Research to Practice
Should Male Infants Be Circumcised?

It is a routine practice in both the Jewish and Islamic faiths: circumcision of male infants soon after birth, a procedure in which the skin covering the end of the penis is removed. But are there medical reasons to perform the practice?

According to the American Academy of Pediatrics (2000a), the answer is no. Admittedly, some minor health benefits are associated with circumcision, including a slightly lower risk of urinary tract infections and sexually transmitted diseases (including AIDS), a lower risk of cancer of the penis (a disease for which the risk is already very low), and easier genital hygiene.

However, these minor benefits have to be weighed against the risks involved in circumcision. As in any surgery, there is a small risk of complications, such as bleeding, infection, irritation, and botched surgery. It is also possible—although hard to substantiate—that circumcision reduces sexual pleasure.

After analyzing the risks and benefits, the Academy determined that the benefits are not sufficient to recommend that all boys be routinely circumcised—nor that the practice be avoided. Instead, the decision to have male infants circumcised must rest on religious, social, and cultural traditions. For example, some parents may choose circumcision because they want their child to look like the other males in the family, all of whom are circumcised. Or the practice may be an ingrained tradition or a matter of religious practice. The point is that such decisions are not medical, but cultural and psychological (Springen, 2000).

What is clear, though, is that if a male baby is to be circumcised, pain-killers should be used. Local anesthetics can be injected prior to the operation, and topical creams can also be used. The pain of circumcision can—and should—be avoided.

In response to increasing support for the notion that infants experience pain and that its effects may be long-lasting, medical experts now endorse the use of anesthesia and painkillers during surgery for even the youngest infants. According to the American Academy of Pediatrics, painkilling drugs are appropriate in most types of surgery—including, as we consider in the *From Research to Practice* box, the practice of circumcision.

Responding to Touch. It clearly does not take the sting of pain to get an infant's attention. Recall how much Ana Natalia Epstein, the baby described in the chapter prologue, enjoyed her afternoon massage. Even the youngest infants respond to gentle touches, such as a soothing caress, which can calm a crying, fussy infant (Stack & Muir, 1992).

In fact, touch is one of the most highly developed sensory systems in a newborn. It is also one of the first to develop; there is evidence that by 32 weeks after conception, the entire body is sensitive to touch. Furthermore, several of the basic reflexes present at birth, such as the rooting reflex, require touch sensitivity to operate: An infant must sense a touch near the mouth in order to seek automatically a nipple to suck (Haith, 1986).

Infants' abilities in the realm of touch are particularly helpful in their efforts to explore the world. Several theorists have suggested that one of the ways children gain information about the world is through touching. For instance, at the age of 6 months, infants are apt to place almost any object in their mouths, apparently taking in data about its configuration from their sensory responses to the feel of it in their mouths (Ruff, 1989).

In addition, touch plays an important role in an organism's future development, for it triggers a complex chemical reaction that assists infants in their efforts to survive. For example, gentle massage stimulates the production of certain chemicals in an infant's brain that instigate growth. Periodic massage is also helpful in treating several kinds of medical conditions, including premature delivery and the effects of prenatal exposure to AIDS or cocaine. Furthermore, massage is beneficial for infants and even older children whose mothers are depressed and for those who suffer from burns, cancer, asthma, and a

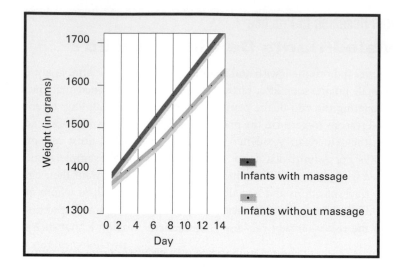

Figure 4-14 Effect of Massage on Weight Gain

The weight gain of premature infants who were systematically massaged is greater than those who did not receive the massage. How can this phenomenon be explained?

(*Source:* T. M. Field, 1988.)

variety of other medical conditions (Schanberg et al., 1993; Field, 1995a, 1995b, 1999; Hernandez-Reif et al., 1999).

In one study that illustrates the benefits of massage, a group of preterm infants who were massaged for 15 minutes three times a day gained weight some 50 percent faster than a group of preterm infants of the same age who were not stroked (see Figure 4-14). The massaged infants also were more active and responsive to stimuli. Ultimately, the preterm infants who were massaged were discharged earlier from the hospital, and the costs of their medical care were significantly lower than for infants in the unmassaged group (Field, 1988a, 1995).

Multimodal Perception: Combining Individual Sensory Inputs

When Eric Pettigrew was 7 months old, his grandparents presented him with a squeaky rubber doll. As soon as he saw it, he reached out for it, grasped it in his hand, and listened as it squeaked. He seemed delighted with the gift.

One way of considering Eric's sensory reaction to the doll is to focus on each of the senses individually: what the doll looked like to Eric, how it felt in his hand, and what it sounded like. In fact, this approach has dominated the study of sensation and perception in infancy.

However, let's consider another approach: We might examine how the various sensory responses are integrated with one another. Instead of looking at each individual sensory response, we could consider how the responses work together and are combined to produce Eric's ultimate reaction. The **multimodal approach to perception** considers how information that is collected by various individual sensory systems is integrated and coordinated.

Although the multimodal approach is a relatively recent innovation in the study of how infants understand their sensory world, it raises some fundamental issues about the development of sensation and perception. For instance, some researchers argue that sensations are initially integrated with one another in the infant, while others maintain that the infant's sensory systems are initially separate and that brain development leads to increasing integration (Quinn & Eimas, 1996; Lickliter & Bahrick, 2000; De Gelder, 2000).

We do not know yet which view is correct. However, it does appear that by an early age infants are able to relate what they have learned about an object through one sensory channel to what they have learned about it through another. For instance, even one-month-old infants are able to recognize by sight objects that they have previously held in their mouths but never seen (Meltzoff, 1981; Steri & Spelke, 1988). Clearly, some crosstalk between various sensory channels is already possible a month after birth.

multimodal approach to perception the approach that considers how information that is collected by various individual sensory systems is integrated and coordinated

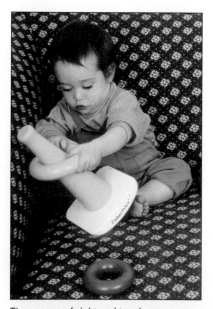

The senses of sight and touch are integrated by infants through multimodal perception.

Becoming an Informed Consumer of Development

Exercising Your Infant's Body and Senses

We've seen how the experiences infants encounter as they grow are reflected in their motor and sensory development. For instance, recall how cultural expectations and environments affect the age at which various physical milestones, such as the first step, occur. Does this suggest that parents are well advised to try to accelerate their infants' timetables?

Although experts disagree, most feel that such acceleration yields little advantage. No data suggest that a child who walks at 10 months ultimately has any advantage over one who walks at 15 months.

On the other hand, parents should ensure that their infants receive sufficient physical and sensory stimulation. There are several specific ways to accomplish this goal:

▶ Carry a baby in different positions—in a backpack, in a frontpack, or in a football hold with the infant's head in the palm of your hand and its feet lying on your arm.

▶ Let infants explore their environment. Don't contain them too long in a barren environment. Let them crawl or wander around—after first making the environment "childproof" by removing dangerous objects.

▶ Engage in "rough-and-tumble" play. Wrestling, dancing, and rolling around on the floor—if not violent—are activities that are fun and that stimulate older infants' motor and sensory systems.

▶ Let babies touch their food and even play with it. Infancy is too early to start teaching table manners.

▶ Provide toys that stimulate the senses, particularly toys that can stimulate more than one sense at a time. For example, brightly colored, textured toys with movable parts are enjoyable and help hone infants' senses.

The success of infants at multimodal perception is another example of the sophisticated perceptual abilities of infants, which continue to grow throughout the period of infancy. Such perceptual growth is aided by infants' discovery of **affordances**, the action possibilities that a given situation or stimulus provides. For example, infants learn that they might potentially fall when walking down a steep ramp—that is, the ramp affords the possibility of falling. Such knowledge is crucial as infants make the transition from crawling to walking. Similarly, infants learn that an object shaped in a certain way can slip out of their hands if not grasped correctly. For example, Eric is learning that his toy has several affordances: He can grab it and squeeze it, listen to it squeak, and even chew comfortably on it if he is teething (Adolph, Eppler, & Gibson, 1993; Adolph, 1997; McCarty & Ashmead, 1999).

affordances the action possibilities that a given situation or stimulus provides

Review and Rethink

REVIEW

■ Sensation refers to the activation of the sense organs by external stimuli. Perception is the analysis, interpretation, and integration of sensations.

■ Infants' sensory abilities are surprisingly well developed at or shortly after birth. Their perceptions help them explore and begin to make sense of the world.

■ Very early, infants can see depth and motion, distinguish colors and patterns, localize and discriminate sounds, and recognize the sound and smell of their mothers.

■ Infants are sensitive to pain and touch, and most medical authorities now subscribe to procedures, including anesthesia, that minimize infants' pain.

■ Infants also have a keen ability to integrate information from more than one sense.

RETHINK

■ Are the processes of sensation and perception always linked? Is it possible to sense without perceiving? To perceive without sensing? How?

■ Persons who are born without the use of one sense often develop unusual abilities in one or more other senses. Do you think this phenomenon might relate to the argument about whether integration of the senses precedes differentiation, or vice versa? How?

Looking Back

How do the human body and nervous system develop?

■ Human babies grow rapidly in height and weight, especially during the first 2 years of life.

■ Major principles that govern human growth include the cephalocaudal principle, the proximodistal principle, the principle of hierarchical integration, and the principle of the independence of systems.

■ The nervous system contains a huge number of neurons, more than will be needed as an adult. For neurons to survive and become useful, they must form interconnections with other neurons based on the infant's experience of the world. "Extra" connections and neurons that are not used are eliminated as an infant develops.

Does the environment affect the pattern of development?

■ Brain development, largely predetermined genetically, also contains a strong element of plasticity—a susceptibility to environmental influences.

■ Many aspects of development occur during sensitive periods when the organism is particularly susceptible to environmental influences.

What developmental tasks must infants undertake in this period?

■ One of the primary tasks of the infant is the development of rhythms—cyclical patterns that integrate individual behaviors. An important rhythm pertains to the infant's state—the degree of awareness it displays to stimulation.

■ Reflexes are unlearned, automatic responses to stimuli that help newborns survive and protect themselves. Some reflexes also have value as the foundation for future, more conscious behaviors.

■ The development of gross and fine motor skills proceeds along a generally consistent timetable in normal children, with substantial individual and cultural variations.

What is the role of nutrition in physical development?

■ Adequate nutrition is essential for physical development. Malnutrition and undernutrition affect physical aspects of growth and also may affect IQ and school performance.

■ Breast-feeding has distinct advantages over bottle-feeding, including the nutritional completeness of breast milk, its provision of a degree of immunity to certain childhood diseases, and its easy digestibility. In addition, breast-feeding offers significant physical and emotional benefits to both child and mother.

What sensory capabilities do infants possess?

■ Sensation, the stimulation of the sense organs, differs from perception, the interpretation and integration of sensed stimuli.

■ Infants' visual and auditory perception are rather well developed, as are the senses of smell and taste. Infants use their highly developed sense of touch to explore and experience the world. In addition, touch plays an important role in the individual's future development, which is only now being understood.

EPILOGUE

In this chapter, we discussed the nature and pace of infants' physical growth and the pace of less obvious growth in the brain and nervous system and in the regularity of infants' patterns and states.

We next looked at motor development, the development and uses of reflexes, the role of environmental influences on the pace and shape of motor development, and the importance of nutrition.

We closed the chapter with a look at the senses, observing how sophisticated is the infant's ability to use the senses and to combine data from multiple sensory sources.

Turn back for a moment to the prologue of this chapter, about 7-month-old Ana Natalia Epstein's encounters with a variety of sensory stimuli, and answer these questions.

1. How do researchers find out whether various forms of sensory stimulation are pleasurable to infants? Do you think there is a danger of overinterpretation of infants' reactions?

2. Are the reactions that a baby produces in response to a piece of music or a backrub examples of *sensation* or *perception?* Why? How would a researcher explore this question?

3. Which principle or principles of growth (i.e., cephalocaudal, proximodistal, hierarchical integration, independence of systems) might underlie the development of the senses?

4. In addition to her physical development, do you think Ana Natalia's home environment might affect other aspects of her development, such as her intellectual and social development? How?

Key Terms and Concepts

cephalocaudal principle (p. 119)
proximodistal principle (p. 120)
principle of hierarchical integration
 (p. 120)
principle of the independence of systems
 (p. 120)
neuron (p. 120)
synapse (p. 121)
myelin (p. 122)
cerebral cortex (p. 122)

plasticity (p. 122)
sensitive period (p. 123)
rhythms (p. 124)
state (p. 124)
rapid eye movement (REM) sleep
 (p. 126)
sudden infant death syndrome (SIDS)
 (p. 127)
reflexes (p. 129)
norms (p. 133)

Brazelton Neonatal Behavioral Assessment Scale (NBAS) (p. 133)
marasmus (p. 136)
kwashiorkor (p. 136)
nonorganic failure to thrive (p. 137)
sensation (p. 140)
perception (p. 140)
multimodal approach to perception
 (p. 146)
affordances (p. 147)

Cognitive Development in Infancy

PROLOGUE: PAIGE

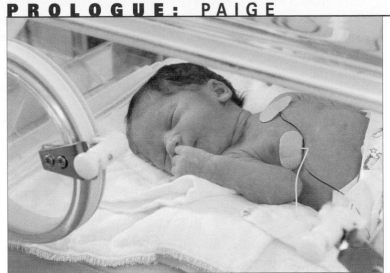

Language development can be affected by a variety of factors, such as premature birth, as illustrated by the case of Paige Arbeiter.

Paige Arbeiter was a 2-pound 7-ounce preemie when she earned the nickname "Little Houdini" 6 years ago. A day and a half after delivery, she pulled the tube off her face to breathe on her own. And she dazzled her intensive-care nurses by inching across her incubator to hang a tiny foot out the door.

When Paige went home after 6 weeks, her parents noticed that loud noises didn't faze her. The pediatrician told them repeatedly not to worry, but when Paige was 10 months old they took her to New York's Long Island Jewish Speech and Hearing Center for tests. The verdict: She was nearly deaf in both ears.

"Most people we told said, 'Oh, you caught it so early, she'll be just fine,'" her mom recalls, "but we learned we'd missed a very important period in her speech and language development." (Cowley, 2000, p. 12)

Looking Ahead   With the help of an ear implant that improves her hearing, and with speech therapy, Paige now counts to 10—but her overall language proficiency lags far behind that of other children her age.

Why is early exposure to language critical to subsequent language development? To answer that question, developmental researchers have focused on cognitive development during the first 2 years of life—the topic of this chapter. We examine the work of developmental researchers who seek to understand and explain the enormous strides that infants make in their understanding of the world and their ability to communicate with others.

We begin by discussing the work of Swiss psychologist Jean Piaget, whose theory of developmental stages served as a highly influential impetus for a considerable amount of research on cognitive development. We'll look at both the limitations and the contributions of this important developmental theorist.

We then turn to the basic processes by which cognitive growth occurs. After considering how learning takes place, we examine memory in infants and the ways in which infants process, store, and retrieve information. We discuss the controversial issue of the recollection of events that occurred during infancy. We also address individual differences in intelligence.

Finally, we consider language, the medium by which we all communicate with others. We look at the roots of language in prelinguistic speech and trace the milestones indicating the development of language skills in the progression from baby's first words to phrases and sentences. We also look at the characteristics of communication addressed to infants, and examine some surprising universals in the nature of such communication across different cultures.

After reading this chapter, you'll be able to answer these questions:

▶ **What are the fundamental features of Piaget's theories of cognitive development?**

▶ **How do infants process information?**

▶ **How is infant intelligence measured?**

▶ **By what processes do children learn to use language?**

▶ **How do children influence adults' language?**

Swiss psychologist Jean Piaget

Piaget's Approach to Cognitive Development

Olivia's dad is wiping up the mess around the base of her high chair—for the third time today! Lately, the 14-month-old Olivia seems to take great delight in dropping food from the high chair. She also drops toys, spoons, anything it seems, just to watch how it hits the floor. She almost appears to be experimenting to see what kind of noise or what size of splatter is created by each different thing she drops.

Swiss psychologist Jean Piaget (1896–1980) probably would have said that Olivia's dad is right in theorizing that Olivia is conducting her own series of experiments to learn more about the workings of her world. Piaget's views of the ways infants learn could be summed up in a simple equation: Action = Knowledge. He argued that infants do not acquire knowledge from facts communicated by others, nor through sensation and perception. Instead,

Piaget suggested that knowledge is the product of direct motor behavior. Although many of his basic explanations and propositions have been challenged by subsequent research, as we'll discuss later, the view that in significant ways infants learn by doing remains unquestioned (Piaget, 1952, 1962, 1983; Bullinger, 1997).

Key Elements of Piaget's Theory

As we first noted in Chapter 1, Piaget's theory is based on a stage approach to development. He assumed that all children pass through a series of four universal stages in a fixed order from birth through adolescence: sensorimotor, preoperational, concrete operational, and formal operational. He also suggested that movement from one stage to the next occured when a child reaches an appropriate level of physical maturation *and* is exposed to relevant types of experience. Without such experience, children are assumed to be incapable of reaching their cognitive potential. Furthermore, in contrast to approaches to cognition that focus on changes in the *content* of children's knowledge about the world, Piaget argued that it was critical to also consider the changes in the *quality* of children's knowledge and understanding as they move from one stage to another.

For instance, as they develop cognitively, infants experience changes in their understanding about what can and cannot occur in the world. Consider a baby who participates in an experiment during which she is exposed to an impossible event. Through some clever trickery with mirrors, she sees three identical versions of her mother all at the same time. A 3-month-old infant shows no disturbance over the multiple apparitions and in fact will interact happily with each. However, by 5 months of age, the child becomes quite agitated at the sight of multiple mothers. Apparently by this time the child has figured out that she has but one mother, and viewing three at a time is thoroughly alarming (Bower, 1977). To Piaget, such reactions indicate that a baby is developing a mastery of underlying principles regarding the way the world operates.

Piaget believed that the basic building blocks of the way we understand the world are mental structures called **schemes,** organized patterns of functioning, that adapt and change with mental development. Although at first schemes are related to physical, or sensorimotor, activity, as children develop their schemes move to a mental level, reflecting thought. Schemes are similar to computer software: They direct and determine how data from the world, such as new events or objects, are considered and dealt with (Achenbach, 1992).

If you give a baby a new cloth book, for example, he or she will touch it, mouth it, perhaps try to tear it or bang it on the floor. To Piaget, each of these actions may represent a scheme, and they are the infant's way of gaining knowledge and understanding of this new object. Adults, on the other hand, would use a different scheme upon encountering the book. Rather than picking it up and putting it in their mouths or banging it on the floor, they would probably be drawn to the letters on the page, seeking to understand the book through the meaning of the printed words—a very different approach.

Piaget suggested that two principles underlie the growth in children's schemes: assimilation and accommodation. **Assimilation** is the process in which people understand an experience in terms of their current stage of cognitive development and way of thinking. Assimilation occurs, then, when a stimulus or event is acted upon, perceived, and understood in accordance with existing patterns of thought. For example, an infant who tries to suck on any toy in the same way is assimilating the objects to her existing sucking scheme. Similarly, a child who encounters a flying squirrel at a zoo and calls it a "bird" is assimilating the squirrel to his existing scheme of bird.

In contrast, when we make changes in our existing ways of thinking, understanding, or behaving in response to encounters with new stimuli or events, **accommodation** takes

scheme an organized pattern of sensorimotor functioning

assimilation the process in which people understand an experience in terms of their current stage of cognitive development and way of thinking

accommodation changes in existing ways of thinking that occur in response to encounters with new stimuli or events

place. For instance, when a child modifies the way she sucks on a toy according to the particular shape of the toy, she is accommodating her sucking scheme to the special characteristics of the toy. In the same way, a child who sees a flying squirrel and calls it "a bird with a tail" is beginning to accommodate to new knowledge, modifying his scheme of bird.

Piaget believed that the earliest schemes are primarily limited to the reflexes with which we are all born, such as sucking and rooting. Infants start to modify these simple early schemes almost immediately, through the processes of assimilation and accommodation, in response to their sensorimotor exploration of the environment. Schemes quickly become more sophisticated as infants become more advanced in their motor capabilities—to Piaget, a signal of the potential for more advanced cognitive development. Because the sensorimotor stage of development begins at birth and continues until the child is about 2 years old, we consider it here in detail. (In future chapters, we'll discuss development during the other stages.)

cw

sensorimotor stage (of cognitive development) Piaget's initial major stage of cognitive development, which can be broken down into six substages

The Sensorimotor Period: Charting the Course of Early Cognitive Growth

Piaget suggests that the **sensorimotor stage,** the initial major stage of cognitive development, can be broken down into six substages. These are summarized in Table 5-1, and we'll consider them in more detail. However, it is important to keep in mind that although the specific substages of the sensorimotor period may at first appear to unfold with great regularity, as infants reach a particular age and smoothly proceed into the next substage, the reality of cognitive development is somewhat different. First, the ages at which infants actually reach a particular stage vary a good deal among different children. The exact timing of a stage reflects an interaction between the infant's level of physical maturation and the nature of the social environment in which the child is being raised. Consequently, although Piaget contended that the order of the substages does not change from one child to the next, he admitted that the timing can and does vary to some degree.

Furthermore, Piaget argued that development is a more gradual process than the demarcation of different stages might seem to imply. Specifically, infants do not go to sleep one night in one substage and wake up the next morning in the next one. Instead, there is a rather steady shift in behavior as a child moves toward the next stage of cognitive development. Infants also pass through periods of transition, in which some aspects of their behavior reflect the next higher stage, while other aspects indicate their current stage (see Figure 5-1).

Figure 5-1 **Transitions**

Infants do not suddenly shift from one stage of cognitive development to the next. Instead, Piaget argues that there is a period of transition in which some behavior reflects one stage, while other behavior reflects the more advanced stage. Does this gradualism argue against Piaget's interpretation of stages?

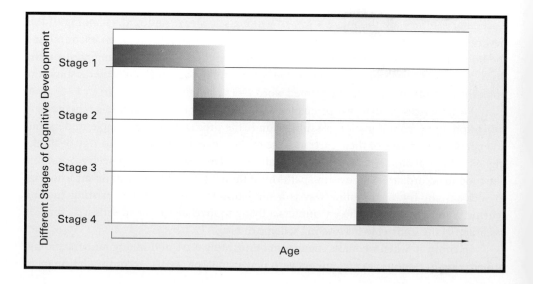

Table 5-1

PIAGET'S SIX SUBSTAGES OF THE SENSORIMOTOR STAGE

Substage	Age	Description	Example
SUBSTAGE 1: Simple reflexes	First month of life	During this period, the various reflexes that determine the infant's interactions with the world are at the center of its cognitive life.	The sucking reflex causes the infant to suck at anything placed in its lips.
SUBSTAGE 2: First habits and primary circular reactions	From 1 to 4 months	At this age infants begin to coordinate what were separate actions into single, integrated activities.	An infant might combine grasping an object with sucking on it, or staring at something with touching it.
SUBSTAGE 3: Secondary circular reactions	From 4 to 8 months	During this period, infants take major strides in shifting their cognitive horizons beyond themselves and begin to act on the outside world.	A child who repeatedly picks up a rattle in her crib and shakes it in different ways to see how the sound changes is demonstrating her ability to modify her cognitive scheme about shaking rattles.
SUBSTAGE 4: Coordination of secondary circular reactions	From 8 to 12 months	In this stage infants begin to use more calculated approaches to producing events, coordinating several schemes to generate a single act. They achieve object permanence during this stage.	An infant will push one toy out of the way to reach another toy that is lying, partially exposed, under it.
SUBSTAGE 5: Tertiary circular reactions	From 12 to 18 months	At this age infants develop what Piaget regards as the deliberate variation of actions that bring desirable consequences. Rather than just repeating enjoyable activities as in Substage 4, infants appear to carry out miniature experiments to observe the consequences.	A child will drop a toy repeatedly, varying the position from which he drops it, carefully observing each time to see where it falls.
SUBSTAGE 6: Beginnings of thought	From 18 months to 2 years	The major achievement of Substage 6 is the capacity for mental representation or symbolic thought. Piaget argued that only at this stage can infants imagine where objects that they cannot see might be.	Children can even plot in their heads unseen trajectories of objects, so that if a ball rolls under a piece of furniture, they can figure out where it is likely to emerge on the other side.

Substage 1: Simple Reflexes. The first substage of the sensorimotor period is *Substage 1: Simple reflexes*, encompassing the first month of life. During this time, the various inborn reflexes, described in Chapters 3 and 4, are at the center of a baby's cognitive life, determining the nature of his or her interactions with the world. For example, the sucking reflex causes the infant to suck at anything placed in his or her lips. This sucking behavior, according to Piaget, provides the newborn with information about objects—information that paves the way to the next substage of the sensorimotor period.

At the same time, some of the reflexes become modified as a result of the infant's experience with the nature of the world. For instance, an infant who is being breast-fed, but who also receives supplemental bottles, may start to change the way he or she sucks, depending on whether a nipple is on a breast or a bottle.

Substage 2: First Habits and Primary Circular Reactions. *Substage 2: First habits and primary circular reactions*, the second substage of the sensorimotor period, occurs from 1 to 4 months of age. In this period, infants begin to coordinate what were separate actions into single, integrated activities. For instance, an infant might combine grasping an object with sucking on it, or staring at something while touching it.

If an activity engages a baby's interests, he or she may repeat it over and over, simply for the sake of continuing to experience it. This repetition of a chance motor event helps the baby start building cognitive shemes through a process known as a **circular reaction.** *Primary circular reactions* are schemes reflecting an infant's repetition of interesting or enjoyable actions, just for the enjoyment of doing them. Piaget referred to these schemes as *primary* because the activities they involve focus on the infant's own body. Thus, when an infant first puts his thumb in his mouth and begins to suck, it is a mere chance event. However, when he repeatedly sucks his thumb in the future, it represents a primary circular reaction, which he is repeating because the sensation of sucking is pleasurable.

Substage 3: Secondary Circular Reactions. *Substage 3: Secondary circular reactions* occurs from 4 to 8 months of age. During this period, infants take major strides in shifting their cognitive horizons beyond themselves and begin to act upon the outside world. For instance, infants now seek to repeat enjoyable events in their environments if they happen to produce them through chance activities. A child who repeatedly picks up a rattle in her crib and shakes it in different ways to see how the sound changes is demonstrating her ability to modify her cognitive scheme about shaking rattles. She is engaging in what Piaget calls secondary circular reactions.

Secondary circular reactions are schemes regarding repeated actions that bring about a desirable consequence. The major difference between primary circular reactions and secondary circular reactions is whether the infant's activity is focused on the infant and his or her own body (primary circular reactions), or involves actions relating to the world outside (secondary circular reactions).

During the third substage, the degree of vocalization increases substantially as infants come to notice that if they make noises, other people around them will respond with noises of their own. Similarly, infants begin to imitate the sounds made by others. Vocalization becomes a secondary circular reaction that ultimately helps lead to the development of language and the formation of social relationships.

Substage 4: Coordination of Secondary Circular Reactions. One of the major leaps forward in terms of cognitive development comes as infants move through the next substage, *Substage 4: Coordination of secondary circular reactions,* which lasts from around 8 months to 12 months. Before this stage, behavior involved direct action on objects. When something happened by chance that caught an infant's interest, she attempted to repeat the event using a single scheme. However, in Substage 4, infants begin to use more calculated approaches to producing events. They employ **goal-directed behavior,** in which several schemes are combined and coordinated to generate a single act to solve a problem. For instance, they will push one toy out of the way to reach another toy that is lying, partially exposed, under it. They also begin to anticipate upcoming events. For instance, Piaget tells of his son Laurent, who at 8 months "recognizes by a certain noise caused by air that he is nearing the end of his feeding and, instead of insisting on drinking to the last drop, he rejects his bottle . . ." (Piaget, 1952, pp. 248–249).

Infants' newfound purposefulness, their ability to use means to attain particular ends, and their skill in anticipating future circumstances, owe their appearance in part to the developmental achievement of object permanence that emerges in Substage 4. **Object permanence** is the realization that people and objects exist even when they cannot be seen. It is a simple principle, but its mastery has profound consequences.

Consider, for instance, 7-month-old Chu, who has yet to learn the idea of object permanence. Chu's father shakes a rattle in front of him, then takes the rattle and places it

circular reaction an activity that permits the construction of cognitive schemes through the repetition of a chance motor event

goal-directed behavior behavior in which several schemes are combined and coordinated to generate a single act to solve a problem

object permanence the realization that people and objects exist even when they cannot be seen

Infants in substage 4 can coordinate their secondary circular reactions, displaying an ability to plan or calculate how to produce a desired outcome.

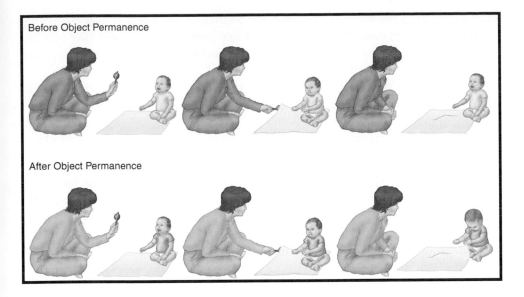

Before Object Permanence

After Object Permanence

***Figure 5-2* Object Permanence**

Before an infant has understood the idea of object permanence, he will not search for an object that has been hidden right before his eyes. But several months later, he will search for it, illustrating that he has attained object permanence. Why is the concept of object permanence important?

under a blanket. To Chu, who has not mastered the concept of object permanence, the rattle no longer exists. He will make no effort to look for it.

Several months later, when he is in Substage 4, the story is quite different (see Figure 5-2). This time, as soon as his father places the rattle under the blanket, Chu tries to toss the cover aside, eagerly searching for the rattle. Chu clearly has learned that the object continues to exist even when it cannot be seen. For the infant who achieves an understanding of object permanence, then, out of sight is decidedly not out of mind.

The attainment of object permanence extends not only to inanimate objects, but to people, too. It gives Chu the security that his father and mother still exist even when they have left the room. This awareness is likely a key element in the development of social attachments, which we consider in Chapter 6. The recognition of object permanence also feeds infants' growing assertiveness: As they realize that an object taken away from them doesn't just cease to exist, but is merely somewhere else, their only-too-human reaction may be to want it back—and quickly.

Although the understanding of object permanence emerges in Substage 4, it is only a rudimentary understanding. It takes several months for the concept to be fully comprehended, and infants continue for several months to make certain kinds of errors relating to object permanence. For instance, they often are fooled when a toy is hidden first under one blanket and then under a second blanket. In seeking out the toy, Substage 4 infants most often turn to the first hiding place, ignoring the second blanket under which the toy is currently located—even if the hiding was done in plain view.

Substage 5: Tertiary Circular Reactions. *Substage 5: Tertiary circular reactions* is reached at around the age of 12 months and extends to 18 months. As the name of the stage indicates, during this period infants develop what Piaget labeled *tertiary circular reactions,* schemes regarding the deliberate variation of actions that bring desirable consequences. Rather than just repeating enjoyable activities, as they do with secondary circular reactions, infants appear to carry out miniature experiments to observe the consequences.

For example, Piaget observed his son Laurent dropping a toy swan repeatedly, varying the position from which he dropped it, carefully observing each time to see where it fell. Instead of just repeating the action each time (as in a secondary circular reaction), Laurent made modifications in the situation to learn about their consequences. As you may recall from our discussion of research methods in Chapter 1, this behavior represents the essence of the scientific method: An experimenter varies a situation in a laboratory to learn the effects of the variation. To infants in Substage 5, the world is their laboratory, and they spend their days leisurely carrying out one miniature experiment after another. Olivia, the baby described earlier who enjoyed dropping things from her high chair, is another little scientist in action.

What is most striking about infants' behavior during Substage 5 is their interest in the unexpected. Unanticipated events are treated not only as interesting, but also as something to be explained and understood. Infants' discoveries can lead to newfound skills, some of which may cause a certain amount of chaos, as Olivia's dad realized while cleaning up around her high chair.

Substage 6: Beginnings of Thought. The final stage of the sensorimotor period is *Substage 6: Beginnings of thought*, which lasts from around 18 months to 2 years. The major achievement of Substage 6 is the capacity for mental representation, or symbolic thought. A **mental representation** is an internal image of a past event or object. Piaget argued that by this stage infants can imagine where objects might be that they cannot see. They can even plot in their heads unseen trajectories of objects, so if a ball rolls under a piece of furniture, they can figure out where it is likely to emerge on the other side.

Because of children's new abilities to create internal representations of objects, their understanding of causality also becomes more sophisticated. For instance, consider Piaget's description of his son Laurent's efforts to open a garden gate:

> Laurent tries to open a garden gate but cannot push it forward because it is held back by a piece of furniture. He cannot account either visually or by any sound for the cause that prevents the gate from opening, but after having tried to force it he suddenly seems to understand; he goes around the wall, arrives at the other side of the gate, moves the armchair which holds it firm, and opens it with a triumphant expression. (Piaget, 1954, p. 296)

The attainment of mental representation also permits another important development: the ability to pretend. Using the skill of what Piaget refers to as **deferred imitation,** in which a person who is no longer present is imitated later, children are able to pretend that they are driving a car, feeding a doll, or cooking dinner long after they have witnessed such scenes played out in reality. To Piaget, deferred imitation provided clear evidence that children form internal mental representations.

mental representation an internal image of a past event or object

deferred imitation an act in which a person who is no longer present is imitated by children who have witnessed a similar act

With the attainment of the cognitive skill of deferred imitation, children are able to imitate people and scenes they have witnessed in the past.

Appraising Piaget: Support and Challenges

Most developmental researchers would probably agree that in many significant ways, Piaget's descriptions of how cognitive development proceeds during infancy are quite accurate (Harris, 1983, 1987). Yet, there is substantial disagreement over the validity of the theory and many of its specific predictions.

Let's start with what is clearly correct about the Piagetian approach. Piaget was a masterful reporter of children's behavior, and his descriptions of growth during infancy remain a monument to his powers of observation. Furthermore, literally thousands of studies have supported Piaget's view that children learn much about the world by acting on objects in their environment. Finally, the broad outlines sketched out by Piaget of the sequence of cognitive development and the increasing cognitive accomplishments that occur during infancy are generally accurate (Gratch & Schatz, 1987).

On the other hand, specific aspects of the theory have come under increasing scrutiny—and criticism—in the decades since Piaget carried out his pioneering work. For example, some researchers question the stage conception that forms the basis of Piaget's theory. Although, as we noted earlier, even Piaget acknowledged that children's transitions between stages are gradual, critics contend development proceeds in a much more continuous fashion. Rather than showing major leaps of competence at the end of one stage and the beginning of the next, improvement comes in more gradual increments, growing step-by-step in a skill-by-skill manner.

For instance, developmental researcher Robert Siegler suggests that cognitive development proceeds not in stages but in "waves." According to him, children don't one day drop a mode of thinking and the next take up a new form. Instead, there is an ebb and flow of cognitive approaches that children use to understand the world. One day children may use one form of cognitive strategy, while another day they may choose a less advanced strategy—moving back and forth over a period of time. Although one strategy may be used most frequently at a given age, children still may have access to alternative ways of thinking. Siegler thus sees cognitive development as in constant flux (Siegler, 1995).

Other critics dispute Piaget's notion that cognitive development is grounded in motor activities. Some developmental specialists charge that such a view ignores the importance of the sophisticated sensory and perceptual systems that are present from a very early age in infancy—systems about which Piaget knew little, since so much of the research illustrating their sophistication was done relatively recently (Butterworth, 1994). Some research studies have also involved children born without arms and legs (due to their mothers' unwitting use of teratogenic drugs during pregnancy, as described in Chapter 2). Critics of Piaget point out that these studies show that such children display normal cognitive development, despite their lack of practice with motor activities (Decarrie, 1969).

To bolster their views, Piaget's critics also point to recent studies that cast doubt on Piaget's view that infants are incapable of mastering the concept of object permanence until they are close to a year old. For instance, some work suggests that younger infants may not appear to understand object permanence because the techniques used to test their abilities are too insensitive (Baillargeon & DeVos, 1991; Munakata et al., 1997).

It may be that a 4-month-old doesn't search for a rattle hidden under a blanket because she hasn't learned the motor skills necessary to do the searching—not because she doesn't understand that the rattle still exists. Similarly, the apparent inability of young infants to comprehend object permanence may reflect more about their memory deficits than their lack of understanding of the concept: The memories of young infants may be poor enough that they simply do not recall the earlier concealment of the toy. In fact, when more age-appropriate tasks were employed, some researchers found indications of object permanence in children as young as 3 1/2 months (Baillargeon, 1987; Mandler, 1990; Spelke, 1991).

Other types of behavior likewise seem to emerge earlier than Piaget suggested. For instance, recall the ability of neonates to imitate basic facial expressions of adults just hours after birth, as we discussed in Chapter 3. The presence of such skill at such an early age contradicts Piaget's view that initially infants are able to imitate only behavior that they see in others, using parts of their own body that they can plainly view—such as their hands and feet. In fact, facial imitation suggests that humans are born with a basic, innate capability for imitating others' actions, a capability that depends on certain kinds of environmental experiences (Meltzoff & Moore, 1989), but one that Piaget believed develops later in infancy.

Some of the most powerful evidence against Piaget's views emerges from work with children in non-Western cultures. For instance, some evidence suggests cognitive skills emerge on a different timetable for children in non-Western cultures than for children living in Europe and the United States. Infants raised in the Ivory Coast of Africa, for example, reach the various substages of the sensorimotor period at an earlier age than infants reared in France (Dasen et al., 1978). This is not altogether surprising, since parents in the Ivory Coast tend to emphasize motor skills more heavily than parents in Western societies, thereby providing greater opportunity for practice of those skills (Dasen et al., 1978; Rogoff & Chavajay, 1995).

Despite these problems regarding Piaget's view of the sensorimotor period, even his most passionate critics concede that he has provided us with a masterful description of the broad outlines of sensorimotor development during infancy. His failings seem to be in underestimating the capabilities of younger infants and in his claims that sensorimotor skills develop in a consistent, fixed pattern. Still, his influence has been enormous, and although the focus of many contemporary developmental researchers has shifted to newer information-processing approaches that we discuss next, Piaget remains a towering and pioneering figure in the field of development (Siegler, 1994; Fischer & Hencke, 1996; Roth, Slone, & Dar, 2000).

Review and Rethink

REVIEW

- Jean Piaget's theory of human cognitive development involves a succession of stages through which children progress from birth to adolescence.
- As humans move from one stage to another, the way they understand the world changes.
- The sensorimotor stage, from birth to about 2 years, involves a gradual progression through simple reflexes, single coordinated activities, interest in the outside world, purposeful combinations of activities, manipulation of actions to produce desired outcomes, and symbolic thought.

- Piaget is respected as a careful observer of children's behavior and a generally accurate interpreter of the way human cognitive development proceeds.

RETHINK

- Name some examples of the principles of assimilation and accommodation at work in child development. Do these principles function in adult human learning?
- In general, what are some implications for child-rearing practices of Piaget's observations about the ways children gain an understanding of the world?

Information-Processing Approaches to Cognitive Development

At the age of 3 months, Amber Nordstrom breaks into a smile as her brother Marcus stands over her crib, picks up a doll, and makes a whistling noise through his teeth. In fact, Amber never seems to tire of Marcus's efforts at making her smile, and soon whenever Marcus appears and simply picks up the doll, her lips begin to curl into a smile.

Clearly, Amber remembers Marcus and his humorous ways. But how does she remember him? And how much else can Amber remember?

To answer questions such as these, we need to diverge from the road that Piaget laid out for us. Rather than seeking to identify the universal, broad milestones in cognitive development through which all infants pass, as Piaget tried to do, we must consider the specific processes by which individual babies acquire and use the information to which they are exposed. We need, then, to focus less on the qualitative changes in infants' mental lives and consider more closely their quantitative capabilities.

Information-processing approaches to cognitive development seek to identify the way that individuals take in, use, and store information (Siegler, 1998). According to this approach, the quantitative changes in infants' abilities to organize and manipulate information represent the hallmarks of cognitive development.

Taking this perspective, cognitive growth is characterized by increasing sophistication, speed, and capacity in information processing. Earlier, we compared Piaget's idea of schemes to computer software, which directs the computer in how to deal with data from the world. We might compare the information-processing perspective on cognitive growth to the improvements that come from the use of more efficient programs that lead to increased speed and sophistication in the processing of information. Information-processing approaches, then, focus on the types of "mental programs" that people use when they seek to solve problems (Mehler & DuPoux, 1994; Reyna, 1997).

Because infants and children, like all people, are exposed to massive amounts of information, they are able to encode selectively, choosing what they will pay attention to without being overwhelmed.

information-processing approaches the model that seeks to identify the way that individuals take in, use, and store information

Encoding, Storage, and Retrieval: The Foundations of Information Processing

Information processing has three basic aspects: encoding, storage, and retrieval (see Figure 5-3). *Encoding* is the process by which information is initially recorded in a form usable to memory. Infants and children—indeed, all people—are exposed to a massive amount of information; if they tried to process it all, they would be overwhelmed. Consequently, they encode selectively, picking and choosing the information to which they will pay attention.

Even if someone has been exposed to the information initially and has encoded it in an appropriate way, there is still no guarantee that he or she will be able to use it in the future. Information must also have been stored in memory adequately. *Storage* refers to the maintenance of material saved in memory. Finally, success in using the material in the future depends on retrieval processes. *Retrieval* is the process by which material in memory storage is located, brought into awareness, and used.

We can use our comparison to computers again here. Information-processing approaches suggest that the processes of encoding, storage, and retrieval are analogous to different parts of a computer. Encoding can be thought of as a computer's keyboard, through which one inputs information; storage is the computer's hard drive, where information is stored; and retrieval is analogous to a computer's screen, where information is

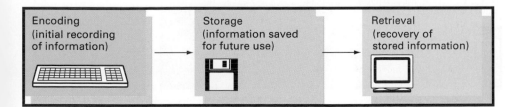

Encoding (initial recording of information)	Storage (information saved for future use)	Retrieval (recovery of stored information)

Figure 5-3 **Information Processing**

The process by which information is encoded, stored, and retrieved.

displayed. Only when all three processes are operating—encoding, storage, and retrieval—can information be processed.

Automatization. In some cases, encoding, storage, and retrieval are relatively automatic, while in other cases they are deliberate. *Automatization* is the degree to which an activity requires attention. Processes that require relatively little attention are automatic; processes that require relatively large amounts of attention are controlled. For example, some activities that may be automatic for you, but that required your full attention at first, might include walking, eating with a fork, or reading.

Automatic mental processes help children in their initial encounters with the world by enabling them to easily and "automatically" process information in particular ways. For instance, by the age of 5, children automatically encode information in terms of frequency. Without a lot of attention to counting or tallying, they become aware, for example, of how often they have encountered various people, permitting them to differentiate familiar from unfamiliar people (Hasher & Zacks, 1984).

Furthermore, without intending to and without being aware of it, infants and children develop a sense of how often different stimuli are found together simultaneously. This permits them to develop an understanding of *concepts*, categorizations of objects, events, or people that share common properties. For example, by encoding the information that four legs, a wagging tail, and barking are often found together, we learn very early in life to understand the concept of "dog." Children—as well as adults—are rarely aware of how they learn such concepts, and they are often unable to articulate the features that distinguish one concept (such as a dog) from another (such as cat). Instead, learning tends to occur automatically.

Some of the things we learn automatically are unexpectedly complex. For example, infants have the ability to learn subtle statistical patterns and relationships; these results are consistent with a growing body of research showing that the mathematical skills of infants are surprisingly sophisticated. For instance, infants as young as 5 months are able to calculate the outcome of simple addition and subtraction problems. In a study by developmental psychologist Karen Wynn, infants first were shown an object—a 4-inch-high Mickey Mouse statuette (see Figure 5-4). A screen was then raised, hiding the statuette. Next, the experimenter showed the infants a second, identical Mickey Mouse, and then placed it behind the same screen (Wynn, 1992, 1995, 2000).

Finally, depending on the experimental condition, one of two outcomes occurred. In the "correct addition" condition, the screen dropped, revealing the two statuettes (anal-

Figure 5-4 **Mickey Mouse Math**

Researcher Dr. Karen Wynn found that 5-month-olds like Michelle Follet, pictured here, reacted differently according to whether the number of Mickey Mouse statuettes they saw represented correct or incorrect addition. Do you think this ability is unique to humans? How would you find out?

ogous to 1 + 1 = 2). But in the "incorrect addition" condition, the screen dropped to reveal just one statuette (analogous to the incorrect 1 + 1 = 1).

Because infants look longer at unexpected occurrences than at expected ones, the researchers examined the pattern of infants' gazes in the different conditions. In support of the notion that infants can distinguish between correct and incorrect addition, the infants in the experiment gazed longer at the incorrect result than at the correct one. In a similar procedure, infants looked longer at incorrect subtraction problems than at correct ones. The conclusion: Infants have rudimentary mathematical skills.

The results of this research suggest that infants have an innate ability to comprehend certain basic mathematical functions and statistical patterns. This inborn proficiency is likely to form the basis for learning more complex mathematics and statistical relationships later in life, as well as to pave the way for language acquisition (Wakeley, Rivera, & Langer, 2000; Wynn, 2000).

We turn now to several aspects of information processing, focusing on memory and individual differences in intelligence.

Memory During Infancy: They Must Remember This . . .

Simona Young was fated to spend her infancy with virtually no human contact. For up to 20 hours each day, she was left alone in a crib in a squalid Romanian orphanage. Cold bottles of milk were propped above her small body, which she would clutch to get nourishment. She would rock back and forth, rarely feeling any soothing touch or hearing words of comfort. Alone in her bleak surroundings, she would rock back and forth for hours on end.

Simona's story, however, has a happy ending. After being adopted by a Canadian couple when she was two, Simona's life is now filled with the usual activities of childhood involving friends, classmates, and above all, a loving family. In fact, now, at age six, she can remember almost nothing of her miserable life in the orphanage. It is as if she has entirely forgotten the past. (Blakeslee, 1995, p. C1)

How likely is it that Simona truly remembers nothing of her infancy? And if she ever does recall her first 2 years of life, how accurate will her memories be? To answer these questions, we need to consider the qualities of memory that exist during infancy.

Memory Capabilities in Infancy. Certainly, infants have **memory** capabilities, defined as the process by which information is initially recorded, stored, and retrieved. As we've seen, the ability of infants to distinguish new stimuli from old, as illustrated by habituation, implies that some memory of the old must be present. Unless the infants had some memory of an original stimulus, it would be impossible for them to recognize that a new stimulus differed from the earlier one (Newcombe, Drummey, & Lie, 1995).

However, infants' capability to habituate and show other basic forms of learning tells us little about how age brings about changes in the capacities of memory and in its fundamental nature. Do infants' memory capabilities increase as they get older? The answer is clearly affirmative. In one study, infants were taught that they could move a mobile hanging over the crib by kicking (see Figure 5-5). It took only a few days for 2-month-old infants to forget their training, but 6-month-old infants still remembered for as long as 3 weeks (Rovee-Collier, 1993, 1999).

Furthermore, infants who were later prompted to recall the association between kicking and moving the mobile showed evidence that the memory continued to exist even longer. Infants who had received just two training sessions lasting 9 minutes each still recalled about a week later, as illustrated by the fact that they began to kick when placed in

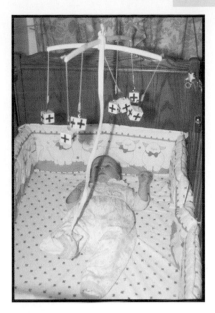

Figure 5-5 **Early Signs of Memory**

Infants who had learned the association between a moving mobile and kicking showed surprising recall ability if they were exposed to a reminder.

memory the process by which information is initially recorded, stored, and retrieved

the crib with the mobile. Two weeks later, however, they made no effort to kick, suggesting that they had forgotten entirely.

But they hadn't: When the babies saw a reminder—a moving mobile—their memories were apparently reactivated. In fact, the infants could remember the association, following prompting, for as long as an additional month (Sullivan, Rovee-Collier, & Tynes, 1979). Other evidence confirms these results, suggesting that hints can reactivate memories that at first seem lost, and that the older the infant, the more effective such prompting is (Rovee-Collier & Hayne, 1987; Hayne & Rovee-Collier, 1995; Rovee-Collier & Gerhardstein, 1997).

Is the nature of memory in infants different from that in older children and adults? Some researchers suggest that memory during infancy is dependent on particular neurological systems in the brain—specifically, the hippocampus—and that memory in later life involves additional structures of the brain (Nelson, 1995).

Other researchers suggest, however, that information is processed similarly throughout the life span even though the particular information changes and different parts of the brain may be used. According to memory expert Carolyn Rovee-Collier, people, regardless of their age, gradually lose memories, although, just like babies, they may regain them if reminders are provided. Moreover, the more times a memory is retrieved, the more enduring the memory becomes (Rovee-Collier, 1999).

The Duration of Memories. Although the processes that underlie memory retention and recall seem similar throughout the life span, the quantity of information stored and recalled does differ markedly as infants develop. Older infants can retrieve information more rapidly, and they can remember it longer. But just how long? Can memories from infancy be recalled, for example, when babies become grown up?

Researchers disagree on the age from which memories can be retrieved. Older research supports the notion of **infantile amnesia,** the lack of memory for experiences that occurred prior to 3 years of age. For instance, consider whether you can recall the birth of a younger brother or sister. For most college students, if the birth happened before they reached the age of 3, they can remember virtually nothing about it (Sheingold & Tenney, 1982).

However, more recent research shows surprising retention in infants. For example, Nancy Myers and her colleagues exposed a group of 6-month-old children to an unusual series of events in a laboratory, such as intermittent periods of light and dark and unusual sounds. When the children were later tested at the age of 1 1/2 years or 2 1/2 years, they demonstrated clear evidence that they had some memory of their participation in the earlier experience. Their behavior, such as reaching for things, reflected their earlier participation. They also seemed more familiar with the testing situation itself, showing more willingness to remain in a potentially unnerving situation than a control group of same-age children (Myers, Clifton, & Clarkson, 1987; Mandler & McDonough, 1995; Jusczyk & Hohne, 1997).

Such findings are consistent with evidence that the physical record of a memory in the brain appears to be relatively permanent, suggesting that memories, even from infancy, may be enduring. However, because memories may be stored somewhere in the recesses of the brain, they may not be easily, or accurately, retrieved. Memories are susceptible to interference from other, newer information, which may displace or block out the older information, thereby preventing its recall. Furthermore, recall of memories is sensitive to the environmental context in which the memories were initially formed. If changes have occurred in the context relating to the initial memories, then recall may be difficult, if not impossible (Ceci & Hembrooke, 1993; Bauer et al., 2000). Since people acquire a considerable amount of new information after infancy and are unlikely to experi-

infantile amnesia the lack of memory for experiences that occurred prior to 3 years of age

Though researchers disagree as to the age from which memories can be retrieved, people generally cannot remember events or experiences that occurred before the age of three.

ence the same environment they did as babies (for example, you probably cannot fit into your baby crib), it is hardly surprising that most adults cannot retrieve memories from their infant days.

Ultimately, the question of whether memories formed during infancy are retained into adulthood remains an open—and controversial—issue. Although infants' memories may be highly detailed and can be enduring if the infants experience repeated reminders, it is still not clear how accurate those memories remain over the course of the life span. In fact, research shows that early memories are susceptible to misrecollection if people are exposed to related, and contradictory, information following the initial formation of the memory. Not only does such new information potentially impair recall of the original material, but the new material may be inadvertently incorporated into the original memory, thereby corrupting its accuracy (Fivush, 1995; Bauer, 1996; DuBreuil, Garry, & Loftus, 1998).

In sum, the data suggest that, at least theoretically, it is possible for memories to remain intact from a very young age—if subsequent information does not interfere with them. This is a big "if" because most memories are likely to involve experiences that are somehow related to subsequent experiences and therefore are susceptible to interference. Ultimately, it may be that the validity of recollections of memories from infancy needs to be evaluated on a case-by-case basis.

Individual Differences in Intelligence: Is One Infant Smarter Than Another?

Maddy Rodriguez is a bundle of curiosity and energy. At 6 months of age, she cries heartily if she can't reach a toy, and when she sees a reflection of herself in a mirror, she gurgles and seems, in general, to find the situation quite amusing.

***

Jared Lynch, at 6 months, is a good deal more inhibited than Maddy. He doesn't seem to care much when a ball rolls out of his reach, losing interest in it rapidly. And, unlike Maddy, when he sees himself in a mirror, he pretty much ignores the reflection.

As anyone who has spent any time at all observing more than one baby can tell you, not all infants are alike. Some are full of energy and life, apparently displaying a natural-born curiosity, while others seem, by comparison, somewhat less interested in the world around them. Does this mean that such infants differ in intelligence?

Answering questions about how and to what degree infants vary in their underlying intelligence is not easy. Although it is clear that different infants show significant variations in their behavior, the issue of just what types of behavior may be related to cognitive ability is complicated. Interestingly, the examination of individual differences between infants was the initial approach taken by developmental specialists to understand cognitive development, and such issues still represent an important focus within the field.

What Is Infant Intelligence? Before we can address whether and how infants may differ in intelligence, we need to consider what is meant by the term "intelligence." Educators, psychologists, and other experts on development have yet to agree upon a general definition of intelligent behavior, even among adults. Is it the ability to do well in scholastic endeavors? Proficiency in business negotiations? Competence in navigating across treacherous seas, such as that shown by peoples of the South Pacific, who have no knowledge of Western navigational techniques?

Defining intelligence in infants is even more problematic than with adults. Is it the speed with which a new task is learned through classical or operant conditioning? How fast a baby becomes habituated to a new stimulus? The age at which an infant learns to

Determining what is meant by intelligence in infants represents a major challenge for developmentalists.

crawl or walk? Furthermore, even if we are able to identify particular behaviors that seem validly to differentiate one infant from another in terms of intelligence during infancy, we need to address a further, and probably more important, issue: How well do measures of infant intelligence relate to eventual adult intelligence?

Clearly, such questions are not simple, and no simple answers have been found. However, developmental specialists have devised several approaches (summarized in Table 5-2) to illuminate the nature of individual differences in intelligence during infancy.

Developmental Scales. Developmental psychologist Arnold Gesell formulated the earliest measure of infant development, which was designed to screen out normally developing babies from those with atypical development (Gesell, 1946). Gesell based his scale on examinations of hundreds of babies. He compared their performance at different ages to learn what behaviors were most common at a particular age. If an infant varied significantly from the norms of a given age, he or she was considered to be developmentally delayed or advanced.

Following the lead of researchers who sought to quantify intelligence through a specific score (known as an intelligence quotient, or IQ, score), Gesell developed a developmental quotient, or DQ. The **developmental quotient** is an overall developmental score that relates to performance in four domains: motor skills (for example, balance and sitting), language use, adaptive behavior (such as alertness and exploration), and personal-social (for example, feeding and dressing).

Later researchers have created other developmental scales. For instance, Nancy Bayley developed one of the most widely used measures for infants. The **Bayley Scales of Infant Development** evaluate an infant's development from 2 to 42 months. The Bayley Scales focus on two areas: mental and motor abilities. The mental scale focuses on the senses, perception, memory, learning, problem solving, and language, while the motor scale evaluates fine and gross motor skills (see Table 5-3). Like Gesell's approach, the Bayley yields a developmental quotient (DQ). A child who scores at an average level—meaning average performance for other children at the same age—receives a score of 100 (Bayley, 1969; Black & Matula, 1999; Gagnon & Nagle, 2000).

developmental quotient an overall developmental score that relates to performance in four domains: motor skills, language use, adaptive behavior, and personal-social

Bayley Scales of Infant Development a measure that evaluates an infant's development from 2 to 42 months

Table 5-2

APPROACHES USED TO DETECT DIFFERENCES IN INTELLIGENCE DURING INFANCY

Development quotient	Formulated by Arnold Gesell, the developmental quotient is an overall developmental score that relates to performance in four domains: motor skills (balance and sitting), language use, adaptive behavior (alertness and exploration), and personal-social (feeding and dressing).
Bayley Scales of Infant Development	Developed by Nancy Bayley, the Bayley Scales of Infant Development evaluate an infant's development from 2 to 42 months. The Bayley Scales focus on two areas: mental (senses, perception, memory, learning, problem solving, and language) and motor abilities (fine and gross motor skills).
Visual-recognition memory measurement	Measures of visual-recognition memory, the memory of and recognition of a stimulus that has been previously seen, also relate to intelligence. The more quickly an infant can retrieve a representation of a stimulus from memory, the more efficient, presumably, is that infant's information processing.

Table 5-3

SAMPLE ITEMS FROM THE BAYLEY SCALES OF INFANT DEVELOPMENT

Age	Mental Scale	Motor Scale
2 months	Turns head to sound	Holds head erect/steady for 15 seconds
	Reacts to disappearance of face	Sits with support
6 months	Lifts cup by handle	Sits alone for 30 seconds
	Looks at pictures in book	Grasps foot with hands
12 months	Builds tower of 2 cubes	Walks with help
	Turns pages of book	Grasps pencil in middle
17–19 months	Imitates crayon stroke	Stands alone on right foot
	Identifies objects in photo	Walks up stairs with help
23–25 months	Matches pictures	Laces 3 beads
	Imitates a 2-word sentence	Jumps distance of 4 inches
38–42 months	Names 4 colors	Copies circle
	Uses past tense	Hops twice on 1 foot
	Identifies gender	Walks down stairs, alternating feet

Source: Bayley, N. (1993). Bayley scales of infant development (BSID-II), 2nd Ed. San Antonio, TX: The Psychological Corporation.

The virtue of approaches such as those taken by Gesell and Bayley is that they provide a good snapshot of an infant's current developmental level. Using these scales, we can tell in an objective manner whether a particular infant falls behind or is ahead of his or her same-age peers. They are particularly useful in identifying infants who are substantially behind their peers, and who therefore need immediate special attention (Culbertson & Gyurke, 1990).

On the other hand, except in extreme cases, such scales are not very good at all in predicting a child's future course of development. A child whose development at the age of 1 year is relatively slow, as identified by these measures, does not necessarily display slow development at age 5, or 12, or 25. The association between most measures of behavior during infancy and adult intelligence, then, is minimal (Siegel, 1989; DiLalla et al., 1990; Molese & Acheson, 1997).

Because of the difficulties in using developmental scales to obtain measures of infant intelligence that are related to later intelligence, investigators have turned in the last decade to other techniques that may help assess intelligence in a meaningful way. Some have proven to be quite useful.

Information-Processing Approaches to Individual Differences in Intelligence. When we speak of intelligence in everyday parlance, we often differentiate between "quick" individuals and those who are "slow." Actually, according to research on the speed of information processing, such terms hold some truth. Contemporary approaches to infant intelligence suggest that the speed with which infants process information may correlate most strongly with later intelligence, as measured by IQ tests administered during adulthood (Rose & Feldman, 1997; Sigman, Cohen, & Beckwith, 1997).

How can we tell if a baby is processing information quickly or not? Most researchers use habituation tests. Infants who process information efficiently ought to be able to learn about stimuli more quickly. Consequently, we would expect that they would turn their

visual-recognition memory the memory and recognition of a stimulus that has been previously seen

cross-modal transference the ability to identify a stimulus that previously has been experienced only through one sense by using another sense

attention away from a given stimulus more rapidly than those who are less efficient at information processing, leading to the phenomenon of habituation. Similarly, measures of **visual-recognition memory,** the memory and recognition of a stimulus that has been previously seen, also relate to IQ. The more quickly an infant can retrieve a representation of a stimulus from memory, the more efficient, presumably, is that infant's information processing (Tamis-Lemonda & Bornstein, 1993; Canfield et al., 1997).

Research using an information-processing framework is clear in suggesting a relationship between information processing and cognitive abilities: Measures of how quickly infants lose interest in stimuli that they have previously seen, as well as their responsiveness to new stimuli, correlate moderately well with later measures of intelligence. Infants who are more efficient information processors during the 6 months following birth tend to have higher intelligence scores between 2 and 12 years of age, as well as higher scores on other measures of cognitive competence (Rose & Feldman, 1995; Slater, 1995; Sigman et al., in press).

Other research suggests that abilities related to the *multimodal approach to perception,* which we considered in Chapter 4, may offer clues about later intelligence. For instance, the information-processing skill of cross-modal transference is associated with intelligence. **Cross-modal transference** is the ability to identify a stimulus that previously has been experienced through only one sense by using another sense. For instance, a baby who is able to recognize by sight a screwdriver that she has previously only touched, but not seen, is displaying cross-modal transference. Research has found that the degree of cross-modal transference displayed by an infant at age 1—which requires a high level of abstract thinking—is associated with intelligence scores several years later (Rose & Ruff, 1987; Spelke, 1987; Rose et al., 1991).

Although information-processing efficiency and cross-modal transference abilities during infancy relate moderately well to later IQ scores, we need to keep in mind two qualifications. First, even though there is an association between early information-processing capabilities and later measures of IQ, the correlation is only moderate in strength. Other factors, such as the degree of environmental stimulation, also play a crucial role in helping to determine adult intelligence. Consequently, we should not assume that intelligence is somehow permanently fixed in infancy.

Second, and perhaps even more important, intelligence measured by traditional IQ tests relates to a particular type of intelligence, one that emphasizes abilities that lead to academic, and certainly not artistic or professional, success. Consequently, predicting that a child may do well on IQ tests later in life is not the same as predicting that the child will be successful later in life.

Still, the relatively recent finding that an association exists between efficiency of information processing and later IQ scores has changed how we view the consistency of cognitive development across the life span. Whereas the earlier reliance on scales such as the Bayley led to the misconception that little continuity existed, the more recent information-processing approaches suggest that cognitive development unfolds in a more orderly, continuous manner from infancy to the later stages of life.

Assessing Information-Processing Approaches. In considering information-processing perspectives on cognitive development during infancy, we've seen an approach that is very different from Piaget's. Rather than focusing on broad explanations of the *qualitative* changes that occur in infants' capabilities, as Piaget does, information processing looks at *quantitative* change. Piaget sees cognitive growth occurring in fairly sudden spurts; information processing sees more gradual, step-by-step growth. (Think of the difference between a track and field runner leaping hurdles versus a slow but steady marathon racer.)

What Can You Do to Promote Infants' Cognitive Development?

All parents want their children to reach their full cognitive potential, but sometimes efforts to reach this goal take a bizarre path. For instance, some parents spend hundreds of dollars enrolling in workshops with titles such as "How to Multiply Your Baby's Intelligence" and buying books with titles such as *How to Teach Your Baby to Read* (Sharpe, 1994).

Do such efforts ever succeed? Although some parents swear they do, there is no scientific support for the effectiveness of such programs. For example, despite the many cognitive skills of infants, no infant can actually read. Furthermore, "multiplying" a baby's intelligence is impossible, and such organizations as the American Academy of Pediatrics and the American Academy of Neurology have denounced programs that claim to do so.

On the other hand, certain things can be done to promote cognitive development in infants. The following suggestions, based upon findings of developmental researchers, offer a starting point (Meyerhoff & White, 1986; Schwebel, Maher, & Fagley, 1990; Schulman, 1991):

▶ *Provide infants the opportunity to explore the world.* As Piaget suggests, children learn by doing, and they need the opportunity to explore and probe their environment. Make sure the environment contains a variety of toys, books, and other sources of stimulation. (Also see the *Speaking of Development* box.)

▶ *Be responsive to infants on both a verbal and a nonverbal level.* Try to speak *with* babies, as opposed to *at* them. Ask questions, listen to their responses, and provide further communication.

▶ *Read to your infants.* Although they may not understand the meaning of your words, they will respond to your tone of voice and the intimacy provided by the activity. Reading together also begins to create a lifelong reading habit.

▶ *Keep in mind that you don't have to be with an infant 24 hours a day.* Just as infants need time to explore their world on their own, parents and other caregivers need time off from childcare activities.

Even if they don't understand the meaning of the words, infants still benefit from being read to.

▶ *Don't push infants and don't expect too much too soon.* Your goal should not be to create a genius; it should be to provide a warm, nurturing environment that will allow an infant to reach his or her potential.

Because information-processing researchers consider cognitive development in terms of a collection of individual skills, they are often able to use more precise measures of cognitive ability, such as processing speed and memory recall, than proponents of Piaget's approach. Still, the very precision of these individual measures makes it harder to get an overall sense of the nature of cognitive development, something at which Piaget was a master. It's as if information-processing approaches focus more on the individual pieces of the puzzle of cognitive development, while Piagetian approaches focus more on the whole puzzle.

Ultimately, both Piagetian and information-processing approaches are critical in providing an account of cognitive development in infancy. Coupled with advances in the biochemistry of the brain and theories that consider the effects of social factors on learning and cognition (which we'll discuss in the next chapter), the two approaches will continue to help us paint a full picture of cognitive development.

SPEAKING OF DEVELOPMENT

Helen Shwe, Toy Designer Consultant

EDUCATION: BA, Cognitive Science, University of Rochester, New York; MA & PhD, Developmental Psychology, Stanford University, California.

HOME: Redwood City, California

Toys have traditionally been provided to children for entertainment, but over the years it has become apparent that what were once considered mere playthings have become important components of a child's development. As a result, toy researchers and designers, like Helen Shwe, are designing toys not only for specific age groups, but also to encourage development.

"First you have to decide on the age group for whom the toy is targeted, and make sure that the range is not too broad," said Shwe, who is a consultant to a number of toy designers. "Because their cognitive and social development changes very much, you have to keep their interest. A three-year-old is very different from a four-year-old."

While color, texture, and shape are most important for very young children, according to Shwe, toy designs for older children consider the social aspect.

For children around age 3, Shwe explained, you try to have a toy that will "allow multiple children to play with it: a toy that will encourage social interaction and cooperation. Fantasy and pretend play is popular, and you would want to bring some of that into the design.

"For example, a social action toy will allow children to compose a song together. One would push a button to add one phrase, and the other child would add another musical phrase," she said.

One area of toy design that has grown quickly over the past 5 years has been that of incorporating technology into toys.

"Today, more than 50 percent of toys have some type of electronics or technology," said Shwe. "Technology toys have refreshed content in that a parent can connect to a Web site and download new content for the toy as the child grows," she added.

While the combination of developmental psychologists and high technology can provide some interesting and sophisticated playthings for children, Shwe notes that there will always be room for more traditional toys.

"There is definitely room for both types of toys, because they foster different abilities," she added.

Review and Rethink

REVIEW

- Information-processing approaches consider quantitative changes in children's abilities to organize and use information. Cognitive growth is regarded as the increasing sophistication of encoding, storage, and retrieval.
- Infants clearly have memory capabilities from a very early age, although the duration and accuracy of such memories are unresolved questions.
- Traditional measures of infant intelligence focus on behavioral attainments, which can help identify developmental delays or advances but are not strongly related to measures of adult intelligence.
- Information-processing approaches to assessing intelligence rely on variations in the speed and quality with which infants process information.

RETHINK

- What information from this chapter could you use to refute the claims of books or educational programs that promise to help parents multiply their babies' intelligence or instill advanced intellectual skills in infants?
- In what ways is the use of such developmental scales as Gesell's or Bayley's helpful? In what ways is it dangerous? How would you maximize the helpfulness and minimize the danger?

The Roots of Language

Vicki and Dominic were engaged in a friendly competition over whose name would be the first word their baby, Maura, said. "Say 'mama,'" Vicki would coo, before handing Maura over to Dominic for a diaper change. Grinning, he would take her and coax, "No, say 'daddy.'" Both parents ended up losing—and winning—when Maura's first word sounded more like "baba," and seemed to refer to her bottle.

Mama. No. Cookie. Dad. Jo. Most parents can remember their baby's first word, and no wonder. It's an exciting moment. When an infant utters his or her first word, no matter what it is, it marks the start of a transformation: from an entity seemingly not so different from animals of many other species to an entity who can now use a skill that is, arguably, unique to human beings.

But those initial words are just the first and most obvious manifestations of language. Many months earlier, infants began using language to comprehend the world around them. How does this linguistic ability develop? What is the pattern and sequence of language development? And how does the use of language mark a transformation in the cognitive world of infants and their parents? We consider these questions, and others, as we address the development of language during the first years of life.

The Fundamentals of Language: From Sounds to Symbols

Language, the systematic, meaningful arrangement of symbols, provides the basis for communication. But it does more than this: It is closely tied to the way infants think and understand the world. It enables them to reflect on people and objects, and to convey their thoughts to others.

Language has several formal characteristics that must be mastered as linguistic competence is developed. They include:

■ *Phonology.* Phonology refers to the basic sounds of language, called *phonemes,* that can be combined to produce words and sentences. For instance, the "a" in "mat" and the "a" in "mate" represent two different phonemes in English. Although English employs just 40 phonemes to create every word in the language, other languages have as many as 85 phonemes—and some as few as 15 (Akmajian, Demers, & Harnish, 1984).

■ *Morphemes.* A morpheme is the smallest language unit that has meaning. Some morphemes are complete words, while others add information necessary for interpreting a word, such as the endings "-s" for plural and "-ed" for past tense.

■ *Semantics.* Semantics are the rules that govern the meaning of words and sentences. As their knowledge of semantics develops, children are able to understand the subtle distinction between "Ellie was hit by a car" (an answer to the question of why Ellie has not been in school for the last week) and "A car hit Ellie" (used to announce an emergency situation).

In considering the development of language, we need to distinguish between linguistic *comprehension,* the understanding of speech, and linguistic *production,* the use of language to communicate. One principle underlies the relationship between the two: Comprehension precedes production. An 18-month-old may be able to understand a complex series of directions ("pick up your coat from the floor and put it on the chair by the fireplace") but may not yet have strung more than two words together when speaking

language the systematic, meaningful arrangement of symbols, which provides the basis for communication

cw

for herself. Comprehension, then, begins earlier than production, and throughout infancy comprehension increases at a faster rate than production. For instance, during infancy, comprehension of words expands at a rate of 22 new words a month, while production of words increases at a rate of about 9 new words a month, once they start talking. Other forms of language ability show the same pattern, with comprehension consistently preceding production (Benedict, 1979; Tincoff & Jusczyk, 1999; see Figure 5-6).

Prelinguistic Communication. Consider the following "dialogue" between a mother and her 3-month-old child (Snow, 1977a):

Mother	*Infant*
	[Smiles]
Oh, what a nice little smile!	
Yes, isn't that pretty?	
There now.	
There's a nice little smile.	
	[Burps]
What a nice wind as well!	
Yes, that's better, isn't it?	
Yes.	
Yes.	
	[Vocalizes]
Yes!	
There's a nice noise.	

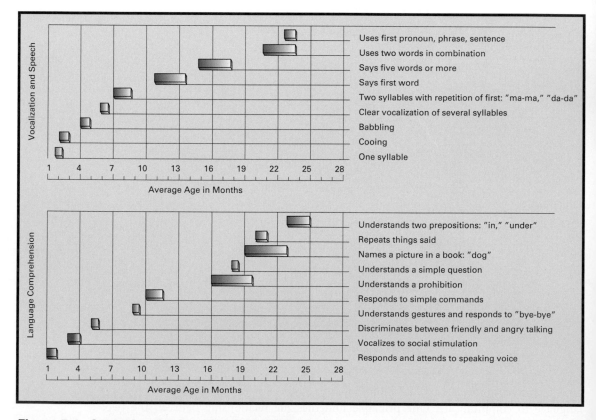

Figure 5-6   Comprehension Precedes Production

Throughout infancy, the comprehension of speech precedes the production of speech.

(*Source:* Adapted from Bornstein & Lamb, 1992a.)

Although we tend to think of language in terms of the production of words and then groups of words, infants can begin to communicate linguistically well before they say their first word.

Although we tend to think of language in terms of the production first of words and then of groups of words, infants actually begin to communicate linguistically well before they say their first word. Spend 24 hours with even a very young infant and you will hear a variety of sounds: cooing, crying, gurgling, murmuring, and assorted types of other noises. These sounds, although not meaningful in themselves, play an important role in linguistic development, paving the way for true language (Bloom, 1993). It is this very early period of linguistic development that Paige Arbeiter, whom we met in the prologue, appears to have missed almost entirely.

Prelinguistic communication is communication through sounds, facial expressions, gestures, imitation, and other nonlinguistic means. When a father responds to his daughter's "ah" with an "ah" of his own, and then the daughter repeats the sound, and the father responds once again, they are engaged in prelinguistic communication. Clearly, the "ah" sound has no particular meaning. However, its repetition, which mimics the give-and-take of conversation, teaches the infant something about turn-taking (Dromi, 1993).

The most obvious manifestation of prelinguistic communication is babbling. **Babbling,** making speechlike but meaningless sounds, starts at the age of 2 or 3 months and continues until around the age of 1 year. When they babble, infants repeat the same vowel sound over and over, changing the pitch from high to low (as in "ee-ee-ee," repeated at different pitches). After the age of 5 months, the sounds of babbling begin to expand, reflecting the addition of consonants (such as "bee-bee-bee-bee").

Babbling is a universal phenomenon, accomplished in the same way throughout all cultures. While they are babbling, infants spontaneously produce all of the sounds found in every language, not just the language they hear people around them speaking. In fact, as we discuss in the *From Research to Practice* box, even deaf children display their own form of babbling: Infants who cannot hear and who are exposed to sign language babble with their hands instead of their voices (Petitto & Marentette, 1991; Locke, 1994; Cormier, Mauk, & Repp, 1998).

The form of babbling follows a progression from sounds that are the simplest to make to more complex sounds. Furthermore, although initially exposure to a particular language does not seem to influence babbling, experience eventually does make a difference. By the age of 6 months, babbling differs according to the language to which infants are exposed (Blake & Boysson-Bardies, 1992). The difference is so noticeable that even untrained listeners can distinguish between babbling infants who have been raised in cul-

prelinguistic communication communication through sounds, facial expressions, gestures, imitation, and other nonlinguistic means

babbling making speechlike but meaningless sounds

cw

From Research to Practice

Do Gestures Hold the Key to Understanding the Origins of Human Language?

One chimp sits in the group, contentedly eating fruit in her natal African forest. As she does, a second, younger chimp approaches, but not too close, and extends her hand in a cupping gesture. She is asking the first chimp to share the food. Another chimp, this one at a research center outside Atlanta, eyes a banana just beyond reach, outside and to the left of his cage. When a scientist approaches, the chimp gestures with his right hand, extending it in what's called a whole-hand point, looking back and forth between the scientist and the banana: Would you mind passing the chow, big guy? (Begley, 1999, p. 56)

As language goes, these examples are not all that sophisticated. But gestures such as these may provide clues to understanding how language evolved in human beings and how infants use gestures to make themselves understood.

Researchers have begun to extend findings from studies of chimps to studies of human infants who can neither hear nor speak. According to an increasing body of research on such deaf-mute children, language based upon gestures may be innate in the human brain. Going even further, some scientists argue that language may have evolved directly from the use of hand gestures (Corballis, 1999; Corballis & Lea, 1999; Azar, 2000).

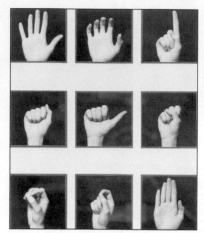

Deaf infants who are exposed to sign language do their own type of babbling, related to the use of signs.

Evidence for this theory comes from several sources. For one thing, blind children gesture in much the same way that sighted children do, suggesting that the use of gestures is a natural part of development. Second, research shows that gesturing follows a set of sophisticated rules that are similar to the rules of verbal language. In fact, children who are deaf have invented numerous forms of sign language, and their gestural babbling is analogous to the verbal babbling of children who can speak (see photo). Furthermore, as shown in Figure 5-7, the areas of the brain activated during the production of hand gestures are similar to the areas activated during speech production (Corballis, 2000; Mayberry & Nicoladis, 2000).

The theory that gestures form a kind of sophisticated, silent language helps explain the relatively quick evolution of spoken language in humans. According to fossil evidence, the ability to speak—signaled by the emergence of vocal tracts—did not develop until around 150,000 years ago; we also know that civilizations with spoken language emerged around 5,000 years ago. The time span between the emergence of vocal tracts and the use of spoken language is remarkably quick—the blink of an eye in evolutionary terms. However, if humans already had developed a sophisticated use of gestures that included the formal attributes of language, the quick leap to a spoken language begins to make sense.

The idea that spoken language evolved from gestural languages remains a theory. Still, it does help explain the universal nature of gesturing, and it also helps us to understand how human babies develop the ability to use the spoken word.

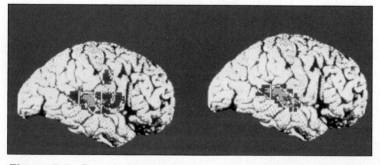

Figure 5-7 Broca's Area

Areas of the brain that are activated during speech are similar to the areas activated during the production of hand gestures.

(*Source:* American Scientist, 1999.)

tures in which French, Arabic, or Cantonese languages are spoken (Locke, 1983; Vihman, 1991; Oller et al., 1997).

Babbling may be the most obviously language-like achievement of early infancy, but there are other indications of prelinguistic speech. For instance, consider 5-month-old Marta, who spies her red ball just beyond her reach. After reaching for it and finding that she is unable to get to it, she makes a cry of anger that alerts her parents that something is amiss, and her mother hands it to her. Communication, albeit prelinguistic, has occurred.

Four months later, when Marta faces the same situation, she no longer bothers to reach for the ball and doesn't respond in anger. Instead, she holds out her arm in the direction of the ball, and with great purpose, seeks to catch her mother's eye. When her mother sees the behavior, she knows just what Marta wants. Clearly, Marta's communicative skills—although still prelinguistic—have taken a leap forward.

Even these prelinguistic skills are supplanted in just a few months, when the gesture gives way to a new communicative skill: producing an actual word. Marta's parents clearly hear her say "ball."

First Words. When a mother and father first hear their child say "Mama" or "Dada," or even "baba," the first word of Maura, the baby described earlier in this section, it is hard to be anything but delighted. But their initial enthusiasm may be dampened a bit when they find that the same sound is used to ask for a cookie, a doll, and a ratty old blanket.

First words generally are spoken somewhere around the age of 10 to 14 months, but may occur as early as 9 months. Linguists differ on just how to recognize that a first word has actually been uttered. Some say it is when an infant clearly understands words and can produce a sound that is close to a word spoken by adults, such as a child who uses "mama" for any request she may have. Other linguists use a stricter criterion for the first word; they restrict "first word" to cases in which children give a clear, consistent name to a person, event, or object. In this view, "mama" counts as a first word only if it is consistently applied to the same person, seen in a variety of situations and doing a variety of things, and is not used to label other people (Kamhi, 1986; Bornstein & Tamis-LeMonda, 1989; Hollich et al., 2000).

Although there is disagreement over when we can say a first word has been uttered, no one disputes that once an infant starts to produce words, the rate of increase in vocabulary is rapid. By the age of 15 months, the average child has a vocabulary of 10 words. The child's vocabulary methodically expands until the one-word stage of language development ends at around 18 months. Around that time, a sudden spurt in vocabulary occurs. In just a short period—a few weeks somewhere between 16 and 24 months of age—a child's vocabulary typically increases from 50 to 400 words (Bates, Bretherton, & Snyder, 1988; Gleitman & Landau, 1994; Fernald et al., 1998).

As you can see from the list in Table 5-4, the first words in children's early vocabularies typically regard objects and things, both animate and inanimate. Most often they refer to people or objects who constantly appear and disappear ("Mama"), to animals ("kitty"), or to temporary states ("wet"). These first words are often **holophrases,** one-word utterances that stand for a whole phrase, whose meaning depends on the particular context in which they are used. For instance, a youngster may use the phrase "ma" to mean, depending on the context, "I want to be picked up by Mom" or "I want something to eat, Mom" or "Where's Mom?" (Nelson, 1981; Clark, 1983; Dromi, 1987).

holophrases one-word utterances that stand for a whole phrase, whose meaning depends on the particular context in which they are used

Culture has an effect on the type of first words spoken. For example, unlike North American English-speaking infants, who are more apt to use nouns initially, Chinese Mandarin-speaking infants use more verbs than nouns (Tardif, 1996).

First Sentences. When Aaron was 19 months old, he heard his mother coming up the back steps, as she did every day just before dinner. Aaron turned to his father and distinctly

Table 5-4

THE TOP FIFTY: THE FIRST WORDS CHILDREN UNDERSTAND AND SPEAK

	Comprehension Percentage	Production Percentage
1. Nominals (Words referring to "things")	56	61
Specific (people, animals, objects)	17	11
General (words referring to all members of a category)	39	50
Animate (objects)	9	13
Inanimate (objects)	30	37
Pronouns (e.g., this, that, they)	1	2
2. Action words	36	19
Social action games (e.g., peek-a-boo)	15	11
Events (e.g., "eat")	1	NA
Locatives (locating or putting something in specific location)	5	1
General action and inhibitors (e.g., "don't touch")	15	6
3. Modifiers	3	10
Status (e.g., "all gone")	2	4
Attributes (e.g., "big")	1	3
Locatives (e.g., "outside")	0	2
Possessives (e.g., "mine")	1	1
4. Personal-social	5	10
Assertions (e.g., "yes")	2	9
Social expressive (e.g., "bye-bye")	4	1

Note: Percentage refers to percentage of children who include this type of word among their first 50 words.
(*Source:* Adapted from Benedict, 1979.)

By the age of two, most children use two-word phrases, such as "ball play."

said, "Ma come." In stringing those two words together, Aaron took a giant step in his language development.

The increase in vocabulary that comes at around 18 months is accompanied by another accomplishment: the linking together of individual words into sentences that convey a single thought. Although there is a good deal of variability in the time at which children first create two-word phrases, it is generally around 8 to 12 months after they say their first word.

The linguistic advance represented by two-word combinations is important because the linkage not only provides labels for things in the world but also indicates the relations between them. For instance, the combination may declare something about possession ("Mama key") or recurrent events ("Dog bark"). Interestingly, most early sentences don't represent demands or even necessarily require a response. Instead, they are often merely comments and observations about events occurring in the child's world (Slobin, 1970; Halliday, 1975).

Two-year-olds using two-word combinations tend to employ particular sequences that are similar to the ways in which adult sentences are constructed. For instance, sentences in English typically follow a pattern in which the subject of the sentence comes first, followed by the verb, and then the object ("Josh threw the ball"). Children's speech most often uses a similar order, although not all the words are initially included. Consequently, a child might say "Josh threw" or "Josh ball" to indicate the same thought. What is significant is that the order is typically not "threw Josh" or "ball Josh," but rather the usual order of English, which makes the utterance much easier for an English speaker to comprehend (Brown, 1973; Maratsos, 1983; Hirsh-Pasek & Michnick-Golinkoff, 1995).

Although the creation of two-word sentences represents an advance, the language used by children still is by no means adultlike. As we've just seen, 2-year-olds tend to leave out words that aren't critical to the message similar to the way we might write a telegram for which we were paying by the word. For that reason, their talk is often called **telegraphic speech.** Rather than saying, "I showed you the book," a child using telegraphic speech might say, "I show book." "I am drawing a dog" might become "Drawing dog" (see Table 5-5).

Early language has other characteristics that differentiate it from the language used by adults. For instance, consider Sarah, who refers to the blanket she sleeps with as "blankie." When her Aunt Ethel gives her a new blanket, Sarah refuses to call the new one a "blankie," restricting the word to her original blanket.

Sarah's inability to generalize the label of "blankie" to blankets in general is an example of **underextension,** using words too restrictively, which is common among children just mastering spoken language. Underextension occurs when language novices think that a word refers to a specific instance of a concept, instead of to all examples of the concept (Caplan & Barr, 1989).

As infants like Sarah grow more adept with language, the opposite phenomenon sometimes occurs. In **overextension,** words are used too broadly, overgeneralizing their meaning. For example, when Sarah refers to buses, trucks, and tractors as "cars," she is guilty of overextension, making the assumption that any object with wheels must be a car. Although overextension reflects speech errors, it also shows that advances are occurring in the child's thought processes: The child is beginning to develop general mental categories and concepts (Behrend, 1988).

Infants also show individual differences in the style of language they use. For example, some use a **referential style,** in which language is used primarily to label objects. Others tend to use an **expressive style,** in which language is used primarily to express feelings and needs about oneself and others (Bates et al., 1994; Nelson, 1996).

Language styles reflect, in part, cultural factors. For example, mothers in the United States label objects more frequently than do Japanese mothers, encouraging a more referential style of speech. In contrast, mothers in Japan are more apt to speak about social interactions, encouraging a more expressive style of speech (Fernald & Morikawa, 1993).

telegraphic speech speech in which words not critical to the message are left out

underextension the overly restrictive use of words, common among children just mastering spoken language

overextension the overly broad use of words, overgeneralizing their meaning

referential style a style of language use in which language is used primarily to label objects

expressive style a style of language use in which language is used primarily to express feelings and needs about oneself and others

Table 5-5

CHILDREN'S IMITATION OF SENTENCES SHOWING DECLINE OF TELEGRAPHIC SPEECH

	Eve, 25.5 Months	Adam, 28.5 Months	Helen, 30 Months	Ian, 31.5 Months	Jimmy, 32 Months	June, 35.5 Months
I showed you the book.	I show book.	(I show) book.	C	I show you the book.	C	Show you the book.
I am very tall.	(My) tall.	I (very) tall.	I very tall.	I'm very tall.	Very tall.	I very tall.
It goes in a big box.	Big box.	Big box.	In big box.	It goes in the box.	C	C
I am drawing a dog.	Drawing dog.	I draw dog.	I drawing dog.	Dog.	C	C
I will read the book.	Read book.	I will read book.	I read the book.	I read the book.	C	C
I can see a cow.	See cow.	I want see cow.	C	Cow.	C	C
I will not do that again.	Do–again.	I will that again.	I do that.	I again.	C	C

C = correct imitation.
(*Source:* Adapted from R. Brown & C. Fraser, 1963.)

learning theory approach the theory that language acquisition follows the basic laws of reinforcement and conditioning

nativist approach the theory that a genetically determined, innate mechanism directs language development

universal grammar Noam Chomsky's theory that all the world's languages share a similar underlying structure

language-acquisition device (LAD) a neural system of the brain hypothesized to permit understanding of language

The Origins of Language Development. The immense strides in language development during the preschool years raise a fundamental question: How does proficiency in language come about? Linguists are deeply divided on how to answer this question.

One response comes from the basic principles of learning. According to the **learning theory approach,** language acquisition follows the basic laws of reinforcement and conditioning discussed in Chapter 1. For instance, a child who articulates the word "da" may be hugged and praised by her father, who jumps to the conclusion that she is referring to him. This reaction reinforces the child, who is more likely to repeat the word. In sum, the learning theory perspective on language acquisition suggests that children learn to speak by being rewarded for making sounds that approximate speech. Through the process of *shaping,* language becomes more and more similar to adult speech (Skinner, 1957).

There's a problem, though, with the learning theory approach. It doesn't seem to explain adequately how readily children acquire the rules of language. For instance, novice users of language are reinforced not only when they use grammatically impeccable language, but also when they make errors. Parents are apt to be just as responsive if their child says, "Why the dog won't eat?" as they are if the child phrases the question more correctly ("Why won't the dog eat?"). Both forms of the question are understood correctly, and both elicit the same response; reinforcement is provided for both correct and incorrect language usage. Under such circumstances, learning theory is hard-put to explain how children learn to speak properly.

Still other problems exist with learning theory explanations. For instance, research shows that children are able to move beyond specific utterances they have heard, and produce novel phrases, sentences, and constructions. Furthermore, children can apply rules to nonsense words. In one study, 4-year-old children heard the nonsense verb "to pilk" in the sentence "the bear is pilking the horse." Later, when asked what was happening to the horse, they responded by placing the nonsense verb in the correct tense and voice: "He's getting pilked by the bear."

Such conceptual difficulties with the learning theory approach have led to the development of an alternative, championed by the linguist Noam Chomsky and known as the nativist approach (1968, 1978, 1991, 1999). The **nativist approach** argues that there is a genetically determined, innate mechanism that directs the development of language. According to Chomsky, people are born with an innate capacity to use language, which emerges, more or less automatically, due to maturation.

Chomsky's analysis of different languages suggests that all the world's languages share a similar underlying structure, which he calls **universal grammar.** In this view, the human brain is wired with a neural system called the **language-acquisition device,** or **LAD,** that both permits the understanding of language structure and provides a set of strategies and techniques for learning the particular characteristics of the language to which a child is exposed. In this view, language is uniquely human, made possible by a genetic predisposition to both comprehend and produce words and sentences (Lust, Suner, & Whitman, 1995; Lillo-Martin, 1997; Nowak, Komarova, & Niyogi, 2001).

Like the learning theory approach, the view that language represents an innate ability unique to humans has its critics. For instance, some researchers argue that certain primates are able to learn at least the basics of language, an ability that calls into question the uniqueness of the human linguistic capacity. Other critics suggest that we must identify mechanisms other than either a language-acquisition device or learning theory principles if we are to understand fully the processes that underlie language development (MacWhinney, 1991; Savage-Rumbaugh et al., 1993).

Given that neither the learning theory nor the nativist perspective provides an explanation that is fully supported by research, some theorists have turned to a theory that combines both schools of thought. The *interactionist perspective* suggests that language development is produced through a combination of genetically determined predispositions and environmental events.

The interactionist perspective accepts that innate factors shape the broad outlines of language development. However, interactionists also argue that the specific course of language development is determined by the language to which children are exposed and the reinforcement they receive for using language in particular ways. Social factors are considered to be key to development, since the motivation provided by one's membership in a society and culture and one's interactions with others leads to the use of language and the growth of language skills (Bohannon, 1993).

Just as there is support for some aspects of learning theory and nativist positions, the interactionist perspective has also received some support. We don't know, at the moment, which of these positions will ultimately provide the best explanation. More likely, different factors play different roles at different times during childhood. The full explanation for language acquisition, then, remains to be found.

Speaking to Children: The Language of Infant-Directed Speech

Say the following sentence aloud: Do you like the apple dumpling?

Now pretend that you are going to ask the same question of an infant, and speak it as you would for the child's ears.

Chances are several things happened when you translated the phrase for the infant. First of all, the wording probably changed, and you may have said something like, "Does baby like the apple dumpling?" At the same time, the pitch of your voice probably rose, your general intonation most likely had a singsong quality, and you probably separated your words carefully.

Infant-Directed Speech. The shift in your language was due to your use of **infant-directed speech,** a style of speech directed toward infants. This type of speech pattern was previously called *motherese*, because it was assumed that it applied only to mothers. However, that assumption was wrong, and the gender-neutral term *infant-directed speech* is now used more frequently.

Infant-directed speech is characterized by short, simple sentences. Pitch becomes higher, the range of frequencies increases, and intonation is more varied. There is also repetition of words, and topics are restricted to items that are assumed to be comprehensible to infants, such as concrete objects in the baby's environment.

Sometimes infant-directed speech includes amusing sounds that are not even words, imitating the prelinguistic speech of infants. In other cases, it has little formal structure, but is similar to the kind of telegraphic speech that infants use as they develop their own language skills.

Infant-directed speech changes as children become older. Around the end of the first year, infant-directed speech takes on more adultlike qualities. Sentences become longer and more complex, although individual words are still spoken slowly and deliberately. Pitch is also used to focus attention on particularly important words.

Infant-directed speech plays an important role in infants' acquisition of language. Newborns prefer such speech to regular language, a fact that suggests that they may be particularly receptive to it. Furthermore, some research suggests that unusually extensive exposure to infant-directed speech early in life is related to the comparatively early appearance of first words and earlier linguistic competence in other areas (Hampson & Nelson, 1993; Cooper & Aslin, 1990, 1994; Gogate, Bahrick, & Watson, 2000).

Motherese, or, more precisely, infant-directed speech, includes the use of short, simple sentences and is said in a pitch that is higher than that used with older children and adults.

infant directed speech a type of speech directed toward infants, characterized by short, simple sentences

Developmental Diversity

Is Infant-Directed Speech Similar Across All Cultures?

Do mothers in the United States, Sweden, and Russia speak the same way to their infants?

In some respects, they clearly do. Although the words themselves differ across languages, the way the words are spoken is quite similar. According to a growing body of research, there are basic similarities across cultures in the nature of infant-directed speech (Grieser & Kuhl, 1988; Papousek & Papousek, 1991; Rabain-Jamin & Sabeau-Jouannet, 1997).

Consider, for instance, the comparison in Table 5-6 of the major characteristics of speech directed at infants used by native speakers of English and Spanish. Of the 10 most frequent features, 6 are common to both: exaggerated intonation, high pitch, lengthened vowels, repetition, lower volume, and instructional emphasis (that is, heavy stress on certain key words, such as emphasizing the word "ball" in the sentence, "No, that's a *ball*") (Blount, 1982). Similarly, mothers in the United States, Sweden, and Russia all exaggerate and elongate the pronunciation of the three vowel sounds of "ee," "ah," and "oh" when speaking to infants in similar ways, despite differences in the languages in which the sounds are used (Kuhl et al., 1997).

Even deaf mothers use a form of infant-directed speech: When communicating with their infants, deaf mothers use signed language at a significantly slower tempo than when communicating with adults, and they frequently repeat the signs (Swanson, Leonard, & Gandour, 1992; Masataka, 1996; 1998; 2000).

The cross-cultural similarities in infant-directed speech are so great, in fact, that they appear in some facets of language specific to particular types of interactions. For instance, evidence comparing American English, German, and Mandarin Chinese speakers shows that in each of the languages, pitch rises when a mother is attempting to get an infant's attention or produce a response, while pitch falls when she is trying to calm an infant (Papousek & Papousek, 1991).

Table 5-6

THE MOST COMMON FEATURES OF INFANT-DIRECTED SPEECH IN ENGLISH AND SPANISH

English	Spanish
1. Exaggerated intonation	1. Exaggerated intonation
2. Breathiness	2. Repetition
3. High pitch	3. High pitch
4. Repetition	4. Instructional
5. Lowered volume	5. Attentionals
6. Lengthened vowel	6. Lowered volume
7. Creaky voice	7. Raised volume
8. Instructional	8. Lengthened vowel
9. Tenseness	9. Fast tempo
10. Falsetto	10. Personal pronoun substitution

(*Source:* Adapted from B. G. Blount, 1982.)

Why do we find such similarities across very different languages? One hypothesis is that the characteristics of infant-directed speech activate innate responses in infants. As we have noted, infants seem to prefer infant-directed speech over adult-directed speech, suggesting that their perceptual systems may be more responsive to such characteristics. Another explanation is that infant-directed speech facilitates language development, providing cues as to the meaning of speech before infants have developed the capacity to understand the meaning of words (Fernald & Kuhl, 1987; Fernald, 1989; Fisher & Tokura, 1996; Kuhl et al., 1997).

Despite the similarities in the style of infant-directed speech across diverse cultures, there are some important cultural differences in the *quantity* of speech that infants hear from their parents. For example, although the Gusii of Kenya care for their infants in an extremely close, physical way, they speak to them less than American parents do (LeVine, 1994).

There are also some stylistic differences related to cultural factors in the U.S. A major factor, it seems, might be gender. ▢

Gender Differences. To a girl, a bird is a birdie, a blanket a blankie, and a dog a doggy. To a boy, a bird is a bird, a blanket a blanket, and a dog a dog.

At least that's what parents of boys and girls appear to think, as illustrated by the language they use toward their sons and daughters. Virtually from the time of birth, the language parents employ with their children differs depending on the child's sex, according to research conducted by developmental psychologist Jean Berko Gleason (Gleason et al., 1994; Gleason, 1987).

Gleason found that, by the age of 32 months, girls hear twice as many diminutives (words such as "kitty" or "dolly" instead of "cat" or "doll") as boys hear. Although the use of diminutives declines with increasing age, their use consistently remains higher in speech directed at girls than in that directed at boys (see Figure 5-8).

Parents also are more apt to respond differently to children's requests depending on the child's gender. For instance, when turning down a child's request, mothers are likely to respond with a firm "no" to a male child, but to soften the blow to a female child by providing a diversionary response ("Why don't you do this instead?") or by somehow making the refusal less direct. Consequently, boys tend to hear firmer, clearer language, while girls are exposed to warmer phrases, often referring to inner emotional states (Perlmann & Gleason, 1990).

Do such differences in language directed at boys and girls during infancy affect their behavior as adults? Although there is no direct evidence that plainly supports such an association, it is clear that men and women use different sorts of language as adults. For instance, as adults, women tend to use more tentative, less assertive language than men. While we don't know if these differences are a reflection of early linguistic experiences, such findings are certainly intriguing (Matlin, 1987; Tannen, 1991; Leaper, Anderson, & Sanders, 1998).

Figure 5-8 **Diminishing Diminutives**

While the use of diminutives toward both male and female infants declines with age, they are consistently used more often in speech directed at females. What do you think is the cultural significance of this?

(*Source:* Gleason et al., 1991.)

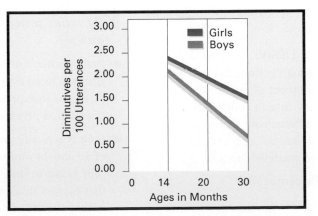

Review and Rethink

REVIEW

- Before they speak, infants understand many adult utterances and engage in several forms of prelinguistic communication, including the use of facial expressions, gestures, and babbling.

- Children typically produce their first words between 10 and 14 months, and rapidly increase their vocabularies from that point on, especially during a spurt at about 18 months.

- Children's language development proceeds through a pattern of holophrases, two-word combinations, and telegraphic speech.

- Learning theorists believe that basic learning processes account for language development, whereas Noam Chomsky and his followers argue that humans have an innate language capacity. The interactionists suggest that language is a consequence of both environmental and innate factors.

- When talking to infants, adults of all cultures tend to use infant-directed speech.

RETHINK

- What are some ways in which children's linguistic development reflects their acquisition of new ways of interpreting and dealing with their world?

- What are some implications of differences in the ways adults speak to boys and girls? How might such speech differences contribute to later differences not only in speech, but also in attitudes?

Looking Back

What are the fundamental features of Piaget's theories of cognitive development?

- Jean Piaget's stage theory asserts that children pass through stages of cognitive development in a fixed order. The stages represent changes not only in the quantity of infants' knowledge, but in the quality of that knowledge as well.

- According to Piaget, all children pass gradually through the four major stages of cognitive development (sensorimotor, preoperational, concrete operational, and formal operational) and their various substages when the children are at an appropriate level of maturation and are exposed to relevant types of experiences.

- In the Piagetian view, children's understanding grows through assimilation of their experiences into their current way of thinking or through accommodation of their current way of thinking to their experiences.

- During the sensorimotor period (birth to about 2 years) with its six substages, infants progress from the use of simple reflexes, through the development of repeated and integrated actions that gradually increase in complexity, to the ability to generate purposeful effects from their actions. By the end of the sixth substage of the sensorimotor period, infants are beginning to engage in symbolic thought.

How do infants process information?

- Information-processing approaches to the study of cognitive development seek to learn how individuals receive, organize, store, and retrieve information. Such approaches differ from Piaget's by considering quantitative changes in children's abilities to process information.

- Infants have memory capabilities from their earliest days, although the accuracy of infant memories is a matter of debate.

How is infant intelligence measured?

- Traditional measures of infant intelligence, such as Gesell's developmental quotient and the Bayley Scales of Infant Development, focus on average behavior observed at particular ages in large numbers of children.

- Information-processing approaches to assessing intelligence rely on variations in the speed and quality with which infants process information.

By what processes do children learn to use language?

- Prelinguistic communication involves the use of sounds, gestures, facial expressions, imitation, and other nonlinguistic means to express thoughts and states. Prelinguistic communication prepares the infant for speech.

- Infants typically produce their first words between the ages of 10 and 14 months. At around 18 months, children typically begin to link words together into primitive sentences that express single thoughts. Beginning speech is characterized by the use of holophrases, telegraphic speech, underextension, and overextension.

■ The learning theory approach to language acquisition assumes that adults and children use basic behavioral processes—such as conditioning, reinforcement, and shaping—in language learning. A different approach proposed by Chomsky holds that humans are genetically endowed with a language-acquisition device, which permits them to detect and use the principles of universal grammar that underlie all languages.

▶ *How do children influence adults' language?*

■ Adult language is influenced by the children to whom it is addressed. Infant-directed speech takes on characteristics, surprisingly invariant across cultures, that make it appealing to infants and that probably encourage language development.

■ Adult language also exhibits differences based on the gender of the child to whom it is directed, which may have effects that emerge later in life.

EPILOGUE

In this chapter we looked at infants' cognitive development from the perspective of Jean Piaget, focusing on the substages of the sensorimotor stage through which infants pass in the first 2 years of life. We also looked at a different perspective on infant development based on information-processing theory. We examined infant learning, memory, and intelligence, and we concluded the chapter with a look at language.

Turn to the prologue of this chapter, about Paige Arbeiter, an infant with a hearing disorder, and answer the following questions.

1. Paige's hearing disorder was not properly diagnosed until she was 10 months old. What elements of linguistic development did Paige probably miss?

2. Do you think a child who misses the first year of linguistic development because of a disorder, and then completely recovers from the disorder, will learn to speak? In what ways will her development be different from others'? Why?

3. Do you think Paige, who could apparently make sounds despite her imperfect hearing, babbled verbally during her first year? Did she babble in any other way? Why?

4. If Paige had been raised by deaf parents who used sign language, do you think Paige would have developed sign language as a normal aspect of her development?

5. Do hearing children raised by deaf parents learn to use sign language through the same process as other children learn to speak? Do you think such children also develop spoken language? Why?

Key Terms and Concepts

scheme (p. 153)
assimilation (p. 153)
accommodation (p. 153)
sensorimotor stage (of cognitive development) (p. 154)
circular reaction (p. 156)
goal-directed behavior (p. 156)
object permanence (p. 156)
mental representation (p. 158)
deferred imitation (p. 158)
information-processing approaches (p. 161)

memory (p. 163)
infantile amnesia (p. 164)
developmental quotient (p. 166)
Bayley Scales of Infant Development (p. 166)
visual-recognition memory (p. 168)
cross-modal transference (p. 168)
language (p. 171)
prelinguistic communication (p. 173)
babbling (p. 173)
holophrases (p. 175)

telegraphic speech (p. 177)
underextension (p. 177)
overextension (p. 177)
referential style (p. 177)
expressive style (p. 177)
learning theory approach (p. 178)
nativist approach (p. 178)
universal grammar (p. 178)
language-acquisition device (LAD) (p. 178)
infant-directed speech (p. 179)

Social and Personality Development in Infancy

PROLOGUE: THE VELCRO CHRONICLES

Infants not only learn desirable behaviors, but less positive ones (like shoe removal techniques), through observation of their more "expert" peers.

It was during the windy days of March that the problem in the child care center first arose. Its source: 10-month-old Russell Ruud. Otherwise a model of decorum, Russell had somehow learned how to unzip the Velcro chin strap to his winter hat. He would remove the hat whenever he got the urge, seemingly oblivious to the potential health problems that might follow.

But that was just the start of the real difficulty. To the chagrin of the teachers in the child-care center, not to speak of the children's parents, soon other children were following his lead, removing their own caps at will.

Russell's mother, made aware of the anarchy at the child care center—and the other parents' distress over Russell's behavior—pleaded innocent. "I never showed Russell how to unzip the Velcro," claimed his mother, Judith Ruud, an economist with the Congressional Budget Office in Washington, D.C. "He learned by trial and error, and the other kids saw him do it one day when they were getting dressed for an outing." (Goleman, 1993, C10)

By then, though, it was too late for excuses: Russell, it seems, was an excellent teacher. Keeping the children's hats on their heads proved to be no easy task. Even more ominous was the thought that if the infants could master the Velcro straps on their hats, would they soon be unfastening the Velcro straps on their shoes and removing *them*?

Looking Ahead   Russell's behavior embodies what recent research suggests is a heretofore unsuspected outcome of infants' participation in child care: the acquisition of new skills and abilities from more "expert" peers. Infants, as we will see, have an amazing capacity to learn from other children, and their interactions with others can play a central role in their developing social and emotional worlds.

In this chapter we consider social and personality development in infancy. We begin by examining the emotional lives of infants, considering which emotions they feel and how well they can decode others' emotions. We also consider how infants use others to shape their own reactions and how they view their own and others' mental lives.

We then turn to a consideration of infants' social relationships. We look at how they forge bonds of attachment and the ways they interact with family members and peers.

Finally, we cover the characteristics that differentiate one infant from another. We'll discuss differences in the way children are treated depending on their gender. We'll consider the nature of family life as the 21st century begins and discuss how it differs from earlier eras. The chapter closes with a look at the advantages and disadvantages of infant child care outside the home, a child-care option that today's families increasingly employ.

After reading this chapter, you will be able to answer these questions:

▶ **What sort of emotional lives do infants have?**

▶ **What sort of mental lives do infants have?**

▶ **What is attachment in infancy and how does it relate to the future social competence of individuals?**

▶ **What roles do other people play in infants' social development?**

▶ **What sorts of individual differences do infants display?**

▶ **Is child care beneficial or harmful for infants?**

Forming the Roots of Sociability

Germaine smiles when he catches a glimpse of his mother. Tawanda looks angry when her mother takes away the spoon that she is playing with. Sydney scowls when a loud plane flies overhead.

A smile. A look of anger. A scowl. The emotions of infancy are written all over a baby's face. Yet do infants experience emotions in the same way that adults do? When do they become capable of understanding what others are experiencing emotionally? And how do they use others' emotional states to make sense of their environment? We consider some of these questions as we seek to understand how infants develop emotionally and socially.

Emotions in Infancy: Do Infants Experience Emotional Highs and Lows?

Anyone who spends any time at all around infants knows they display facial expressions that seem indicative of their emotional states. In situations in which we expect them to be happy, they seem to smile; when we might assume they are frustrated, they show anger; and when we might expect them to be unhappy, they look sad.

In fact, these basic facial expressions are remarkably similar across the most diverse cultures. Whether we look at babies in India, the United States, or the jungles of New

Guinea, the expression of basic emotions is the same (see Figure 6-1). Furthermore, the nonverbal expression of emotion, called *nonverbal encoding,* is fairly consistent throughout the life span. These consistencies have led researchers to conclude that we are born with the capacity to display basic emotions (Feldman, 1982; Camras, Malatesta, & Izard, 1991; Ekman & O'Sullivan, 1991; Izard et al., 1995).

Infants appear to display a fairly wide range of emotional expressions. According to research on what mothers see in their children's nonverbal behavior, almost all think that by the age of 1 month, their babies have expressed interest and joy. In addition, 84 percent of mothers think their infants have expressed anger, 75 percent surprise, 58 percent fear, and 34 percent sadness (Johnson et al., 1982; Sroufe, 1996).

Although infants display similar *kinds* of emotions, the *degree* of emotional expressivity varies between different infants. In fact, reliable differences in expressivity are found between children in different cultures, even during infancy. For example, developmental psychologist Linda Camras and colleagues have found that at the age of 11 months, Chinese infants are generally less expressive than European, American, and Japanese infants (Camras et al., 1998; Kochanska et al., 1998; Eisenberg et al., 2000).

Experiencing Emotions. Does the capability of infants to express emotions nonverbally in a consistent, reliable manner mean that they actually *experience* emotions, and—if they do—is the experience similar to that of adults? These questions are not easy to answer.

The fact that children display nonverbal expressions in a manner similar to that of adults does not necessarily mean that the actual experience is identical. In fact, if the nature of such displays is innate, or inborn, it is possible that facial expressions can occur without any accompanying emotional experience. Nonverbal expressions, then, might be emotionless in young infants, in much the same way that your knee reflexively jerks forward when a physician taps it, without the involvement of emotions (Soussignan et al., 1997).

However, most developmental researchers think otherwise: They argue that the nonverbal expressions of infants represent emotional experiences. In fact, developmental psy-

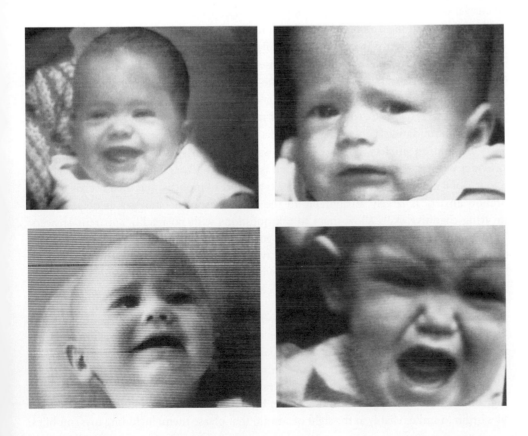

Figure 6-1 **Universals in Facial Expressions**

Across every culture, infants show similar facial expressions relating to basic emotions. Do you think such expressions are similar in nonhuman animals?

differential emotions theory Izard's theory that emotional expressions reflect emotional experiences and help in the regulation of emotion itself

stranger anxiety the caution and wariness displayed by infants when encountering an unfamiliar person

separation anxiety the distress displayed by infants when a customary care provider departs

chologist Carroll Izard suggests in his **differential emotions theory** that emotional expressions not only reflect emotional experiences, but also help regulate the emotion itself. Izard suggests that infants are born with an innate repertoire of emotional expressions, reflecting basic emotional states. As infants and children grow older, they expand and modify these basic expressions and become more adept at controlling their nonverbal behavioral expressions. Furthermore, Izard suggests that in addition to becoming able to express a wider variety of emotions, we also become able to experience a wider array of emotions (Izard & Malatesta, 1987; Camras, Malatesta, & Izard, 1991; Buss & Goldsmith, 1998).

In sum, infants do appear to experience emotions, although the range of emotions at birth is fairly restricted. However, as they get older, infants both display and experience a wider range of increasingly complex emotions (Fox, 1994; Sroufe, 1996).

Stranger Anxiety and Separation Anxiety. "She used to be such a friendly baby," thought Erika's mother. "No matter who she encountered, she had a big smile. But now, I don't know what's happened. Almost the day she turned 7 months old, she began to react to strangers as if she were seeing a ghost. Her face crinkles up with a frown, and she either turns away or stares at them with suspicion. And she doesn't want to be left with anyone she doesn't already know. It's as if she has undergone a personality transplant."

What happened to Erika is, in fact, quite typical. By the end of the first year, infants often develop both stranger anxiety and separation anxiety. **Stranger anxiety** is the caution and wariness displayed by infants when encountering an unfamiliar person. Such anxiety typically appears in the second half of the first year.

What brings on stranger anxiety? One basic cause is the increased cognitive abilities of infants, allowing them to separate the people they know from the people they don't. The same cognitive advances that allow them to respond so positively to those people with whom they are familiar also give them the ability to recognize people who are unfamiliar. Furthermore, between 6 and 9 months, infants begin trying to make sense of their world. When something happens that they can't make sense of—such as with the appearance of an unknown person—they experience fear. It's as if an infant has a question but is unable to answer it (Ainsworth, 1973; Kagan, Kearsley, & Zelazo, 1978).

Although stranger anxiety is common after the age of 6 months, significant differences exist between children. Some infants, particularly those who have a lot of experience with strangers, tend to show less anxiety than those whose experience with strangers is limited. Furthermore, not all strangers evoke the same reaction. For instance, infants tend to show less anxiety with female strangers than with male strangers. In addition, they react more positively to strangers who are children than to strangers who are adults, perhaps because their size is less intimidating (Lenssen, 1973; Brooks & Lewis, 1976; Thompson & Limber, 1990).

Separation anxiety is the distress displayed by infants when a customary care provider departs. Separation anxiety, which is universal across cultures, usually begins at about 7 or 8 months (see Figure 6-2). It peaks around 14 months, and then decreases. Separation anxiety is largely attributable to the same reasons as stranger anxiety. Infants' growing cognitive skills allow them to ask questions with no readily apparent answers: "Why is my mother leaving?" "Where is she going?" and "Will she come back?"

Stranger anxiety and separation anxiety represent important social progress. They reflect both cognitive advances and the growing emotional and social bonds between infants and their caregivers—bonds that we'll consider later in the chapter when we discuss infants' social relationships.

Smiling. As Luz lay sleeping in her crib, her mother and father caught a glimpse of the most beautiful smile crossing her face. Her parents were sure that Luz was having a pleasant dream. Were they right?

Probably not. The earliest smiles expressed during sleep probably have little meaning, although no one can be absolutely sure. However, by 6 to 9 weeks it is clear that babies begin to smile reliably at the sight of stimuli that please them, including toys, mobiles,

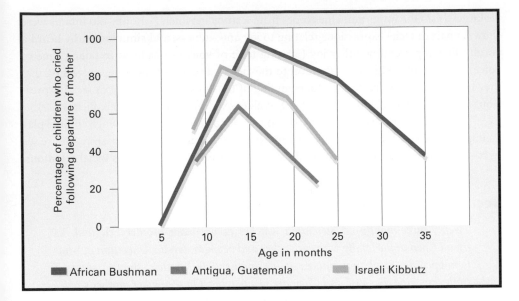

Figure 6-2 **Separation Anxiety**

Separation anxiety, the distress displayed by infants when their usual care provider leaves their presence, is a universal phenomenon beginning at around the age of 7 or 8 months. It peaks at around the age of 14 months and then begins to decline. Does separation anxiety have survival value for humans?

(*Source:* Kagan, Kearsley, & Zelazo, 1978.)

and—to the delight of parents—people. The first smiles tend to be relatively indiscriminate, as infants first begin to smile at the sight of almost anything they find amusing. However, as they get older, they become more selective in their smiles.

A baby's smile in response to another person, rather than to nonhuman stimuli, is considered a **social smile.** As babies get older, their social smiles become directed toward particular individuals, not just anyone (Wolff, 1963). By the age of 18 months, social smiling, directed more toward mothers and other caregivers, becomes more frequent than smiling directed toward nonhuman objects. Moreover, if an adult is unresponsive to a child, the amount of smiling decreases. In short, by the end of the second year children are quite purposefully using smiling to communicate their positive emotions, and they are sensitive to the emotional expressions of others (Toda & Fogel, 1993; Dickson, Walker, & Fogel, 1997; Messinger & Fogel, 1998; Carvajal & Iglesias, 2000; Fogel et al., 2000).

social smile smiling in response to other individuals

Decoding Others' Facial and Vocal Expressions. You may recall from Chapter 3 that neonates are able to imitate adults' facial expressions, a capability that is apparent even minutes after birth (Kaitz et al., 1988; Reissland, 1988). Although their imitative abilities certainly do not imply that they can understand the meaning of others' facial expressions, such imitation does pave the way for *nonverbal decoding* abilities, which begin to emerge fairly soon. Using these abilities, infants can interpret others' facial and vocal expressions that carry emotional meaning (Slater & Butterworth, 1997; Walker-Andrews, 1997).

Infants seem to be able to discriminate vocal expressions of emotion at a slightly earlier age than they discriminate facial expressions. Although relatively little attention has been given to infants' perception of vocal expressions, it does appear that they are able to discriminate happy and sad vocal expressions at the age of 5 months (Walker-Andrews & Lennon, 1991; Soken & Pick, 1999).

Scientists know more about the *sequence* in which nonverbal facial decoding ability progresses. In the first 6 to 8 weeks, infants' visual precision is sufficiently limited that they cannot pay much attention to others' facial expressions. But they soon begin to discriminate among different facial expressions of emotion and even seem to be able to respond to differences in emotional intensity conveyed by facial expressions. They also respond to unusual facial expressions. For instance, they show distress when their mothers pose bland, unresponsive, neutral facial expressions (Lamb, Morrison, & Malkin, 1987; Nelson, 1987).

By the time they reach the age of 4 months, infants may already have begun to understand the emotions that lie behind the facial and vocal expressions of others. How do

When infants smile at a person, rather than a nonhuman stimulus, they are displaying a social smile.

we know this? One important clue comes from a study in which 7-month-old infants were shown a pair of facial expressions relating to joy and sadness, and simultaneously heard a vocalization representing either joy (a rising tone of voice) or sadness (a falling tone of voice). The infants paid more attention to the face that matched the tone, suggesting that they had at least a rudimentary understanding of the emotional meaning of facial expressions and voice tones (Phillips et al., 1990; Walker-Andrews, 1997; Soken & Pick, 1999).

In sum, infants learn early both to produce and to decode emotions. Such abilities play an important role not only in helping them experience their own emotions, but—as we see next—in using others' emotions to understand the meaning of ambiguous social situations.

Social Referencing: Feeling What Others Feel

Twenty-three-month-old Stephania watches as her older brother Eric and his friend Chen argue loudly with each other and begin to wrestle. Uncertain of what is happening, Stephania glances at her mother. Her mother, though, wears a smile, knowing that Eric and Chen are just playing. On seeing her mother's reaction, Stephania smiles too, mimicking her mother's facial expression.

Like Stephania, most of us have been in situations in which we feel uncertain. In such cases, we sometimes turn to others to see how they are reacting. This reliance on others, known as social referencing, helps us decide what an appropriate response ought to be.

social referencing the intentional search for information about others' feelings to help explain the meaning of uncertain circumstances and events

Social referencing is the intentional search for information about others' feelings to help explain the meaning of uncertain circumstances and events. Social referencing is used to clarify the meaning of a situation by reducing our uncertainty about what is occurring.

Social referencing first tends to occur around the age of 8 or 9 months. It is a fairly sophisticated social ability: Infants need it not only to understand the significance of others' behavior, such as their facial expressions, but also to realize that others' behavior has meaning with reference to specific circumstances (Waldon & Ogan, 1988; Rosen, Adamson, & Bakeman, 1992).

Infants make particular use of facial expressions in their social referencing, the way Stephania did when she noticed her mother's smile. For instance, in one study infants were given an unusual toy to play with. The amount of time they played with it depended on their mothers' facial expressions. When their mothers displayed disgust, they played with it significantly less than when their mothers appeared pleased. Furthermore, when given the opportunity to play with the same toy later, the infants revealed lasting consequences of their mothers' earlier behavior, despite the mothers' now neutral-appearing facial reactions (Hornik & Gunnar, 1988).

Although it is clear that social referencing begins fairly early in life, researchers are still not certain *how* it operates. Consider, for instance, one possibility: It may be that observing someone else's facial expression brings about the emotion the expression represents. That is, an infant who views someone looking sad may come to feel sad herself, and her behavior may be affected. On the other hand, it may be the case that viewing another's facial expression simply provides information. In this case, the infant does not experience the particular emotion represented by another's facial expression; she simply uses the display as data to guide her own behavior.

Both explanations for social referencing have received support, and so we still don't know which is correct. What we do know is that social referencing is most likely to occur when a situation breeds uncertainty and ambiguity. Furthermore, infants who reach the age when they are able to use social referencing become quite upset if they receive conflicting nonverbal messages from their mothers and fathers. Mixed messages, then, are a real source of stress for an infant (Walden & Baxter, 1989; Hirshberg, 1990; Hirshberg & Svejda, 1990; Camras & Sachs, 1991).

The Development of Self: Do Infants Know Who They Are?

Elysa, 8 months old, crawls past the full-length mirror that hangs on a door in her parents' bedroom. She barely pays any attention to her reflection as she moves by. On the other hand, her cousin Brianna, who is almost 2 years old, stares at herself in the mirror as she passes, and laughs as she sees, and then rubs, a smear of jelly on her forehead.

Perhaps you have had the experience of catching a glimpse of yourself in a mirror and noticing a hair out of place. You probably reacted by attempting to push the unruly hair back into place. Your reaction shows more than that you care about how you look. It implies that you have a sense of yourself, the awareness and knowledge that you are an independent social entity to which others react, and which you attempt to present to the world in ways that reflect favorably upon you.

However, we are not born with the knowledge that we exist independently from others and the larger world. Although it is difficult to demonstrate, the youngest infants do not seem to have a sense of themselves as individuals. They do not recognize likenesses of themselves, whether in photos or in mirrors, and they show no evidence of being able to distinguish themselves from other people (Gallup, 1977).

The roots of **self-awareness,** knowledge of oneself, begin to grow at around the age of 12 months. We know this from a simple but ingenious experimental technique known as the *mirror-and-rouge task.* In it, an infant's nose is secretly colored with a dab of red rouge, and the infant is seated in front of a mirror. If infants touch their noses or attempt to wipe off the rouge, we have evidence that they have at least some knowledge of their physical characteristics. For them, this awareness is one step in developing an understanding of themselves as independent objects. For instance, Brianna, in the example at the beginning of this section showed her awareness of her independence when she tried to rub the jam off her forehead.

self-awareness knowledge of oneself

Although some infants as young as 12 months seem startled on seeing the rouge spot, for most a reaction does not occur until between 17 and 24 months of age. It is also around this age that children begin to show awareness of their own capabilities. For instance, infants who participate in experiments when they are between the ages of 23 and 25 months sometimes begin to cry if the experimenter asks them to imitate a complicated sequence of behaviors involving toys, although they readily accomplish simpler sequences.

Research suggests that this 18-month-old is exhibiting a clearly developed sense of self.

According to developmental psychologist Jerome Kagan (1981), their reaction suggests that they are conscious that they lack the capability to carry out difficult tasks and are unhappy about it—a reaction that provides a clear indication of self-awareness (Asendorpf, Warkentin, & Baudonniere, 1996; Legerstee, 1998).

In sum, by the age of 18 to 24 months, infants have developed at least the rudiments of awareness of their own physical characteristics and capabilities, and they understand that their appearance is stable over time. Although it is not clear how far this awareness extends, it is becoming increasingly evident that, as we discuss next, infants have not only a basic understanding of themselves, but also the beginnings of an understanding of how the mind operates—what has come to be called a "theory of mind" (Moore, 1996; Legerstee, Anderson, & Schaffer, 1998; Mitchell & Riggs, 1999).

Theory of Mind: Infants' Perspectives on the Mental Lives of Others—and Themselves

theory of mind children's knowledge and beliefs about their mental world

empathy an emotional response that corresponds to the feelings of another person

What are infants' thoughts about thinking? According to developmental psychologist John Flavell, infants begin to understand certain things about the mental processes of themselves and others at quite an early age. Flavell has investigated children's **theory of mind,** their knowledge and beliefs about the mental world. Theories of mind are the explanations that children use to explain how others think. For instance, cognitive advances during infancy permit older infants to come to see people in very different ways from how they view other objects. They learn to see others as *compliant agents,* beings similar to themselves who behave under their own power and who have the capacity to respond to infants' requests (Flavell, Green, & Flavell, 1995; Rochat, 1999). Eighteen-month-old Chris, for example, has come to realize that he can ask his father to get him more juice.

In addition, children's capacity to understand intentionality and causality grows during infancy. They begin to understand that others' behaviors have some meaning and that the behaviors they see people enacting are designed to accomplish particular goals, in contrast to the "behaviors" of inanimate objects (Parritz, Mangelsdorf, & Gunnar, 1992; Gelman & Kalish, 1993; Golinkoff, 1993).

By the age of 2, infants begin to demonstrate the rudiments of empathy. **Empathy** is an emotional response that corresponds to the feelings of another person. At 24 months of age, infants sometimes comfort others or show concern for them. In order to do this, they need to be aware of others' emotional states. Further, during their second year, infants begin to use deception, both in games of "pretend" and in outright attempts to fool others. A child who plays "pretend" and who uses falsehoods must be aware that others hold beliefs about the world—beliefs that can be manipulated. In short, by the end of infancy children have developed the rudiments of their own personal theory of mind. It helps them understand the actions of others and it affects their own behavior (Moses & Chandler, 1992; Zahn-Waxler, Robinson, & Emde, 1992; Lee & Homer, 1999).

Review and Rethink

REVIEW

- Infants appear to express and to experience emotions, which broaden in range to reflect increasingly complex emotional states.
- Infants from different cultures use similar facial expressions to express basic emotional states.
- Infants begin to experience stranger anxiety at about 6 months and separation anxiety at around 8 months of age.

- The ability to decode the nonverbal facial and vocal expressions of others develops early in infants. The use of nonverbal decoding to clarify situations of uncertainty and determine appropriate responses is called *social referencing.*
- Infants develop self-awareness, the knowledge that they exist separately from the rest of the world, after about 12 months of age.
- By the age of 2, children have developed the rudiments of a theory of mind.

The foundations of empathy, emotional responses that correspond to the feelings of another person, are forged in the early years of life.

RETHINK

■ If the facial expressions that convey basic emotions are similar across cultures, how do such expressions arise? Can you think of facial expressions that are culture-specific? How do they arise?

■ In what situations do adults rely on social referencing to work out appropriate responses? How might social referencing be used to manipulate individuals' responses?

Forging Relationships

Louis Moore became the center of attention on the way home [from the hospital]. His father brought Martha, aged 5, and Tom, aged 3, to the hospital with him when Louis and his mother were discharged. Martha rushed to see "her" new baby and ignored her mother. Tom clung to his mother's knees in the reception hall of the hospital.

A hospital nurse carried Louis to the car. . . . The two older children immediately climbed over the seat and swamped mother and baby with their attention. Both children stuck their faces into his, smacked at him, and talked to him. They soon began to fight over him with loud voices. The loud argument and the jostling of his mother upset Louis, and he started to cry. He let out a wail that came like a shotgun blast into the noisy car. The children quieted immediately and looked with awe at this new infant. His insistent wails drowned out their bickering. He had already asserted himself in their eyes. Martha's lip quivered as she watched her mother attempt to comfort Louis, and she added her own soft cooing in imitation of her mother. Tom squeezed even closer to his mother, put his thumb in his mouth, and closed his eyes to shut out the commotion. (Brazelton, 1983, p. 48)

The arrival of a newborn brings a dramatic change to a family's dynamics. No matter how welcome a baby's birth, it causes a fundamental shift in the roles that people play within the family. Mothers and fathers must start to build a relationship with their infant, and older children must adjust to the presence of a new member of the family and build their own alliance with their infant brother or sister.

Although the process of social development during infancy is neither simple nor automatic, it is crucial: The bonds that grow between infants and their parents, family, and others provide the foundation for a lifetime's worth of social relationships.

cw

attachment the positive emotional bond that develops between a child and a particular individual

Attachment: Forming Social Bonds

The most important form of social development that takes place during infancy is attachment. **Attachment** is the positive emotional bond that develops between a child and a particular, special individual. When children experience attachment to a given person, they feel pleasure when they are with them and feel comforted by their presence at times of distress. As we'll see when we consider social development in early adulthood (Chapter 14), the nature of our attachment during infancy affects how we relate to others throughout the rest of our lives (Beckwith, Cohen, & Hamilton, 1999; Hamilton, 2000; Waters et al., 2000; Waters, Weinfield, & Hamilton, 2000).

To understand attachment, the earliest researchers turned to the bonds that form between parents and children in the nonhuman animal kingdom. For instance, ethologist Konrad Lorenz (1965) observed newborn goslings, who have an innate tendency to follow their mother, the first moving object to which they typically are exposed after birth. Lorenz found that goslings whose eggs were raised in an incubator and who viewed him just after hatching would follow his every movement, as if he were their mother. As we discussed in Chapter 3, he labeled this process *imprinting:* behavior that takes place during a critical period and involves attachment to the first moving object that is observed.

Lorenz's findings suggested that attachment was based on biologically determined factors, and other theorists agreed. For instance, Freud suggested that attachment grew out of a mother's ability to satisfy a child's oral needs.

It turns out, however, that the ability to provide food and other physiological needs may not be as crucial as Freud and other theorists first thought. In a classic study, psychologist Harry Harlow gave infant monkeys the choice of cuddling a wire "monkey" that provided food or a soft, terry cloth monkey that was warm but did not provide food (see Figure 6-3). Their preference was clear: They would spend most of their time clinging to the cloth monkey, although they made occasional expeditions to the wire monkey to nurse. Harlow suggested that the preference for the warm cloth monkey provided *contact comfort* (Harlow & Zimmerman, 1959).

Harlow's work clearly illustrates that food alone is insufficient to bring about attachment. Furthermore, given that the monkey's preference for the soft cloth "mothers" developed some time after birth, these findings are consistent with the research we discussed in Chapter 3, showing little support for the existence of a critical bonding period between human mothers and infants immediately following birth.

The earliest work on human attachment, which is still highly influential, was carried out by John Bowlby (1951). Bowlby's theorizing about attachment had a biological basis, although it was supplemented by observations of emotionally disturbed children with whom he worked in a London clinic. Consequently, the theory is an *epigenetic theory*, a developmental theory that stresses the reciprocal interaction between genes and the environment.

In Bowlby's view, attachment is based primarily on infants' needs for safety and security—their genetically determined motivation to avoid predators. As they develop, infants come to learn that their safety is best provided by a particular individual. This realization ultimately leads to the development of a special relationship with that individual, who is typically the mother. Bowlby suggests that this single relationship is qualitatively different from the bonds formed with others, including the father—a suggestion that, as we'll see later, has been a source of some subsequent dispute.

Figure 6-3 **Monkey Mothers Matter**

Harlow's research showed that monkeys preferred the warm, soft "mother" over the wire "monkey" that provided food.

Bowlby also argues that attachment—which has its roots in the desire to seek the protective security of the mother—is critical in allowing an infant to explore the world. According to his view, having strong, firm attachment provides a kind of home base. As children become more independent, they can progressively roam further away from their secure base.

Developmental psychologist Mary Ainsworth built on Bowlby' theorizing to develop a widely used experimental technique to measure attachment (Ainsworth et al., 1978). The **Ainsworth Strange Situation** consists of a sequence of staged episodes that illustrate the strength of attachment between a child and (typically) his or her mother. The "strange situation" follows this general eight-step pattern: (1) The mother and baby enter an unfamiliar room; (2) the mother sits down, leaving the baby free to explore; (3) an adult stranger enters the room and converses first with the mother and then with the baby; (4) the mother exits the room, leaving the baby alone with the stranger; (5) the mother returns, greeting and comforting the baby, and the stranger leaves; (6) the mother departs again, leaving the baby alone; (7) the stranger returns; and (8) the mother returns and the stranger leaves (Ainsworth et al., 1978).

Infants' reactions to the various aspects of the Strange Situation vary considerably, depending on the nature of their attachment to their mothers. Onc-year-olds show three major patterns—securely attached, avoidant, and ambivalent (summarized in Table 6-1). Children who have a **secure attachment pattern** use the mother as the kind of home base that Bowlby described. These children seem at ease in the Strange Situation as long as their mothers are present. They explore independently, returning to her occasionally. Although they may or may not appear upset when she leaves, securely attached children immediately go to her when she returns and seek contact. Most children—about two-thirds—fall into the securely attached category.

In contrast, children with an **avoidant attachment pattern** do not seek proximity to the mother, and after she has left, they typically do not seem distressed. Furthermore, they seem to avoid her when she returns. It is as if they are indifferent to her behavior. Some 20 percent of 1-year-old children are in the avoidant category.

Finally, the last group, those with an **ambivalent attachment pattern,** display a combination of positive and negative reactions to their mothers. Initially, ambivalent children are in such close contact with the mother that they hardly explore their environment. They appear anxious even before the mother leaves, and when she does leave, they show great distress. But upon her return, they show ambivalent reactions, seeking to be close to her but also hitting and kicking, apparently in anger. About 12 percent of 1-year-olds fall into the ambivalent classification (Cassidy & Berlin, 1994).

Although Ainsworth identified only three categories, a more recent expansion of her work suggests that there is a fourth category: disorganized-disoriented. Children who have a **disorganized-disoriented attachment pattern** show inconsistent, often contradictory behavior, such as approaching the mother when she returns but not looking at her. Their confusion suggests that they may be the least securely attached children of all (Egeland & Farber, 1984; O'Connor, Sigman, & Brill, 1987; Mayseless, 1996; Ofra, 1996).

A child's attachment style would be of only minor consequence were it not for the fact that the nature of attachment between infants and their mothers has significant consequences for relationships at later stages of life. For example, boys who are securely attached at the age of 1 year show fewer psychological difficulties at older ages than do avoidant or ambivalent children. Similarly, children who are securely attached as infants tend to be more socially and emotionally competent later, and others view them more positively. Adult romantic relationships are associated with the kind of attachment style developed during infancy (Schneider, Atkinson, & Tardif, 2001).

On the other hand, we cannot say that children who do not have a secure attachment style during infancy invariably experience difficulties later in life, nor that those with

Mary Ainsworth, who devised the Strange Situation to measure infant attachment.

Ainsworth Strange Situation a sequence of staged episodes that illustrate the strength of attachment between a child and (typically) his or her mother

secure attachment pattern a style of attachment in which children use the mother as a kind of home base and are at ease when she is present; when she leaves, they become upset and go to her as soon as she returns

avoidant attachment pattern a style of attachment in which children do not seek proximity to the mother; after the mother has left, they seem to avoid her when she returns as if they are angered by her behavior

ambivalent attachment pattern a style of attachment in which children display a combination of positive and negative reactions to their mothers; they show great distress when the mother leaves, but upon her return they may simultaneously seek close contact but also hit and kick her

disorganized-disoriented attachment pattern a style of attachment in which children show inconsistent, often contradictory behavior, such as approaching the mother when she returns but not looking at her; they may be the least securely attached children of all

In this illustration of the strange situation, the infant first explores the playroom on his own, as long as his mother is present. But when she leaves, he begins to cry. On her return, however, he is immediately comforted and stops crying. The conclusion: he is securely attached.

a secure attachment at age 1 always have good adjustment later on. In fact, some evidence suggests that children with avoidant and ambivalent attachment—as measured by the Strange Situation—do quite well (Vondra & Barnett, 1999; Weinfield, Sroufe, & Egeland, 2000; Lewis, Feiring, & Rosenthal, 2000).

Producing Attachment: The Roles of the Mother and Father

As 5-month-old Annie cries passionately, her mother comes into the room and gently lifts her from her crib. After just a few moments, as her mother rocks Annie and speaks softly, Annie's cries cease, and she cuddles in her mother's arms. But the moment her mother places her back in the crib, Annie begins to wail again, leading her mother to pick her up once again.

The pattern is familiar to most parents. The infant cries, the parent reacts, and the child responds in turn. Such seemingly insignificant sequences as these, repeatedly occurring in the lives of infants and parents, help pave the way for the development of relationships between children, their parents, and the rest of the social world. We'll consider how each of the major caregivers and the infant play a role in the development of attachment.

Mothers and Attachment. Sensitivity to their infants' needs and desires is the hallmark of mothers of securely attached infants. Such a mother tends to be aware of her child's

Table 6-1

CLASSIFICATIONS OF INFANT ATTACHMENT

	CLASSIFICATION CRITERIA				
Label	Seeking Proximity with Caregiver	Maintaining Contact with Caregiver	Avoiding Proximity with Caregiver	Resisting Contact with Caregiver	
Avoidant	Low	Low	High	Low	Low (pre-separation), high or low (separation), low (reunion)
Secure	High	High (if distressed)	Low	Low	Low (pre-separation), high or low (separation), low (reunion)
Ambivalent	High	High (often pre-separation)	Low	High	Occasionally (pre-separation), high (separation), moderate to high (reunion)

(*Source:* Waters, 1978.)

moods, and she takes into account her child's feelings as they interact. She is also responsive during face-to-face interactions, provides feeding "on demand," and is warm and affectionate to her infant (Ainsworth, 1993; DeWolff & van IJzendoorn, 1997).

It is not only a matter of responding in *any* fashion to their infants' signals that separates mothers of securely attached and insecurely attached children. Mothers of secure infants tend to provide the appropriate level of response. In fact, research has shown that overly responsive mothers are just as likely to have insecurely attached children as underresponsive mothers. In contrast, mothers whose communication involves *interactional synchrony*, in which caregivers respond to infants appropriately and both caregiver and child match emotional states, are more likely to produce secure attachment (Belsky, Rovine, & Taylor, 1984; Kochanskya, 1998).

The research showing the correspondence between mothers' sensitivity to their infants and the security of the infants' attachment is consistent with Ainsworth's arguments that attachment depends on how mothers react to their infants' social overtures. Ainsworth suggests that mothers of securely attached infants respond rapidly and positively to their infants. For example, Annie's mother responds quickly to her cries by cuddling and comforting her. In contrast, the way for mothers to produce insecurely attached infants, according to Ainsworth, is to ignore their behavioral cues, to behave inconsistently with them, and to ignore or reject their social efforts.

But how do mothers know how to respond to their infants' cues? One answer is that they learn from their own mothers. For instance, mothers tend to have attachment styles that are similar to those developed by their infants. In fact, some research finds substantial stability in attachment patterns from one generation to the next (Boit & Parker, 1994).

In part, mothers' (and others') behavior toward infants is a reaction to the children's ability to provide effective cues. A mother may not be able to respond effectively to a child whose own behavior is unrevealing, misleading, or ambiguous. The kind of signals an infant sends may in part determine how successful the mother will be in responding.

Fathers and Attachment. Up to now, we've barely touched upon one of the key players involved in the upbringing of a child: the father. In fact, if you looked at the early theorizing and research on attachment, you'd find little mention of the father and his potential contributions to the life of the infant (Russell & Radojevic, 1992; Tamis-LeMonda & Cabrera, 1999).

There are at least two reasons for this absence. First, John Bowlby, who provided the initial theory of attachment, suggested that there was something unique about the mother–child relationship. He believed the mother was uniquely equipped, biologically, to provide sustenance for the child, and he concluded that this capability led to the development of a special relationship between mothers and children. Second, the early work on attachment was influenced by the traditional social views of the time, which considered it "natural" for the mother to be the primary caregiver, while the father's role was to work outside the home to provide a living for his family.

Several factors led to the demise of this view. One was that societal norms changed, and fathers began to take a more active role in childrearing activities. More important, it became increasingly clear from research findings that—despite societal norms that relegated fathers to secondary childrearing roles—some infants formed their primary initial relationship with their fathers (Lamb, 1982b; Goossens & van IJzendoorn, 1990; Volling & Belsky, 1992).

In addition, a growing body of research showed the critical importance of fathers' demonstrations of love for their children, revealed by fathers' nurturance, warmth, affection, support, and concern. In fact, certain kinds of psychological disorders, such as substance abuse and depression, have been found to be related more to fathers' than mothers'

A growing body of research highlights the importance of a father's demonstration of love for his children. In fact, certain disorders such as depression and substance abuse have been found to be more related to fathers' than mothers' behavior.

behavior. In short, evidence of the importance of fathers' behavior has been growing (Rohner, 1998; Tamis-LeMonda & Cabrera, 1999).

Other research reveals that infants may develop strong attachment relationships with multiple individuals simultaneously. For example, one study found that although most infants formed their first primary relationship with one person, around one-third had multiple relationships, and it was difficult to determine which attachment was primary. Furthermore, by the time the infants were 18 months old, most had formed multiple relationships. In sum, infants may develop attachments not only to their mothers, but to a variety of others as well (Fox, Kimmerly, & Schafer, 1991; Rosen & Burke, 1999; Silverstein & Auerbach, 1999).

Are There Differences in Attachment to Mothers and Fathers? Although infants are fully capable of forming attachments to both mother and father—as well as other individuals—the nature of attachment between infants and mothers, on the one hand, and infants and fathers, on the other hand, is not identical. For example, when they are in unusually stressful circumstances, most infants prefer to be soothed by their mothers rather than by their fathers (Lamb, 1977; Cox et al., 1992; Pipp, Easterbrooks, & Brown, 1993).

One reason for qualitative differences in attachment involves the differences in what fathers and mothers do with their children. Mothers spend a greater proportion of their time feeding and directly nurturing their children. In contrast, fathers spend more time, proportionally, playing with infants. Almost all fathers do contribute to child care: Surveys show that 95 percent say they do some child-care chores every day. But on average they still do less than mothers. For instance, 30 percent of fathers with wives who work do 3 or more hours of daily child care. In comparison, 74 percent of employed married mothers spend that amount of time every day in child-care activities (Jacobsen & Edmondson, 1993; Bailey, 1994; Grych & Clark, 1999; Kazura, 2000).

Furthermore, the nature of fathers' play with their babies is often quite different from that of mothers. Fathers engage in more physical, rough-and-tumble activities with their children. In contrast, mothers play traditional games such as peek-a-boo and games with more verbal elements (Lamb, 1986; Parke, 1990, 1996).

The differences in the ways that fathers and mothers play with their children occur even in families in which the father is the primary caregiver. Based on this observation, how does culture affect attachment?

These differences in the ways that fathers and mothers play with their children occur even in the minority of families in the United States in which the father is the primary caregiver. Moreover, the differences occur in very diverse cultures: Fathers in Australia, Israel, India, Japan, Mexico, and even in the Aka Pygmy tribe in central Africa all engage more in play than in caregiving, although the amount of time they spend with their infants varies widely. For instance, Aka fathers spend more time caring for their infants than members of any other known culture, holding and cuddling their babies at a rate some five times higher than anywhere else in the world (Lamb, 1987; Roopnarine, 1992; Engle & Breaux, 1998).

These similarities and differences in child-rearing practices across different societies raise an important question: How does culture affect attachment?

Developmental Diversity

Does Attachment Differ Across Cultures?

Recall that the work on attachment was initially inspired by John Bowlby's observations of the biologically motivated efforts of the young of other species to seek safety and security. From these observations, Bowlby suggested that seeking attachment was a biological universal, one that we should find not only in other species, but among humans as well. Such reasoning suggests that we should see attachment strivings in all humans, regardless of their culture.

However, research has brought this contention into question. For example, one study of German infants showed that most fell into the avoidant category. Other studies, conducted in Israel and Japan, have found a smaller proportion of infants who were securely attached than in the United States. Finally, comparisons of Chinese and Canadian children show that Chinese children are more inhibited than Canadians in the Strange Situation (Grossmann et al., 1982; Takahashi, 1986; Chen et al., 1998).

Other cross-cultural analyses confirm not only that there are differences in the proportions of infants who fall into the various attachment categories, but that subcultural differences also exist even within particular societies (Sagi, van IJzendoorn, & Koren-Karie, 1991; Sagi et al., 1994, 1995; Rothbaum et al., 2000). Do such findings suggest that we should abandon the notion that attachment is a universal biological tendency?

Not necessarily. On the one hand, it is possible that Bowlby's claim that the desire for attachment is universal was too strongly stated. On the other hand, most of the data on attachment have been obtained by using the Ainsworth Strange Situation, which may not be the most appropriate measure in non-Western cultures. For example, Japanese parents seek to avoid separation and stress during infancy, and they don't strive to foster independence to the same degree as parents in many Western societies. Because of their relative lack of prior experience in separation, then, infants placed in the Strange Situation may experience unusual stress—producing the appearance of less secure attachment in Japanese children. If a different measure of attachment were used, one that might be administered later in infancy, more Japanese infants could likely be classified as secure (Nakagawa, Lamb, & Miyaki, 1992; Mizuta et al., 1996; Vereijken et al., 1997).

More recent approaches view attachment as not entirely biologically determined, but rather as susceptible to cultural norms and expectations. Cross-cultural and within-cultural differences in attachment reflect the nature of the measure employed. Specifically, some developmental specialists suggest that attachment should be viewed as a general tendency, but one that is modifiable according to how actively caregivers in a society seek to

Japanese parents seek to avoid separation and stress during infancy and do not foster independence. As a result, Japanese children often have the appearance of being less securely attached according to the Strange Situation, but using other measurement techniques they may well score higher in attachment.

instill independence in their children. Consequently, secure attachment may be seen earliest in cultures that promote independence, but may be delayed in societies in which independence is a less important cultural value (Harwood, Miller, & Irizarry, 1995; Rothbaum et al., 2000). ☐

Infant Interactions: Developing a Working Relationship

Research on attachment is clear in showing that infants may develop multiple attachment relationships, and that over the course of time the specific individuals with whom the infant is primarily attached may change. These variations in attachment highlight the fact that the development of relationships is an ongoing process, not only during infancy, but throughout our lifetimes.

Which processes underlie the development of relationships during infancy? One answer comes from studies that examine how parents interact with their children. For instance, across almost all cultures, mothers behave in typical ways with their infants. They tend to exaggerate their facial and vocal expressions—the nonverbal equivalent of the infant-directed speech that they use when they speak to infants (as we discussed in Chapter 5). Similarly, they often imitate their infants' behavior, responding to distinctive sounds and movements by repeating them. There are even types of games, such as peek-a-boo, itsy-bitsy spider, and pat-a-cake, that are nearly universal (Field, 1979, 1990; Kochanska, 1997).

mutual regulation model the model in which infants and parents learn to communicate emotional states to one another and to respond appropriately

According to the **mutual regulation model,** infants and parents learn to communicate emotional states to one another and to respond appropriately. For instance, both infant and parent act jointly to regulate turn-taking behavior, with one individual waiting until the other completes a behavioral act before starting another. Consequently, at the age of 3 months, infants and their mothers have about the same influence on each other's behavior. Interestingly, by the age of 6 months, infants have more control over turn-taking, although by the age of 9 months both partners once again become roughly equivalent in terms of mutual influence (Cohn & Tronick, 1989; Tronick, 1998).

One of the ways infants and parents signal each other when they interact is through facial expressions. As we saw earlier in this chapter, even quite young infants are able to read, or decode, the facial expressions of their caregivers, and they react to those expressions (Lelwica & Haviland, 1983; Camras, Malatesta, & Izard, 1991; Anisfeld, 1996).

For example, an infant whose mother, during an experiment, displays a stony, immobile facial expression reacts by making a variety of sounds, gestures, and facial expressions of her own in response to such a puzzling situation—and possibly to elicit some new response from her mother. Infants also show more happiness themselves when their mothers appear happy, and they look at their mothers longer. On the other hand, infants are apt to respond with sad looks and to turn away when their mothers display unhappy expressions (Termin & Izard, 1988).

In short, the development of attachment in infants does not merely represent a reaction to the behavior of the people around them. Instead, there is a process of **reciprocal socialization,** in which infants' behaviors invite further responses from parents and other caregivers. In turn, the caregivers' behaviors bring about a reaction from the child, continuing the cycle. Recall, for instance, Annie, the baby who kept crying to be picked up when her mother put her in her crib. Ultimately, the actions and reactions of parents and child lead to an increase in attachment, forging and strengthening bonds between infants and caregivers. Figure 6-4 summarizes the sequence of infant–caregiver interaction (Bell & Ainsworth, 1972; Ainsworth & Bowlby, 1991; Bradley & Caldwell, 1995).

> **reciprocal socialization** a process in which infants' behaviors invite further responses from parents and other caregivers, which in turn bring about further responses from the infants

Infants' Sociability with Their Peers: Infant–Infant Interaction

How sociable are infants with other children? Although it is clear that they do not form "friendships" in the traditional sense, they do react positively to the presence of peers from early in life, and they engage in rudimentary forms of social interaction (Field, 1990).

Infants' sociability is expressed in several ways. From the earliest months of life, they smile, laugh, and vocalize while looking at their peers. They show more interest in peers than in inanimate objects and pay greater attention to other infants than they do to a mirror image of themselves (Legerstee, Anderson, & Schaffer, 1998). They also begin to show

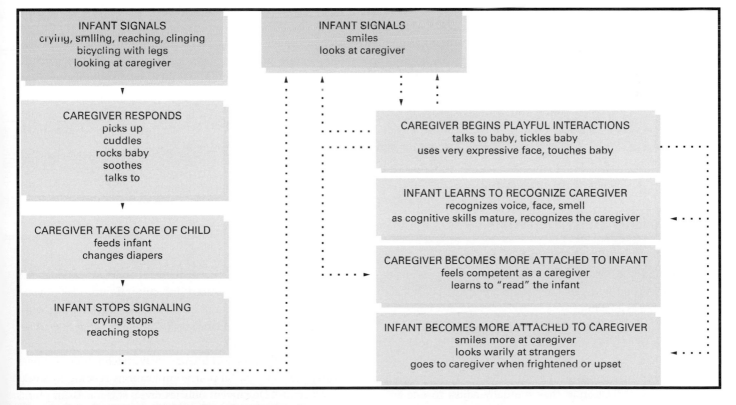

Figure 6-4 **Sequence of Infant–Caregiver Interaction**

The actions and reactions of caregivers and infants influence each other in complex ways. Do you think a similar pattern shows up in adult–adult interactions?

(Adapted from Bell & Ainsworth, 1972; Tomlinson-Keasey, 1985.)

preferences for people with whom they are familiar compared with those they do not know. For example, studies of identical twins show that twins exhibit a higher level of social behavior toward each other than toward an unfamiliar infant (Fogel, 1980; Field & Roopnarine, 1982; Field, 1981, 1990).

Infants' level of sociability generally rises with age. Nine- to twelve-month-olds mutually present and accept toys, particularly if they know each other. They also play social games, such as peek-a-boo or crawl-and-chase (Vincze, 1971; Endo, 1992). Such behavior is important, as it serves as a foundation for future social exchanges in which children will try to elicit responses from others and then offer reactions to those responses (Brownell, 1986; Howes, 1987). These kinds of exchanges are important to learn, since they continue even into adulthood. For example, someone who says, "Hi, what's up?" may be trying to elicit a response to which he or she can then reply.

Finally, as infants age, they begin to imitate each other (Russon & Waite, 1991). For instance, 14-month-old infants who are familiar with one another sometimes reproduce each other's behavior (Mueller & Vandell, 1979). Such imitation serves a social function and can also be a powerful teaching tool. For example, recall the story of 10-month-old Russell Ruud in the chapter prologue, who showed the other children in his child care center how he could remove his hat by unfastening its Velcro straps, and soon had others following his lead.

According to Andrew Meltzoff, a developmental psychologist at the University of Washington, Russell's ability to impart this information is only one example of how so-called "expert" babies are able to teach skills and information to other infants. According to the research of Meltzoff and his colleagues, the abilities learned from the "experts" are retained and later utilized to a remarkable degree. Moreover, learning by exposure starts early in life. For example, recent evidence shows that even 6-week-old infants perform delayed imitation of a novel stimulus to which they have earlier been exposed, such as an adult sticking the tongue out the side of the mouth (Hanna & Meltzoff, 1993; Barr & Hayne, 1999; Meltzoff & Moore, 1994; 1999).

Finding that infants learn new behaviors, skills, and abilities due to exposure to other children has several implications. For one thing, it suggests that interactions between infants provide more than social benefits; they may have an impact on children's future cognitive development as well. Even more important, these findings illustrate a possible benefit that infants derive from participation in child-care centers (which we consider later in this chapter). Although we don't know for sure, the opportunity to learn from their peers may prove to be a lasting advantage for infants in group child-care settings.

Review and Rethink

REVIEW

- Attachment, the positive emotional bond between an infant and a significant individual, relates to a person's later social competence as an adult.
- By the amount of emotion they display nonverbally, infants help determine the nature and quality of their caregivers' responses to them.
- Infants and the persons with whom they interact engage in reciprocal socialization as they mutually adjust to one another's interactions.
- Infants react differently to other children than to inanimate objects, and gradually they engage in increasing amounts of peer social interaction.

RETHINK

- In what sort of society might the attachment style labeled "avoidant" be encouraged by cultural attitudes toward childrearing? In such a society, would characterizing the infant's consistent avoidance of its mother as anger be an accurate interpretation?
- Does the importance of infants' early attachment to primary caregivers have social policy implications relating to working parents? Do current policies reveal societal assumptions pertaining to the different roles of mothers and fathers?

Differences Among Infants

Lincoln was a difficult baby, his parents both agreed. For one thing, it seemed like they could never get him to sleep at night. He cried at the slightest noise, a problem since his crib was near the windows facing a busy street. Worse yet, once he started crying, it seemed to take forever to calm him down again. One day his mother, Aisha, was telling her mother-in-law, Mary, about the challenges of being Lincoln's mom. Mary recalled that her own son, Lincoln's father Malcom, had been much the same way. "He was my first child, and I thought this was how all babies acted. So, we just kept trying different ways until we found out how he worked. I remember, we put his crib all over the apartment until we finally found out where he could sleep, and it ended up being in the hallway for a long time. Then his sister, Maleah, came along, and she was so quiet and easy, I didn't know what to do with my extra time!"

As the story of Lincoln's family shows, babies are not all alike, and neither are their families. In fact, as we'll see, some of the differences among people seem to be present from the moment we are born. The differences among infants include overall personality and temperament, and differences in the lives they lead—differences based on their gender, the nature of their families, and the ways in which they are cared for.

Personality Development: The Characteristics That Make Infants Unique

The origins of **personality,** the sum total of the enduring characteristics that differentiate one individual from another, stem from infancy. From birth onward, infants begin to show unique, stable traits and behaviors that ultimately lead to their development as distinct, special individuals (Caspi, 2000; Kagan, 2000).

According to psychologist Erik Erikson, whose approach to personality development we first discussed in Chapter 1, infants' early experiences are responsible for shaping one of the key aspects of their personalities: whether they will be basically trusting or mistrustful.

Erikson's theory of psychosocial development considers how individuals come to understand themselves and the meaning of others'—and their own—behavior (Erikson, 1963). The theory suggests that developmental change occurs throughout people's lives in eight distinct stages, the first of which occurs in infancy.

According to Erikson, during the first 18 months of life, we pass through the **trust-versus-mistrust stage.** During this period, infants develop a sense of trust or mistrust, largely depending on how well their needs are met by their caregivers. Mary's attention to Malcom's needs, in the example above, probably helped him develop a basic sense of trust in the world. Erikson suggests that if infants are able to develop trust, they experience a sense of hope, which permits them to feel as if they can fulfill their needs successfully. On the other hand, feelings of mistrust lead infants to see the world as harsh and unfriendly, and they may have later difficulties in forming close bonds with others.

During the end of infancy, children enter the **autonomy-versus-shame-and-doubt stage,** which lasts from around 18 months to 3 years. During this period, children develop independence and autonomy if parents encourage exploration and freedom within safe boundaries. However, if children are restricted and overly protected, they feel shame, self-doubt, and unhappiness.

Erikson argues that personality is primarily shaped by infants' experiences. However, as we discuss next, other developmentalists concentrate on consistencies of behavior that are present at birth, even before the experiences of infancy. These consistencies are viewed as largely genetically determined and as providing the raw material of personality.

personality the sum total of the enduring characteristics that differentiate one individual from another

Erikson's theory of psychosocial development the theory that considers how individuals come to understand themselves and the meaning of others'—and their own—behavior

trust-versus-mistrust stage according to Erikson, the period during which infants develop a sense of trust or mistrust, largely depending on how well their needs are met by their caregivers

autonomy-versus-shame-and-doubt stage the period during which, according to Erikson, toddlers (aged 18 months to 3 years) develop independence and autonomy if they are allowed the freedom to explore, or shame and self-doubt if they are restricted and overprotected

According to Erikson, children from 18 months to 3 years develop independence and autonomy if parents encourage exploration and freedom, within safe boundaries. What does Erikson theorize if children are restricted and overly protected at this stage?

Temperament: Stabilities in Infant Behavior

Sarah's parents thought there must be something wrong. Unlike her older brother Josh, who had been so active as an infant that he seemed never to be still, Sarah was much more placid. She took long naps and was easily soothed on those relatively rare occasions when she became agitated. What could be producing her extreme calmness?

The most likely answer: The difference between Sarah and Josh reflected differences in temperament. As we first discussed in Chapter 2, **temperament** encompasses patterns of arousal and emotionality that are consistent and enduring characteristics of an individual (Rothbart, Ahadi, & Evans, 2000).

Temperament refers to *how* children behave, as opposed to *what* they do or *why* they do it. Infants show temperamental differences in general disposition from the time of birth, largely due initially to genetic factors, and temperament tends to be fairly stable well into adolescence. On the other hand, temperament is not fixed and unchangeable: Childrearing practices can modify temperament significantly. In fact, some children show little consistency in temperament from one age to another (Rothbart & Bates, 1998; Lemery et al., 1999; McCrae et al., 2000; Rothbart, Derryberry, & Hershey, 2000).

Temperament is reflected in several dimensions of behavior. One central dimension is *activity level,* which reflects the degree of overall movement. Some babies (like Sarah and Maleah, in the earlier examples) are relatively placid, and their movements are slow and almost leisurely. In contrast, the activity level of other infants (like Josh) is quite high, with strong, restless movements of the arms and legs.

Another important dimension of temperament is the nature and quality of an infant's mood, and in particular a child's *irritability*. Like Lincoln, who was described in the example at the beginning of this section, some infants are easily disturbed and cry easily, while others are relatively easygoing. Irritable infants fuss a great deal, and they are easily upset. They are also difficult to soothe when they do begin to cry. Such irritability is relatively stable: Researchers find that infants who are irritable at birth remain irritable at the age of 1, and even at age 2 they are still more easily upset than infants who were not irritable just after birth (Worobey & Bajda, 1989). (Other aspects of temperament are listed in Table 6-2.)

Categorizing Temperament: Easy, Difficult, and Slow-to-Warm Babies. Because temperament can be viewed along so many dimensions, some researchers have asked whether there are broader categories that can be used to describe children's overall behavior. According to Alexander Thomas and Stella Chess, who carried out a large-scale study of a group of infants that has come to be known as the *New York Longitudinal Study*, babies can be described according to one of several profiles:

- Easy babies. **Easy babies** have a positive disposition. Their body functions operate regularly, and they are adaptable. They are generally positive, showing curiosity about new situations, and their emotions are moderate or low in intensity. This category applies to about 40 percent (the largest number) of infants.

- Difficult babies. **Difficult babies** have more negative moods and are slow to adapt to new situations. When confronted with a new situation, they tend to withdraw. About 10 percent of infants belong in this category.

- Slow-to-warm babies. **Slow-to-warm babies** are inactive, showing relatively calm reactions to their environment. Their moods are generally negative, and they withdraw from new situations, adapting slowly. Approximately 15 percent of infants are slow-to-warm.

As for the remaining 35 percent, they cannot be consistently categorized. These children show a variety of combinations of characteristics. For instance, one infant may have

temperament patterns of arousal and emotionality that are consistent and enduring characteristics of an individual

easy babies babies who have a positive disposition; their body functions operate regularly, and they are adaptable

difficult babies babies who have negative moods and are slow to adapt to new situations; when confronted with a new situation, they tend to withdraw

slow-to-warm babies babies who are inactive, showing relatively calm reactions to their environment; their moods are generally negative, and they withdraw from new situations, adapting slowly

Table 6-2

DIMENSIONS OF TEMPERAMENT

Dimension	Definition
Activity level	Proportion of active time periods to inactive time periods
Approach-withdrawal	The response to a new person or object, based on whether the child accepts the new situation or withdraws from it
Adaptability	How easily the child is able to adapt to changes in his or her environment
Quality of mood	The contrast of the amount of friendly, joyful, and pleasant behavior with unpleasant, unfriendly behavior
Attention span and persistence	The amount of time the child devotes to an activity and the effect of distraction on that activity
Distractibility	The degree to which stimuli in the environment alter behavior
Rhythmicity (regularity)	The regularity of basic functions such as hunger, excretion, sleep, and wakefulness
Intensity of reaction	The energy level or reaction of the child's response
Threshold of responsiveness	The intensity of stimulation needed to elicit a response

(*Source:* Thomas, Chess & Birch, 1968.)

relatively sunny moods, but react negatively to new situations, or another may show little stability of any sort in terms of general temperament.

The Consequences of Temperament: Does Temperament Matter? One obvious question to emerge from the findings of the relative stability of temperament is whether a particular kind of temperament is beneficial. The answer seems to be that no single type of temperament is invariably good or bad. Instead, children's long-term adjustment depends on the **goodness-of-fit** of their particular temperament and the nature and demands of the environment in which they find themselves. For instance, children with a low activity level and low irritability may do particularly well in an environment in which they are left to explore on their own and are allowed largely to direct their own behavior. In contrast, high-activity-level, highly irritable children may do best with greater direction, which permits them to channel their energy in particular directions (Thomas & Chess, 1977, 1980; Mangelsdorf et al., 1990; Strelau, 1998). Mary, the grandmother in the earlier example, found ways to adjust the environment for her son, Malcom. Malcom and Aisha may need to do the same for their own son, Lincoln.

Some research does suggest that certain temperaments are, in general, more adaptive than others. For instance, Thomas and Chess found that difficult children, in general, were more likely to show behavior problems by school age than those who were classified in infancy as easy children (Thomas, Chess, & Birch, 1968). But not all difficult children experience problems. The key determinant seems to be the way parents react to their infants' difficult behavior. If they react by showing anger and inconsistency—responses that their child's difficult, demanding behavior readily evokes—then the child is ultimately more likely to experience behavior problems. On the other hand, parents who display more warmth and consistency in their responses are more likely to have children who avoid later problems (Belsky, Fish, & Isabella, 1991; Teerikangas et al., 1998).

goodness-of-fit the notion that development is dependent on the degree of match between children's temperament and the nature and demands of the environment in which they are being raised

Furthermore, temperament seems to be at least weakly related to infants' attachment to their adult caregivers. For example, infants vary considerably in how much emotion they display nonverbally. Some are "poker-faced," showing little expressivity, while others' reactions tend to be much more easily decoded. More expressive infants may provide more easily discernible cues to others, thereby easing the way for caregivers to be more successful in responding to their needs and facilitating attachment (Feldman & Rimé, 1991; Goldsmith & Harman, 1994; Seifer, Schiller, & Sameroff, 1996).

Cultural differences also have a major influence on the consequences of a particular temperament. For instance, children who would be described as "difficult" in Western cultures actually seem to have an advantage in the East African Masai culture. The reason? Mothers offer their breast to their infants only when they fuss and cry; therefore, the irritable, more difficult infants are apt to receive more nourishment than the more placid, easy infants. Particularly when environmental conditions are bad, such as during a drought, difficult babies may have an advantage (deVries, 1984).

Recent approaches to temperament grow out of the framework of behavioral genetics that we discussed in Chapter 2. For instance, David Buss and Robert Plomin (1984) argue that temperamental characteristics represent inherited traits that are fairly stable during childhood and across the entire life span. These traits are seen as making up the core of personality and playing a substantial role in future development.

Gender: Why Do Boys Wear Blue and Girls Wear Pink?

"It's a boy." "It's a girl."

One of these two statements, or some variant, is probably the first announcement made after the birth of a child. From the moment of birth, girls and boys are treated differently. Their parents send out different kinds of birth announcements. They are dressed in different clothes and wrapped in different-colored blankets. They are given different toys. (Bridges, 1993; Coltrane & Adams, 1997).

Parents play with them differently: From birth on, fathers tend to interact more with sons than daughters, while mothers interact more with daughters (Parke & Sawin, 1980; Leaper, Anderson, & Sanders, 1998). Because, as we noted earlier in the chapter, mothers and fathers play in different ways (with fathers typically engaging in more physical, rough-and-tumble activities and mothers in traditional games such as peek-a-boo), male and female infants are clearly exposed to different styles of activity and interaction from their parents (Power & Parke, 1982; Lamb, 1986; Parke, 1990; Grant, 1994).

The behavior exhibited by girls and boys is interpreted in very different ways by adults. For instance, in one experiment researchers showed adults a video of an infant whose name was given as either "John" or "Mary" (Condry & Condry, 1976). Although it was the same baby performing a single set of behaviors, adults perceived "John" as adventurous and inquisitive, while "Mary" was fearful and anxious. Clearly, adults view the behavior of children through the lens of gender. **Gender** refers to our sense of being male or female. The term "gender" is often used to mean the same thing as "sex," but they are not actually the same. Sex typically refers to sexual anatomy and sexual behavior, while gender refers to the perceptions of maleness or femaleness. All cultures prescribe *gender roles* for males and females, but these roles differ greatly between one culture to another.

Although to some extent boys and girls live in at least partially different worlds due to their gender, there is a considerable amount of argument over both the extent and causes of such gender differences. Some gender differences are fairly clear from the time of birth. For example, male infants tend to be more active and fussier than female infants. Boys' sleep tends to be more disturbed than that of girls. Boys grimace more, although no gender difference exists in the overall amount of crying. There is also some evidence that male newborns are more irritable than female newborns, although the findings are inconsistent (Phillips, King, & DuBois, 1978; Eaton & Enns, 1986).

gender the sense of being male or female

Differences among male and female infants, however, are generally minor. In fact, in most ways infants seem so similar that usually adults cannot discern whether a baby is a boy or girl, as the "John" and "Mary" video research shows. Furthermore, it is important to keep in mind that there are much larger differences among individual boys and among individual girls than there are, on average, between boys and girls. (Unger & Crawford, 1996).

Gender differences emerge more clearly as children age—and become increasingly influenced by the gender roles that society sets out for them. For instance, by the age of 1 year, infants are able to distinguish between males and females. Girls at this age prefer to play with dolls or stuffed animals, while boys seek out blocks and trucks. Often, of course, these are the only options available to them, due to the choices their parents and other adults have made in the toys they provide (Poulin-Dubois et al., 1994; Caldera & Sciaraffa, 1998; Serbin et al., 2001).

Children's preferences for certain kinds of toys are reinforced by their parents, although parents of boys are more apt to be concerned about their child's choices than are parents of girls. For example, 1-year-old boys receive more positive reactions for playing with transportation and building toys than do girls. Moreover, the amount of reinforcement boys receive for playing with toys that society deems appropriate increases with age. On the other hand, girls who play with toys seen by society as "masculine" are less discouraged for their behavior than boys who play with toys seen as "feminine" (Eisenberg et al., 1985; Fagot & Hagan, 1991).

By the time they reach the age of 2, boys behave more independently and less compliantly than girls. Much of this behavior can be traced to parental reactions to earlier behavior. For instance, when a child takes his or her first steps, parents tend to react differently, depending on the child's gender: Boys are encouraged more to go off and explore the world, while girls are hugged and kept close. In general, exploratory behavior tends to be encouraged more in boys than in girls. It is hardly surprising, then, that by the age of 2, girls tend to show less independence and greater compliance (Fagot, 1978; Brooks-Gunn & Matthews, 1979; Kuczynski & Kochanska, 1990).

Societal encouragement and reinforcement do not, however, completely explain differences in behavior between boys and girls. For example, as we'll discuss further in Chapter 8, one study examined girls who were exposed before birth to abnormally high levels of *androgen*, a male hormone, because their mothers unwittingly took a drug containing the hormone while pregnant. Later, these girls were more likely to play with toys stereotypically preferred by boys (such as cars) and less likely to play with toys stereotypically

Parents of girls who play with toys related to activities associated with boys are apt to be less concerned than parents of boys who play with toys associated with girls.

The number of single-parent families has increased dramatically over the past twenty years. If the current trend continues, 60 percent of all children will live at some time with a single parent.

associated with girls (such as dolls). Although there are many alternative explanations for these results—you can probably think of several yourself—one possibility is that exposure to male hormones affected the brain development of the girls, leading them to favor toys that involve certain kinds of preferred skills (Levine et al., 1999; Mealey, 2000).

In sum, differences in behavior between boys and girls begin in infancy, and—as we will see in future chapters—continue throughout childhood (and beyond). Although gender differences have complex causes, representing some combination of innate, biologically related factors and environmental factors, they play a profound role in the social and emotional development of infants.

Family Life in the 21st Century

A look back at television shows of the 1950s (such as *Leave It to Beaver*) finds a world of families portrayed in a way that today seems oddly old-fashioned and quaint: mothers and fathers, married for years, and their good-looking children making their way in a world that seems to have few, if any, serious problems.

As we discussed in Chapter 1, even in the 1950s such a view of family life was overly romantic and unrealistic. Today, however, it is broadly inaccurate, representing only a minority of families in the United States. A quick review tells the story:

■ The number of single-parent families has increased dramatically in the last two decades, as the number of two-parent households has declined. Some 27 percent of all families with children are headed by single parents. Sixty-five percent of African American children and 37 percent of Hispanic children live in single-parent households (U.S. Bureau of the Census, 1998; ChildStats.gov, 2000).

■ The average size of families is shrinking. Today, on average, there are 2.6 persons per household, compared to 2.8 in 1980. The number of people living in nonfamily households (without any relatives) is close to 30 million.

■ In 1960, 5 percent of all births in the United States were to unmarried mothers. By the 1990s, more than 25 percent of births were to unmarried mothers.

High quality infant child care seems to produce only minor differences from home care in most respects, and some aspects of development may even be enhanced. What aspects of development might be enhanced by participation in infant child care outside the home?

From Research to Practice

Infant Child Care: Assessing the Consequences

Should infants be placed in group child-care settings, such as the one described in the chapter prologue, where Russell Ruud was leading the Velcro revolt? For many parents, there is little choice: Economic realities, or the desire to maintain a career, require that their children be left in the care of others for a portion of the day, typically in infant child-care settings. In fact, recent figures indicate that almost 30 percent of preschool children whose mothers work outside the home spend their days in child-care centers (see Figure 6-5), and overall, more than 80 percent of infants are cared for by people other than their mothers during their first year of life. The majority of these infants begin child care outside the home before the age of 4 months and are enrolled for almost 30 hours per week (NICHD Early Child Care Research Network, 1997). Do such arrangements have any discernible effects on infant development?

The answer is reassuring. According to the findings of a large study supported by the U.S. National Institute of Child Health and Development, high-quality child care outside the home produces only minor differences from home care in most respects, and may even enhance certain aspects of development. For example, most research finds little or no difference in the strength or nature of parental attachment bonds of infants who have been in high quality child care compared with infants raised solely by their parents. On the other hand, the research found that infants are less secure when they are placed in low-quality child care, if they are placed in multiple child-care arrangements, or if their mothers are relatively insensitive and unresponsive (NICHD Early Child Care Research Network, 1997, 1999).

The study also found an unexpected gender difference: Boys who experienced high levels of care and girls who had minimal amounts of care were somewhat less apt to be securely attached—although the meaning of this finding is unclear. Overall, though, there is little evidence that even extensive and continuous enrollment in child care outside the home is related to undesirable outcomes.

In fact, various studies have found clear benefits from participation in child care outside the home. For instance, children who participate in Early Head Start—a program that serves at-risk infants and toddlers in high-quality child-care centers—later are better able to solve problems, pay greater attention to others, and use language more effectively than poor children who do not participate in the programs. In addition, their parents (who are also involved in the program) benefit from their participation. Participating parents talk and read more to their children, and they are less likely to spank them (*HHS News*, 2001).

In addition to the direct benefits from use of child care outside the home, there are indirect ones. For example, although parental employment itself has been shown to have little effect on children's later functioning, children in lower income households and those whose mothers are single may actually benefit from the higher income produced by parental employment (Harvey, 1999).

It is important to note, however, that not all research on group child care provides such good news. Some studies on the outcomes of infant child-care centers have yielded mixed, or even negative, results, finding lower attachment on the part of children in child care. Still other research shows virtually no difference between children receiving care from their mothers compared with nonmaternal care. Ultimately, more research is needed on just who makes use of child care and how it is used by members of different segments of society to fully understand its consequences (Belsky & Rovine, 1988; Erel, Oberman & Yirmiya, 2000; Hungerford, Brownell, & Campbell, 2000)

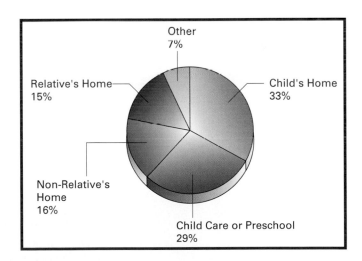

Figure 6-5 **Where Are Children Cared For?**

Most children spend their days at home, but almost 30 percent of children younger than 5 years of age whose mothers work outside the home spend their days in child-care centers.

(*Source*: U.S. Bureau of the Census, 1997; ChildHealth, 1998.)

Becoming an Informed Consumer of Development
Choosing the Right Infant Care Provider

If there is one finding that emerges with crystal clarity from research conducted on the consequences of infant child care programs, it is that benefits occur only when child care is of high quality. But what distinguishes high-quality child care from low-caliber programs? The American Psychological Association suggests that parents consider these questions in choosing a program (Zigler & Styfco, 1994; Committee on Children, Youth and Families, 1994):

▶ Are there enough providers? A desirable ratio is one adult for every three infants, although one to four can be adequate.

▶ Are group sizes manageable? Even with several providers, a group of infants should not be larger than eight.

▶ Has the center complied with all governmental regulations, and is it licensed?

▶ Do the people providing the care seem to like what they are doing? What is their motivation? Is child care just a temporary job, or is it a career? Are they experienced? Do they seem happy in the job, or is offering child care just a way to earn money?

▶ What do the caregivers do during the day? Do they spend their time playing with, listening and talking to, and paying attention to the children? Do they seem genuinely interested in the children, rather than merely going through the motions of caring for them?

▶ Are the children safe and clean? Does the environment allow infants to move around safely? Is the equipment and furniture in good repair? Do the providers adhere to the highest levels of cleanliness? After changing a baby's diaper, do providers wash their hands?

▶ What training do the providers have in caring for children? Do they demonstrate a knowledge of the basics of infant development and an understanding of how normal children develop? Do they seem alert to signs that development may depart from normal patterns?

▶ Finally, is the environment happy and cheerful? Child care is not just a babysitting service: For the time an infant is there, it is the child's whole world. You should feel fully comfortable and confident that the child-care center is a place where your infant will be treated as an individual.

In addition to following these guidelines, you may contact the National Association for the Education of Young Children, from which you may be able to get the name of a resource and referral agency in your area. Write (enclosing a self-addressed, stamped envelope) to NAEYC Information Service, 1834 Connecticut Avenue NW, Washington, DC 20009; or call (800) 424-2460.

■ Every minute, an adolescent in the United States gives birth.

■ More than 5 million children under the age of 3 are cared for by other adults while their parents work, and more than half of mothers of infants work outside the home.

■ One in 6 children lives in poverty in the United States. The rates are even higher for African American and Hispanic families, and for single-parent families of young children. More children under 3 live in poverty than do older children, adults, or the elderly (National Center for Children in Poverty, 2000).

Most of these statistics are disheartening. At the very least, they suggest that infants are being raised in environments in which substantial stressors are present, factors that make an unusually difficult task of raising children—never easy even under the best circumstances.

On the other hand, society is adapting to the new realities of family life in the 21st century. Several kinds of social support exist for the parents of infants, and society is evolving new institutions to help in their care. One example is the growing array of child-care arrangements available to help working parents, discussed in the *Research to Practice* box. Some guidelines for parents who choose group child care are included in the *Becoming an Informed Consumer of Development* section.

Review and Rethink

REVIEW

- According to Erikson, during infancy individuals move from the trust-versus-mistrust stage of psychosocial development to the autonomy-versus-shame-and-guilt stage.
- Temperament encompasses enduring levels of arousal and emotionality that are characteristic of an individual.
- Gender differences become more pronounced as infants age.
- Child care outside of the home can have neutral, positive, or negative effects on the social development of children, depending largely on its quality.
- Research on the effects of child care must take into account the varying quality of different child-care settings and the social characteristics of the parents who tend to use child care.

RETHINK

- What are some social implications of the changes in family life described in this chapter? What sorts of family policies might be instituted to address these changes?
- Why does society frown less on girls playing with "boy's" toys than boys playing with "girl's" toys? What does this suggest about our gender values?

Looking Back

What sort of emotional lives do infants have?

- Infants display a variety of facial expressions, which are similar across cultures and appear to reflect basic emotional states.

- By the end of the first year, infants often develop both stranger anxiety, wariness around an unknown person, and separation anxiety, distress displayed when a customary care provider departs.

- Early in life, infants develop the capability of nonverbal decoding: determining the emotional states of others based on their facial and vocal expressions.

- Through social referencing, infants from the age of 8 or 9 months use the expressions of others to clarify ambiguous situations and learn appropriate reactions to them.

What sort of mental lives do infants have?

- Infants begin to develop self-awareness at about the age of 12 months.

- They also begin to develop a theory of mind at this time: knowledge and beliefs about how they and others think.

What is attachment in infancy, and how does it relate to the future social competence of individuals?

- Attachment, a strong, positive emotional bond that forms between an infant and one or more significant persons, is a crucial factor in enabling individuals to develop social relationships.

- Infants display one of four major attachment patterns: securely attached, avoidant, ambivalent, and disorganized-disoriented. Research suggests an association between an infant's attachment pattern and his or her adult social and emotional competence.

What roles do other people play in infants' social development?

- Mothers' interactions with their babies are particularly important for social development. Mothers who respond effectively to their babies' social overtures appear to contribute to the babies' ability to become securely attached.

- Through a process of reciprocal socialization, infants and caregivers interact and affect one another's behavior, which strengthens their mutual relationship.

- From an early age, infants engage in rudimentary forms of social interaction with other children, and their level of sociability rises as they age.

What sorts of individual differences do infants display?

- The origins of personality, the sum total of the enduring characteristics that differentiate one individual from another, arise during infancy.

- Temperament encompasses enduring levels of arousal and emotionality that are characteristic of an individual. Temperamental differences underlie the broad classification of infants into easy, difficult, and slow-to-warm categories.

- As infants age, gender differences become more pronounced, mostly due to environmental influences. Differences are accentuated by parental expectations and behavior.

▶ *Is child care beneficial or harmful for infants?*

- Child care, a societal response to the changing nature of the family, can be beneficial to the social development of children, fostering social interaction and cooperation, if it is of high quality.

EPILOGUE

In this chapter we looked at the ways infants develop as social individuals, decoding and encoding emotions using social referencing and a "theory of mind." We considered the attachment patterns that infants display and their potential long-term effects. We examined personality, taking a close look at Erik Erikson's theory of psychosocial development. We also discussed temperament and explored the nature and causes of gender differences. We concluded with a discussion of infant day care.

Return to the prologue of this chapter, about Russell Ruud's Velcro discovery, and answer the following questions.

1. Is this episode evidence of self-awareness on the part of Russell or his child-care companions? Why or why not?

2. What role do you think social referencing might have played in this scenario? If Russell's care providers had reacted with obvious negativity, would this have stopped the other children from imitating Russell?

3. How does this story relate to the sociability of infants?

4. Can we form any opinion about Russell's personality based on this event? Why or why not?

5. Do you think Russell's actions might have brought a different response from his adult care providers if he had been a girl? Would the response from his peers have been different? Why or why not?

Key Terms and Concepts

differential emotions theory (p. 188)
stranger anxiety (p. 188)
separation anxiety (p. 188)
social smile (p. 189)
social referencing (p. 190)
self-awareness (p. 191)
theory of mind (p. 192)
empathy (p. 192)
attachment (p. 194)
Ainsworth Strange Situation (p. 195)

secure attachment pattern (p. 195)
avoidant attachment pattern (p. 195)
ambivalent attachment pattern (p. 195)
disorganized-disoriented attachment pattern (p. 195)
mutual regulation model (p. 200)
reciprocal socialization (p. 201)
personality (p. 203)
Erikson's theory of psychosocial development (p. 203)

trust-versus-mistrust stage (p. 203)
autonomy-versus-shame-and-doubt stage (p. 203)
temperament (p. 204)
easy babies (p. 204)
difficult babies (p. 204)
slow-to-warm babies (p. 204)
goodness-of-fit (p. 205)
gender (p. 206)

Bridges

In Part Two, we looked at three aspects of infants' development. First, we discussed the ways in which they grow physically, examining their remarkably rapid progress from largely instinctual beings to individuals with a range of complex physical and motor abilities. We'll see next how preschoolers use their physical skills to further their explorations of the world and as the basis for building even more complex skills.

Second, we encountered Piaget and the notion of "stages" of development, as well as some alternative views on cognitive development. We evaluated how well these views explain the amazing growth in learning, memory, and—especially—language that infants experience. Language development is far from complete as children become preschoolers, however. In Part Three, we'll see how preschoolers learn to apply the rules of language to create sentences and to communicate better with others.

The last phase of development we examined was social and personality development. We observed how gender differences are a matter of both genes and environment. We saw how infants begin to develop as social beings, moving from interactions with their parents to relations with other adults and children. Next, we'll see how, as preschoolers, children continue to expand their social circles through play and friendships and begin to make decisions on issues of right and wrong.

Above all, we got a preview of the ways in which factors that date from infancy continue to influence the individual into adulthood. In Parts Six and Seven, for example, we'll see how temperament and personality remain uncannily constant throughout the life span, how infant attachment patterns can have lasting effects, and how the earliest social influences can define even gender roles for life. As we proceed, keep in mind how the seeds of our futures appear in many cases to be present in our earliest beginnings.

THE PRESCHOOL YEARS

Physical and Cognitive Development in the Preschool Years

PROLOGUE: THE LONG GOODBYE

The first day of school raises emotion in both children and their parents.

The night before my younger child, Will, started kindergarten, neither he nor I could sleep. Mingled with his excitement was, I imagined, concern over some of the worries that he had expressed to my husband and me: Would he be smart enough? Would he be able to read? Would there be enough time at school to play? Similar doubts haunted my own dreams like the Wild Things; I wondered whether I should have left Will in preschool for another year (with an August birthday, he would be one of the youngest in his class), whether his skills would be as advanced as the other children's, whether his teacher would appreciate his charms, tolerate his mishaps, and love him no matter what, as we do—and how I would survive without a little one at my heels.

The next morning, I helped Will get dressed in the new outfit that we had bought weeks earlier and carefully laid out the night before. To avoid last-minute panic, I'd packed his favorite lunch and his backpack the night before. After a photo session, we set off together. Although he clutched my hand on the walk to the classroom, Will lined up with his classmates as if he had been doing it for years, and trotted into the class with nary a backward glance. (Fishel, 1993, p. 165)

Looking Ahead   For both children and their parents, the experience of attending school for the first time produces a combination of apprehension, exhilaration, and anticipation. It marks the start of an intellectual as well as social journey that will continue for many years and shape the development of children in significant ways.

Traditionally, the preschool years are a time of preparation: a period spent anticipating and getting ready for the start of a child's formal education, through which society will begin the process of passing on its intellectual tools to a new generation.

But it is a mistake to take the label "preschool" too literally. The years between 3 and 6 are hardly a mere way station in life, an interval spent waiting for the next, more important period to start. Instead, the preschool years are a time of tremendous change and growth, where physical, intellectual, and social development proceeds at a rapid pace.

In this chapter, we focus on the physical, cognitive, and linguistic growth that occurs during the preschool years. We begin by considering the nature of physical change during those years. We discuss weight and height, nutrition, and health and wellness. We consider changes in the brain and its neural byways, and touch on some intriguing findings relating to gender differences in the way that the brain functions. We also look at how both gross and fine motor skills change over the preschool years.

Intellectual development is the focus of much of the remainder of the chapter. We examine the major approaches to cognitive development, including Piaget's theory, information-processing approaches, and Vygotsky's view of cognitive development, which takes culture into account.

Finally, the chapter considers the important advances in language development that occur during the preschool years. We end with a discussion of several factors that influence cognitive development, including exposure to television and participation in childcare and preschool programs.

After reading this chapter, you will be able to answer the following questions:

▶ **What is the state of children's bodies and overall health during the preschool years?**

▶ **How do preschool children's brains and physical skills develop?**

▶ **How does Piaget interpret cognitive development during the preschool years?**

▶ **How do other views of cognitive development differ from Piaget's?**

▶ **How does children's language develop in the preschool years?**

▶ **What effects does television have on preschoolers?**

▶ **What kinds of preschool educational programs are available?**

Physical Growth

It is an unseasonably warm spring day at the Cushman Hill Preschool, one of the first nice days after a long winter. The children in Mary Scott's class have happily left their winter coats in the classroom for the first time this spring, and they are excitedly playing outside. Jessie plays a game of catch with Germaine, while Sarah and Molly climb on the jungle gym. Craig and Marta chase one another, while Jesse and Bernstein try, with gales of giggles, to play leap-frog. Virginia and Ollie sit across from each other on the teeter-totter, successively bumping it so hard into the ground that they both are in danger of being knocked off. Erik, Jim, Scott, and Paul race around the perimeter of the playground, running for the sheer joy of it.

These same children, now so active and mobile, were unable even to crawl or walk just a few years earlier. The advances in their physical abilities that have occurred in such a short time are nothing short of astounding. Just how far they have developed is apparent when we look at the specific changes they have undergone in their size, shape, and physical abilities.

The Growing Body

Two years after birth, the average child in the United States weighs in at around 25 to 30 pounds and is close to 36 inches tall—around half the height of the average adult. Children grow steadily during the preschool period, and by the time they are 6 years old, they weigh, on average, about 46 pounds and stand 46 inches tall (see Figure 7-1).

Individual Differences in Height and Weight. These averages mask great individual differences in height and weight. For instance, 10 percent of 6-year-olds weigh 55 pounds or more, and 10 percent weigh 36 pounds or less. Furthermore, average differences in height and weight between boys and girls increase during the preschool years. Although at age 2 the differences are relatively small, boys start becoming taller and heavier, on average, than girls.

Furthermore, profound differences in height and weight exist between children in economically developed countries and those in developing countries. The better nutrition and health care received by children in developed countries translates into significant differences in growth. For instance, the average Swedish 4 year old is as tall as the average 6-year-old in Bangladesh (United Nations, 1991).

Differences in height and weight reflect economic factors within the United States, as well. For instance, children in families whose incomes are below the poverty level are far more likely to be unusually short than children raised in more affluent homes (Barrett & Frank, 1987; Egan, 1994; Sherry et al., 1992).

Changes in Body Shape and Structure. If we compare the bodies of a 2-year-old and a 6-year-old, we find that the bodies vary not only in height and weight, but also in shape. During the preschool years, boys and girls become less chubby and roundish and more slender. They begin to burn off some of the fat they have carried from their infancy, and they no longer have a pot-bellied appearance. Moreover, their arms and legs lengthen, and the size relationship between the head and the rest of the body becomes more adultlike. In fact, by the time children reach 6 years of age, their proportions are quite similar to those of adults.

The changes in size, weight, and appearance we see during the preschool years are only the tip of the iceberg. Internally, other physical changes are occurring. Children grow stronger as their muscle size increases and their bones become sturdier. The sense organs continue their development. For instance, the *eustachian tube* in the ear, which carries sounds from the external part of the ear to the internal part, moves from a position that is almost parallel to the ground at birth to a more angular position. This change sometimes leads to an increase in the frequency of earaches during the preschool years.

Nutrition: Eating the Right Foods. Nutritional needs change during the preschool years. Because the rate of growth during this period is slower than during infancy, preschoolers need less food to maintain their growth. The change in food consumption may be so noticeable that parents sometimes worry that their preschooler is not eating enough. However, children tend to be quite adept at maintaining an appropriate intake of food, if provided with

Providing preschoolers with a variety of foods helps insure good nutrition.

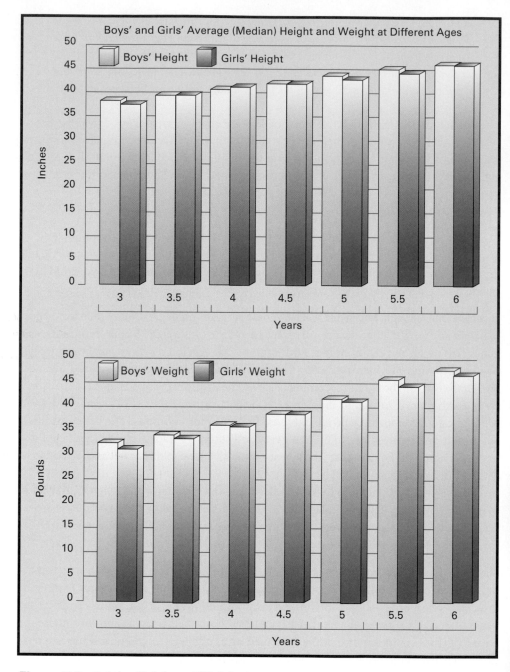

Figure 7-1 **Gaining Height and Weight**

The preschool years are marked by steady increases in height and weight. The figures show the median point for boys and girls at each age, in which 50 percent of children in each category are above this height or weight level and 50 percent are below.

(Adapted from Lowrey, 1978.)

obesity body weight more than 20 percent higher than the average weight for a person of a given age and height

nutritious meals. In fact, anxiously encouraging children to eat more than they seem to want naturally may lead them to increase their food intake beyond an appropriate level.

Ultimately, some children's food consumption can become so high as to lead to **obesity,** which is defined as a body weight more than 20 percent higher than the average weight for a person of a given age and height. The prevalence of obesity among older preschoolers has increased significantly over the last 20 years. (We'll discuss the causes of obesity in Chapter 9.)

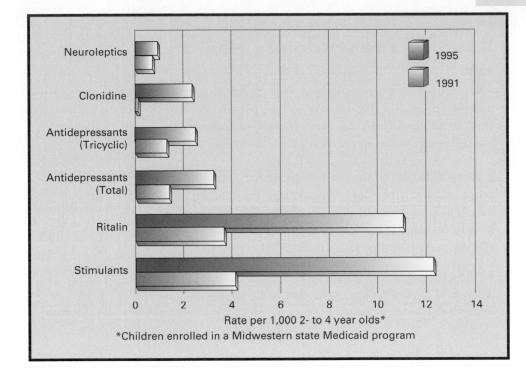

Figure 7-2 **Numbers of Preschool Children Taking Medication for Behavioral Problems**

Although there is no clear explanation why the use of stimulants and antidepressants has increased among children, some experts believe it is a quick-fix solution for behavior problems that may be normal difficulties.

(*Source:* Zito et al., 2000.)

How do parents ensure that their children have good nutrition without turning mealtimes into a tense, adversarial situation? In most cases, the best strategy is to make sure that a variety of foods, low in fat and high in nutritional content, is available. Foods that have a relatively high iron content are particularly important: Iron deficiency anemia, which causes chronic fatigue, is one of the prevalent nutritional problems in developed countries such as the United States. High-iron foods include dark green vegetables (such as broccoli), whole grains, and some kinds of meat (Ranade, 1993).

On the other hand, preschool children, like adults, will not find all foods equally appealing, and children should be given the opportunity to develop their own natural preferences. As long as their overall diet is adequate, no single food is indispensable (L. Shapiro, 1997).

Health and Illness. For the average child in the United States, a runny nose due to the common cold is the most frequent—and happily, the most severe—kind of health problem during the preschool years. In fact, the majority of children in the United States are reasonably healthy during this period (Kalb, 1997).

Although physical illness is typically a minor problem during the preschool years, an increasing number of children are being treated with drugs for emotional disorders. In fact, the use of drugs such as antidepressants and stimulants doubled and sometimes tripled between 1991 and 1995 (see Figure 7-2). Although it is not clear why the increase has occurred, some experts believe that parents and preschool teachers may be seeking a quick fix for behavior problems that may, in fact, represent normal difficulties (Marshall, 2000; Pear, 2000; Zito et al., 2000).

Injuries During the Preschool Years: Playing It Safe

Aaron, an energetic 3-year-old, was trying to stretch far enough to reach the bowl of cookies sitting on the kitchen counter. Because the bowl was just beyond his grasp, he pushed a chair from the kitchen table over to the counter and was able to pick out a cookie. As he tried to get down, however, the chair slid away from

Becoming an Informed Consumer of Development

Keeping Preschoolers Healthy

There is no way around it: Even the healthiest preschooler occasionally gets sick. Social interaction with others ensures that illnesses will be passed from one child to another. However, some diseases are preventable, and others can be minimized if simple precautions are taken:

▶ Preschoolers should eat a well-balanced diet containing the proper nutrients, particularly foods containing sufficient protein. (The recommended energy intake for children at age 24 months is about 1,300 calories a day, and for those aged 4 to 6, it is around 1,700 calories a day.)

▶ Children should get as much sleep as they wish. Being run-down from lack of either nutrition or sleep makes children more susceptible to illness.

▶ Children should avoid contact with others who are ill. Parents should make sure that children wash their hands after playing with other kids who are obviously sick.

▶ Ensure that children follow an appropriate schedule of immunizations. As illustrated in Table 7-1, current recommendations state that a child should have received nine different vaccines and other preventive medicines in five to seven separate visits to the doctor.

▶ Finally, if a child does get ill, remember this: Minor illnesses during childhood sometimes provide immunity to more serious illnesses later on.

Table 7-1

RECOMMENDED CHILDHOOD IMMUNIZATION SCHEDULE

Vaccines are listed under routinely recommended ages. Bars indicate range of recommended ages for immunization. Any dose not given at the recommended age should be given as a "catch-up" immunization at any subsequent visit when indicated and feasible. Ovals indicate vaccines to be given if previously recommended doses were missed or given earlier than the recommended minimum age.

Age ▶ Vaccine ▼	Birth	1 mo	2 mos	4 mos	6 mos	12 mos	15 mos	18 mos	24 mos	4–6 yrs	11–12 yrs	14–18 yrs
Hepatitis B		Hep B #1	Hep B #2		Hep B #3						Hep B	
Diphtheria, Tetanus, Pertussis			DTaP	DTaP	DTaP		DTaP			DTaP	Td	
H. influenzae type b			Hib	Hib	Hib	Hib						
Inactivated Polio			IPV	IPV	IPV					IPV		
Pneumococcal Conjugate			PCV	PCV	PCV	PCV						
Measles, Mumps, Rubella						MMR				MMR	MMR	
Varicella						Var					Var	
Hepatitis A									Hep A-in selected areas			

Approved by the Advisory Committee on Immunization Practices (ACIP), the American Academy of Pediatrics (AAP), and the American Academy of Family Physicians (AAFP).

For additional information about the vaccines listed above, please visit the National Immunization Program Home Page at www.cdc.gov/nip or call the National Immunization Hotline at 800-232-2522 (English) or 800-232-0233 (Spanish).

(*Source:* American Academy of Pediatrics, 2000)

the counter, and Aaron fell to the floor, twisting and fracturing his arm. His wails brought his father on the run from the next room.

In some ways, Aaron was lucky, for some injuries sustained by preschoolers are far more serious, resulting in permanent disfigurement or even death. In fact, statistically speaking, the greatest risk that preschoolers face comes from neither illness nor nutritional problems but from accidents: Before the age of 10, children have twice the likelihood of dying from an injury than from an illness. In fact, children in the United States have a 1 in 3 chance every year of receiving an injury that requires medical attention (National Safety Council, 1989).

The danger of injuries during the preschool years is in part a result of the children's high levels of physical activity. A 3-year-old might think that it is perfectly reasonable to climb on an unsteady chair to get something that is out of reach, and a 4-year-old might enjoy holding on to a low tree branch and swinging her legs up and down. At the same time, children lack the judgment to know that their activities may hold some danger, and they are less likely than older children to be careful.

Furthermore, some children are more apt to take risks than others, and such preschoolers are more likely to be injured than their more cautious peers. Boys, who are more active than girls and tend to take more risks, have a higher rate of injuries (Morrongiello, 1997). Ethnic differences, probably due to differences in cultural norms about how closely children need to be supervised, can also be seen in accident rates. Asian American children in the United States, who tend to be supervised particularly strictly by their parents, have one of the lowest accident rates for children. Economic factors also play a role. Children raised under conditions of poverty in urban areas, whose inner-city neighborhoods may contain more hazards than more affluent areas, are two times more likely to die of injuries than children living in affluence.

The range of dangers that preschoolers face is wide. Injuries come from falls, burns from stoves and fires, drowning in bathtubs indoors and standing water outdoors, and suffocation in places such as abandoned refrigerators. Auto accidents also account for a large number of injuries. Finally, children face injuries from poisonous substances, such as household cleaners.

Parents and caregivers of preschoolers can take several precautions to prevent injuries, although, as we've seen, none of these measures eliminates the need for close supervision of active preschoolers. Caregivers can start by "child-proofing" preschoolers' homes and classrooms to the extents possible with covers for electrical outlets and child locks on cabinets where poisons are kept, for example. Child car seats and bike helmets can help prevent injuries in case of accidents. Parents and teachers also need to be aware of the dangers from long-term hazards, such as lead poisoning.

The Silent Danger: Lead Poisoning in Young Children

At the age of 3, Tory couldn't sit still. He was unable to watch a television show for more than 5 minutes, and sitting still while his mother read to him seemed to be an impossibility. He was often irritable, and he impulsively took risks when he was playing with other children.

When his behavior reached a point where his parents thought there was something seriously wrong with him, they took him to a pediatrician for a thorough physical examination. After testing Tory's blood, the pediatrician found that his parents were right: Tory was suffering from lead poisoning.

Some 14 million children are at risk for lead poisoning due to exposure to potentially toxic levels of lead, according to the Centers for Disease Control. Although there are now strin-

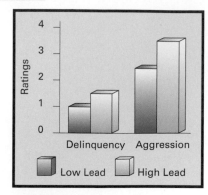

Figure 7-3 **The Consequence of Lead Poisoning**

High levels of lead have been linked to higher levels of antisocial behavior, including aggression and delinquency, in school-age children

(*Source:* Needleman et al., 1996.)

lateralization the process in which certain cognitive functions are located more in one hemisphere of the brain than in the other

The urban environment in which poor children often live make them especially susceptible to lead poisoning.

gent legal restrictions on the amount of lead in paint and gasoline, lead is still found on painted walls and window frames—particularly in older homes, and in gasoline, ceramics, lead-soldered pipes, and even dust and water. People who live in areas of substantial air pollution due to automobile and truck traffic may also be exposed to high levels of lead. The U.S. Department of Health and Human Services has called lead poisoning the most hazardous health threat to children under the age of 6 (Centers for Disease Control, 1991; Tesman & Hills, 1994).

Even tiny amounts of lead can permanently harm children. Exposure to lead has been linked to lower intelligence, problems in verbal and auditory processing, and—as in the case of Tory—hyperactivity and distractibility. High lead levels have also been linked to higher levels of antisocial behavior, including aggression and delinquency in school-age children (see Figure 7-3). At yet higher levels of exposure, lead poisoning results in illness and death (Thomson et al., 1989; Leviton et al., 1993; Needleman et al., 1996).

Poor children are particularly susceptible to lead poisoning, and the results of poisoning tend to be worse for them than for children from more affluent families. Children living in poverty are more apt to reside in housing that contains peeling and chipping lead paint, or to live near heavily trafficked urban areas with high levels of air pollution. At the same time, many families living in poverty may be less stable and unable to provide consistent opportunities for intellectual stimulation that might serve to offset some of the cognitive problems caused by the poisoning. Consequently, lead poisoning is especially harmful to poorer children (Harvey et al., 1984; Tesman & Hills, 1994; Duncan & Brooks-Gunn, 2000).

Efforts to reduce the incidence of lead poisoning have taken many forms. One approach is through legislation that mandates the removal of paint that contains lead in dwellings in which children reside. Another is through parent education (Porter, 1997; Serwint, Dias, & White, 2000).

Still, the problem of potentially dangerous levels of lead in many children's surroundings persists. The questions that must be addressed are how to remove such dangers and what the costs will be. Clearly, there is no easy solution to the problem.

The Growing Brain

The brain grows at a faster rate than any other part of the body. Two-year-olds have brains that are about three-quarters the size and weight of an adult brain. By age 5, children's brains weigh 90 percent of average adult brain weight. In comparison, the average 5-year-old's total body weight is just 30 percent of average adult body weight (Schuster & Ashburn, 1986; Lowrey, 1986; Nihart, 1993).

Why does the brain grow so rapidly? One reason is an increase in the number of interconnections among cells, as we saw in Chapter 4. These interconnections allow for more complex communication between neurons, and they permit the rapid growth of cognitive skills that we'll discuss later in the chapter. In addition, the amount of myelin—protective insulation that surrounds parts of neurons—increases, which speeds the transmission of electrical impulses along brain cells but also adds to brain weight.

By the end of the preschool period, some parts of the brain have undergone particularly significant growth. For example, the *corpus callosum*, a bundle of nerve fibers that connect the two hemispheres of the brain, becomes considerably thicker, developing as many as 800 million individual fibers that help coordinate brain functioning between the two hemispheres (Branch & Heller, 1998).

Brain Lateralization. The two halves of the brain also begin to become increasingly differentiated and specialized. **Lateralization,** the process in which certain functions are located more in one hemisphere than the other, becomes more pronounced during the preschool years.

For most people, the left hemisphere concentrates on tasks that necessitate verbal competence, such as speaking, reading, thinking, and reasoning. The right hemisphere develops its own strengths, especially in nonverbal areas such as comprehension of spatial relationships, recognition of patterns and drawings, music, and emotional expression (Zaidel, 1994; Fiore & Schooler, 1998; McAuliffe & Knowlton, 2001; see Figure 7-4).

Each of the two hemispheres also begins to process information in a slightly different manner. Whereas the left hemisphere considers information sequentially, one piece of data at a time, the right hemisphere processes information in a more global manner, reflecting on it as a whole (Gazzaniga, 1983; Springer & Deutsch, 1989; Leonard et al., 1996).

Despite the specialization of the hemispheres, we need to keep in mind that in most respects the two hemispheres act in tandem. They are interdependent, and the differences between the two are minor. Furthermore, the fact that each hemisphere specializes in certain tasks does not mean that it alone functions in any particular area. In fact, each hemisphere can perform most of the tasks of the other. For example, the right hemisphere does some language processing and plays an important role in language comprehension (Beeman & Chiarello, 1998; Knecht et al., 2000).

In addition, many individual differences exist in the nature of lateralization. For example, many of the 10 percent of people who are left-handed or ambidextrous (able to use both hands interchangeably) have language centered in their right hemispheres or have no specific language center (Banich & Nicholas, 1998).

Even more intriguing are differences in lateralization related to gender and culture. For instance, starting during the first year of life and continuing in the preschool years, boys and girls show some hemispheric differences associated with lower body reflexes and the processing of auditory information (Shucard et al., 1981; Grattan et al., 1992). Furthermore, males clearly tend to show greater lateralization of language in the left hemisphere; among females, language is more evenly divided between the two hemispheres (Gur et al., 1982). Such differences may help explain why—as we'll see later in the chapter—females' language development proceeds at a more rapid pace during the preschool years than males' language development.

We still don't know the source of the difference in lateralization between females and males. One explanation is genetic: that female and male brains are predisposed to function in slightly different ways. Such a view is supported by data suggesting that there are minor structural differences between males' and females' brains. For instance, a section of the corpus callosum is proportionally larger in women than in men. Furthermore, studies conducted among other species, such as primates, rats, and hamsters, have found size and structural differences in the brains of males and females (Hammer, 1984; Witelson, 1989; Highley et al., 1999).

Before we accept a genetic explanation for the differences between female and male brains, we need to consider an equally plausible alternative: It may be that verbal abilities emerge earlier in girls because girls receive greater encouragement for verbal skills than boys do. For instance, some evidence suggests that even as infants, girls are spoken to more than boys. Such higher levels of verbal stimulation may produce growth in particular areas of the brain that does not occur in boys. Consequently, environmental factors rather than genetic ones may lead to the gender differences we find in brain lateralization. Most likely, a combination of genetics and environment is at work, as it is with many of our other human characteristics. Once again, we find that teasing out the relative impact of heredity and environment is a challenging task.

The Links Between Brain Growth and Cognitive Development. Neuroscientists are just beginning to understand the ways in which brain development is related to cognitive development. For example, it appears that there are periods during childhood in which the brain

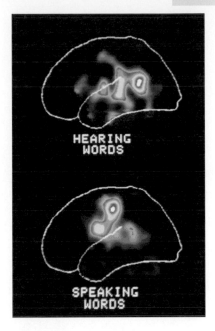

Figure 7-4 **Looking Into the Brain**

These scans show how different parts of the brain are activated during particular tasks, illustrating the specialization of different areas of the brain. If one part of the brain is injured, will the functions associated with it be permanently lost?

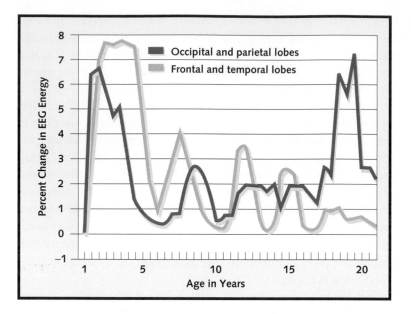

Figure 7-5 **Brain Growth Spurt**

According to one study, electrical activity in the brain has been linked to advances in cognitive abilities at various stages across the life span. In this graph activity increases dramatically between a year-and-half and 2 years, a period during which language rapidly develops.

(*Source:* Fischer & Rose, 1995.)

shows unusual growth spurts, and these periods are linked to advances in cognitive abilities. One study that measured electrical activity in the brain across the life span found unusual spurts at between a year-and-a-half and 2 years, a time when language abilities increase rapidly. Other spurts occurred around other ages when cognitive advances are particularly intense (see Figure 7-5; Fischer & Rose, 1995).

Other research has suggested that increased myelination in particular areas of the brain may be related to preschooler's growing cognitive capabilities. For example, myelination of the reticular formation, an area of the brain associated with attention and concentration, is completed by the time children are about 5. This may be associated with children's growing attention spans as they approach school age. The improvement in memory that occurs during the preschool years may also be associated with myelination: During the preschool years, myelination is completed in the hippocampus, an area associated with memory (Rolls, 2000).

We do not yet know the direction of causality (does brain development produce cognitive advances, or do cognitive accomplishments fuel brain development?). However, it is clear that increases in our understanding of the physiological aspects of the brain will eventually have important implications for parents and teachers.

Motor Development

Anya sat in the sandbox at the park, chatting with the other parents and playing with her two children, 5-year-old Nicholai and 13-month old Smetna. While she chatted, she kept a close eye on Smetna, who would still put sand in her mouth sometimes if she wasn't stopped. Today, however, Smetna seemed content to run the sand through her hands and try to put it into a bucket. Nicholai, meanwhile, was busy with two other boys, rapidly filling and emptying the other sand buckets to build an elaborate sand city, which they would then destroy with toy trucks.

When children of different ages gather at a playground, it's easy to see that preschool children have come a long way in their motor development since infancy. Both their gross and fine motor skills have become increasingly fine-tuned. Smetna, for example, is still mastering putting sand into a bucket, while her brother Nicolai uses that skill easily as part of his larger goal of building a sand city.

During the preschool years, children grow in both gross and fine motor skills.

Gross Motor Skills. By the time they are 3, children have mastered a variety of skills: jumping, hopping on one foot, skipping, and running. By 4 and 5, their skills have become more refined as they have gained increasing control over their muscles. For instance, at 4 they can throw a ball with enough accuracy that a friend can catch it, and by age 5 they can toss a ring and have it land on a peg 5 feet away. Five-year-olds can learn to ride bikes, climb ladders, and ski downhill—activities that all require considerable coordination (Clark & Humphrey, 1985). (Table 7-2 summarizes major gross motor skills that emerge during the preschool years.)

These achievements may be related to brain development and myelination of neurons in areas of the brain related to balance and coordination. Another reason that motor skills develop at such a rapid clip during the preschool years is that children spend a great deal of time practicing them. During this period, the general level of activity is extraordinarily high: Preschoolers seem to be perpetually in motion. In fact, the activity level is higher at age 3 than at any other point in the entire life span (Eaton & Yu, 1989; Poest et al., 1990).

Girls and boys differ in certain aspects of gross motor coordination, in part because of differences in muscle strength, which is somewhat greater in boys than in girls. For instance, boys can typically throw a ball better and jump higher. Furthermore, a boy's overall activity level tends to be greater than a girl's (Eaton & Yu, 1989). On the other hand, girls generally surpass boys in tasks that involve the coordination of limbs. For instance, at the age of 5, girls are better than boys at jumping jacks and balancing on one foot (Cratty, 1979).

Table 7-2

MAJOR GROSS MOTOR SKILLS IN EARLY CHILDHOOD

3-Year-Olds	4-Year-Olds	5-Year-Olds
Cannot turn or stop suddenly or quickly	Have more effective control of stopping, starting, and turning	Start, turn, and stop effectively in games
Jump a distance of 15 to 24 inches	Jump a distance of 24 to 33 inches	Can make a running jump of 28 to 36 inches
Ascend a stairway unaided, alternating the feet	Descend a long stairway alternating the feet, if supported	Descend a long stairway alternating the feet
Can hop, using largely an irregular series of jumps with some variations added	Hop 4 to 6 steps on one foot	Easily hop a distance of 16 feet

(*Source:* C. Corbin, 1973.)

From Research to Practice

Potty Wars:
When—and How—Should Children Be Toilet Trained?

Ann Wright, of University Park, Maryland, woke up on a sweltering night in June at 3 a.m., her head spinning as she re-enacted the previous day's parenting trauma: She and her husband, Oliver, had told their 4-year-old daughter, Elizabeth, on Thursday night that it was time for her to stop using her pull-up training pants. For the next 18 hours, the girl had withheld her urine, refusing to use the toilet.

"We had been talking to her for months about saying goodbye to the pull-ups, and she seemed ready," says Wright. "But on the day of the big break she refused to sit on the toilet. Two hours before she finally went, she was crying and constantly moving, clearly uncomfortable."

Eventually the child wet herself. (Gerhardt, 1999, p. C1)

Few child-care issues raise so much concern among parents as toilet training. And on few issues are there so many opposing opinions from experts and laypersons. Often, the various viewpoints are played out in the media and even take on political overtones. For instance, the well-known pediatrician T. Berry Brazelton suggests a flexible approach to toilet training, advocating that it be put off until the child shows signs of readiness (Brazelton, 1997; Brazelton et al., 1999). On the other hand, psychologist John Rosemond, known primarily for his media advocacy of a conservative, traditional stance to childrearing, argues for a more rigid approach, saying that toilet training should be done early and quickly.

What is clear is that the age at which toilet training takes place has been rising over the last few decades. For example, in 1957, 92 percent of children were toilet trained by the age of 18 months. In 1999, only 25 percent were toilet trained at that age, and just 60 percent of 36-month-olds were toilet trained. Some 2 percent were still not toilet trained at the age of 4 years (Goode, 1999).

Current guidelines of the American Academy of Pediatrics support Brazelton's position, suggesting that there is no single time to begin toilet training and that training should begin only when children show that they are ready. Children younger than 12 months have no bladder or bowel control, and only slight control for 6 months longer. Although some children show signs of readiness for toilet training between 18 and 24 months, some are not ready until 30 months or older (American Academy of Pediatrics, 1999; Stadtler, Gorski, & Brazelton, 1999).

The signs of readiness include staying dry at least two hours at a time during the day or waking up dry after naps; regular and predictable bowel movements; an indication, through facial expressions or words, that urination or a bowel

Among the signs that a child is ready to give up diapers is evidence that he or she is able to follow directions and can get to the bathroom and undress on his or her own.

movement is about to occur; the ability to follow simple directions; the ability to get to the bathroom and undress alone; discomfort with soiled diapers; asking to use the toilet or potty chair; and the desire to wear underwear. Furthermore, children must be ready not only physically, but emotionally, and if they show strong signs of resistance to toilet training, like Elizabeth in the example above, toilet training should be put off (American Academy of Pediatrics, 1999).

Even after children are toilet trained during the day, it often takes months or years before they are able to achieve control at night. Around three-quarters of boys and most girls are able to stay dry after the age of 5 years.

Complete toilet training eventually occurs in almost all children as they mature and attain greater control over their muscles. However, delayed toilet training can be a cause for concern if a child is upset about it or if it makes the child a target of ridicule from siblings or peers. In such cases, several types of treatments have proven effective. In particular, treatments in which children are rewarded for staying dry or are awakened by a battery device that senses when they have wet the bed are often effective (Wagner, Smith, & Norris, 1988; American Psychiatric Association, 1994).

Another aspect of muscular skills—one that parents of toddlers often find most problematic—is bowel and bladder control. As we discuss in the *From Research to Practice* box, toilet training can be a controversial issue.

Fine Motor Skills. At the same time gross motor skills are developing, children are progressing in their ability to use fine motor skills, which involve more delicate, smaller body movements. These skills encompass such varied activities as using a fork and spoon, cutting with scissors, tying one's shoelaces, and playing the piano.

The skills involved in fine motor movements require a good deal of practice, as anyone knows who has watched a 4-year-old struggling painstakingly to copy letters of the alphabet. Yet fine motor skills show clear developmental patterns. At the age of 3, children are already able to draw a circle and square with a crayon, and they can undo their clothes when they go to the bathroom. They can put a simple jigsaw puzzle together, and they can fit blocks of different shapes into matching holes. However, they do not show much polish in accomplishing such tasks: For instance, they may try to force puzzle pieces into place.

By the age of 4, their fine motor skills are considerably better. They can draw a person that looks like a person, and they can fold paper into triangular designs. And by the time they are 5, they are able to hold and manipulate a thin pencil properly.

Handedness. How do preschoolers decide which hand to hold the pencil in as they work on their copying and other fine motor skills? For many, their choice was established soon after birth.

Beginning in early infancy, many children show signs of a preference for the use of one hand over another—the development of **handedness.** For instance, young infants may show a preference for one side of their bodies over another. By the age of 7 months, some infants seem to favor one hand by grabbing more with it than the other (Ramsay, 1980; Michel, 1981).

handedness the preference of using one hand over another

Most children display a clear-cut tendency to use one hand over the other by the end of the preschool years. Some 90 percent are right-handed and 10 percent are left-handed. Furthermore, there is a gender difference: More boys than girls are left-handed.

Much speculation has been devoted to the meaning of handedness, fueled in part by longstanding myths about the sinister nature of left-handedness. (In fact, the word "sinister" itself is derived from the Latin word meaning "on the left.") In Islamic cultures, for instance, the left hand is generally used in going to the toilet, and it is considered uncivilized to serve food with that hand. Many artistic portrayals of the devil show him as left-handed.

However, there is no scientific basis for myths that suggest that there is something wrong with being left-handed. In fact, some evidence exists that left-handedness may be associated with certain advantages. For example, a study of 100,000 students who took the Scholastic Aptitude Test (SAT) showed that 20 percent in the highest-scoring category were left-handed, double the proportion of left-handed people in the general population. Moreover, such individuals as Michelangelo, Leonardo da Vinci, Benjamin Franklin, and Pablo Picasso were left-handed (Bower, 1985).

Although some educators of the past tried to force left-handed children to use the right hand, particularly when learning to write, thinking has changed. Most teachers now encourage children to use the hand they prefer. Still, most left-handed people will agree that the design of desks, scissors, and most other everyday objects favors those who are right-handed. In fact, the world is so "right-biased" that it may prove to be a dangerous place for those who are left-handed: Left-handed people have more accidents and are at greater risk of dying younger than right-handed people (Coren & Halpern, 1991; Ellis & Engh, 2000; Mackenzie & Peters, 2000).

Review and Rethink

REVIEW

- The preschool period is marked by steady physical growth.
- Preschoolers tend to eat less than they did as babies, but generally regulate their food intake appropriately, given nutritious options and the freedom to develop their own choices and controls.
- Brain growth is rapid during the preschool years. In addition, the brain develops lateralization, a tendency of the two hemispheres to adopt specialized tasks.
- The preschool period is generally the healthiest time of life, with only minor illnesses threatening children. Accidents and environmental hazards are the greatest threats to preschoolers' health. Parents and caregivers need to be aware of steps they can take to keep preschoolers healthy and prevent injuries.
- Gross and fine motor development also advances rapidly during the preschool years. Boys' and girls' gross motor skills begin to diverge, and children develop handedness.

RETHINK

- How might biology and environment combine to affect the physical growth of a child adopted as an infant from a developing country and taken to a more industrialized country to live?
- Aside from obesity, to what other sorts of eating problems might overly controlling parents contribute? How?

Intellectual Development

> *Three-year-old Sam was talking to himself. As his parents listened with amusement from another room, they could hear him using two very different voices. "Find your shoes," he said in a low voice. "Not today. I'm not going. I hate the shoes," he said in a higher-pitched voice. The lower voice answered, "You are a bad boy. Find the shoes, bad boy." The higher-voiced response was "No, no, no."*
>
> *Sam's parents realized that he was playing a game with his imaginary friend, Gill. Gill was a bad boy who often disobeyed his mother, at least in Sam's imagination. In fact, according to Sam's musings, Gill often was guilty of the very same misdeeds for which his parents blamed Sam.*

In some ways, the intellectual sophistication of 3-year-olds is astounding. Their creativity and imagination leap to new heights, their language is increasingly sophisticated, and they reason and think about the world in ways that would have been impossible even a few months earlier. But what underlies the dramatic advances in intellectual development that start in the preschool years and continue throughout that period? We can consider several approaches, starting with a look at Piaget's findings on the cognitive changes that occur during the preschool years.

Piaget's Stage of Preoperational Thinking

The Swiss psychologist Jean Piaget, whose stage approach to cognitive development we discussed in Chapter 5, saw the preschool years as a time of both stability and great change. He suggests that the preschool years fit entirely into a single stage of cognitive development—the preoperational stage—which lasts from the age of 2 years until around 7 years.

During the **preoperational stage,** children's use of symbolic thinking grows, mental reasoning emerges, and the use of concepts increases. Children become better at representing events internally, and they grow less dependent on the use of direct sensorimotor

preoperational stage according to Piaget, the stage from approximately age 2 to age 7 in which children's use of symbolic thinking grows, mental reasoning emerges, and the use of concepts increases

activity to understand the world around them. Yet they are still not capable of **operations:** organized, formal, logical mental processes. It is only at the end of the preoperational stage that the ability to carry out operations comes into play.

According to Piaget, a key aspect of preoperational thought is *symbolic function,* the ability to use a mental symbol, a word, or an object to stand for, or represent, something that is not physically present. For example, during this stage, preschoolers can use a mental symbol for a car (the word "car"), and they likewise understand that a small toy car is representative of the real thing. Because of their ability to use symbolic function, children have no need to get behind the wheel of an actual car to understand its basic purpose and use.

The Relation Between Language and Thought. Symbolic function is at the heart of one of the major advances that occurs in the preoperational period: the increasingly sophisticated use of language. As we discuss later in this chapter, children make substantial progress in language skills during the preschool period.

Piaget suggests that language and thinking are inextricably intertwined and that the advances in language that occur during the preschool years offer several improvements over the type of thinking that is possible during the earlier sensorimotor period. For instance, thinking embedded in sensorimotor activities is relatively slow, since it depends on actual movements of the body that are bound by human physical limitations. In contrast, the use of symbolic thought allows preschoolers to represent actions symbolically, permitting much greater speed.

Even more important, the use of language allows children to think beyond the present to the future. Consequently, rather than being grounded in the immediate here-and-now, preschoolers can imagine future possibilities through language.

Do the increased language abilities of preschoolers lead to increased thinking proficiency, or do the improvements in thinking during the preoperational period lead to enhancements in language ability? This question—whether thought determines language or language determines thought—is one of the enduring and most controversial questions within the field of psychology. Piaget's answer is that language grows out of cognitive advances, rather than the other way around. He argues that improvements during the earlier sensorimotor period are necessary for language development and that continuing growth in cognitive ability during the preoperational period provides the foundation for language ability. Consequently, Piaget suggests that language development is based on the development of more sophisticated modes of thinking—and not the other way around.

Centration: What You See Is What You Think. Place a dog mask on a cat and what do you get? According to 3- and 4-year-old preschoolers, a dog. To them, a cat with a dog mask ought to bark like a dog, wag its tail like a dog, and eat dog food. In every respect, the cat has been transformed into a dog (deVries, 1969).

Piaget suggests that the root of this belief is centration, a key element, and limitation, of the thinking of children in the preoperational period. **Centration** is the process of concentrating on one limited aspect of a stimulus and ignoring other aspects.

Preschoolers are unable to consider all available information about a stimulus. Instead, they focus on superficial, obvious elements that are within their sight. These external elements come to dominate preschoolers' thinking, leading to inaccuracy in thought.

For example, consider what preschoolers say when they are shown two rows of buttons, one with 10 buttons that are closely spaced together, and the other with 8 buttons spread out to form a longer row (see Figure 7-6). If asked which of the rows contains more buttons, children who are 4 or 5 usually choose the row that looks longer rather than the one that actually contains more buttons. This occurs in spite of the fact that children this age know quite well that 10 is more than 8.

operations organized, formal, logical mental processes

centration the process of concentrating on one limited aspect of a stimulus and ignoring other aspects

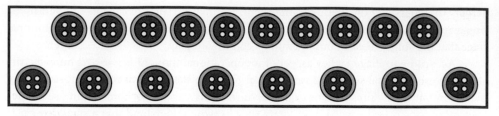

Figure 7-6 **Which Row Contains More Buttons?**

When preschoolers are shown these two rows and asked which row has more buttons, they usually respond that the lower row of buttons contains more, because it looks longer. They answer in this way even though they know quite well that 10 is greater than 8. Do you think preschoolers can be *taught* to answer correctly?

The cause of the children's mistake is that the visual image dominates their thinking. Rather than taking into account their understanding of quantity, they focus on appearance. To a preschooler, appearance is everything. Preschoolers' focus on appearances might be related to another aspect of preoperational thought, the lack of conservation.

Conservation: Learning That Appearances Are Deceiving. Consider the following scenario:

> *Four-year-old Jaime is shown two drinking glasses of different shapes. One is short and broad, the other tall and thin. A teacher half-fills the short, broad glass with apple juice. The teacher then pours the juice into the tall, thin glass. The juice fills the tall glass almost to the brim. The teacher asks Jaime a question: Is there more juice in the second glass than there was in the first?*

If you view this as an easy task, so do children like Jaime. They have no trouble answering the question. However, they almost always get the answer wrong.

Most 4-year-olds respond that there is more apple juice in the tall, thin glass than there was in the short, broad one. In fact, if the juice is poured back into the shorter glass, they are quick to say that there is now less juice than there was in the taller glass (see Figure 7-7).

The reason for the error in judgment is that children of this age have not mastered conservation. **Conservation** is the knowledge that quantity is unrelated to the arrangement and physical appearance of objects. During the preoperational period, preschoolers are unable to understand that changes in one dimension (such as appearance) do not necessarily mean that other dimensions (such as quantity) are changed.

Children who do not yet understand the principle of conservation feel quite comfortable in asserting that the amount of liquid changes as it is poured between glasses of

conservation the knowledge that quantity is unrelated to the arrangement and physical appearance of objects

Figure 7-7 **Which Glass Contains More?**

Most 4-year-old children believe that the amount of liquid in these two glasses differs because of the differences in the containers' shapes, even though they may have seen equal amounts of liquid being poured into each.

different sizes. They simply are unable to realize that the transformation in appearance does not imply a transformation in quantity.

The inability to conserve manifests itself in several ways during the preoperational period. For example, if 5-year-olds are shown a row of checkers and asked to build a row that is "the same," the row they typically build will be identical in length—but it may vary in the number of checkers. Similarly, if shown two rows of checkers, each with the same number of checkers, but one with the checkers more spread out, children in the preoperational stage will reason that the two rows are not equal.

The lack of conservation also manifests itself in children's understanding of area, as illustrated by Piaget's cow-in-the-field problem (Piaget, Inhelder, & Szenubsjam, 1960). In the problem, two sheets of green paper, equal in size, are shown to a child, and a toy cow is placed in each field. Next, a toy barn is placed in each field, and children are asked which cow has more to eat. The typical—and, so far, correct—response is that the cows have the same amount.

In the next step, a second toy barn is placed in each field. But in one field, the barns are placed adjacent to one another, while in the second field, they are separated from one another. Children who have not mastered conservation usually say that the cow in the field with the adjacent barns has more grass to eat than the cow in the field with the separated barns. In contrast, children who can conserve answer, correctly, that the amount available is identical. (Some other conservation tasks are shown in Figure 7-8).

Why do children in the preoperational stage make errors on tasks that require conservation? Piaget suggests that the main reason is that their tendency toward centration prevents them from focusing on the relevant features of the situation. Furthermore, they cannot follow the sequence of transformations that accompanies changes in the appearance of a situation.

Incomplete Understanding of Transformation. Children in the preoperational period are unable to understand the notion of transformation. **Transformation** is the process in which one state is changed into another. For instance, adults know that if a pencil that is held upright is allowed to fall down, it passes through a series of successive stages until it reaches its final, horizontal resting spot (see Figure 7-9). In contrast, children in the preoperational period are unable to envision or recall the successive transformations that the pencil followed in moving from the upright to the horizontal position. If asked to reproduce the sequence in a drawing, they draw the pencil upright and lying down, with nothing in between. Basically, they ignore the intermediate steps.

Similarly, a preoperational child who sees several worms during a walk in the woods may believe that they are all the same worm. The reason: She views each sighting in isolation and is unable to reconstruct the transformation it would take for the worm to move quickly from one sighting to the next, and realize that worms can't perform that transformation.

Egocentrism: The Inability to Take Others' Perspectives. Another hallmark of the preoperational period is egocentric thinking. **Egocentric thought** is thinking that does not take into account the viewpoints of others. Preschoolers do not understand that others have different perspectives from their own. Egocentric thought takes two forms: the lack of awareness that others see things from a different physical perspective and the failure to realize that others may hold thoughts, feelings, and points of view that differ from theirs. (Note what egocentric thought does *not* imply: that preoperational children intentionally think in a selfish or inconsiderate manner.)

Egocentric thinking underlies children's lack of concern over their nonverbal behavior and the impact it has on others. For instance, a 4-year-old who is given an unwanted gift of socks when he was expecting something more desirable may frown and scowl as he

transformation the process in which one state is changed into another

egocentric thought thinking that does not take into account the viewpoints of others

Type of Conservation	Modality	Change in Physical Appearance	Average Age Invariance Is Grasped
Number	Number of elements in a collection	Rearranging or dislocating elements	6–7 years
Substance (mass)	Amount of a malleable substance (e.g., clay or liquid)	Altering shape	7–8 years
Length	Length of a line or object	Altering shape or configuration	7–8 years
Area	Amount of surface covered by a set of plane figures	Rearranging the figures	8–9 years
Weight	Weight of an object	Altering shape	9–10 years
Volume	Volume of an object (in terms of water displacement)	Altering shape	14–15 years

Figure 7-8 **Common Tests of Children's Understanding of the Principle of Conservation**

Why is a sense of conservation important?

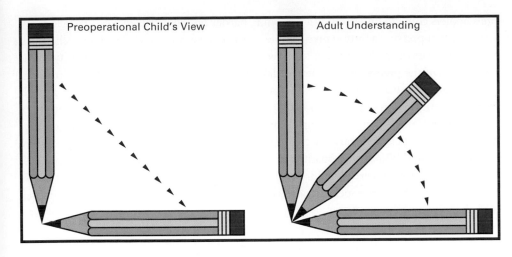

Preoperational Child's View   Adult Understanding

Figure 7-9 The Falling Pencil

Children in Piaget's preoperational stage do not understand that as a pencil falls from the upright to the horizontal position it moves through a series of intermediary steps. Instead, they think that there are no intermediate steps in the change from the upright to horizontal position.

opens the package, unaware that his face can be seen by others, and may reveal his true feelings about the gift (Feldman, 1992).

Egocentrism lies at the heart of several types of behavior during the preoperational period. For instance, preschoolers may talk to themselves, even in the presence of others, and at times they simply ignore what others are telling them. Rather than being a sign of eccentricity, such behavior illustrates the egocentric nature of preoperational children's thinking: the lack of awareness that their behavior acts as a trigger to others' reactions and responses. Consequently, a considerable amount of verbal behavior on the part of preschoolers has no social motivation behind it but is meant for the preschoolers' own consumption.

Similarly, egocentrism can be seen in hiding games with children during the preoperational stage. In a game of hide-and-seek, 3-year-olds may attempt to hide by covering their faces with a pillow—even though they remain in plain view. Their reasoning: If they cannot see others, others cannot see them. They assume that others share their view.

The Emergence of Intuitive Thought. Because Piaget labeled the preschool years as the "*preoperational period*," it is easy to assume that this is a period of marking time, waiting for the more formal emergence of operations. As if to support this view, many of the characteristics of the preoperational period highlight deficiencies, cognitive skills that the preschooler has yet to master. However, the preoperational period is far from idle. Cognitive development proceeds steadily, and in fact several new types of ability emerge. A case in point: the development of intuitive thought.

Intuitive thought refers to preschoolers' use of primitive reasoning and their avid acquisition of knowledge about the world. From about age 4 through 7, children's curiosity blossoms. They constantly seek out the answers to a wide variety of questions.

At the same time, children may act as if they are authorities on particular topics, feeling certain that they have the correct—and final—word on an issue. If pressed, they are unable to back up their reasoning, and they are inattentive to how they know what they know. In other words, their intuitive thought leads them to believe that they know answers to all kinds of questions, but there is little or no logical basis for this confidence in their understanding of the way the world operates.

On the other hand, the intuitive thinking that children display in the late stages of the preoperational period has certain qualities that prepare them for more sophisticated forms of reasoning. For example, by the end of the preoperational stage, preschoolers begin to understand the notion of functionality. *Functionality* refers to the concept that actions, events, and outcomes are related to one another in fixed patterns. For instance,

intuitive thought thinking that reflects preschoolers' use of primitive reasoning and their avid acquisition of knowledge about the world

preschoolers come to understand that pushing harder on the pedals makes a bicycle move faster, or that pressing a button on a remote control makes the television change channels.

Furthermore, children begin to show an awareness of the concept of identity in the later stages of the preoperational period. *Identity* is the understanding that certain things stay the same, regardless of changes in shape, size, and appearance. For instance, knowledge of identity allows one to understand that a lump of clay contains the same amount of clay regardless of whether it is clumped into a ball or stretched out like a snake. Comprehension of identity is necessary for children to develop an understanding of conservation, the ability to understand that quantity is not related to physical appearances, as we discussed earlier. Piaget regarded children's development of conservation as a skill that marks the transition from the preoperational period to the next stage, concrete operations, which we will discuss in Chapter 9.

Evaluating Piaget's Approach to Cognitive Development. Piaget, a masterful observer of children's behavior, provides a detailed portrait of preschoolers' cognitive abilities. His rich description of how children view the world is simply unmatched by most other accounts of cognitive development. The broad outlines of his approach provide us with a useful means of thinking about the advances in cognitive ability that occur during the preschool years (Siegal, 1997).

However, it is important to consider Piaget's approach to cognitive development within the appropriate historical context and in light of more recent research findings. Recall, as we discussed in Chapter 5, that his theory is based on extensive observations of relatively few children. Despite his insightful and groundbreaking observations, recent experimental investigations suggest that in certain regards, Piaget underestimated children's capabilities.

Take, for instance, Piaget's views of how children in the preoperational period understand numbers. He contends that preschoolers' thinking is seriously handicapped, as evidenced by their performance on tasks involving conservation and reversibility, the understanding that a transformation can be reversed to return something to its original state. Yet more recent experimental work suggests otherwise. For instance, developmental psychologist Rochel Gelman has found that children as young as 3 can readily discern the difference between rows of two and three toy animals, regardless of the animals' spacing. Furthermore, older children are able to note differences in number, performing tasks such as identifying which of two numbers is larger and indicating that they understand some rudiments of addition and subtraction problems (Gelman, 1972; Wynn, 1992; Sophian, Garyantes, & Chang, 1997).

Based on such evidence, Gelman concludes that children have an innate ability to count, one akin to the ability to use language that some theorists see as universal and genetically determined. Such a conclusion is clearly at odds with Piagetian notions, which suggest that children's numerical abilities do not blossom until after the preoperational period.

Some developmentalists (particularly those who favor the information-processing approach, as we'll see later in the chapter) also believe that cognitive skills develop in a more continuous manner than Piaget's stage theory implies. Rather than thought changing in quality, as Piaget argues, critics of Piaget suggest that developmental changes are more quantitative in nature. The underlying processes that produce cognitive skill are regarded by such critics as undergoing only minor changes with age (Gelman & Baillargeon, 1983; Case, 1991).

There are further difficulties with Piaget's view of cognitive development. His contention that conservation does not emerge until the end of the preoperational period, and in some cases even later, has not stood up to careful experimental scrutiny. For instance, performance on conservation tasks can be improved by providing preoperational children with certain kinds of training and experiences. The mere possibility of enhancing performance argues against the Piagetian view that children in the preoperational period have not reached a level of cognitive maturity that would permit them to understand conservation (Field, 1987; Siegler, 1995).

Clearly, children are more capable at an earlier age than Piaget's account would lead us to believe. Why did Piaget underestimate children's cognitive abilities? One answer is that his questioning of children used language that was too difficult to allow children to answer in a way that would provide a true picture of their skills. In addition, as we've seen, Piaget tended to concentrate on preschoolers' *deficiencies* in thinking, focusing his observations on children's lack of logical thought. In contrast, more recent theorists have focused more on children's competence. By shifting the question, they have found increasing evidence for a surprising degree of competence in preschoolers.

Information-Processing Approaches to Cognitive Development

Even as an adult, Paco has clear recollections of his first trip to a farm, which he took when he was 3 years old. He was visiting his godfather, who lived in Puerto Rico, and the two of them went to a nearby farm. Paco recounts seeing what seemed like hundreds of chickens, and he clearly recalls his fear of the pigs, who seemed huge, smelly, and frightening. Most of all, he recalls the thrill of riding on a horse with his godfather.

That Paco has a clear memory of his farm trip is not surprising: Most people have unambiguous, and seemingly accurate, memories dating as far back as the age of 3. But are the processes used to form memories during the preschool years similar to those that operate later in life? More broadly, what general changes in the processing of information occur during the preschool years?

Information-processing approaches view the changes that occur in children's cognitive abilities during the preschool years as analogous to the way a computer program becomes more sophisticated as a programmer modifies it on the basis of experience. These approaches focus on changes in the kinds of "mental programs" that children invoke when approaching problems. In fact, for many child developmentalists, information-processing approaches represent the dominant, most comprehensive, and ultimately the most accurate explanation of how children develop cognitively (Siegler, 1994; Mehler & DuPoux, 1994).

We'll focus on two domains that highlight the approach taken by information processing theorists: understanding of numbers and memory development during the preschool years.

Preschoolers' Understanding of Numbers. As we saw earlier, one of the flaws critics have noticed in Piaget's theory is that preschoolers have a greater understanding of numbers than Piaget thought. Researchers using information-processing approaches to cognitive development have found increasing evidence for the sophistication of preschoolers' understanding of numbers. The average preschooler is able not only to count, but to do so in a fairly systematic, consistent manner (Siegler, 1998).

For instance, developmental psychologist Rochel Gelman suggests that preschoolers follow a number of principles in their counting. When shown a group of several items, they know they should assign just one number to each item and that each item should be counted only once. Moreover, even when they get the *names* of numbers wrong, they are consistent in their usage. For instance, a 4-year-old who counts three items as "1, 3, 7" will say "1, 3, 7" when counting another group of different items. And she will probably say that there are 7 items in the group, if asked how many there are (Gelman & Gallistel, 1978; Gelman, 1972).

In short, preschoolers may demonstrate a surprisingly sophisticated understanding of numbers, although their understanding is not totally firm. Still, by the age of 4, most are able to carry out simple addition and subtraction problems by counting, and they are able to compare different quantities quite successfully (Donlan, 1998).

Memory: Recalling the Past. Think back to your own earliest memory. If you are like Paco, described earlier, and most other people too, it probably is of an event that occurred after the age of 3. According to Katherine Nelson (1989), **autobiographical memory,** memory of particular events from one's own life, achieves little accuracy until after 3 years of age. Accuracy then increases gradually and slowly throughout the preschool years (Nelson, 1989, 1992; Gathercole, 1998).

Preschool children's recollections of events that happened to them are sometimes, but not always, accurate. For instance, 3-year-olds can remember fairly well central features of routine occurrences, such as the sequence of events involved in eating at a restaurant. In addition, preschoolers are typically accurate in their responses to open-ended questions, such as "What rides did you like best at the amusement park?" (Nelson, 1986; Goodman & Reed, 1986; Price & Goodman, 1990).

One determinant of the accuracy of preschoolers' memories is how soon they are assessed. Unless an event is particularly vivid or meaningful, it is not likely to be remembered at all. Moreover, not all autobiographical memories last into later life. For instance, Will, the 5-year-old described in the chapter prologue, may remember the first day of kindergarten 6 months or a year later, but later in his life, he might not remember that day at all.

Preschoolers' autobiographical memories not only fade, but the ones that are remembered may not be wholly accurate. For example, if an event happens often, it may be hard to remember one specific time it happened. Preschoolers' memories of familiar events are often organized in terms of **scripts,** broad representations in memory of events and the order in which they occur. For example, a young preschooler might represent eating in a restaurant in terms of a few steps: talking to a waitress, getting the food, and eating. With age, the scripts become more elaborate: getting in the car, being seated at the restaurant, ordering, waiting for the food to come, eating, ordering dessert, and paying for the food. Because events that are frequently repeated tend to be melded into scripts, particular instances of a scripted event are recalled with less accuracy than those that are unscripted in memory (Farrar & Goodman, 1992; Fivush, Kuebli, & Clubb, 1992).

There are other reasons why preschoolers may not have entirely accurate autobiographical memories. Preschoolers have difficulty describing certain kinds of information, such as complex causal relationships, and may oversimplify recollections. And, as we consider next, their memories are also susceptible to the suggestions of others. This is a special concern when children are called upon to testify in legal situations, such as when abuse is suspected.

Children's Eyewitness Testimony: Memory on Trial

I was looking and then I didn't see what I was doing and it got in there somehow. . . . The mousetrap was in our house because there's a mouse in our house. . . . The mousetrap is down in the basement, next to the firewood. . . . I was playing a game called "Operation" and then I went downstairs and said to Dad, "I want to eat lunch," and then it got stuck in the mousetrap. . . . My daddy was down in the basement collecting firewood. . . . [My brother] pushed me [into the mousetrap]. . . . It happened yesterday. The mouse was in my house yesterday. I caught my finger in it yesterday. I went to the hospital yesterday. (Ceci & Bruck, 1993, p. A23)

autobiographical memory memory of particular events from one's own life

scripts broad representations in memory of events and the order in which they occur

This preschooler may recall this ride in six months, but by the time she is 12, it will probably be forgotten. Can you explain why?

Despite the detailed account by this 4-year-old boy of his encounter with a mousetrap and subsequent trip to the hospital, there's a problem: The incident never happened, and the memory is entirely false.

The 4-year-old's explicit recounting of a mousetrap incident that had not actually occurred was the product of a study on children's memory. Each week for 11 weeks, the 4-year-old boy was told, "You went to the hospital because your finger got caught in a mousetrap. Did this ever happen to you?"

The first week, the child quite accurately said, "No. I've never been to the hospital." But by the second week, the answer changed to, "Yes, I cried." In the third week, the boy said, "Yes. My mom went to the hospital with me." By the eleventh week, the answer had expanded to the quote above (Ceci & Bruck, 1993).

The embellishment of a completely false incident is characteristic of the fragility and inaccuracy of memory in young children. Young children may recall things quite mistakenly, but with great conviction, contending that events occurred which never really happened, and forgetting events that did occur.

Furthermore, children's memories are susceptible to the suggestions of adults asking them questions. This is particularly true of preschoolers, who are considerably more vulnerable to suggestion than either adults or school-age children. Preschoolers are also more prone to make inaccurate inferences about the reasons behind others' behavior and are less able to draw appropriate conclusions based on their knowledge of a situation (Ceci & Huffman, 1997; Loftus, 1997; Thompson, Clarke-Stewart, & Lepore, 1997; Bruck & Ceci, 1999).

Of course, preschoolers recall many things accurately; as we discussed earlier in the chapter, children as young as 3 recall some events in their lives without distortion. However, not all recollections are accurate, and some events that are recalled with seeming accuracy never actually occurred.

The error rate for children is further heightened when the same question is asked repeatedly (Cassel, Roebers, & Bjorklund, 1996). Furthermore, false memories—of the type reported by the 4-year old who "remembered" going to the hospital after his finger was caught in a mousetrap—in fact may be more persistent than actual memories (Brainerd, Reyna, & Brandse, 1995).

In addition, when questions are highly suggestive (that is, when questioners attempt to lead a person to particular conclusions), children are more apt to make mistakes in recall (Ceci & Huffman, 1997). For instance, consider the following excerpt, which presents an extreme example of a preschool child being questioned. It comes from an actual case involving a teacher, Kelly Michaels, who was accused of sexually molesting children in a preschool:

Preschool teacher Kelly Michaels may have been convicted of sexually molesting several preschool children as the result of highly suggestive questions posed to the children.

Social worker: Don't be so unfriendly. I thought we were buddies last time.
Child: Nope, not any more.
Social worker: We have gotten a lot of other kids to help us since I last saw you…. Did we tell you that Kelly is in jail?
Child: Yes. My mother already told me.
Social worker: Did I tell you that this is the guy (pointing to the detective) that arrested her?… Well, we can get out of here real quick if you just tell me what you told me the last time, when we met.
Child: I forgot.
Social worker: No you didn't. I know you didn't.
Child: I did! I did!
Social worker: I thought we were friends last time.
Child: I'm not your friend any more!
Social worker: How come?
Child: Because I hate you!
Social worker: You have no reason to hate me. We were buddies when you left.
Child: I hate you now!

Social worker: Oh, you do not, you secretly like me, I can tell.

Child: I hate you.

Social worker: Oh, come on. We talked to a few more of your buddies. And everyone told me about the nap room, and the bathroom stuff, and the music room stuff, and the choir stuff, and the peanut butter stuff, and everything. . . . All your buddies [talked]. . . . Come on, do you want to help us out? Do you want to keep her in jail? I'll let you hear your voice and play with the tape recorder; I need your help again. Come on. . . . Real quick, will you just tell me what happened with the wooden spoon? Let's go.

Child: I forgot.

Detective: Now listen, you have to behave.

Social worker: Do you want me to tell him to behave? Are you going to be good boy, huh? While you are here, did he [the detective] show you his badge and his handcuffs? (Ceci & Bruck, 1993, p. 422–423).

Clearly, the interview is filled with leading questions, not to mention social pressure to conform ("all your buddies talked"), bribery ("I'll let you hear your voice and play with the tape recorder"), and even implicit threats ("did the detective show you his badge and handcuffs?").

How can children be questioned to produce the most accurate recollections? One way is to question them as soon as possible after an event has occurred. The longer the time between the actual event and questioning, the less firm are children's recollections. Furthermore, more specific questions are answered more accurately than more general ones. Asking the questions outside of a courtroom is also preferable, as the courtroom setting can be intimidating and frightening (Saywitz & Nathanson, 1993; Ceci & Bruck, 1995; Poole & Lamb, 1998; also see Table 7-3).

Although some experts have advocated the use of anatomically correct dolls, on which children can point out where they have may have experienced sexual contact, careful research has not been supportive of the technique. In fact, in some instances children, using anatomically correct dolls, claimed that they had touched another person in particular places that are wholly implausible—such as when a child claims to have touched a female's penis (Wolfner, Faust, & Dawes, 1993; Bruck et al., 1995). A more recent study on anatomically correct doll use found that African American and white nonabused preschoolers

Table 7-3

ELICITING ACCURATE RECOLLECTIONS FROM CHILDREN

Recommended Practice

PLAY DUMB
INTERVIEWER *Now that I know you a little better, tell me why you are here today.*

ASK FOLLOW-UP QUESTIONS
CHILD *Bob touched my private.*
INTERVIEWER *Tell me everything about that.*

ENCOURAGE CHILDREN TO DESCRIBE EVENTS
INTERVIEWER *Tell me everything that happened at Bob's house from the beginning to the end.*

AVOID SUGGESTING THAT INTERVIEWERS EXPECT DESCRIPTIONS OF PARTICULAR KINDS OF EVENTS

AVOID OFFERING REWARDS OR EXPRESSING DISAPPROVAL

(*Source:* Poole & Lamb, 1998.)

demonstrated behaviors that are associated with sexual abuse (Geddie, Dawson, & Weunsch, 1998). Based on this research, the use of anatomically correct dolls does not appear to be the best way to interview preschool-aged children (Bruck, Ceci, & Francoeur, 2000).

Ultimately, no foolproof way exists to test the accuracy of children's recollections. Testimony needs to be evaluated on a case-by-case basis, and judges must ensure that children are questioned in a low-key, nonthreatening manner by impartial questioners (Bruck, Ceci, & Hembrooke, 1998; Gordon, Baker-Ward, & Ornstein, 2001).

Information Processing in Perspective. According to information-processing approaches, cognitive development consists of gradual improvements in the ways people perceive, understand, and remember information. With age and practice, preschoolers process information more efficiently and with greater sophistication, and they are able to handle increasingly complex problems. In the eyes of proponents of information-processing approaches, it is these quantitative advances in information processing—and not the qualitative changes suggested by Piaget—that constitute cognitive development (Case & Okamoto, 1996; Goswami, 1998; Chen & Siegler, 2000).

For supporters of information-processing approaches, the reliance on well-defined processes that can be tested, with relative precision, by research is one of the perspective's most important features. Rather than relying on concepts that are somewhat vague, such as Piaget's notions of assimilation and accommodation, information-processing approaches provide a comprehensive, logical set of concepts.

For instance, dramatic changes in the nature of attention occur as preschoolers grow older: They have longer attention spans, can monitor and plan what they are attending to more effectively, and become increasingly aware of their cognitive limitations. As we discussed earlier in this chapter, these advances may be due to brain development. Such increasing attentional abilities place some of Piaget's findings in a different light. For instance, increased attention allows older children to attend to both the height *and* the width of tall and short glasses into which liquid is poured. This permits them to understand that the amount of liquid in the glasses stays the same when it is poured back and forth. Preschoolers, in contrast, are unable to attend to both dimensions simultaneously, and thus are less able to conserve (Miller & Seier,1994; Hudson, Sosa, & Shapiro, 1997).

Proponents of information-processing theory have also been successful in focusing on important cognitive processes to which alternative approaches traditionally have paid little attention, such as memory and attention. They suggest that information processing provides a clear, logical, and full account of cognitive development.

Yet information-processing approaches have their detractors, who raise significant points. For one thing, the focus on a series of single, individual cognitive processes leaves out of consideration some important factors that appear to influence cognition. For instance, information-processing theorists pay relatively little attention to social and cultural factors—a deficiency that Vygotsky's approach, which we'll consider next, attempts to remedy.

An even more important criticism is that information-processing approaches "lose the forest for the trees." In other words, information-processing approaches pay so much attention to the detailed, individual sequence of processes that compose cognitive processing and development that they never adequately paint a whole, comprehensive picture of cognitive development—which Piaget clearly did quite well.

Developmentalists using information-processing approaches have responded to such criticisms. They contend that their model of cognitive development has the advantage of being precisely stated and capable of leading to testable hypotheses. They also argue that there is far more research supporting their approach than there is for alternative theories of cognitive development. In short, they suggest that their approach provides a more accurate account than any other.

Russian developmental psychologist Lev Vygotsky proposed that the focus of cognitive development should be on a child's social and cultural world, as opposed to the Piagetian approach concentrating on individual performance.

cw

Information-processing approaches have been highly influential over the past several decades. They have inspired a tremendous amount of research that has helped explain how children develop cognitively. Furthermore, it is clear that the information-processing perspective will continue to be an important guide to understanding how children make such remarkable cognitive strides as they develop.

Vygotsky's View of Cognitive Development: Taking Culture into Account

As her daughter watches, a member of the Chilcotin Indian tribe prepares a salmon for dinner. When the daughter asks a question about a small detail of the process, the mother takes out another salmon and repeats the entire process. According to the tribal view of learning, understanding and comprehension can come only from grasping the total procedure, and not from learning about the individual subcomponents of the task. (Tharp, 1989)

The Chilcotin view of how children learn about the world contrasts with the prevalent view of Western society, which assumes that only by mastering the separate parts of a problem can one fully comprehend it. Do differences in the ways particular cultures and societies approach problems influence cognitive development? According to Russian developmental psychologist Lev Vygotsky, who lived from 1896 to 1934, the answer is a clear "yes."

In an increasingly influential view, Vygotsky argues that the focus of cognitive development should be on a child's social and cultural world. Instead of concentrating on individual performance, as do Piagetian and many alternative approaches, Vygotsky focuses on the social aspects of development and learning. He holds that cognitive development proceeds as a result of social interactions in which partners jointly work to solve problems. Because of the assistance that such adult and peer partners provide, children gradually grow intellectually and begin to function on their own (Vygotsky, 1979;1926/1997; Wertsch & Tulviste, 1992).

Vygotsky contends that the nature of the partnership that adults and peers provide is determined largely by cultural and societal factors. For instance, culture and society establish the institutions, such as preschools and play groups—and the kindergarten that young Will, introduced in the chapter prologue, is about to enter—that promote development by providing opportunities for cognitive growth. Furthermore, by emphasizing particular tasks, culture and society shape the nature of specific cognitive advances. Unless we look at what is important and meaningful to members of a given society, we may seriously underestimate the nature and level of cognitive abilities that ultimately will be attained (Belmont, 1995; Tappan, 1997).

Vygotsky's approach is therefore quite different from that of Piaget. Where Piaget looked at developing children and saw junior scientists, working by themselves to develop an independent understanding of the world, Vygotsky saw cognitive apprentices, learning from master teachers the skills that are important in the child's culture. In Vygotsky's view, children's cognitive development is dependent on interaction with others. Vygotsky argued that it is only through partnership with other people—peers, parents, teachers, and other adults—that children can fully develop their knowledge, thinking processes, beliefs, and values (Kitchener, 1996; Fernyhough, 1997).

The Zone of Proximal Development and Scaffolding: Foundations of Cognitive Development. Vygotsky proposed that children's cognitive abilities increase through exposure to information that resides within the child's zone of proximal development. The **zone of proximal development, or ZPD,** is the level at which a child can *almost,* but not fully, perform a task independently, but can do so with the assistance of someone more competent. When appropriate instruction is offered within the zone of proximal development, children are able to increase their understanding and master new tasks. In order for cognitive develop-

zone of proximal development or **ZPD** according to Vygotsky, the level at which a child can *almost,* but not fully, perform a task independently, but can do so with the assistance of someone more competent

ment to occur, then, new information must be presented—by parents, teachers, or more skilled peers—within the zone of proximal development. For example, a preschooler might not be able to figure out by herself how to get a handle to stick on the clay pot she's building, but she could do it with some advice from her child-care teacher (Rogoff, 1990; Steward, 1995; Blank & White, 1999).

The concept of the zone of proximal development suggests that even though two children might be able to achieve the same amount without help, if one child receives aid, he or she may improve substantially more than the other. The greater the improvement that comes with help, the larger is the zone of proximal development (see Figure 7-10).

The assistance provided by others has been termed scaffolding (Wood, Bruner, & Ross, 1976). **Scaffolding** is the support for learning and problem solving that encourages independence and growth. To Vygotsky, the process of scaffolding not only helps children solve specific problems, but also aids in the development of their overall cognitive abilities.

Scaffolding takes its name from the scaffolds that are put up to aid in the construction of a building and removed once the building is complete. In education, scaffolding involves, first of all, helping children think about and frame a task in an appropriate manner. In addition, a parent or teacher is likely to provide clues to task completion that are appropriate to the child's level of development and to model behavior that can lead to completion of the task (Radiszewska & Rogoff, 1988; Rogoff, 1995). As in construction, the scaffolding that more competent people provide, which facilitates the completion of identified tasks, is removed once children are able to solve a problem on their own. For example, after suggesting some ideas for different ways to make a handle for a clay pot, the teacher might leave the child alone to try out the handle she likes best.

In some societies parental support for learning differs by gender. In one study, Mexican mothers were found to provide more scaffolding than fathers (Tenenbaum & Leaper, 1998). A possible explanation is that mothers may be more aware of their children's cognitive abilities than are fathers.

The aid that more accomplished individuals provide to learners comes in the form of cultural tools. *Cultural tools* are actual, physical items (e.g., pencils, paper, calculators, computers, and so forth), as well as an intellectual and conceptual framework for solving problems. The intellectual and conceptual framework available to learners includes the language that is used within a culture, its alphabetical and numbering schemes, its mathematical and scientific systems, and even its religious systems. These cultural tools provide a structure that can be used to help children define and solve specific problems, as well as an intellectual point of view that encourages cognitive development.

For example, consider how people talk about distance. In cities, distance is usually measured in blocks ("the store is about 15 blocks away"). To a child from a rural background, such a unit of measurement is meaningless, and more meaningful distance-related terms may be used, such as yards, miles, such practical rules of thumb as "a stone's throw,"

scaffolding the support for learning and problem solving that encourages independence and growth

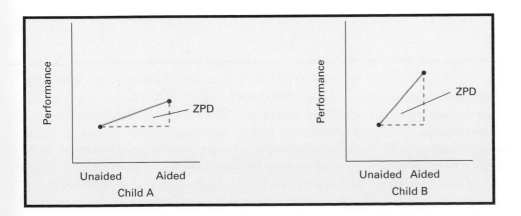

Figure 7-10 **Sample Zones of Proximal Development (ZPD) for Two Children**

Although the two children's performance is similar when working at a task without aid, Child B benefits more from aid and therefore has a larger ZPD. Is there any way to measure a child's ZPD? Can it be enlarged?

or references to known distances and landmarks ("about half the distance to town"). To make matters more complicated, "how far" questions are sometimes answered in terms not of distance, but of time ("it's about 15 minutes to the store"), which will be understood variously to refer to walking or riding time, depending on context—and, if riding time, to different forms of riding (e.g., ox cart, bicycle, bus, train, automobile, airplane), again depending on cultural context. Obviously, the nature of the tools available to children to solve problems and perform tasks is highly dependent on the culture in which they live.

Evaluating Vygotsky's Contributions. Vygotsky's view—that the specific nature of cognitive development can be understood only by taking into account cultural and social context—has become increasingly influential in the last decade. In some ways, this is surprising, in light of the fact that Vygotsky died over six decades ago at the young age of 37 (Van Der Veer & Valsiner, 1993, 1994).

Several factors explain Vygotsky's growing influence. One is that until recently he was largely unknown to developmentalists. His writings are only now becoming widely disseminated in the United States due to the growing availability of good English translations. In fact, for most of the 20th century Vygotsky was not widely known even within his native land. His work was banned for some time, and it was not until the breakup of the Soviet Union that it became freely available in the formerly Soviet countries. Thus, Vygotsky, long hidden from his fellow developmentalists, emerged onto the scene only long after his death.

Even more important, though, is the quality of Vygotsky's ideas. They represent a consistent theoretical system and help explain a growing body of research attesting to the importance of social interaction in promoting cognitive development. The idea that children's comprehension of the world is an outcome of their interactions with their parents, peers, and other members of society is both appealing and well supported by research findings. It is also consistent with a growing body of multicultural and cross-cultural research, which finds evidence that cognitive development is shaped, in part, by cultural factors (Beilin, 1996; Daniels, 1996).

Of course, not every aspect of Vygotsky's theorizing has been supported, and he can be criticized for a lack of precision in his conceptualization of cognitive growth. For instance, such broad concepts as the zone of proximal development are not terribly precise, and they do not always lend themselves to experimental tests (Wertsch, 1999).

Furthermore, Vygotsky was largely silent on how basic cognitive processes such as attention and memory develop and how children's natural cognitive capabilities unfold. Because of his emphasis on broad cultural influences, he did not focus on how individual bits of information are processed and synthesized. These processes, which must be taken into account if we are to have a complete understanding of cognitive development, are more directly addressed by information-processing theories.

Still, Vygotsky's melding of the cognitive and social worlds of children has been an important advance in our understanding of cognitive development. We can only imagine what his impact would have been if he had lived a longer life.

Review and Rethink

REVIEW

- According to Piaget, children in the preoperational stage develop symbolic function, a qualitative change in their thinking that is the foundation of further cognitive advances.

- Preoperational children use intuitive thought to explore and draw conclusions about the world, and their thinking begins to encompass the important notions of functionality and identity.

- Recent developmentalists, while acknowledging Piaget's gifts and contributions, take issue with his emphasis on children's limitations and his underestimation of their capabilities.

- Proponents of information-processing approaches argue that quantitative changes in children's processing skills largely account for their cognitive development.

- Vygotsky believes that children develop cognitively within a context of culture and society through such processes as scaffolding, the temporary support that children need to help them frame and complete tasks.

RETHINK

■ In your view, how do thought and language interact in preschoolers' development? Is it possible to think without language? How do children who have been deaf from birth think?

■ If children's cognitive development is dependent on interactions with others, what obligations does the broader society have regarding such social settings as preschools, schools, and neighborhoods?

The Growth of Language and Learning

I tried it out and it was very great!
This is a picture of when I was running through the water with Mommy.
Where you are going when I go to the fireworks with Mommy and Daddy?
I didn't know creatures went on floats in pools.
We can always pretend we have another one.
And the teacher put it up on the counter so no one could reach it.
I really want to keep it while we're at the park.
You need to get your own ball if you want to play "hit the tree."
When I grow up and I'm a baseball player, I'll have my baseball hat, and I'll put
it on, and I'll play baseball. (Schatz, 1994, p. 179)

Listen to Ricky, at the age of 3. In addition to recognizing most letters of the alphabet, printing the first letter of his name, and writing the word "HI," he is readily capable of producing the complex sentences quoted above.

During the preschool years, children's language skills reach new heights of sophistication. They begin the period with reasonable linguistic capabilities, although with significant gaps in both comprehension and production. In fact, no one would mistake the language used by a 3-year-old for that of an adult. However, by the end of the preschool years, they can hold their own with adults, both comprehending and producing language that has many of the qualities of adults' language. How does this transformation occur?

Language Development

The two-word utterances of the 2-year-old soon increase in both number of words and scope. Indeed, language blooms so rapidly between the late twos and the mid-threes that researchers have yet to understand the exact pattern. What is clear is that sentence length increases at a steady pace, and the ways in which children at this age combine words and phrases to form sentences—known as **syntax**—doubles each month. By the time a preschooler is 3, the various combinations reach into the thousands (see Table 7-4 for an example of one child's growth in the use of language; Pinker, 1994; Wheeldon, 1999).

In addition to the increasing complexity of sentences, there are enormous leaps in the number of words children use. By age 6, the average child has a vocabulary of around 14,000 words. To reach this number, preschoolers acquire vocabulary at a rate of nearly one new word every 2 hours, 24 hours a day (Clark, 1983). They manage this feat through a process known as **fast mapping,** in which new words are associated with their meaning after only a brief encounter (Fenson et al., 1994).

By the age of 3, preschoolers routinely use plurals and possessive forms of nouns (such as "boys" and "boy's"), employ the past tense (adding "-ed" at the end of words), and use articles ("the" and "a"). They can ask, and answer, complex questions ("Where did you say my book is?" and "Those are trucks, aren't they?").

Preschoolers' skills extend to the appropriate formation of words that they have never before encountered. For example, in one classic experiment, preschool children

syntax the way in which an individual combines words and phrases to form sentences

fast mapping instances in which new words are associated with their meaning after only a brief encounter

Table 7-4

GROWING SPEECH CAPABILITIES

Over the course of just a year, the sophistication of the language of a boy named Adam increases amazingly, as these speech samples show:

2 years, 3 months:	Play checkers. Big drum. I got horn. A bunny-rabbit walk.
2 years, 4 months:	See marching bear go? Screw part machine. That busy bulldozer truck.
2 years, 5 months:	Now put boots on. Where wrench go? Mommy talking bout lady. What that paper clip doing?
2 years, 6 months:	Write a piece of paper. What that egg doing? I lost a shoe. No, I don't want to sit seat.
2 years, 7 months:	Where piece a paper go? Ursula has a boot on. Going to see kitten. Put the cigarette down. Dropped a rubber band. Shadow has hat just like that. Rintintin don't fly, Mommy.
2 years, 8 months:	Let me get down with the boots on. Don't be afraid a horses. How tiger be so healthy and fly like kite? Joshua throw like a penguin.
2 years, 9 months:	Where Mommy keep her pocket book? Show you something funny. Just like turtle make mud pie.
2 years, 10 months:	Look at that train Ursula brought. I simply don't want put in chair. You don't have paper. Do you want little bit, Cromer? I can't wear it tomorrow.
2 years, 11 months:	That birdie hopping by Missouri in bag. Do want some pie on your face? Why you mixing baby chocolate? I finish drinking all up down my throat. I said why not you coming in? Look at that piece of paper and tell it. Do you want me tie that round? We going turn light on so you can't see.
3 years, 0 months:	I going come in fourteen minutes. I going wear that to wedding. I see what happens. I have to save them now. Those are not strong mens. They are going sleep in wintertime. You dress me up like a baby elephant.
3 years, 1 month:	I like to play with something else. You know how to put it back together. I gon' make it like a rocket to blast off with. I put another one on the floor. You went to Boston University? You want to give me some carrots and some beans? Press the button and catch it, sir. I want some other peanuts. Why you put the pacifier in his mouth? Doggies like to climb up.
3 years, 2 months:	So it can't be cleaned? I broke my racing car. Do you know the light wents off? What happened to the bridge? When it's got a flat tire it's need a go to the station. I dream sometimes. I'm going to mail this so the letter can't come off. I want to have some espresso. The sun is not too bright. Can I have some sugar? Can I put my head in the mailbox so the mailman can know where I are and put me in the mailbox? Can I keep the screwdriver just like a carpenter keep the screwdriver?

(*Source:* Pinker, 1994.)

were shown cards with drawings of a cartoon-like bird, such as those shown in Figure 7-11 (Berko, 1958). The experimenter told the children that the figure was a "wug," and then showed them a card with two of the cartoon figures. "Now there are two of them," the children were told, and they were then asked to supply the missing word in the sentence, "There are two ____" (the answer to which, as *you* no doubt know, is "wugs").

Not only did children show that they knew rules about the plural forms of nouns, but they understood possessive forms of nouns and the third-person singular and past-tense forms of verbs—all for words that they never had previously encountered, since they were nonsense words with no real meaning.

Preschoolers also learn what *cannot* be said as they acquire the principles of grammar. **Grammar** is the system of rules that determine how our thoughts can be expressed. For instance, preschoolers come to learn that "I am sitting" is correct, while the similarly structured "I am knowing [that]" is incorrect. Although they still make frequent mistakes of one sort or another, 3-year-olds follow the principles of grammar most of the time. Some errors are very noticeable—such as the use of "mens" and "catched"—but these er-

grammar the system of rules that determine how our thoughts can be expressed

rors are actually quite rare, occurring between one-tenth of a percent and eight percent of the time. Put another way, more than 90 percent of the time, young preschoolers are correct in their grammatical constructions (deVilliers & deVilliers, 1992; Pinker, 1994; Hirsh-Pasek & Michnick-Golinkoff, 1996).

Private Speech and Social Speech. In even a short visit to a preschool, you're likely to notice some children talking to themselves during play periods. A child might be reminding a doll that the two of them are going to the grocery store later, or another child, while playing with a toy racing car, might speak of an upcoming race. In some cases, the talk is sustained, as when a child, working on a puzzle, says things like, "This piece goes here. . . . Uh-oh, this one doesn't fit. . . . Where can I put this piece? . . . This can't be right."

Some developmentalists suggest that **private speech,** speech by children that is spoken and directed to themselves, performs an important function. For instance, Vygotsky suggests that private speech is used as a guide to behavior and thought. By communicating with themselves through private speech, children are able to try out ideas, acting as their own sounding boards. In this way, private speech facilitates children's thinking and helps them control their behavior. (Have you ever said to yourself, "Take it easy" or "Calm down" when trying to control your anger over some situation?) In Vygotsky's view, then, private speech ultimately serves an important social function, allowing children to solve problems and reflect upon difficulties they encounter (Winsler, Diaz, & Montero, 1997). He suggests further that private speech is a forerunner to the internal dialogues that we use when we reason with ourselves during thinking.

In addition, private speech may foster the development of preschoolers' pragmatic abilities. **Pragmatics** is the aspect of language relating to communicating effectively and appropriately with others. The development of pragmatic abilities permits children to understand the basics of conversations—turn-taking, sticking to a topic, and what should and should not be said, according to the conventions of society. When children are taught that the appropriate response to receiving a gift is "thank you," or that they should use different language in various settings (on the playground with their friends versus in the classroom with their teacher), they are learning the pragmatics of language.

The preschool years also mark the growth of social speech. **Social speech** is speech directed toward another person and meant to be understood by that person. Before the age of 3, children may seem to be speaking only for their own entertainment, apparently uncaring whether anyone else can understand. However, during the preschool years, children begin to direct their speech to others, wanting others to listen and becoming frustrated when they cannot make themselves understood. As a result, they begin to adapt their speech to others through pragmatics, as discussed above. Recall that Piaget contended that most speech during the preoperational period was egocentric: Preschoolers were seen as taking little account of the effect their speech was having on others. However, more recent experimental evidence suggests that children are somewhat more adept in taking others into account than Piaget initially suggested.

Poverty and Language Development. The language that preschoolers hear at home has profound implications for future cognitive success, according to results of a landmark study by psychologists Betty Hart and Todd Risley (1995). The researchers studied the language used over a 2-year period by a group of parents of varying levels of affluence as they interacted with their children. Their examination of some 1,300 hours of everyday interactions between parents and children produced several major findings:

- The greater the affluence of the parents, the more they spoke to their children. As shown in Figure 7-12, the rate at which language was addressed to children varied significantly according to the economic level of the family.

Figure 7-11 Appropriate Formation of Words

Even though no preschooler—like the rest of us—is likely to have ever before encountered a wug, they are able to produce the appropriate word to fill in the blank (which, for the record, is *wugs*).

(Adapted from Berko, 1958.)

private speech speech by children that is spoken and directed to themselves

pragmatics the aspect of language that relates to communicating effectively and appropriately with others

social speech speech directed toward another person and meant to be understood by that person

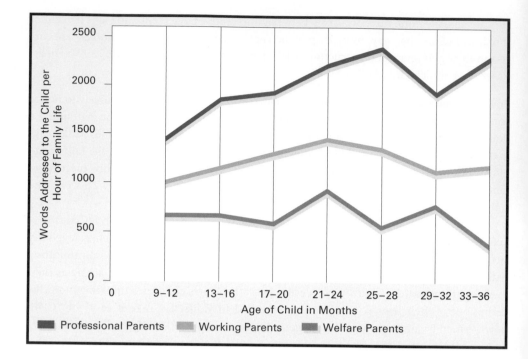

Figure 7-12 **Different Language Exposure**

Parents at differing levels of economic affluence provide different language experiences. Professional parents and working parents address more words to their children, on average, than parents on welfare. Why do you think this is so?

(*Source:* Hart & Risley, 1995.)

■ In a typical hour, parents classified as professionals spent almost twice as much time interacting with their children as parents who received welfare assistance.

■ By the age of 4, children in families that received welfare assistance were likely to have been exposed to some 13 million fewer words than those in families classified as professionals.

■ The kind of language used in the home differed among the various types of families. Children in families that received welfare assistance were apt to hear prohibitions ("no" or "stop," for example) twice as frequently as those in families classified as professionals.

Ultimately, the study found that the type of language to which children were exposed was associated with their performance on tests of intelligence. The greater the number and variety of words children heard, for instance, the better their performance at age 3 on a variety of measures of intellectual achievement.

Although the findings are correlational, and thus cannot be interpreted in terms of cause-and-effect, they clearly suggest the importance of early exposure to language, in terms of both quantity and variety. They also suggest that intervention programs that teach parents to speak to their children more often and use more varied language may be useful in alleviating some of the potentially damaging consequences of poverty.

The research is also consistent with an increasing body of evidence that family income and poverty have powerful consequences for children's general cognitive development and behavior. By the age of 5, children raised in poverty tend to have lower IQ scores and perform less well on other measures of cognitive development than children raised in affluence. Furthermore, the longer children live in poverty, the more severe are the consequences. Poverty not only reduces the educational resources available to children, it also has such negative effects on *parents* that it limits the psychological support they can provide their families. In short, the consequences of poverty are severe, and they linger (McLoyd, 1998; Ramey & Ramey, 1998; Evans, Maxwell, & Hart, 1999; Whitehurst & Fischel, 2000).

Television: Learning from the Media

It's a Thursday afternoon at Unitel Studio on Ninth Avenue, where Sesame Street *is taping its nineteenth season. Hanging back in the wings is a newcomer on the set, a compact young woman with short blonde hair named Judy Sladky. Today is her screen test. Other performers come to New York aspiring to be actresses, dancers, singers, comedians. But Sladky's burning ambition is to be Alice, a shaggy mini-mastodon who will make her debut later this season as the devoted baby sister of Aloysius Snuffle-upagus, the biggest creature on the show. (Hellman, 1987, p. 50)*

Ask almost any preschooler, and she or he will be able to identify Snuffle-upagus, as well as Big Bird, Bert, Ernie, and a host of other characters: the members of the cast of *Sesame Street*. *Sesame Street* is the most successful television show in history targeted at preschoolers; its audience is in the millions.

But *Sesame Street* is not all that preschoolers are watching, for television plays a central role in many U.S. households. In fact, it is one of the most potent and widespread stimuli to which children are exposed, with the average preschooler watching more than 21 hours of TV a week. More than a third of households with children 2 to 7 years of age say that television is on "most of the time" in their homes. In comparison, preschoolers spend three-quarters of an hour reading on the average day (see Figure 7-13; Robinson & Bianchi, 1997; Roberts et al., 1999).

Television: Controlling Exposure. Despite the introduction of a number of high-quality educational programs over the past decade, many children's programs are not of high quality or are not appropriate for a preschool audience. Accordingly, the American Academy of Pediatrics recommends that exposure to television should be limited. They suggest that until the age of 2, children watch *no* television, and after that age, no more than 1 to 2 hours of quality programming each day (American Academy of Pediatrics, 1999).

What are the limits of preschoolers' "television literacy"? When they do watch television, preschool children often do not fully understand the plots of the stories they are viewing, particularly in longer programs. They are unable to recall significant story details after viewing a program, and the inferences they make about the motivations of characters are

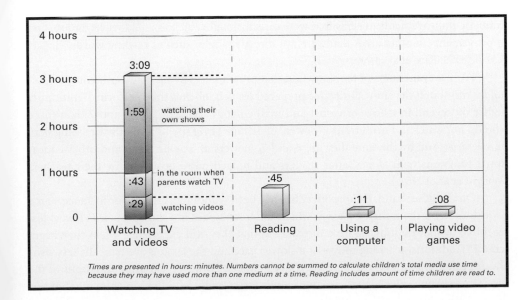

Times are presented in hours: minutes. Numbers cannot be summed to calculate children's total media use time because they may have used more than one medium at a time. Reading includes amount of time children are read to.

Figure 7-13 **Television Time**

While 2- to 7-year olds spend more time reading than playing video games or using a computer, they spend considerably more time watching television.

(*Source:* Roberts et al., 1999.)

limited and often erroneous. Moreover, preschool children may have difficulty separating fantasy from reality in television programming (Rule & Ferguson, 1986; Wright et al., 1994).

On the other hand, some kinds of information are likely to be understood relatively well by children. For instance, preschoolers are able to decode the facial expressions they see on television. Perhaps this is related to the fact that the television shows viewed most frequently by children include surprisingly high rates of nonverbal displays of emotion. However, the emotional displays that children view on TV differ from what they find in the everyday, nontelevised world. Certain emotions (such as happiness and sadness) are displayed considerably more frequently than others (for instance, fear and disgust). (Houle & Feldman, 1991; Coats & Feldman, 1995).

In short, the world to which preschoolers are exposed on TV is imperfectly understood and unrealistic. As they get older and their information-processing capabilities improve, preschoolers' understanding of the material they see on television improves. They remember things more accurately, and they become better able to focus on the central message of a show. This suggests that the powers of the medium of television may be harnessed to bring about cognitive gains—exactly what the producers of *Sesame Street* set out to do (Weisninger, 1998; Levine & Waite, 2000; Singer & Singer, 2000).

***Sesame Street:* A Teacher in Every Home?**   *Sesame Street* is, without a doubt, the most popular educational program for children in the United States. Almost half of all preschoolers in the United States watch the show, and it is broadcast in almost 100 different countries and in 13 foreign languages. Characters like Big Bird and Elmo have become familiar throughout the world to both adults and preschoolers (Liebert & Sprafkin, 1988; Bickham, Wright, & Huston, 2000).

Sesame Street was devised with the express purpose of providing an educational experience for preschoolers. Its specific goals include teaching letters and numbers, increasing vocabulary, and teaching preliteracy skills. Has *Sesame Street* achieved its goals? Most evidence suggests that it has.

For example, a 2-year longitudinal study compared three groups of 3- and 5-year-olds: those who watched cartoons or other programs, those who watched the same amount of *Sesame Street,* and those who watched little or no TV. Children who watched *Sesame Street* had significantly larger vocabularies than those who watched other programs or those who watched little television. These findings held regardless of the children's gender, family size, and parent education and attitudes. Such findings are consistent with earlier evaluations of the program, which concluded that viewers showed dramatic improvements in skills that were directly taught, such as alphabet recitation, and improvements in other areas that were not directly taught, such as reading words (Bogatz & Ball, 1972; Rice et al., 1990).

Formal evaluations of the show find that preschoolers living in lower income households who watch the show are better prepared for school, and they perform significantly higher on several measures of verbal and mathematics ability at ages 6 and 7 than those who do not watch it. Furthermore, viewers of *Sesame Street* spend more time reading than nonviewers. And by the time they are 6 and 7, viewers of *Sesame Street* and other educational programs tend to be better readers and judged more positively by their teachers (Wright et al., 1995).

On the other hand, *Sesame Street* has not been without its critics. For instance, some educators claim the frenzied pace at which different scenes are shown makes viewers less receptive to the traditional forms of teaching that they will experience when they begin school. Traditional teaching moves at a slower pace and the lessons are typically less visually appealing than those presented on *Sesame Street.* However, careful evaluations of the program find no evidence that viewing *Sesame Street* leads to declines in enjoyment of traditional schooling (Van Evra, 1990).

Early Childhood Education: Taking the "Pre" Out of the Preschool Period

The term "preschool period" is something of a misnomer: Almost three-quarters of children in the United States are enrolled in some form of care outside the home, much of which is designed either explicitly or implicitly to teach skills that will enhance intellectual as well as social abilities (see Figure 7-14). There are several reasons for this increase, but one major factor—as we considered in Chapter 6 when we discussed infant care centers—is the rise in the number of families in which both parents work outside the home. For instance, a high proportion of fathers work outside the home, and close to 60 percent of women with children under 6 are employed, most of them full-time (Gilbert, 1994; Borden, 1998).

However, there is another reason, one less tied to the practical considerations of child care: Developmental psychologists have found increasing evidence that children can benefit substantially from involvement in some form of educational activity before they enroll in formal schooling, which typically takes place at age 5 or 6 in the United States. When compared to children who stay at home and have no formal educational involvement, those children enrolled in *good* preschools experience clear cognitive and social benefits (Haskins, 1989; Clarke-Stewart, 1993; NICHD Early Child Care Research Network, 1998, 1999).

The Varieties of Early Education. The variety of early education alternatives is vast. Some outside-the-home care for children is little more than babysitting, while other options are designed to promote intellectual and social advances. Among the major choices of the latter type are the following:

- Child-care centers. **Child-care centers** typically provide care for children all day, while their parents are at work. (Child-care centers were previously referred to as *day care centers*. However, because a significant number of parents work nonstandard schedules and therefore require care for their children at times other than the day, the preferred label has changed to child-care centers.)

- Although many child-care centers were first established as safe, warm environments where children could be cared for and could interact with other children, today their purpose tends to be broader, aimed at providing some form of intellectual stimulation. Still, their primary purpose tends to be more social and emotional than cognitive.

- Some child care is provided in family child-care centers, small operations run in private homes. Because centers in some areas are unlicensed, the quality of care can be uneven, and parents should consider whether a family child-care center is licensed before enrolling their children. In contrast, providers of center-based care, which is offered in institutions such as school classrooms, community centers, and churches

child-care centers places that typically provide care for children all day while their parents are at work

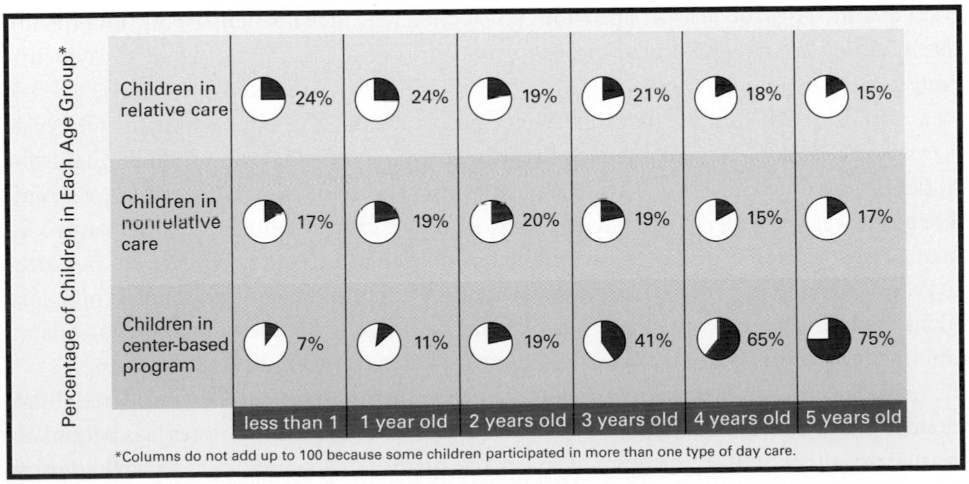

Figure 7-14 **Care Outside the Home**

Approximately 75 percent of children in the United States are enrolled in some form of care outside the home—a trend that is the result of more parents employed full time. Evidence suggests that children can benefit from early childhood education.

(*Source:* U.S. Department of Education, National Center)

Children in relative care: less than 1: 24%, 1 year old: 24%, 2 years old: 19%, 3 years old: 21%, 4 years old: 18%, 5 years old: 15%

Children in nonrelative care: less than 1: 17%, 1 year old: 19%, 2 years old: 20%, 3 years old: 19%, 4 years old: 15%, 5 years old: 17%

Children in center-based program: less than 1: 7%, 1 year old: 11%, 2 years old: 19%, 3 years old: 41%, 4 years old: 65%, 5 years old: 75%

Percentage of Children in Each Age Group*

*Columns do not add up to 100 because some children participated in more than one type of day care.

and synagogues, are typically licensed and regulated by governmental authorities. Because teachers in such programs are more often trained professionals than those who provide family child care, the quality of care is often higher and more stable.

- Preschools or nursery schools. **Preschools** (or **nursery schools**) are more explicitly designed to provide intellectual and social experiences for children. Because they tend to be more limited in their schedules, typically providing care for only 3 to 5 hours per day, preschools mainly serve children from middle and higher socioeconomic levels.

- Like child-care centers, preschools vary enormously in the activities they provide. Some emphasize social skills, while others focus on intellectual development. Some do both. For instance, Montessori preschools, which use a method developed by Italian educator Maria Montessori, employ a carefully designed set of materials to create an environment that fosters sensory, motor, and language development.

- School child care. **School child care** is provided by some local school systems in the United States. Almost half the states in the United States fund prekindergarten programs for 4-year-olds, often targeted at disadvantaged children. Because they typically are staffed by better-trained teachers than less-regulated child-care centers, school child-care programs are often of higher quality than other early education alternatives.

preschools (or **nursery schools**) child-care facilities designed to provide intellectual and social experiences for children

school child care child-care facility provided by some local school systems in the United States

cw

How effective are such programs? Most research suggests that preschoolers enrolled in child-care centers show intellectual development that at least matches that of children at home, and often is better. For instance, some studies find that preschoolers in child care are more verbally fluent, show memory and comprehension advantages, and even achieve higher IQ scores than at-home children. Other studies find that early and long-term participation in child care is particularly helpful for children from impoverished home environments or who are otherwise at risk (Clarke-Stewart, 1993; Ramey & Ramey, 1999; Erel, Oberman, & Yirmiya, 2000).

Analogous advantages are found in social development. Children in high-quality programs tend to be more self-confident, independent, and knowledgeable about the social world in which they live than those who do not participate. On the other hand, not all the outcomes of outside-the-home care are positive: Children in child care have been found to be less polite, less compliant, less respectful of adults, and sometimes more competitive and aggressive than their peers (Belsky, Steinberg, & Walker, 1982; Thornburg et al., 1990; Bates et al., 1991).

It is important to keep in mind that not all early childhood care programs are equally effective. As we observed of infant child care in Chapter 6, one key factor is program *quality:* High-quality care provides intellectual and social benefits, while low-quality care not only is unlikely to furnish benefits, but poor programs actually may harm children (Ramey & Ramey, 1999; NICHD Early Child Care Research Network, 1999).

How can we define "high quality"? Several characteristics are important; they are analogous to those that pertain to infant child care (see Chapter 6). For example, high-quality facilities have well-trained care providers. Furthermore, both the overall size of the group and the ratio of care providers to children are critical. Single groups should not have many more than 14 to 20 children, and there should be no more than five to ten 3-year-olds per caregiver, or seven to ten 4- or 5-year-olds per caregiver. Finally, the curriculum of a child-care facility should not be left to chance, but should be carefully planned out and coordinated among the teachers (National Research Council, 1991; Cromwell, 1994; Scarr, 1997).

No one knows how many programs in the United States can be considered "high quality," but there are many fewer than desirable. In fact, the United States lags behind almost every other industrialized country in the quality of its child care as well as in its quantity and affordability (Zigler & Finn-Stevenson, 1995; Scarr, 1998).

Developmental Diversity

Preschools Around the World

In France and Belgium, access to preschool is a legal right. In Sweden and Finland, preschoolers whose parents work have child care provided, if it is wanted. Russia has an extensive system of state-run *yasli-sads,* nursery schools and kindergartens, attended by 75 percent of children age 3 to 7 in urban areas.

In contrast, the United States has no coordinated national policy on preschool education—or on the care of children in general. There are several reasons for this. For one, decisions about education have traditionally been left to the states and local school districts. For another, the United States has no tradition of teaching preschoolers, unlike other countries in which preschool-age children have been enrolled in formal programs for decades. Finally, the status of preschools in the United States has been traditionally low. Consider, for instance, that preschool and nursery school teachers are the lowest paid of all teachers. (Teacher salaries increase as the age of students rises. Thus, college and high school teachers are paid most, while preschool and elementary school teachers are paid least.)

Preschools also differ significantly from one country to another according to the views that different societies hold of the purpose of early childhood education (Lamb et al., 1992). For instance, in a cross-country comparison of preschools in China, Japan, and the United States, researchers found that parents in the three countries view the purpose of preschools very differently. Whereas parents in China tend to see preschools primarily as a way of giving children a good start academically, Japanese parents view them primarily as a way of giving children the opportunity to be members of a group. In the United States, in comparison, parents regard the primary purpose of preschools as making children more independent and self-reliant, although obtaining a good academic start and having group experience are also important (see Figure 7-15; Tobin, Wu, & Davidson, 1989; Huntsinger et al., 1997). ☐

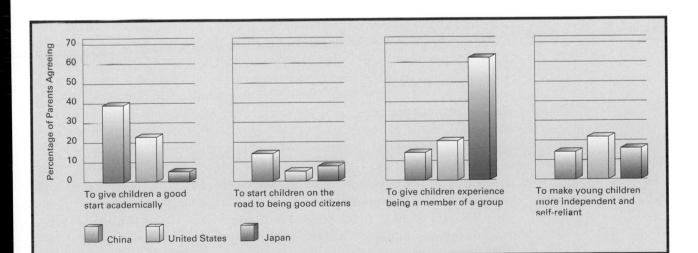

Figure 7-15 **The Purpose of Preschool**

To parents in China, Japan, and the United States, the main purpose of preschools is very different. Whereas parents in China see preschools mainly as a way of giving children a good start academically, parents in Japan see them primarily as a means of giving children the experience of being a member of a group. In contrast, parents in the United States view preschools as a way of making children more independent, although obtaining a good academic start and group experience are also important. How do you interpret these findings?

(*Source:* Based on Tobin, Wu, & Davidson, 1989.)

Preparing Preschoolers for Academic Pursuits: Does Head Start Truly Provide a Head Start? Although many programs designed for preschoolers focus primarily on social and emotional factors, some are geared primarily toward promoting cognitive gains and preparing preschoolers for the more formal instruction they will experience when they start kindergarten. In the United States, the best-known program designed to promote future academic success is Head Start. Born in the 1960s when the United States declared a War on Poverty, the program has served over 13 million children and their families. The program, which stresses parental involvement, was designed to serve the "whole child," including children's physical health, self-confidence, social responsibility, and social and emotional development (Zigler, Styfco, & Gilman, 1993; Zigler & Styfco, 1994; Ripple et al., 1999).

Whether Head Start is seen as successful or not depends on the lens through which one is looking. If, for instance, the program is expected to provide long-term increases in IQ scores, it is a disappointment. Although graduates of Head Start programs tend to show immediate IQ gains, these increases do not last. On the other hand, it is clear that Head Start is meeting its goal of getting preschoolers ready for school. Preschoolers who participate in Head Start are better prepared for future schooling than those who do not. Furthermore, graduates of Head Start programs have better future school adjustment than their peers, and they are less likely to be in special education classes or to be retained in grade. Finally, some research suggests that ultimately Head Start graduates show higher academic performance at the end of high school, although the gains are modest (Galper, Wigfield, & Seefeldt, 1997; Ramey & Ramey, 1999; Schnur & Belanger, 2000).

In addition, results from other types of preschool readiness programs indicate that those who participate and graduate are less likely to repeat grades, and they complete school more frequently than those who are not in the program. Moreover, according to a cost-benefit analysis of one preschool readiness program, for every dollar spent on the program, taxpayers saved seven dollars by the time the graduates reached the age of 27 (Schweinhart, Barnes, & Weikart, 1993).

The most recent comprehensive evaluation of early intervention programs suggests that, taken as a group, preschool programs can provide significant benefits, and that government funds invested early in life may ultimately lead to a reduction in future costs. For instance, compared with children who did not participate in early intervention programs, participants in various programs showed gains in emotional or cognitive development, better educational outcomes, increased economic self-sufficiency, reduced levels of criminal activity, and improved health-related behaviors. Of course, not every program produced all these benefits, and not every child benefited to the same extent. Furthermore, some researchers argue that less expensive programs are just as good as relatively expensive ones, such as Head Start. Still, the results of the evaluation were promising, suggesting that the potential benefits of early intervention can be substantial (Scarr, 1996, 1998; Karoly et al., 1998; Campbell et al., 2001). (For more on preschool programs from the perspective of a caregiver, see the Speaking of Development interview.)

Should We Seek to Improve Cognitive Skills During the Preschool Years? Not everyone agrees that programs that seek to enhance academic skills during the preschool years are a good thing. In fact, according to developmental psychologist David Elkind, U.S. society tends to push children so rapidly that they begin to feel stress and pressure at a young age (Elkind, 1984, 1988).

Elkind argues that academic success is largely dependent upon factors out of parents' control, such as inherited abilities and a child's rate of maturation. Consequently, children of a particular age cannot be expected to master educational material without taking into account their current level of cognitive development. In short, children require **developmentally appropriate educational practice,** which is education that is based on both typical development and the unique characteristics of a given child (Bredekamp, 1989; Cromwell, 1994).

developmentally appropriate educational practice education that is based on both typical development and the unique characteristics of a given child

Roberto Recio, Jr., Preschool Teacher

EDUCATION: Associates Degree, early childhood education, Daley College, Chicago, Illinois

HOME: Chicago

For Robert Recio, head teacher at the Christopher House Uptown preschool in Chicago, each day offers new challenges as he seeks to enhance children's development.

Recio tries to be more of a role model, guide, and facilitator than a teacher, he says. "I try to prepare the environment to provide stimulating and challenging material. For children to fully understand what is going on, the information you provide has to be meaningful for them. If it's not relevant, they won't be motivated and will not get it."

Recio, who along with two assistants is responsible for 20 children ages 3 to 5, uses a lot of hands-on approaches to learning.

"The other day we were taking about fishing, so I went to the market and bought an actual fish and brought it in the next day," Recio said. "You should have seen the smiles on their faces as they were touching it and smelling it. Most of these children have never seen a real fish. We later used it in an art project, making prints with it," he said.

Recio is constantly interacting with the children and challenging them, even when doing chores.

"When they set tables for lunch, I will ask them how many utensils need to be used. Or when setting up chairs, I will put out fewer than the number of children we have, and I'll have them figure out how many more are needed," he said.

While math, science, and art are all covered in Recio's class on a daily basis, one additional area he feels is particularly important is making the children aware of the diversity within their community.

"We have a lot of cultural diversity in our class," he said. At the same time, "I like to have them understand that we are all the same inside," he added.

Rather than arbitrarily expecting children to master material at a particular age, Elkind suggests that a better strategy is to provide an environment in which learning is encouraged, but not pushed. By creating an atmosphere in which learning is facilitated—for instance, by reading to preschoolers—parents will allow children to proceed at their own pace rather than at one that pushes them beyond their limits (Reese & Cox, 1999).

Although Elkind's suggestions are appealing—it is certainly hard to disagree that increases in children's anxiety levels and stress should be avoided—they are not without their detractors. For instance, some educators have argued that pushing children is largely a phenomenon of the middle and higher socioeconomic levels, possible only if parents are relatively affluent. For poorer children, whose parents may not have substantial resources available to push their children nor the easy ability to create an environment that promotes learning, the benefits of formal programs that promote learning are likely to outweigh their drawbacks.

Review and Rethink

REVIEW

- In the preschool years, children rapidly increase in linguistic ability, developing an improved sense of grammar and shifting gradually from private to social speech.
- Poverty can affect children's language development by limiting the opportunities for parents and other caregivers to interact linguistically with children.
- Preschoolers watch television at high levels. The effects of television on preschoolers are mixed, with benefits from some programs and clear disadvantages due to other aspects of viewing.
- Preschool educational programs are beneficial if they are of high quality, with trained staff, good curriculum, proper group sizes, and small staff-student ratios.

■ Preschool children are likely to benefit from a developmentally appropriate, individualized, and supportive environment for learning.

RETHINK

■ Is private speech egocentric or useful? Do adults ever use private speech? What functions does it serve?

■ Do you accept the view that children in U.S. society are "pushed" academically to the extent that they feel too much stress and pressure at a young age? Why?

Looking Back

▶ What is the state of children's bodies and overall health during the preschool years?

■ In addition to gaining height and weight, the bodies of preschool children undergo changes in shape and structure. Children grow more slender, and their bones and muscles strengthen.

■ Children in the preschool years are generally quite healthy. Obesity in these years is caused by genetic and environmental factors. The greatest health threats are accidents and environmental factors.

▶ How do preschool children's brains and physical skills develop?

■ Brain growth is particularly rapid during the preschool years, with the number of interconnections among cells and the amount of myelin around neurons increasing greatly. The halves of the brain begin to specialize in somewhat different tasks—a process called lateralization.

■ Both gross and fine motor skills advance rapidly during the preschool years. Gender differences begin to emerge, fine motor skills are honed, and handedness begins to assert itself.

▶ How does Piaget interpret cognitive development during the preschool years?

■ During the stage that Piaget has described as *preoperational*, children are not yet able to engage in organized, formal, logical thinking. However, their development of symbolic function permits quicker and more effective thinking as they are freed from the limitations of sensorimotor learning.

■ According to Piaget, children in the preoperational stage engage in intuitive thought for the first time, actively applying rudimentary reasoning skills to the acquisition of world knowledge.

▶ How do other views of cognitive development differ from Piaget's?

■ A different approach to cognitive development is taken by proponents of information-processing theories, who focus on preschoolers' storage and recall of information and on quantitative changes in information-processing abilities (such as attention).

■ Lev Vygotsky proposed that the nature and progress of children's cognitive development are dependent on the children's social and cultural context.

▶ How does children's language develop in the preschool years?

■ Children rapidly progress from two-word utterances to longer, more sophisticated expressions that reflect their growing vocabularies and emerging grasp of grammar.

■ The development of linguistic abilities is affected by socioeconomic status. The result can be lowered linguistic—and ultimately academic—performance by poorer children.

▶ What effects does television have on preschoolers?

■ The effects of television are mixed. Preschoolers' sustained exposure to emotions and situations that are not representative of the real world have raised concerns. On the other hand, preschoolers can derive meaning from such targeted programs as *Sesame Street*, which are designed to bring about cognitive gains.

▶ What kinds of preschool educational programs are available?

■ Early childhood educational programs, offered as center-based or school-based child care or as preschool, can lead to cognitive and social advances.

■ The United States lacks a coordinated national policy on preschool education. The major federal initiative in U.S. preschool education has been the Head Start program, which has yielded mixed results.

E P I L O G U E

In this chapter, we looked at children in the preschool years, focusing on their physical development, growth, nutritional needs, overall health, brain growth, and advances in gross and fine motor skills. We discussed cognitive development from the Piagetian perspective, with its description of the characteristics of thought in the preoperational stage, and from the perspective of information-processing theorists and Lev Vygotsky. We then discussed the burst in linguistic ability that occurs during the preschool years and the influence of television on preschoolers' development. We concluded with a discussion of preschool education and its effects.

Return to the prologue, which describes Will's preparation for his first day of kindergarten, and answer these questions.

1. According to Piaget, what sorts of understandings—and limitations to his understandings—will Will have as he enters school?

2. From a broad developmental perspective (including physical and cognitive development), what is Will now able to do that he couldn't do a year or two ago?

3. Can you discuss from an information-processing perspective the likely course of Will's cognitive development during his preschool years? What most likely changed as he progressed toward kindergarten, and why?

4. In what ways is kindergarten likely to affect Will's sense of the pragmatics of language that govern communications with others?

5. To what aspects of the school "culture" that Will is joining do Vygotsky's theories apply? What features of the typical kindergarten program would a follower of Vygotsky emphasize?

Key Terms and Concepts

obesity (p. 218)
lateralization (p. 222)
handedness (p. 227)
preoperational stage (p. 228)
operations (p. 229)
centration (p. 229)
conservation (p. 230)
transformation (p. 231)
egocentric thought (p. 231)

intuitive thought (p. 233)
autobiographical memory (p. 236)
scripts (p. 236)
zone of proximal development (ZPD) (p. 240)
scaffolding (p. 241)
syntax (p. 243)
fast mapping (p. 243)
grammar (p. 244)

private speech (p. 245)
pragmatics (p. 245)
social speech (p. 245)
child-care centers (p. 249)
preschools (or nursery schools) (p. 250)
school child care (p. 250)
developmentally appropriate educational practice (p. 252)

OUTLINE

Social and Personality Development in the Preschool Years

PROLOGUE: FEELING HIS MOTHER'S PAIN

During the preschool years a child's ability to understand others' emotions begins to grow.

When Alison Gopnik got home from the lab one day, she was overcome with the feeling that she was a lousy teacher, an incompetent scientist, and a bad mother. A student had argued about a grade, a grant proposal had been rejected, and the chicken legs she'd planned for dinner were still in the freezer. So the University of California, Berkeley, developmental psychologist collapsed on the couch and started to cry. Her son, almost 2, sized up the situation like a little pro. He dashed to the bathroom, fumbled around for what he needed, and returned with Band-Aids—which he proceeded to stick all over his sobbing (and now startled) mother, figuring that eventually he would find the place that needed patching. (Begley, 2000, p. 25)

Looking Ahead   Like most 2-year-olds, Gopnik's son not only could share his mother's pain, but was able to try to soothe it. During the preschool years, children's ability to understand others' emotions begins to grow, and it colors their relationships with others.

In this chapter we address social and personality development during the preschool period, a time of enormous growth and change. We begin by examining how preschool-age children continue to form a sense of self, focusing on how they develop their self-concepts. We especially examine issues of self relating to gender, a central aspect of children's views of themselves and others.

Preschoolers' social lives are the focus of the next part of the chapter. We look at how children play with one another, examining the various types of play. We consider how parents and other authority figures use discipline to shape children's behavior.

Finally, we examine two key aspects of preschool-age children's social behavior: moral development and aggression. We consider how children develop a notion of right and wrong, and how that development can lead them to be helpful to others. We also look at the other side of the coin—aggression—and examine the factors that lead preschool-age children to behave in a way that hurts others. We end on an optimistic note: considering how we may help preschool-age children to be more moral, and less aggressive, individuals.

After reading this chapter, you'll be able to answer these questions:

▶ **How do preschool-age children develop a concept of themselves?**

▶ **How do children develop their sense of racial identity and gender?**

▶ **In what sorts of social relationships do preschool-age children engage?**

▶ **What sorts of disciplinary styles do parents employ, and what effects do they have?**

▶ **What factors contribute to child abuse and neglect?**

▶ **How do children develop a moral sense?**

▶ **How does aggression develop in preschool-age children?**

Forming a Sense of Self

Although the question "Who am I?" is not explicitly posed by most preschool-age children, it underlies a considerable amount of development during the preschool years. During this period, children wonder about the nature of the self, and the way they answer the "Who am I?" question may affect them for the rest of their lives.

Psychosocial Development: Resolving the Conflicts

MaryAlice's preschool teacher raised her eyebrows slightly when the 4-year-old took off her coat. MaryAlice, usually dressed in well-matched play suits, was a medley of prints. She had on a pair of flowered pants along with a completely clashing plaid top. The outfit was accessorized with a striped headband, socks in an animal print, and MaryAlice's polka-dotted rain boots. MaryAlice's mom gave a slightly embarrassed shrug. "MaryAlice got dressed all by herself this

The view of the self that preschoolers develop depends in part on the culture in which they grow up.

morning," she explained as she handed over a bag containing spare shoes, just in case the rain boots became uncomfortable during the day.

Psychoanalyst Erik Erikson may well have praised MaryAlice's mother for helping MaryAlice develop a sense of initiative (if not of fashion). The reason: Erickson (1963) suggested that, during the preschool years, children face a key conflict relating to psychosocial development that involves the development of initiative.

As we discussed in Chapter 6, **psychosocial development** encompasses changes both in the understandings individuals have of themselves as members of society and in their comprehension of the meaning of others' behavior. Erikson suggests that throughout life, society and culture present particular challenges, which shift as people age. As we noted in Chapter 6, Erikson suggests that people pass through eight distinct stages, each of which necessitates resolution of a crisis or conflict. Our experiences as we try to resolve these conflicts lead us to develop ideas about ourselves that can last for the rest of our lives.

In the early part of the preschool period, children are ending the autonomy-versus-shame-and-doubt stage, which lasts from around 18 months to 3 years. In this period, children either become more independent and autonomous if their parents encourage exploration and freedom or they experience shame and self-doubt if they are restricted and overprotected.

The preschool years largely encompass the **initiative-versus-guilt stage,** which lasts from around age 3 to age 6. It is during this period that children's views of themselves undergo major change as preschool-age children face conflicts between, on the one hand, the desire to act independently of their parents and, on the other hand, the guilt that comes from the unintended consequences of their actions. In essence, preschool-age children come to realize that they are persons in their own right, and they begin to make decisions and to shape the kind of persons that they will become.

Parents, such as MaryAlice's mother, who react positively to this transformation toward independence can help their children resolve the opposing feelings that are characteristic of this period. By providing their children with opportunities to act self-reliantly, while still giving them direction and guidance, parents can support and encourage their

psychosocial development according to Erikson, development that encompasses changes both in the understandings individuals have of themselves as members of society and in their comprehension of the meaning of others' behavior

initiative-versus-guilt stage according to Erikson, the period during which children aged 3 to 6 years experience conflict between independence of action and the sometimes negative results of that action

children's initiative. On the other hand, parents who discourage their children's efforts to seek independence may contribute to a sense of guilt that persists throughout their lives as well as affects their self-concept, which begins to develop during this period.

Self-Concept in the Preschool Years: Thinking About the Self

If you ask preschool-age children to specify what makes them different from other kids, they readily respond with answers like, "I'm a good runner" or "I like to color" or "I'm a big girl." Such answers relate to **self-concept**—their identity, or their set of beliefs about what they are like as individuals (Pipp-Siegel & Foltz, 1997; Brown, 1998; Tessor, Felson, & Suls, 2000).

The statements that describe children's self-concepts are not necessarily accurate. In fact, preschool children typically overestimate their skills and knowledge across all domains of expertise. Consequently, their view of the future is quite rosy: They expect to win the next game they play, to beat all opponents in an upcoming race, to write great stories when they grow up. Even when they have just experienced failure at a task, they are likely to expect to do well in the future. This optimistic view is held, in part, because they have not yet started to compare themselves and their performance against others (Stipek & Hoffman, 1980; Ruble, 1983; Damon & Hart, 1988).

Preschool-age children also begin to develop a view of self that reflects the way their particular culture considers the self. For example, many Asian societies tend to have a **collectivistic orientation**, promoting the notion of interdependence. People in such cultures tend to regard themselves as parts of a larger social network in which they are interconnected with others. In contrast, children in Western cultures are more likely to develop an independent view of the self, reflecting an **individualistic orientation** that emphasizes personal identity and the uniqueness of the individual. They are more apt to see themselves as self-contained and autonomous, in competition with others for scarce resources. Consequently, children in Western cultures are more likely to focus on their uniqueness and what sets them apart from others—what makes them special.

Such views pervade a culture, sometimes in subtle ways. For instance, one well-known saying in Western cultures states that "the squeaky wheel gets the grease." Preschoolers who are exposed to this perspective come to understand that they should seek to get the attention of others by standing out and making their needs known. On the other hand, children in Asian cultures are exposed to a different perspective; they are told that "the nail that stands out gets pounded down." This perspective suggests to preschoolers that they should attempt to blend in and refrain from making themselves distinctive (Markus & Kitayama, 1991; Triandis, 1995).

Preschoolers' developing self-concepts can also be affected by their culture's attitudes toward various racial and ethnic groups, as we'll see next.

Developmental Diversity

Developing Racial and Ethnic Awareness

The preschool years mark an important turning point for children. Their answer to the question of who they are begins to take into account their racial and ethnic identity.

For most preschool-age children, racial awareness comes relatively early. Certainly, even infants are able to distinguish different skin colors; their perceptual abilities allow for such color distinctions quite early in life. However, it is only later that children begin to attribute meaning to different racial characteristics. By the time they are 3 or 4 years of age,

---

self-concept a person's identity, or set of beliefs about what one is like as an individual

collectivistic orientation a philosophy that promotes the notion of interdependence

individualistic orientation a philosophy that emphasizes personal identity and the uniqueness of the individual

preschool-age children distinguish between African Americans and whites and begin to understand the significance that society places on racial membership (Signorella, Bigler & Liben, 1993; Sheets & Hollins, 1999).

At the same time, some preschool-age children start to experience ambivalence over the meaning of their racial and ethnic identity. Some preschoolers experience **race dissonance,** the phenomenon in which minority children indicate preferences for majority values or people. For instance, some studies find that as many as 90 percent of African American children, when asked about their reactions to drawings of black and white children, react more negatively to the drawings of black children than to those of white children. However, these negative reactions did not translate into lower self-esteem for the African American subjects. Instead, their preferences appear to be a result of the powerful influence of the dominant white culture rather than a disparagement of their own racial characteristics (Holland, 1994).

Ethnic identity emerges somewhat later. For instance, in one study of Mexican American ethnic awareness, preschoolers displayed only a limited knowledge of their ethnic identity. However, as they became older, their understanding of their racial background grew in both magnitude and complexity. In addition, those preschoolers who were bilingual, speaking both Spanish and English, were most apt to be aware of their racial identity (Bernal, 1994).

race dissonance the phenomenon in which minority children indicate preferences for majority values or people

Gender Identity: Developing Femaleness and Maleness

Boys' awards: Very Best Thinker, Most Eager Learner, Most Imaginative, Most Enthusiastic, Most Scientific, Best Friend, Mr. Personality, Hardest Worker, Best Sense of Humor.

Girls' awards: All-Around Sweetheart, Sweetest Personality, Cutest Personality, Best Sharer, Best Artist, Biggest Heart, Best Manners, Best Helper, Most Creative.

What's wrong with this picture? To one parent, whose daughter received one of the girls' awards during a kindergarten graduation ceremony, quite a bit. While the girls were getting pats on the back for their pleasing personalities, the boys were receiving awards for their intellectual and analytic skills (Deveny, 1994).

Such a situation is not rare: Girls and boys often live in very different worlds. Differences in the ways males and females are treated begin at birth (as we noted in Chapter 6), continue during the preschool years, and—as we'll see later—extend into adolescence and beyond (Coltrane & Adams, 1997; Maccoby, 1999).

Gender, the sense of being male or female, is well established by the time children reach the preschool years. (As we first noted in Chapter 6, "gender" and "sex" do not mean the same thing. *Sex* typically refers to sexual anatomy and sexual behavior, while *gender* refers to the perception of maleness or femaleness related to membership in a given society). By the age of 2, children consistently label themselves and those around them as male or female (Signorella, Bigler, & Liben, 1993; Fagot & Leinbach, 1993; Poulin-Dubois et al., 1994.)

One way gender is manifested is in play. During the preschool years, boys spend more time than girls in rough-and-tumble play, while girls spend more time than boys in organized games and role-playing. Furthermore, boys begin to play more with boys, and girls play more with girls, a trend that increases during middle childhood. Actually, girls begin the process of preferring same-sex playmates a little earlier than boys. Girls first have a clear preference for interacting with other girls at age 2, while boys don't show much preference for same-sex partners until age 3 (Fagot, 1991; Ramsey, 1995; Braza et al., 1997).

During the preschool period, differences in play, relating to gender, become more pronounced. In addition, boys tend to play with boys, and girls with girls.

Such same-sex preferences appear in many cultures. For instance, studies of kindergartners in mainland China show no examples of mixed-gender play. Similarly, gender "outweighs" ethnic variables when it comes to play: A Hispanic boy would rather play with a white boy than with a Hispanic girl (Whiting & Edwards, 1988; Fishbein & Imai, 1993; Martin, 1993).

Preschool-age children also begin to hold expectations about appropriate behavior for girls and boys. In fact, their expectations about gender-appropriate behavior are even more rigid and gender-stereotyped than those of adults and may be less flexible during the preschool years than at any other point in the life span. For instance, beliefs in gender stereotypes become more pronounced up to age 5 and have already started to become somewhat less rigid by age 7, although they do not disappear altogether. In fact, the content of gender stereotypes held by preschoolers is similar to that held traditionally by adults in society (Urberg, 1982; Golombok & Fivush, 1994; Yee & Brown, 1994).

And what is the nature of preschoolers' gender expectations? Like adults, preschoolers expect that males are more apt to have traits involving competence, independence, forcefulness, and competitiveness. In contrast, females are viewed as more likely to have traits such as warmth, expressiveness, nurturance, and submissiveness. Although these are *expectations,* and say nothing about the way that men and women actually behave, such expectations provide the lens through which preschool-age children view the world. Preschoolers' views and expectations affect their own behavior as well as the way they interact with peers and adults (Signorella, Bigler, & Liben, 1993; Durkin & Nugent, 1998).

The prevalence and strength of preschoolers' gender expectations, and differences in behavior between boys and girls, have proven puzzling. Why should gender play such a powerful role during the preschool years (as well as during the rest of the life span)? Developmentalists have proposed several explanations.

Biological Perspectives on Gender. Recall that gender relates to the sense of being male or female, while sex refers to the physical characteristics that differentiate males and females. It would hardly be surprising to find that the physical characteristics associated with sex might themselves lead to gender differences, and this in fact has been shown to be true.

Hormones are one such biological characteristic. Some research has focused on girls whose mothers had taken drugs that contained high levels of *androgens* (male hormones) to treat medical problems they had before they realized that they were pregnant. These androgen-exposed girls are more likely to display behaviors associated with male stereotypes than are their sisters who were not exposed to androgens (Money & Ehrhardt, 1972). Androgen-exposed girls preferred boys as playmates and spent more time than other girls playing with toys associated with the male role, such as cars and trucks. Similarly, boys prenatally exposed to unusually high levels of female hormones are apt to display more behaviors that are stereotypically female than is usual (Berenbaum & Hines, 1992; Hines & Kaufman, 1994).

Moreover, as we first noted in Chapter 7, some research suggests that biological differences exist in the structure of female and male brains. For instance, part of the *corpus callosum*, the bundle of nerves that connects the hemispheres of the brain, is proportionally larger in women than in men (Whitelson, 1989). To some theoreticians, evidence such as this suggests that gender differences may be produced by biological factors (Benbow, Lubinski, & Hyde, 1997).

Before accepting such contentions, however, it is important to note that alternative explanations abound. For example, it may be that the *corpus callosum* is proportionally larger in women as a result of certain kinds of experiences that influence brain growth in particular ways. If this is true, environmental experience produces biological change—and not the other way around.

Other developmentalists see gender differences as reflecting the goal of survival of the species through reproduction. Basing their work on an evolutionary approach, these theorists suggest that our male ancestors who showed more stereotypically masculine qualities, such as forcefulness and competitiveness, may have been able to attract females who were able to provide them with hardy offspring. Females who excelled at stereotypically feminine tasks, such as nurturing, may have been valuable partners because they could increase the likelihood that children would survive the dangers of childhood (Geary, 1998).

As in other domains that involve the interaction of inherited biological characteristics and environmental influences, it is difficult to attribute behavioral characteristics unambiguously to biological factors. Because of this problem, we must consider other explanations for gender differences.

According to social learning approaches, children observe the behavior of same-sex adults and come to imitate it.

Psychoanalytic Perspectives. You may recall from Chapter 1 that Freud's psychoanalytic theory suggests that we move through a series of stages related to biological urges. To Freud, the preschool years encompass the *phallic stage*, in which the focus of a child's pleasure relates to genital sexuality.

Freud argued that the end of the phallic stage is marked by an important turning point in development: the Oedipal conflict. According to Freud, the *Oedipal conflict* occurs at around the age of 5, when the anatomical differences between males and females become particularly evident. Boys begin to develop sexual interests in their mothers, viewing their fathers as rivals. As a consequence, boys conceive a desire to kill their fathers—just as Oedipus did in the ancient Greek tragedy. However, because they view their fathers as all-powerful, boys develop a fear of retaliation, which takes the form of *castration anxiety*. In order to overcome this fear, boys repress their desires for their mothers and instead begin to identify with their fathers, attempting to be as similar to them as possible. **Identification** is the process in which children attempt to be similar to their same-sex parent, incorporating the parent's attitudes and values.

Girls, according to Freud, go through a different process. They begin to feel sexual attraction toward their fathers and experience *penis envy*—a view that not unexpectedly has led to accusations that Freud viewed women as inferior to men. In order to resolve their penis envy, girls ultimately identify with their mothers, attempting to be as similar to them as possible.

In the cases of both boys and girls, the ultimate result of identifying with the same-sex parent is that the children adopt their parents' gender attitudes and values. In this way,

identification the process in which children attempt to be similar to their same-sex parent, incorporating the parent's attitudes and values

says Freud, society's expectations about the ways females and males "ought" to behave are perpetuated into new generations.

If you are like many people, you may find it difficult to accept Freud's elaborate explanation of gender differences. So do most developmentalists, who believe that gender development is best explained by other mechanisms. In part, they base their criticisms of Freud on the lack of scientific support for his theories. For example, children learn gender stereotypes much earlier than the age of 5. Furthermore, this learning occurs even in single-parent households. However, some aspects of psychoanalytic theory have been supported, such as findings indicating that preschool-age children whose same-sex parents support sex-stereotyped behavior tend to demonstrate that behavior also. Still, far simpler processes can account for this phenomenon, and many developmentalists have searched for explanations of gender differences other than Freud's (Mussen, 1969; Maccoby, 1980).

Social Learning Approaches. According to social learning approaches, children learn gender-related behavior and expectations from their observation of others. In this view, children watch the behavior of their parents, teachers, siblings, and even peers. Their observation of the rewards that these others attain for acting in a gender-appropriate manner leads them to conform to such behavior themselves (Rust et al., 2000).

Books and the media, and in particular television and video games, also play a role in perpetuating traditional views of gender-related behavior from which preschoolers may learn. Analyses of the most popular television shows, for example, find that male characters outnumber female characters by 2 to 1. Furthermore, females are more apt to appear with males, whereas female–female relationships are relatively uncommon.

Television also presents men and women in traditional gender roles. For instance, television shows typically define female characters in terms of their relationships with males. Also, females appear as victims far more often than do males (Wright et al., 1995; Turner-Bowker, 1996). Furthermore, women are much less likely to be illustrated as decision-makers or productive individuals, and more likely to be portrayed as characters interested in romance, their homes, and their families. Such models, according to social learning theory, are apt to have a powerful influence on preschoolers' definitions of appropriate behavior (VandeBerg & Streckfuss, 1992; Browne, 1998).

In some cases, learning of social roles does not involve models, but occurs more directly. For example, most of us have heard preschool-age children being told by their parents to act like a "little girl" or "little man." What this generally means is that girls should behave politely and courteously, or that boys should be tough and stoic—traits associated with society's traditional stereotypes of men and women. Such direct training sends a clear message about the behavior expected of a preschool-age child (Witt, 1997).

Cognitive Approaches. In the view of some theorists, the desire to form a clear sense of identity leads children to establish a **gender identity,** a perception of themselves as male or female. To do this, they develop a **gender schema,** a cognitive framework that organizes information relevant to gender (Lobel et al., 2000; Martin, 2000).

Gender schemas are developed early in life, forming a lens through which preschoolers view the world. For instance, preschoolers use their increasing cognitive abilities to develop "rules" about what is right and what is inappropriate for males and females. Thus, some girls decide that wearing pants is inappropriate for a female and apply the rule so rigidly that they refuse to wear anything but dresses. Or a preschool boy may reason that since makeup is typically worn by females, it is inappropriate for him to wear makeup even when he is in a preschool play and all the other boys and girls are wearing it.

According to *cognitive-developmental theory,* proposed by Lawrence Kohlberg, this rigidity is in part an outcome of changes in preschoolers' understanding of gender (Kohlberg, 1966). Initially, gender schemas are influenced by erroneous beliefs about sex differences. Specifically, young preschoolers believe that sex differences are based not on

gender identity the perception of oneself as male or female

gender schema a cognitive framework that organizes information relevant to gender

biological factors but on differences in appearance or behavior. Employing this view of the world, a girl may reason that she can be a father when she grows up, or a boy may think he could turn into a girl if he put on a dress and tied his hair in a ponytail. However, by the time they reach the age of 4 or 5, children develop an understanding of **gender constancy,** the belief that people are permanently males or females, depending on fixed, unchangeable biological factors.

Although research has supported the notion that the understanding of gender constancy changes during the preschool period, it has been less supportive of the idea that this understanding is the cause of gender-related behavior. In fact, the appearance of gender schemas occurs well before children understand gender constancy. Even young preschool-age children assume that certain behaviors are appropriate—and others are not—on the basis of stereotypic views of gender (Maccoby, 1990; Bussey & Bandura, 1992; Warin, 2000).

Can we reduce the objectionable consequences of viewing the world in terms of gender schemas? According to Sandra Bem (1987), one way is to encourage children to be **androgynous,** a state in which gender roles encompass characteristics thought typical of both sexes. For instance, parents and caregivers can encourage preschool children to adopt a gender schema through which they see males as assertive (typically viewed as a male-appropriate trait) but at the same time warm and tender (usually viewed as female-appropriate traits). Similarly, girls might be encouraged to see the female role as both empathetic and tender (typically seen as female-appropriate traits) and competitive, assertive, and independent (typical male-appropriate traits).

Like the other approaches to gender development (summarized in Table 8-1), the cognitive perspective does not imply that differences between the two sexes are in any way improper or inappropriate. Instead, it suggests that preschoolers should be taught to treat others as individuals. Furthermore, preschoolers need to learn the importance of fulfilling their own talents, acting as individuals and not as representatives of a particular gender.

gender constancy the belief that people are permanently males or females, depending on fixed, unchangeable biological factors

androgynous a state in which gender roles encompass characteristics thought typical of both sexes

Table 8-1

FOUR APPROACHES TO GENDER DEVELOPMENT

Perspective	Key Concepts	Applying the Concepts to Preschool Children
Biological	Our ancestors who behaved in ways that are now stereotypically feminine or masculine may have been more successful in reproducing. Brain differences may lead to gender differences.	Girls may be genetically "programmed" by evolution to be more expressive and nurturing, while boys are "programmed" to be more competitive and forceful. Hormone exposure before birth has been linked to both boys and girls behaving in ways typically expected of the other gender.
Psychoanalytic	Gender development is the result of identification with the same-sex parent, achieved by moving through a series of stages related to biological urges.	Girls and boys whose parents of the same sex behave in stereotypically masculine or feminine ways are likely to do so, too, perhaps because they identify with those parents.
Social Learning	Children learn gender-related behavior and expectations from their observation of others' behavior.	Children notice that other children and adults are rewarded for behaving in ways that conform to standard gender stereotypes—and sometimes punished for violating those stereotypes.
Cognitive	Through the use of gender schemas, developed early in life, preschoolers form a lens through which they view the world. They use their increasing cognitive abilities to develop "rules" about what is appropriate for males and females.	Preschoolers are more rigid in their rules about proper gender behavior than people at other ages, perhaps because they have just developed gender schemas that don't yet permit much variation from stereotypical expectations.

Review and Rethink

REVIEW

- According to Erikson's psychosocial development theory, preschool-age children move from the autonomy-versus-shame-and-doubt stage to the initiative-versus-guilt stage.
- During the preschool years, children develop their self-concepts, beliefs about themselves that they derive from their own perceptions, their parents' behaviors, and society.
- Racial and ethnic awareness begins to form in the preschool years.
- Gender awareness also develops in the preschool years. Explanations of this phenomenon include biological, psychoanalytical, learning, and cognitive approaches.

RETHINK

- How would you relate Erikson's stages of trust versus mistrust, autonomy versus shame and doubt, and initiative versus guilt to the issue of secure attachment discussed in an earlier chapter?
- What are the distinctions among gender differences, gender expectations, and gender stereotypes? How are they related?

Friends and Family: Preschoolers' Social Lives

When Juan was 3, he had his first best friend, Emilio. Juan and Emilio, who lived in the same apartment building in San Jose, were inseparable. They played incessantly with toy cars, racing them up and down the apartment hallways until some of the neighbors began to complain about the noise. They pretended to read to one another, and sometimes they slept over at each other's home—a big step for a 3-year-old. Neither boy seemed more joyful than when he was with his "best friend"—the term each used of the other.

An infant's family can provide nearly all the social contact he or she needs. As preschoolers, however, many children, like Juan and Emilio, begin to discover the joys of friendship with their peers. Although they may expand their social circles considerably, parents and family nevertheless remain very influential in the lives of preschoolers. Let's take a look at both these sides of preschoolers' social development, friends and family.

The Development of Friendships

Before the age of 3, most social activity involves simply being in the same place at the same time, without real social interaction. However, at around the age of 3, children begin to develop real friendships like Juan and Emilio's. Peers come to be seen not as miniature, less powerful adults, but as individuals who hold some special qualities and rewards. While preschoolers' relations with adults reflect children's needs for care, protection, and direction, their relations with peers are based more on the desire for companionship, play, and entertainment.

Furthermore, as they get older, preschoolers' conception of friendship gradually evolves. With age, they come to view friendship as a continuing state, a stable relationship that has meaning beyond the immediate moment and that bears implications for future activity (Snyder, Horsch, & Childs, 1997; Harris, 1998, 2000).

The quality of interactions that children have with friends changes during the preschool period. The focus of friendship in 3-year-olds is the enjoyment of carrying out shared activities—doing things together and playing jointly, as when Juan and Emilio played with their toy cars in the hallway. Older preschoolers, however, pay more attention to abstract concepts such as trust, support, and shared interests (Park, Lay, & Ramsay, 1993). Playing together, however, remains an important part of all preschoolers' friendships. Like friendships, play patterns change during the preschool years.

Playing by the Rules: The Work of Play

In Rosie Graiff's class of 3-year-olds, Minnie bounces her doll's feet on the table as she sings softly to herself. Ben pushes his toy car across the floor, making motor noises. Sarah chases Abdul around and around the perimeter of the room.

Play is more than what children of preschool age do to pass the time. Instead, play serves an important purpose, helping preschoolers develop socially, cognitively, and physically (Pelligrini & Smith, 1998; Power, 2000).

Categorizing Play. At the beginning of the preschool years, children engage in **functional play**—simple, repetitive activities typical of 3-year-olds. Functional play may involve objects, such as dolls or cars, or repetitive muscular movements like skipping, jumping, or rolling and unrolling a piece of clay. Functional play, then, involves doing something for the sake of being active rather than with the aim of creating some end product (Rubin, Fein, & Vandenberg, 1983).

As children get older, functional play declines. By the time they are 4, children become involved in a more sophisticated form of play. In **constructive play** children manipulate objects to produce or build something. A child who builds a house out of Legos or puts a puzzle together is involved in constructive play: He or she has an ultimate goal—to produce something. Such play is not necessarily aimed at creating something novel, since children may repeatedly build a house of blocks, let it fall into disarray, and then rebuild it.

Constructive play permits children to test their developing physical and cognitive skills and to practice their fine muscle movements. They gain experience in solving problems about the ways and the sequences in which things fit together. They also learn to cooperate with others—a development we observe as the social nature of play shifts during the preschool period. Consequently, it's important for adults who care for preschoolers to provide a variety of toys that allow for both functional and constructive play (Tegano et al., 1991; Fromberg, 1998; Power, 1999; Edwards, 2000).

The Social Aspects of Play. If two preschoolers are sitting at a table side by side, each putting a different puzzle together, are they engaged jointly in play?

According to pioneering work done by Mildred Parten (1932), the answer is "yes." She suggests that these preschoolers are engaged in **parallel play,** in which children play with similar toys, in a similar manner, but do not interact with each other. Parallel play is typical for children during the early preschool years. Preschoolers also engage in another form of play, a highly passive one: onlooker play. In **onlooker play,** children simply watch others at play, but do not actually participate themselves. They may look on silently, or they may make comments of encouragement or advice.

As they get older, however, preschool-age children engage in more sophisticated forms of social play that involve a greater degree of interaction. In **associative play** two or more children actually interact with one another by sharing or borrowing toys or materials, although they do not do the same thing. In **cooperative play,** children genuinely play

As preschoolers get older, their conception of friendship evolves and the quality of their interactions changes.

functional play play that involves simple, repetitive activities typical of 3-year-olds

constructive play play in which children manipulate objects to produce or build something

parallel play action in which children play with similar toys, in a similar manner, but do not interact with each other

onlooker play action in which children simply watch others at play, but do not actually participate themselves

associative play play in which two or more children actually interact with one another by sharing or borrowing toys or materials, although they do not do the same thing

cooperative play play in which children genuinely interact with one another, taking turns, playing games, or devising contests

According to Russian developmentalist Lev Vygotsky, children are able, through make-believe play, to practice activities that are a part of their particular culture and broaden their understanding of the way the world functions.

with one another, taking turns, playing games, or devising contests. (The various types of play are summarized in Table 8-2).

Although associative and cooperative play do not typically become prevalent until children reach the end of the preschool years, the amount and kind of social experience children have had significantly influences the nature of play. For instance, children who have had substantial preschool experience are apt to engage in more social forms of behavior, such as associative and cooperative play, fairly early in the preschool years than those with less experience (Roopnarine, Johnson, & Hooper, 1994).

Furthermore, solitary and onlooker play continue in the later stages of the preschool period. There are simply times when children prefer to play by themselves. And when newcomers join a group, one strategy for becoming part of the group—often successful—is to engage in onlooker play, waiting for an opportunity to join the play more actively (Smith, 1978; Howes, Unger, & Seidner, 1989; Hughes, 1995).

The nature of pretend, or make-believe, play also changes during the preschool period. In some ways, pretend play becomes increasingly *un*realistic, as preschoolers change from using only realistic objects to using less concrete ones. Thus, at the start of the preschool period, children may pretend to listen to a radio only if they actually have a plastic radio that looks realistic. Later, however, they are more likely to use an entirely different object, such as a large cardboard box, as a pretend radio (Bornstein et al., 1996).

Russian developmentalist Lev Vygotsky (1930/1978) argued that pretend play, particularly if it involves social play, is an important means for expanding preschool-age chil-

Table 8-2

PRESCHOOLERS' PLAY

Type of Play	Description	Examples
Functional play	Simple, repetitive activities typical of 3-year-olds. May involve objects or repetitive muscular movements.	Moving dolls or cars repetitively. Skipping, jumping, rolling or unrolling a piece of clay.
Constructive play	More sophisticated play in which children manipulate objects to produce or build something. Developed by age 4, constructive play lets children test physical and cognitive skills and practice fine muscle movements.	Building a doll house or car garage out of Legos, putting together a puzzle, making an animal out of clay.
Parallel play	Children use similar toys in a similar manner at the same time, but do not interact with each other. Typical of children during the early preschool years.	Children sitting side by side, each playing with his or her own toy car, putting together his or her own puzzle, or making an individual clay animal.
Onlooker play	Children simply watch others at play, but do not actually participate. They may look on silently or they may make comments of encouragement or advice. Common among preschoolers and can be helpful when a child wishes to join a group already at play.	One child watches as a group of others play with dolls, cars, or clay; build with Legos; or work on a puzzle together.
Associative play	Two or more children interact, sharing or borrowing toys or materials, although they do not do the same thing.	Two children, each building his or her own Lego garage, may trade bricks back and forth.
Cooperative play	Children genuinely play with one another, taking turns, playing games, or devising contests.	A group of children working on a puzzle may take turns fitting in the pieces. Children playing with dolls or cars may take turns making the dolls talk or may agree on rules to race the cars.

In parallel play, children play with similar toys, in a similar manner, but don't necessarily interact with one another.

dren's cognitive skills. Through make-believe play, children are able to "practice" activities that are a part of their particular culture and broaden their understanding of the way the world functions.

Children's cultural backgrounds also result in different styles of play. For example, comparisons of Korean Americans and Anglo-Americans find that Korean American children engage in a higher proportion of parallel play than their Anglo-American counterparts, while Anglo-American preschoolers are involved in more pretend play (see Figure 8-1; Farver, Kim, & Lee-Shin, 1995; Haight et al., 1999; Farver & Lee-Shin, 2000).

Preschoolers' Theory of Mind: Understanding What Others Are Thinking

One reason behind the developmental changes in children's play is the continuing development of preschoolers' theory of mind. As we first discussed in Chapter 6, *theory of mind* refers to knowledge and beliefs about the mental world. Using their theory of mind,

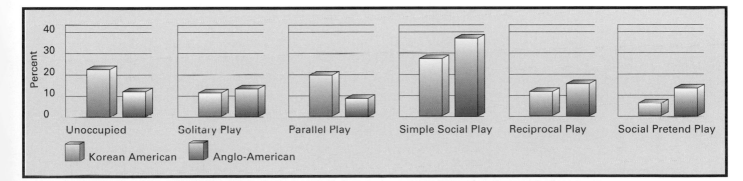

Figure 8-1 **Comparing Play Complexity**

An examination of Korean American and Anglo-American preschoolers' play complexity finds clear differences in patterns of play. Can you think of any explanation for this finding?

(*Source:* Adapted from Farver, Kim, & Lee, 1995.)

Children with authoritative parents tend to be well adjusted, in part because the parents are supportive and take the time to explain things. What are the consequences of parents who are too permissive? Too authoritarian? Too uninvolved?

children are able to come up with explanations for how others think and the reasons for their behaving in the way they do.

During the preschool years, children increasingly can see the world from others' perspectives. Even children as young as 2 are able to understand that others have emotions, as did Alison Gopnik's son, whose efforts to soothe his mother's pain were described in the chapter prologue. By the age of 3 or 4, preschoolers can distinguish between mental phenomena and physical actuality. For instance, 3-year-olds know that they can imagine something that is not physically present, such as a pretend animal, and that others can do the same. They can also pretend that something has happened and react as if it really had occurred. And they know that others have the same capability (Denham, 1998; Cadinu & Kiesner, 2000).

Preschool-age children also understand that people have motives and reasons for their behavior. A child at this age can understand that his mother is angry because she was late for an appointment, even if the child himself hasn't seen her be late. Furthermore, by the age of 4, preschool-age children's understanding that people can be fooled and that they can be mistaken by physical reality becomes surprisingly sophisticated. This increase in understanding helps children become more socially skilled (Fischer & Rose, 1994; Nguyen & Frye, 1999).

The Emergence of Theory of Mind.   What factors are involved in the emergence of theory of mind? Certainly, brain maturation and the development of language skills play a role. In particular, the ability to understand the meaning of words such as "think" and "know" is important in helping preschool-age children understand the mental lives of others.

Opportunities for social interaction and make-believe play are also critical in promoting the development of theory of mind. For example, preschool-age children with older siblings (who provide high levels of social interaction) have more sophisticated theories of mind than those without older siblings (Moore, Pure, & Furrow, 1990; Ruffman et al., 1998; Watson, 2000).

Cultural factors also play an important role in the development of theory of mind. For example, children in more industrialized Western cultures may be more likely to regard others' behavior as due to the kind of people they are, seeing it as a function of their personal traits and characteristics. In contrast, children in non-Western cultures may see others' behavior as produced by forces that are less under their personal control, such as unhappy gods or bad fortune (Lillard, 1998).

As we've seen, preschooler's family situations can influence their theory of mind. In fact, families provide a major influence on all aspects of preschoolers' development. What is family life like for today's young children?

Preschoolers' Family Lives

Four-year-old Benjamin was watching TV while his mom cleaned up after dinner. After a while, he wandered in and grabbed a towel, saying, "Mommy, let me help you do the dishes." Surprised by this unprecedented behavior, she asked him, "Where did you learn to do dishes?"

"I saw it on Leave It to Beaver," *he replied, "Only it was the dad helping. Since we don't have a dad, I figured I'd do it."*

For an increasing number of preschool-age children, life does not mirror what we see in reruns of *Leave it to Beaver*. Many face the realities of an increasingly complicated world. For instance, as we noted in Chapter 6 and will discuss in greater detail in Chapter 10, children are increasingly likely to live with only one parent. In 1960, less than 10 percent of all children under the age of 18 lived with one parent; by 1989, almost a quarter lived in a single-parent household. In fact, in the 1990s, almost 50 percent of all children experienced their parents' divorce and lived with one parent for an average of 5 years (Carnegie Task Force, 1994).

Still, for most children the preschool years are not a time of upheaval and turmoil. Instead, the period encompasses a growing interaction with the world at large. As we've seen, for instance, preschoolers begin to develop genuine friendships with other children, in which close ties emerge. One central factor leading preschoolers to develop friendships is when parents provide a warm, supportive home environment. A good deal of research finds that strong, positive relationships between parents and children encourage children's relationships with others. How do parents nurture that relationship? For a discussion of effective parenting, see the *From Research to Practice* box.

Child Abuse and Psychological Maltreatment: The Grim Side of Family Life

To Nicole and Diana Schoo, the movie Home Alone *probably didn't seem too funny. For them, the tale of a child mistakenly left behind by his vacationing parents was all too similar to their own experience. In their case, though, their abandonment was no comic error: Their parents intentionally left them behind.*

Diana, age 4, and her older sister Nicole, age 9, were found at home— alone—while their parents were on a 9-day vacation in Acapulco, Mexico. It was not the first time the girls had been left unattended; their parents had left them unaccompanied while they went off on a 4-day visit to Massachusetts the previous summer.

Local authorities who learned of the girls' plight arrested the Schoo parents on their return from Acapulco. The Schoos faced charges on two felony counts of child abandonment and cruelty to children and a misdemeanor charge of child endangerment.

authoritarian parents parents who are controlling, punitive, rigid, and cold, and whose word is law. They value strict, unquestioning obedience from their children and do not tolerate expressions of disagreement

permissive parents parents who provide lax and inconsistent feedback and require little of their children

authoritative parents parents who are firm, setting clear and consistent limits, but who try to reason with their children, giving explanations for why they should behave in a particular way

uninvolved parents parents who show almost no interest in their children and indifferent, rejecting behavior

The Schoos faced charges of child abandonment, cruelty to children, and child endangerment for leaving their children Diana, 4, and Nicole, 9, home alone while they vacationed.

From Research to Practice
Effective Parenting: Teaching Children Desired Behavior

While she thinks no one is looking, Maria goes into her brother Alejandro's bedroom, where he has been saving the last of his Halloween candy. Just as she takes his last Reese's Peanut Butter Cup, the children's mother walks into the room and immediately takes in the situation.

If you were Maria's mother, which of the following reactions seems most reasonable?

(1) Tell Maria that she must go to her room and stay there for the rest of the day, and that she is going to lose access to her favorite blanket, the one she sleeps with every night and during naps.

(2) Mildly tell Maria that what she did was not such a good idea, and she shouldn't do it in the future.

(3) Explain why her brother Alejandro was going to be upset, and tell her that she must go to her room for an hour as punishment.

(4) Forget about it, and let the children sort it out themselves.

Each of these four alternative responses represents one of the major parenting styles identified by Diana Baumrind (1971, 1980) and updated by Eleanor Maccoby and colleagues (Baumrind, 1971, 1980; Maccoby & Martin, 1983). **Authoritarian parents** are controlling, punitive, rigid, cold. Their word is law, and they value strict, unquestioning obedience from their children. They also do not tolerate expressions of disagreement.

Permissive parents, in contrast, provide lax and inconsistent feedback. They require little of their children, and they don't see themselves as holding much responsibility for how their children turn out. They place little or no limits or control on their children's behavior.

Authoritative parents are firm, setting clear and consistent limits. Although they tend to be relatively strict, like authoritarian parents, they are loving and emotionally supportive. They also try to reason with their children, giving explanations for why they should behave in a particular way and communicating the rationale for any punishment they may impose. Authoritative parents encourage their children to be independent.

Finally, **uninvolved parents** show virtually no interest in their children, displaying indifferent, rejecting behavior. They are detached emotionally and see their role as no more than feeding, clothing, and providing shelter for their child. In its most extreme form, uninvolved parenting results in *ne-*

glect, a form of child abuse. (The four patterns are summarized in Table 8-3.)

Does the particular style of discipline that parents use result in differences in children's behavior? The answer is very much yes—although, as you might expect, there are many exceptions.

Children of authoritarian parents tend to be withdrawn, showing relatively little sociability. They are not very friendly, often behaving uneasily around their peers. Girls who are raised by authoritarian parents are especially dependent on their parents, whereas boys are unusually hostile.

Permissive parents have children who, in many ways, share the undesirable characteristics of children of authoritarian parents. Children with permissive parents tend to be dependent and moody, and they are low in social skills and self-control.

Children of authoritative parents fare best. They generally are independent, friendly with their peers, self-assertive, and cooperative. They have strong motivation to achieve, and they are typically successful and likable. They regulate their own behavior effectively, both in terms of their relationships with others and emotional self-regulation.

Some authoritative parents also display several characteristics that have come to be called *supportive parenting*, including parental warmth, proactive teaching, calm discussion during disciplinary episodes, and interest and involvement in children's peer activities. Children whose parents engage in such supportive parenting show better adjustment and are protected from the consequences of later adversity (Pettit, Bates, & Dodge, 1997; Belluck, 2000; Kaufmann et al., 2000).

Children whose parents show uninvolved parenting styles are the worst off. Their parents' lack of involvement disrupts their emotional development considerably, leading them to feel unloved and emotionally detached, and affects their physical and cognitive development as well.

Clearly, authoritative, supportive parents appear to be the most likely to produce successful children. But not always. For instance, in a significant number of cases the children of authoritarian and permissive parents develop quite successfully. Moreover, parents are not entirely consistent: Although the authoritarian, permissive, authoritative, and uninvolved patterns describe general styles, sometimes parents switch from their dominant mode to one of the others. For instance, when a child darts into the street, even the most laid-back and permissive parent is likely to react in a harsh, authoritarian manner, laying down strict demands about safety. In such cases, authoritarian styles may be most effective (Janssens & Dekovic,1997; Holden & Miller, 1999).

Table 8-3

PARENTING STYLES

	How Demanding Parents Are of Children	
	Demanding	**Undemanding**
Highly Responsive	*Authoritative*	*Permissive*
	Characteristics: firm, setting clear and consistent limits	**Characteristics:** lax and inconsistent feedback
	Relationship with Children: Although they tend to be relatively strict, like authoritarian parents, they are loving and emotionally supportive and encourage their children to be independent. They also try to reason with their children, giving explanations for why they should behave in a particular way, and communicate the rationale for any punishment they may impose.	**Relationship with Children:** They require little of their children, and they don't see themselves as holding much responsibility for how their children turn out. They place little or no limits or control on their children's behavior.
Low Responsive	*Authoritarian*	*Uninvolved*
	Characteristics: controlling, punitive, rigid, cold	**Characteristics:** displaying indifferent, rejecting behavior
	Relationship with Children: Their word is law, and they value strict, unquestioning obedience from their children. They also do not tolerate expressions of disagreement.	**Relationship with Children:** They are detached emotionally and see their role as only providing food, clothing, and shelter. In its extreme form, this parenting style results in *neglect,* a form of child abuse.

How Responsive Parents Are to a Child

(*Sources:* Based on Baumrind, 1971; Maccoby & Martin, 1983.)

Furthermore, the findings regarding childrearing styles are chiefly applicable to Western societies. The style of parenting that is most successful may depend quite heavily on the norms of a particular culture—and what parents in a particular culture are taught regarding appropriate childrearing practices (Papps et al., 1995; Rubin, 1998).

For example, the Chinese concept of *chiao shun* suggests that parents should be strict, firm, and in tight control of their children's behavior. Parents are seen to have a duty to train their children to adhere to socially and culturally desirable standards of behavior, particularly those manifested in good school performance. Children's acceptance of such an approach to discipline is seen as a sign of parental respect (Chao, 1994).

Parents in China are typically highly directive with their children, pushing them to excel and controlling their behavior to a considerably higher degree than parents typically do in Western countries. And it works: Children of Asian parents tend to be quite successful, particularly academically (Steinberg, Dornbusch, & Brown, 1992).

In contrast, U.S. parents are generally advised to use authoritative methods and explicitly to avoid authoritarian measures. Interestingly, it wasn't always this way. Until World War II, the point of view that dominated the advice literature was authoritarian, apparently founded on Puritan religious influences that suggested that children had "original sin" or that they needed to have their wills broken (Smuts & Hagen, 1985).

In short, the childrearing practices that parents are urged to follow reflect cultural perspectives about the nature of children as well as about the appropriate role of parents. No single parenting pattern or style, then, is likely to be universally appropriate or likely invariably to produce successful children. Instead, cultural context must be taken into account (Harwood et al., 1996; Hart et al., 1998).

Despite common wisdom, the use of physical punishment of any sort is not recommended by child care experts. While parents rarely mean to abuse their children, a spanking begun in anger can escalate easily to abuse.

The figures are gloomy and disheartening: At least five children are killed by their parents or caretakers every day, and 140,000 others are physically injured every year. Overall, more than three million children are abused or neglected in the United States each year. The abuse takes several forms, ranging from actual physical abuse to psychological mistreatment (see Figure 8-2; Mones, 1995; U.S. Advisory Board on Child Abuse and Neglect, 1995; Briere et al., 1997; Parnell & Day, 1998).

Physical Abuse. Although child abuse can occur in any household, regardless of economic well-being or the social status of the parents, it is most frequent in families living in stressful environments. Conditions of poverty, single-parent households, and families with higher-than-average levels of marital conflict create such environments. Stepfathers are more likely to commit abuse against stepchildren than genetic fathers are against their own offspring. Child abuse is also related to the presence of violence between spouses (Daly & Wilson, 1996; Emery & Laumann-Billings, 1998; Fantuzzo & Mohr, 1999; Slep, Smith, & O'Leary, 2001). (Table 8-4 lists some of the warning signs of abuse).

Children with certain characteristics are more prone to be the victims of child abuse. Abused children are more likely to be fussy, resistant to control, and not readily adaptable to new situations. They have more headaches and stomachaches, experience more bed-wetting, are generally more anxious, and may show developmental delays. Moreover, victims are most vulnerable to abuse at certain ages: Three- and 4-year-olds, as well as 15- to 17-year-olds, are the most likely to be abused by their parents (Straus & Gelles, 1990; Ammerman & Patz, 1996; Haugaard, 2000).

It is critical to keep in mind that labeling children as being at higher risk for receiving abuse does not make them responsible for their abuse; the family members who carry out the abuse are at fault. Statistical findings simply suggest that children with such characteristics are more at risk of being the recipients of family violence.

Why does physical abuse occur? Most parents certainly do not intend to hurt their children. In fact, most parents who abuse their children later express bewilderment and dismay at their own behavior.

One reason for child abuse is the vague demarcation between permissible and impermissible forms of physical violence. Societal folklore says that spanking is not merely acceptable, but often necessary and desirable. For example, one survey found that almost half of mothers with children less than 4 years of age had spanked their child in the previous week, and close to 20 percent of mothers believe it is appropriate to spank a child less than 1 year of age (Socolar & Stein, 1995, 1996).

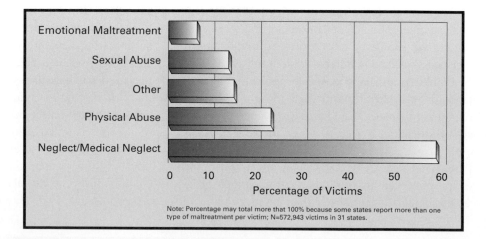

Figure 8-2 **Types of Child Abuse**

Becoming an Informed Consumer of Development

Disciplining Children

The question of how best to discipline children has been raised for generations. Answers from developmentalists today include the following advice (Grusec & Goodnow, 1994a; Wierson & Forehand, 1994; O'Leary, 1995):

◗ For most children in Western cultures, authoritative parenting works best. Parents should be firm and consistent, providing clear direction for desirable behavior. Authoritative disciplinarians provide rules, but they explain why those rules make sense, using language that children can understand.

◗ Spanking is *never* an appropriate discipline technique, according to the American Academy of Pediatrics. Not only is spanking less effective than other techniques in curbing undesirable behavior, but it leads to additional, unwanted outcomes, such as the potential for more aggressive behavior (American Academy of Pediatrics, 1998).

◗ Use *time-out* for punishment, in which children are removed from a situation in which they have misbehaved and not permitted to engage in enjoyable activities for a set period of time.

◗ Tailor parental discipline to the characteristics of the child and the situation. Try to keep the child's particular personality in mind, and adapt discipline to it.

◗ Use routines (such as a bath routine or a bedtime routine) to avoid noncompliance. For instance, bedtime can be the source of a nightly struggle between a resistant child and an insistent parent. Parental strategies for gaining compliance that involve making the situation predictably enjoyable—such as routinely reading a bedtime story or engaging in a nightly "wrestling" match with the child—can defuse potential battles.

Unfortunately, the line between "spanking" and "beating" is not clear, and spankings begun in anger can escalate easily into abuse. Furthermore, despite common wisdom, the use of physical punishment of any sort is *not* recommended by child care experts, according to the American Academy of Pediatrics (American Academy of Pediatrics, 1998). (The *Becoming an Informed Consumer of Development* section offers more guidelines on child discipline.)

Table 8-4

WHAT ARE THE WARNING SIGNS OF CHILD ABUSE?

Because child abuse is typically a secret crime, identifying the victims of abuse is particularly difficult. Still, there are several signs in a child that indicate that he or she is the victim of violence (Robbins, 1990):

■ visible, serious injuries that have no reasonable explanation
■ bite or choke marks
■ burns from cigarettes or immersion in hot water
■ feelings of pain for no apparent reason
■ fear of adults or care providers
■ inappropriate attire in warm weather (long sleeves, long pants, high necked garments)—possibly to conceal injuries to the neck, arms, and legs
■ extreme behavior—highly aggressive, extremely passive, extremely withdrawn
■ fear of physical contact

If you suspect a child is a victim of aggression, it is your responsibility to act. Call your local police or the department of social services in your city or state, or call the National Center on Child Abuse and Neglect (Washington, DC) at (202)245-2856. Talk to a teacher or a member of the clergy. Remember, by acting decisively you can literally save someone's life.

Many other societies do not differentiate between acceptable violence and abuse as we do in the United States. For instance, Sweden outlaws *any* form of physical punishment directed toward a child. In many other countries, such as China, social norms work against the use of physical punishment, and its use is rare. In contrast, the values of personal freedom and responsibility prevalent in the United States foster a social climate in which high levels of child abuse occur (Kessen, 1979; Durant, 1999).

Another factor that leads to high rates of abuse is the privacy with which child care is conducted in Western societies. Unlike other cultures, in which childrearing is seen as the joint responsibility of several people and even society as a whole, in most Western cultures—and particularly the United States—children are raised in private, isolated households. Because child care is seen as the sole responsibility of the parent, other people are typically not available when a parent's patience is tested.

One additional source of abuse is insensitivity to age norms on the part of parents. Abusive caregivers may have unrealistically high expectations regarding children's abilities to be quiet and compliant at a particular age. Their children's failure to meet these unrealistic expectations may provoke abuse (Peterson, 1994).

Finally, abuse inflicted on children is often associated with violence that the abusers themselves have suffered as children. According to the **cycle of violence hypothesis,** the abuse and neglect that children suffer predispose them as adults to abuse and neglect their own children (Dodge, Bates, & Pettit, 1990; Maxfield & Widom, 1996; Miller-Perrin & Perrin, 1999; Widom, 2000).

The cycle of violence hypothesis suggests that victims of abuse have learned from their childhood experiences that violence is an appropriate and acceptable form of discipline. Violence is consequently perpetuated from one generation to another, as each generation learns to behave abusively through its participation in an abusive, violent family (Straus & Gelles, 1990; Ney, Fung, & Wickett, 1993; Straus, Sugarman, & Giles-Sims, 1997; Blumenthal, 2000).

On the other hand, although there are many cases in which abusive parents have themselves suffered abuse as children, being abused as a child does not inevitably lead to abuse of one's own children. In fact, statistics show that only about one-third of people who were abused or neglected as children abuse their own children; the remaining two-thirds of people abused as children do not turn out to be child abusers. Clearly, suffering abuse as a child is not the full explanation for child abuse in adults (Cicchetti, 1996; Straus & McCord, 1998).

Psychological Maltreatment. Children may also be the victims of psychological maltreatment. **Psychological maltreatment** occurs when parents or other caregivers harm children's behavioral, cognitive, emotional, or physical functioning. Psychological maltreatment may occur through either overt behavior or neglect (Hart, Brassard, & Karlson, 1996).

For example, abusive parents may frighten, belittle, or humiliate their children, thereby intimidating and harassing them. Children may be made to feel like disappointments or failures, or they may be constantly reminded that they are a burden to their parents. Parents may tell their children that they wish they had never had children and specifically that they wish that their children had never been born. Children may be threatened with abandonment or even death. In other instances, older children may be exploited. They may be forced to seek employment and then to give their earnings to their parents.

In other cases of psychological maltreatment, the abuse takes the form of neglect. Parents may ignore their children or act emotionally unresponsive to them. In such cases,

cycle of violence hypothesis the theory that the abuse and neglect that children suffer predispose them as adults to abuse and neglect their own children

psychological maltreatment abuse that occurs when parents or other caregivers harm children's behavioral, cognitive, emotional, or physical functioning

children may be given unrealistic responsibilities or may be left to fend for themselves, as in the case of the Schoo children.

No one is certain how much psychological maltreatment occurs each year, because figures separating psychological maltreatment from other types of abuse are not routinely gathered. Most maltreatment occurs in the privacy of people's homes. Furthermore, psychological maltreatment typically causes no physical damage, such as bruises or broken bones, to alert physicians, teachers, and other authorities. Consequently, many cases of psychological maltreatment probably are not identified. However, it is clear that profound neglect that involves children who are unsupervised or uncared for is the most frequent form of psychological maltreatment (Hewitt, 1997).

What are the consequences of psychological maltreatment? Although some children are sufficiently resilient to survive the abuse and grow into psychologically healthy adults, in many cases lasting damage results. For example, psychological maltreatment has been associated with low self-esteem, lying, misbehavior, and underachievement in school. In extreme cases, it can produce criminal behavior, aggression, and murder. In other instances, children who have been psychologically maltreated become depressed and even commit suicide (Perez & Widom, 1994; Leiter & Johnsen, 1997; Shonk & Cicchetti, 2001).

Resilience: Overcoming the Odds

Not all children succumb to the mistreatment and abuse that life thrusts on them. In fact, some do surprisingly well, considering the type of problems they have encountered. What enables some children to overcome stress and trauma that in most cases scars others for life?

Resilience refers to the ability to overcome circumstances that place a child at high risk for psychological or physical damage. Several factors seem to reduce and, in certain cases, eliminate some children's reactions to difficult circumstances—such as extremes of poverty, prenatal stress, or homes that are racked with violence or other forms of social disorder—that in others produce profoundly negative consequences.

resilience the ability to overcome circumstances that place a child at high risk for psychological or physical damage

According to developmental psychologist Emmy Werner (1995), resilient children have temperaments that evoke positive responses from a wide variety of caregivers. They tend to be affectionate, easy-going, and good-natured. They are easily soothed as infants, and they are able to elicit care from the most nurturant people in any environment in which they find themselves. In a sense, then, resilient children are successful in making their own environments by drawing out behavior in others that is necessary for their own development.

Similar traits are associated with resilience in older children. The most resilient school-age children are those who are socially pleasant, outgoing, and have good communication skills. They tend to be relatively intelligent, and they are independent, feeling that they can shape their own fate and are not dependent on others or luck (Werner & Smith, 1992; Werner, 1993, 1995; Eisenberg et al., 1997).

The characteristics of resilient children suggest ways to improve the prospects of children who are at risk from a variety of developmental threats. For instance, in addition to decreasing their exposure to factors that put them at risk in the first place, we need to increase their competence and teach them ways to deal with their situation. In fact, programs that have been successful in helping especially vulnerable children have a common thread: They provide competent and caring adult models who can teach the children problem-solving skills and help them to communicate their needs to those who are in a position to help them (Zimmerman & Arunkumar, 1994; Haggerty et al., 1994; Hetherington & Blechman, 1996; Masten & Coatsworth, 1998).

Review and Rethink

REVIEW

- In the preschool years, children develop their first true friendships on the basis of personal characteristics, trust, and shared interests.
- The character of preschoolers' play changes over time, growing more sophisticated, interactive, and cooperative, and relying increasingly on social skills.
- There are several distinct childrearing styles, including authoritarian, permissive, authoritative, and uninvolved.
- Childrearing styles show strong cultural influences.
- Some children suffer abuse from their own family members.

RETHINK

- Are the styles and strategies of preschool-age children's play, such as parallel play and onlooker play, mirrored in adult life in realms of interaction other than play?
- What cultural and environmental factors in the United States may have contributed to the shift in the dominant childrearing style from authoritarian to authoritative since World War II? Is another shift under way?

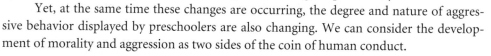

Moral Development and Aggression

During snack time at preschool, playmates Jan and Meg inspected the goodies in their lunch boxes. Jan found two appetizing cream-filled cookies. Meg's snack offered less tempting carrot and celery sticks. As Jan began to munch on one of her cookies, Meg looked at the cut-up vegetables and burst into tears. Jan responded to Meg's distress by offering her companion one of her cookies, which Meg gladly accepted. Jan was able to put herself in Meg's place, understand Meg's thoughts and feelings, and act compassionately. (Katz, 1989, p. 213)

In this short scenario we see many of the key elements of morality, as it is played out among preschool-age children. Changes in children's views of morality and their helpfulness to others are an important element of growth during the preschool years.

Yet, at the same time these changes are occurring, the degree and nature of aggressive behavior displayed by preschoolers are also changing. We can consider the development of morality and aggression as two sides of the coin of human conduct.

Developing Morality: Following Society's Rights and Wrongs

moral development the changes in people's sense of justice and of what is right and wrong, and in their behavior related to moral issues

Moral development refers to changes in people's sense of justice and of what is right and wrong, and in their behavior related to moral issues. Developmentalists have considered moral development in terms of children's reasoning about morality, their attitudes toward moral transgressions, and their behavior when faced with moral issues. In the process of studying moral development, several approaches have evolved (Langford, 1995; Grusec & Kuczynski, 1997).

heteronomous morality the stage of moral development in which rules are seen as invariant and unchangeable

Piaget's View of Moral Development. Child psychologist Jean Piaget was one of the first to study questions of moral development. He suggested that moral development, like cognitive development, proceeds in stages (Piaget, 1932). The earliest stage is a broad form of moral thinking known as **heteronomous morality,** in which rules are seen as invariant and unchangeable. During this stage, which lasts from about age 4 through age 7, children play games rigidly, assuming that there is one, and only one, way to play and that every other way is wrong. At the same time, though, preschool-age children may not even fully grasp game rules. Consequently, a group of children may be playing together, with each child playing according to a slightly different set of rules. Nevertheless, they enjoy playing with others. Piaget suggests that every child may "win" such a game, because winning is equated with having a good time, as opposed to truly competing with others.

Heteronomous morality ultimately is replaced by two later stages of morality: incipient cooperation and autonomous cooperation. In the *incipient cooperation stage,* which lasts from around age 7 to age 10, children's games become more clearly social. Children actually learn the formal rules of games, and they play according to this shared knowledge. Consequently, rules are still seen as largely unchangeable. There is a "right" way to play the game, and children play according to these formal rules.

It is not until the *autonomous cooperation stage,* which begins at about age 10, that children become fully aware that formal game rules can be modified if the people who play them agree. The later transition into more sophisticated forms of moral development—which we will consider in Chapter 12—also is reflected in school-age children's understanding that rules of law are created by people and are subject to change according to the will of people.

Until these later stages are reached, however, children's reasoning about rules and issues of justice is bounded in the concrete. For instance, consider the following two stories:

A little boy who is called John is in his room. He is called to dinner. He goes into the dining room. But behind the door there was a chair, and on the chair there was a tray with fifteen cups on it. John couldn't have known there was all this behind the door. He goes in, the door knocks against the tray, bang go the fifteen cups, and they all get broken!

Once there was a little boy whose name was Marcello. One day when his mother was out he tried to get some jam out of the cupboard. He climbed up on to a chair and stretched out his arm. But the jam was too high up and he couldn't reach it and have any. But while he was trying to get it he knocked over a cup. The cup fell down and broke. (Piaget, 1932, p. 122)

Piaget found that a preschool child in the heteronomous morality stage judges the child who broke the 15 cups worse than the one who broke just one. In contrast, children who have moved beyond the heteronomous morality stage consider the child who broke the one cup naughtier. The reason: Children in the heteronomous morality stage do not take *intention* into account.

Children in the heteronomous stage of moral development also believe in immanent justice. **Immanent justice** is the notion that rules that are broken earn immediate punishment. Preschool children believe that if they do something wrong, they will be punished instantly—even if no one sees them carrying out their misdeeds. In contrast, older children understand that punishments for misdeeds are determined and meted out by people. Children who have moved beyond the heteronomous morality stage have come to notice that authority figures make judgments about the severity of a transgression and that they take intentionality into account in determining the nature of the penalty to be imposed.

immanent justice the notion that rules that are broken earn immediate punishment

Evaluating Piaget's Approach to Moral Development. Recent research suggests that although Piaget was on the right track in his description of how moral development proceeds, his approach suffers from the same problem we encountered in his theory of cognitive development. Specifically, Piaget underestimated the age at which children's moral skills are honed.

It is now clear that preschool-age children understand the notion of intentionality by about age 3, and this allows them to make judgments based on intent at an earlier age than Piaget supposed. Specifically, when provided with moral questions that emphasize intent, preschool children judge someone who is intentionally bad as more "naughty" than someone who is unintentionally bad, but who creates more objective damage. Moreover, by the age of 4, they judge intentional lying wrong (Yuill & Perner, 1988; Bussey, 1992).

Social Learning Approaches to Morality. Social learning approaches to moral development stand in stark contrast to Piaget's approach. While Piaget emphasizes how limitations in preschoolers' cognitive development lead to particular forms of moral *reasoning*, social learning approaches focus more on how the environment in which preschoolers operate produces **prosocial behavior,** helping behavior that benefits others (Eisenberg et al., 1999).

Social learning approaches build upon the behavioral approaches that we first discussed in Chapter 1. They acknowledge that some instances of children's prosocial behavior stem from situations in which they have received positive reinforcement for acting in a morally appropriate way. For instance, when Claire's mother tells her she has been a "good girl" for sharing a box of candy with her brother Dan, Claire's behavior has been reinforced. As a consequence, she is more likely to engage in sharing behavior in the future.

However, social learning approaches go a step further, arguing that not all prosocial behavior has to be directly performed and subsequently reinforced for learning to occur. According to social learning approaches, children also learn moral behavior more indirectly by observing the behavior of others, called *models* (Bandura, 1977). Children imitate models who receive reinforcement for their behavior, and ultimately they learn to perform the behavior themselves. For example, when Claire's friend Jake watches Claire share her candy with her brother, and Claire is praised for her behavior, Jake is more likely to engage in sharing behavior himself at some later point.

Quite a few studies illustrate the power of models and of social learning more generally in producing prosocial behavior in preschool-age children. For example, experiments have shown that children who view someone behaving generously or unselfishly are apt to follow the model's example, subsequently behaving in a generous or unselfish manner themselves when put in a similar situation (Midlarsky & Bryan, 1972; Kim & Stevens, 1987). The opposite also holds true: If a model behaves selfishly, children who observe such behavior tend to behave more selfishly themselves (Staub, 1971; Grusec, 1982, 1991).

Not all models are equally effective in producing prosocial responses. For instance, preschoolers are more apt to model the behavior of warm, responsive adults than of adults who appear colder. Furthermore, models viewed as highly competent or high in prestige are more effective than others (Yarrow, Scott, & Waxler, 1973; Bandura, 1977).

Children do more than simply mimic unthinkingly behavior that they see rewarded in others. By observing moral conduct, they are reminded of society's norms about the importance of moral behavior as conveyed by parents, teachers, and other powerful authority figures. They notice the connections between particular situations and certain kinds of behavior. This increases the likelihood that similar situations will elicit similar behavior in the observer.

Consequently, modeling paves the way for the development of more general rules and principles in a process called **abstract modeling**. Rather than always modeling the particular behavior of others, older preschoolers begin to develop generalized principles that underlie the behavior that they observe. After observing repeated instances in which a model is rewarded for acting in a morally desirable way, children begin the process of inferring and learning the general principles of moral conduct (Bandura, 1991).

Piaget believed at the heteronomous morality stage, this child would find the degree to which she had done the wrong thing to be directly related to the number of items broken.

prosocial behavior helping behavior that benefits others

abstract modeling the process in which modeling paves the way for the development of more general rules and principles

Empathy and Moral Behavior. According to some developmentalists, **empathy**—the understanding of what another individual feels—lies at the heart of some kinds of moral behavior. Think back to the example in this chapter's prologue of Alison Gopnik's son who used Band-Aids to try to heal the "owie" that was making his mother cry. In order for her son to understand that Alison needed comforting, it was necessary for him to feel empathy with her unhappiness. Although he may have been confused about the source of her pain, Alison's son realized that she seemed hurt and warranted sympathy.

The roots of empathy grow early. One-year-old infants cry when they hear other infants crying. By 2 and 3, toddlers will offer gifts and spontaneously share toys with other children and adults, even if they are strangers (Stanjek, 1978; Radke-Yarrow, Zahn-Waxler, & Chapman, 1983; Zahn-Wexler & Radke-Yarrow, 1990).

During the preschool years, empathy continues to grow. Some theorists believe that increasing empathy—as well as other positive emotions, such as sympathy and admiration—leads children to behave in a more moral fashion. In addition, some negative emotions—such as anger at an unfair situation or shame over previous transgressions—also may promote moral behavior (Damon, 1988; Farver & Branstetter, 1994; Miller & Jansen op de Haar, 1997).

The notion that negative emotions may promote moral development is one that Freud first suggested in his theory of psychoanalytic personality development. Recall from Chapter 1 that Freud argued that a child's *superego*, the part of the personality that represents societal do's and don'ts, is developed through resolution of the *Oedipal conflict*. Children come to identify with their same-sex parent, incorporating that parent's standards of morality in order to avoid unconscious guilt raised by the Oedipal conflict.

Whether or not we accept Freud's account of the Oedipal conflict and the guilt it produces—and most developmentalists do not, as we saw in Chapter 1—it is consistent

empathy the understanding of what another individual feels

The roots of empathy grow early, and by the time children reach the age of 2 or 3 are able to offer gifts and spontaneously share toys with other children and adults.

with more recent findings. These suggest that preschoolers' attempts to avoid experiencing negative emotions sometimes lead them to act in more moral, helpful ways. For instance, one reason children help others is to avoid the feelings of personal distress that they experience when they are confronted with another person's unhappiness or misfortune (Eisenberg & Fabes, 1991).

Aggression and Violence in Preschoolers: Sources and Consequences

Four-year-old Duane could not contain his anger and frustration any more. Although he usually was mild-mannered, when Eshu began to tease him about the split in his pants and kept it up for several minutes, Duane finally snapped. Rushing over to Eshu, Duane pushed him to the ground and began to hit him with his small, closed fists. Because he was so distraught, Duane's punches were not terribly effective, but they were severe enough to hurt Eshu and bring him to tears before the preschool teachers could intervene.

Although violence of this sort is relatively rare among preschool-age children, aggression is not uncommon. The potential for verbal hostility, shoving matches, kicking, and other forms of aggression is present throughout the preschool period, although the degree to which aggression is acted out changes as children become older.

Aggression is intentional injury or harm to another person (Berkowitz, 1993). Infants don't act aggressively; it is hard to contend that their behavior is *intended* to hurt others, even if they inadvertently manage to do so. On the other hand, by the time they reach preschool age, children demonstrate true aggression.

During the early preschool years, some of the aggression is addressed at attaining a desired goal, such as getting a toy away from another person or using a particular space

aggression intentional injury or harm to another person

"Have you been a moral child?"

Aggression, both physical and verbal, is present throughout the preschool period.

occupied by another person. Consequently, in some ways the aggression is inadvertent, and minor scuffles may in fact be a typical part of early preschool life. It is the rare child who does not demonstrate at least an occasional act of aggression.

On the other hand, extreme and sustained aggression is a cause of concern. In most children, the amount of aggression declines as they move through the preschool years. Typically, the frequency and average length of episodes of aggressive behavior decline in the preschool years (Cummings, Iannotti, & Zahn-Waxler, 1989).

Advances in personality and social development contribute to the decline in aggression. Throughout the preschool years, children are increasingly able to control the emotions that they are experiencing. **Emotional self-regulation** is the capability to adjust emotions to a desired state and level of intensity. Starting at age 2, children are able to talk about their feelings, and they engage in strategies to regulate them. As they get older, they develop more effective strategies, learning to better cope with negative emotions. In addition to their increasing self-control, children are also, as we've seen, developing sophisticated social skills. Most learn to use language to express their wishes, and they become increasingly able to negotiate with others (Eisenberg & Zhou, 2000).

Although declines in aggression are typical, some children remain aggressive throughout the preschool period. Furthermore, aggression is a relatively stable characteristic: The most aggressive preschoolers tend to be the most aggressive children during the school-age years, and the least aggressive preschoolers tend to be the least aggressive school-age children (Kellam et al., 1998; Rosen, 1998; Tremblay, 2001).

The Roots of Aggression. How can we explain the aggression of preschoolers? Some theoreticians suggest that to behave aggressively is an instinct, part and parcel of the human condition. For instance, Freud's psychoanalytic theory suggests that we all have a death drive, which leads us to act aggressively toward others as we turn our inward hostility outward (Freud, 1920). According to ethologist Konrad Lorenz, an expert in animal behavior, animals—including humans—share a fighting instinct that stems from primitive urges to preserve territory, maintain a steady supply of food, and weed out weaker animals (Lorenz, 1966, 1974).

emotional self-regulation the capability to adjust emotions to a desired state and level of intensity

Similar arguments are made by evolutionary theorists and *sociobiologists*, scientists who consider the biological roots of social behavior. They argue that aggression leads to reproductive success, increasing the likelihood that one's genes will be passed on to future generations. Furthermore, aggression may help to strengthen the species and its gene pool as a whole. Ultimately, then, aggressive instincts promote the survival of one's genes to pass on to future generations (McKenna, 1983; Reiss, 1984).

Although instinctual explanations of aggression are logical, most developmentalists believe they are not the whole story (Bandura, 1978). Not only do instinctual explanations fail to take into account the increasingly sophisticated cognitive abilities that humans develop as they get older, but they also have relatively little experimental support. Moreover, they provide little guidance in determining when and how children, as well as adults, will behave aggressively, other than noting that aggression is an inevitable part of the human condition. Consequently, developmentalists have turned to other approaches to explain aggression and violence.

Social Learning Approaches to Aggression. The day after Duane lashed out at Eshu, Lynn, who had watched the entire scene, got into an argument with Ilya. They verbally bickered for a while, and suddenly Lynn balled her hand into a fist and tried to punch Ilya. The preschool teachers were stunned: It was rare for Lynn to get upset, and she had never displayed aggression before.

Is there a connection between the two events? Most of us would answer yes, particularly if we subscribed to the view, suggested by social learning approaches, that aggression is largely a learned behavior. Social learning approaches to aggression contend that aggression is based on prior learning. To understand the causes of aggressive behavior, then, we should look at the system of rewards and punishments that exists in a child's environment.

Social learning approaches to aggression emphasize how social and environmental conditions teach individuals to be aggressive. They grow out of behavioral perspectives, which suggest that aggressive behavior is learned through direct reinforcement. For instance, preschool-age children may learn that they can continue to play with the most desirable toys by declining aggressively their classmates' requests for sharing. In the parlance

Social learning explanations of aggression suggest that children's observation of aggression on television can result in actual aggression.

of traditional learning theory, they have been reinforced for acting aggressively, and they are more likely to behave aggressively in the future.

But social learning approaches suggest that reinforcement also comes in less direct ways. A good deal of research suggests that exposure to aggressive models leads to increased aggression, particularly if the observers are themselves angered, insulted, or frustrated. For example, Albert Bandura and his colleagues illustrated the power of models in a classic study of preschool-age children (Bandura, Ross, & Ross, 1962). One group of children watched a film of an adult playing aggressively and violently with a Bobo doll (a large, inflated plastic dummy that always returns to an upright position after being pushed down). In comparison, children in another condition watched a film of an adult playing sedately with a set of Tinkertoys (see Figure 8-3). Later, the preschool-age children were allowed to play with a number of toys, which included both the Bobo doll and the Tinkertoys. But first, the children were led to feel frustration by being refused the opportunity to play with a favorite toy.

Consistent with social learning approaches, the preschool-age children modeled the behavior of the adult. Those who had seen the aggressive model playing with the Bobo doll were considerably more aggressive than those who had watched the calm, unaggressive model playing with the Tinkertoys.

Later research has supported this early study, and it is clear that exposure to aggressive models increases the likelihood that aggression on the part of observers will follow (Farver et al., 1997). These findings have profound consequences, particularly for children who live in communities in which violence is prevalent. For instance, one survey con-

Figure 8-3 **Modeling Aggression**

This series of photos is from Albert Bandura's classic Bobo doll experiment, designed to illustrate social learning of aggression. The photos clearly show how the adult model's aggressive behavior (in the first row) is imitated by children who had viewed the aggressive behavior (second and third rows).

ducted in a city public hospital found that 1 in 10 children under the age of 6 said they had witnessed a shooting or stabbing. Other research indicates that one-third of the children in some urban neighborhoods have seen a homicide and that two-thirds have seen a serious assault (Groves et al., 1993; Osofsky, 1995b; Farver & Frosch, 1996).

Even children who are not witnesses to real-life violence—the majority of preschool-age children—are typically exposed to aggression via the medium of television, particularly in light of the high levels of viewing in which most preschool-age children engage. The average preschooler watches 3 hours of television each day, and even children whose parents don't own television sets watch from 1 to 2 hours a day—at friends' homes (Condry, 1989).

Although television has a clear impact on cognitive development, as we discussed in Chapter 7, it has other, and perhaps even more important, consequences for frequent viewers. In particular, because it contains so much violent content (see Figure 8-4), the medium can have a powerful influence on the subsequent aggressive behavior of viewers (Liebert & Sprafkin, 1988; Wood, Wong, & Chachere, 1991; Sanson & diMuccio, 1993; Huesmann, Moise, & Podolski, 1997).

Programs such as the *Mighty Morphin Power Rangers* and *Pokemon* are watched by millions of preschoolers, who later imitate violent behavior during play. This is no surprise, given social learning theory. But does the playful enactment of aggression later turn into the real thing, producing children (and later adults) who demonstrate more actual—and ultimately deadly—aggression?

It is hard to answer the question definitively, primarily because no true experiments outside laboratory settings have been conducted. Although it is clear that laboratory observation of aggression on television leads to higher levels of aggression, evidence showing that real-world viewing of aggression is associated with subsequent aggressive behavior is correlational. (Think, for a moment, of how we might conduct a true experiment involv-

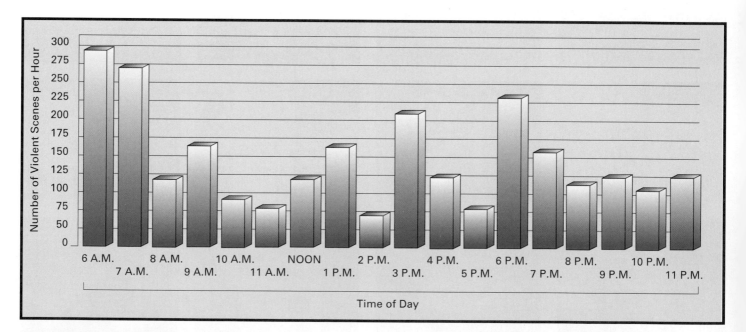

Figure 8-4   Acts of Violence

A survey of the violence shown on the major TV networks and several cable channels in Washington, D.C., on one particular weekday found acts of violence during every time period. Do you think depictions of violence on TV should be regulated?

(*Source:* Center for Media and Public Affairs, 1995).

ing children's viewing habits. It would require that we control children's viewing of television in their homes for extended periods, exposing some to a steady diet of violent shows and others to nonviolent ones—something that most parents would not agree to.)

Despite the fact that the results are primarily correlational and therefore inconclusive, the weight of research evidence is clear in suggesting that observation of televised aggression does lead to subsequent aggression. For example, in one longitudinal study, children's preferences for violent television shows at age 8 were related to the seriousness of criminal convictions by age 30 (Huesmann, 1986). Other evidence supports the notion that observation of media violence can lead to a greater readiness to act aggressively and to an insensitivity to the suffering of victims of violence (Linz, Donnerstein, & Penrod, 1988; Gadow & Sprafkin, 1993; Kremar & Greene, 2000).

Fortunately, the same principles of social learning theory that lead preschoolers to learn aggression from television suggest ways to reduce the negative influence of the medium. For instance, children can be explicitly taught critical viewing skills that influence their interpretation of televised models. In such training, they are taught that violence is not representative of the real world, that the viewing of violence is objectionable, and that they should refrain from imitating the behavior they have seen on television (Huesmann et al., 1983; Eron & Huesmann, 1985; Zillman, 1993; Farhi, 1995).

Furthermore, just as exposure to aggressive models leads to aggression, observation of *non*aggressive models can *reduce* aggression. Preschoolers don't learn from others only how to be aggressive; they can also learn how to avoid confrontation and to control their aggression, as we'll discuss later.

Cognitive Approaches to Aggression: The Thoughts Behind Violence. Two children, waiting for their turn in a game of kickball, inadvertently knock into one another. One child's reaction is to apologize; the other's is to shove, saying angrily, "Cut it out."

Despite the fact that each child bears the same responsibility for the minor event, very different reactions result. The first child interprets the event as an accident, while the second sees it as a provocation and reacts with aggression.

The cognitive approach to aggression suggests that the key to understanding moral development is to examine preschoolers' interpretations of others' behavior and of the environmental context in which a behavior occurs. According to developmental psychologist Kenneth Dodge and his colleagues, some children are more prone than others to assume that actions are aggressively motivated. They are unable to pay attention to the appropriate cues in a situation and unable to interpret the behaviors in a given situation accurately. Instead, they assume—often erroneously—that what is happening is related to others' hostility. Subsequently, in deciding how to respond, they base their behavior on their inaccurate interpretation of behavior. In sum, they may behave aggressively in response to a situation that never in fact existed (Dodge & Coie, 1987; Dodge & Crick, 1990).

Although the cognitive approach to aggression provides a description of the process that leads some children to behave aggressively, it is less successful in explaining how certain children come to be inaccurate perceivers of situations in the first place. Furthermore, it fails to explain why such inaccurate perceivers so readily respond with aggression, and why they assume that aggression is an appropriate and even desirable response.

On the other hand, cognitive approaches to aggression are useful in pointing out a means to reduce aggression: By teaching preschool-age children to be more accurate interpreters of a situation, we can induce them to be less prone to view others' behavior as motivated by hostility, and consequently less likely to respond with aggression themselves. The guidelines in the accompanying *Becoming an Informed Consumer of Development* feature are based on the various theoretical perspectives on aggression and morality that we've discussed in this chapter.

▶ Becoming an Informed Consumer of Development

Increasing Moral Behavior and Reducing Aggression in Preschool-age Children

Based on our discussions of moral development and the roots of aggression, we can identify several methods for encouraging preschoolers' moral conduct and reducing the incidence of aggression. Among the most practical and readily accomplished are the following (Bullock, 1988):

▶ Provide opportunities for preschool-age children to observe others acting in a cooperative, helpful, prosocial manner. Furthermore, encourage them to interact with peers in joint activities in which they share a common goal. Such cooperative activities can teach the importance and desirability of working with—and helping—others.

▶ Do not ignore aggressive behavior. Parents and teachers should intervene when they see aggression in preschoolers, and send a clear message that aggression is an unacceptable means to resolve conflicts.

▶ Help preschoolers devise alternative explanations for others' behavior. This is particularly important for children who are prone to aggression and who may be apt to view others' conduct as more hostile than it actually is. Parents and teachers should help such children see that the behavior of their peers has several possible interpretations.

▶ Monitor preschoolers' television viewing, particularly the violence that they view. There is good evidence that observation of televised aggression results in subsequent increases in children's levels of aggression. At the same time, encourage preschoolers to watch particular shows that are designed, in part, to increase the level of moral conduct, such as *Sesame Street, Mr. Rogers' Neighborhood,* and *Barney.*

▶ Help preschoolers understand their feelings. When children become angry—and there are times when almost all children do—they need to learn how to deal with their feelings in a constructive manner. Tell them *specific* things they can do to improve the situation ("I see you're really angry with Jake for not giving you a turn. Don't hit him, but tell him you want a chance to play with the game.")

▶ Explicitly teach reasoning and self-control. Preschoolers can understand the rudiments of moral reasoning, and they should be reminded why certain behaviors are desirable. For instance, explicitly saying "If you take all the cookies, others will have no dessert" is preferable to saying, "Good children don't eat all the cookies."

Review and Rethink

REVIEW

- Piaget believed that preschoolers are in the heteronomous morality stage of moral development.
- Social learning approaches to moral development emphasize the importance of reinforcement for moral actions and the observation of models of moral conduct. Psychoanalytical and other theories focus on children's empathy with others and their wish to help others so they can avoid unpleasant feelings themselves.
- Aggression typically declines in frequency and duration as children become more able to regulate their emotions and to use language to negotiate disputes.
- Ethologists and sociobiologists regard aggression as an innate human characteristic, while proponents of social learning and cognitive approaches focus on learned aspects of aggression.

RETHINK

- If high-prestige models of behavior are particularly effective in influencing moral attitudes and actions, are there implications for individuals in such industries as sports, advertising, and entertainment?
- If television and aggression are ever conclusively linked, what will be the social policy implications? Why do children enjoy watching acts of aggression and violence on television?

Looking Back

▶ *How do preschool-age children develop a concept of themselves?*

■ According to Erik Erikson, preschool-age children initially are in the autonomy-versus-shame-and-doubt stage (18 months to 3 years) in which they develop independence and mastery over their physical and social worlds or feel shame, self-doubt, and unhappiness. Later, in the initiative-versus-guilt stage (ages 3 to 6), preschool-age children face conflicts between the desire to act independently and the guilt that comes from the unintended consequences of their actions.

■ Preschoolers' self-concepts are formed partly from their own perceptions and estimations of their characteristics, partly from their parents' behavior toward them, and partly from cultural influences.

▶ *How do children develop a sense of racial identity and gender?*

■ Preschool-age children form racial attitudes largely in response to their environment, including parents and other influences. Gender differences emerge early in the preschool years as children form expectations—which generally conform to social stereotypes—about what is appropriate and inappropriate for each sex.

■ The strong gender expectations held by preschoolers are explained in different ways by different theorists. Some point to genetic factors as evidence for a biological explanation of gender expectations. Freud's psychoanalytic theories use a framework based on the subconscious. Social learning theorists focus on environmental influences, including parents, teachers, peers, and the media, while cognitive theorists propose that children form gender schemas, cognitive frameworks that organize information that the children gather about gender.

▶ *In what sorts of social relationships and play do preschoolers engage?*

■ Preschool social relationships begin to encompass genuine friendship, which takes on a dimension of stability and trust.

■ Older preschoolers engage in more constructive play than functional play. They also engage in more associative and cooperative play than younger preschoolers, who do more parallel and onlooker playing.

▶ *What sorts of disciplinary styles do parents employ, and what effects do they have?*

■ Disciplinary styles differ both individually and culturally. In the United States and other Western societies, parents' styles tend to be mostly authoritarian, permissive, uninvolved, and authoritative, the last regarded as the most effective. Children of authoritarian and permissive parents may develop dependency, hostility, and low self-control, while children of uninvolved parents may feel unloved and emotionally detached. Children of authoritative parents tend to be more independent, friendly, self-assertive, and cooperative.

▶ *What factors contribute to child abuse and neglect?*

■ Child abuse, which may be either physical or psychological, occurs especially in stressful home environments. Firmly held notions regarding family privacy and the use of physical punishment in childrearing contribute to the high rate of abuse in the United States. Moreover, the cycle of violence hypothesis points to the likelihood that persons who were abused as children may turn into abusers as adults.

▶ *How do children develop a moral sense?*

■ Piaget believed that preschool-age children are in the heteronomous morality stage of moral development, characterized by a belief in external, unchangeable rules of conduct and sure, immediate punishment for all misdeeds.

■ In contrast, social learning approaches to morality emphasize interactions between environment and behavior in moral development in which models of behavior play an important role in development.

■ Some developmentalists believe that a child's development of empathy, which begins early in life, underlies many kinds of moral behavior. Other emotions, including the negative emotions of anger and shame, may also promote moral behavior.

▶ *How does aggression develop in preschool-age children?*

■ Aggression, which involves intentional harm to another person, begins to emerge in the preschool years. As children age and improve their language skills, acts of aggression typically decline in frequency and duration.

■ Some ethologists, such as Konrad Lorenz, believe that aggression is simply a biological fact of human life, a belief held also by many sociobiologists, who focus on competition within species to pass genes on to the next generation.

■ Social learning theorists focus on the role of the environment, including models of behavior and social reinforcement.

■ The cognitive approach to aggression emphasizes the role of interpretations of the behaviors of others in determining aggressive or nonaggressive responses.

E P I L O G U E

In this chapter, we examined the social and personality development of preschool-age children, including their development of self-concept. We looked at the social relationships of preschool-age children and the changing nature of play. We considered typical styles of parental discipline and their effects later in life, and we examined the factors that lead to child abuse. We discussed the development of a moral sense from several developmental perspectives, and we concluded with a discussion of aggression.

Reread the prologue to this chapter, about Alison Gopnik's son, and answer the following questions.

1. In what ways do the actions of Alison Gopnik's son indicate that he is developing a theory of mind?

2. Is Erikson's framework of moral development helpful in interpreting the boy's actions in this instance? Why or why not?

3. Do you think the boy's reaction would have been different if his father had collapsed on the couch after a bad day, instead of his mother? Why or why not? Can you think of a hypothesis to test based on this question? Could an experiment be devised to examine the hypothesis?

4. How might social learning approaches to morality and the concept of empathy explain the son's actions in helping his mother?

5. Can you discuss the boy's actions in terms of emotional self-regulation?

Key Terms and Concepts

psychosocial development (p. 259)
initiative-versus-guilt stage (p. 259)
self-concept (p. 260)
collectivistic orientation (p. 260)
individualistic orientation (p. 260)
race dissonance (p. 261)
identification (p. 263)
gender identity (p. 264)
gender schema (p. 264)
gender constancy (p. 265)
androgynous (p. 265)

functional play (p. 267)
constructive play (p. 267)
parallel play (p. 267)
onlooker play (p. 267)
associative play (p. 267)
cooperative play (p. 267)
authoritarian parents (p. 271)
permissive parents (p. 271)
authoritative parents (p. 271)
uninvolved parents (p. 271)
cycle of violence hypothesis (p. 276)

psychological maltreatment (p. 276)
resilience (p. 277)
moral development (p. 278)
heteronomous morality (p. 278)
immanent justice (p. 280)
prosocial behavior (p. 280)
abstract modeling (p. 281)
empathy (p. 281)
aggression (p. 282)
emotional self-regulation (p. 283)

Bridges

In Part Three, we extended our discussion of physical, cognitive, social, and personality development into the preschool years. We saw that these years bring great improvements in children's motor skills, thinking, and language, and in their social awareness and development of morality.

Children begin the preschool years as somewhat wobbly toddlers with few words at their command. They emerge with an array of skills for sports and games, learning, communicating, and making new friends. These skills will all help them as they move into middle childhood—the part of the life span discussed in Part Four. For example, we'll see how important friendships become to children during their school years.

In Part Three, we discussed many theories of cognitive and social development, and encountered some of the groundbreaking ideas—and great controversies—associated with such giants in the field of development as Piaget, Vygotsky, Freud, and Erikson. All of these theorists stressed the importance of early developments as a foundation for later growth, whether in cognitive skills or personality development. In Part Four, we'll explore how children's sociocultural environments during the preschool years might relate to their success in school. We will also introduce you to the controversies surrounding intelligence and how early development may affect it.

The progress that preschoolers make is transformed into a remarkable capacity for social functioning in middle childhood. As you study middle childhood, keep in mind the milestones of infancy and preschool, and think about how they are related to one another.

OUTLINE

Physical and Cognitive Development in Middle Childhood

PROLOGUE: LA-TOYA PANKEY AND *THE WITCHES*

La-Toya Pankey

There are few books in La-Toya Pankey's apartment on 102nd Street near Amsterdam Avenue in Manhattan, and even fewer places for an 8-year-old girl to steal away to read them.

There is no desk, no bookshelf, no reading lamp or even a bureau in La-Toya's small room, one of only two bedrooms in the apartment she shares with seven other people: her mother, her five sisters and her infant brother.

At night, there is little light, save a couple of bare bulbs mounted on the peeling, beige walls. And there are few places to sit, except a lone, wooden chair at a battered kitchen table, which La-Toya must wait her turn to occupy.

Yet there was La-Toya, on a rainy evening earlier this month, leaning against that table and reading aloud, flawlessly, to her mother from the Roald Dahl classic *The Witches,* which she had borrowed from the makeshift library in her third-grade classroom. (Steinberg, 1997, p. B1)

Looking Ahead

It was a significant moment for La-Toya. It marked a shift from the first-grade-level books that she had previously chosen to read to a far more challenging one, written at a grade level two years higher than her own.

Middle childhood is characterized by a procession of moments such as these, as children's physical, cognitive, and social skills ascend to new heights. Beginning at age 6 and continuing to the start of adolescence at around age 12, the period of middle childhood is often referred to as the "school years" because it marks the beginning of formal education for most children. Sometimes the physical and cognitive growth that occurs during middle childhood is gradual; other times it is sudden; but always it is remarkable.

We begin our consideration of middle childhood by examining physical and motor development. We discuss how children's bodies change and the twin problems of malnutrition and—the other side of the coin—childhood obesity. We also consider both typical development and some of the special needs that affect exceptional children's sensory and physical abilities.

Next, we turn to cognitive development in middle childhood. We examine several approaches, including Piagetian and information-processing theories and the important ideas of Lev Vygotsky. We look at language development and the critical questions revolving around bilingualism—an increasingly pressing social issue in the United States due to the growing diversity of the school-age population.

Finally, we consider several issues involving schooling. After discussing the scope of education throughout the world, we examine the critical skill of reading and the nature of multicultural education. The chapter ends with a discussion of intelligence, a characteristic closely tied to school success. We look at the nature of IQ tests and at the education of children who are either significantly below or above the intellectual norm.

After reading this chapter, you will be able to answer these questions:

▶ **In what ways do children grow during the school years, and what factors influence their growth?**

▶ **What are the main health concerns of school-age children?**

▶ **What sorts of special needs may become apparent in children at this age, and how can they be met?**

▶ **In what ways do children develop cognitively during these years, according to major theoretical approaches?**

▶ **How does language develop during the middle childhood period?**

▶ **What are some trends in schooling today?**

▶ **How can intelligence be measured, and how are exceptional children educated?**

Physical Development

Cinderella, dressed in yella, went upstairs to kiss her fellah
But she made a mistake and she kissed a snake. How many doctors did it take?
One, two, . . .

While the other girls chanted the classic jump-rope rhyme, Kat proudly displayed her newly developed ability to jump backwards. In second grade, Kat was starting to get quite good at jumping rope. In first grade, she simply had not been able to master it. But over the summer, she had spent many hours practicing, and now that practice seemed to be paying off.

As Kat is gleefully experiencing, middle childhood is a time when children make great physical strides, mastering all kinds of new skills as they grow bigger and stronger. How does this progress occur? We'll first consider typical physical growth during middle childhood and then turn our attention to a look at exceptional children

The Growing Body

Slow but steady. If three words could characterize the nature of growth during middle childhood, it would be these. Especially when compared to the swift growth during the first 5 years of life and the remarkable growth spurt characteristic of adolescence, middle childhood is relatively tranquil. On the other hand, the body has not shifted into neutral. Physical growth continues, although at a more stately pace than it did during the preschool years.

Height and Weight Changes. While they are in elementary school, children in the United States grow, on average, 2 to 3 inches a year. By the age of 11, the average height for girls is 4 feet, 10 inches and the average height for boys is slightly shorter at 4 feet, 9 1/2 inches. This is the only time during the life span when girls are, on average, taller than boys. This height difference reflects the slightly more rapid physical development of girls, who start their adolescent growth spurt around the age of 10.

Weight gain follows a similar pattern. During middle childhood, both boys and girls gain around 5 to 7 pounds a year. Weight also becomes redistributed. As the rounded look of "baby fat" disappears, children's bodies become more muscular and their strength increases.

Average height and weight increases disguise significant individual differences, as anyone who has seen a line of fourth-graders walking down a school corridor has doubtless noticed. It is not unusual to see children of the same age who are six or seven inches apart in height.

Cultural Patterns of Growth. Most children in North America receive sufficient nutrients to grow to their full potential. In other parts of the world, however, inadequate nutrition and disease take their toll, producing children who are shorter and who weigh less than they would if they had sufficient nutrients. The discrepancies can be dramatic: Children in poorer areas of cities such as Calcutta, Hong Kong, and Rio de Janeiro are smaller than their counterparts in affluent areas of the same cities.

In the U.S., most variations in height and weight are the result of different people's unique genetic inheritance, including genetic factors relating to racial and ethnic background. For instance, children from Asian and Oceanic Pacific backgrounds tend to be shorter, on average, than those with northern and central European heritages (Meredith, 1971). However, even within particular racial and ethnic groups, there is significant variation between individuals. Furthermore, we cannot attribute racial and ethnic differences solely to inherited factors, because dietary customs as well as possible variations in levels of affluence also may contribute to the differences.

Promoting Growth with Hormones: Should Short Children Be Made to Grow? Being tall is considered an advantage in most of U.S. society. Because of this cultural preference, parents sometimes worry about their children's growth if their children are short. To the manufacturers of Protropin, an artificial human growth hormone that can make short children

cw

Variations of six inches in height between children of the same age are not unusual and well within normal ranges.

taller, there's a simple solution: Administer the drug to make the children grow taller than they naturally would. (Kolata, 1994).

Should children be given such drugs? The question is a relatively new one: Artificial hormones to promote growth have become available only in the last two decades. Although tens of thousands of children who have insufficient natural growth hormone are taking such drugs, some observers question whether shortness is a serious enough problem to warrant the use of the drug. Certainly, one can function well in society without being tall. Furthermore, the drug is costly and has potentially dangerous side effects. In some cases, the drug may lead to the premature onset of puberty, which may—ironically—restrict later growth.

On the other hand, there is no denying that artificial growth hormones are effective in increasing children's height, in some cases adding well over a foot in height to extremely short children, placing them within normal height ranges. Ultimately, parents and medical personnel must carefully weigh the pros and cons before administering the drug to their children.

Nutrition. We discussed the rather obvious relationship between size and nutrition earlier in this chapter. However, children's levels of nutrition significantly affect many other aspects of their lives as well. For instance, longitudinal studies over many years in Guatemalan villages show that children's nutritional backgrounds are related to several dimensions of social and emotional functioning at school age. Children who had received more nutrients were more involved with their peers, showed more positive emotion, had less anxiety, and had more moderate activity levels than their peers who had received less adequate nutrition. Furthermore, the children with a better nutritional history were more eager to explore new environments, showed more persistence in frustrating situations, were more alert on some types of activities, and generally displayed higher energy levels and more self-confidence (Barrett & Frank, 1987; see Figure 9-1).

Nutrition is also linked to cognitive performance. For instance, in one study, children in Kenya who were well nourished performed better on a test of verbal abilities and on other cognitive measures than those who had mild to moderate undernutrition. Other research suggests that malnutrition may influence cognitive development by dampening children's curiosity, responsiveness, and motivation to learn (Ricciuti, 1993; McDonald et al., 1994; Brown & Pollitt, 1996).

Figure 9-1 **Nutritional Benefits**

Children who received higher levels of nutrients had more energy and felt more self-confident than those whose nutritional intake was lower. What policy implications does this finding suggest?

(Adapted from Barrett & Radke-Yarrow, 1985.)

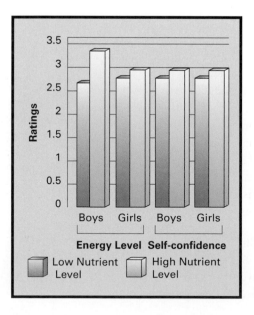

Although undernutrition and malnutrition clearly lead to physical, social, and cognitive difficulties, in some cases *over*nutrition—the intake by a child of too many calories—presents problems of its own, particularly when it leads to childhood obesity.

Childhood Obesity. When Ruthellen's mother asks if she would like a piece of bread with her meal, Ruthellen replies that she better not—she thinks that she may be getting fat. Ruthellen, who is of normal weight and height, is 6 years old.

Although height can be of concern to both children and parents during middle childhood, maintaining the appropriate weight is an even greater worry for some. In fact, concern about weight can border on an obsession, particularly among girls. For instance, many 6-year-old girls worry about becoming "fat," and some 40 percent of 9- and 10-year-olds are trying to lose weight. Why? Their concern is most often the result of the U.S. preoccupation with being slim, which permeates every sector of society (Schreiber et al., 1996).

In spite of this widely held view that thinness is a virtue, however, increasing numbers of children are becoming obese. *Obesity* is defined as body weight that is more than 20 percent above the average for a person of a given age and height. By this definition, some 10 percent of all children are obese—a proportion that is growing. In fact, since the 1960s, obesity among children aged 6 to 11 has risen by 54 percent (Lamb, 1984; Gortmaker et al., 1987; Troiano et al., 1995).

Obesity is caused by a combination of genetic and social characteristics. Particular inherited genes are related to obesity and predispose certain children to be overweight. For example, adopted children tend to have weights that are more similar to those of their birth parents than to those of their adoptive parents (Zhang et al., 1994; Whitaker et al., 1997).

Social factors also enter into children's weight problems. For example, parents who are particularly controlling and directive regarding their children's eating may produce children who lack internal controls to regulate their own food intake (Brownell & Rodin, 1994; Johnson & Birch, 1994; Faith, Johnson, & Allison, 1997).

Children's poor diets also can contribute to obesity. Despite their knowledge that certain foods are necessary for a balanced, nutritious diet, most children eat too few fruits and vegetables and more fats and sweets than recommended (see Figure 9-2).

Another important social factor that determines obesity is exercise—or rather, the lack of exercise. School-age children, by and large, tend to engage in relatively little exercise and are not particularly fit (Wolf et al., 1993). For instance, around 40 percent of boys 6 to 12 are unable to do more than one pull-up, and a quarter can't do any. Furthermore, school fitness surveys reveal that children in the United States have shown little or no

"Can Johnny come out and eat?"

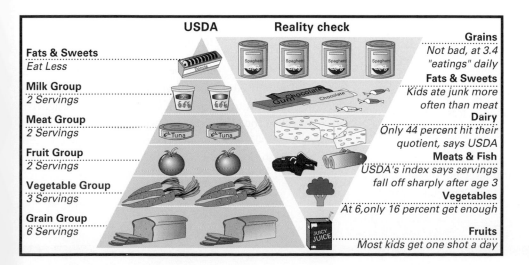

USDA		Reality check	
Fats & Sweets Eat Less			**Grains** *Not bad, at 3.4 "eatings" daily*
Milk Group 2 Servings			**Fats & Sweets** *Kids ate junk more often than meat*
Meat Group 2 Servings			**Dairy** *Only 44 percent hit their quotient, says USDA*
Fruit Group 2 Servings			**Meats & Fish** *USDA's index says servings fall off sharply after age 3*
Vegetable Group 3 Servings			**Vegetables** *At 6, only 16 percent get enough*
Grain Group 6 Servings			**Fruits** *Most kids get one shot a day*

Figure 9-2 Balanced Diet?

Recent studies have found that the diet of children is almost the opposite of that recommended by the U.S. Department of Agriculture, a situation which can lead to an increase in obesity. The typical 10-year-old is 10 pounds heavier than a decade ago.

(*Source:* NPD Group, 1998; USDA, 1999.)

improvement in the amount of exercise they get, despite national efforts to increase the level of fitness of school-age children. From the ages of 6 to 18, boys decrease their physical activity by 24 percent and girls by 36 percent (Ungrady, 1992; Murray, 1996).

Why, when our visions of childhood include children running happily on school playgrounds, playing sports, and chasing one another in games of tag, is the actual level of exercise relatively low? One answer is that many kids are inside their homes, watching television.

The correlation between television viewing and obesity is significant: The more television children watch, the more likely they are to be overweight. There are several reasons for this pattern. For one thing, television viewing is a sedentary activity; few people engage in vigorous exercise while watching TV. Another factor is that children tend to snack while watching television, thereby increasing their caloric intake beyond nutritional need. It is even possible that frequent exposure to commercials for food products entices habitual television viewers to be overly interested in food and eating (Gortmaker et al., 1996; Harrell et al., 1997; Gable & Lutz, 2000). Some tips for easing sedentary kids into a more active lifestyle are included in *The Informed Consumer of Development* section, next.

The Informed Consumer of Development

Keeping Children Fit

Here is a brief portrait of a contemporary American: Sam works all week at a desk and gets no regular physical exercise. On weekends he spends many hours sitting in front of the TV, often snacking on sodas and sweets. Both at home and at restaurants, his meals feature high-calorie, fat-saturated foods. (Segal & Segal, 1992, p. 235)

Although this sketch could apply to many adult men and women, Sam is actually a 6-year-old. He is one of many school-age children in the United States who get little or no regular exercise and who consequently are physically unfit and at risk for obesity and other health problems.

However, several approaches can be taken to encourage children to become more physically active (Squires, 1991; O'Neill, 1994):

▶ Make exercise fun. In order for children to build the habit of exercising, they need to find it enjoyable. Activities that keep children on the sidelines or that are overly competitive may give children with inferior skills a lifelong distaste for exercise.

▶ Be an exercise role model. Children who see that exercise is a regular part of the lives of their parents, teachers, or adult friends may come to think of fitness as a regular part of their lives, too.

▶ Gear activities to the child's physical level and motor skills. For instance, use child-size equipment that can make participants feel successful.

▶ Encourage the child to find a partner. It could be a friend, a sibling, or a parent. Exercising can involve a variety of activities, such as roller skating or hiking, but almost all activities are carried out more readily if someone else is doing them too.

▶ Start slowly. Sedentary children—those who haven't habitually engaged in physical activity—should start off gradually. For instance, they could start with 5 minutes of exercise a day, 7 days a week. Over ten weeks, they could move toward a goal of 30 minutes of exercise 3 to 5 days a week.

▶ Urge participation in organized sports activities, but do not push too hard. Not every child is athletically inclined, and pushing too hard for involvement in organized sports may backfire. Make participation and enjoyment the goals of such activities, not winning.

▶ Don't make physical activity, such as jumping jacks or push-ups, a punishment for unwanted behavior.

▶ Schools and parents should encourage children to participate in an organized physical fitness program. For instance, the Cooper Institute for Aerobics Research has designed a program called the "Fitnessgram," which is used by 2 million children in 3,000 schools around the United States. (For more information, write Cooper Institute for Aerobics Research, 12330 Preston Road, Dallas, Texas 75230.)

During middle childhood, children master many types of skills that earlier they could not perform well, such as riding a bike, ice skating, swimming, and skipping rope. Is this the same for children of other cultures?

Motor Development

The fact that the fitness level of school-age children is not as high as we would desire does not mean that such children are physically incapable. In fact, even without regular exercise, children's gross and fine motor skills develop substantially over the course of the school years.

Gross Motor Skills. One important improvement in gross motor skills is in the realm of muscle coordination. Watching a softball player pitch a ball past a batter to her catcher, a runner reach the finish line in a race, or Kat, the jump-roper described earlier in the chapter, we are struck by the huge strides that these children have made since the more awkward days of preschool.

During middle childhood, children master many types of skills that earlier they could not perform well. For instance, most school age children can readily learn to ride a bike, ice skate, swim, and skip rope (Cratty, 1986; see Figure 9-3).

Do boys and girls differ in their motor skills? Traditionally, developmentalists have concluded that gender differences in gross motor skills become increasingly pronounced during these years, with boys outperforming girls (Espenschade, 1960). However, more recent research casts some doubt on this conclusion. When comparisons are made between boys and girls who regularly take part in similar activities—such as softball—gender variations in gross motor skills are minimized (Hall & Lee, 1984).

Why? Performance differences were probably found in the first place because of differences in motivation and expectations. Society told girls that they would do worse than boys in sports, and the girls' performance reflected that message.

Today, however, society's message has changed, at least officially. For instance, the American Academy of Pediatrics suggests that boys and girls should engage in the same sports and games, and that they can do so together in mixed-gender groups. There is no reason to separate the sexes in physical exercise and sports until puberty, when the smaller size of females begins to make them more susceptible to injury in contact sports (American Academy of Pediatrics, 1989).

Fine Motor Skills. Typing at a computer keyboard. Writing in cursive with pen and pencil. Drawing detailed pictures.

These are just some of the accomplishments that depend on improvements in fine motor coordination that occur during early and middle childhood. Six- and 7-year-olds

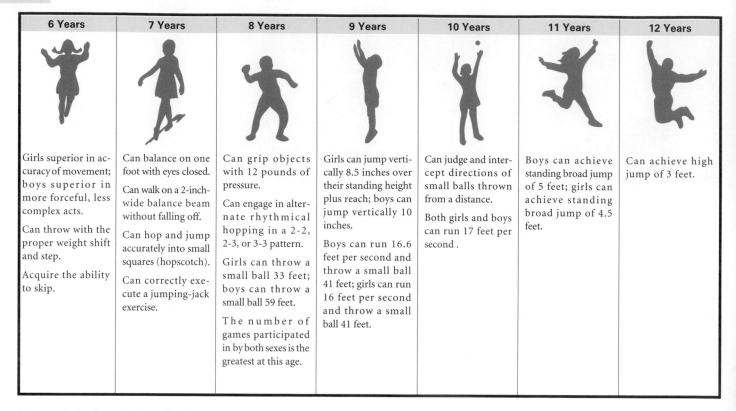

6 Years	7 Years	8 Years	9 Years	10 Years	11 Years	12 Years
Girls superior in accuracy of movement; boys superior in more forceful, less complex acts. Can throw with the proper weight shift and step. Acquire the ability to skip.	Can balance on one foot with eyes closed. Can walk on a 2-inch-wide balance beam without falling off. Can hop and jump accurately into small squares (hopscotch). Can correctly execute a jumping-jack exercise.	Can grip objects with 12 pounds of pressure. Can engage in alternate rhythmical hopping in a 2-2, 2-3, or 3-3 pattern. Girls can throw a small ball 33 feet; boys can throw a small ball 59 feet. The number of games participated in by both sexes is the greatest at this age.	Girls can jump vertically 8.5 inches over their standing height plus reach; boys can jump vertically 10 inches. Boys can run 16.6 feet per second and throw a small ball 41 feet; girls can run 16 feet per second and throw a small ball 41 feet.	Can judge and intercept directions of small balls thrown from a distance. Both girls and boys can run 17 feet per second .	Boys can achieve standing broad jump of 5 feet; girls can achieve standing broad jump of 4.5 feet.	Can achieve high jump of 3 feet.

Figure 9-3 Gross Motor Skills

Gross motor skills developed by children between the ages of 6 and 12 years.

(Adapted from Cratty, 1979, p. 222.)

are able to tie their shoes and fasten buttons; by age 8, they can use each hand independently; and by 11 and 12, they can manipulate objects with almost as much capability as they will show in adulthood.

One of the reasons for advances in fine motor skills is that the amount of myelin in the brain increases significantly between the ages of 6 and 8 (Lecours, 1982). *Myelin* provides protective insulation that surrounds parts of nerve cells. Because increased levels of myelin raise the speed at which electrical impulses travel between neurons, messages can reach muscles more rapidly and control them better.

Health During Middle Childhood

Imani was miserable. Her nose was running, her lips were chapped, and her throat was sore. Although she had been able to stay home from school and spend the day watching old reruns on TV, she still felt that she was suffering mightily.

Despite her misery, Imani's situation is not so bad. She'll get over the cold in a few days and be no worse for having experienced it. In fact, she may be a little *better* off, for she is now immune to the specific cold germs that made her ill in the first place.

Imani's cold may end up being the most serious illness that she gets during middle childhood. For most children, this is a period of robust health, and most of the ailments they do contract tend to be mild and brief. Routine immunizations during childhood have produced a considerably lower incidence of the life-threatening illnesses that 50 years ago claimed the lives of a significant number of children.

On the other hand, illness is not uncommon. For instance, more than 90 percent of children are likely to have at least one serious medical condition over the 6-year period of middle childhood, according to the results of one large survey. And, although most children have short-term illnesses, about one in nine has a chronic, persistent condition, such as repeated migraine headaches (Starfield, 1991). And some illnesses are actually becoming more prevalent.

Asthma. Asthma is among the diseases that have shown a significant increase in prevalence over the last several decades. **Asthma** is a chronic condition characterized by periodic attacks of wheezing, coughing, and shortness of breath. More than 15 million U.S. children suffer from the disorder, and worldwide the number is more than 150 million (see Figure 9-4 ; Vogel, 1997; Doyle, 2000).

Asthma occurs when the airways leading to the lungs constrict, partially blocking the passage of oxygen. Because the airways are obstructed, more effort is needed to push air through them, making breathing more difficult. As air is forced through the obstructed airways, it makes the whistling sound called wheezing.

Not surprisingly, children are often exceedingly frightened by asthma attacks, and the anxiety and agitation produced by their breathing difficulties may actually make the attack worse. In some cases, breathing becomes so difficult that further physical symptoms develop, including sweating, an increased heart rate, and—in the most severe cases—a blueness in the face and lips due to a lack of oxygen.

Asthma attacks are triggered by a variety of factors. Among the most common are respiratory infections (such as colds or flu), allergic reactions to airborne irritants (such as pollution, cigarette smoke, dust mites, and animal dander and excretions), stress, and exercise. Sometimes, even a sudden change in air temperature or humidity is enough to bring on an attack.

Although asthma can be serious, treatment is increasingly effective for those who suffer from the disorder. Some children who experience frequent asthma attacks use a small aerosol container with a special mouthpiece to spray drugs into the lungs. Other patients take tablets or receive injections (Klinnert, McQuaid, & Gavin, 1997).

One of the most puzzling questions about asthma is why more and more children have been suffering from it over the last two decades. Some researchers suggest that increasing air pollution has led to the rise; others believe that cases of asthma that might have been missed in the past are simply being identified more accurately. Still others have suggested that exposure to "asthma triggers," such as dust, may be increasing, because new buildings are more weatherproof—and therefore less drafty—than old ones, and consequently the flow of air within them is more restricted.

Finally, poverty may play an indirect role. Children living in poverty have a higher incidence of asthma than other children, probably due to poorer medical care and less sanitary living conditions. For instance, poor youngsters are more likely than more afflu-

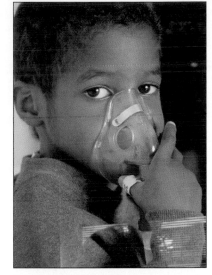

The incidence of asthma, a chronic respiratory condition, has increased dramatically over the last several decades.

asthma a chronic condition characterized by periodic attacks of wheezing, coughing, and shortness of breath

cw

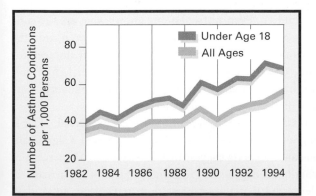

Figure 9-4 **Rising Rates of Asthma**

Since the early 1980s, the rate of asthma among children has almost doubled. A number of factors explain the rise, including increased air pollution and better means of detecting the disease.

(*Source:* National Center for Health Statistics, 1997.)

ent ones to be exposed to triggering factors that are associated with asthma, such as dust mites, cockroach feces and body parts, and rodent feces and urine (Nossiter, 1995).

Psychological Disorders. Jackson had always been a quiet child and had, since his days as a toddler, seemed less exuberant than most other children. But when his third-grade teacher called his parents to report that Jackson seemed increasingly withdrawn from his classmates and had to be coaxed into going out to the playground, the parents thought they might have a serious problem on their hands. They took Jackson to a psychologist, who diagnosed Jackson as suffering from *childhood depression*.

For years most people neglected the symptoms of childhood depression, and even today parents and teachers may overlook its presence. In part, their neglect is due to the fact that its symptoms are not entirely consistent with the ways adults express depression. Rather than being manifested in a profound sadness or hopelessness, a negative outlook on life, and, in extreme cases, suicidal thoughts, as adult depression is, childhood depression may instead be characterized by the expression of exaggerated fears, clinginess, or avoidance of everyday activities. In older children, childhood depression may produce sulking, school problems, and even acts of delinquency (Mitchell et al., 1988; Prieto, Cole, & Tageson, 1992; Wenar, 1994).

It is important to keep in mind that all children are occasionally sad, and short periods of unhappiness should not be mistaken for childhood depression. The distinguishing characteristics of childhood depression are its depth, which can be truly profound, and its duration, which can extend for days or even weeks (Besseghini, 1997; Bandura et al., 1999).

Like adult depression, childhood depression can be treated effectively through a variety of approaches. In addition to psychological counseling, drugs are sometimes prescribed, although their use is controversial. For example, the use of Prozac has become a popular—if highly controversial—treatment for a variety of childhood psychological disorders. By the late 1990s, 200,000 prescriptions were written annually for children between the ages of 6 and 12 (Strauch, 1997).

Surprisingly, though, the drug has never been approved by governmental regulators for use with children. In fact, no antidepressant drug has ever received approval for use by children or adolescents. Still, because the drug has received approval for adult use, it is perfectly legal for physicians to write prescriptions for children.

Proponents of the increased use of Prozac as well as other antidepressants, such as Zoloft and Paxil, for children suggest that depression and other psychological disorders can be treated quite successfully using drug therapies. In many cases, more traditional nondrug therapies that largely employ verbal methods simply are ineffective. In such cases, drugs can provide the only form of relief. Furthermore, at least one clinical test has shown that the drugs are effective with children (Emslie et al., 1997).

Critics, on the other hand, contend that there is little evidence for the long-term effectiveness of antidepressants with children. Even worse, no one knows what are the consequences of the use of antidepressants on the developing brains of children, nor the long-term consequences more generally. Little is known about the correct dosages for children of given ages. Finally, some observers suggest that the use of special children's versions of the drugs, in orange- or mint-flavored syrups, might lead to overdoses or perhaps eventually encourage the use of illegal drugs (Strauch, 1997).

Although the use of antidepressant drugs to treat children is controversial, what is clear is that childhood depression and other psychological disorders remain a significant problem for many children. For instance, experts suggest that between 2 and 5 percent of school-age children suffer from childhood depression. In some children it is particularly severe: About 1 percent are so depressed that they express unmistakable suicidal ideas (Larsson & Melin, 1992; Cohen et al., 1993). Furthermore, some 8 to 9 percent of children suffer from *anxiety disorders*, in which they experience intense, uncontrollable anxiety about situations that most people would not find bothersome. For instance, some children have strong fears about specific stimuli—such as germs or school—while others have bouts of generalized anxiety, the source of which they cannot pinpoint (Wenner, 1994; Ollendick et al., 1996).

Childhood psychological disorders must not be ignored. Not only are the disorders disruptive during childhood, but those who suffer from psychological problems as children are at risk for future disorders during adulthood (Harrington et al., 1990; Kazdin, 1990; Alloy, Acocella, & Bootzin, 1996).

As we'll see next, adults also need to pay attention to other, ongoing special needs that affect many school age children.

Children with Special Needs

> *Andrew Mertz was a very unhappy little boy . . . . Third grade was a disaster, the culmination of a crisis that had been building since he entered kindergarten in suburban Maryland. He couldn't learn to read, and he hated school. "He would throw temper tantrums in the morning because he didn't want to go," recalls his mother, Suzanne. The year before, with much prodding from Suzanne, the school had authorized diagnostic tests for Andrew. The results revealed a host of brain processing problems that explained why he kept mixing up letters and sounds. Andrew's problem now had a label—he was officially classified as learning disabled—and he was legally entitled to help. (Wingert & Kantrowitz, 1997)*

Andrew joined millions of other children who are classified as learning disabled, one of several types of special needs that children can have. Although every child has different specific capabilities, children with *special needs* differ significantly from typical children in terms of physical attributes or learning abilities. Furthermore, their needs present major challenges for both care providers and teachers.

We turn now to the most prevalent exceptionalities that affect children of normal intelligence: sensory difficulties, learning disabilities, and attention deficit disorders. (We will consider the special needs of children who are significantly below and above average in intelligence later in the chapter.)

Sensory Difficulties: Visual, Auditory, and Speech Problems. Anyone who has temporarily lost his or her eyeglasses or a contact lens has had a glimpse of how difficult even rudimentary, everyday tasks must be for those with sensory impairments. To function with less than typical vision, hearing, or speech can be a tremendous challenge.

Visual impairment can be considered in both a legal and an educational sense. The definition of legal impairment is quite straightforward: *Blindness* is visual acuity of less than 20/200 after correction (meaning the inability to see even at 20 feet what a typical person can see at 200 feet), while *partial sightedness* is visual acuity of less than 20/70 after correction.

visual impairment a difficulty in seeing that may include blindness or partial sightedness

Even when the legal limits of impairment are not reached, however, visual impairment in an educational sense can be present. For one thing, the legal criterion pertains solely to distance vision, while most educational tasks require close-up vision. In addition, the legal definition does not consider abilities in the perception of color, depth, and light—all of which might influence a student's educational success. About one student in a thousand requires special education services relating to a visual impairment.

Although most severe visual problems are identified fairly early, it sometimes happens that an impairment goes undetected. Furthermore, visual problems can emerge gradually as children develop physiologically and changes occur in the visual apparatus of the eye. Parents and teachers must be aware of the signals of visual problems in children. Frequent eye irritation (redness, sties, or infection), continual blinking and facial contortions when reading, holding reading material unusually close to the face, difficulty in writing, and frequent headaches, dizziness, or burning eyes are some of the signs of visual problems.

Another relatively frequent special need relates to **auditory impairment**. Auditory impairments can cause academic problems, and they can produce social difficulties as well, since considerable peer interaction takes place through informal conversation. Hearing loss, which affects some 1 to 2 percent of the school-age population, is not simply a matter of not hearing enough. Rather, auditory problems can vary along a number of dimensions (U.S. Department of Education, 1987; Harris, VanZandt, & Rees, 1997).

In some cases of hearing loss, only a limited range of frequencies, or pitches, is affected. For example, the loss may be great at pitches in the normal speech range yet quite minor in other frequencies, such as those of very high or low sounds. A child with this kind of loss may require different levels of amplification at different frequencies; a hearing aid that indiscriminately amplifies all frequencies equally may be ineffective.

The age of onset of a hearing loss is critical in determining the degree to which a child can adapt to the impairment. If the loss of hearing occurs in infancy, the effects will probably be much more severe than if it occurs after the age of 3. The reason relates to the critical role that hearing plays in the development of language. Children who have had little or no exposure to the sound of language are unable to understand or produce oral language themselves. On the other hand, loss of hearing after a child has learned language will not have serious consequences on subsequent linguistic development.

Severe and early loss of hearing is also associated with difficulties in abstract thinking. Because hearing-impaired children may have limited exposure to language, abstract concepts that can be understood fully only through the use of language may be less well understood than concrete concepts that can be illustrated visually (Hewett & Forness, 1974).

Auditory difficulties are sometimes accompanied by speech impairments. A speech impairment is one of the most public types of exceptionality: Every time the child speaks aloud, the impairment is obvious to listeners. In fact, the definition of **speech impairment** suggests that speech is impaired when it deviates so much from the speech of others that it calls attention to itself, interferes with communication, or produces maladjustment in the speaker (Van Riper, 1972). In other words, if a child's speech sounds impaired, it probably is. Speech impairments are present in around 3 to 5 percent of the school-age population (U.S. Department of Education, 1987).

auditory impairment a special need that involves the loss of hearing or some aspect of hearing

speech impairment speech that deviates so much from the speech of others that it calls attention to itself, interferes with communication, or produces maladjustment in the speaker

Auditory impairments can produce both academic and social difficulties, and they may lead to speech difficulties.

Stuttering, which entails substantial disruption in the rhythm and fluency of speech, is the most common speech impairment. Despite a great deal of research on the topic, no single cause has been identified. Although the disfluencies of stuttering are relatively normal in young children—and occasionally occur in normal adults—chronic stuttering can be a severe problem. Not only does stuttering hinder communication, but it can produce embarrassment and stress in children, who may become inhibited from conversing with others and speaking aloud in class (Whaley & Parker, 2000).

Parents and teachers can adopt several strategies for dealing with stuttering. For starters, attention should not be drawn to the stuttering, and children should be given sufficient time to finish what they begin to say, no matter how protracted the statement becomes. It does not help stutterers to finish their sentences for them or otherwise correct their speech (Onslow, 1992).

stuttering substantial disruption in the rhythm and fluency of speech; the most common speech impairment

learning disabilities difficulties in the acquisition and use of listening, speaking, reading, writing, reasoning, or mathematical abilities

Learning Disabilities: Discrepancies Between Achievement and Capacity to Learn. Like Andrew Mertz, who was described at the beginning of this section, some 2.6 million school-age children in the United States are officially labeled as having learning disabilities. **Learning disabilities** are characterized by difficulties in the acquisition and use of listening, speaking, reading, writing, reasoning, or mathematical abilities. A somewhat ill-defined, grab-bag category, learning disabilities are diagnosed when there is a discrepancy between children's actual academic performance and their apparent potential to learn (Roush, 1995; Lyon, 1996; Wong, 1996).

Such a broad definition encompasses a wide and heterogeneous variety of difficulties. For instance, some children suffer from *dyslexia*, a reading disability that can result in the misperception of letters during reading and writing, unusual difficulty in sounding out letters, confusion between left and right, and difficulties in spelling. Although the causes of dyslexia are not fully understood, one likely explanation is a problem in the part of the brain responsible for breaking words into the sound elements that make up language (Shaywitz, 1996; Pugh et al., 2000; Snowling, 2000).

The causes of learning disabilities are not well understood. Although they are generally attributed to some form of brain dysfunction, probably due to genetic factors, some experts suggest that they are produced by such environmental causes as poor early nutrition or allergies (Mercer, 1992).

Attention-Deficit Hyperactivity Disorder

Dusty Nash, an angelic-looking blond child of 7, awoke at five one recent morning in his Chicago home and proceeded to throw a fit. He wailed. He kicked. Every muscle in his 50-pound body flew in furious motion. Finally, after about 30 minutes, Dusty pulled himself together sufficiently to head downstairs for breakfast. While his mother bustled about the kitchen, the hyperkinetic child pulled a box of Kix cereal from the cupboard and sat on a chair.

But sitting still was not in the cards this morning. After grabbing some cereal with his hands, he began kicking the box, scattering little round corn puffs across the room. Next he turned his attention to the TV set, or rather, the table supporting it. The table was covered with checkerboard Con-Tact paper, and Dusty began peeling it off. Then he became intrigued with the spilled cereal and started stomping it to bits. At this point his mother interceded. In a firm but calm voice she told her son to get the stand-up dust pan and broom and clean up the mess. Dusty got out the dust pan but forgot the rest of the order. Within seconds he was dismantling the plastic dust pan, piece by piece. His next project: grabbing three rolls of toilet paper from the bathroom and unraveling them around the house (Wallis, 1994, p. 43)

It was only 7:30 a.m.

Seven-year-old Dusty Nash's high energy and low attention span is due to attention-deficit hyperactivity disorder, which occurs in 3 to 5 percent of the school-age population.

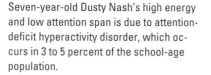

attention-deficit hyperactivity disorder (ADHD) a learning disability marked by inattention, impulsiveness, a low tolerance for frustration, and generally a great deal of inappropriate activity

Dusty suffers from a disorder that no one had heard of just a few decades ago—attention-deficit hyperactivity disorder. **Attention-deficit hyperactivity disorder,** or **ADHD,** is marked by inattention, impulsiveness, a low tolerance for frustration, and generally a great deal of inappropriate activity. Although all children show such traits some of the time, for those diagnosed with ADHD, such behavior is common and interferes with their home and school functioning (Barkley, 1997b; American Academy of Pediatrics, 2000a).

Although it is hard to know how many children have the disorder, most estimates put the number at from 3 to 5 percent of the school-age population, or some 3.5 million Americans under the age of 18. What is clear is that a child with ADHD is physically active, has limited self-control, is easily distracted, and is likely to have difficulty staying on task and working toward goals. An ADHD child like Dusty can be a whirlwind of activity, exhausting the energy and patience of parents, teachers, and even peers (Baker, 1994; Hinshaw et al., 1997; Barkley, 1997a).

The treatment of children with ADHD has been a source of considerable controversy. Because it has been found that doses of Ritalin or Dexadrine (which, paradoxically, are stimulants) reduce activity levels in hyperactive children, many physicians routinely prescribe drug treatment (Greenhill, Halperin, & Abikoff, 1999; Volkow et al., 2001).

Although in many cases such drugs are effective in increasing attention span and compliance, in some cases the side effects are considerable, and the long-term health consequences of this treatment are unclear. Furthermore, although in the short run drugs often help scholastic performance, the long-term evidence for continuing improvement is mixed. In fact, some studies suggest that after a few years, children treated with drugs do not perform academically any better than untreated children with ADHD. Furthermore, the drug is prescribed far more frequently in the United States than in other countries, suggesting it may be overprescribed (see Figure 9-5; McDaniel, 1986; Weber, Frankenberger, & Heilman, 1992; Marshall, 2000).

What are the most common signs of ADHD? Although it is often difficult to distinguish between children who simply have a high level of activity and those with ADHD, some of the most common symptoms include persistent difficulty in finishing tasks, following instructions, and organizing work; inability to watch an entire television program; frequent interruption of others; and a tendency to jump into a task before hearing all the

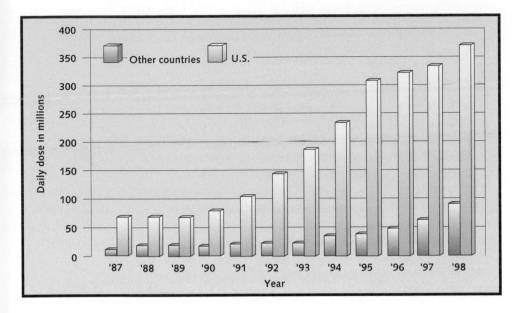

Figure 9-5 **Overprescribing Ritalin?**

Compared with other countries, health care providers in the United States prescribe the drug Ritalin for children diagnosed with attention-deficit hyperactivity disorder more frequently. Some experts argue that the drug may be overprescribed

(*Source*: Marshall, 2000.)

instructions. If a child is suspected of having ADHD, he or she should be evaluated by a specialist. (Parents can receive support from the Center for Hyperactive Child Information, PO Box 66272, Washington, DC 20035).

Review and Rethink

REVIEW

■ During the middle childhood years, the body grows at a slow but steady pace that is influenced by both genetic and social factors.

■ Adequate nutrition is important for physical, social, and cognitive development, but overnutrition may lead to obesity.

■ Children substantially improve their gross and fine motor skills during the school years, with muscular coordination and manipulative skills advancing to near-adult levels.

■ The incidence of asthma and childhood depression has increased significantly over the last several decades.

■ Many school-age children have special needs, particularly in the areas of vision, hearing, and speech. Some also have learning disabilities.

■ Attention deficit hyperactivity disorder, marked by attention, organization, and activity problems, affects between 3 and 5 percent of the school-age population. Treatment through the use of drugs is highly controversial.

RETHINK

■ Under what circumstances would you recommend the use of a growth hormone such as Protropin? Is shortness primarily a physical or a cultural problem?

■ In general, are social attitudes toward people with speech impairments supportive? How would you advise parents to treat a child with a noticeable speech impairment?

Intellectual Development

Jared's parents were delighted when he came home from kindergarten one day and explained that he had learned why the sky was blue. He talked about the earth's atmosphere—although he didn't pronounce the word correctly—and how tiny bits of moisture in the air reflected the sunlight. Although his explanation had rough edges (he couldn't quite grasp what the "atmosphere" was), he still had the general idea, and that, his parents felt, was quite an achievement for their 5-year-old.

***

Fast-forward six years. Jared, now 11, had already spent an hour laboring over his evening's homework. After completing a two-page worksheet on multiplying and dividing fractions, he had begun work on his U.S. Constitution project. He was taking notes for his report, which would explain what political factions had been involved in the writing of the document and how the Constitution had been amended since its creation.

Jared is not alone in having made vast intellectual advances during middle childhood. During this period, children's cognitive abilities broaden, and they become increasingly able to understand and master complex skills. At the same time, though, their thinking is still not fully adultlike.

What are the advances, and the limitations, in thinking during childhood? Several perspectives explain what goes on cognitively during middle childhood.

Piagetian Approaches to Cognitive Development

Let's return for a moment to Jean Piaget's view of the preschooler, which we considered in Chapter 7. From Piaget's perspective, the preschooler thinks *preoperationally*. This type of thinking is largely egocentric, and preoperational children lack the ability to use *operations*—organized, formal, logical mental processes.

concrete operational stage the period of cognitive development between 7 and 12 years of age, which is characterized by the active, and appropriate, use of logic

decentering the ability to take multiple aspects of a situation into account

The Rise of Concrete Operational Thought. All this changes, according to Piaget, during the concrete operational period, which coincides with the school years. The **concrete operational stage,** which occurs between 7 and 12 years of age, is characterized by the active, and appropriate, use of logic. Concrete operational thought involves applying *logical operations* to concrete problems. For instance, when children in the concrete operational stage are confronted with a conservation problem (such as determining whether the amount of liquid poured from one container to another container of a different shape stays the same), they use cognitive and logical processes to answer, no longer being influenced solely by appearance. Consequently, they easily—and correctly—solve conservation problems. Because they are less egocentric, they can take multiple aspects of a situation into account, an ability known as **decentering.** Jared, the sixth-grader described at the beginning of this section, was using his decentering skills to consider the views of the different factions involved in creating the U.S. Constitution.

The shift from preoperational thought to concrete operational thought does not happen overnight, of course. During the 2 years before children move firmly into the concrete operational period, they shift back and forth between preoperational and concrete operational thinking. For instance, they typically pass through a period when they can answer conservation problems correctly but can't articulate why they did so. When asked to explain the reasoning behind their answers, they may respond with an unenlightening, "Because."

However, once concrete operational thinking is fully engaged, children show several cognitive advances. For instance, they attain the concept of *reversibility*, which is the notion that processes that transform a stimulus can be reversed, returning it to its original form. Grasping reversibility permits children to understand that a ball of clay that has been squeezed into a long, snake-like rope can be returned to its original state. More abstractly, it allows school-age children to understand that if 3 + 5 equals 8, then 5 + 3 also equals 8—and, later during the period, that 8 − 3 equals 5.

Cognitive development makes substantial advances in middle childhood.

Concrete operational thinking also permits children to understand such concepts as the relationship between time and speed. For instance, consider the problem shown in Figure 9-6, in which two cars start and finish at the same points in the same amount of time, but travel different routes. Children who are just entering the concrete operational period reason that the cars are traveling at the same speed. However, between the ages of 8 and 10, children begin to draw the right conclusion: that the car traveling the longer route must be moving faster if it arrives at the finish point at the same time as the car traveling the shorter route.

Despite the advances that occur during the concrete operational stage, children still experience one critical limitation in their thinking. They remain tied to concrete, physical reality. Furthermore, they are unable to understand truly abstract or hypothetical questions, or ones that involve formal logic.

Piaget in Perspective: Piaget Was Right, Piaget Was Wrong. As we learned in our prior consideration of Piaget's views in chapters 5 and 7, researchers following in Piaget's footsteps have found much to cheer about—as well as much to criticize.

Piaget was a virtuoso observer of children, and his many books contain pages of brilliant, careful observations of children at work and play. Furthermore, his theories have

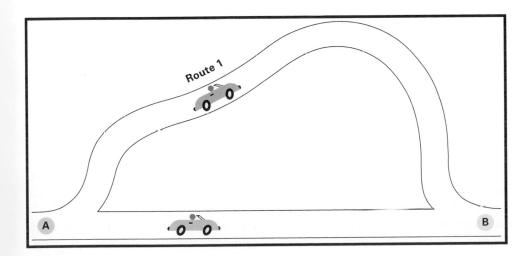

Figure 9-6 **Routes to Conservation**

After being told that the two cars traveling the Routes 1 and 2 start and end their journeys in the same amount of time, children who are just entering the concrete operational period still reason that the cars are traveling at the same speed. Later, however, they reach the correct conclusion: that the car traveling the longer route must be moving at a higher speed if it starts and ends its journey at the same time as the car traveling the shorter route.

Research conducted in such places as remote areas of Australia shows that, contrary to Piaget's assertion, not everyone reaches the concrete operational stage.

powerful educational implications, and many schools employ principles derived from his views to guide the nature and presentation of instructional materials (Flavell, 1985, 1996; Ravitch, 1985; Siegler & Ellis, 1996).

In some ways, then, Piaget's approach was quite successful in describing cognitive development (Lourenco & Machado, 1996). At the same time, though, critics have raised compelling and seemingly legitimate grievances about his approach. As we have noted before, many researchers argue that Piaget underestimated children's capabilities, in part because of the limited nature of the mini-experiments he conducted. When a broader array of experimental tasks is used, children show less consistency within stages than Piaget would predict (Siegler, 1994; Bjorklund, 1997b).

Furthermore, Piaget seems to have misjudged the age at which children's cognitive abilities emerge. As might be expected from our earlier discussions of Piaget's stages, increasing evidence suggests that children's capabilities emerge earlier than Piaget envisioned. Some children show evidence of a form of concrete operational thinking before the age of 7, the time at which Piaget suggested these abilities first appear.

Still, we cannot dismiss the Piagetian approach. Although some early cross-cultural research seemed to imply that children in certain cultures never left the preoperational stage, failing to master conservation and to develop concrete operations, more recent research suggests otherwise. For instance, with proper training in conservation, children in non-Western cultures who do not conserve can readily learn to do so. For instance, in one study, urban Australian children—who develop concrete operations on the same timetable as Piaget suggested—were compared to rural Aborigine children, who typically do not demonstrate an understanding of conservation at the age of 14 (Dasen, Ngini, & Lavallee, 1979). When the rural Aborigine children were given training, they showed conservation skills similar to their urban counterparts, although with a time lag of around 3 years (see Figure 9-7).

Furthermore, when children are interviewed by researchers from their own culture, who know the language and customs of the culture well and who use reasoning tasks that are related to domains important to the culture, the children are considerably more likely to display concrete operational thinking (Nyiti, 1982; Jahoda, 1983). Ultimately, such research suggests that Piaget was right when he argued that concrete operations were universally achieved during middle childhood. Although school-age children in some cultures may differ from Westerners in the demonstration of certain cognitive skills, the most probable ex-

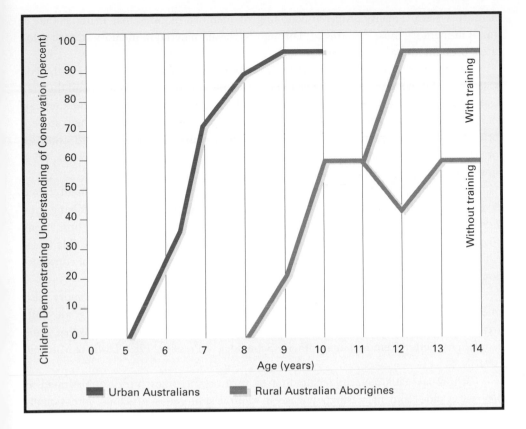

Figure 9-7 **Conservation Training**

Rural Australian Aborigine children trail their urban counterparts in the development of their understanding of conservation; with training, they later catch up. Without training, around half of 14-year-old Aborigines do not have an understanding of conservation. What can be concluded from the fact that training influences the understanding of conservation?

(Adapted from Dasen, Ngini, & Lavallee, 1979.)

planation of the difference is that the non-Western children have had different sorts of experiences from those that permit children in Western societies to perform well on Piagetian measures of conservation and concrete operations. The progress of cognitive development, then, cannot be understood without looking at the nature of a child's culture (Jahoda & Lewis, 1988; Beilin & Pufall, 1992; Berry et al., 1992; Mishra, 1997).

Information Processing in Middle Childhood

It is a significant achievement for first-graders to learn basic math tasks, such as addition and subtraction of single-digit numbers, as well as the spelling of simple words such as "dog" and "run." But by the time they reach the sixth grade, children are able to work with fractions and decimals, like the fractions worksheet that Jared, the boy in the example at the start of this section, completed for his sixth-grade homework. They can also spell such words as "exhibit" and "residence."

According to *information-processing approaches*, children become increasingly sophisticated in their handling of information. Like computers, they can process more data as the size of their memories increases and the "programs" they use to process information become increasingly sophisticated (Kuhn et al., 1995).

Memory. As we saw in Chapter 5, **memory** in the information-processing model is the ability to encode, store, and retrieve information. For a child to remember a piece of information, the three processes must all function properly. Through *encoding*, the child initially records the information in a form usable to memory. Children who were never taught that 5 + 6 = 11, or who didn't pay attention when they were exposed to this fact, will never be able to recall it. They never encoded the information in the first place.

But mere exposure to a fact is not enough; the information also has to be *stored*. In our example, the information that 5 + 6 = 11 must be placed and maintained in the

memory the process by which information is initially recorded, stored, and retrieved

memory system. Finally, proper functioning of memory requires that material that is stored in memory must be *retrieved*. Through retrieval, material in memory storage is located, brought into awareness, and used.

During middle childhood, short-term memory capacity improves significantly. For instance, children are increasingly able to hear a string of digits ("1-5-6-3-4") and then repeat the string in reverse order ("4-3-6-5-1"). At the start of the preschool period, they can remember and reverse only about two digits; by the beginning of adolescence, they can perform the task with as many as six digits. In addition, they use more sophisticated strategies for recalling information, which can be improved with training (Ardila & Rosselli, 1994; Bjorklund et al., 1994; Halford et al., 1994; Roodenrys, Hulme, & Brown, 1993).

Memory capacity may shed light on another issue in cognitive development. Some developmental psychologists suggest that the difficulty children experience in solving conservation problems during the preschool period may stem from memory limitations (Siegler & Richards, 1982). They argue that young children simply may not be able to recall all the necessary pieces of information that enter into the correct solution of conservation problems.

metamemory an understanding about the processes that underlie memory, which emerges and improves during middle childhood

Metamemory, an understanding about the processes that underlie memory, also emerges and improves during middle childhood. By the time they enter first grade, children have a general notion of what memory is, and they are able to understand that some people have better memories than others (Schneider & Pressley, 1989; Lewis & Mitchell, 1994).

School-age children's understanding of memory becomes more sophisticated as they grow older and increasingly engage in *control strategies*—conscious, intentionally used tactics to improve cognitive processing. For instance, school-age children are aware that rehearsal, the repetition of information, is a useful strategy for improving memory, and they increasingly employ it over the course of middle childhood. Similarly, they progressively make more effort to organize material into coherent patterns, a strategy that permits them to recall it better. For instance, when faced with remembering a list including cups, knives, forks, and plates, older school-age children are more likely to group the items into coherent patterns—cups and plates, forks and knives—than children just entering the school-age years (Howe & O'Sullivan, 1990; Pressley & Van Meter, 1993; Weed, Ryan, & Day, 1990).

Improving Memory. Can children be trained to be more effective in the use of control strategies? The answer is decidedly yes. School-age children can be taught to apply particular strategies, although such teaching is not a simple matter. For instance, children need to know not only how to use a memory strategy, but also when and where to use it most effectively. But if such information is conveyed by teachers and parents, it can be a genuine boon to children (O'Sullivan, 1993).

Take, for example, an innovative technique called the keyword strategy, which can help students learn the vocabulary of a foreign language, the capitals of the states, or other information in which two sets of words or labels are paired. In the *keyword strategy*, one word is paired with another that sounds like it. For instance, in learning foreign language vocabulary, a foreign word is paired with a common English word that has a similar sound. The English word is the keyword. Thus, to learn the Spanish word for duck (*pato*, pronounced *pot-o*), the keyword might be "pot"; for the Spanish word for horse (*caballo*, pronounced *cob-eye-yo*), the keyword might be "eye." Once the keyword is chosen, children then form a mental image of the two words interacting with one another. For instance, a student might use an image of a duck taking a bath in a pot to remember the word *pato*, or a horse with bulging eyes to remember the word *caballo* (Pressley & Levin, 1983; Pressley, 1987).

Vygotsky's Approach to Cognitive Development and Classroom Instruction

Recall from Chapter 7 that Russian developmentalist Lev Vygotsky proposed that cognitive advances occur through exposure to information within a child's *zone of proximal development*, or ZPD. The ZPD is the level at which a child can almost, but not quite, understand or perform a task.

Vygotsky's approach has been particularly influential in the development of several classroom practices based on the proposition that children should actively participate in their educational experiences (e.g., Holzman, 1997). Consequently, classrooms are seen as places where children should have the opportunity to experiment and try out new activities (Vygotsky, 1926/1997).

Specifically, Vygotsky suggests that education should focus on activities that involve interaction with others. Both child–adult and child–child interactions can provide the potential for cognitive growth. Yet the nature of the interactions must be carefully structured to fall within each individual child's zone of proximal development.

Several noteworthy educational innovations have borrowed heavily from Vygotsky's work. For example, *cooperative learning*, in which children work together in groups to achieve a common goal, incorporates several aspects of Vygotsky's theory. Students working in cooperative groups benefit from the insights of others, and if they get off onto the wrong track, they may be brought back to the correct course by others in their group. On the other hand, not every peer is equally helpful to members of a cooperative learning group: As Vygotsky's approach would imply, individual children benefit most when at least some of the other members of the group are more competent at the task and can act as experts (Azmitia, 1988; Slavin, 1995; Karpov & Haywood, 1998).

Reciprocal teaching is another educational practice that reflects Vygotsky's approach to cognitive development. *Reciprocal teaching* is a technique to teach reading comprehension strategies. Students are taught to skim the content of a passage, raise questions about its central point, summarize the passage, and finally predict what will happen next. A key to this technique is its reciprocal nature. In the beginning, teachers lead students through the comprehension strategies. Gradually, students progress through their zones of proximal development, taking more and more control over use of the strategies, until

Students working in cooperative groups benefit from the insights of others.

the students are able to take on a teaching role. The method has shown impressive success in raising reading comprehension levels, particularly for students experiencing reading difficulties (Lysynchuk, Pressley, & Vye, 1990; Palincsar & Klenk, 1992; Palincsar, Brown, & Campione, 1993).

Language Development: What Words Mean

If you listen to what school-age children say to one another, their speech, at least at first hearing, sounds not too different from that of adults. However, the apparent similarity is deceiving. The linguistic sophistication of children—particularly at the start of the school-age period—still requires refinement to reach adult levels of expertise.

Mastering the Mechanics of Language. Vocabulary continues to increase during the school years. Although children know thousands of words, they continue to add new words to their vocabularies, and at a fairly rapid clip. For instance, the average 6-year-old has a vocabulary of from 8,000 to 14,000 words, whereas the vocabulary grows by another 5,000 words between the ages of 9 and 11.

Furthermore, school-age children's mastery of grammar improves. For instance, the use of the passive voice is rare during the early school-age years (as in "The dog was walked by Jon," compared with the active-voice "Jon walked the dog"). Six- and 7-year-olds only infrequently use conditional sentences, such as "If Sarah will set the table, I will wash the dishes." However, over the course of middle childhood, the use of both passive voice and conditional sentences increases. In addition, children's understanding of *syntax,* the rules that indicate how words and phrases can be combined to form sentences, grows during middle childhood.

By the time they reach first grade, most children pronounce words quite accurately. However, certain *phonemes,* units of sound, remain troublesome. For instance, the ability to pronounce *j, v, th,* and *zh* sounds develops later than the ability to pronounce other phonemes.

School-age children also may have difficulty decoding sentences when the meaning depends on *intonation,* or tone of voice. For example, consider the sentence, "George gave a book to David and he gave one to Bill." If the word "he" is emphasized, the meaning is "George gave a book to David and David gave a different book to Bill." But if the intonation emphasizes the word "and," then the meaning changes to "George gave a book to David and George also gave a book to Bill." School-age children cannot easily sort out subtleties such as these (Moshman, Glover, & Bruning, 1987; Woolfolk, 1993).

Children also become more competent during the school years in their use of *pragmatics,* the rules governing the use of language to communicate in a social context. Pragmatics concern children's ability to use appropriate and effective language in a given social setting.

For example, although children are aware of the rules of conversational turn-taking at the start of the early childhood period, their use of these rules is sometimes primitive. Consider the following conversation between 6-year-olds Yonnie and Max:

> Yonnie: My dad drives a FedEx truck.
> Max: My sister's name is Molly.
> Yonnie: He gets up really early in the morning.
> Max: She wet her bed last night.

Later, however, conversations show more give-and-take, with the second child actually responding to the comments of the first. For instance, this conversation between 11-year-olds Mia and Josh reflects a more sophisticated mastery of pragmatics:

> Mia: I don't know what to get Claire for her birthday.
> Josh: I'm getting her earrings.

Mia: She already has a lot of jewelry.
Josh: I don't think she has that much.

Metalinguistic Awareness. One of the most significant developments in middle childhood is the increasing metalinguistic awareness of children. **Metalinguistic awareness** is an understanding of one's own use of language. By the time children are 5 or 6, they understand that language is governed by a set of rules. Whereas in the early years they learn and comprehend these rules implicitly, during middle childhood children come to understand them more explicitly (Kemper & Vernooy, 1994).

Metalinguistic awareness helps children achieve comprehension when information is fuzzy or incomplete. For instance, when preschoolers are given ambiguous or unclear information, they rarely ask for clarification, and they tend to blame themselves if they do not understand. By the time they reach the age of 7 or 8, children realize that miscommunication may be due to factors attributable not only to themselves, but to the person communicating with them as well. Consequently, school-age children are more likely to ask for clarifications of information that is unclear to them (Beal & Belgrad, 1990; Kemper & Vernooy, 1993).

How Language Promotes Self-Control. The growing sophistication of their language helps school-age children control their behavior. For instance, in one experiment, children were told that they could have one marshmallow treat if they chose to eat one immediately, but two treats if they waited. Most of the children, who ranged in age from 4 to 8, chose to wait, but the strategies they used while waiting differed significantly.

The 4-year-olds often chose to look at the marshmallows while waiting, a strategy that was not terribly effective. In contrast, 6- and 8-year-olds used language to help them overcome temptation, although in different ways. The 6-year-olds spoke and sang to themselves, reminding themselves that if they waited they would get more treats in the end. The 8-year-olds focused on aspects of the marshmallows that were not related to taste, such as their appearance, which helped them to wait.

Bilingualism: Speaking in Many Tongues

For picture day at New York's P.S. 217, a neighborhood elementary school in Brooklyn, the notice to parents was translated into five languages. That was a nice gesture, but insufficient: More than 40 percent of the children are immigrants whose families speak any one of twenty-six languages, ranging from Armenian to Urdu. (Leslie, 1991, p. 56)

From the smallest towns to the biggest cities, the voices with which children speak are changing. In seven states, including Texas, New York, and Colorado, more than a quarter of the students are not native English speakers. In fact, English is the second language for more than 32 million Americans. **Bilingualism**—the use of more than one language—is growing increasingly common (U.S. Bureau of the Census, 1993; see Figure 9-8).

Children with little, or even no, English proficiency present a challenge to educators. One approach to educating non-English speakers is *bilingual education*, in which children are initially taught in their native language, while at the same time learning English. With bilingual instruction, students are able to develop a strong foundation in basic subject areas using their native language. The ultimate goal of most bilingual education programs is to shift instruction into English.

An alternative approach is to immerse students in English, teaching solely in that language. To proponents of this approach, initially teaching students in a language other than English hinders students' efforts to learn English and slows their integration into society.

metalinguistic awareness an understanding of one's own use of language

bilingualism the use of more than one language

In immersion programs, students receive instruction only in English. Immersion programs contrast with bilingual education, in which children are initially taught in their own language, while also learning English.

The two quite different approaches have been highly politicized, with some politicians arguing in favor of "English-only" laws. Still, the psychological research is clear in suggesting that knowing more than one language offers several cognitive advantages. For instance, speakers of two languages show greater cognitive flexibility. Because they have a wider range of linguistic possibilities to choose from as they assess a situation, they can solve problems with greater creativity and versatility. Furthermore, some research suggests that learning in one's native tongue is associated with higher self-esteem in minority students (Romaine, 1994; Wright & Taylor, 1995).

Bilingual students often have greater metalinguistic awareness, understanding the rules of language more explicitly. They even may score higher on tests of intelligence, according to some research. For example, one survey of French- and English-speaking schoolchildren in Canada found that bilingual students scored significantly higher on both verbal and nonverbal tests of intelligence than those who spoke only one language (Lambert & Peal, 1972; Ricciardelli, 1992; Genesee, 1994; Bochner, 1996).

Figure 9-8 **The Voices of America**

The number of U.S. residents over the age of 5 who speak at home a language other than English.

(*Source:* U.S. Census Bureau, 1993.)

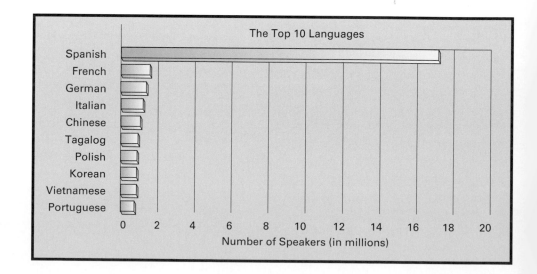

Finally, because many linguists contend that universal processes underlie language acquisition, as we noted in Chapter 5, instruction in a native language may enhance instruction in a second language. In fact, as we discuss next, many educators believe that second-language learning should be a regular part of elementary schooling for *all* children (Lindholm, 1991; Perozzi & Sanchez, 1992; Yelland, Pollard, & Mercuri, 1993; Kecskes & Papp, 2000).

Developmental Diversity

The Benefits of Bilingualism: Children Do Swimmingly in Language-Immersion Programs

One by one, the first graders recite the characters the teacher has drawn on the board. Only it's not the ABCs that these six- and seven-year-olds are rattling off but the hiragana characters of the Japanese language.

The students in this inner-city public-school classroom have no Japanese heritage. In fact, almost all of them are African-American. But all day long, they hear only Japanese from their teachers. They recite their math problems in Japanese. Their language readers open from left to right as in Japan. When the teacher asks in Japanese, "Do you understand?" the children chirp, "Hai." (Reitman, 1994, B1)

These students, enrolled in Detroit's Foreign Language Immersion and Cultural Studies School, are participating in a program designed to capitalize on younger children's ability to learn second languages with relative ease. The school represents a sharp departure from traditional language instruction. In what is called a *language immersion program,* the school teaches all of its subjects in a foreign language.

Children in language immersion programs make rapid advances with the foreign language in which they are being taught, for several reasons. One is that, unlike older children, they have not learned to be frightened by the task of learning a language. Furthermore, they feel relatively little embarrassment if they mispronounce words or make grammatical errors.

For those enrolled in language immersion programs, learning a second language provides several benefits beyond command of the language. It can raise self-esteem due to the sense of mastery that comes from achieving proficiency in a difficult subject. It can make students more sensitive to other cultures. Furthermore, although parents sometimes worry that their children's progress in English will be limited by their concentration on a foreign language, such concerns seem misplaced. Research suggests that children in immersion programs perform as well as their peers, and sometimes even better, in English grammar, reading comprehension, and tests of English vocabulary (Larsen-Freeman & Long, 1991).

On the other hand, not all language immersion programs are successful. The most positive results have come from programs in which majority group children are learning languages that are not spoken by the dominant culture. In contrast, when minority group children who enter school knowing only a language other than English are immersed in English-only programs, the results are less positive. In fact, children from minority language backgrounds enrolled in English-only programs sometimes perform worse in both English *and* their native languages than same-age peers (Genesee, 1994).

Clearly, the effectiveness of language immersion programs varies widely. Furthermore, such programs are difficult to operate administratively. Finding an adequate number of bilingual teachers can be difficult, and teacher and student attrition can be a problem. Still, the results of participation in immersion programs can be impressive, particularly as knowledge of multiple languages becomes less of a luxury and more of a necessity in today's multicultural world. (See also the *Speaking of Development* interview). ☐

The Ebonics Controversy: Is Black English a Separate Language from Standard English?

Although the word *Ebonics* had been in use since the 1970s, few people had heard of it before the Oakland, California, school board declared it a distinctive language. Their decision affirmed that Ebonics—a word derived from a combination of the words *ebony* and *phonics*—was a language separate from English. According to the school board's declaration, Ebonics was a distinct language with roots in Africa, one spoken by many African Americans in inner cities. The school board ordered that students who spoke Ebonics

SPEAKING OF DEVELOPMENT

Lauro Cavazos, Former U.S. Secretary of Education

EDUCATION: B.A., M.A., Texas Tech University; Ph.D., Iowa State University; numerous honorary degrees

POSITION: United States Secretary of Education, 1988–1990

HOME: Concord, MA

As the 21st century dawns, many facets of society in America will change, and much of that change will be the result of education, according to Lauro F. Cavazos, who served as Secretary of Education (1988–90) in the administration of President George H. Bush.

In his cabinet position Cavazos worked toward three main goals: raising the expectations of students, teachers and parents; providing access to quality education for all students, especially those most at risk of failing; and promoting the notion that quality education is the responsibility of every member of society. This was a tremendous task, considering the growing diversity of the student population.

"First of all, we're finally starting to recognize that there is cultural diversity and acknowledge it in a serious fashion," says the sixth-generation Texan. "Already some 30 percent of the students in elementary and secondary public education are Hispanic or African American, and these numbers are going to continue to grow."

Noting the increase in bilingual students, Cavazos points out that the trend will have an impact on the areas of literature,

history, geography, and economics, among others—all contributing to the changing of American society.

"We need to recognize that diversity is a bonus in America," he notes. "I'm a strong supporter of bilingual education, but certain conditions need to be met in order for it to work. First, I think non-English-speaking students need to learn English as quickly as possible, hopefully within a year, but at most three years. Second, they should retain their original language, whatever that language is—Cambodian, Spanish, or whatever. And third, each group should be expected to add to the culture of America, because America is an amalgamation of many different cultures. We need to recognize that America is already a pluralistic society."

Maintaining that one of America's biggest problems is an education deficit, Cavazos stresses the importance of the educational development of children.

"Some 27 million Americans are illiterate, and 40 to 50 million Americans read at the fourth-grade level," he says. "We have 600,000 to 700,000 youngsters who drop out of school each year, and we haven't had a significant increase in SAT scores in years. I call that the education deficit.

"Our first major goal is to help those students who are in need—the minorities, handicapped, students in special education, and so forth. Our second central goal is to support good research. I've had tremendous resistance to some of the things I've said, and some people really take offense," Cavazos states. "But if we don't change things, in one or two generations this nation is going to be in serious trouble."

should receive their initial classroom instruction using Ebonics, and not standard English (Applebome, 1997).

The school board's decision provoked a national controversy, and within a month the board had reversed its decision. Members of the board said that they had never meant for students to learn anything other than standard English, and that they had merely wanted recognition for the fact that many African American students needed instruction to make the leap from the Ebonics they spoke at home to standard English.

The controversy raised several issues, none of which have had definitive resolutions. For instance, linguists vary in their views of the legitimacy of Ebonics as a language. According to linguist Dennis Baron, most linguists consider what they call African American Vernacular English, or sometimes Black English, to be a dialect or variety of standard English. Although it has some characteristics that are derived from African languages, it can be understood fairly well by speakers of standard English. Furthermore, certain features of Ebonics, such as the use of different conjugations of the verb "to be" (as in "I be going") are evidence that it is not a separate language, but a dialect of English (Baron, 1997; Sanchez, 1997).

On the other hand, it is also clear that Black English operates according to a set of consistent rules and conventions. Although in the past African American Vernacular English has been treated as a form of speech disability, one that required the intervention of speech pathologists or special education teachers, today educators have become more accepting. Probably most educators would argue that any such nonstandard English is not an *inferior* form of language, but one that is *different*—an important distinction. Furthermore, they point out that many words that have their origins in Black English have entered the mainstream of standard English, including "hip," "cool," "chill out," "slick," and "rip-off" (Sanchez, 1997).

Still, the issues revolving around the use of Ebonics or Black English or African American Vernacular English—or whatever else it may be called—in schools are not likely to go away soon. The controversy raises important issues that are social as well as linguistic (Seymour, Abdulkarim, & Johnson, 1999). As we'll see in the remainder of the chapter, language is only one of the social issues related to schooling in the U.S.

Review and Rethink

REVIEW

- According to Piaget, school-age children are in the concrete operational stage, characterized by the application of logical processes to concrete problems.
- Information-processing approaches focus on quantitative improvements in memory and in the sophistication of the mental programs that the school-age child can handle.
- Vygotsky's approach holds that children in the school years should have the opportunity to experiment and participate actively with their colleagues in their educational experiences.
- The memory processes—encoding, storage, and retrieval—come under increasing control during the school years, and the development of metamemory improves cognitive processing and memorization.

- Language development is characterized by improvements in vocabulary, syntax, and pragmatics; by the growth of metalinguistic awareness; and by the use of language as a self-control device.
- Bilingualism can produce improvements in cognitive flexibility, metalinguistic awareness, and even IQ test performance.

RETHINK

- Do you think a non-Western Piaget working in a different culture might have developed a theory of stages involving cognitive tasks that Western children would have difficulty performing without explicit instruction? Why?
- Do adults use language as a self-control device? How?

Schooling: The Three Rs (and More) of Middle Childhood

As the eyes of the six other children in his reading group turned to him, Glenn shifted uneasily in his chair. Reading had never come easily to him, and he always felt anxious when it was his turn to read aloud. But as his teacher nodded in encouragement, he plunged in, hesitantly at first, then gaining momentum as he read the story about a mother's first day on a new job. He found that he could read the passage quite nicely, and he felt a surge of happiness and pride at his accomplishment. When he was done, he broke into a broad smile as his teacher said simply, "Well done, Glenn."

Small moments such as these, repeated over and over, make—or break—a child's educational experience. Schooling marks a time when society formally attempts to transfer to new generations its accumulated body of knowledge, beliefs, values, and wisdom. The success with which this transfer is managed determines, in a very real sense, the future fortunes of the world.

Schooling Around the World: Who Gets Educated?

In the United States, as in most developed countries, a primary school education is both a universal right and a legal requirement. Virtually all children are provided with a free education through the twelfth grade.

Children in other parts of the world are not so fortunate. More than 160 million of the world's children do not have access to even a primary school education (World Conference on Education for All, 1990; International Literacy Institute, 2001). An additional 100 million children do not progress beyond a level comparable to our elementary-school education, and overall close to a billion individuals (two-thirds of them women) are illiterate throughout their lives (see Figure 9-9).

In almost all developing countries, fewer females than males receive formal education, a discrepancy found at every level of schooling. Even in developed countries, women lag be-

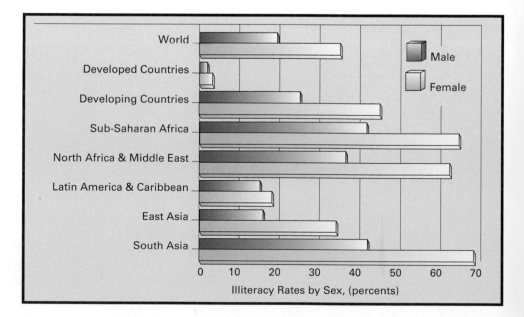

Figure 9-9 **The Plague of Illiteracy**

Illiteracy remains a significant problem worldwide, particularly for women. Across the world, close to a billion people were illiterate throughout their lives.

(*Source:* UNESCO, 1990.)

hind men in their exposure to science and technological topics. These differences reflect widespread and deeply held cultural and parental biases that favor males over females. Educational levels in the U.S. are more nearly equal between men and women, and especially in the early years of school, boys and girls share equal access to educational opportunities.

What Makes Children Ready for School?

Many parents have a hard time deciding exactly when to enroll their children in school for the first time. Do children who are younger than most of the other children in their grade suffer as a result of the age difference? According to traditional wisdom, the answer is yes. Because younger children are assumed to be slightly less advanced developmentally than their peers, it has been assumed that such children would be at a competitive disadvantage. In some cases, teachers have recommended that students delay entry into kindergarten in order to cope better academically and emotionally.

However, recent research has begun to dispel this view. According to a massive study conducted by developmental psychologist Frederick Morrison, children who are among the youngest in first grade progress at the same rate as the oldest. Although they were slightly behind older first-graders in reading, the difference was negligible. It was also clear that parents who chose to hold their children back in kindergarten, thereby ensuring that they would be among the oldest in first grade and after, were not doing their children a favor. These older children did no better than their younger classmates (Morrison, 1993; DeAngelis, 1994).

Other research even has identified some delayed negative reaction to delayed entry. For example, one longitudinal study examined adolescents whose entrance into kindergarten was delayed by a year. Even though many seemed to show no ill effects from the delay during elementary school, during adolescence a surprising number of these children had emotional and behavioral problems (Byrd, Weitzman, & Auinger, 1997).

In short, delaying children's entry into school does not necessarily provide an advantage, and in some cases may actually be harmful. Ultimately age, per se, is not a critical indicator of when children should begin school. Instead, the start of formal schooling is more reasonably tied to overall developmental readiness, the product of a complex combination of several factors. Family support is one of the factors that affects children's likelihood of success in school, as described next in *The Informed Consumer of Development* section.

Reading: Learning to Decode the Meaning Behind Words

The efforts of La-Toya Pankey (described in the chapter prologue) to improve her reading are no small matter, for there is no other task that is more fundamental to schooling than learning to read. Reading involves a significant number of skills, from low-level cognitive skills (the identification of single letters and associating letters with sounds) to higher-level skills (matching written words with meanings located in long-term memory and using context and background knowledge to determine the meaning of a sentence).

Development of reading skill generally occurs in several broad, frequently overlapping, stages (see Table 9-1; Chall, 1979). In *Stage 0*, which lasts from birth to the start of first grade, children learn the essential prerequisites for reading, including identification of the letters in the alphabet, sometimes writing their names and reading a few very familiar words (such as their own names or "stop" on a stop sign).

Stage 1 brings the first real type of reading, but it largely involves *phonological recoding* skill. At this stage, which usually encompasses the first and second grade, children can sound out words by blending the letters together. Children also complete the job of learning the names of letters and the sounds that go with them.

The Informed Consumer of Development

Creating an Atmosphere That Promotes School Success

What makes children succeed in school? Although there are many factors, some of which we'll be discussing in the next chapter, there are several practical steps that can be taken to maximize children's chances of success. Among them:

▶ Promote a "literacy environment." Parents should read to their children and familiarize them with books and reading. Adults should provide reading models: Children should see that reading is an important activity in the lives of the adults with whom they interact.

▶ Talk to children. Discuss events in the news, talk about their friends, and share hobbies. Getting children to think about and discuss the world around them is one of the best preparations for school.

▶ Provide a place for children to work. This can be a desk, a corner of a table, or an area of a room. What's important is that it be a separate, designated area.

▶ Encourage children's problem-solving skills. To solve a problem, they should learn to identify their goal, what they know, and what they don't know; to design and carry out a strategy; and finally to evaluate their result.

In *Stage 2*, typically around second and third grades, children learn to read aloud with fluency. However, they do not attach much meaning to the words, because the effort involved in simply sounding out words is usually so great that relatively few cognitive resources are left over to process the meaning of the words. LaToya's flawless reading of *The Witches* shows that she has reached at least this stage of reading development.

The next period, *Stage 3*, extends from fourth to eighth grades. Reading becomes a means to an end—in particular, a way to learn. Whereas earlier reading was an accomplishment in and of itself, by this point children use reading to learn about the world. However, understanding gained from reading is not complete. For instance, one limitation children have at this stage is that they are able to comprehend information only when it is presented from a single perspective.

In the final period, *Stage 4*, children are able to read and process information that reflects multiple points of view. This ability, which begins during the transition into high school, permits children to develop a far more sophisticated understanding of material.

Beginning around the fourth grade, children begin to use reading as a primary source of learning.

Table 9-1

DEVELOPMENT OF READING SKILLS

Stage	Age	Key Characteristics
Stage 0	Birth to start of first grade	learns prerequisites for reading, such as identification of the letters
Stage 1	First and second grades	learns phonological recoding skills; starts reading
Stage 2	Second and third grades	reads aloud fluently, but without much meaning
Stage 3	Fourth to eighth grades	uses reading as a means for learning
Stage 4	Eighth grade and beyond	understands reading in terms of reflecting multiple points of view

(*Source:* Based on Chall, 1979.)

This explains why great works of literature are not read at an earlier stage of education. It is not so much that younger children do not have the vocabulary to understand such works (although this is partially true); it is that they lack the ability to understand the multiple points of view that sophisticated literature invariably presents.

Educators have long been engaged in an ongoing debate regarding the most effective means of teaching reading. At the heart of this debate is a disagreement about the nature of the mechanisms by which information is processed during reading. According to proponents of *code-based approaches to reading*, reading should be taught by presenting the basic skills that underlie reading. Code-based approaches emphasize the components of reading, such as the sounds of letters and their combinations—phonics—and how letters and sounds are combined to make words. They suggest that reading consists of processing the individual components of words, combining them into words, and then using the words to derive the meaning of written sentences and passages (Rayner & Pollatsek, 1989; Vellutino, 1991).

In contrast, some educators argue that reading is taught most successfully by using a whole-language approach. In *whole-language approaches to reading,* reading is viewed as a natural process, similar to the acquisition of oral language. According to this view, children should learn to read through exposure to complete writing—sentences, stories, poems, lists, charts, and other examples of actual uses of writing. Instead of being taught to painstakingly sound out words, children are encouraged to make guesses about the meaning of words based on the total context in which they appear. Through such a trial-and-error approach, children come to learn whole words and phrases at a time, gradually becoming proficient readers. To encourage this process, children are immersed in literature and encouraged to take informed guesses as they work through it. As their skill increases, they are better able to quickly look at a word and automatically retrieve its meaning from long-term memory (Smith, 1992; Graham & Harris, 1997).

Research has not been able to ascertain whether the whole-language or code-based approach to reading instruction is better. Both seem to be effective not only in developing proficient readers, but in producing the same level of positive attitudes toward reading. In fact, the National Research Council, in a landmark 1998 report, argued that the optimum approach was to use a combination of elements of code-based and whole-language approaches. Still, the debate continues to rage (Pressley, 1994; McKenna, Kear, & Ellsworth, 1995; Steinberg, 1998).

Educational Trends: Beyond the Three Rs

Schooling in the early 2000s is very different from what it was as recently as a decade ago. In fact, U.S. schools are experiencing a definite return to the educational fundamentals embodied in the traditional three Rs (reading, writing, and arithmetic). As can be seen in the model curriculum promoted by the New Jersey Department of Education (Table 9-2), the emphasis on educational basics is strong. This trend marks a departure from the 1970s and 1980s, when the emphasis was on socioemotional issues and on allowing students to choose study topics on the basis of their interests instead of in accordance with a set curriculum (Short & Talley, 1997).

Elementary school classrooms today also stress individual accountability, both for teachers and students. Teachers are more likely to be held responsible for their students' learning, and both students and teachers are more likely to be required to take tests, developed at the state or national level, to assess their competence. Many schools push students to succeed more vigorously than in previous eras, using such strategies as assigning large quantities of homework—sometimes with mixed results, as we discuss in the *From Research to Practice* box.

Table 9-2

NEW JERSEY CORE CURRICULUM STANDARDS

This set of core curriculum standards was set by the state of New Jersey. They describe what all students should know and be able to do upon completion of a 13-year public education. (New Jersey Department of Education, 1999).

Cross-Content Workplace Readiness

Standard 1: All students will develop career planning and workplace readiness skills.
Standard 2: All students will use technology, information, and other tools.
Standard 3: All students will use critical thinking, decision-making, and problem-solving skills.
Standard 4: All students will demonstrate self-management skills.
Standard 5: All students will apply safety principles.

Visual and Performing Acts

Standard 1.1: All students will acquire knowledge and skills that increase aesthetic awareness in dance, music, theater, and visual arts.
Standard 1.2: All students will refine perceptual, intellectual, physical, and technical skills through creating dance, music, theater, and/or visual arts.
Standard 1.3: All students will utilize arts elements and arts media to produce artistic products and performances.
Standard 1.4: All students will demonstrate knowledge of the process of critique.
Standard 1.5: All students will identify the various historical, social, and cultural influences and traditions, which have generated artistic accomplishments throughout the ages and which continue to shape contemporary arts.
Standard 1.6: All students will develop design skills for planning the form and function of space, structures, objects, and events.

Comprehensive Health and Physical Education

Standard 2.1: All students will learn health promotion and disease prevention concepts and health-enhancing behaviors.
Standard 2.2: All students will learn health-enhancing personal, interpersonal, and life skills.
Standard 2.3: All students will learn the physical, mental, emotional, and social effects of the use and abuse of alcohol, tobacco, and other drugs.
Standard 2.4: All students will learn the biological, social, cultural, and psychological aspects of human sexuality and family life.
Standard 2.5: All students will learn and apply movement concepts and skills that foster participation in physical activities throughout life.
Standard 2.6: All students will learn and apply health-related fitness concepts.

Language and Arts Literacy

Standard 3.1: All students will speak for a variety of real purposes and audiences.
Standard 3.2: All students will listen actively in a variety of situations to information from a variety of sources.
Standard 3.3: All students will write in clear, concise, organized language that varies in content and form for different audiences and purposes.
Standard 3.4: All students will read various materials and texts with comprehension and critical analysis.
Standard 3.5: All students will view, understand, and use nontextual visual information.

Mathematics

Standard 4.1: All students will develop the ability to pose and solve mathematical problems in mathematics, other disciplines, and everyday experiences.
Standard 4.2: All students will communicate mathematically through written, oral, symbolic, and visual forms of expression.
Standard 4.3: All students will connect mathematics to other learning by understanding the interrelationships of mathematical ideas and the roles that mathematics and mathematical modeling play in other disciplines and in life.
Standard 4.4: All students will develop reasoning ability and will become self-reliant, independent mathematical thinkers.
Standard 4.5: All students will regularly and routinely use calculators, computers, manipulatives, and other mathematical tools to enhance mathematical thinking, understanding, and power.
Standard 4.6: All students will develop number sense and an ability to represent numbers in a variety of forms and use numbers in diverse situations.
Standard 4.7: All students will develop spatial sense and an ability to use geometric properties and relationships to solve problems in mathematics and in everyday life.
Standard 4.8: All students will understand, select, and apply various methods of performing numerical operations.
Standard 4.9: All students will develop an understanding of and will use measurement to describe and analyze phenomena.
Standard 4.10: All students will use a variety of estimation strategies and recognize situations in which estimation is appropriate.

Standard 4.11: All students will develop an understanding of patterns, relationships, and functions and will use them to represent and explain real-world phenomena.

Standard 4.12: All students will develop an understanding of statistics and probability and will use them to describe sets of data, model situations, and support appropriate inferences and arguments.

Standard 4.13: All students will develop an understanding of algebraic concepts and processes and will use them to represent and analyze relationships among variable quantities and to solve problems.

Standard 4.14: All students will apply the concepts and methods of discrete mathematics to model and explore a variety of practical situations.

Standard 4.15: All students will develop an understanding of the conceptual building blocks of calculus and will use them to model and analyze natural phenomena.

Standard 4.16: All students will demonstrate high levels of mathematical thought through experiences which extend beyond traditional computation, algebra, and geometry.

Science

Standard 5.1: All students will learn to identify systems of interacting components and understand how their interactions combine to produce the overall behavior of the system.

Standard 5.2: All students will develop problem-solving, decision-making and inquiry skills, reflected by formulating usable questions and hypotheses, planning experiments, conducting systematic observations, interpreting and analyzing data, drawing conclusions, and communicating results.

Standard 5.3: All students will develop an understanding of how people of various cultures have contributed to the advancement of science and technology, and how major discoveries and events have advanced science and technology.

Standard 5.4: All students will develop an understanding of technology as an application of scientific principles.

Standard 5.5: All students will integrate mathematics as a tool for problem-solving in science, and as a means of expressing and/or modeling scientific theories.

Standard 5.6: All students will gain an understanding of the structure, characteristics, and basic needs of organisms.

Standard 5.7: All students will investigate the diversity of life.

Standard 5.8: All students will gain an understanding of the structure and behavior of matter.

Standard 5.9: All students will gain an understanding of natural laws as they apply to motion, forces, and energy transformations.

Standard 5.10: All students will gain an understanding of the structure, dynamics, and geophysical systems of the earth.

Standard 5.11: All students will gain an understanding of the origin, evolution, and structure of the universe.

Standard 5.12: All students will develop an understanding of the environment as a system of interdependent components affected by human activity and natural phenomena.

Social Studies

Standard 6.1: All students will learn democratic citizenship and how to participate in the constitutional system of government of the United States.

Standard 6.2: All students will learn democratic citizenship through the humanities by studying literature, art, history and philosophy, and related fields.

Standard 6.3: All students will acquire historical understanding of political and diplomatic ideas, forces, and institutions throughout the history of New Jersey, the United States, and the world.

Standard 6.4: All students will acquire historical understanding of societal ideas and forces throughout the history of New Jersey, the United States, and the world.

Standard 6.5: All students will acquire historical understanding of varying cultures throughout the history of New Jersey, the United States, and the world.

Standard 6.6: All students will acquire historical understanding of economic forces, ideas, and institutions throughout the history of New Jersey, the United States, and the world.

Standard 6.7: All students will acquire geographical understanding by studying the world in spatial terms.

Standard 6.8: All students will acquire geographical understanding by studying human systems in geography.

Standard 6.9: All students will acquire geographical understanding by studying the environment and society.

Word Languages

Standard 7.1: All students will be able to communicate at a basic literacy level in at least one language other than English.

Standard 7.2: All students will be able to demonstrate an understanding of the interrelationship between language and culture for at least one world language in addition to English.

(*Source*: New Jersey Department of Education, 1999.)

From Research to Practice

Homework in Middle Childhood: Forget It?

Adam's homework began in the first grade . . . . It was just a little in the beginning—maybe 15 minutes a night, plus reading. Now, in fourth grade, it has soared to three hours a night, and Adam, identified as a gifted student, "is completely frustrated," says his mother. "Last night he was up until 10:15 finishing a project, and he is crying more and more often. He asks me, 'I work hard six hours a day in school—how much do I have to do?' He is even having trouble focusing in school, and I suspect it's because he is exhausted." (Begley, 1998a, p. 48)

If the homework Adam struggles over each night boosted his academic performance, perhaps his frustration might be worthwhile. However, the reality, according to a growing body of evidence, is that homework yields few benefits during middle childhood.

This surprising conclusion comes from studies examining the consequences of homework on student achievement. Although gains from homework begin to be seen in students in junior high and middle school, until then most studies show no benefits from homework for children in elementary school. Furthermore, homework's intended nonacademic benefits—that it fosters discipline and self-responsibility—also do not hold up when tested by research (Corno, 1996).

In fact, some research finds that homework actually *hurts* the academic performance of elementary school children, with children who spend more time on homework performing the worst. The reason? Students for whom homework takes the greatest amount of time are frequently taking so long because they are struggling with the material. If school is already difficult for them, piling on more of the same unpleasant experience at home is demoralizing and can reinforce negative attitudes about schooling (Cooper, 1989; Begley, 1998b).

Research into homework during middle childhood also dispels other myths about its importance. Homework often does not support what children are taught in class. Instead, it only reinforces learning if the student has an appropriate home environment and the ability and work habits to make it effective. Furthermore, homework that is too difficult or frustrating makes children less able learners and lowers their motivation to succeed. Homework that is given as punishment—as it sometimes is—can lead to resentment and anger (Corno, 1996).

Of course, not all homework is bad. After children enter adolescence, homework has demonstrable advantages, producing clear benefits on standardized tests. But until then, the value of homework is questionable.

The research on homework has clear implications for educational policymakers. Although small amounts of carefully targeted homework in elementary school may be beneficial, substantial amounts should be avoided. Furthermore, homework should be different from what occurs in class. It should help students hone their study skills, and it should help them develop a love of education and make learning a lifelong enterprise (Cooper, 1989; Begley, 1998b).

Furthermore, increased attention is being paid to issues involving student diversity and multiculturalism. And with good reason: The demographic makeup of students in the United States is undergoing an extraordinary shift. For instance, the proportion of Hispanics will in all likelihood more than double in the next 50 years. Moreover, by the year 2050, non-Hispanic Caucasians will likely become a minority of the total population of the United States (U.S. Bureau of the Census, 2001; see Figure 9-10). Consequently, educators have been increasingly serious about multicultural concerns.

Developmental Diversity

Multicultural Education

Since the earliest period of formal education in the United States, classrooms have been populated by individuals from a broad range of backgrounds and experiences. Yet it is only relatively recently that variations in student backgrounds have been viewed as one of the major challenges—and opportunities—that educators face.

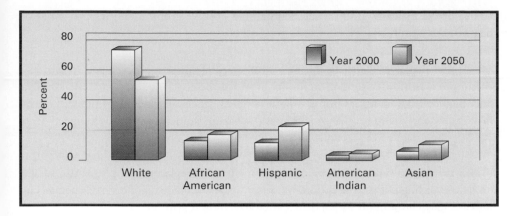

Figure 9-10 **Changes in the Face of America**

Current projections of the population makeup of the United States show that by the year 2050, the proportion of non-Hispanic whites will decline as the proportion of minority group members increases.

(*Source:* U.S. Census Bureau, 1993.)

In fact, the diversity of background and experience in the classroom relates to a fundamental objective of education, which is to provide a formal mechanism to transmit the information a society holds important. As the famous anthropologist Margaret Mead once said, "In its broadest sense, education is the cultural process, the way in which each newborn human infant, born with a potentiality for learning greater than that of any other mammal, is transformed into a full member of a specific human society, sharing with the other members of a specific human culture" (Mead, 1942, p. 633).

Culture, then, can be thought of as a set of behaviors, beliefs, values, and expectations shared by members of a particular society. But although culture is often thought of in a relatively broad context (as in "Western culture" or "Asian culture"), it is also possible to focus on particular *subcultural* groups within a larger, more encompassing culture. For example, we can consider particular racial, ethnic, religious, socioeconomic, or even gender groups within the United States as manifesting characteristics of a subculture.

Membership in a cultural or subcultural group might be of only passing interest to educators were it not for the fact that students' cultural backgrounds have a substantial impact on the way that they—and their peers—are educated. In fact, in recent years a considerable amount of thought has gone into establishing **multicultural education,** a form of education in which the goal is to help minority students develop competence in the

multicultural education a form of education in which the goal is to help minority students develop competence in the culture of the majority group while maintaining positive group identities that build on their original cultures

Pupils and teachers exposed to a diverse group could better understand the world and gain a greater sensitivity to the values and needs of others. What are some ways of developing greater sensitivity in the classroom?

culture of the majority group while maintaining positive group identities that build on their original cultures. ☐

Cultural Assimilation or Pluralistic Society? Multicultural education developed in part as a reaction to a **cultural assimilation model** in which the goal of education is to assimilate individual cultural identities into a unique, unified American culture. In practical terms this meant, for example, that non-English speaking students were discouraged from speaking their native tongues and were totally immersed in English.

In the early 1970s, however, educators and members of minority groups began to suggest that the cultural assimilation model ought to be replaced by a **pluralistic society model.** According to this conception, American society is made up of diverse, coequal cultural groups that should preserve their individual cultural features.

The pluralistic society model grew in part from the belief that teachers, by discouraging children's use of their native tongues, denigrated their cultural heritages and lowered their self-esteem. Furthermore, because instructional materials inevitably feature culture-specific events and understandings, children who were denied access to their own cultural materials might never be exposed to important aspects of their backgrounds. For example, English-language texts rarely present some of the great themes that appear throughout Spanish literature and history (such as the search for the Fountain of Youth and the Don Juan legend). Hispanic students immersed in such texts might never come to understand important components of their own heritage.

Ultimately, educators began to argue that the presence of students representing diverse cultures enriched and broadened the educational experience of all students. Pupils and teachers exposed to people from different backgrounds could better understand the world and gain greater sensitivity to the values and needs of others.

Fostering a Bicultural Identity. Today, most educators agree that the pluralistic society model is the most valid one for schooling and that minority children should be encouraged to develop a **bicultural identity.** They recommend that children be supported in maintaining their original cultural identities while they integrate themselves into the dominant culture. This view suggests that an individual can live as a member of two cultures, with two cultural identities, without having to choose one over the other (Garcia, 1988; LaFromboise, Coleman, & Gerton, 1993).

However, the means of achieving the goal of biculturalism are far from clear. Consider, for example, children who enter a school speaking only Spanish. The traditional "melting-pot" technique would be to immerse the children in classes taught in English while providing a crash course in English language instruction (and little else) until the children demonstrate a suitable level of proficiency. Unfortunately, the traditional approach has a considerable drawback: Until the children master English, they fall further and further behind their peers who entered school already knowing English (First & Cardenas, 1986).

More contemporary approaches emphasize a bicultural strategy in which children are encouraged to maintain simultaneous membership in more than one culture. In the case of Spanish-speaking children, for example, instruction begins in the child's native language and shifts as rapidly as possible to include English. This element of the bicultural strategy is essentially the bilingual education approach discussed earlier in this chapter; but there is more to bicultural education.

Even after the children have mastered English, some instruction in the native language continues. At the same time, the school conducts a program of multicultural education for all students, in which teachers present material on the cultural backgrounds and traditions of all the students in the school. Such instruction is designed to enhance the

cultural assimilation model the model that fostered the view of American society as the proverbial melting pot

pluralistic society model the concept that American society is made up of diverse, coequal cultural groups that should preserve their individual cultural features

bicultural identity Maintaining one's original cultural identity while integrating oneself into the dominant culture

self-image of speakers from both majority and minority cultures (Boriel, 1993; Wright & Taylor, 1995).

Successful bicultural programs also attempt to bring aspects of multiple cultures into the context of everyday social interactions. In schools where many of the students have a language other than English, for example, children are encouraged to use a variety of languages in their social relationships and to become equally adept at several languages.

Although most educational experts favor bicultural approaches, the general public does not always agree. For instance, the national "English-only" movement mentioned earlier in the chapter has as one of its goals the prohibition of school instruction in any language other than English. Whether such a perspective will prevail remains to be seen.

Intelligence: Determining Individual Strengths

"Why should you tell the truth?" "How far is Los Angeles from New York?" "A table is made of wood; a window of _____."

As 10-year-old Hyacinth sat hunched over her desk, trying to answer a long series of questions like these, she tried to guess the point of the test she was taking in her fifth-grade classroom. Clearly, the test didn't cover material that her teacher, Ms. White-Johnston, had talked about in class.

"What number comes next in this series: 1, 3, 7, 15, 31, ___?"

As she continued to work her way through the questions, she gave up trying to guess the rationale for the test. She'd leave that to her teacher, she sighed to herself. Rather than attempting to figure out what it all meant, she simply tried to do her best on the individual test items.

Hyacinth was taking an intelligence test. She might be surprised to learn that she was not alone in questioning the meaning and import of the items on the test. Intelligence test items are painstakingly prepared, and intelligence tests show a strong relationship to success in school (for reasons we'll soon discuss). Many developmentalists, however, would admit to harboring their own doubts as to whether questions such as those on Hyacinth's test are entirely appropriate to the task of assessing intelligence.

Understanding just what is meant by the concept of intelligence has proven to be a major challenge for researchers interested in delineating what separates intelligent from unintelligent behavior. Although nonexperts have their own conceptions of intelligence (one survey found, for instance, that laypersons believe that intelligence consists of three components: problem-solving ability, verbal ability, and social competence), it has been more difficult for experts to concur (Sternberg et al., 1981; Howe, 1997). Still, a general definition of intelligence is possible: **Intelligence** is the capacity to understand the world, think with rationality, and use resources effectively when faced with challenges (Wechsler, 1975).

intelligence the capacity to understand the world, think with rationality, and use resources effectively when faced with challenges

Part of the difficulty in defining intelligence stems from the many—and sometimes unsatisfactory—paths that have been followed over the years in the quest to distinguish more intelligent people from less intelligent ones. To understand how researchers have approached the task of devising batteries of assessments, called *intelligence tests*, we need to consider some of the historical milestones in the area of intelligence.

Intelligence Benchmarks: Differentiating the Intelligent from the Unintelligent

The Paris school system was faced with a problem at the turn of the 20th century: A significant number of children were not benefiting from regular instruction. Unfortunately, these children—many of whom we would now call mentally retarded—were generally not identified early enough to shift them to special classes. The French minister of instruction approached psychologist Alfred Binet with this problem and asked him to devise a technique for the early identification of students who might benefit from instruction outside the regular classroom.

Binet tackled his task in a thoroughly practical manner. His years of observing school-aged children suggested to him that previous efforts to distinguish intelligent from unintelligent students—some of which were based on reaction time or keenness of sight—were off the mark. Instead, he launched a trial-and-error process in which items and tasks were administered to students who had been previously identified by teachers as being either "bright" or "dull." Tasks that the bright students completed correctly and the dull students failed to complete correctly were retained for the test. Tasks that did not discriminate between the two groups were discarded. The end result of this process was a test that reliably distinguished students who had previously been identified as fast or slow learners.

Binet's pioneering efforts in intelligence testing left three important legacies. The first was his pragmatic approach to the construction of intelligence tests. Binet did not have theoretical preconceptions about what intelligence was. Instead, he used a trial-and-error approach to psychological measurement that continues to serve as the predominant approach to test construction today. His definition of intelligence as *that which his test measured* has been adopted by many modern researchers, and it is particularly popular among test developers who respect the widespread utility of intelligence tests but wish to avoid arguments about the underlying nature of intelligence.

Our second inheritance from Binet stems from his focus on linking intelligence and school success. Binet's procedure for constructing an intelligence test ensured that intelligence—defined as performance on the test—and school success would be virtually one and the same. Thus, Binet's intelligence test, and today's tests that follow in Binet's footsteps, have become reasonable indicators of the degree to which students possess attributes that contribute to successful school performance. Unfortunately, they do not provide particularly useful information regarding a vast number of other attributes that are largely unrelated to academic proficiency.

Finally, Binet developed a procedure of linking each intelligence test score with a **mental age,** the age of the children taking the test who, on average, achieved that score. For example, if a 6-year-old girl received a score of 30 on the test, and this was the average score received by 10-year-olds, her mental age would be considered 10 years. Similarly, a 15-year-old boy who scored a 90 on the test—thereby matching the mean score for 15-year-olds—would be assigned a mental age of 15 years.

Although assigning a mental age to students provides an indication of whether or not they are performing at the same level as their peers, it does not permit adequate comparisons between students of different **chronological (or physical) ages.** By using mental age alone, for instance, it would be assumed that a 15-year-old responding with a mental age of 17 years would be as bright as a 6-year-old responding with a mental age of 8 years, when actually the 6-year-old would be showing a much greater *relative* degree of brightness.

A solution to this problem comes in the form of the **intelligence quotient,** or **IQ,** a score that takes into account a student's mental *and* chronological age. The traditional method of calculating an IQ score uses the following formula, in which MA stands for mental age and CA for chronological age:

$$\text{IQ score} = \frac{\text{MA}}{\text{CA}} \times 100$$

As a bit of trial-and-error with this formula demonstrates, people whose mental age (MA) is equal to their chronological age (CA) will always have an IQ of 100. Furthermore, if the chronological age exceeds the mental age—implying below-average intelligence—the score will be below 100; and if the chronological age is lower than the mental age—suggesting above-average intelligence—the score will be above 100.

mental age the typical intelligence level found for people at a given chronological age

chronological (or physical) age the actual age of the child taking the intelligence test

intelligence quotient (or IQ score) a measure of intelligence that takes into account a student's mental *and* chronological age

cw

Using this formula, we can return to our earlier example of a 15-year-old who scores at a 17-year-old mental age. This student's IQ is $\frac{17}{15} \times 100$, or 113. In comparison, the IQ of a 6-year-old scoring at a mental age of 8 is $\frac{8}{6} \times 100$, or 133—a higher IQ score than the 15-year-old's.

While the basic principles behind the calculation of an IQ score still hold, scores today are calculated in a more mathematically sophisticated manner and are known as *deviation IQ scores*. The average deviation IQ score remains set at 100, but tests are now devised so that the degree of deviation from this score permits the calculation of the proportion of people who have similar scores. For instance, approximately two-thirds of all people fall within 15 points of the average score of 100, achieving scores between 85 and 115. As scores rise or fall beyond this range, the percentage of people in the same score category drops significantly.

Measuring IQ: Present-day Approaches to Intelligence. Since the time of Binet, tests of intelligence have become increasingly sophisticated in terms of the accuracy with which they measure IQ. However, most of them can still trace their roots to his original work in one way or another. For example, one of the most widely used tests—the **Stanford-Binet Intelligence Scale**—began as an American revision of Binet's original test. The test consists of a series of items that vary according to the age of the person being tested. For instance, young children are asked to answer questions about everyday activities or to copy complex figures. Older people are asked to explain proverbs, solve analogies, and describe similarities between groups of words. The test is administered orally and test-takers are given progressively more difficult problems until they are unable to proceed.

The **Wechsler Intelligence Scale for Children-Revised (WISC-III)** and its adult version, the **Wechsler Adult Intelligence Scale-Revised (WAIS-III),** are two other widely used intelligence tests. The tests provide separate measures of verbal and performance (or nonverbal) skills, as well as a total score. As you can see from the sample items in Figure 9-11, the verbal tasks are traditional word problems testing skills such as understanding a passage, while typical nonverbal tasks are copying a complex design, arranging pictures in a logical order, and assembling objects. The separate portions of the test allow for easier identification of any specific problems a test-taker may have. For example, significantly

Stanford-Binet Intelligence Scale a test that consists of a series of items that vary according to the age of the person being tested

Wechsler Intelligence Scale for Children-Revised (WISC-III) a test for children that provides separate measures of verbal and performance (or nonverbal) skills, as well as a total score

Wechsler Adult Intelligence Scale-Revised (WAIS-III) a test for adults that provides separate measures of verbal and performance (or nonverbal) skills, as well as a total score

The Wechsler Intelligence Scale for Children-Revised (WISC-III) is widely used as an intelligence test that measures verbal and performance (nonverbal) skills.

NAME	GOAL OF ITEM	EXAMPLE
VERBAL SCALE		
Information	Assess general information	Where does honey come from?
Comprehension	Assess understanding and evaluation of social norms and past experience	Why do we use an umbrella when it rains?
Arithmetic	Assess math reasoning through verbal problems	Alice found three baseballs in a field. She gives two to her friend Jocelyn. How many baseballs does Alice have left?
Similarities	Test understanding of how objects or concepts are alike, tapping abstract reasoning	In what way are birds and airplanes alike?
PERFORMANCE SCALE		
Digit symbol	Assess speed of learning	Match symbols to numbers using key. 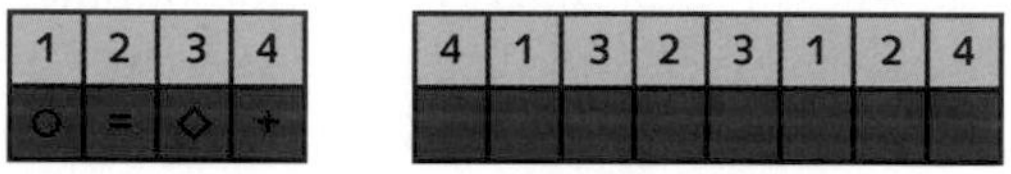
Picture completion	Visual memory and attention	Identify what is missing. 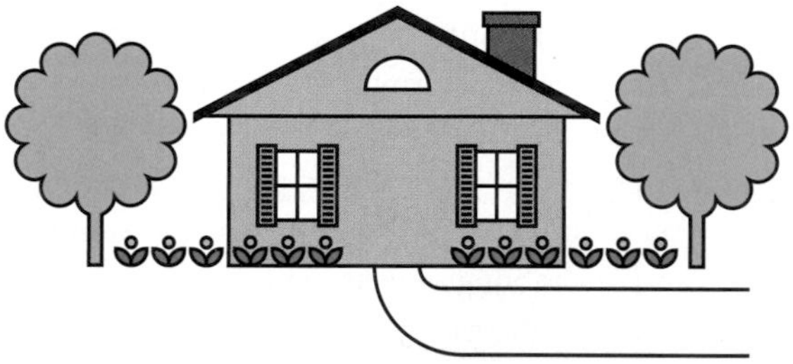
Object assembly	Test understanding of relationship of parts to wholes	Put pieces together to form a whole. 

Figure 9-11   **Measuring intelligence**

The Wechsler Intelligence Scales for Children (WISC-III) includes items such as these. What do such items cover? What do they miss?

higher scores on the performance part of the test than on the verbal part may indicate difficulties in linguistic development.

The **Kaufman Assessment Battery for Children (K-ABC)** takes a different approach than the Stanford-Binet, WISC-III, and WAIS-III. In it, children are tested on their ability to integrate different kinds of stimuli simultaneously and to use step-by-step thinking. A special virtue of the K-ABC is its flexibility. It allows the person giving the test to use alternative wording or gestures, or even to pose questions in a different language, in order to maximize a test-taker's performance. This capability of the K-ABC makes testing more valid and equitable for children to whom English is a second language.

What do the IQ scores derived from IQ tests mean? For most children, IQ scores are reasonably good predictors of their school performance. That's not surprising, given that the initial impetus for the development of intelligence tests was to identify children who were having difficulties in school.

But when it comes to performance outside of academic spheres, the story is different. For instance, although people with higher IQ scores are apt to finish more years of schooling, once this is statistically controlled for, IQ scores are not closely related to income and later success in life. Furthermore, IQ scores are frequently inaccurate when it comes to predicting a particular individual's future success. For example, two people with different IQ scores may both finish their bachelor's degrees at the same college, and the person with a lower IQ might end up with a higher income and a more successful career. Because of these difficulties with traditional IQ scores, researchers have turned to alternative approaches to intelligence (McClelland, 1993).

What IQ Tests Don't Tell: Alternative Conceptions of Intelligence. The intelligence tests used most frequently in school settings today share an underlying premise: Intelligence is composed of a single, unitary mental ability factor. This one main attribute has commonly been called *g* (Spearman, 1927). The *g* factor is assumed to underlie performance on every aspect of intelligence, and it is the *g* factor that intelligence tests presumably measure.

However, many theorists dispute the notion that intelligence is unidimensional (Anderson, 1999; Neisser, 1999). For example, some developmentalists suggest that in fact two kinds of intelligence exist: fluid intelligence and crystallized intelligence (Catell, 1967; 1987). **Fluid intelligence** reflects information processing capabilities, reasoning, and memory. For example, a student asked to group a series of letters according to some criterion or to remember a set of numbers would be using fluid intelligence. In contrast, **crystallized intelligence** is the accumulation of information, skills, and strategies that people have learned through experience and that they can apply in problem-solving situations. A student would likely be relying on crystallized intelligence to solve a puzzle or deduce the solution to a mystery, in which it was necessary to draw on past experience.

Other theorists divide intelligence into an even greater number of parts. For example, psychologist Howard Gardner suggests that we have eight distinct intelligences, each relatively independent (see Table 9-3). Gardner suggests that these separate intelligences operate not in isolation, but together, depending on the type of activity in which we are engaged (Gardner, 2000).

The Russian psychologist Lev Vygotsky, whose approach to cognitive development we first discussed in Chapter 1, takes a very different approach to intelligence. He suggests that to assess intelligence, we should look not only at those cognitive processes that are fully developed, but at those that are currently being developed as well. To do this, Vygotsky contends that assessment tasks should involve cooperative interaction between the individual who is being assessed and the person who is doing the assessment—a process called *dynamic assessment*. In short, intelligence is seen as being reflected not only in how

Kaufman Assessment Battery for Children (K-ABC) an intelligence test that measures children's ability to integrate different stimuli simultaneously and step-by-step thinking

fluid intelligence intelligence that reflects information processing capabilities, reasoning, and memory

crystallized intelligence the accumulation of information, skills, and strategies that people have learned through experience and that they can apply in problem-solving situations

Table 9-3

GARDNER'S EIGHT INTELLIGENCES

1. *Musical intelligence* (skills in tasks involving music). Case example:
   When he was 3, Yehudi Menuhin was smuggled into the San Francisco Orchestra concerts by his parents. The sound of Louis Persinger's violin so entranced the youngster that he insisted on a violin for his birthday and Louis Persinger as his teacher. He got both. By the time he was 10 years old, Menuhin was an international performer.

2. *Bodily kinesthetic intelligence* (skills in using the whole body or various portions of it in the solution of problems or in the construction of products or displays, exemplified by dancers, athletes, actors, and surgeons). Case example:
   Fifteen-year-old Babe Ruth played third base. During one game, his team's pitcher was doing poorly and Babe loudly criticized him from third base. Brother Mathias, the coach, called out, "Ruth, if you know so much about it, *you* pitch!" Babe was surprised and embarrassed because he had never pitched before, but Brother Mathias insisted. Ruth said later that at the very moment he took the pitcher's mound, he *knew* he was supposed to be a pitcher.

3. *Logical mathematical intelligence* (skills in problem solving and scientific thinking). Case example:
   Barbara McClintock won the Nobel Prize in medicine for her work in microbiology. She describes one of her breakthroughs, which came after thinking about a problem for half an hour . . . : "Suddenly I jumped and ran back to the [corn] field. At the top of the field [the others were still at the bottom] I shouted, 'Eureka, I have it!'"

4. *Linguistic intelligence* (skills involved in the production and use of language). Case example:
   At the age of 10, T.S. Elliot created a magazine called *Fireside,* to which he was the sole contributor. In a 3-day period during his winter vacation, he created eight complete issues.

5. *Spatial intelligence* (skills involving spatial configurations, such as those used by artists and architects). Case example:
   Navigation around the Caroline Islands . . . is accomplished without instruments. . . . During the actual trip, the navigator must envision mentally a reference island as it passes under a particular star and from that he computes the number of segments completed, the proportion of the trip remaining, and any corrections in heading.

6. *Interpersonal intelligence* (skills in interacting with others, such as sensitivity to the moods, temperaments, motivations, and intentions of others). Case example:
   When Anne Sullivan began instructing the deaf and blind Helen Keller, her task was one that had eluded others for years. Yet, just 2 weeks after beginning her work with Keller, Sullivan achieved a great success. In her words, "My heart is singing with joy this morning. A miracle has happened! The wild little creature of 2 weeks ago has been transformed into a gentle child."

7. *Intrapersonal intelligence* (knowledge of the internal aspects of oneself; access to one's own feelings and emotions). Case example:
   In her essay "A Sketch of the Past," Virginia Woolf displays deep insight into her own inner life through these lines, describing her reaction to several specific memories from her childhood that still, in adulthood, shock her: "Though I still have the peculiarity that I receive these sudden shocks, they are now always welcome; after the first surprise, I always feel instantly that they are particularly valuable. And so I go on to suppose that the shock-receiving capacity is what makes me a writer."

8. *Naturalist intelligence* (ability to identify and classify patterns in nature). Case example:
   In prehistoric periods, hunter-gatherers required naturalist intelligence in order to identify what types of plants were edible.

(*Source:* Adapted from Walters & Gardner, 1986.)

children can perform on their own, but in terms of how well they perform when helped by adults (Vygotsky, 1927/1976; Daniels, 1996; Brown & Ferrara, 1999).

Taking yet another approach, psychologist Robert Sternberg (1987, 1990) suggests that intelligence is best thought of in terms of information processing. In this view, the way in which people store material in memory and later use it to solve intellectual tasks provides the most precise conception of intelligence. Rather than focusing on the various subcomponents that make up the *structure* of intelligence, then, information-processing approaches examine the *processes* that underlie intelligent behavior.

Researchers who have broken tasks and problems into their component parts have noted critical differences in the nature and speed of problem-solving processes between those who score high and those who score low on traditional IQ tests. For instance, when verbal problems such as analogies are broken into their component parts, it becomes clear that people with higher intelligence levels differ from others not only in the number of problems they ultimately are able to solve, but in their method of solving the problems as well. People with high IQ scores spend more time on the initial stages of problem-solving, retrieving relevant information from memory. In contrast, those who score lower on traditional IQ tests tend to spend less time on the initial stages, instead skipping ahead and making less informed guesses. The processes used in solving problems, then, may reflect important differences in intelligence (Sternberg, 1982, 1990).

Sternberg's work on information-processing approaches to intelligence has led him to develop the **triarchic theory of intelligence.** According to this model, intelligence consists of three aspects of information processing: the componential element, the experiential element, and the contextual element. The componential aspect of intelligence reflects how efficiently people can process and analyze information. Efficiency in these areas allows people to infer relationships among different parts of a problem, solve the problem, and then evaluate their solution. People who are strong on the componential element score highest on traditional tests of intelligence (Sternberg, 1996).

The experiential element is the insightful component of intelligence. People who have a strong experiential element can easily compare new material with what they already know and can combine and relate facts that they already know in novel and creative ways. Finally, the contextual element of intelligence concerns practical intelligence, or ways of dealing with the demands of the everyday environment.

In Sternberg's view, people vary in the degree to which each of these three elements is present. Our level of success at any given task reflects the match between the task and our own specific pattern of strength on the three components of intelligence (Sternberg, 1985a, 1991).

triarchic theory of intelligence a model that states that intelligence consists of three aspects of information processing: the componential element, the experiential element, and the contextual element

Group Differences in IQ

A "jontry" is an example of a
   (a) rulpow
   (b) flink
   (c) spudge
   (d) bakwoe

If you were to find an item composed of nonsense words such as this on an intelligence test, your immediate—and quite legitimate—reaction would likely be to complain. How could a test that purports to measure intelligence include test items that incorporate meaningless terminology?

Yet for some people, the items actually used on traditional intelligence tests might appear equally nonsensical. To take a hypothetical example, suppose children living in rural areas were asked details about subways, while those living in urban areas were asked about the mating practices of sheep. In both cases, we would expect that the previous experiences of test-takers would have a substantial effect on their ability to answer the questions. And if questions about such matters were included on an IQ test, the test could rightly be viewed as a measure of prior experience rather than of intelligence.

Although the questions on traditional IQ tests are not so blatantly dependent upon test-takers' prior experiences our examples, cultural background and experience do have the potential to play a crucial role in determining intelligence test scores. In fact, many educators suggest that traditional measures of intelligence are subtly biased in favor of

Bodily kinesthetic intelligence, as displayed by dancers, ballplayers and gymnasts is one of Gardner's eight intelligences. What are some examples of other Gardner intelligences?

white, upper- and middle-class students and against groups with different cultural experiences.

Explaining Racial Differences in IQ. The issue of how cultural background and experience influence IQ test performance has led to considerable debate among researchers. The debate has been fueled by the finding that IQ scores of certain racial groups are consistently lower, on average, than the IQ scores of other groups. For example, the mean score of African Americans tends to be about 15 IQ points lower than the mean score of whites—although the measured difference varies a great deal depending on the particular IQ test employed (e.g., Vance, Hankins, & Brown, 1988; Fish, 2001).

The question that emerges from such differences, of course, is whether they reflect actual differences in intelligence or, instead, are caused by bias in the intelligence tests themselves in favor of majority groups and against minorities. For example, if whites perform better on an IQ test than African Americans because of their greater familiarity with the language used in the test items, the test hardly can be said to provide a fair measure of the intelligence of African Americans. Similarly, an intelligence test that solely used African American Vernacular English could not be considered an impartial measure of intelligence for whites.

The question of how to interpret differences between intelligence scores of different cultural groups lies at the heart of one of the major controversies in child development: To what degree is an individual's intelligence determined by heredity, and to what degree by environment? The issue is important because of its social implications. For instance, if intelligence is primarily determined by heredity and is therefore largely fixed at birth, attempts to alter cognitive abilities later in life, such as schooling, will meet with limited success. On the other hand, if intelligence is largely environmentally determined, modifying social and educational conditions is a more promising strategy for bringing about increases in cognitive functioning (Sternberg & Grigorenko, 1996; Suzuki & Valencia, 1997).

The Bell Curve **Controversy.** Although investigations into the relative contributions of heredity and environment to intelligence have been conducted for decades, the smoldering debate became a raging fire with the publication in 1994 of a book by Richard J. Herrnstein and Charles Murray, titled *The Bell Curve*. In the book, Herrnstein and Murray argue that the average 15-point IQ difference between whites and African Americans is due primarily to heredity rather than environment. Furthermore, they argue that this IQ difference accounts for the higher rates of poverty, lower employment, and higher use of welfare among minority groups as compared with majority groups (Herrnstein & Murray, 1994).

The conclusions reached by Herrnstein and Murray raised a storm of protest, and many researchers who examined the data reported in the book came to conclusions that were quite different. Most developmentalists and psychologists responded by arguing that the differences between races in measured IQ can be explained by environmental differences between the races. In fact, when a variety of indicators of economic and social factors are statistically taken into account simultaneously, mean IQ scores of black and white children turn out to be actually quite similar. For instance, children from similar middle-class backgrounds, whether African American or white, tend to have similar IQ scores (Brooks-Gunn, Klebanov, & Duncan, 1996).

Furthermore, critics maintained that there is little evidence to suggest that IQ is a cause of poverty and other social ills. In fact, some critics suggested, as mentioned earlier in this discussion, that IQ scores were unrelated in meaningful ways to later success in life (e.g., McClelland, 1993; Nisbett, 1994; Sternberg, 1995, 1997a; Reifman, 2000).

Finally, members of cultural and social minority groups may score lower than members of the majority group due to the nature of the intelligence tests themselves. It is clear that traditional intelligence tests may discriminate against minority groups who have not had exposure to the same environment as majority group members have experienced.

Although certain IQ tests (such as the *System of Multicultural Pluralistic Assessment,* or *SOMPA*) have been designed to be equally valid regardless of the cultural background of test-takers, no test can be completely without bias (Sandoval et al., 1998).

In short, most experts in the area of IQ were not convinced by *The Bell Curve* contention that differences in group IQ scores are largely determined by genetic factors. Still, we cannot put the issue to rest, largely because it is impossible to design a definitive experiment that can determine the cause of differences in IQ scores between members of different groups. (Thinking about how such an experiment might be designed shows the futility of the enterprise: One cannot ethically assign children to different living conditions to find the effects of environment, nor would one wish to genetically control or alter intelligence levels in unborn children.)

In practical terms, however, it ultimately may be less important to know the absolute degree to which intelligence is determined by genetic and environmental factors than it is to learn how to improve children's living conditions and educational experiences. By enriching the quality of children's environments, we will be in a better position to permit all children to reach their full potential and to maximize their contributions to society, whatever their individual levels of intelligence (Wachs, 1996; Wickelgren, 1999).

Below and Above Intelligence Norms: Mental Retardation and the Intellectually Gifted

Although Connie kept pace with her classmates in kindergarten, by the time she reached first grade, she was academically the slowest in almost every subject. It was not that she didn't try, but rather that it took her longer than other students to catch on to new material, and she regularly required special attention to keep up with the rest of the class.

On the other hand, in some areas she excelled: When asked to draw or produce something with her hands, she not only matched her classmates' performance but exceeded it, producing beautiful work that was much admired by her classmates. Although the other students in the class felt that there was something different about Connie, they were hard-pressed to identify the source of the difference, and in fact they didn't spend much time pondering the issue.

Connie's parents and teacher, though, knew what made her special. Extensive testing in kindergarten had shown that Connie's intelligence was well below normal, and she was officially classified as a special needs student.

If Connie had been attending school before 1975, she would most likely have been removed from her regular class as soon as her low IQ was identified, and placed in a class taught by a special needs teacher. Often consisting of students with a hodgepodge of afflictions, including emotional difficulties, severe reading problems, and physical disabilities such as multiple sclerosis, such classes were traditionally kept separate and apart from the regular educational process.

However, all that changed in 1975 when Congress passed Public Law 94-142, the Education for All Handicapped Children Act. The intent of the law—an intent that has been largely realized—was to ensure that children with special needs received a full education in the **least restrictive environment,** the setting most similar to that of children without special needs (Yell, 1995).

least restrictive environment the setting that is most similar to that of children without special needs

In practice, the law has meant that children with special needs must be integrated into regular classrooms and regular activities to the greatest extent possible, as long as doing so is educationally beneficial. Children are to be isolated from the regular classroom only for those subjects that are specifically affected by their exceptionality; for all other subjects, they are to be taught with nonexceptional children in regular classrooms. Of course, some children with severe handicaps still need a mostly or entirely separate education, depending on the extent of their condition. But the goal of the law is to integrate exceptional children and typical children to the fullest extent possible (Yell, 1995).

This educational approach to special education, designed to end the segregation of exceptional students as much as possible, has come to be called mainstreaming. In **mainstreaming,** exceptional children are integrated as much as possible into the traditional educational system and are provided with a broad range of educational alternatives (Hocutt, 1996).

Ending Segregation by Intelligence Levels: The Benefits of Mainstreaming. In many respects, the introduction of mainstreaming—while clearly increasing the complexity of classroom teaching—was a reaction to failures of traditional special education. For one thing, there was little research support for the advisability of special education for exceptional students. Research that examined such factors as academic achievement, self-concept, social adjustment, and personality development generally failed to discern any advantages for special needs children placed in special, as opposed to regular, education classes. Furthermore, systems that compel minorities to be educated separately from majorities historically tend to be less effective—as an examination of schools that were once segregated on the basis of race clearly demonstrates (Wang, Peverly, & Catalano, 1987; Wang, Reynolds, & Walberg, 1996).

Ultimately, though, the most compelling argument in favor of mainstreaming is philosophical: Because special needs students must ultimately function in a normal environment, greater experience with their peers ought to enhance their integration into society, as well as positively affect their learning. Mainstreaming, then, provides a mechanism to equalize the opportunities available to all children. The ultimate objective of mainstreaming is to ensure that all persons, regardless of ability or disability, will have—to the greatest extent possible—opportunities to choose their goals on the basis of a full education, enabling them to obtain a fair share of life's rewards (Fuchs & Fuchs, 1994).

Does the reality of mainstreaming live up to its promise? To some extent, the benefits extolled by proponents have been realized. However, classroom teachers must receive substantial support in order for mainstreaming to be effective. It is not easy to teach a class in which students' abilities are significantly different from one another (Kauffman, 1993; Daly & Feldman, 1994; Scruggs & Mastropieri, 1994).

The benefits of mainstreaming have led some professionals to promote an alternative educational model known as full inclusion. *Full inclusion* is the integration of all students, even those with the most severe disabilities, into regular classes. In such a system, separate special education programs would cease to operate. Full inclusion is controversial, and it remains to be seen how widespread such a practice will become (Hocutt, 1996; Siegel, 1996; Kavale & Forness, 2000).

Below the Norm: Mental Retardation. Approximately 1 to 3 percent of the school-age population is considered to be mentally retarded (U.S. Department of Education, 1987). Estimates vary so widely because the most widely accepted definition of mental retardation is one that leaves a great deal of room for interpretation. According to the American Association on Mental Retardation (AAMR), **mental retardation** refers to "substantial limitations in present functioning" characterized by "significantly subaverage intellectual functioning, existing concurrently with related limitations in two or more of the following applicable adaptive skill areas: communication, self-care, home living, social skills, community use, self direction, health and safety, functional academics, leisure and work. Mental retardation manifests before age 18" (AAMR, 1992).

While "subaverage intellectual functioning" can be measured in a relatively straightforward manner—using standard IQ tests—it is more difficult to determine how to gauge limitations in "applicable adaptive skills." Ultimately, this imprecision leads to a lack of

---

mainstreaming an educational approach in which exceptional children are integrated to the extent possible into the traditional educational system and are provided with a broad range of educational alternatives

mental retardation a significantly subaverage level of intellectual functioning which occurs with related limitations in two or more skill areas

This boy, who has been identified as mentally retarded, is mainstreamed into this fifth grade class.

uniformity in the ways experts apply the label of "mental retardation." Furthermore, it has resulted in significant variation in the abilities of people who are categorized as mentally retarded. Accordingly, mentally retarded people range from those who can be taught to work and function with little special attention to those who are virtually untrainable and who never develop speech or such basic motor skills as crawling or walking (Matson & Mulick, 1991).

In addition, even when objective measures such as IQ tests are used to identify mentally retarded individuals, discrimination may occur against children from ethnically diverse backgrounds. Most traditional intelligence tests are standardized using white, English-speaking, middle-class populations. As a result, children from different cultural backgrounds may perform poorly on the tests—not because they are retarded, but because the tests use questions that are culturally biased in favor of majority group members. In fact, one classic study found that in one California school district, Mexican American students were 10 times more likely than whites to be placed in special education classes (Mercer, 1973). More recent findings show that nationally twice as many African American students as white students are classified as mildly retarded, a difference that experts attribute primarily to cultural bias and poverty (Reschly, 1996; Terman et al., 1996).

The vast majority of the mentally retarded—some 90 percent—have relatively low levels of deficits. Classified with **mild retardation,** they score in the range of 50 or 55 to 70 on IQ tests. Typically, their retardation is not even identified before they reach school, although their early development often is slower than average. Once they enter elementary school, their retardation and their need for special attention usually become apparent, as it did with Connie, the first-grader profiled at the beginning of this discussion. With appropriate training, these students can reach a third- to sixth-grade educational level, and although they cannot carry out complex intellectual tasks, they are able to hold jobs and function quite independently and successfully.

Intellectual and adaptive limitations become more apparent, however, at higher levels of mental retardation. People whose IQ scores range from around 35 or 40 to 50 or 55 are classified with **moderate retardation.** Composing between 5 and 10 percent of those classified as mentally retarded, the moderately retarded display distinctive behavior early in their lives. They are slow to develop language skills, and their motor development is also affected. Regular schooling is usually not effective in training people with moderate retardation to acquire academic skills, because generally they are unable to progress beyond the second-grade level. Still, they are capable of learning occupational and social

mild retardation retardation in which IQ scores fall in the range of 50 or 55 to 70

moderate retardation retardation in which IQ scores range from around 35 or 40 to 50 or 55

skills, and they can learn to travel independently to familiar places. Typically, they require moderate levels of supervision.

severe retardation retardation in which IQ scores range from around 20 or 25 to 35 or 40

profound retardation retardation in which IQ scores fall below 20 or 25

gifted and talented children who show evidence of high performance capability in areas such as intellectual, creative, artistic, leadership capacity, or specific academic fields

At the most significant levels of retardation—those who are classified with **severe retardation** (IQs ranging from around 20 or 25 to 35 or 40) and **profound retardation** (IQs below 20 or 25)—the ability to function is severely limited. Usually, such people have little or no speech, have poor motor control, and may need 24-hour nursing care. At the same time, though, some people with severe retardation are capable of learning basic self-care skills, such as dressing and eating, and they may even develop the potential to become partially independent as adults. Still, the need for relatively high levels of care continues throughout the life span, and most severely and profoundly retarded people are institutionalized for the majority of their lives.

Above the Norm: The Gifted and Talented. Consider this situation:

> I was standing at the front of the room explaining how the earth revolves and how, because of its huge size, it is difficult for us to realize that it is actually round. All of a sudden, Spencer blurted out, "The earth isn't round." I curtly replied, "Ha, do you think it's flat?" He matter-of-factly said, "No, it's a truncated sphere." I quickly changed the subject. Spencer said the darndest things. (Payne et al., 1974, p. 94)

It sometimes strikes people as curious that the gifted and talented are considered to have a form of exceptionality. Yet—as the above quote suggests—the 3 to 5 percent of school-age children who are gifted and talented present special challenges of their own.

Which students are considered to be **gifted and talented?** Because of the breadth of the term, little agreement exists among researchers on a single definition. However, the federal government considers the term *gifted* to include "children who give evidence of high performance capability in areas such as intellectual, creative, artistic, leadership capacity, or specific academic fields, and who require services or activities not ordinarily provided by the school in order to fully develop such capabilities" (Sec 582, P.L. 97-35). Intellectual capabilities, then, represent only one type of exceptionality; unusual potential in areas outside the academic realm are also included in the concept. Gifted and talented children have so much potential that they, no less than students with low IQs, warrant special concern (Azar, 1995; Winner, 1997; Robinson, Zigler, & Gallagher, 2000; Pfeiffer & Stocking, 2000).

Although the stereotypic description of the gifted—particularly those with exceptionally high intelligence—would probably include adjectives such as "unsociable," "poorly adjusted," and "neurotic," such a view is far off the mark. In fact, most research suggests that highly intelligent people also tend to be outgoing, well adjusted, and popular (Southern, Jones, & Stanley, 1993; Gottfried et al., 1994; Field et al., 1998).

For instance, one landmark, long-term study of 1,500 gifted students, which began in the 1920s, found that the gifted did better in virtually every dimension studied. Not only were they smarter than average, but they were healthier, better coordinated, and psychologically better adjusted than their less intelligent classmates. Furthermore, their lives played out in ways that most people would envy. The subjects received more awards and distinctions, earned more money, and made many more contributions in art and literature than the average person. For instance, by the time they had reached the age of 40, they had collectively produced more than 90 books, 375 plays and short stories, and 2,000 articles, and they had registered more than 200 patents. Perhaps not surprisingly, they reported greater satisfaction with their lives than the nongifted (Sears, 1977; Terman & Oden, 1959; Shurkin, 1992).

Yet being gifted and talented is no guarantee of success in school, as we can see if we consider the particular components of the category. For example, the verbal abilities that allow the eloquent expression of ideas and feelings can equally permit the expression of glib and persuasive statements that happen to be inaccurate. Furthermore, teachers may sometimes misinterpret the humor, novelty, and creativity of unusually gifted children, considering their intellectual fervor to be disruptive or inappropriate. And peers are not always sympathetic: Some very bright children try to hide their intelligence in an effort to fit in better with other students (Feldman, 1982).

Two main approaches to educating the gifted and talented have been devised: acceleration and enrichment (Feldhusen, Haeger & Pellegrino, 1989). **Acceleration** allows gifted students to move ahead at their own pace, even if this means skipping to higher grade levels. The materials that students receive under acceleration programs are not necessarily different from what other students receive; they simply are provided at a faster pace than for the average student.

An alternative approach is **enrichment,** through which students are kept at grade level but are enrolled in special programs and given individual activities to allow greater depth of study on a given topic. In enrichment, the material provided to gifted students differs not only in the timing of its presentation, but in its sophistication as well. Thus, enrichment materials are designed to provide an intellectual challenge to the gifted student, encouraging higher-order thinking.

Acceleration programs can be remarkably effective. Most studies have shown that gifted students who begin school even considerably earlier than their age-mates do as well as or better than those who begin at the traditional age (Rimm & Lovance, 1992). One of the best illustrations of the benefits of acceleration is the "Study of Mathematically Precocious Youth," an ongoing program at Johns Hopkins University in Baltimore. In this program, seventh- and eighth-graders who have unusual abilities in mathematics participate in a variety of special classes and workshops. The results have been nothing short of sensational, with students successfully completing college courses and sometimes even enrolling in college early. Some students have even graduated from college before the age of 18 (Stanley & Benbow, 1983; Brody & Benbow, 1987).

> **acceleration** special programs that allow gifted students to move ahead at their own pace, even if this means skipping to higher grade levels

> **enrichment** an approach through which students are kept at grade level but are enrolled in special programs and given individual activities to allow greater depth of study on a given topic

Review and Rethink

REVIEW

- The development of reading skill generally occurs in several stages. A combination of elements from code-based (i.e., phonics) approaches and whole language approaches appears to offer the most promise.
- Multicultural education is in transition from a melting pot model of cultural assimilation to a pluralistic society model.
- The measurement of intelligence has traditionally been a matter of testing skills that promote academic success.
- Recent theories of intelligence suggest that there may be several distinct intelligences or several components of intelligence that reflect different ways of processing information.
- U.S. educators are attempting to deal with substantial numbers of exceptional persons whose intellectual and other skills are significantly lower or higher than normal.

RETHINK

- Is an educational focus on the basic academic skills appropriate? How does the theory that there are multiple intelligences relate to this issue?
- How do fluid intelligence and crystallized intelligence interact? Which of the two is likely to be more influenced by genetic factors, and which by environmental factors? Why?

Looking Back

▶ *In what ways do children grow during the school years, and what factors influence their growth?*

■ The middle childhood years are characterized by slow and steady growth. Weight is redistributed as baby fat disappears. In part, growth is genetically determined, but societal factors such as affluence, dietary habits, nutrition, and disease also contribute significantly.

■ During the middle childhood years, great improvements occur in gross motor skills. Cultural expectations appear to underlie most gross motor skill differences between boys and girls. Fine motor skills also develop rapidly.

▶ *What are the main health concerns of school-age children?*

■ Adequate nutrition is important because of its contributions to growth, health, social and emotional functioning, and cognitive performance.

■ Obesity is partially influenced by genetic factors, but is also associated with with children's failure to develop internal controls over eating, overindulgence in sedentary activities such as television viewing, and lack of physical exercise.

■ Asthma and childhood depression are fairly prevalent among children of school age.

▶ *What sorts of special needs first become apparent in children of this age, and how can they be met?*

■ Visual, auditory, and speech impairments, as well as other learning disabilities, can lead to academic and social problems and must be handled with sensitivity and appropriate assistance.

■ Children with attention-deficit hyperactivity disorder exhibit another form of special need. ADHD is characterized by inattention, impulsiveness, failure to complete tasks, lack of organization, and excessive amounts of uncontrollable activity. Treatment of ADHD by drugs is highly controversial because of unwanted side effects and doubts about long-term consequences.

▶ *In what ways do children develop cognitively during these years, according to major theoretical approaches?*

■ According to Piaget, school-age children enter the concrete operational period and for the first time become capable of applying logical thought processes to concrete problems.

■ According to information-processing approaches, children's intellectual development in the school years can be attributed to substantial increases in memory capacity and the sophistication of the "programs" children can handle.

■ Vygotsky recommends that students focus on active learning through child–adult and child–child interactions that fall within each child's zone of proximal development.

▶ *How does language develop during the middle childhood period?*

■ The language development of children in the school years is substantial, with improvements in vocabulary, syntax, and pragmatics. Children learn to control their behavior through linguistic strategies, and they learn more effectively by seeking clarification when they need it.

■ Bilingualism can be beneficial in the school years. Children who are taught all subjects in the first language, with simultaneous instruction in English, appear to experience few deficits and several linguistic and cognitive advantages.

▶ *What are some trends in schooling today?*

■ Schooling, which is available to nearly all children in most developed countries, is not as accessible to children, especially girls, in many less developed countries.

■ The development of reading skill, which is fundamental to schooling, generally occurs in several stages: identifying letters, reading highly familiar words, sounding out letters and blending sounds into words, reading words with fluency but with little comprehension, reading with comprehension and for practical purposes, and reading material that reflects multiple points of view.

■ Multiculturalism and diversity are significant issues in U.S. schools, where the melting pot society, in which minority cultures were assimilated to the majority culture, is being replaced by the pluralistic society, in which individual cultures maintain their own identities while participating in the definition of a larger culture.

▶ *How can intelligence be measured, and how are exceptional children educated?*

■ Intelligence testing has traditionally focused on factors that differentiate successful academic performers from unsuccessful ones. The intelligence quotient, or IQ, reflects the ratio of a person's mental age to his or her chronological age. Other conceptualizations of intelligence focus on different types of intelligence or on different aspects of the information processing task.

■ In today's schools, exceptional children—including intellectual deficits—are to be educated in the least restrictive environment, typically the regular classroom. If done properly,

this strategy can benefit all students and permit the exceptional student to focus on strengths rather than weaknesses.

■ Gifted and talented children can benefit from special educational programs, including acceleration programs and enrichment programs.

EPILOGUE

In this chapter, we discussed children's physical and cognitive development during the middle childhood years. We considered physical growth, nutrition, and health concerns, as well as intellectual growth as interpreted by Piaget, information-processing approaches, and Lev Vygotsky. We noted children's increased capabilities in memory and language, which facilitate and support gains in many other areas. We looked at some aspects of schooling worldwide and, especially, in the United States, concluding with an examination of intelligence: how it is defined, how it is tested, and how children who fall significantly below or above the intellectual norm are educated and treated.

Look back to the prologue, about La-Toya Pankey's development of reading skills, and answer the following questions.

1. Judging from the cues provided in the prologue, how would you have estimated La-Toya's chances for academic success before you learned about her ability to read? Why?

2. If you wished to isolate the factors in La-Toya's genetic or environmental background that contributed to her interest and ability in reading, how would you proceed? Which factors would you examine? Which questions would you ask?

3. Given her circumstances, what threats to academic accomplishment does La-Toya still face? What advantages does she seem to have?

4. Discuss La-Toya's situation in light of the premises of the authors of *The Bell Curve*. If La-Toya succeeds academically, outperforming students of higher socioeconomic status, how would the authors explain this phenomenon? How do you explain it?

Key Terms and Concepts

asthma (p. 301)
visual impairment (p. 303)
auditory impairment (p. 304)
speech impairment (p. 304)
stuttering (p. 305)
learning disabilities (p. 305)
attention-deficit hyperactivity disorder (ADHD) (p. 306)
concrete operational stage (p. 308)
decentering (p. 308)
memory (p. 311)
metamemory (p. 312)
metalinguistic awareness (p. 315)
bilingualism (p. 315)

multicultural education (p. 327)
cultural assimilation model (p. 328)
pluralistic society model (p. 328)
bicultural identity (p. 328)
intelligence (p. 329)
mental age (p. 330)
chronological (or physical) age (p. 330)
intelligence quotient (or IQ score) (p. 330)
Stanford-Binet Intelligence Scale (p. 331)
Wechsler Intelligence Scale for Children-Revised (WISC-III) (p. 331)
Wechsler Adult Intelligence Scale-Revised (WAIS-III) (p. 331)
Kaufman Assessment Battery for Children (K-ABC) (p. 333)

fluid intelligence (p. 333)
crystallized intelligence (p. 333)
triarchic theory of intelligence (p. 335)
least restrictive environment (p. 337)
mainstreaming (p. 338)
mental retardation (p. 338)
mild retardation (p. 339)
moderate retardation (p. 339)
severe retardation (p. 340)
profound retardation (p. 340)
gifted and talented (p. 340)
acceleration (p. 341)
enrichment (p. 341)

Social and Personality Development in Middle Childhood

PROLOGUE: PLAY TIME

During middle childhood, play involves the development of friendships and social relationships.

On a bright weekday afternoon, six boys are playing under the endless Nevada sky. Bryan and Christopher Hendrickson are third-graders, 9-year-old twins, and as on so many afternoons, their garage is headquarters.

The twins, their younger brother, Andrew, and three friends pull two enormous boxes from the garage—one each from a recently purchased washer and dryer—and set to work transforming them.

"We're making our spaceship," says Bryan. "With guns included."

Why does the spaceship need guns?

"For evil, don't you know?" says Bryan. He sprays machine gun sounds.

As the sun sets, an ever-larger clan of kids, now including the twins' older sister, Lindsay, invades the backyard. The boxes become forts, the group divides in two, and a furious round of capture-the-stuffed-tiger ensues. . . .

Around 6 o'clock, mom Judy summons all the kids—now nearly a dozen—inside for dinner of pizza and juice. Later, the game resumes for another hour or so by moonlight before exhausting itself. Some children wander home. Others are picked up by their parents. (Fishman, 1999, p. 56)

Looking Ahead

For Bryan and Christopher, afternoons like these represent more than just a way of passing time. They also pave the way for the formation of friendships and social relationships, a key developmental task during middle childhood.

In this chapter, we focus on social and personality development during middle childhood. It is a time when children's views of themselves undergo significant changes, they form new bonds with friends and family, and they become increasingly attached to social institutions outside the home.

We start our consideration of personality and social development during middle childhood by examining the changes that occur in the ways children see themselves. We discuss how they view their personal characteristics, and we examine the complex issue of self-esteem.

Next, the chapter turns to relationships during middle childhood. We discuss the stages of friendship and the ways gender and ethnicity affect how and with whom children interact. We also examine how to improve children's social competence.

The last part of the chapter explores the central societal institution in children's lives: the family. We consider the consequences of divorce, self-care children, and the phenomenon of group care.

After reading this chapter, you will be able to answer the following questions:

▶ **In what ways do children's views of themselves change during middle childhood?**

▶ **Why is self-esteem important during these years?**

▶ **Through what stages does moral development proceed as children age?**

▶ **What sorts of relationships and friendships are typical of middle childhood?**

▶ **How do gender and ethnicity affect friendships?**

▶ **How do today's diverse family and care arrangements affect children?**

▶ **How do social and emotional factors contribute to school outcomes?**

The Developing Self

Nine-year-old Karl Haglund is perched in his eagle's nest, a treehouse built high in the willow that grows in his backyard. Sometimes he sits there alone among the tree's spreading branches, his face turned toward the sky, a boy clearly enjoying his solitude. . . .

This morning Karl is busy sawing and hammering. "It's fun to build," he says. "I started the house when I was 4 years old. Then when I was about 7, my dad built me this platform. 'Cause all my places were falling apart and they were crawling with carpenter ants. So we destroyed them and then built me a deck.

*And I built on top of it. It's stronger now. You can have privacy here, but it's a
bad place to go when it's windy 'cause you almost get blown off." (Kotre & Hall,
1990, p. 116)*

Karl's growing sense of competence is reflected in the passage above, as he describes how
he and his father built his treehouse. Conveying what psychologist Erik Erikson calls "industriousness," Karl's quiet pride in his accomplishment illustrates one of the ways in
which children's views of themselves evolve.

Psychosocial Development in Middle Childhood: Industry Versus Inferiority

According to Erik Erikson, whose approach to psychosocial development we last discussed
in Chapter 8, middle childhood encompasses the **industry-versus-inferiority stage.** Lasting from roughly age 6 to age 12, the industry-versus-inferiority stage is characterized by a
focus on efforts to attain competence in meeting the challenges presented by parents,
peers, school, and the other complexities of the modern world.

As they move through middle childhood, children direct their energies not only to
mastering what they are presented in school—an enormous body of information—but to
making a place for themselves in their social worlds. Success in this stage brings with it
feelings of mastery and proficiency and a growing sense of competence, like those expressed by Karl when he talks about his building experience. On the other hand, difficulties in this stage lead to feelings of failure and inadequacy. As a result, children may
withdraw both from academic pursuits, showing less interest and motivation to excel, and
from interactions with peers.

Children such as Karl may find that attaining a sense of industry during the middle
childhood years has lasting consequences. For example, one study examined how childhood industriousness and hard work were related to adult behavior by following a group
of 450 men over a 35-year period, starting in early childhood. The men who were most industrious and hard-working during childhood were most successful as adults, both in occupational attainment and in their personal lives. In fact, childhood industriousness was
more closely associated with adult success than was intelligence or family background
(Vaillant & Vaillant, 1981).

Understanding One's Self: A New Response to "Who Am I?"

During middle childhood, children continue their efforts to answer the question "Who
am I?" as they seek to understand the nature of the self. Although the question does not
yet have the urgency it will assume in adolescence, elementary-school-age children still
seek to pin down their place in the world.

The Shift in Self-Understanding from the Physical to the Psychological. Several changes in children's views of themselves during middle childhood illustrate the quest for self-
understanding. For one thing, they begin to view themselves less in terms of external,
physical attributes and more in terms of psychological traits (Aboud & Skerry, 1983;
Marsh, Craven, & Debus, 1998).

For instance, 6-year-old Carey describes herself as "a fast runner and good at drawing"—both characteristics dependent on skill in external activities relying on motor skills.
In contrast, 11-year-old Meiping characterizes herself as "pretty smart, friendly, and helpful to my friends." Meiping's portrayal is based on psychological characteristics, inner
traits that are more abstract than the younger child's descriptions. The use of inner traits

industry-versus-inferiority stage the period from age 6 to 12 characterized by a
focus on efforts to attain competence in
meeting the challenges presented by
parents, peers, school, and the other
complexities of the modern world

As children become older, they begin to
characterize themselves in terms of their
psychological attributes as well as their
physical achievements.

to determine self-concept results from the child's increasing cognitive skills, a development that we discussed in Chapter 9.

In addition to shifting focus from external characteristics to internal, psychological traits, children's views of self become more differentiated. In Erikson's view, children are seeking out endeavors where they can be successfully industrious. As they get older, children discover that they may be good at some things and not so good at others. Ten-year-old Ginny, for instance, comes to understand that she is good at arithmetic but not very good at spelling; 11-year-old Alberto determines that he is good at softball but doesn't have the stamina to play soccer very well.

Children's self-concepts become divided into personal and academic spheres. In fact, as can be seen in Figure 10-1, self-concept in each of the four domains can be broken down even further. For instance, the nonacademic self-concept includes the components of physical appearance, peer relations, and physical ability. Academic self-concept is similarly divided. Research on students' self-concepts in English, mathematics, and nonacademic realms has found that the separate self-concepts are not always correlated, although there is overlap among them (Marsh, 1990; Marsh & Holmes, 1990; Burnett, 1996).

Social Comparison. If someone asks you how good you are at math, how would you respond? Most of us would compare our performance to others who are roughly of the same age and educational level. It is unlikely that we'd answer the question by comparing ourselves either to Albert Einstein or to a kindergartner just learning about numbers.

Elementary-school-age children begin to follow the same sort of reasoning when they seek to understand how able they are. Whereas earlier they tended to consider their abilities in terms of absolutes, now they begin to use social comparison processes to determine their levels of accomplishment during middle childhood (Weiss, Ebbeck, & Horn, 1997).

social comparison the desire to evaluate one's own behavior, abilities, expertise, and opinions by comparing them to those of others

Social comparison is the desire to evaluate one's own behavior, abilities, expertise, and opinions by comparing them to those of others. According to a theory first suggested by psychologist Leon Festinger (1954), when concrete, objective measures of ability are lacking, people turn to *social reality* to evaluate themselves. Social reality refers to understanding that is derived from how others act, think, feel, and view the world.

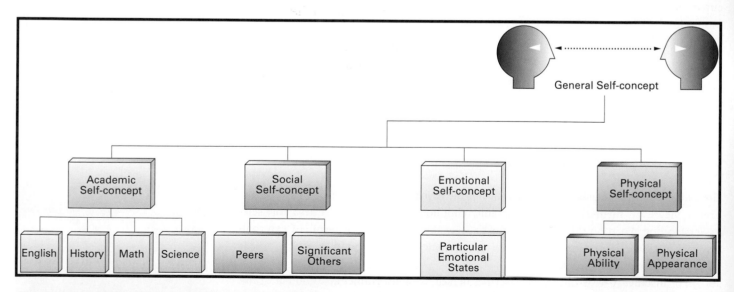

Figure 10-1 **Looking Inward: The Development of Self**

As children get older, their views of self become more differentiated, comprising several personal and academic spheres. What cognitive changes make this possible?

(Adapted from Shavelson, Hubner, & Stanton, 1976.)

According to Erik Erikson, middle childhood encompasses the industry-versus-inferiority stage, characterized by a focus on meeting the challenges presented by the world.

But who provides the most adequate comparison? Generally, children compare themselves to persons who are similar along relevant dimensions. Consequently, when they cannot objectively evaluate their ability, children during middle childhood increasingly look to others who are similar to themselves (Ruble et al., 1989; Wood, 1989; Suls & Wills, 1991).

Although children typically compare themselves to similar others, in some cases—particularly when their self-esteem is at stake—they choose to make *downward social comparisons* with others who are obviously less competent or successful (Pyszczynski, Greenberg & LaPrelle, 1985).

Downward social comparison protects self-image. By comparing themselves to those who are less able, children ensure that they will come out on top and thereby preserve an image of themselves as successful.

Downward social comparison helps explain why some students in elementary schools with low achievement levels are found to have stronger academic self-esteem than very capable students in schools with high achievement levels. The reason seems to be that students in the low-achievement schools observe others who are not doing terribly well academically, and they feel relatively good by comparison. In contrast, students in the high-achievement schools may find themselves competing with a more academically proficient group of students, and their perception of their performance may suffer in comparison. In some ways, then, it is better to be a big fish in a small pond than a small fish in a big one (Marsh & Parker, 1984).

Self-Esteem: Developing a Positive—or Negative—View of Oneself

Children don't dispassionately view themselves just in terms of an itemization of physical and psychological characteristics. Instead, they make judgments about themselves as being good or bad in particular ways. **Self-esteem** is an individual's overall and specific positive and negative self-evaluation. Whereas self-concept reflects beliefs and cognitions about the self, self-esteem is more emotionally oriented (Baumeister, 1993).

Self-esteem develops in important ways during middle childhood. As we've noted, children increasingly compare themselves to others, and as they do, they assess how well

self-esteem an individual's overall and specific positive and negative self-evaluation

they measure up to society's standards. In addition, they increasingly develop their own internal standards of success, and they can see how well they compare to those.

One of the advances that occurs during middle childhood is an increasing differentiation of self-esteem. At the age of 7, most children have self-esteem that reflects a global, undifferentiated view of themselves. If their overall self-esteem is positive, they assume that they are relatively good at all things. Conversely, if their overall self-esteem is negative, they assume that they are inadequate at most things (Marsh & Shavelson, 1985; Harter, 1990b). As children progress into the middle childhood years, however, their self-esteem, like their self-concept, becomes differentiated: higher for some areas that they evaluate and lower for others.

Change and Stability in Self-Esteem.   Generally, the self-esteem of most children tends to increase during middle childhood, with a brief decline around the age of 12. Although there are probably several reasons for the decline, the main one appears to be the school transition that typically occurs around this age: Students leaving elementary school and entering either middle school or junior high school show a decline in self-esteem, which then gradually rises again (Eccles et al., 1989).

Children with chronically low self-esteem face a tough road, in part because their self-esteem becomes enmeshed in a cycle of failure that grows increasingly difficult to break. Assume, for instance, that Harry, a student with chronically low self-esteem, is facing an important test. Because of his low self-esteem, he expects to do poorly. As a consequence, he is quite anxious—so anxious that he is unable to concentrate well and study effectively. Furthermore, he may decide not to study much, because he figures that if he's going to do badly anyway, why bother studying?

Ultimately, of course, Harry's high anxiety and lack of effort bring about the result he expected: He does poorly on the test. This failure, which confirms Harry's expectation, reinforces his low self-esteem, and the cycle of failure continues (see Figure 10-2).

Parents can help break the cycle of failure by promoting their child's self-esteem. The best way to do this is through the use of the *authoritative* child-rearing style that we discussed in Chapter 8. Authoritative parents are warm and emotionally supportive, while still setting clear limits for their children's behavior. In contrast, other parenting styles have less positive effects on self-esteem. Parents who are highly punitive and controlling send a message to their children that they are untrustworthy and unable to make good decisions—a message that can undermine children's sense of adequacy, and highly indulgent

Figure 10-2 **A Cycle of Low Self-Esteem**

Because children with low self-esteem may expect to do poorly on a test, they may experience high anxiety and not work as hard as those with higher self-esteem. As a result, they actually do perform badly on the test, which in turn confirms their negative view of themselves. Can this cycle be broken?

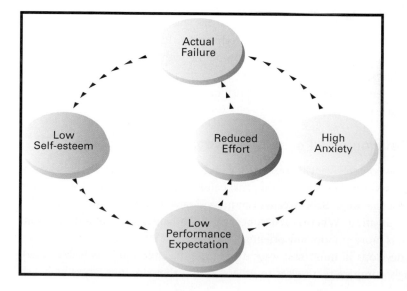

In pioneering research conducted several decades ago, African American girls' preference for white dolls was viewed as an indication of low self-esteem. More recent evidence, however, suggest that whites and African American children show little difference in self-esteem.

parents can create a false sense of self-esteem in their children, which ultimately may be just as damaging to children (Damon, 1995).

Ethnicity and Self-Esteem. If you were a member of a minority group whose members routinely experienced prejudice and discrimination, how might your self-esteem be affected?

For many decades, developmentalists hypothesized—and found supportive evidence for the notion—that members of minority groups would feel lower self-esteem than members of majority groups. In particular, the evidence seemed clear that African Americans had lower self-esteem than whites (Deutsch, 1967).

Some of the first evidence was found in a set of pioneering studies a generation ago in which African American children were shown a black doll and a white doll (Clark & Clark, 1947). In the study, the children received a series of requests, including "Give me the doll that looks bad" and "Give me the doll that is a nice color." In every case, the African American children preferred white dolls over black ones. The interpretation that was drawn from the study: The self-esteem of the African American children was low.

Subsequent research in the 1950s and 1960s supported the notion that children showed lower self-esteem as a consequence of being members of minority groups that were discriminated against. In fact, some research even suggested that members of minority groups preferred members of majority groups to members of their own groups, and that they rejected membership in their own groups, showing a form of self-hatred due to minority-group status (Milner, 1983).

More recent theorizing, however, sheds a different light on the issue of self-esteem and racial group membership. According to *social identity theory,* members of a minority group are likely to accept the negative views held by a majority group only if they perceive that there is little realistic possibility of changing the power and status differences between the groups. If minority group members feel that prejudice and discrimination can potentially be reduced, and they blame society for the prejudice and not themselves, self-esteem should not differ between majority and minority groups (Tajfel, 1982; Turner & Onorato, 1999).

In fact, as group pride and ethnic awareness on the part of minority group members has grown, differences in self-esteem between members of different ethnic groups have narrowed. This trend has further been supported by an increased sensitivity to the importance of multiculturalism (Harter, 1990a; Duckitt, 1994; Goodstein & Ponterotto, 1997).

Developmental Diversity

Are Children of Immigrant Families Well Adjusted?

Immigration to the United States has undergone a significant rise in the last 30 years. More than 13 million children in the U.S. are either foreign born or the children of immigrants—some one-fifth of the total population of children.

How well are these children of immigrants faring? Quite well. In fact, in some ways they are better off than their nonimmigrant peers. For example, they tend to have equal or better grades in school and better health-related adjustment than children whose parents were born in the United States. Psychologically, they also do quite well, showing similar levels of self-esteem to nonimmigrant children, although they do report feeling less popular and less in control of their lives (Kao & Tienda, 1995; Kao, in press; Harris, in press).

Why is the adjustment of immigrant children so generally positive? One answer is that often their socioeconomic status is relatively higher. In spite of stereotypes that immigrant families come from lower social classes, many in fact are well educated and come to the U.S. seeking greater opportunities.

But socioeconomic status is only part of the story, for many immigrant children are not financially well off. However, they are often more highly motivated to succeed and place greater value on education than do children in nonimmigrant families. In addition, many immigrant children come from societies that emphasize collectivism, and consequently they may feel more obligation and duty towards their family to succeed. Finally, having a strong cultural identity relating to their country of origin may prevent immigrant children from adopting undesirable behaviors—perceived as "American"—such as materialism or selfishness (Fuligni, Tseng, & Lam, 1999).

In short, during the middle childhood years, children in immigrant families typically do quite well in the United States. The story is less clear, however, when immigrant children reach adolescence and adulthood. Although some research suggests that the longer an individual has been in the U.S., the lower the level of adjustment, the findings are far from definitive. Research is just beginning to clarify the process by which adjustment changes over the course of the life span (Fulgini, 1998).

Immigrant children tend to fare quite well in the United States, partly because many come from societies that emphasize collectivism, and consequently may feel more obligation and duty to their family to succeed. What are some other cultural differences that can support the success of immigrant children?

Moral Development

Your wife is near death from an unusual kind of cancer. One drug exists that the physicians think might save her—a form of radium that a scientist in a nearby city has recently developed. The drug, though, is expensive to manufacture, and the scientist is charging ten times what the drug costs him to make. He pays $1,000 for the radium and charges $10,000 for a small dose. You have gone to everyone you know to borrow money, but you can get together only $2,500—one-quarter of what you need. You've told the scientist that your wife is dying and asked him to sell it more cheaply or let you pay later. But the scientist has said, "No, I discovered the drug and I'm going to make money from it." In desperation, you consider breaking into the scientist's laboratory to steal the drug for your wife. Should you do it?

According to developmental psychologist Lawrence Kohlberg and his colleagues, the answer that children give to this question reveals central aspects of their sense of morality and justice. He suggests that people's responses to moral dilemmas such as this one reveal the stage of moral development they have attained—as well as yield information about their general level of cognitive development (Kohlberg, 1984; Colby & Kohlberg, 1987).

Kohlberg contends that people pass through a series of stages in the evolution of their sense of justice and in the kind of reasoning they use to make moral judgments. Primarily due to cognitive characteristics that we discussed earlier, younger school-age children tend to think either in terms of concrete, unvarying rules ("It is always wrong to steal" or "I'll be punished if I steal") or in terms of the rules of society ("Good people don't steal" or "What if everyone stole?").

By the time they reach adolescence, however, individuals are able to reason on a higher plane, typically having reached Piaget's stage of formal operations. They are capable of comprehending abstract, formal principles of morality, and they consider cases such as the one presented above in terms of broader issues of morality and of right and wrong ("Stealing may be justifiable if you are following your own standards of conscience").

Kohlberg suggests that moral development can best be understood within the context of a three-level sequence, which is further subdivided into six stages (see Table 10-1). At the lowest level, *preconventional morality* (Stages 1 and 2), people follow unvarying rules based on punishments or rewards. For example, a student at the preconventional level might evaluate the moral dilemma posed in the story by saying that it was not worth stealing the drug because if you were caught, you would go to jail.

In the next level, that of *conventional morality* (Stages 3 and 4), people approach moral problems in terms of their own position as good, responsible members of society. Some students at this level would decide *against* stealing the drug because they think they would feel guilty or dishonest for violating social norms. Other students would decide *in favor* of stealing the drug because if they did nothing in this situation, they would be unable to face others. All of these students would be reasoning at the conventional level of morality.

Finally, individuals using *postconventional morality* (Level 3; Stages 5 and 6) invoke universal moral principles that are considered broader than the rules of the particular society in which they live. Students who feel that they would condemn themselves if they did not steal the drug because they would not be living up to their own moral principles would be reasoning at the postconventional level.

Kohlberg's theory proposes that people move through the periods of moral development in a fixed order and that they are unable to reach the highest stage until adolescence, due to deficits in cognitive development that are not overcome until then (Kurtines & Gewirtz, 1987). However, not everyone is presumed to reach the highest stages: Kohlberg found that postconventional reasoning is relatively rare.

Although Kohlberg's theory provides a fairly good account of the development of moral *judgments*, it is less adequate in predicting moral *behavior*. A good deal of research,

Table 10-1

KOHLBERG'S SEQUENCE OF MORAL REASONING

| | | SAMPLE MORAL REASONING | |
| | | In Favor of Stealing | Against Stealing |
Level	**Stage**		
LEVEL 1 Preconventional morality: At this level, the concrete interests of the individual are considered in terms of rewards and punishments.	*STAGE 1* Obedience and punishment orientation: At this stage, people stick to rules in order to avoid punishment, and obedience occurs for its own sake.	"If you let your wife die, you will get in trouble. You'll be blamed for not spending the money to save her, and there'll be an investigation of you and the druggist for your wife's death."	"You shouldn't steal the drug because you'll get caught and sent to jail if you do. If you do get away, your conscience will bother you thinking how the police will catch up with you at any minute."
	STAGE 2 Reward orientation: At this stage, rules are followed only for a person's own benefit. Obedience occurs because of rewards that are received.	"If you do happen to get caught, you could give the drug back and you wouldn't get much of a sentence. It wouldn't bother you much to serve a little jail term, if you have your wife when you get out."	"You may not get much of a jail term if you steal the drug, but your wife will probably die before you get out, so it won't do much good. If your wife dies, you shouldn't blame yourself; it isn't your fault she has cancer."
LEVEL 2 Conventional morality: At this level, people approach moral problems as members of society. They are interested in pleasing others by acting as good members of society.	*STAGE 3* "Good boy" morality: Individuals at this stage show an interest in maintaining the respect of others and doing what is expected of them.	"No one will think you're bad if you steal the drug, but your family will think you're an inhuman husband if you don't. If you let your wife die, you'll never be able to look anybody in the face again."	"It isn't just the druggist who will think you're a criminal; everyone else will, too. After you steal the drug, you'll feel bad thinking how you've brought dishonor on your family and yourself; you won't be able to face anyone again."
	STAGE 4 Authority and social-order-maintaining morality: People at this stage conform to society's rules and consider that "right" is what society defines as right.	"If you have any sense of honor, you won't let your wife die just because you're afraid to do the only thing that will save her. You'll always feel guilty that you caused her death if you don't do your duty to her."	"You're desperate and you may not know you're doing wrong when you steal the drug. But you'll know you did wrong after you're sent to jail. You'll always feel guilty for your dishonesty and law-breaking."
LEVEL 3 Postconventional morality: At this level, people use moral principles which are seen as broader than those of any particular society.	*STAGE 5* Morality of contract, individual rights, and democratically accepted law: People at this stage do what is right because of a sense of obligation to laws which are agreed upon within society. They perceive that laws can be modified as part of changes in an implicit social contract.	"You'll lose other people's respect, not gain it, if you don't steal. If you let your wife die, it will be out of fear, not out of reasoning. So you'll just lose self-respect and probably the respect of others, too."	"You'll lose your standing and respect in the community and violate the law. You'll lose respect for yourself if you're carried away by emotion and forget the long-range point of view."
	STAGE 6 Morality of individual principles and conscience: At this final stage, a person follows laws because they are based on universal ethical principles. Laws that violate the principles are disobeyed.	"If you don't steal the drug, and if you let your wife die, you'll always condemn yourself for it afterward. You won't be blamed and you'll have lived up to the outside rule of the law, but you won't have lived up to your own standards of conscience."	"If you steal the drug, you won't be blamed by other people, but you'll condemn yourself because you won't have lived up to your own conscience and standards of honesty."

(*Source:* Adapted from Kohlberg, 1969.)

for example, suggests that aspects of moral conduct are clearly related to Kohlberg's levels of moral reasoning, but the results are often complex and not easy to interpret. For instance, children who reason at Stage 1 and Stage 3 tend to be the best behaved in school, while those who reason at Stage 2 are more apt to exhibit poor social behavior in school settings (Richards et al., 1992; Langford, 1995; Carpendale, 2000).

In another example, one experiment found that 15 percent of students who reasoned at the postconventional level of morality—the highest category—cheated on a task, although they were not as likely to cheat as those at lower levels, where more than half of the students cheated. Clearly, though, knowing what is morally right does not always mean acting that way (Malinowski & Smith, 1985; Snarey, 1985; Killen & Hart, 1995).

Kohlberg's theory has also been criticized because of his reliance on members of Western cultures. In fact, cross-cultural research finds that members of more industrialized, technologically advanced cultures move through the stages more rapidly than members of nonindustrialized countries. Why? One explanation is that Kohlberg's higher stages are based on moral reasoning involving governmental and societal institutions. In less industrialized areas, morality may be based more on relationships between people in a particular village. In short, the nature of morality may differ in diverse cultures, and Kohlberg's theory is more suited for Western cultures (Snarey, 1995).

An aspect of Kohlberg's theory that has proved even more problematic is the difficulty it has explaining *girls'* moral judgments. Because the theory initially was based largely on data from males, some researchers have argued that it does a better job describing boys' moral development than girls' moral development. This would explain the surprising finding that women typically score at a lower level than men on tests of moral judgments using Kohlberg's stage sequence. This result has led to an alternative account of moral development for girls.

Moral Development in Girls. Psychologist Carol Gilligan (1982; 1987) has suggested that differences in the ways boys and girls are raised in our society lead to basic distinctions in how men and women view moral behavior. According to her, boys view morality primarily in terms of broad principles such as justice or fairness, while girls see it in terms of responsibility toward individuals and willingness to sacrifice themselves to help specific individuals within the context of particular relationships. Compassion for individuals, then, is a more prominent factor in moral behavior for women than it is for men (Gilligan, Ward, & Taylor, 1988; Gilligan, Lyons, & Hammer, 1990; Gump, Baker, & Roll, 2000).

Some critics feel the differences between Gilligan's and Kohlberg's stages are too pronounced, particularly in light of research showing that males and females both use "justice" and "care" orientation in making moral judgments.

Table 10-2

GILLIGAN'S THREE STATES OF MORAL DEVELOPMENT FOR WOMEN

Stage	Characteristics	Example
Stage 1 Orientation toward individual survival	Initial concentration is on what is practical and best for self. Gradual transition from selfishness to responsibility, which includes thinking about what would be best for others.	A first-grader may insist on playing only games of her own choosing when playing with a friend.
Stage 2 Goodness as self-sacrifice	Initial view is that a woman must sacrifice her own wishes to what other people want. Gradual transition from "goodness" to "truth," which takes into account needs of both self and others.	Now older, the same girl may believe that to be a good friend, she must play the games her friend chooses, even if she herself doesn't like them.
Stage 3 Morality of nonviolence	A moral equivalence is established between self and others. Hurting anyone—including one's self—is seen as immoral. Most sophisticated form of reasoning, according to Gilligan.	The same girl may realize that both friends must enjoy their time together and look for activities that both she and her friend can enjoy.

Gilligan views morality as developing among females in a three-stage process (summarized in Table 10-2). In the first stage, called "orientation toward individual survival," females first concentrate on what is practical and best for them, gradually making a transition from selfishness to responsibility, in which they think about what would be best for others. In the second stage, termed "goodness as self-sacrifice," females begin to think that they must sacrifice their own wishes to what other people want. Ideally, women make a transition from "goodness" to "truth," in which they take into account their own needs plus those of others. This transition leads to the third stage, "morality of nonviolence," in which women come to see that hurting anyone is immoral—including hurting themselves. This realization establishes a moral equivalence between themselves and others and represents, according to Gilligan, the most sophisticated level of moral reasoning.

It is obvious that Gilligan's sequence of stages is quite different from Kohlberg's, and some developmentalists have suggested that her rejection of Kohlberg's work is too sweeping and that gender differences are not as pronounced as first thought (Colby & Damon, 1987). For instance, some research has found that both males and females use similar "justice" and "care" orientations in making moral judgments. Clearly, the question of how boys and girls differ in their moral orientations, as well as the nature of moral development in general, is far from settled (Kahn, 1997; Wygant, 1997; Chiu et al., 1997; Cassidy, Chu, & Dahlsgaard, 1997).

Review and Rethink

REVIEW

■ According to Erikson, children at this time are in the industry-versus-inferiority stage.

■ In the middle childhood years, children begin to use social comparison and self-concepts based on psychological rather than physical characteristics.

■ During the middle childhood years, self-esteem is based on comparisons with others and internal standards of success; if self-esteem is low, the result can be a cycle of failure.

■ According to Kohlberg, moral development proceeds from a concern with rewards and punishments, through a focus on social conventions and rules, toward a sense of universal moral principles. Gilligan has suggested, however, that girls may follow an alternative progression of moral development.

RETHINK

■ What is an example of the relationship between low self-esteem and the cycle of failure in an area other than academics? How might the cycle of failure be broken?

■ Kohlberg and Gilligan each suggest the existence of three major levels of moral development. Are any of their levels comparable? In which level of either theory do you think that the largest discrepancy between males and females would be observed?

Relationships: Building Friendship in Middle Childhood

In Lunch Room Number Two, Jamillah and her new classmates chew slowly on sandwiches and sip quietly on straws from cartons of milk. . . . Boys and girls look timidly at the strange faces across the table from them, looking for someone who might play with them in the schoolyard, someone who might become a friend.

For these children, what happens in the schoolyard will be just as important as what happens in the school. And when they're out on the playground, there will be no one to protect them. No child will hold back to keep from beating them at a game, humiliating them in a test of skill, or harming them in a fight. No one will run interference or guarantee membership in a group. Out on the playground, it's sink or swim. No one automatically becomes your friend. (Kotre & Hall, 1990, pp. 112–113)

As Jamillah and her classmates demonstrate, friendship comes to play an increasingly important role during middle childhood. Children grow progressively more sensitive to the importance of friends, and building and maintaining friendships becomes a large part of children's social lives.

The formation of friendships influences children's development in several ways. For instance, friendships provide children with information about the world and other people as well as about themselves. Friends provide emotional support that allows children to respond more effectively to stress. They also provide support by helping children avoid being the target of aggression.

Recall the Hendrickson twins described in the chapter prologue. They and their neighborhood friends are experiencing all of these benefits—and more. They are learning that friends can teach children how to manage and control their emotions and help them interpret their own emotional experiences. Friendships also provide a training ground for communicating and interacting with others, and they can foster intellectual growth. Finally, friendships allow children to practice their skills in forming close relationships with others—skills that will become increasingly important in their future lives (Asher & Parker, 1991; Hartup & Stevens, 1997; Harris, 1998; Nangle & Erdley, 2001).

Although friends and other peers become increasingly influential throughout middle childhood, their influence does not become greater than the influence of parents and other family members. Most developmentalists reject the argument that peers are the primary influence on psychological functioning, instead suggesting that it is a combination of factors that determines children's development during middle childhood (Harris, 2000; Vandell, 2000). For that reason, we'll talk more about the influence of family later in this chapter.

Mutual trust is considered to be the centerpiece of friendship during middle childhood.

Stages of Friendship: Changing Views of Friends

During middle childhood, a child's conception of the nature of friendship undergoes some profound changes. According to developmental psychologist William Damon, a child's view of friendship passes through three distinct stages (Damon, 1977; Damon & Hart, 1988).

In the first stage, which ranges from around 4 to 7 years of age, children see friends as others who like them and with whom they share toys and other activities. They view the children with whom they spend the most time as their friends. For instance, a kindergartner who was asked, "How do you know that someone is your best friend?" responded in this way:

> I sleep over at his house sometimes. When he's playing ball with his friends he'll let me play. When I slept over, he let me get in front of him in 4-squares. He likes me. (Damon, 1983, p. 140)

What children in this first stage don't do much of, however, is to take others' personal qualities into consideration. For instance, they don't see their friendships as being based upon their peers' unique positive personal traits. Instead, they use a very concrete approach to deciding who is a friend, primarily dependent upon others' behavior. They like those who share and with whom they can share, while they don't like those who don't share, who hit, or who don't play with them. In sum, in the first stage, friends are viewed largely in terms of presenting opportunities for pleasant interactions.

In the next stage, however, children's view of friendship becomes more complicated. Lasting from around age 8 to age 10, this stage covers a period in which children take others' personal qualities and traits as well as the rewards they provide into consideration. But the centerpiece of friendship in this second stage is mutual trust. Friends are seen as those who can be counted on to help out when they are needed. This means that violations of trust are taken very seriously, and friends cannot make amends for such violations just by engaging in positive play, as they might at earlier ages. Instead, the expectation is that formal explanations and formal apologies must be provided before a friendship can be reestablished.

The third stage of friendship begins toward the end of middle childhood, from 11 to 15 years of age. During this period, children begin to develop the view of friendship that they hold during adolescence. Although we'll discuss this perspective in detail in Chapter 12, the main criteria for friendship shift toward intimacy and loyalty. Friendship is characterized by psychological closeness, mutual disclosure, and exclusivity. By the time they reach the end of middle childhood, children seek out friends who will be loyal, and they come to view friendship not so much in terms of shared activities as in terms of the psychological benefits that friendship brings (Newcomb & Bagwell, 1995).

Children also develop clear ideas about which behaviors they seek in their friends—and which they dislike. As can be seen in Table 10-3, fifth- and sixth-graders most enjoy others who invite them to participate in activities and who are helpful, both physically and psychologically. In contrast, displays of physical or verbal aggression, among other behaviors, are disliked.

Individual Differences in Friendship: What Makes a Child Popular?

Why is it that some children, like the Hendrickson twins described in the chapter prologue, are the schoolyard equivalent of the life of the party, while others are social isolates whose overtures toward their peers are dismissed or disdained?

Developmentalists have attempted to answer this question by examining individual differences in popularity, seeking to identify the reasons why some children climb the ladder of popularity while others remain firmly on the ground.

Table 10-3

THE MOST-LIKED AND LEAST-LIKED BEHAVIORS THAT CHILDREN NOTE IN THEIR FRIENDS, IN ORDER OF IMPORTANCE

Most-Liked Behaviors	Least-Liked Behaviors
Having a sense of humor	Verbal aggression
Being nice or friendly	Expressions of anger
Being helpful	Dishonesty
Being complimentary	Being critical or criticizing
Inviting one to participate in games, etc.	Being greedy or bossy
Sharing	Physical aggression
Avoiding unpleasant behavior	Being annoying or bothersome
Giving one permission or control	Teasing
Providing instructions	Interfering with achievements
Loyalty	Unfaithfulness
Performing admirably	Violating of rules
Facilitating achievements	Ignoring others

(*Source*: Adapted from Zarbatany, Hartmann, & Rankin, 1990.)

Status Among School-Age Children: Establishing One's Position. Who's on top? Although school-age children are not likely to articulate such a question, the reality of children's friendships is that they exhibit clear hierarchies in terms of status. **Status** is the evaluation of a role or person by other relevant members of a group. Children who have higher status have greater access to available resources, such as games, toys, books, and information. In contrast, lower-status children are more likely to follow the lead of children of higher status. Thinking back to the children in the chapter prologue, for example, when Bryan Hendrickson declared that the cardboard boxes would become spaceships, the other boys seemed willing to follow his direction.

status the evaluation of a role or person by other relevant members of a group

Status is an important determinant of children's friendships. High-status children tend to form friendships with higher-status individuals, while lower-status children are more likely to have friends of lower status. Status is also related to the number of friends a child has: Higher-status children are more apt to have a greater number of friends than those of lower status. Consider, for example, the large group of friends that hang around the Hendrickson boys' house.

But it is not only the quantity of social interactions that separates high-status children from lower-status children; the nature of their interactions is also different. Higher-status children are more likely to be viewed as friends by other children. They are more likely to form cliques, groups that are viewed as exclusive and desirable, and they tend to interact with a greater number of other children. In contrast, children of lower status are more likely to play with younger or less popular children (Ladd, 1983).

In short, popularity is a reflection of children's status. School-age children who are mid to high in status are more likely to initiate and coordinate joint social behavior, making their general level of social activity higher than that of children low in social status (Erwin, 1993).

What Personal Characteristics Lead to Popularity? Popular children share several personality characteristics. They are usually helpful, cooperating with others on joint projects. Again, consider the Hendrickson twins and their cooperative games with the cardboard boxes.

A variety of factors lead some children to be unpopular and socially isolated from their peers.

social competence the collection of social skills that permit individuals to perform successfully in social settings

social problem-solving the use of strategies for solving social conflicts in ways that are satisfactory both to oneself and to others

Popular children are also funny, tending to have good senses of humor and to appreciate others' attempts at humor. Compared with children who are less popular, they are better able to understand others' emotional experiences by more accurately reading their nonverbal behavior. They also can control their nonverbal behavior more effectively, thereby presenting themselves well. In short, popular children are high in **social competence,** the collection of individual social skills that permit individuals to perform successfully in social settings (Feldman, Philippot, & Custrini, 1991; Feldman, Tomasian, & Coats, 1999).

Generally speaking, then, popular children are typically friendly, open, and cooperative. On the other hand, some popular children have a very different profile. For example, one significant subgroup of popular boys displays an array of negative behaviors. Despite acting aggressive, being disruptive, and causing trouble, they are seen as cool and tough by their peers, and they are remarkably popular (Rodkin et al., 2000).

Social Problem-Solving Abilities. Another factor that relates to children's popularity is their skill at social problem-solving. **Social problem-solving** refers to the use of strategies for solving social conflicts in ways that are satisfactory both to oneself and to others. Because social conflicts among school-age children are a not infrequent occurrence—even among the best of friends—successful strategies for dealing with them are an important element of social success (Laursen, Hartup, & Koplas, 1996; Rose & Asher, 1999).

According to developmental psychologist Kenneth Dodge, successful social problem-solving proceeds through a series of steps that correspond to children's information-processing strategies (see Figure 10-3). Dodge argues that the manner in which children solve social problems is a consequence of the decisions that they make at each point in the sequence (Dodge, 1985a; Dodge & Crick, 1990; Dodge & Price, 1994).

By carefully delineating each of the stages, Dodge provides a means by which interventions can be targeted toward a specific child's deficits. For instance, some children routinely misinterpret the meaning of other children's behavior (Step 2), and then respond according to their misinterpretation.

Consider, for example, Frank, a fourth-grader, who is playing a game with Bill. While playing the game, Bill begins to get angry because he is losing. If Frank mistakenly assumes that Bill is angry not because he is losing but because of something that Frank has

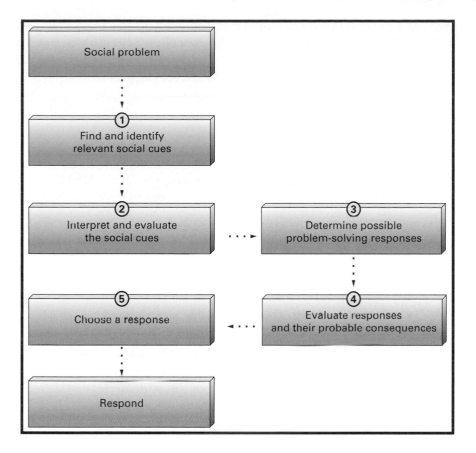

Figure 10-3 **Problem-Solving Steps**

Children's problem-solving proceeds through several steps involving different information-processing strategies.

(*Source:* Based on Dodge, 1985.)

done, Frank's misunderstanding may lead *him* to react with anger, making the situation more volatile. If Frank interprets the source of Bill's anger more accurately, Frank may be able to behave in a more effective manner, thereby defusing the situation.

Generally, children who are popular are better at interpreting the meaning of others' behavior. Furthermore, they possess a wider inventory of techniques for dealing with social problems. In contrast, less popular children tend to be less effective at understanding the causes of others' behavior, and their strategies for dealing with social problems are more limited (Vitaro & Pelletier, 1991; Rose & Asher, 1999).

Teaching Social Competence. Can anything be done to help unpopular children learn social competence? Happily, the answer appears to be yes. Several programs have been developed to teach children a set of social skills that seem to underlie general social competence. For example, in one experimental program, a group of unpopular fifth- and sixth-graders were taught the skills that underlie such abilities as holding a conversation with friends. They were taught ways to disclose material about themselves, to learn about others by asking questions, and to offer help and suggestions to others in a nonthreatening way.

Compared with a group of children who did not receive such training, the children who were in the experiment interacted more with their peers, held more conversations, developed higher self-esteem, and—most critically—were more accepted by their peers than before training (Bierman & Furman, 1984; Asher & Rose, 1997).

Gender and Friendships: The Sex Segregation of Middle Childhood

Boys are idiots. Girls have cooties.

At least, those are the typical views offered by boys and girls regarding members of the opposite sex during the elementary school years. Avoidance of the opposite sex becomes quite pronounced during those years, to the degree that the social networks of most

Though same-sex groupings dominate in middle childhood, when boys and girls do make occasional forays into each others' territory, there are often romantic overtones. Such behavior has been termed "border work."

boys and girls consist almost entirely of same-sex groupings (Gottman, 1986; Adler, Kless, & Adler, 1992; Lewis & Phillipsen, 1998). For example, the Hendrickson twins, described in the chapter prologue, spent much of the day with their all-boy group of friends before allowing their older sister and some other girls and boys to join them.

Interestingly, the segregation of friendships according to gender occurs in almost all societies. In nonindustrialized societies, same-gender segregation may be the result of the types of activities that children engage in. For instance, in many cultures, boys are assigned one type of chore and girls another (Harkness & Super, 1985; Whiting & Edwards, 1988). Participation in different activities may not provide the whole explanation for sex segregation, however: Even children in more developed countries, who attend the same schools and participate in many of the same activities, still tend to avoid members of the other gender.

When boys and girls make occasional forays into the other gender's territory, the action often has romantic overtones. For instance, girls may threaten to kiss a boy, or boys might try to lure girls into chasing them. Such behavior, termed "border work," helps to emphasize the clear boundaries that exist between the two sexes. In addition, it may pave the way for future interactions that do involve romantic or sexual interests, when school-age children reach adolescence and cross-sex interactions become more socially endorsed (Thorne, 1986; Beal, 1994).

The lack of cross-gender interaction in the middle childhood years means that boys' and girls' friendships are restricted to members of their own gender. Furthermore, the nature of friendships within these two gender groups is quite different.

Boys typically have larger networks of friends than girls, and they tend to play in groups, rather than pairing off. The status hierarchy is usually fairly blatant, with an acknowledged leader and members falling into particular levels of status. Because of the fairly rigid rankings that represent the relative social power of those in the group, known as the **dominance hierarchy,** members of higher status can safely question and oppose children lower in the hierarchy (Beal, 1994).

dominance hierarchy rankings that represent the relative social power of those in a group

Boys tend to be concerned with their place in the status hierarchy, and they attempt to maintain their status and improve upon it. This makes for a style of play known as *restrictive*. In restrictive play, interactions are interrupted when a child feels that his status is challenged. Thus, a boy who feels that he is unjustly challenged by a peer of lower status may attempt to end the interaction by scuffling over a toy or otherwise behaving assertively. Consequently, boys' play tends to come in bursts, rather than in more extended, tranquil episodes (Boulton & Smith, 1990; Benenson & Apostoleris, 1993).

The language of friendship used among boys reflects their concern over status and challenge. For instance, consider this conversation between two boys who were good friends:

> Child 1: Why don't you get out of my yard?
> Child 2: Why don't you *make* me get out the yard?
> Child 1: I *know* you don't want that.
> Child 2: You're not gonna make me get out the yard cuz you can't.
> Child 1: Don't force me.
> Child 2: You can't. Don't force me to hurt you (*snickers*). (Goodwin, 1990, p. 37)

Friendship patterns among girls are quite different. Rather than having a wide network of friends, school-age girls focus on one or two "best friends" who are of relatively equal status. In contrast to boys, who seek out status differences, girls profess to avoid differences in status, preferring to maintain friendships at equal-status levels.

Conflicts among school-age girls are usually solved through compromise, by ignoring the situation, or by giving in, rather than by seeking to make one's own point of view prevail. In sum, the goal is to smooth over disagreements, making social interaction easy and nonconfrontational (Goodwin, 1990).

According to developmental psychologist Carole Beal, the motivation of girls to solve social conflict indirectly does not stem from a lack of self-confidence or from apprehension over the use of more direct approaches. In fact, when school-age girls interact with other girls who are not considered friends or with boys, they can be quite confrontational. However, among friends their goal is to maintain equal-status relationships—ones lacking a dominance hierarchy (Beal, 1994).

The language used by girls tends to reflect their view of relationships. Rather than blatant demands ("Give me the pencil"), girls are more apt to use language that is less confrontational and directive. Girls tend to use indirect forms of verbs, such as "Let's go to the movies" or "Would you want to trade books with me?" rather than "I want to go to the movies" or "Let me have these books" (Goodwin, 1980, 1990).

As children age there is a decline in the number of and depth of friendships outside their own racial group. What are some ways in which schools can foster mutual acceptance?

Cross-Race Friendships: Integration In and Out of the Classroom

Are friendships color-blind? For the most part, the answer is no. Children's closest friendships tend largely to be with others of the same race. In fact, as children age there is a decline in the number and depth of friendships outside their own racial group. By the time they are 11 or 12, it appears that African American children become particularly aware of and sensitive to the prejudice and discrimination directed toward members of their race, and they are more apt to make ingroup–outgroup distinctions (Singleton & Asher, 1979; Hartup, 1983; Bigler, Jones, & Lobliner, 1997).

For instance, when third-graders from one long-time integrated school were asked to name a best friend, around one-quarter of white children and two-thirds of African American children chose a child of the other race. In contrast, by the time they reached tenth grade, less than 10 percent of whites and 5 percent of African Americans named a different-race best friend (Singleton & Asher, 1979; Asher, Singleton, & Taylor, 1982).

On the other hand, although they may not choose each other as best friends, whites and African Americans—as well as members of other minority groups—can show a high degree of mutual acceptance. This pattern is particularly true in schools with ongoing integration efforts. This makes sense: A good deal of research supports the notion that contact between majority and minority group members can reduce prejudice and discrimination (Gaertner et al., 1990; Wells & Crain, 1994; Kerner & Aboud, 1998).

Stopping the Torment: Dealing with Schoolyard Bullies

For some children, school represents a virtual battleground in which they live in constant fear of being the victim of a bully. In fact, according to the National Association of School Psychologists, 160,000 U.S. schoolchildren stay home from school each day because they are afraid of being bullied (Bosworth, Espelage, & Simon, 1999).

The victims of bullies typically share several characteristics. Most often they are loners who are fairly passive. They often cry easily, and they tend to lack the social skills that might otherwise defuse a bullying situation with humor. But even children without these characteristics are bullied at some point in their school careers: Some 90 percent of middle-school students report being bullied at some point in their time at school, beginning as early as the preschool years (Schwartz et al., 1997; Egan & Perry, 1998).

About 15 percent of students bully others at one time or another. About half of all bullies come from abusive homes—meaning, of course, that half don't. They tend to watch more television containing violence, and they misbehave more at home and at school than non-bullies. When their bullying gets them into trouble, they may try to lie their way out of the situation, and they show little remorse for their victimization of

The Informed Consumer of Development
Increasing Children's Social Competence

It is clear that building and maintaining friendships is critical in children's lives. Is there anything that parents and teachers can do to increase children's social competence?

The answer is a clear yes. Among the strategies that can work are the following:

▶ Encourage social interaction. Teachers can devise ways in which children are led to take part in group activities, and parents can encourage membership in such groups as Brownies and Cub Scouts or participation in team sports.

▶ Teach listening skills to children. Show them how to listen carefully and respond to the underlying meaning of a communication as well as its overt content.

▶ Make children aware that people display emotions and moods nonverbally and that consequently they should pay attention to others' nonverbal behavior, not only to what they are saying on a verbal level.

▶ Teach conversational skills, including the importance of asking questions and self-disclosure. Encourage students to use "I" statements in which they clarify their own feelings or opinions, and avoid making generalizations about others.

▶ Don't ask children to choose teams or groups publicly. Instead, assign children randomly: It works just as well in ensuring a distribution of abilities across groups and avoids the public embarrassment of a situation in which some children are chosen last.

others. Furthermore, bullies, compared with their peers, are more likely to break the law as adults. Although bullies are sometimes popular among their peers, some ironically find themselves victims of bullying themselves (Olweus, 1995; Boulton, 1999; Kaltiala-Heino et al., 2000; Haynie et al., 2001).

Despite the prevalence of bullying, it is possible to stop the behavior. Victims of bullying can be taught skills that help them defuse difficult circumstances that might otherwise lead to being victimized. They can be taught to protect themselves by leaving situations in which bullying can occur. They also need to increase their tolerance, understanding that they should not get upset by a bully's taunts and realizing that they are not responsible for the bully's behavior (Garrity, Jens, & Porter, 1996).

Of course, changing the behavior of the bully is also a good way to address the problem of bullying. For instance, bullies and their classmates need to be taught the importance of creating a caring, warm environment. By attempting to change the norms of the school to ones in which bullying is not tolerable and by helping children in general to exercise positive social skills, social pressures on bullies can help to keep their bullying in check (Seppa, 1996).

Review and Rethink

REVIEW

■ Children's understanding of friendship changes from the sharing of enjoyable activities, through the consideration of personal traits that can meet their needs, to a focus on intimacy and loyalty.

■ Friendships in childhood display status hierarchies. Improvements in social problem-solving and social information processing can lead to better interpersonal skills and greater popularity.

■ Boys and girls engage increasingly in same-sex friendships, with boys' friendships involving group relationships and girls' friendships characterized by equal-status pairings.

■ Interracial friendships decrease in frequency as children age, but equal-status contacts among members of different races can promote mutual acceptance and appreciation.

■ Many children are the victims of bullies during their school years, but both victims and bullies can be taught to reduce bullying.

RETHINK

■ Do you think the stages of friendship are a childhood phenomenon, or do adults' friendships display similar stages?

■ How might it be possible to decrease the segregation of friendships along racial lines? What factors would have to change in individuals or in society?

Family and School: Shaping Children's Behavior in Middle Childhood

Tamara's mother, Brenda, waited outside the door of her second-grade classroom for the end of the school day. Tamara came over to greet her mother as soon as she spotted her. "Mom, can Anna come over to play today?" Tamara demanded. Brenda had been looking forward to spending some time alone with Tamara, who had spent the last three days at her dad's house. But, Brenda reflected, Tamara hardly ever got to ask kids over after school, so she agreed to the request. Unfortunately, it turned out today wouldn't work for Anna's family, so they tried to find an alternate date. "How about Thursday?" Anna's mother suggested. Before Tamara could reply, her mother reminded her, "You'll have to ask your dad. You're at his house that night." Tamara's expectant face fell. "OK," she mumbled.

How will Tamara's adjustment be affected from splitting her time between the two homes where she lives with her divorced parents? What about the adjustment of her friend, Anna, who lives with both her parents, who both work outside the home? These are just a few of the questions we need to consider as we look at the ways that children's schooling and home life affect their lives during middle childhood.

Family: The Changing Home Environment

The original plot goes like this: First comes love. Then comes marriage. Then comes Mary with a baby carriage. But now there's a sequel: John and Mary break up. John moves in with Sally and her two boys. Mary takes the baby Paul. A year later Mary meets Jack, who is divorced with three children. They get married. Paul, barely 2 years old, now has a mother, a father, a stepmother, a stepfather, and five stepbrothers and stepsisters—as well as four sets of grandparents (biological and step) and countless aunts and uncles. And guess what? Mary's pregnant again. (Katrowitz & Wingert, 1990, p. 24)

We've already noted in earlier chapters the changes that have occurred in the structure of the family over the last few decades. With an increase in the number of parents who both work outside of the home, a soaring divorce rate, and a rise in single-parent families, the environment faced by children passing through middle childhood in the 21st century is very different from the one prior generations faced.

One of the basic challenges facing children and their parents is to navigate the independence that increasingly characterizes children's behavior during middle childhood. During the period, children move from being almost completely controlled by their parents to increasingly controlling their own destinies—or at least their everyday conduct. Middle childhood, then, is a period of **coregulation** in which children and parents jointly control behavior. Increasingly, parents provide broad, general guidelines for conduct, while children have control over their everyday behavior. For instance, parents may urge

coregulation a period in which parents and children jointly control children's behavior

their daughter to buy a balanced, nutritious school lunch each day, but their daughter's decision to regularly buy pizza and two desserts is very much her own.

Family Life. During the middle years of childhood, children spend significantly less time with their parents. Still, parents remain the major influence in their children's lives, and they are seen as providing essential assistance, advice, and direction (Furman & Buhrmester, 1992).

Siblings also have an important influence on children during middle childhood, for good and for bad. Although brothers and sisters can provide support, companionship, and a sense of security, they can also be a source of strife.

Sibling rivalry can occur, with siblings competing or quarreling with one another. Such rivalry can be most intense when siblings are similar in age and of the same gender (Howe & Ross, 1990). Parents may intensify sibling rivalry by being perceived as favoring one child over another. Such perceptions may or may not be accurate. For example, older siblings may be permitted more freedom, which the younger sibling may interpret as favoritism. In some cases, perceived favoritism not only leads to sibling rivalry, but may damage the self-esteem of the younger sibling (Ciricelli, 1995).

What about children who have no siblings? Although only children have no opportunity to develop sibling rivalry, they also miss out on the benefits that siblings can bring. Still, despite the stereotype that only children are spoiled and self-centered, the reality is that they are as well-adjusted as children with brothers and sisters. In fact, in some ways, only children are better-adjusted, often having higher self-esteem and stronger motivation to achieve. This is particularly good news for parents in the People's Republic of China, where a strict one-child policy is in effect. Studies there show that Chinese only-children often perform better than children with siblings (Falbo, 1992; Jiao, Ji, & Jing, 1996).

When Both Parents Work: How Do Children Fare? In most cases, children whose parents both work full-time outside of the home fare quite well. Children whose parents are loving, are sensitive to their children's needs, and provide appropriate substitute care typically develop no differently from children in families in which one of the parents does not work (Hoffman, 1989; Harvey, 1999).

The good adjustment of children whose mothers and fathers both work relates to the psychological adjustment of the parents, especially mothers. In general, women who are satisfied with their lives tend to be more nurturing with their children. When work provides a high level of satisfaction, then, mothers who work outside of the home may be more psychologically supportive of their children. Thus, it is not so much a question of whether a mother chooses to work full-time, to stay at home, or to arrange some combination of the two. What matters is how satisfied she is with the choices she has made (Scarr, Phillips, & McCartney, 1989; Barnett & Rivers, 1992; Gilbert, 1994).

Although we might expect that children whose parents both work would spend comparatively less time with their parents than children with one parent at home full-time, research suggests otherwise. Children with mothers and fathers who work full-time spend essentially the same amount of time with family, in class, with friends, and alone as children in families where one parent stays at home (Galambos & Dixon, 1984; Richards & Duckett, 1991, 1994).

What are children doing during the day? The activities that take the most time are sleeping and school. The next most frequent activities are watching television and playing, followed closely by personal care and eating. This has changed little over the past 20 years (see Figure 10-4). What has changed is the amount of time spent in supervised, structured settings. In 1981, 40 percent of a child's day was free time; by the late 1990s, only 25 percent of a child's day was unscheduled (Hofferth & Sandberg, 1998). (For another view of what children do with their time, see the *From Research to Practice* box.)

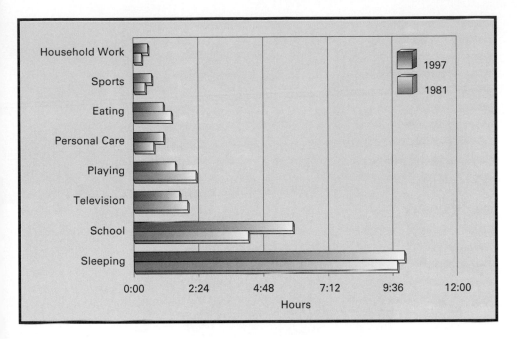

Figure 10-4 **How Kids Spend Their Time**

While the amount of time spent on some activities of children have remained constant over the years, others, such as playing and eating, have shown significant changes. What might account for these changes?

(*Source:* Hofferth & Sandberg, 1998.)

Divorce. Having divorced parents, like Tamara, the second-grader who was described earlier, is no longer very distinctive. Only around half the children in the United States spend their entire childhoods living in the same household with both their parents. The rest will

self-care children children who let themselves into their homes after school and wait alone until their caretakers return from work; previously known as *latchkey children*

From Research to Practice

Home and Alone: What Do Children Do?

When 10-year-old Johnetta Colvin comes home after finishing a day at Martin Luther King Elementary School, the first thing she does is grab a few cookies and turn on the computer. She takes a quick look at her email, and then goes over to the television and typically spends the next hour watching. During commercials, she takes a look at her homework.

What she doesn't do is chat with her parents, neither of whom are there. She's home alone.

Johnetta is a **self-care child,** the term for children who let themselves into their homes after school and wait alone until their parents return from work. She is far from unique. Some 12 to 14 percent of children in the United States between the ages of 5 and 12 spend some time alone after school, without adult supervision (Lamorey et al., 1998; Berger, 2000).

In the past, concern about self-care children centered on their lack of supervision and the emotional costs of being alone. In fact, such children were previously called *latchkey children,* raising connotations of sad, pathetic, and neglected children. However, a new view of self-care children is emerg-

ing. According to sociologist Sandra Hofferth, given the hectic schedule of many children's lives, a few hours alone may provide a helpful period of decompression. Furthermore, it may provide the opportunity for children to develop a greater sense of autonomy (Hofferth & Sandberg, 2001).

Research has identified few differences between self-care children and children who return to homes with parents. Although some children report negative experiences while at home by themselves (such as loneliness), they seem emotionally undamaged by the experience. In addition, if they stay at home by themselves rather than "hanging out" unsupervised with friends, they may avoid involvement in activities that can lead to difficulties (Long & Long, 1983; Belle, 1999; Goyette-Ewing, 2000).

In sum, the consequences of being a self-care child are not necessarily harmful. In fact, children may develop an enhanced sense of independence and competence. Furthermore, the time spent alone provides an opportunity to work uninterrupted on homework and school or personal projects. Some findings even suggest that children with employed parents can have higher self-esteem because they feel they are contributing to the household in significant ways (Hoffman, 1989).

Based on current trends almost three-quarters of American children will spend some portion of their lives in a single-parent family. What are some possible consequences for a child in a single-parent family?

The consequences of being a self-care child are not necessarily harmful, and may even lead to a greater sense of independence and competence.

live in single-parent homes or with stepparents, grandparents, or other nonparental relatives; and some will end up in foster care (Cherlin, 1992).

How do children react to divorce? The answer depends on how soon you ask the question following a divorce as well as how old the children are at the time. Immediately after a divorce, the results can be quite devastating. Both children and parents may show several types of psychological maladjustment for a period that may last from 6 months to 2 years. For instance, children may be anxious, experience depression, or show sleep disturbances and phobias. Even though children most often live with their mothers following a divorce, the quality of the mother–child relationship declines in the majority of cases (Gottman, 1993; Holyrod & Sheppard, 1997; Wallerstein, Lewis, & Blakeslee, 2000).

During the early stage of middle childhood, children whose parents are divorcing often blame themselves for the breakup. By the age of 10, children feel pressure to choose sides, taking the position of either the mother or the father. They thereby experience some degree of divided loyalty (Wallerstein & Blakeslee, 1989; Shaw, Winslow, & Flanagan, 1999).

The consequences of divorce become less destructive from 18 months to 2 years later. After reaching a low point approximately a year after the divorce, most children begin to return to their predivorce state of psychological adjustment. Still, twice as many children of divorced parents require psychological counseling as children from intact families, and the effects may linger. For example, people who have experienced parental divorce are more at risk for experiencing divorce themselves later in life (Tucker et al., 1997; Wallerstein, Lewis, & Blakeslee, 2000).

Several factors relate to how children react to divorce. One is the economic standing of the family the child is living with. In many cases, divorce brings a decline in both parents' standards of living. When this occurs, children may be thrown into poverty, which can have a negative effect on many aspects of their upbringing.

In other cases, the negative consequences of divorce are less severe than they might otherwise be because the divorce reduces the hostility and anger in the home. If the predivorce household was overflowing with parental strife, the greater calm of a postdivorce household may be beneficial to children. This is particularly true for children who maintain a close, positive relationship with the parent with whom they do not live. Consequently, for some children, living with parents who have an intact but unhappy marriage, high in conflict, has more and stronger negative consequences than experiencing a parental divorce (Booth & Edwards, 1989; Cherlin, 1993; Gelles, 1994; Davies & Cummings, 1994; Gottfried & Gottfried, 1994).

Single-Parent Families. Almost one-quarter of all children under the age of 18 in the United States live with only one parent. If present trends continue, almost three-quarters of American children will spend some portion of their lives in a single-parent family before they are 18 years old. For minority children, the numbers are even higher: Some 60 percent of African American children and 35 percent of Hispanic children under the age of 18 live in single-parent homes (Demo & Acock, 1991; U.S. Bureau of the Census, 1994; Usdansky, 1996; see Figure 10-5).

In most cases of single-parent households, no spouse was ever present (that is, the mother never married), the spouses have divorced, or the spouse is absent. In the vast majority of cases, the single parent who is present is the mother.

What consequences are there for children living in homes with just one parent? This is a difficult question to answer. Much depends on whether a second parent was present earlier and the nature of the parents' relationship at that time. Furthermore, the economic status of the single-parent family plays a role in determining the consequences for children. Single-parent families are often less well-off financially than two-parent families, and living in relative poverty has a negative impact on children (Gongla & Thompson, 1987; Gottman & Katz, 1989).

In sum, the impact of living in a single-parent family is not, by itself, invariably negative or positive. Given the large number of single-parent households, the stigma that

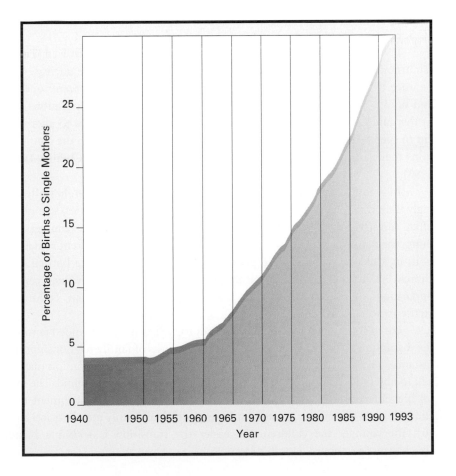

Figure 10-5 **Increase of Single Mothers, 1940–1993**

The number of mothers without spouses has increased significantly over the last five decades.

(*Source:* National Center for Health Statistics, 1996.)

"Blended" families occur when previously married husbands and wives with children remarry.

once existed toward such families has largely declined. The ultimate consequences for children depend on a variety of factors that accompany single parenthood, such as the economic status of the family, the amount of time that the parent is able to spend with the child, and the degree of stress in the household.

Living in Blended Families. For many children, the aftermath of divorce includes the subsequent remarriage of one or both parents. In fact, more than 10 million households in the United States contain at least one spouse who has remarried. More than 5 million married couples have at least one stepchild living with them in what have come to be called **blended families.** Overall, 17 percent of all children in the U.S. live in blended families (U.S. Bureau of the Census, 2001).

Living in a blended family is challenging for the children involved. There often is a fair amount of *role ambiguity,* in which roles and expectations are unclear. Children may be uncertain about their responsibilities, how to behave to stepparents and stepsiblings, and how to make a host of decisions that have wide-ranging implications for their role in the family. For instance, a child in a blended family may have to choose which parent to spend each vacation and holiday with, or to decide between the conflicting suggestions they have received from biological parent and stepparent (Cherlin, 1993; Dainton, 1993).

In many cases, however, school-age children in blended families often do surprisingly well. In comparison to adolescents, who have more difficulties, school-age children often adjust relatively smoothly to blended arrangements, for several reasons. For one thing, the family's financial situation is often improved after a parent remarries. In addition, in a blended family more people are available to share the burden of household chores. Finally, the simple fact that the family contains more individuals can increase the opportunities for social interaction (Hetherington, Stanley-Hagan, & Anderson, 1989; Hetherington & Clingempeel, 1992).

On the other hand, not all children adjust well to life in a blended family. Some find the disruption of routine and of established networks of family relationships difficult. For instance, a child who is used to having her mother's complete attention may find it difficult to observe her mother showing interest and affection to a stepchild. The most successful blending of families occurs when the parents create an environment that supports children's self-esteem and creates a culture in which all family members feel a part. Generally, the younger the children, the easier the transition is within a blended family (Buchanan, Maccoby, & Dornbusch, 1996).

blended families a remarried couple that has at least one stepchild living with them

Group Care: Orphanages in the 21st Century

The term "orphanage" evokes images of pitiful youngsters clothed in rags, eating porridge out of tin cups, and housed in huge, prisonlike institutions.

The reality today is different. Even the term *orphanage* is rarely used, having been replaced by *group home* or *residential treatment center*. Typically housing a relatively small number of children, group homes are used for children whose parents are no longer able to care for them adequately.

Group care has grown significantly in the last decade. In fact, in the 5-year period from 1995 to 2000, the number of children in foster care increased by more than 50 percent. Today, more than one-half million children in the United States live in foster care (Carnegie Task Force on Meeting the Needs of Young Children, 1994; Berrick, 1998; Roche, 2000).

About three-quarters of children in group care were the victims of neglect and abuse in their homes. Most of them can be returned to their homes following intervention with their families by social service agencies. But the remaining one-quarter are so psychologically damaged due to abuse or other causes that once they are placed in group care, they are likely to remain there throughout childhood. Children who have developed severe problems, such as high levels of aggression or anger, have difficulty finding adoptive families, and in fact it is often difficult to find even temporary foster families who are able to cope with their emotional and behavior problems (Sugden, 1995; Nickman, 1996; Rosenfeld et al., 1997).

Although some politicians have suggested that an increase in group care is a solution to complex social problems associated with unwed mothers who become dependent on welfare, experts in providing social services and psychological treatment are not so sure. For one thing, group homes cannot always consistently provide the support and love potentially available in a family setting. Moreover, group care is hardly cheap: It can cost some $40,000 per year to support a child in group care—about ten times the cost of maintaining a child in foster care or on welfare (Fanshel, Finch, & Grundy, 1990, 1992; Roche, 2000). Other experts argue that group care is inherently neither good nor bad. Instead, the consequences of living away from one's family may be quite positive, depending on the particular characteristics of the staff of the group home and whether child and youth care

Although the orphanages of the early 1900s were crowded and institutional (left), today the equivalent, called group homes or residential treatment centers (right), are much more pleasant.

workers are able to develop an effective, stable, and strong emotional bond with a specific child. On the other hand, if a worker is unable to form a meaningful relationship with a child in a group home, the results may well be unfavorable (Shealy, 1995; McKenzie, 1997; Reddy & Pfeiffer, 1997). (Table 10-4 shows the personal characteristics of the best—and worst—child and youth care workers.)

School: The Academic Environment

Where do children spend most of their time? During the school year, at least, children spend more of their day in the classroom than anywhere else. It is not surprising, then, that schools have a profound impact on children's lives, shaping and molding not only their ways of thinking but the ways they view the world. We turn now to a number of critical aspects of schooling in middle childhood.

How Children Explain Academic Success and Failure. Most of us, at one time or another, have done poorly on a test. Think back to how you felt when you received a bad grade. Did you feel shame? Anger at the teacher? Fear of the consequences? According to psychologist Bernard Weiner (1985, 1994), your response in such situations is determined largely by the particular causes to which you attribute your failure. And the kinds of attributions you make ultimately determine how hard you strive to do well on future tests.

Weiner has proposed a theory of motivation based on people's **attributions,** their explanations for the reasons behind their behavior. He suggests that people attempt to determine the causes of their academic success or failure by considering three basic dimensions:

attributions people's explanations for the reasons behind their behavior

Table 10-4

PERSONAL CHARACTERISTICS OF THE BEST AND WORST CHILD AND YOUTH CARE WORKERS

The best workers:	*The worst workers:*
Flexible	Exhibit pathology
Mature	Selfish
Integrity	Defensive
Good judgment	Dishonest
Common sense	Abusive
Appropriate values	Abuse drugs/alcohol
Responsible	Uncooperative
Good self-image	Poor self-esteem
Self-control	Rigid
Responsive to authority	Irresponsible
Interpersonally adept	Critical
Stable	Passive-aggressive
Unpretentious	Inappropriate boundaries
Predictable/consistent	Unethical
Nondefensive	Authoritarian/coercive
Nurturant/firm	Inconsistent/unpredictable
Self-aware	Avoidant
Empowering	Don't learn from experience
Cooperative	Poor role model
Good role model	Angry/explosive

(*Source:* Adapted from Shealy, 1995.)

(1) whether the cause is internal (dispositional) or external (situational); (2) whether the cause is stable or unstable; and (3) whether the cause is controllable or uncontrollable.

Consider, for instance, a student named Henry who gets a 98, the highest score in the class, on an exam. To what can he attribute his success? He might think it is a result of his ability, his effort in studying for the test, or the fact that he was rested and relaxed when he took the test. Because each of these factors is related to what Henry is or has done, they are internal attributions. But note how they differ on the other two dimensions: Ability is a stable, enduring factor, while study effort and degree of relaxation are both unstable and can fluctuate from one test to another. Finally, study effort and degree of relaxation differ from each other in terms of controllability: While amount of effort is controllable, degree of relaxation may not be.

How people feel about their performance in a situation is a factor of the attributions they make for that performance. For example, the internal–external dimension can be linked to esteem-related emotions. When a success is attributed to internal factors, students tend to feel pride; but failure attributed to internal factors causes shame. The stability dimension determines future expectations about success and failure. Specifically, when students attribute success or failure to factors that are relatively stable and invariant, they are apt to expect similar performance in the future. In contrast, when they attribute performance to unstable factors such as effort or luck, their expectations about future performance are relatively unaffected.

Finally, the controllability dimension affects emotions that are directed toward others. If children feel that failure was due to factors within their control—e.g., lack of effort—they are apt to experience anger at themselves and others; but if the failure was uncontrollable, they are likely to feel sadness.

Cultural Comparisons: Individual Differences in Attribution. Not everyone comes to the same conclusions about the sources of success and failure. In fact, among the strongest influences on people's attributions are their race, ethnicity, and socioeconomic status. Because different experiences give us different perceptions about the ways things in the world fit together, it is not surprising that there are subcultural differences in how achievement-related behaviors are understood and explained.

One important difference is related to racial factors: African Americans are less likely than whites to attribute success to internal rather than external causes. Specifically, African American children sometimes feel that task difficulty and luck (external causes)

Doonesbury © 1988, G. B. Trudeau. Reprinted with permission of Universal Press Syndicate. All rights reserved.

are the major determinants of their performance outcomes. They may believe that even if they put in maximum effort, prejudice and discrimination will prevent them from succeeding (Friend & Neale, 1972; Ogbu, 1988; Graham, S., 1990, 1994).

Such an attributional pattern, one that overemphasizes the importance of external causes, can cause problems. Attributions to external factors reduce a student's sense of personal responsibility for success or failure. But when attributions are based on internal factors, they suggest that a change in behavior—such as increased effort—can bring about a change in success (Graham, 1986; 1990; Glasgow et al., 1997).

African Americans are not the only group susceptible to maladaptive attributional patterns. Women, for example, often attribute their unsuccessful performance to low ability, an uncontrollable factor. Ironically, though, they do not attribute successful performance to high ability, but to factors outside their control. A belief in this pattern suggests the conclusion that even with future effort, success will be unattainable. Females who hold these views may be less inclined to expend the effort necessary to improve their rate of success (Dweck & Bush, 1976; Dweck, 1991; Phillips & Zimmerman, 1990; Nelson & Cooper, 1997).

Developmental Diversity

Cultural Differences in Attributions for Academic Performance: Explaining Asian Academic Success

Consider two students, Ben and Hannah, each performing poorly in school. Suppose you thought that Ben's poor performance was due to unalterable, stable causes, such as a lack of intelligence, while Hannah's was produced by temporary causes, such as a lack of hard work. Who would you think would ultimately do better in school?

If you are like most people, you'd probably predict that the outlook was better for Hannah. After all, Hannah could always work harder, but it is hard for someone like Ben to develop higher intelligence.

Research shows that teachers' expectations regarding student performance can create a self-fulfilling prophecy. In what ways is the child affected by the self-fulfilling prophecy? The teacher?

According to psychologist Harold Stevenson, this reasoning lies at the heart of the superior school performance of Asian students compared with students in the United States. Stevenson's research suggests that teachers, parents, and students in the United States are likely to attribute school performance to stable, internal causes, while people in Japan, China, and other East Asian countries are more likely to see temporary, situational factors as the cause of their performance. The Asian view, which stems in part from ancient Confucian writings, tends to accentuate the necessity of hard work and perseverance.

This cultural difference in attributional styles is displayed in several ways. For instance, surveys show that mothers, teachers, and students in Japan and Taiwan all believe strongly that students in a typical class tend to have the same amount of ability. In contrast, mothers, teachers, and students in the United States are apt to disagree, arguing that there are significant differences in ability among the various students (see Figure 10-6).

It is easy to imagine how such different attributional styles can influence teaching approaches. If, as in the United States, students and teachers seem to believe that ability is fixed and locked in, poor academic performance will be greeted with a sense of failure and reduced motivation to work harder to overcome it. In contrast, Japanese teachers and students are apt to see failure as a temporary setback due to their lack of hard work. After making such an attribution, they are more apt to expend increased effort on future academic activities.

Some developmentalists have suggested that these different attributional orientations may explain the fact that Asian students frequently outperform American students in international comparisons of student achievement (Linn, 1997; Wheeler, 1998). Because Asian students tend to assume that academic success results from hard work, they may put greater effort into their schoolwork than American students, who believe that their inherent ability determines their performance. These arguments suggest that the attributional style of students and teachers in the United States might well be maladaptive. They also argue that the attributional styles taught to children by their parents may have a significant effect on their future success (Chen & Stevenson, 1995; Chao, 1996; Geary, 1996; Eaton & Dembo, 1997, Little & Lopez, 1997). □

As we've seen, students' attributional styles are related to the expectations and beliefs of their teachers and parents. Let's take a closer look at how expectations can affect school-age children.

Expectation Effects: How Others' Expectancies Influence Children's Behavior. Imagine yourself as an elementary school teacher. Suppose you were told at the beginning of a new school year that the children in your class had taken a test described in this way:

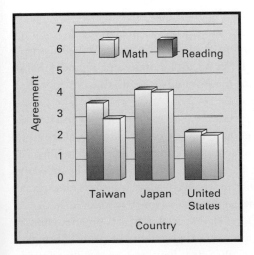

Figure 10-6 **Mothers' Beliefs in Children's Ability**

Compared to mothers in Taiwan and Japan, U.S. mothers were less apt to believe that all children have the same degree of underlying, innate ability. Subjects responded using a 7-point scale, where 1 = strongly disagree and 7 = strongly agree. What are the implications of this finding for schooling in the United States?

(*Source:* Stevenson & Lee, 1990.)

All children show hills, plateaus, and valleys in their scholastic progress. A study being conducted at Harvard with the support of the National Science Foundation is interested in those children who show an unusual forward spurt of academic progress. These spurts can and do occur at any level of academic and intellectual functioning. When these spurts occur in children who have not been functioning too well academically, the result is familiarly referred to as "late blooming."

As part of our study we are further validating a test which predicts the likelihood that a child will show an inflection point or "spurt" within the near future. This test which will be administered in your school will allow us to predict which youngsters are most likely to show an academic spurt. . . . The development of the test for predicting inflections or "spurts" is not yet such that *every* one of the top 20 percent will show the spurt or "blooming" effect. But the top 20 percent of the children *will* show a more significant inflection or spurt within the next year or less than will the remaining 80 percent of the children. (Rosenthal & Jacobson, 1968, p. 66)

Consider your reaction to the children on the list of "bloomers" identified by the test. Would you treat them differently from the children who were not so designated?

If the results of a classic but controversial study are any guide, your answer should be affirmative: Teachers do in fact seem to treat children for whom they have expectations of improvement differently from those for whom they have no such expectations (Rosenthal & Jacobson, 1968). In the experiment, elementary school teachers were told at the beginning of a new school year that five children in their classes would be likely to "bloom" in the upcoming year, based on the test described above. In reality, however, the information was bogus: The names of the children had simply been picked at random, although the teachers didn't know that. The teachers received no further details from the experimenters for the rest of the year.

At the end of the year, the children completed an intelligence test that was identical to one taken a year earlier. According to the experimenters, the results showed that clear differences existed in the intellectual growth of the so-called "bloomers" compared with that of the other members of their classes. Those randomly designated as likely to make significant gains did in fact improve more than the other children. However, the results were not uniform: The greatest differences were found for children in first and second grades, with smaller differences for children in grades three through six.

When the findings of the experiment, reported in a book dubbed *Pygmalion in the Classroom,* were published, they caused an immediate stir among educators—and among the public at large. The reason for this furor was the implication of the results: If merely holding high expectations is sufficient to bring about gains in achievement, wouldn't holding low expectations lead to slowed achievement? And since teachers sometimes may hold low expectations about children from lower socioeconomic and minority backgrounds, did this mean that children from such backgrounds were destined to show low achievement throughout their educational careers?

Although the original experiment has been criticized on methodological and statistical grounds (Snow, 1969; Wineburg, 1987), enough new evidence has been amassed to make it clear that the expectations of teachers are communicated to their students and can in fact bring about the expected performance. The phenomenon has come to be called the **teacher expectancy effect**—the cycle of behavior in which a teacher transmits an expectation about a child and actually brings about the expected behavior (Babad, 1992).

The teacher expectancy effect can be viewed as a special case of a broader concept known as the *self-fulfilling prophecy,* in which a person's expectation is capable of bringing about an outcome (Snyder, 1974). For instance, physicians have long known that provid-

teacher expectancy effect the cycle of behavior in which a teacher transmits an expectation about a child and thereby actually brings about the expected behavior

ing patients with placebos (fake, inactive drugs) can sometimes "cure" them, simply because the patients expect the medicine to work.

In the case of teacher expectancy effects, the basic explanation seems to be that teachers, after forming an initial expectation about a child's ability, transmit it to the child through a complex series of verbal and nonverbal cues. These communicated expectations in turn indicate to the child what behavior is appropriate, and the child behaves accordingly (Harris & Rosenthal, 1986; Rosenthal, 1987, 1994).

Once teachers have developed expectations about a child, by what method do they transmit them? Generally, four major factors relate to the transmission of expectations (Harris & Rosenthal, 1986; Rosenthal, 1994):

- *Classroom social-emotional climate.* Teachers create a warmer, more accepting environment for children for whom they hold high expectations than for those they expect less from. They convey more positive attitudes by smiling and nodding more often, and they look at high-expectation children more frequently.

- *Input to children.* Children who are expected to do well receive greater quantities of material from their teachers, and they are asked to complete more difficult material. Consequently, they are given more opportunities to perform well.

- *Output from teachers.* Teachers initiate more contacts with high-expectation children, and the overall number of contacts between teachers and high-expectation children is higher than with low-expectation children. As a result, high-expectation children have more opportunities to respond in class.

- *Feedback.* When teachers hold high expectations for a child, they provide more positive evaluations of the child's work and they are more accepting of the child's ideas. In contrast, low-expectation children receive more criticism and little or no feedback in some situations. Even when low-expectation children do well, the kind of feedback teachers offer is less positive than when a high-expectation child does well.

The final link in the chain of events that encompasses the teacher expectation effect is the child. And given the range of teacher behaviors brought about by teacher expectations, it is hardly surprising that children's performance would be significantly affected. Clearly, children who encounter a warm social-emotional climate, who are given more material to complete, who have more contact with teachers, and who are the recipients of more feedback from their teachers are going to develop more positive self-concepts, be more motivated, and work harder than those who receive negative treatment or neglect. Ultimately, the high-expectation children are likely to perform better in class.

The cycle, then, is complete: A teacher who expects a child to do better treats that child more positively. The child responds to such treatment and eventually performs in accord with the teacher's expectations. But note that the cycle does not stop there: Once children behave congruently with the teacher's expectations, the expectations are reinforced. As a consequence, a child's behavior ultimately may cement the expectation initially held by the teacher (see Figure 10-7).

Expectations are an omnipresent phenomenon in classrooms and are not the province of teachers alone. For instance, children develop their own expectations about their teacher's competence, based on rumors and other bits of information, and they communicate their expectations to those teachers. In the end, a teacher's behavior may be brought about in significant measure by children's expectations (Feldman & Prohaska, 1979; Feldman & Theiss, 1982; Jamieson et al., 1987).

Finally, remember that the classroom is not the only place in which expectations operate. *Any* setting in which one person holds an expectation about a child, and vice versa,

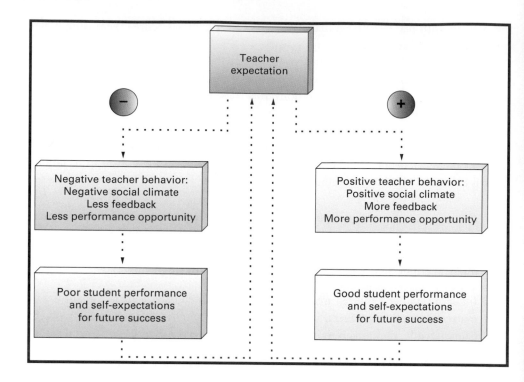

Figure 10-7 **Teacher Expectations and Student Performance**

Teachers' expectations about their students—positive or negative—can actually bring about positive or negative performance from their students. How does this relate to what we know about self-esteem?

emotional intelligence the set of skills that underlie the accurate assessment, evaluation, expression, and regulation of emotions

may produce analogous expectancy effects. Clearly, children's views of themselves and of their behavior are in part a consequence of what others expect of them (Eden, 1990; Harris et al., 1992).

Beyond the 3Rs: Should Schools Teach Emotional Intelligence? In many elementary schools, the hottest topic in the curriculum has little to do with the traditional 3Rs. Instead, a significant educational trend for educators in many elementary schools throughout the United States is the use of techniques to increase students' **emotional intelligence,** the set of skills that underlie the accurate assessment, evaluation, expression, and regulation of emotions (Goleman, 1995; Mayer & Salovey, 1997; Salovey & Sluyter, 1997; Mayer, Salovey, & Caruso, 2000; Mayer, 2001; Pfeiffer, 2001).

Psychologist Daniel Goleman (1995), who wrote a best-seller entitled *Emotional Intelligence,* argues that emotional literacy should be a standard part of the school curriculum. He points to several programs that are effective in teaching students to manage their emotions more effectively. For instance, in one program, children are provided with lessons in empathy, self-awareness, and social skills. In another, children are taught about caring and friendship as early as first grade through exposure to stories.

Programs meant to increase emotional intelligence have not been met with universal acceptance. Critics suggest that the nurturance of emotional intelligence is best left to students' families and that schools ought to concentrate on more traditional curriculum matters. Others suggest that adding emotional intelligence to an already crowded curriculum may reduce time spent on academics. Finally, some critics argue that there is no well-specified set of criteria for what constitutes emotional intelligence, and consequently it is difficult to develop appropriate, effective curriculum materials.

Still, most people consider emotional intelligence to be something that is worthy of nurturance. Certainly, it is clear that emotional intelligence is quite different from traditional conceptions of intelligence. For example, most of us can think of individuals who, while quite intelligent in a traditional sense, are also insensitive and socially unskilled. The goal of emotional intelligence training is to produce people who are not only cognitively sophisticated but able to manage their emotions effectively (Schulman & Mekler, 1994; Sleek, 1997).

Review and Rethink

REVIEW

- Self-care children may develop independence and enhanced self-esteem from their experience.
- The consequences of divorce depend on such factors as financial circumstances and the comparative levels of tension in the family before and after the divorce.
- The effects of being raised in a single-parent household depend on financial circumstances, the amount of parent–child interaction, and the level of tension in the family.
- People's attributional patterns differ along individual, cultural, and gender dimensions.
- Expectancies can affect behavior and produce outcomes that reflect and confirm the expectancies.

- Emotional intelligence is becoming accepted as an important aspect of social intelligence.

RETHINK

- How might the development of self-esteem in middle childhood be affected by a divorce? By a family situation characterized by constant hostility and tension between parents?
- Politicians often speak of "family values." How does this term relate to the diverse family situations covered in this chapter, including divorced parents, single parents, blended families, working parents, self-care children, abusive families, and group care?

Looking Back

In what ways do children's views of themselves change during the middle childhood years?

- According to Erikson, children in the middle childhood years are in the industry-versus-inferiority stage, focusing on achieving competence and responding to a wide range of personal challenges.

- Children in the middle childhood years begin to view themselves in terms of psychological characteristics and to differentiate their self-concepts into separate areas. They use social comparison to evaluate their behavior, abilities, expertise, and opinions.

Why is self-esteem important during these years?

- Children in these years are developing self-esteem; those with chronically low self-esteem can become trapped in a cycle of failure in which low self-esteem feeds on itself by producing low expectations and poor performance.

Through what stages does moral development proceed as children age?

- According to Kohlberg, people pass from preconventional morality (motivated by rewards and punishments), through conventional morality (motivated by social reference), to postconventional morality (motivated by a sense of universal moral principles). Gilligan has sketched out an alternative progression for girls, from an orientation toward individual survival, through goodness as self-sacrifice, to the morality of nonviolence.

What sorts of relationships and friendships are typical of middle childhood years?

- Children's friendships display status hierarchies, and their understanding of friendship passes through stages, from a focus on mutual liking and time spent together, through the consideration of personal traits and the rewards that friendship provides, to an appreciation of intimacy and loyalty.

- Popularity in children is related to traits that underlie social competence. Because of the importance of social interactions and friendships, developmental researchers have engaged in efforts to improve social problem-solving skills and the processing of social information.

How do gender and ethnicity affect friendships?

- Boys and girls in middle childhood increasingly prefer same-gender friendships. Male friendships are characterized by groups, status hierarchies, and restrictive play. Female friendships tend to involve one or two close relationships, equal status, and a reliance on cooperation.

- Cross-race friendships diminish in frequency as children age. Equal-status interactions among members of different racial groups can lead to improved understanding, mutual respect and acceptance, and a decreased tendency to stereotype.

▶ *How do today's diverse family and care arrangements affect children?*

■ Children in families in which both parents work outside the home generally fare well. "Self-care children" who fend for themselves after school may develop independence and a sense of competence and contribution.

■ Immediately after a divorce, the effects on children in the middle childhood years can be serious, depending on the financial condition of the family and the hostility level between spouses before the divorce.

■ The consequences of living in a single-parent family depend on the financial condition of the family and, if there had been two parents, the level of hostility that existed between them.

■ Blended families present challenges to the child, but can also offer opportunities for increased social interaction.

■ Children in group care tend to have been victims of neglect and abuse. Many can be helped and placed with their own or other families, but about 25 percent of them will spend their childhood years in group care.

▶ *How do social and emotional factors contribute to school outcomes?*

■ People attach attributions to their academic successes and failures. Differences in attributional patterns are not only individual, but appear to be influenced by culture and gender as well.

■ The expectancies of others, particularly teachers, can produce outcomes that conform to those expectancies by leading students to modify their behavior.

■ Emotional intelligence is the set of skills that permit people to manage their emotions effectively.

E P I L O G U E

In this chapter we considered social and personality development in the middle childhood years, looking at self-esteem and moral development. We discussed relationships and friendships, and we looked at the ways gender and race can affect friendships. We considered the changing nature of family arrangements and the effects of these changes on social and personality development. We concluded with a discussion of attributions of success and failure, expectancies, and emotional intelligence.

Return to the prologue—about Bryan and Christopher Hendrickson—and answer the following questions.

1. In what ways do the Hendrickson twins' activities exemplify Erikson's industry-versus-inferiority stage of development?

2. How does the children's play with the boxes differ from the way they would have played during the preschool years?

3. What would you expect is the basis of the friendship between the twins and the other kids in the prologue?

4. What educated guesses can you make about the popularity, status, and social competence of the twins based on the information in the prologue?

Key Terms and Concepts

industry-versus-inferiority stage (p. 347)
social comparison (p. 348)
self-esteem (p. 349)
status (p. 359)
social competence (p. 360)

social problem-solving (p. 360)
dominance hierarchy (p. 362)
coregulation (p. 365)
self-care children (p. 367)
blended families (p. 370)

attributions (p. 372)
teacher expectancy effect (p. 376)
emotional intelligence (p. 378)

Bridges

In Part Four, we saw how children use their expanded physical and cognitive abilities to negotiate new ways of solving problems, understanding their roles in the world, and dealing with people more effectively. We observed the foundation of many future developments that will become more evident in adolescence and adulthood. In our discussion of adolescence, for example, we'll see that children's concepts of themselves continue to become more differentiated and that they develop varied levels of self-esteem for different areas of their lives.

We continued our consideration of the major developmental theorists—Piaget, Erikson, Vygotsky, and others—and their explanations of the key events and milestones that children experience during these years, and we extended our discussion of the influences that society exerts on children through phenomena associated with family life, divorce, schooling, popularity, and friendship. The major theorists will figure heavily in our discussion of adolescence too, and we'll explore the pressures of society that adolescents face. We will see how cognitive and physical development affect adolescents' school achievement, drug use, and mental health.

In brief, what we can see in the middle childhood period is a tremendous outward expansion of the individual as she or he begins the personal redefinition process that will continue, with even more noticeable effects, in adolescence. As we move on into adolescence, we'll see how negotiating relationships between individuals and the society in which they live becomes more complicated.

OUTLINE

PHYSICAL MATURATION

**COGNITIVE DEVELOPMENT
AND SCHOOLING**

*From Research to Practice:
Preventing School Violence*

**THREATS TO ADOLESCENTS'
WELL-BEING**

*Speaking of Development: Doreen
Gail Branch, Substance Abuse
Researcher*

*The Informed Consumer
of Development: Hooked on Drugs
or Alcohol?*

*Developmental Diversity: Selling
Death: Pushing Smoking to the Less
Advantaged*

ADOLESCENCE

Physical and Cognitive Development in Adolescence

PROLOGUE: AGAINST THE ODDS

Students in inner-city, poor neighborhoods face extraordinary challenges.

Recently, a student was shot dead by a classmate during lunch period outside Frank W. Ballou Senior High. It didn't come as much of a surprise to anyone at the school, in this city's most crime-infested ward. Just during the current school year, one boy was hacked by a student with an ax, a girl was badly wounded in a knife fight with another female student, five fires were set by arsonists, and an unidentified body was dumped next to the parking lot.

But all is quiet in the echoing hallways at 7:15 a.m., long before classes start on a spring morning. The only sound comes from the computer lab, where 16-year-old Cedric Jennings is already at work on an extra-credit project, a program to bill patients at a hospital. Later, he will work on his science-fair project, a chemical analysis of acid rain.

He arrives every day this early and often doesn't leave until dark. The high-school junior with the perfect grades has big dreams: He wants to go to Massachusetts Institute of Technology. (Suskind, 1994, p. 1; Suskind, 1999)

Looking Ahead

Cedric Jennings was one of a tiny group of students who had an average of B or better at their huge inner-city high school in Washington, D.C. These achievers were a lonely group, the frequent target of threats and actual violence. Yet Cedric persevered, intent on getting a college education and succeeding academically and, ultimately, in life—something that he would ultimately accomplish.

How do students such as Cedric overcome the extremes of poverty and violence that they face, while others are less successful? More broadly, how do all adolescents navigate the challenges that each of them faces?

In this chapter and the next, we consider the basic issues and questions that underlie adolescence. **Adolescence** is the developmental stage that lies between childhood and adulthood. It begins and ends imprecisely, starting just before the teenage years and ending just after them. This imprecision reflects the nature of society's treatment of the period: Adolescents are considered no longer children, but not yet adults. Clearly, though, adolescence is a time of considerable physical and psychological growth and change.

This chapter focuses on physical and cognitive growth during adolescence. We begin by considering the extraordinary physical maturation that occurs during adolescence, triggered by the onset of puberty. We discuss the consequences of early and late maturation, as well as nutrition and eating disorders.

Next, we turn to a consideration of cognitive development during adolescence. After reviewing several approaches to understanding changes in cognitive capabilities, we examine school performance, focusing on the ways that socioeconomic status, ethnicity, and race affect scholastic achievement.

The chapter concludes with a discussion of several of the major threats to adolescents' well-being. We will focus on drug, alcohol, and tobacco use as well as sexually transmitted diseases.

After reading this chapter, you will be able to answer the following questions:

adolescence the developmental stage between childhood and adulthood

▶ **What physical changes do adolescents experience?**

▶ **What are the consequences of early and late maturation?**

▶ **What nutritional needs and concerns do adolescents have?**

▶ **In what ways does cognitive development proceed during adolescence?**

▶ **What factors affect adolescent school performance?**

▶ **What dangerous substances do adolescents use and why?**

▶ **What dangers do adolescent sexual practices present, and how can these dangers be avoided?**

Physical Maturation

For the male members of the Awa tribe, the beginning of adolescence is signaled by an elaborate and—to Western eyes—gruesome ceremony marking the transition from childhood to adulthood. First, the boys are whipped for two or three days with sticks and prickly branches. Through the whipping, the boys atone for their previous infractions and honor tribesmen who were killed in warfare.

But that's just for starters. In the next phase of the ritual, sharpened sticks are punched into the boys' nostrils, producing a considerable amount of blood. Then, adults force a five-foot length of vine into the boys' throats, causing them to choke and vomit. Finally, deep cuts are made in the boys' genitals. Jeering onlookers poke at the cuts to make them bleed even more.

Most of us probably feel gratitude that we did not have to endure such physical trials when we entered adolescence. But members of Western cultures do have their own rites of passage into adolescence, admittedly less fearsome, such as bar mitzvahs and bat mitzvahs at age 13 for Jewish boys and girls, and confirmation ceremonies in many Christian denominations (Dunham, Kidwell, & Wilson, 1986; Delaney, 1995; Herdt, 1998).

Regardless of the nature of the ceremonies celebrated by various cultures, their underlying purpose tends to be similar from one culture to the next: symbolically celebrating the onset of the physical changes that take a child to the doorstep of adulthood.

Growth During Adolescence: The Rapid Pace of Physical and Sexual Maturation

The growth in height and weight during adolescence can be breathtaking. In only a few months, an adolescent can grow several inches and require a virtually new wardrobe. In fact, in a period of only 4 years, boys and girls undergo a transformation, at least in physical appearance, from children to young adults.

The dramatic changes during adolescence constitute the adolescent growth spurt, a period of very rapid growth in height and weight. During the adolescent growth spurt, height and weight increase as quickly as they did during infancy. On average, boys grow 4.1 inches a year and girls 3.5 inches a year. Some adolescents grow as much as 5 inches in a single year (Tanner, 1972).

Boys' and girls' adolescent growth spurts begin at different times. On average, girls start their spurts 2 years earlier than boys, and they complete them earlier as well. As you can see in Figure 11-1, girls begin their spurts around age 10, while boys start at about age 12. For the 2-year period starting at age 11, girls tend to be a bit taller than boys. This soon changes, however: By the age of 13, boys, on average, are taller than girls—a state of affairs that persists for the remainder of the life span.

Note the changes that have occurred in just a few years in these pre- and post-puberty photos of the same boy.

Puberty: The Start of Sexual Maturation

Like the growth spurt, **puberty,** the period during which the sexual organs mature, begins earlier for girls than for boys. Girls start puberty at around age 11 or 12, and boys begin at around age 13 or 14. However, there are wide variations among individuals. For example, some girls begin puberty as early as 7 or 8 or as late as 16 years of age.

Puberty begins when the pituitary gland in the brain signals other glands in children's bodies to begin producing the sex hormones, androgens (male hormones) or estrogens (female hormones), at adult levels. The pituitary gland also signals the body to increase production of growth hormones that interact with the sex hormones to cause the growth spurt and puberty.

Puberty in Girls. What triggers the start of puberty in girls? Although we know what happens when it begins, no one has yet identified the reason that it begins at a particular time. However, it is clear that environmental and cultural factors play a role. For example, **menarche,** the onset of menstruation and probably the most conspicuous signal of puberty in girls, varies greatly in different parts of the world. In poorer, developing countries, menstruation begins later than in more economically advantaged countries. Even within

puberty the period during which the sexual organs mature, beginning earlier for girls than for boys

menarche the onset of menstruation

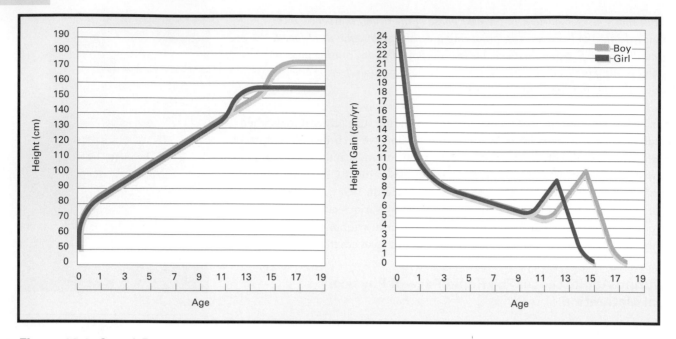

Figure 11-1   **Growth Patterns**

Patterns of growth are depicted in two ways. The first figure shows height at a given age, while the second shows the height *increase* that occurs from birth through the end of adolescence. Notice that girls begin their growth spurt around age 10, while boys begin the growth spurt at about age 12. However, by the age of 13, boys tend to be taller than girls. What are the social consequences of being taller or shorter than average for boys and girls?

(Adapted from Cratty, 1986.)

secular trend a statistical tendency observed over several generations

primary sex characteristics characteristics associated with the development of the organs and structures of the body that directly relate to reproduction

secondary sex characteristics the visible signs of sexual maturity that do not directly involve the sex organs

wealthier countries, girls in more affluent groups begin to menstruate earlier than less affluent girls (see Figure 11-2). Consequently, it appears that girls who are better nourished and healthier are more apt to start menstruation at an earlier age than those who suffer from malnutrition or chronic disease. In fact, some studies have suggested that weight or the proportion of fat to muscle in the body play a role in the timing of menarche. For example, in the U.S., athletes with a low percentage of body fat may start menstruating later than less active girls (Richards, 1996; Vizmanos & Marti-Henneberg, 2000).

Other factors can affect the timing of menarche. For instance, environmental stress due to such factors as parental divorce or high levels of family conflict can bring about an early onset (Graber, Brooks-Gunn, & Warren, 1995; Hulanicka, 1999; Kim & Smith, 1999).

Over the past 100 years or so, girls in the U.S. and other cultures have been experiencing puberty at earlier ages. Near the end of the 19th century, menstruation began, on average, around age 14 or 15, compared with today's 11 or 12. Other indictors of puberty, such as the age at which adult height and sexual maturity are reached, have also appeared at earlier ages, probably due to reduced disease and improved nutrition. The earlier start of puberty is an example of a significant **secular trend,** a statistical tendency observed over several generations.

Menstruation is just one of several changes in puberty that are related to the development of primary and secondary sex characteristics. **Primary sex characteristics** are associated with the development of the organs and structures of the body that directly relate to reproduction. In contrast, **secondary sex characteristics** are the visible signs of sexual maturity that do not involve the sex organs directly.

For instance, girls experience the development of primary sex characteristics through changes in the vagina and uterus as a result of maturation. Secondary sex characteristics include the development of breasts and pubic hair. Breasts begin to grow at

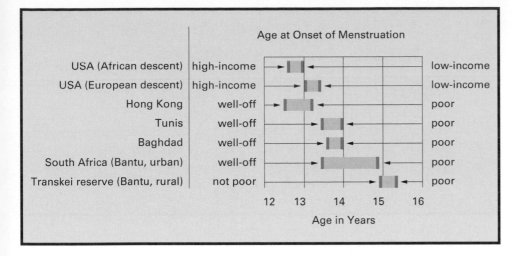

Age at Onset of Menstruation

		Age in Years
USA (African descent)	high-income	low-income
USA (European descent)	high-income	low-income
Hong Kong	well-off	poor
Tunis	well-off	poor
Baghdad	well-off	poor
South Africa (Bantu, urban)	well-off	poor
Transkei reserve (Bantu, rural)	not poor	poor

12   13   14   15   16

Age in Years

Figure 11-2 **Onset of Menstruation**

The onset of menstruation occurs earlier in more economically advantaged countries than in those that are poorer. But even in wealthier countries, girls living in more affluent circumstances begin to menstruate earlier than those living in less affluent situations. Why is this the case?

(Adapted from Eveleth & Tanner, 1976.)

around the age of 10, and pubic hair begins to appear at about age 11. Underarm hair appears about 2 years later.

For some girls, indications of puberty start unusually early. One out of 7 Caucasian girls develops breasts or pubic hair by age 8. Even more surprisingly, the figure is 1 out of 2 for African American girls. The reasons for this earlier onset of puberty are unclear, and the demarcation between normal and abnormal onset of puberty is a point of controversy among specialists (Lemonick, 2000; The Endocrine Society, 2001).

Puberty in Boys. Boys' sexual maturation follows a somewhat different course. In terms of primary sex characteristics, the penis and scrotum begin to grow at an accelerated rate around the age of 12, and they reach adult size about 3 or 4 years later. As boys' penises enlarge, the prostate gland and seminal vesicles, which produce semen (the fluid that carries sperm) also grow. This sets the stage for the first ejaculation, known as *spermarche*. Spermarche usually occurs around the age of 13, although the body has already been producing sperm for more than a year. Initially, the semen contains relatively few sperm, but the amount of sperm increases significantly with age. At the same time, there is development in secondary sex characteristics. Pubic hair begins to grow around the age of 12, followed by the growth of underarm and facial hair. Finally, boys' voices deepen as the vocal cords become longer and the larynx larger. (Figure 11-3 summarizes the changes that occur in sexual maturation during early adolescence.)

The surge in production of hormones that triggers the start of adolescence also may lead to rapid swings in mood. For example, boys may have feelings of anger and annoyance that are associated with higher hormone levels. In girls, the emotions produced by hormone production are somewhat different: Higher levels of hormones are associated with anger and depression (Buchanan, Eccles, & Becker, 1992).

Body Image: Reactions to Physical Changes in Adolescence

Many parents notice that adolescents seem to suddenly develop a habit of spending inordinate amounts of time in the bathroom grooming and gazing at themselves. Unlike infants, who also undergo extraordinarily rapid growth, adolescents are well aware of what is happening to their bodies, and they may react with horror or joy. Few, though, are neutral about the changes they are witnessing (Mehran, 1997).

For instance, menarche produces several psychological consequences. In the past, Western society has emphasized the more negative aspects of menstruation, such as the potential of cramps and messiness, and girls tended to react to menarche with anxiety (Ruble

Boys who mature early tend to be more successful in athletics, and have a more positive self-concept. Explain why there can be a downside to early maturation.

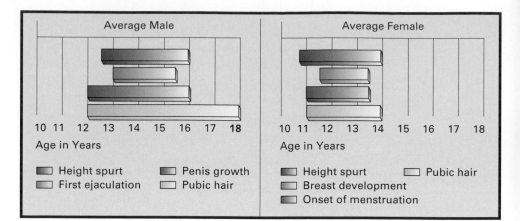

Figure 11-3 **Sexual Maturation**

The changes in sexual maturation that occur for males and females during early adolescence.

(Adapted from Tanner, 1978.)

& Brooks-Gunn, 1982). Today, however, society's view of menstruation tends to be more positive, in part because menstruation has been demystified and discussed more openly. (For instance, television commercials for tampons are commonplace.) As a consequence, menarche is typically accompanied by an increase in self-esteem, a rise in status, and greater self-awareness (Brooks-Gunn & Reiter, 1990; Johnson, Roberts, & Worell, 1999).

In some ways, a boy's first ejaculation is roughly equivalent to menarche in a girl. However, while girls generally tell their mothers about the onset of menstruation, boys rarely mention their first ejaculation to either their parents or their friends (Stein & Reiser, 1994). Why? One reason is that boys see the first ejaculation as an indication of their budding sexuality, an area about which they are quite uncertain and which they are therefore reluctant to discuss with others.

Menstruation and ejaculations generally occur privately, but changes in body shape and size are quite public. Consequently, teenagers entering puberty are frequently embarrassed by the changes that are occurring.

Girls, in particular, are often unhappy with their new bodies. This dissatisfaction is likely due to strong societal pressures regarding the ideal female shape, which frequently has little to do with the reality of mature women's bodies. Specifically, ideals of beauty in many western countries call for an unrealistic thinness that is quite different from the actual shape of most women. Puberty brings a considerable increase in the amount of fatty tissue, as well as enlargement of the hips and buttocks—a far cry from the slenderness that society seems to demand (Attie & Brooks-Gunn, 1989; Unger & Crawford, 1996).

How children react to the onset of puberty depends in part on when it happens. Girls and boys who mature either earlier or later than most of their peers are especially affected by the timing of puberty.

The Timing of Puberty: The Consequences of Early and Late Maturation. What are the social consequences of early or late maturation? One of the most persistent questions addressed by developmentalists who specialize in adolescence is whether early and late maturation bring with them any particular advantages or disadvantages. The answer, it turns out, differs for boys and girls.

For boys, early maturation is largely a plus. Early-maturing boys tend to be more successful at athletics, presumably because of their larger size. Furthermore, they tend to be more popular and to have a more positive self-concept.

On the other hand, early maturation in boys does have a downside. Boys who mature early are more apt to have difficulties in school, and they are more likely to become involved in delinquency and substance abuse. The reason: Their larger size makes it more likely that they will seek out the company of older boys who may involve them in activities that are inappropriate for their age. Furthermore, although early-maturers are more responsible and cooperative in later life, they are also more conforming and lacking in humor. Overall, though, the pluses seem to outweigh the minuses for early maturing boys (Livson & Peskin, 1980; Duncan et al., 1985; Andersson & Magnusson, 1990).

The story is a bit different for early-maturing girls. For them, the obvious changes in their bodies—such as the development of breasts—may lead them to feel uncomfortable and different from their peers (Lee, 1997; Williams & Currie, 2000). Moreover, because girls, in general, mature earlier than boys, early maturation tends to come at a very young age in the girl's life. Early-maturing girls may have to endure ridicule from their less mature classmates.

On the other hand, early maturation is not a completely negative experience for girls. Girls who mature earlier tend to be sought after more as potential dates, and their popularity may enhance their self-concepts. Still, they may not be socially ready to participate in the kind of dating situations that most girls deal with at a later age, and such situations may be psychologically challenging for early-maturing girls. Moreover, the conspicuousness of their deviance from their later-maturing classmates may have a negative effect on them (Simmons & Blyth, 1987).

Whether girls face difficulties with early maturation depends in part on cultural norms and standards. For instance, in the United States, the notion of female sexuality is looked upon with a degree of ambivalence. Consequently, the outcome of early maturation may be negative. In countries in which attitudes about sexuality are more liberal, the results of early maturation may be more positive. For example, in Germany, which has a more open view of sex, early-maturing girls have higher self-esteem than such girls in the United States. Furthermore, the consequences of early maturation vary even within the United States, depending on the views of girls' peer groups and on prevailing community standards regarding sex (Silbereisen et al., 1989; Richards et al., 1990; Petersen, 2000).

As with early maturation, the situation with late maturation is mixed, although in this case boys fare worse than girls. For instance, boys who are smaller and lighter than their more mature peers tend to be viewed as less attractive. Because of their smaller size, they are at a disadvantage when it comes to sports activities. Furthermore, because of the social convention that boys should be taller than their dates, the social lives of late-maturing boys may suffer. Ultimately, these difficulties may lead to a decline in self-concept. If this happens, the disadvantages of late maturation for boys could extend well into adulthood (Mussen & Jones, 1957; Livson & Peskin, 1980). On the other hand, coping with the challenges of late maturation may actually help males in some ways. Late-maturing boys grow up to have several positive qualities such as assertiveness and insightfulness, and they are more creatively playful than early maturers.

The picture for late-maturing girls is a bit more complicated. Girls who mature later may be overlooked in dating and other mixed-sex activities during junior high school and middle school, and they may have relatively low social status (Apter et al., 1981; Clarke-Stewart & Friedman, 1987). However, by the time they are in tenth grade and have begun to mature visibly, late-maturing-girls' satisfaction with themselves and their bodies may be greater than that of early-maturers. In fact, late-maturing girls may end up with fewer emotional problems. The reason? Late-maturing girls are more apt to fit the societal ideal of a slender, "leggy" body type than early-maturers, who tend to look heavier in comparison (Simmons & Blythe, 1987; Petersen, 1988).

In sum, the reactions to early and late maturation present a complex picture. Some developmentalists suggest that the concern over early and later maturation, and over the effects of puberty in general, may have been overemphasized in the past (Petersen & Crockett, 1985; Paikoff & Brooks-Gunn, 1990). Rather than focusing on the growth spurt and sexual maturation that occur during adolescence, they suggest that other factors, such as changes in peer groups, family dynamics, and particularly schools and other societal institutions, may be more pertinent in determining an adolescent's behavior. As we have

This young woman suffers from anorexia nervosa, a severe eating disorder in which people refuse to eat, while denying that their behavior and appearance are out of the ordinary.

anorexia nervosa a severe eating disorder in which individuals refuse to eat, while denying that their behavior and appearance, which may become skeletal, are out of the ordinary

Obesity has become the most common nutritional concern during adolescence. In addition to issues of health, what are some psychological concerns about obesity in adolescence?

seen repeatedly, we need to take into consideration the complete constellation of factors affecting individuals in order to understand their development.

Nutrition, Food, and Eating Disorders: Fueling the Growth of Adolescence

A rice cake in the afternoon, an apple for dinner. That was Heather Rhodes's typical diet her freshman year at St. Joseph's College in Rensselaer, Indiana, when she began to nurture a fear (exacerbated, she says, by the sudden death of a friend) that she was gaining weight. But when Rhodes, now 20, returned home to Joliet, Illinois, for summer vacation a year and a half ago, her family thought she was melting away. "I could see the outline of her pelvis in her clothes . . ." says Heather's mother . . . , so she and the rest of the family confronted Heather one evening, placing a bathroom scale in the middle of the family room. "I told them they were attacking me and to go to hell," recalls Heather, who nevertheless reluctantly weighed herself. Her 5'7" frame held a mere 85 pounds—down 22 pounds from her senior year in high school. "I told them they rigged the scale," she says. It simply didn't compute with her self-image. "When I looked in the mirror," she says, "I thought my stomach was still huge and my face was fat." (Sandler, 1994, p. 56)

Heather's problem: a severe eating disorder, anorexia nervosa.

The rapid physical growth of adolescence is fueled by an increase in food consumption. Particularly during the growth spurt, adolescents eat substantial quantities of food, increasing their intake of calories rather dramatically. During the teenage years, the average girl requires some 2,200 calories a day, and the average boy 2,800.

Of course, not just any calories help nourish adolescents' growth. Several key nutrients are essential, including in particular calcium and iron. The calcium provided by milk helps bone growth, which may prevent the later development of osteoporosis—the thinning of bones—that affects 25 percent of women later in their lives. Similarly, iron is necessary to prevent iron-deficiency anemia, an ailment that is not uncommon among teenagers.

For most adolescents, the major nutritional issue is ensuring the consumption of a sufficient balance of appropriate foods. But for a substantial minority, nutrition can be a major concern and can create a real threat to health. Among the most prevalent problems: obesity and eating disorders like the one afflicting Heather Rhodes.

Obesity. The most common nutritional concern during adolescence is obesity. One in 5 adolescents is overweight, and 1 in 20 can be formally classified as obese (body weight that is more than 20 percent above average) (Gans, 1990; Brook & Tepper, 1997).

Although adolescents are obese for the same reasons as younger children, the psychological consequences may be particularly severe during a time of life when body image is of special concern. Furthermore, the potential health consequences of obesity during adolescence are also problematic. For instance, obesity taxes the circulatory system, increasing the likelihood of high blood pressure and diabetes. Finally, obese adolescents stand an 80 percent chance of becoming obese adults.

Anorexia Nervosa and Bulimia. The desire to avoid obesity sometimes becomes so strong that it turns into a problem. For instance, Heather Rhodes suffered from anorexia nervosa. **Anorexia nervosa** is a severe eating disorder in which individuals refuse to eat, while denying that their behavior and appearance, which may become skeletal, are out of the ordinary.

Anorexia is a severe psychological disorder; some 15 to 20 percent of its victims literally starve themselves to death. It primarily afflicts women between the ages of 12 and 40; those most susceptible are intelligent, successful, and attractive white adolescent girls from affluent homes. Anorexia is also becoming a problem for more boys. About 10 percent of victims are male, a percentage that is increasing (Hsu, 1990; Button, 1993; Crosscope-Happel, et al., 2000).

In the early stages, anorexics' lives become centered on food. Even though they eat little, they may go shopping often, collect cookbooks, talk about food, or cook huge meals for others. Although they may be incredibly thin, their body images are so distorted that they see their reflections in mirrors as disgustingly fat and try to lose more and more weight. Even when they look like skeletons, they are unable to see what they have become.

Bulimia, another eating disorder, is characterized by binges on large quantities of food, followed by purges of the food through vomiting or the use of laxatives. Bulimics may eat an entire gallon of ice cream or a whole package of tortilla chips. But after such a binge, sufferers experience powerful feelings of guilt and depression, and they intentionally rid themselves of the food.

bulimia an eating disorder characterized by binges on large quantities of food, followed by purges of the food through vomiting or the use of laxatives

Although the weight of a person with bulimia remains fairly normal, the disorder is quite hazardous. The constant vomiting and diarrhea of the binge-and-purge cycles may produce a chemical imbalance that can lead to heart failure.

The exact reasons for the occurrence of eating disorders are not clear, although several factors appear to be implicated. Dieting often precedes the development of eating disorders, as even normal-weight individuals are spurred on by societal standards of slenderness to seek to lower their weight. Furthermore, girls who mature earlier than their peers and who have a higher level of body fat are more susceptible to eating disorders during later adolescence. In addition, adolescents who are clinically depressed are more likely to develop eating disorders later (Cauffman & Steinberg, 1996; Striegel-Moore, 1997; Gardner, et al., 2000).

Some theorists suggest that a biological cause lies at the root of both anorexia nervosa and bulimia. In fact, there appear to be genetic components to the disorders, and in some cases doctors have found hormonal imbalances in sufferers (Condit, 1990; Irwin, 1993; Treasure & Tiller, 1993).

Other attempts to explain the eating disorders emphasize psychological and social factors. For instance, some experts suggest that the disorders are a result of overdemanding parents or byproducts of other family difficulties. Culture also plays a role. Anorexia nervosa, for instance, is found only in cultures that idealize slender female bodies. Because in most places such a standard does not hold, anorexia is not prevalent outside the United States. For instance, there is no anorexia in all of Asia, with two interesting exceptions: the upper classes of Japan and of Hong Kong, where Western influence is greatest. Furthermore, anorexia nervosa is a fairly recent disorder. It was not seen in the 17th and 18th centuries, when the ideal of the female body was a plump corpulence. The increasing number of boys with anorexia in the U.S. may be related to a growing emphasis on a muscular male physique that features little body fat (Miller, McCluskey-Fawcett, & Irving, 1993; Keel, Leon, & Fulkerson, 2001).

Because anorexia nervosa and bulimia are products of both biological and environmental causes, treatment typically involves multiple approaches. For instance, both psychological therapy and dietary modifications are likely to be needed for successful treatment (Walsh & Devlin, 1998; Gilbert, 2000; Miller & Mizes, 2000; Porzelius, Dinsmore, & Staffelbach, 2001).

Brain Development and Thought: Paving the Way for Cognitive Growth

Continuing physical development of the brain paves the way for the significant advances that occur in cognitive abilities during adolescence, as we'll consider in the next part of the chapter. The number of neurons (the cells of the nervous system) continue to grow, and their interconnections become more complex (Thompson & Nelson, 2001).

One specific area of the brain that undergoes considerable development throughout adolescence is the prefrontal cortex, which is not fully developed until around the age

The prefrontal cortex, the area of the brain responsible for impulse control is biologically immature during adolescence, leading to some of the risk and impulsive behavior associated with this age group.

of 20. The *prefrontal cortex* is the part of the brain that allows people to think, evaluate, and make complex judgments in a uniquely human way.

The prefrontal cortex also is the area of the brain that provides for impulse control. Rather than simply reacting to emotions such as anger or rage, an individual with a fully developed prefrontal cortex is able to inhibit the desire for action that stems from such emotions. However, because during adolescence the prefrontal cortex is biologically immature, the ability to inhibit impulses is not fully developed—leading to some of the risky and impulsive behaviors that are characteristic of adolescence and which we'll discuss later in the chapter (Weinberger, 2001).

Review and Rethink

REVIEW

- Adolescence is a period of rapid physical growth, including the changes associated with puberty. Girls typically begin their growth spurts and puberty about 2 years earlier than boys.
- Puberty can cause reactions in adolescents ranging from confusion to increased self-esteem.
- Early or late maturation can bring advantages and disadvantages, depending on gender as well as emotional and psychological maturity.
- Adequate nutrition is essential in adolescence because of the need to fuel physical growth. Changing physical needs and environmental pressures can induce obesity or eating disorders.
- The two most common eating disorders are anorexia nervosa and bulimia. Both must be treated with a combination of physical and psychological therapies.

RETHINK

- Why do you think the passage to adolescence is regarded in many cultures as such a significant transition that it calls for unique ceremonies?
- How can societal and environmental influences contribute to the emergence of an eating disorder?

Cognitive Development and Schooling

Mrs. Kirby smiled as she read a particularly creative paper. As part of her eighth-grade American Government class every year, she asked students to write about what their lives would be like if America had not won its war for independence from Britain. She had tried something similar with her sixth-graders, but many of them seemed unable to imagine anything different from what they already knew. By eighth grade, however, they were able to come up with some very interesting scenarios.

What is it that sets adolescents' thinking apart from that of younger children? One of the major changes is the ability to think beyond the concrete, current situation to what *might* or *could* be. Adolescents are able to keep in their heads a variety of abstract possibilities, and they can see issues in relative, as opposed to absolute, terms. Instead of viewing problems as having black-and-white solutions, they are capable of perceiving shades of gray (Keating, 1980, 1990).

As was the case with other stages of life, we can use several approaches to explain adolescents' cognitive development. We'll begin by returning to Piaget's theory, which has had a significant influence on how developmentalists think about thinking during adolescence.

Piagetian Approaches to Cognitive Development: Using Formal Operations

Fourteen-year-old Aleigh is asked to solve a problem that anyone who has seen a grandfather's clock may have pondered: What determines the speed at which a pendulum moves back and forth? In the version of the problem that she is asked to solve, Aleigh is given a weight hanging from a string. She is told that she can vary several things: the length of the string, the weight of the object at the end of the string, the amount of force used to push the string, and the height to which the weight is raised in an arc before it is released.

Aleigh doesn't remember, but she was asked to solve the same problem when she was 8 years old, as part of a longitudinal research study. At that time, she was in the concrete operational period, and her efforts to solve the problem were not very successful. She approached the problem haphazardly, with no systematic plan of action. For instance, she simultaneously tried to push the pendulum harder *and* shorten the length of the string *and* increase the weight on the string. Because she was varying so many factors at once, when the speed of the pendulum changed she had no way of knowing which factor or factors made a difference.

Now, however, Aleigh is much more systematic. Rather than immediately beginning to push and pull at the pendulum, she stops a moment and thinks. Then, just like a scientist conducting an experiment, she varies only one factor at a time. By examining each variable separately and systematically, she is able to come to the correct solution: The length of the string determines the speed of the pendulum.

Using Formal Operations to Solve Problems. Aleigh's approach to the pendulum question, a problem devised by Piaget, illustrates that she has moved into the formal operational period of cognitive development (Piaget & Inhelder, 1958). The **formal operational stage** is the stage at which people develop the ability to think abstractly. Piaget suggested that people reach it at the start of adolescence, around the age of 12.

By bringing formal principles of logic to bear on problems they encounter, adolescents in the formal operational stage are able to consider problems in the abstract rather than only in concrete terms. They are able to test their understanding by systematically carrying out rudimentary experiments on problems and situations, and observing what their experimental "interventions" bring about.

Adolescents in the formal operational stage use *hypothetico-deductive reasoning,* in which they start with a general theory about what produces a particular outcome, and then deduce explanations for specific situations in which they see that particular outcome. Like scientists who form hypotheses, they can then test their theories. What distinguishes this kind of thinking from earlier cognitive stages is the ability to start with abstract

formal operational period the stage at which people develop the ability to think abstractly

Like scientists who form hypotheses, adolescents in the formal operational stage use hypothetico-deductive reasoning. They start with a general theory about what produces a particular outcome, and then deduce explanations for specific situations in which they see that particular outcome.

possibilities and move to the concrete; in previous stages, children are tied to the concrete here-and-now. For example, at age 8, Aleigh just started moving things around to see what would happen in the pendulum problem, a concrete approach. At age 12, however, she started with the abstract idea that each variable—the string, the size of the weight, and so forth—should be tested separately.

In addition to using hypothetico-deductive reasoning, adolescents also can employ propositional thought during the formal operational stage. *Propositional thought* is reasoning that uses abstract logic in the absences of concrete examples. For example, propositional thinking allows adolescents to understand that if certain premises are true, then a conclusion must also be true. For example, consider the following:

All men are mortal.   *[premise]*

Socrates is a man.   *[premise]*

Therefore, Socrates is mortal.   *[conclusion]*

Not only can adolescents understand that if both premises are true, then so is the conclusion, but they are also capable of using similar reasoning when premises and conclusions are stated more abstractly, as follows:

All As are B.   *[premise]*

C is an A.   *[premise]*

Therefore, C is a B.   *[conclusion]*

Although Piaget proposed that children enter the formal operational stage at the beginning of adolescence, you may recall that he also hypothesized that—as with all the stages of cognitive development—full capabilities do not emerge suddenly, at one stroke. Instead, they gradually unfold through a combination of physical maturation and environmental experiences. According to Piaget, it is not until adolescents are around 15 years old that they are fully settled in the formal operational stage.

In fact, some evidence suggests that a sizable proportion of people hone their formal operational skills at a later age, and in some cases, never fully employ formal operational thinking at all. For instance, most studies show that only 40 to 60 percent of college students and adults achieve formal operational thinking completely, and some estimates run as low as 25 percent. But many of those adults who do not show formal operational thought in every domain are fully competent in *some* aspects of formal operations (Keating & Clark, 1980; Sugarman, 1988).

One of the reasons adolescents differ in their use of formal operations relates to the culture in which they were raised. For instance, people who live in isolated, scientifically unsophisticated societies and who have little formal education are less likely to perform at the formal operational level than formally educated persons living in more technologically sophisticated societies (Jahoda, 1980; Segall et al., 1990).

Does this mean that adolescents (and adults) from cultures in which formal operations tend not to emerge are incapable of attaining them? Not at all. A more probable conclusion is that the scientific reasoning that characterizes formal operations is not equally valued in all societies. If everyday life does not require or promote a certain type of reasoning, it is unreasonable to expect people to employ that type of reasoning when confronted with a problem (Greenfield, 1976; Shea, 1985; Gauvain, 1998).

Adolescents ability to reason abstractly leads them to be able to question accepted rules and explanations.

The Consequences of Adolescents' Use of Formal Operations. Adolescents' ability to reason abstractly, embodied in their use of formal operations, leads to a change in their everyday behavior. Whereas earlier they may have unquestioningly accepted rules and explanations set out for them, their increased abstract reasoning abilities may lead them to question their parents and other authority figures far more strenuously.

In general, adolescents become more argumentative, sometimes for the sake of being argumentative. They enjoy using abstract reasoning to poke holes in others' explanations, and their increased abilities to think critically make them acutely sensitive to parents' and teachers' perceived shortcomings (Elkind, 1996).

Coping with the increased argumentativeness of adolescents can be challenging for parents, teachers, and other adults who deal with adolescents. But it also makes adolescents more interesting, as they actively seek to understand the values and justifications that they encounter in their lives.

Evaluating Piaget's Approach. Each time we've considered Piaget's theory in previous chapters, several concerns have cropped up. Let's summarize some of the issues here:

■ Piaget suggests that cognitive development proceeds in universal, step-like advances that occur at particular stages. Yet we find significant differences in cognitive abilities from one person to the next, especially when we compare individuals from different cultures. Furthermore, we find inconsistencies even within the same individual. People may be able to accomplish some tasks that indicate they have reached a certain level of thinking, but not others. If Piaget were correct, a person ought to perform uniformly well once she or he reaches a given stage (Siegler, 1994).

■ The notion of stages proposed by Piaget suggests that cognitive abilities do not grow gradually or smoothly. Instead, the stage point of view implies that cognitive growth is typified by relatively rapid shifts from one stage to the next. In contrast, many developmentalists argue that cognitive development proceeds in a more continuous fashion, increasing not so much in qualitative leaps forward as in quantitative accumulations. They also contend that Piaget's theory is better at *describing* behavior at a given stage than *explaining* why the shift from one stage to the next occurs (Gelman & Baillargeon, 1983; Case, 1991).

■ Because of the nature of the tasks Piaget employed to measure cognitive abilities, critics suggest that he underestimated the age at which certain capabilities emerge. It is now widely accepted that infants and children are more sophisticated at an earlier age than Piaget asserted (Bornstein & Sigman, 1986).

■ Piaget had a relatively narrow view of what is meant by *thinking* and *knowing*. To Piaget knowledge consists primarily of the kind of understanding displayed in the pendulum problem. However, as we discussed in Chapter 9, developmentalists such as Howard Gardner suggest that we have many kinds of intelligence, separate from and independent of one another (Gardner, 2000).

■ Finally, some developmentalists argue that formal operations do not represent the epitome of thinking and that more sophisticated forms of thinking do not actually emerge until early adulthood. For instance, developmental psychologist Giesela Labouvie-Vief (1980, 1986) argues that the complexity of society requires thought that is not necessarily based on pure logic. Instead, a kind of thinking is required that is flexible, allows for interpretive processes, and reflects the fact that reasons behind events in the real world are subtle—something that Labouvie-Vief calls *postformal thinking.* (We'll examine Labouvie-Vief's ideas on postformal thinking in more detail in Chapter 13).

These criticisms and concerns regarding Piaget's approach to cognitive development have considerable merit. On the other hand, Piaget made momentous contributions to our understanding of cognitive development, and his work remains highly influential. He was a brilliant observer of children's and adolescents' behavior, and his portrayal of children as actively constructing and transforming information about their world has had a substantial impact on the way we view children and their cognitive capabilities.

Piaget's theory has been the impetus for an enormous number of studies on the development of thinking capacities and processes, and it also spurred a good deal of classroom reform. Finally, his bold statements about the nature of cognitive development provided a fertile soil from which many opposing positions on cognitive development bloomed, such as the information-processing perspective, to which we turn next (Demetriou, Shayer, & Efklides, 1993; Zigler & Gilman, 1998).

Information-Processing Perspectives: Gradual Transformations in Abilities

information-processing perspective the model that seeks to identify the way that individuals take in, use, and store information

metacognition the knowledge that people have about their own thinking processes, and their ability to monitor their cognition

To proponents of information-processing approaches to cognitive development, growth in mental abilities proceeds gradually and continuously. Unlike Piaget's view that the increasing cognitive sophistication of the adolescent is a reflection of stage-like spurts, the **information-processing perspective** sees changes in cognitive abilities as gradual transformations in the capacity to take in, use, and store information.

In this view, developmental advances are brought about by progressive changes in the ways people organize their thinking about the world, develop strategies for dealing with new situations, sort facts, and achieve advances in memory capacity and perceptual abilities (Burbules & Lin, 1988; Wellman & Gelman, 1992; Pressley & Schneider, 1997).

The cognitive strides made during adolescence are considerable. Although general intelligence—as measured by traditional IQ tests—remains stable, dramatic improvements evolve in the specific mental abilities that underlie intelligence. Verbal, mathematical, and spatial abilities increase. Memory capacity grows, and adolescents become more adept at effectively dividing their attention across more than one stimulus at a time—such as simultaneously studying for a biology test and listening to a Ricky Martin CD.

Furthermore, as Piaget noted, adolescents grow increasingly sophisticated in their understanding of problems, their ability to grasp abstract concepts and to think hypothetically, and their comprehension of the possibilities inherent in situations.

Adolescents know more about the world, too; their store of knowledge increases as the amount of material to which they are exposed grows and their memory capacity enlarges (Pressley, 1987). Taken as a whole, the mental abilities that underlie intelligence show a marked improvement during adolescence, peaking at around age 20.

According to information-processing explanations of cognitive development during adolescence, one of the most important reasons for advances in mental abilities is the growth of metacognition. **Metacognition** is the knowledge that people have about their own thinking processes, and their ability to monitor their cognition. Although school-age children can use some metacognitive strategies, adolescents are much more adept at understanding their own mental processes.

For example, as adolescents improve their understanding of their memory capacity, they get better at gauging how long they need to study a particular kind of material to memorize it for a test. Furthermore, they can judge when they have fully memorized the material considerably more accurately than when they were younger. These improvements in metacognitive abilities permit adolescents to comprehend and master school material more effectively (Nelson, 1994; Kuhn, 2000).

On the other hand, advances in metacognition do not always produce positive results. For instance, metacognition may make adolescents particularly introspective and self-conscious—two hallmarks of the period which, as we see next, may produce a high degree of egocentrism.

Egocentrism in Thinking: Adolescents' Self-Absorption

Carlos is furious at his parents. He sees them as totally unfair because, when he borrows their car, they insist that he call home and let them know where he is. Eleanor is angry at Molly because Molly, by chance, bought earrings just like hers, and Molly insists on sometimes wearing them to school. Lu is upset with his biology teacher, Ms. Sebastian, for giving a long, difficult midterm exam on which he didn't do well.

Each of these adolescents is furious, angry, or upset over what may seem like not-so-unreasonable behavior on the part of others. Why? One cause may lie in the egocentrism that sometimes dominates adolescents' thinking. **Adolescent egocentrism** is a state of self-absorption in which the world is viewed from one's own point of view. Egocentrism makes adolescents highly critical of authority figures such as parents and teachers, unwilling to accept criticism, and quick to find fault with others' behavior (Elkind, 1967, 1985; Ryeck et al., 1998).

The kind of egocentrism we see in adolescence helps explain why adolescents sometimes perceive that they are the focus of everyone else's attention. In fact, adolescents may develop what has been called an **imaginary audience,** fictitious observers who pay as much attention to the adolescents' behavior as adolescents do themselves.

Because of adolescents' newly sophisticated metacognitive abilities, they readily imagine that others are thinking about them, and they may construct elaborate scenarios about others' thoughts. The imaginary audience is usually perceived as focusing on the one thing that adolescents think most about: themselves. Unfortunately, these scenarios may suffer from the same kind of egocentrism as the rest of their thinking. For instance, a student sitting in a class may be sure a teacher is focusing on her, and a teenager at a basketball game may just know that everyone around is focusing on the pimple on his chin.

Egocentrism leads to a second distortion in thinking: the notion that one's experiences are unique. Adolescents develop **personal fables,** the view that what happens to them is unique, exceptional, and shared by no one else. For instance, teenagers whose romantic relationships have ended may feel that no one has ever experienced the hurt they feel, that no one has ever been treated so badly, that no one can understand what they are going through.

Personal fables also may make adolescents feel invulnerable to the risks that threaten others (Klacynski, 1997). Much of adolescents' risk-taking may well be traced to the personal fables they construct for themselves (Lightfoot, 1997; Ponton, 1999; Greene et al., 2000). They may think that there is no need to use condoms during sex because, in the personal fables they construct, pregnancy and sexually transmitted diseases such as AIDS only happen to other kinds of people, not to them. They may drive after drinking, because their personal fables paint them as careful drivers, always in control.

adolescent egocentrism a state of self-absorption in which the world is viewed from one's own point of view

imaginary audience an adolescent's belief that his or her own behavior is a primary focus of others' attentions and concerns

personal fables the view held by some adolescents that what happens to them is unique, exceptional, and shared by no one else

School Performance

Do the advances that occur in metacognition, reasoning, and other cognitive abilities during adolescence translate into improvements in school performance? If we use students' grades as the measure of school performance, the answer is no. On average, students' grades *decline* during the course of schooling (Schulenberg, Asp, & Petersen, 1984; Simmons & Blyth, 1987).

The reasons for this decline are not entirely clear. Obviously, the nature of the material to which students are exposed becomes increasingly complex and sophisticated over the course of adolescence. But the growing cognitive abilities of adolescents might be expected to compensate for the increased sophistication of the material. Thus, we need to look to other explanations to account for the grade decline.

A better explanation seems to relate not to student performance but to teachers' grading practices. It turns out that teachers grade older adolescents more stringently than younger ones. Consequently, even though students may be demonstrating greater competence as they continue with their schooling, their grades don't necessarily reflect the improvement because teachers are grading them more strictly (Simmons & Blyth, 1987).

The decline in grades may also reflect broader difficulties in educational achievement, particularly that of students in the United States. For example, over the past four decades, the U.S. high school graduation rate has slipped from first place in the world to 24th and now stands at 72 percent (see Figure 11-4; OECD, 1998).

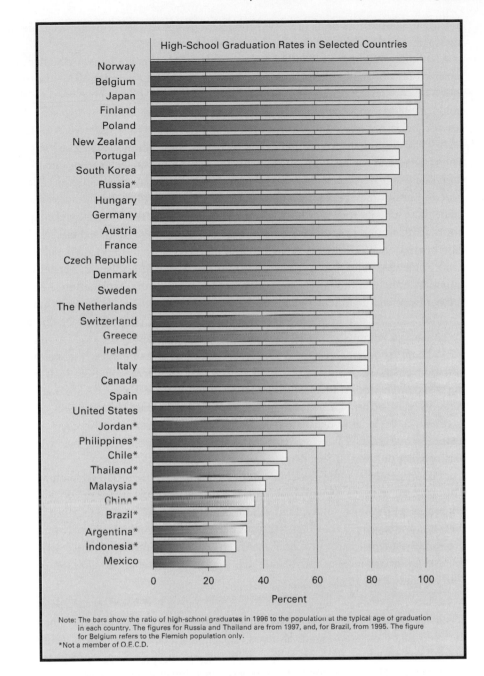

High-School Graduation Rates in Selected Countries

Norway
Belgium
Japan
Finland
Poland
New Zealand
Portugal
South Korea
Russia*
Hungary
Germany
Austria
France
Czech Republic
Denmark
Sweden
The Netherlands
Switzerland
Greece
Ireland
Italy
Canada
Spain
United States
Jordan*
Philippines*
Chile*
Thailand*
Malaysia*
China*
Brazil*
Argentina*
Indonesia*
Mexico

0   20   40   60   80   100

Percent

Note: The bars show the ratio of high-school graduates in 1996 to the population at the typical age of graduation in each country. The figures for Russia and Thailand are from 1997, and, for Brazil, from 1995. The figure for Belgium refers to the Flemish population only.
*Not a member of O.E.C.D.

Figure 11-4 **High School Graduation Rates**

Previously at the top in the percentage of the population who graduates from high school, the United States is now 24th when compared to other industrialized countries.

(*Source:* OECD, 1998.)

Furthermore, the performance of students in the United States on math and science is poor when compared to that of students in other industrialized countries, and performance in geography is only average. There is no single reason for this gap in the educational achievement of U.S. students, but a combination of factors, such as less time spent in classes and less intensive instruction, are at work. For example, the broad diversity of the U.S. school population may affect performance relative to other countries, in which the population attending school is more homogeneous and affluent. Certainly, as we discuss next, differences in socioeconomic status are reflected in school performance within the United States.

Socioeconomic Status and School Performance: Individual Differences in Achievement

Despite the ideal that all students are entitled to the same opportunity in the classroom, it is very clear that certain groups have more educational advantages than others. One of the most telling indicators of this reality is the relationship between educational achievement and socioeconomic status (SES).

Middle- and high-SES students, on average, earn higher grades, score higher on standardized tests of achievement, and complete more years of schooling than students from lower-SES homes. Of course, this disparity does not start in adolescence; the same findings hold for children in lower grades. However, by the time students are in high school, the effects of socioeconomic status become even more pronounced (Garbarino & Asp, 1981).

Why do students from middle- and high-SES homes show greater academic success? There are several explanations, most involving environmental factors. For one thing, children living in poverty lack many of the advantages enjoyed by other children. Their nutrition and health may be less adequate. Often living in crowded conditions and attending inadequate schools, they may have few places to do homework. Their homes may lack the books and computers commonplace in more economically advantaged households (Caldas & Bankston, 1997; Adams & Singh, 1998; Bowen & Bowen, 1999).

Some researchers point to genetic factors as a source of SES differences in educational attainment, although most developmentalists reject this explanation. According to the controversial argument put forward by the authors of *The Bell Curve* (discussed in Chapter 9), lower school performance of children living in poverty may be due to inherited differences in intelligence levels (Herrnstein & Murray, 1994).

There are several reasons to reject this reasoning. For one thing, there is substantial variation in school performance *within* a particular SES level—often, in fact, more than the variation *between* students of different SES. Put another way, there are many low-SES students who perform far better than the average performance of higher-SES students; we have only to consider Cedric Jennings, described in the prologue to this chapter, for an illustration of this fact. Likewise, many higher-SES students perform well below the average performance of lower-SES students.

More important, the consequences of environment are particularly potent. Students from impoverished backgrounds may be at a disadvantage from the day they begin their schooling. As they grow older, their school performance may continue to lag, and in fact their disadvantage may snowball. Because later school success builds heavily on basic skills presumably learned early in school, children who experience problems early may find themselves falling increasingly behind the academic eight ball as adolescents (Huston, 1991; Phillips et al., 1994).

Ethnic and Racial Differences in School Achievement. Achievement differences between ethnic and racial groups are significant, and they paint a troubling picture of American education. For instance, data on school achievement indicate that, on average, African American and Hispanic students tend to perform at lower levels, receive lower grades, and score lower on standardized tests of achievement than Caucasian students (see Table 11-1). In contrast, Asian American students tend to receive higher grades than Caucasian students (Dornbusch, Ritter, & Steinberg, 1992; NCES, 2000).

What is the source of such ethnic and racial differences in academic achievement? Clearly, much of the difference is due to socioeconomic factors: Because more African American and Hispanic families live in poverty, their economic disadvantage may be reflected in their school performance. In fact, when we take socioeconomic levels into account by comparing different ethnic and racial groups at the same socioeconomic level, achievement differences diminish (Steinberg, Dornbusch, & Brown, 1992; Luster & McAdoo, 1994; Meece & Kurtz-Costes, 2001).

But socioeconomic factors are not the full story. For instance, anthropologist John Ogbu (1988, 1992) argues that members of certain minority groups may perceive school success as relatively unimportant. They may believe that societal prejudice in the workplace will dictate that they will not succeed, no matter how much effort they expend. The conclusion is that hard work in school will have no eventual payoff.

Children living in poverty often attend inadequate and crowded schools. Their homes may lack the books and computers that are commonplace in more economically advantaged households. What type of action can be taken to provide equal advantage for children living in poverty?

Furthermore, Ogbu suggests that members of minority groups who enter a new culture voluntarily are more likely to be successful in school than those who are brought into a new culture against their will. For instance, he notes that Korean children who are the sons and daughters of voluntary immigrants to the United States tend to be, on average, quite successful in school. On the other hand, Korean children in Japan, whose parents were forced to immigrate during World War II and work as forced laborers, tend to do relatively poorly in school. The reason for the disparity? The process of involuntary immigration apparently leaves lasting scars, reducing the motivation to succeed in subsequent generations. Ogbu suggests that in the U.S. the involuntary immigration, as slaves, of the ancestors of many African American students might be related to their motivation to succeed (Ogbu, 1992; Gallagher, 1994).

Table 11-1

PERFORMANCE ON TESTS OF ACHIEVEMENT

Reading 1998	4th Graders	8th Graders	12th Graders
National Average	217	264	291
White	227	272	298
Black	194	243	270
Hispanic	196	244	275
Asian/Pacific Islander	225	271	289
American Indian	202	248	276
Mathematics 2000	**4th Graders**	**8th Graders**	**12th Graders**
National Average	228	275	301
White	236	286	308
Black	205	247	274
Hispanic	212	253	283
Asian/Pacific Islander	232*	289	319
American Indian	216	255	293

*1996 Figure
(*Source:* National Center for Education Statistics, National Assessment of Educational Progress (NAEP), 1999, 2001.)

Another factor in the differential success of various ethnic and racial group members has to do with attributions for academic success. As we discussed in Chapter 10, students from many Asian cultures tend to view achievement as the consequence of temporary situational factors, such as how hard they work. In contrast, African American students are more apt to view success as the result of external causes over which they have no control, such as luck or societal biases. Students who subscribe to the belief that effort will lead to success, and then expend that effort, are more likely to do better in school than students who believe that effort makes less of a difference (Stevenson & Stigler, 1992; Stevenson, Chen, & Lee, 1992; Fuligni, 1997).

Ethnic disparities in adolescent performance may also be due to differences in adolescents' beliefs about the consequences of not doing well in school. Specifically, it may be that African American and Hispanic students tend to believe that they can succeed *despite* poor school performance. This belief may cause them to put less effort into their studies. In contrast, Asian American students tend to believe that if they do not do well in school, they are unlikely to get good jobs and be successful. Asian Americans, then, are motivated to work hard in school by a fear of the consequences of poor academic performance (Steinberg, Dornbusch, & Brown, 1992).

Dropping Out of School

Although most students complete high school, some half million students each year drop out prior to graduating. Adolescents who leave school do so for a variety of reasons. Some leave because of pregnancy or problems with the English language. Some must leave for economic reasons, needing to support themselves or their families.

As shown in Figure 11-5, the dropout rate differs according to ethnicity. For instance, although the dropout rate for all ethnicities has been declining somewhat over the last two decades, Hispanics and African American students still are more likely to leave high school before graduating than non-Hispanic white students. On the other hand, not all minority groups show higher dropout rates: Asians, for instance, drop out at a lower rate than Caucasians (NCES, 2000; Canedy, 2001).

Twenty-three percent of students who live in households with the lowest 20 percent of income levels drop out. This rate is nearly eight times greater than the 3 percent of dropout students in households with incomes in the highest 20 percent. Because economic success is so dependent on education, dropping out often perpetuates a cycle of poverty (U.S. National Center for Education Statistics, 1997). (For another aspect of schooling, see the *From Research to Practice* box.)

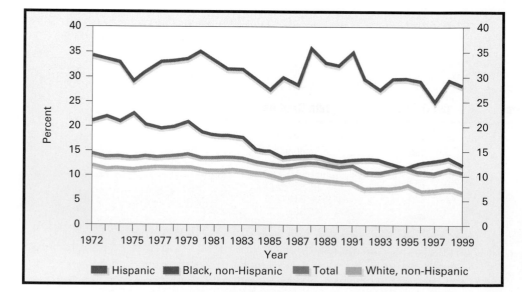

Figure 11-5   **Dropout Rates Differ According to Ethnicity**

Hispanic and African American students are still more likely not to graduate in spite of lower dropout rates.

(*Source:* National Center for Education Statistics, 2000.)

From Research to Practice
Preventing School Violence

When two students went on a rampage at Littleton, Colorado's Columbine High School one bright April morning, the result was shocking. The killers, who targeted blacks and athletes, murdered 13 fellow students and a teacher, and they planted dozens of bombs around the school. As the two ran through the school, laughing, students hid in storage rooms, offices, and closets to escape the danger. At the end of the shooting spree, they took their own lives.

In retrospect, the signs of impending violence seemed obvious. One of the pair created a Web page containing death threats, and the two had made a video for a class that foreshadowed the massacre. One had a bedroom filled with Nazi and hate literature and explosives. They threatened fellow students, saying, "just wait" to those who made fun of the black trenchcoats they wore as members of the "Trenchcoat Mafia." Minor disagreements with others turned into threats of violence. In a philosophy class, one spoke incessantly about purchasing a gun.

Still, no one could predict the direction their anger would take.

The Columbine shooting is one of a number of significant acts of violence that have occurred in U.S. schools. Since 1974, there have been about 100 incidents of school violence. The good news is that despite the public perception that school violence is on the upswing, in fact there has been a decline in overall violence. Even in the year of the Columbine shooting, the number of deaths in school-related incidents dropped 40 percent from the previous year (Spencer, J., 2001).

Although statistically the likelihood of injury from a school shooting is tiny, and school is actually one of the safest places for children, parents and their children still worry about safety issues. For example, after a school shooting in Jonesboro, Arkansas, almost three-quarters of respondents said they felt that a shooting was "likely" or "very likely" in their own community.

Why do some students behave in violent ways? In an analysis of school shootings, the Federal Bureau of Investigation has identified several characteristics of individuals who are at risk for carrying out violence in schools. They include a low tolerance for frustration, poor coping skills, a lack of resiliency, failed love relationships, resentment over perceived injustices, depression, self-centeredness, and alienation (O'Toole, 2000).

According to psychologist Elliot Aronson, students who carry out violence in schools frequently were the targets of bullying or have been rejected in some way. He notes that there are tremendous status differences in schools, and students who have been taunted and humiliated by students of higher status (or by their parents or other adults) may lash out in frustration (Aronson, 2000).

To respond to the potential of violence, many schools have taken significant steps to prevent a shooting. Some have installed metal detectors and security cameras and conduct surprise searches of student lockers. Others have a "zero tolerance" policy that mandates that students are suspended if they bring to school anything—such as a penknife—that could potentially be a weapon. Some schools even make students wear identification tags and carry clear plastic backpacks.

Unfortunately, there is little evidence that such security measures are effective. What seems to work better are programs that moderate the cultures of schools. For instance, programs involving cooperative learning, peer mediation, and communication skills training appear to be helpful. In addition, teaching students, parents, and educators to take threats seriously is important; many students who become violent threaten to commit violence before they actually do. Ultimately, schools need to be places where students feel comfortable discussing their feelings and problems, rather than sources of alienation and rejection (Aronson, 2000; Spencer, J., 2001).

Review and Rethink

REVIEW

■ Adolescence corresponds to Piaget's formal operations period, a stage characterized by abstract reasoning and an experimental approach to problems.

■ According to the information processing perspective, the cognitive advances of adolescence are quantitative and gradual, involving improvements in many aspects of thinking and memory. Improved metacognition enables the monitoring of thought processes and of mental capacities.

■ Adolescents are susceptible to adolescent egocentrism and the perception that their behavior is constantly observed by an imaginary audience. They also construct personal fables that stress their uniqueness and immunity to harm.

■ Academic performance is linked in complex ways to socioeconomic status and to race and ethnicity.

RETHINK

■ When faced with complex problems, do you think most adults spontaneously apply formal operations like those used to solve the pendulum problem? Why or why not?

■ In what ways does adolescent egocentrism complicate adolescents' social and family relationships? Do adults entirely outgrow egocentrism and personal fables?

Threats to Adolescents' Well-Being

Like most parents, I had thought of drug use as something you worried about when your kids got to high school. Now I know that, on the average, kids begin using drugs at 11 or 12, but at the time that never crossed our minds. Ryan had just begun attending mixed parties. He was playing Little League. In the eighth grade, Ryan started getting into a little trouble—one time he and another fellow stole a fire extinguisher, but we thought it was just a prank. Then his grades began to deteriorate. He began sneaking out at night. He would become belligerent at the drop of a hat, then sunny and nice again. . . .

It wasn't until Ryan fell apart at 14 that we started thinking about drugs. He had just begun McLean High School, and to him, it was like going to drug camp every day. Back then, everything was so available. He began cutting classes, a common tip-off, but we didn't hear from the school until he was flunking everything. It turned out that he was going to school for the first period, getting checked in, then leaving and smoking marijuana all day (Shafer, 1990, p. 82).

Ryan's parents learned all too soon that marijuana was not the only drug Ryan was using. As his friends later admitted, Ryan was what they called a "garbage head." He would try anything. Despite efforts to curb his use of drugs, he never succeeded in stopping. He died at the age of 16, hit by a passing car after wandering into the street during an episode of drug use.

Although most cases of adolescent drug use produce far less extreme results, the use of drugs, as well as other kinds of substance use and abuse, represents a primary threat to health during adolescence, which otherwise is usually one of the healthiest periods of life. While the extent of risky behavior is difficult to gauge, preventable problems such as drug, alcohol, and tobacco use, as well as sexually transmitted diseases, represent serious threats to adolescents' well-being.

Illegal Drugs

How common is illegal drug use during adolescence? Very. For instance, the most recent annual survey of nearly 50,000 U.S. students shows that almost 40 percent of high school seniors and more than a third of eighth-graders report having used marijuana within the past year. Furthermore, these figures have been steadily increasing since the early 1990s (Johnston, Bachman, & O'Malley, 2000; see Figure 11-6).

The use of other illegal drugs is also on the rise. Although drug use by adolescents is less prevalent than it was during parts of the 1970s and 1980s, drug use began to rise during the early 1990s. Furthermore, usage rates for some illegal drugs, such as Ecstasy, increased considerably at the end of the 1990s and the beginning of the 21st century.

Why do adolescents use drugs? There are multiple reasons. Some relate to the perceived pleasurable experience drugs may provide, and others to the escape from the pres-

The use of marijuana among high school students has increased significantly since the early 1990s.

sures of everyday life that drugs temporarily permit. Some adolescents try drugs simply for the thrill of doing something illegal. The alleged drug use of well-known role models, such as movie star Robert Downey, Jr., may also contribute. Finally, peer pressure plays a role: Adolescents, as we'll discuss in greater detail in Chapter 12, are particularly susceptible to the perceived standards of their peer groups (Petraitis, Flay, & Miller, 1995; Jenkins, 1996; Bogenschneider et al., 1998).

The use of illegal drugs is dangerous in several respects. For instance, some drugs are addictive. **Addictive drugs** are drugs that produce a biological or psychological dependence in users, leading to increasingly powerful cravings for them. When drugs produce a biological addiction, their presence in the body becomes so common that the body is unable to function in their absence. Drugs can also produce a psychological addiction. In such cases, people grow to depend on drugs to cope with the everyday stress of life.

In addition, if drugs are used as an escape, they may prevent adolescents from confronting—and potentially solving—the problems that led them to drug use in the first

addictive drugs drugs that produce a biological or psychological dependence in users, leading to increasingly powerful cravings for them

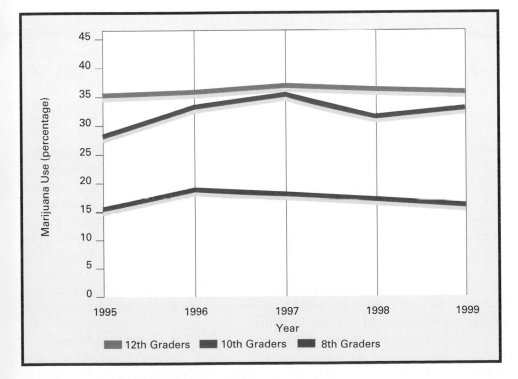

Figure 11-6 **Going to Pot**

According to the most recent annual survey, marijuana use over the last twelve months has increased since 1995 for 10th and 12th graders, but dropped slightly for 8th graders.

(*Source:* Johnston, Bachman, & O'Malley, 2000)

SPEAKING OF DEVELOPMENT

Doreen Gail Branch, Substance Abuse Researcher

BORN: 1958

EDUCATION: Howard University, Washington, D.C., B.S. and M.A. in psychology

POSITION: Research Associate for the National Public Service Research Institute

HOME: Greenbelt, Maryland

People of many ages abuse alcohol, tobacco, and drugs, but one group that is particularly vulnerable to the allure of drugs is adolescents. In an effort to create effective preventive programs, Doreen Branch is working on a project with a community services coalition in Maryland's Prince George's County. The coalition serves adolescents between the ages of 12 and 18.

"We are currently looking at the community and how the different parts can band together to battle alcohol, tobacco, and other drug abuse problems, as well as those associated with their use," says Branch.

One major goal of her work is to provide youth with alternatives to using drugs by introducing them to other activities. "Many people are familiar with midnight basketball programs," she says, "but our efforts go beyond them. For instance, one of the things we are developing is a tennis program that not only teaches tennis, but also provides mentoring to at-risk adoles-

cents." She notes that such a program emphasizes that there are other things to do with one's time than use drugs.

"We have to educate students on drugs, and we need to inform them of the dangers of even a little drug use. Many adolescents that we deal with do not believe that marijuana, and sometimes even cocaine, are harmful," Branch adds.

Branch is also studying how tobacco and alcohol manufacturers use advertising to influence teenagers. "One of the things that we are trying to do is to change local policies in terms of billboards that cater to the advertising of cigarettes and alcohol. While many of these advertisements are in the poorest sections of town, all teenagers can be influenced by them," she notes.

One tactic she has used to deter drug use by adolescents has been to ask them to write, produce, and act in their own commercials on the dangers of drug and alcohol abuse. Another has been to provide funding for a large meeting, the "Kiamsha Youth Empowerment Conference." With some help from adult mentors, Maryland adolescents organized the meeting largely by themselves.

"The issues discussed at the conference included drugs, sex, violence, and spirituality," says Branch. "The whole conference was planned and conducted by teenagers. They hit on a lot of issues that kids have to deal with, and—in part because it was planned by the adolescents themselves—it was a great success."

---

place. Finally, drugs may be dangerous because even casual users of less hazardous drugs can escalate to more dangerous forms of substance abuse. For instance, those who smoke marijuana are 85 times more likely to use cocaine than those who do not (Toch, 1995; Segal & Stewart, 1996). (Also see the *Speaking of Development* interview.)

Alcohol: Use and Abuse

More than 75 percent of college students have something in common: They've consumed at least one alcoholic drink during the last 30 days. More than 40 percent say they've had 5 or more drinks within the past 2 weeks, and some 16 percent drink 16 or more drinks per week. High school students, too, are drinkers: Some 76 percent of high school seniors report having had an alcoholic drink in the last year, and in some subgroups—such as male athletes—the proportion of drinkers is even higher (NIAAA, 1990; Carmody, 1990; Center on Addiction and Substance Abuse, 1994; Carr, Kennedy, & Dimick, 1996).

One of the most troubling patterns is the frequency of binge drinking in college students. Binge drinking is defined for men as drinking five or more drinks in one sitting; for women, who tend to weigh less and whose bodies absorb alcohol less efficiently, binge drinking is defined as four drinks in one sitting.

Recent surveys find that some 50 percent of male college students and 39 percent of female college students say they participated in binge drinking during the previous 2 weeks (see Figure 11-7). Even for lighter drinkers and nondrinkers, the high level of

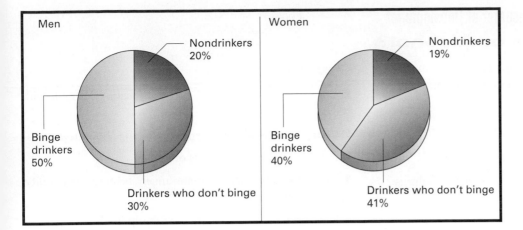

Figure 11-7 Binge Drinking Among College Students

For men, binge drinking was defined as consuming five or more drinks in one sitting; for women, the total was four or more. Why is binge drinking popular?

(*Source:* Wechsler et al., 2000.)

drinking among their peers affects their college experience. For instance, two-thirds of lighter drinkers reported that they had been disturbed by drunken students while sleeping or studying. Around a third had been insulted or humiliated by a drunken student, and 25 percent of women said they had been the target of an unwanted sexual advance by a drunk classmate (Wechsler et al., 2000).

Why do adolescents start to drink? Some believe it is the "adult" thing to do. For some—especially male athletes, whose rate of drinking tends to be higher than that of the adolescent general population—drinking is seen as a way of maintaining a "macho" image. Others drink for the same reason that they use drugs: It releases inhibitions and tension and reduces stress. Finally, some adolescents drink because of a *false consensus effect,* in which they assume that everyone is drinking at high levels due to a few conspicuous examples (Carr, Kennedy, & Dimick, 1996; Pavis, Cunningham-Burley, & Amos, 1997).

For some adolescents, alcohol use becomes a habit that cannot be controlled. **Alcoholics, those with alcohol problems, learn to depend on alcohol and are unable to control their drinking.** They also become increasingly immune to the consequences of drinking, and therefore need to drink ever larger amounts of liquor in order to bring about the positive effects they crave. Some drink throughout the day, while others go on binges in which they consume huge quantities of alcohol (NIAAA, 1990; Morse & Flavin, 1992).

The reasons that some adolescents become alcoholics are not fully known. Genetics plays a role: Alcoholism runs in families. On the other hand, not all alcoholics have family members with alcohol problems. For those adolescents, alcoholism may be triggered by efforts to deal with environmental stress (Bushman, 1993; Boyd, Howard, & Zucker, 1995).

No matter what the origins of an adolescent's problems with alcohol or drugs, parents, teachers, and friends can help the teen find help—if they realize there is a problem. How can concerned friends and family members tell if an adolescent they know is having difficulties with alcohol or drugs? Some of the telltale signs are described next.

alcoholics persons with alcohol problems who have learned to depend on alcohol and are unable to control their drinking

Tobacco: The Dangers of Smoking

Most adolescents are well aware of the dangers of smoking, but many still indulge in it. While recent figures show that, overall, a smaller proportion of adolescents smoke than in prior decades, the numbers remain substantial. Furthermore, within certain groups the numbers are increasing. For instance, smoking is more prevalent among girls, and in several countries, including Austria, Norway, and Sweden, the proportion of girls who smoke is higher than the proportion of boys. There are racial differences, as well: White children and children in lower socioeconomic status households are more likely to experiment with cigarettes and to start smoking earlier than African American children and children living in higher socioeconomic status households. Also, smoking among white males of high school age is significantly greater than among African American males in high school,

The portrayal of Joe Camel as a hip and smooth character helped to maintain the image of smoking as a "cool" activity.

The Informed Consumer of Development
Hooked on Drugs or Alcohol?

Although it is not always easy to determine if an adolescent has a drug or alcohol abuse problem, there are some signals. Among them:

Identification with the drug culture

▶ Drug-related magazines or slogans on clothing

▶ Conversation and jokes that are preoccupied with drugs

▶ Hostility discussing drugs

▶ Collection of beer cans

Signs of physical deterioration

▶ Memory lapses, short attention span, difficulty concentrating

▶ Poor physical coordination, slurred or incoherent speech

▶ Unhealthy appearance, indifference to hygiene and grooming

▶ Bloodshot eyes, dilated pupils

Dramatic changes in school performance

▶ Marked downturn in grades—not just from C's to F's, but from A's to B's and C's; assignments not completed

▶ Increased absenteeism or tardiness

Changes in behavior

▶ Chronic dishonesty (lying, stealing, cheating); trouble with the police

▶ Changes in friends; evasiveness in talking about new ones

▶ Possession of large amounts of money

▶ Increasing and inappropriate anger, hostility, irritability, secretiveness

▶ Reduced motivation, energy, self-discipline, self-esteem

▶ Diminished interest in extracurricular activities and hobbies (Adapted from Franck & Brownstone, 1991, p. 593–594.)

If an adolescent—or anyone else, for that matter—fits any of these descriptors, help is probably needed. It is possible to get advice from a national hotline. For alcohol difficulties, call the National Council on Alcoholism at (800) 622-2255; for drug problems, call the National Institute on Drug Abuse at (800) 662-4357. In addition, those who need advice can find a local listing for Alcoholics Anonymous or Narcotics Anonymous in the telephone book. Finally, for help with alcohol and drug problems, contact the National Council on Alcoholism and Drug Dependence at 12 West 21 Street, New York, NY 10010.

---

although the differences have narrowed in recent years (Griesler & Kandel, 1998; Harrell et al., 1998; Stolberg, 1998).

Adolescents smoke despite growing social sanctions against the habit. As the dangers of secondhand smoke become more apparent, many people look down on smokers. More places, including schools and places of business, have become "smoke-free," a trend that makes it increasingly difficult to find a place to smoke. Furthermore, the health dangers of smoking are hardly in dispute: Every package of cigarettes carries a warning that smoking is linked to a higher mortality rate, and even adolescents who smoke admit that they know the dangers.

Why, then, do adolescents begin to smoke and then maintain the habit? One reason is that smoking is still considered sexy and hip. Advertisements for cigarettes depict attractive individuals smoking, and clever ads, such as the highly successful "Joe Camel" series, make an effective pitch to young males. In fact, before Joe Camel commercials were withdrawn from use, children as young as 6 could identify Joe Camel as readily as Mickey Mouse (Lipman, 1992; Ono, 1995; Bartecchi, MacKenzie, & Schrier, 1995; Urberg, Degirmencioglu, & Pilgrim, 1997).

There are other reasons, too. Nicotine, the active chemical ingredient of cigarettes, can produce biological and psychological dependency: Smoking produces a pleasant emotional state that smokers seek to maintain (Pomerleau & Pomerleau, 1989; Nowak, 1994b). Furthermore, exposure to parents and peers who smoke increases the chances that an adolescent will take up the habit (Botvin, et al., 1994; Webster, Hunter, & Keats, 1994). Finally, smoking is sometimes seen as an adolescent rite of passage: Trying cigarettes is looked upon as a sign of growing up. Although one or two cigarettes do not usually produce a lifetime smoker, it takes only a little more to start the habit. In fact, people who smoke as few as 10 cigarettes early in their lives stand an 80 percent chance of becoming habitual smokers (Salber, Freeman, & Abelin, 1968; Bowen et al., 1991; Stacy et al., 1992).

Developmental Diversity

Selling Death: Pushing Smoking to the Less Advantaged

In Dresden, Germany, three women in miniskirts offer passers-by a pack of Lucky Strikes and a leaflet that reads "You just got hold of a nice piece of America." Says a local doctor, "Adolescents time and again receive cigarettes at such promotions."

A Jeep decorated with the Camel logo pulls up to a high school in Buenos Aires. A woman begins handing out free cigarettes to 15- and 16-year-olds during their lunch recess.

At a video arcade in Taipei, free American cigarettes are strewn atop each game. At a disco filled with high school students, free packs of Salems are on each table (Ecenbarger, 1993, p. 50).

If you are a cigarette manufacturer and you find that the number of people using your product is declining, what do you do? U.S. companies have sought to carve out new markets by turning to the least advantaged groups of people, both at home and abroad. For instance, in the early 1990s the R.J. Reynolds tobacco company designed a new brand of cigarettes it named "Uptown." The advertising used to herald its arrival made clear who the target was: African Americans living in urban areas (Quinn, 1990). Because of subsequent protests, the tobacco company withdrew "Uptown" from the market.

In addition to seeking new converts in the United States, tobacco companies aggressively recruit adolescent smokers abroad. In many developing countries the number of smokers is still low. Tobacco companies are seeking to increase this number through marketing strategies designed to hook adolescents on the habit by means of free samples. In addition, in countries where American culture and products are held in high esteem, advertising suggests that the use of cigarettes is an American—and consequently prestigious—habit (Sesser, 1993).

The strategy is effective. For instance, in some Latin American cities as many as 50 percent of teenagers smoke. According to the World Health Organization, smoking will prematurely kill some 200 million of the world's children and adolescents, and overall, 10 percent of the world's population will die because of smoking (Ecenbarger, 1993). ☐

Sexually Transmitted Diseases: One Cost of Sex

In the fall of 1990, Krista Blake was 18 and looking forward to her first year at Youngstown State University in Ohio. She and her boyfriend were talking about getting married. Her life was, she says, "basic, white-bread America." Then she went to the doctor, complaining about a backache, and found out she had the AIDS virus.

Blake had been infected with HIV, the virus that causes AIDS, two years earlier by an older boy, a hemophiliac. "He knew that he was infected, and he didn't tell me," she says. "And he didn't do anything to keep me from getting infected, either." (Becahy, 1992, p. 49)

Krista Blake contracted AIDS at the age of 16. She later died from the disease.

acquired immunodeficiency syndrome (AIDS) a sexually transmitted disease, produced by the HIV virus, that has no cure and ultimately causes death

sexually transmitted disease (STD) a disease that is spread through sexual contact

chlamydia the most common sexually transmitted disease, caused by a parasite

AIDS. Krista Blake, who later died from the disorder, was not alone: **Acquired immunodeficiency syndrome,** or **AIDS,** is one of the leading causes of death among young people. AIDS has no cure and ultimately brings death to those who are infected with the HIV virus that produces the disease.

Because AIDS is spread primarily through sexual contact, it is classified as a **sexually transmitted disease (STD).** Although it began as a problem that primarily afflicted homosexuals, it has spread to other populations, including heterosexuals and intravenous drug users. Minorities have been particularly hard hit: African Americans and Hispanics account for some 40 percent of AIDS cases, although they make up only 18 percent of the population. Already, 16 million people have died due to AIDS, and the number of people living with the disease numbers 34 million worldwide (see Figure 11-8).

AIDS and Adolescent Behavior. It is no secret how AIDS is transmitted—through the exchange of bodily fluids, including semen and blood. However, motivating teenagers to employ safer sex practices that can prevent its spread has proven difficult. On the one hand, the use of condoms during sexual intercourse has increased, and people are less likely to engage in casual sex with new acquaintances (Kalichman, 1998; Everett, et al., 2000).

On the other hand, the use of safer sex practices is far from universal. Adolescents, who—as we discussed earlier in the chapter—are prone to engage in risky behavior due to feelings of invulnerability, are likely to believe that their chances of contracting AIDS are minimal. This is particularly true when adolescents perceive that their partner is "safe"—someone they know well and with whom they are involved in a relatively long-term relationship (Serovich & Greene, 1997; Freiberg, 1998; Lefkowitz, Sigman, & Kit-fong Au, 2000).

Unfortunately, unless an individual knows the complete sexual history and HIV status of a partner, unprotected sex remains risky business. And learning a partner's complete sexual history is difficult. It is often inaccurately communicated because of embarrassment, a sense of privacy, or simply forgetfulness.

Short of celibacy, a solution regarded as improbable for many adolescents involved in relationships, there is no certain way to avoid AIDS. However, health experts suggest several strategies for making sex safer; these are listed in Table 11-2.

Other Sexually Transmitted Diseases. Although AIDS is the deadliest of sexually transmitted diseases, others are far more common (see Figure 11-9). In fact, one out of four adolescents contracts an STD before graduating from high school. Overall, around 2.5 million teenagers contract an STD, such as the ones listed here, each year. (Alan Guttmacher Institute, 1993a; Ubell, 1996; Leary, 1996).

Figure 11-8 **AIDS Around the World**

The number of people carrying the AIDS virus varies substantially by geographic region. By far the most cases are found in Africa and the Middle East, although the disease is a growing problem in Asia.

(*Source:* United Nations AIDS Program, 1999.)

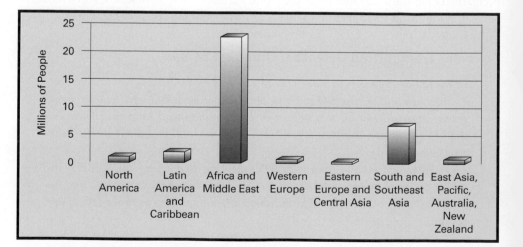

Table 11-2

SAFER SEX: PREVENTING THE TRANSMISSION OF AIDS

Health psychologists and educators have devised several guidelines to help prevent the spread of AIDS. Among them are the following:

- **Use condoms.** The use of condoms greatly reduces the risk of transmission of the virus that produces AIDS, which occurs through exposure to bodily fluids such as semen or blood.

- **Avoid high-risk behaviors.** Such practices as unprotected anal intercourse or the exchange of needles used in drug use greatly increase the risk of AIDS.

- **Know your partner's sexual history.** Knowing your sexual partner and his or her sexual history can help you to evaluate the risks of sexual contact.

- **Consider abstinence.** Although not always a practical alternative, the only certain way of avoiding AIDS is to refrain from sexual activity altogether.

Chlamydia, a disease caused by a parasite, is the most common STD. Initially it has few symptoms, but later it causes burning urination and a discharge from the penis or vagina. It can lead to pelvic inflammation and even to sterility. Although not bacterial in origin, chlamydial infections can be treated successfully with antibiotics. Unfortunately, many adolescents are not aware of chlamydia, and those who have heard of it are typically unaware of the problems it causes (Nockels & Oakshott, 1999).

Another common STD is **genital herpes,** a virus not unlike the cold sores that sometimes appear around the mouth. The first symptoms of herpes are often small blisters or sores around the genitals, which may break open and become quite painful. Although the sores may heal after a few weeks, the disease often recurs after an interval, and the cycle repeats itself. When the sores reappear, the disease, for which there is no cure, is contagious.

Several other STDs are frequent among adolescents. *Trichomoniasis,* an infection in the vagina or penis, is caused by a parasite. Initially without symptoms, it can eventually cause a painful discharge. *Gonorrhea* and *syphilis* are the STDs that have been recognized for the longest time; cases were recorded by ancient historians. Until the advent of antibiotics, both diseases were deadly; today both can be treated quite effectively.

Even though many STDs are treatable, they remain a serious health concern. Furthermore, contracting an STD is not only an immediate problem during adolescence, but could become a problem later in life, too. Some diseases increase the chances of future infertility and cancer.

genital herpes a common sexually transmitted disease which is a virus and not unlike cold sores that sometimes appear around the mouth

cw

---

3 million teenagers, about 1 person in 8 aged 13–19 and about 1 in 4 of those who have had sexual intercourse, acquire an STD every year. Among the most common:

Chlamydia: Chlamydia is more common among teenagers than among older men and women; in some studies, 10 to 29 percent of sexually active adolescent girls and 10 percent of teenage boys have been found to be infected with chlamydia.

Genital herpes: A viral disease that is incurable, often indicated first by small blisters or sores around the genitals. It is periodically contagious.

Trichomoniasis: An infection of the vagina or penis, caused by a parasite.

Gonorrhea: Adolescents aged 15–19 have higher rates of gonorrhea than do sexually active men and women in any 5-year age group between 20–44.

Syphilis: Infectious syphilis rates more than doubled between 1986 and 1990 among women aged 15–19.

***Figure 11-9* Sexually Transmitted Diseases (STDs) Among Adolescents**

Why are adolescents in particular in danger of contracting an STD?

(*Source:* Alan Guttmacher Institute, 1993a.)

Review and Rethink

REVIEW

■ Illegal drug use is prevalent among adolescents as a way to find pleasure, avoid pressure, or gain the approval of peers.

■ The use of alcohol is also popular among adolescents, often to appear adult or to lessen inhibitions.

■ Despite the well-known dangers of smoking, adolescents often smoke to enhance their images or emulate adults.

■ AIDS is the most serious of the sexually transmitted diseases, ultimately causing death. Safe sex practices or sexual abstinence can prevent AIDS, although adolescents often ignore these strategies.

■ Other sexually transmitted diseases affect adolescents, such as chlamydia, genital herpes, trichomoniasis, gonorrhea, and syphilis.

RETHINK

■ How do adolescents' concerns about self-image and their perception that they are the center of attention contribute to smoking and alcohol use?

■ Why do adolescents' increased cognitive abilities, including the ability to reason and to think experimentally, fail to deter them from irrational behavior such as drug and alcohol abuse, tobacco use, and unsafe sex practices?

Looking Back

What physical changes do adolescents experience?

■ The adolescent years are marked by a physical growth spurt, which for girls begins around age 10, and for boys, around age 12.

■ Puberty begins in girls at around 11 and in boys at around 13. The physical changes of puberty often have psychological effects, such as an increase in self-esteem and self-awareness, as well as confusion and uncertainty about sexuality.

What are the consequences of early and late maturation?

■ For boys, early maturation can lead to increased athleticism, greater popularity, and a more positive self-concept. For girls, early maturation can lead to increased popularity and an enhanced social life, but also embarrassment over their bodies. Early maturation can lead boys and girls into situations for which they are not adequately prepared.

■ For boys, late maturation can be a physical and social disadvantage that affects self-concept. Girls who mature late may suffer neglect by their peers, but ultimately they appear to suffer no lasting ill effects and may even benefit.

What nutritional needs and concerns do adolescents have?

■ While most adolescents have no greater nutritional worries other than fueling their growth with appropriate foods,

some are obese or overweight. Excessive concern about obesity can cause some adolescents, especially girls, to contract an eating disorder such as anorexia nervosa or bulimia.

In what ways does cognitive development proceed during adolescence?

■ Cognitive growth during adolescence is rapid, with gains in abstract thinking, reasoning, and the ability to view possibilities in relative rather than absolute terms.

■ Adolescence coincides with Piaget's formal operations period of development, when people begin to engage in abstract thought and experimental reasoning.

■ According to information-processing approaches, cognitive growth during adolescence is gradual and quantitative, involving improvements in memory capacity, mental strategies, metacognition, and other aspects of cognitive functioning.

■ Another major area of cognitive development is the growth of metacognition, which permits adolescents to monitor their thought processes and accurately assess their cognitive capabilities.

■ Adolescent egocentrism is a self-absorption that makes it hard for adolescents to accept criticism and tolerate authority figures. Adolescents may play to an imaginary audience of critical observers, and they may develop personal fables.

▶ *What factors affect adolescent school performance?*

■ School performance declines during the adolescent years. School achievement is linked with socioeconomic status, race, and ethnicity. While many academic achievement differences are due to socioeconomic factors, attributional patterns regarding success factors and belief systems regarding the link between school success and success in life also play a part.

▶ *What dangerous substances do adolescents use, and why?*

■ The use of illicit drugs, alcohol, and tobacco is very prevalent among adolescents, who are motivated by pleasure-seeking, pressure-avoidance, the desire to flout authority, or the imitation of role models.

▶ *What dangers do adolescent sexual practices present, and how can these dangers be avoided?*

■ AIDS is one of the leading causes of death among young people, affecting minority populations with particular severity. Adolescent behavior patterns and attitudes, such as shyness, self-absorption, and a belief in personal invulnerability, militate against the use of safe sex practices that can prevent the disease.

■ Other sexually transmitted diseases, including chlamydia, genital herpes, trichomoniasis, gonorrhea, and syphilis, occur frequently among the adolescent population and can also be prevented by safe sex practices or abstinence.

EPILOGUE

In this chapter, we began our examination of adolescence, a period of great change in people's lives. We looked at the significant physical, psychological, and cognitive changes that adolescents undergo and at some of the consequences of entering and living through adolescence.

Before turning to the next chapter, return for the moment to the opening prologue of this one, about Cedric Jennings. In light of what you now know about adolescence, consider the following questions about Cedric.

1. What are the main threats to physical health and well-being that confront an adolescent boy such as Cedric?

2. What other types of threats would face a student such as Cedric, attending a large school in an environment where crime is prevalent?

3. Why would Cedric and other students like him be the target of threats and violence at school? What would motivate the aggressors, assuming they were also adolescents?

4. How might advances in Cedric's cognitive development have helped him to meet the many challenges he faced?

5. To what do you think Cedric and his family probably attribute academic success? Is this typical of his peer group?

Key Terms and Concepts

adolescence (p. 384)
puberty (p. 385)
menarche (p. 385)
secular trend (p. 386)
primary sex characteristics (p. 386)
secondary sex characteristics (p. 386)
anorexia nervosa (p. 390)
bulimia (p. 391)

formal operational stage (p. 393)
information-processing perspective (p. 396)
metacognition (p. 396)
adolescent egocentrism (p. 397)
imaginary audience (p. 397)
personal fables (p. 397)
addictive drugs (p. 405)

alcoholics (p. 407)
acquired immunodeficiency syndrome (AIDS) (p. 410)
sexually transmitted disease (STD) (p. 410)
chlamydia (p. 410)
genital herpes (p. 411)

Social and Personality Development in Adolescence

Chapter 12

PROLOGUE: FIRST FORMAL

In spite of the rebel stereotype, the majority of adolescents pass through the period in relative tranquility.

Slim and dark, with a passing resemblance to actress Demi Moore, Leah is dressed up and ready to go to the first real formal dance of her life. True, the smashing effect of her short, beaded black dress is marred slightly by the man's shirt she insists on wearing to cover her bare shoulders. And she is in a sulk. Her boyfriend, Sean Moffitt, is four minutes late, and her mother, Linda, refuses to let her stay out all night at a coed sleep-over party after the dance.

When Sean arrives with his mother, Pam, Leah reluctantly sheds the work shirt. She greets Sean shyly, not sure he'll approve of that afternoon's makeover by hairdresser and manicurist. Sean, an easygoing youth with dimples and rosy cheeks, squirms in his tuxedo. Leah recombs his hair and makes him remove his earring. "None of the guys are wearing them to the dance," she declares. (She's wrong. A few moments later, their friends Melissa and Erik arrive, and Erik is wearing his earring.)

Leah's father, George, suggests a 2 A.M. curfew: Leah hoots incredulously. Sean pitches the all-nighter, stressing that the party will be chaperoned. Leah's mother has already talked to the host's mother, mortifying Leah with her off-hand comment that a coed sleep-over seemed "weird." Rolling her eyes, Leah persists: "It's not like anybody's really going to sleep!" Sean asks his mother for another $20. "Why did the amount suddenly jump?" she asks, digging into her purse. (Graham, 1995, p. B1)

Looking   Ahead

This snapshot of the life of 16-year-old Leah Brookner of Norwalk, Connecticut, provides a glimpse of some of the complex, interdependent relationships in which adolescents are involved. As Leah juggles parents, friends, and romantic partners, her life—and those of other adolescents—seems, at times, like an intricate jigsaw puzzle in which not all the pieces fit together perfectly.

Leah's life, which is focused around friends, parents, and school, is surprisingly similar to that of most adolescents. She is not a rebel, and she has good relations with her parents—like most of her peers. For despite the reputation of adolescence as a time of confusion and rebellion, research shows that most people pass through the period without much turmoil. Although they may "try on" different roles and flirt with activities that their parents find objectionable, the majority of adolescents pass through the period in relative tranquility (Peterson, 1988; Steinberg, 1993).

This is not to say that the transitions adolescents pass through are less than highly challenging. As we shall see in this chapter, in which we examine the personality and social developments of the period, adolescence brings about major changes in the ways in which individuals must deal with the world (Takanishi, Hamburg, & Jacobs, 1997; Hersch, 1999).

We begin by considering how adolescents form their views of themselves. We look at self-concept, self-esteem, and identity development. We also examine two major psychological difficulties: depression and suicide.

Next, we discuss relationships during adolescence. We consider how adolescents reposition themselves within the family and how the influence of family members declines in some spheres as peers take on new importance. We also examine the ways in which adolescents interact with their friends, and the determinants of popularity and rejection.

Finally, the chapter considers dating and sexual behavior. We look at the role of dating in adolescents' lives, and we consider sexual behavior and the standards that govern adolescents' sex lives. We conclude by looking at teenage pregnancy and at programs that seek to prevent unwanted pregnancy.

After reading this chapter, you will be able to answer these questions:

▶ **How does the development of self-concept, self-esteem, and identity proceed during adolescence?**

▶ **What dangers do adolescents face as they deal with the stresses of adolescence?**

▶ **How does the quality of relationships with family and peers change during adolescence?**

▶ **What are gender, race, and ethnic relations like in adolescence?**

▶ **What does it mean to be popular and unpopular in adolescence, and how do adolescents respond to peer pressure?**

▶ **What are the functions and characteristics of dating during adolescence?**

▶ **How does sexuality develop in the adolescent years?**

▶ **Why is teenage pregnancy a particular problem in the United States?**

Identity: Asking "Who Am I?"

"Thirteen is a hard age, very hard. A lot of people say you have it easy, you're a kid, but there's a lot of pressure being 13—to be respected by people in your school, to be liked, always feeling like you have to be good. There's pressure to do drugs, too, so you try not to succumb to that. But you don't want to be made fun of, so you have to look cool. You gotta wear the right shoes, the right clothes—if you have Jordans, then it's all right." —Carlos Quintana (1998, p. 66)

The thoughts of 13-year-old Carlos Quintana demonstrate a clear awareness—and self-consciousness—regarding his newly forming place in society and life. During adolescence, questions like "Who am I?" and "Where do I belong in the world?" begin to take a front seat.

Why should issues of identity become so important during adolescence? One reason is that adolescents' intellectual capacities become more adultlike. They now understand and appreciate such abstract issues as the importance of establishing their position in society and the need to form a sense of themselves as individuals. Another reason is that the dramatic physical changes during puberty make adolescents acutely aware of their own bodies and aware that others are reacting to them in ways to which they are unaccustomed. Whatever the cause, adolescence often brings substantial changes in teenagers' self-concepts and self-esteem—in sum, their notions of their own identity.

Self-Concept: Characterizing One's Self

Ask Louella to describe herself, and she says, "Others look at me as laid-back, relaxed, and not worrying too much. But really, I'm often nervous and emotional."

The fact that Louella distinguishes others' views of her from her own perceptions represents a developmental advance of adolescence. In childhood, Louella would have characterized herself according to a list of traits that would not differentiate her view of herself and others' perspectives. However, adolescents are able to make the distinction, and when they try to describe who they are, they take both their own and others' views into account (Harter, 1990a).

This broadening view of themselves is one aspect of adolescents' increasing discernment and perception in their understanding of who they are. The view of the self becomes more organized and coherent, and they can see various aspects of the self simultaneously. Furthermore, they look at the self from a psychological perspective, viewing traits not as concrete entities but as abstractions (Adams, Montemayor, & Gullotta, 1996). For example, teenagers are more likely than younger children to describe themselves in terms of their ideology (saying something like "I'm an environmentalist") than in terms of physical characteristics (such as "I'm the fastest runner in my class").

In some ways, however, the increasing differentiation of self-concept is a mixed blessing, especially during the earlier years of adolescence. At that time, adolescents may be troubled by the multiple aspects of their personalities. During the beginning of adolescence, for instance, teenagers may want to view themselves in a certain way ("I'm a sociable person and love to be with people"), and they may become concerned when their behavior is inconsistent with that view ("Even though I want to be sociable, sometimes I can't stand being around my friends and just want to be alone"). By the end of adolescence, however, teenagers accept that different situations elicit different behaviors and feelings (Harter, 1990b; Pyryt & Mendaglio, 1994).

Adolescents' self-concept is sufficiently broad that they can distinguish between how they see themselves and how others see them. Why are issues of identity so important during adolescence?

Self-Esteem: Evaluating Oneself

Knowing who you are and *liking* who you are represent two different things. Although adolescents become increasingly accurate in understanding who they are (their self-concept), this knowledge does not guarantee that they like themselves (their self-esteem) any better. In fact, their increasing accuracy in understanding themselves permits them to see themselves fully—warts and all.

The same cognitive sophistication that allows adolescents to differentiate various aspects of the self also leads them to evaluate those aspects in different ways (Chan, 1997; Cohen, J., 1999). For instance, an adolescent may have high self-esteem in terms of academic performance, but lower self-esteem in terms of relationships with others. Or it may be just the opposite, as articulated by this adolescent:

> How much do I *like* the kind of person I am? Well, I like some things about me, but I don't like others. I'm glad that I'm popular since it's really important to me to have friends. But in school I don't do as well as the really smart kids. That's OK, because if you're too smart you'll lose your friends. So being smart is just not that important. Except to my parents. I feel like I'm letting them down when I don't do as well as they want. (Harter, 1990b, p. 364)

Gender Differences in Self-Esteem. What determines an adolescent's self-esteem? Several factors make a difference. One is gender: Particularly during early adolescence, girls' self-esteem tends to be lower and more vulnerable than boys' (Watkins, Dong, & Xia, 1997; Byrne, 2000; Miyamoto et al., 2000).

One reason is that, compared to boys, girls are more highly concerned about physical appearance and social success—in addition to academic achievement. Although boys are also concerned about these things, their attitudes are often more casual. Moreover, traditional societal messages may be interpreted as suggesting that female academic achievement is a roadblock to social success. Girls hearing such messages, then, are in a difficult bind: If they do well academically, they jeopardize their social success. No wonder that the self-esteem of adolescent girls is more fragile than that of boys (Hess-Biber, 1996; Mendelson, White, & Mendelson, 1996; Unger & Crawford, 1996).

Socioeconomic Status and Race Differences in Self-Esteem. Socioeconomic status (SES) and race also influence self-esteem. Adolescents of higher SES generally have higher self-esteem than those of lower SES, particularly during middle and later adolescence. It may be that the social status factors that especially enhance one's standing and self-esteem—such as having more expensive clothes or a car—become more conspicuous in the later periods of adolescence (Savin-Williams & Demo, 1983; Van Tassel-Baska, Olszewski-Kubilius, & Kulieke, 1994).

Race also plays a role in self-esteem, although the findings are not entirely consistent. Early studies argued that minority status would lead to lower self-esteem. This finding led to the hypothesis—initially supported—that African Americans and Hispanics would have lower self-esteem than Caucasians. Researchers' explanations for this finding were straightforward: Societal prejudice would be incorporated into the self-concepts of the targets of the prejudice, making them feel disliked and rejected.

However, more recent research paints a different picture. Most findings now suggest that African Americans differ little from whites in their levels of self-esteem (Harter, 1990b). Why should this be? One explanation is that social movements within the African American community that bolster racial pride help support African American adolescents. In fact, research finds that a stronger sense of racial identity is related to a higher level of self-esteem in African Americans and Hispanics (Phinney, Lochner, & Murphy, 1990; Gray-Little & Hafdahl, 2000).

Another reason for overall similarity in self-esteem levels between minority and majority adolescents is that teenagers in general focus their preferences and priorities on those aspects of their lives at which they are best. Consequently, African American youths may concentrate on the things that they find most satisfying and gain self-esteem from being successful at them (Hunt & Hunt, 1975; Phinney & Alipura, 1990).

Current research has found that minority status does not necessarily lead to low self-esteem. In fact, a strong sense of racial identity is tied to higher levels of self-esteem.

Finally, self-esteem may be influenced not by race alone, but by a complex combination of factors. For instance, some developmentalists have considered race and gender simultaneously, coining the term *ethgender* to refer to the joint influence of race and gender. One study that simultaneously took both race and gender into account found that African American and Hispanic males had the highest levels of self-esteem, while Asian and Native American females had the lowest levels (Martinez & Dukes, 1991; Dukes & Martinez, 1994).

Identity Formation in Adolescence: Change or Crisis?

According to Erik Erikson, whose theory we last discussed in Chapter 10, the search for identity inevitably leads some adolescents into substantial psychological difficulties as they encounter the adolescent identity crisis (Erikson, 1963). Erikson's theory regarding this stage, which is summarized with his other stages in Table 12-1, suggests that adolescence is the time of the **identity-versus-identity-confusion stage.**

During the identity-versus-identity-confusion stage, teenagers seek to determine what is unique and distinctive about themselves. They strive to discover their particular strengths and weaknesses and the roles they can best play in their future lives. This discovery process often involves "trying on" different roles or choices to see if they fit an adolescent's capabilities and views about himself or herself. Through this process, adolescents seek to understand who they are by narrowing and making choices about their personal, occupational, sexual, and political commitments.

In Erikson's view, adolescents who stumble in their efforts to find a suitable identity may follow several dysfunctional courses. They may adopt socially unacceptable roles, such as that of deviant, or they may have difficulty forming and maintaining long-lasting close personal relationships later on in life. In general, their sense of self becomes "diffuse," failing to organize around a central, unified core identity.

On the other hand, those who are successful in forging an appropriate identity set a course that provides a foundation for future psychosocial development. They learn their unique capabilities, and they develop an accurate sense of who they are. They are prepared to set out on a path that takes full advantage of what their unique strengths permit them to do (Kahn et al., 1985; Blustein, & Palladino, 1991; Archer & Waterman, 1994).

cw

identity-versus-identity-confusion stage
the period during which teenagers seek to determine what is unique and distinctive about themselves

During the identity-versus-identity-confusion stage, teenagers seek to understand who they are by narrowing and making choices about their personal, occupational, sexual, and political commitments. Can this stage be applied to teenagers in other cultures? Why or why not?

Table 12-1

A SUMMARY OF ERIKSON'S STAGES

Stage	Approximate Age	Positive Outcomes	Negative Outcomes
1. Trust versus mistrust	Birth–1.5 years	Feelings of trust from environmental support	Fear and concern regarding others
2. Autonomy versus shame and doubt	1.5–3 years	Self-sufficiency if exploration is encouraged	Doubts about self, lack of independence
3. Initiative versus guilt	3–6 years	Discovery of ways to initiate actions	Guilt from actions and thoughts
4. Industry versus inferiority	6–12 years	Development of sense of competence	Feelings of inferiority, no sense of mastery
5. Identity versus identity confusion	Adolescence	Awareness of uniqueness of self, knowledge of role to be followed	Inability to identify appropriate roles in life
6. Intimacy versus isolation	Early adulthood	Development of loving, sexual relationships and close friendships	Fear of relationships with others
7. Generativity versus stagnation	Middle adulthood	Sense of contribution to continuity of life	Trivialization of one's activities
8. Ego-integrity versus despair	Late adulthood	Sense of unity in life's accomplishments	Regret over lost opportunities of life

(*Source:* Erikson, 1963.)

Societal pressures are high during the identity-versus-identity-confusion stage, as any student knows who has been repeatedly asked by parents and friends "What's your major?" and "What are you going to do when you graduate?" Adolescents feel pressure to decide whether their post-high-school plans include work or college and, if they choose work, which occupational track to follow. These are new choices, because up to this point in their development, U.S. society lays out a universal educational track. However, the track ends at high school, and consequently, adolescents face difficult choices about which of several possible future paths they will follow (Kidwell et al., 1995).

During the identity-versus-identity-confusion period, adolescents increasingly rely on their friends and peers as sources of information. At the same time, their dependence on adults declines. As we discuss later in the chapter, this increasing dependence on the peer group enables adolescents to forge close relationships. It also helps them clarify their own identities as they compare themselves to others.

The importance of peers in helping adolescents define their identities and learn to form relationships points out a link between this stage of psychosocial development and the next stage Erikson proposed, known as intimacy versus isolation. It also relates to the subject of gender differences in identity formation. When Erikson developed his theory, he suggested that males and females move through the identity-versus-identity-confusion period differently. He argued that males are more likely to proceed through the social development stages in the order they are shown in Table 12-1, developing a stable identity before committing to an intimate relationship with another person. In contrast, he suggested that females reverse the order, seeking intimate relationships and then defining their identities through these relationships. These ideas largely reflect the social conditions at the time he was writing, when women were less likely to go to college or establish their own careers and instead often married early. Today, however, the experiences of boys and girls seem relatively similar during the identity-versus-confusion period.

Because of the pressures of the identity-versus-identity-confusion period, Erikson suggested that many adolescents pursue a "psychological moratorium." The *psychological moratorium* is a period during which adolescents take time off from the upcoming responsibilities of adulthood and explore various roles and possibilities. For example, many college students take a semester or year off to travel, work, or find some other way to examine their priorities.

On the other hand, many adolescents cannot, for practical reasons, pursue a psychological moratorium involving a relatively leisurely exploration of various identities. Some adolescents, for economic reasons, must work part-time after school and then take jobs immediately after graduation from high school. As a result, they have little time to experiment with identities and engage in a psychological moratorium. Does this mean such adolescents will be psychologically damaged in some way? Probably not. In fact, the satisfaction that can come from successfully holding a part-time job while attending school may be a sufficient psychological reward to outweigh the inability to try out various roles.

Marcia's Approach to Identity Development: Updating Erikson

Using Erikson's theory as a springboard, psychologist James Marcia (1966, 1980) suggests that identity can be seen in terms of four categories, called statuses. The identity statuses depend on whether each of two characteristics—crisis and commitment—is present or absent. *Crisis* is a period of identity development in which an adolescent consciously chooses between various alternatives and makes decisions. *Commitment* is psychological investment in a course of action or an ideology.

By conducting lengthy interviews with adolescents, Marcia proposed four categories of adolescent identity (see Table 12-2).

identity achievement the status of adolescents who commit to a particular identity following a period of crisis during which they consider various alternatives

1. Identity achievement. Teenagers within this identity status have successfully explored and thought through who they are and what they want to do. Following a period of crisis during which they considered various alternatives, these adolescents have committed to a particular identity. Teens who have reached this identity status tend to be the most

Table 12-2

MARCIA'S FOUR CATEGORIES OF ADOLESCENT DEVELOPMENT

		COMMITMENT	
		PRESENT	ABSENT
EXPLORATION	PRESENT	Identity achievement	Moratorium
	ABSENT	Identity foreclosure	Identity diffusion

(*Source:* Marcia, 1980.)

psychologically healthy, higher in achievement motivation and moral reasoning than adolescents of any other status.

2. Identity foreclosure. These are adolescents who have committed to an identity, but who did not do it by passing through a period of crisis in which they explored alternatives. Instead, they accepted others' decisions about what was best for them. Typical adolescents in this category are a son who enters the family business because it is expected of him, and a daughter who decides to become a physician simply because her mother is one. Although foreclosers are not necessarily unhappy, they tend to have what can be called "rigid strength": Happy and self-satisfied, they also have a high need for social approval and tend to be authoritarian.

3. Moratorium. Although adolescents in the moratorium category have explored various alternatives to some degree, they have not yet committed themselves. As a consequence, they show relatively high anxiety and experience psychological conflict. On the other hand, they are often lively and appealing, seeking intimacy with others. Adolescents of this status typically settle on an identity, but only after something of a struggle.

4. Identity diffusion. Some adolescents in this category consider various alternatives, but never commit to one. Others in this group never even get that far, not even considering their options in any conscious way. They tend to be flighty, shifting from one thing to the next. While they may seem carefree, their lack of commitment impairs their ability to form close relationships. In fact, they are often socially withdrawn.

It is important to note that adolescents are not necessarily stuck in one of the four categories. For instance, even though a forecloser may have settled upon a career path during early adolescence with little active decision making, he or she may reassess the choice later and move into another category. For some individuals, then, identity formation may take place beyond the period of adolescence. However, identity gels in the late teens and early twenties for most people (Waterman, 1982; Meeus, 1996; Kroger, 2000).

Identity, Race, and Ethnicity

Although the path to forming an identity is difficult for all adolescents, it presents a particular challenge for members of racial and ethnic minority groups. One part of the problem stems from contradictory societal values. On the one hand, adolescents are told that society should be color blind, that race and ethnic background should not matter in terms of opportunities and achievement. Based on a traditional *cultural assimilation model,* this view holds that individual cultural identities should be assimilated into a unified culture in the United States—the proverbial melting pot model.

On the other hand, the *pluralistic society model* suggests that U.S. society is made up of diverse, coequal cultural groups that should preserve their individual cultural features. The pluralistic society model grew in part from the belief that the cultural assimilation model denigrates the cultural heritage of minorities and lowers their self-esteem. According to this view, then, racial and ethnic factors become a central part of adolescents' identity and are not submerged in an attempt to assimilate into the majority culture.

There is a middle ground. Some observers suggest that identity in minority adolescents is facilitated by the formation of *bicultural identity* in which adolescents draw from their own cultural identity while integrating themselves into the dominant culture. This view suggests that an individual can live as a member of two cultures, with two cultural identities, without having to choose one over the other (Garcia, 1988; LaFromboise, Coleman, & Gerton, 1993). The choice of a bicultural identity is increasingly common. In fact, the number of individuals who think of themselves as belonging to more than one race is considerable, according to data from the 2000 U.S. census (see Figure 12-1; Schmitt, 2001).

Teenagers who have successfully attained what Marcia termed identity achievement tend to be the most psychologically healthy and higher in achievement motivation than adolescents of any other status.

identity foreclosure the status of adolescents who prematurely commit to an identity without adequately exploring alternatives

moratorium the status of adolescents who may have explored various identity alternatives to some degree, but have not yet committed themselves

identity diffusion the status of adolescents who consider various identity alternatives, but never commit to one or never even consider identity options in any conscious way

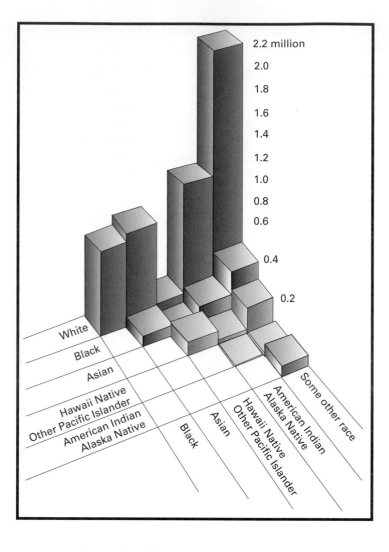

Figure 12-1 Increase in Bicultural Identity

On the 2000 census, almost 7 million people indicated they were multiracial.

(*Source:* U.S. Bureau of the Census, 2000.)

Regardless of which path to identity a member of a minority group chooses, the process of identity formation is not likely to be simple. Racial and ethnic identity takes time to form, and for some individuals it may occur over a prolonged period. Still, the ultimate result can be the formation of a rich, multifaceted identity (Cross, 1991; Tatum, 1997; Roberts et al., 1999).

Depression and Suicide: Psychological Difficulties in Adolescence

Although by far the majority of teenagers weather the search for identity—as well as the other challenges presented by the period—without major psychological difficulties, some find adolescence particularly stressful. Some, in fact, develop severe psychological problems. Two of the most serious are adolescent depression and suicide (Besseghini, 1997).

Adolescent Depression. No one is immune to periods of sadness and bad moods, and adolescents are no exception. The end of a relationship, failure at an important task, the death of a loved one—all may produce profound feelings of sadness, loss, and grief. In situations such as these, depression is a fairly typical reaction.

How common are feelings of depression in adolescence? Although figures are hard to come by, some estimates suggest that 20 to 35 percent of boys and 25 to 40 percent of girls report having experienced depressed moods in the previous 6 months. Reports of feeling "sad and hopeless" are even higher: Almost two-thirds of teenagers say they have experienced such feelings at one time or another. On the other hand, only a small minority of adolescents—some 3 percent—experience *major depression,* a full-blown psychological disorder in which depression is severe and lingers for long periods (Culp, Clyman, & Culp, 1995; Cicchetti & Toth, 1998).

Gender, ethnic, and racial differences also are found in depression rates. As is the case among adults, adolescent girls, on average, experience depression more often than boys. Furthermore, some studies have found that African American adolescents have higher rates of depression than white adolescents, although not all research supports this conclusion. Native Americans, too, appear to have higher rates of depression (Fleming & Offord, 1990; Nettles & Pleck, 1990).

Depression has several causes. In cases of severe, long-term depression, biological factors are often involved. Some adolescents, for instance, seem to be genetically predisposed to experience depression (Ehlers, Frank, & Kupfer, 1988; Brooks-Gunn, Petersen, & Compas, 1994).

However, environmental and social factors relating to the extraordinary changes in the social lives of adolescents are also an important cause. An adolescent who experiences the death of a loved one, for example, or one who grows up with a depressed parent, is at a higher risk of depression. In addition, being unpopular, having few close friends, and experiencing rejection are associated with adolescent depression (Aseltine, Gore, & Colten, 1994; Hammond & Romney, 1995; Lau & Kwok, 2000).

One of the most puzzling questions about depression is why its incidence is higher among girls than boys. Hormones do not seem to be the reason. Little evidence links hormonal production in adolescent girls to depression (Petersen, Sarigiani, & Kennedy, 1991; Nolen-Hoeksema & Girgus, 1994; Lewinsohn et al., 1994).

Some psychologists speculate that stress is more pronounced for girls than for boys in adolescence due to the many, sometimes contradictory, aspects of the traditional female gender role. Recall, for instance, the plight of the adolescent girl who was quoted in our discussion of self-esteem. Accepting traditional gender roles, she is worried both about doing well in school and about being popular. If she feels that academic success undermines her popularity, she is placed in a difficult bind.

There may also be other causes of girls' generally higher levels of depression during adolescence. They may be more apt than boys to react to stress by turning inward, thereby experiencing a sense of helplessness and hopelessness. In contrast, boys more often react by externalizing the stress and acting more impulsively or aggressively, or by turning to drugs and alcohol.

Adolescent Suicide. Elyssa Drazin was 16. Although her grades had gone down in the previous 6 months, she was still a pretty good student. Her social life had picked up over the last 2 years, and she had been involved with Hector Segool. In the past month, however, the relationship had cooled considerably, and Hector had told her he wanted to date other girls. Elyssa was devastated, and—as she wrote in a note that was found on her desk—she could not bear the thought of seeing Hector holding hands with another girl. She took a large quantity of sleeping pills and became one of the thousands of adolescents who take their own lives each year.

The rate of adolescent suicide in the United States has tripled in the last 30 years. In fact, one teenage suicide occurs every 90 minutes, for an annual rate of 12.2 suicides per 100,000 adolescents. Moreover, the reported rate may actually understate the true number of suicides; parents and medical personnel are often reluctant to report a death as suicide, preferring to label it an accident. Even with underreporting, suicide is the third most common cause of death in the 15-to-24-year-old age group, after accidents and homicide (Henry et al., 1993; Healy, 2001).

Between 25 and 40 percent of girls, and 20 to 35 percent of boys, experience occasional episodes of depression during adolescence, although the incidence of major depression is far lower.

The rate of adolescent suicide has tripled in the last 30 years. These girls console one another following the suicide of a classmate.

The rate of suicide is higher for boys than girls, although girls *attempt* suicide more frequently. Suicide attempts among males are more likely to result in death because of the methods they use: Boys tend to use more violent means, such as guns, while girls are more apt to choose the more peaceful strategy of drug overdose. Some estimates suggest that there are as many as 200 attempted suicides for every successful one (Hawton, 1986; Berman & Jobes, 1991; Gelman, 1994).

The reasons behind the increase in adolescent suicide over past decades are unclear. The most obvious explanation is that the stress experienced by teenagers has increased, leading those who are most troubled to be more likely to commit suicide (Elkind, 1984). But why should stress have increased only for adolescents? The suicide rate for other segments of the population has remained fairly stable over the same time period. (And it's important to keep in mind that although the rate of suicide for adolescents has risen more than for other age groups, suicide is still more common among adults than it is among younger people.)

Although an explanation for the increase in adolescent suicide has not been found, it is clear that certain factors heighten the risk of suicide. One factor is depression. Depressed teenagers who are experiencing a profound sense of hopelessness are at greater risk of committing suicide (although most depressed individuals do not commit suicide). In addition, social inhibition, perfectionism, and a high level of stress and anxiety are related to a greater risk of suicide (Lewinsohn, Rohde, & Seeley, 1994; Beautrais, Joyce, & Muilder, 1996; Huff, 1999).

Some cases of suicide are associated with family conflicts and adjustment difficulties (Pillay & Wassanaar, 1997). Others follow a history of abuse and neglect. The rate of suicide among drug and alcohol abusers is also relatively high. As can be seen in Figure 12-2, teens who called in to a hotline because they were thinking of killing themselves mentioned several other factors as well (Brent et al., 1994; Garnefski & Arends, 1998; Lyon et al., 2000).

Some suicides appear to be caused by exposure to the suicide of others. In **cluster suicide,** one suicide leads to attempts by others to kill themselves. For instance, some high schools have experienced a series of suicides following a well-publicized case. As a result,

cluster suicide a situation in which one suicide leads to attempts by others to kill themselves

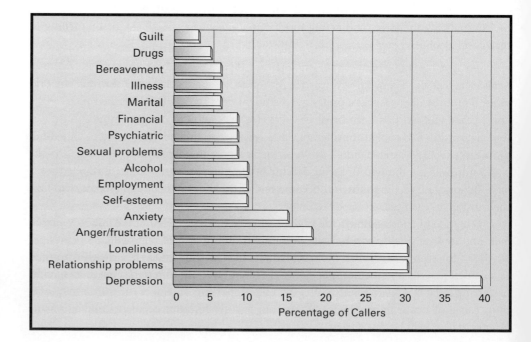

Figure 12-2 **Adolescent Difficulties**

These problems were the ones most frequently cited by callers to a suicide-prevention hotline who were contemplating suicide.

(*Source:* Boston Samaritans, 1991.)

The Informed Consumer of Development
Deterring Adolescent Suicide

If you suspect that an adolescent, or anyone else for that matter, is contemplating suicide, don't stand idly by. Act! Here are several suggestions:

▶ Talk to the person, listen without judging, and give the person an understanding forum in which to try to talk things through.

▶ Talk specifically about suicidal thoughts, such as: Does the person have a plan? Has he or she bought a gun? Where is it? Has he or she stockpiled pills? Where are they? The Public Health Service notes that, "contrary to popular belief, such candor will not give a person dangerous ideas or encourage a suicidal act."

▶ Evaluate the situation, trying to distinguish between general upset and more serious danger, as when suicide plans *have* been made. If the crisis is acute, *do not leave the person alone.*

▶ Be supportive, let the person know you care, and try to break down his or her feelings of isolation.

▶ Take charge of finding help, without concern about invading the person's privacy. Do not try to handle the problem alone; get professional help immediately.

▶ Make the environment safe, removing from the premises (not just hiding) weapons such as guns, razors, scissors, medication, and other potentially dangerous household items.

▶ Do not keep suicide talk or threats secret; these are calls for help and warrant immediate action.

▶ Do not challenge, dare, or use verbal shock treatment. They can have tragic effects.

▶ Make a contract with the person, getting a promise or commitment, preferably in writing, not to make any suicidal attempt until you have talked further.

▶ Beware of elevated moods and seemingly quick recoveries; sometimes they are illusory, reflecting the relief of finally deciding to commit suicide or the temporary release of talking to someone, though the underlying problems have not been resolved.

For immediate help with a suicide-related problem, call (800) 621-4000, a national hotline staffed with trained counselors.

---

many schools have established crisis intervention teams to counsel students when one student commits suicide (Hazell, 1993).

There are several warning signs that should sound an alarm regarding the possibility of suicide. Among them:

■ Direct or indirect talk about suicide, such as "I wish I were dead" or "You won't have me to worry about any longer"

■ School difficulties, such as missed classes or a decline in grades

■ Making arrangements as if preparing for a long trip, such as giving away prized possessions or arranging for the care of a pet

■ Writing a will

■ Loss of appetite or excessive eating

■ General depression, including a change in sleeping patterns, slowness and lethargy, and uncommunicativeness

■ Dramatic changes in behavior, such as a shy person suddenly acting outgoing

■ Preoccupation with death in music, art, or literature.

Talking about suicide, contrary to popular opinion, does not encourage it. In fact, it actually helps to provide support and breaks down the sense of isolation many suicidal people have.

Review and Rethink

REVIEW

- Self-concept during adolescence grows more differentiated as the view of the self becomes more organized, broader, and more abstract, and takes account of the views of others.

- Self-esteem, too, grows increasingly differentiated as the adolescent develops the ability to place different values on different aspects of the self.

- Both Erikson's identity-versus-identity-confusion stage and Marcia's four identity statuses focus on the adolescent's struggle to determine an identity and a role in society.

- One of the dangers that adolescents face is depression, which affects girls more than boys.

- Suicide is the third most common cause of death among 15- to 24-year-olds.

RETHINK

- What are some consequences of the shift from reliance on adults to reliance on peers? Are there advantages? Dangers?

- Do you believe that all four of Marcia's identity statuses can lead to reassessment and different choices later in life? Do you think some statuses are more likely than others to produce this type of rethinking? Why?

Relationships: Family and Friends

"Keep the Hell Out of my Room!" says a sign on Trevor's bedroom wall, just above an unmade bed, a desk littered with dirty T-shirts and candy wrappers, and a floor covered with clothes. Is there a carpet? "Somewhere," he says with a grin. "I think it's gold." Trevor is the third of four sons of Richard Kelson, 56, a retired truck driver, and his wife, JoAnn, 46, a medical tape transcriber. The family lives in a four-bedroom home across from Hunter Junior High School, where Trevor is in ninth grade. He spent the summer volunteering in a leadership-training program at the Sugar House Boys & Girls Club in Salt Lake City. "I guess it gives you a good feeling to help somebody else," he says. In off-hours, he played Nintendo with pal Andy Muhlestein, 15. "When we don't have anything else to do, and we're tired of playing videos," he says, "we sit around and talk about girls." (Fields-Meyer, 1995, p. 53)

The social world of adolescents is considerably wider than that of younger children. As adolescents' relationships with people outside the home grow increasingly important, their interactions with their families evolve and take on a new, and sometimes difficult, character (Montemayor, Adams, & Gulotta, 1994; Collins, Gleason, & Sesma, 1997).

Family Ties: Reassessing Relations with Relations

When Pepe Lizzagara entered junior high school, his relationship with his parents changed drastically. Although relations were quite good previously, by the middle of seventh grade, tensions grew. In Pepe's view, his parents always seemed to be "on his case." Instead of giving him more freedom, which he felt he deserved at age 13, they actually seemed to be getting more restrictive.

Pepe's parents would probably suggest that they were not the source of the tension in the household—Pepe was. From their point of view, Pepe, with whom they'd established what seemed to be a stable relationship throughout much of his childhood, suddenly seemed transformed. To his parents, Pepe presented novel, and often bewildering, behavior.

Adolescents increasingly seek autonomy, independence, and a sense of control over their lives.

The Quest for Autonomy. Parents are sometimes angered, and even more frequently puzzled, by adolescents' conduct. Children who have previously accepted their parents' judgments, declarations, and guidelines begin to question—and sometimes rebel against—their parents' views of the world.

One reason for these clashes is the shift in the roles that both children and parents must deal with during adolescence. Adolescents increasingly seek **autonomy,** independence and a sense of control over their lives. Most parents intellectually realize that this shift is a normal part of adolescence, representing one of the primary developmental tasks of the period, and in many ways they welcome it as a sign of their children's growth. However, in many cases the day-to-day realities of adolescents' increasing autonomy may prove difficult for them to deal with (Smetana, 1995).

In most families, teenagers' autonomy grows gradually over the course of adolescence. For instance, one study of changes in adolescents' views of their parents found that increasing autonomy led them to perceive parents less in idealized terms and more as persons in their own right. At the same time, adolescents came to depend more on themselves and to feel more like separate individuals (see Figure 12-3).

The increase in adolescent autonomy is reflected in the relationship between parents and teenagers. At the start of adolescence, the relationship tends to be asymmetrical: Parents hold most of the power and influence over the relationship. By the end of adolescence, however, power and influence have become more balanced, and parents and children end up in a more symmetrical, or egalitarian, relationship. Power and influence are shared, although parents typically retain the upper hand.

The degree of autonomy that is eventually achieved varies from one family to the next. Furthermore, cultural factors play an important role. In Western societies, which tend to value individualism, adolescents seek autonomy at a relatively early stage of adolescence. In contrast, Asian societies are *collectivistic;* they promote the idea that the well-being of the group is more important than that of the individual. In such societies, adolescents' aspirations to achieve autonomy are less pronounced (Feldman & Rosenthal, 1990; Kim et al., 1994).

Adolescents from different cultural backgrounds also vary in the degree of obligation to their family that they feel. Those in more collectivistic cultures tend to feel greater obligation to their families, in terms of their expectations about their duty to provide assistance, show respect, and support their families in the future, than those from more individualistic societies (see Figure 12-4; Fuligni, Tseng, & Lam, 1999).

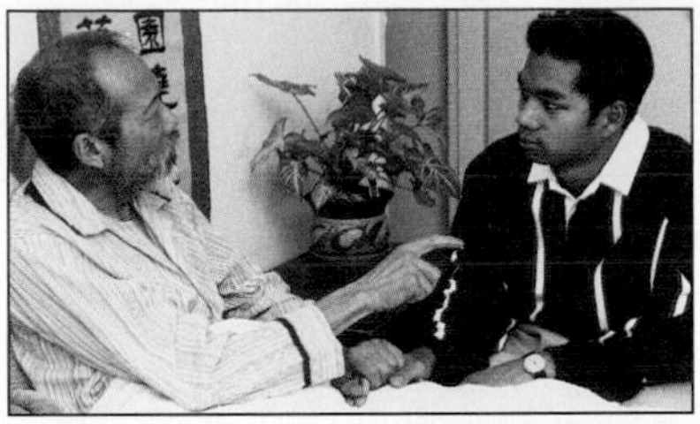

Adolescents from more collectivistic cultures tend to feel greater obligation to their families, in terms of their expectations about their duty to provide assistance, show respect, and support their families in the future, than those from more individualistic societies.

autonomy having independence and a sense of control over one's life

The Myth of the Generation Gap. Teen movies often depict adolescents and their parents with totally opposing points of view about the world. For example, the parent of an environmentalist teen might turn out to own a polluting factory. These exaggerations are often funny because we assume there is a kernel of truth in them, in that parents and teenagers often don't

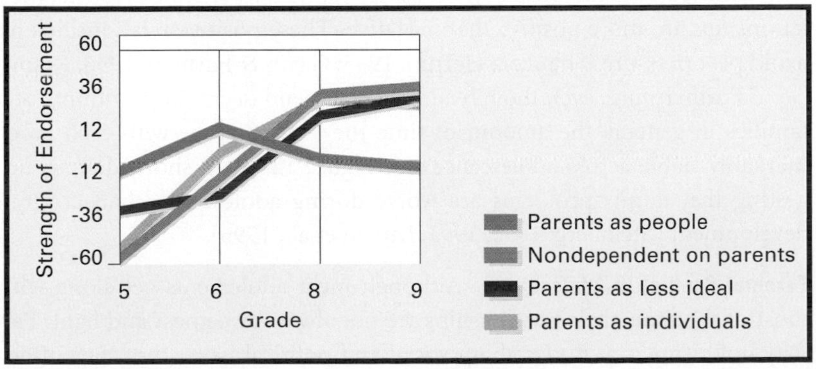

Figure 12-3 **Changing Views of Parents**

As adolescents become older, they come to perceive their parents in less idealized terms and more as individuals. What effects is this likely to have on family relations?

(Adapted from Steinberg & Silverberg, 1986.)

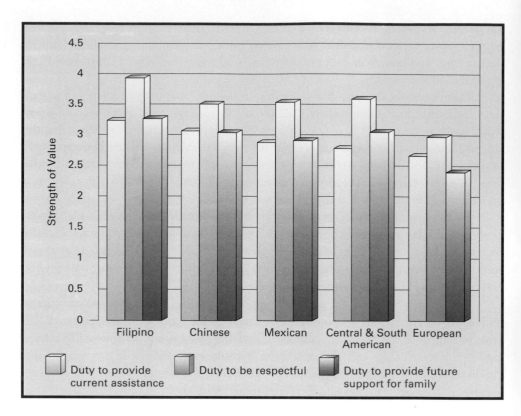

Figure 12-4 **Family Obligations**

Adolescents from Asian and Latin American groups felt a greater sense of respect and obligation toward their families than those adolescents with European backgrounds.

(*Source:* Fulgini, Tseng, & Lam, 1999.)

generation gap a divide between parents and adolescents in attitudes, values, aspirations, and world views

see things the same way. According to this argument, there is a **generation gap,** a deep divide between parents and children in attitudes, values, aspirations, and world views.

The reality, however, is quite different. The generation gap, when it exists, is really quite narrow. Adolescents and their parents tend to see eye-to-eye in a variety of domains. Republican parents generally have Republican children; members of the Christian right have children who espouse similar views; parents who advocate for abortion rights have children who are pro-abortion. On social, political, and religious issues, parents and adolescents tend to be in synch, and children's worries mirror those of their parents. Adolescents' concerns about society's problems (see Figure 12-5) are ones with which most adults would probably agree (Youniss, 1989; Chira, 1994; PRIMEDIA/Roper National Youth Survey, 1998).

Similarly, there is typically no generation gap in the value that parents and adolescents place on the relationship they have with one another. As we observed in the chapter prologue about Leah's first formal dance, despite their quest for autonomy and independence, most adolescents have deep love, affection, and respect for their parents—reciprocating the feelings that their parents have for them. Although there are notable exceptions, with some parent–adolescent relationships marked by significant strife, the majority of relationships are more positive than negative. These positive relationships help adolescents avoid peer pressure (Shantz & Hartup, 1995; Gavin & Furman, 1996; Resnick et al., 1997).

Furthermore, even though adolescents spend decreasing amounts of time with their families in general, the amount of time they spend alone with each parent remains remarkably stable across adolescence (see Figure 12-6). In short, there is no evidence suggesting that family problems are worse during adolescence than at any other stage of development (Steinberg, 1990, 1993; Larson et al., 1996).

Parental Conflict in Adolescence. Although most adolescents get along with their parents most of the time, their relationships are not always sweetness and light. Parents and teens may hold similar attitudes about social and political issues, but they often hold different views on matters of personal taste, such as music preferences and styles of dress. Also, as

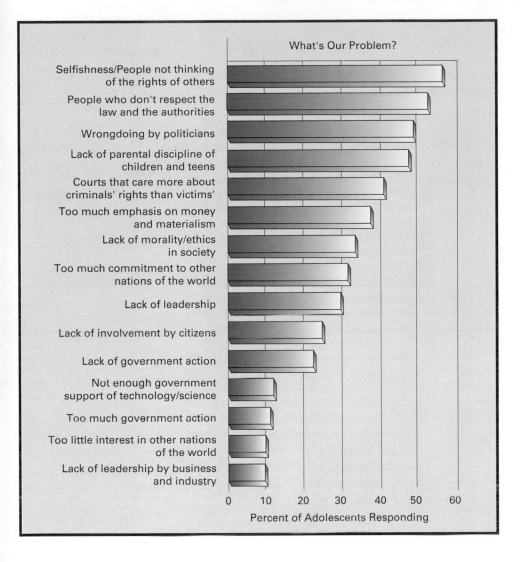

What's Our Problem?

- Selfishness/People not thinking of the rights of others
- People who don't respect the law and the authorities
- Wrongdoing by politicians
- Lack of parental discipline of children and teens
- Courts that care more about criminals' rights than victims'
- Too much emphasis on money and materialism
- Lack of morality/ethics in society
- Too much commitment to other nations of the world
- Lack of leadership
- Lack of involvement by citizens
- Lack of government action
- Not enough government support of technology/science
- Too much government action
- Too little interest in other nations of the world
- Lack of leadership by business and industry

0   10   20   30   40   50   60

Percent of Adolescents Responding

Figure 12-5 **What's the Problem?**

Adolescents' view of society's ills are ones with which their parents would be likely to agree.

(*Source:* PRIMEDIA/Roper National Youth Survey, 1999.)

we've seen, parents and children may run into disagreements when children seek to achieve autonomy and independence. Consequently, parent–child conflicts are more likely to occur during adolescence, particularly during the early stages, although it's important to remember that not every family is affected to the same degree (Laursen, Coy, & Collins, 1998; Arnett, 2000; Sagrestano et al., 1999).

Why should strife be greater during early adolescence than at later stages of the period? According to developmental psychologist Judith Smetana, the reason involves differing definitions of, and rationales for, appropriate and inappropriate conduct. Parents may feel, for instance, that getting one's ear pierced in three places is inappropriate because society traditionally deems it inappropriate. On the other hand, adolescents may view the issue in terms of personal choice (Smetana, 1988, 1989; Smetana, Yau, & Hanson, 1991).

Furthermore, the newly sophisticated reasoning of adolescents (discussed in the previous chapter) leads teenagers to think about parental rules in more complex ways. Arguments that were convincing to a school-age child ("Do it because I tell you to do it") are less compelling to an adolescent.

The argumentativeness and assertiveness of early adolescence at first may lead to an increase in conflict, but in many ways they play an important role in the evolution of parent–child relationships. While parents may initially react defensively to the challenges that their children present, and may grow inflexible and rigid, in most cases they eventually come to realize that their children *are* growing up.

The argumentativeness of adolescents can bring about an evolution in parent–child relationships, as parents can at times see that some of their child's arguments are not unreasonable.

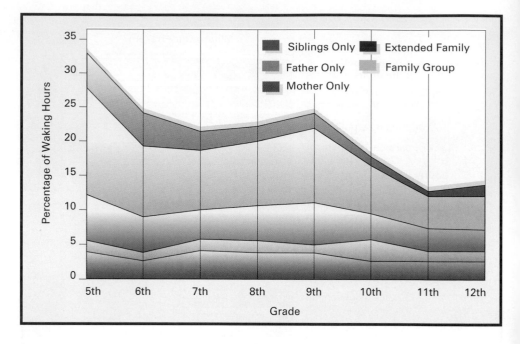

Figure 12-6 Time Spent by Adolescents with Parents

Despite their quest for autonomy and independence, most adolescents have deep love, affection, and respect for their parents, and the amount of time they spend alone with each parent remains remarkably stable across adolescence.

(*Source:* Larson, Richards, Moneta, Holmbeck, & Duckett, 1996.)

Parents also come to see that their adolescent children's arguments are often compelling and not so unreasonable, and that their daughters and sons can in fact be trusted with more freedom. Consequently, they become more yielding, allowing and eventually perhaps even encouraging independence. As this process occurs during the middle stages of adolescence, the combativeness of early adolescence declines.

Of course, this pattern does not apply for all adolescents. Although the majority of teenagers maintain stable relations with their parents throughout adolescence, as many as 20 percent pass through a fairly rough time (Dryfoos, 1990).

Cultural Differences in Parent–Child Conflicts During Adolescence. Although parent–child conflicts are found in every culture, the amount of conflict seems lower in "traditional," preindustrial cultures. In fact, teenagers in traditional cultures also experience fewer mood swings and instances of risky behavior that are often seen during adolescence (Schlegel & Barry, 1991; Arnett, 2000).

Why? The answer may relate to the degree of independence that adolescents expect and adults permit. In more industrialized societies, in which the value of individualism is typically high, independence is an expected component of adolescence. Consequently, adolescents and their parents must negotiate the amount and timing of the adolescent's increasing independence—a process that often leads to strife.

In contrast, in more traditional societies, individualism is not valued as highly, and therefore adolescents are less inclined to seek out independence. With diminished independence-seeking on the part of adolescents, the result is less parent–child conflict (Dasen, in press).

Relationships with Peers: The Importance of Belonging

In the eyes of numerous parents, the most fitting symbol of adolescence is the telephone. For many of their sons and daughters, it appears to be an indispensable lifeline, sustaining ties to friends with whom they may have already spent many hours earlier in the day.

The seemingly compulsive need to communicate with friends demonstrates the role that peers play in adolescence. Continuing the trend that began in middle childhood, adolescents spend increasing amounts of time with their peers, and the importance of peer relationships grows as well. In fact, there is probably no period of life in which peer relationships are as important as they are in adolescence (Youniss & Haynie, 1992).

There are several reasons for the prominence of peers during adolescence. For one thing, peers provide the opportunity to compare and evaluate opinions, abilities, and even physical changes—a process called *social comparison*. Because physical and cognitive changes are so pronounced, especially during the early stages of puberty, adolescents turn increasingly to others who share, and consequently can shed light on, their own experiences (Weiss, Ebbeck, & Horn, 1997; Paxton et al., 1999).

Parents are unable to provide social comparison. Not only are they well beyond the changes that adolescents undergo, but adolescents' questioning of adult authority and their motivation to become more autonomous make parents, other family members, and adults in general inadequate and invalid sources of knowledge. Who is left to provide such information? Peers.

Finally, adolescence is a time of experimentation, of trying out new roles and conduct. Peers provide information about what roles and behavior are most acceptable by serving as a reference group. **Reference groups** are groups of people with whom one compares oneself.

Reference groups present a set of *norms*, or standards, against which adolescents can judge their social success. An adolescent need not even belong to a group for it to serve as a reference group. For instance, unpopular adolescents may find themselves belittled and rejected by members of a popular group, yet use that more popular group as a reference group (Berndt, 1999).

Cliques and Crowds: Belonging to a Group. Even if they do not belong to the group they use for reference purposes, adolescents typically are part of some identifiable group. In fact, one of the consequences of the increasing cognitive sophistication of adolescents is the ability to group others in more discriminating ways. Rather than defining people in concrete terms relating to what they do ("football players" or "musicians"), adolescents use more abstract terms packed with greater subtleties ("jocks" or "the artsy craftsy crowd") (Brown, 1990; Montemayor, Adams, & Gulotta, 1994).

What are the typical groups to which adolescents belong? There are actually two types: cliques and crowds. **Cliques** are groups of from 2 to 12 people whose members have frequent social interactions with one another. In contrast, **crowds** are larger, comprising individuals who share particular characteristics but who may not interact with one another. For instance, "jocks" and "nerds" are representative of crowds found in many high schools.

Choice of membership in particular cliques and crowds is often determined by the degree of similarity with members of the group. One of the most important dimensions of similarity relates to substance use; adolescents tend to choose friends who use alcohol and other drugs to the same extent that they do. Their friends are also often similar in terms of their academic success, although this is not always true. For instance, during early adolescence, attraction to peers who are particularly well behaved seems to decrease while, at the same time, those who behave more aggressively become more attractive (Bukowski, Sippola, & Newcomb, 2000; Hamm, 2000).

Gender Relations. As children enter adolescence from middle childhood, their groups of friends are composed almost universally of same-sex individuals. Boys hang out with boys; girls hang out with girls. Technically, this sex segregation is called the **sex cleavage**.

However, the situation changes in short order as members of both sexes enter puberty. Boys and girls experience the hormonal surge that marks puberty and causes the maturation of the sex organs. At the same time, societal pressures suggest that the time is appropriate for romantic involvement. These developments lead to a change in the ways adolescents view the opposite sex. Rather than seeing every member of the opposite sex as "annoying" and "a pain," boys and girls begin to regard each other with greater interest in terms of both personality and sexuality.

reference groups groups of people with whom one compares oneself

cliques groups of from 2 to 12 people whose members have frequent social interactions with one another

crowds larger groups than cliques, composed of individuals who share particular characteristics but who may not interact with one another

sex cleavage sex segregation in which boys interact primarily with boys and girls primarily with girls

The sex segregation of childhood continues during the early stages of adolescence. However, by the time of middle adolescence, this segregation decreases, and boys' and girls' cliques begin to converge.

When this change occurs, boys' and girls' cliques, which previously had moved along parallel but separate tracks, begin to converge. Adolescents begin to attend boy–girl dances or parties, although most of the time the boys still spend their time with boys, and the girls with girls (Csikszentmihalyi & Larson, 1984). (Think back to your own early adolescence, and perhaps you'll recall dances with boys lined up on one side of the room and girls on the other.)

A little later, however, adolescents increasingly spend time with members of the opposite sex (Dunphy, 1963). New cliques emerge, composed of both males and females. Not everyone participates initially: Early on, the teenagers who are leaders of the same-sex cliques and who have the highest status pilot the way. Eventually, however, most adolescents find themselves in cliques that include boys and girls.

Cliques and crowds undergo yet another transformation at the end of adolescence: They become less powerful and may in fact succumb to the increased pairing off that occurs between males and females. Rather than the clique being the center of adolescents' social lives, then, boy–girl interaction becomes the focus.

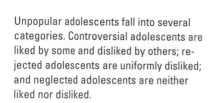

Unpopular adolescents fall into several categories. Controversial adolescents are liked by some and disliked by others; rejected adolescents are uniformly disliked; and neglected adolescents are neither liked nor disliked.

Developmental Diversity

Race Segregation:
The Great Divide of Adolescence

When Philip McAdoo, a [student] at the University of North Carolina, stopped one day to see a friend who worked on his college campus, a receptionist asked if he would autograph a basketball for her son. Because he was African American and tall, "she just assumed that I was on the basketball team," recounted McAdoo.

Jasme Kelly, an African American sophomore at the same college, had a similar story to tell. When she went to see a friend at a fraternity house, the student who answered the door asked if she was there to apply for the job of cook.

White students, too, find racial relations difficult and in some ways forbidding. For instance, Jenny Johnson, a white 20-year-old junior, finds even the most basic conversation with African American classmates difficult. She describes a conversation in which African American friends "jump at my throat because I used the word 'black' instead of African American. There is just such a huge barrier that it's really hard . . . to have a normal discussion." (Sanoff & Minerbrook, 1993, p. 58)

The pattern of race segregation found at the University of North Carolina is repeated over and over in schools and colleges throughout the United States: Even when they attend desegregated schools with a high proportion of minority students, people of different ethnicities and races interact very little. Moreover, even if they have a friend of a different ethnicity within the confines of a school, most adolescents don't interact with that friend outside of school (DuBois & Hirsch, 1990).

It doesn't start out this way. During elementary school and even during early adolescence, there is a fair amount of integration among students of differing ethnicities. However, by middle and late adolescence, the amount of segregation is striking (Shrum, Cheek, & Hunter, 1988; Spencer & Dornbusch, 1990; Spencer, 1991; Ennett & Bauman, 1996).

Why should racial and ethnic segregation be the rule, even in schools that have been desegregated for some time? One reason is that minority students may actively seek support from others who share their minority status. Furthermore, by associating primarily with other members of their own minority group, they are able to affirm their own identity.

Other explanations for campus segregation are less positive. For instance, socioeconomic status (SES) differences between people of different races and ethnicities may keep integration at low levels. Racial and ethnic differences tend to mirror SES differences: People from minority groups are overrepresented in lower SES groups (Coleman, 1961), just as people from the majority group are overrepresented in higher SES groups. Because cliques tend to be comprised members who are of similar SES, they also display very little racial integration. It is possible, then, that apparent ethnic differences in interaction patterns are really due to SES characteristics, and not to ethnicity per se.

Another explanation for the lack of interaction between members of different racial and ethnic groups relates to differences in academic performance. Because minority group members tend to experience less school success than members of the majority group, as we discussed in Chapter 10, it may be that ethnic and racial segregation is based not on ethnicity itself, but on academic achievement.

Specifically, some students attend schools in which classes are assigned on the basis of students' prior levels of academic success. If minority group members experience less success, they may find themselves in classes with proportionally fewer majority group members. Similarly, majority students may be in classes with few minority students. Such class assignment practices, then, may inadvertently maintain and promote racial and ethnic segregation. This pattern would be particularly prevalent in schools where rigid academic tracking is practiced, with students assigned to "low," "medium," and "high" tracks depending on their prior achievement (Hallinan & Williams, 1989).

Finally, the lack of racial and ethnic interaction in school may reflect negative attitudes held by both majority and minority students. Minority students may feel that the white majority is prejudiced, discriminatory, and hostile, and they may prefer to stick to same-race groups. Conversely, majority students may assume that minority group members are antagonistic and unfriendly. Such mutually destructive attitudes reduce the likelihood that meaningful interaction can take place (Miller & Brewer, 1984; Phinney, Ferguson, & Tate, 1997).

Is the voluntary segregation along racial and ethnic lines found during adolescence inevitable? No. For instance, adolescents who have had extensive interactions with members of different races earlier in their lives are more likely to have friends of different races. Furthermore, schools that actively promote contact between members of different ethnicities in mixed-ability classes may create an environment in which cross-race friendships can flourish (Schofield & Francis, 1982).

Still, the task is daunting. Many societal pressures act to keep members of different races from interacting with one another. Furthermore, cliques may actively promote norms that discourage group members from crossing racial and ethnic lines to form new friendships. ☐

Popularity and Rejection: Adolescent Likes and Dislikes

Most adolescents have well-tuned antennae when it comes to determining who is popular and who is not. In fact, for some teenagers, concerns over popularity—or lack of it—may be a central focus of their lives. Think back, for example, to the girl quoted earlier in the chapter, who felt that having friends was more important than school success.

Actually, the social world of adolescents is divided not only into popular and unpopular individuals; the differentiations are more complex (see Figure 12-7). For instance, some adolescents are controversial; in contrast to *popular* adolescents, who are mostly liked, **controversial adolescents** are liked by some and disliked by others. Furthermore, there are **rejected adolescents,** who are uniformly disliked, and **neglected adolescents,** who are neither liked nor disliked. In most cases, popular and controversial adolescents tend to be similar in that their overall status is higher, while rejected and neglected adolescents share a generally lower status.

Popular and controversial adolescents have more close friends, engage more frequently in activities with their peers, and disclose more about themselves to others than less popular students. They are also more involved in extracurricular school activities. In addition, they are well aware of their popularity, and they are less lonely than their less popular classmates (Franzoi, Davis, & Vasquez-Suson, 1994; Englund et al., 2000).

In contrast, the social world of rejected and neglected adolescents is considerably more negative. They have fewer friends, engage in social activities less frequently, and have less contact with the opposite sex. They see themselves—accurately, it turns out—as less popular, and they are more likely to feel lonely.

Conformity: Peer Pressure in Adolescence

Whenever Aldos Henry said he wanted to buy a particular brand of sneakers or a certain style of shirt, his parents complained that he was just giving in to peer pressure and told him to make up his own mind about things.

In arguing with Aldos, his parents were subscribing to a view of adolescence that is quite prevalent in U.S. society: that teenagers are highly susceptible to **peer pressure,** the influence of one's peers to conform to their behavior and attitudes. Were his parents correct?

controversial adolescents children who are liked by some peers and disliked by others

rejected adolescents children who are actively disliked, and whose peers may react to them in an obviously negative manner

neglected adolescents children who receive relatively little attention from their peers in the form of either positive or negative interactions

peer pressure the influence of one's peers to conform to their behavior and attitudes

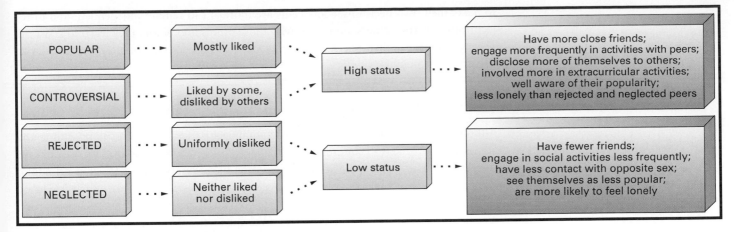

Figure 12-7 **The Social World of Adolescence**

An adolescent's popularity can fall into one of four categories, depending on the opinions of his or her peers. Popularity is related to differences in status, behavior, and adjustment.

The research suggests that it all depends. In some cases, adolescents *are* highly susceptible to the influence of their peers. For instance, when considering what to wear, whom to date, and what movies to see, adolescents are apt to follow the lead of their peers. On the other hand, when it comes to many nonsocial matters, such as choosing a career path or trying to solve a problem, they are more likely to turn to an experienced adult (Phelan, Yu, & Davidson, 1994).

In short, particularly in middle and late adolescence, teenagers turn to those they see as experts on a given dimension (Young & Ferguson, 1979). If they have social concerns, they turn to the people most likely to be experts—their peers. If the problem is one about which parents or other adults are most likely to have expertise, teenagers tend to turn to them for advice and are most susceptible to their opinions.

Overall, then, it does not appear that susceptibility to peer pressure suddenly soars during adolescence. Instead, adolescence brings about a change in the people to whom an individual conforms. Whereas children conform fairly consistently to their parents during childhood, in adolescence conformity shifts to include the peer group, in part because pressures to conform increase.

Ultimately, however, adolescents conform less to both peers *and* adults as they develop increasing autonomy over their lives. As they grow in confidence and in the ability

As they grow more confident of their own decisions, adolescents become less likely to conform to peers and parents.

to make their own decisions, adolescents are more apt to remain independent and to reject pressures from others, no matter who those others are. Before they learn to resist the urge to conform to their peers, however, teenagers may get into trouble, often along with their friends (Steinberg, 1993; Crockett & Crouter, 1995).

Juvenile Delinquency: The Crimes of Adolescence

Although the vast majority of them are law-abiding citizens, adolescents, along with young adults, are more likely to commit crimes than any other age group. Some of the reasons for this state of affairs have to do with the definition of certain behaviors (such as drinking), which are illegal for adolescents but not for older individuals. But even when such crimes are disregarded, adolescents are disproportionately involved in violent crimes, such as murder, assaults, and rape, and in property crimes involving theft, robbery, and arson.

Although the number of violent crimes committed by U.S. adolescents over the past decade has shown a decline, probably due to the strength of the economy, delinquency among some teenagers remains a significant problem (Juvenile Justice Clearinghouse, 1995; Pope & Bierman, 1999). Overall, a quarter of all serious violent crime involves an adolescent. Almost 20 percent of serious violent crimes are committed by adolescents, either alone or in groups. Another 8 percent are committed by adolescents in conjunction with older offenders.

Why do adolescents become involved in criminal activity? Some offenders are known as **undersocialized delinquents,** adolescents who are raised with little discipline or with harsh, uncaring parental supervision. These children have never been appropriately socialized and simply have not learned standards of conduct to regulate their own behavior. Undersocialized delinquents typically begin criminal activities at an early age, well before the onset of adolescence.

Undersocialized delinquents share several characteristics. They tend to be relatively aggressive and violent fairly early in life, characteristics that lead to rejection by peers and academic failure. They also are more likely to have been diagnosed with attention deficit disorder as children, and they tend to be less intelligent than average (Gullotta et al., 1995; Henry et al., 1996; Silverthorn & Frick, 1999).

Undersocialized delinquents often suffer from psychological difficulties, and as adults fit a psychological pattern called antisocial personality disorder. They are relatively unlikely to be successfully rehabilitated, and many undersocialized delinquents live on the margins of society throughout their lives (Lewis et al., 1994; Tate, Reppucci, & Mulvey, 1995; Rönkä & Pulkkinen, 1995; Lynam, 1996).

On the other hand, most adolescent offenders are socialized delinquents. **Socialized delinquents** know and subscribe to the norms of society; they are fairly normal psychologically. For them, transgressions committed during adolescence do not lead to a life of crime. Instead, most socialized delinquents pass through a period during adolescence when they engage in some petty crimes, but they do not continue lawbreaking into adulthood.

Socialized delinquents are typically highly influenced by their peers, and their delinquency often occurs in groups. In addition, some research suggests that parents of socialized delinquents supervise their children's behavior less closely than other parents (Dornbusch et al., 1985; Windle, 1994; Fletcher et al., 1995; Thornberry & Krohn, 1997).

undersocialized delinquents adolescent delinquents who are raised with little discipline or with harsh, uncaring parental supervision

socialized delinquents adolescent delinquents who know and subscribe to the norms of society and who are fairly normal psychologically

cw

Review and Rethink

■ The search for autonomy may cause a readjustment in relations between teenagers and their parents, but the generation gap is less wide than is generally thought.

■ Cliques and crowds serve as reference groups in adolescence and offer a ready means of social comparison. Sex cleavage gradually diminishes, until boys and girls begin to pair off.

- Racial separation increases during adolescence, bolstered by socioeconomic status differences, different academic experiences, and mutually distrustful attitudes.
- Degrees of popularity in adolescence include popular, controversial, neglected, and rejected adolescents.
- Adolescents tend to conform to their peers in areas in which they regard their peers as experts, and to adults in areas of perceived adult expertise.
- Adolescents are disproportionately involved in criminal activities, although most do not commit crimes. Juvenile delinquents can be categorized as undersocialized or socialized delinquents.

RETHINK

- In what ways do you think parents with different styles—authoritarian, authoritative, and permissive—tend to react to attempts to establish autonomy during adolescence?
- How do the findings about conformity and peer pressure reported in this chapter relate to adolescents' developing cognitive abilities?

Dating, Sexual Behavior, and Teenage Pregnancy

It took him almost a month, but Sylvester Chiu finally got up the courage to ask Jackie Durbin to go to the movies. It was hardly a surprise to Jackie, though. Sylvester had first told his friend Erik about his resolve to ask Jackie out, and Erik had told Jackie's friend Cynthia about Sylvester's plans. Cynthia, in turn, had told Jackie, who was primed to say "yes" when Sylvester finally did call.

Welcome to the complex world of dating, an important ritual of adolescence. We'll consider dating, as well as several other aspects of adolescents' relationships with one another, in the remainder of the chapter.

Dating: Boy Meets Girl in the 21st Century

By the time most girls are 12 or 13, and boys 13 or 14, they begin to engage in dating. By the age of 16, more than 90 percent of teenagers have had at least one date, and by the end of high school, some three-quarters of adolescents have dated someone steadily (Dickenson, 1975; McCabe, 1984).

The Functions of Dating. Although on the surface dating may seem to be simply part of a pattern of courtship that can potentially lead to marriage, it actually serves other functions as well. For instance, dating is a way to learn how to establish intimacy with other individuals. Furthermore, it can provide entertainment and, depending on the status of the person one is dating, prestige. It even can be used to develop a sense of one's own identity (Skipper & Nass, 1966; Savin-Williams & Berndt, 1990; Sanderson & Cantor, 1995). For example, Leah Brookner and her boyfriend Sean Moffitt, described in the chapter prologue, are definitely finding entertainment, and probably learning something about themselves, as they attend their first formal dance.

Just how well dating serves such functions, particularly the development of psychological intimacy, is an open question. What specialists in adolescence do know, however, is surprising: Dating in early and middle adolescence is not terribly successful at facilitating intimacy. On the contrary, dating is often a superficial activity in which the participants so rarely let down their guards that they never become truly close and never expose themselves emotionally to each other. Psychological intimacy may be lacking even when sexual activity is part of the relationship (Douvan & Adelson, 1966; Savin-Williams & Berndt, 1990).

True intimacy becomes more common during later adolescence. At that point, the dating relationship may be taken more seriously by both participants, and it may be seen as a way to select a mate and as a potential prelude to marriage (an institution we consider in Chapter 14).

Just how well dating serves such functions as the development of psychological intimacy is still an open question.

Dating in Minority Groups. Cultural influences affect dating patterns among minority adolescents, particularly those whose parents have come to the United States from other countries. Minority parents may try to control their children's dating behavior in an effort to preserve the minority group's traditional values (Spencer & Dornbusch, 1990).

For example, Asian parents may be especially conservative in their attitudes and values, in part because they themselves may have had no experience of dating. (In many cases, the parents' marriage was arranged by others, and the entire concept of dating is unfamiliar.) They may insist that dating be conducted with chaperones, or not at all. As a consequence, they may find themselves involved in substantial conflict with their children (Sung, 1985).

Sexual Relationships: Permissiveness with Affection

The maturation of the sexual organs during the start of adolescence opens a new range of possibilities in relations with others: sexuality. In fact, sexual behavior and thoughts are among the central concerns of adolescents. Almost all adolescents think about sex, and many think about it a good deal of the time (Kelly, 2001).

Masturbation. For most adolescents, their initiation into sexuality comes from **masturbation,** sexual self-stimulation. Almost half of all adolescent boys and a quarter of adolescent girls report that they have engaged in masturbation. The frequency of masturbation shows a sex difference: Male masturbation is most frequent in the early teens and then begins to decline, while females begin more slowly and reach a maximum later (Oliver & Hyde, 1993; Schwartz, 1999).

masturbation sexual self-stimulation

Although masturbation is widespread, it still may produce feelings of shame and guilt. There are several reasons for this. One is that adolescents may believe that masturbation signifies the inability to find a sexual partner—an erroneous assumption, since statistics show that three-quarters of married men and 68 percent of married women report masturbating between 10 and 24 times a year (Hunt, 1974). Another reason is the legacy of shame remaining from misguided past views. For instance, 19th-century physicians and lay persons warned of horrible effects of masturbation, including "dyspepsia, spinal disease, headache, epilepsy, various kinds of fits . . . , impaired eyesight, palpitation of the heart, pain in the side and bleeding at the lungs, spasm of the heart, and sometimes sudden death" (Gregory, 1856). Suggested remedies included bandaging the genitals, covering them with a cage, tying the hands, male circumcision without anesthesia (so that it might better be remembered), and for girls, the administration of carbolic acid to the clitoris. One physician, J. W. Kellogg, believed that certain grains would be less likely to provoke sexual excitation—leading to his invention of corn flakes (Hunt, 1974; Michael et al., 1994).

The reality is different. Today, experts on sexual behavior view masturbation as a normal, healthy, and harmless activity (Leitenberg, Detzer, & Srebnik, 1993). In fact, some suggest that it provides a useful way to learn about one's own sexuality.

Sexual Intercourse. Although it may be preceded by many different types of sexual intimacy, including deep kissing, massaging, petting, and oral sex, sexual intercourse remains a major milestone in the perceptions of most adolescents. Consequently, the focus of researchers investigating sexual behavior has been on the act of intercourse.

The age at which adolescents first have sexual intercourse has been steadily declining over the last 50 years. Overall, around half of adolescents begin having intercourse between the ages of 15 and 18, and at least 80 percent have had sex before the age of 20 (see Figure 12-8). Some 7 percent of high school students report having had intercourse before the age of 13 (Seidman & Reider, 1994; Centers for Disease Control & Prevention, 1998).

Overall, sexual activities are taking place earlier during adolescence than they did in prior eras (Warren et al., 1997). This is in part a result of a change in societal norms governing sexual conduct. The prevailing norm several decades ago was the *double standard* in which premarital sex was considered permissible for males but not for females. Women were told by society that "nice girls don't," while men heard that premarital sex was permissible—although they should be sure to marry virgins.

Today, however, the double standard has largely been supplanted by a new norm, called *permissiveness with affection*. According to this standard, premarital intercourse is viewed as permissible for both men and women if it occurs in the context of a long-term, committed, or loving relationship (Reiss, 1960; Hyde, 1994).

On the other hand, the demise of the double standard is far from complete. Attitudes toward sexual conduct are typically more lenient for males than for females, even in relatively socially liberal cultures. And in some cultures, the standards for men and women are quite distinct. For example, in North Africa, the Middle East, and the majority of Asian countries, most women conform to societal norms suggesting that they abstain from sexual intercourse until they are married. In Mexico, where there are strict standards against premarital sex, males are also considerably more likely than females to have premarital sex (Liskin, 1985; Spira et al., 1992; Johnson et al., 1992). On the other hand, in Sub-Saharan Africa, women are more likely to have sexual intercourse prior to marriage, and intercourse is common among unmarried teenage women.

Sexual Orientation: Heterosexuality and Homosexuality

When we consider adolescents' sexual development, the most frequent pattern is *heterosexuality*, sexual attraction and behavior directed to the opposite sex. Yet some teenagers do not follow this path. Instead, some experience *homosexual* feelings, sexual attraction to members of their own sex.

At one time or another, around 20 to 25 percent of adolescent boys and 10 percent of adolescent girls have at least one same-sex sexual encounter. However, many fewer adolescents become exclusively homosexual. Although accurate figures are difficult to obtain, estimates range from a low of 1.1 percent to a high of 10 percent. Most experts believe that between 4 and 10 percent of both men and women are exclusively homosexual during extended periods of their lives (Kinsey, Pomeroy, & Martin, 1948; McWhirter, Sanders, & Reinisch, 1990; Alan Guttmacher Institute, 1993; Michael et al., 1994).

The difficulty in determining the proportion of people who are homosexual is due in part to the fact that homosexuality and heterosexuality are not completely distinct

The stresses of adolescence are magnified for homosexuals, who often face societal prejudice. Eventually, however, most adolescents come to grips with their sexual orientation, as these students at a symposium exemplify.

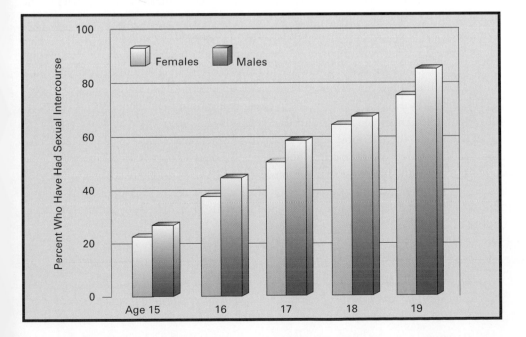

Figure 12-8 **Adolescents and Sexual Activity**

The age at which adolescents have sexual intercourse for the first time is declining, and 80 percent have had sex before the age of 20.

(*Source:* Kantrowitz & Wingert, 1999.)

sexual orientations. Alfred Kinsey, a pioneer sex researcher, argued that sexual orientation should be viewed as a continuum in which "exclusively homosexual" is at one end and "exclusively heterosexual" at the other (Kinsey, Pomeroy, & Martin, 1948). In between are people who show both homosexual and heterosexual behavior.

The determination of sexual preference is further complicated by confusion between sexual orientation and gender identity (Hunter & Mallon, 2000). While sexual orientation relates to the object of one's sexual interests, *gender identity* is the gender a person believes he or she is psychologically. There is no relationship between sexual orientation and gender identity: A man who has a strong masculine gender identity may be attracted to other men. Furthermore, the extent to which men and women enact traditional "masculine" or "feminine" behavior is unrelated to their sexual orientation or gender identity.

The factors that induce people to develop as heterosexual or homosexual are not well understood. Increasing evidence suggests that genetic and biological factors may play an important role. For instance, evidence from studies of twins shows that identical twins are more likely to both be homosexual than pairs of siblings who don't share their genetic makeup. Other research finds that various structures of the brain are different in homosexuals and heterosexuals, and hormone production also seems to be linked to sexual orientation (LeVay, 1993; Gladue, 1994; Berenbaum & Snyder, 1995; Meyer-Bahlburg et al., 1995).

On the other hand, evidence of a biological cause is not yet conclusive, given that most findings are based on small samples (Byne & Parsons, 1994). Consequently, some researchers have suggested that family or peer environmental factors play a role. For example, Freud argued that homosexuality was the result of inappropriate identification with the opposite-sex parent (Freud, 1922/1959).

The difficulty with Freud's theoretical perspective and other, similar perspectives that followed is that there simply is no evidence to suggest that any particular family dynamic or childrearing practice is consistently related to sexual orientation. Similarly, explanations based on learning theory, which suggest that homosexuality arises because of rewarding, pleasant homosexual experiences and unsatisfying heterosexual ones, do not appear to be the complete answer (Bell & Weinberg, 1978; Isay, 1990; Golombok & Tasker, 1996).

In short, there is no accepted explanation of why some adolescents develop a heterosexual orientation and others a homosexual orientation. Most experts believe that sexual orientation develops out of a complex interplay of genetic, physiological, and environmental factors (Gladue, 1994).

What is clear is that adolescents who find themselves attracted to members of the same sex may face a more difficult time than other teens. U.S. society still harbors great ignorance and prejudice regarding homosexuality, persisting in the belief that people have a choice in the matter—which they do not. Gay and lesbian teens may be rejected by their family or peers, or even harassed and assaulted if they are open about their orientation. The result is that adolescents who find themselves to be homosexual are at greater risk for depression, and suicide rates are significantly higher for homosexual adolescents than heterosexual adolescents (Henning-Stout, 1996; Refaedi et al., 1998).

Ultimately, though, most people are able to come to grips with their sexual orientation. Once they are past adolescence, homosexuals have the same overall degree of mental and physical health as heterosexuals. Homosexuality is not considered a psychological disorder by any of the major psychological or medical associations, and all of them endorse efforts to reduce discrimination against homosexuals (Bersoff & Ogden, 1991; Herek, 1993; Patterson, 1994).

Teenage Pregnancy

Night has eased into day, but it is all the same for Tori Michel, 17. Her 5-day-old baby, Caitlin, has been fussing for hours, though she seems finally to have settled into the pink-and-purple car seat on the living-room sofa. "She wore herself out," explains Tori, who lives in a two-bedroom duplex in this St. Louis suburb with her mother, Susan, an aide to handicapped adults. "I think she just had gas."

Motherhood was not in Tori's plans for her senior year at Fort Zumwalt South High School—not until she had a "one-night thing" with James, a 21-year-old she met through friends. She had been taking birth-control pills but says she stopped after breaking up with a long-term boyfriend. "Wrong answer," she now says ruefully. (Gleick, Reed, & Schindehette, 1994)

This 16-year-old mother and her child are representative of a major social problem: teenage pregnancy. Why is teenage pregnancy a greater problem in the U.S. than in other countries?

Feedings at 3:00 a.m., diaper changes, and visits to the pediatrician are not part of most people's vision of adolescence. Yet, every year, tens of thousands of adolescents in the United States give birth. Figure 12-9 shows that although the birth rate for U.S. teenagers of different ethnic groups has declined over the past four decades and is at near-record lows, about 5 percent of girls age 15 to 19 still become mothers each year (Darroch & Singh, 1999).

Despite the decline in teenage births, the problem remains a severe one, particularly when the rate of teenage pregnancy in the United States is compared to that of other industrialized countries, which are much lower. Although it might be suspected that the higher rates of pregnancy in the United States are due to more frequent or earlier sexual activity, that is not the case. For instance, there is little difference among industrialized countries in the age at which adolescents first have sexual intercourse.

What does differ is the use of birth control. Many adolescent pregnancies are unintended and happen because teenagers do not use effective contraceptives. Girls in the United States are much less likely to use contraception than teenagers in other countries. And even when they do use birth control, teenagers in the United States are less likely to use effective methods (Musick, 1993).

However, ineffective birth control is only part of the answer. An additional factor is that despite increasing rates of premarital sexual behavior, people in the United States remain basically intolerant of premarital sex, and they are unwilling to provide sex education that includes information on contraception, which might reduce the rate of teenage pregnancies.

Consequently, sex education is considerably more limited in the United States than in other industrialized countries. And because sex remains a contentious topic, with many political ramifications, effective sex education programs are difficult to develop and implement (Rauch-Elnekave, 1994; Allen et al., 1997). Many pregnancy prevention efforts focus on abstinence, encouraging teens to avoid or delay having intercourse. The *From Research to Practice* box evaluates one popular strategy.

The results of an unintended pregnancy can be devastating to both mother and child. In comparison to earlier times, teenage mothers today are much less likely to be

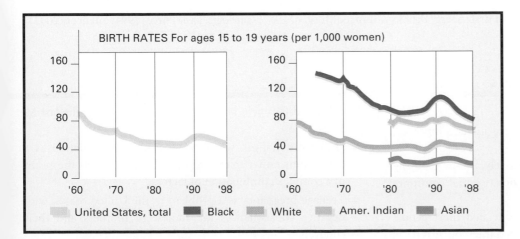

Figure 12-9 **Teenage Pregnancy Rates**

The rate of teenage pregnancy in the United States has declined significantly over the last decades among all ethnic groups.

(*Source:* National Center for Health Statistics, 1998.)

From Research to Practice

Taking the Pledge: Do Virginity Pledges Delay Premarital Sex Among Teenagers?

Does taking a pledge of virginity delay the incidence of premarital sex among teenagers?

Yes, at least under some circumstances. Recent research suggests that teenagers who make a public pledge to refrain from premarital sex delay intercourse significantly longer than those who do not make a public commitment. One study, sponsored by the National Institute of Child Health and Human Development, looked at 6,800 students from 141 schools in the United States. Adolescents who took a pledge to defer sexual intercourse until marriage delayed sex about 18 months longer than those who had never taken such a pledge (Bearman & Bruckner, 2001).

But before those intent on delaying sexual intercourse until marriage begin printing up pledge cards, they need to keep in mind the limitations to pledges. First, the study examined only people who had voluntarily taken a public pledge; the results tell us nothing about whether people who are bullied through social pressure into making a pledge are more likely to remain virgins. Furthermore, the effectiveness of pledging depended on a student's age. For older adoles-

cents, 18 years old and above, taking a pledge had no effect. Pledges were effective only for 16- and 17-year-olds.

Finally, the pledges were effective only when a *minority* of people in a school took such a pledge. When more than 30 percent took such a pledge, the effectiveness of the pledge diminished substantially. The reason for this somewhat suprising finding relates to why virginity pledges work in the first place: They offer adolescents a sense of identity, similar to the way joining a club does. When a minority of students take a virginity pledge, they feel part of a special group, and they are more likely to adhere to the norms of that group—in this case, remaining a virgin. In contrast, if a majority of students take a pledge of virginity, the pledge becomes less unique and adherence is less likely.

The study also examined whether breaking the pledge had an effect on pledgers' self-esteem. The answer: No. Despite previous research that found that girls who broke a virginity pledge had slightly lower self-esteem as a result, this study found that breaking the pledge had no effect on how teenagers viewed themselves (Bearman & Bruckner, 2001).

---

married. In a high percentage of cases, mothers care for their children without the help of the father (Coley & Chase-Lansdale, 1998; National Center for Health Statistics, 1998). Without financial or emotional support, a mother may have to abandon her own education, and consequently she may be relegated to unskilled, poorly paying jobs for the rest of her life. In other cases, she may develop long-term dependency on welfare. An adolescent mother's physical and mental health may suffer as she faces unrelenting stress due to continual demands on her time (Ambuel, 1995; Barratt et al., 1996).

The children of teenage mothers also do not fare well when compared to children of older mothers. They are more likely to suffer from poor health and to show poorer school performance. Later, they are more likely to become teenage parents themselves, creating a cycle of pregnancy and poverty from which it is very difficult to extricate themselves (Furstenberg, Brooks-Gunn, & Morgan, 1987; Carnegie Task Force, 1994; Spencer, 2001)

Review and Rethink

REVIEW

■ The functions of dating in adolescence include intimacy, entertainment, and prestige.

■ Masturbation, once viewed very negatively, is now generally regarded as a normal and harmless practice that continues into adulthood.

■ Sexual intercourse is a major milestone that most people reach during adolescence. The age of first intercourse reflects

cultural differences and has been declining over the last 50 years.

■ Sexual orientation, which is most accurately viewed as a continuum rather than categorically, develops as the result of a complex combination of factors.

■ Teenage pregnancy is a problem in the United States, with negative consequences for adolescent mothers and their children.

RETHINK

■ Which factors in early and middle adolescence work against the achievement of true intimacy in dating?

■ How might the interplay of genetic, physiological, and environmental factors influence sexual orientation?

Looking Back

How does the development of self-concept, self-esteem, and identity proceed during adolescence?

■ During adolescence, self-concept differentiates to encompass others' views as well as one's own and to include multiple aspects simultaneously. Differentiation of self-concept can cause confusion as behaviors reflect a complex definition of the self.

■ Adolescents also differentiate their self-esteem, evaluating particular aspects of themselves differently.

■ According to Erik Erikson, adolescents are in the identity-versus-identity-confusion stage, seeking to discover their individuality and identity. They may become confused and exhibit dysfunctional reactions, and they may rely for help and information more on friends and peers than on adults.

■ James Marcia identifies four identity statuses that individuals may experience in adolescence and in later life: identity achievement, identity foreclosure, identity diffusion, and moratorium.

■ The formation of an identity is challenging for members of racial and ethnic minority groups, many of whom appear to be embracing a bicultural identity approach.

What dangers do adolescents face as they deal with the stresses of adolescence?

■ Many adolescents have feelings of sadness and hopelessness, and some experience major depression. Biological, environmental, and social factors contribute to depression, and there are gender, ethnic, and racial differences in its occurrence.

■ The rate of adolescent suicide is rising, with suicide now the third most common cause of death in the 15- to 24-year-old bracket.

How does the quality of relationships with family and peers change during adolescence?

■ Adolescents' quest for autonomy often brings confusion and tension to their relationships with their parents, but the actual "generation gap" between parents' and teenagers' attitudes is usually small.

■ Peers are important during adolescence because they provide social comparison and reference groups against which to judge social success. Relationships among adolescents are characterized by the need to belong.

What are gender, race, and ethnic relations like in adolescence?

■ During adolescence, boys and girls begin to spend time together in groups and, toward the end of adolescence, to pair off.

■ In general, segregation between people of different races and ethnicities increases in middle and late adolescence, even in schools with a diverse student body.

What does it mean to be popular and unpopular in adolescence, and how do adolescents respond to peer pressure?

■ Degrees of popularity during adolescence include popular and controversial adolescents (on the high end of popularity) and neglected and rejected adolescents (on the low end).

■ Peer pressure is not a simple phenomenon. Adolescents conform to their peers in areas of peer expertise, and to adults in areas of adult expertise. As adolescents grow in confidence, their conformity to both peers and adults declines.

■ Although most adolescents do not commit crimes, adolescents are disproportionately involved in criminal activities. Juvenile delinquents can be categorized as undersocialized or socialized delinquents.

What are the functions and characteristics of dating during adolescence?

■ During adolescence, dating provides intimacy, entertainment, and prestige. Achieving psychological intimacy, difficult at first, becomes easier as adolescents mature, gain confidence, and take relationships more seriously.

▶ *How does sexuality develop in the adolescent years?*

■ For most adolescents, masturbation serves as the first step into sexuality. The age of first intercourse, which is now in the teens, has declined as the double standard has faded and the norm of permissiveness with affection has gained ground.

■ Most people's sexual orientation is largely or entirely heterosexual, with between 4 and 10 percent being mostly or exclusively homosexual. Sexual orientation apparently develops out of a complex interplay of genetic, physiological, and environmental factors.

▶ *Why is teenage pregnancy a particular problem in the United States?*

■ In the United States, about 5 percent of girls under 20 give birth each year. The incidence of both contraception and sex education is comparatively low in the United States, a situation that contributes to the high rate of adolescent pregnancy.

EPILOGUE

We continued our consideration of adolescence in this chapter, discussing the highly important social and personality issues of self-concept, self-esteem, and identity. We looked at adolescents' relationships with family and peers, and at gender, race, and ethnic relations during adolescence. Our discussion concluded with a look at dating, sexuality, and pregnancy.

Return to the prologue, in which we looked at a moment in the life of 16-year-old Leah Brookner, who is about to head out to her first formal. In light of what you now know about adolescent social and personality development, consider the following questions.

1. In what ways does Leah appear to be dealing with the issues of self-concept, self-esteem, and identity?

2. How is she dealing with the issues of belonging and relationships with peers?

3. In what ways is Leah's behavior an example of the quest for autonomy? Is this evidence of a large generation gap in Leah's family?

4. What aspects of adolescent dating practices are evident in this scene? If Leah wants advice on dating or sexuality, is she more likely to seek it from her parents or her peers? Why?

Key Terms and Concepts

identity-versus-identity-confusion stage (p. 420)
identity achievement (p. 422)
identity foreclosure (p. 423)
moratorium (p. 423)
identity diffusion (p. 423)
cluster suicide (p. 426)

autonomy (p. 429)
generation gap (p. 430)
reference groups (p. 433)
cliques (p. 433)
crowds (p. 433)
sex cleavage (p.433)
controversial adolescents (p. 436)

rejected adolescents (p. 436)
neglected adolescents (p. 436)
peer pressure (p. 436)
undersocialized delinquents (p. 438)
socialized delinquents (p. 438)
masturbation (p. 440)

Bridges

Adolescence is the bridge between childhood and adulthood. In Part Five, we've seen how growth in different domains intertwines to help adolescents in the progression from child to adult. As we turn to early adulthood in the next section of the book, we'll observe how the development foundations that already have been laid continue to contribute to the unfolding of life as an adult.

The myth of adolescence in U.S. culture is that it is a time of intense emotional difficulties and intergenerational conflict. We've seen, however, that although making the transition to adulthood is challenging for everyone, reality diverges from this myth.

Physically, adolescents experience extraordinary maturation with the onset of puberty, and they must cope with the awkward changes associated with it. Adolescents' physical development is accompanied by cognitive advances that bring sophistication in the use of formal reasoning and abstract thought, as well as an increasing ability—and tendency—to question authority. In Part Six, we'll see that although some theorists believe that we reach the peak of cognitive development in adolescence, others suggest that adults continue to develop new ways of thinking.

Teenagers' thoughts are often focused on themselves as they cross the bridge to adulthood. Maybe this helps them deal with one of the most important developmental tasks of the period: refining their view of themselves. We observed, for example, how adolescents use their increasingly sophisticated cognitive skills to differentiate their self-concept and self-esteem into component parts, a process they began during the school years and will continue throughout adulthood.

We discussed adolescents' relationships with peers and parents. As we go on, we'll see that the quest for autonomy, which is one of the hallmarks of adolescence, is finally resolved, for most people, in the next phase of their lives, as young adults.

OUTLINE

EARLY ADULTHOOD

Physical and Cognitive Development in Early Adulthood

PROLOGUE: A TALE OF TWO STUDENTS

College campuses, like the rest of society, reflect increasing diversity.

For Enrico Vasquez, there was never any doubt: He was headed for college. Enrico, the son of a wealthy Cuban immigrant who had made a fortune in the medical supply business after fleeing Cuba 5 years before Enrico's birth, had had the importance of education constantly drummed into him by his family. In fact, the question was never *whether* he would go to college, but what college he would be able to get into. As a consequence, Enrico found high school to be a pressure cooker: Every grade and extracurricular activity was seen as helping—or hindering—his chances of admission to a "good" college.

***

Armando Williams' letter of acceptance to Dallas County Community College is framed on the wall of his mother's apartment. To her, the letter represents nothing short of a miracle, an answer to her prayers. Growing up in a neighborhood saturated with drugs and drive-by shootings, Armando had always been a hard worker and a "good boy," in his mother's view. But when he was growing up, she never even entertained the possibility of his making it to college. To see him reach this stage in his education fills her with joy.

Looking Ahead

Although Enrico Vasquez's and Armando Williams's lives have followed two very different paths, they share the single goal of obtaining a college education. They represent the increasing diversity in family background, socioeconomic status, race, and ethnicity that is coming to characterize college populations today.

Whether they attend college or not, people in early adulthood are at the height of their cognitive abilities. Physically, too, they are at their peak. The body acts as if it's on automatic pilot: Physical health and fitness are never better.

At the same time, though, considerable development goes on during early adulthood, which starts at the end of adolescence (around age 20) and continues until roughly the start of middle age (around age 40). As we see throughout this and the following chapter, significant changes occur as new opportunities arise and people choose to take on (or to forgo) a new set of roles as spouse, parent, and worker.

This chapter focuses on physical and cognitive development. It begins with a look at the physical changes that extend into early adulthood. We will see not only that growth continues, but that various motor skills change as well. We look at diet and weight, examining the prevalence of obesity. We also consider stress and coping during the early years of adulthood.

The chapter then turns to cognitive development. Although traditional approaches to cognitive development regarded adulthood as an inconsequential plateau, we will examine some new theories that suggest that significant cognitive growth occurs during adulthood. We also consider the nature of adult intelligence and how life events are reflected in cognitive development.

Finally, the last part of the chapter considers college, the institution that shapes intellectual growth for those who attend. After taking a look at who goes to college, we will consider how gender and race are related to achievement. We end by looking at some reasons why students drop out of college and examining some of the adjustment problems that college students face.

After reading this chapter, you will be able to answer these questions:

▶ **How does the body develop during early adulthood, and to what risks are young adults exposed?**

▶ **What are the effects of stress, and what can be done about it?**

▶ **Does cognitive development continue in young adulthood?**

▶ **How is intelligence defined today, and what causes cognitive growth in young adults?**

▶ **Who attends college today, and how is the college population changing?**

▶ **What do students learn in college, and what difficulties do they face?**

Physical Development and Stress

Grady McKinnon grinned as his mountain bike left the ground briefly. The 27-year-old financial auditor was delighted to be out for the camping and biking weekend with four of his college buddies. Grady had been worried that an upcoming deadline at work would make him miss this trip. When they were still in school, Grady and his friends used to go biking nearly every weekend. But jobs, marriage—

and even a child for one of the guys—started taking up a lot of their attention. This was their only trip this summer. He was sure glad he hadn't missed it.

Grady and his friends were probably in the best physical condition of their lives when they first started to go mountain biking regularly in college. Even now, as Grady's life becomes more complicated and sports starts to take a back seat to work and other personal demands, he is still enjoying one of the healthiest periods of his life. As we will see, although most people, like Grady, reach the height of their physical capacities in young adulthood, at the same time, they must try to cope with the stress produced by the challenges of their adult lives.

Physical Development and the Senses

In most respects, physical development and maturation are complete at early adulthood. Most people are at the peak of their physical capabilities. They have attained their full height, and their limbs are proportional to their size, rendering the gangliness of adolescence a memory. People in their early 20s tend to be healthy, vigorous, and energetic. Although **senescence,** or biological aging, the natural physical decline brought about by increasing age, has begun, age-related changes are not usually very obvious to people until later in their lives.

senescence the natural physical decline brought about by aging

On the other hand, not all growth is complete. Some people, particularly late maturers, continue to gain height in their early 20s. Furthermore, certain parts of the body do not fully mature until early adulthood. For instance, the brain continues to grow in both size and weight, reaching its maximum during early adulthood. Brain wave patterns also reveal change during early adulthood, although many people in their early 20s show mature patterns (Haug, 1991; Scheibel, 1992; Friedman, Berman, & Hamberger, 1993; Robinson, 1997).

The senses are as sharp as they will ever be. Although there are changes in the elasticity of the eye—a continuation of an aging process that may begin as early as 10—they are so minor that they produce no deterioration in vision. It is not until the 40s that eyesight changes sufficiently to be noticeable—as we will see in Chapter 15.

Hearing, too, is at its peak. However, a gender difference emerges: Women can detect higher tones more readily than men (McGuinness, 1972). In general, though, the

People in their early twenties tend to be healthy, vigorous, and energetic, but they also tend to experience quite a bit of stress.

Professional athletes, like tennis player Jana Novotna, are at the peak of their psychomotor abilities during early adulthood.

hearing of both men and women is quite good. Under quiet conditions, the average young adult can hear the ticking of a watch 20 feet away.

The other senses, including taste, smell, and sensitivity to touch and pain, are quite good, and they remain that way throughout early adulthood. These senses do not begin to deteriorate until the 40s or 50s.

Motor Functioning, Fitness, and Health: Staying Well

If you are a professional athlete, most people probably consider you to be over the hill by the time you leave your 20s. Although there are notable exceptions (think of baseball star Nolan Ryan, who continued playing into his 40s, for instance), even athletes who train constantly tend to lose their physical edge once they reach their 30s. In some sports, the peak passes even earlier. In swimming, for instance, women reach their peak at age 18, and men at age 20 (Schultz & Curnow, 1988).

Most professional athletes—as well as the rest of us—are at the peak of their psychomotor abilities during early adulthood. Reaction time is quicker, muscle strength is greater, and eye-hand coordination is better than at any other period (Sliwinski et al., 1994; Salthouse, 1993).

Physical Fitness. The physical prowess that typically characterizes early adulthood doesn't come naturally, however; nor does it come to everyone. In order to reach their physical potential, people must exercise and maintain a proper diet.

The benefits of exercise are hardly secret: In the United States, jazzercise and aerobics classes, NordicTraks and Nautilus workouts, and jogging and swimming are common and seemingly ubiquitous activities. Yet the conspicuousness of exercise activities is misleading. Less than 10 percent of Americans are involved in sufficient regular exercise to keep them in good physical shape, and less than a quarter engage in even moderate regular exercise (MMWR, 1989; Kaplan, Sallis, & Patterson, 1993). Furthermore, the opportunity to exercise is largely an upper- and middle-class phenomenon; people of lower socioeconomic status (SES) often have neither the time nor the money to engage in regular exercise (Atkins et al., 1990).

The amount of exercise required to yield significant health benefits is not enormous (Dunn & Blair, 1997). According to recommendations from the American College of Sports Medicine and the Centers for Disease Control and Prevention, people should accumulate at least 30 minutes of moderate physical activity at least 5 days a week. The time spent exercising can be continuous or occur in bouts of at least 10 minutes, as long as it totals 30 minutes each day. Moderate activity includes walking briskly at 3 to 4 mph, biking at speeds up to 10 mph, golfing while carrying or pulling clubs, fishing by casting from shore, playing ping pong, or canoeing at 2 to 4 mph. Even common household chores, such as weeding, vacuuming, and mowing with a power mower provide moderate exercise (American College of Sports Medicine, 1997).

The advantages to those who do become involved in regular exercise programs are many. Exercise increases cardiovascular fitness, meaning that the heart and circulatory system operate more efficiently. Furthermore, lung capacity increases, raising endurance. Muscles become stronger, and the body is more flexible and maneuverable. The range of movement is greater, and the muscles, tendons, and ligaments are more elastic. Moreover, exercise during this period helps reduce *osteoporosis,* the thinning of the bones, in later life.

Exercise also may optimize the immune response of the body, helping it fight off disease. Exercise may even decrease stress and anxiety and reduce depression (Mutrie, 1997). It can provide people with a sense of control over their bodies, as well as impart a feeling of accomplishment (Brown, 1991; Gross, 1991).

Regular exercise provides another, ultimately more important, reward: It increases longevity. In brief, the higher the level of fitness, the lower the death rate (see Figure 13-1; Blair et al., 1989).

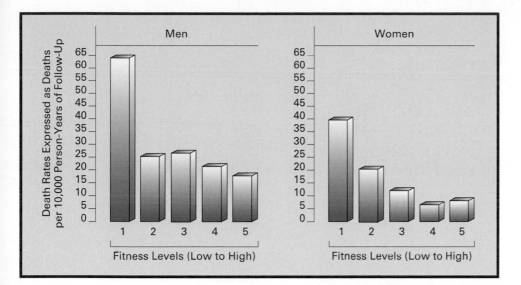

Figure 13-1 **The Result of Fitness: Longevity**

The greater the fitness level, the lower the death rate tends to be for both men and women.

(*Source:* Blair et al., 1989.)

Health. Although a lack of exercise may produce poor health (and worse), health risks in general are relatively slight during early adulthood. During this period, people are less susceptible to colds and other minor illnesses than they were as children, and when they do come down with illnesses, they usually get over them quickly.

Adults in their 20s and 30s stand a higher risk of dying from accidents, primarily those involving automobiles, than from most other causes. But there are other killers: Among the leading sources of death for people 25 to 34 are AIDS, cancer, heart disease, and suicide. Amid the grim statistics of mortality, the age 35 represents a significant milestone. It is at that point that illness and disease overtake accidents as the leading cause of death—the first time this is true since infancy.

Not all people fare equally well during early adulthood. Lifestyle choices, including the use—or abuse—of alcohol, tobacco, or drugs or engaging in unprotected sex, can hasten *secondary aging,* physical declines brought about by environmental factors or individual choices. These substances can also increase a young adult's risk of dying from one of the leading causes mentioned above.

As the definition of secondary aging implies, cultural factors, including gender and race, are also related to the risk of dying in young adulthood. For instance, men are more apt to die than women, primarily due to their higher involvement in automobile accidents. Furthermore, African Americans have twice the death rate of Caucasians, and minorities in general have a higher likelihood of dying than the Caucasian majority.

Another major cause of death for men is violence, particularly in the United States. The murder rate is significantly higher in the United States than in any other developed country (see Figure 13-2). Compare, for instance, the U.S. murder rate of 21.9 per 100,000 men to Japan's 0.5 murders per 100,000 men—a difference in magnitude of more than 4,000 percent. Statistics like this one have led some observers to conclude that violence is "as American as apple pie" (Fingerhut & Kleinman, 1990; Berkowitz, 1993).

Murder rates also depend significantly on racial factors. Although murder is the fifth most frequent cause of death for young adult white Americans, it is *the* most likely cause of death for African Americans, and it is a significant factor for Hispanic Americans. In some areas of the country, a young black male has a higher probability of being murdered than a soldier in the Vietnam War had of being killed. Overall, an African American male has a 1 in 21 chance of being murdered during his lifetime. In contrast, a white male has a 1 in 131 chance of being murdered (Centers for Disease Control, 1991; Berkowitz, 1993; Triandis, 1994).

Cultural factors influence not only causes of death, but also young adult's lifestyles and health-related behavior—in wellness or illness.

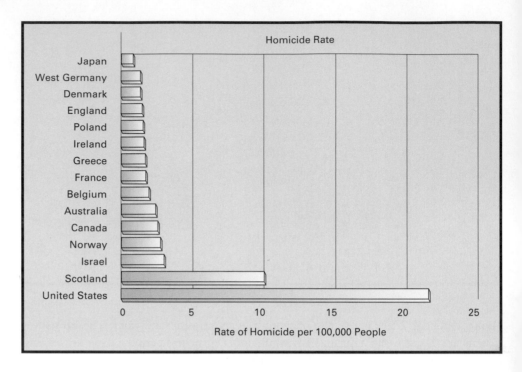

Homicide Rate

Rate of Homicide per 100,000 People

Figure 13-2 **Tracking Murder**

The murder rate (per 100,000 men) is far higher in the United States than in any other developed country. What features of U.S. society contribute to this state of affairs?

(*Source:* Fingerhut & Kleinman, 1990.)

 D e v e l o p m e n t a l   D i v e r s i t y

How Cultural Health Beliefs Influence Use of Health Care

Manolita recently suffered a heart attack. She was advised by her doctor to change her eating and activity habits or face the risk of another life-threatening heart attack. During the period that followed, Manolita dramatically changed her eating and activity habits. She also began going to church and praying extensively. After a recent check-up, Manolita is in the best shape of her life. What are some of the reasons for Manolita's amazing recovery? (Murguia, Peterson, & Zea, 1997, p. 16)

The murder rate in the United States is significantly higher than in any other developed country.

After reading the passage above, would you conclude that Manolita recovered her health because (a) she changed her eating and activity habits; (b) she became a better person; (c) God was testing her faith; or (d) her doctor prescribed the correct changes?

In response to a survey asking this question, more than two-thirds of Latino immigrants from Central America, South America, or the Caribbean believed that "God was testing her faith" had a moderate or great effect on her recovery, although most also agreed that a change in eating and activity habits was important (Murguia, Peterson, & Zea, 1997).

The findings are significant because they help explain why Latinos are the least likely of any Western ethnic group to seek the help of a physician when they are ill. According to psychologists Alejandro Murguia, Rolf Peterson, and Maria Zea (1997), cultural health beliefs, along with demographic and psychological barriers, reduce people's use of physicians and medical care.

Specifically, they suggest that Latinos, as well as members of some other non-Western groups, are more likely than non-Hispanic whites to believe in supernatural causes of illness. For instance, members of these groups may attribute illness to a punishment from God, a lack of faith, or a hex. Such beliefs may reduce the motivation to seek medical care from a physician (Landrine & Klonoff, 1994). Demographic barriers, such as lower socioeconomic status, also reduce the ability to rely on traditional medical care, which is expensive. In addition, the lower level of involvement in the mainstream culture that is characteristic of recent immigrants to the United States is associated with a lower likelihood of visiting a physician and obtaining mainstream medical care (Wells, Golding, & Hough, 1989; Pachter & Weller, 1993).

In order to ensure that members of every group receive adequate health care, physicians and other health care providers must take cultural health beliefs into account. For example, if a patient believes that the source of his or her illness is a spell cast by a jealous romantic rival, the patient may not comply with medical regimens that ignore that perceived source. To provide effective health care, then, health care providers must be sensitive to such cultural health beliefs. ☐

Eating, Nutrition, and Obesity: A Weighty Concern

Most young adults know which foods are nutritionally sound and how to maintain a balanced diet; they just don't bother to follow the rules—even though the rules are not all that difficult to follow.

Good Nutrition. According to guidelines provided by the U.S. Department of Agriculture, people can achieve good nutrition by eating foods that are low in fat, including vegetables, fruits, whole grain foods, fish, poultry, lean meats, and low-fat dairy products. In addition, whole grain foods and cereal products, vegetables (including dried beans and peas), and fruit are beneficial in another way: They help people raise the amount of complex carbohydrates and fiber they ingest. Milk and other sources of calcium are also needed to prevent osteoporosis. Finally, people should reduce salt intake (U.S.D.A., 1992).

During adolescence, a poor diet does not always present a significant problem. For instance, teenagers don't suffer too much from a diet high in junk foods and fat, because they are undergoing such tremendous growth. The story changes when they reach young adulthood, however. With growth tapering off, young adults must reduce the caloric intake they were used to during adolescence.

Many do not. Although most people enter young adulthood with bodies of average height and weight, they gradually put on weight if their poor dietary habits remain unchanged (Insel & Roth, 1991).

Obesity. The adult population of the United States is growing—in more ways than one. Obesity, defined as body weight that is 20 percent or more above the average weight for a

Obesity increased 6 percent between 1998 and 1999. It is estimated that 12 percent of those age 18 to 29 are obese, and the numbers increase throughout adulthood.

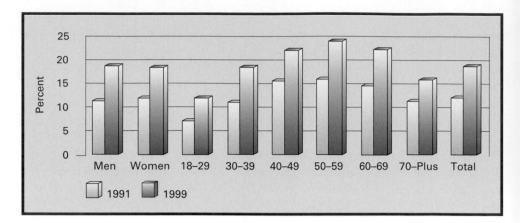

Figure 13-3 **Obesity on the Rise**

In spite of greater awareness of the importance of good nutrition, obesity among American adults has risen dramatically over the past decade. Why do you think this rise has occurred?

(Centers for Disease Control and Prevention, 2000.)

person of a given height, is on the rise in the United States. In just the 1-year period from 1998 to 1999, obesity increased 6 percent. Some 12 percent of those age 18 to 29 are obese, and the numbers edge up throughout adulthood: As age increases, more and more people are classified as obese (see Figure 13-3; Centers for Disease Control and Prevention, 2000).

Weight control is a difficult, and often losing, battle for many young adults. Most people who diet ultimately regain the weight they have lost, and they become involved in a seesaw cycle of weight gain and loss. In fact, some obesity experts now argue that the rate of dieting failure is so great that people may want to avoid dieting altogether. Instead, if people eat the foods they really want in moderation, they may be able to avoid the binge eating that often occurs when diets fail. Even though obese people may never reach their desired weight, they may, according to this reasoning, ultimately control their weight more effectively (Polivy & Herman, 1991; Heatherton, Polivy, & Herman, 1991; Lowe, 1993).

Physical Disabilities: Coping with Physical Challenge

Spotting him as he emerges from beneath a shady tree, the coach goes over and places one arm across the runner's sweaty back. Even though Tony Gorczyca has just claimed an Olympic victory in the 5,000 meters, his coach is not about to let it go to his head.

"It sure got boring watching you run around in circles," the coach, Dave Landau, says as he squints against the blazing sun. "You looked like a gerbil out there."

Gorczyca pauses momentarily, letting Landau's words sink in, then shoots back his reply: "Anytime you want to race, let me know."

It is a warm retort, made of friendship. After a spring of training together, these two Montgomery County [Maryland] residents have established a bond of respect that extends far beyond the white lanes of the track. And while he himself is a marathoner, Landau knows Gorczyca could pose a challenge were they to race—even though Gorczyca is mentally retarded and suffers from a disease that has left him with an under-developed right leg and arm, blind in one eye, and prone to violent seizures. (Wisnia, 1994, p. D5)

Most young adults do not face the physical challenges—let alone the mental hurdles—that Tony Gorczyca faces. However, over 50 million people in the United States are physically or mentally challenged, according to the official definition of *disability*—a condition that substantially limits a major life activity such as walking or vision. People with disabilities face a difficult, challenging path.

Statistics paint a grim picture of a minority group that is undereducated and underemployed. Fewer than 10 percent of people with major handicaps have finished high

The physically-challenged face a variety of obstacles, despite the passage of the Americans with Disabilities Act in 1990, which mandates full access to public establishments.

school, fewer than 25 percent of disabled men and 15 percent of disabled women work full-time, and unemployment rates are high. Furthermore, even if people with disabilities do find work, the positions they find are often routine and low-paying (Schaefer & Lamm, 1992).

Individuals with disabilities face several kinds of barriers to leading full lives that are completely integrated into the broader society. Some barriers are physical. Despite passage in 1990 of the landmark Americans with Disabilities Act (ADA), which mandates full access to public establishments such as stores, office buildings, hotels, and theaters, people in wheelchairs still cannot gain access to many older buildings.

Another barrier—sometimes harder to overcome than a physical one—is prejudice and discrimination. People with disabilities sometimes face pity or avoidance from nondisabled people. Some nondisabled people focus so much on the disability that they overlook other characteristics, reacting to a person with a disability only as a problem category and not as an individual. Others treat people with disabilities as if they were children (Heward & Orlansky, 1988). Ultimately, such treatment can take its toll on the way people with disabilities think about themselves (French & Swain, 1997).

Stress and Coping: Dealing with Life's Challenges

It's 5:00 p.m. Rosa Convoy, a 25-year-old single mother, has just finished her work as a receptionist at a dentist's office and is on her way home. She has exactly 2 hours to pick up her daughter Zoe from child care, get home, make and eat dinner, pick up and return with a babysitter from down the street, say goodbye to Zoe, and get to her 7 o'clock programming class at a local community college. It's a marathon she runs every Tuesday and Thursday night, and she knows she doesn't have a second to spare if she wants to reach the class on time.

It doesn't take an expert to know what Rosa Convoy is experiencing: **stress,** the response to events that threaten or challenge us. Like those of other young adults, Rosa's days pass in a blur of activity, sometimes, it seems, taxing her body—and mind—to the breaking point. How well Rosa, and everyone, can cope with stress depends on a complex interplay between physical and psychological factors (Hetherington & Blechman, 1996).

Stress is a part of nearly everyone's existence, and our lives are crowded with events and circumstances, known as *stressors,* that produce threats to our well-being. Stressors need not be unpleasant events: Even the happiest events, such as starting a long-sought job or planning a wedding, can produce stress (Sarason, Johnson, & Siegel, 1978; Brown & McGill, 1989).

Researchers in the new field of **psychoneuroimmunology (PNI)**—the study of the relationship among the brain, the immune system, and psychological factors—have found that stress produces several outcomes. The most immediate is typically a biological reaction, as certain hormones, secreted by the adrenal glands, cause a rise in heart rate, blood pressure, and respiration rate, and sweating. In some situations, these immediate effects may be beneficial because they produce an "emergency reaction" in the sympathetic nervous system by which people are better able to defend themselves from a sudden, threatening situation (Parkes, 1997).

On the other hand, long-term, continuous exposure to stressors may result in a reduction of the body's ability to deal with stress. As stress-related hormones are constantly secreted, the heart, blood vessels, and other body tissues may deteriorate. As a consequence, people become more susceptible to diseases as their ability to fight off germs declines (Kiecolt-Glaser & Glaser, 1986; Cohen, Tyrrell, & Smith, 1997; see also the *Speaking of Development* box).

stress the response to events that threaten or challenge an individual

psychoneuroimmunology (PNI) the study of the relationship among the brain, the immune system, and psychological factors

SPEAKING OF DEVELOPMENT

Patricia Norris, Psychoneuroimmunologist

BORN: 1932

EDUCATION: University of California at Santa Barbara, B.A. in psychology; Union Institute, Cincinnati, Ohio, Ph.D. in psychology

POSITION: Director of psychoneuroimmunology at the Life Sciences Institute of Mind–Body Health

HOME: Topeka, Kansas

After 14 years as director of biofeedback and psychophysiology at the Menninger Clinic in Topeka, Kansas, Patricia Norris went into private practice in 1994.

Today she works at the Life Sciences Institute of Mind–Body Health, where she is director of psychoneuroimmunology—the study of the relationship between the body's immune system and psychological factors. Norris works with people who face stress and pain in their everyday lives.

"Just about everyone would agree that any patient who goes to a doctor is experiencing stress on several levels, whether the stress is psychological or physical," she says. "Our main work here focuses on teaching self-regulation, helping people discover their own powers to respond differently—in helpful or unhelpful ways—to all types of things, including panic, anxiety, pain, and life's events. Self-regulation is the bottom line."

Through *biofeedback,* which uses electronic devices to provide people with information about their bodily functions,

Norris teaches patients how to control their muscles and blood flow, a strategy that she has found works well in helping relieve both pain and stress.

"Biofeedback is a technique that people can observe and use. They can watch their hearts actually beat slower," she notes, "and then they can learn to use their knowledge as a tool for self-regulation."

"If we think of stress as what is going on in our lives, there isn't much that we can do about it. But if we think of stress as a response, there's a lot we can do. We can actually learn to change the response on a physiological and psychological level," she explains.

"We start with learning to change reactions. It's not your life that is killing you, it's your reactions to it," Norris says. "People aren't capable of dealing with stress until they learn internal strategies for changing their reactions. Once they are able to change their reactions, they can decide to make bigger and more central changes.

"For instance, people with high blood pressure know they should exercise and cut out salt, but because of their tension, they don't do it. Once they're able to manage their stress, they can begin to make the changes they need in their lives to treat the high blood pressure itself.

"Many times people's stress patterns come out of their early developmental history. As they start to change some of their stress reactions, they often get in touch with very early life events, beliefs, or 'scripts' they wrote for themselves. Probably all of our stress patterns are developmental in nature."

The Origins of Stress. Experienced job interviewers, college counselors, and owners of bridal shops all know that not everyone reacts the same way to a potentially stressful event. What makes the difference in people's reactions? According to psychologists Arnold Lazarus and Susan Folkman, people move through a series of stages, depicted in Figure 13-4, that determine whether they will experience stress (Lazarus & Folkman, 1984; Lazarus, 1968, 1991).

primary appraisal the assessment of an event to determine whether its implications are positive, negative, or neutral

Primary appraisal is the first step—the individual's assessment of an event to determine whether its implications are positive, negative, or neutral. If a person sees the event as primarily negative, he or she appraises it in terms of the harm that it has caused in the past, how threatening it is likely to be, and how likely it is that the challenge can be resisted successfully.

secondary appraisal the assessment of whether one's coping abilities and resources are adequate to overcome the harm, threat, or challenge posed by the potential stressor

Secondary appraisal follows. **Secondary appraisal** is the individual's assessment of whether one's coping abilities and resources are adequate to overcome the harm, threat, or challenge posed by the potential stressor. At this point in the process, people try to de-

Although we commonly think of negative events, such as auto mishaps, leading to stress, even welcome events can be stressful.

termine if they will be able to meet the dangers in the situation. If resources are lacking, and the potential threat is great, they will experience stress.

Clearly, stress is a very personal response. For most of us, hang gliding and rock climbing would cause a great deal of stress. However, for some people in early adulthood, such activities would be diverting and entertaining.

Still, some general principles help predict when an event will be appraised as stressful. Psychologist Shelley Taylor (1991) suggests the following:

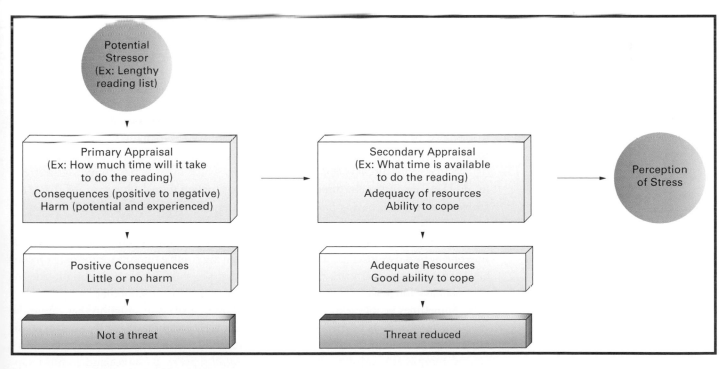

Figure 13-4   **Steps in the Perception of Stress**

The way an individual appraises a potential stressor determines whether the individual will experience stress.

(Adapted from Kaplan, Sallis, & Patterson, 1993.)

■ Events and circumstances that produce negative emotions are more likely to lead to stress than events that are positive. For example, planning for the adoption of a new baby produces less stress than dealing with the illness of a loved one.

■ Situations that are uncontrollable or unpredictable are more likely to produce stress than those that can be controlled and predicted. Professors who give surprise quizzes in their classes, then, produce more stress than those whose quizzes are scheduled in advance.

■ Events and circumstances that are ambiguous and confusing produce more stress than those that are unambiguous and clear. If people cannot easily understand a situation, they must struggle simply to comprehend it, rather than dealing with it directly. Taking a new job that does not have a clear job description is likely to produce more stress than starting in well-defined position.

■ People who must accomplish simultaneously many tasks that strain their capabilities are more likely to experience stress than those who have fewer things to do. A graduate student who is expecting her first child during the same month she is scheduled to take her dissertation oral exam is likely to be feeling quite a bit of stress, for example.

The Consequences of Stress. Over the long run, the constant wear and tear caused by the physiological arousal that occurs as the body tries to fight off stress produces negative effects. If enough stress is experienced it can have formidable costs. For instance, headaches, backaches, skin rashes, indigestion, chronic fatigue, and even the common cold are stress-related illnesses (Cohen, Tyrrell, & Smith, 1993, 1997; Suinn, 2001).

psychosomatic disorders medical problems caused by the interaction of psychological, emotional, and physical difficulties

coping the effort to control, reduce, or learn to tolerate the threats that lead to stress

Stress may also lead to **psychosomatic disorders,** medical problems caused by the interaction of psychological, emotional, and physical difficulties. For instance, ulcers, asthma, arthritis, and high blood pressure may—although not invariably—be produced by stress (Lepore, Palsane, & Evans, 1991).

In sum, stress affects people in a number of ways. It can increase the risk of becoming ill, it may actually produce illness, it makes it more difficult to recover from illness, and it may reduce one's ability to cope with future stress. (To get a sense of how much stress you have in your own life, complete the questionnaire in Table 13-1).

Coping with Stress. Some young adults are better than others at **coping,** the effort to control, reduce, or learn to tolerate the threats that lead to stress. What is the key to successful coping?

Some people use *problem-focused coping,* by which they attempt to manage a stressful problem or situation by directly changing the situation to make it less stressful. For example, a man who is having on-the-job difficulties may speak to his boss and ask that his responsibilities be modified.

Other people employ *emotion-focused coping,* which involves the conscious regulation of emotion. For instance, a mother who is having trouble finding appropriate care for her child while she is at work may tell herself that she should look at the bright side: At least she has a job in a difficult economy (Folkman & Lazarus, 1980; 1988).

Sometimes people acknowledge that they are in a stressful situation that cannot be changed, but they cope by managing their reactions. For example, they may take up meditation or exercise to reduce their physical reactions.

Coping is also aided by the presence of *social support,* assistance and comfort supplied by others. Turning to others in the face of stress can provide both emotional support (in the form of a shoulder to cry on) and practical, tangible support (such as a temporary loan) (Croyle & Hunt, 1991; Lepore, Palsane, & Evans, 1991; Spiegel, 1993).

Table 13-1

HOW STRESSED ARE YOU?

Test your level of stress by answering these questions, and adding the score from each box. Questions apply to the last month only. A key below will help you determine the extent of your stress.

1. How often have you been upset because of something that happened unexpectedly?

   ☐ 0 = never, 1 = almost never, 2 = sometimes, 3 = fairly often, 4 = very often

2. How often have you felt that you were unable to control the important things in your life?

   ☐ 0 = never, 1 = almost never, 2 = sometimes, 3 = fairly often, 4 = very often

3. How often have you felt nervous and "stressed"?

   ☐ 0 = never, 1 = almost never, 2 = sometimes, 3 = fairly often, 4 = very often

4. How often have you felt confident about your ability to handle your personal problems?

   ☐ 4 = never, 3 = almost never, 2 = sometimes, 1 = fairly often, 0 = very often

5. How often have you felt that things were going your way?

   ☐ 4 = never, 3 = almost never, 2 = sometimes, 1 = fairly often, 0 = very often

6. How often have you been able to control irritations in your life?

   ☐ 4 = never, 3 = almost never, 2 = sometimes, 1 = fairly often, 0 = very often

7. How often have you found that you could not cope with all the things that you had to do?

   ☐ 0 = never, 1 = almost never, 2 = sometimes, 3 = fairly often, 4 = very often

8. How often have you felt that you were on top of things?

   ☐ 4 = never, 3 = almost never, 2 = sometimes, 1 = fairly often, 0 = very often

9. How often have you been angered because of things that were outside your control?

   ☐ 0 = never, 1 = almost never, 2 = sometimes, 3 = fairly often, 4 = very often

10. How often have you felt difficulties were piling up so high that you could not overcome them?

    ☐ 0 = never, 1 = almost never, 2 = sometimes, 3 = fairly often, 4 – very often

How You Measure Up

Stress levels vary among individuals—compare your total score to the averages below:

AGE		GENDER	
18–29	14.2	Men	12.1
30–44	13.0	Women	13.7
45–54	12.6		
55–64	11.9		
65 & over	12.0		

MARITAL STATUS	
Widowed	12.6
Married or living with	12.4
Single or never wed	14.1
Divorced	14.7
Separated	16.6

(*Source:* Shelden Cohen, Dept. of Psychology, Carnegie Mellon Univ.)

Finally, even if people do not consciously cope with stress, some psychologists suggest that they may use unconscious defensive coping mechanisms of which they are unaware and which aid in stress reduction. *Defensive coping* involves unconscious strategies that distort or deny the true nature of a situation. For instance, people may deny the seriousness of a threat, trivializing a life-threatening illness, or they may say to themselves that academic failure on a series of tests is unimportant. If defensive coping becomes a habitual response to stress, it can be problematic. Instead of dealing with the reality of the situation, it merely avoids or ignores the problem.

Another problematic set of coping strategies involve escaping from stressful situations with the aid of drugs or alcohol. Drinking and drug use do not help address the situation causing the stress, and they can increase a person's difficulties. For example, people may become addicted to the substances that initially provided them with a pleasurable sense of escape.

Assistance and comfort by others in times of stress as social support can provide both emotional and practical support.

Table 13-2

HOW TO ELICIT THE RELAXATION RESPONSE

Some general advice on regular practice of the relaxation response:

■ Try to find 10 to 20 minutes in your daily routine; before breakfast is a good time.

■ Sit comfortably.

■ For the period you will practice, try to arrange your life so you won't have distractions. Put the phone on the answering machine, and ask someone else to watch the kids.

■ Time yourself by glancing periodically at a clock or watch (but don't set an alarm). Commit yourself to a specific length of practice, and try to stick to it.

There are several approaches to eliciting the relaxation response. Here is one standard set of instructions:

Step 1. Pick a focus word or short phrase that's firmly rooted in your personal belief system. For example, a nonreligious individual might choose a neutral word like *one* or *peace* or *love*. A Christian person desiring to use a prayer could pick the opening words of Psalm 23, *The Lord is my shepherd*; a Jewish person could choose *Shalom*.

Step 2. Sit quietly in a comfortable position.

Step 3. Close your eyes.

Step 4. Relax your muscles.

Step 5. Breathe slowly and naturally, repeating your focus word or phrase silently as you exhale.

Step 6. Throughout, assume a passive attitude. Don't worry about how well you're doing. When other thoughts come to mind, simply say to yourself, "Oh, well," and gently return to the repetition.

Step 7. Continue for 10 to 20 minutes. You may open your eyes to check the time, but do not use an alarm. When you finish, sit quietly for a minute or so, at first with your eyes closed and later with your eyes open. Then do not stand for one or two minutes.

Step 8. Practice the technique once or twice a day.

(*Source:* Benson, 1993.)

The Informed Consumer of Development

Coping with Stress

Although no single formula can cover all cases of stress, some general guidelines can help all of us cope with the stress that is part of our lives. Among them are the following (Holahan & Moos, 1987, 1990; Sacks, 1993; Greenglass & Burke, 1991; Kaplan, Sallis, & Patterson, 1993).

▶ Seek control over the situation producing the stress. Putting yourself in charge of a situation that is producing stress can take you a long way toward coping with it.

▶ Redefine "threat" as "challenge." Changing the definition of a situation can make it seem less threatening. "Look for the silver lining" is not bad advice.

▶ Get social support. Almost any difficulty can be faced more easily with the help of others. Friends, family members, and even telephone hot lines staffed by trained counselors can provide significant support. (For help in identifying appropriate hot lines, the U.S. Public Health Service maintains a "master" toll-free number that can provide phone numbers and addresses of many national groups. Call 800-336-4794.)

▶ Use relaxation techniques. Procedures that reduce the physiological arousal brought about by stress can be particularly effective. A variety of techniques that produce relaxation, such as transcendental meditation, Zen and yoga, progressive muscle relaxation, and even hypnosis, have been shown to be effective in reducing stress. One that works particularly well was devised by physician Herbert Benson and is illustrated in Table 13-2 (Benson, 1993).

▶ Try to maintain a healthy lifestyle that will reinforce your body's natural coping mechanisms. Exercise, eat nutritiously, get enough sleep, avoid or moderate use of alcohol, tobacco, or other drugs.

▶ If all else fails, keep in mind that a life without any stress at all would be a dull one. Stress is a natural part of life, and successfully coping with it can be a gratifying experience.

Review and Rethink

REVIEW

- By young adulthood, the body and the senses are at their peak, but growth is proceeding, particularly in the brain.
- Young adults are generally as fit and healthy as they will ever be, and accidents present the greatest risk of death. In the United States, violence is also a significant risk, particularly for non-white males.
- Health must be maintained by proper diet and exercise. Obesity is increasingly a problem for young adults.
- People with physical disabilities face not only physical barriers, but also psychological barriers caused by prejudice and stereotyping.

- Stress, which is a healthy reaction in small doses, can be harmful to body and mind if it is frequent or of long duration.

RETHINK

- Why is violence so prevalent in the United States, compared with other societies?
- What sorts of interpersonal barriers do people with disabilities face? How can those barriers be removed?

Cognitive Development

Ben is known to be a heavy drinker, especially when he goes to parties. Tyra, Ben's wife, warns him that if he comes home drunk one more time, she will leave him and take the children. Tonight Ben is out late at an office party. He comes home drunk. Does Tyra leave Ben?

According to Giesela Labouvie-Vief, the nature of thought changes qualitatively during early adulthood.

An adolescent who hears this situation (drawn from research by Adams and Labouvie-Vief, 1986) may find the case to be open-and-shut: Tyra leaves Ben. But in early adulthood, the answer becomes a bit less clear. As people enter adulthood, they become less concerned with the sheer logic of situations and instead take into account real-life concerns that may influence and temper behavior in particular instances.

Intellectual Growth in Early Adulthood

If cognitive development were to follow the same pattern as physical development, we would expect to find little new intellectual growth in early adulthood. In fact, Piaget, whose theory of cognitive development played such a prominent role in our earlier discussions of intellectual change, argued that by the time people left adolescence, their thinking, at least qualitatively, had largely become what it would be for the rest of their lives. People might gather more information, but the ways in which they think about it would not change.

Was Piaget's view correct? Increasing evidence suggests that arguments like his might well be flawed.

Postformal Thought

Developmental psychologist Giesela Labouvie-Vief (1980, 1986) suggests that the nature of thinking changes qualitatively during early adulthood. She asserts that thinking based solely on formal operations (Piaget's final stage, reached during adolescence) is insufficient to meet the demands placed on young adults. The complexity of society, which requires specialization, and the increasing challenge of finding one's way through all that complexity require thought that is not necessarily based on pure logic.

Instead, Labouvie-Vief suggests that adaptive thinking during adulthood would involve several tasks that go beyond pure logic: using analogies and metaphors to make comparisons, confronting society's paradoxes, and becoming comfortable with a more subjective understanding. Such thinking is more flexible; it allows for interpretive processes and reflects the fact that reasons behind events in the real world are subtle, painted in shades of gray rather than in black and white (Labouvie-Vief, 1990; Sinnott, 1998).

To demonstrate how this sort of thinking develops, Labouvie-Vief presented experimental subjects, ranging in age from 10 to 40, with scenarios similar to the Ben and Tyra scenario at the beginning of this section. Each story had a clear, logical conclusion. However, the story could be interpreted differently if real-world demands and pressures were taken into account.

In responding to the scenarios, adolescents relied heavily on the logic inherent in formal operations. For instance, they would predict that Tyra would immediately pack up her bags and leave with the children when Ben came home drunk. After all, that's what she said she would do.

In contrast, young adults were less prone to use strict logic in determining a character's likely course of action. Instead, they would consider various possibilities that might come into the picture in a real-life situation: Would Ben be apologetic and beg Tyra not to leave? Did Tyra really mean it when she said she would leave? Does Tyra have some alternative place to go?

Young adults exhibited what Labouvie-Vief calls postformal thinking. **Postformal thought** is thinking that goes beyond Piaget's formal operations. Rather than being based on purely logical processes, with absolutely right and wrong answers to problems, postformal thought acknowledges that adult predicaments must sometimes be solved in relativistic terms.

Postformal thought also encompasses *dialectical thinking,* an interest in and appreciation for argument, counter-argument, and debate (Basseches, 1984). Dialectical thinking

postformal thought thinking that acknowledges that adult predicaments must sometimes be solved in relativistic terms accepts that issues are not always clear-cut, and that answers to questions are not always absolutely right or wrong but must sometimes be negotiated.

In short, postformal thought and dialectical thinking acknowledge a world that sometimes lacks clearly right and wrong solutions to problems, a world in which logic may fail to resolve complex human questions. Instead, finding the best resolution to difficulties may involve drawing upon and integrating prior experiences.

Schaie's Stages of Development

Developmental psychologist K. Warner Schaie (1977/1978) offers another perspective on postformal thought (Schaie et al., 1989; Schaie & Willis, 1993). Taking up where Piaget left off, Schaie suggests that adults' thinking follows a set pattern of stages (illustrated in Figure 13-5). But Schaie focuses on the ways in which information is *used* during adulthood, rather than on changes in the acquisition and understanding of new information, as in Piaget's approach.

Schaie suggests that before adulthood, the main cognitive developmental task is acquisition of information. Consequently, he labels the first stage of cognitive development, which encompasses all of childhood and adolescence, the **acquisitive stage.** Information gathered before we grow up is largely squirreled away for future use. In fact, much of the rationale for education during childhood and adolescence is to prepare people for future activities.

The situation changes considerably in early adulthood, however. Instead of targeting the future use of knowledge, the focus shifts to the here-and-now. Schaie suggests that young adults enter the **achieving stage,** in which intelligence is applied to specific situations involving the attainment of long-term goals regarding careers, family, and societal contributions. During the achieving stage, young adults must confront and resolve several major issues, and the decisions they make—such as what job to take and whom to marry—have implications for the rest of their lives.

During the late stages of early adulthood and in middle adulthood, people move into the responsible and executive stages. In the **responsible stage,** the major concerns of middle-aged adults relate to their personal situations: protecting and nourishing their spouses, families, and careers.

Sometime later, during middle adulthood, many people (but not all) enter the executive stage. In the **executive stage,** people take a broader perspective that includes

acquisitive stage according to Schaie, the first stage of cognitive development, encompassing all of childhood and adolescence, in which the main developmental task is to acquire information

achieving stage the point reached by young adults in which intelligence is applied to specific situations involving the attainment of long-term goals regarding careers, family, and societal contributions

responsible stage the stage where the major concerns of middle-aged adults relate to their personal situations, including protecting and nourishing their spouses, families, and careers

executive stage the period in middle adulthood when people take a broader perspective than earlier, including concerns about the world

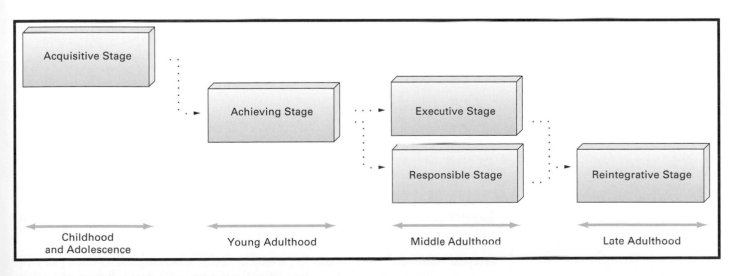

Figure 13-5 **Schaie's Stages of Adult Development**
(*Source:* Schaie, 1977/1978.)

During childhood and adolescence the main cognitive challenge is acquisition of knowledge, while in early adulthood the focus shifts to using knowledge to attain long-term goals.

reintegrative stage the period of late adulthood during which the focus is on tasks that have personal meaning

triarchic theory of intelligence Sternberg's theory that intelligence is made up of three major components: componential, experiential, and contextual

concerns about the world (Sinnott, 1997). Rather than focusing only on their own lives, people in the executive stage also put energy into nourishing and sustaining societal institutions. They may become involved in town government, religious congregations, service clubs, charitable groups, factory unions—organizations that have a larger purpose in society. People in the executive stage, then, look beyond their individual situations.

Old age marks entry into the final period, the reintegrative stage. The **reintegrative stage** is the period of late adulthood during which the focus is on tasks that have personal meaning. In this stage, people no longer focus on acquiring knowledge as a means of solving potential problems that they may encounter. Instead, their information acquisition is directed toward particular issues that specifically interest them. Furthermore, they have less interest in—and patience for—things that they do not see as having some immediate application to their lives. Thus, the abstract issue of whether the federal budget should be balanced may be of less concern to an elderly individual than whether the government should provide universal health care.

Intelligence: What Matters in Early Adulthood?

> *Your year on the job has been generally favorable. Performance ratings for your department are at least as good as they were before you took over, and perhaps even a little better. You have two assistants. One is quite capable. The other just seems to go through the motions and is of little real help. Even though you are well liked, you believe that there is little that would distinguish you in the eyes of your superiors from the nine other managers at a comparable level in the company. Your goal is rapid promotion to an executive position. (Based on Wagner & Sternberg, 1985, p. 447)*

How do you meet your goal?

The way adults answer this question has a great deal to do with their future success, according to psychologist Robert Sternberg. The question is one of a series designed to assess a particular type of intelligence that may have more of an impact on future success than the type of intelligence measured by traditional IQ tests (of the sort we discussed in Chapter 9).

In his **triarchic theory of intelligence,** Sternberg suggests that intelligence is made up of three major components: componential, experiential, and contextual (see Figure 13-6). The *componential* aspect involves the mental components involved in analyzing data used in solving problems, especially problems involving rational behavior. It relates to people's ability to select and use formulas, to choose appropriate problem-solving strategies, and in general to make use of what they have been taught. The *experiential* component refers to the relationship between intelligence, people's prior experience, and their ability to cope with new situations. This is the insightful aspect of intelligence, which allows people to relate what they already know to a new situation and an array of facts never before encountered. Finally, the *contextual* component of intelligence involves the degree of success people demonstrate in facing the demands of their everyday, real-world environments. For instance, the contextual component is involved in adapting to on-the-job professional demands (Sternberg, 1985a; 1991).

Traditional intelligence tests, which yield an IQ score, tend to focus on the componential aspect of intelligence. Yet increasing evidence suggests that a more useful measure, particularly when one is looking for ways to compare and predict adult success, is the contextual component—the aspect of intelligence that has come to be called practical intelligence.

Practical and Emotional Intelligence. According to Robert Sternberg, the IQ score that most traditional tests produce relates quite well to academic success. However, IQ seems to be unrelated to other types of achievement, such as career success. For example, although it is clear that success in business settings requires some minimal level of the sort of intelli-

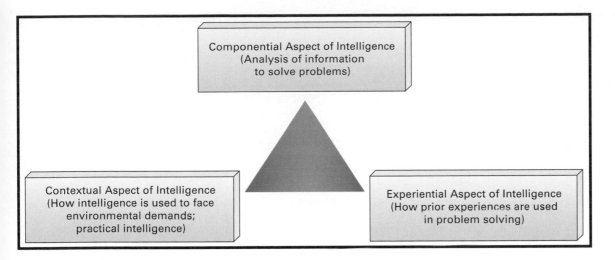

Figure 13-6 **Sternberg's Triarchic Theory of Intelligence**
(Based on Sternberg, 1985a, 1991.)

gence measured by IQ tests, the rate of career advancement and the ultimate success of business executives is only marginally related to IQ scores (Wagner & Sternberg, 1991; Sternberg & Wagner, 1986; 1993; McClelland, 1993).

Sternberg contends that success in a career necessitates a type of intelligence—called **practical intelligence**—that is substantially different from that involved in traditional academic pursuits (Sternberg et al., 1997). While academic success is based on knowledge of particular types of information, obtained largely from reading and listening, practical intelligence is learned primarily by observing others and modeling their behavior. People who are high in practical intelligence can extract and deduce broad principles and norms about appropriate behavior and apply them in particular situations. (See Figure 13-7 for sample items from a test of practical intelligence).

Another type of intelligence involves emotional domains. **Emotional intelligence** is the set of skills that underlie the accurate assessment, evaluation, expression, and regulation of emotions (Goleman, 1995; Salovey & Sluyter, 1997; Davies , Stankov, & Roberts, 1998). Emotional intelligence underlies the ability to get along well with others, to understand what others are feeling and experiencing, and to respond appropriately to the needs of others. It permits people to tune into others' feelings, allowing them to respond appropriately. Emotional intelligence is also of obvious value to career and personal success as a young adult.

Creativity: Novel Thought. The hundreds of musical compositions of Wolfgang Amadeus Mozart, who died at the age of 35, were largely written during early adulthood. The same is true of many other creative individuals: Their major works were produced during early adulthood (Dennis, 1966a; see Figure 13-8).

One reason for the higher productivity of early adulthood may be that after early adulthood, creativity can be stifled by a situation that psychologist Sarnoff Mednick (1963) described as "Familiarity breeds rigidity." By this he meant that the more people know about a subject, the less likely they are to be creative in that area. According to such reasoning, people in early adulthood may be at the peak of their creativity because many of the problems they encounter on a professional level are novel—or at least new to them. As they get older, however, and become more familiar with the problems, their creativity may be stymied.

On the other hand, not everybody seems to have this problem. Many people do not reach their pinnacle of creativity until much later in life. For instance, Buckminster Fuller did not devise his major contribution, the geodesic dome, until he was in his 50s. Frank

practical intelligence according to Sternberg, intelligence that is learned primarily by observing others and modeling their behavior

emotional intelligence the set of skills that underlie the accurate assessment, evaluation, expression, and regulation of emotions

Management

You are responsible for selecting a contractor to renovate several large buildings. You have narrowed the choice to two contractors on the basis of their bids and after further investigation, you are considering awarding the contract to the Wilson & Sons Company. Rate the importance of the following pieces of information in making your decision to award the contract to Wilson & Sons.

_____ The company has provided letters from satisfied former customers.

_____ The Better Business Bureau reports no major complaints about the company.

_____ Wilson & Sons has done good work for your company in the past.

_____ Wilson & Sons' bid was $2000 less than the other contractor's (approximate total cost of the renovation is $325,000).

_____ Former customers whom you have contacted strongly recommended Wilson & Sons for the job.

Sales

You sell a line of photocopy machines. One of your machines has relatively few features and is inexpensive, at $700, although it is not the least expensive model you carry. The $700 photocopy machine is not selling well and it is overstocked. There is a shortage of the more elaborate photocopy machines in your line, so you have been asked to do what you can to improve sales of the $700 machine. Rate the following strategies for maximizing your sales of the slow-moving photocopy machine.

_____ Stress to potential customers that although this model lacks some desirable features, the low price more than makes up for it.

_____ Stress that there are relatively few models left at this price.

_____ Arrange as many demonstrations as possible of the machine.

_____ Stress simplicity of use, since the machine lacks confusing controls that other machines may have.

Academic Psychology

It is your second year as an assistant professor in a prestigious psychology department. This past year you published two unrelated empirical articles in established journals. You don't, however, believe there is yet a research area that can be identified as your own. You believe yourself to be about as productive as others. The feedback about your first year of teaching has been generally good. You have yet to serve on a university committee. There is one graduate student who has chosen to work with you. You have no external source of funding, nor have you applied for any.

Your goals are to become one of the top people in your field and to get tenure in your department. The following is a list of things you are considering doing in the next two months. You obviously cannot do them all. Rate the importance of each by its priority as a means of reaching your goals.

_____ Improve the quality of your teaching.

_____ Write a grant proposal.

_____ Begin a long-term research project that may lead to a major theoretical article.

_____ Concentrate on recruiting more students.

_____ Begin several related short-term research projects, each of which may lead to an empirical article.

_____ Participate in a series of panel discussions to be shown on the local public television station.

College Student Life

You are enrolled in a large introductory lecture course. Requirements consist of three exams and a final. Please indicate how characteristic it would be of your behavior to spend time doing each of the following if your goal were to receive an A in the course.

_____ Attend class regularly.

_____ Attend optional weekly review sections with the teaching fellow.

_____ Read assigned text chapters thoroughly.

_____ Take comprehensive class notes.

_____ Speak with the professor after class and during office hours.

Figure 13-7   Sample Items From a Test That Taps Four Domains of Practical Intelligence
(*Source:* Sternberg, 1993.)

Lloyd Wright designed the Guggenheim Museum in New York at age 70. Charles Darwin and Jean Piaget were still writing influential works well into their 70s, and Picasso was painting in his 90s. Furthermore, when we look at overall productivity, as opposed to the period of a person's most important output, we find that productivity remains fairly steady throughout adulthood, particularly in the humanities (Dennis, 1966b; Simonton, 1989).

Overall, the study of creativity reveals few consistent developmental patterns. One reason for this is the difficulty of determining just what constitutes an instance of **creativity,** which is defined as combining responses or ideas in novel ways. Because definitions of what is "novel" may vary from one person to the next, it is hard to identify a particular behavior unambiguously as creative (Isaksen & Murdock, 1993; Sasser-Coen, 1993).

creativity the combination of responses or ideas in novel ways

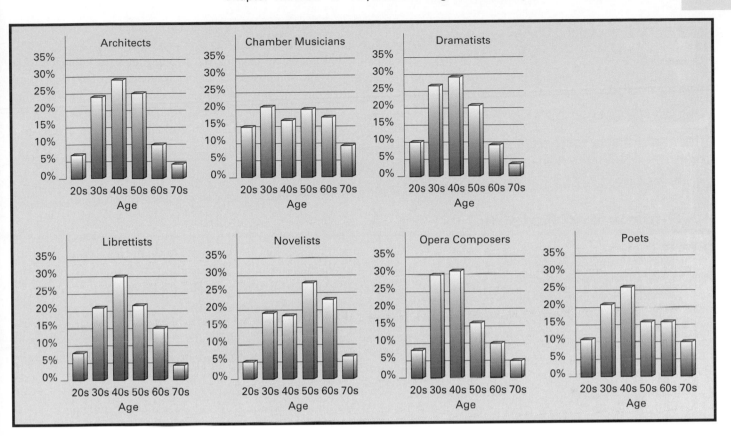

Figure 13-8 Creativity and Age

The period of maximum creativity differs depending on the particular field. The percentages refer to the percent of total lifetime major works produced during the particular age period. Why do poets peak earlier than novelists?
(Based on Dennisa, 1966.)

That ambiguity hasn't stopped psychologists from trying. For instance, one important component of creativity is a person's willingness to take risks that may result in potentially high payoffs (Sternberg & Lubart, 1992). Creative people are analogous to successful stock market investors, who try to follow the "buy low, sell high" rule. Creative people develop and endorse ideas that are unfashionable or regarded as wrong ("buying low"). They assume that eventually others will see the value of the ideas and embrace them ("selling high"). According to this theory, one approach to remaining creative throughout adulthood is to take a fresh look at ideas or problem solutions that might initially be discarded, particularly if the problem is a familiar one.

Life Events and Cognitive Development

Marriage. The death of a parent. Starting a first job. The birth of a child. Buying a house.

The course of life comprises many events such as these—important milestones on the path through the life span. Such occurrences, whether they are welcome or unwanted, clearly may bring about stress, as we saw earlier in this chapter. But do they also cause cognitive growth?

Although the research is still spotty and largely based on case studies, some evidence suggests that major life events may lead to cognitive growth. For instance, the birth of a child—a profound event—may trigger fresh insights into the nature of one's relationships with relatives and ancestors, one's broader place in the world, and the role one has in perpetuating humanity. Similarly, the death of a loved one may cause people to reevaluate

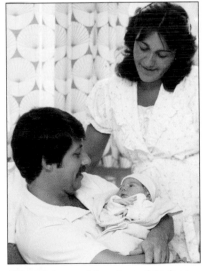

Although research is not complete, it appears that profound events such as the birth of a child, or the death of a loved one, can stimulate cognitive development by offering us an opportunity to reevaluate our place in the world. What are some other profound events that might stimulate cognitive development?

what is important to them and to look anew at the manner in which they lead their lives (Feldman, Biringen, & Nash, 1981; Haan, 1985).

In sum, the ups and downs of life events may lead young adults to think about the world in novel, more complex and sophisticated, and often less rigid ways. Rather than applying formal logic to situations—a strategy of which they are fully capable—they instead apply the broader perspective of postformal thought that we described earlier in this chapter. Such thinking allows them to deal more effectively with the complex social worlds (discussed in Chapter 14) of which they are a part.

Review and Rethink

REVIEW

- Cognitive development continues into young adulthood with the emergence of postformal thought, which goes beyond logic to encompass interpretive and subjective thinking.
- According to Schaie, people pass through five stages in the way they use information: acquisitive, achieving, responsible, executive, and reintegrative.
- New views of intelligence encompass the triarchic theory, practical intelligence, and emotional intelligence.
- Creativity seems to peak during early adulthood, with young adults viewing even longstanding problems as novel situations.

- Major life events contribute to cognitive growth by providing opportunities and incentives to rethink one's self and one's world.

RETHINK

- Can you think of situations that you would deal with differently as an adult than as an adolescent? Do the differences reflect postformal thinking?
- What does "familiarity breeds rigidity" mean? Can you think of examples of this phenomenon from your own experience?

College: Pursuing Higher Education

It's 4:30 in the morning. Marion Mealey, a college student who has returned to school at the age of 27, looks in on her son, walks her dogs, and begins to study for a biology exam.

By 6:00 a.m., she leaves the house, taking her breakfast and lunch that she had readied the night before. Her son and her mother are still asleep. Her mother, who helps care for Mealey's son, will soon wake up herself, and get her grandson off to school.

Before she returns home at the end of the day, Mealey will have spent four hours in transit, fitting in some additional study time along the way, four hours in class, and three hours at a job that pays her family's living expenses. After spending a few hours with her family, she still has to read for classes tomorrow. (Adapted from Dembner, 1995a)

Marion Mealey, one of the one-third of college students who are above the age of 24, faces unusual challenges as she pursues the goal of a college degree. Older students like her represent the increasing diversity in family background, socioeconomic status, race, and ethnicity that characterizes college campuses today. We noted this phenomenon in the chapter prologue, in which we met Enrico Vasquez and Armando Williams, two students who might never have been able to attend college just a few years ago.

Marion Mealey, one of the 25 percent of college students who are over the age of 25. Copyright 1995 Globe Newspaper Company, Inc. Republished with permission of Globe Newspaper Company, Inc.

For any student, though, attending college is a significant accomplishment. Although students already enrolled may feel that college attendance is nearly universal, this is not the case at all: Nationwide, only a minority of high school graduates enter college.

The Demographics of Higher Education

What kinds of students enter college? Like the population as a whole, college students are primarily white and middle class, although the percentage of minorities has increased significantly over the last several decades. Total minority enrollment now comprises a quarter of the total college enrollment (see Figure 13-9). In fact, at some colleges, such as the University of California at Berkeley, whites have shifted from the majority to the minority as what is traditionally called "minority" representation has increased significantly.

These trends reflect changes in the racial and ethnic composition of the United States, and are important, since higher education remains an important way for families to improve their economic well-being. Just 3 percent of adults who have a college education live below the poverty line. Compare that with high school dropouts: They are 10 times more likely to be living in poverty (see Figure 13-10; O'Hare, 1997).

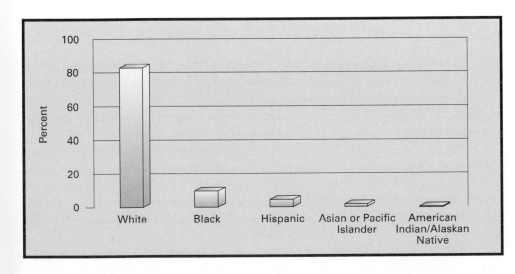

Figure 13-9 **College Enrollment by Racial Group**

The proportion of nonwhites who attend college have increased in the last few decades.

(*Source:* National Center for Education Statistics, 2000.)

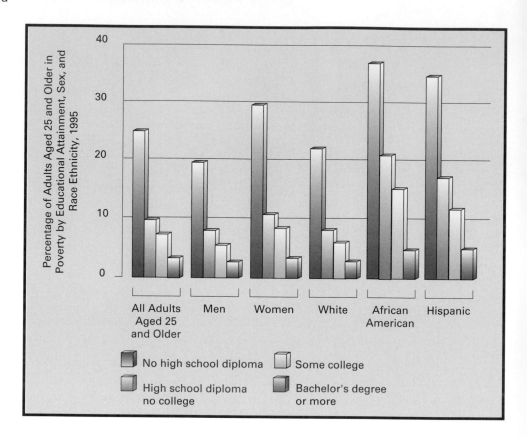

Figure 13-10 Education and Economic Security

Education provides more than knowledge; it is also an important means to attain economic security for both men and women.

(*Source:* Current Population Survey, Census Bureau, March 1996.)

cw

A greater availability of higher paying jobs that do not require a college education is one reason why enrollment of men in college is increasing more slowly than women.

In addition to a greater proportion of minorities attending college, the proportion of women, relative to men, is also increasing. There are now more women than men enrolled in college, and by the year 2007, women's enrollment is expected to increase 30 percent from the level reached in 1995, whereas men's enrollment is projected to increase only 13 percent.

Why is men's enrollment increasing at a slower pace than women's? It may be that men have more opportunities to earn money when they graduate from high school. For instance, the military, trade unions, and jobs that require physical strength may be more attractive to men, and consequently more men than women may perceive that good options other than college are available. Furthermore, as affirmative action has become less a factor in admissions, women often have better high school academic records than men, and they may be admitted to college at greater rates (Dortch, 1997).

The Changing College Student: Never Too Late to Go to College?

If the words "average college student" bring to mind an image of a 19-year-old, you should begin to rethink your view. Increasingly, students are older. In fact, more than a third of students taking college courses for credit in the United States are 25 years old or older, like Marion Mealy, the 27-year-old student profiled at the beginning of this section. The average age of community college students is 31 (U.S. Bureau of the Census, 1995; Dortch, 1997).

Why are so many older, nontraditional students taking college courses? One reason is economic. As a college degree becomes increasingly important in obtaining a job, some workers feel compelled to get the credential. Furthermore, some employers encourage or require workers to undergo training to learn new skills or update their old ones. Finally, older students sometimes enroll in college classes simply for the joy of learning; they appreciate the opportunity for intellectual stimulation.

According to developmental psychologist Sherry Willis (1985), several broad goals underlie adults' participation in learning experiences. First, adults may be seeking to under-

From Research to Practice
What Do First-Year College Students Believe?

How closely were first-year college students watching the back-and-forth of the Bush–Gore presidential election in the fall of 2000?

If the results of a comprehensive nationwide survey of first-year college students are any indication, they weren't paying much attention at all. The survey of almost 270,000 students at 434 U.S. colleges and universities found that only 28 percent of first-year students said that "keeping up to date with political affairs" was an interest of theirs (Sax et al., 2000).

What are first-year students interested in? Mostly themselves and their own personal circumstances. The survey found that compared with previous years, students tended to be more focused on attaining their own personal goals. Tops among those goals: earning a great deal of money. Of a list of objectives that students could endorse, the greatest agreement came on the objective of "being very well off financially," with almost three-quarters of students feeling it was essential or very important.

At the same time that personal wealth grew in importance, concerns about status declined. Fewer students than in previous years were interested in becoming professionally recognized as authorities in their fields.

First-year students are also far more likely to be computer-savvy than students in the past. More than three-fourths of students used computers regularly before they attended college. In addition, a gender gap between women's and men's use of computers is steadily eroding, with women's rates of use nearly matching those of men. Still, despite the fact that first-year college women are using computers at the same rates as men, there is a huge gap in confidence regarding skill levels between male and female students. Men are considerably more likely than women to rate their computer skills as "above average" or within the "top 10 percent" (23 percent for women compared with 46 percent for men).

stand their own aging. As they get older, they try to figure out what is happening to them and what to expect in the future. Second, adults seek education in order to understand more fully the rapid technological and cultural changes that characterize modern life.

Furthermore, adult learners may be seeking a practical edge in combating obsolescence on the job. Some individuals also may be attempting to acquire new vocational skills. Finally, adult educational experiences may be seen as helpful in preparing for future retirement. As adults get older, they become increasingly concerned with shifting from a work orientation to a leisure orientation, and they may see education as a means of broadening their possibilities. (For further discussion of the changing attitudes of college students, see the *From Research to Practice* box.)

College Adjustment: Reacting to the Demands of College Life

When you began college, did you feel depressed, lonely, anxious, and withdrawn from others? If you did, you weren't alone. Many students, particularly those who are recent high school graduates and who are living away from home for the first time, experience difficulties in adjustment during their first year in college. The **first-year adjustment reaction** is a cluster of psychological symptoms relating to the college experience. Although any first-year student may suffer from one or more of the symptoms of first-year adjustment reaction, it is particularly likely to occur among students who have been unusually successful, either academically or socially, in high school. When they begin college, their sudden change in status may cause them distress.

Most often, first-year adjustment reaction passes as students make friends, experience academic success, and integrate themselves into campus life. In other cases, though, the problems remain and may fester, leading to more serious psychological difficulties.

first-year adjustment reaction a cluster of psychological symptoms, including loneliness, anxiety, withdrawal, and depression, relating to the college experience suffered by first-year college students

The Informed Consumer of Development

When Do College Students Need Professional Help with Their Problems?

A college friend comes to you and says that she has been feeling depressed and unhappy and can't seem to shake the feeling. She doesn't know what to do and thinks that she may need professional help. How do you answer her?

Although there are no hard-and-fast rules, several signals can be interpreted to determine if professional help is warranted. Among them (Engler & Goleman, 1992):

▶ psychological distress that lingers and interferes with a person's sense of well-being and ability to function

▶ feelings that one is unable to cope effectively with the stress

▶ hopeless or depressed feelings, with no apparent reason

▶ the inability to build close relationships with others

▶ physical symptoms that have no apparent underlying cause

If some of these signals are present, discussions with some kind of help-provider—such as a counseling psychologist, clinical psychologist, or other mental health worker—are warranted. (College students can find an appropriate provider by starting with their campus medical center; others can turn to their personal physicians or to local boards of health for referrals.)

Several other problems are common to college students (Duke & Nowicki, 1979). As Table 13-3 shows, male students are most likely to be concerned with their grades, social lives, and vocational decisions. In contrast, female students are concerned most with what to do with their lives, relationships, and the strain of too much work.

How prevalent are these concerns? Surveys find that almost half of college students report having at least one significant psychological issue, and certain groups of students show particular problems. For example, overweight students report more psychological concerns, and minority women report having a higher frequency of problems relating to motivation than white women (Wechsler, Rohman, Solomon, 1981; American Council on Education, 1995).

Students who have been successful and popular in high school are particularly vulnerable to first-year adjustment reaction in college. Counseling, as well as increasing familiarity with campus life, can help a student adjust.

Table 13-3

COLLEGE STUDENTS' PROBLEMS

Among the most prevalent problems of college students are the following:

For male students:	*For female students:*
Grades	What to do with their lives
Social life	Developing sexual and emotional relationships
Vocational decisions	Strain from too much work
The future	Grades
Sexual relationships	Adjustment
Peer pressures	Gaining independence
Adjusting to a new environment	Identity
Leaving family for the first time	Pressure from parents
Competition	Peer pressures
Depression	Morals

(*Source:* Wechsler, Rohman, & Solomon, 1981.)

What Do College Students Learn?

The response to this question is not only "math" or "hotel management" or even "lifespan development," although that is part of the answer. Clearly, students gain a body of knowledge that may help them function more effectively in the world. However, college is more than that: It is a period of developmental growth that encompasses mastery not just of particular bodies of knowledge, but of ways of understanding the world.

For example, psychologist William Perry (1970) examined the ways in which students grew intellectually and morally during college. In comprehensive interviews with a group of students at Harvard University, he found that students entering college tended to use *dualistic thinking* in their views of the world. For instance, they reasoned that something was right, or it was wrong; people were good, or they were bad; and others were either for them, or against them.

However, as they encountered new ideas and points of view from other students and their professors, their dualistic thinking declined. Consistent with the increase in postformal thinking that we discussed earlier, students increasingly realized that issues can have more than one plausible side. Furthermore, they understood more clearly that it is possible to hold multiple perspectives on an issue. This *multiple thinking* was characterized by a shift in the way the students viewed authorities: Instead of presupposing that experts had all the answers, they began to assume that their own thinking on an issue had validity if their position was well argued and rational.

In fact, they had entered a stage in which knowledge and values were regarded as *relativistic*. Rather than seeing the world as having absolute standards and values, they argued that different societies, cultures, and individuals could have different standards and values, all of them equally valid.

Gender and College Performance

I registered for a calculus course my first year at DePauw. Even twenty years ago I was not timid, so on the very first day I raised my hand and asked a question. I still have a vivid memory of the professor rolling his eyes, hitting his head with his

As a result of the powerful influence of gender stereotypes in the world of education, women are dramatically underrepresented in the areas of physical science, math, and engineering. What can be done to reverse this trend?

hand in frustration, and announcing to everyone, "Why do they expect me to teach calculus to girls?" I never asked another question. Several weeks later I went to a football game, but I had forgotten to bring my ID. My calculus professor was at the gate checking IDs, so I went up to him and said, "I forgot my ID but you know me, I'm in your class." He looked right at me and said, "I don't remember you in my class." I couldn't believe that someone who changed my life and whom I remember to this day didn't even recognize me. (Sadker & Sadker, 1994, p. 162)

Although such incidents of blatant sexism are less likely to occur today, prejudice and discrimination directed at women are still a fact of college life. For instance, the next time you are in class, consider the gender of your classmates—and the subject matter of the class. Although men and women attend college in roughly equal proportions, there is significant variation in the classes they take. Classes in education and the social sciences, for instance, typically have a larger proportion of women than men; and classes in engineering, the physical sciences, and mathematics tend to have more men than women.

Even women who start out in mathematics, engineering, and the physical sciences are more likely than men to drop out. For instance, the attrition rate for women in such fields during the college years is two-and-a-half times greater than the rate for men. Ultimately, although white women make up 43 percent of the U.S. population and, as we saw, a majority of the college-student population, they earn just 22 percent of the bachelor of science degrees and 13 percent of the doctorates, and they hold only 10 percent of the jobs in physical science, math, and engineering (Hewitt & Seymour, 1991).

The differences in gender distribution and attrition rates across subject areas are no accident. They reflect the powerful influence of gender stereotypes that operate throughout the world of education—and beyond. For instance, when women in their first year of college are asked to name a likely career choice, they are much less apt to choose careers that have traditionally been dominated by men, such as engineering or computer programming, and more likely to choose professions that have traditionally been populated by women, such as nursing and social work (Glick, Zion, & Nelson, 1988; CIRE, 1990).

Women also expect to earn less than men, both when they start their careers and when they are at their peaks (Major & Konar, 1984; Martin, 1989; Jackson, Gardner, & Sullivan, 1992; Desmarais & Curtis, 1997). These expectations jibe with reality: On average, women earn 72 cents for every dollar that men earn. Moreover, women who are members of minority groups do even worse: African American women earn 62 cents for every dollar men make, while for Hispanic women the figure is 54 cents (U.S. Bureau of Labor Statistics, 1999).

Male and female college students also have different expectations regarding their areas of competence. For instance, one survey asked first-year college students whether they were above or below average on a variety of traits and abilities. As shown in Figure 13-11, men were more likely than women to think of themselves as above average in overall academic and mathematical ability, competitiveness, and emotional health.

Both male and female college professors treat men and women differently in their classes, even though the different treatment is largely unintentional and the professors are unaware of their actions. For instance, professors call on men in class more frequently than women, and they make more eye contact with men than with women. Furthermore, male students are more likely to receive extra help from their professors than women. Finally, the quality of the responses received by male and female students differs, with male students receiving more positive reinforcement for their comments than female students—exemplified by the startling illustration in Table 13-4 (Epperson, 1988; AAUW, 1992; Sadker & Sadker, 1994).

Benevolent Sexism: When Being Nice Is Not So Nice. Although some cases of unequal treatment of women represent *hostile sexism* in which people treat women in a way that is overtly harmful, in other cases women are the victims of benevolent sexism. *Benevolent sexism* is a form of sexism in which women are placed in stereotyped and restrictive roles that appear, on the surface, to be positive.

Benevolent sexism even seems, at first, to be beneficial to women. For instance, a male college professor may compliment a female student on her good looks or offer to give her an easier research project so she won't have to work so hard. While the professor may feel that he is merely being thoughtful, in fact he may be making the woman feel that she is not taken seriously and undermining her view of her competence. In short, benevolent sexism can be just as harmful as hostile sexism (Glick et al., 2000).

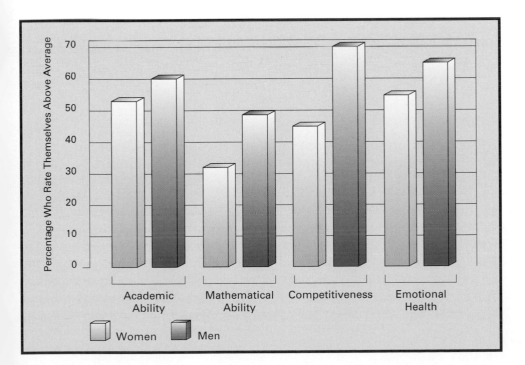

Figure 13-11 The Great Gender Divide

During their first year of college, men, compared to women, are more apt to view themselves as above average on several spheres relevant to academic success. What is the root of this difference?

(*Source:* The American Freshman: National Norms for Fall, 1990; Astin, Korn, & Berz. Higher Education Research Institute, UCLA.)

Table 13-4

GENDER BIAS IN THE CLASSROOM

The course on the U.S. Constitution is required for graduation, and more than 50 students, approximately half male and half female, file in. The professor begins by asking if there are questions on next week's midterm. Several hands go up.

BERNIE: Do you have to memorize names and dates in the book? Or will the test be more general?

PROFESSOR: You do have to know those critical dates and people. Not every one but the important ones. If I were you, Bernie, I would spend time learning them. Ellen?

ELLEN: What kind of short-answer questions will there be?

PROFESSOR: All multiple choice.

ELLEN: Will we have the whole class time?

PROFESSOR: Yes, we'll have the whole class time. Anyone else?

BEN (calling out): Will there be an extra-credit question?

PROFESSOR: I hadn't planned on it. What do you think?

BEN: I really like them. They take some of the pressure off. You can also see who is doing extra work.

PROFESSOR: I'll take it under advisement. Charles?

CHARLES: How much of our final grade is this?

PROFESSOR: The midterm is 25 percent. But remember, class participation counts as well. Why don't we begin?

The professor lectures on the Constitution for 20 minutes before he asks a question about the electoral college. The electoral college is not as hot a topic as the midterm, so only four hands are raised. The professor calls on Ben.

BEN: The electoral college was created because there was a lack of faith in the people. Rather than have them vote for the president, they voted for the electors.

PROFESSOR: I like the way you think. (He smiles at Ben, and Ben smiles back.) Who could vote? (Five hands go up, five out of fifty.) Angie?

ANGIE: I don't know if this is right, but I thought only men could vote.

BEN (calling out): That was a great idea. We began going downhill when we let women vote. (Angie looks surprised but says nothing. Some of the students laugh, and so does the professor. He calls on Barbara.)

BARBARA: I think you had to be pretty wealthy, own property—

JOSH (not waiting for Barbara to finish, calls out): That's right. There was a distrust of the poor, who could upset the democracy. But if you had property, if you had something at stake, you could be trusted not to do something wild. Only property owners could be trusted.

PROFESSOR: Nice job, Josh. But why do we still have electors today? Mike?

MIKE: Tradition, I guess.

PROFESSOR: Do you think it's tradition? If you walked down the street and asked people their views of the electoral college, what would they say?

MIKE: Probably they'd be clueless. Maybe they would think that it elects the Pope. People don't know how it works.

PROFESSOR: Good, Mike. Judy, do you want to say something? (Judy's hand is at "half-mast," raised but just barely. When the professor calls her name, she looks a bit startled.)

JUDY (speaking very softly): Maybe we would need a whole new constitutional convention to change it. And once they get together to change that, they could change anything. That frightens people, doesn't it? (As Judy speaks, a number of students fidget, pass notes, and leaf through their books; a few even begin to whisper.)

(*Source:* Sadker & Sadker, 1994.)

Disidentification with School: Do Social Stereotypes Depress the Academic Performance of Women and African Americans?

Women lack ability in math and science. African Americans don't do well in academic pursuits.

So say erroneous, damaging, and yet persistent stereotypes about women and African Americans. And in the real world these stereotypes play out in vicious ways. For instance, even though boys and girls perform virtually identically on standardized math tests in elementary school and middle school, this all changes when they reach high school. At that level, and even more in college, men tend to do better in math than women. In fact, when women take college math, science, and engineering courses, they are more likely to do poorly than men who enter college with the same level of preparation and identical SAT scores. Strangely, though, this phenomenon does not hold true for other areas of the curriculum, where men and women perform at similar levels (Hyde, Fennema, & Lamon, 1990).

Analogously, when African Americans start elementary school, their standardized test scores are only slightly lower than those of Caucasian students, and yet a 2-year gap emerges by the sixth grade. And even though more African American high school graduates are enrolling in college, the increase has not been as large as for other groups (American Council on Education, 1995–1996).

According to psychologist Claude Steele, the reason behind the declining levels of performance for both women and African Americans is the same: *academic disidentification,* a lack of personal identification with an academic domain. For women, disidentification is specific to math and science; for African Americans, it is more generalized across academic domains. In both cases, negative societal stereotypes produce a state of "stereotype threat" in which members of the group fear that their behavior will indeed confirm the stereotype (Steele, 1997).

For instance, women seeking to achieve in nontraditional fields that rely on math and science may be hindered as they become distracted by worries about the failure that society predicts for them. In some cases, a woman may decide that failure in a male-dominated field, because it would confirm societal stereotypes, presents such great risks that, paradoxically, the struggle to succeed is not worth the effort. In that instance, the woman may not even try very hard (Inzlicht & Ben-Zeev, 2000).

Similarly, African Americans may work under the pressure of feeling that they must disconfirm the negative stereotype regarding their academic performance. The pressure can be anxiety-provoking and threatening, and can reduce their performance below their true ability level. Ironically, stereotype threat may be most severe for better, more confident students, who have not internalized the negative stereotype to the extent of questioning their own abilities (Steele, 1997).

Rather than ignoring negative stereotypes, women and African Americans may perform less well and, ultimately, disidentify with schooling and academic pursuits relevant to the stereotype.

In support of such reasoning, Steele and colleagues (Spencer, Quinn, & Steele, 1997) devised an experiment using a group of male and female college students and a very difficult math test. Some of the participants were told that the test typically showed gender differences. This instruction was meant to imply that because of their supposed lower math ability, women might experience difficulty in taking the test. Other participants were told that the test showed no gender differences. The implication here was that the gender stereotype was irrelevant to participants' performance. The researchers hypothesized that stereotype threat would be minimized in this condition.

The results fully supported the stereotype threat hypothesis. When women thought the test showed a gender difference, they scored considerably worse than men taking the same test. But when the test was portrayed as being typically gender-neutral, there was no gender difference: Men and women performed virtually the same (see Figure 13-12; Spencer, Quinn, & Steele, 1997).

In short, the evidence from this study, as well as from other experiments, clearly suggests that women are vulnerable to expectations regarding their future success, whether the expectations come from societal stereotypes or from information about the prior performance of women on similar tasks. Other research yields similar results for members of other groups who are stereotyped. For example, when racial stereotypes are emphasized, the performance of African American and other minority students is depressed (Steele & Aronson, 1995; Cheryan & Bodenhausen, 2000).

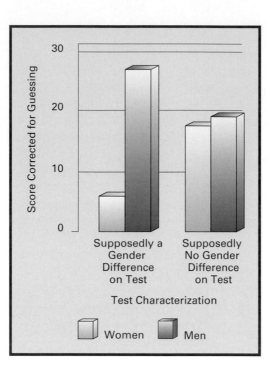

Figure 13-12 **Stereotype Threat**

Evidence from several studies, including this one, have indicated that women are vulnerable to expectations regarding their future success, whether the expectations come from societal stereotypes or from information about the prior performance of women on similar tasks. Does this study suggest a remedy for this situation?

(*Source:* Spencer, Steele, & Quinn, 1997.)

Dropping Out of College

Not everyone who enters colleges completes it. In fact, only around 45 percent of those who start college finish 4 years later with a degree. Although about half of those who don't receive a degree in 4 years eventually do finish, the other half never get a college degree. For minorities, the picture is even more bleak: The national dropout rate for African American college students stands at 70 percent (Minorities in Higher Education, 1990).

Why is the college dropout rate so high? There are several reasons. One has to do with finances: Given the high cost of college, many students are unable to afford the continued expense. Other people leave college because of changes in their life situations, such as marriage, the birth of a child, or the death of a parent.

Academic difficulties also may play a role. Some students simply find that they are not successful in their studies, and they are either forced by academic authorities to drop out or they leave on their own. However, in most cases students who drop out are not in academic jeopardy (Rotenberg & Morrison, 1993).

College students who drop out—intending to return one day, but never making it back because they become enmeshed in the nitty-gritty of everyday life—can experience real difficulties. They may become riveted as young adults to undesirable, low-paying jobs for which they are intellectually overqualified. A college education becomes a lost opportunity.

On the other hand, dropping out is not always a step backward on a person's life path. In some cases, it gives people breathing room to reassess their goals. For instance, students who view the college experience as simply marking time until they can get on with their "real" lives by earning a living can sometimes benefit from a period of full-time work. During the hiatus from college, they often get a different perspective on the realities of both work and school. Other individuals simply benefit by having some time off from school in which to mature socially or psychologically, as we'll discuss further in the next chapter.

Review and Rethink

REVIEW

- Rates of college enrollment differ across racial and ethnic lines.
- The average age of college students is steadily increasing as more adults return to college.
- New students often find the transition to college difficult and experience first-year adjustment reaction.
- In college, students learn not only a body of knowledge, but also a way of understanding the world that generally accepts more viewpoints and sees values in relativistic terms.
- Gender differences in treatment and expectations cause men and women to make different choices and engage in different behaviors in college.

- The phenomena of academic disidentification and stereotype threat help explain the lower performance of women and African Americans in certain academic domains.

RETHINK

- Why do college professors behave differently toward male and female students? What factors contribute to this phenomenon? Can this situation be changed?
- How are older students likely to affect the college classroom, given what you know about human development? Explain.

Looking Back

How does the body develop during early adulthood, and to what risks are young adults exposed?

- The body and the senses generally reach their peak in early adulthood. Health risks are minimal, with accidents presenting the greatest risk of death, followed by AIDS. In the United States, violence is a significant cause of death, particularly among nonwhite segments of the population.

- Many young adults begin to put on weight because they fail to change poor eating habits developed earlier, and the percentage of obese adults increases with every year of aging.

- People with physical disabilities face physical and material difficulties as well as psychological difficulties, including prejudice and stereotyping.

What are the effects of stress, and what can be done about it?

- Moderate, occasional stress is biologically healthy, but long exposure to stressors produces damaging physical and psychosomatic effects. In reacting to potentially stressful situations, people pass through primary appraisal of the situation itself and secondary appraisal of their own coping abilities.

- People cope with stress in a number of healthy and unhealthy ways, including problem-focused coping, emotion-focused coping, social support, and defensive coping.

Does cognitive development continue in young adulthood?

- Some theorists find increasing evidence of postformal thought, which goes beyond formal logic to produce more flexible and subjective thinking that takes account of real-world complexity and yields subtler answers than those found during adolescence.

- According to Schaie, the development of thinking follows a set pattern of stages: the acquisitive stage, the achieving stage, the responsible stage, the executive stage, and the reintegrative stage.

How is intelligence defined today, and what causes cognitive growth in young adults?

- Traditional views that equated IQ with intelligence are being questioned. According to Sternberg's triarchic theory, intelligence is made up of componential, experiential, and contextual components. Practical intelligence seems to be related most closely with career success, and emotional intelligence underlies social interactions and responsiveness to others' needs.

■ Creativity often peaks in young adulthood, possibly because young people view problems in novel ways rather than in the familiar ways of their older peers.

■ Important life events, such as births and deaths, seem to contribute to cognitive growth by generating new insights into the self and revised views of the world.

▶ Who attends college today, and how is the college population changing?

■ The profile of the U.S. college student has been changing, with many students beyond the traditional 19- to 22-year-old age range. Compared to white high school graduates, a smaller percent of African American and Hispanic American high school graduates enter college.

▶ What do students learn in college, and what difficulties do they face?

■ Many college students, particularly those who experience a decline in status from their high school days, fall victim to the first-year adjustment reaction—feelings of depression, anxiety, and withdrawal that typically pass quickly as the students integrate themselves into their new surroundings.

■ In college, students learn different ways of understanding the world, shifting from dualistic thinking to multiple thinking and to a more relativistic view of values.

■ Gender differences exist in the fields of study chosen by students, students' expectations regarding their future careers and earnings, and professors' treatment of students.

■ Academic disidentification is the tendency of some students (especially females and African Americans) to abandon personal identification with an academic domain because of negative stereotypes that predict their failure in that domain. The concept of stereotype threat, the fear of confirming the negative stereotypes, may explain this phenomenon.

EPILOGUE

In this chapter we discussed physical and cognitive development in early adulthood. We looked at overall health and fitness and at intellectual growth, which proceeds through stages that profit from young adults' increasing experience and subtlety. We also looked at college, noting demographic trends and differences in treatment and academic performance that affect some groups of college students. We discussed the advantages of college and the adjustment reaction that some first-year college students experience as they encounter the new realities of college life.

Return to the prologue of this chapter, in which we met college students Enrico Vasquez and Armando Williams. In light of what you now know about physical and cognitive development in early adulthood, answer the following questions.

1. How do you think family expectations about education affected the two students' decisions to enroll in college?

2. As a Hispanic American student from a wealthy background, what challenges is Enrico likely to encounter if he enters a college in which Hispanic students are a small minority?

3. Is academic disidentification likely to be a problem for Armando, with his "mean streets" background? Why or why not?

4. How does the phenomenon of stereotype threat affect both Enrico and Armando?

5. Which student do you think may have the more difficult adjustment to college? Which is more likely to drop out of college? Why?

Key Terms and Concepts

senescence (p. 451)

stress (p. 457)

psychoneuroimmunology (PNI) (p. 457)

primary appraisal (p. 458)

secondary appraisal (p. 458)

psychosomatic disorders (p. 460)

coping (p. 460)

postformal thought (p. 464)

acquisitive stage (p. 465)

achieving stage (p. 465)

responsible stage (p. 465)

executive stage (p. 465)

reintegrative stage (p. 466)

triarchic theory of intelligence (p. 466)

practical intelligence (p. 467)

emotional intelligence (p. 467)

creativity (p. 468)

first-year adjustment reaction (p. 473)

OUTLINE

Social and Personality Development in Early Adulthood

PROLOGUE: LOVE WITHOUT BORDERS

Grace Tsuyuki, Richard, and her father.

Ah, the weddings. The hair, the makeup, the layers of fabric. They're enough to frazzle the calmest of brides. But when Taiwanese-American Grace Tsai married Japanese-Canadian Richard Tsuyuki, she took wedding-day stress to a whole new level. After a Roman Catholic ceremony in a New Jersey church, the wedding party dashed to a banquet hall in Philadelphia's Chinatown. There was the waltz, the cake, and the bouquet toss. Then the new Mrs. Tsuyuki rushed to a back room, took off her white gown and returned in a slim-fitting, high-necked Chinese *chipao* dress for a customary tea ceremony. As guests dug into a 13-course Chinese meal, she dashed out, changed into an elaborate Japanese kimono and reappeared for a sake-drinking ritual. By the time the bride raised her tiny cup of Japanese wine, she was ready for a drink. "It was totally crazy and exhausting," she says. "But it was important for us to meld together our different cultures." (Clemetson, 2000, p. 62)

Looking Ahead

Life hasn't gotten any less complicated for Grace and Richard. Expecting their first child, they are outfitting the baby' room with the ABCs on one wall, Chinese characters on another, and Japanese characters on a third.

Early adulthood, as Grace and Richard are discovering, is a period during which we face a variety of developmental tasks (see Table 14-1). During this period, we come to grips with the notion that we are no longer other people's children. We begin to perceive ourselves as adults, full members of society with significant responsibilities (Arnett, 2000).

In this chapter, we will examine these challenges, concentrating on the development and course of relationships with others. We will consider first how we establish and maintain love for others, distinguishing between liking and loving, and among different types of love. The chapter will look at how people choose partners and how their choices are influenced by societal and cultural factors.

Next, the chapter turns to relationships during early adulthood. We will examine the choice of whether to marry and the factors that influence the course and success of marriage. We also consider how the arrival of a child influences a couple's happiness and the kinds of roles children play within a marriage. Families today come in all shapes and sizes, representing the complexity of relationships that are the stuff of life for most people during early adulthood.

Finally, the chapter considers careers. We see how identity during early adulthood is often tied to one's job and how people decide on the kind of work they wish to do. The

Table 14-1

THE DEVELOPMENT TASKS OF ADULTHOOD

Adulthood (Ages 20–40)	Middle Adulthood (Ages 40–60)	Late Adulthood (Ages 60+)
1. Psychological separation from parents.	1. Dealing with body changes or illness and altered body image.	1. Maintaining physical health.
2. Accepting responsibility for one's own body.	2. Adjusting to middle-life changes in sexuality.	2. Adapting to physical infirmities or permanent impairment.
3. Becoming aware of one's personal history and time limitation.	3. Accepting the passage of time.	3. Using time in gratifying ways.
4. Integrating sexual experience (homosexual or heterosexual).	4. Adjusting to aging.	4. Adapting to losses of partner and friends.
5. Developing a capacity for intimacy with a partner.	5. Living through illness and death of parents and contemporaries.	5. Remaining oriented to present and future, not preoccupied with the past.
6. Deciding whether to have children.	6. Dealing with realities of death.	6. Forming new emotional ties.
7. Having and relating to children.	7. Redefining relationship to spouse or partner.	7. Reversing roles of children and grandchildren (as caretakers).
8. Establishing adult relationships with parents.	8. Deepening relations with grown children or grandchildren.	8. Seeking and maintaining social contacts: companionship vs. isolation and loneliness.
9. Acquiring marketable skills.	9. Maintaining long-standing friendships and creating new ones.	9. Attending to sexual needs and (changing) expressions.
10. Choosing a career.	10. Consolidating work identity.	10. Continuing meaningful work and play (satisfying use of time).
11. Using money to further development.	11. Transmitting skills and values to the young.	11. Using financial resources wisely, for self and others.
12. Assuming a social role.	12. Allocating financial resources effectively.	12. Integrating retirement into new lifestyle.
13. Adapting ethical and spiritual values.	13. Accepting social responsibility.	
	14. Accepting social change.	

(*Source:* Colarusso & Nemiroff, 1981.)

chapter ends with a discussion of the reasons people work—not only to earn money—and techniques for choosing a career.

After reading this chapter, you will be able to answer the following questions:

▶ **How do young adults form loving relationships, and how does love change over time?**

▶ **How do people choose spouses, and what makes relationships work and cease working?**

▶ **How does the arrival of children affect a relationship?**

▶ **Why is choosing a career such an important issue for young adults, and what factors influence the choice of a career?**

▶ **Why do people work, and what elements of a job bring satisfaction?**

Forging Relationships: Intimacy, Liking, and Loving During Early Adulthood

Asia Kaia Linn, whose parents chose her name while looking through a world atlas, met Chris Applebaum about six years ago at Hampshire College in Massachusetts and fell in love with him one Saturday night while they were dancing.

Although many women might swoon over a guy with perfect hair and fluid dance steps, it was his silly haircut and overall lack of coordination that delighted her. "He's definitely a funny dancer, and he spun me around and we were just being goofy," Ms. Linn recalled. "I realized how much fun we were having, and I thought this is ridiculous and fabulous and I love him." (Brady, 1995, p. 47)

Asia followed her first instincts: Ultimately, she and Chris were married in an unconventional wedding ceremony at an art gallery, with guests wearing a psychedelic mélange of clothes, and a ring-bearer delivering the wedding ring by steering a remote-control truck down the aisle of the gallery.

Not everyone falls in love quite as easily as Asia. For some, the road to love is tortuous, meandering through soured relationships and fallen dreams; for others, it is a road never taken. For some, love leads to marriage and a life befitting society's storybook view of home, children, and long years together as a couple. For many, it leads to a less happy ending, prematurely concluding in divorce and custody battles.

It is clear that intimacy and the formation of relationships are major considerations during early adulthood. Young adults' happiness stems, in part, from their relationships, and many worry about whether or not they are developing serious relationships "on time."

The Components of Happiness: Fulfillment of Psychological Needs

Think back over the last seven days of your life. What made you happiest?

According to research on young adults, it probably wasn't money or material objects that brought you happiness. Instead, happiness usually is derived from feelings of independence, competence, self-esteem, or relatedness (Sheldon et al., 2001).

When asked to recall a time when they were happy, people in early adulthood focus on the satisfaction of psychological needs rather than material needs. Conversely, when

Chris Applebaum and Asia Linn.

they recall times when they were least satisfied, they usually mention incidents in which basic psychological needs were left unsatisfied.

It's interesting to compare these findings, based on research in the United States, with studies conducted in Asian countries. For example, young adults in Korea more often associate satisfaction with experiences involving other people, whereas young adults in the United States experienced satisfaction from experiences relating to the self and self-esteem. Apparently, culture influences which psychological needs are most important in determining happiness (Sheldon et al., 2001).

The Social Clocks of Adulthood

Having children. Receiving a promotion. Getting divorced. Changing jobs. Becoming a grandparent. Each of these events marks a moment on what has been called the social clock of life.

social clock the psychological time-piece that records the major milestones in people's lives

The **social clock** is an expression used to describe the psychological timepiece that records the major milestones in people's lives. Each of us has such a social clock; it provides us with a sense of whether we have reached the major benchmarks of life early, late, or right on time in comparison to our peers.

Until the middle of the 20th century, the social clocks of adulthood were fairly uniform—at least for upper-class and middle-class people. Most people moved through a series of developmental stages closely aligned with particular ages. For example, the typical man completed his education by his early 20s, started a career, married in his mid-20s, and was working to provide for a growing family by the time he was in his 30s. Women also followed a set pattern, which focused on getting married and raising children—but not, in most cases, entering a profession and developing a career.

Today, there is considerably more heterogeneity in the social clocks of both men and women. The timing at which major life events occur has changed considerably. Furthermore, as we consider next, women's social clocks have changed dramatically as a result of social and cultural changes.

Women's Social Clocks. Developmental psychologist Ravenna Helson and colleagues suggest that people have several social clocks from which to choose, and the selection they make has substantial implications for personality development during middle adulthood. Focusing on a sample of women who graduated from college during the early 1960s, Helson's longitudinal research has examined women whose social clocks were focused either on their families, on careers, or on a more individualistic target (Helson & Moane, 1987).

Helson found several broad patterns. Over the course of the study, which assessed participants at the ages of 21, 27, and 43, the women who were studied generally became more self-disciplined and committed to their duties. They also felt greater independence and confidence, and they were able to cope with stress and adversity more effectively.

Measures of traditional feminine behavior changed over time. Although traditional feminine behavior increased from age 21 to age 27, it showed a decrease between the ages of 27 and 43. Helson speculates that the increase was related to a rise in sex-role specialization as the women became more involved in mothering. In contrast, the subsequent decline was likely a result of a decrease in child-care responsibilities as the women's children became older.

Helson's work also identified some intriguing similarities in personality development between women who chose to focus on family and those who focused on career. Both groups tended to show generally positive changes. In contrast, the women who had no strong focus on either family or career tended to show either little change or more negative shifts in personality development.

Helson's conclusion is that the particular social clock that a woman chooses may not be the critical factor in determining the course of personality development. Instead, just proceeding according to some socially acceptable and justifiable social-clock pattern may be the key. Furthermore, it is important to keep in mind that social clocks are culturally determined (Helson, Stewart, & Ostrove, 1995; Stewart & Ostrove, 1998).

Despite changes in the nature of women's (and men's) social clocks, one aspect of adulthood still remains a central feature: the development and maintenance of relationships with others. As we consider next, those relationships are a key part of development during early adulthood.

Always culturally determined, women's social clocks have changed over the years.

Seeking Intimacy: Erikson's View of Young Adulthood

Erik Erikson regards young adulthood as the time of the **intimacy-versus-isolation stage.** As we first noted in Chapter 12 (see Table 12-1), the intimacy-versus-isolation stage spans the period of postadolescence into the early 30s. During this period, the focus is on developing close, intimate relationships with others.

Erikson's idea of intimacy comprises several aspects. One is a degree of selflessness, involving the sacrifice of one's own needs to those of another. A further component involves sexuality, the experience of joint pleasure from focusing not just on one's own gratification but also on that of one's partner. Finally, there is deep devotion, marked by efforts to fuse one's identity with the identity of a partner.

Erikson suggests that those who experience difficulties during this stage are often lonely, isolated, and fearful of relationships with others. Their difficulties may stem from an earlier failure to develop a strong identity. In contrast, young adults who successfully resolve the crisis of the stage are able to form intimate relationships with others on a physical, intellectual, and emotional level.

Although Erikson's approach has been influential, some aspects of his theory trouble today's developmentalists. For instance, Erikson's view of healthy intimacy was limited to adult heterosexuality, the goal of which was to produce children. Consequently, homosexual partnerships, couples who were childless by choice, and other relationships that deviated from what Erikson saw as the ideal were thought of as less than satisfactory. Furthermore, Erikson focused more on men's development than on women's, greatly limiting the applicability of his theory.

intimacy-versus-isolation stage according to Erikson, the period of postadolescence into the early 30s that focuses on developing close relationships with others

People are most attracted to those who can keep confidences, and are loyal, warm, and affectionate.

Still, Erikson's work has been influential historically because of its emphasis on examining the continued growth and development of personality throughout the life span. Furthermore, it inspired other developmentalists to consider psychosocial growth during young adulthood and the range of intimate relationships we develop, from friendship to mates for life.

Friendship

Most of our relationships with others involve friends, and for most people maintaining such relationships is an important part of adult life. Why? One reason is that there is a basic *need for belongingness* that leads people in early adulthood to establish and maintain at least a minimum number of relationships with others. Most people are driven toward forming and preserving relationships that allow them to experience a sense of belonging with others (Manstead, 1997; Rice, 1999).

But how do particular people end up becoming our friends? One of the most important reasons is simple proximity—people form friendships with others who live nearby and with whom they come in contact most frequently. Because of their accessibility, people who are in close proximity can obtain rewards of friendship, such as companionship, social approval, and the occasional helping hand, at relatively little cost.

Similarity also plays an important role in friendship formation. Birds of a feather *do* flock together: People are more attracted to others who hold attitudes and values similar to their own (McCaul et al., 1995).

The importance of similarity becomes particularly evident when we consider cross-race friendships. As we noted in Chapter 12, by the time of adolescence, the number of cross-race close friendships dwindles, a pattern that continues throughout the remainder of the life span. In fact, although most adults claim on surveys to have a close friend of a different race, when they are queried regarding the names of close friends, few include a person of a different race (see Figure 14-1).

We also choose friends on the basis of their personal qualities. What's most important? According to results of surveys, people are most attracted to others who keep confi-

Figure 14-1 **Rephrasing the Question**

Although a relatively high percentage of whites and blacks claim to have a close friend who is a member of a different race, only a small majority actually name a person of the another race or ethnicity when asked to list the names of their close friends.

(*Source:* General Social Survey, 1998.)

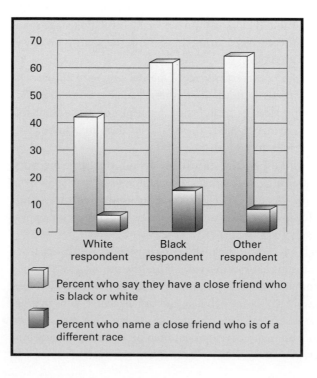

dences and are loyal, warm, and affectionate. In addition, people like those who are supportive, frank, and have a good sense of humor (Parlee, 1979; Hartup & Stevens, 1999).

Falling in Love: When Liking Turns to Loving

After a few chance encounters at the laundromat where they wash their clothes each week, Rebecca and Jerry begin to talk with one another. They find they have a lot in common, and they begin to look forward to what are now semi-planned meetings. After several weeks, they go out on their first official date and discover that they are well suited to each other.

If such a pattern seems predictable, it is: Most relationships develop in a fairly similar way, following a surprisingly regular progression (Burgess & Huston, 1979; Berscheid, 1985):

- Two people interact with each other more often and for longer periods of time. Furthermore, the range of settings increases.

- The two people increasingly seek out each other's company.

- They open up to each other more and more, disclosing more intimate information about themselves. They begin to share physical intimacies.

- The couple are more willing to share both positive and negative feelings, and they may offer criticism in addition to praise.

- They begin to agree on the goals they hold for the relationship.

- Their reactions to situations become more similar.

- They begin to feel that their own psychological well-being is tied to the success of the relationship, viewing it as unique, irreplaceable, and cherished.

- Finally, their definition of themselves and their behavior changes: They begin to see themselves and act as a couple, rather than as two separate individuals.

The evolution of a relationship can be seen in terms of what psychologist Bernard Murstein calls stimulus-value-role theory (Murstein, 1976, 1986, 1987). According to **stimulus-value-role (SVR) theory,** relationships proceed in a fixed order of three stages.

In the first stage, the *stimulus stage,* relationships are built on surface, physical characteristics such as the way a person looks. Usually, this represents just the initial encounter. The second stage, the *value stage,* usually occurs between the second and the seventh encounter. In the value stage, the relationship is characterized by increasing similarity of values and beliefs. Finally, in the third stage, the *role stage,* the relationship is built on specific roles played by the participants. For instance, the couple may define themselves as boyfriend–girlfriend or husband–wife.

Although stimulus, value, and role factors each dominate at a particular stage, they also contribute at other junctures in the developing relationship. For instance, consider Figure 14-2, which illustrates the course of a typical relationship.

Of course, not every relationship follows a similar pattern, and this has led to criticism of SVR theory (Gupta & Singh, 1982; Sternberg, 1986). For instance, there seems to be no logical reason why value factors, rather than stimulus factors, could not predominate early in a relationship. Two people who first encounter each other at a political meeting, for example, could be attracted to each other's views of current issues. Consequently, additional approaches have been devised to explain the course of relationship development.

stimulus-value-role (SVR) theory the theory that relationships proceed in a fixed order of three stages: stimulus, value, and role

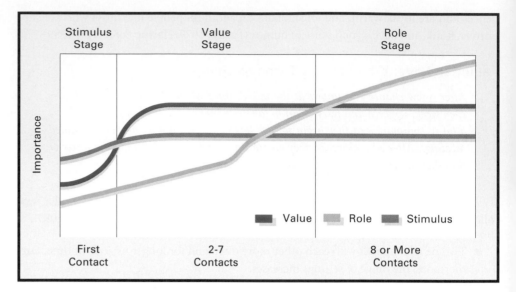

Figure 14-2 **The Path of Relationships**

According to stimulus-value-role (SVR) theory, relationships proceed through a fixed series of stages.

(*Source:* Murstein, 1987.)

passionate (or romantic) love a state of powerful absorption in someone

companionate love the strong affection for those with whom our lives are deeply involved

labeling theory of passionate love the theory that individuals experience romantic love when two events occur together: intense physiological arousal and situational cues suggesting that the arousal is due to love

Passionate and Companionate Love: The Two Faces of Love

Is "love" just a lot of "liking"? Most developmental psychologists would answer negatively; love not only differs quantitatively from liking, it represents a qualitatively different state. For example, love, at least in its early stages, involves relatively intense physiological arousal, an all-encompassing interest in another individual, recurrent fantasies about the other individual, and rapid swings of emotion (Lamm & Wiesman, 1997). As distinct from liking, love includes elements of closeness, passion, and exclusivity (Walster & Walster, 1978; Hendrick & Hendrick, 1989).

Not all love is the same, however. We don't love our mothers the same way we love girlfriends or boyfriends, brothers or sisters, or lifelong friends. What distinguishes these different types of love? Some psychologists suggest that our love relationships can fall into two different categories: passionate or companionate.

Passionate (or romantic) love is a state of powerful absorption in someone. It includes intense physiological interest and arousal, and caring for another's needs. In comparison, **companionate love** is the strong affection that we have for those with whom our lives are deeply involved (Hatfield, 1988; Hecht, Marston, & Larkey, 1994; Lamm & Wiesman, 1997).

What is it that fuels the fires of passionate love? According to one theory, anything that produces strong emotions—even negative ones such as jealousy, anger, or fear of rejection—may be the source of deepening passionate love.

In psychologists Elaine Hatfield and Ellen Berscheid's **labeling theory of passionate love,** individuals experience romantic love when two events occur together: intense physiological arousal and situational cues that indicated that "love" is the appropriate label for the feelings they are experiencing (Berscheid & Walster, 1974a). The physiological arousal can be produced by sexual arousal, excitement, or even negative emotions such as jealousy. Whatever the cause, if that arousal is subsequently labeled as "I must be falling in love" or "she makes my heart flutter" or "he really turns me on," then the experience is attributed to passionate love.

The theory is particularly useful in explaining why people may feel deepened love even when they experience continual rejection or hurt from their assumed lover. It suggests that such negative emotions can produce strong physiological arousal. If this arousal is interpreted as being caused by "love," then people may decide that they are even more in love than they were before they experienced the negative emotions.

But why should people label an emotional experience as "love" when there are so many possible alternatives? One answer is that in Western cultures, passionate love is seen as possible, acceptable, desirable—an experience to be sought. The virtues of passion are extolled in love ballads, commercials, television shows, and films. Consequently, young adults are primed and ready to experience love in their lives (Dion & Dion, 1988; Hatfield & Rapson, 1993).

It is interesting to note that this is not the way it is in every culture. For instance, in many cultures, passionate, romantic love is a foreign concept. Marriages may be arranged on the basis of economic and status considerations. Even in Western cultures, the concept of love is of relatively recent origin. For instance, the notion that couples need to be in love was not "invented" until the Middle Ages, when social philosophers first suggested that love ought to be a requirement for marriage. Their goal in making such a proposal: to provide an alternative to the raw sexual desire that had served as the primary basis for marriage before (Lewis, 1958; Xiaohe & Whyte, 1990).

Sternberg's Triangular Theory: The Three Faces of Love

To psychologist Robert Sternberg, love is more complex than a simple division into passionate and companionate types. He suggests instead that love is made up of three components: intimacy, passion, and decision/commitment. The **intimacy component** encompasses feelings of closeness, affection, and connectedness. The **passion component** comprises the motivational drives relating to sex, physical closeness, and romance. This component is exemplified by intense, physiologically arousing feelings of attraction. Finally, the third aspect of love, the **decision/commitment component,** embodies both the initial cognition that one loves another person and the longer-term determination to maintain that love (Sternberg, 1986, 1988, 1997b).

By jointly considering whether each of the three components is either present or missing from a relationship, eight unique combinations of love can be formed (see Table 14-2). For instance, *nonlove* refers to people who have only the most casual of relationships; it consists of the absence of the three components of intimacy, passion, and decision/commitment. *Liking* develops when only intimacy is present; *infatuated love* exists when only passion is felt; and *empty love* exists when only decision/commitment is present.

Other types of love are more complex. For instance, *romantic love* occurs when intimacy and passion are present, and *companionate love* when intimacy and decision/commitment occur jointly. When two people experience romantic love, they are drawn together physically and emotionally, but they do not necessarily view the relationship as lasting. Companionate love, on the other hand, may occur in long-lasting relationships in which physical passion has taken a backseat.

Fatuous love exists when passion and decision/commitment, without intimacy, are present. Fatuous love is a kind of mindless loving in which there is no emotional bond between the partners.

Finally, the eighth kind of love is *consummate love.* In consummate love, all three components of love are present. Although we might assume that consummate love represents the "ideal" love, such a view may well be mistaken. Many long-lasting and entirely satisfactory relationships are based on types of love other than consummate love. Furthermore, the type of love that predominates in a relationship varies over time. As shown Figure 14-3, in strong, loving relationships the level of decision/commitment peaks and remains fairly stable. By contrast, passion tends to peak early in a relationship, but then declines and levels off. Intimacy also increases fairly rapidly, but can continue to grow over time.

The idea of romantic or passionate love is predominately a western concept. How do other cultures view romantic or passionate love?

intimacy component the component of love that encompasses feelings of closeness, affection, and connectedness

passion component the component of love that comprises the motivational drives relating to sex, physical closeness, and romance

decision/commitment component the third aspect of love that embodies both the initial cognition that one loves another person and the longer-term determination to maintain that love

Table 14-2

THE COMBINATIONS OF LOVE

	Component			
Type of Love	**Intimacy**	**Passion**	**Decision/ Commitment**	**Example**
Nonlove	Absent	Absent	Absent	The way you might feel about the person who takes your ticket at the movies.
Liking	Present	Absent	Absent	Good friends who have lunch together at least once or twice a week.
Infatuated love	Absent	Present	Absent	A "fling" or short-term relationship based only on sexual attraction.
Empty Love	Absent	Absent	Present	An arranged marriage or a couple who have decided to stay married "for the sake of the children."
Romantic love	Present	Present	Absent	A couple who have been happily dating a few months, but have not made any plans for a future together.
Companionate love	Present	Absent	Present	A couple who enjoy each other's company and their relationship, although they no longer feel much sexual interest in each other.
Fatuous love	Absent	Present	Present	A couple who decides to move in together after knowing each other for only two weeks.
Consummate love	Present	Present	Present	A loving, sexually vibrant, long-term relationship.

Sternberg's triangular theory of love emphasizes both the complexity of love and its dynamic, evolving quality. As people and relationships develop and change over time, so does their love.

Choosing a Partner: Recognizing Mr. or Ms. Right

For many young adults, the search for a partner is a major pursuit during early adulthood. Certainly society offers a great deal of advice on how to succeed in this endeavor, as a glance at the array of magazines at any supermarket check-out counter confirms. Despite

Fatuous love is kind of mindless love in which there is no emotional bond between individuals.

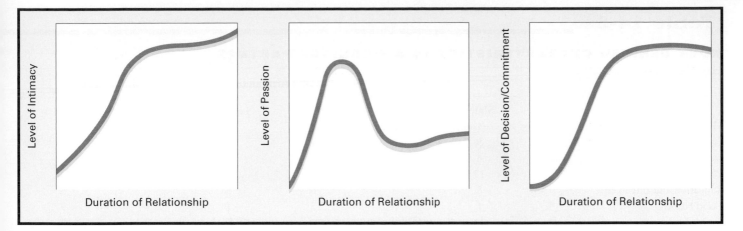

Figure 14-3 **The Shape of Love**

Over the course of a relationship, the three aspects of love—intimacy, passion, and decision/commitment—vary in strength. How do these change as a relationship develops?

(*Source:* Sternberg, 1986.)

all the counsel, however, the road to identifying an individual to share one's life is not always easy.

Seeking a Spouse: Is Love the Only Thing That Matters? Most people have no hesitation in articulating that the major factor in choosing a husband or wife is love. Most people in the United States, that is: If we ask people in other societies, love becomes a secondary consideration. For instance, consider the results of a survey in which college students were asked if they would marry someone they did not love. Hardly anyone in the United States, Japan, or Brazil would consider it. On the other hand, a goodly proportion of college students in Pakistan and India would find it acceptable to marry without love (Levine, 1993).

If love is not the only important factor, what else matters? The characteristics differ considerably from one culture to another (see Table 14-3). For instance, a survey of nearly 10,000 people from around the world found that although people in the United States believed that love and mutual attraction were the primary characteristics, in China men ranked good health most important and women rated emotional stability and maturity most critical. In contrast, in South Africa men from a Zulu background rated emotional stability first, and women rated dependable character of greatest concern (Buss et al., 1990).

On the other hand, there are commonalities across cultures. For instance, love and mutual attraction, even if not at the top of a specific culture's list, were relatively highly desired across all cultures. Furthermore, traits such as dependability, emotional stability, pleasing disposition, and intelligence were highly valued almost universally.

Certain gender differences in the preferred characteristics of a mate were similar across cultures—findings that have been confirmed by other surveys (e.g., Sprecher, Sullivan, & Hatfield, 1994). Men, more than women, prefer a potential marriage partner who is physically attractive. In contrast, women, more than men, prefer a potential spouse who is ambitious and industrious.

One explanation for cross-cultural similarities in gender differences rests on evolutionary factors. According to psychologist David Buss and colleagues (Buss et al., 1990), human beings, as a species, seek out certain characteristics in their mates that are likely to maximize the availability of beneficial genes. He argues that males in particular are genetically programmed to seek out mates with traits that indicate they have high reproductive capacity. Consequently, physically attractive, younger women might be more desirable since they are more capable of having children over a longer time period.

Table 14-3

MOST DESIRED CHARACTERISTICS IN A MARRIAGE PARTNER

	China		South African (Zulu)		United States	
	Males	Females	Males	Females	Males	Females
Mutual Attraction—Love	4	8	10	5	1	1
Emotional Stability and Maturity	5	1	1	2	2	2
Dependable Character	6	7	3	1	3	3
Pleasing Disposition	13	16	4	3	4	4
Education and Intelligence	8	4	6	6	5	5
Good Health	1	3	5	4	6	9
Sociability	12	9	11	8	8	8
Desire for Home and Children	2	2	9	9	9	7
Refinement, Neatness	7	10	7	10	10	12
Ambition and Industriousness	10	5	8	7	11	6
Good Looks	11	15	14	16	7	13
Similar Education	15	12	12	12	12	10
Good Financial Prospects	16	14	18	13	16	11
Good Cook and Housekeeper	9	11	2	15	13	16
Favorable Social Status or Rating	14	13	17	14	14	14
Similar Religious Background	18	18	16	11	15	15
Chastity (no prior sexual intercourse)	3	6	13	18	17	18
Similar Political Background	17	17	15	17	18	17

Note: numbers indicate rank ordering of characteristics.
(*Source:* Buss et al., 1990.)

In contrast, women are genetically programmed to seek out men who have the potential to provide scarce resources in order to increase the likelihood that their offspring will survive. Consequently, they are attracted to mates who offer the highest potential of providing economic well-being (Feingold, 1992; Walter, 1997; Kasser & Sharma, 1999).

Although the evolutionary explanation makes logical sense, not everyone agrees. For instance, critics suggest that the similarities across cultures relating to different gender preferences may simply reflect similar patterns of gender stereotyping that have nothing to do with evolution. Such critics point out that although some differences in what men and women prefer are consistent across cultures, there are several inconsistencies as well.

Filtering Models: Sifting Out a Spouse. While surveys assist in identifying the characteristics that are highly valued in a potential spouse, they are less helpful in determining how a specific individual is chosen as a partner. One approach that helps explain this is the filtering model developed by psychologists Louis Janda and Karen Klenke-Hamel (1980). They suggest that people seeking a mate screen potential candidates through successively finer-grained filters, just as we sift flour in order to remove undesirable material (see Figure 14-4).

The model assumes that people first filter for factors relating to broad determinants of attractiveness. Once these early screens have done their work, more sophisticated types of screening are used. The end result is a choice based on compatibility between the two individuals.

What determines compatibility? It is not only a matter of pleasing personality characteristics; several cultural factors also play an important role. For instance, people often marry according to the principle of homogamy. **Homogamy** is the tendency to marry someone who is similar in age, race, education, religion, and other basic demographic characteristics.

homogamy the tendency to marry someone who is similar in age, race, education, religion, and other basic demographic characteristics

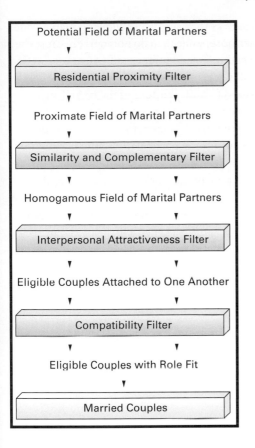

Figure 14-4   Filtering Potential Marriage Partners

According to one approach, we screen potential mates through successively finer-grained filters in order to settle on an appropriate spouse.

(Adapted from Janda & Klenke-Hamel, 1980.)

Homogamy has traditionally been the dominant standard for most marriages in the United States. On the other hand, the importance of homogamy is declining, as we observed in the wedding of Taiwanese-American Grace and Japanese-Canadian Richard, described in the prologue. As of 1999, about 3 million marriages crossed ethnic and racial lines, an increase of more than 50 percent since 1980 (see Figure 14-5 ; Suro, 1999).

The marriage gradient represents another societal standard that determines who marries whom. The **marriage gradient** is the tendency for men to marry women who are slightly younger, smaller, and lower in status, and women to marry men who are slightly older, larger, and higher in status (Bernard, 1982).

The marriage gradient, which has a powerful influence on marriage in the United States, has important, and insidious, effects on partner choice. For one thing, it limits the

marriage gradient the tendency for men to marry women who are slightly younger, smaller, and lower in status, and women to marry men who are slightly older, larger, and higher in status

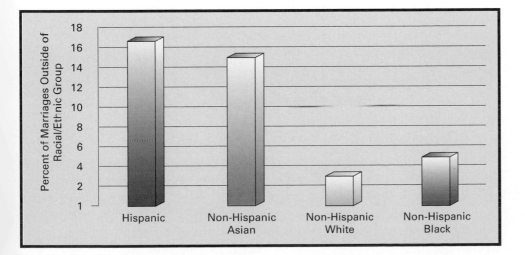

Figure 14-5   Marriage Outside of Racial/Ethnic Group

Although homogamy has been the standard for most marriages in the United States, the rate of marriages crossing ethnic and racial lines has been increasing. What factors contribute to this shift?

(*Source:* Based on data from William H. Grey, Milken Institute, reported in *American Demographics*, Nov. 1999.)

Some psychologists believe that our attachment style as infants is repeated in the quality of our intimate relationships as adults.

number of potential mates for women, especially as they age, while allowing men a wider choice of partners as their age increases. Furthermore, some men do not marry because they cannot find women of low enough status to meet the demands of the gradient, or cannot find women of the same or higher status who are willing to accept them as mates. Consequently, they are, in the words of sociologist Jessie Bernard (1982), "bottom of the barrel" men. On the other hand, some women will be unable to marry because they are higher in status than anyone in the available pool of men—"cream of the crop" women, in Bernard's words.

The marriage gradient makes finding a spouse particularly difficult for well-educated African American women. Fewer African American men attend college than African American women, making the potential pool of men who are suitable—as defined by society and the marriage gradient—relatively small. Consequently, relative to women of other races, African American women are more apt to marry men who are less educated than they are—or not marry at all (Taylor et al., 1991; Tucker & Mitchell-Kernan, 1995; Kiecolt & Fossett, 1997).

Attachment Styles and Romantic Relationships: Do Adult Loving Styles Reflect Attachment in Infancy?

"I want a girl just like the girl that married dear old Dad." So go the lyrics of an old song, suggesting that the songwriter would like to find someone who loves him as much as his mother did. Is this just a corny tune, or is there a kernel of truth in this sentiment? Put more broadly, is the nature of attachment that people display during infancy reflected in their adult romantic relationships?

Increasing evidence suggests that it very well may be. As you may recall, attachment refers to the positive emotional bond that develops between a child and a particular individual (see Chapter 6). Most infants fall into one of three attachment categories: *securely attached* children, who have healthy, positive, trusting relationships with their caregivers; *avoidant* infants, who are relatively indifferent to caregivers and who avoid interactions with them; and *anxious-ambivalent* infants, who show great distress when separated from a caregiver, but who appear angry upon the caregiver's return.

According to psychologist Phillip Shaver and colleagues, the influence of infants' attachment styles continues into adulthood and affects the nature of their romantic relationships (Hazan & Shaver, 1987; Shaver, Hazan, & Bradshaw, 1988; Shaver, 1994; Koski & Shaver, 1997). For instance, consider the following statements:

(1) I find it relatively easy to get close to others and am comfortable depending on them and having them depend on me. I don't often worry about being abandoned or about someone getting too close to me.

(2) I am somewhat uncomfortable being close to others; I find it difficult to trust them completely, difficult to allow myself to depend on them. I am nervous when anyone gets too close, and often love partners want me to be more intimate than I feel comfortable being.

(3) I find that others are reluctant to get as close as I would like. I often worry that my partner doesn't really love me or won't want to stay with me. I want to merge completely with another person, and this desire sometimes scares people away. (Shaver, Hazan, & Bradshaw, 1988)

According to Shaver's research, agreement with the first statement reflects a secure attachment style. Adults who agree with this statement readily enter into relationships and feel happy and confident about the future success of their relationships. Most young adults—just over half—display the secure style of attachment (Hazan & Shaver, 1987).

In contrast, adults who agree with the second statement typically display the avoidant attachment style. These individuals, who make up about a quarter of the population, tend to be less invested in relationships, have higher break-up rates, and often feel lonely.

Finally, agreement with the third category is reflective of an anxious-ambivalent style. Adults with an anxious-ambivalent style have a tendency to become overly invested in relationships, have repeated break-ups with the same partner, and have relatively low self-esteem. Around 20 percent of adults fall into this category (Simpson, 1990).

Recent research indicates that attachment style is also related to the nature of caregiving that adults give to their romantic partners when they need assistance. For instance, secure adults tend to provide sensitive caregiving, while anxious adults are more likely to provide compulsive, intrusive caregiving to partners (Shaver, 1994; Feeney & Noller, 1996).

It seems clear that there are continuities between infants' attachment styles and their behavior as adults. People who are having difficulty in relationships might well look back to their infancy to identify the root of their problem (Brennan & Shaver, 1995). Insight into the roots of our current behavior can sometimes help us learn more adaptive skills as adults.

The quality of lesbian and gay relationships differs little from that of heterosexual relationships.

Developmental Diversity

Gay and Lesbian Relationships: Men with Men and Women with Women

Most research conducted by developmental psychologists has examined heterosexual relationships, but an increasing number of studies have looked at relationships involving gay men and those involving lesbian women. The findings suggest that gay relationships are quite similar to relationships between heterosexuals.

For example, gay men describe successful relationships in ways that are similar to heterosexual couples' descriptions. They believe that successful relationships involve greater appreciation for the partner and the couple as a whole, less conflict, and more positive feelings toward the partner. Similarly, lesbian women in a relationship show high levels of attachment, caring, intimacy, affection, and respect (Peplau, Padesky, & Hamilton, 1982; Brehm, 1992).

Furthermore, the age preferences expressed in the marriage gradient for heterosexuals also extend to partner preferences for homosexual men. Like heterosexual men, homosexual men prefer partners who are the same age or younger. On the other hand, lesbians' age preferences fall somewhere between those of heterosexual women and heterosexual men (Kenrick et al., 1995).

Finally, despite the stereotype that gay males, in particular, find it difficult to form relationships and are interested in only sexual alliances, the reality is different. Most gays and lesbians seek loving, long-term, and meaningful relationships that differ little qualitatively from those desired by heterosexuals (Peplau & Cochran, 1990; Kurdek, 1991, 1992; Division 44, 2000). □

Review and Rethink

REVIEW

- According to Erikson, young adults are in the intimacy-versus-isolation stage.
- The course of relationships typically follows a pattern of increasing interaction, intimacy, and redefinition. SVR theory regards relationships as passing successively though stimulus, value, and role stages.
- According to the labeling theory of passionate love, people experience love when intense physiological arousal is ac-

companied by situational cues that the experience should be labeled "love."

- Types of love include passionate and companionate love. Sternberg's triangular theory identifies three basic components (intimacy, passion, and decision/commitment).
- In many Western cultures, love is the most important factor in selecting a partner.
- According to filtering models, people apply increasingly fine filters to potential partners, eventually choosing a mate

according to the principles of homogamy and the marriage gradient.

■ Attachment styles in infants appear to be linked to the ability to form romantic relationships in adulthood.

■ In general, the values applied to relationships by heterosexual, gay, and lesbian couples are more similar than different.

RETHINK

■ What has to change for a relationship to move from passionate to companionate love? From companionate to passionate love? In which direction is it more difficult for a relationship to move? Why?

■ How do the principles of homogamy and the marriage gradient work to limit options for high-status women? How do they affect men's options?

The Course of Relationships

He wasn't being a chauvinist or anything, expecting me to do everything and him nothing. He just didn't volunteer to do things that obviously needed doing, so I had to put down some ground rules. Like if I'm in a bad mood, I may just yell: "I work eight hours just like you. This is half your house and half your child, too. You've got to do your share!" Jackson never changed the kitty litter box once in four years, but he changes it now, so we've made great progress. I just didn't expect it to take so much work. We planned this child together and we went through Lamaze together, and Jackson stayed home for the first two weeks. But then— wham—the partnership was over (Cowan & Cowan, 1992, p. 63).

cohabitation couples living together without being married

Relationships, like the individuals who make them up, face a variety of challenges. As men and women move through early adulthood, they encounter significant changes in their lives as they work at starting and building their careers, having children, and establishing, maintaining, and sometimes ending relationships with others. One of the primary questions young adults face is whether and when to marry.

Marriage, POSSLQ, and Other Relationship Choices: Sorting Out the Options of Early Adulthood

For some people, the primary issue is not identifying a potential spouse, but whether to marry at all. Although surveys show that most heterosexuals say they want to get married, a significant number choose some other route. For instance, the past three decades have seen a dramatic rise in couples living together without being married, a status known as **cohabitation** (see Figure 14-6). These people, whom the census bureau calls *POSSLQs*, or *persons of the opposite sex sharing living quarters,* now make up around 4 percent of all couples in the United States—over 7.5 million people (Fields & Casper, 2001).

POSSLQs, or Persons of the Opposite Sex Sharing Living Quarters, now make up about 4 percent of all couples in the United States—almost 7.5 million people.

POSSLQs tend to be young: Almost a quarter of cohabiting women and over 15 percent of cohabiting men are under 25. Although most are white, African Americans are more likely to cohabit than whites. Other countries have even higher cohabitation rates. In Sweden, for instance, around a quarter of all couples cohabit (Bianchi & Spain, 1986; Popenoe, 1987; Tucker & Mitchell-Kernan, 1995).

Why do some couples choose to cohabit rather than to marry? Some feel they are not ready to make a lifelong commitment. Others feel that cohabitation provides "practice" for marriage. Some reject the institution of marriage altogether, maintaining that marriage is outmoded and that it is unrealistic to expect a couple to spend a lifetime together (Sarantakos, 1991; Hobart & Grigel, 1992; Cunningham & Antill, 1994).

Those who feel that cohabiting increases their subsequent chances of a happy marriage are incorrect. On the contrary, the chances of divorce are somewhat higher for those

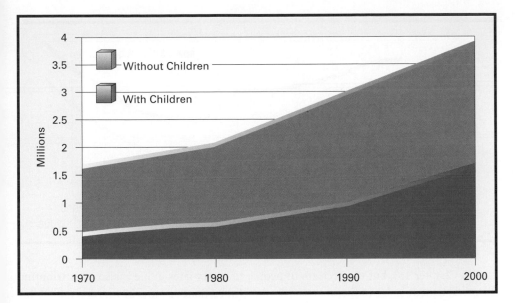

Figure 14-6 POSSLQs

The number of POSSLQs, or persons of the opposite sex sharing living quarters, has risen considerably in the last three decades. Why do you think this is the case?

(*Source:* U.S. Bureau of the Census, 2001.)

who have previously cohabited, according to data collected in both the United States and western Europe. However, it's unclear why this is true. It may be that people who decide to cohabit have personal characteristics that would already predispose them to marriage problems (DeMaris & Rao, 1992; McRae, 1997).

Despite the prevalence of cohabitation, marriage remains the preferred alternative for most people during early adulthood. Many see marriage as the appropriate culmination of a loving relationship, while others feel it is the "right" thing to do after reaching a particular age in early adulthood. Others seek marriage because of the various roles that a spouse can fill. For instance, a spouse can play an economic role, providing security and financial well-being. Spouses also fill a sexual role, offering a means of sexual gratification and fulfillment that is fully accepted by society. Another role is therapeutic and recreational: Spouses provide a sounding board to discuss one another's problems and act as partners for activities. Marriage also offers the only means of having children that is fully accepted by all segments of society (Waite, 1995; Furstenberg, 1996; DeVita, 1996).

Although marriage remains important, it is not a static institution. For example, fewer U.S. citizens are now married (62 percent) than at any time since the late 1890s. Part of this decline in marriage statistics is attributable to higher divorce rates (which we dis-

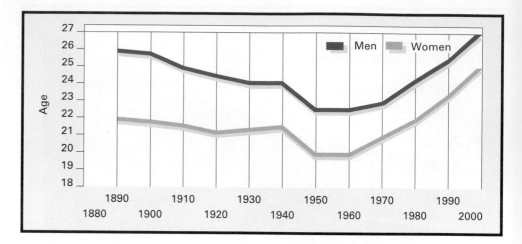

Figure 14-7 **Postponing Marriage**

The age at which women and men first marry is the highest since national statistics were first collected in the late 1800s. What factors account for this?

(*Source:* U.S. Bureau of the Census, 2001.)

cuss in Chapter 16), but the decision of people to marry later in life is also a contributing factor. The median age of first marriage in the United States is now 27 for men and 25 for women—the oldest age for women since national statistics were first collected in the 1880s (see Figure 14-7; U.S. Census Bureau, 2001; Usdansky, 1992; Furstenberg, 1996).

Does this mean that marriage is losing its viability as a social institution? Probably not. Most people—some 90 percent—eventually do marry, and national polls find that almost everyone endorses the notion that a good family life is important. In fact, almost nine out of ten 18- to 29-year-olds believe that a happy marriage is an ingredient of a good life (Roper Starch Worldwide, 1997).

Why are people getting married later in life? The delay in part reflects economic concerns and the commitment to establishing a career. Choosing and starting a career presents an increasingly difficult series of decisions for young adults, and some feel that until they get a foothold on a career path and begin to earn an adequate salary, marriage plans should be put on hold (Dreman, 1997).

What Makes Marriage Work?

Partners in successful marriages display several characteristics. They visibly show affection to one another and communicate relatively little negativity. Happily married couples tend to perceive themselves as part of an interdependent couple rather than as one of two independent individuals. For example, Grace and Richard, the couple described in the prologue, made their wedding a symbol of their desire to think as a couple by working to meld their cultural traditions together. They also experience *social homogamy,* a similarity in leisure activity and role preferences. They hold similar interests, and they agree on a distribution of roles—such as who takes out the garbage and who takes care of the children (Gottman, Fainsilber-Katz, & Hooven, 1996; Carrere et al., 2000; Huston et al., 2001).

However, our awareness of the characteristics displayed by husbands and wives in successful marriages has not helped prevent what can only be called an epidemic of divorce. The statistics on divorce are grim: Only about half of all marriages in the United States remain intact. Over a million marriages end in divorce each year, and there are 4.2 divorces for every 1,000 individuals. This figure actually represents a decline from the peak in the mid-1970s of 5.3 divorces per 1,000 people, and most experts think that the rate is leveling off (National Center for Health Statistics, 2001).

Divorce is not just a problem in the United States. Countries around the world, both rich and poor, have shown increases in divorce during the last several decades (see Figure 14-8).

Although we discuss the consequences of divorce in greater detail in Chapter 16 when we consider middle age, divorce is a problem that has its roots in early adulthood and the early years of marriage. In fact, most divorces occur during the first 10 years of marriage.

In part, love involves companionship and mutual enjoyment of various activities.

Early Marital Conflict. According to some statistics, nearly half of newly married couples experience a significant degree of conflict. One of the major reasons is that partners may initially idealize one another, perceiving each other through the proverbial "starry eyes." However, as the realities of day-to-day living together and interacting begin to sink in, they become more aware of flaws, like the wife whose quotation began this section of the chapter. In fact, perceptions of marital quality on the part of both wives and husbands show a decline in the early years of marriage, followed by a period of stabilization, and then additional decline over the first 10 years of marriage (see Figure 14-9; Pauker & Arond, 1989; Kurdek, 1999; Huston et al., 2001).

Several factors may lead to marital conflict. For example, husbands and wives may have difficulty making the status transition from children of their parents to autonomous adults. Others have difficulty developing an identity apart from their spouses, while some struggle to find a satisfactory allocation of time to share with the spouse, compared with time spent with friends and other family members (Cohan & Bradbury, 1997; Fincham et al., 1997; Fincham, 1998).

On the other hand, most married couples view the early years of marriage as deeply satisfying. For them, marriage can be a kind of extension of courtship. As they negotiate changes in their relationship and learn more about each other, many couples find themselves more deeply in love than before marriage. In fact, the newlywed period is for many couples one of the happiest of their entire married lives (Bird & Melville, 1994; Orbuch et al., 1996).

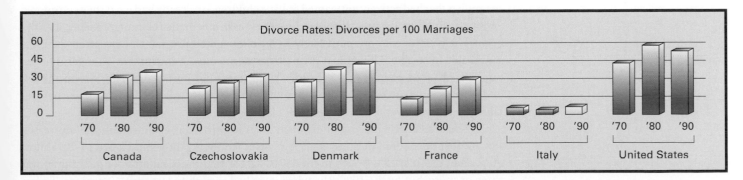

Figure 14-8 **Divorce Around the World**

Increases in divorce rates are not just a U.S. phenomenon: Data from other countries also show significant increases.

(*Source:* Population Council, 1995.)

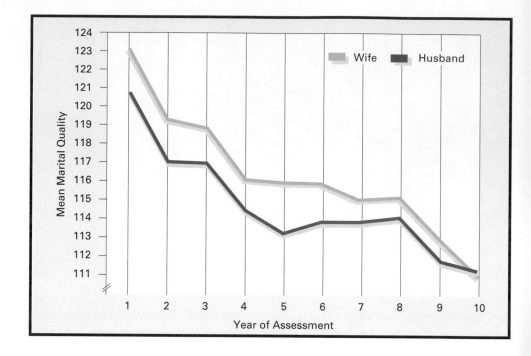

Figure 14-9 **Perceptions of Marital Quality**

At the beginning of marriage, partners see each other in a more idealized manner. But as time passes, the perception of the quality of the marriage declines.

(*Source:* Kurdek, 1999.)

Parenthood: Choosing to Have Children

Deciding whether to have children is one of the most important decisions couples make. What makes a couple decide to have children? Childrearing certainly isn't economically advantageous: According to one estimate, a middle-class family with two children spends around $100,000 for each child by the time the child reaches the age of 18. Add in the costs of college and the figure comes to over $200,000 per child (Belkin, 1985; Cutler, 1990).

Instead, young adults typically cite psychological reasons for having children. They expect to derive pleasure from watching their children grow, fulfillment from their children's accomplishments, satisfaction from seeing them become successful, and enjoyment from forging a close bond with their children. But there also may be a self-serving element in the decision to have children. For example, parents-to-be may hope that their children will provide for them in their old age, maintain a family business or farm, or simply offer companionship. Others have children because to do so is such a strong societal norm: More than 90 percent of all married couples have at least one child (Mackey, White, & Day, 1992).

For some couples, the decision to have children is inadvertent. Due to the failure of birth control methods, some children are born without the benefit of being planned. In some cases, the family had been planning to have children at some point in the future, and so the pregnancy is not regarded as particularly undesirable and may even be welcomed. But in families that had actively *not* wanted to have children, or already had what they considered "enough" children, the pregnancy can be viewed as problematic (Clinton & Kelber, 1993).

The couples who are most likely to have unwanted pregnancies are often the most vulnerable in society. Unplanned pregnancies occur most frequently in younger, poorer, and less educated couples. On the other hand, there has been a dramatic rise in the use and effectiveness of contraceptives, and the incidence of undesired pregnancies has declined in the last several decades (Pratt et al., 1984).

The availability and use of effective contraceptives has also dramatically decreased the number of children in the average American family. As shown in Figure 14-10, almost 70 percent of Americans polled in the 1930s agreed that the ideal number of children was three or more, but by the 1990s the percentage had shrunk to less than 40 percent. Today, most families seek to have no more than two children—although most say that three or more is ideal if money is no object (CNN/USA Today/Gallup, 1997; Kate, 1998).

These preferences have been translated into changes in the actual birth rate. In 1957, the *fertility rate* reached a post-World War II peak in the United States of 3.7 children per woman and then began to decline. Today, the rate remains below 2.0 children per woman, which is less than the *replacement level,* the number of children that one generation must produce to be able to replenish its numbers (Exter, 1990).

What has produced this decline in the fertility rate? In addition to the availability of more reliable birth control methods, one reason is that increasing numbers of women have joined the workforce. The pressures of simultaneously holding a job and raising a child have convinced many women to have fewer children. Furthermore, many women who work outside the home are choosing to have children later in their childbearing years in order to develop their careers. In fact, women between the ages of 30 and 34 are the only ones whose rate of births has actually increased over earlier decades. Still, because women who have their first children in their 30s have fewer years in which to have children, they ultimately cannot have as many children as women who begin childbearing in their 20s.

In addition, some of the traditional incentives for having children—such as their potential for providing economic support in old age—may no longer be as attractive. Potential parents may view Social Security and other pensions as a more predictable means of support when they are elderly. Furthermore, the sheer cost of raising a child, particularly the well-publicized increase in the cost of college, may act as a disincentive for bearing larger numbers of children (Bird & Melville, 1994).

Finally, some couples avoid having children because they simply don't want the work involved in childrearing. Women may also fear that they will share a disproportionate amount of the effort involved in childrearing—a perception that may be an accurate reading of reality, as we consider next.

Dual-Earner Couples. One of the major historical shifts that began in the last half of the 20th century is the increase in families in which both parents work. Close to three-quarters of married women with school aged children are employed outside the home, and more than half of mothers with children under 6 are working. In the mid-1960s, only 17 percent of mothers of 1-year-olds worked full time; now, more than 50 percent do (Darnton, 1990; Carnegie Task Force, 1994).

Although the income that is generated when both partners work provides economic benefits, it takes a toll, particularly on women. Even when both spouses work similar hours, the wife generally spends more time taking care of the children than the husband

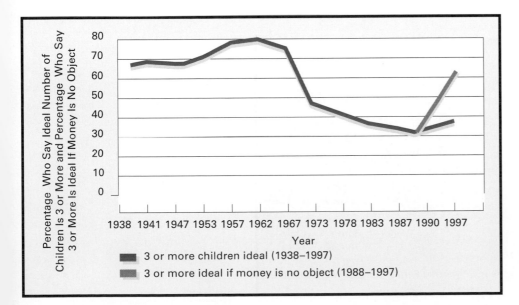

Figure 14-10 **Shrinking Families**

In the 1930s close to 70 percent of Americans felt the ideal number of children was three or more. By the late 1990s, that figure dropped to less than 40 percent. What are some societal developments that contributed to this change?

(CNN/USA Today/Gallup Poll, 1998.)

The fertility rate has been dropping since just after World War II. Today the rate remains below 2.0 children, less than the replacement level. What are some factors that has contributed to the falling rate of fertility?

does (Huppe & Cyr, 1997). And even though men are spending more time with their children than in the past (the amount of time has increased by one-quarter in the last 20 years), wives still spend more time with their children than husbands do (Families and Work Institute, 1998).

Furthermore, the nature of husbands' contributions to the household often differs from wives'. For instance, husbands tend to carry out chores such as mowing the lawn or house repairs that are more easily scheduled in advance (or sometimes postponed), while women's household chores tend to be devoted to things that need immediate attention, such as child care and meal preparation. As a result, wives experience greater levels of anxiety and stress (Biernat & Wortman, 1991; Kurdek, 1993; Barnett & Shen, 1997; see Figure 14-11).

Whatever the reasons, choosing to have children produces tremendous changes in family dynamics, as we consider in the *From Research to Practice* box.

Gay and Lesbian Parents

In increasing numbers, children are being raised in families in which there are two Moms or two Dads. Rough estimates suggest that some 20 percent of gay men and lesbian women are parents (Falk, 1989; Turner, Scadden, & Harris, 1990).

Figure 14-11 **Division of Labor**

Although husbands and wives generally work at their paying jobs a similar number of hours each week, wives are apt to spend more time than their husbands doing home chores and in child care activities. Why do you think this pattern exists?

(Googans & Burden, 1987.)

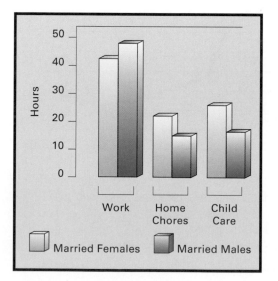

From Research to Practice

The Impact of Children on Parents: Two's a Couple, Three's a Crowd?

We had no idea what we were getting into when our first child was born. We certainly prepared for the event, reading magazine articles and books and even attending a class on child care. But when Sheanna was actually born, the sheer enormity of the task of taking care of her, her presence at every moment of the day, and the awesome responsibility of raising another human being weighed on us like nothing else we'd ever faced. Not that it was a burden. But it did make us look at the world with an entirely different perspective.

Like many parents, this couple was unable, before the fact, to grasp fully the tremendous and sometimes overwhelming nature of childrearing. The arrival of a child alters virtually every aspect of family life, in positive and, sometimes, negative ways.

Traditionally, it was assumed that for many couples, marital satisfaction takes a dive (Figley, 1973; Tucker & Aron, 1993). Before the birth of children, spouses are able to focus their attention on each other. They are able to respond to one another's needs, and they see their partners, as well as themselves, as autonomous individuals.

The birth of a child brings about a dramatic shift in the roles spouses must play. They are suddenly placed in new roles—"mother" and "father"—and these new positions may overwhelm their ability to respond in their older, although continuing, roles of "wife" and "husband." Consequently, for many couples, the strains accompanying the birth of a child produce the lowest level of marital satisfaction of any point in their marriage. This is particularly true for women, who tend to be more dissatisfied than men with their marriages after the arrival of children. The most likely reason for this gender difference is that wives typically experience a greater increase in their responsibilities than husbands do (Glenn & Weaver, 1990; Levy-Shiff, 1994).

On the other hand, recent evidence suggests that not all couples experience a decrease in marital satisfaction upon the birth of a child. According to work by John Gottman and colleagues (Shapiro, Gottman, & Carrère, 2000), marital satisfaction can stay steady, and actually rise, with the birth of a child. They identified three factors that permitted couples to successfully weather the increased stress that follows the birth of a child:

▶ Working to build fondness and affection towards one's partner

Parenthood expands the roles of both husbands and wives into that of fathers and mothers, a process that can have profound effects on couples' relationships.

▶ Remaining aware of events in one's spouse's life, and responding to those events

▶ Considering problems as controllable and solvable.

In particular, those couples who were well satisfied with their marriages as newlyweds were more likely to continue to be satisfied as they raised their children. Couples who harbor realistic expectations regarding the extent of childrearing effort and other household responsibilities they face when children are born also tend to be more satisfied after they become parents.

In short, having children can well lead to greater marital satisfaction—at least for couples who are already satisfied with their marriage. For marriages in which satisfaction is low, having children may make a bad situation worse (Hackel & Ruble, 1992; Shapiro, Gottman, & Carrère, 2000).

How do lesbian and gay households compare to heterosexual households? To answer the question, we first need to consider some characteristics of gay and lesbian couples without children. According to studies comparing gay, lesbian, and heterosexual couples, labor tends to be divided more evenly in homosexual households than in heterosexual households. Each partner in a homosexual relationship is more likely to carry out approximately the same number of different chores, compared with heterosexual partners. Furthermore, gay and lesbian couples cling more strongly to the ideal of an egalitarian

"If Heather has two mommies, and each of them has two brothers, and one of those brothers has another man for a 'roommate,' how many uncles does Heather have?"

allocation of household work than heterosexual couples do (Kurdek, 1993; Patterson, 1992, 1994; Parks, 1998).

However, as with heterosexual couples, the arrival of a child (usually through adoption or artificial insemination) changes the dynamics of household life considerably in homosexual couples. As in heterosexual unions, a specialization of roles develops. According to recent research on lesbian mothers, for instance, childrearing tends to fall more to one member of the couple, while the other spends more time in paid employment. Although both partners usually say they share household tasks and decision-making equally, biological mothers are more involved in child care. Conversely, the nonbiological mother in the couple is more likely to report spending greater time in paid employment (Patterson, 1995).

In short, research appears to indicate that the evolution of homosexual couples when children arrive is more similar to that of heterosexual couples than dissimilar, particularly in the increased role specialization occasioned by the requirements of child care. Of course, such research does not answer the question of what the consequences are for children being raised by homosexual parents. Most research suggests that children raised in households in which the parents are homosexual show no differences in terms of eventual adjustment from those raised in heterosexual households. Although they may face greater challenges from a society in which the roots of prejudice against homosexuality are deep, children who have two Moms or two Dads ultimately seem to fare well (Patterson & Redding, 1996; Tasker & Golombok, 1997).

Review and Rethink

REVIEW

- Cohabitation is an increasingly popular option for young adults, but most still choose marriage.
- Divorce is prevalent in the United States, particularly within the first 10 years of marriage.
- Couples overwhelmingly desire to produce children, although the availability of contraception and changes in women's roles in the workplace have combined to decrease average family size.
- Children bring pressures to both heterosexual and homosexual relationships, causing changes in focus, roles, and responsibilities.

RETHINK

- In what ways do you think cognitive changes in early adulthood (e.g., the emergence of postformal thought and practical intelligence) affect how young adults deal with questions of marriage, divorce, and childrearing?
- Why do you think society has established such a powerful norm in favor of marriage? What effects might such a norm have on a person who prefers to remain single?

Work: Choosing and Embarking on a Career

Why did I decide that I wanted to be a lawyer? The answer is a bit embarrassing. When I got to my senior year of college, I began to worry about what I was going to do when I graduated. My parents were asking, with increasing frequency, what kind of work I was thinking about, and I felt the pressure rising with each phone call from home. So I began to think seriously about the problem. At the time, the O. J. Simpson trial was in the news all the time, and it got me to thinking about what it might be like to be an attorney. I had always been fascinated by L.A. Law when it had been on television, and I could envision myself in one of those big corner offices with a view of the city. For these reasons, and just about none other, I decided to take the law boards and apply to law school.

For almost all of us, early adulthood is a period of decisions with lifelong implications. One of the most critical is choosing a career path. The choice we make goes well beyond determining how much money we will earn; it also relates to our status, our sense of self-worth, and the contribution that we will make in life. In sum, decisions about work go to the very core of a young adult's identity.

Identity During Young Adulthood: The Role of Work

According to psychiatrist George Vaillant, young adulthood is marked by a stage of development called career consolidation. During **career consolidation,** a stage that begins between the ages of 20 and 40, young adults become centered on their careers. Based on a comprehensive longitudinal study of a large group of male graduates of Harvard, begun when they were freshmen in the 1930s, Vaillant found a general pattern of psychological development (Vaillant, 1977; Vaillant & Vaillant, 1990).

In their early 20s, the men tended to be influenced by their parents' authority. But in their late 20s and early 30s, they started to act with greater autonomy. They married and began to have and raise children. At the same time, they started and began to focus on their careers—the period of career consolidation.

Based on his data, Vaillant drew a relatively uninspiring portrait of people in the career consolidation stage. The participants in his study worked very hard because they were working their way up the corporate ladder. They tended to be rule-followers who sought to conform to the norms of their professions. Rather than showing the independence and questioning that they had displayed earlier, while still in college, they threw themselves unquestioningly into their work.

Vaillant argues that work played such an important role in the lives of the men he studied that the career consolidation stage should be seen as an addition to Erikson's intimacy-versus-isolation stage of psychosocial identity. In Vaillant's view, career concerns come to supplant the focus on intimacy, and the career consolidation stage marks a bridge between Erikson's intimacy-versus-isolation stage and Erikson's next period, that of generativity versus stagnation. (Generativity refers to an individual's contribution to society, as we discuss in Chapter 16.)

However, the reaction to Vaillant's viewpoint has been mixed. Critics point out, for instance, that Vaillant's sample, although relatively large, comprised a highly restricted, unusually bright group of people, all of them men. It is hard to know how generalizable the results are. Furthermore, societal norms have changed considerably since the time the study was begun in the late 1930s, and people's views of the importance of work may have shifted. Finally, the lack of women in the sample and the fact that there have been major changes in the role of work in *women's* lives make Vaillant's conclusions even less generalizable.

Still, it is hard to argue about the importance of work in most people's lives, and current research suggests that it makes up a significant part of both men's and women's identity—if for no other reason than that many people spend more time working than they do on any other activity (Deaux et al., 1995). We turn now to how people decide what careers to follow—and the implications of that decision.

Picking an Occupation: Choosing Life's Work

Some people know from childhood that they want to be physicians or firefighters or to go into business, and they follow invariant paths toward their goals. For others, the choice of a career is very much a matter of chance, of turning to the want ads and seeing what's available. Many of us fall somewhere between these two depictions.

Ginzberg's Career Choice Theory. According to Eli Ginzberg (1972), people typically move through a series of stages in choosing a career. The first stage is the **fantasy period,** which

career consolidation a stage that is entered between the ages of 20 and 40, when young adults become centered on their careers

fantasy period according to Ginzberg, the period, lasting until about age 11, when career choices are made, and discarded, without regard to skills, abilities, or available job opportunities

According to one theory, people move through a series of life stages in choosing a career. The first stage is the fantasy period, which lasts until a person is around 11 years old.

lasts until a person is around 11. During the fantasy period, career choices are made, and discarded, without regard to skills, abilities, or available job opportunities. Instead, choices are made solely on the basis of what sounds appealing. Thus, a child may decide she wants to be a veterinarian—despite the fact that she is allergic to dogs and cats.

People begin to take practical considerations into account during the tentative period. During the **tentative period,** which spans adolescence, people begin to think in pragmatic terms about the requirements of various jobs and how their own abilities might fit with them. They also consider their personal values and goals, exploring how well a particular occupation might satisfy them.

Finally, in early adulthood, people enter the realistic period. In the **realistic period,** young adults explore specific career options either through actual experience on the job or through training for a profession. After initially exploring what they might do, people begin to narrow their choices to a few alternative careers and eventually make a commitment to a particular one.

Although Ginzberg's theory makes sense, critics have charged that it oversimplifies the process of choosing a career. Because Ginzberg's research was based on subjects from middle socioeconomic levels, it may overstate the choices and options available to people in lower socioeconomic levels. Furthermore, the ages associated with the various stages may be too rigid. For instance, a person who does not attend college but begins to work immediately after high school graduation is likely to be making serious career decisions at a much earlier point than a person who attends college. In addition, economic shifts have caused many people to change careers at different points in their adult lives.

Holland's Personality Type Theory.   Other theories of career choice emphasize how an individual's personality affects decisions about a career. According to John Holland, for instance, certain personality types match particularly well with certain careers. If the correspondence between personality and career is good, people will enjoy their careers more and be more likely to stay in them; but if the match is poor, they will be unhappy and more likely to shift into other careers (Holland, 1973, 1987; Gottfredson & Holland, 1990).

According to Holland, six personality types are important in career choice:

- Realistic. These people are down-to-earth, practical problem-solvers, and physically strong, but their social skills are mediocre. They make good farmers, laborers, and truck drivers.

- Intellectual. Intellectual types are oriented toward the theoretical and abstract. Although not particularly good with people, they are well suited to careers in math and science.

- Social. The traits associated with the social personality type are related to verbal skills and interpersonal relations. Social types are good at working with people, and consequently make good salespersons, teachers, and counselors.

- Conventional. Conventional individuals prefer highly structured tasks. They make good clerks, secretaries, and bank tellers.

- Enterprising. These individuals are risk-takers and take-charge types. They are good leaders and may be particularly effective as managers or politicians.

- Artistic. Artistic types use art to express themselves, and they often prefer the world of art to interactions with people. They are best suited to occupations involving art.

Although Holland's enumeration of personality types is sensible, it suffers from a central flaw: Not everyone fits neatly into particular personality types. Furthermore, there

---

tentative period   the second stage of Ginzberg's theory, which spans adolescence, when people begin to think in pragmatic terms about the requirements of various jobs and how their own abilities might fit with them

realistic period   the third stage of Ginzberg's theory, which occurs in early adulthood, when people begin to explore specific career options, either through actual experience on the job or through training for a profession, and then narrow their choices and make a commitment

are certainly exceptions to the typology, with jobs being held by people who don't have the particular personality that Holland would predict. Still, the basic notions of the theory have been validated, and they form the foundation of several of the "job quizzes" that people can take to see what occupations they might especially enjoy (Randahl, 1991).

Gender and Career Choices: Women's Work

WANTED: Full-time employee for small family firm. DUTIES: Including but not limited to general cleaning, cooking, gardening, laundry, ironing and mending, purchasing, bookkeeping and money management. Child care may also be required. HOURS: Avg. 55/wk but standby duty required 24 hours/day, 7 days/wk. Extra workload on holidays. SALARY AND BENEFITS: No salary, but food, clothing, and shelter provided at employer's discretion; job security and benefits depend on continued good will of employer. No vacation. No retirement plan. No opportunities for advancement. REQUIREMENTS: No previous experience necessary, can learn on the job. Only women need apply. (Unger & Crawford, 1992, p. 446)

A generation ago, many women entering early adulthood assumed that this admittedly exaggerated job description matched the work for which they were best suited and to which they aspired: housewife. Even those women who sought work outside the home were relegated to certain professions. For instance, until the 1960s, employment ads in newspapers throughout the United States were almost always divided into two sections: "Help Wanted: Male" and "Help Wanted: Female." The men's job listings encompassed such professions as police officer, construction worker, and legal counsel; the women's listings were for secretaries, teachers, cashiers, and librarians.

The breakdown of jobs deemed appropriate for men and women reflected society's traditional view of what the two genders were best suited for. Traditionally, women were considered most appropriate for **communal professions,** occupations associated with relationships. In contrast, men were perceived as best suited for agentic professions. **Agentic professions** are associated with getting things accomplished. It is probably no coincidence that communal professions typically have lower status and pay than agentic professions (Eagly & Steffen, 1984, 1986; Hattery, 2000).

Although discrimination based on gender is far less blatant today than it was several decades ago—it is now illegal, for instance, to advertise a position specifically for a man or a woman—remnants of traditional gender role prejudice persist (Pratto et al., 1997). As we discussed in Chapter 13, women are less likely to be found in traditionally male-dominated professions such as engineering and computer programming. As shown in Figure 14-12, in 97 percent of the occupations for which data have been collected, women's weekly earnings are less than men's. In fact, women in many professions earn significantly less than men in identical jobs (U.S. Bureau of Labor, Women's Bureau, 1998; U.S. Bureau of the Census, 2001).

Despite status and pay that are often lower than men's, more women are working outside the home than ever before. Between 1950 and 1990, the percent of the female population (aged 16 and over) in the U.S. labor force increased from around 35 percent to nearly 60 percent, and women today make up around 55 percent of the labor force, a figure comparable to their presence in the general population. Almost all women expect to earn a living, and almost all do at some point in their lives. Furthermore, in about one-half of U.S. households, women earn about as much as their husbands (Lewin, 1995).

Furthermore, opportunities for women are in many ways considerably greater than they were in earlier years. Women are more likely to be physicians, lawyers, insurance agents, and bus drivers than they were in the past. However, within specific job categories,

cw

communal professions occupations that are associated with relationships

agentic professions occupations that are associated with getting things accomplished

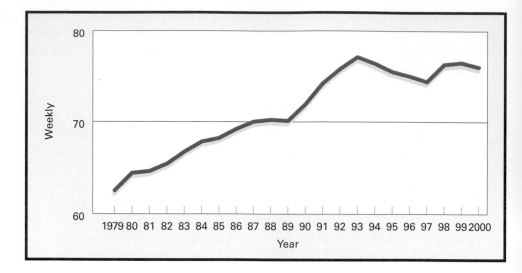

Figure 14-12 **The Gender–Wage Gap**

Women's weekly earnings as a percent of men's has increased since 1979, but still is only a bit more than 75% and has remained steady over the past three years.

(*Source:* U.S. Bureau of the Census, 2001.)

there are still notable gender differences. For example, female bus drivers are more apt to have part-time school bus routes, while men hold better-paying full-time routes in cities. Similarly, female pharmacists are more likely to work in hospitals, while men work in higher-paying jobs in retail stores (England & McCreary, 1987; Unger & Crawford, 1996).

In the same way, women (and minorities, too) in high-status, visible professional roles may hit what has come to be called the *glass ceiling.* The glass ceiling is an invisible barrier within an organization that, because of discrimination, prevents individuals from being promoted beyond a certain level. It operates subtly, and often the people responsible for keeping the glass ceiling in place are unaware of how their actions perpetuate discrimination against women and minorities.

Why Do People Work? More Than Earning a Living

This may seem an easy question to answer: People work to earn a living. Yet the reality is different, for young adults express many reasons for seeking a job.

extrinsic motivation motivation that drives people to obtain tangible rewards, such as money and prestige

intrinsic motivation motivation that causes people to work for their own enjoyment, not for the rewards work may bring

status the evaluation of a role or person by other relevant members of a group or society

Intrinsic and Extrinsic Motivation. Certainly, people work in order to obtain various concrete rewards, or out of extrinsic motivation. **Extrinsic motivation** drives people to obtain tangible rewards, such as money and prestige (Singer, Stacey, & Lange, 1993).

On the other hand, people also work for factors relating to intrinsic motivation. **Intrinsic motivation** causes people to work for their own enjoyment, not for the rewards work may bring. For instance, people in many Western societies tend to subscribe to the *Puritan work ethic,* the notion that work is important in and of itself. According to this view, working is a meaningful act that brings psychological and (at least in the traditional view) even spiritual well-being and satisfaction.

Work also brings a sense of personal identity. Consider, for instance, what people say about themselves when they first meet someone. After mentioning their names and where they live, they very typically tell what they do for a living. What people do is a large part of who they are.

Work also may be a central element in people's social lives. Because so much time is spent in work settings, work can be a source of young adults' friends and social activities. Social relationships forged at work may spill over into other parts of people's lives. In addition, there are often social obligations—dinner with the boss, or the annual seasonal party in December—that are related to work.

Finally, the kind of work that people do is a factor in determining status. **Status** is the evaluation by society of the role a person plays. Various jobs are associated with a cer-

Extrinsic motivation drives people to obtain tangible rewards, such as money, prestige, or a fancy automobile. How would another culture view extrinsic motivation? Intrinsic motivation?

tain status, as indicated in Table 14-4. For instance, physicians and college teachers are near the top of the status hierarchy, while ushers and shoe shiners fall to the bottom.

Satisfaction on the Job. The status associated with particular jobs affects people's satisfaction with their work. As might be expected, the higher the status of the job, the more satisfied people tend to be (Yankelovich, 1974). Furthermore, the status of the job of the major wage-earner can affect the status of the other members of the family.

Table 14-4

STATUS HIERARCHY OF VARIOUS PROFESSIONS

Occupation	Score	Occupation	Score
Physician	82	Bank teller	50
College teacher	78	Electrician	49
Lawyer	76	Police officer	48
Dentist	74	Insurance agent	47
Bank officer	72	Secretary	46
Airline pilot	70	Air traffic controller	43
Clergy	69	Mail carrier	42
Sociologist	66	Owner of a farm	41
Secondary school teacher	63	Restaurant manager	39
Registered nurse	62	Automobile mechanic	37
Pharmacist	61	Baker	34
Elementary school teacher	60	Salesclerk	29
Accountant	56	Gas station attendant	22
Painter	56	Waiter and waitress	20
Librarian	55	Laundry operator	18
Actor	55	Garbage collector	17
Funeral director	52	Janitor	16
Athlete	51	Usher	15
Reporter	51	Shoe shiner	12

(*Source:* NORC, 1990.)

Of course, status isn't everything: Worker satisfaction depends on a number of factors, not the least of which is the nature of the job itself (Ting, 1997). For example, consider the plight of Patricia Alford, who worked at the Equitable Life Assurance Company. Her job consisted of entering data into a computer 9 hours each day except for two 15-minute breaks and an hour off for lunch. She never knew how much she was earning, because her salary depended on how many insurance claims she entered into the computer each day. The pay standards were so complicated that her pay varied from $217 to $400 a week, providing her with a weekly surprise at paycheck time (Booth, 1987).

Other people who work at computers are monitored on a minute-by-minute basis; supervisors can consistently see how many keystrokes they are entering. In some firms in which workers use the telephone for sales or to take customer orders, their conversations are monitored by supervisors. Workers' Internet use and email are also monitored or restricted by a large number of employers. Not surprisingly, such forms of management produce worker dissatisfaction.

On the other hand, job satisfaction increases when workers have input into the nature of their jobs. Furthermore, variety is the spice of job life: People enjoy jobs that require several different types of skills more than those that require only a minimal number. Finally, the more influence employees have over others, either directly as supervisors or more informally, the greater their job satisfaction (Katzell & Guzzo, 1983; Steers & Porter, 1991).

The Informed Consumer of Development
Choosing a Career

One of the greatest challenges people face in early adulthood is making a decision that will have lifelong implications: the choice of a career. Although there is no single correct choice—most people can be happy in any of several different jobs—the options can be daunting. Here are some guidelines for at least starting to come to grips with the question of what occupational path to follow.

▶ Systematically evaluate a variety of choices. Libraries contain a wealth of information about potential career paths, and most colleges and universities have career centers that can provide occupational data and guidance.

▶ Know yourself. Evaluate your strengths and weaknesses, perhaps by completing a questionnaire at a college career center that can provide insight into your interests, skills, and values.

▶ Create a "balance sheet," listing the potential gains and losses that you will incur from a particular profession. First list the gains and losses that you will experience directly, and then list gains and losses for others, such as family members.

Next, write down your projected self-approval or self-disapproval from the potential career. Finally, write down the projected social approval or disapproval you are likely to receive from others. By systematically evaluating a set of potential careers according to each of these criteria, you will be in a better position to compare different possibilities.

▶ "Try out" different careers through paid or unpaid internships. By seeing a job first-hand, interns are able to get a better sense of what an occupation is truly like.

▶ Remember that if you make a mistake, you can change careers. In fact, people today increasingly change careers in early adulthood and even beyond. No one should feel locked into a decision made earlier in life. As we have seen throughout this book, people develop substantially over the course of their lives.

▶ It is reasonable to expect that shifting values, interests, abilities, and life circumstances might make a different career more appropriate later in life than the one chosen during early adulthood.

Review and Rethink

- Choosing a career is an important step in early adulthood, so important that George Vaillant considers career consolidation a developmental stage on a par with Erikson's intimacy-versus-isolation stage.
- According to Eli Ginzberg, people pass through three stages in considering careers: the fantasy period, the tentative period, and the realistic period.
- Other theories of career choice, such as John Holland's, attempt to match personality types to suitable careers.
- Gender stereotypes are changing, but women still experience subtle prejudice in career choices, roles, and wages.

- People work because of both extrinsic and intrinsic motivation factors.

RETHINK

- If Vaillant's study were performed today on women, in what ways do you think the results would be similar to or different from those of the original study?
- How does the division of jobs into communal and agentic relate to traditional views of male–female differences?

Looking Back

▶ *How do young adults form loving relationships, and how does love change over time?*

- Young adults face Erikson's intimacy-versus-isolation stage, with those who resolve this conflict able to develop intimate relationships with others.

- According to stimulus-value-role theory, relationships pass through the consideration of surface characteristics, values, and finally the roles played by the participants.

- Passionate love is characterized by intense physiological arousal, intimacy, and caring, while companionate love is characterized by respect, admiration, and affection.

- Psychologist Robert Sternberg suggests that three components of love (intimacy, passion, and decision/commitment) combine to form eight types of love, through which a relationship can dynamically evolve.

▶ *How do people choose spouses, and what makes relationships work and cease working?*

- Although in Western cultures love tends to be the most important factor in selecting a partner, other cultures emphasize other factors.

- According to filtering models, people filter potential partners initially for attractiveness and then for compatibility, generally conforming to the principle of homogamy and the marriage gradient.

- Gay men and lesbian women generally seek the same qualities in relationships as heterosexual men and women: attachment, caring, intimacy, affection, and respect.

- In young adulthood, while cohabitation is popular, marriage remains the most attractive option. The median age of first marriage is rising for both men and women.

- Divorce is prevalent in the United States, affecting nearly half of all marriages.

▶ *How does the arrival of children affect a relationship?*

- More than 90 percent of married couples have at least one child, but the size of the average family has decreased, due partly to birth control and partly to the changing roles of women in the workforce.

- Children bring pressures to any marriage, shifting the focus of the marriage partners, changing their roles, and increasing their responsibilities. Gay and lesbian couples with children experience similar changes in their relationships.

▶ *Why is choosing a career such an important issue for young adults, and what factors influence the choice of a career?*

- According to George Vaillant, career consolidation is a developmental stage in which young adults are involved in defining their careers and themselves.

■ A model developed by Eli Ginzberg suggests that people typically move through three stages in choosing a career: the fantasy period of youth, the tentative period of adolescence, and the realistic period of young adulthood.

■ Other theories attempt to match people's personality types with suitable careers. This sort of research underlies most career-related inventories and measures used in career counseling.

■ Gender role prejudice and stereotyping remain a problem in the workplace and in preparing for and selecting careers. Women tend to be pressured into certain occupations and out of others, and they earn less money for the same work.

▶ *Why do people work, and what elements of a job bring satisfaction?*

■ People are motivated to work by both extrinsic factors, such as the need for money and prestige, and intrinsic factors, such as the enjoyment of work and its personal importance. Work helps determine a person's identity, social life, and status.

■ Job satisfaction is the result of many factors, including the nature and status of one's job, the amount of input one has into its nature, the variety of one's responsibilities, and the influence one has over others.

E P I L O G U E

In this chapter we looked at some of the most significant issues of early adulthood: forming relationships, falling in love and potentially getting married, and finding a career. We explored the factors that lead to loving relationships, the considerations that affect the choice of whether and whom to marry, and the characteristics of good—and not so good—marriages. We also discussed factors that people consider in choosing careers and the features of careers that make them satisfying.

Before we move on to middle adulthood in the next chapter, recall the prologue that began this chapter, about the marriage of Grace Tsai and Richard Tsuyuki. In light of your knowledge of relationships and careers in early adulthood, answer the following questions.

1. How does this couple's insistence on performing three ceremonies underline the cultural importance of marriage?

2. How does the concept of homogamy relate to Grace and Richard's marriage? In what ways are the two individuals similar, and in what ways are they different?

3. Assuming that Grace and Richard are typical, what steps did their courtship probably follow?

4. What advice would you give Grace and Richard about keeping their marriage happy once their baby arrives?

Key Terms and Concepts

social clock (p. 488)
intimacy-versus-isolation stage (p. 489)
stimulus-value-role (SVR) theory (p. 491)
passionate (or romantic) love (p. 492)
companionate love (p. 492)
labeling theory of passionate love (p. 492)
intimacy component (p. 493)
passion component (p. 493)

decision/commitment component (p. 493)
homogamy (p. 496)
marriage gradient (p. 497)
cohabitation (p. 500)
career consolidation (p. 509)
fantasy period (p. 509)
tentative period (p. 510)

realistic period (p. 510)
communal professions (p. 511)
agentic professions (p. 511)
extrinsic motivation (p. 512)
intrinsic motivation (p. 512)
status (p. 512)

Bridges

Our examination of early adulthood revealed a period less dramatic than others in terms of evident growth, but no less important or less characterized by change and development. We witnessed individuals at the peak of health and the height of their intellectual powers entering a period of their lives in which true independence is the challenge and the goal.

We saw that in this period individuals typically making the big choices that will have the deepest and longest-lasting impact on their lives: the choice of friends, partners in love and marriage, whether to have children and how many children to have, and what career to pursue. We noted that an individual's background, and maybe even genetic inheritance, affects his or her choices during this period. For example, adults' romantic attachments seem to mirror the attachments they had to their caregivers when they were babies.

Even the smaller, day-to-day choices that people make as young adults can have lasting effect. We saw, for example, that some physical capabilities can begin to decline already during this stage of life. But we also saw that healthy lifestyle choices, such as a commitment to exercise and a healthy diet, along with avoiding tobacco and other drugs, can slow these changes. We'll see, as we continue our discussion, that the importance of lifestyle choices only grows as adults age.

In Part Seven we will continue our journey as we see how the decisions made and challenges met in young adulthood are consolidated, extended, and sometimes reversed in middle adulthood.

517

1 2 3 4 5 6 7 8 9 10

OUTLINE

PHYSICAL DEVELOPMENT

*From Research to Practice:
Pregnancy After Menopause:
What Are the Ethics?*

HEALTH

*Developmental Diversity: Individual
Variation in Health: Ethnic and
Gender Differences*

COGNITIVE DEVELOPMENT

*Becoming an Informed Consumer
of Development: Effective
Strategies for Remembering*

MIDDLE ADULTHOOD

Physical and Cognitive Development in Middle Adulthood

PROLOGUE: LIFE OFF THE GRIDIRON

Pro football star Brian Sipes during his playing years.

I thought I got better as I got older. I found out that wasn't the case in a real hurry last year. After going twelve years in professional football and twelve years before that in amateur football without ever having surgery performed on me, the last two seasons of my career I went under the knife three times. It happened very quickly and without warning, and I began to ask myself, "Is this age? Is this what's happening?" Because up until that moment, I'd never realized that I was getting older. . . .

In professional football I was constantly asked, "What are you gonna do when it's over? What are you gonna do when it's over?" And I used to manufacture answers, because I thought that these people need to know that the quarterback of their football team has something else going. He's not just a dumb jock. In reality, I've always wanted to walk out of football and have the curtain come down and say, "Okay, here's life. Here's life without football. It's been sports all my life, and here's a new life." What a great opportunity! How many people have a chance to do that? (Kotre & Hall, 1990, pp. 257, 259–260)

L o o k i n g   A h e a d

For former professional football player Brian Sipes, entry into middle adulthood occurred with unusual clarity. As he witnessed his body's gradual inability to keep up with the rigors of professional athletics, Sipes faced the challenge of transition that all of us, at some point during middle adulthood, encounter.

In this chapter, we consider both physical and cognitive development during middle adulthood, roughly defined as the period from 40 to 60 years of age. For many people, it is a period when the passage of time becomes increasingly conspicuous as their bodies and, to some extent, their cognitive abilities begin to change in unwelcome ways, perhaps for the first time in their lives. Yet at the same time, as we see in this and the following chapter, it is a period when many individuals are at the height of their capabilities, when they are engaged in the process of shaping their lives as never before.

We begin the chapter by considering physical development. We consider changes in height, weight, and strength, and discuss the subtle decline in acuity of the senses. We also look at the role of sexuality in middle adulthood.

Next, we consider health. We examine both wellness and illness during middle age, and pay particular attention to two of the major health problems of the period, heart disease and cancer.

Finally, the chapter focuses on cognitive development in middle age. We ask whether intelligence declines during the period, and we consider the difficulty of answering the question fully. We also look at memory, examining the ways in which memory capabilities change during middle adulthood.

After reading this chapter, you will be able to answer these questions:

▶ **What sorts of physical changes affect people in middle adulthood?**

▶ **What changes in sexuality do middle-aged men and women experience?**

▶ **Is middle adulthood a time of health or disease for men and women?**

▶ **What sorts of people are likely to get coronary heart disease?**

▶ **What causes cancer, and what tools are available to diagnose and treat it?**

▶ **What happens to a person's intelligence in middle adulthood?**

▶ **How does aging affect memory, and how can memory be improved?**

Physical Development

It crept up gradually on Sharon Boker-Tov. Soon after reaching the age of 40, she noticed that it took her a bit longer to bounce back from minor illnesses such as colds and the flu. Then she became conscious of changes in her eyesight: She needed more light to read fine print, and she had to adjust how far she held newspapers from her face in order to read them easily. Finally, she couldn't help but notice that the strands of gray hair on her head, which had begun to appear gradually in her late 20s, were becoming a virtual forest.

Physical Transitions: The Gradual Change in the Body's Capabilities

Middle adulthood is the time when most people first become aware of the gradual changes in their bodies that mark the aging process. As we saw in Chapter 13, some of the aging that people experience is the result of senescence, or naturally occurring declines related to age.

Other changes, however, are the result of lifestyle choices, such as diet, exercise, smoking, and alcohol or drug use. As we'll see throughout this chapter, people's lifestyle choices can have a major impact on their physical, and even cognitive, fitness during middle age.

Of course, physical changes occur throughout the entire life span. Yet these changes take on new significance during middle adulthood, particularly in Western cultures that place a high value on youthful appearance. For many people, the psychological significance of such changes far exceeds the relatively minor and gradual changes that they are experiencing.

People's reactions to the physical changes of middle adulthood depend in part on their self-concepts. For those whose self-image is tied closely to their physical attributes—such as highly athletic men and women or those who are physically quite attractive—middle adulthood can be particularly difficult. This is one of the realities that former football player Brian Sipes, whom we met in the prologue, is working hard to come to terms with. On the other hand, because most people's views of themselves are not so closely tied to physical attributes, middle-aged adults generally report no less satisfaction with their body images than younger adults (Berscheid, Walster, & Bohrnstedt, 1973).

Still, physical appearance plays an important role in determining how people view themselves, as well as how they are viewed by others. This is particularly the case for women in Western cultures, who face especially strong societal pressures to retain a youthful appearance. In fact, society applies a double standard to men and women in terms of appearance: Whereas older women tend to be viewed in unflattering terms, aging men are more frequently perceived as displaying a maturity that enhances their stature (Nowak, 1977; Katchadourian, 1987; Harris, 1994).

Height, Weight, and Strength: The Benchmarks of Change

Most people reach their maximum height during their 20s and remain relatively close to that height until around age 55. At that point, people begin a "settling" process in which the bones attached to the spinal column become less dense. Although the loss of height is very slow, ultimately women average a 2-inch decline and men a 1-inch decline over the rest of the life span (Rossman, 1977).

Women are more prone to a decline in height because of their greater risk of osteoporosis. **Osteoporosis,** a condition in which the bones become brittle, fragile, and thin, is often brought about by a lack of calcium in the diet. As we discuss further in Chapter 17, osteoporosis, although it has a genetic component, is one of the aspects of aging that can be affected by a person's lifestyle choices. Women—and men, for that matter—can reduce the risk of osteoporosis by maintaining a diet high in calcium (which is found in milk, yogurt, cheese, and other dairy products) and by exercising regularly (Prince et al., 1991).

Both men and women continue to gain weight during middle adulthood, and the amount of body fat likewise tends to grow in the average person. "Middle-age spread" is a visible symptom of this problem, as even those who have been relatively slim all their lives may begin to put on weight. Because height is not increasing, and actually may be declining, these weight and body fat gains lead to an increase in the numbers of people who become obese.

The typical gains in weight that occur during middle adulthood are hardly preordained by genetic factors. Lifestyle choices play a major role. In fact, people who maintain an exercise program during middle age tend to avoid obesity, as do individuals living in cultures where the typical life is more active and less sedentary than that of many Western cultures.

Changes in height and weight are also accompanied by declines in strength. Throughout middle adulthood, strength gradually decreases, particularly in the back and

cw

osteoporosis a condition in which the bones become brittle, fragile, and thin, often brought about by a lack of calcium in the diet

Beginning at around the age of 40, visual acuity, the ability to discern fine spatial detail, begins to drop. Most people begin to suffer from presbyopia, a decline in near vision.

presbyopia a nearly universal change in eyesight during middle adulthood that results in some loss of near vision

glaucoma a condition in which pressure in the fluid of the eye increases, either because the fluid cannot drain properly or because too much fluid is produced

leg muscles. By the time they are 60, people have lost, on average, about 10 percent of their maximum strength. Still, such a loss in strength is relatively minor, and most people are easily able to compensate for it (Troll, 1985; Spence, 1989). Again, lifestyle choices can make a difference. People who exercise regularly are likely to feel stronger and to have an easier time compensating for any losses than those who are sedentary.

The Senses: The Sights and Sounds of Middle Age

Sharon Boker-Tov's experiences with needing extra light to read and holding the newspaper a little farther away are so common that bifocals have become almost a stereotypical emblem of middle age. Like Sharon, most people notice unmistakable changes in the sensitivity, not only of their eyes, but also of other sense organs. Although all the organs seem to shift at roughly the same rate, the changes are particularly noticeable in vision and hearing.

Vision. Starting at around age 40, *visual acuity*—the ability to discern fine spatial detail in both close and distant objects—begins to decline (see Figure 15-1). One major reason is a change in the shape and elasticity of the eye's lens, which makes it harder to focus images sharply onto the retina. Furthermore, the lens becomes less transparent, which reduces the amount of light that passes through the eye (Pitts, 1982; DiGiovanna, 1994).

A nearly universal change in eyesight during middle adulthood is the loss of near vision, called **presbyopia.** Even people who have never needed glasses or contact lenses find themselves holding reading matter at an increasing distance from their eyes in order to bring it into focus. Eventually, they need reading glasses. For those who were previously nearsighted, presbyopia may require bifocals or two sets of glasses (Kline & Schieber, 1985).

Other changes in vision also begin in middle adulthood. For instance, declines occur in depth perception, distance perception, and the ability to view the world in three dimensions. Furthermore, adaptation to darkness, which allows people to see in dimly lit environments, also declines. Such visual reductions may make it more difficult to climb stairs or to navigate around a dark room (Artal et al., 1993; Spear, 1993).

Although changes in vision are most often brought about by the gradual processes of normal aging, in some cases disease is involved. One of the most frequent causes of eye problems is glaucoma, which may, if left untreated, ultimately produce blindness. **Glaucoma** occurs when pressure in the fluid of the eye increases, either because the fluid cannot drain properly or because too much is produced. Around 1 to 2 percent of people over

Figure 15-1 **The Decline of Visual Acuity**

Beginning around the age of 40, the ability to discern fine detail begins to drop.

(Adapted from Pitts, 1982.)

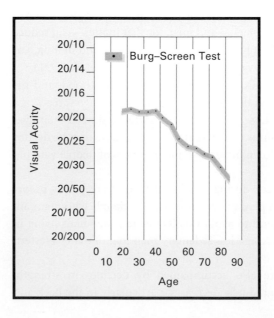

the age of 40 are afflicted by the disorder, and African Americans are particularly susceptible (Wilson, 1989).

Initially, the increased pressure in the eye may constrict the neurons involved in peripheral vision and lead to tunnel vision. Ultimately, the pressure can become so high that
all nerve cells are constricted, which causes complete blindness. Fortunately, glaucoma can
be treated if it is detected early enough. Medication can reduce the pressure in the eye, as
can surgery to restore normal drainage of eye fluid.

Hearing. Like vision, hearing undergoes a gradual decline in acuity starting in middle adulthood. For the most part, however, the changes are less evident than those involving eyesight.

Some of the hearing losses of middle adulthood result from environmental factors.
For instance, people whose professions keep them near loud noises—such as airplane mechanics and construction workers—are more apt to suffer debilitating and permanent
hearing loss.

However, many changes are simply related to aging. For instance, age brings a loss
of *hair cells* in the inner ear, which transmit neural messages to the brain when vibrations
bend them. Furthermore, the eardrum becomes less elastic with age, further reducing
sound sensitivity (Olsho, Harkins, & Lenhardt, 1985).

The primary sort of loss is for sounds of high frequency, a problem called **presbycusis.** About 12 percent of people between 45 and 65 suffer from presbycusis. There is also a
gender difference: Men are more prone to hearing loss than women, starting at around
age 55. People who have hearing difficulties may also have problems due to diminished
sound localization, the process by which the origin of a sound is identified (Schneider,
1997). This is true because sound localization depends on comparing the discrepancy in
sound perceived by the two ears, and hearing loss may not affect both ears equally (DiGiovanna, 1994).

presbycusis loss of the ability to hear
sounds of high frequency

Despite these physiological changes, declines in sensitivity to sounds do not
markedly affect most people in middle adulthood. Most people are able to compensate for
the losses that do occur relatively easily— by asking people to speak up, turning up the volume of a television set, or paying greater attention to what others are saying.

Reaction Time: Not-so-slowing Down

One common concern about aging is the notion that people begin to slow down once they
reach middle adulthood. How valid is such a worry?

In most cases, not very. Although there is an increase in reaction time (meaning that
it takes longer to react to a stimulus), usually the increase is fairly mild and hardly noticeable (Nobuyuki, 1997). For instance, reaction time on simple tasks increases by around 20
percent from age 20 to 60. More complex tasks, which require the coordination of various
skills—such as driving a car—show less of an increase. Still, it takes a bit more time for
drivers to move the foot from the gas pedal to the brake when they are faced with an emergency situation. Increases in reaction time are largely produced by changes in the speed
with which the nervous system processes nerve impulses (DiGiovanna, 1994). The injuries
sustained by Brian Sipes, the football player quoted in the chapter prologue, may have
been related to slower reaction times.

On the other hand, because complex skills are often heavily practiced, or rehearsed,
major drops in actual performance are generally avoided. In fact, middle-aged drivers
tend to have fewer accidents than younger ones. Why would this be? Part of the reason is
that older drivers tend to be more careful and to take fewer risks than younger ones. Much
of the cause for their better performance, however, is older drivers' greater amount of
practice in the skill. In the case of reaction time, then, practice may indeed make perfect
(Birren, Woods, & Williams, 1980; Siegler & Costa, 1985).

Part of the reason that middle-aged drivers tend to have fewer accidents than younger ones is that drivers tend to be more careful and take fewer risks, as well as having a greater amount of experience in the skill.

Can slowing down be slowed down? In many cases, the answer is yes. Lifestyle choices once more come into play. Specifically, involvement in an active exercise program retards the effects of aging, producing several important outcomes (see Figure 15-2). "Use it or lose it" is an aphorism with which developmental psychologists would agree.

Sex in Middle Adulthood: The Ongoing Sexuality of Middle Age

Common wisdom, particularly among those under 40, suggests that sex is an activity of youth and early adulthood that generally fades away with age.

Figure 15-2 **The Benefits of Exercise**

There are many benefits from maintaining a high level of physical activity throughout life.

(*Source:* DiGiovanna, 1994.)

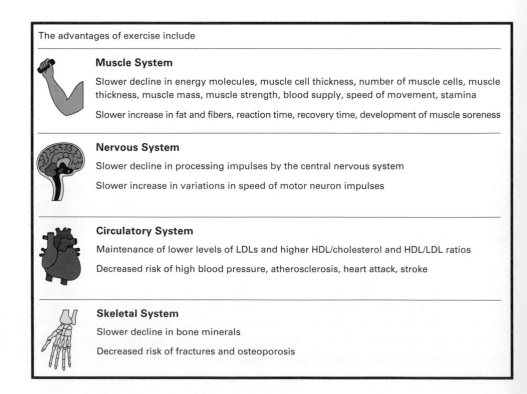

The advantages of exercise include

Muscle System

Slower decline in energy molecules, muscle cell thickness, number of muscle cells, muscle thickness, muscle mass, muscle strength, blood supply, speed of movement, stamina

Slower increase in fat and fibers, reaction time, recovery time, development of muscle soreness

Nervous System

Slower decline in processing impulses by the central nervous system

Slower increase in variations in speed of motor neuron impulses

Circulatory System

Maintenance of lower levels of LDLs and higher HDL/cholesterol and HDL/LDL ratios

Decreased risk of high blood pressure, atherosclerosis, heart attack, stroke

Skeletal System

Slower decline in bone minerals

Decreased risk of fractures and osteoporosis

Most middle-aged people would tell a different story. Although it is true that the frequency of sexual intercourse declines with age (see Figure 15-3), sexual activities of various sorts remain a vital part of most middle-aged adults' lives. About half of men and women age 45 to 59 report having sexual intercourse about once a week or more (Michael et al., 1994; Shaw, 1994; Budd, 1999).

In fact, many people experience a kind of sexual enjoyment and freedom that they lacked during their earlier lives. With their children grown and away from home, middle-aged married couples may have more time to engage in uninterrupted sexual activities. Furthermore, if the female partner has passed through menopause, they may be liberated from the fear of pregnancy and may no longer need to employ birth control techniques (Sherwin, 1991; Lamont, 1997).

Both men and women can face some challenges to their sexuality during middle adulthood. For instance, a man typically needs more time to achieve an erection, and it takes longer after an orgasm to have another. The volume of fluid that is ejaculated declines. Finally, the production of *testosterone*, the male sex hormone, declines with age (Hyde, 1994).

Sexuality continues to be a vital part of most couples' lives in middle adulthood.

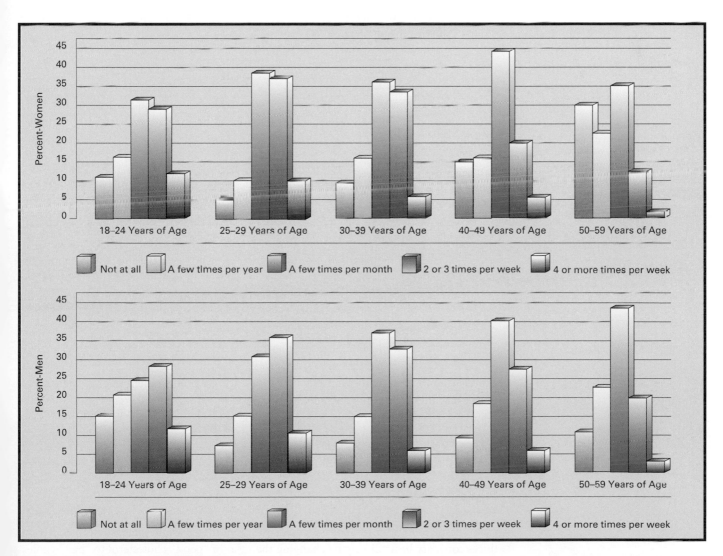

Figure 15-3 **Frequency of Sexual Intercourse**

As people age, the frequency of sexual intercourse declines.

(Adapted from Michael et al., 1994.)

While women in some cultures look forward to menopause with dread, Mayan women have no notion of hot flashes, and they generally look forward to the end of their childbearing years.

cw

female climacteric the period that marks the transition from being able to bear children to being unable to do so

menopause the cessation of menstruation

For women, the walls of the vagina become thinner and less elastic. The vagina shrinks and its entrance becomes compressed, potentially making intercourse painful. Most women, however, seem to be able to avoid this problem. In fact, in one national survey, women in their 50s were less likely than younger women to report pain during intercourse (Laumann, Paik, & Rosen, 1999).

The Female Climacteric and Menopause. Starting at around age 45, women enter a period known as the climacteric that lasts for some 15 to 20 years. The **female climacteric** marks the transition from being able to bear children to being unable to do so.

The most notable sign of the female climacteric is menopause. **Menopause** is the cessation of menstruation. For most women, menstrual periods begin to occur irregularly and less frequently during a 2-year period starting at around age 47 or 48, although this process may begin as early as age 40 or as late as age 60. After a year goes by without a menstrual period, menopause is said to have occurred.

Menopause is important for several reasons. For one thing, it marks the point at which a traditional pregnancy is no longer possible (although, as we will discuss later, eggs implanted in a postmenopausal woman can produce a pregnancy). In addition, the production of estrogen and progesterone, the female sex hormones, begins to drop, producing a variety of hormone-related age changes (Hyde, 1994; DiGiovanna, 1994; Wise, Krajnak, & Kashon, 1996).

The changes in hormone production may produce a variety of symptoms, although the degree to which a woman experiences them varies significantly. One of the best-known and most prevalent symptoms is "hot flashes," in which a woman senses an unexpected feeling of heat from the waist up. A woman may get red and begin to sweat when a hot flash occurs. Afterwards, she may feel chilled. Some women experience hot flashes several times a day; others, not at all.

Other symptoms may mark menopause. For instance, headaches, feelings of dizziness, heart palpitations, and aching joints are relatively common during the period. However, such complaints are far from universal. In one survey, for instance, only half of the women reported experiencing hot flashes. In general, only about one-tenth of all women experience severe distress during menopause. And many—perhaps as many as half—have no significant symptoms at all (McKinlay & Jeffreys, 1974; Hyde, 1994).

For many women, symptoms of menopause may begin a decade before menopause actually occurs. *Perimenopause* is the period beginning around 10 years prior to menopause when hormone production begins to change. Perimenopause is marked by sometimes radical fluctuations in hormone production, resulting in some of the same symptoms that are found in menopause.

Symptoms of menopause also differ by race. Compared with Caucasians, Japanese and Chinese women generally report fewer overall symptoms. African American women experience more hot flashes and night sweats, and Hispanic women report a higher level of several other symptoms, including heart pounding and vaginal dryness. Although the reason for these differences is unclear, it may be related to systematic racial differences in hormonal levels (Deutsch, 2000; Avis et al., 2001).

Hormone Replacement Therapy (HRT). For women who do experience significant distress during menopause, one treatment is to take substitute hormones. In *hormone replacement therapy* (HRT), estrogen and progesterone are administered to alleviate the worst of the symptoms experienced by menopausal women. HRT reduces a variety of problems, such as hot flashes and loss of skin elasticity. In addition, there is some suggestion that HRT reduces coronary heart disease by changing the ratio of "good" cholesterol to "bad" cholesterol. HRT also decreases the thinning of the bones related to osteoporosis, which, as discussed, becomes a problem for many people in late adulthood. Furthermore, some studies show that the risk of stroke declines, and there may be a decreased risk of colon cancer. Estrogen may even slow the mental deterioration found in people suffering from Alzheimer's disease. Finally, increased estrogen may lead to a greater sex drive (Stahl, 1997; Morrison & Tweedy, 2000; Sarrel, 2000).

But what is also clear is that hormone replacement therapy may have a dark side, and that the positive results may come at a price that some women may find too high to pay. The most daunting problem is research suggesting that the risk of breast cancer rises with estrogen use. For instance, some studies, such as one involving 70,000 nurses, indicate that there is a greater risk of breast cancer in women taking replacement hormones. Other risks include abnormal blood clots, cancer of the uterine lining, and an increase in benign fibroid tumors in the uterus (Colditz et al., 1995).

These uncertainties make the routine use of HRT controversial, and many women face difficult choices in deciding whether the benefits of the treatment outweigh the potential dangers (Swan, 1997; Sheffield, 1997; Kittell & Mansfield, 2000).

The Psychological Consequences of Menopause. Does menopause produce psychological problems? Traditionally, experts, as well as the general population, believed that menopause was linked directly to depression, anxiety, crying spells, lack of concentration, and irritability. In fact, some researchers estimated that as many as 10 percent of menopausal women suffered severe depression. It was assumed that physiological changes in menopausal women's bodies brought about such disagreeable outcomes (Schmidt & Rubinow, 1991).

Today, however, most researchers view menopause from a different perspective. It now seems more reasonable to regard menopause as a normal part of aging that does not, by itself, produce psychological symptoms. Certainly, some women experience psychological difficulties, but they do at other points in life as well (Dell & Stewart, 2000; Matthews et al., 2000).

Furthermore, research indicates that the expectations women have about menopause make a significant difference in their experience of it. Women who expect to have difficulties during menopause are more likely to attribute every physical symptom and emotional swing to it. On the other hand, those with more positive attitudes toward menopause may be less apt to attribute physical sensations to menopausal physiological changes. A woman's attribution of physical symptoms, then, affects her perception of the rigors of menopause—and ultimately her actual experience of the period (Leiblum, 1990; Dell & Stewart, 2000).

The nature and extent of menopausal symptoms also differ according to a woman's ethnic and cultural background. In fact, women in non-Western cultures often have vastly different menopausal experiences from those in Western cultures. For instance, women of high castes in India report few symptoms of menopause. In fact, they look forward to menopause because being postmenopausal produces several social advantages, such as an end to taboos associated with menstruation and a perception of increased wisdom due to age. Similarly, Mayan women have no notion of hot flashes, and they generally look forward to the end of their childbearing years (Flint, 1989; Beck, 1992; Avis et al., 2001).

Although by definition menopause marks the end of natural childbearing years, new technologies have begun to change that limitation. For one thing, research with animals has shown that it is possible to alter genes that retard aging associated with reproduction—at least in mice. Furthermore, as we discuss in the *From Research to Practice* box, it is now possible for postmenopausal women to deliver children—a prospect that raises considerable ethical questions (Morita & Tilly, 2000).

The Male Climacteric. Do men experience the equivalent of menopause? Not really: Because they have never weathered anything akin to menstruation, they would have difficulty experiencing its discontinuation. On the other hand, men experience some changes during middle age that are collectively referred to as the male climacteric. The **male climacteric** is the period of physical and psychological change in the reproductive system that occurs during late middle age.

male climacteric the period of physical and psychological change relating to the male reproductive system that occurs during late middle age

From Research to Practice
Pregnancy After Menopause: What Are the Ethics?

Sophia sits in a booth in a dimly lighted Chinese restaurant, reluctantly talking about the details of her life. She is beyond tired, as she has been for several months, and as she is likely to be for several more. The weathered brown of her hair, the weary brown shadows under her eyes, even the muted brown of her maternity dress over her very pregnant lap—all of these things somehow magnify her exhaustion.

It is a Friday night, and she did not leave the office until nearly 6:30, working until the last moment, tying up the loose ends in her high-powered job. On Monday, she will have a Caesarean section, which she scheduled months ago because her doctor did not think her body could withstand the rigors of labor....

Sophia is having her first baby. She is 51 years old. (Belkin, 1997, p. 35)

Sophia, a woman in her early 50s, with her newborn infant.

Sophia is not the oldest woman to become pregnant—not by a long shot. That record belongs to a 63-year-old woman who gave birth to a healthy baby girl in 1997 (Kolata, 1997).

Despite earlier thinking that the environment of the uterus of postmenopausal women was inhospitable to eggs even from much younger women, the successful pregnancy of the 63-year-old suggests that any woman, no matter her age, may be able to become pregnant with a donated egg, providing the donor is young enough. If the sperm used to fertilize the egg is from the husband or partner of the woman seeking to be pregnant, then the baby will receive half its genetic endowment from him.

The possibility of older women becoming pregnant raises both medical and ethical questions. One is whether the pregnancy will be too physically taxing for the woman, and whether—once the baby is born—she will have the energy to care for the child adequately. Furthermore, there is the issue of who should determine if an older woman should be implanted with a younger egg: the woman, physicians, medical boards, or legislatures (Klock & Greenfeld, 2000).

The source of an egg also raises issues, particularly when younger women are paid a fee for providing an egg. Furthermore, it is unclear whether the woman who donates the egg should have any legal or financial responsibility or ties to the child. Because the technology that allows for pregnancies in older women is so new, none of these questions has been sorted out (Belkin, 1997; Kolata, 1997; Abu-Heija, Jallad, & Abukteish, 2000).

Because the changes happen gradually, it is hard to pinpoint the exact period of the male climacteric. For instance, despite progressive declines in the production of testosterone and sperm, men continue to be able to father children throughout middle age. Furthermore, it is no easier in men than in women to attribute psychological symptoms to subtle physiological changes.

One physical change that does occur quite frequently is enlargement of the *prostate gland.* By the age of 40, around 10 percent of men have enlarged prostates, and the percentage increases to half of all men by the age of 80. Enlargement of the prostate produces problems with urination, including difficulty starting urination or a need to urinate frequently at night.

Although the physical changes associated with middle age are unequivocal, whether they are the direct cause of any particular psychological symptoms or changes is unclear. Men, like women, clearly undergo psychological development during middle adulthood, but the extent to which psychological changes—which we discuss more in the next chapter—are associated with changes in reproductive or other physical capabilities remains an open question.

Review and Rethink

REVIEW

- People in middle adulthood experience gradual changes in physical characteristics and appearance.
- The acuity of the senses, particularly vision and hearing, and speed of reaction decline slightly during middle age.
- Sexuality in middle adulthood changes slightly, but middle-aged couples, freed from concerns about children, can often progress to a new level of intimacy and enjoyment.
- Physiological changes relating to sexuality occur in both men and women. Both the female climacteric, which includes menopause, and the male climacteric seem to have physical and perhaps psychological symptoms.

- Controversy attends the emerging medical areas of estrogen replacement therapy and induced pregnancy in older women through implantation of the eggs of much younger women.

RETHINK

- What cultural factors in the United States might contribute to a woman's negative experience of menopause? How?
- Would you rather fly on an airplane with a middle-aged pilot or a young one? Why?

Health

It was an average exercise session for Jerome El-Neel. After the alarm went off at 5:30 a.m., he climbed onto his exercise bike and began vigorously peddling, trying to maintain, and exceed, his average speed of 14 miles per hour. Stationed in front of the television set, he used the remote control to tune to the morning business news. Occasionally glancing up at the television, he began reading a report he had not finished the night before, swearing under his breath at some of the poor sales figures he was finding in the report. By the time he had completed exercising a half-hour later, he had gotten through the report, had managed to sign a few letters his secretary had typed for him, and had even left two voice-mail messages for some colleagues.

Most of us would be ready to head back to bed after such a packed half-hour. For Jerome El-Neel, however, it was routine: He consistently tried to accomplish several activities at the same time. Jerome thought of such behavior as efficient. Developmental psychologists might view it in another light, however: as symptomatic of a style of behavior that makes Jerome a likely candidate for coronary heart disease.

Although most people are relatively healthy in middle adulthood, they also become increasingly susceptible to a variety of health-related concerns. We will consider some of the typical health problems of middle age, focusing in particular on coronary heart disease and cancer.

Wellness and Illness: The Ups and Downs of Middle Adulthood

Health concerns become increasingly important to people during middle adulthood. In fact, surveys asking adults what they worry about show health—as well as safety and money—to be an issue of concern. For instance, more than half of adults surveyed say they are either "afraid" or "very afraid" of having cancer (see Figure 15-4).

For most people, however, middle age is a period of health. According to census figures, the vast majority of middle-aged adults report no chronic health difficulties and face no limitations on their activities.

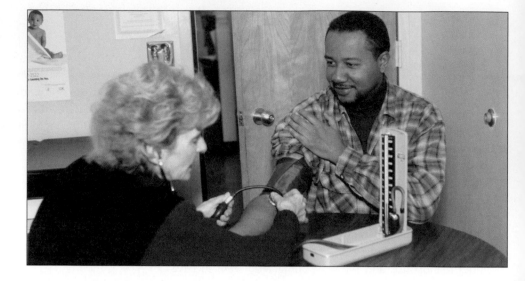

Hypertension, or high blood pressure, is sometimes referred to as the silent killer since it has no symptoms and often leads to heart disease. Regular monitoring is important.

In fact, in some ways people are better off, healthwise, in middle adulthood than in earlier periods of life. People between the ages of 45 and 65 are less likely than younger adults to experience infections, allergies, respiratory diseases, and digestive problems. They may contract fewer of these diseases now because they may have already experienced them and built up immunities during younger adulthood (Sterns, Barrett, & Alexander, 1985).

On the other hand, during middle adulthood people can become particularly susceptible to chronic diseases. Arthritis typically begins after the age of 40, and diabetes is most likely to occur in people between the ages of 50 and 60, particularly if they are overweight. Hypertension (high blood pressure) is one of the most frequent chronic disorders found in middle age. Sometimes called the "silent killer" because it is symptomless, hypertension, if left untreated, greatly increases the risk of strokes and heart disease. For such

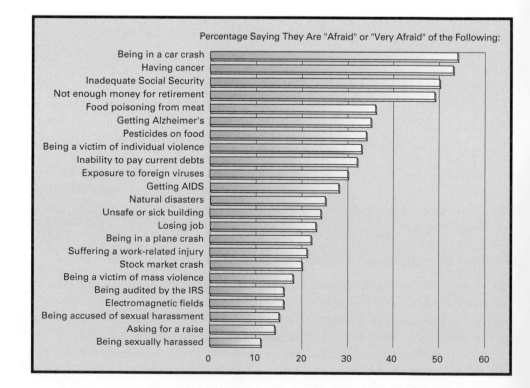

Figure 15-4 **Worries of Adulthood**

As people enter middle adulthood, health and safety concerns become increasingly important, followed by financial worries.

(*Source: USA Weekend*, Aug. 22–24, 1997.)

Table 15-1

SELECTED PREVENTION AND SCREENING RECOMMENDATIONS FOR OLDER ADULTS

Blood pressure	Every exam, at least every 1–2 years
Mammogram	The American Cancer Society recommends annually after age 40, although other groups say every other year is OK.* From 70 to 85, screening can be every 1–3 years if a doctor deems it appropriate. Screening is unnecessary after that.
Physician breast exam	Annually after age 40
Pelvic exam/Pap	Every 2–3 years after 3 negative annual exams. Can decrease or discontinue after age 65–69.
Prostate/PSA	The American Cancer Society recommends annually after age 50, but other groups say this is only an option that should be discussed between patient and physician.
Cholesterol	Adults every 5 years; less certain for elderly
Rectal exam	Annually after age 40
Fecal occult blood test	Annually after age 50
Sigmoidoscopy	Every 3–5 years after age 50
Thyroid function	Prudent for elderly, especially women
Electrocardiogram	Periodically from 40s onward
Tetanus vaccine	Booster every 10 years

*This controversy is addressed later in this chapter.
(*Source:* Adapted from *Journal of the American Geriatrics Society,* March 1997.)

reasons, a variety of preventive and diagnostic medical tests are routinely recommended for adults during middle adulthood (see Table 15-1).

As a result of this greater susceptibility to disease, the death rate among middle-aged individuals is higher than it is in earlier periods of life. Still, death remains a rare occurrence: Statistically, only three out of every hundred 40-year-olds would be expected to die before the age of 50, and eight out of every hundred 50-year-olds would be expected to die before the age of 60. Furthermore, the death rate for people between 40 and 60 has declined dramatically over the past 50 years. For instance, the death rate now stands at just half of what it was in the 1940s (Smedley & Syme, 2000).

Developmental Diversity

Individual Variation in Health: Ethnic and Gender Differences

Masked by the overall figures describing the health of middle-aged adults are vast individual differences. While most people are relatively healthy, some are beset by a variety of ailments. Part of the cause is genetic. For instance, hypertension often runs in families.

Some of the causes of poor health are more insidious, however; they are related to social and environmental factors. For instance, the death rate for middle-aged African Americans in the United States is twice the rate for Caucasians. Why should this be true?

The answer seems to lie not in race per se, but in socioeconomic status (SES) differences between majority and minority groups. For instance, when whites and African Amer-

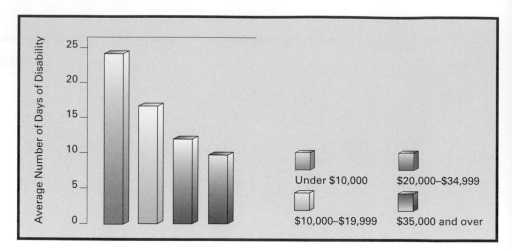

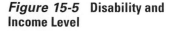

Figure 15-5 **Disability and Income Level**

Workers living in poverty are more likely to become disabled than those with higher income levels. Why?

(*Source:* U.S. Bureau of the Census, 1990b.)

icans of the same SES level are compared, the death rate for African Americans actually falls below that of whites. Furthermore, the lower a family's income, the more likely it is that a member will experience a disabling illness. Similarly, people living in lower SES households are more apt to work in occupations that are dangerous, such as mining or construction work. Ultimately, then, a higher incidence of accidents and poor health, and ultimately a higher death rate, are linked to lower levels of income (U.S. Bureau of the Census, 1990b; Fingerhut & Makuc, 1992; Dahl & Birkelund, 1997; see Figure 15-5).

Gender, like ethnicity and race, also makes a difference in health. Even though women's overall mortality rate is lower than men's—a trend that holds true from the time of infancy—the incidence of illness among middle-aged women is higher than it is among men.

Why are women more apt to be sick, but at the same time less likely to die? The answer is that women are more likely to experience minor, short-term illness and chronic, but non-life-threatening diseases, and men are more apt to experience more serious illnesses. Furthermore, the rate of cigarette smoking is lower among women than men, which reduces their susceptibility to cancer and heart disease; women drink less alcohol than men, which reduces the risk of cirrhosis of the liver and auto accidents; and they work at less dangerous jobs (Verbrugge, 1985; Schaefer & Lamm, 1992).

One might reason that the higher incidence of illness in women would be accompanied by greater medical research targeted toward the types of disorders from which they

The discrepancies in the lives of people of higher and lower socioeconomic status are associated with differences in death rates between the two groups.

suffer. However, this is not the case. In fact, the vast majority of medical research money is aimed at preventing life-threatening diseases faced mostly by men rather than at chronic conditions that may cause disability and suffering, but not necessarily death. Even when research is carried out on diseases that strike both men and women, much of it has focused on men as subjects rather than on women. Although this bias is specifically being addressed in initiatives announced by the U.S. National Institutes of Health, the historical pattern has been one of gender discrimination by the traditionally male-dominated research community (Shumaker & Smith, 1994). ☐

Stress in Middle Adulthood

Stress continues to have a significant impact on health during middle adulthood, as it did in young adulthood, although the nature of what is stressful may have changed. For example, parents may experience stress over their adolescent children's potential drug use rather than worry about whether their toddlers are ready to be weaned.

Despite the change in the events that trigger stress, the results are similar. According to *psychoneuroimmunologists,* who study the relationship between the brain, the immune system, and psychological factors, stress produces three main consequences, summarized in Figure 15-6. First, stress has direct physiological outcomes, ranging from increased blood pressure to hormonal activity. Second, stress leads people to engage in unhealthy behaviors, such as cutting back on sleep, smoking, drinking, or taking other drugs. Finally, stress has indirect effects on health-related behavior. People under a lot of stress may be less likely to seek out good medical care or to comply with medical advice (Baum, 1994; Suinn, 2001). All of these can lead to serious health conditions. One of the most serious conditions affecting middle-aged adults is heart disease.

The A's and B's of Coronary Heart Disease: Linking Health and Personality

More men die in middle age from diseases relating to the heart and circulatory system than from any other cause. Women are less vulnerable, as we'll see, but they are not immune. Each year such diseases kill around 200,000 people under the age of 65, and they are responsible for more loss of work and disability days due to hospitalization than any other cause (American Heart Association, 1988).

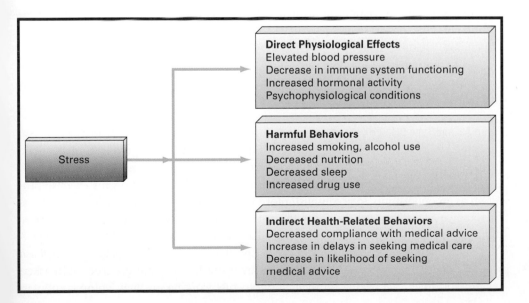

Figure 15-6 The Consequences of Stress

Stress produces three major consequences: direct physiological effects, harmful behaviors, and indirect health-related behaviors.

(Adapted from Baum, 1994.)

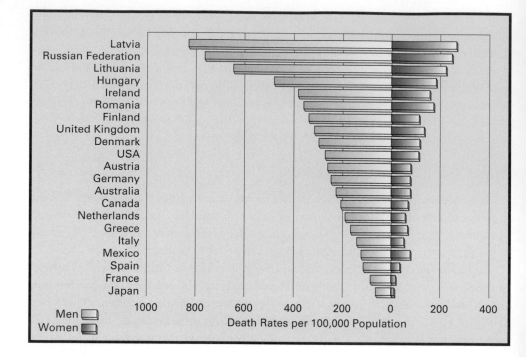

***Figure 15-7*   Death from Heart Disease Worldwide**

The risk of dying from cardiovascular disease differs significantly depending on the country in which one lives. What cultural or environmental factors might help to explain this fact?

(*Source:* World Health Organization, 1999.)

Risk Factors for Heart Disease.   Although heart and circulatory diseases are a major problem, they are not an equal threat for all people—some people have a much lower risk than others. For instance, the death rate in some countries, such as Japan, is only a quarter the rate in the United States. A few other countries have a considerably higher death rate (see Figure 15-7). Why should this be true?

The answer is that both genetic and experiential characteristics are involved. Some people seem genetically predisposed to develop heart disease. If a person's parents suffered from it, the likelihood is greater that she or he will too. Similarly, sex and age are risk factors: Men are more likely to suffer from heart disease than women, and the risk rises as people age.

However, environment and lifestyle choices are also linked to several risk factors. For instance, cigarette smoking, a diet high in fats and cholesterol, and a relative lack of physical exercise all increase the likelihood of heart disease. Such factors may explain country-to-country variations in incidence. For example, the relatively low death rate attributable to heart disease in Japan may be due to differences in diet: The typical diet in Japan is much lower in fat than the typical diet in the United States.

In addition, increasing evidence suggests that psychological factors may be associated with heart disease. In particular, a set of personality characteristics appears to be related to the development of coronary heart disease—the Type A behavior pattern.

Type A's and Type B's.   For a certain proportion of adults, waiting patiently in a long line at the grocery store is a near impossibility. Sitting in their cars at a long red light makes them seethe. And an encounter with a slow, inept clerk at a retail store turns them furious.

People like this—and those similar to Jerome El-Neel, who uses his exercise program as an opportunity to accomplish more work—have a set of personality characteristics known as the Type A behavior pattern. The **Type A behavior pattern** is characterized by competitiveness, impatience, and a tendency toward frustration and hostility. Type A people are driven to accomplish more than others, and they engage in *polyphasic activities*—multiple activities carried out simultaneously. They are the true multitaskers whom you might see talking on their phones while working on their laptop computers

Type A behavior pattern behavior characterized by competitiveness, impatience, and a tendency toward frustration and hostility

while riding the commuter train—and eating breakfast. They are easily angered and become both verbally and nonverbally hostile if they are prevented from reaching a goal they seek to accomplish.

In contrast to the Type A behavior pattern, many people have virtually the opposite characteristics in a pattern known as the Type B behavior pattern. The **Type B behavior pattern** is characterized by noncompetitiveness, patience, and a lack of aggression. In contrast to Type A's, Type B's experience little sense of time urgency, and they are rarely hostile.

Although most adults are not purely Type A's or Type B's, they do tend to fall predominantly into one of the two categories. Which category they fall into is of some importance, because a great deal of research suggests that the distinction is related to the incidence of coronary heart disease. For example, Type A men have twice the rate of coronary heart disease, a greater number of fatal heart attacks, and five times as many heart problems overall as Type B men (Rosenman, 1990; Strube, 1990).

Although it is not certain why Type A behavior increases the risk of heart problems, the most likely explanation is that when Type A's are in stressful situations, they become excessively aroused physiologically. Heart rate and blood pressure rise, and production of the hormones epinephrine and norepinephrine increases. Undue wear and tear on the body's circulatory system ultimately produces coronary heart disease (Matthews, 1982; Suarez & Williams, 1992; Blascovich & Katkin, 1993; Lyness, 1993; Raikkonen et al., 1995; Sundin et al., 1995).

On the other hand, the links between Type A behavior and coronary heart disease are correlational, and no definitive evidence has been found that Type A behavior *causes* coronary heart disease. In fact, some evidence suggests that only certain components of Type A behavior are most involved in producing disease, and not the entire constellation of behaviors associated with the pattern. For instance, there is a growing consensus that the hostility and anger related to the Type A behavior pattern may be the central link to coronary heart disease (Lassner, Matthews, & Stoney, 1994; Jiang et al., 1996; Whiteman et al., 2000).

Although the relationship between at least some Type A behaviors and heart disease is clear, this does not mean that all middle-aged adults who can be characterized as Type A's are destined to suffer from coronary heart disease. For one thing, almost all the research conducted to date has focused on men, primarily because the incidence of coronary heart disease is much higher for males than for females. Consequently, until more research involving women is done, the findings that link the Type A behavior pattern to coronary heart disease apply primarily to men.

Furthermore, Type A men can learn to behave differently. For example, several programs have taught Type A's to slow their pace, to be less competitive, and in general to be more patient and less hostile with others. Such training is linked to declines in the risk of coronary heart disease (Cottreaux, 1993; Thoresen & Bracke, 1997).

In addition to being characterized as competitive, people with Type A personalities also tend to engage in polyphasic activies, or doing a number of things at once. Does a Type A personality deal with stress differently than a Type B personality?

Type B behavior pattern behavior characterized by noncompetitiveness, patience, and a lack of aggression

The Threat of Cancer

Brenda surveyed the crowd as she stood in line to start the annual "Race for the Cure," a running and walking event that raised funds to fight breast cancer. It was a sobering sight. She spotted a group of five women, all wearing the bright pink shirts that marked them as cancer survivors. Several other racers had photos of loved ones who had lost their battles with the disease pinned to their jerseys.

Few diseases are as frightening as cancer, and many middle-aged individuals view a cancer diagnosis as a death sentence. Although the reality is different—many forms of cancer respond quite well to medical treatment, and 40 percent of people diagnosed with the disease are still alive 5 years later—the disease raises many fears. And there is no denying that cancer is the second-leading cause of death in the United States (Smedley & Syme, 2000).

The precise trigger for cancer is still not known, but the process by which cancer spreads is straightforward. For some reason, particular cells in the body begin to multiply uncontrollably and rapidly. As they increase in number, these cells form tumors. If left unimpeded, they draw nutrients from healthy cells and body tissue. Eventually, they destroy the body's ability to function properly.

Like heart disease, cancer is associated with a variety of risk factors, some genetic and others environmental. Some kinds of cancer have clear genetic components. For example, a family history of breast cancer—which is the most common cause of cancer death among women—raises the risk for a woman.

However, several environmental and behavioral factors are also related to the risk of cancer. For instance, poor nutrition, smoking, alcohol use, exposure to sunlight, exposure to radiation, and particular occupational hazards (such as exposure to certain chemicals or asbestos) are all known to increase the chances of developing cancer.

After a diagnosis of cancer, several forms of treatment are possible, depending on the type of cancer. One treatment is *radiation therapy,* in which the tumor is the target of radiation designed to destroy it. Patients undergoing *chemotherapy* ingest controlled doses of toxic substances meant, in essence, to poison the tumor. Finally, surgery may be used to remove the tumor (and often the surrounding tissue). The exact form of treatment is a function of how far the cancer has spread throughout a patient's body when it is first identified.

Because early cancer detection improves a patient's chances, diagnostic techniques that help identify the first signs of cancer are of great importance. This is particularly true during middle adulthood, when the risk of contracting certain kinds of cancer increases. Consequently, physicians urge that women routinely examine their breasts and men regularly check their testicles for signs of cancer. Furthermore, mammograms, which provide internal scans of women's breasts, also help identify early-stage cancer. However, the question of when women should begin to routinely have the procedure is highly controversial.

Routine Mammograms: At What Age Should Women Start?   Consider the following case:

> *I found the lump in February 1990. Buried deep in my left breast, it was rock-hard, the size of a BB, and it hurt. I wondered if it might be cancer. Like blue eyes and a sense of humor, the disease runs in my family. But not breast cancer. And not me. I was too young. OK. I had recently turned 40, but I was healthy. I worked out three times a week and I was almost a vegetarian. My next physical was only a month away. I'd have it checked then. (Driedger, 1994, p. 46)*

For Sharon Driedger, feeling healthy, exercising, and eating a good diet was not enough: She did have cancer. But she was also lucky. After aggressive treatment with radiation therapy, she stands a good chance of a full recovery.

In part, her good luck is a result of the early identification of her cancer. Statistically, the earlier breast cancer is diagnosed, the better a woman's chances of survival. But just how to accomplish early identification has become a major source of contention in the medical field, pitting one medical expert against another, and sometimes patients against physicians. Specifically, the controversy surrounds the use of mammograms, pictures produced by a process called mammography, in which a weak X-ray is used to examine breast tissue.

Mammograms are among the best means of detecting breast cancer in its earliest stages. The technique allows physicians to identify tumors while they are still very small. Patients have time for treatment before the tumor grows and spreads to other parts of the body. Mammograms have the potential for saving many lives, and nearly all medical professionals suggest that women over the age of 50 routinely obtain them.

Women should routinely examine their breasts for signs of breast cancer.

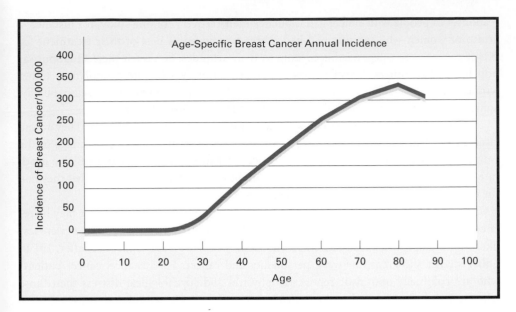

Figure 15-8 Age and the Risk of Breast Cancer

Starting around the age of 30, the risk of breast cancer becomes increasingly likely, as these annual incidence figures show.

(Adapted from Kaplan, Sallis & Patterson, 1993.)

But what about younger women? As shown in Figure 15-8, the risk of breast cancer does not suddenly rise at the age of 50. Instead, it begins to grow at around the age of 30 and then becomes increasingly more likely. For instance, the incidence of breast cancer in women between the ages of 40 and 44 is 112 out of 100,000, while the number almost doubles between the ages of 50 and 54 (Sondik, 1988). What, then, is so special about the age of 50?

To many observers, nothing much. According to them, women should have routine mammograms beginning at age 40, and some advocate the routine use of mammography even earlier. However, others dispute this advice because of two considerations. First, there is the problem of *false positives,* instances in which the test suggests something is wrong when in fact there is no problem. Because the breast tissue of younger women is denser than that of older women, younger women are more likely to have false positives. In fact, some estimates suggest that as many as a third of all younger women who have repeated mammograms are likely to have a false positive that necessitates further testing or a biopsy. Furthermore, the opposite problem also may occur: *false negatives,* in which a mammogram does not detect indications of cancer (Miller, 1991; Baines et al., 1997).

A second problem with routine mammograms for women under 50 is cost. The average mammogram costs $100. If the incidence of breast cancer at age 40 is 112 cases out of 100,000, this means that it will cost $10 million to detect just 112 cases. Although one can argue that even one life saved is worth any financial cost, the medical establishment, plagued with increasing costs, is unlikely to find such reasoning compelling (Kaplan, Sallis, & Patterson, 1993).

In sum, the use of mammograms raises some difficult issues involving medical, developmental, and societal considerations. It pits one medical group against another: For instance, the American Cancer Society and American Medical Association both recommend annual mammograms for women aged 40 to 49, while the American College of Physicians and National Cancer Institute do not recommend them. Whether the current recommendation that only those over 50 undergo routine mammograms will evolve remains to be seen (Taubes, 1997; Rimer et al., 2001).

Psychological Factors Relating to Cancer: Mind Over Tumor? Increasing evidence suggests that cancer is related not only to physiological causes, but to psychological factors as well (Edelman & Kidman, 1997). In particular, some research indicates that the emotional responses of people with cancer can influence their recovery. In one study, for instance, a group of women who recently had had a breast removed as part of their treatment for breast cancer were categorized according to their attitudes. Some felt their situation was hopeless, while others stoically accepted their cancer, voicing no complaints. Other women expressed a "fighting spirit," contending that they would lick the disease. Finally, some simply denied that they had cancer, refusing to accept the diagnosis.

Ten years later, the researchers looked again at the group of women. They found clear-cut evidence that initial attitude was related to survival. A larger percentage of the women who had stoically accepted their cancer or had felt hopeless had died. The death rate was much lower for those who had a "fighting spirit" or who had denied that they had the disease (Pettingale et al., 1985; see Figure 15-9).

Other studies suggest that the degree of social support people experience may be related to cancer. For example, some research finds that people with close family ties are less likely to develop cancer than those without them (Thomas, Duszynski, & Schaffer, 1979). Other studies show links between personality and cancer. For instance, cancer patients who are habitually optimistic report less physical and psychological distress than those who are less optimistic (Baltrusch, Stangel, & Tirze, 1991; Carver & Scheier, 1993; Bolger et al., 1996).

Finally, recent evidence suggests that participation in psychological therapy may give cancer patients an edge in treatment success. According to the preliminary results of a study done by psychologist David Spiegel, women in the advanced stages of breast cancer who participated in group therapy lived at least 18 months longer than those who did not participate in therapy. Furthermore, the women who participated also experienced less anxiety and pain (Spiegel et al., 1989; Spiegel, 1993, 1996).

How, exactly, might a person's psychological state become linked to his or her prognosis with cancer? One possibility is that patients who have the most positive attitudes and are involved in therapy might be more likely to adhere to intricate, complex, and often unpleasant medical treatments for cancer. Consequently, such patients are more likely to experience treatment success (Holland & Lewis, 1993).

However, there is another possibility. It may be that a positive psychological outlook benefits the body's *immune system,* the natural line of defense against disease. Ac-

Figure 15-9 **Attitude and Surviving Cancer**

Fighting spirit pays off. A woman's psychological reaction three months after her cancer operation was clearly associated with whether she was alive 10 years later. What does this suggest about potential treatment approaches?

(*Source:* Pettingale et al., 1985.)

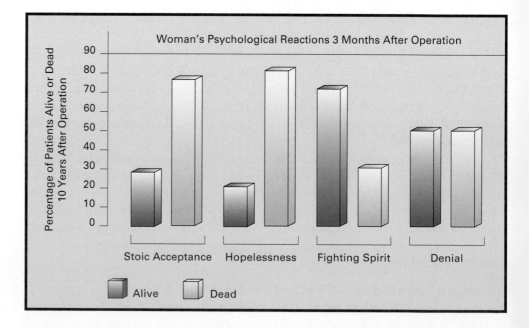

Research has found that social support and cancer support groups like this one, can help prolong life.

cording to this perspective, a positive emotional outlook bolsters the immune system, energizing the production of "killer" cells that fight the cancerous cells. In contrast, negative emotions and attitudes may impair the ability of the body's natural killer cells to fight off the cancer (Andersen, Kiecolt-Glaser, & Glaser, 1994; Seligman, 1995; Fawzey, 1994).

It is important to keep in mind that the link between attitudes and emotions, on the one hand, and cancer, on the other, is far from proven. Furthermore, we need to avoid blaming cancer patients for their cancer. It is unjustified and unfair to assume that a cancer patient would be doing better if only he or she had a more positive attitude. On the other hand, it is reasonable to suggest that psychological therapy might be warranted as a routine component of cancer treatment, even if it does nothing more than improve the patient's psychological state and raise his or her morale (Zevon & Corn, 1990; Holland & Lewis, 1993).

Review and Rethink

REVIEW

- In general, middle adulthood is a period of good health, although susceptibility to chronic diseases, such as arthritis, diabetes, and hypertension, increases.
- Heart disease is a risk for middle-aged adults. Both genetic and environmental factors contribute to heart disease, including the Type A behavior pattern.
- The incidence of cancer begins to be significant in middle adulthood.
- Therapies such as radiation therapy, chemotherapy, and surgery can successfully treat cancer, and psychological factors, such as a fighting attitude and a refusal to accept the finality of cancer, can influence survival rates.
- The issue of the age at which women should begin to have regular mammograms is controversial.

RETHINK

- Why is the incidence of disabling illness higher in lower-SES groups? Are there social policy implications to this fact?
- Does the effect of psychological attitude on cancer survival suggest that nontraditional healing techniques might have a place in cancer treatment? Why or why not?

Cognitive Development

It began innocently enough. Forty-five-year-old Bina Clingman couldn't remember whether she had mailed the letter that her husband had given her, and she wondered, in passing, whether this was a sign of aging. The very next day, her feelings were reinforced when she had to spend 20 minutes looking for a phone number that she knew she had written down on a piece of paper—somewhere. By the time she had found it, she was surprised and even a little anxious. "Am I losing my memory?" she asked herself, with both annoyance and some degree of concern.

Many people in their 40s will tell you that they feel more absentminded than they did 20 years earlier and that they harbor at least some concern about becoming less mentally able than when they were younger. Certainly, common wisdom suggests that people lose some cognitive nimbleness as they age. But how accurate is common wisdom?

Does Intelligence Decline in Adulthood?

For years, psychologists provided a clear, unwavering response when asked whether intelligence declined during adulthood. It was a response that most adults were not happy to hear: Intelligence peaks at age 18, stays fairly steady until the mid-20s, and then begins a gradual decline that continues until the end of life (Yerkes, 1923).

The Difficulties in Answering the Question. The conclusion that intelligence starts to diminish in the mid-20s was based on extensive research. In particular, *cross-sectional studies*—which test people of different ages at the same point in time—clearly showed that older subjects were more likely to score less well than younger subjects on traditional intelligence tests, of the sort we first discussed in Chapter 9.

But consider the drawbacks of cross-sectional research—in particular the possibility that it may suffer from *cohort effects.* Recall from Chapter 1 that cohort effects are influences associated with growing up at a particular historical time that affect persons of a particular age. For instance, suppose that compared to the younger people, the older people in a cross-sectional study had had less adequate educations, were exposed to less stimulation in their jobs, or were relatively less healthy. In that case, the lower IQ scores of the older group could hardly be attributed solely, or perhaps even partially, to differences in intelligence between younger and older individuals. In sum, because they do not control for cohort effects, cross-sectional studies may well *underestimate* intelligence in older subjects.

In an effort to overcome the cohort problems of cross-sectional studies, psychologists began to turn to *longitudinal studies,* in which the same people are studied periodically over a span of time. These studies began to reveal a different developmental pattern for intelligence: Adults tended to show fairly stable and even increasing intelligence test scores until they reached their mid-30s, and in some cases up to their 50s. At that point, though, scores began to decline (Bayley & Oden, 1955).

But let's step back a moment and consider the drawbacks of longitudinal studies. For instance, people who take the same intelligence test repeatedly may perform better simply because they become more familiar—and comfortable—with the testing situation. Similarly, because they have been exposed to the same test regularly over the years, they may even begin to remember some of the test items. Consequently, practice effects may account for the relatively superior performance of people on longitudinal measures of intelligence as opposed to cross-sectional measures.

Furthermore, it is difficult for researchers using longitudinal studies to keep their samples intact. Participants in a study may move away, decide they no longer want to participate, or become ill and die. In fact, as time goes on, the participants who remain in the study may represent a healthier, more stable, and more psychologically positive group of people than those who are no longer part of the sample. If this is the case, then longitudinal studies may mistakenly *overestimate* intelligence in older subjects.

Crystallized and Fluid Intelligence. The ability of developmental psychologists to draw conclusions about age-related changes in intelligence faces still more hurdles, some of which are common to both cross-sectional and longitudinal studies. For instance, many IQ tests include sections based on physical performance, such as arranging a group of blocks. Many tests also contain timed sections that are scored on the basis of how quickly a question is completed. If older people take longer on physical tasks—and remember that reaction time slows with age, as we discussed earlier in the chapter—then their poorer performance on IQ tests may be a result of physical rather than cognitive changes (Schaie, 1991; Nettlebeck & Rabbit, 1992).

To complicate the picture even further, many researchers believe that there are two kinds of intelligence: fluid intelligence and crystallized intelligence (Cattell, 1967, 1987). As we first noted in Chapter 9, **fluid intelligence** reflects information processing capabilities, reasoning, and memory. For instance, a person who is asked to arrange a series of letters according to some rule or to memorize a set of numbers uses fluid intelligence. In contrast, **crystallized intelligence** is the accumulation of information, skills, and strategies that people have learned through experience and that they can apply in problem-solving situations. Someone who is solving a crossword puzzle or attempting to identify the murderer in a mystery story is using crystallized intelligence, relying on his or her past experience as a resource.

> **fluid intelligence** reflects information-processing capabilities, reasoning, and memory
>
> **crystallized intelligence** the accumulation of information, skills, and strategies that people have learned through experience and that they can apply in problem-solving situations

Initially, researchers believed that fluid intelligence was largely determined by genetic factors, and crystallized intelligence primarily by experiential, environmental factors. However, they later abandoned this distinction, largely because they found that crystallized intelligence is determined in part by fluid intelligence. For instance, a person's ability to solve a crossword puzzle (which involves crystallized intelligence) is a result of that person's proficiency with letters and patterns (a manifestation of fluid intelligence).

When developmental psychologists looked at the two kinds of intelligence separately, they arrived at a new answer to the question of whether intelligence declines with age. Actually, they arrived at two answers: yes and no. Yes, because in general, fluid intelli-

Although he is in his 90s, orchestra leader and vibraphonist Lionel Hampton displays the accumulated skills that make up crystallized intelligence.

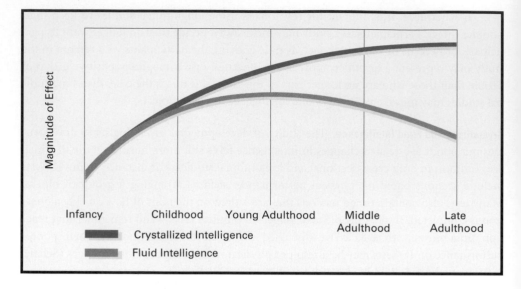

Figure 15-10 **Changes in Crystallized and Fluid Intelligence**

Although crystallized intelligence increases with age, fluid intelligence begins to decline in middle age. What are the implications for general competence in middle adulthood?

(*Source:* Schaie, 1985.)

gence does show declines with age; no, because crystallized intelligence holds steady and in some cases actually improves (Schaie, 1993; Isingrini & Vazou, 1997; Ryan, Sattler, & Lopez, 2000; see Figure 15-10).

In fact, according to developmental psychologist K. Warner Schaie (1994), who has conducted extensive longitudinal research on the course of adult intellectual development, the broad division of intelligence into the fluid and crystallized categories masks true age-related differences and developments in intelligence. He argues that researchers should instead consider many particular types of ability, such as spatial orientation, numeric ability, verbal ability, and so on.

When looked at in this way, the question of how intelligence changes in adulthood yields yet another answer, but a more specific one. Schaie finds that certain abilities, such as inductive reasoning, spatial orientation, perceptual speed, and verbal memory, start a gradual decline at around age 25 and continue to decline through old age. On the other hand, numeric and verbal abilities show a quite different pattern. For instance, numeric ability tends to increase until the mid-40s, is lower at age 60, and then stays steady throughout the rest of life. Verbal ability rises until about the start of middle adulthood, around age 40, and stays fairly steady throughout the rest of the life span (Schaie, 1994).

Reframing the Issue: What Is the Source of Competence During Middle Adulthood? It is clear that there is no simple answer to the question of whether intelligence declines during middle and later adulthood. The issue remains controversial; we will return to it when we consider older people in Chapter 17.

What is apparent is that even though overall IQ, as measured by traditional intelligence tests, drops in middle adulthood, almost all people in middle age show no apparent decline in general cognitive competence (Cunningham & Hamen, 1992). In fact, it is during the middle part of the life span that people come to hold some of the most important and powerful positions in society. How can we explain such continuing, and even growing, intellectual competence in the face of apparently ongoing declines in certain cognitive skills?

One answer comes from psychologist Timothy Salthouse (1989, 1990, 1994a), who suggests that there are four reasons why this discrepancy exists. For one thing, it is possible that typical measures of cognitive skills tap a different type of cognition than what is required to be successful in particular occupations. Recall the discussion of practical intelligence in Chapter 13, in which we found that traditional IQ tests fail to measure cognitive abilities that are related to occupational success. Perhaps we would find no discrepancy between intelligence and cognitive abilities in middle adulthood if we used measures of practical intelligence rather than traditional IQ tests to assess intelligence.

A second factor also relates to the measurement of IQ and occupational success. It is possible that the most successful middle-aged adults are not representative of middle-aged adults in general. It may be that only a small proportion of people are highly successful, and the rest, who experience only moderate or little success, may have changed occupations, retired, or become sick and died. If we look at highly successful people, then, we are examining an unrepresentative sample of individuals.

It is also conceivable that the degree of cognitive ability required for professional success is simply not that high. According to this argument, people can be quite successful professionally and still be on the decline in certain kinds of cognitive abilities. In other words, their cognitive declines are not all that important; they have brains to spare.

Finally, it may be that older people are successful because they have developed specific kinds of expertise and particular competencies. Whereas IQ tests measure reactions to novel situations, occupational success may be influenced by very specific sorts of well-practiced abilities. Consequently, although their overall intellectual skills may show a decline, middle-aged individuals may maintain and even expand the distinctive talents they need for professional accomplishment. This explanation has generated a whole area of research on expertise, as we'll see later in the chapter.

For example, developmental psychologists Paul Baltes and Margaret Baltes have studied a strategy called selective optimization. **Selective optimization** is the process by which people concentrate on particular skill areas to compensate for losses in other areas. Baltes suggests that cognitive development during middle and later adulthood is a mixture of growth and decline. As people begin to lose certain abilities due to biological deterioration, they also advance in other areas by strengthening their skills. Ultimately, they are able to compensate for their losses, and they avoid showing any practical deterioration (Perlmutter, Kaplan, & Nyquist, 1990; Staudinger, Marsiske, & Baltes, 1993; Baltes, 1987, 1993). Overall cognitive competence, then, remains quite intact.

For instance, recall that reaction time lengthens as people get older. Because reaction time is a component of typing skill, we would expect that older typists would be slower than younger ones. However, this is not the case. Why? The answer is that while their reaction time is increasing, older typists look further ahead in the material they are to type. This allows them to compensate for their lengthier reaction time (Salthouse, 1984). Selective optimization is only one of the strategies experts in various fields use to maintain high performance. What are some other characteristics of experts?

The Development of Expertise: Separating Experts from Novices

If you were ill and needed a diagnosis, would you rather visit a newly minted young physician who had just graduated from medical school, or a more experienced, middle-aged physician?

If you chose the older physician, it's probably because you assumed that he or she would have a higher level of expertise. **Expertise** is the acquisition of skill or knowledge in a particular area. More focused than broader intelligence, expertise develops as people devote attention and practice to particular domains, either because of their profession or because they simply enjoy a given area. For example, physicians simply become better at diagnosing the symptoms of a medical problem in their patients as they gain experience. Similarly, a person who enjoys cooking and does a lot of it begins to know beforehand how a recipe will taste if certain modifications are made.

What separates experts from those who are less skilled in a given area? While beginners use formal procedures and rules, often following them very strictly, experts rely on experience and intuition, and they often bend the rules. Because experts have so much

Cognitive development during middle and later adulthood is a mixture of growth and decline. As people begin to lose certain abilities due to biological deterioration, they also advance in other areas by strengthening their skills.

selective optimization the process by which people concentrate on particular skill areas to compensate for losses in other areas

expertise the acquisition of skill or knowledge in a particular area

Expertise develops as people become more experienced in a particular domain and so are flexible with procedures and rules.

experience, their behavior is often automatic, performed without the need for much thought. Experts are often not very articulate in explaining how they draw conclusions; their solutions often just seem right to them—and *are* more likely to be right. Finally, experts develop better strategies than nonexperts, and they're more flexible in approaching problems. Their experience has provided them with alternative routes to the same problem, and this increases the probability of success (Willis, 1996; Clark, 1998).

Of course, not everyone develops expertise in some particular area during middle adulthood. Professional responsibilities, amount of leisure time, educational level, income, and marital status all affect the development of expertise.

Memory: You Must Remember This

Whenever Mary Donovan can't find her car keys, she mutters to herself that she is "losing her memory." Like Bina Clingman, who was worried about forgetting things like letters and phone numbers, Mary probably believes that memory loss is pretty common in middle age.

However, if she fits the pattern of most people in middle adulthood, her assessment is not necessarily accurate. According to research on memory changes in adulthood, most people show only minimal memory losses, and many exhibit none at all, during middle adulthood. Furthermore, because of societal stereotypes about aging, people in middle adulthood may be prone to attribute their absentmindedness to aging, even though they have been absentminded throughout their lives. Consequently, it is the *meaning* they give to their forgetfulness that changes, rather than their actual ability to remember (Erber, Rothberg, & Szuchman, 1991).

Types of Memory. To understand the nature of memory changes, it is necessary to consider the different types of memory. Memory is traditionally viewed in terms of three sequential components: sensory memory, short-term memory (also called working memory), and long-term memory. *Sensory memory* is an initial, momentary storage of information that lasts only an instant. Information is recorded by an individual's sensory system as a raw, meaningless stimulus. Next, information moves into *short-term memory*, which holds it for 15 to 25 seconds. Finally, if the information is rehearsed, it is moved into *long-term memory*, where it is stored on a relatively permanent basis.

Effective Strategies for Remembering

All of us, at one time or another, are forgetful. However, there are techniques that can enhance our memories and make it less likely that we will forget things that we wish to remember. **Mnemonics** (pronounced "nee-MON-iks") are formal strategies for organizing material in ways that make it more likely to be remembered. Among the mnemonics that work not only in middle adulthood, but at other points of the life span, are the following (Mastropieri & Scruggs, 1991; Bellezza, Six, & Phillips, 1992; Guttman, 1997).

▶ *Get organized.* For people who have trouble keeping track of where they left their keys or remembering appointments, the simplest approach is for them to become more organized. Using an appointment book, hanging one's keys on a hook, or using Post-It notes can help jog one's memory.

▶ *Pay attention.* People can improve their recall by initially paying attention when they are exposed to new information, by purposefully thinking that they wish to recall it in the future. If you are particularly concerned about remembering something, such as where you parked your car, pay particular attention at the moment you park the car, and remind yourself that you really want to remember.

▶ *Use the encoding specificity phenomenon.* According to the encoding specificity phenomenon, people are most likely to recall information in environments that are similar to those in which they initially learned ("encoded") it (Tulving & Thompson, 1973). For instance, people are best able to recall information on a test if the test is held in the room in which they studied.

▶ *Visualize.* Making mental images of ideas can help recall them later. For example, if you want to remember that global warming may lead to rising oceans, think of yourself on a beach on a hot day, with the waves coming closer and closer to where you've set out your beach blanket.

▶ *Rehearse.* In the realm of memory, practice makes perfect, or if not perfect, at least better. Adults of all ages can improve their memories if they expend more effort in rehearsing what they want to remember. By practicing what they wish to recall, people can substantially improve their recall of the material.

The different types of memory storage vary with age in different ways. Both sensory memory and short-term memory show virtually no weakening during middle adulthood. The story is a bit different for long-term memory, which, for some people, shows some decline with age. However, the reason for the decline does not appear to be a fading or a complete loss of memory, but rather that with age, people get less efficient at initially registering and storing information. Furthermore, memory declines may also be related to a reduction in the efficiency of information retrieval from memory. In other words, even if the information was stored efficiently in long-term memory, it may become more difficult to locate or isolate it (Schieber et al., 1992; Salthouse, 1994b).

It is important to keep in mind that memory declines in middle age are relatively minor, and most can be compensated for by various cognitive strategies. For instance, paying greater attention to material when it is first encountered can aid in its later recall. Losing one's keys, for instance, may have relatively little to do with memory declines; instead, it may be the result of inattentiveness at an earlier moment.

People may find it hard to pay attention to particular things because they are used to using a memory shortcut, *schemas,* to ease the burden of remembering all the many things that each of us experiences every day.

Memory Schemas. During adulthood, we recall material through the use of schemas. **Schemas** are organized bodies of information stored in memory. Schemas help people represent the way the world is organized, and allow them to categorize and interpret new information (Rumelhart, 1984; Fiske & Taylor, 1991).

mnemonics formal strategies for organizing material in ways that make it more likely to be remembered

schemas organized bodies of information stored in memory

Understanding a tale told by Native American storytellers requires familiarity with the culture, due to the existence of particular schemas.

People hold schemas for particular individuals (such as one's mother, wife, or child) as well as for categories of people (mail carriers, lawyers, or professors) and behaviors or events (dining in a restaurant or visiting the dentist). People's schemas serve to organize their behavior into coherent wholes and help them to interpret social events. For instance, psychologists Susan Fiske and Shelley Taylor (1991) give an example of an old Native American folktale in which the hero participates with several companions in a battle and is shot by an arrow. However, he feels no pain from the arrow. When he returns to his home and tells the story, something black emerges from his mouth, and he dies the next morning.

This tale is puzzling to many people because they are unschooled in the particular Native American culture to which the story belongs. People from Western societies tend to add, change, and omit details to fit their own existing schemas. However, to someone familiar with the Native American culture, the story makes perfect sense. The hero feels no pain because his companions are ghosts, and the "black thing" coming from his mouth is his departing soul.

In short, people's previous experiences within the context of a particular culture allow them to construct schemas in memory. In turn, their schemas allow them to comprehend and interpret new encounters. Furthermore, memory schemas influence people's recall of new information to which they are exposed. Material that is consistent with existing schemas is more likely to be recalled than material that is inconsistent (Laszlo, 1986; Hansen, 1989; Van Manen & Pietromonaco, 1993). For example, a person who usually puts her keys in a certain spot may lose them because she doesn't recall putting them down somewhere other than in the usual place.

Review and Rethink

REVIEW

- The question of whether intelligence declines in middle adulthood is complicated by limitations in cross-sectional studies and longitudinal studies.
- Intelligence appears to be divided into components, some of which decline while others hold steady or even improve.
- In general, cognitive competence in middle adulthood holds fairly steady despite declines in some areas of intellectual functioning.
- Memory may appear to decline in middle age, but in fact long-term memory deficits are probably due to ineffective strategies of storage and retrieval.

RETHINK

- How might crystallized and fluid intelligence work together to help middle-aged people deal with novel situations and problems?
- How do you explain the apparent discrepancy between declining IQ scores and continuing cognitive competence in middle adulthood?

Looking Back

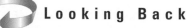

▶ **What sorts of physical changes affect people in middle adulthood?**

- During middle adulthood, roughly the period from 40 to 60, people typically decline slowly in height and strength,

and gain in weight. Height loss, especially in women, may be associated with osteoporosis, a thinning of the bones brought about by a lack of calcium in the diet. The best antidote for physical and psychological deterioration appears to be a healthful lifestyle, including regular exercise.

■ Visual acuity declines during this period as the eye's lens changes. People in middle adulthood tend to experience declines in near vision, depth and distance perception, adaptation to darkness, and the ability to perceive in three dimensions. In addition, the incidence of glaucoma, a disease that can cause blindness, increases in middle adulthood.

■ Hearing acuity also declines slightly in this period, typically involving some loss of the ability to hear high-frequency sounds and a deterioration of sound localization.

■ Reaction time of middle-aged people begins to increase gradually, but slower reactions are largely offset in complex tasks by increased skill due to years of task rehearsal.

► *What changes in sexuality do middle-aged men and women experience?*

■ Adults in middle age experience changes in sexuality, but these are less dramatic than commonly supposed, and many middle-aged couples experience new sexual freedom and enjoyment.

■ Women in middle age experience the female climacteric, the change from being able to bear children to no longer being able to do so. The most notable sign is menopause, which is often accompanied by physical and emotional discomfort. Therapies and changing attitudes toward menopause appear to be lessening women's fears and experience of difficulty regarding menopause.

■ Hormone replacement therapy (HRT) is a popular but controversial therapy that aims to decrease symptoms related to menopause and slow the deterioration associated with aging by replacing the female body's estrogen. Despite evidence of positive effects, some studies have suggested that HRT can increase the risk of breast cancer and other health problems.

■ Men also undergo changes in their reproductive systems, sometimes referred to as the male climacteric. Generally, the production of sperm and testosterone declines and the prostate gland enlarges, causing difficulties with urination.

► *Is middle adulthood a time of health or disease for men and women?*

■ Middle adulthood is generally a healthy period, but people become more susceptible to chronic diseases, including arthritis, diabetes, and hypertension, and they have a higher death rate than before. However, the death rate among people in middle adulthood in the United States has been steadily declining.

■ Overall health in middle adulthood varies according to socioeconomic status and gender. People of higher SES are healthier and have lower death rates than people of lower SES. Women have a lower mortality rate than men, but a higher incidence of illness. Researchers have generally paid more attention to the life-threatening diseases experienced by men than to the less fatal but chronic diseases typical of women.

► *What sorts of people are likely to get coronary heart disease?*

■ Heart disease begins to be a significant factor in middle adulthood. Genetic characteristics, such as age, gender, and a family history of heart disease, are associated with the risk of heart disease, as are environmental and behavioral factors, including smoking, a diet high in fats and cholesterol, and a lack of exercise.

■ Psychological factors also play a role in heart disease. A pattern of behaviors associated with competitiveness, impatience, frustration, and particularly hostility—called the Type A behavior pattern—is associated with a high risk of heart problems.

► *What causes cancer, and what tools are available to diagnose and treat it?*

■ Like heart disease, cancer becomes a threat in middle adulthood and is related to genetic and environmental factors. Treatments include radiation therapy, chemotherapy, and surgery.

■ Psychological factors appear to play a role in cancer. Cancer patients who refuse to accept that they have the disease or who fight back against it seem to have a higher survival rate than patients who stoically accept their diagnosis or fall into hopelessness. Furthermore, persons with strong family and social ties appear to be less likely to develop cancer than persons who lack such ties.

■ Breast cancer is a significant risk for women in middle adulthood. Mammography can help identify cancerous tumors early enough for successful treatment, but the age at which women should begin to have routine mammograms—40 or 50—is a matter of controversy.

► *What happens to a person's intelligence in middle adulthood?*

■ The question of whether intelligence declines in middle adulthood is challenging to answer because the two basic methods of addressing it have significant limitations. Cross-sectional methods, which study many subjects of different ages at one point in time, suffer from cohort effects. Longitudinal studies, which focus on the same subjects at several different points in time, are plagued by the difficulty of keeping a sample of subjects intact over many years.

■ Because intelligence appears to have several components, the question of intellectual declines is complex. Those who divide intelligence into two main types—fluid and crystallized—generally find that fluid intelligence slowly declines through middle adulthood while crystallized intelligence holds steady or even improves. Those who divide intelligence into greater numbers of components find an even more complicated pattern.

■ People in middle adulthood generally display a high degree of overall cognitive competence despite demonstrated declines in particular areas of intellectual functioning. People tend to focus on and exercise specific areas of competence that generally compensate for areas of loss, a strategy known as selective optimization.

■ Experts maintain, and even increase, cognitive competence through attention and practice to a particular subject. Experts process information about their field significantly differently from novices.

▶ *How does aging affect memory, and how can memory be improved?*

■ Memory in middle adulthood may seem to be on the decline, but the problem is not with either sensory memory or short-term memory. Even apparent problems with long-term memory appear to relate to people's storage and retrieval strategies rather than to overall memory deterioration, and the problems are minor and relatively easy to overcome.

■ People interpret, store, and recall information in the form of memory schemas, which organize related bits of information to set up expectations and add meaning to phenomena. Prior experience contributes to memory schemas and facilitates interpretation of new situations and recall of information that fits the schema.

■ Mnemonic devices can help people improve their ability to recall information by forcing them to pay attention to information as they store it (the keyword technique), to use cues to enable retrieval (the encoding specificity phenomenon), or to practice information retrieval (rehearsal).

EPILOGUE

We began our consideration of middle adulthood with a look at physical development, health, and sexuality. Despite slow changes, people's physical abilities and health are generally still good. The incidence of chronic and life-threatening diseases increases, especially heart disease and cancer. In the cognitive realm we found very gradual declines in some areas of intelligence and memory, but compensatory strategies and gains in other areas. We concluded with a look at some ways to improve memorization.

Return to the prologue of this chapter, about Brian Sipes's physical declines, and answer these questions.

1. In what ways might changes in sensory functions have affected Brian's performance in football? What adjustments could he have made to compensate?

2. Why might accepting the physical changes of middle adulthood be more difficult for Brian than for a person who was not a professional football player?

3. If Brian returns to school in middle adulthood, what cognitive challenges will he face compared with his younger classmates?

4. What advantages will Brian most likely have in completing his studies? Why?

Key Terms and Concepts

osteoporosis (p. 521)

presbyopia (p. 522)

glaucoma (p. 522)

presbycusis (p. 523)

female climacteric (p. 526)

menopause (p. 526)

male climacteric (p. 527)

Type A behavior pattern (p. 534)

Type B behavior pattern (p. 535)

fluid intelligence (p. 542)

crystallized intelligence (p. 542)

selective optimization (p. 543)

expertise (p. 544)

mnemonics (p. 545)

schemas (p. 545)

Social and Personality Development in Middle Adulthood

PROLOGUE: FIRES IN THE FAMILY

Mother and daughter Johanna Hoagland &
Erika Enslin-Franklin

"She'd come home from fires tired and excited," says Erika Enslin-Franklin. "And I'd think, 'Yeah, when everyone else runs out of the house, she runs in.'" In their teenage years, Erika and younger sister Janna worried that their mother might be killed. Newly divorced at 40, Johanna Hoagland was working in a video store to support her family when a customer suggested she volunteer at the fire station. She did, and 15 years ago she was hired as a combination community services officer and firefighter in Rohnert Park, California. "I was gung ho," says Johanna, now 57. "I knew at the time I was setting an example for my kids."

Still, Johanna would not have predicted that her rebellious track-and-field-star daughter would follow her so closely. After high school Erika joined the volunteers supporting her mother's corps and took fire science courses at a local college. "I got hooked," she says. "I remember lying on the floor at the academy and watching the fire roll over the top of us and thinking, 'This is so cool!'" (*Life,* 1999, p. 50.)

Looking Ahead

Firefighter may seem like an out-of-the-ordinary career choice for a woman, and even more when the choice is first made during middle adulthood. But maybe Johanna Hoagland's life is not so unusual: Few lives follow a set, predictable pattern through middle age. In fact, one of the remarkable characteristics of middle adulthood is its diversity, as the paths that different people travel continue to diverge.

In this chapter the focus is on the personality and social development that occurs in midlife. We begin by considering personality development, examining the personality changes that typify this period. We also explore some of the controversies that underlie developmental psychologists' understandings of midlife, including whether the midlife crisis, a phenomenon popularized in modern society, is fact or fiction.

We then turn to the relationships that evolve during middle adulthood. We consider the various familial ties that bind people together (or come unglued) during this period, including marriage, divorce, the empty nest, and grandparenting. We also look at a bleaker side of family relations: family violence, which is surprisingly prevalent.

Finally, the chapter considers the role of work and leisure during middle adulthood. We will examine the changing role of work in people's lives and some of the difficulties associated with work, such as burnout and unemployment. The chapter concludes with a discussion of leisure time, which gains increasing importance during middle age.

After reading this chapter, you will be able to answer the following questions:

▶ **In what ways does personality develop during middle adulthood?**

▶ **Is there continuity in personality development during adulthood?**

▶ **What are typical patterns of marriage and divorce in middle adulthood?**

▶ **What changing family situations do middle-aged adults face?**

▶ **What are the causes and characteristics of family violence in the United States?**

▶ **What are the characteristics of work and career in middle adulthood?**

Personality Development

My 40th birthday was not an easy one. It's not that I woke up one morning and felt different—that's never been the case. But what did happen during my 40th year was that I came to the realization of the finiteness of life, and that the die was cast. I began to understand that I probably wasn't going to be president of the United States—a secret ambition—or even a captain of industry. Time was no longer on my side, but something of an adversary. But it was curious: Rather than following my traditional pattern of focusing on the future, planning to do this or do that, I began to appreciate what I had. I looked around at my life, was pretty well satisfied with some of my accomplishments, and began to focus on the things that were going right, not the things that I was lacking. But this state of mind didn't happen in a day; it took several years after turning 40 before I felt this way. Even now, it is hard to fully accept that I am middle-aged.

In Western society, turning 40 represents an important milestone.

As this 47-year-old man suggests, the realization that one has entered middle adulthood does not always come easily. In many Western societies, the age of 40 has special meaning, bringing with it the inescapable fact that one is now middle-aged—at least in the view of others—and the suggestion, embodied in everyday common wisdom, that one is about to experience the throes of a "midlife crisis" (Gergen, 1990). Is this view correct? As we'll see, it depends on your perspective.

Two Perspectives on Adult Personality Development: Normative-Crisis Versus Life Events

Traditional views of personality development during adulthood have suggested that people move through a fixed series of stages, each tied fairly closely to age. Furthermore, these stages are related to specific crises in which an individual goes through an intense period of questioning and even psychological turmoil. This traditional perspective is a feature of normative-crisis models of personality development. **Normative-crisis models** see personality development in terms of fairly universal stages, tied to a sequence of age-related crises. We'll discuss three normative-crisis theories of adult development. Erik Erikson's psychosocial theory predicts a series of stages and crises throughout the life span. Roger Gould believes that adults experience seven predictable transformations from adolescence to middle age. Daniel Levinson's theory suggests that adults experience alternating periods of relative stability and crisis or change.

Keep in mind, however, that some critics suggest that normative-crisis models may be outmoded. They arose at a time when society had fairly rigid and uniform roles for people. Traditionally, men were expected to work and support a family; women were expected to stay at home, be housewives, and take care of the children. And the roles of men and women played out at relatively uniform ages.

Today, however, there is considerably more flexibility in people's roles, not only occupationally, but also in the timing of major life events. For example, although some women follow the traditional model of bearing children in their early 20s and then staying home to raise them, many others are continuing their jobs and having children later. In sum, changes in society have called into question normative-crisis models that are tied closely to age (Fugate & Mitchell, 1997).

Consequently, theorists such as Ravenna Helson focus on what may be called life events approaches. **Life events models** suggest that it is the particular events in an adult's life, rather than age per se, that determines the course of personality development. For instance, a woman who has her first child at age 21 may experience psychological forces similar to those experienced by a woman who has her first child at age 39. The result is that the two women, despite their very different ages, share certain commonalities of personality development (Neugarten, 1979; Hagestad & Neugarten, 1985; Helson & Wink, 1992).

It is not clear whether the normative-crisis view or the life events perspective will ultimately paint the more accurate picture of personality development and change during the course of adulthood. What is clear is that developmental theorists from a range of perspectives would all agree that middle adulthood is a time of continuing psychological growth (Helson & Roberts, 1994).

Erikson's Stage of Generativity Versus Stagnation

As we first discussed in Chapter 12, psychoanalyst Erik Erikson suggests that middle adulthood encompasses the period of **generativity versus stagnation.** Generativity refers to an individual's contribution to family, community, work, and society as a whole. Generative people strive to play a role in guiding and encouraging future generations. Often, people find generativity through parenting, but other roles can fill this need too. People may work directly with younger individuals, acting as mentors, or they may satisfy their need for generativity through creative and artistic output, seeking to leave a lasting contribution. The focus of those who experience generativity, then, is beyond themselves, as they

cw

normative-crisis models the approach to personality development that is based on fairly universal stages tied to a sequence of age-related crises

life events models the approach to personality development that is based on the timing of particular events in an adult's life rather than on age per se

generativity versus stagnation according to Erikson, the stage during middle adulthood in which people consider their contributions to family and society

look toward the continuation of their own lives through others (McAdams & de St. Aubin, 1998; Pratt et al., 2001).

On the other hand, a lack of psychological success in this period means that people become stagnant. Focusing on the triviality of their own activity, people may come to feel that they have made only limited contributions to the world, that their presence has counted for little. In fact, some individuals find themselves floundering, still seeking new and potentially more fulfilling careers. Others become frustrated and bored.

Although Erikson provides a broad overview of personality development, some psychologists have suggested that we need a more precise look at changes in personality during middle adulthood. For example, adult developmental psychologist George Vaillant (1977) has suggested that an important period during middle adulthood is "keeping the meaning versus rigidity." *Keeping the meaning versus rigidity* occurs between about ages 45 and 55. During that period, adults seek to extract the meaning from their lives, and they seek to "keep the meaning" by developing an acceptance of the strengths and weaknesses of others. Although they recognize the shortcomings of the world, they strive to preserve their world, and they are relatively content. The man quoted at the beginning of this section, for example, seems to be content with the meaning he has found in his life. People who are not able to keep the meaning in their lives risk becoming rigid and increasingly isolated from others.

Gould's Transformations

Psychiatrist Roger Gould (1975, 1980) offers another alternative to Erikson's view. While he agrees that people move through a series of stages and potential crises, his account of the specific developmental transformations differs from that of Erikson. For example, he suggests that adults pass through a series of seven stages associated with specific age periods (see Table 16-1). According to Gould, people in their late 30s and early 40s begin to feel a sense of urgency in terms of attaining life's goals as they realize that their time is limited. Coming to grips with the reality that life is finite can propel people towards adult maturity.

Gould based his model of adult development on a relatively small sample and relied heavily on his own clinical judgments. In fact, little research has supported his description

Table 16-1

GOULD'S TRANSFORMATION IN ADULT DEVELOPMENT

Stage	Approximate Age	Development(s)
1	16 to 18	Desire to escape parental control
2	18 to 22	Leaving the family; peer group orientation
3	22 to 28	Developing independence; commitment to a career and to children
4	29 to 34	Questioning self; role confusion; marriage and career vulnerable to dissatisfaction
5	35 to 43	Period of urgency to attain life's goals; awareness of time limitation; realignment of life's goals
6	43 to 53	Settling down; acceptance of one's life
7	53 to 60	More tolerance; acceptance of past; less negativism; general mellowing

(*Source:* From Gould, R. L., & Gould, M. D. (1978). *Transformations.* NY: Simon & Schuster.)

of the various stages, which was heavily influenced by the psychoanalytic perspective. Daniel Levinson's theory has received more attention.

Levinson's Seasons of Life

According to psychologist Daniel Levinson (1986, 1992), the early 40s are a period of transition and crisis. He based his contention on a comprehensive study of 40 men. Despite the relatively small sample size and the fact that the study included no women, Levinson's view has been influential. It provided one of the first and most far-reaching descriptions of the stages through which people pass during adulthood.

Levinson suggests that adult men pass through a series of stages beginning with their entry into early adulthood at around age 20 and continuing into middle adulthood (see Figure 16-1). The beginning stages have to do with leaving one's family and entering the adult world. During this time of early adulthood, people construct what Levinson calls "The Dream," a broad, comprehensive vision of the future. "The Dream" encompasses an individual's goals and aspirations, whether they entail becoming a captain of industry, a parent, or an elementary school teacher.

In early adulthood people make, and sometimes discard, career choices as they come to grips with their capabilities and ultimately commit to long-term decisions, which leads to a period—the late 30s—of settling down. They establish themselves and move toward the vision of "The Dream."

However, at around age 40 or 45, people move into a period that Levinson calls the midlife transition. The *midlife transition* is a time of questioning. People begin to focus on the finite nature of life, and they begin to question some of their everyday, fundamental assumptions. They experience the first signs of aging, and they confront the knowledge that they will be unable to accomplish all their aims before they die.

In Levinson's view, this period of assessment may lead to a midlife crisis. The **midlife crisis** is a stage of uncertainty and indecision brought about by the realization that life is finite. Facing signs of physical aging, men may also discover that even the accomplishments of which they are proudest have brought them less satisfaction than they expected. Looking toward the past, they may seek to define what went wrong and look for

cw

midlife crisis a stage of uncertainty and indecision brought about by the realization that life is finite

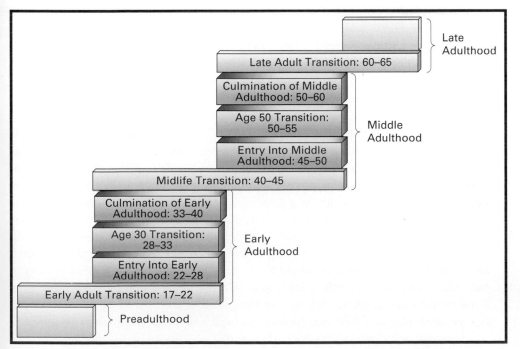

Figure 16-1 **Men's Stages of Adulthood**

According to Levinson, men pass through a series of stages and crises. However, not everyone accepts the universality of these stages, and their applicability to women has not been established. Can you think of groups of men for whom these stages are not typical?

(Adapted from Levinson, 1986.)

In spite of there being no strong evidence to support the concept of people universally experiencing "midlife crisis," the belief that it is commonplace remains, probably because symbols of it tend to be quite noticeable. How would you explain why someone would purchase a fancy sports car once in middle age?

ways to correct their past mistakes. The midlife crisis, then, is a painful and tumultuous period of questioning.

Although his initial theory was built upon interviews with men, Levinson later interviewed a sample of women and found some gender differences. For example, he suggests that women have greater difficulty than men in "The Dream" stage, experiencing trouble clearly articulating what their futures will encompass. The reason, Levinson argues, is that women are more subject than men to conflict between the goals of having a career and raising a family (Levinson, 1992).

Levinson's view is that most people are susceptible to a fairly profound midlife crisis. But before accepting his view, we need to go back to some critical drawbacks in his research. First, his initial theorizing was based on a group of only 40 men, and his later work with women was carried out years after his initial formulation and once again on only a small sample. Furthermore, Levinson overstated the consistency and generality of the patterns he found in the samples he used to derive his theory (McCrae & Costa, 1990; Stewart & Ostrove, 1998).

The Midlife Crisis: Reality or Myth? Central to Levinson's model of the seasons of life is the concept of midlife crisis, a period in the early 40s presumed to be marked by intense psychological turmoil. The notion has taken on a life of its own: There is a general expectation in U.S. society that the age of 40 represents an important psychological juncture (Sheehy, 1976).

There's a problem, though, with such a view: The evidence for a widespread midlife crisis is simply lacking. In fact, most research suggests that for most people, the passage into middle age is relatively tranquil. The majority of people regard midlife as a particularly rewarding time. If they are parents, for example, their children often have passed the period when childrearing is physically demanding, and in some cases children have left the home altogether, allowing parents the opportunity to rekindle an intimacy that they may have lost. Many middle-aged people find that their careers have blossomed—as we discuss later in this chapter—and far from being in crisis, they may feel quite content with their lot in life. Rather than looking toward the future, they focus on the present, seeking to maximize their ongoing involvement with family, friends, and other social groups. Even those people who experience regrets over the course of their lives may be motivated to change the direction of their lives (perhaps through a new job, like Johanna Hoagland in the chapter prologue), and those who do change their lives end up better off psychologically (Stewart & Vandewater, 1999).

Furthermore, by the time they approach and enter middle adulthood, most people feel younger than they actually are, as can be seen in Figure 16-2 (Miller, Hemesath, & Nelson, 1997; Wethington, Cooper, & Holmes, 1997).

In short, the evidence for a midlife crisis experienced by most people is no more compelling than the evidence for a stormy adolescence that we discussed in Chapter 12. Yet, like that notion, the idea that the midlife crisis is nearly universal seems unusually well entrenched in "common wisdom." Why is this the case? One reason may be that people who do experience turmoil during middle age tend to be perceptually obvious and easily remembered by observers. For instance, a 40-year-old man who divorces his wife, replaces his sedate Ford Taurus station wagon with a red Saab convertible, and marries a much younger woman is likely to be more conspicuous than a happily married man who remains with his spouse (and Taurus) throughout middle adulthood. As a consequence, we attend to, and recall, marital difficulties more readily than the lack of them. In such ways is the myth of a blustery and universal midlife crisis perpetuated. The reality, though, is quite different: For most people, a midlife crisis is more the stuff of fiction than of reality. In fact, for some people midlife may not bring many changes at all.

Stability Versus Change in Personality

Harry Hennesey, age 53 and a vice president of an investment banking firm, says that inside, he still feels like a kid.

Many middle-aged adults would agree with such a sentiment. Although most people tend to say that they have changed a good deal since they reached adolescence—and mostly for the better—many also contend that in terms of basic personality traits, they perceive important similarities between their present selves and their younger selves.

The degree to which personality is stable across the life span or changes as we age is one of the major issues of personality development during middle adulthood. Theorists such as Erikson and Levinson clearly suggest that there is substantial change over time. Erikson's stages and Levinson's seasons describe set patterns of change. The change may be predictable and age-related, but it is substantial.

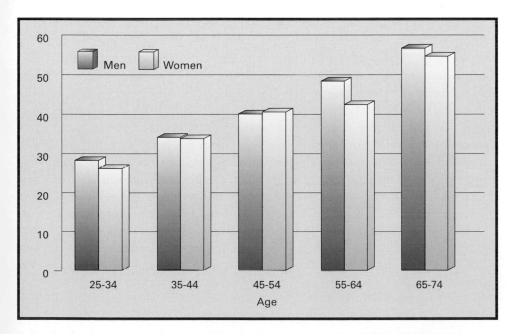

Figure 16-2 **What Age Do You Feel Most of the Time?**

Throughout adulthood, most people say they feel younger than they actually are.

(*Source:* The John D. and Catherine T. MacArthur Foundation Research Network on Successful Midlife Development, 1999.)

While Erikson and Levinson suggest there is substantial personality change over time, other research has shown that personality in terms of individual traits remains stable over the lifespan. How many of these high school swimmers do you think are still physically active after 40 years? Why?

On the other hand, an impressive body of research suggests that at least in terms of individual traits, personality is quite stable and continuous over the life span. Developmental psychologists Paul Costa and Robert McCrae find remarkable stability in particular traits. Even-tempered 20-year-olds are even-tempered at age 75; affectionate 25-year-olds become affectionate 50-year-olds; and disorganized 26-year-olds are still disorganized at age 60. Similarly, self-concept at age 30 is a good indication of self-concept at age 80 (Costa & McCrae, 1989, 1997; McCrae & Costa, 1990; Herbst et al., 2000: also see Figure 16-3).

Furthermore, there is evidence that people's traits actually become more ingrained as they age. For instance, some research suggests that confident adolescents become more confident in their mid-50s, while diffident people become more diffident over the same time frame.

Quite a bit of research has centered on the personality traits that have come to be known as the "Big Five"—because they represent the five major clusters of personality characteristics. These include neuroticism, the degree to which a person is moody, anxious, and self-critical; extraversion, how outgoing or shy a person is; openness, a person's level of curiosity and interest in new experiences; agreeableness, how easygoing and helpful a person tends to be; and conscientiousness, a person's tendencies to be organized and responsible. The majority of studies find that the Big Five traits are relatively stable past the age of 30, although there are some variations in specific traits. In particular, neuroticism, extraversion, and openness to experience decline somewhat from early adulthood through middle adulthood, while the agreeableness and conscientiousness increase to a degree—findings that are consistent across cultures. The basic pattern, however, is one of stability through adulthood (Haan, Millsap, & Hartka, 1986).

Does evidence for the stability of personality traits contradict the perspective of personality change championed by theorists such as Erikson, Gould, and Levinson? Not necessarily, for on closer inspection the contradictions of the two approaches may be more apparent than real.

It is likely that general personality is in fact relatively stable over time. People's basic traits do appear to show great continuity, particularly over the course of their adult lives. On the other hand, people are also susceptible to changes in their lives, and adulthood is

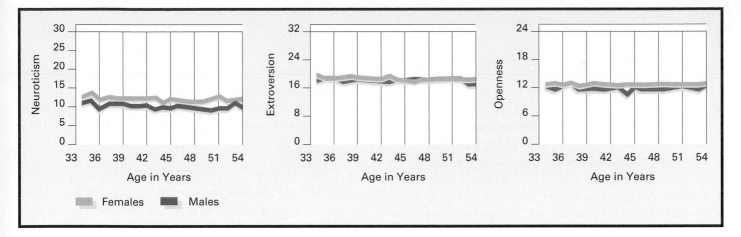

Figure 16-3 **The Stability of Personality**

According to Paul Costa and Robert McCrae, basic personality traits such as openness, extroversion, and neuroticism are stable and consistent throughout adulthood.

(Adapted from Costa et al., 1986, p. 148.)

jam-packed with major events, such as changes in family status, career, and even the economy. Furthermore, physical changes due to aging can provide the impetus for changes in the ways people view themselves and the world at large (Krueger & Heckhausen, 1993).

In sum, personality development is marked by both stability and change. The challenge for developmental psychologists is to determine under what conditions and for which traits stability and change prevail. One area in which psychologists have been studying our levels of stability versus change is happiness. Some interesting research on what makes people happy is described in the *From Research to Practice* box.

From Research to Practice

If You Became a Millionaire, Would You Be Happier? Subjective Well-Being Across the Life Span

If you hit it big on *Who Wants to Be a Millionaire?*, would you be a happier person?

For most people, the answer would be no. According to a growing body of research, adults' sense of *subjective well-being* or general happiness remains stable over their lives. Even winning the lottery doesn't do much to change happiness; despite an initial surge of subjective well-being, one year later people's happiness tends to return to pre-lottery levels (Diener et al., 2000).

The steadiness of subjective well-being suggests that most people have a general "set point" for happiness, a level of happiness that is consistent despite the day-to-day ups and downs of life. Although specific events may temporarily elevate or depress a person's mood (for example, a surprisingly high job evaluation or being laid off from work), people eventually return to their general level of happiness.

Most people's happiness set points seem to be fairly high. For example, some 30 percent of people in the United States rate themselves as "very happy," while only 10 percent rate themselves as "not too happy." Most people say they are "pretty happy." These findings are similar across different social groups. Men and women rate themselves as equally happy, and African Americans rate themselves as "very happy" at only slightly lower rates than whites. Regardless of where they stand economically, residents of countries across the world have similar levels of happiness (Mroczek & Kolarz, 1998; Schkade & Kahneman, 1998; Staudinger, Fleeson, & Baltes, 1999; Diener, 2000).

Ultimately, it seems clear that people generally feel they are happy, regardless of their economic situation. The conclusion: Money doesn't buy happiness.

Review and Rethink

- Normative-crisis models portray people as passing through age-related stages of development; life events models focus on specific changes in response to varying life events.
- According to Erikson, middle adulthood is the "generativity versus stagnation" stage, while Vaillant sees it as the "keeping the meaning versus rigidity" period.
- Gould suggests that people move through seven stages during adulthood.
- Levinson argues that the midlife transition can lead to a midlife crisis, but there is little evidence for this in the majority of middle-aged people.

- Broad personality characteristics are relatively stable, although more specific aspects of personality change in response to life events.

RETHINK

- How do you think the midlife transition is different for a middle-aged person whose child has just entered adolescence versus a middle-aged person who has just become a parent for the first time?
- In what ways might normative-crisis models of personality development be culture-specific?

Relationships: Family in Middle Age

For Kathy and Bob, accompanying their son Jon to his college orientation was like nothing they had ever experienced in the life of their family. When Jon had been accepted at a college on the other side of the country, the reality that he would be leaving home was still fairly abstract. But the months flew by rapidly, and when the time came to leave him on his new campus, it was a wrenching experience. Not only did Kathy and Bob worry about their son in the way that parents always worry about their children, but they felt a sense of profound loss—a sense that their family would be changing in ways they could barely fathom, and that, to a large extent, their job of raising their son was over. Now he was largely on his own. It was a thought that filled them with pride and anticipation for his future, but with great sadness as well. They would miss him.

For members of many non-Western cultures who live in traditional extended families in which multiple generations spend their lives in the same household or village, middle adulthood is not particularly special. This is most decidedly not the case in Western cultures, where family dynamics undergo significant change during middle adulthood. It is in middle age that most parents experience major changes in their relationships not only with their children, but with other family members as well. It is a period of shifting role relationships that, in 21st century Western cultures, encompass an increasing number of combinations and permutations. We'll start by looking at the developmental trajectory of marriage and then consider some of the many alternative forms that family life takes today (Kaslow, 2001).

Marriage

Fifty years ago, midlife was similar for most people. Men and women who had married during early adulthood were still married to one another. One hundred years ago, when life expectancy was much shorter than it is today, people in their 40s were most likely married—but not to the same persons they had first married. Because the death of a spouse was not an infrequent occurrence, people were often well into their second marriage by the time of middle age.

Indian women view their life course not on the basis of chronological age, but on the nature of one's social responsibility, family management issues, and moral sense at a given period.

Today, however, the story is different and more complex. More people are single during middle adulthood, having never married. Single people may live alone or with a partner. Gay and lesbian adults, for example, may have committed relationships even though marriage is typically not an option for them. Among heterosexuals, some have divorced, lived alone, and then remarried. During middle adulthood, many people's marriages end in divorce, and many families are in "blended" households, containing children and stepchildren from previous marriages. On the other hand, many couples still spend between 40 and 50 years together, the bulk of those years during middle adulthood. Furthermore, many people experience the peak of marital satisfaction during middle age.

The Ups and Downs of Marriage. Even for happily married couples, marriage has its ups and downs, with satisfaction rising and falling over the course of the marriage (Karney & Bradbury, 1995). The most frequent pattern of satisfaction is the U-shaped configuration shown in Figure 16-4 (Figley, 1973). Marital satisfaction begins to decline just after the marriage, and it continues to fall until it reaches its lowest point following the births of the couple's children. However, at that point, satisfaction begins to grow, eventually returning to the same level that it held before the marriage (Noller, Feeney, & Ward, 1997).

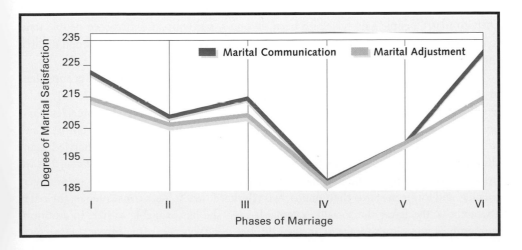

Figure 16-4 **The Phases of Marital Satisfaction**

For many couples, marital satisfaction falls and rises in a U-shaped configuration. It begins to decline after the wedding and continues to fall until it reaches its lowest point following the births of the couple's children. Satisfaction begins to increase when the youngest child leaves home. Why do you think communication improves so markedly in the last phase?

(*Source:* Adapted from Figley, 1973.)

Middle-aged couples cite several sources of particular satisfaction (Levenson, Carstensen, & Gottman, 1993). For instance, in response to one survey, both men and women stated that their spouse was "their best friend" and that they liked their spouses as people. They also tended to view marriage as a long-term commitment and to agree on their aims and goals. Finally, most also felt that their spouses had grown more interesting over the course of the marriage (Lauer & Lauer, 1985).

Although sexual satisfaction is related to general marital satisfaction, what matters is not how often married people have sex (Spence, 1997). (If the amount of sex were critical, most couples would be dissatisfied: Frequency of intercourse tends to decline with age.) Instead, for both men and women, being in agreement about their sex lives leads to satisfaction (Tavris & Sadd, 1977; Lauer & Lauer, 1985; Goleman, 1985).

Divorce. For certain couples marital satisfaction, instead of rising again after the initial decline, continues to fall. For some, their dissatisfaction leads to divorce. Just as with younger couples, today's divorce rate for middle-aged couples is higher than in earlier decades. For instance, about one woman in eight who is in her first marriage will get divorced after the age of 40 (Uhlenberg, Cooney, & Boyd, 1990; Stewart et al., 1997).

Why do marriages unravel? There are many causes. One is that people are more individualistic, spending less time together than in earlier years. Today, many people feel concerned with their own personal happiness, and if their marriage is not bringing them happiness, they feel that divorce may be the answer. In addition, divorce is more socially acceptable than in the past, and legally it is often an easy—if not inexpensive—course of action (Wallerstein, Lewis, & Blakeslee, 2000).

Another reason for divorce is that feelings of romantic, passionate love may subside over time. Because Western culture emphasizes the importance of romance and passion, members of marriages in which passion has declined may feel that that is a sufficient reason to divorce. Finally, there is a great deal of stress in households in which both parents work. Much of the energy directed towards families in the past is now directed towards work and other institutions outside the home (Macionis, 2001).

Whatever the causes, divorce can be especially difficult for women in midlife, particularly if they have followed the traditional female role of staying with their children and never performing substantial work outside the home. They also may face prejudice against older workers, finding that they are less likely to be hired than younger people, even in jobs with minimal requirements. Without a good deal of training and support, these divorced women, lacking recognized job skills, may remain virtually unemployable (Clarke-Stewart & Bailey, 1990; Morgan, 1991; Stewart et al., 1997).

Remarriage. Despite problems with an earlier marriage, many of the people who divorce—some 75 to 80 percent—end up marrying again, usually within 2 to 5 years. They are most likely to marry people who have also been divorced, partly because divorced people tend to be the ones in the available pool, but also because those who have gone through divorce share similar experiences (DeWitt, 1992).

Although the overall rate of remarriage is high, it is far higher in some groups than in others. For instance, it is harder for women to remarry than men, particularly older women. Whereas 90 percent of women under the age of 25 remarry after divorce, less than one-third of women over the age of 40 remarry. In addition, while 75 percent of white women remarry, less than half of African American women eventually get married again (Bumpass, Sweet, & Martin, 1990). The reason stems from the *marriage gradient* that we first discussed in Chapter 14: Societal norms push men to marry women who are younger, smaller, and lower in status than themselves (Bernard, 1982). As a consequence, the older a woman is, the fewer the socially acceptable men she has available to her. In addition, women have the disadvantage of societal double standards regarding physical attractiveness. Older women tend to be perceived as unattractive, while older men tend to be seen as "distinguished" and "mature" (Hatfield & Sprecher, 1986).

Still, remarriage is common. There are several reasons divorced people may find getting married again more appealing than remaining single. One motivation to remarry is to avoid the social consequences of divorce. Even in the early 21st century, when the breakup of marriages is common, divorce carries with it a certain stigma that people may attempt to overcome by remarrying.

Furthermore, divorced people miss the companionship that marriage provides. Divorced men in particular report feeling lonely and experience an increase in physical and mental health problems following divorce. Finally, marriage provides clear economic benefits (Ross, Microwsky, & Goldsteen, 1991; Stewart et al., 1997).

Second marriages are not the same as first marriages. Older couples tend to be more mature and realistic. They tend to look at marriage in less romantic terms than younger couples, and they are more cautious. Furthermore, they show greater flexibility in terms of roles and duties; they share household chores more equitably and make decisions in a more participatory manner (Guisinger, Cowan, & Schuldberg, 1989; Hetherington, 1999).

Unfortunately, though, this doesn't make second marriages more durable than first ones. In fact, the divorce rate for second marriages is slightly higher than for first marriages. Several factors explain this phenomenon. One is that second marriages may be subject to stresses that are not present in first marriages, such as the strain of blending different families. For another, having experienced and survived divorce before, partners in second marriages may be more ready to walk away from unsatisfactory relationships (Cherlin, 1993; Warshak, 2000).

Despite the high divorce rate for second marriages, many people settle into remarriage quite successfully. In such cases, people report as great a degree of satisfaction as people who are in successful first marriages (Glenn & Weaver, 1977; Bird & Melville, 1994).

Leaving their youngest child at college marks the start of a significant transition for parents, who face an "empty nest."

Family Evolutions: From Full House to Empty Nest

For many parents, a major transition that typically occurs during middle adulthood is the departure of children, who may be either going to college, getting married, joining the military, or taking a job far from home. Even people who become parents at relatively late ages are likely to experience this transition at some point during middle adulthood, since the period spans nearly a quarter century. As we saw in the description of Kathy and Bob, a child's departure can be a wrenching experience—so wrenching, in fact, that it has been labeled the "empty nest syndrome." The **empty nest syndrome** refers to instances in which parents experience unhappiness, worry, loneliness, and depression from their children's departure from home (Lauer & Lauer, 1999).

Many parents report that major adjustments are required. Particularly for women who have followed the traditional societal model and stayed home to rear their children, the loss can be difficult. Certainly, if traditional homemakers have little or nothing else in their lives except their children, they do face a challenging period.

On the other hand, even mothers who have not worked outside the home have many other outlets for their physical and psychological energies, such as community or recreational activities. When the children leave, they may have more time for such activities. Moreover, they may feel that they now have the opportunity to get a job or to go back to school. Finally, many mothers find that the period of motherhood is not easy; surveys show that most people feel that being a mother is harder than it used to be (Heubusch, 1997). Such mothers may now feel liberated from a comparatively difficult set of responsibilities.

Consequently, for most people the empty nest syndrome is more myth than reality. There is little, if any, evidence to suggest that the departure of children produces anything

empty nest syndrome the experience that relates to parents' feelings of unhappiness, worry, loneliness, and depression resulting from their children's departure from home more than temporary feelings of sadness and distress. This is especially true for women who have been working outside the home (Raup & Myers, 1989).

In fact, there are some discernible benefits when children leave home. Married spouses have more time for one another. Married or unmarried people can throw themselves into their own work without having to worry about helping the kids with homework, carpools, and the like. The house stays neater, and the telephone rings less often.

It is important to keep in mind that most research examining the so-called empty nest syndrome has focused on women. Because men traditionally are not as involved as women in childrearing, it was assumed that the transition when children left home would be relatively smooth for men. However, at least some research suggests that men experience some degree of loss when their children depart, although the nature of that loss may be different from that experienced by women.

For example, one survey found that although most fathers expressed either happy or neutral feelings about the departure of their children, almost a quarter felt unhappy (Lewis, Freneau, & Roberts, 1979). Primarily, they bemoaned lost opportunities, regretting things that they had not done with their children. For instance, some felt that they had been too busy for their children or hadn't been sufficiently nurturing or caring.

The concept of the empty nest syndrome first arose at a time when children, after growing up, tended to leave home for good. However, times change, and the empty nest frequently becomes replenished with what have been called "boomerang children," as we discuss next.

Boomerang Children: Refilling the Empty Nest.

Carole Olis doesn't know what to make of her 23-year-old son, Rob. He has been living at home since his graduation from college more than 2 years ago. Her six older children returned to the nest for just a few months and then bolted.

"I ask him, 'Why don't you move out with your friends?'" says Mrs. Olis, shaking her head. Rob has a ready answer: "They all live at home, too."

Carole Olis is not alone in being surprised and somewhat perplexed by the return of her son. There has been a significant increase in the United States in the number of young adults who come back to live in the homes of their middle-aged parents.

boomerang children young adults who return, after leaving home for some period, to live in the homes of their middle-aged parents

Known as **boomerang children**, these returning offspring typically cite economic issues as the main reason for returning. Because of a difficult economy, many younger individuals are unable to find jobs after college, or the positions they do find pay so little that they have difficulty making ends meet. Others return home after the breakup of a marriage (Mogelonsky, 1996; Bianchi & Casper, 2000).

Parents' reactions to the return of their children vary, largely according to the reasons for it. If their children are unemployed, their return to the previously empty nest may be a major irritant. Fathers in particular may not grasp the realities of the difficult job market that college graduates may encounter, and may be decidedly unsympathetic to their children's return. Moreover, there may be some subtle parent–child rivalry for the attention of the spouse (Gross, 1991; Wilcox, 1992).

In contrast, mothers tend to be more sympathetic to children who are unemployed. Single mothers in particular may welcome the help and security provided by returning children. Furthermore, both mothers and fathers feel fairly positive about returning sons and daughters who work and contribute to the functioning of the household (Quinn, 1993).

In short, parents' reactions to boomerang children are both positive and negative. However, most middle-aged parents would probably agree with the sentiments expressed by comedian Bill Cosby: "Your parents want you out of the house. They really want you out of the house. They are worried about you. They love you but, God, they want you out of the house" (Wilcox, 1992, p. 83).

The Sandwich Generation: Between Children and Parents. At the same time children are leaving the nest, or perhaps even returning as boomerang children, many middle-aged adults face another challenge: growing responsibility for the care of their aging parents. Many people feel squeezed between two generations, a fact that causes them to be called the sandwich generation. The term **sandwich generation** refers to those who in middle adulthood must fulfill the needs of both their children and their aging parents.

sandwich generation couples who in middle adulthood must fulfill the needs of both their children and their aging parents

Being part of the sandwich generation is a relatively new phenomenon, produced by several converging trends. First, both men and women are marrying later and having children at an older age. At the same time, people are living longer. Consequently, the likelihood is growing that those in middle adulthood will simultaneously have children who still require a significant amount of nurturing and parents who are still alive and in need of care.

The care of aging parents can be psychologically tricky. For one thing, there is a significant degree of role reversal (Merrill, 1997). As we'll discuss further in Chapter 18, elderly people, who were previously independent, may resent and resist their children's efforts to help. They certainly do not want to be burdens on their children. For instance, almost all elderly people who live alone report that they do not wish to live with their children (CFCEPLA, 1986).

People in middle adulthood provide a range of care for their parents. In some cases, the care is merely financial, such as helping them make ends meet on meager pensions. In other situations, it takes the form of help in managing a household, such as taking down storm windows in the spring or shoveling snow in the winter.

In more extreme cases, parents may be invited to live in the home of a son or daughter. Such a situation can present the greatest difficulties, as roles are renegotiated. Suddenly, the children—who are no longer children—are in charge of the situation, and both they and their parents must find some common ground in making decisions. The loss of independence on the part of an elderly parent can be particularly difficult (Walker, Thompson, & Morgan, 1987; Mancini & Blieszner, 1991).

In many cases, the burden of caring for aging parents is not shared equally, with the larger share most often taken on by women. Even in married couples where both husband and wife are in the labor force, middle-aged women tend to be more involved in the day-to-day care of aging parents (Dean et al., 1989; Walker & Pratt, 1991; Green, 1991; Spitze & Logan, 1990).

Despite the burden of being sandwiched in the middle of two generations, which can stretch the caregiving child's resources, there are also significant rewards. The psychological attachment between middle-aged children and their elderly parents can continue to grow. Both partners in the relationship can see each other more realistically. They can become closer, more accepting of each other's weaknesses and more appreciative of each other's strengths (Troll, 1989; Mancini & Blieszner, 1991).

Becoming a Grandparent: Who, Me?

When her eldest son and daughter-in-law had their first child, Leah couldn't believe it. At age 54, she had become a grandmother! She kept telling herself that she felt far too young to be considered anybody's grandparent.

Middle adulthood often brings one of the unmistakable symbols of aging: becoming a grandparent. Grandparenting tends to fall into different styles (Cherlin & Furstenberg, 1986). *Involved* grandparents are actively engaged in grandparenting and have influence over their grandchildren's lives. They hold clear expectations about the ways their grand-

One reason that African American grandparents are more involved with their grandchildren than white grandparents is the greater prevalence of three-generation families living together in African Amercian households.

children should behave. A retired grandmother or grandfather who takes care of a grandchild several days a week while her parents are at work is an example of an involved grandparent.

In contrast, *companionate* grandparents are more relaxed. Rather than taking responsibility for their grandchildren, companionate grandparents act as supporters and buddies to them. Grandparents who visit and call frequently, and perhaps occasionally take their grandchildren on vacations or invite them to visit without their parents, are practicing the companionate style of grandparenting. Finally, the most aloof type of grandparents are *remote*. Remote grandparents are detached and distant, and they show little interest in their grandchildren. Remote grandparents, for example, would rarely make visits to see their grandchildren and might complain about their childish behavior when they did see them.

There are marked gender differences in the extent to which people enjoy grandparenthood. Generally, grandmothers are more interested and experience greater satisfaction than grandfathers, particularly when they have a high level of interaction with younger grandchildren (Thomas, 1986; Smith, 1995).

Furthermore, African American grandparents are more apt to be involved with their grandchildren than white grandparents. The most likely explanation for this phenomenon is that the prevalence of three-generation families who live together is greater among African Americans than among Caucasians. In addition, African American families, which are more likely than white families to be headed by single parents, often rely substantially on the help of grandparents in everyday child care, and cultural norms tend to be highly supportive of grandparents taking an active role (Budris, 1998; Baydar & Brooks-Gunn, 1998; Baird, John, & Hayslip, 2000).

Family Violence: The Hidden Epidemic

After finding an unidentified earring, the wife accused her husband of being unfaithful. His reaction was to throw her against the wall of their apartment, and then to toss her clothes out the window. In another incident, the husband became angry. Screaming at his wife, he threw her against a wall, and then picked her up and literally threw her out of the house. Another time, the wife called 911, begging for the police to protect her. When the police came, the woman, with a black eye, a cut lip, and swollen cheeks, hysterically screamed, "He's going to kill me."

If nothing else was clear about what was called the murder trial of the century, there is ample evidence that the spousal abuse described above was an ingredient in the lives of O.J. Simpson and Nicole Brown Simpson. The allegations of abuse that came out during the trial were both chilling and yet all too familiar.

The Prevalence of Spousal Abuse. Domestic violence is one of the ugly truths about marriage in the United States, occurring at epidemic levels. Some form of violence happens in one-fourth of all marriages, and more than half the women who were murdered in one recent 10-year period were murdered by a partner. Between 21 and 34 percent of women will be slapped, kicked, beaten, choked, or threatened or attacked with a weapon at least once by an intimate partner. In fact, close to 15 percent of all marriages in the United States are characterized by continuing, severe violence (Straus & Gelles, 1990; Browne, 1993; Walker, 1999).

No segment of society is immune from spousal abuse. Violence occurs across social strata, races, ethnic groups, and religions. Both gay and straight partnerships can be damaged by abuse. It also occurs across genders: Although in the vast majority of cases of

Parents who abuse their own spouses and children were often victims of abuse themselves as children, reflecting a cycle of violence.

abuse a husband batters a wife, in about 8 percent of the cases wives physically abuse their husbands (Emery & Laumann-Billings, 1998; de Anda & Becerra, 2000; Harway, 2000).

Certain factors increase the likelihood of abuse. For instance, families of lower socioeconomic status (SES), in which there is continuing economic concern, a high level of verbal aggression, and large family size, are more likely to be involved in spousal abuse than families in which such factors are not present. Furthermore, husbands and wives who grew up in families where violence was present are more likely to be violent themselves (Straus & Gelles, 1990; Straus & Yodanis, 1996).

The factors that put a family at risk are similar to those associated with child abuse, another form of family violence. Child abuse occurs most frequently in stressful environments, in lower socioeconomic levels, in single-parent families, and in situations with high levels of marital conflict. Families with four or more children have higher rates of abuse, and those with incomes lower than $15,000 a year have abuse rates that are seven times higher than families with higher incomes. But not all types of abuse are higher in poorer families: Incest is more likely to occur in affluent families (Dodge, Bates, & Pettit, 1990; APA, 1996).

According to psychologists Neil Jacobson and John Gottman, husbands who abuse their wives fall into two categories, which they call "pit bulls" and "cobras." "Pit bulls" confine violence to those whom they love, and they strike out in rage against their wives when they feel jealous or when their fear of abandonment is aroused. In contrast, "cobras" are likely to be aggressive to everyone, not just their spouses, and their violence is more likely to involve weapons such as knives or guns. "Cobras" are more calculating and show surprisingly little emotion or physiological arousal when they are acting aggressively (Jacobson & Gottman, 1998).

Marital aggression by a husband typically occurs in three stages (Walker, 1984, 1989; see Figure 16-5). The first is the *tension building* stage in which a batterer becomes upset and shows dissatisfaction initially through verbal abuse. He may also show some preliminary physical aggression in the form of shoving or grabbing. The wife may be desperately trying to avoid the impending violence, attempting to placate her spouse or withdraw from the situation. Such behavior may serve only to enrage the husband, who senses his wife's vulnerability.

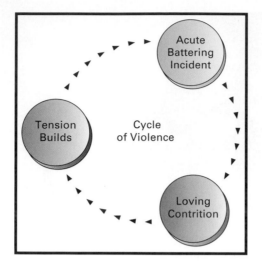

Figure 16-5 The Stages
of Violence
(Adapted from Walker, 1979, 1984; Gondolf, 1985.)

The next stage consists of an *acute battering incident,* when the physical abuse actually occurs. It may last from several minutes to hours. Wives may be shoved against walls, choked, slapped, punched, kicked, and stepped on. Their arms may be twisted or broken, they may be shaken severely, thrown down a flight of stairs, or burned with cigarettes or scalding liquids. About a quarter of wives are forced to engage in sexual activities during this period, which takes the form of aggressive sexual acts and rape.

Finally, in some—but not all—cases, the episode moves into the *loving contrition* stage. At this point, the husband feels remorse and apologizes for his actions. He may minister to his wife, providing first aid and sympathy, and assuring her that he will never act violently again. Because wives may feel that in some way they were partly at fault in triggering the aggression, they may be motivated to accept the apology and forgive their husbands. They want to believe that the aggression will never occur again.

The loving contrition stage helps explain why many wives remain with abusive husbands and are the continuing victims of abuse. Wishing desperately to keep their marriages intact, and believing that they have no good alternatives, some wives remain out of a vague sense that they are responsible for the abuse. Others remain out of fear: They are afraid their husbands may come after them if they leave.

The Cycle of Violence. Still other wives stay with batterers because they, like their husbands, have learned a seemingly unforgettable lesson from childhood: that violence is an acceptable means of settling disputes.

cycle of violence hypothesis the theory that abuse and neglect of children leads them to be predisposed to abusiveness as adults

Individuals who abuse their spouses and children were often as children the victims of abuse themselves. According to the **cycle of violence hypothesis,** abuse and neglect of children leads them to be predisposed to abusiveness as adults (Dodge, Bates, & Pettit, 1990; McCloskey & Bailey, 2000). In line with social learning theory, the cycle of violence hypothesis suggests that family aggression is perpetuated from one generation to another as family members follow the lead of the previous generation. It is a fact that individuals who abuse their wives often have been raised in households in which they have witnessed spousal abuse, just as parents who abuse their children frequently have been the victims of abuse themselves as children (Straus, Gelles, & Steinmetz, 1980; Feshbach, 1980; McCloskey & Bailey, 2000).

However, growing up in a home where abuse occurs does not invariably lead to abusiveness as an adult. For instance, only about one-third of people who were abused or neglected as children abuse their own children as adults, and fully two-thirds of abusers were not themselves abused as children. The cycle of violence, then, does not tell the full story of abuse (Kaufman & Zigler, 1987; Jacobson & Gottman, 1998).

Becoming an Informed Consumer of Development

Dealing with Spousal Assault

Despite the fact that spousal abuse occurs in some 25 percent of all marriages, efforts to deal with victims of abuse are underfunded and inadequate to meet current needs. In fact, some psychologists argue that the same factors that led society to underestimate the magnitude of the problem for many years now hinder the development of effective interventions. Still, there are several measures to help the victims of spousal abuse (Dutton, 1988, 1992; Browne, 1993; Koss et al., 1993).

◗ Teach both wives and husbands a basic premise: Physical violence is *never,* under *any* circumstances, an acceptable means of resolving disagreements.

◗ Call the police. It is against the law to assault another person, including a spouse. Although it may be difficult to involve law enforcement officers, this is a realistic way of dealing with domestic abuse. Judges can also issue restraining orders requiring abusive husbands to stay away from their wives.

◗ Understand that the remorse shown by a spouse, no matter how heartfelt, may have no bearing on the possibility of future violence. Even if a husband shows loving regret after a battering session and vows that he will never be violent again, such a promise is no guarantee against future abuse.

◗ If you are the victim of abuse, seek a safe haven. Many communities have shelters for the victims of domestic violence that can house women and their children. Because addresses of shelters are kept confidential, an abusive spouse will not be able to find you. Telephone numbers are listed in the yellow or blue pages of phone books, and local police should also have the numbers.

◗ If you feel in danger from an abusive partner, seek a restraining order from a judge in court. Under a restraining order a spouse is forbidden to come near you, under penalty of law.

◗ Call the National Domestic Violence Hotline at 1-800-799-7233 for immediate advice.

Spousal Abuse and Society: The Cultural Roots of Violence. Consider these scenarios:

> *After Dong Lu Chen beat his wife to death, he was sentenced to five years probation. He had confessed to the act but claimed that his wife had been unfaithful to him. His lawyer (and an anthropologist) had argued in court that traditional Chinese values might have led to his violent reaction to his wife's purported infidelity.*
>
> *After Lee Fong, a Laotian immigrant, had abducted a 16-year-old girl, he was acquitted of kidnapping, sexual assault, and menacing. During his trial, his lawyer argued that "bride stealing" is a traditional custom among the Hmong people of Laos.*
>
> *Both cases were decided in courts in the United States. In both cases, lawyers based their arguments on the claim that in the Asian countries from which the defendants had emigrated, the use of violence against women was common and may even have received social approval. The juries obviously agreed with this "cultural defense" justification. (Findlen, 1990)*

Although the tendency often is to see marital violence and aggression as a particularly North American phenomenon, in fact other cultures have traditions that establish an atmosphere in which violence is regarded as acceptable (Rao, 1997). For instance, wife battering is particularly prevalent in cultures in which women are viewed as inferior to men.

In fact, in Western societies too, legal traditions suggested at one time that wife beating was acceptable. According to English common law, which formed the foundation of the legal system in the United States, husbands were allowed to beat their wives. In the

1800s this law was modified to permit only certain kinds of beating. Specifically, a husband could not beat his wife with a stick or rod that was thicker than his thumb—the origin of the phrase "rule of thumb." It was not until the late 19th century that this law was removed from the books in the United States (Davidson, 1977).

Some experts on abuse suggest that the traditional power structure under which women and men function is a root cause of abuse. They argue that the more a society differentiates between men and women in terms of status, the more likely it is that abuse will occur (Pence & Shepard, 1988).

As evidence, they point to research examining the legal, political, educational, and economic roles of women and men. For example, some research has compared battering statistics across the various states in the United States. The findings are that states in which women's status is either relatively low or relatively high compared with women's status in other states show the highest levels of spousal abuse. Apparently, relatively low status makes women easy targets of violence. Conversely, unusually high status may make husbands feel threatened and consequently more likely to behave abusively (Yllo, 1983; Yllo & Bograd, 1988; Dutton, 1994).

Review and Rethink

REVIEW

- For most couples, marital satisfaction rises during middle adulthood.

- Family changes in middle adulthood include the departure of children. In recent years, the phenomenon of "boomerang children" has emerged.

- Middle-aged adults often have increasing responsibilities for their aging parents.

- A further change is grandparenthood. Typically, grandparents may be involved, companionate, or remote.

- Marital violence tends to pass through three stages: tension building, an acute battering incident, and loving contrition.

- The incidence of family violence is highest in families of lower socioeconomic status. A "cycle of violence" affords a partial explanation. Cultural norms may also play a role.

RETHINK

- How does the experience of divorce differ for women with outside careers versus women who have stayed home to rear children? How does the marriage gradient affect women with outside careers?

- Are the phenomena of the empty nest, boomerang children, the sandwich generation, and grandparenting culturally dependent? Why might such phenomena be different in societies where multigenerational families are the norm?

Work and Leisure

Enjoying a weekly game of golf . . . starting a neighborhood watch program . . . coaching a Little League baseball team . . . joining an investment club . . . traveling . . . taking a cooking class . . . attending a theater series . . . running for the local town council . . . going to the movies with friends . . . hearing lectures on New Age mysticism . . . fixing up a porch in the back of the house . . . chaperoning a high school class on an out-of-state trip . . . lying on a beach in Duck, North Carolina, reading a book during an annual vacation . . .

When we look at what people in the middle years of adulthood actually do, we find activities as varied as the individuals themselves. Although for most people middle adulthood represents the peak of on-the-job success and earning power, it is also a time when people throw themselves into leisure and recreational activities. In fact, middle age may be the period when work and leisure activities are balanced most easily. No longer feeling that they must prove themselves on the job, and increasingly valuing the contributions they are able to make to family, community, and—more broadly—society, middle-aged adults may find that work and leisure complement one another in ways that enhance overall happiness.

Work and Careers: Jobs at Midlife

For many, middle age is the time of greatest productivity, success, and earning power. It is also a time when occupational success may become considerably less alluring than it once was. This is particularly the case for those who may not have reached their goals, achieving less occupational success than they anticipated when they began their careers. In such cases, work becomes less valued, while family and other off-the-job interests become more important (Howard, 1992; Simonton, 1997).

The factors that make a job satisfying often undergo a transformation during middle age. Whereas younger adults are more interested in abstract and future-oriented concerns, such as the opportunity for advancement or the possibility of recognition and approval, middle-aged employees care more about the here-and-now qualities of work. For instance, they are more concerned with pay, working conditions, and specific policies, such as the way vacation time is calculated. Furthermore, as at earlier stages of life, changes in overall job quality are associated with changes in stress levels for both men and women (Rosenfeld & Owens, 1965; Barnett et al., 1995; Hattery, 2000).

In general, though, the relationship between age and work seems to be positive: The older workers are, the more overall job satisfaction they experience. This pattern is not altogether surprising, since younger adults who are dissatisfied with their positions will quit them and find new positions that they like better. Furthermore, older workers have fewer opportunities to change positions. Consequently, they may learn to live with what they have, and accept that the position they have is the best they are likely to get. Such acceptance may ultimately be translated into satisfaction (Doering, Rhodes, & Schuster, 1983; Schulz & Ewen, 1988).

burnout a situation that occurs when highly trained professionals experience dissatisfaction, disillusionment, frustration, and weariness from their jobs

Challenges of Work: On-the-Job Dissatisfaction

Job satisfaction is not universal in middle adulthood. For some people, in fact, work becomes increasingly stressful as dissatisfaction with working conditions or with the nature of the job mounts. In some cases, conditions become so bad that the result is burnout or a decision to change jobs (Remondet & Hansson, 1991; Buunk & Janssen, 1992).

Burnout. For 44-year-old Peggy Augarten, early-morning shifts in the intensive care unit of the suburban hospital where she worked were becoming increasingly difficult. Although it had always been hard to lose a patient, recently she found herself breaking into tears over her patients at the strangest moments: while she was doing the laundry, washing the dishes, or watching TV. When she began to dread going to work in the morning, she knew that her feelings about her job were undergoing a fundamental change.

Augarten's response can probably be traced to the phenomenon of burnout. **Burnout** occurs when highly trained professionals experience dissatisfaction, disillusionment, frustration, and weariness from their jobs. It occurs most often in jobs that involve helping others, and it often strikes those who initially were the most idealistic and driven. In some ways, in fact, such workers may be overcommitted to their jobs, and the realization that they can make only minor dents in huge societal problems such as poverty and medical care is disappointing and demoralizing (Freudenberger & Richelson, 1980; Maslach, 1982; Hales, 1992; Lavanco, 1997).

One of the consequences of burnout is a growing cynicism about one's work, as well as indifference and lack of concern about how well one does it. The idealism with which a

Burnout occurs when a professional experiences dissatisfaction, disillusionment, frustration, or weariness from his or her job. Those who experience it grow increasingly cynical or indifferent toward their work.

worker may have entered a profession is replaced by pessimism and the attitude that it is impossible to provide any kind of meaningful solution to a problem (Lock, 1992).

People can combat burnout, even those in professions with high demands and seemingly insurmountable burdens. For example, providing workers with realistic expectations about what can and cannot be accomplished lets them focus on what is practical and doable. Furthermore, jobs can be structured so that although the "big picture" of disease, poverty, racism, and an inadequate educational system may look gloomy, workers experience small victories in their daily work.

Unemployment: The Dashing of the Dream

The dream is gone—probably forever. And it seems like it tears you apart. It's just disintegrating away. You look alongside the river banks . . . there's all flat ground. There used to be a big scrap pile there where steel and iron used to be melted and used over again, processed. That's all leveled off. Many a time I pass through and just happen to see it. It's hard to visualize it's not there anymore. (Kotre & Hall, 1990, p. 290)

It is hard not to view 52-year-old Matt Nort's description of an obsolete Pittsburgh steel mill as symbolic of his own life. Because he has been unemployed for several years, Matt's dreams for occupational success in his own life have died as much as the mill in which he once worked.

For many workers, unemployment is a hard reality of life, and the implications of not being able to find work are as much psychological as they are economic. For those who have been fired, laid-off by corporate downsizing, or forced out of jobs by technological advances, being out of work can be psychologically and even physically devastating (Sharf, 1992).

People who are unemployed frequently suffer from insomnia and feel anxious, depressed, and irritable. Their self-confidence may plummet, and they may be unable to concentrate. In fact, according to one analysis, every time the unemployment rate goes up 1 percent, there is a 4 percent rise in suicide, and admissions to psychiatric facilities go up by some 4 percent for men and 2 percent for women (Walker & Mann, 1987; Kates, Grieff, & Hagen, 1990; Connor, 1992).

Even aspects of unemployment that might at first seem positive, such as having more time to spend with one's family, often produce disagreeable consequences. For instance, unemployed people are less apt to participate in community activities, use libraries, and read than employed people. Furthermore, they are more likely to be late for appointments and even for meals (Jahoda, 1982; Fryer & Payne, 1986).

And these problems may linger. Middle-aged adults who lose their jobs tend to stay unemployed longer than younger workers, and people have fewer opportunities for gratifying work as they age. Furthermore, employers may discriminate against older job applicants and make it more difficult to obtain new employment (Allan, 1990). Ironically, such discrimination is not only illegal, but is based on misguided assumptions: Research finds that older workers show less absenteeism than younger ones, hold their jobs longer, are more reliable, and are more willing to learn new skills (Birsner, 1991; Connor, 1992).

In sum, midlife unemployment is a shattering experience. And for some people, especially those who never find meaningful work again, it taints their entire view of the world. For people forced into such involuntary—and premature—retirement, the loss of a job can lead to pessimism, cynicism, and despondency. Overcoming such feelings requires a major investment of psychological resources on the part of both the unemployed individuals and their families (Trippet, 1991). There are challenges for those who *do* find a new career, too.

Switching—and Starting—Careers at Midlife

For some people, middle adulthood brings with it a hunger for change. For such individuals, who may be experiencing dissatisfaction with their jobs, switching careers after a period of unemployment, or simply returning to a job market they left years before, their developmental paths lead to new careers.

People who change careers in middle adulthood do so for several reasons. It may be that their jobs offer little challenge; they have achieved mastery, and what was once difficult is now routine. Other people change because their jobs have changed in ways they do not like. They may be asked to accomplish more with fewer resources, or technological advances may have made such drastic changes in their day-to-day activities that they no longer enjoy what they do.

Still others are unhappy with the status they have achieved and wish to make a fresh start. Some are burned out or feel that they are on a treadmill. In addition, some people simply do not like to think of themselves doing the same thing for the rest of their lives. For them, middle age is seen as the last point at which they can make a meaningful occupational change (Steers & Porter, 1991).

Finally, a significant number of people, almost all of them women, return to the job market after having taken time off to raise children. Some, like Johanna Hoagland, described in the chapter prologue, may need to find paying work after a divorce. Since the mid-1980s, the number of women in the workforce who are in their 50s has grown significantly. Around 65 percent of women between the ages of 50 and 60—and 80 percent of those who graduated from college—are now in the workforce, with three-quarters in full-time jobs (see Figure 16-6). (For a discussion of the of the special challenges faced by women returning to work, see the *Speaking of Development* box.)

For those who switch or start new careers, the outcome can be quite positive. They may feel invigorated by their work, and because of their prior work experience and their high level of motivation and enthusiasm, they may be especially valued employees (Connor, 1992; Adelmann, Antonucci, & Crohan, 1990; Bromberger & Matthews, 1994).

In other cases, the outcome is not so positive. People may enter new professions with unrealistically high expectations and be disappointed by the realities of the situation. Furthermore, middle-aged people who start new careers may find themselves in entry-level positions. As a consequence, their peers on the job may be considerably younger than they are (Sharf, 1992).

Still, for those people who change careers in middle adulthood, the potential rewards are great. In fact, some visionaries suggest that career changes may become the rule rather than the exception. According to this point of view, technological advances will occur so rapidly that people will be forced periodically to change dramatically what they do to earn a living. In such a scenario, people will have not one, but several, careers during

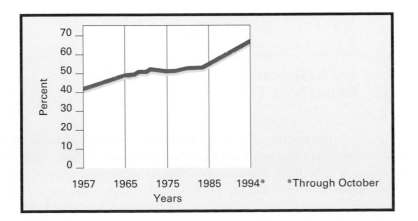

Figure 16-6 **Women at Work**

The percentage of women aged 50 to 60 who are in the labor force has steadily increased over the last 40 years.

(*Source:* U. S. Bureau of Labor Statistics, 1995.)

SPEAKING OF DEVELOPMENT

Cindy Marano, Career Advisor

EDUCATION: Northwestern University and George Mason University, B.A. in English

POSITION: Executive director, Wider Opportunities for Women

HOME: Washington, D.C.

Pursuing a career in today's highly competitive workforce can be a demanding and intimidating process, but few groups find the going as rough as women who, in middle age, must return to work.

Over the years Cindy Marano, executive director of Wider Opportunities for Women (WOW)—which serves 150 women each year in the Washington, D.C., area—has refined a process that she feels has been successful in helping women reenter the workforce in viable and well-paying jobs.

According to Marano, the first step in working with women trying to make the transition is evaluating labor market information. "Many women have a limited notion as to what the job market is, especially the current job market. Because women have been allowed so few job options, their perspective is narrowed. Consequently, you have to find out what the woman's interests are, given the current job market.

"The next step is a personal assessment, where you look at her paid work experience, volunteer experiences, and hobbies. You have to find out the kind of transferable experiences in her life that can be translated into work," Marano adds.

Marano notes that a number of barriers also have to be overcome, such as personal fears, family responsibilities, educational and literacy skills, and the lack of transportation.

"Does she have four little children under 5, and what are the child-care implications?" Marano adds. "It is almost like taking a photograph of this entire person and then digging beneath the surface. It is common to find a person with low self-esteem because of a lack of well-paid work experience. She may have had enormous personal leadership experience as a volunteer, or high skills in arts and crafts, but feels it is worthless in terms of the labor market."

In the third step of the process, WOW tries to look at the mesh between the labor market and the financial needs of the individual, according to Marano. Each woman participates in a 13-week prevocational program that builds basic skills and explores a variety of high-wage, nontraditional careers. Many of the jobs—in such fields as cable installation, repair maintenance, and the construction trades—have been predominantly filled by men.

"We do have problems finding good skills training or getting financial assistance for education, and we struggle with sending women into a hostile work environment, but we do projects with unions and management to make the environment more hospitable," she adds.

The two final steps are to identify the training needs of the individual and to help her market herself with practice interviewing and the development of a proper résumé.

"I have found that women tend to do this process best in groups. In fact, the development of a support system during the process of transition is the best thing the program can offer," Marano says.

their lifetimes. This is especially true for those who make the major change of immigrating to America as adults.

Developmental Diversity

Immigrants on the Job: Making It in America

Seventeen years ago, Mankekolo Mahlangu-Ngcobo was placed in solitary confinement for 21 days in South Africa's Moletsane police station, falsely accused of terrorism. In 1980, once again in danger of imprisonment for her anti-apartheid protests, she fled to Botswana, leaving her 12-year-old son Ratijawe with her

Mankekolo Mahlangu-Ngcobo, who fled Botswana, is now a lecturer and minister in the United States.

mother. She came to the U.S. in 1981, won political asylum in 1984 and now lives with her 13-year-old daughter Ntokozo in a $60,000 Baltimore row house. Her experiences left her with a deep appreciation of her adopted land. "If you have never lived somewhere else," she says, "you cannot know how much freedom you have here."

Ngcobo also found prosperity here. As with many of her fellow immigrants, the key was education. Since her arrival, she has earned a bachelor's degree, two master's and a doctorate in theology—which she paid for largely with scholarships or with her own money. Her academic credentials and dedication to helping others have won her two soul-satisfying careers, as a lecturer in public health at Baltimore's Morgan State University and as assistant minister at the Metropolitan African Methodist Episcopal Church in Washington, D.C. (Kim, 1995, p. 133)

If we rely solely on public opinion, we would probably view immigrants to the United States as straining the educational, health care, welfare, and prison systems while contributing little to U.S. society. But—as the story of Mankekolo Mahlangu-Ngcobo exemplifies—the assumptions that underlie anti-immigrant sentiment are in fact quite wrong.

With the number of immigrants entering the United States hovering around one million each year, residents born outside the country now represent close to 10 percent of the population, a percentage nearly twice what it was in 1980. In some states, almost a quarter of the population is foreign-born. (The proportion of foreign-born residents is still smaller than during the immigration wave in the early part of the century, when it reached 15 percent of the U.S. population.)

Critics of immigration contend that today's immigrants are somehow "different" from the earlier wave. In some ways, they are right. Only 38 percent are white, compared with 88 percent of immigrants who arrived before 1960. Critics also argue that new immigrants lack the skills that will allow them to make a contribution to the high-tech economy of the 21st century.

However, the critics are wrong in many fundamental respects. For instance, consider the following data (Topolnicki, 1995):

▶ Most legal *and* illegal immigrants are doing quite well financially. For example, U.S. Census Bureau figures show that immigrants who arrived in the United States prior to 1980 and have had a chance to establish themselves actually have a higher family income than native-born Americans.

▶ Only a few immigrants come to the United States to get on welfare. Instead, most say they come because of opportunities to work and prosper in the United States. Non-refugee immigrants who are old enough to work are less likely to be on welfare than native-born U.S. citizens.

▶ Given time, immigrants contribute more to the economy than they take away. Although initially costly to the government, often because they hold low-paying jobs and therefore pay no income taxes, immigrants become more productive as they get older. Ultimately, immigrants pay $25 billion to $30 billion a year more in taxes than they use in government services.

In short, the reality is that the vast majority of immigrants ultimately become contributing members of U.S. society. Furthermore, their contributions serve to invigorate not only the economy but the broader society as well. ☐

Leisure Time: Life Beyond Work

With the typical work week hovering between 35 and 40 hours—and becoming shorter for most people—most middle-aged adults have some 70 waking hours per week at their disposal (Kacapyr, 1997). What do they do with their leisure time?

For one thing, they watch an awful lot of television. On average, middle-aged people watch around 15 hours of television each week. But middle-aged adults do much more with their leisure time than watch television. In fact, for many people middle adulthood represents a renewed opportunity to become involved in activities outside the home. As children leave home, parents have substantial time freed up to participate more extensively in leisure activities. Consequently, adults in the United States spend some 6 hours each week socializing. Their involvement in community activities also may be significant (Robinson & Godbey, 1997).

Some of the motivation for developing leisure activities during middle adulthood comes from the desire to prepare for retirement. In fact, a significant number of people find the allure of leisure so great that they take early retirement. An increasing percentage of people in their 50s have voluntarily retired from their jobs. For those who make such a choice, and who have adequate financial resources to last the dozens of years that likely remain to them, life can be quite gratifying (Cliff, 1991; Ransom, Sutch, & Williamson, 1991).

Although middle adulthood presents the opportunity for more leisure activities, most people report that the pace of their lives does not appear slower. In fact, because much of their greater free time is scattered throughout the week in 15- and 30-minute chunks, it may seem that they have experienced no increase in leisure activity—despite a documented increase of 5 hours of weekly leisure time since 1965 (Robinson & Godlbey, 1997).

And while leisure time is increasing in the United States, the pace of life is still considerably faster than in many countries. For instance, research has examined the tempo of living in a variety of countries by assessing the length of time average pedestrians cover 60 feet, the time it takes for a customer to purchase a stamp, and the accuracy of public clocks. According to a composite of these measures, the United States has a quicker tempo than many other countries, particularly Latin American, Asian, Middle Eastern, and African countries. On the other hand, many countries outpace the United States. For example, Western European countries and Japan operate more quickly than the United States, with Switzerland ranking first (see Table 16-2; Levine, 1997a, 1997b).

Table 16-2

PACE OF LIFE WORLDWIDE

	Overall Pace	Walking 60 Feet	Postal Service	Public Clock
Switzerland	1	3	2	1
Ireland	2	1	3	11
Germany	3	5	1	8
Japan	4	7	4	6
Italy	5	10	12	2
England	6	4	9	13
Sweden	7	13	5	7
Austria	8	23	8	3
Netherlands	9	2	14	25
Hong Kong	10	14	6	14
France	11	8	18	10
Poland	12	12	15	8
Costa Rica	13	16	10	15
Taiwan	14	18	7	21
Singapore	15	25	11	4
United States	16	6	23	20
Canada	17	11	21	22
South Korea	18	20	20	16
Hungary	19	19	19	18
Czech Republic	20	21	17	23
Greece	21	14	13	29
Kenya	22	9	30	24
China	23	24	25	12
Bulgaria	24	27	22	17
Romania	25	30	29	5
Jordan	26	28	27	19
Syria	27	29	28	27
El Salvador	28	22	16	31
Brazil	29	31	24	28
Indonesia	30	26	26	30
Mexico	31	17	31	26

(Rank of 31 countries for overall pace of life and for three measures: minutes downtown pedestrians take to walk 60 feet; minutes it takes a postal clerk to complete a stamp purchase transaction; and accuracy in minutes of public clocks)
(*Source:* Adapted from Levine, 1997a.)

Review and Rethink

REVIEW

■ People in middle age look at their jobs differently than before, placing more emphasis on short-term factors and less on career striving and ambition.

■ Job satisfaction tends to be high for most middle-aged people, but some are dissatisfied because of disappointment with their accomplishments and for other reasons. Burnout is a factor, especially for people in the helping professions.

■ Unemployment in midlife can have negative economic, psychological, and physical effects.

■ Midlife career changes are becoming more prevalent, motivated usually by dissatisfaction, the need for more challenge or status, or the desire to return to the workforce after child-rearing.

■ People in middle adulthood usually have more leisure time than previously. Often they use it to become more involved outside the home in recreational and community activities.

RETHINK

■ Why might striving for occupational success be less appealing in middle age than before? What cognitive and personality changes might contribute to this phenomenon?

■ Why do you think immigrants' ambition and achievements are widely underestimated? Does the occurrence of conspicuous negative examples play a role (as it does in perceptions of the midlife crisis and stormy adolescence)?

Looking Back

▶ In what ways does personality change during middle adulthood?

■ A developmental controversy concerns whether people pass through age-related developmental stages in a more or less uniform progression, as normative-crisis models indicate, or respond to a varying series of major life events at different times and in different orders, as life events models suggest.

■ Erik Erikson suggests that the developmental conflict of the age is generativity versus stagnation, involving a shift in focus from oneself to the world beyond. George Vaillant views the main developmental issue as keeping the meaning versus rigidity, in which people seek to extract meaning from their lives and accept the strengths and weaknesses of others.

■ Roger Gould suggests that people move through seven stages during adulthood. Daniel Levinson's theory of the seasons of life focuses on the creation of "The Dream"—a global vision of one's future—in early adulthood, followed by the midlife transition of the early 40s, during which people confront their mortality and question their accomplishments, often inducing a midlife crisis. Levinson's has been criticized for the methodological limitations of his study, which focused on a small sample of men.

■ The notion of the midlife crisis has been discredited for lack of evidence. Furthermore, the concept of a distinct "middle age" appears to be cultural in nature, achieving significance in some cultures and not in others.

▶ Is there continuity in personality development during middle adulthood?

■ It appears that, in general, the broad personality may be relatively stable over time, with particular aspects changing in response to life changes.

▶ What are typical patterns of marriage and divorce in middle adulthood?

■ Middle adulthood is, for most married couples, a time of satisfaction, but for many couples marital satisfaction declines steadily and divorce results.

■ Most people who divorce remarry, usually to another divorced person. Because of the marriage gradient, women over 40 find it harder to remarry than men.

■ People who marry for a second time tend to be more realistic and mature than people in first marriages, and to share roles and responsibilities more equitably. However, second marriages end in divorce even more often than first marriages.

▶ *What changing family situations do middle-aged adults face?*

- The empty nest syndrome, a supposed psychological upheaval following the departure of children, is probably exaggerated. The permanent departure of children is often delayed as "boomerang" children return home for a number of years after having faced the harsh realities of economic life.

- Adults in the middle years often face responsibilities for their children and for their aging parents. Such adults, who have been called the sandwich generation, face significant challenges.

- Many middle-aged adults become grandparents for the first time. Researchers have identified three grandparenting styles: involved, companionate, and remote. Styles tend to differ by gender and race.

▶ *What are the causes and characteristics of family violence in the United States?*

- Family violence in the United States has reached epidemic proportions, with some form of violence occurring in a quarter of all marriages. The likelihood of violence is highest in families that are subject to economic or emotional stresses. In addition, people who were abused as children have a higher likelihood of becoming abusers as adults—a phenomenon termed the "cycle of violence."

- Marital aggression typically proceeds through three stages: a tension building stage, an acute battering incident, and a loving contrition stage. Despite contrition, abusers tend to remain abusers unless they get effective help.

▶ *What are the characteristics of work and career in middle adulthood?*

- For most persons, midlife is a time of job satisfaction. For middle-aged workers, career ambition becomes less of a force in their lives, and outside interests begin to be more valued.

- Job dissatisfaction can result from disappointment with one's achievements and position in life or from the feeling that one has failed to make a difference in the insurmountable problems of the job. This latter phenomenon, termed "burnout," often affects those in the helping professions.

- Some people in middle adulthood must face unexpected unemployment, which brings economic, psychological, and physical consequences.

- A growing number of people voluntarily change careers in midlife, some to increase job challenge, satisfaction, and status, and others to return to a workforce they left years earlier to rear children.

- Middle-aged people have substantial leisure time at their disposal, which many spend in social, recreational, and community activities. Leisure activities in midlife serve as a good preparation for retirement.

E P I L O G U E

In this chapter we have looked at the ways in which personality and social development continues throughout midlife. We examined theories of the stages of midlife development and viewed some of the major controversies of this period. We also examined the status of relationships during middle adulthood, particularly relationships with children, parents, and spouses. Finally, we discussed work and leisure time during midlife, when career and retirement issues are especially important.

Recall the prologue to this chapter, about Johanna Hoagland's decision to become a firefighter, and answer these questions.

1. Does Johanna Hoagland display any of the signs of a midlife crisis? Why or why not?

2. How might Hoagland's formation of what Levinson calls "The Dream" have occurred? Do you think she followed the same pattern that a man of her age might have followed? Why or why not?

3. Can you interpret Hoagland's life more accurately in terms of a normative-crisis model of personality development or a life events model? Why?

4. If Hoagland had become a firefighter at age 20 instead of age 40, how might her goals for the job have differed? Why?

5. In what ways is Hoagland typical of people who change jobs in middle adulthood? In what ways is she different?

Key Terms and Concepts

normative-crisis models (p. 553)   midlife crisis (p. 555)   sandwich generation (p. 565)
life events models (p. 553)   empty nest syndrome (p. 563)   cycle of violence hypothesis (p. 568)
generativity versus stagnation (p. 553)   boomerang children (p. 564) burnout (p. 571)

Bridges

Despite the lingering beliefs that middle adulthood is a time of stagnation, crisis, and dissatisfaction, we have seen that people continue to grow and change during this period. Physically, they experience gradual declines and become more susceptible to some diseases. Lifestyle choices people made during their early adult years may affect their health now, but positive actions during middle age can often reduce the risk of disease and slow the effects of physical declines. And, as we'll see in Part Eight, healthy lifestyle choices in middle age can also benefit people during later adulthood.

Cognitively, middle-aged adults experience both gains in some areas and losses in others, and generally they learn to compensate rather well for any declining capacities. As we go on, we'll see that the strategies people learn to compensate for declining capacities will continue to be used as they face further declines during their later years.

As for the realm of social and personality development, we witnessed people facing and dealing successfully with a large number of changes in family relationships and work life. We also saw that to characterize this as a time of crisis is to overstate the negative and to ignore the positive aspects of the period, which is usually characterized by satisfaction and successful adjustment. People in middle age most typically successfully fill many roles, engaging with others from many periods of the life span, including their children, parents, spouses, friends, and coworkers.

Far from being a time of threat and decline, then, middle adulthood is actually a stimulating and exciting time in which people find considerable satisfaction and begin to reap the rewards of life. They also begin to develop traits and habits that will help them deal successfully with the last stage of life—late adulthood, to which we turn in the next and final part of the book.

OUTLINE

LATE ADULTHOOD

Physical and Cognitive Development

PROLOGUE: 100 AND COUNTING

Gerontologists have found that people in late adulthood can be as vigorous and active as those many years younger.

*L*enore Schaeffer, Age 100: She took up dancing after being widowed at 82 and hasn't stopped since. Her home is filled with trophies for the fox trot, the rumba and the merengue. "I've danced from Santa Monica to Miami," says Schaeffer, who learned to waltz at Jane Addams' Hull House, the famous turn-of-the-century school. "Ballroom dancing gave me a whole new life." (Cowley, 1997, p. 58)

****

Anselmo Medina, Age 102: His family calls him "Mr. Party" because he never misses a birthday, wedding or anniversary celebration. He lives alternately with two of his daughters, moving back and forth across the street. Medina "eats everything" and likes an occasional drink of Jim Beam bourbon. He stays fit by shoveling snow and moving the furniture when it's time to vacuum the house. (Cowley, 1997, p. 59)

***

Philip Carret, Age 100: Last year, he cut back to a three-day week at Carret & Company, the money-management firm he founded in 1963. He's written three books on investments; a widower, he plans another on marriage. "Keep active and keep a positive outlook on life," he says. "Pessimism is a deadly poison. I have known several pessimists. They all died prematurely." (Cowley, 1997, p. 67)

Looking Ahead

Lenore Schaeffer, Anselmo Medina, and Philip Carret are hardly alone in reaching the century mark. There are more than 60,000 people in the United States who are 100 or more years old, and by 2020, there will probably be well over 200,000. With the mean life expectancy of people in Western countries continuing to rise, reaching the age of 100 may be the reality for increasing numbers of us.

gerontologists specialists who study aging

Old age used to be equated with loss: loss of brain cells, loss of intellectual capabilities, loss of energy, loss of sex drive. Increasingly, however, that view is being displaced as **gerontologists,** specialists who study aging, paint a very different picture of late adulthood. Rather than being viewed through the single lens of decline, late adulthood is now seen as a period of considerable diversity in which people continue to change—to grow in some areas and, yes, to decline in others.

Even the definition of "old" is changing, for many of those in the period of late adulthood, which begins at around age 60 and continues to death, are as vigorous and involved with life as people several decades younger. The reality, then, is that we cannot define old age by chronological years alone; we also must take into account people's physical and psychological well-being, their *functional ages.* Some researchers of aging divide people into three groups according to their functional ages: the *young old* are healthy and active; the *old old* have some health problems and difficulties with daily activities; and the *oldest old* are frail and in need of care. Although a person's chronological age can predict which group they are most likely to fall into, it is not a sure thing; an active, healthy 90-year-old or the people we met in the chapter prologue, would be considered young old. In comparison, a 65-year-old in the late stages of emphysema would be considered among the oldest old, according to functional age (Neugarten & Neugarten, 1987). In this chapter, we will consider both physical and cognitive development during late adulthood. We begin with a discussion of the myths and realities behind aging, examining some of the stereotypes that color our understanding of late adulthood. We look at the outward and inward signs of aging and the ways the nervous system and senses change with age.

Next, we consider health and well-being in late adulthood. After examining some of the major disorders that affect older people, we consider what factors determine wellness and the relationship between aging and disease. We also focus on various theories that seek to explain the aging process, as well as on gender, race, and ethnic differences in life expectancy.

Finally, the chapter discusses intellectual development during late adulthood. We look at the nature of intelligence in older people and the various ways cognitive abilities change. We also assess how different types of memory fare during late adulthood, and we consider ways to reverse intellectual declines in older people.

After reading this chapter, you will be able to answer the following questions:

▶ **What is it like to grow old in the United States today?**

▶ **What sorts of physical changes occur in old age?**

▶ **How are the senses affected by aging?**

▶ **What is the general state of health of older people, and to what disorders are they susceptible?**

▶ **Can wellness and sexuality be maintained in old age?**

▶ **How long can people expect to live, and why do they die?**

▶ **How well do older people function intellectually?**

▶ **Do people lose their memories in old age?**

Physical Development in Late Adulthood

One of the newest NASA astronauts is also its oldest: Senator John Glenn, who was 77 years old when launched into space as part of a 10-day space shuttle mission. Although the magnitude of Glenn's accomplishment sets him apart from most others, many people lead active, vigorous lives during late adulthood, and they are fully engaged with life.

Aging: Myth and Reality

Late adulthood holds a unique distinction among the periods of human life: Because people are living longer, late adulthood is actually increasing in length. Whether we peg the start of the period at age 60, 65, or 70, there is today a greater proportion of people alive in late adulthood than at any time in world history. In fact, because the period has begun to last so long for so many people, demographers have taken to dividing their measurements of the elderly population by age. They use the same terms as researchers who refer to functional aging, but with different meanings (so be sure to clarify if someone is using one of these terms). For demographers, the *young old* are those 65 to 74 years old. The *old old* are between 75 and 84, and the *oldest old* are people 85 and older.

The Demographics of Late Adulthood. At the start of the 20th century, approximately 6 percent of the population of the United States was age 60 or older. By 1990, the comparable figure was more than 17 percent. And projections suggest that by the year 2050, nearly one-quarter of the population will be age 65 and above. The number of people over the age of 85 is projected to increase from the current 4 million to 18 million by 2050 (see Figure 17-1; Schneider, 1999).

When a woman reaches the age of 65, her life expectancy is 19.2 years, and a man can expect to live another 15.5 years. In fact, the fastest growing segment of the population

cw

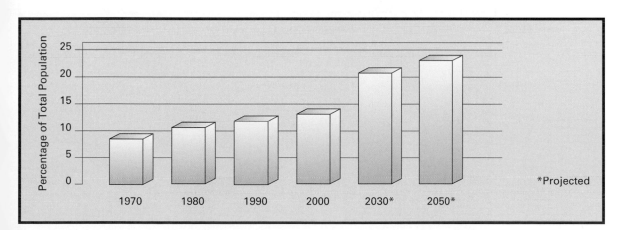

Figure 17-1 **The Flourishing Elderly**

The percentage of people over the age of 65 is projected to rise to almost 25 percent of the population by the year 2050. Can you name two factors that contribute to this?

(Adapted from U.S. Bureau of the Census, 2000.)

is the oldest old—people who are 85 or older. In the last two decades, the size of this group has nearly doubled.

The population explosion among older people is not limited to the United States. In fact, the rate of increase is much higher in developing countries. For instance, in recent years, developing countries have shown over a 100 percent increase in the number of people over the age of 60, as compared with an increase of just over 50 percent in previously developed nations. Similarly, by the year 2025 the number of people age 80 and older will increase by 415 percent in developing countries and 132 percent in already developed countries. As can be seen in Figure 17-2, the sheer numbers of elderly are increasing substantially in countries around the globe (Turner & Helms, 1993; Wilmoth et al, 1999; Sandis, 2000).

Ageism: Confronting the Stereotypes of Late Adulthood. Crotchety. Old codger. Old coot. Senile. Old geezer. Old hag.

Such are the labels of late adulthood. If you find that they don't draw a pretty picture, you're right: Such words are demeaning and biased, representing both overt and subtle ageism. **Ageism** is prejudice and discrimination directed at older people.

Ageism is manifested in several ways. It is found in widespread negative attitudes toward older people, suggesting that they are in less than full command of their mental faculties. For example, the results of many attitude studies have found that older adults are viewed more negatively than younger ones on a variety of traits, particularly those having to do with general competence and attractiveness (Secouler, 1992; Palmore & Maddox, 1999).

Furthermore, identical behavior carried out by an older and a younger person often is interpreted quite differently. For example, older adults who show memory lapses are viewed as chronically forgetful and likely to be suffering from some mental disorder. Similar behavior on the part of young adults is judged more charitably, merely as evidence of temporary forgetfulness produced by having too much on their minds (Erber, Szuchman, & Rothberg, 1990).

In addition, a negative view of older people is supported by the reverence of youth and youthful appearance that characterizes many Western societies. It is the rare advertisement that includes an elderly person, unless it is for a product specifically designed for

ageism prejudice and discrimination directed at older people

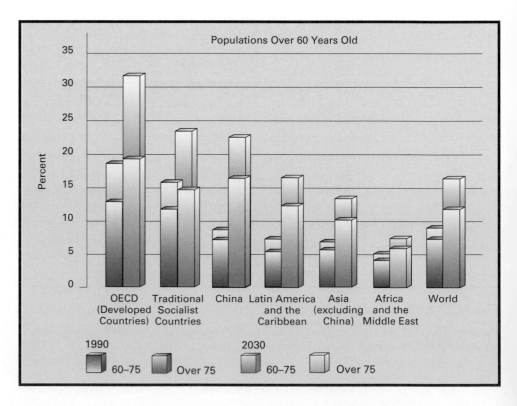

Figure 17-2 **The Elderly Population Worldwide**

Longer life is transforming population profiles worldwide with the number of elderly predicted to increase substantially by the year 2030.

(*Source:* World Bank Report, 1994.)

older adults. And when older persons are portrayed in television programming, they are often presented as someone's mother, father, grandmother, or grandfather rather than as individuals in their own right (Vernon, 1990).

The ageism that produces such negative views of older people is reflected in their treatment. For instance, elderly individuals seeking jobs may face open prejudice, being told in job interviews that the job would be better filled by people who are "less set in their ways" or "better equipped to compete in today's fast-paced world." Similarly, older applicants have been told that they have no business seeking positions that should be filled by younger persons with families to support. Such job discrimination persists even though it is illegal.

Even older people who are not employed experience ageist treatment. Older adults in nursing homes, for example, are often the recipients of "baby talk," the language and tone of voice that adults use to speak to infants (the type we discussed in Chapter 5). An 84-year-old woman might be addressed as "honey" or "baby," for example, and told that she has to go "night-night" (Whitbourne & Wills, 1993).

The ageism directed toward people in late adulthood is, in some ways, a peculiarly modern and Western cultural phenomenon. In the colonial period of U.S. history, a long life was an indication that a person had been particularly virtuous, and older people were held in high esteem. Similarly, people in most Asian societies venerate those who have reached old age because elders have attained special wisdom as a consequence of living so long. Likewise, many Native American societies traditionally have viewed older people as storehouses of information about the past (Cowgill, 1972; Palmore & Maddox, 1999).

Today, however, negative views of older people prevail in U.S. society, and they are based on widespread misinformation. For instance, to test your knowledge about aging, try answering the questions posed in Table 17-1. Most people score no higher than chance on the items, averaging about 50 percent correct (Palmore, 1988, 1992).

Given the prevalence of ageist stereotypes in Western societies today, it is reasonable to ask how accurate these views are. Is there a kernel of truth in them?

The answer is largely no. As we have seen in the cases of the centenarians Lenore Schaeffer, Anselmo Medina, and Philip Carret, whom we met in the prologue, and as will see in the remainder of this and the next chapter, aging produces consequences that vary greatly from one person to the next. Although some elderly people are in fact physically frail, have cognitive difficulties, and require constant care, others are vigorous and independent—and sharp, brilliant, and shrewd thinkers. Furthermore, some problems that seem at first glance attributable to old age are actually a result of illness, improper diet, or insufficient nutrition. As we will see, then, the autumn and winter of life can bring change and growth on a par with—and sometimes even better than—earlier periods of the life span (Whitbourne, 1996).

Physical Transitions in Older People

"Feel the burn." That's what the Jane Fonda exercise tape says, and many of the 14 women in the group are doing just that. As the exercise tape continues through a variety of drills, the women participate to varying degrees. Some stretch and reach vigorously, while others mostly appear to be just swaying in time to the pounding beat of the music. It's not much different from thousands of exercise classes all over the United States. Yet to a youthful observer, there is one surprise: The youngest woman in this exercise group is 66 years old, and the oldest, dressed in sleek Spandex leotards, is 81.

The surprise registered by this observer reflects a popular stereotype of elderly persons. Many people view those over 60 as sedentary and sedate, an image that certainly does not incorporate involvement in vigorous exercise.

Table 17-1

THE MYTHS OF AGING

1. The majority of old people (age 65 and older) are senile (have defective memory, are disoriented, or demented). **T or F?**
2. The five senses (sight, hearing, taste, touch, and smell) all tend to weaken in old age. **T or F?**
3. The majority of old people have no interest in, nor capacity for, sexual relations. **T or F?**
4. Lung vital capacity tends to decline in old age. **T or F?**
5. The majority of old people feel miserable most of the time. **T or F?**
6. Physical strength tends to decline in old age. **T or F?**
7. At least one-tenth of the aged are living in long-stay institutions (such as nursing homes, mental hospitals, and homes for the aged.) **T or F?**
8. Aged drivers have fewer accidents per driver than those under age 65. **T or F?**
9. Older workers usually cannot work as effectively as younger workers. **T or F?**
10. Over three-fourths of the aged are healthy enough to carry out their normal activities. **T or F?**
11. The majority of old people are unable to adapt to change. **T or F?**
12. Old people usually take longer to learn something new. **T or F?**
13. It is almost impossible for the average old person to learn something new. **T or F?**
14. Older people tend to react slower than do younger people. **T or F?**
15. In general, old people tend to be pretty much alike. **T or F?**
16. The majority of old people say they are seldom bored. **T or F?**
17. The majority of old people are socially isolated. **T or F?**
18. Older workers have fewer accidents than do younger workers. **T or F?**

Scoring
All odd-numbered statements are false; all even-numbered statements are true. Most college students miss about six, and high school students miss about nine. Even college instructors miss an average of about three.

(*Source:* Palmore, 1988.)

The reality, however, is different. Although the physical capabilities of elderly people are not the same as they were in earlier stages of life, many older persons remain remarkably agile and physically fit in later life (Paffenbarger et al., 1994; Fiatarone & Garnett, 1997).

Still, the changes in the body that began subtly during middle adulthood become unmistakable during old age. Both the outward indications of aging and those related to internal functioning become incontestable.

Even in late adulthood, exercise is possible—and beneficial.

Although gray hair is often characterized as "distinguished" in men, the same trait in women is viewed more often as a sign of being "over the hill"—a clear double standard.

As we discuss aging, it is important to remember the distinction, introduced in chapters 13 and 15, between primary and secondary aging. **Primary aging,** or *senescence,* involves the universal and irreversible changes that occur as people get older due to genetic preprogramming. It reflects the inevitable changes that all of us experience from the time we are born. In contrast, **secondary aging** encompasses changes that are due to illness, health habits, and other individual differences, but which are not due to increased age itself and are not inevitable. Although the physical and cognitive changes that involve secondary aging are more common as people become older, they are potentially avoidable and can sometimes be reversed.

Outward Signs of Aging. One of the most obvious signs of aging is the hair. Most people's hair becomes distinctly gray and eventually white, and it may thin out. The face and other parts of the body become wrinkled as the skin loses elasticity and *collagen,* the protein that forms the basic fibers of body tissue (Bowers & Thomas, 1995; Medina, 1996).

People may become noticeably shorter, with some shrinking as much as four inches. Although this shortening is partially due to changes in posture, the primary cause is that the cartilage in the disks of the backbone has become thinner. This is particularly true for women, who are more susceptible than men to **osteoporosis,** or thinning of the bones.

Osteoporosis, which affects 25 percent of women over the age of 60, is a primary cause of broken bones among elderly people. It is also largely preventable if people's calcium and protein intake are sufficient in earlier parts of life and if they have engaged in sufficient exercise (Perlmutter & Hall, 1992; Guralnik et al., 1995).

Although negative stereotypes against appearing old operate for both men and women, they are particularly potent for women. In fact, in Western cultures there is a *double standard* for appearance, by which women who show signs of aging are judged more harshly than men. For instance, gray hair in men is often viewed as "distinguished," a sign of character; the same characteristic in women is a signal that they are "over the hill" (Sontag, 1979; Bell, 1989).

As a consequence of the double standard, women are considerably more likely than men to feel compelled to hide the signs of aging. For instance, older women are much more likely than men to dye their hair and to have cosmetic surgery, and women's use of cosmetics is designed to make them look younger than their years (Unger & Crawford, 1992). There are recent signs that men are becoming more interested in maintaining a youthful appearance. For example, more cosmetic products, such as wrinkle creams, are

primary aging aging that involves universal and irreversable changes that, due to genetic preprogramming, occur as people get older

secondary aging changes in physical and cognitive functioning that are due to illness, health habits, and other individual differences, but which are not due to increased age itself and are not inevitable

osteoporosis a condition in which the bones become brittle, fragile, and thin, often brought about by a lack of calcium in the diet

available for men. This may be interpreted as a sign that the double standard is easing or that ageism is becoming more of a concern for both sexes.

Internal Aging. As the outward physical signs of aging become increasingly apparent, significant changes occur in the internal functioning of the organ systems. The capacities of many functions decline with age (see Figure 17-3; Turner & Helms, 1994; Whitbourne, 2001).

The brain becomes smaller and lighter with age, although, in the absence of disease, it retains its structure and function. As the brain shrinks, it pulls away from the skull, and the amount of space between brain and skull doubles from age 20 to age 70. Furthermore, there is a reduction in the flow of blood within the brain, which also uses less oxygen and glucose. The number of neurons, or brain cells, declines in some parts of the brain, although not as much as was once thought. For instance, recent research suggests that the number of cells in the brain's cortex may drop only minimally or not at all (Scheibel, 1992; Wickelgren, 1996; Morrison & Hof, 1997; see Figure 17-4).

The reduced flow of blood in the brain reflects in part reductions in the capacity of the heart to pump blood throughout the circulatory system. Because of hardening and shrinking of blood vessels throughout the body, the heart is forced to work harder, and it is typically unable to compensate fully. Consequently, 75-year-old men are able to pump less than three-quarters of the blood that they were able to pump during early adulthood (Shock, 1962; Kart, 1990).

Other bodily systems work at lower capacity than they did earlier in life. For instance, the efficiency of the respiratory system declines with age, and the digestive system produces less digestive juice and is less efficient in pushing food through the system—

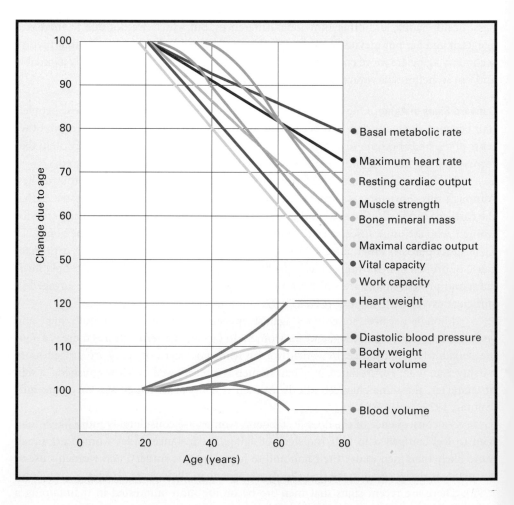

Figure 17-3 **Changing Physical Capacities**

As people age, there are significant changes in the functioning of various systems of the body.

(*Source:* Whitbourne, 2001.)

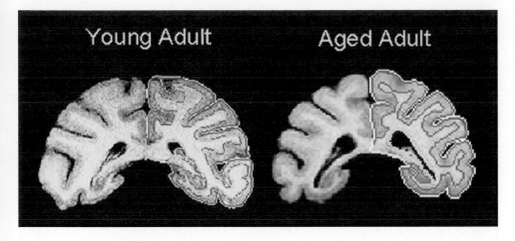

Figure 17-4 **Brain Cell Decline**

These MRI images show loss of white, but not gray, matter in the brain of a 32-year-old rhesus monkey (right). The young adult is 5 years old.

(*Source:* Rosene et al., 1996.)

which produces a higher incidence of constipation. Some hormones are produced at lower levels with increasing age. Furthermore, muscle fibers decrease both in size and in amount, and they become less efficient at using oxygen from the bloodstream and storing nutrients (Fiatarone & Garnett, 1997; Lamberts, van den Beld, & van der Lely, 1997).

Although all of these changes are the normal processes of primary aging, they can occur more quickly in people who have less healthy lifestyles. For example, smoking speeds declines in cardiovascular capacity at any age. It may be possible that lifestyle factors could also slow these changes. For example, people whose exercise program includes weightlifting may lose muscle fiber at a slower rate than those who are sedentary.

Slowing Reaction Time

Karl winced as the "game over" message came up on his grandson's video game system. He enjoyed trying out their games, but he just couldn't shoot down those bad guys as quickly as his grandkids could.

As people get older, they take longer: longer to put on a tie, longer to reach a ringing phone, longer to press the buttons in a video game. One reason for this slowness is a lengthening of reaction time. As we discussed first in Chapter 15, reaction time begins to increase in middle age, and by late adulthood the rise can be significant (Fozard et al., 1994; Sliwinski et al., 1994).

It is not clear why people slow down. One explanation, known as the **peripheral slowing hypothesis,** suggests that overall processing speed declines in the peripheral nervous system. According to this notion, the peripheral nervous system, which encompasses the nerves that branch out from the spinal cord and brain and reach the extremities of the body, becomes less efficient with age. Because of this decrease in efficiency, it takes longer for information from the environment to reach the brain and longer for commands from the brain to be transmitted to the body's muscles (Salthouse, 1989).

Other researchers have proposed an alternative explanation. According to the **generalized slowing hypothesis,** processing in all parts of the nervous system, including the brain, is less efficient. As a consequence, slowing occurs throughout the body, including the processing of both simple and complex stimuli and the transmission of commands to the muscles of the body (Cerella, 1990).

Although we don't know which explanation provides the more accurate account, it is clear that the slowing of reaction time and general processing results in a higher incidence of accidents for elderly persons. Because their reaction and processing time is slowed, they are unable to efficiently receive information from the environment that may indicate a dangerous situation, their decision-making processes may be slower, and ultimately their ability to

peripheral slowing hypothesis the theory that suggests that overall processing speed declines in the peripheral nervous system with increasing age

generalized slowing hypothesis the theory that processing in all parts of the nervous system, including the brain, is less efficient

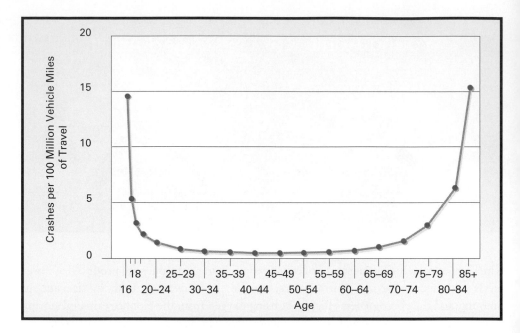

remove themselves from harm's way is impaired. As evidence of this fact, drivers over the age of 70 have as many fatal accidents as teenagers when accidents are figured in terms of miles of driving (Whitbourne, Jacobo, & Munoz-Ruiz, 1996; see Figure 17-5).

Although it takes older individuals longer to respond, the *perception* of time seems to increase with age. The days and weeks seem to go by more quickly; generally time seems to rush by faster for older adults than younger ones. The reason may be due to changes in the way the brain coordinates its internal time clock (Mangan, 1997).

The Senses: Sight, Sound, Taste, and Smell

Old age brings with it distinct declines in the sense organs of the body, although in this area there is a great deal of variation. Sensory declines are of major psychological consequence because the senses serve as people's link with the world outside the mind.

Vision. Age-related changes in the physical apparatus of the eye—the cornea, lens, retina, and optic nerve—lead to a decrease in visual abilities. For instance, the lens becomes less transparent and the pupil shrinks. Even the optic nerve becomes less efficient in transmitting nerve impulses (Scheiber, 1992).

As a result, vision declines along several dimensions. Vision of distant objects becomes less acute, more light is needed to see clearly, and it takes longer to adjust from dark to light places and vice versa.

The changes in vision produce everyday difficulties. For instance, driving, particularly at night, becomes more challenging (Ball & Rebok, 1994). Similarly, reading requires more lighting, and eye strain occurs more easily. On the other hand, eyeglasses and contact lenses can correct many of these problems, and the majority of older people can see reasonably well (Akutsu, 1991; Horowitz, 1994; Orr, 1991).

Several eye diseases become more common during late adulthood. For instance, *cataracts*—cloudy or opaque areas on the lens of the eye that interfere with passing light—frequently develop. People with cataracts have blurred vision and tend to experience glare in bright light. If cataracts are left untreated, the lens becomes milky white and blindness is the eventual result. However, cataracts can be surgically removed, and eyesight can be restored through the use of eyeglasses, contact lenses, or *intraocular lens implants,* in which a plastic lens is permanently placed in the eye.

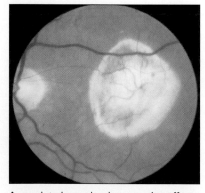

Age-related macular degeneration affects the macula, a yellowish area of the eye located near the retina. Eyesight gradually deteriorates once the portion of the macula thins and degenerates.

Another serious problem that afflicts many elderly individuals is glaucoma. As we noted first in Chapter 15, *glaucoma* occurs when pressure in the fluid of the eye increases, either because the fluid cannot drain properly or because too much fluid is produced. Glaucoma, too, can be treated by drugs or surgery if it is detected early enough.

The most common cause of blindness in people over the age of 60 is *age-related macular degeneration (AMD)*. This disorder affects the *macula,* a yellowish area of the eye located near the retina at which visual perception is most acute. When a portion of the macula thins and degenerates, the eyesight gradually deteriorates. If diagnosed early, macular degeneration can sometimes be treated with lasers. In addition, there is some evidence that a diet rich in antioxidant vitamins (C, E, and A) can reduce the risk of the disease (Frishman, 1997a; Smith et al., 1999; Mayo Clinic, 2000).

Hearing. Hearing loss is fairly common among elderly people. Around 30 percent of adults between the ages of 65 and 74 have some degree of hearing loss, and the figure rises to 50 percent among people over the age of 75. Overall, more than 10 million elderly people in the United States have hearing impairments of one kind or another (Hudson, 1990; HHL, 1997).

The ability to hear higher frequencies is particularly affected during old age. Loss of these frequencies makes it hard to hear conversations when there is considerable background noise or when several people are speaking simultaneously. Furthermore, some elderly persons actually find loud noises painful.

Although hearing aids can help compensate and would probably be helpful in around 75 percent of the cases of permanent hearing loss, only 20 percent of elderly people wear them. One reason is that hearing aids are far from perfect. They amplify background noises as much as they amplify conversations, making it difficult for wearers to separate what they want to hear from other sounds. Moreover, there is a stigma attached to wearing a hearing aid; many elderly people feel that the use of hearing aids makes them appear even older than they really are and causes them to be treated as if their minds were disabled (Hudson, 1990; Patterson, Dancer, & Clark, 1990).

A hearing loss can particularly harm the social lives of older people. Unable to hear conversations fully, some elderly people with hearing problems withdraw from others, avoiding situations in which many people are present. They may also be unwilling to respond to others, since they are unsure of what was said to them. In addition, such hearing losses can lead to feelings of paranoia; able to catch only fragments of conversations, a hearing-impaired older adult can easily feel left out and lonely (Knutson & Lansing, 1990).

Taste and Smell. Elderly people who have enjoyed eating throughout their lives may experience a real decline in the quality of life because of changes in sensitivity to taste and smell. Both senses become less discriminating in old age, causing food to taste and smell less appetizing than it did earlier (Matteson, 1988; Myslinski, 1990; Scheiber, 1992; de Graaf, Polet, & van Staveren, 1994; Kaneda et al., 2000).

The reason for the decrease in taste and smell sensitivity can be traced to physical changes. Most older people have fewer taste buds in the tongue than they did when they were younger. Furthermore, the olfactory bulbs in the brain begin to shrivel, which reduces the ability to smell. Because smell is responsible in part for taste, the shrinkage of the olfactory bulbs makes food taste even more bland.

The loss of taste and smell sensitivity has an unfortunate side effect: Because food does not taste as good, people eat less and open the door to malnutrition. Furthermore, to compensate for the loss of taste buds, older people may oversalt their food, thereby increasing their chances of developing *hypertension,* or high blood pressure, one of the most common health problems of old age (Stevens et al., 1991).

Review and Rethink

REVIEW

- Older people are often the victims of ageism—prejudice and discrimination against old people.
- Old age brings external changes—thinning and graying hair, wrinkles, and shorter stature—and internal changes—decreased brain size, reduced blood flow within the brain, and diminished efficiency in circulation, respiration, and digestion.
- The two main hypotheses to explain the increase in reaction time in old age are the peripheral slowing hypothesis and the generalized slowing hypothesis.
- Vision may become more difficult at distances, in dim light, and when moving from darkness to light and vice versa.

- Hearing, especially of high frequencies, may diminish, causing social and psychological difficulties, and taste and smell may become less discriminating, leading to nutritional problems.

RETHINK

- When older people win praise and attention for being "vigorous," "active," and "youthful," is this a message that combats or supports ageism?
- Should strict examinations for renewal of driver's licenses be imposed on older people? What issues should be taken into consideration?

Health and Wellness in Late Adulthood

Like an actor settled into a long-running show, he continues to play the familiar role almost by rote: chopping wood, riding horses, visiting his office where, these days, the only business that awaits are letters from well-wishers and a jar of jelly beans. But nearly four months after his poignant handwritten note informing the world that he was suffering from Alzheimer's disease, former President Ronald Reagan, 84, is increasingly forgetting his lines and missing his cues. "About six months ago, he stopped recognizing me," Reagan's biographer, Edmund Morris, wrote recently. "Now I no longer recognize him." (Lambert, Armstrong, & Wagner, 1995, p. 32)

Former president Ronald Reagan became one of the 4 million Americans who suffer from Alzheimer's disease, a debilitating condition that saps both the physical and mental powers of its victims. In some ways, his disease symbolizes our view of elderly people, who, according to popular stereotypes, are more apt to be ill than healthy.

However, the reality is different: Most elderly people are in relatively good health for most of old age. According to surveys conducted in the United States, almost three-quarters of people 65 years old and above rate their health as good, very good, or excellent (USDHHS, 1990; Rowe & Kahn, 1998).

On the other hand, to be old is to be susceptible to a host of diseases. We now consider some of the major physical and psychological problems that beset older people.

Health Problems in Older People: Physical and Psychological Disorders

Most of the illnesses and diseases found in late adulthood are not peculiar to old age; people of all ages suffer from cancer and heart disease, for instance. However, the incidence of these and many other diseases rises with age, raising the odds that an elderly person will be ill during the period. Moreover, while younger people can readily rebound from a variety

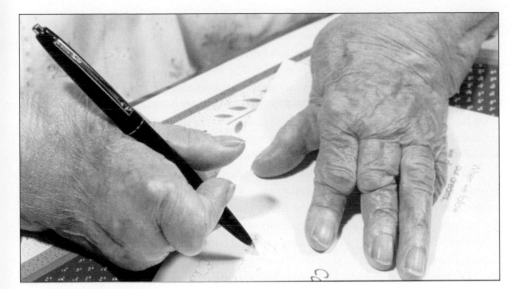

Arthritis can produce swelling and inflammation in the joints of the hands.

of health problems, older persons bounce back more slowly from illnesses. And ultimately, the illness may get the best of an older person, preventing a full recovery.

Common Physical Disorders. The leading causes of death in elderly people are heart disease, cancer, and stroke. Close to three-quarters of people in late adulthood die from these problems. Because aging is associated with a weakening of the body's immune system, older adults are also more susceptible to infectious diseases (Feinberg, 2000).

In addition to their risk of fatal diseases and conditions, most older people have at least one chronic, long-term condition (AARP, 1990). For instance, *arthritis*, an inflammation of one or more joints, is common, striking around half of older people. Arthritis can cause painful swelling in various parts of the body, and it can be disabling. Sufferers can find themselves unable to carry out the simplest of everyday activities, such as unscrewing the cap of a jar of food or turning a key in a lock. Although aspirin and other drugs can relieve some of the swelling and reduce the pain, the condition cannot be cured (Burt & Harris, 1994).

Around one-third of older people have *hypertension*, or high blood pressure. Many people who have high blood pressure are unaware of their condition because it does not have any symptoms, which makes it more dangerous. Over time, higher tension within the circulatory system can result in deterioration of the blood vessels and heart, and can raise the risk of cerebrovascular disease, or stroke, if it is not treated.

Psychological and Mental Disorders. Like people in other age groups, older adults are susceptible to a variety of psychological disorders. Some 15 to 25 percent of those over age 65 are thought to show some symptoms of psychological disorder (Haight, 1991).

One of the more prevalent problems is major depression, which is characterized by intense sadness, pessimism, and hopelessness. One obvious reason older people may become depressed is the cumulative losses they experience with the death of spouses and friends, often of the same age and sometimes even younger. Furthermore, declining health and physical capabilities, which may rob older people of a sense of control, may contribute to the prevalence of depression (Bruce & Hoff, 1994; Penninx et al., 1998).

On the other hand, it is not clear that depression is a significantly worse problem in late adulthood than it is earlier in life. In fact, some studies suggest that the rate of depression actually may be lower during late adulthood. One reason for this puzzling finding is that there may be two kinds of depression in older adulthood: depression that continues from earlier stages of life and depression that occurs as a result of aging (Gatz, 1997).

Some elderly people may suffer from drug-induced psychological disorders brought about combinations of drugs they may be taking for various medical conditions. Because of changes in metabolism, a dose of a particular drug that would be appropriate for a 25-year-old might be much too large for a person of 75. The effects of drug interactions can be subtle, and they can manifest themselves in a variety of psychological symptoms, such as drug intoxication or anxiety. Because of these possibilities, older people who take medications must be on guard, informing their physicians and pharmacists of every drug they take. They should also avoid medicating themselves with over-the-counter drugs, because a combination of nonprescription and prescription drugs may be dangerous, or even deadly.

The most common mental disorder of elderly people is dementia. **Dementia** is a broad category covering several diseases, each of which includes serious memory loss accompanied by declines in other mental functioning. Although dementia has many causes, the symptoms are similar: declining memory, lessened intellectual abilities, and impaired judgment. The chances of experiencing dementia increase with age. For example, although less than 2 percent of people between 60 and 65 years are diagnosed with dementia, the percentages double for every 5-year period past 65. Consequently, almost one-third of people over the age of 85 suffer from some sort of dementia. There are some ethnic differences, too, with African Americans and Hispanics showing higher levels of dementia than Caucasians (National Research Council, 1997).

Dementia is hardly inevitable, and most people do not suffer from the disorder during late adulthood. Still, it strikes a significant number of people, particularly in its most common form: Alzheimer's disease. Alzheimer's represents one of the most serious mental health problems faced by the aging population.

Alzheimer's Disease. **Alzheimer's disease,** a progressive brain disorder that produces loss of memory and confusion, leads to the deaths of 100,000 people in the United States each year. Nineteen percent of people 75 to 84 have Alzheimer's, and almost 50 percent of people over the age of 85 are affected by the disease. In fact, unless a cure is found, some 14 million people will be victims of Alzheimer's by 2050—more than three times more than the current number (Cowley, 2000).

The symptoms of Alzheimer's disease develop gradually. Generally, the first sign is unusual forgetfulness. A person may stop at a grocery store several times during the week, forgetting that he or she has already done the shopping. People may also have trouble recalling particular words during conversations. At first, recent memories are affected, and then older memories fade. Eventually, people with the disease are totally confused, unable to speak intelligibly or to recognize even their closest family and friends. In the final stages of the disease, they lose voluntary control of their muscles and are bedridden. Because victims of the disorder are initially aware that their memories are failing and often understand quite well the future course of the disease, they may suffer from anxiety, fear, and depression—emotions not difficult to understand, given the grim prognosis.

Biologically, Alzheimer's occurs when production of the protein *beta amyloid precursor protein*—a protein that normally helps the production and growth of neurons—goes awry, producing large clumps of cells that trigger inflammation and deterioration of nerve cells. The brain shrinks, and several areas of the hippocampus and frontal and temporal lobes show deterioration. Furthermore, certain neurons die, which leads to a shortage of various neurotransmitters, such as acetylcholine (Cooper et al., 2000; George-Hyslop, 2000; Lanctot, Herrmann, & Mazzotta, 2001).

Although the physical changes in the brain that produce the symptoms of Alzheimer's are clear, what is not known is what triggers the problem in the first place. Several explanations have been advanced. For instance, as we saw in Chapter 2, genetics clearly plays a role, with some families showing a much higher incidence of Alzheimer's than others. In fact, in certain families half the children appear to inherit the disease from

dementia the most common mental disorder of the elderly, it covers several diseases, each of which includes serious memory loss accompanied by declines in other mental functioning

Alzheimer's disease a progressive brain disorder that produces loss of memory and confusion

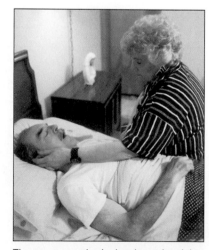

The enormous physical and emotional demands of caring for an Alzheimer patient leads many caregivers to frustration, anger and exhaustion. What can ease the stress of the caregiver?

their parents. Furthermore, years before the actual symptoms of Alzheimer's emerge, people who are genetically at high risk for the disease show differences in brain functioning when they are trying to recall information, as illustrated in the brain scans in Figure 17-6 (Bertram et al., 2000; Bookheimer et al., 2000).

Although most evidence suggests that Alzheimer's is an inherited disorder, recent research implies that nongenetic factors such as high blood pressure or diet may increase susceptibility to the disease. In one cross-cultural study, poor Black residents in a Nigerian town were less likely to develop Alzheimer's than a comparable sample of Blacks living in the United States. The researchers speculate that variations in diet between the two groups—the residents of Nigeria ate mainly vegetables—might account for the differences in the Alzheimer's rates (Hendrie et al., 2001).

Other explanations for the disease have also been investigated. For example, scientists are studying certain kinds of viruses, dysfunctions of the immune system, and hormone imbalances that may produce the disease. Other studies have found that lower levels of linguistic ability in the early 20s are associated with declines in cognitive capabilities due to Alzheimer's much later in life (Small et al., 1995; Snowdon et al., 1996).

At the present time, there is no cure for Alzheimer's disease; treatment deals only with the symptoms. Although understanding of the causes of Alzheimer's is incomplete, several drug treatments for Alzheimer's appear promising, although none is effective in the long term. The most promising drugs are related to the loss of the neurotransmitter acetylcholine (Ach) that occurs in some forms of Alzheimer's disease. Tacrine (Cognex) and Aricept have been found to inhibit an enzyme that breaks down Ach, and they seem to alleviate some of the symptoms of the disease. Still, they are effective in only about 20 percent of Alzheimer's patients (Corliss, 1996).

Other drugs being studied include anti-inflammatory drugs, which may reduce the brain inflammation that occurs in Alzheimer's. In addition, the chemicals in vitamins C and E are being tested, since some evidence suggests that people who take such vitamins are at lower risk for developing the disorder. Still, at this point, it is clear that no drug treatment is truly effective (TIMHE, 1995).

Ultimately, caregivers must provide total care for victims of Alzheimer's. As victims lose the ability to feed and clothe themselves, or even to control bladder and bowel functions, they must be cared for 24 hours a day. Because such care is typically impossible for even the most dedicated families, most Alzheimer's victims end their lives in nursing homes. Patients with Alzheimer's make up some two-thirds of those in nursing homes (Gray, Farish, & Dorevitch, 1992; Rovner & Katz, 1993).

People who care for the victims of Alzheimer's often become secondary victims of the disease. It is easy to become frustrated, angry, and exhausted by the demands of Alzheimer's patients, whose needs may be overpowering. In addition to the physical chore of providing total care, caregivers face the loss of a loved one, who may be visibly deteriorating. The burdens of caring for a person with Alzheimer's can be overwhelming (Talkington-Boyer & Snyder, 1994; Williamson & Schulz, 1993; Schulz, 2000).

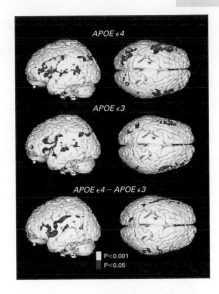

Figure 17-6   A Different Brain?

Brain scans during memory recall tasks show differences between the brains of people who have an inherited tendency toward Alzheimer's disease and those who do not. The brains at the top are a composite of those at risk; the brains in the middle are a composite of normal brains. The bottom row indicates areas of difference between the first two rows.

(*Source:* Bookheimer et al., 2000.)

Wellness in Late Adulthood:
The Relationship Between Aging and Illness

Is getting sick an inevitable part of old age? Not necessarily. Whether an older person is ill or well depends less on age than on a variety of factors, including genetic predisposition, past and present environmental factors, and psychological factors.

Certain diseases, such as cancer and heart disease, have a clear genetic component. Some families have a higher incidence of breast cancer, for instance, than others. At the same time, though, a genetic predisposition does not automatically mean that a person will get a particular illness. People's lifestyles—whether or not they smoke, the nature of

Becoming an Informed Consumer of Development
Caring for People with Alzheimer's Disease

Alzheimer's disease is one of the most difficult illnesses to deal with, as a friend or loved one inexorably deteriorates both mentally and physically. However, several steps can be taken to help both patient and caregiver deal with Alzheimer's.

▶ Make patients feel secure in their home environments by keeping them occupied in everyday tasks of living as long as possible.

▶ Provide labels for everyday objects, furnish calendars and detailed but simple lists, and give oral reminders of time and place.

▶ Keep clothing simple: Provide clothes with few zippers and buttons, and lay them out in the order in which they should be put on.

▶ Put bathing on a schedule. People with Alzheimer's may be afraid of falling and of hot water, and may therefore avoid needed bathing.

▶ Prevent people with the disease from driving. Although patients often want to continue driving, their accident rate is high—some 20 times higher than average.

▶ Monitor the use of the telephone. Alzheimer patients who answer the phone have been victimized by agreeing to requests of telephone salespeople and investment counselors.

▶ Provide opportunities for exercise, such as a daily walk. This prevents muscle deterioration and stiffness.

▶ Caregivers should remember to take time off. Although caring for an Alzheimer's patient can be a full-time chore, caregivers need to lead their own lives. Seek out support from community service organizations.

▶ Call or write the Alzheimer's Association, which can provide support and information. The Association can be reached at 919 North Michigan Avenue, Suite 1000, Chicago, Illinois 60611-1676; Tel. 1-800-272-3900; *http://www.alz.org*.

---

their diets, their exposure to cancer-causing agents such as sunlight or asbestos—may raise or lower their chances of coming down with such a disease.

Furthermore, economic well-being also plays a role. For instance, as at all stages of life, living in poverty restricts access to medical care. Even relatively well-off people may have difficulties finding affordable health care. In 1997, for example, older individuals averaged almost $3,000 in out-of-pocket health care expenditures, a rise of 35 percent since 1990. Furthermore, older people spend 12 percent of their total expenditures on health care, three times more than younger individuals. Because the United States lacks a health care insurance system that provides for universal medical coverage, many elderly individuals face grave financial burdens in obtaining affordable health care. As a result, many receive inadequate care. They are less likely to have regular checkups, and when they finally go for treatment, their illnesses may be more advanced (AARP, 1997).

Finally, psychological factors play an important role in determining people's susceptibility to illness—and ultimately the likelihood of death. For example, having a sense of control over one's environment, even in terms of making choices involving everyday matters, leads to a better psychological state and superior health outcomes (Taylor, 1991).

People can do specific things to enhance their physical well-being—as well as their longevity—during old age. It is probably no surprise that the right things to do are no different from what people should do during the rest of the life span: Eat a proper diet, exercise, and avoid obvious threats to health, such as smoking (see Figure 17-7). Medical and social services providers who work with elderly people have begun to emphasize the importance of these lifestyle choices for older adult. The goal of many such professionals has become not just to keep older adults from illness and death, to extend people's *active life spans,* the amount of time they remain healthy and able to enjoy their lives (Wannamethee et al., 1998; Burns, 2000; Resnick, 2000).

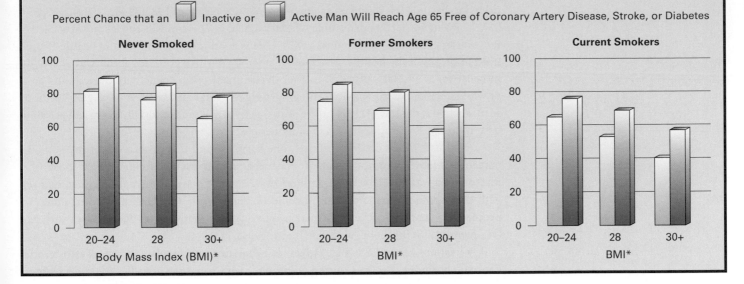

Figure 17-7 **Benefits of Exercise and a Healthy Diet**

A recent study of more than 7,000 men, aged 40 to 59, found that not smoking, keeping weight down, and exercising regularly can greatly reduce the risk of coronary heart disease, stroke, and diabetes. Although the study included only men, a healthy lifestyle can benefit women too. *To find your body mass index (BMI) multiply your weight in pounds by 705. Divide the result by your height in inches, then divide by your height again.

(Adapted from Wannamethee, et al., 1998.)

Sometimes, however, older people experience difficulties that prevent them from following even these simple guidelines. For instance, varying estimates suggest that between 16 and 50 percent of elderly people do not have adequate nutrition, and several million experience hunger every day (Manson & Shea, 1991; McCarthy, 1994; Burt & Harris, 1994).

The reasons for such malnutrition and hunger are varied. Some elderly people are too poor to purchase adequate food, and some are too infirm to shop or cook for themselves. Others feel little motivation to prepare and eat proper meals, particularly if they live alone. For those who have experienced significant declines in taste and smell sensitivity, eating well-prepared food may no longer be enjoyable. And some older people may never have eaten well-balanced meals in earlier periods of their lives (Ponza & Wray, 1990; Horwath, 1991).

Obtaining sufficient exercise may also prove problematic for older persons. Physical activity increases muscle strength and flexibility, reduces blood pressure and the risk of heart attack, and produces several other benefits, but many older people do not get sufficient exercise to experience any of these benefits.

For instance, illness may prevent older adults from exercising, and even inclement weather during the winter may restrict a person's ability to get out of the house. Furthermore, problems can combine: A poor person with insufficient money to eat properly may as a consequence have little energy to put into physical activity.

Sexuality in Old Age: Use It or Lose It

Do your grandparents have sex?

Quite possibly, yes. Although the answer may surprise you, increasing evidence suggests that people are sexually active well into their 80s and 90s. This happens in spite of societal stereotypes suggesting that it is somehow improper for two 75-year-olds to have sexual intercourse, and even worse for a 75-year-old to masturbate. Such negative attitudes are a function of societal expectations in the United States. In many other cultures, elderly people are expected to remain sexually active, and in some societies, people are expected to become less inhibited as they age (Winn & Newton, 1982; Hyde, 1994).

Two major factors determine whether an elderly person will engage in sexual activity (Masters, Johnson, & Kolodny, 1982). One is good physical and mental health. People need to be physically healthy and to hold generally positive attitudes about sexual activity in order for sex to take place. The other determinant of sexual activity during old age is previous regular sexual activity. The longer elderly men and women have gone without sexual activity, the less likely is future sexual activity. "Use it or lose it" seems an accurate description of sexual functioning in older people.

And use it they do. For instance, one survey found that 43 percent of men and 33 percent of women over the age of 70 masturbated. The average frequency for those who masturbated was once per week. Around two-thirds of married men and women had sex with their spouses, again averaging around once per week. In addition, the percentage of people who view their sexual partners as physically attractive actually increases with age (see Figure 17-8; Brecher et al., 1984; Budd, 1999).

Of course, there are some changes in sexual functioning related to age. Testosterone, the male hormone, declines during adulthood, with some research finding a decrease of approximately 30 to 40 percent from the late 40s to the early 70s. It takes a longer time, and more stimulation, for men to get a full erection. The refractory period—the time following an orgasm during which men are unable to become aroused again—may last as long as a day or even several days. Women's vaginas become thin and inelastic, and they produce less natural lubrication, making intercourse more difficult (Frishman, 1996).

Despite these changes in sexual functioning, sexual expression remains a full possibility (Kellett, 1993; Crose & Drake, 1993; Schiavi, 1990; Gelfand, 2000; Kellett, 2000). In fact, sexual activity can continue throughout the life span. Furthermore, there's some intriguing evidence that having sex may have some unexpected side benefits: One study found that having sex regularly is associated with a lower risk of death (Purdy, 1995; Davey, Frankel, & Yarnell, 1997)!

Approaches to Aging: Why Is Death Inevitable?

Hovering over our discussion of health in late adulthood is the specter of death. At some point, no matter how healthy we have been throughout life, we know that we will experience physical declines and that life will end. But why?

Theories of Aging. There are two major approaches to explaining why we undergo physical deterioration and death: genetic preprogramming theories and wear-and-tear theories.

genetic preprogramming theories of aging theories that suggest that our body's DNA genetic code contains a built-in time limit for the reproduction of human cells

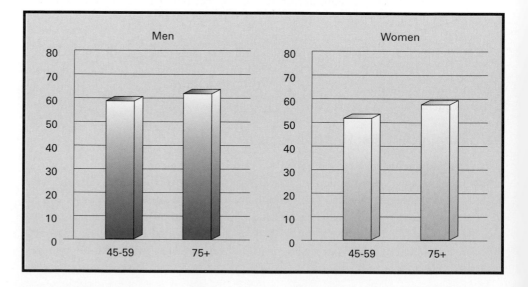

Figure 17-8 **Attractiveness Over Time**

More than 50 percent of Americans over 45 find their partners attractive, and as time goes on, more attractive.

(*Source:* AARP/Modern Maturity Sexuality Study, August, 1999.)

Genetic preprogramming theories of aging suggest that our body's DNA genetic code contains a built-in time limit for the reproduction of human cells. After a certain amount of time has gone by—determined genetically—the cells are no longer able to divide, and the individual begins to deteriorate (Jazwinski, 1996; Finch & Tanzi, 1997).

There are actually several variations of the genetic preprogramming approach. One is that the genetic material contains a "death gene" that is programmed to direct the body to deteriorate and die. Researchers who take an evolutionary viewpoint, described first in Chapter 1, suggest that survival of the species would require that people live long enough to reproduce. A long life span after the reproductive years, however, would be unnecessary. According to this view, genetically related diseases that tend to strike later in life would continue to exist, because they allow people time to have children, thus passing along genes that are "programmed" to cause diseases and death.

Another variation of the genetic preprogramming view is that the cells of the body can only duplicate a certain number of times. Throughout our lives, new cells are being made, through cell duplication, to repair and replenish all of our various tissues and organs. According to this view, however, the genetic instructions for running the body can be read only a certain number of times before they become illegible. (Think of a computer disk containing a program that is used over and over and eventually just gives out.) As these instructions become incomprehensible, cells stop reproducing. Because the body is not being renewed at the same rate, people begin to experience bodily deterioration and ultimately death (Hayflick, 1974; Pereira-Smith et al., 1988; Finch, 1990).

The second class of explanations for physical declines are wear-and-tear theories of aging. **Wear-and-tear theories** argue that the mechanical functions of the body simply wear out—the way cars and washing machines do. In addition, some wear-and-tear theorists suggest that the body's constant manufacture of energy to fuel its activities creates by-products. These by-products, combined with the toxins and threats of everyday life (such as radiation, chemical exposure, accidents, and disease), eventually reach such high levels that they impair the body's normal functioning. The ultimate result is deterioration and death.

One specific category of by-products that have been related to aging includes *free radicals*, electrically charged molecules or atoms that are produced by the cells of the body. Because of their electrical charge, free radicals may cause negative effects on other cells of the body. A great deal of research suggests that oxygen free radicals may be implicated in a number of age-related problems, including cancer, heart disease, and diabetes (Brody,

wear-and-tear theories the theory that the mechanical functions of the body simply wear out with age

According to genetic preprogramming theories of aging, people's DNA genetic code contains a built-in limit on the length of life. Scientists are seeking to crack the code.

1994b; Vajragupta et al., 2000). (The *From Research to Practice* box later in the chapter discusses the implications of this research for prolonging life.)

Genetic preprogramming theories and wear-and-tear theories make different suggestions about the inevitability of death. Genetic preprogramming theories suggest that there is a built-in time limit to life—it's programmed in the genes, after all. On the other hand, wear-and-tear theories, particularly those that focus on the toxins that are built up during the course of life, paint a somewhat more optimistic view. They suggest that if a means can be found to eliminate the toxins produced by the body and by exposure to the environment, aging might well be prevented.

We don't know which class of theories provides the more accurate account of the reasons for aging. Each is supported by some research, and each seems to explain certain aspects of aging. Ultimately, then, just why the body begins to deteriorate and die remains something of a mystery (DiGiovanna, 1994).

life expectancy the average age of death for members of a population

Life Expectancy: How Long Have I Got? Although the reasons for deterioration and death are not fully apparent, conclusions about average life expectancy can be stated quite clearly: Most of us can expect to live into old age. The **life expectancy**—the average age of death for members of a population—of a person born in 1980, for instance, is 74 years of age. This is of course a far cry from the 100+ years achieved by the individuals we met in the chapter prologue, but even that life span is not as uncommon as it once was.

Average life expectancy has been steadily increasing. In 1776, average life expectancy in the United States was just 35. By the early 1900s, it had risen to 47. And in only four decades, between 1950 to 1990, it increased from 68 to over 75 years. Predictions are that it will continue to rise steadily, possibly reaching age 80 by the year 2050 (see Figure 17-9).

There are several reasons for the steady increase in life expectancy over the past 200 years. Health and sanitation conditions are generally better, with many diseases, such as smallpox, wiped out entirely. Other diseases that used to kill people at early ages, such as measles and mumps, are now better controlled through vaccines and preventive measures. People's working conditions are generally better, and many products are safer than they once were. As we've seen, many people are becoming aware of lifestyle choices that can extend their lives. As environmental factors continue to improve, we can predict that life expectancy will continue to increase. Also, as we've seen, many people are becoming aware of the importance of lifestyle choices for extending not just the length of their lives, but their active life spans, the years they spend in health and enjoyment of life.

One major question for gerontologists is just how far the lifespan can be increased. The most common answer is that the upper limit of life hovers around 120 years, the age

Figure 17-9 **Living to Age 100**

If increases in life expectancy continue, it may be a common occurrence for people to live to be 100 by the end of this century. What implications does this have for society?

(*Source:* U.S. Bureau of the Census, 1997.)

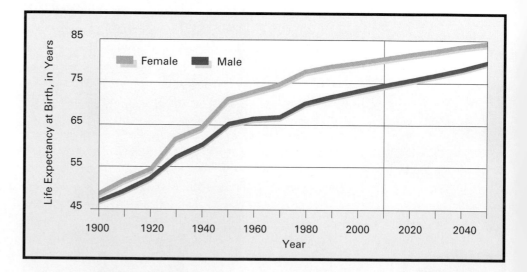

reached by Jeanne Calment, who was the oldest person in the world until she died in 1997 at the age of 122. Living beyond this age would probably require some major genetic alterations in humans, and that seems both technically and ethically improbable. Still, as discussed in the accompanying *From Research to Practice* box, several scientific and technological advances that have occurred in the last decade suggest that significantly extending the life span is not an impossibility.

It is also important to keep in mind that these figures for average life expectancy mask considerable gender, race, and ethnic disparities. These differences have important implications for society at large, as we discuss next.

Developmental Diversity

Gender, Race, and Ethnic Differences in Average Life Expectancy: Separate Lives, Separate Deaths

▶ The average white child born in the United States is likely to live 76 years. The average African American child is likely to live 5 years less.

▶ A child born in Japan has a life expectancy of 79 years; for a child born in Gambia, life expectancy is less than 45 years.

▶ A male born in the United States today is most likely to live to the age of 73; a female will probably live some 7 years longer.

There are several reasons for these discrepancies. Consider, for example, the gender gap in life expectancy, which is particularly pronounced. Across the industrialized world, women live longer than men by some 4 to 10 years (Holden, 1987). This female advantage begins just after conception: Although slightly more males are conceived, males are more likely to die during the prenatal period, infancy, and childhood. Consequently, by the age of 30 there are roughly equal numbers of men and women. But by the age of 65, 84 percent of females and only 70 percent of males are still alive. For those over 85, the gender gap gapes wider: For every male, 2.57 women are still alive (AARP, 1990).

There are several explanations for the gender gap. One is that the naturally higher levels of hormones such as estrogen and progesterone in women provide some protection from diseases such as heart attacks. Another possibility is that because women have been relegated to certain traditional professional roles, they experience less stress than men. It is also possible that women engage in healthier behavior during their lives, such as eating well. However, no conclusive evidence supports any of these explanations fully (DiGiovanna, 1994).

Whatever its cause, the gender gap continued to increase during much of the 20th century. In the early part of the century, there was only a 2-year difference in favor of women. In contrast, the gap grew to 7 years in the 1980s. On the other hand, the size of the gap seems to have leveled off, largely due to the fact that men are more likely than previously to engage in positive health behaviors (such as smoking less, eating better, and exercising more).

The racial and ethnic differences are troubling. They point out the disparities in socioeconomic well-being of various groups in the United States. For example, life expectancy is almost 10 percent greater for Caucasians than for African Americans (see Figure 17-10). Furthermore, in contrast to Caucasians, whose life expectancy keeps edging up, African Americans have actually experienced slight declines in life expectancy in recent years.

From Research to Practice
Postponing Aging: Can Scientists Find the Fountain of Youth?

Are researchers close to finding the scientific equivalent of the mythical fountain of youth that can postpone aging?

They haven't found it yet, but they're getting closer, at least in nonhuman species. Researchers have made significant strides in the last decade in identifying potential ways that aging may be held off. For instance, studies involving nematodes, microscopic, transparent worms that typically live for just 9 days, have found that it is possible to extend their lives to 50 days, which is the equivalent of having a human live to the age of 420 years. Fruit flies' lives have also been extended, doubling their life expectancy (Lakowski & Hekimi, 1996; Ewbank et al., 1997; Whitbourne, 2001).

According to new findings in several areas, humans might well extend our life spans through biochemical and even mechanical means. There is no single mechanism that is likely to postpone aging. Instead, it is probable that a combination of some of the following most promising avenues for increasing the length of life will prove effective (Rose, 1999; Stock & Campbell, 2000):

▶ **Telomere therapy.** Telomeres are tiny, protective areas at the tip of chromosomes that appear to grow shorter each time a cell divides. When a cell's telomere has just about disappeared, the cell stops replicating, making it more susceptible to damage. Some scientists believe that if telomeres could be lengthened, age-related problems could be slowed. Researchers are now attempting to find genes that control the natural production of telomerase, an enzyme that seems to regulate the length of telomeres (Fu et al., 2000; Steinert, Shay, & Wright, 2000; Urquidi, Tarin, & Goodison, 2000).

▶ **Reducing free radicals through antioxidant drugs.** As mentioned earlier, free radicals are unstable molecules that are a by-product of normal cell functioning that may drift through the body, damaging other cells and leading to aging. Although antioxidant drugs that reduce the number of free radicals have not yet been proven to retard free radicals, some scientists think that they may prove effective. Furthermore, someday it may be possible to insert in human cells genes that produce enzymes that act as antioxidants. In the mean-

time, nutritionists urge a diet rich in antioxidant vitamins, which are found in fruits and vegetables (Irani et al., 1997; Bodnar et al., 1998; Vajragupta et al., 2000).

▶ **Restricting calories.** For at least the last decade, researchers have known that laboratory rats who are fed an extremely low-calorie diet, one that provides 30 to 50 percent of their normal intake, often live 30 percent longer than better-fed rats, providing they obtain all the vitamins and minerals that they require. The reason appears to be that fewer free radicals are produced in the hungry rats. Does this mean if we starve ourselves we're likely to live longer? No one knows for sure, because no definitive studies have been done. In addition, no one should try it, since maintaining proper nutrition is extremely tricky. Researchers hope to develop drugs that mimic the effects of calorie restriction without forcing people to feel hungry all the time (Sohal & Weindruch, 1996; Weindruch, 1996; Lee et al., 1999).

▶ **The bionic solution: replacing worn-out organs.** Heart transplants . . . liver transplants . . . lung transplants. We live in an age where the removal of damaged or diseased organs and their replacement with better-functioning ones seems nearly routine. However, despite significant advances in organ transplantation, transplants frequently fail because the body rejects the foreign tissue. To overcome this problem, some researchers suggest that replacement organs can be grown from a recipient's cloned cells, thereby solving the rejection problem. In an even more radical advance, genetically engineered cells from nonhumans that do not evoke rejection could be cloned, harvested, and transplanted into people who require transplants. Finally, it is possible that technical advances permitting the development of artificial organs that can completely replace diseased or damaged ones will become common. In fact, the first self-contained artificial heart, called the AbioCor, was implanted in a Kentucky man, Robert Tools, in 2001. Such artificial organs offer the possibility of significantly extending the human life span in the same way that we can keep automobiles on the road by replacing the parts that break down (Bengston & Schaie, 1999; Rogers & Hayden, 1997).

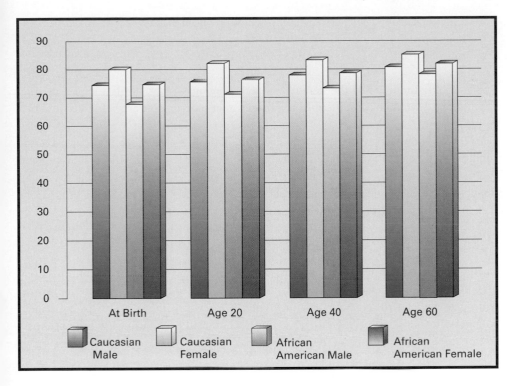

Figure 17-10 **Life Expectancy of African Americans and Whites**

Both male and female African Americans have a shorter life expectancy than male and female Caucasians. Are the reasons for this genetic, cultural, or both?

(*Source:* Anderson, U.S. National Center for Health Statistics, 2001.)

Review and Rethink

REVIEW

■ Although most older people are healthy, the incidence of some serious diseases rises in old age, and most people have at least one chronic ailment before they die.

■ Older people are susceptible to psychological disorders such as depression.

■ The most prevalent and damaging brain disorder among older people is Alzheimer's disease.

■ Proper diet, exercise, and avoidance of health risks can lead to prolonged wellness during old age, and sexuality can continue throughout the life span in healthy adults.

■ Whether death is caused by genetic preprogramming or by general physical wear and tear is an unresolved question.

Life expectancy, which has risen for centuries, varies with gender, race, and ethnicity.

■ New approaches to increasing life expectancy include telomere therapy, reducing free radicals through antioxidant drugs, restricting caloric intake, and replacing worn-out organs.

RETHINK

■ In what ways is socioeconomic status related to wellness in old age and to life expectancy?

■ How might studies be designed to test whether the genetic preprogramming or wear-and-tear theory is more accurate?

Cognitive Development in Late Adulthood

Three women were talking about the inconveniences of growing old.

"Sometimes," one of them confessed, "when I go to my refrigerator, I can't remember if I'm putting something in or taking something out."

"Oh, that's nothing," said the second woman. "There are times when I find myself at the foot of the stairs wondering if I'm going up or if I've just come down."

"Well, my goodness!" exclaimed the third woman. "I'm certainly glad I don't have any problems like that"—and she knocked on wood. "Oh," she said, starting up out of her chair, "there's someone at the door." (Dent, 1984, p. 38)

This old joke summons up the stereotypic view of aging. In fact, not too long ago many gerontologists would have subscribed to the view that older people are befuddled and forgetful.

Today, however, the view has changed dramatically. Researchers no longer see the cognitive abilities of older people as inevitably declining. Overall intellectual ability and specific cognitive skills, such as memory and problem solving, are more likely to remain strong. In fact, with the appropriate practice and exposure to certain kinds of environmental stimuli, cognitive skills can actually improve.

Intelligence in Older People

The notion that older people become less cognitively adept initially arose from misinterpretations of research evidence. As we first noted in Chapter 15, early research on how intelligence changed as a result of aging typically drew a simple comparison between younger and older people's performance on the same IQ test, using traditional cross-sectional experimental methods. For example, a group of 30-year-olds and a group of 70-year-olds might have been given the same test and had their performance compared.

However, there are several drawbacks to such a procedure, as we noted in Chapter 1. One is that cross-sectional methods do not take into account *cohort effects*—influences attributable to growing up in a particular era. For example, if the the younger group—because of when they grew up—has more education, on average, than the older group, we might expect the younger group to do better on the test for that reason alone. Furthermore, because some traditional intelligence tests include timed portions or reaction-time components, the slower reaction time of older people might account for their inferior performance.

To try to overcome such problems, developmental psychologists turned to longitudinal studies, which followed the same individuals for many years. But these studies, too, raise some fundamental interpretive difficulties. Because of repeated exposure to the same test, subjects may, over time, become familiar with the test items, a fact that calls later results into question. Furthermore, participants in longitudinal studies may move away, quit participating, become ill, or die, leaving a smaller and possibly more cognitively

Although some aspects of intelligence decline during late adulthood—as well as throughout earlier adulthood—crystallized intelligence (the store of information, skills, and strategies that people have acquired) remains steady and actually may improve.

skilled group of people. In short, longitudinal studies have their drawbacks, and their use initially led to some erroneous conclusions about older people.

Recent Conclusions about the Nature of Intelligence in Older People

More recent research has attempted to overcome the drawbacks of both cross-sectional and longitudinal methods. In what is probably the most ambitious—and still ongoing—study of intelligence in older people, developmental psychologist K. Warner Schaie has employed cross-sequential methods. As we discussed in Chapter 1, *cross-sequential studies* combine cross-sectional and longitudinal methods by examining several different age groups at a number of points in time.

In Schaie's massive study, carried out in Seattle, Washington, a battery of tests of cognitive ability was given to a group of 500 randomly chosen individuals. The people belonged to different age groups, starting at age 20 and extending at 5-year intervals to age 70. The participants were tested, and continue to be tested, every 7 years, and more people are recruited to participate every year. At this point, more than 5,000 participants have been tested (Schaie, 1994).

The study, along with other research, supports several generalizations about the nature of intellectual change during old age. Among the major ones (Schaie, 1994; Craik & Salthouse, 1999):

- Some abilities gradually decline throughout adulthood, starting at around age 25, while others stay relatively steady (see Figure 17-11). There is no uniform pattern in adulthood of age-related changes across all intellectual abilities. In addition, as we discussed in Chapter 15, fluid intelligence (the ability to deal with new problems and situations) declines with age, while crystallized intelligence (the store of information, skills, and strategies that people have acquired) remains steady and in some cases actually improves (Baltes & Schaie, 1974; Schaie, 1993).

- For the average person, some cognitive declines are found in all abilities by age 67. However, these declines are minimal until the 80s. Even at age 81, less than half of the people tested showed consistent declines over the previous 7 years.

- Significant individual differences are found in the patterns of change in intelligence. Some people begin to show intellectual declines in their 30s, while others do not ex-

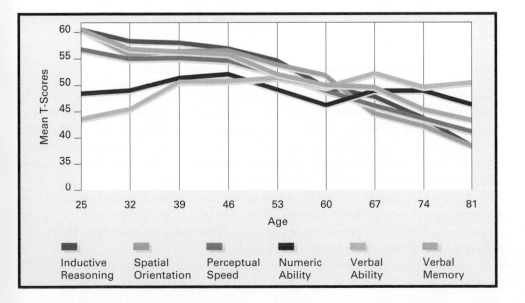

Figure 17-11 **Changes in Intellectual Functioning**

Although some intellectual abilities decline across adulthood, others stay relatively steady.

(*Source:* Schaie, 1994, p. 307.)

perience any decreases until they are in their 70s. In fact, around a third of those in their 70s score higher than the average young adult.

■ Certain environmental and cultural factors are related to greater or lesser degrees of intellectual decline. People who showed less decline were likely to share several other characteristics, including the absence of chronic diseases, higher socioeconomic status (SES), involvement in an intellectually stimulating environment, a flexible personality style, being married to a bright spouse, maintenance of good perceptual processing speed, and feelings of self-satisfaction with one's accomplishments in midlife or early old age.

The relationship between environmental factors and intellectual skills suggested to Schaie and his colleagues that it might be possible to develop procedures to help older adults maintain their information-processing skills. Schaie and Sherry L. Willis have carried out several studies examining methods of enhancing elderly people's cognitive skills. In one experiment, 229 older men and women participated in a 5-hour training program on reasoning and spatial skills (Schaie & Willis, 1986). The participants' average was 73. Some of them had already experienced declines in their cognitive skills, according to tests. All participants were taught general strategies for dealing with problems, and they also completed a series of practice test items similar to those used to measure cognitive skills.

After completing the training, participants were tested on a variety of skills. Of those people who had shown earlier declines in reasoning and spatial skills, most began to improve. Furthermore, the training boosted the performance of those elderly people whose abilities had remained relatively stable. Specifically, more than half of the subjects with prior declines in intellectual functioning showed significant improvement, and more than a third of the stable subjects improved significantly following training.

Subsequent research shows that cognitive training can have lasting effects. For example, one group of subjects received training three times over a 7-year period. By the end of the 7 years, many of the subjects performed at a significantly higher level than they did at the start of the study. Furthermore, the study found that even adults in their late 70s showed significant improvement due to training (Willis & Nesselroade, 1990).

Even more important than these people's improvements on the experimental tests was that the training seemed to help them in everyday life. Growth in cognitive abilities was related to improvements in practical intelligence and on tasks associated with daily living. Such **plasticity,** or modifiability of behavior, suggests that there is nothing fixed about the changes that may occur in intellectual abilities during late adulthood. With the proper stimulation, practice, and motivation, older people can maintain their mental abilities. In mental life, then, as in so many other areas of human development, the motto "use it or lose it" is quite fitting (Willis et al., 1992; Garnett, 1996; Sinnott, 1998).

Memory: Remembrance of Things Past—and Present

Composer Aaron Copland summed up what had happened to his memory in old age by remarking, "I have no trouble remembering everything that had happened 40 or 50 years ago—dates, places, faces, music. But I'm going to be 90 my next birthday, November 14th, and I find I can't remember what happened yesterday" (*Time,* 1980, p. 57). Our confidence in the accuracy of Copland's analysis is strengthened by an error in his statement: On his next birthday, he would be only 80 years old!

Is memory loss an inevitable part of aging? Not necessarily. For instance, cross-cultural research reveals that in societies where older people are held in relatively high esteem, such as in China, people are less likely to show memory losses than in societies where they are held in less regard (Levy & Langer, 1994).

Furthermore, even when memory declines that can be directly traced to aging do occur, they are limited primarily to *episodic memories,* which relate to specific life experiences. In contrast, other types of memory, such as *semantic memories* (general knowledge

plasticity the degree to which a developing structure or behavior is susceptible to experience

and facts) and *implicit memories* (memories about which people are not consciously aware), are largely unaffected by age (Russo & Parkin, 1993; Nilsson et al., 1997).

Still, it is clear that memory capacities change during old age. For instance, *short-term memory* slips gradually during adulthood until age 70, when the decline becomes more pronounced. The largest drop is for information that is presented quickly and verbally, such as when someone staffing a computer helpline rattles off a series of complicated steps for fixing a problem with a computer. In addition, information about things that are completely unfamiliar is more difficult to recall. For example, declines occur in memory for prose passages, names and faces of people, and even such critical information as the directions on a medicine label, possibly because new information is not registered and processed effectively when it is initially encountered. Although these age-related changes are generally minor, and their impact on everyday life negligible (because most elderly people automatically learn to compensate for them), memory losses are real (Cherry & Park, 1993; Carroll, 2000; Light, 2000).

Autobiographical Memory: Recalling the Days of Our Lives. When it comes to **autobiographical memory,** memories of information about one's own life, older people are subject to some of the same principles of recall as younger individuals. For instance, memory recall frequently follows the *Pollyanna principle,* in which pleasant memories are more likely to be recalled than unpleasant memories. Similarly, people tend to forget information about their past that is not congruent with the way they currently see themselves and are more likely to make the material that they do recall "fit" their current conception of themselves (Friedman, 1993; Rubin 1996; Eacott, 1999).

Furthermore, particular periods of life are remembered better than others. As can be seen in Figure 17-12, 70-year-olds tend to recall autobiographical details from their 20s and 30s best. In contrast, 50-year-olds are likely to have more memories of their teenage years and their 20s. In both cases, recall of earlier years is better than recall of somewhat more recent decades, but not as complete as recall of very recent events (Fromholt & Larsen, 1991; Rubin, 1985, 2000).

Explaining Memory Changes in Old Age. Explanations for apparent changes in memory among older people tend to focus on three main categories: environmental factors, information processing deficits, and biological factors.

■ *Environmental factors.* Certain transitory factors that cause declines in memory may be found more frequently in older people. For example, older people are more apt than younger ones to take the kinds of prescription drugs that hinder memory. The lower performance of older people on memory tasks may be related to drug taking and not to age per se.

Memory loss is not as common among Chinese elderly as it is in the West. What are some factors that contribute to cultural differences in memory loss of the elderly?

autobiographical memory memories of information about one's own life

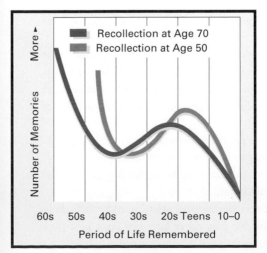

Figure 17-12 **Remembrances of Things Past**

Recall of autobiographical memories varies with age, with 70-year-olds recalling details from their 20s and 30s best, and 50-year-olds recalling memories from their teenage years and 20s. People of both ages also recall more recent memories best of all.

(*Source:* Rubin, 1986.)

Similarly, declines in memory can sometimes be traced to life changes in late adulthood. For instance, retirees, no longer facing intellectual challenges from their jobs, may become less practiced in using memory. Also, their motivation to recall information may be lower than previously, accounting for lower performance on tasks involving memory. They also may be less motivated than younger people to do their best in testing situations in experiments.

■ *Information processing deficits.* Other explanations assume that memory declines not because of environmental factors, such as changes in lifestyle or motivation, but because of changes in information processing capabilities. For example, one approach suggests that as we reach later adulthood, our ability to inhibit irrelevant information and thoughts may decrease, and that the presence of irrelevant thoughts interferes with successful problem solving. Similarly, some research suggests that the speed of information processing declines, perhaps in a similar way to the slowing of reaction times that we discussed earlier, leading to the memory impairments observed in old age (Salthouse, 1991; Hartley, 1993; Bashore, Ridderinkhof, & van der Molen, 1998).

The information-processing-deficit approach that has received the most research support suggests that memory declines are due to changes in the ability to pay attention to and organize tasks involving memory skills. In this view, older adults concentrate less effectively than younger individuals and have greater difficulty paying attention to appropriate stimuli and organizing material in memory. Furthermore, older people use less efficient processes to retrieve information from memory. These information-processing deficits subsequently lead to declines in recall abilities (Light, 1991; Craik, 1984, 1994).

■ *Biological factors.* The last of the major approaches to explaining changes in memory during late adulthood concentrates on biological factors. According to this view, memory changes are a result of brain and body deterioration.

For instance, declines in episodic memory may be related to the deterioration of the frontal lobes of the brain. Furthermore, some studies show a loss of cells in the hippocampus, which is critical to memory. In addition, estrogen loss may be a factor in memory deficits. However, specific sorts of memory deficits occur in many older people without any evidence of underlying biological deterioration, and the evidence of a decline in cells in the hippocampus is increasingly being questioned (Wickelgren, 1996; Morrison & Hof, 1997; Shaywitz et al., 1999).

Learning in Later Life: Never Too Late to Learn

The University of Arkansas campus is buzzing with talk of midterms and football. In a cafeteria, students are grousing about the food.

"Where are the dinner rolls?" says one. "I'm a vegetarian, and all they have is meat," complains another. Soon, though, everyone has moved on to complaining about classes.

A typical college scene—except for all the canes, hearing aids and white hair in evidence. This is Elderhostel, a program for people 60 and older run by a Boston nonprofit organization, formed in 1975, that recruits colleges to conduct weeklong educational sessions in everything from genealogy to the archaeology of ancient Egypt. . . .

Dorothy McAlpin, 63, is one of the program's most devoted students. A little more than a year ago, as she prepared to retire from a job as a correctional officer in a medium-security men's prison in Clarinda, Iowa, her biggest fear was "waking up in the morning alone and with nothing to do."

Rather than "play bridge and put on church bake sales," as older folks do in Clarinda, the grandmother, who wears her long silver hair tied back in a pink bow, decided to spend her retirement attending Elderhostel programs.

She studied the thick course directory and mapped out a route that allowed her to attend a different one in a different place just about every week. . . . Then, Mrs. McAlpin, who was divorced three years ago, became a vagabond. She gave up her apartment, bought a second-hand Winnebago and traveled around the country, from campus to campus.

In 52 weeks, Mrs. McAlpin, a community-college graduate, attended 45 Elderhostel programs, from Boston to Florida, Texas to Minnesota (Stern, 1994, p. A1).

Dorothy McAlpin is just one of the more than 250,000 people who enroll annually in thousands of classes organized by the Elderhostel program, the largest educational program for people in late adulthood. Represented on college campuses across the world, the Elderhostel movement is among the increasing evidence that intellectual growth and change continue to be important throughout people's lives, including late adulthood (Miller, 1997; Sack, 1999). In fact, as we saw in our examination of research on cognitive training, exercising specific cognitive skills may be especially important to older adults who want to maintain their intellectual functioning.

The popularity of programs such as Elderhostel attests to a growing trend among older people: the continuation of their education throughout late adulthood. Because the majority of older people have retired, they have time to delve into subjects in which they have always been interested, but which they have not previously been able to pursue.

Although sometimes classes are specially designed for older adults (as with Elderhostel), in other cases older people enroll in regular courses. For instance, many colleges encourage senior citizens to enroll in classes by providing them with free tuition.

Not everyone in late adulthood is able to take advantage of such educational opportunities. Because Elderhostels charge tuition, students who enroll in them tend to be of higher socioeconomic status, and the majority have postcollege graduate training of some sort (Beck, 1991).

In addition, some elderly people are doubtful about their intellectual capabilities and consequently avoid regular college classes in which they might have to compete with younger students. Their concern is largely misplaced, however: Older adults often have no trouble maintaining their standing in rigorous college classes. Furthermore, professors and other students generally find the presence of older people, with their varied and substantial life experiences, a real educational benefit (Shevron & Lumsden, 1985).

Review and Rethink

REVIEW

- Cross-sectional and longitudinal studies that found lower intellectual functioning among elderly people have been called into question.
- Cross-sequential studies indicate that different aspects of intellectual functioning change in different ways.
- Studies also reveal that the intellect retains considerable plasticity and can be maintained with stimulation, practice, and motivation.
- Declines in memory affect mainly episodic memories and short-term memory.

- Explanations of memory changes in old age have focused on environmental factors, information processing declines, and biological factors.

RETHINK

- Do you think steady or increasing crystallized intelligence can partially or fully compensate for declines in fluid intelligence? Why or why not?
- How might cultural factors, such as the esteem in which a society holds its older members, work to affect an older person's memory performance?

Looking Back

▶ **What is it like to grow old in the United States today?**

■ The number and proportion of older people in the United States and many other countries are larger than ever, and elderly people are the fastest growing segment of the U.S. population. Older people as a group are subjected to stereotyping and discrimination, a phenomenon referred to as "ageism."

▶ **What sorts of physical changes occur in old age?**

■ Old age is a period in which outward physical changes unmistakably indicate aging, but many older people remain fit, active, and agile well into the period.

■ Inwardly, older people experience a decrease in brain size and a reduction of blood flow (and oxygen) to all parts of the body, including the brain. The circulatory, respiratory, and digestive systems all work with less efficiency.

■ Slowed reaction time is explained by the peripheral slowing hypothesis (processing speed in the peripheral nervous system slows down) and the generalized slowing hypothesis (processing in all parts of the nervous system slows down).

▶ **How are the senses affected by aging?**

■ Physical changes in the eye bring declines in vision, and several eye diseases become more prevalent in old age, including cataracts, glaucoma, and age-related macular degeneration (AMD).

■ Hearing also declines, particularly the ability to hear higher frequencies. Hearing loss has psychological and social consequences, since it discourages older people from engaging in social interactions. Declines in the senses of taste and smell can have health consequences.

▶ **What is the general state of health of older people, and to what disorders are they susceptible?**

■ Although most older people are healthy, the incidence of certain serious diseases rises in old age and the ability to recuperate declines. Most older people suffer from at least one long-term ailment. The leading causes of death in old age are heart disease, cancer, and stroke.

■ Older people are also susceptible to psychological disorders, such as depression and brain disorders, especially Alzheimer's disease.

▶ **Can wellness and sexuality be maintained in old age?**

■ Psychological and lifestyle factors can influence wellness in old age. A sense of control over one's life and environment can have positive effects, as can a proper diet, exercise, and the avoidance of risk factors, such as smoking.

■ Despite some changes in sexual functioning, sexuality continues throughout old age, provided both physical and mental health are good.

▶ **How long can people expect to live, and why do they die?**

■ The inevitability of death is unquestioned but unexplained. Genetic preprogramming theories claim that the body has a built-in time limit on life, while wear-and-tear theories maintain that the body simply wears out.

■ Life expectancy has been rising steadily for centuries and continues to do so, with differences according to gender, race, and ethnicity. The life span may be further increased by technological advances such as telomere therapy, the use of antioxidant drugs to reduce free radicals, development of low-calorie diets, and organ replacement.

▶ **How well do older people function intellectually?**

■ According to cross-sequential studies, such as those conducted by K. Warner Schaie, intellectual abilities tend to decline slowly throughout old age, but different abilities change in different ways. Training, stimulation, practice, and motivation can help older people maintain their mental abilities.

▶ **Do people lose their memories in old age?**

■ Loss of memory in old age is not general, but specific. Episodic memories are most affected, while semantic and implicit memories are largely unaffected. Short-term memory declines gradually until age 70, then deteriorates quickly.

■ Explanations of memory changes may focus on environmental factors, information-processing declines, and biological factors. Which approach is most accurate is not entirely settled.

EPILOGUE

In this chapter we began by reviewing the demographics of old age and looking at the phenomenon of ageism. We discussed health and wellness during late adulthood and found that older people can extend their well-being through good diet, good habits, and good exercise. We also discussed the length of the life span and explored some of the reasons why life expectancy has been increasing. We ended with an examination of cognitive abilities, finding many discrepancies between reality and stereotypical views of older people's intellectual abilities and memory.

Return to the prologue of this chapter, about Lenore Schaeffer, Anselmo Medina, and Philip Carret, and answer the following questions.

1. In what ways do Schaeffer, Medina, and Carret contradict the stereotypes of older people and life in old age?

2. What elements of these three lives may have contributed to their longevity? What do you think they were like as younger people?

3. What are common elements in the lives of Shaeffer, Medina, and Carret? What elements are different? Can any hypotheses be drawn about the key to long life? How could these hypotheses be tested?

4. Would it be reasonable to administer an IQ test to any of these three people and interpret the results according to the current IQ scale? Why or why not?

5. According to predictions regarding memory in late adulthood, are Shaeffer, Medina, and Carret more likely to recall accurately the events of World War I (1914–1918) or World War II (1939–1945)? Why?

Key Terms and Concepts

gerontologists (p. 584)
ageism (p. 586)
primary aging (p. 589)
secondary aging (p. 589)
osteoporosis (p. 589)
peripheral slowing hypothesis (p. 591)

generalized slowing hypothesis (p. 591)
dementia (p. 596)
Alzheimer's disease (p. 596)
genetic preprogramming theories of aging (p. 600)
wear-and-tear theories (p. 601)

life expectancy (p. 602)
plasticity (p. 608)
autobiographical memory (p. 609)

1 2 3 4 5 6 7 8 9 10

Social and Personality Development in Late Adulthood

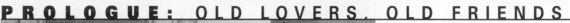
PROLOGUE: OLD LOVERS, OLD FRIENDS

Eva and Joseph Solymosi, married for close to 80 years.

"Well, I tell you," says Eva Solymosi, and so she does, starting at the beginning when she first met Joseph. The youngest of 13, she was a poor cook in Hungary, befriended by an old woman who shared this advice: "When a kind face comes by, keep him."

Eva saw Joseph, an 18-year-old chimney sweep, getting a drink of cold water by the public well. "He had a kind face. So that's it," she says and shrugs. They married the next year, moved to the U.S., and have been together since. She is 97 and he is 93. . . .

They are partners. When one is telling a story, the other quietly gets up and fetches a pertinent picture or letter. They share the chores and praise the other's efforts. . . .

They have been blessed, they say, not only with each other but with good friends. Look, they say. There's the dining room table from Hazel's grandmother, and the perfume from a lawyer and his wife who, before they died years ago, drove 70 miles to visit them every Sunday. . . .

When Joseph is shopping or watching the news, Eva will spend hours going through her dozen photo albums. There is Joseph as a young man reading the newspaper, Eva eating an ear of corn in the 1920s, their first Christmas tree . . . She comes across a picture of him when he was 18. "Ah ha, that is the kind face I fell in love with. In my eyes he is still as handsome." He says nothing, but gently taps her cane with his. (Ansberry, 1995, p. A1, a17)

615

Looking Ahead The warmth and affection between Joseph and Eva are unmistakable. Their relationship, spanning almost eight decades, continues to bring them quiet joy, and their mutual love and admiration reach the heights of human interconnectedness.

We turn in this chapter to the social and emotional aspects of late adulthood. We begin by considering how personality continues to develop in elderly individuals, and then turn to an examination of various ways people can age successfully.

Next, we consider how various societal factors affect the day-to-day living conditions of older adults. We discuss options in living arrangements, as well as ways economic and financial issues influence people's lives. We also look at how culture governs the way we treat older people, and we examine the influence of work and retirement on elderly individuals, considering the ways retirement can be optimized.

Finally, we consider relationships in late adulthood, not only among married couples, but also among other relatives and friends. We will see how the social networks of late adulthood continue to play an important—and sustaining—role in people's lives. We examine how events such as the divorce of a parent, decades earlier, can still have a critical impact on the course of people's lives. We end with a discussion of the growing phenomenon of elder abuse.

After reading this chapter, you will be able to answer the following questions:

▶ **In what ways does personality develop during late adulthood?**

▶ **How do people deal with aging?**

▶ **In what circumstances do older people live, and what difficulties do they face?**

▶ **What is it like to retire?**

▶ **How do marriages in late adulthood fare?**

▶ **What happens when an elderly spouse dies?**

▶ **What sorts of relationships are important in late adulthood?**

Personality Development and Successful Aging

Greta Roach has a puckish manner, a habit of nudging you when she is about to say something funny. This happens often, because that is how she views the world. Even last year's knee injury, which forced her to drop out of her bowling league and halted the march of blue-and-chrome trophies across her living-room table, is not—in her mind—a frailty of age.

Roach, 93, takes the same spirited approach to life in her 90s as she did in her 20s, something not all elders can do. . . . "I enjoy life. I belong to all the clubs. I love to talk on the telephone. I write to my old friends." She pauses. "Those that are still alive." (Pappano, 1994, pp. 19, 30)

In many ways, Roach, with her wit, high spirits, and enormous activity level, is much the same person she was in earlier years. Yet for other older adults, time and circumstances seem to bring changes in their outlook on life, in their views of themselves, and perhaps even in their basic personalities. In fact, one of the fundamental questions asked by developmental psychologists concerns the degree to which personality either remains stable or changes in later adulthood.

Continuity and Change in Personality During Late Adulthood

Is personality relatively stable throughout adulthood, or does it vary in significant ways? The answer, it turns out, depends on which facets of personality we wish to consider. According to developmental psychologists Paul Costa and Robert McCrae, whose work we first discussed in Chapter 16, the "big five" basic personality traits are remarkably stable across adulthood. For instance, even-tempered people at age 20 are still even-tempered at age 75, and people who hold positive self-concepts early in adulthood still view themselves positively in late adulthood (Costa & McCrae, 1988, 1989, 1997; McCrae & Costa, 1990). At 93, Greta Roach is still active and humorous, as she was in her 20s. Similarly, other longitudinal investigations have found that the big five basic personality traits remain quite stable (agreeableness, satisfaction, intellect, extroversion, and energy). Such research suggests that there is a fundamental continuity to personality (Field & Millsap, 1991).

On the other hand, the existence of stable basic personality traits does not preclude the possibility of change over time. As we noted in Chapter 16, the profound changes that occur throughout adulthood in people's social environments may produce fluctuations and changes in personality. What is important to a person at age 80 is not necessarily the same as what was important at age 40.

Consequently, some theorists have focused their attention on the discontinuities of development. As we'll see next, the work of Erik Erikson, Robert Peck, Daniel Levinson, and Bernice Neugarten has focused on the changes in personality that occur as a result of new challenges that appear in later adulthood.

Ego Integrity Versus Despair: Erikson's Final Stage. Psychoanalyst Erik Erikson's final word on personality concerns late adulthood, the time, he suggested, when elderly people move into the last of life's eight stages of psychosocial development. Labeled the **ego-integrity-versus-despair stage,** this last period is characterized by a process of looking back over one's life, evaluating it, and coming to terms with it.

People who are successful in this stage of development experience a sense of satisfaction and accomplishment, which Erikson terms "integrity." When people achieve integrity, they feel that they have realized and fulfilled the possibilities that have come their way in life, and they have few regrets. On the other hand, some people look back on their lives with dissatisfaction. They may feel that they have missed important opportunities and have not accomplished what they wished, and their lives may lack integration. Such individuals may be unhappy, depressed, angry, or despondent over what they have done, or failed to do, with their lives—in short, they despair.

Peck's Developmental Tasks. Although Erikson's approach provides a picture of the broad possibilities of later adulthood, other theorists offer a more differentiated view of what occurs in the final stage of life. For instance, Robert Peck (1968) suggests that personality development in elderly people is occupied by three major developmental tasks or challenges.

In Peck's view, the first task is a **redefinition of self versus preoccupation with work-role,** in which those in old age must redefine themselves in ways that do not relate to their work-roles or occupations. As we will see when we discuss retirement, the changes that occur when people stop working can trigger a difficult adjustment that has a major impact on the way people view themselves. Peck suggests that people must adjust their value systems to achieve a self-concept and a sense of self-esteem in which work is not involved.

The second major developmental task in late adulthood is **body transcendence versus body preoccupation.** As we saw in Chapter 17, elderly individuals can undergo significant changes in their physical capabilities as a result of aging. In the body transcendence

cw

ego-integrity-versus-despair stage Erikson's final stage of life, characterized by a process of looking back over one's life, evaluating it, and coming to terms with it

redefinition of self versus preoccupation with work-role the theory that those in old age must redefine themselves in ways that do not relate to their work-roles or occupations

body transcendence versus body preoccupation a period in which people must learn to cope with and move beyond changes in physical capabilities as a result of aging

Some aspects of personality remain quite stable throughout the life span. For example, this cartoon suggests that baby boomers will still indulge in their stereotypical excesses when they are older.

versus body preoccupation stage, people must learn to cope with and move beyond those physical changes (transcendence). If they don't, they become preoccupied with their physical deterioration, to the detriment of their personality development. Greta Roach, who just gave up bowling in her 90s, is an example of someone who is coping with the physical changes of aging.

Finally, the third developmental task faced by those in old age is **ego transcendence versus ego preoccupation,** in which elderly people must come to grips with their coming death. They need to understand that although death is inevitable, and probably not too far off, they have made contributions to society. If people in late adulthood see these contributions, which can take the form of children or work- and civic-related activities, as lasting beyond their own lives, they will experience ego transcendence. If not, they may become preoccupied with the question of whether their lives had value and worth to society.

ego transcendence versus ego preoccupation the period in which elderly people must come to grips with their coming death

Levinson's Final Season: The Winter of Life. Daniel Levinson's theory of adult development does not focus as much as Erikson's and Peck's theories on the challenges that aging adults must overcome. Instead, he looks at the processes that can lead to personality change as we grow old. According to Daniel Levinson, people enter late adulthood by passing through a transition stage that typically occurs around age 60 to 65 (Levinson, 1986, 1992). During this transition period, people come to view themselves as entering late adulthood—or, ultimately, as being "old." Knowing full well what society's stereotypes about elderly individuals are, and how negative they can be, people struggle with the notion that they are now in this category.

According to Levinson, a recognition that comes with age is that one is no longer on the center stage of life, but is increasingly playing bit parts. This loss of power, respect, and authority may be difficult for individuals accustomed to having control in their lives.

On the other hand, people in late adulthood can serve as resources to younger individuals, and they may find themselves regarded as "venerated elders" whose advice is sought and relied upon. Furthermore, old age can bring with it a new freedom to do things for the simple sake of the enjoyment and pleasure they bring, rather than because they are obligations.

Coping with Aging: Neugarten's Study. Rather than focusing on the commonalities of aging, or the processes and tasks involved in aging, Bernice Neugarten (1972, 1977)—in what became a classic study—examined results, the different ways that people cope with aging. Neugarten found four different personality types in her research on people in their 70s:

Older adults may become "venerated elders," whose advice is sought and relied upon.

■ *Disintegrated and disorganized personalities.* These people are unable to accept aging, and they experience despair as they get older. They often end up in nursing homes or are hospitalized.

■ *Passive-dependent personalities.* These individuals lead lives filled with fear—fear of falling ill, fear of the future, fear of their own inability to cope. They are so fearful that they may seek out help, even when they don't need it.

■ *Defended personalities.* Rather than accepting aging, individuals in this category seek to ward it off. They may attempt to act young, exercising vigorously, and engaging in youthful activities. Unfortunately, they may set up unrealistic expectations for themselves and feel disappointed as a result.

■ *Integrated personalities.* The most successful individuals cope comfortably with aging. They accept becoming older and maintain a sense of self dignity.

Neugarten found that the majority of the people she studied fell into the final category. They acknowledged aging and were able to look back at their lives and gaze into the future with acceptance.

Life Review and Reminiscence: The Common Theme of Personality Development. Erikson, Peck, Neugarten, and Levinson all suggest that a major characteristic of personality development in old age is looking backward. In fact, **life review,** in which people examine and evaluate their lives, is a common theme for most personality theorists who focus on late adulthood.

life review the point in life in which people examine and evaluate their lives

According to gerontologist Robert Butler, life review is triggered by the increasingly obvious prospect of one's death (Butler, 1968, 1990; Butler & Lewis, 1981). As people age, they look back on their lives, remembering and reconsidering what has happened to them (Andrews, 1997). We might at first suspect that such reminiscence may be harmful, as people relive the past, wallow in past problems, and revive old wounds, but this is not the case at all. By reviewing the events of their lives, elderly people often come to a better understanding of their past. They may be able to resolve lingering problems and conflicts, and they may feel they can face their current lives with greater serenity (McDougall, Blixen, & Suen, 1997).

There are other benefits from the process of life review. For example, reminiscence may lead to a sense of sharing and mutuality, a feeling of interconnectedness with others. Moreover, it can be a source of social interaction, as older adults seek to share their prior experiences with others (Unruh, 1989; Sherman, 1991).

Reminiscence may even have cognitive benefits, serving to improve memory in older people. By reflecting on the past, people activate a variety of memories about people and events in their lives. In turn, these memories may trigger other, related memories, and may bring back sights, sounds, and even smells of the past (Thorsheim & Roberts, 1990; Kartman, 1991).

On the other hand, the outcomes of life review and reminiscence are not always positive. People who become obsessive about the past, reliving old insults and mistakes that cannot be rectified, may end up feeling guilt, depression, and anger against people from the past who may not even still be alive. In such cases, reminiscence produces declines in psychological functioning (DeGenova, 1993).

Overall, though, the process of life review and reminiscence can play an important role in the ongoing lives of elderly individuals. It provides continuity between past and present, and may increase awareness of the contemporary world. It also can provide new insights into the past and into others, allowing people to continue personality growth and to function more effectively in the present (Stevens-Ratchford, 1993; Turner & Helms, 1994).

Age Stratification Approaches to Late Adulthood

Age, like race and gender, provides a way of ranking people within a given society. **Age stratification theories** suggest that economic resources, power, and privilege are distributed unequally among people at different stages of the life course. Such inequality is particularly pronounced during late adulthood.

> **age stratification theories** the view that an unequal distribution of economic resources, power, and privilege exists among people at different stages of the life course

Even as advances in medical technologies have led to a longer life span, power and prestige for the elderly have eroded, at least in industrialized societies. For example, the peak earning years are the 50s; later, earnings tend to decline. Further, younger people have more independence and are often physically removed from their elders, making them less dependent on older adults. In addition, rapidly changing technology causes older adults to be seen as lacking important skills. Ultimately, older adults are seen as not particularly productive members of society and in some cases simply irrelevant (Cohn, 1982; Macionis, 2001). As Levinson's theory emphasizes, people are certainly aware of the declines in status that accompany growing old in Western societies. Levinson considers adjusting to them to be the major transition of late adulthood.

Age stratification theories help explain why aging is viewed more positively in less industrialized societies. For example, in cultures in which agricultural activities predominate, older people can accumulate control over important resources such as animals and land. In such societies, in which the concept of retirement is unknown, older individuals (especially older males) are exceptionally respected, in part because they continue to be involved in daily activities central to the society. Furthermore, because agricultural practices change at a less rapid pace than the technological advances that characterize more industrialized societies, people in late adulthood are seen as possessing considerable wisdom. Cultural values that stress respect for elders are not limited to less industrialized countries. They shape how elderly adults are treated in a variety of societies.

Developmental Diversity

How Culture Shapes the Way We Treat People in Late Adulthood

The elderly Eskimo grandmother is bundled up in a parka, placed in a boat, and rowed to a large ice floe floating in the sea. She leaves the boat, walks out onto the ice. The boat pulls away, leaving her to die a certain and lonely death.

The situation described above has reached the level of folklore, with some people assuming that the Arctic Ocean is full of aged Eskimos waiting to die on ice floes. But this view is just plain wrong: Although isolated cases of abandonment are reported, the truth is that it rarely happens (Fry, 1985).

Now consider another scene relating to the treatment of elderly individuals, drawn from a different society:

> The elderly grandmother is seated at the head of the table, in a place of honor, as the Chinese family sits down to dinner. She is given the first choice of food and is fussed over throughout the meal. At the end of the meal, she rises and leaves, making no effort to help clean up. No one expects her to—she is held in such high regard by her family and Chinese society that she never has to lift a finger.

Such veneration of aging people in Asian families seems hardly surprising to most people in Western cultures. Most of us have been taught that citizens of many non-

Western cultures hold older individuals in far greater esteem than citizens of Western cultures, treating them at all times with the utmost respect and consideration.

Yet in some ways, this view of the treatment of elderly individuals is as overdrawn as the folklore about elderly Eskimos. In neither society is the treatment of older adults invariably bad or invariably good.

Even those societies that articulate strong ideals regarding the treatment of older adults do not always live up to those standards. For instance, careful research on the Chinese people, whose admiration, respect, and even worship for individuals in late adulthood are strong, shows that people's actual behavior, in almost every segment of the society except for the most elite, fails to be as positive as their attitudes are. Furthermore, it is typically sons and their wives who are expected to care for elderly parents; parents with just daughters may find themselves with no one to care for them in late adulthood. In short, conduct toward elderly people in particular cultures is quite variable, and we must be careful not to make broad, global statements about how older adults are treated in a given society (Sankar, 1981; Harrell, 1981; Fry, 1985).

On the other hand, some generalizations can be supported. For example, Asian societies, in general, do hold elderly people, particularly members of their own families, in higher esteem than Western cultures tend to. Although the strength of this standard has been declining in areas of Asia in which industrialization has been increasing rapidly, such as Japan, the view of aging and the treatment of people in late adulthood still tend to be more positive than in Western cultures (Fry, 1985; Ikels, 1989).

What is it about Asian cultures that leads to higher levels of esteem for old age? In general, cultures that hold the elderly in high regard are relatively homogeneous in socioeconomic terms. In addition, the roles that people play in those societies entail greater responsibility with increasing age, and elderly people control resources to a relatively large extent.

Moreover, roles display continuity throughout the life span, and older adults continue to engage in activities that are valued by society. Finally, cultures in which older adults are held in higher regard tend to be organized around extended families in which the older generations are well integrated into the family structure (Press & McKool, 1972; Fry, 1985; Sangree, 1989). In such an arrangement, younger family members may come to see older members as having accumulated a great deal of wisdom, which they can share. ☐

Does Age Bring Wisdom?

Most of us could agree that people such as Socrates and Solomon were wise. But does the average person have wisdom, and do people gain wisdom as they become older?

wisdom expert knowledge in the practical aspects of life

Although it seems reasonable to believe that we get wiser as we get older, we don't know for sure, because the concept of **wisdom**—expert knowledge in the practical aspects of life—has, until recent years, received little attention from gerontologists and other researchers. In part, this lack of attention stems from the difficulty in defining and measuring the concept, which is unusually vague.

Developmentalists disagree on whether we should expect a relationship between wisdom and aging. For instance, some developmentalists argue, consistent with the view of some Eastern philosophies such as Taoism, that wisdom is a trait of the young and actually declines with age. On the other hand, other researchers suggest that wisdom reflects an accumulation of knowledge, experience, and contemplation, and that older age may be necessary to acquire true wisdom (Baltes et al., 1995; Baltes & Staudinger, 2000).

Another challenge for developmentalists has been to distinguish wisdom from intelligence. Some researchers suggest that a primary distinction is related to timing: While knowledge that is derived from intelligence is related to the here-and-now, wisdom is a more timeless quality. Furthermore, while intelligence may permit a person to think logically and systematically, wisdom provides an understanding of human behavior. According to psychologist Robert Sternberg, who has conducted research related to practical intelligence, as we discussed in Chapter 13, intelligence permits humans to invent the atom bomb, while wisdom prevents them from using it (Seppa, 1997).

Measuring wisdom has proven to be a difficult task. However, research by Ursula Staudinger and Paul Baltes (2000) has shown that it is possible to assess people reliably on the concept. For example, in one study, pairs of people ranging in age from 20 to 70 years discussed difficulties relating to life events. One problem involved someone who gets a phone call from a good friend who says that he or she is planning to commit suicide. Another involved a 14-year-old girl who wanted to move out of her family home immediately. Participants were asked what they should do and consider.

Although there were no absolute right or wrong answers to these problems, the responses were evaluated against several criteria, including the amount of factual knowledge the participants brought to bear on the problem; their procedural knowledge about decision-making strategies; how well the participants considered the problem within the context of the central character's life span and the values that the central character may hold; and whether or not the participants recognized that there may not be a single, absolute solution.

Using these criteria, participants' responses were rated as relatively wise or unwise. For instance, an example of a response to the suicide problem rated as particularly wise is the following:

> On the one hand this problem has a pragmatic side, one has to react one way or other. On the other hand, it also has a philosophical side whether human beings are allowed to kill themselves etc. . . . . First one would need to find out whether this decision is the result of a longer process or whether it is a reaction to a momentary life situation. In the latter case, it is uncertain how long this condition will last. There can be conditions that make suicide conceivable. But I think no one should be easily released from life. They should be forced to "fight" for their death if they really want it. . . . . It seems that one has a responsibility to try to show the person alternative pathways. Currently, for example, there seems to be a trend in our society that it becomes more and more accepted that old people commit suicide. This can also be viewed as dangerous. Not because of the suicide itself but because of its functionality for society. (Staudinger & Baltes, 1996, p. 762)

Studies such as this show that wisdom is not in the sole territory of late adulthood; people of other ages can be wise as well. On the other hand, the Staudinger and Baltes study also found that the older participants benefited more from an experimental condition designed to promote wise thinking, and other research suggests that the very wisest individuals may be older adults.

Other research has looked at wisdom in terms of the development of theory of mind. In this view, wisdom is represented by the ability to make inferences about others' thoughts, feelings, and intentions—their mental states. According to this work, older adults' abilities with respect to theory of mind are actually superior to those of younger individuals. These findings suggest that one component of wisdom may be a more sophisticated theory of mind (Happe, Winner, & Brownell, 1998).

Successful Aging: What Is the Secret?

At age 77, Elinor Reynolds spends most of her time at home, leading a quiet, routine existence. Never married, Elinor receives visits from her two sisters every few weeks, and some of her nieces and nephews stop by on occasion. But for the most part, she keeps to herself. When asked, she says she is quite happy.

In contrast, Carrie Masterson, also 77, is involved in something different almost every day. If she is not visiting the senior center, participating in some kind of activity, she is out shopping. Her daughter complains that Carrie is "never home" when she tries to reach her by phone, and Carrie replies that she has never been busier—or happier.

Clearly, there is no single way to age successfully (Hersen & VanHasselt, 1996; Schultz & Heckhausen, 1996; Rowe & Kahn, 1998). How people age depends on personality factors and the circumstances in which they find themselves. Two major approaches provide alternative explanations: disengagement theory and activity theory.

disengagement theory the period in late adulthood that marks a gradual withdrawal from the world on physical, psychological, and social levels

Disengagement Theory: Gradual Retreat. According to **disengagement theory,** late adulthood marks a gradual withdrawal from the world on physical, psychological, and social levels (Cummings & Henry, 1961). On a physical level, elderly people have lower energy levels and tend to slow down progressively. Psychologically, they begin to withdraw from others, showing less interest in the world around them and spending more time looking inward. Finally, on a social level, they engage in less interaction with others, in terms of both day-to-day, face-to-face encounters and participation in society as a whole. Older adults also become less involved and invested in the lives of others (Quinnan, 1997).

Disengagement theory suggests that withdrawal is a mutual process. Because of norms and expectations about aging, society in general begins to disengage from those in late adulthood. For example, mandatory retirement ages compel elderly people to withdraw from work-related roles, thereby accelerating the process of disengagement.

Contrary to what we might expect, such withdrawal is not necessarily a negative experience for those in old age. In fact, most theorists who subscribe to disengagement theory argue that the outcomes of disengagement are largely positive. According to this view, the gradual withdrawal of people in late adulthood permits them to become more reflective about their own lives and less constrained by social roles. Furthermore, people can become more discerning in their social relationships, focusing on those who best meet their needs. In a sense, then, disengagement can be liberating (Johnson & Barer, 1992; Carstensen, 1995).

Similarly, decreased emotional investment in others can be viewed as beneficial. By investing less emotional energy in their social relationships with others, people in late adulthood are better able to adjust to the increasing frequency of serious illness and death among their peers.

Does disengagement theory provide an accurate account of late adulthood? An initial study, examining close to 300 people aged 50 to 90, found clear evidence for disengagement (Cummings & Henry, 1961). For instance, the researchers found that specific events, such as retirement or the death of a spouse, were accompanied by a gradual disengagement in which the level of social interaction with others plummeted.

However, later research has not been so supportive of disengagement theory. For example, a follow-up study involving about half the subjects in the original study found contradictory results. In this second look at the subjects, researchers found that although some of the subjects were happily disengaged, others, who had remained quite involved and active, were as happy as those who showed signs of disengagement, and sometimes even happier (Havighurst, Neugarten, & Tobin, 1968; Havighurst, 1973; Bergstrom & Holmes, 2000).

Other evidence argues against disengagement theory. In many non-Western cultures, for instance, people remain engaged, active, and busy throughout old age. In such cultures, where late adulthood is viewed as little different from earlier periods of life, the expectation is that people will remain actively involved in everyday life (Palmore, 1975). Clearly, then, disengagement is not an automatic, universal process for all people in late adulthood.

Given the limitations of disengagement theory, gerontologists have developed an alternative approach. This has come to be known as activity theory.

While disengagement theory suggests that people in late adulthood begin to gradually withdraw from the world, activity theory argues that successful aging occurs when people maintain their involvement with others.

Activity Theory: Continued Involvement. According to activity theory, the people who are most likely to be happy in late adulthood are those who are fully involved and engaged with the world. **Activity theory** suggests that successful aging occurs when people maintain the interests and activities they pursued during middle age and resist any decrease in the amount and type of social interaction they have with others (Blau, 1973; Palmore, 1979).

In the view of activity theorists, happiness and satisfaction with life are assumed to spring from a high level of involvement with the world. Moreover, successful aging occurs when older adults adapt to inevitable changes in their environments not by withdrawing, but by resisting reductions in their social involvement (Bell, 1978; Charles, Reynolds, & Gatz, 2001).

Activity theory suggests, then, that late adulthood should reflect a continuation of activities in which elderly people participated earlier. Furthermore, in cases in which it is no longer possible to participate in certain activities—such as work, following retirement—activity theory argues that successful aging occurs when replacement activities are found.

Like disengagement theory, activity theory has drawn critics. For one thing, activity theory makes little distinction between various types of activities. Surely not every activity will have an equal impact on a person's happiness and satisfaction with life, and being involved in various activities just for the sake of remaining engaged is unlikely to be satisfying. In sum, the specific nature and quality of the activities in which people engage are likely to be more critical than the mere quantity or frequency of their activities (Gubrium, 1973; Burrus-Bammel & Bammel, 1985).

A more significant criticism is that for some people in late adulthood, the principle of "less is more" clearly holds. For such individuals, less activity brings greater enjoyment of life. They are able to slow down and do only the things that bring them the greatest satisfaction (Ward, 1984). In fact, some people view the ability to moderate their pace as one of the bounties of late adulthood. For them, a relatively inactive, and perhaps even solitary, existence is welcomed (Hansson & Carpenter, 1994).

In short, neither disengagement theory nor activity theory provides a complete picture of successful aging. For some people, a gradual disengagement occurs, and this leads to relatively high levels of happiness and satisfaction. For others, preserving a significant level of activity and involvement leads to greater satisfaction. (Johnson & Barer, 1992; Rapkin & Fischer, 1992).

In fact, some theorists have suggested a compromise between disengagement theory and activity theory, known as continuity theory. According to **continuity theory,** people

activity theory the theory suggesting that successful aging occurs when people maintain the interests, activities, and social interactions with which they were involved during middle age

continuity theory the theory suggesting that people need to maintain their desired level of involvement in society in order to maximize their sense of well being and self-esteem

need to maintain their desired level of involvement in society in order to maximize their sense of well-being and self-esteem (Atchley, 1989; Whitbourne, 2001).

Ultimately, the best predictor of whether disengagement or activity will lead to successful aging may be one's behavior prior to late adulthood (Maddox & Campbell, 1985). Highly socially involved younger adults may be the ones for whom activity leads to the greatest satisfaction. In contrast, for those people who were relatively socially independent, uninvolved, or withdrawn as young adults, disengagement during late adulthood may be perfectly satisfying.

Whichever pattern occurs, most older adults experience positive emotions as frequently as younger individuals. Of course, certain factors enhance feelings of happiness. For instance, good physical and mental health are clearly important in determining an elderly person's overall sense of well-being. Similarly, having enough financial security to provide for basic needs, including food, shelter, and medical care, is critical. In addition, a sense of autonomy, independence, and personal control over one's life is a significant advantage (Abeles, Gift, & Ory, 1994; Rowe & Kahn, 1997; Carstensen et al., 2000).

Finally, the way elderly people perceive old age can influence their happiness and satisfaction. Those who view late adulthood in terms of positive attributes—such as the possibility of gaining knowledge and wisdom—are apt to perceive themselves in a more positive light than those who view old age in a more pessimistic and unfavorable way (Heckhausen, Dixon, & Baltes, 1989; Thompson, 1993).

Selective Optimization with Compensation: A General Model of Successful Aging. In considering the factors that lead to successful aging, developmental psychologists Paul Baltes and Margret Baltes focus on the "selective optimization with compensation" model. As we first noted in Chapter 15, the assumption underlying the model is that late adulthood brings with it changes and losses in underlying capabilities, which vary from one person to another. However, it is possible to overcome such shifts in capabilities through selective optimization.

selective optimization the process by which people concentrate on selected skills areas to compensate for losses in other areas

Selective optimization is the process by which people concentrate on particular skill areas to compensate for losses in other areas. They do this by seeking to fortify their general motivational, cognitive, and physical resources, while also, through a process of selection, focusing on particular areas of special interest (Staudinger, Marsiske, & Baltes, 1993; Baltes, 1995; Smith & Baltes, 1997). A person who has run marathons all her life may have to cut back or give up entirely other activities in order to increase her training. By giving up other activities, she may be able to maintain her running skills through concentration on them.

At the same time, the model suggests that elderly individuals engage in compensation for the losses that they have sustained due to aging. Compensation may take the form, for instance, of employing a hearing aid to offset losses in hearing.

Piano virtuoso Arthur Rubinstein provides another example of selective optimization with compensation. In his later years, he maintained his concert career and was acclaimed for his playing. To manage this, he used several strategies that illustrate the model of selective optimization with compensation.

First, Rubinstein reduced the number of pieces he played at concerts—an example of being selective in what he sought to accomplish. Second, he practiced those pieces more often, thus using optimization. Finally, in an example of compensation, he slowed down the tempo of musical passages immediately preceding faster passages, thereby fostering the illusion that he was playing just as fast as he had ever played (Baltes & Baltes, 1990).

In short, the model of selective optimization with compensation (summarized in Figure 18-1) illustrates the fundamentals of successful aging. Although late adulthood may bring about various changes in underlying capabilities, people who focus on optimizing their achievements in particular areas may well be able to compensate for any limitations and losses that do occur. The outcome is a life that is reduced in some areas, but is also transformed and modified and, ultimately, is effective and successful.

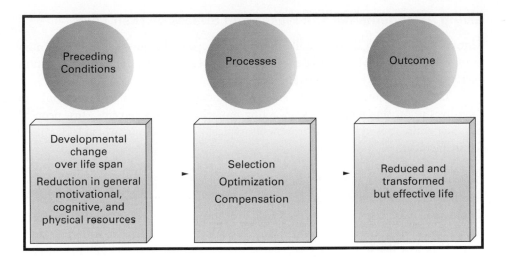

Figure 18-1 **Selective Optimization with Compensation**

According to the model proposed by Paul Baltes and Margret Baltes, successful aging occurs when an older adult focuses on his or her most important areas of functioning and compensates for losses in other areas. Is this unique to old age?

(Adapted from Baltes & Baltes, 1990.)

Review and Rethink

REVIEW

■ While some aspects of personality remain stable, others change to reflect the social environments through which people pass as they age.

■ Erikson calls older adulthood the ego-integrity-versus-despair stage, while Peck focuses on three tasks that define the period.

■ According to Levinson, after struggling with the notion of being old, people can experience liberation and self-regard. Neugarten focuses on the ways people cope with aging.

■ Age stratification theories suggest that the unequal distribution of economic resources, power, and privilege becomes particularly pronounced during late adulthood.

■ Societies in which elderly people are respected are generally characterized by social homogeneity, extended families, responsible roles for older people, and control of significant resources by older people.

■ Disengagement theory suggests that older people gradually withdraw from the world, which can lead to reflection and satisfaction. In contrast, activity theory suggests that the happiest people continue to be engaged with the world.

■ The most successful model for aging may be selective optimization with compensation.

RETHINK

■ How might personality traits account for success or failure in achieving satisfaction through the life review process?

■ How might cultural factors affect an older person's likelihood of pursuing either the disengagement strategy or the activity strategy?

The Daily Life of Late Adulthood

I hear all these retired folks complaining that they don't have this and they don't have that. . . . I'm not pinched. . . . My house is paid for. My car is paid for. Both my sons are grown up. I don't need many new clothes. Every time I go out and eat somewhere, I get a senior citizen's discount. This is the happiest period of my life. These are my golden years. (Gottschalk, 1983, p. 1)

This positive view of life in late adulthood was expressed by a 74-year-old retired shipping clerk. Although the story is certainly not the same for all retirees, many, if not most, find their postwork lives happy and involving. We will consider some of the ways in which people lead their lives in late adulthood, beginning with where they live.

Living in a multigenerational setting with children and their families can be rewarding and helpful for those in late adulthood. Are there any disadvantages to this type of situation? What are some solutions?

Living Arrangements: The Places and Spaces of Their Lives

Think "old age," and if you are like most people, your thoughts soon turn to nursing homes. Popular stereotypes place most elderly people in lonely, unpleasant, institutional surroundings, under the care of strangers.

The reality, however, is quite different. Although it is true that some people finish their lives in nursing homes, they are a tiny minority—only 5 percent. Most people live out their entire lives in home environments, typically in the company of at least one other family member.

Living at Home. A large number of older adults live alone. People over 65 represent a quarter of America's 9.6 million single-person households. However, even more live with family members. Roughly two-thirds of people over the age of 65 live with other members of the family. In most cases they live with spouses. Some older adults live with their siblings, and others they live in multigenerational settings with their children, grandchildren, and even occasionally great-grandchildren.

The consequences of living with a family member are quite varied, depending on the nature of the setting. For married couples, living with a spouse represents continuity with earlier life. On the other hand, for people who move in with their children, the adjustment to life in a multigenerational setting can be jarring. Not only is there a potential loss of independence and privacy, but older adults may feel uncomfortable with the way their children are raising their grandchildren. Unless there are some ground rules about the specific roles that people are to play in the household, friction can ensue (Sussman & Sussman, 1991).

For some groups, living in extended families is more typical than for other groups. For instance, African Americans are more likely than whites to live in multigenerational families. Furthermore, the amount of influence that family members have over one another and the interdependence of extended families are generally greater in African American, Asian American, and Hispanic families than in Caucasian families (Gibson, 1986; McAdoo, 1988).

Specialized Living Environments. For some 10 percent of those in late adulthood, home is an institution. As we'll see, there is a broad range of different types of specialized environments in which elderly people live (Moos & Lemke, 1985).

One of the most recent innovations in living arrangements is the **continuing-care community.** Such communities typically offer an environment in which all the residents are of retirement age or older. They may need various levels of care, which is provided by the community. Residents sign contracts under which the community makes a commitment to provide care at whatever level is needed. In many such communities, people start out living in separate houses or apartments, either independently or with occasional home care. As they age and their needs increase, residents may eventually move into *assisted living,* in which people live in independent housing but are supported by medical providers to the extent required. Continuing care ultimately extends all the way to full-time nursing care, which is often provided at an on-site nursing home.

Continuing-care communities tend to be fairly homogeneous in terms of religious, racial, and ethnic backgrounds, and they are often organized by private or religious organizations. Because joining may involve a substantial initial payment, members of such communities tend to be relatively well-off financially (Forrest & Forrest, 1991; Barton, 1997).

Several types of nursing institutions exist, ranging from those that provide part-time day care to homes that offer 24-hour-a-day, live-in care. In **adult day-care facilities,** elderly individuals receive care only during the day, but spend nights and weekends in their own homes. During the time that they are at the facility, people receive nursing care, take their meals, and participate in scheduled activities. Sometimes adult facilities are combined with infant and child day-care programs, an arrangement that allows for interaction between the old and the young (Kocarnik & Ponzetti, 1991; Quade, 1994).

continuing-care community a community that offers an environment in which all the residents are of retirement age or older and need various levels of care

adult day-care facilities a facility in which elderly individuals receive care only during the day, but spend nights and weekends in their own homes

Other institutional settings provide more extensive care. The most intensive institutions are **skilled-nursing facilities,** which provide full-time nursing care for people who have chronic illnesses or are recovering from a temporary medical condition. Although skilled-nursing facilities, which are traditional nursing homes, hold only 5 percent of the population over 65, the percentage increases with age. For instance, just over 1 percent of people between the ages of 64 and 74 are in nursing homes, while for those 85 and older, the proportion climbs to 25 percent (USDHHS, 1990).

The greater the extent of nursing home care, the greater the adjustment required of residents. Although some newcomers adjust relatively rapidly, the loss of independence brought about by institutional life may lead to difficulties. In addition, elderly people are as susceptible as other members of society to society's stereotypes about nursing homes, and their expectations may be particularly negative. They may see themselves as just marking time until they eventually die, forgotten and discarded by a society that venerates youth (Biedenharn & Normoyle, 1991; Baltes, 1996).

Although such fears may be exaggerated, they can lead to **institutionalism,** a psychological state in which people develop apathy, indifference, and a lack of caring about themselves (Butler & Lewis, 1981). Institutionalism is brought about, in part, by a sense of *learned helplessness,* a belief that one has no control over one's environment.

The sense of helplessness brought about by institutionalism can literally have deadly consequences. Consider, for instance, what happens when people enter nursing homes in late adulthood. One of the most conspicuous changes from their independent past is that they no longer have control over their most basic activities (Kane et al., 1997). They may be told when and what to eat, their sleeping schedules may be arranged by others, and even their visits to the bathroom may be regulated.

A classic experiment showed the consequences of such a loss of control. In the study, psychologists Ellen Langer and Irving Janis (1979) divided elderly residents of a nursing home into two groups. In one group, the residents were encouraged to make a variety of choices about their day-to-day activities; in the other, the residents were given no choices and were encouraged to let the nursing home staff care for them. The results were clear. The participants who had choices were not only happier, they were also healthier. In fact, 18 months after the experiment began, only 15 percent of the choice group had died—compared to 30 percent of the comparison group.

In short, the loss of control experienced by residents of nursing homes and other institutions can have a profound effect on their sense of well-being. At the same time, however, some nursing homes are considerably better than others. The best go out of their way to permit residents to make basic life decisions, and they attempt to give people in late adulthood a sense of control over their lives.

Financial Issues: The Economics of Late Adulthood

People in late adulthood range from one end of the socioeconomic spectrum to the other. In many ways, in fact—including financial condition—they are not much different from younger populations. Like the man quoted earlier in this section of the chapter, those who were relatively affluent during their working years tend to remain relatively affluent, while those who were poor at earlier stages of life tend to remain poor when they reach late adulthood.

However, the social inequities that various groups experience during their earlier lives become magnified with increasing age (Duncan & Smith, 1989; Ben-Porath, 1991). At the same time, people who reach late adulthood today may experience growing economic pressure as a result of the ever-increasing human life span.

Some 11 percent of people age 65 and older live below the poverty line, a proportion that is quite close to that for people less than age 65. However, there are significant differences in gender and racial groups. For instance, women are almost twice as likely as men to be living in poverty. Of those elderly women living alone, around one-fourth live on

skilled-nursing facilities a facility that provides full-time nursing care for people who have chronic illnesses or are recovering from a temporary medical condition

institutionalism a psychological state in which people in nursing homes develop apathy, indifference, and a lack of caring about themselves

cw

During late adulthood, the range of socioeconomic well-being mirrors that of earlier years.

incomes below the poverty line. A married woman may also slip into poverty if she becomes widowed, for she may have used up savings to pay for her husband's final illness, and the husband's pension may cease with his death (Burkhauser, Holden, & Feaster, 1988; Grambs, 1989).

Furthermore, while only 7 percent of whites in late adulthood live below the poverty level, 18 percent of Hispanic men and a quarter of African American men live in poverty. Minority women fare the worst of any category. For example, divorced black women aged 65 to 74 had a poverty rate of 47 percent (Rank & Hirschl, 1999; Federal Interagency Forum on Age-Related Statistics, 2000).

One source of financial vulnerability for people in late adulthood is the reliance on a fixed income for support. Unlike that of a younger person, the income of an elderly person, which typically comes from a combination of Social Security benefits, pensions, and savings, rarely keeps up with inflation. Consequently, as inflation drives up the price of goods such as food and clothing, income does not rise as quickly. What may have been a reasonable income at age 65 is worth much less 20 years later, as the elderly person gradually slips into poverty (Brock, 1991).

Another important source of financial vulnerability in older adults is rising health care costs. During the mid-1990s, Congress made efforts to curb the growing cost to the U.S. Treasury by making cuts in government payments for medical care and medical care insurance entitlements such as Medicare, which provides health care insurance to elderly people.

Even before any Medicare cuts, people in late adulthood were hardly protected: By the late 1980s, the average older person was spending close to 20 percent of his or her income for health care costs. Moreover, for those elderly individuals who require care in nursing home facilities, the financial costs can be staggering, running an average of $30,000 to $40,000 a year (Hess, 1990).

To complicate the problem even further, unless major changes are made in the way that Social Security and Medicare are financed, the costs borne by younger U.S. citizens in the workforce must rise significantly. Increasing expenditures mean that a larger proportion of younger people's pay must be taxed to fund benefits for the elderly. Such a situation is apt to lead to increasing friction and segregation between younger and older generations. Indeed, as we'll see, Social Security payments are one key factor in many people's decisions about how long to work.

Work and Retirement in Late Adulthood

When to retire is a major decision faced by the majority of individuals in late adulthood. Although for some the decision is easy, many people experience a fair amount of difficulty in making the identity shift from "worker" to "retiree." For others, though, retirement

Retirement is a different journey for each individual. Some are content with a more sedate lifestyle, while others continue to remain active and in some cases pursue new activities. Can you explain why many non-Western cultures do not follow the disengagement theory of retirement?

represents a major opportunity, offering the chance to lead, perhaps for the first time in adulthood, a life of leisure.

Because the typical retirement age is moving downward, toward age 60, and because people's life spans are expanding, people spend far more time in retirement than in previous generations. Moreover, because the number of people in late adulthood continues to increase, retirees are an increasingly significant and influential segment of the U.S. population.

Older Workers: Combating Age Discrimination. Although the number of retirees is on the rise, many people continue to work, either full- or part-time, for some part of late adulthood. They can do so largely because of legislation that was passed in the late 1970s, in which mandatory retirement ages were made illegal in almost every profession. Part of broader legislation that makes age discrimination illegal, these laws gave most workers the opportunity either to remain in jobs they held previously or to begin working in entirely different fields (Borgatta, 1991).

Age discrimination remains a reality despite laws making it illegal. Some employers encourage older workers to leave their jobs in order to replace them with younger employees whose salaries will be considerably lower. Furthermore, some employers believe that older workers are not up to the demands of the job or are less willing to adapt to a changing workplace—stereotypes about the elderly that are enduring, despite legislative changes (Moss, 1997).

The reality is that there is little evidence to support supposed declines in older workers' ability to perform their jobs. In many fields, such as art, literature, science, politics, or even entertainment, it is easy to find examples of people who have made some of their greatest contributions during late adulthood. Even in those few professions that were specifically exempted from laws prohibiting mandatory retirement ages—those involving public safety—the evidence does not support the notion that workers should be retired at an arbitrary age. For instance, one large-scale, careful study of older police officers, firefighters, and prison guards came to the conclusion that age did not predict well whether a worker was likely to be incapacitated on the job, or the level of his or her general work performance. Instead, a case-by-case analysis of individual workers' performance was a more accurate predictor (Landy, 1994).

Ongoing age discrimination as well as several other factors have led to a marked decline over the last three decades in the number of people who continue working in late adulthood. Part of the reason for the decline is that Social Security and other pensions provide workers with enough income to live sufficiently well to make retirement an appealing option. Another reason is that a disincentive for working is built into the Social Security laws: Workers who are collecting Social Security are taxed both on their earnings *and* on their Social Security pensions. They may be left with minimal earnings after paying these taxes. Such factors increase the probability that the later years of life will be spent in retirement rather than work.

Retirement: Filling a Life of Leisure. Why do people decide to retire? Although the basic reason seems apparent—to stop working—the retirement decision is actually based on a variety of factors. For instance, sometimes workers are burned out after a lifetime of work; they seek a respite from the tension and frustration of their jobs and from the sense that they are not accomplishing as much as they once wished they could. Others retire because their health has declined, and still others because they are offered incentives by their employers in the form of bonuses or increased pensions if they retire by a certain age. Finally, some people have planned for years to retire and intend to use their increased leisure to travel, study, or spend more time with their children and grandchildren (Mutran, Reitzes, & Fernandez, 1997; Beehr et al., 2000).

Whatever the reason they retire, people often pass through a series of retirement stages, summarized in Table 18-1 (Atchley, 1982, 1985). Retirement may begin with a *honeymoon* period, in which former workers engage in a variety of activities, such as travel, that were previously hindered by full-time work. The next phase may be *disenchantment*, in which retirees conclude that retirement is not all they thought it would be. They may miss the stimulation of their previous jobs, or they may find it hard to keep busy.

The next phase is *reorientation*, in which retirees reconsider their options and become engaged in new, more fulfilling activities. If successful, this leads to the *retirement routine* stage, in which they come to grips with the realities of retirement and feel fulfilled in this new phase of life. Not all people reach this stage; some may feel disenchanted with retirement for years.

Finally, the last phase of the retirement process is *termination*. Although some people terminate retirement by going back to work, termination for most people results from major physical deterioration. In this case, health becomes so bad that the person can no longer function independently.

Obviously, not everyone passes through all these stages, and the sequence is not universal. In large measure, a person's reactions to retirement stem from the reasons he or she retired in the first place. For example, a person forced into retirement for health reasons will have a very different experience from a person who eagerly chose to retire at a

Table 18-1

STAGES OF RETIREMENT

Stage	Characteristic
Honeymoon	In this period, former workers engage in a variety of activities, such as travel, that were previously hindered by working full-time.
Disenchantment	In this stage, retirees feel that retirement is not all that they thought it would be. They may miss the stimulation of a job or may find it difficult to keep busy.
Reorientation	At this point, retirees reconsider their options and become engaged in new, more fulfilling activities. If successful, it leads them to the next stage.
Retirement Routine	Here the retiree comes to grips with the realities of retirement and feels fulfilled with this new phase of life. Not all reach this stage; some may feel disenchanted with retirement for years.
Termination	Although some people terminate retirement by going back to work, termination occurs for most people because of major physical deterioration where their health becomes so bad they can no longer function independently.

(*Source*: Atchley, 1982.)

Becoming an Informed Consumer of Development

Planning For—and Living—a Good Retirement

What makes for a good retirement? Gerontologists suggest that several factors are related to success (Kreitlow & Kreitlow, 1997; Rowe & Kahn, 1998).

▶ Plan ahead financially. Because most financial experts suggest that Social Security pensions will be inadequate in the future, personal savings are critical. Similarly, having adequate health care insurance is essential.

▶ Consider tapering off from work gradually. Sometimes it is possible to enter into retirement by shifting from full-time to part-time work. Such a transition may be helpful in preparing for eventual full-time retirement.

▶ Explore your interests before you retire. Assess what you like about your current job and think how that might be translated into leisure activities.

▶ If you are married or in a long-term partnership, spend some time discussing your views of the ideal retirement with your partner. You may find that you need to negotiate a vision that will suit you both.

▶ Consider where you want to live. Try out, temporarily, a community to which you are thinking of moving.

▶ Determine the advantages and disadvantages of downsizing your current home.

▶ Plan to volunteer your time. People who retire have an enormous wealth of skills, and these are often needed by non-profit organizations and small businesses. Organizations such as the Retired Senior Volunteer Program or the Foster Grandparent Program can help match your skills with people who need them.

particular age. Similarly, the retirement of people who loved their jobs may be a quite different experience from that of people who despised their work.

In short, the psychological consequences of retirement vary a great deal from one individual to the next. For many people, though, retirement is a continuation of a life well-lived, and they use it to the fullest.

Review and Rethink

REVIEW

- Elderly people live in a variety of settings.
- Financial issues can trouble older people, largely because their incomes are fixed, health care costs are increasing, and the life span is lengthening.
- Retired people may pass through stages, including a honeymoon period, disenchantment, reorientation, retirement routine, and termination.

RETHINK

- What policies might a nursing home institute to minimize the chances that its residents will develop "institutionalism"? Why are such policies relatively uncommon?
- How does the marriage gradient contribute to the likelihood that a woman will fall into poverty when she reaches old age?

Relationships: Old and New

Philip Cassidy, 88, and Viola Cassidy, 85, live in the 1 1/2-story Needham Cape that Philip's uncle built in 1930, when the couple were first married. They have no health problems and take no daily medications. Together they do arts-and-crafts projects and make Christmas ornaments for their grandchildren. In June, they traveled to Alaska for two weeks. They socialize at the Needham Council on Aging and are regulars at Thursday cribbage games. Viola volunteers at her

Philip and Viola Cassidy lead an active life together.

church and takes ceramics classes. Philip is a member of the hospitality committee of the Retired Men's Club and plays golf.

"This is an easy time," says Viola. "You don't have to do all the things you do when you are younger. You don't have to get up early. It's a different life altogether." (Pappano, 1994, p. 28)

The life the Cassidys lead is the sort that many couples envision for themselves: time for family, friends, travel, and doing the things that they were unable to do before they retired. Yet it is also something of a rarity for those in the last stage of life. For every older person who is part of a couple, many more are alone.

What is the nature of the social world of people in late adulthood? To answer the question, we will first consider the nature of marriage in that period.

Marriage in the Later Years: Together, Then Alone

It's a man's world—at least when it comes to marriage after the age of 65. The proportion of men who are married is far greater than that of women (see Figure 18-2). One reason for this disparity is that 70 percent of women outlive their husbands by at least a few years. Because there are fewer men available (many have died), these women are unlikely to remarry (Barer, 1994).

Figure 18-2 **Living Patterns of Older Americans**

What, if anything, do these patterns suggest about the relative health and adjustment of men and women?

(*Source:* Federal Interagency Forum on Age-Related Statistics, 2000.)

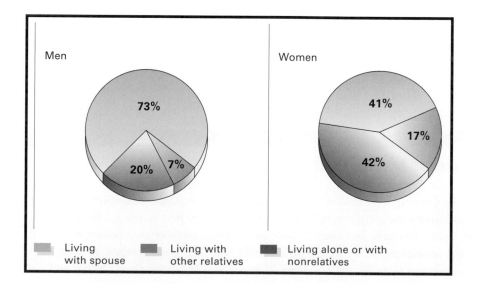

Furthermore, the marriage gradient that we first discussed in Chapter 14 is still a powerful influence. Reflecting societal norms that suggest that women should marry men older than themselves, the marriage gradient works to keep women single even in the later years of life. At the same time, it makes remarriage for men much easier, since the available pool of eligible partners is much larger (Treas & Bengtson, 1987; AARP, 1990).

The vast majority of people who are still married in later life report that they are satisfied with their marriages. Like Eva and Joseph Solymosi, whom we met in the prologue, they indicate that their partners provide substantial companionship and emotional support. Because at this period in life they have typically been together for a long time, they have great insight into their partners (Brubaker, 1991; Levenson, Cerstensen, & Gottman, 1993).

At the same time, not every aspect of marriage is equally satisfying, and marriages may undergo severe stress as spouses experience changes in their lives. For instance, the retirement of one or both spouses can bring about a shift in the nature of a couple's relationship (Askham, 1994).

For some couples, the stress is so great that one spouse or the other seeks a divorce. Although the exact numbers are hard to come by, at least 2 percent of divorces in the United States involve women over the age of 60 (Uhlenberg, Cooney, & Boyd, 1990).

The reasons for divorce at such a late stage of life are varied. Often, women who divorce do so because their husbands are abusive or alcoholic. But in the more frequent case of a husband seeking a divorce from his wife, the reason is often that he has found a younger woman. Often the divorce occurs soon after retirement, when men who have been highly involved in their careers are in psychological turmoil (Cain, 1982).

Divorce so late in life is particularly difficult for women. Due to the marriage gradient and the limited size of the potential pool of eligible men, it is unlikely that a late divorced woman will remarry. Furthermore, for many women, marriage has been their primary role and the center of their identities, and they may view divorce as a major failure. As a consequence, happiness and the quality of life for divorced women often plummet (Chiriboga, 1982; Burrus-Bammel & Bammel, 1985; Goldscheider, 1994). (Another aspect of divorce is considered in the *From Research to Practice* box.)

It is important to keep in mind that some people enter late adulthood having never married. For those who have remained single throughout their lives—about 5 percent of the population—late adulthood may bring fewer transitions, since the status of living alone does not change. In fact, never-married individuals report feeling less lonely than do most people their age, and they have a greater sense of independence (Gubrium, 1975; Essex & Nam, 1987; Newston & Keith, 1997).

Dealing with Retirement: Too Much Togetherness? When Morris Abercrombie finally stopped working full-time, his wife, Roxanne, found some aspects of his increased presence at home troubling. Although their marriage was strong, his intrusion into her daily routine and his constant questioning about whom she was on the phone with and where she was going when she went out were irksome. Finally, she began to wish he would spend less time around the house. It was an ironic thought: She had passed much of Morris's preretirement years wishing that he would spend more time at home.

The situation in which Morris and Roxanne found themselves is not unique. For many couples, retirement means that relationships need to be refashioned. In some cases, retirement results in a couple's spending more time together than at any other point in their marriage. In others, retirement provides an opportunity to alter the longstanding distribution of household chores, with men taking on more responsibility than before for the everyday functioning of the household.

In fact, research suggests that it is not unusual for gender-stereotyped roles to become reversed in late adulthood. In contrast to the early years of marriage, when wives, more than husbands, typically desire greater companionship with their spouses, in late

From Research to Practice
The Lasting Influence of Childhood: Evidence from the Terman Study

It was more than three-quarters of a century ago that psychologist Lewis M. Terman searched California's schools for children who tested in the genius range on his then newly devised intelligence test. The group of 1,500 children that he found are still being studied in what is probably the longest-running longitudinal study in the field of psychology.

The people in the study—who began to refer to themselves as "Termites" as the study wore on—are still being tested every 5 years or so. Although dwindling in number—most who are still living are in their 80s and 90s—they continue to provide a wealth of new information, and previous data continue to be mined for nuggets of understanding about the course of human development.

Recent analyses have examined the impact that several types of psychological stresses experienced by the participants during childhood have had on their current lives—and deaths. One of the most unexpected findings from a recent analysis of the data reveals that participants whose parents divorced faced a one-third greater risk of an earlier death than participants whose parents remained married at least until the participants reached age 21 (Friedman et al., 1995a, 1995b).

Specifically, the average age of death was 76 for men whose parents divorced during their childhoods—and 80 for men whose parents did not divorce. For women, the average age of death for those whose parents divorced was 82; those whose parents did not divorce lived to an average age of 86 (Schwartz et al., 1995).

To gather the data, psychologist Howard Friedman tracked down the death certificates of the participants in the study who had died, and then examined their backgrounds. He suggests that the surprising findings are due to the greater stigma attached to divorce during the childhoods of the study participants, who were born about 1910.

Further analyses also revealed that the children of divorce also tended to have greater marital instability themselves during their adult years. Such marital instability was also linked to an increased risk of premature death (Winger, 1993).

Other analyses of the Terman findings shows that earlier death is related to occupational choice. Specifically, both men and women who chose more male-typical occupational preferences showed higher mortality rates than those who chose occupations that were more typical for females. Although the exact explanation for these findings is not clear, it is apparent that the Terman longitudinal study continues to yield important and interesting findings, even as the study itself moves through a healthy old age (Lippa, Martin, & Friedman, 2000).

---

adulthood husbands' companionship needs tend to be greater than their wives'. The power structure of marriage also changes: Men become more affiliative and less competitive following retirement. At the same time, women become more assertive and autonomous (Blumstein & Schwartz, 1989; Bird & Melville, 1994).

Caring for an Aging Spouse. The shifts in health that accompany late adulthood sometimes require women and men to care for their spouses in ways that they never envisioned. Consider, for example, one woman's comments of frustration:

> I cry a lot because I never thought it would be this way. I didn't expect to be mopping up the bathroom, changing him, doing laundry all the time. I was taking care of babies at twenty; now I'm taking care of my husband. (Doress et al., 1987, pp. 199–200)

At the same time, some people view caring for an ailing and dying spouse in a more positive light, regarding it in part as a final opportunity to demonstrate love and devotion. In fact, some caregivers report feeling quite satisfied as a result of fulfilling what they see as their responsibility to their spouse. And some of those who experience emotional distress initially find that the distress declines as they successfully adapt to the stress of caregiving (Lawton et al., 1989; Townsend et al., 1989; Zarit & Reid, 1994).

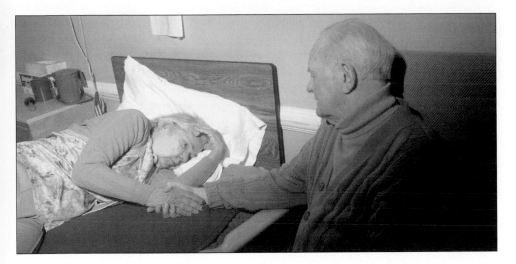

One of the most difficult responsibilities of later adulthood is caring for one's ill spouse.

Yet even if giving care is viewed in such a light, there is no getting around the fact that it is an arduous chore, made more difficult by the fact that the spouses providing the care are probably not in the peak of physical health themselves. In fact, caregiving may be detrimental to the provider's own physical and psychological health. For instance, caregivers report lower levels of satisfaction with life than do noncaregivers (Vitaliano, Dougherty, & Siegler, 1994).

In most cases, it should be noted, the spouse who provides the care is the wife. Just under three-quarters of people who provide care to a spouse are women. Part of the reason is demographic: Men tend to die earlier than women, and consequently they contract the diseases leading to death earlier than women. A second reason, though, relates to society's traditional gender roles, which view women as "natural" caregivers. As a consequence, health care providers may be more likely to suggest that a wife care for her husband than that a husband care for his wife (Polansky, 1976; Unger & Crawford, 1992).

The Death of a Spouse: Becoming Widowed. Hardly any event is more painful and stressful than the death of one's spouse. Especially for those who married young, the death of a spouse leads to profound feelings of loss and often brings about drastic changes in economic and social circumstances. If the marriage has been a good one, the death of the partner means the loss of a companion, a lover, a confidante, a helper.

Upon a partner's death, spouses suddenly assume a new and unfamiliar societal role: widowhood. At the same time, they lose the role with which they were most familiar: spouse. Suddenly, widowed people are no longer part of a couple; instead they are viewed by society, and themselves, solely as individuals. All this occurs as they are dealing with profound and sometimes overwhelming grief (which we discuss more in Chapter 19).

Widowhood brings a variety of new demands and concerns. There is no longer a companion with whom to share the day's events. If the deceased spouse primarily carried out household chores, the surviving spouse must learn how to do these tasks and must perform them every day. Although initially family and friends provide a great deal of support, this assistance quickly fades into the background, and newly widowed people are left to make the adjustment to being single on their own (Wortman & Silver, 1990).

Following the death of a spouse, people's social lives often change drastically. Typically, married couples tend to socialize with other married couples; widowed individuals may feel like "fifth wheels" as they seek to maintain the friendships they enjoyed as couples. Eventually, such friendships may cease, although they may be replaced by friendships with other single people (van den Hoonaard, 1994).

Economic issues are of major concern to many widowed people. Although many have insurance, savings, and pensions to provide economic security, some individuals, most often women, experience a decline in their economic well-being as the result of a spouse's death, as we noted earlier in this chapter. In such cases, the change in financial status can force wrenching decisions, such as selling the house in which the couple spent their entire married lives (O'Bryant & Morgan, 1989; Hoskins, 1992).

According to sociologists Gloria Heinemann and Patricia Evans (1990), the process of adjusting to widowhood encompasses three stages (see Figure 18-3). In the first stage, *preparation,* spouses prepare, in some cases years and even decades ahead of time, for the eventual death of the partner. Consider, for instance, the purchase of life insurance, the preparation of a will, and the decision to have children who may eventually provide care in one's old age. Each of these actions helps prepare for the eventuality that one will be widowed and will require some degree of assistance (Heinemann & Evans, 1990).

The second stage of adjustment to widowhood, *grief and mourning,* is an immediate reaction to the death of a spouse. It starts with the shock and pain of loss and continues as the survivor works through the period of grief and mourning. The length of time a person

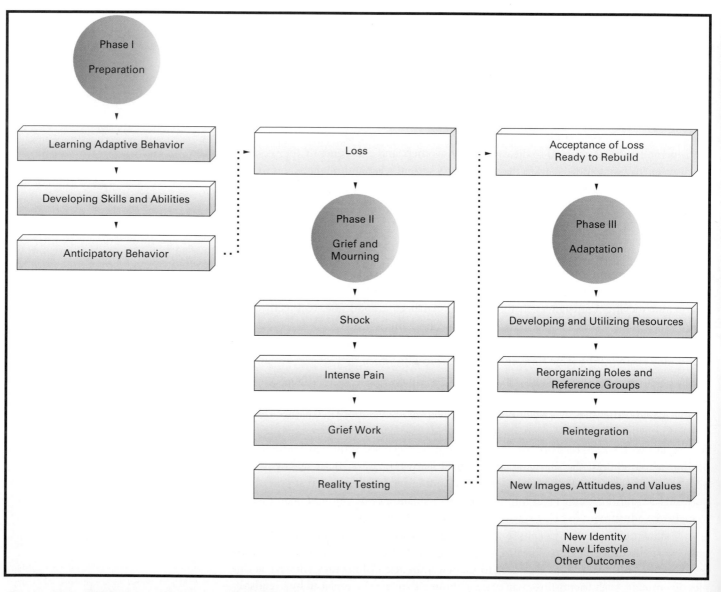

Figure 18-3 **The Process of Adjustment to Widowhood**

Is the process identical for men and women?

(Based on Heinemann & Evans, 1990.)

spends in this period depends on the degree of support received from others, as well as on personality factors. In some cases, the grief and mourning period may extend for years, while in others it lasts a few months.

The last stage of adjustment is *adaptation*. In adaptation, the widowed individual starts a new life. The period begins with the acceptance of one's loss and continues with the reorganization of roles and the formation of new friendships. The adaptation stage also encompasses a period of reintegration in which a new identity—as an unmarried person—is developed.

For most people, life returns to normal and becomes enjoyable once again. For others, life is viewed as all right, but just barely: The life they had before their spouse's death is seen as qualitatively better than their current existence. And for a minority of those who are widowed, there is no recovery; they constantly experience a strong sense of loss that overwhelms their current efforts at achieving happiness.

It is important to keep in mind that the model of loss and change proposed by Heinemann and Evans (1990) may not apply to everyone. Certainly, there are vast individual differences in the ways people react to the death of a spouse. Furthermore, the timing of the various stages in the model differs substantially from one person to the next.

Without fail, however, the death of a spouse is a profound event in any period of life. During late adulthood, its implications are particularly powerful, since it can be seen as a forewarning of one's own mortality (Howie, 1993).

The Social Networks of Late Adulthood

Elderly people enjoy friends as much as younger people do, and friendships play an important role in the lives of those in late adulthood. In fact, time spent with friends is often valued more highly during late adulthood than time spent with family, and friends are often seen as more important providers of support than family members. Furthermore, around a third of older persons report that they made a new friend within the past year, and many older adults engage in significant interaction (see Figure 18-4; Hartshorne, 1994; Hansson & Carpenter, 1994; Ansberry, 1997).

Friendship: Why Friends Matter in Late Adulthood. One reason for the importance of friendship relates to the element of control. In friendship relationships, unlike family relationships, we choose whom we like and whom we dislike, meaning that we have considerable control. Because late adulthood may bring with it a gradual loss of control in other areas, such as in one's health, the ability to maintain friendships may take on more importance than in other stages of life (Marshall, 1986; Chappell, 1991; Krause & Borawski-Clark, 1994).

In addition, friendships—especially ones that have developed recently—may be more flexible than family ties, given that recent friendships are not likely to have a history of obligations and past conflicts. In contrast, family ties may have a long and sometimes stormy record that can reduce the emotional sustenance they provide (Hartshorne, 1994; Magai & McFadden, 1996).

Another reason for the importance of friendships in late adulthood relates to the increasing likelihood, over time, that one will be without a marital partner. When a spouse dies, people typically seek out the companionship of friends to help deal with their loss and also to replace some of the social functions that were provided by the deceased spouse.

Of course, it isn't only spouses who die during old age; friends die too. The way adults view friendship in late adulthood determines how vulnerable they are to the death of a friend. If the friendship has been defined as irreplaceable, then the loss of the friend may be quite difficult. On the other hand, if the friendship is defined as a role relationship that fulfills companionship needs, then the death of a friend may be less traumatic. In such cases, older adults are more likely to become involved subsequently with new friends (Hartshorne, 1994).

It has been found that the benefits of social support are considerable, benefiting both the provider and receiver. What is the importance of reciprocity as a factor of social support?

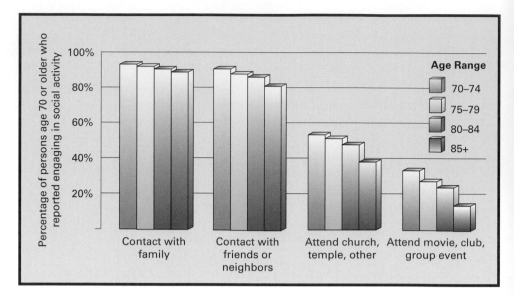

Figure 18-4 **Social Activity in Late Adulthood**

Friends and family play an important role in the social activity of the elderly.

(*Source:* Federal Interagency Forum on Age-Related Statistics, 2000.)

social support assistance and comfort supplied by another person or a network of caring, interested people

Social Support: The Significance of Others. Friendships also provide one of the basic social needs: social support. **Social support** is assistance and comfort supplied by a network of caring, interested people. Such support plays a critical role in successful aging (Antonucci, 1990; Antonucci & Akiyama, 1991).

The benefits of social support are considerable. For instance, people can provide emotional support by lending a sympathetic ear and providing a sounding board for one's concerns. Furthermore, social support from people who are experiencing similar problems—such as the loss of a spouse—can provide an unmatched degree of understanding and a pool of helpful suggestions for coping strategies that would be less credible coming from others.

Finally, people can furnish material support, such as helping with rides or picking up groceries. They can provide help in solving problems, such as dealing with a difficult landlord or fixing a broken appliance.

The benefits of social support extend not only to the recipient of the support, but to the provider. People who offer support experience feelings of usefulness and heightened self-esteem, knowing that they are making a contribution to others' welfare.

What kinds of social support are most effective and appropriate? It depends on the situation, but one factor is that a mechanism should exist whereby those who receive support can reciprocate in some fashion. In Western societies, older adults—like younger people—value relationships in which reciprocity is possible. *Reciprocity* is the expectation that if someone provides something positive to another person, a return benefit ought to be received. Conversely, someone who receives something of benefit from another individual expects to provide something in return (Clark, Mills, & Corcoran, 1989; Clark & Mills, 1993).

On the other hand, with increasing age, it may be progressively more difficult to reciprocate the social support that one receives. As a consequence, relationships may become more asymmetrical, placing the recipient in a difficult psychological position (Roberto, 1987; Selig, Tomlinson, & Hickey, 1991).

Family Relationships: The Ties that Bind

Even after the death of a spouse, most older adults are part of a larger family unit. Connections with siblings, children, grandchildren, and even great-grandchildren continue, and they may provide an important source of comfort to adults in the last years of their lives.

Siblings may provide unusually strong emotional support during late adulthood. Because they often share old, pleasant memories of childhood, and because they usually represent the oldest existing relationships a person has, siblings provide important assistance. While not every memory of childhood may be pleasant, continuing interaction with brothers and sisters still provides substantial emotional support during late adulthood (Bengston, Rosenthal, & Burton, 1990; Moyer 1992).

Children. Even more important than siblings, however, are children and grandchildren. Even in an age in which geographic mobility is high, most parents and children remain fairly close, both geographically and psychologically. Some 75 percent of children live within a 30-minute drive of their parents, and parents and children visit and talk with one another frequently. However, daughters tend to be in more frequent contact with their parents than sons. Furthermore, mothers tend to be the recipients of communication more frequently than fathers (Hoffman, McManus, & Brackbill, 1987; Field & Minkler, 1988; Krout, 1988).

Because the great majority of older adults have at least one child who lives fairly close, family members still provide significant aid to one another. Moreover, parents and children tend to share similar views of how adult children should behave toward their parents (see Table 18-2). In particular, they expect that children should help their parents understand their resources, provide emotional support, and talk over matters of importance (Hamon & Blieszner, 1990). Furthermore, it is most often children who end up caring for their aging parents when they require assistance (Eggebeen & Hogan, 1990; Wolfson et al., 1993).

The bonds between parents and children are sometimes asymmetrical, with parents seeking a closer relationship and children a more distant one. Parents have a greater *developmental stake* in close ties, since they see their children as perpetuating their beliefs,

Table 18-2

PARENTS AND CHILDREN SHARE SIMILAR VIEWS OF HOW ADULT CHILDREN SHOULD BEHAVE TOWARD THEIR PARENTS

Item	Children's Rank	Parent's Rank
Help understand resources	1	2
Give emotional support	2	3
Discuss matters of importance	3	1
Make room in home in emergency	4	7
Sacrifice personal freedom	5	6
Care when sick	6	9
Be together on special occasions	7	5
Provide financial help	8	13
Give parents advice	9	4
Adjust family schedule to help	10	10
Feel responsible for parent	11	8
Adjust work schedule to help	12	12
Believe that parent should live with child	13	15
Visit once a week	14	11
Live close to parent	15	16
Write once a week	16	14

(*Source:* Adapted from Hamon & Blieszner, 1990.)

values, and standards. On the other hand, children are motivated to maintain their autonomy and live independently from their parents. These divergent perspectives make parents more likely to minimize conflicts they experience with their children, and children more likely to maximize them (Bengston et al., 1985; O'Connor, 1994).

For parents, their children remain a source of great interest and concern. Some surveys show, for instance, that even in late adulthood parents talk about their children nearly every day, particularly if the children are having some sort of problem. At the same time, children may turn to their elderly parents for advice, information, and sometimes tangible help, such as money (Greenberg & Becker, 1988).

Grandchildren and Great-Grandchildren. As we discussed first in Chapter 16, not all grandparents are equally involved with their grandchildren. Even those grandparents who take great pride in their grandchildren may be relatively detached from them, avoiding any direct care role (Cherlin & Furstenberg, 1986).

As we saw, grandmothers tend to be more involved with their grandchildren than grandfathers; similarly, there are gender differences in the feelings grandchildren have toward their grandparents. Specifically, most young adult grandchildren feel closer to their grandmothers than to their grandfathers. In addition, most express a preference for their maternal grandmothers over their paternal grandmothers (Kalliopuska, 1994; Chan & Elder, 2000; Hayslip, Shore, & Henderson, 2000).

Furthermore, African American grandparents tend to be more involved with their grandchildren than white grandparents, and African American grandchildren often feel closer to their grandparents. Moreover, grandfathers seem to play a more central role in the lives of African American children than in the lives of white children. The reason for these racial differences probably stems in large measure from the higher proportion of multigenerational families among African Americans than among whites. In such families, grandparents usually play a central role in childrearing (Beck & Beck, 1989; Kivett, 1991; Taylor et al., 1991).

Great-grandchildren play less of a role in the lives of both white and African American great-grandparents. Most great-grandparents do not have close relationships with their great-grandchildren. Close relationships tend to occur only when the great-grandparents and great-grandchildren live relatively near one another (Doka & Mertz, 1988).

There are several explanations for the relative lack of involvement of great-grandparents with great-grandchildren. One is that by the time they reach great-grandparenthood, elderly adults are so old that they do not have much physical or psychological energy to expend on forming relationships with their great-grandchildren. Another is that there may be so many great-grandchildren that great-grandparents do not feel strong emotional ties to them. In fact, it is not uncommon for a great-grandparent who has had a large number of children to have so many great-grandchildren that they are difficult to keep track of. For example, when President John Kennedy's mother, Rose Kennedy (who had given birth to a total of nine children), died at the age of 104, she had 30 grandchildren and 41 great-grandchildren!

Still, even though most great-grandparents may not have close relationships with their great-grandchildren, they still profit emotionally from the mere fact that they have great-grandchildren. For instance, great-grandparents may see their great-grandchildren as representing both their own and their family's continuation, as well as providing a concrete sign of their longevity (Doka & Mertz, 1988).

Elder Abuse: Relationships Gone Wrong

With good health and a sizable pension, 76-year-old Mary T. should have been enjoying a comfortable retirement. But in fact, her life was made miserable by a seemingly endless barrage of threats, insults, and indignities from her live-in adult son.

A habitual gambler and drug user, the son was merciless: he spat at Mary, brandished a knife in her face, stole her money, and sold her possessions. After several emergency room trips and two hospitalizations, social workers convinced Mary to move out and join a support group of other elderly people abused by their loved ones. With a new apartment and understanding friends, Mary finally had some peace. But her son found her, and feeling a mother's guilt and shame, Mary took him back—and opened another round of heartache. (Minaker & Frishman, 1995, p. 9)

It would be easy to assume that such cases are rare. The truth of the matter, however, is that they are considerably more common than we would like to believe. According to some estimates, **elder abuse,** the physical or psychological mistreatment or neglect of elderly individuals, may affect as many as 2 million people above the age of 60 each year. Even these estimates may be too low, since people who are abused are often too embarrassed or humiliated to report their plight. And as the number of elderly people increases, experts believe that the number of cases of elder abuse will also rise (Brubaker, 1991).

Elder abuse is most frequently directed at family members and particularly at elderly parents. Those most at risk are likely to be less healthy and more isolated than the average person in late adulthood, and they are more likely to be living in a caregiver's home. Although there is no single cause for elder abuse, it often is the result of a combination of economic, psychological, and social pressures on caregivers who must provide high levels of care 24 hours a day. Thus, people with Alzheimer's disease or other sorts of dementia are particularly likely to be targets of abuse (Williams & Griffen, 1991; Choi & Mayer, 2000; Dyer et al., 2000).

The best approach to dealing with elder abuse is to prevent it from occurring in the first place. Family members caring for an older adult should take occasional breaks. Social support agencies can be contacted; they can provide advice and concrete support. For instance, the National Family Caregivers Association (800-896-3650) maintains a caregivers' network and publishes a newsletter. Furthermore, anyone suspecting that an elderly person is being abused should contact local authorities, such as their state's Adult Protective Services or Elder Protective Services.

cw

elder abuse the physical or psychological mistreatment or neglect of elderly individuals

Review and Rethink

REVIEW

- While marriages in older adulthood are generally happy, stresses due to aging can bring divorce.
- Retirement often causes a reworking of power relationships within the marriage.
- The death of a spouse brings highly significant psychological, social, and material changes to the survivor.
- Friendships are very important in later life.
- Family relationships are a continuing part of most older people's lives, especially relationships with siblings and children.
- Elder abuse typically involves a socially isolated elderly parent in poor health and a caregiver who feels burdened by the parent.

RETHINK

- What are some factors that can combine to make older adulthood a more difficult time for women than for men?
- What are some ways the retirement of a spouse can bring stress to a marriage? Is retirement less stressful in households where both spouses work, or twice as stressful?

Looking Back

▶ *In what ways does personality develop during late adulthood?*

■ In Erikson's ego-integrity-versus-despair stage of psychosocial development, as people reflect on their lives, they may feel either satisfaction, which leads to integration, or dissatisfaction, which can lead to despair and a lack of integration.

■ Robert Peck identifies the three main tasks of this period as redefinition of self versus preoccupation with work-role, body transcendence versus body preoccupation, and ego transcendence versus ego preoccupation.

■ Daniel Levinson identifies a transitional stage that people pass through on the way to late adulthood, during which they struggle with being "old" and with societal stereotypes. A successful transition can lead to liberation and self-respect.

■ Bernice Neugarten identified four personality types according to the way they cope with aging: disintegrated and disorganized, passive-dependent, defended, and integrated.

■ Life review, a common theme of developmental theories of late adulthood, can help people resolve past conflicts and achieve wisdom and serenity, but some people become obsessive about past errors and slights.

■ Age stratification theories suggest that the unequal distribution of economic resources, power, and privilege is particularly pronounced during late adulthood. In general, Western societies do not hold elderly people in as high esteem as many Asian societies.

▶ *How do people deal with aging?*

■ Disengagement theory and activity theory present opposite views of ways to deal successfully with aging. People's choices depend partly on their prior habits and personalities.

■ The model of selective optimization with compensation involves focusing on personally important areas of functioning and compensating for ability losses in those areas.

▶ *In what circumstances do older people live, and what difficulties do they face?*

■ Living arrangement options include staying at home, living with family members, participating in adult day-care, residing in continuing-care communities, and living in skilled-nursing facilities.

■ Elderly people may become financially vulnerable because they must cope with rising health care and other costs on a fixed income.

▶ *What is it like to retire?*

■ People who retire must fill an increasingly longer span of leisure time. Those who are most successful plan ahead and have varied interests.

■ People who retire often pass through stages, including a honeymoon period, disenchantment, reorientation, a retirement routine stage, and termination.

▶ *How do marriages in late adulthood fare?*

■ Marriages in later life generally remain happy, although stresses brought about by major life changes that accompany aging can cause rifts. Divorce is usually harder on the woman than the man, partly because of the continuing influence of the marriage gradient.

■ Deterioration in the health of a spouse can cause the other spouse—typically the wife—to become a caregiver, which can bring both challenges and rewards.

▶ *What happens when an elderly spouse dies?*

■ The death of a spouse forces the survivor to assume a new societal role, accommodate to the absence of a companion and chore-sharer, create a new social life, and resolve financial problems.

■ Sociologists Gloria Heinemann and Patricia Evans have identified three stages in adjusting to widowhood: preparation, grief and mourning, and adaptation. Some people never reach the adaptation stage.

▶ *What sorts of relationships are important in late adulthood?*

■ Friendships are important in later life because they offer personal control, companionship, and social support.

■ Family relationships, especially with siblings and children, provide a great deal of emotional support for people in later life.

■ In the increasingly prevalent phenomenon of elder abuse, parents who are socially isolated and in poor health may be abused by children who are forced to serve as caregivers.

EPILOGUE

In this chapter we examined social and personality development in the last years of life. We focused on the question of change versus stability in personality and debunked a few stereotypes as we looked at the ways older people live and at the effects of retirement. We discussed relationships, especially marital and family relationships, but also friendships and social networks. We concluded with a consideration of elder abuse.

Turn back to the prologue to this chapter, about the long marriage of Joseph and Eva Solymosi, and answer the following questions.

1. What aspects of Joseph's and Eva's personalities can be deduced from the prologue? Do you think any of those traits have changed substantially since Joseph and Eva lived in Hungary? Why or why not?

2. Based on evidence in the prologue, how do you think Eva and Joseph are managing what Erikson calls the ego-integrity-versus-despair stage? How about Peck's developmental tasks?

3. In what ways are Joseph and Eva accomplishing life review? Does this process appear to be harmful or helpful to them?

4. If Eva and Joseph chose disengagement as a strategy in late adulthood, what would you expect their lives to be like? What if they chose the activity strategy? Is there evidence to suggest which approach they are taking?

5. Joseph and Eva still live together in their own home. In what ways might their lives differ from those of other elderly individuals who have lost a spouse or live under different circumstances?

Key Terms and Concepts

ego-integrity-versus-despair stage (p. 617)
redefinition of self versus preoccupation with work-role (p. 617)
body transcendence versus body preoccupation (p. 617)
ego transcendence versus ego preoccupation (p. 619)

life review (p. 620)
age stratification theory (p. 621)
wisdom (p. 622)
disengagement theory (p. 624)
activity theory (p. 625)
continuity theory (p. 625)
selective optimization (p. 626)

continuing-care community (p. 628)
adult day-care facilities (p. 628)
skilled-nursing facilities (p. 629)
institutionalism (p. 629)
social support (p. 640)
elder abuse (p. 643)

ENDINGS

Death and Dying

PROLOGUE: COMING TO GRIPS WITH DEATH

Although Joan Kindy still experiences deep sadness over the death of her husband Hal, she more frequently recalls pleasant memories.

There are moments, such as when she hears the solemn opening chords of the second movement of Dvorak's "From the New World" symphony, when Joan Kindy feels the rush of 30 years of memories and the pain of nearly two years without her husband, Hal.

It was a cherished piece of music that now, like so many things large and small, reminds Mrs. Kindy that she is a widow.

Their son, David, calls with good news about a job, and Hal is not there to share it. An osprey soars over nearby Lake Tarpon, but Hal's binoculars, which he used to bring the bird's sharp talons into focus, sit on a table. Holidays and anniversaries, sunset walks and quiet dinners at home all pass for Mrs. Kindy now without her husband.

"I actually thought I would be a lot more relieved when he died," said Mrs. Kindy, 63 . . . "I thought, once his pain is over . . . "

Her voice trailed off. "That was my prayer, that he would be out of pain and I would feel relief for him, but I didn't. It's like half my anchor is gone." (Cutter, 1999, p. 10)

Looking Ahead

Joan Kindy is getting better. Although the grief she felt immediately after his death still surfaces, more frequently her thoughts are on pleasant memories.

Death is an experience that will befall all of us at some time, as universal to the human condition as birth. As such, it represents a milestone of life that is central to an understanding of the life span. In fact, death is omnipresent throughout every period of life, a possibility from the moment following conception, in infancy and childhood and throughout adulthood, increasingly likely the longer we live.

Despite the ubiquity of death and dying, however, the study of the topic is a relative newcomer to the domain of developmental psychologists. Only in the past several decades has serious study been given to the developmental implications of dying.

In this chapter we discuss death and dying from several perspectives. We begin by considering how we define death—a determination that is more complex than it seems. We then examine how people view and react to death at different points in the life span, beginning in infancy and continuing through late adulthood. And we consider the very different views of death held by various societies.

Next, we look at how people confront their own deaths. We discuss one theory that people move through several stages as they come to grips with their approaching death. We also look at how people seek to control their deaths through the use of living wills and assisted suicide.

Finally, we consider reactions to bereavement (the fact that one has experienced a loss) and grief (the emotional response to a death). We examine the difficulties in distinguishing normal from unhealthy grief, and we discuss the consequences of a loss. The chapter also looks at mourning and funerals, discussing how people can prepare themselves for the inevitability of death.

After reading this chapter, you will be able to answer the following questions:

▶ **What is death, and what does it mean at different stages of the life span?**

▶ **In what ways do people face the prospect of their own death?**

▶ **How do survivors react to and cope with death?**

Dying and Death Across the Life Span

It took them close to a year to do it, but eventually Karen Ann Quinlan's parents won the right to remove her from a respirator. Lying in a hospital bed in New Jersey in what physicians call a "persistent vegetative state," Quinlan was never expected to regain consciousness following an automobile accident. After the state Supreme Court allowed her parents to have the respirator removed, Quinlan lived on in a coma for close to a decade until she died.

Were Quinlan's parents right in asking for the removal of her respirator? Was she already dead when it was turned off? Were her constitutional rights unfairly ignored by her parents' action?

The difficulty of answering such questions illustrates the complexity of what are, literally, matters of life and death. Death is not only a biological event; it involves psychological aspects as well. We need to consider not only issues relating to the definition of death, but also the ways in which our conception of death changes across various points in the life span.

Defining Death: Determining the Point at Which Life Ends

What is death? Although the question seems straightforward, defining the point at which life ceases and death occurs is surprisingly complex. In fact, medicine over the last few decades has advanced to the point where some people who would have been considered dead a few years ago would now be considered alive.

Functional death is defined by an absence of heartbeat and breathing. Although this definition seems unambiguous, it is not completely straightforward. For example, a person whose heart has stopped beating and whose breathing has ceased for as long as five minutes may be resuscitated and suffer little damage as a consequence of the experience. Does this mean that the person who is now alive was dead, as the functional definition would have it?

Because of the ambiguities involved in using heartbeat and respiration to determine the moment of death, medical experts have turned to a measure of brain functioning. In **brain death,** all signs of brain activity, as measured by electrical brain waves, have ceased. When brain death occurs, there is no possibility of restoring brain functioning.

On the other hand, some medical experts suggest that a definition of death that relies solely on a lack of brain waves is inappropriate. Instead, they argue that a lack of the qualities that make people human—the ability to think, reason, feel, and experience the world—may be sufficient to declare a person dead. In this view, which takes psychological considerations into account, a person who suffers irreversible brain damage, who is in a coma, and who will never experience anything approaching a human life can be considered dead. In such a case, the argument goes, death can be judged to have arrived, even if some sort of primitive brain activity is still occurring (Veatch, 1984).

Not surprisingly, such an argument, which moves us from strictly medical criteria to moral and philosophical considerations, is controversial. As a result, the legal definition of death in most localities in the United States relies on the absence of brain functioning, although some laws still include a definition relating to the absence of respiration and heartbeat. The reality is that no matter where a death occurs, in most cases people do not bother to measure brain waves. Usually, the brain waves are closely monitored only in certain circumstances—when the time of death is significant, when organs may potentially be transplanted, or when criminal or legal issues might be involved.

The difficulty in establishing legal and medical definitions of death may reflect some of the changes in understanding and attitudes about death that occur over the course of people's lives.

functional death the absence of a heartbeat and breathing

brain death a diagnosis of death based on the cessation of all signs of brain activity, as measured by electrical brain waves

Death Across the Life Span: Causes and Reactions

Death is something we associate with old age. However, for many individuals, death comes earlier. In such cases, in part because it seems "unnatural" for a younger person to die, the reactions are particularly extreme. In the U.S. today, in fact, some people believe that it is wrong for children to even know much about death. Yet people of every age can experience the death of friends and family members, as well as their own death. How do our reactions to death evolve as we age? We will consider several age groups.

Death in Infancy and Childhood. Despite its economic wealth, the United States has a relatively high infant mortality rate, as we first discussed in Chapter 3. Although the rate has declined since the mid-1960s, the United States ranks behind 22 other industrialized countries in the proportion of infants who die during the first year of life (Wegman, 1993; National Center for Health Statistics, 1993c).

As these statistics indicate, the number of parents who experience the death of an infant is substantial, and their reactions may be profound. They typically experience all the same reactions they would experience on the death of an older person, and sometimes even more severe effects as they struggle to deal with a death at such an early age. One of the most common reactions is extreme depression (DeFrain et al., 1991; Brockington, 1992).

One kind of death that is exceptionally difficult to deal with is prenatal death, or *miscarriage* (McGreal, Evans, & Burrows, 1997). Parents typically form psychological bonds with their unborn child, and consequently they often feel profound grief if it dies before it is born. Moreover, many times friends and relatives do not attribute as much meaning to miscarriage as do the parents, isolating the parents and making them feel their loss all the more keenly.

Another form of death that produces extreme stress, in part because it is so unanticipated, is sudden infant death syndrome. In **sudden infant death syndrome,** or **SIDS,** a seemingly healthy baby stops breathing and dies of unexplained causes. Usually occurring between the ages of 2 and 4 months, SIDS strikes unexpectedly; a robust, hardy baby is placed into a crib at nap time or night time and never wakes up.

Afterwards, parents often feel intense guilt, and acquaintances may be suspicious of the "true" cause of death. As we discussed in Chapter 3, however, there is no known cause for SIDS, which seems to strike randomly, and parents' guilt is unwarranted. (Downey, Silver, & Wortman, 1990).

During childhood, the most frequent cause of death is accidents, most of them due to motor vehicle crashes, fires, and drowning. However, a substantial number of children in the United States are victims of homicides, which have nearly tripled in number since 1960 (Finkelhor, 1997). By the early 1990s, death by homicide had become the fourth leading cause of death for children between the ages of 1 and 9 (National Center for Health Statistics, 1994).

For parents, the death of a child produces the most profound sense of loss and grief. In fact, there is no worse death in the eyes of most parents, including the loss of a spouse or of parents. Parents' extreme reaction is partly based on the sense that the natural order of the world, in which children "should" outlive their parents, has somehow collapsed. Furthermore, parents feel that it is their primary responsibility to protect their children from any harm, and they may feel that they have failed in this task when a child dies (Gilbert, 1997).

sudden infant death syndrome (SIDS)
the unexplained death of a seemingly healthy baby

cw

The most frequent causes of death during childhood are due to motor vehicle crashes, fires, and drowning. However, a substantial number of children in the United States are victims of homicide.

Parents are almost never well equipped to deal with the death of a child, and they may obsessively ask themselves afterward, over and over, why the death occurred. Because the bond between children and parents is so strong, parents sometimes feel that a part of themselves has died as well (Sanders, 1988; Stroebe, Stroebe, & Hansson, 1993).

Children themselves do not really begin to develop a concept of death until around the age of 5. Although they are well aware of death before that time, they are apt to think of it as a temporary state that involves a reduction in living, rather than a cessation. For instance, a preschool-age child might say, "dead people don't get hungry—well, maybe a little" (Kastenbaum, 1985, p. 629).

Some preschool-age children think of death in terms of sleep—with the consequent possibility of waking up, just as Sleeping Beauty was awakened in the fairy tale. For children who believe this, death is not particularly fearsome; rather, it is something of a curiosity. If people merely tried hard enough—by administering medicine, providing food, or using magic—dead people might "return" (Bluebond-Langner, 1977; Lonetto, 1980).

In some cases, children's misunderstanding of death can produce devastating emotional consequences. Children sometimes leap to the erroneous conclusion that they are somehow responsible for a person's death. For instance, they may assume they could have prevented the death by being better behaved. In the same way, they may think that if the person who died really wanted to, she or he could return.

Around the age of 5, the finality and irreversibility of death become better understood. In some cases, children personify death as some kind of ghostlike or devilish figure. At first, though, they do not think of death as universal, but rather as something that happens only to certain people. By about age 9, however, they come to accept the universality of death and its finality (Nagy, 1948). By middle childhood, children also learn about some of the customs involved with death, such as funerals, cremation, and cemeteries.

Death in Adolescence. We might expect the significant advances in cognitive development that occur during adolescence to bring about a sophisticated, thoughtful, and reasoned view of death. However, in many ways, adolescents' views of death are as unrealistic as those of younger children, although along different lines.

While adolescents clearly understand the finality and irreversibility of death, their view includes some of the drawbacks that affect adolescent thinking in general. As we discussed in Chapter 11, adolescents develop a *personal fable,* a set of beliefs that causes them to feel unique and special. Such thinking can lead to quite risky behavior, as personal fables induce a sense of invulnerability, the idea that the adolescent is so special that bad things, even though they happen to other people, are unlikely affect them (Pattison, 1977; Elkind, 1985).

Many times, this risky behavior causes death in adolescence. For instance, the most frequent cause of death among adolescents is accidents, most often involving motor vehicles. Other frequent causes include homicide, suicide, cancer, and AIDS (National Center for Health Statistics, 1994).

When adolescent feelings of invulnerability confront the likelihood of death due to an illness, the results can be shattering. Adolescents who learn that they have a terminal illness often feel angry and cheated—that life has been unjust to them. Because they feel—and act—so negatively, it may be difficult for medical personnel to treat them effectively.

In contrast, some adolescents diagnosed with a terminal illness react with total denial. Feeling indestructible, they may find it impossible to accept the seriousness of their illness. If it does not interfere with their acceptance of medical treatment, some degree of denial may actually be useful, as it allows an adolescent to continue with his or her normal life as long as possible (Blumberg, Lewis, & Susman, 1984).

Death in Young Adulthood. Young adulthood is the time when most people feel primed to begin their lives. Past the preparatory time of childhood and adolescence, they are on the

Adolescents' views of death may be highly romanticized and dramatic.

threshold of making their mark on the world. Because death at such a point in life seems close to unthinkable, its occurrence is particularly difficult. Because they are actively pursuing their goals for life, they are angry and impatient with any illness that threatens their future.

In early adulthood, the leading cause of death continues to be accidents, followed by suicide, homicide, AIDS, and cancer. By the end of early adulthood, however, disease becomes a more prevalent cause of death.

For those people facing death in early adulthood, several concerns are of particular importance. One is the desire to develop intimate relationships and express sexuality, each of which are inhibited, if not completely prevented, by a terminal illness. For instance, people who test positive for the AIDS virus may find it quite difficult to start new relationships. The role of sexual activities within evolving relationships presents even more challenging issues (Rabkin, Remien, & Wilson, 1994).

Another particular concern during young adulthood involves future planning. At a time when most people are mapping out their careers and deciding at what point to start a family, young adults who have a terminal illness face additional burdens. Should they marry, even though it is likely that the partner will soon end up widowed? Should a couple seek to conceive a child if the child is likely to be raised by only one parent? How soon should one's employer be told about a terminal illness, when it is clear that employers sometimes discriminate against unhealthy workers? None of these questions is easily answered.

Like adolescents, young adults sometimes make poor patients. They are outraged at their plight and feel the world is unfair, and they may direct their anger at care providers and loved ones. In addition, they may make the medical staff who provide direct care—nurses and orderlies—feel particularly vulnerable, since the staff themselves are often young (Cook & Oltjenbruns, 1989).

Death in Middle Adulthood. For people in middle adulthood, the shock of a life-threatening disease—which is the most common cause of death in this period—is not so great. In fact, by this point, people are well aware that they are going to die sometime, and they may be able to consider the possibility of death in a fairly realistic manner.

On the other hand, their sense of realism doesn't make the possibility of dying any easier. In fact, fears about death are often greater in middle adulthood than at any time previously—or even in later life. These fears may lead people to look at life in terms of the number of years they have remaining as opposed to their earlier orientation toward the number of years they have already lived (Kalish & Reynolds, 1976; Neugarten, 1967; Levinson, 1992).

The most frequent cause of death in middle adulthood is heart attack or stroke. Although the unexpectedness of such a death does not allow for preparation, in some ways it is easier than a slow, protracted, and painful death from a disease such as cancer. It is certainly the kind of death that most people prefer: When asked, they say they would like an instant and painless death that does not involve loss of any body part (Taylor, 1991).

Death in Late Adulthood. By the time they reach late adulthood, people know with some certainty that their time is coming to an end. Furthermore, they face an increasing number of deaths in their environment. Spouses, siblings, and friends may have already died, a constant reminder of their own mortality.

The most likely causes of death are cancer, stroke, and heart disease during late adulthood. What would happen if these causes of death were eliminated? According to demographers' estimates, the average 70-year-old's life expectancy would increase around 7 years (see Figure 19-1; Hayward, Crimmins, & Saito, 1997).

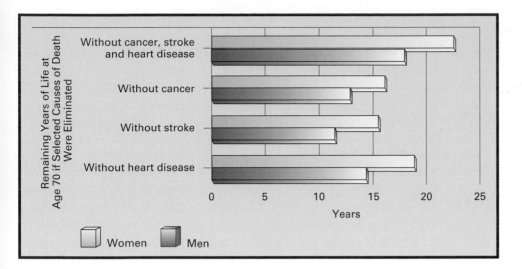

***Figure 19-1* Adding Years**

If the major causes of death were eliminated, the average 70-year-old person would live another 7 years.

(*Source:* Hayward, Crimmins, & Saito, 1997.)

The prevalence of death in the lives of elderly people makes them less anxious about dying than they were at earlier stages of life. This does not mean that people in late adulthood welcome death. Rather, it implies that they are more realistic and reflective about it. They think about death, and they may begin to make preparations for their demise. Some begin to pull away from the world due to diminishing physical and psychological energy (Cummings & Henry, 1961; Gesser, Wong, & Reker, 1988; Turner & Helms, 1994).

Impending death is sometimes accompanied by acceleration of declines in cognitive functioning. In what is known as the *terminal decline*, a significant drop in performance on cognitive tasks may foreshadow death within the next few years (Small & Bäckman, 1999).

Some elderly individuals actively seek out death, turning to suicide. In fact, the suicide rate for men climbs steadily during the course of late adulthood, and no age group has a higher rate of suicide than white men over the age of 85 (De Leo, Conforti, & Carollo, 1997). (Adolescents and young adults commit suicide in greater numbers, but their *rate* of suicide is actually lower.) Suicide is often a consequence of severe depression or some form of dementia, or it can be due to the loss of a spouse. And, as we will discuss later in the chapter, some individuals, struck down with a terminal illness, seek the assistance of others in committing suicide (Blazer, 1991).

One particularly salient issue for older adults suffering from a terminal illness is whether their lives still have value. More than younger individuals, elderly people who are dying harbor concerns that they are burdens to their family or to society. Furthermore, they may be given the message, sometimes inadvertently, that their value to society has ended and that they have attained the status of "dying" as opposed to being "very sick" (Kastenbaum, 2000).

Do older people wish to know if death is impending? The answer, in most cases, is yes. Like younger patients, who usually state that they wish to know the true nature of an ailment, older people want the details of their illnesses (Blumenfield, Levy, & Kaplan, 1979; Miller & Mangan, 1983). Ironically, candor is not something caregivers wish to provide: Physicians usually prefer to avoid telling dying patients that their illnesses are terminal (Feifel, 1963; Kaufman, 1992; Goold, Williams, & Arnold, 2000).

On the other hand, not all people wish to learn the truth about their condition or to know that they are dying. In fact, it is important to keep in mind that individuals react to death in substantially different ways. In part, their reaction is produced by personality factors. For example, a person's general level of anxiety and sense of how quickly time passes have been linked to concerns about death. In addition, there are significant cultural differences in how people view and react to death, as we consider next (Kastenbaum, 2000).

Developmental Diversity
Differing Conceptions of Death

In the midst of a tribal celebration, an older man waits for his oldest son to place a cord around his neck. The older man has been sick, and he is ready to relinquish his ties to this earthly world. He asks that his son lift him to his death, and the son complies.

∗∗∗

To Hindus in India, death is not an ending, but rather part of a continual cycle. Because they believe in reincarnation, death is thought to be followed by rebirth into a new life. Death, then, is seen as a companion to life.

People's responses to death take many forms, particularly in different cultures. But even within Western societies, reactions to death and dying are quite diverse. For instance, consider which is better: for a man to die after a full life in which he has raised a family and been successful in his job, or for a courageous and valiant young soldier to die defending his country in wartime. Has one person died a better death than the other?

The answer depends on one's values, which are largely due to cultural and subcultural teachings, often shared through religious beliefs. For instance, some societies view death as a punishment or as a judgment about one's contributions to the world. Others see death as redemption from an earthly life of travail. Some view death as the start of an eternal life, while others believe that there is no heaven or hell and that an earthly life is all there is.

Given that religious teachings regarding the meaning of life and death are quite diverse, it is not surprising that views of death and dying vary substantially. For instance, one study found that Christian and Jewish 10-year-olds tended to view death from a more "scientific" vantage point than Sunni Moslem and Druze children of the same age. We cannot be sure whether such differences are due to the different religious and cultural backgrounds of the children, or if differences in exposure to dying people influence the rate at which the understanding of death develops. However, it is clear that members of

Differing conceptions of death lead to different rituals, as this ceremony in India illustrates.

the various groups had very different conceptions of death (Florian & Kravetz, 1985; Thorson et al., 1997; Aiken, 2000).

In addition, members of some cultures seem to learn about death at an earlier age than others. For instance, exposure to high levels of violence and death may lead to an awareness of death earlier in some cultures than in cultures in which violence is less a part of everyday life. Research shows that children in Northern Ireland and Israel understood the finality, irreversibility, and inevitability of death at an earlier age than children in the United States and Britain (McWhirter, Young, & Majury, 1983; Atchley, 2000). This chapter's *From Research to Practice* box discusses how children, and adults, might learn more about death in cultures where they are not as likely to be exposed to it. ☐

thanatologists people who study death and dying

From Research to Practice
Can Death Education Prepare Us for the Inevitable?

"When will Mom come back from being dead?"

"Why did Barry have to die?"

"Did Grampa die because I was bad?"

Children's questions such as these illustrate why many developmentalists, as well as **thanatologists,** people who study death and dying, have suggested that death education should be an important component of everyone's schooling. Consequently, a relatively new area of instruction, termed death education, has emerged. *Death education* encompasses programs that teach about death, dying, and grief. Death education is designed to help people of all ages deal better with death and dying—both others' deaths and their own personal mortality.

Why is death education necessary? Probably the most important reason relates to the way we hide death, at least in most Western societies. We typically give hospitals the task of dealing with dying people, and we do not talk to children about death or allow them to go to funerals for fear of disturbing them. Even those most familiar with death, such as emergency workers and medical specialists, are uncomfortable talking about the subject. Because it is discussed so little and is so removed from everyday life, people of all ages may have little opportunity to confront their feelings about death. As a result, death provokes even more anxiety (Pettle & Britten, 1995; Humphrey & Zimpfer, 1996; Kastenbaum, 1999).

Several types of death education programs have been developed. Among the major kinds are the following.

▶ *Crisis intervention education.* When the Oklahoma City federal building was bombed, killing hundreds of people, children in the area were the subjects of several kinds of crisis intervention designed to deal with their anxieties. Because the victims included children in a child-care center in the building, younger children were especially susceptible to feelings that they too might die in a blast. These younger children, whose conceptions of death were shaky at best, needed explanations geared to their levels of cognitive development. In this situation, psychologists provided counseling intervention on an emergency basis. Crisis intervention education is used in less extreme times too. For example, it is common for schools to make emergency counseling available if a student is killed or commits suicide.

▶ *Routine death education.* Although there is relatively little curricular material on death available at the elementary school level, course work in high schools is becoming increasingly common. For instance, some high schools have specific courses on death and dying, and one survey found that the majority of teachers discuss death as part of other lessons (Cappiello & Troyer, 1979). Furthermore, colleges and universities increasingly include courses relating to death in such departments as psychology, human development, sociology, and education.

▶ *Death education for members of the helping professions.* Professionals who will deal with death, dying, and grief as part of their careers have a special need for death education. Almost all medical and nursing schools now offer some form of death education to help their students. The most successful programs not only provide intellectual content regarding death, but also allow students to explore their feelings about the topic (Downe-Wamboldt & Tamlyn, 1997; Kastenbaum, 1999).

Although no single form of death education will be sufficient to demystify death, the kinds of programs described above may help people come to grips more effectively with what is, along with birth, the most universal—and certain—of all human experiences.

Review and Rethink

REVIEW

- Death has been defined as the cessation of heartbeat and respiration (functional death), the absence of electrical brain waves (brain death), and the loss of human qualities.

- The death of an infant or young child can be particularly difficult for parents, and for an adolescent death appears to be unthinkable.

- Death in young adulthood can appear unfair, while people in middle adulthood have begun to understand the reality of death.

- By the time they reach late adulthood, people know they will die and begin to make preparations.

- Cultural differences in attitudes and beliefs about death strongly influence people's reactions to it.

- Thanatologists recommend that death education become a normal part of learning.

RETHINK

- Given their developmental level and understanding of death, how do you think preschool children react to the death of a parent?

- Do you think people who are going to die should be told? Does your response depend on the person's age?

Confronting Death

Helen Reynolds, 63, had undergone operations in January and April to repair and then replace a heart valve that was not permitting a smooth flow of blood. But by May her feet had turned the color of overripe eggplants, their mottled purple black an unmistakable sign of gangrene. . . . In June she chose to have first her right leg, and then her left, amputated in hopes of stabilizing her condition. The doctors were skeptical about the surgery, but deferred to her wishes. . . .

But then Reynolds uncharacteristically began talking about her pain. On that Sunday afternoon in June, a nurse beckoned intern Dr. Randall Evans. Evans, a graduate of the University of New Mexico Medical School who planned a career in the critical-care field, was immensely popular with the nursing staff for his cordial and sympathetic manner. But, unlike the MICU nurses, he had difficulty reading Reynolds's lips (the ventilator made it impossible for her to speak aloud), and asked her to write down her request. Laboriously, she scrawled 16 words on the note pad: "I have decided to end my life as I do not want to live like this." (Begley, 1991, p. 44–45)

Less than a week later, after the ventilator that helped her to breathe had been removed at her request, Helen Reynolds died.

Like other deaths, Reynolds's raises a myriad of difficult questions. Was her request to remove the respirator equivalent to suicide? Should the medical staff have complied with the request? Was she coping with her impending death effectively? How do people come to terms with death, and how do they react and adapt to it? Developmental psychologists and other specialists in death and dying have struggled, with great difficulty, to find answers to such questions.

Understanding the Process of Dying: Are There Steps Toward Death?

No individual has had a greater influence on our understanding of the way people confront death than Elisabeth Kübler-Ross. A psychiatrist, Kübler-Ross developed a theory of death and dying, built on extensive interviews with people who were dying and with those who cared for them (Kübler-Ross, 1969, 1982).

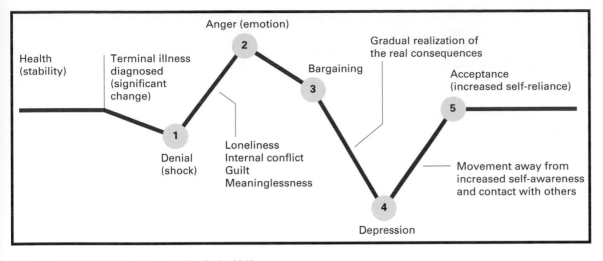

Figure 19-2 **Moving Toward the End of Life**

The steps toward death, according to Kübler-Ross (1975). Do you think there are cultural differences in the steps?

Based on her observations, Kübler-Ross initially suggested that people pass through five basic steps as they move toward death (summarized in Figure 19-2).

Denial. "No, I can't be dying. There must be some mistake." It is typical for people to protest in such a manner on learning that they have a terminal disease. Such objections represent the first stage of dying, *denial*. In denial, people resist the idea that they are going to die. They may argue that their test results have been mixed up, that an X-ray has been read incorrectly, or that their physician does not know what he or she is talking about.

Denial comes in several forms. A patient may flatly reject the diagnosis, simply refusing to believe the news. In extreme cases, memories of weeks in the hospital are forgotten. In other forms of denial, patients fluctuate between refusing to accept the news and at other times confiding that they know they are going to die (Carroll, 1985).

Although we might view the loss of reality implied by denial as a sign of deteriorating mental health, in fact many experts view denial in positive terms. Denial is a defense mechanism that can permit people to absorb the unwelcome news on their own terms, according to their own timetables. Only when they are able to recognize the news can they move on and eventually come to grips with the reality that they are truly going to die.

Anger. After they move beyond denial, people may be likely to express *anger*. A dying person may be angry at everyone: people who are in good health, their spouses and other family members, those who are caring for them, their children. They may lash out at others, and wonder—sometimes aloud—why *they* are dying and not someone else. They may be furious at God, reasoning that they have led good lives and that there are far worse people in the world who should be dying.

It may not be easy to be around people who are going through an anger stage. As they focus their anger on others, they may say and do things that are painful and sometimes unfathomable. Eventually, though, most patients move beyond the anger phase. This may lead to another development—bargaining.

Bargaining. "If you're good, you'll be rewarded." Most people learn this equation in childhood, and many try to apply it to their impending death. In this case, "good" means promising to be a better person, and the "reward" is staying alive.

In *bargaining*, dying people try to negotiate their way out of death. They may declare that they will dedicate their lives to the poor if God saves them. They may promise that if they can just live long enough to see a son married, they will willingly accept death later.

They may say that if just one request is granted to them, they will no longer ask for a postponement of death.

However, the promises that are part of the bargaining process are rarely kept. If one request appears to be granted, people typically seek another, and yet another. Furthermore, they may be unable to fulfill their promises because their illnesses keep progressing and prevent them from achieving what they said they would do.

In some ways, bargaining seems to have positive consequences. Although death cannot be postponed indefinitely, having a goal of attending a particular event or living until a certain time may in fact delay death until then. For instance, death rates of Jewish people fall just before the holiday of Passover, and rise just after it. Similarly, the death rate among older Chinese women falls before and during important holidays, and rises after. It is as if the people involved have negotiated to stay alive until after the holidays have passed (Phillips & Smith, 1990; Philips, 1992).

In the end, of course, all the bargaining in the world is unable to overcome the inevitability of death. When people eventually realize that death is unavoidable, they often move into a stage of depression.

Depression. Many dying people experience phases of *depression*. Realizing that the issue is settled and they cannot bargain their way out of death, people are overwhelmed with a deep sense of loss. They know that they are losing their loved ones and that their lives really are coming to an end.

The depression they experience may be of two types. In *reactive depression,* the feelings of sadness are based on events that have already occurred: the loss of dignity that may accompany medical procedures, the end of a job, or the knowledge that one will never return from the hospital to one's home.

Dying people also experience preparatory depression. In *preparatory depression,* people feel sadness over future losses. They know that death will bring an end to their relationships with others and that they will never see future generations. The reality of death is inescapable in this stage, and it brings about profound sadness over the unalterable conclusion of one's life.

Acceptance. Kübler-Ross suggested that the final step of dying is *acceptance.* People who have developed a state of acceptance are fully aware that death is impending. Unemotional and uncommunicative, they have virtually no feelings—positive or negative—about the present or future. They have made peace with themselves, and they may wish to be left alone. For them, death holds no sting.

Evaluating Kübler-Ross's Theory. Kübler-Ross has had an enormous impact on the way we look at death. As one of the first people to observe systematically how people approach their own deaths, she is recognized as a pioneer. Kübler-Ross was almost single-handedly responsible for bringing into public awareness the phenomenon of death, which previously had languished out of sight in Western societies. Her contributions have been particularly influential among those who provide direct care to the dying.

On the other hand, her work has drawn criticism. For one thing, there are some obvious limitations to her conception of dying. It is largely limited to those who are aware that they are dying and who die in a relatively leisurely fashion. For people who suffer from diseases in which the prognosis is ambiguous as to when or even if they will die, her theory is not applicable.

The most important criticisms, however, concern the stage-like nature of Kübler-Ross's theory. Research on the theory has shown that not every person passes through every step on the way to death, and some people move through the steps in a different sequence. Some people even go through the same steps several times. Depressed patients may show bursts of anger, and an angry patient may bargain for more time (Schulz & Aderman, 1976; Kastenbaum, 1992). This criticism of the theory has been especially important news for medical and other caregivers who work with dying people. Because Kübler-Ross's stages have become so well-known, well-meaning caregivers have sometimes tried to encourage patients to work through the steps in a prescribed order, without enough consideration for their individual needs.

Furthermore, Kübler-Ross may have considered too limited a set of factors when she outlined her theory. For example, other researchers suggest that anxiety plays an important role throughout the process of dying. The anxiety may be about one's upcoming death, or it may relate to fear of the symptoms of the disease. A person with cancer, then, may fear death less than the uncontrollable pain that may be a future possibility (Schulz & Aderman, 1974; Taylor, 1991; Hayslip et al., 1997).

Finally, there are substantial differences in people's reactions to impending death. The specific cause of dying, how long the process of dying lasts, a person's age, sex, and personality, and the social support available from family and friends all influence the course of dying and people's responses to it (Zautra, Reich, & Guarnaccia, 1990; Stroebe, Stroebe, & Hansson, 1993).

In short, there are significant concerns about the accuracy of Kübler-Ross's account of how people react to impending death. In response to some of these concerns, other theorists have developed some alternative ideas. Edwin Shneidman (1983), for example suggests that there are "themes" in people's reactions to dying that can occur—and recur—in any order throughout the dying process. These include such feelings and thoughts as incredulity, a sense of unfairness, fear of pain or even general terror, and fantasies of being rescued.

Another theorist, Charles Corr, suggests that, as in other periods of life, people who are dying face a set of psychological tasks. These include minimizing physical stress, maintaining the richness of life, continuing or deepening their relationships with other people, and fostering hope, often through spiritual searching (Corr, 1991/1992).

Choosing the Nature of Death: Is DNR the Way to Go?

The letters "DNR" written on a patient's medical chart have a simple and clear meaning. Standing for "Do not resuscitate," DNR signifies that rather than administering any and every procedure that might possibly keep a patient alive, no extraordinary means are to be taken. For terminally ill patients, "DNR" may mean the difference between dying immediately or living additional days, months, or even years, kept alive only by the most extreme, invasive, and even painful medical procedures.

The decision to use or not to use extreme medical interventions entails several issues. One is the differentiation of "extreme" and "extraordinary" measures from those that are simply routine. There are no hard-and-fast rules; people making the decision must consider the needs of the specific patient, his or her prior medical history, and factors such as age and even religion. For instance, different standards might apply to a 12-year-old patient and an 85-year-old patient with the same medical condition.

Other questions concern quality of life. How can we determine an individual's current quality of life and whether it will be improved or diminished by a particular medical intervention? Who makes such decisions—the patient, a family member, or medical personnel?

One thing is clear: Medical personnel are reluctant to carry out the wishes of the terminally ill and their families to suspend aggressive treatment. Even when it is certain that a patient is going to die, and patients determine that they do not wish further treatment, physicians often claim to be unaware of their patients' wishes. For instance, although one

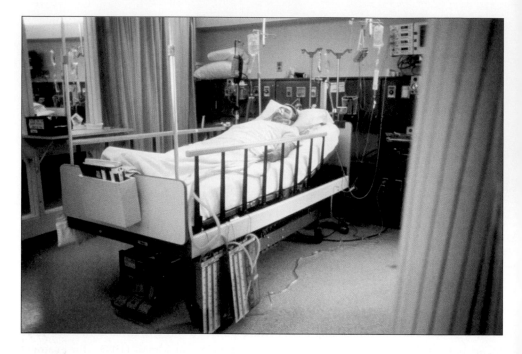

Many terminally ill patients choose "DNR," or "Do Not Resuscitate," as a way to avoid extraordinary medical interventions.

third of the patients ask not to be resuscitated, less than half of these people's physicians state that they know of their patients' preference (see Table 19-1). In addition, only 49 percent of patients have their wishes entered on their medical charts (Knaus et al., 1995; Goold, Williams, & Arnold, 2000).

Living Wills. In order to gain more control over decisions regarding the nature of their death, people are increasingly signing living wills. A **living will** is a legal document that designates the medical treatments a person does or does not want if the person cannot express his or her wishes (see Figure 19-3).

Some living wills designate a specific person, called a *health care proxy*, to act as an individual's representative in making health care decisions. Wills may cover all medical care problems or only terminal illnesses. In such cases, nonterminal problems, such as coma, would not be addressed. As with DNR orders, living wills may not be heeded unless people take steps to make sure their doctors know their wishes. Although they may be reluctant to do so in advance, people should also have frank conversations clarifying their wishes with the representatives they choose as their health care proxies.

living wills legal documents designating what medical treatments people want or do not want if they cannot express their wishes

Table 19-1

DYING HARD: EXPERIENCES OF 4,301 PATIENTS WITH END-OF-LIFE CARE

Terminal patients who did not want resuscitation	31%
Of those patients who did not want resuscitation, percentage whose physicians were aware of their preference	47%
Of those patients who did not want resuscitation, percentage whose preferences were entered on their charts	49%

(*Source:* Knaus et al., 1995.)

MY LIVING WILL

TO MY FAMILY, MY PHYSICIAN, MY LAWYER
AND ALL OTHERS WHOM IT MAY CONCERN

Death is as much a reality as birth, growth, maturity and old age–it is the one certainty of life. If the time comes when I can no longer take part in decisions for my own future, let this statement stand as an expression of my wishes and directions, while I am still of sound mind.

If at such a time the situation should arise in which there is no reasonable expectation of my recovery from extreme physical or mental disability, I direct that I be allowed to die and not be kept alive by medications, artificial means or "heroic measures". I do, however, ask that medication be mercifully administered to me to alleviate suffering even though this may shorten my remaining life.

This statement is made after careful consideration and is in accordance with my strong convictions and beliefs. I want the wishes and directions here expressed carried out to the extent permitted by law. Insofar as they are not legally enforceable, I hope that those to whom this Will is addressed will regard themselves as morally bound by these provisions.

Optional specific provisions to be made in this space.

DURABLE POWER OF ATTORNEY (optional)

I hereby designate _____ to serve as my attorney-in-fact for the purpose of making medical treatment decisions. This power of attorney shall remain effective in the event that I become incompetent or otherwise unable to make such decisions for myself. Optional Notarization:

"Sworn and subscribed to before me this _____ day of _____ , 19 ___ ."

Notary Public
(seal)

Signed _____
Date _____
Witness _____
Address _____
Witness _____
Address _____

Copies of this request have been given to _____

(Optional) My Living Will is registered with Concern for Dying (No. _____)

Figure 19-3 **A Living Will**

What steps can people take to make sure the wishes they write into their living wills are carried out?

Euthanasia and Assisted Suicide. Dr. Jack Kevorkian became well known—and frequently prosecuted—in the early 1990s for his invention and promotion of a "suicide machine," which allows patients to push a button that releases anesthesia and a drug that stops the heart. By supplying the machine and the drugs, which patients administered themselves, Kevorkian was participating in a process known as *assisted suicide,* in which a person provides the means for a terminally ill individual to commit suicide.

Although he was first charged with murder, the initial cases were dismissed. However, the state of Michigan, where the assisted suicides took place, passed a law prohibiting the practice, and new charges were lodged against Kevorkian when he continued to aid people in their deaths. The practice continues to raise bitter conflict in the U.S. and is illegal in most places.

In other countries, however, assisted suicide is an accepted practice. For instance, in the Netherlands medical personnel may help end their patients' lives. However, several conditions must be met to make the practice permissible: At least two physicians must determine that the patient is terminally ill, there must be unbearable physical or mental suffering, the patient must give informed consent in writing, and relatives must be informed beforehand (Joy, 1997; Galbraith & Dobson, 2000; Rosenfeld et al., 2000).

Assisted suicide is one form of **euthanasia,** the practice of assisting terminally ill people to die more quickly. Popularly known as "mercy killing," euthanasia can take a range of forms. *Passive euthanasia* involves removing respirators or other medical equipment that may be sustaining a patient's life, to allow them to die naturally. This happens when medical staff follow a DNR order, for example. In *voluntary active euthanasia* caregivers or medical staff act to end a person's life before death would normally occur, perhaps by administering a dose of pain medication that they know will be fatal. Assisted suicide, as we have seen, lies between passive and voluntary active euthanasia. Euthanasia is an emotional and controversial—although surprisingly widespread—practice.

No one knows how widespread. However, one survey of nurses in intensive care units found that 20 percent had deliberately hastened a patient's death at least once, and other experts assert that euthanasia is far from rare (Asch, 1996).

Euthanasia is highly controversial, in part because it centers on decisions about who should control life. Does the right belong solely to an individual, a person's physicians, his or her dependents, the government, or some deity? Because, at least in the United States, we assume that we all have the absolute right to create lives by bringing children into the world, some people argue that we should also have the absolute right to end our lives (Solomon, 1995; Lester, 1996).

On the other hand, many opponents of euthanasia argue that the practice is morally wrong. In their view, prematurely ending someone's life, no matter how willing that person may be, is the equivalent of murder. Others point out that physicians are often inaccurate in predicting how long a person's life will last. For example, a large-scale study known as SUPPORT—the Study to Understand Prognoses and Preferences for Outcomes and Risks of Treatment—found that patients often outlive physicians' predictions of when they will die. In fact, in some cases, patients have lived for years after being given no more than a 50 percent chance of living for 6 more months (see Figure 19-4).

Other opponents of euthanasia say that even if patients ask or sometimes beg health care providers to help them die, they may be suffering from a form of deep depression. In such cases, patients may be treated with antidepressant drugs that can alleviate the depres-

euthanasia the practice of assisting people who are terminally ill to die more quickly

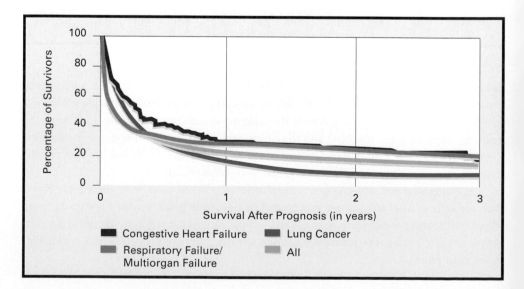

Figure 19-4 **How Long Do "Terminal" Patients Really Live?**

According to the large SUPPORT study, a significant percentage of a group of 3,693 patients given no more than a 50 percent chance of living for 6 months survived well beyond that period. Why do you think this happened?

(*Source:* Lynn, J. et al., 1997.)

sion. Once the depression lifts, patients may change their minds about their earlier wish for death.

The debate over euthanasia is likely to continue. It is a highly personal issue, yet one that society increasingly must face as the world's elderly population increases (Becvar, 2000).

Caring for the Terminally Ill: The Place of Death

Recall the description of Helen Reynolds' last months of life, spent in the intensive care unit of a Boston hospital. Although family members visited her frequently and she seemed to be a favorite of the nurses, Helen also seemed to face a lot of lonely hours watching television as her condition deteriorated. Like Helen Reynolds, most people in the United States die in hospitals, but it need not be that way. In fact, there are several reasons why hospitals are among the least desirable locales in which to face death. Hospitals are typically impersonal, with staff rotating throughout the day. Because visiting hours are limited, people frequently die alone, without the comfort of loved ones at the bedside. Furthermore, hospitals are designed to make people better, not to deal with the dying, and it is extraordinarily expensive to provide custodial care for dying people. In addition, and perhaps more importantly, hospitals typically don't have the resources needed to deal adequately with the emotional requirements of terminally ill patients and their families.

As a consequence, several alternatives to hospitalization have become increasingly popular in the last few decades. In **home care,** dying people stay in their homes and receive treatment from their families and visiting medical staff. Many dying patients prefer home care, because they can spend their final days in a familiar environment, with people they love and a lifetime accumulation of treasures around them (Brescia, Sadof, & Barstow, 1984).

Although the dying may prefer home care, it can be quite difficult for family members. Furnishing final care can offer family members a good deal of emotional solace because they are giving something precious to people they love. But, it is extraordinarily draining, both physically and emotionally, to be on call 24 hours a day. Furthermore, because most relatives are not trained in nursing, they may provide less than optimal medical care. Many people decide they just aren't equipped to care for a dying family member at home.

For these families, another alternative to hospitalization that is becoming increasingly prevalent is hospice care. **Hospice care** is care for the dying provided in institutions devoted to those who are terminally ill. In the Middle Ages, hospices were facilities that provided comfort and hospitality to travelers. Drawing on that concept, today's hospices

home care an alternative to hospitalization in which dying people stay in their homes and receive treatment from their families and visiting medical staff

hospice care care provided for the dying in institutions devoted to those who are terminally ill

A hospice provides a warm and supportive environment for the dying. The emphasis is on making patients' lives as full as possible, not on squeezing out every possible moment of life at any cost. What are the advantages to a society that supports hospices?

SPEAKING OF DEVELOPMENT

Robert P. Picard, R.N., Hospice Services Director

EDUCATION: Community College of Rhode Island, Warwick, Rhode Island, A.S. in science and nursing

POSITION: Director of nurses and hospice services, Visiting Nurse Service of Greater Woonsocket

HOME: Woonsocket, Rhode Island

From the age of 17, when he became a hospital corpsman in the U.S. Navy, Richard P. Picard has been involved in the more intense side of medicine. He worked in emergency medicine, in life support systems, and as a surgical technician before moving into home care in 1988.

Even now his focus is on what many would consider an intense side of life: its end. Picard has spent a number of years with the Visiting Nurse Service of Greater Woonsocket, first as manager of its hospice program and now as director of nurses and hospice services.

"Hospice deals not only with patients who are dying, but with their families as well," he says. "Before gaining admission to hospice, the patient and the family members have made a decision that the patient will be the recipient of no extraordinary act that is curative in nature. They arrive at this decision after two physicians have given a terminal diagnosis and have confirmed that the patient understands that the disease is terminal."

Once admitted to the hospice, the patient is assigned a team that includes a nurse, a social worker, a psychiatric nurse, a member of the clergy, a physician, and volunteers.

"The approach we take is different for each individual, due to the culture of the patient, the family dynamics surrounding the patient, and the patient's understanding of or need for relief of symptoms, as opposed to measures designed to seek a cure.

"When it comes to the family, every case has to be different," he adds. "Some families are disorganized, and some are very close. The nature of the family affects the patient significantly."

Since AIDS has emerged as a major terminal illness, Picard notices great differences in the ways AIDS patients deal with death, as compared with patients who have cancer.

"Patients who are told, as cancer patients are, that based on the best medical knowledge, they will die in 6 to 9 months, regardless of medical intervention, seem to accept the fact more readily," Picard says. "What you hear from the cancer patients is how long it's going to be before they die. We want them to have hope, but we also know that there are some cancers that, no matter how aggressively we treat them, will not be cured.

"It is different with AIDS patients, who are generally between the ages of 20 and 45. With AIDS, we don't have any firm figures on when our patients are going to die, and there is no drug to cure them. Understandably, AIDS patients—mostly younger than cancer patients and hopeful that a cure may be found at any moment—want every medical intervention up to the last minute.

"AIDS patients tend to be more informed than other patients. They do research, they read, they study experimental drugs, and they insist on treatment after treatment," he adds.

One dominating factor that determines how a patient is attended in the hospice is the individual life development of each patient, according to Picard. "You have to respect where the person is coming from, the personal background. You let your patients be themselves.

"Some people are raised to expect that they will have suffering and pain, while others focus on pain avoidance to the extent of overcompensation. But we're not judgmental. We feel that the patient is the only one who knows what the pain level is. My subjective pain, my pain threshold, is different from yours.

"Ultimately, the hospice provides a place to die with dignity. The only person who can define that dignity is the patient," Picard says.

are designed to provide a warm, supportive environment for the dying. They do not focus on extending people's lives, but rather on making their final days pleasant and meaningful. Typically, people who go to hospices are removed from treatments that are painful, and no extraordinary or invasive means are employed to make their lives longer. The emphasis is on making patients' lives as full as possible, not on squeezing out every possible moment of life at any cost (McCracken & Gerdsen, 1991).

Although the research is far from conclusive, hospice patients appear to be more satisfied with the care they receive than those who receive treatment in more traditional settings (Kane et al., 1985). Hospice care, then, provides a clear alternative to traditional hospitalization for the terminally ill. (For more on hospice care, see the accompanying *Speaking of Development* box.)

Review and Rethink

REVIEW

- Elisabeth Kübler-Ross has identified five steps toward dying: denial, anger, bargaining, depression, and acceptance. The stage nature of her theory been criticized, and other theorists have suggested alternatives.

- Issues surrounding dying are highly controversial, including the measures that physicians should apply to keep dying patients alive and who should make the decision. Living wills are a way for people to take some control over the decision.

- Assisted suicide and, more generally, euthanasia are highly controversial and are illegal in most of the United States, although many people believe they should be legalized.

- Although most people in the United States die in hospitals, increasing numbers are choosing home care or hospice care for their final days.

RETHINK

- Do you think Kübler-Ross's five steps of dying might be subject to cultural influences? Age differences? Why or why not?

- Do you think assisted suicide should be permissible? Other forms of euthanasia? Why or why not?

Grief and Bereavement

No one ever told me that grief felt so like fear. I am not afraid, but the sensation is like being afraid. The same fluttering in the stomach, the same restlessness, the yawning. I keep on swallowing.

    At other times it feels like being mildly drunk, or concussed. There is a sort of invisible blanket between the world and me. I find it hard to take in what anyone says. Or perhaps, hard to want to take it in. It is so uninteresting. (Lewis, 1985, p. 394)

For something that is a universal experience, most of us are surprisingly ill-prepared for the grief that follows the death of a loved one. Particularly in Western societies, where life expectancy is long and mortality rates lower than at any time in history, people are apt to view death as an atypical event rather than an expected part of life. This attitude makes grief all the more difficult to bear, particularly when we compare the present day with historical eras in which people lived shorter lives and the death rate was considerably higher (Gluhoski, Leader, & Wortman, 1994; Nolen-Hoeksema & Larson, 1999). The first step in grieving, for most survivors in Western countries, is some sort of funeral.

Mourning and Funerals: Final Rites

Death is a big business in the United States. The average funeral costs $4,000. The purchase of an ornate, polished coffin, transportation to and from the cemetery in a limousine, and preparation of the body for preservation and viewing are among the services that people typically purchase in planning a funeral (Lynwander, 1995).

    In part, the relatively grandiose nature of funerals is due to the vulnerability of those planning the funeral, who are typically close survivors of the deceased. Wishing to demonstrate love and affection, the survivors are susceptible to suggestions to "provide the best" for the deceased.

Because an individual's death represents an important transition, not only for loved ones but for an entire community, the rites associated with death take on an added importance. This combined with the pressure of enterprising salespersons leads many to spend thousands of dollars on a funeral.

But it is not only the pressure of enterprising salespersons that leads many people to spend thousands of dollars on a funeral. In large measure, the nature of funerals is also determined by social norms and customs. Because an individual's death represents an important transition, not only for loved ones but for an entire community, the rites associated with death take on an added importance. In a sense, then, a funeral is not only a public acknowledgment that an individual has died, but a recognition of everyone's ultimate mortality and an acceptance of the cycle of life (DeSpelder & Strickland, 1992).

In Western societies, funeral rituals follow a typical pattern, despite some surface variations. Prior to the funeral, the body is prepared in some way and is dressed in special clothing. Funerals usually include the celebration of a religious rite, the delivery of a eulogy, a procession of some sort, and some formal period, such as the wake for Irish Catholics and shivah for Jews, in which relatives and friends visit the mourning family and pay their respects. Military funerals typically include the firing of weapons and a flag draped over the coffin.

Other cultures include funeral rituals of quite different sorts. For instance, in some societies mourners shave their heads as a sign of grief, while in others they allow the hair to grow and men stop shaving for a period of time. In other cultures, mourners may be hired to wail and grieve. Sometimes noisy celebrations take place at funerals, while in other cultures silence is the norm. Even the nature of emotional displays, such as the amount and timing of crying, are determined culturally (Rosenblatt, 1988).

Historically, some cultures have developed funeral rites that strike us as extreme. For example, in *suttee,* a traditional Hindu practice in India that is now illegal, a widow was expected to throw herself into the fire that consumed her husband's body. In ancient China, servants were sometimes buried (alive) with their masters' bodies.

Ultimately, no matter what the particular ritual, all funerals basically serve the same underlying function: They mark the endpoint for the life of the person who has died—and the starting point for the survivors, from which they can get on with the rest of their lives.

Bereavement and Grief: Adjusting to the Death of a Loved One

bereavement acknowledgment of the objective fact that one has experienced a death

grief the emotional response to one's loss

As we saw in the case of Joan Kindy in the chapter prologue, after the death of a loved one, a painful period of adjustment follows, involving bereavement and grief. **Bereavement** is acknowledgment of the objective fact that one has experienced a death, while **grief** is the

After a death, people move through a painful period of bereavement and grief. These adolescents in Bosnia mourn the loss of a friend who was killed by enemy bombardment.

emotional response to one's loss. Although everyone's grief is different, there are certain similarities in the ways people in Western societies adjust to the loss.

The first stage typically entails shock, numbness, disbelief, or outright denial. People may avoid the reality of the situation, although the pain may break through, causing anguish, fear, and deep sorrow and distress. If the pain is too severe, however, the person may cycle back to numbness. In some ways, such a psychological state may be beneficial, since it permits the survivor to make funeral arrangements and carry out other psychologically difficult tasks. Typically, people pass through this stage in a few days or weeks, although in some cases it lasts longer.

In the next phase, people begin to confront the death and realize the extent of their loss. They fully experience their grief, and they react to the reality that the separation from the dead person will be permanent. In so doing, mourners may suffer deep unhappiness or even depression. They may yearn for the dead individual. Emotions can range from impatient to lethargic. However, they also begin to view their past relationship realistically, good and bad. In so doing, they begin to free themselves from some of the bonds that tied them to their loved ones (de Vries, et al. 1997).

Finally, people who have lost a loved one reach the accommodation stage. They begin to pick up the pieces of their lives and to construct new identities. For instance, rather than seeing herself as someone's widowed spouse, a woman like Joan Kindy, whose husband has died, may come to regard herself as a single person. Still, there are moments when intense feelings of grief occur.

Ultimately, most people are able to live new lives, independent from the person who has died. They form new relationships, and some even find that coping with the death has helped them to grow as individuals. They become more self-reliant and more appreciative of life.

It is important to keep in mind that not everyone passes through the stages of grief in the same manner and in the same order. People display vast individual differences, partly dependent on personality, the nature of the relationship with the deceased, and the post-death opportunities that are available to them for continuing their lives. As with Kübler-Ross's stages of dying, then, the stages of grieving do not unfold in the same way for all people.

Differentiating Unhealthy Grief from Normal Grief. Although ideas abound about what separates normal grief from unhealthy grief, careful research has shown that many of the assumptions that both laypersons and clinicians hold are wrong. For instance, there is no evidence that a particular timetable for grieving exists, especially the common notion that grieving should be complete a year after a spouse has died. Increasing evidence suggests that for some people (but not all) grieving may take considerably longer than a year. Research also contradicts the common assumption that depression is widespread; only 15 to 30 percent of people show relatively deep depression following the loss of a loved one (Wortman & Silver, 1989; Prigerson et al., 1995).

Similarly, it is often assumed that people who show little initial distress over a death are simply not facing up to reality, and that as a consequence they are likely to have problems later. This is not the case. In fact, those who show the most intense distress immediately after a death are the most apt to have adjustment difficulties and health problems later on (Wortman & Silver, 1989; Gluhoski, Leader, & Wortman, 1994).

The Consequences of Grief and Bereavement. In a sense, death is catching, at least in terms of survivors' mortality. A good deal of evidence suggests that widowed people are particularly at risk of death. Some studies find that the risk of death is as much as seven times higher than normal in the first year after the death of a spouse. At particular risk are men and younger women who have been widowed (Gluhoski, Leder, & Wortman, 1994; Martikainen & Valkonen, 1996; Aiken, 2000). Remarriage seems to lower the risk of death for survivors. This is particularly true for men who have lost their wives, although the reasons are not clear.

Several factors increase the likelihood that bereavement will produce negative consequences. For instance, people who are already insecure, anxious, or fearful are less able to cope effectively. Furthermore, people whose relationships were marked by ambivalence before death are more apt to suffer poor post-death outcomes than those who were secure in their relationships. Similarly, those who were highly dependent on the person who died, and who therefore feel more vulnerable without them, are apt to suffer more after the death, as are those who spend a great deal of time reflecting and pondering on a loved one's death and their feelings of grief. Bereaved people who lack social support, and who therefore experience feelings of social loneliness, also are more at risk. Finally, people who are unable to make sense of the death or find meaning in it (such as a new appreciation of

Becoming an Informed Consumer of Development
Helping a Child Cope with Grief

Because of their limited understanding of death, younger children need special help in coping with grief. Among the strategies that can help are the following.

▶ Be honest. Don't say that a dead person is "sleeping" or "on a long trip." Use age-appropriate language to tell children the truth. Gently, but clearly, point out the irreversibility and the final and universal nature of death. For example, you might answer questions about whether grandma will be hungry by pointing out that, "No, after a person dies, their body doesn't work anymore, so it doesn't need food."

▶ Encourage expressions of grief. Don't tell children not to cry or show their feelings. Instead, tell them that it is under-

standable to feel terrible, and that they may always miss the deceased. At the same time, assure them that they will always have good memories of the person who has died.

▶ Reassure children that they are not to blame for the death. Children sometimes attribute a loved one's death to their own behavior—if they had not misbehaved, they mistakenly reason, the person would not have died.

▶ Understand that children's grief may surface in unanticipated ways. Children may show little or no grief at the time of the death, but later they may become upset for no apparent reason. Keep in mind that death can be overwhelming for a child, and try to be consistently loving and supportive.

life) show less overall adjustment (Stroebe et al., 1996; Nolen-Hoeksema, McBraide, & Larson, 1997; Davis, Nolen-Hoeksema, & Larson, 1998).

The suddenness of a loved one's death also appears to affect the course of grieving. People who unexpectedly lose their loved ones are less able to cope than those who were able to anticipate the death. For instance, in one study, people who experienced a sudden death still had not fully recovered four years later. In part, this may be because sudden, unanticipated deaths are often the result of violence, which occurs more frequently among younger individuals (Sanders, 1988; Rando, 1993).

As we noted earlier in the chapter, children may need special help understanding and mourning the death of someone they love.

Review and Rethink

REVIEW

■ Bereavement refers to the loss of a loved one; grief refers to the emotional response to that loss.

■ Funeral rites play a significant role in helping people acknowledge the death of a loved one, recognize their own mortality, and proceed with their lives.

■ For many people, grief passes through denial, sorrow, and accommodation.

■ Children need special help coping with grief.

RETHINK

■ What cultural beliefs in U.S. society do you think contribute to people's reluctance to think about death?

■ Why do you think the risk of death is so high for people who have recently lost a spouse? Why might remarriage lower the risk?

Looking Back

What is death, and what does it mean at different stages of the life span?

■ The precise point of death is difficult to define. Functional death refers to the absence of heartbeat and respiration, from which people can be resuscitated, while brain death refers to the absence of electrical activity in the brain, which is irreversible.

■ The death of an infant or a young child is among the most devastating experiences for parents, largely because it seems unnatural and entirely incomprehensible.

■ Adolescents have an unrealistic sense of invulnerability that makes them susceptible to accidental death. Denial often makes it impossible for terminally ill adolescents to accept the seriousness of their condition.

■ For young adults, death is virtually unthinkable. Young adults who are terminally ill can be difficult patients because of a strong sense of the injustice of their fate.

■ In middle adulthood, disease becomes the leading cause of death, and awareness of the reality of death can lead to a substantial fear of death.

■ People in late adulthood begin to prepare for death. Older people generally prefer to know if death is near, and the main issue they have to deal with is whether their lives continue to have value.

■ Responses to death are in part determined by culture. Death may be regarded as a release from the pains of the world, the beginning of a pleasurable afterlife, a punishment or judgment, or simply the end to life.

■ Death education can help people learn about death and consider their own mortality realistically.

In what ways do people face the prospect of their own death?

■ Elisabeth Kübler-Ross suggests that people pass through five basic stages on their way to death: denial, anger, bargaining, depression, and acceptance. The stage nature of her theory been criticized, and other theorists have suggested alternatives.

▪ A living will is a means of asserting control over decisions surrounding one's death through specification of desired medical treatments in life-threatening situations and designation of a health care proxy to enforce one's wishes.

▪ Assisted suicide, a form of euthanasia, is illegal in most of the United States.

▪ Although most deaths in the United States occur in hospitals, an increasing number of terminal patients are opting for either home care or a hospice.

▸ *How do survivors react to and cope with death?*

▪ Funeral rituals serve a dual function: acknowledging the death of a loved one and recognizing and anticipating the mortality of all who participate.

▪ The death of a loved one brings a period of adjustment involving bereavement and grief. Grief may proceed through stages of shock and denial, the beginning of acceptance, and accommodation. One consequence of bereavement is an increase in the risk of death for the survivor.

▪ Children need particular help in dealing with death, including honesty, encouragement of expressions of grief, reassurance that the death was not due to the child's behavior, and understanding that the child's grief may be delayed and indirect.

EPILOGUE

In this chapter we considered the definition of death and its meaning at various stages in the life span and across cultures. We considered how death education might help people face the topic realistically. We also discussed the ways people confront death and how they try to exert control over death through living wills and euthanasia. We examined the reactions of others to death. We took a look at funeral rites and concluded with some suggestions on how to help children cope with grief.

Return to the chapter prologue, about Joan Kindy's loss of her husband, and answer the following questions.

1. How might Joan Kindy's adjustment differ if her husband had died suddenly in contrast to a slow, lingering death?

2. What stages of bereavement and grief does a person typically pass through following the death of a loved one?

3. What stage is Joan Kindy most likely in now? What evidence is there for your answer?

4. If her husband had died 15 years later, would Joan Kindy's grief be any different? If he had died 15 years earlier? Why or why not?

Key Terms and Concepts

functional death (p. 649)
brain death (p. 649)
sudden infant death syndrome (SIDS) (p. 650)

thanatologists (p. 655)
living wills (p. 660)
euthanasia (p. 662)
home care (p. 663)

hospice care (p. 663)
bereavement (p. 666)
grief (p. 666)

Bridges

In the final part of the book, we focused on late adulthood and the end of life. We saw that genuine physical and cognitive and declines finally become the norm, but that people can continue to lead healthy, engaged lives throughout most of the period—in defiance of stereotypes that characterize them as decrepit and doddering.

As in other periods of the life span, continuity and change are both evident in late adulthood. For example, we noticed that individual differences in cognitive performance, even as they show declines, reflect individual differences that were present in earlier years. We saw that lifestyle choices made earlier, such as exercise participation, contribute to health and longevity during this time.

We also saw that social and personality development can continue throughout late adulthood. We saw that although most people show similar personality traits to their earlier years, late adulthood also affords a unique perspective on the more turbulent years that have gone before. We overturned more stereotypes as we looked closely at the varied ways people live and the rich relationships they sustain in this period. Again, we saw continuity, as elderly people carry on relationships with friends and family members that they have known for years. With age, however, adults in this period often find themselves adapting—usually quite well—to changes in their social lives.

We ended the book with a consideration of the inevitable end of life. Even here, we saw that there are challenges to be faced and satisfaction to be drawn from a graceful departure from life.

In sum, the story of the entire life span is one of fresh challenges and opportunities as we continuously undergo and adjust to physical and cognitive changes and learn to relate to new social situations. Development persists virtually to the point of death, and with preparation, we can appreciate and learn from all parts of the life span.

Glossary

Abstract modeling The process in which modeling paves the way for the development of more general rules and principles (Ch. 8)

Acceleration Special programs that allow gifted students to move ahead at their own pace, even if this means skipping to higher grade levels (Ch. 9)

Accommodation Changes in existing ways of thinking that occur in response to encounters with new stimuli or events (Ch. 1, 5)

Achieving stage The point reached by young adults in which intelligence is applied to specific situations involving the attainment of long-term goals regarding careers, family, and societal contributions (Ch. 13)

Acquired immunodeficiency syndrome (AIDS) A sexually transmitted disease, produced by the HIV virus, that has no cure and ultimately causes death (Ch. 11)

Acquisitive stage According to Schaie, the first stage of cognitive development, encompassing all of childhood and adolescence, in which the main developmental task is to acquire information (Ch. 13)

Active genotype–environment effects Situations in which children focus on those aspects of their environment that are most congruent with their genetically determined abilities (Ch. 2)

Activity theory The theory suggesting that successful aging occurs when people maintain the interests, activities, and social interactions with which they were involved during middle age (Ch. 18)

Addictive drugs Drugs that produce a biological or psychological dependence in users, leading to increasingly powerful cravings for them (Ch. 11)

Adolescence The developmental stage between childhood and adulthood (Ch. 11)

Adolescent egocentrism A state of self-absorption in which the world is viewed from one's own point of view (Ch. 11)

Adult day-care facilities A facility in which elderly individuals receive care only during the day, but spend nights and weekends in their own homes (Ch. 18)

Affordances The action possibilities that a given situation or stimulus provides (Ch. 4)

Age of viability The point at which an infant can survive a premature birth (Ch. 3)

Age stratification theories The view that an unequal distribution of economic resources, power, and privilege exists among people at different stages of the life course (Ch. 18)

Ageism Prejudice and discrimination directed at older people (Ch. 17)

Agentic professions Occupations that are associated with getting things accomplished (Ch. 14)

Aggression Intentional injury or harm to another person (Ch. 8)

Ainsworth Strange Situation A sequence of staged episodes that illustrate the strength of attachment between a child and (typically) his or her mother (Ch. 6)

Alcoholics Persons with alcohol problems who have learned to depend on alcohol and are unable to control their drinking (Ch. 11)

Alzheimer's disease A progressive brain disorder that produces loss of memory and confusion (Ch. 17)

Ambivalent attachment pattern A style of attachment in which children display a combination of positive and negative reactions to their mothers; they show great distress when the mother leaves, but upon her return they may simultaneously seek close contact but also hit and kick her (Ch. 6)

Amniocentesis The process of identifying genetic defects by examining a small sample of fetal cells drawn by a needle inserted into the amniotic fluid surrounding the unborn fetus (Ch. 2)

Androgynous A state in which gender roles encompass characteristics thought typical of both sexes (Ch. 8)

Anorexia nervosa A severe eating disorder in which individuals refuse to eat, while denying that their behavior and appearance, which may become skeletal, are out of the ordinary (Ch. 11)

Anoxia A restriction of oxygen to the baby, lasting a few minutes during the birth process, which can produce brain damage (Ch. 3)

Apgar scale A standard measurement system that looks for a variety of indications of good health in newborns (Ch. 3)

Applied research Research meant to provide practical solutions to immediate problems (Ch. 1)

Artificial insemination A process of fertilization in which a man's sperm is placed directly into a woman's vagina by a physician (Ch. 2)

Assimilation The process in which people understand an experience in terms of their current stage of cognitive development and way of thinking (Ch. 1, 5)

Associative play Play in which two or more children actually interact with one another by sharing or borrowing toys or materials, although they do not do the same thing (Ch. 8)

Asthma A chronic condition characterized by periodic attacks of wheezing, coughing, and shortness of breath (Ch. 9)

Attachment The positive emotional bond that develops between a child and a particular individual (Ch. 6)

Attention-deficit hyperactivity disorder (ADHD) A learning disability marked by inattention, impulsiveness, a low tolerance for frustration, and generally a great deal of inappropriate activity (Ch. 9)

Attributions People's explanations for the reasons behind their behavior (Ch. 10)

Auditory impairment A special need that involves the loss of hearing or some aspect of hearing (Ch. 9)

Authoritarian parents Parents who are controlling, punitive, rigid, and cold, and whose word is law; they value strict, unquestioning obedience from their children and do not tolerate expressions of disagreement (Ch. 8)

Authoritative parents Parents who are firm, setting clear and consistent limits, but who try to reason with their children, giving explanations for why they should behave in a particular way (Ch. 8)

Autobiographical memory Memories of information about one's own life (Ch. 7, 17)

Autonomy Having independence and a sense of control over one's life (Ch. 12)

Autonomy-versus-shame-and-doubt stage The period during which, according to Erikson, toddlers (aged 18 months to 3 years) develop independence and autonomy if they are allowed the freedom to explore, or shame and self-doubt if they are restricted and overprotected (Ch. 6)

Avoidant attachment pattern A style of attachment in which children do not seek proximity to the mother; after the mother has left, they seem to avoid her when she returns as if they are angered by her behavior (Ch. 6)

Babbling Making speechlike but meaningless sounds (Ch. 5)

Bayley Scales of Infant Development A measure that evaluates an infant's development from 2 to 30 months (Ch. 5)

Behavior modification A formal technique for promoting the frequency of desirable behaviors and decreasing the incidence of unwanted ones (Ch. 1)

Behavioral genetics The study of the effects of heredity on behavior (Ch. 2)

Behavioral perspective The approach that suggests that the keys to understanding development are observable behavior and outside stimuli in the environment (Ch. 1)

Bereavement Acknowledgment of the objective fact that one has experienced a death (Ch. 19)

Bicultural identity Maintaining one's original cultural identity while integrating oneself into the dominant culture (Ch. 9)

Bilingualism The use of more than one language (Ch. 9)

Blended families A remarried couple that has at least one stepchild living with them (Ch. 10)

Body transcendence versus body preoccupation A period in which people must learn to cope with and move beyond changes in physical capabilities as a result of aging (Ch. 18)

Bonding Close physical and emotional contact between parent and child during the period immediately following birth, argued by some to affect later relationship strength (Ch. 3)

Boomerang children Young adults who return, after leaving home for some period, to live in the homes of their middle-aged parents (Ch. 16)

Brain death A diagnosis of death based on the cessation of all signs of brain activity, as measured by electrical brain waves (Ch. 19)

Brazelton Neonatal Behavioral Assessment Scale (NBAS) A measure designed to determine infants' neurological and behavioral responses to their environment (Ch. 4)

Bulimia An eating disorder characterized by binges on large quantities of food, followed by purges of the food through vomiting or the use of laxatives (Ch. 11)

Burnout A situation that occurs when highly trained professionals experience dissatisfaction, disillusionment, frustration, and weariness from their jobs (Ch. 16)

Career consolidation A stage that is entered between the ages of 20 and 40, when young adults become centered on their careers (Ch. 14)

Case studies Studies that involve extensive, in-depth interviews with a particular individual or small group of individuals (Ch. 1)

Centration The process of concentrating on one limited aspect of a stimulus and ignoring other aspects (Ch. 7)

Cephalocaudal principle The principle that growth follows a pattern that begins with the head and upper body parts and then proceeds down to the rest of the body (Ch. 4)

Cerebral cortex The upper layer of the brain (Ch. 4)

Cesarean delivery A birth in which the baby is surgically removed from the uterus rather than traveling through the birth canal (Ch. 3)

Child-care centers Places that typically provide care for children all day, while their parents are at work (Ch. 7)

Chlamydia The most common sexually transmitted disease, caused by a parasite (Ch. 11)

Chorionic villus sampling (CVS) A test used to find genetic defects that involves taking samples of hairlike material that surrounds the embryo (Ch. 2)

Chromosomes Rod-shaped portions of DNA that are organized in 23 pairs (Ch. 2)

Chronological (or physical) age The actual age of the child taking the intelligence test (Ch. 9)

Circular reaction An activity that permits the construction of cognitive schemes through the repetition of a chance motor event (Ch. 5)

Classical conditioning A type of learning in which an organism responds in a particular way to a neutral stimulus that normally does not bring about that type of response (Ch. 1, 3)

Cliques Groups of from 2 to 12 people whose members have frequent social interactions with one another (Ch. 12)

Cluster suicide A situation in which one suicide leads to attempts by others to kill themselves (Ch. 12)

Cognitive development Development involving the ways that growth and change in intellectual capabilities influence a person's behavior (Ch. 1)

Cognitive perspective The approach that focuses on the processes that allow people to know, understand, and think about the world (Ch. 1)

Cohabitation Couples living together without being married (Ch. 14)

Cohort A group of people born at around the same time in the same place (Ch. 1)

Collectivistic orientation A philosophy that promotes the notion of interdependence (Ch. 8)

Communal professions Occupations that are associated with relationships (Ch. 14)

Companionate love The strong affection for those with whom our lives are deeply involved (Ch. 14)

Concrete operational stage The period of cognitive development between 7 and 12 years of age, which is characterized by the active, and appropriate, use of logic (Ch. 9)

Conservation The knowledge that quantity is unrelated to the arrangement and physical appearance of objects (Ch. 7)

Constructive play Play in which children manipulate objects to produce or build something (Ch. 8)

Continuing-care community A community that offers an environment in which all the residents are of retirement age or older and need various levels of care (Ch. 18)

Continuity theory The theory suggesting that people need to maintain their desired level of involvement in society in order to maximize their sense of well-being and self-esteem (Ch. 18)

Continuous change Gradual development in which achievements at one level build on those of previous levels (Ch. 1)

Control group The group in an experiment that receives either no treatment or alternative treatment (Ch. 1)

Controversial adolescents Children who are liked by some peers and disliked by others (Ch. 12)

Cooperative play Play in which children genuinely interact with one another, taking turns, playing games, or devising contests (Ch. 8)

Coping The effort to control, reduce, or learn to tolerate the threats that lead to stress (Ch. 13)

Correlational research Research that seeks to identify whether an association or relationship between two factors exists (Ch. 1)

Creativity The combination of responses or ideas in novel ways (Ch. 13)

Critical period A specific time during development when a particular event has its greatest consequences and the presence of certain kinds of environmental stimuli are necessary for development to proceed normally (Ch. 1)

Cross-modal transference The ability to identify a stimulus that previously has been experienced only through one sense by using another sense (Ch. 5)

Cross-sectional research Research in which people of different ages are compared at the same point in time (Ch. 1)

Cross-sequential studies Research in which researchers examine a number of different age groups over several points in time (Ch. 1)

Crowds Larger groups than cliques, composed of individuals who share particular characteristics but who may not interact with one another (Ch. 12)

Crystallized intelligence The accumulation of information, skills, and strategies that people have learned through experience and that they can apply in problem-solving situations (Ch. 9, 15)

Cultural assimilation model The model that fostered the view of American society as the proverbial melting pot (Ch. 9)

Cycle of violence hypothesis The theory that the abuse and neglect that children suffer predispose them as adults to abuse and neglect their own children (Ch. 8, 16)

Decentering The ability to take multiple aspects of a situation into account (Ch. 9)

Decision/commitment component The third aspect of love that embodies both the initial cognition that one loves another person and the longer-term determination to maintain that love (Ch. 14)

Deferred imitation An act in which a person who is no longer present is imitated by children who have witnessed a similar act (Ch. 5)

Dementia The most common mental disorder of the elderly, dementia covers several diseases, each of which includes serious memory loss accompanied by declines in other mental functioning (Ch. 17)

Dependent variable The variable that researchers measure in an experiment and expect to change as a result of the experimental manipulation (Ch. 1)

Developmental quotient An overall developmental score that relates to performance in four domains: motor skills, language use, adaptive behavior, and personal-social (Ch. 5)

Developmentally appropriate educational practice Education that is based on both typical development and the unique characteristics of a given child (Ch. 7)

Differential emotions theory Izard's theory that emotional expressions reflect emotional experiences and help in the regulation of emotion itself (Ch. 6)

Difficult babies Babies who have negative moods and are slow to adapt to new situations; when confronted with a new situation, they tend to withdraw (Ch. 6)

Discontinuous change Development that occurs in distinct steps, or stages, with each stage bringing about behavior that is assumed to be qualitatively different from behavior at earlier stages (Ch. 1)

Disengagement theory The period in late adulthood that marks a gradual withdrawal from the world on physical, psychological, and social levels (Ch. 18)

Disorganized-disoriented attachment pattern A style of attachment in which children show inconsistent, often contradictory behavior, such as approaching the mother when she returns but not looking at her; they may be the least securely attached children of all (Ch. 6)

Dizygotic twins Twins who are produced when two separate ova are fertilized by two separate sperm at roughly the same time (Ch. 2)

DNA (deoxyribonucleic acid) The substance that genes are composed of that determines the nature of every cell in the body and how it will function (Ch. 2)

Dominance hierarchy Rankings that represent the relative social power of those in a group (Ch. 10)

Dominant trait The one trait that is expressed when two competing traits are present (Ch. 2)

Down syndrome A disorder produced by the presence of an extra chromosome on the 21st pair; once referred to as mongolism (Ch. 2)

Easy babies Babies who have a positive disposition; their body functions operate regularly, and they are adaptable (Ch. 6)

Ecological approach The perspective suggesting that different levels of the environment simultaneously influence individuals (Ch. 1)

Ego According to Freud, the part of personality that is rational and reasonable (Ch. 1)

Ego transcendence versus ego preoccupation The period in which elderly people must come to grips with their coming death (Ch. 18)

Egocentric thought Thinking that does not take into account the viewpoints of others (Ch. 7)

Ego-integrity-versus-despair stage Erikson's final stage of life, characterized by a process of looking back over one's life, evaluating it, and coming to terms with it (Ch. 18)

Elder abuse The physical or psychological mistreatment or neglect of elderly individuals (Ch. 18)

Embryonic stage The period from 2 to 8 weeks following fertilization during which significant growth occurs in the major organs and body systems (Ch. 2)

Emotional intelligence The set of skills that underlie the accurate assessment, evaluation, expression, and regulation of emotions (Ch. 10, 13)

Empathy The understanding of what another individual feels (Ch. 6, 8)

Empty nest syndrome The experience that relates to parents' feelings of unhappiness, worry, loneliness, and depression resulting from their children's departure from home (Ch. 16)

Enrichment An approach through which students are kept at grade level but are enrolled in special programs and given individual activities to allow greater depth of study on a given topic (Ch. 9)

Episiotomy An incision sometimes made to increase the size of the opening of the vagina to allow the baby to pass (Ch. 3)

Erikson's theory of psychosocial development The theory that considers how individuals come to understand themselves and the meaning of others'—and their own—behavior (Ch. 6)

Euthanasia The practice of assisting people who are terminally ill to die more quickly (Ch. 19)

Evocative genotype–environment effects Situations in which a child's genes elicit a particular type of environment (Ch. 2)

Evolutionary perspective The theory that seeks to identify behavior that is a result of our genetic inheritance from our ancestors (Ch. 1)

Executive stage The period in middle adulthood when people take a broader perspective than earlier, including concerns about the world (Ch. 13)

Experiment A process in which an investigator, called an experimenter, devises two different experiences for subjects or participants (Ch. 1)

Experimental research Research designed to discover causal relationships between various factors (Ch. 1)

Expertise The acquisition of skill or knowledge in a particular area (Ch. 15)

Expressive style A style of language use in which language is used primarily to express feelings and needs about oneself and others (Ch. 5)

Extrinsic motivation Motivation that drives people to obtain tangible rewards, such as money and prestige (Ch. 14)

Fantasy period According to Ginzberg, the period, lasting until about age 11, when career choices are made, and discarded, without regard to skills, abilities, or available job opportunities (Ch. 14)

Female climacteric The period that marks the transition from being able to bear children to being unable to do so (Ch. 15)

Fertilization The process by which a sperm and an ovum—the male and female gametes, respectively—join to form a single new cell (Ch. 2)

Fetal alcohol effects (FAE) A condition in which children display some, although not all, of the problems of fetal alcohol syndrome due to the mother's consumption of alcohol during pregnancy (Ch. 2)

Fetal alcohol syndrome (FAS) A disorder caused by the pregnant mother consuming substantial quantities of alcohol during pregnancy, potentially resulting in mental retardation and delayed growth in the child (Ch. 2)

Fetal monitor Device that measure the baby's heartbeat during labor (Ch. 3)

Fetal stage The stage that begins at about 8 weeks after conception and continues until birth (Ch. 2)

Fetus A developing child, from 8 weeks after conception until birth (Ch. 2)

Field study A research investigation carried out in a naturally occurring setting (Ch. 1)

First-year adjustment reaction A cluster of psychological symptoms relating to the college experience suffered by first-year college students (Ch. 13)

Fixation Behavior reflecting an earlier stage of development due to an unresolved conflict (Ch. 1)

Fluid intelligence Intelligence that reflects information processing capabilities, reasoning, and memory (Ch. 9, 15)

Formal operations period The stage at which people develop the ability to think abstractly (Ch. 11)

Functional death The absence of a heartbeat and breathing (Ch. 19)

Functional play Play that involves simple, repetitive activities typical of 3-year-olds (Ch. 8)

Gametes The sex cells from the mother and father that form a new cell at conception (Ch. 2)

Gender The sense of being male or female (Ch. 6)

Gender constancy The belief that people are permanently males or females, depending on fixed, unchangeable biological factors (Ch. 8)

Gender identity The perception of oneself as male or female (Ch. 8)

Gender schema A cognitive framework that organizes information relevant to gender (Ch. 8)

Generalized slowing hypothesis The theory that processing in all parts of the nervous system, including the brain, is less efficient (Ch. 17)

Generation gap A divide between parents and adolescents in attitudes, values, aspirations, and world views (Ch. 12)

Generativity versus stagnation According to Erikson, the stage during middle adulthood in which people consider their contributions to family and society (Ch. 16)

Genes The basic unit of genetic information (Ch. 2)

Genetic counseling The discipline that focuses on helping people deal with issues relating to inherited disorders (Ch. 2)

Genetic preprogramming theories of aging Theories that suggest that our body's DNA genetic code contains a built-in time limit for the reproduction of human cells (Ch. 17)

Genital herpes A common sexually transmitted disease which is a virus and not unlike cold sores that sometimes appear around the mouth (Ch. 11)

Genotype The underlying combination of genetic material present (but not outwardly visible) in an organism (Ch. 2)

Germinal stage The first—and shortest—stage of the prenatal period, which takes place during the first 2 weeks following conception (Ch. 2)

Gerontologists Specialists who study aging (Ch. 17)

Gifted and talented Children who show evidence of high performance capability in areas such as intellectual, creative, artistic, leadership capacity, or specific academic fields (Ch. 9)

Glaucoma A condition in which pressure in the fluid of the eye increases, either because the fluid cannot drain properly or because too much fluid is produced (Ch. 15)

Goal-directed behavior Behavior in which several schemes are combined and coordinated to generate a single act to solve a problem (Ch. 5)

Goodness-of-fit The notion that development is dependent on the degree of match between children's temperament and the nature and demands of the environment in which they are being raised (Ch. 6)

Grammar The system of rules that determine how our thoughts can be expressed (Ch. 7)

Grief The emotional response to one's loss (Ch. 19)

Habituation The decrease in the response to a stimulus that occurs after repeated presentations of the same stimulus (Ch. 3)

Handedness The preference of using one hand over another (Ch. 7)

Heteronomous morality The stage of moral development in which rules are seen as invariant and unchangeable (Ch. 8)

Heterozygous Inheriting from parents different forms of a gene for a given trait (Ch. 2)

Holophrases One-word utterances that stand for a whole phrase, whose meaning depends on the particular context in which they are used (Ch. 5)

Home care An alternative to hospitalization in which dying people stay in their homes and receive treatment from their families and visiting medical staff (Ch. 19)

Homogamy The tendency to marry someone who is similar in age, race, education, religion, and other basic demographic characteristics (Ch. 14)

Homozygous Inheriting from parents similar genes for a given trait (Ch. 2)

Hospice care Care provided for the dying in institutions devoted to those who are terminally ill (Ch. 19)

Humanistic perspective The theory that contends that people have a natural capacity to make decisions about their lives and control their behavior (Ch. 1)

Hypothesis A prediction stated in a way that permits it to be tested

Id According to Freud, the raw, unorganized, inborn part of personality, present at birth, that represents primitive drives related to hunger, sex, aggression, and irrational impulses (Ch. 1)

Identification The process in which children attempt to be similar to their same-sex parent, incorporating the parent's attitudes and values (Ch. 8)

Identity achievement The status of adolescents who commit to a particular identity following a period of crisis during which they consider various alternatives (Ch. 12)

Identity diffusion The status of adolescents who consider various identity alternatives, but never commit to one, or never even consider identity options in any conscious way (Ch. 12)

Identity foreclosure The status of adolescents who prematurely commit to an identity without adequately exploring alternatives (Ch. 12)

Identity-versus-identity-confusion stage The period during which teenagers seek to determine what is unique and distinctive about themselves (Ch. 12)

Imaginary audience An adolescent's belief that his or her own behavior is a primary focus of others' attentions and concerns (Ch. 11)

Immanent justice The notion that rules that are broken earn immediate punishment (Ch. 8)

In vitro fertilization (IVF) A procedure in which a woman's ova are removed from her ovaries, and a man's sperm are used to fertilize the ova in a laboratory (Ch. 2)

Independent variable The variable that researchers manipulate in an experiment (Ch. 1)

Individualistic orientation A philosophy that emphasizes personal identity and the uniqueness of the individual (Ch. 8)

Industry-versus-inferiority stage The period from age 6 to 12 characterized by a focus on efforts to attain competence in meeting the challenges presented by parents, peers, school, and the other complexities of the modern world (Ch. 10)

Infant mortality Death within the first year of life (Ch. 3)

Infant-directed speech A type of speech directed toward infants, characterized by short, simple sentences (Ch. 5)

Infantile amnesia The lack of memory for experiences that occurred prior to 3 years of age (Ch. 5)

Infertility The inability to conceive after 12 to 18 months of trying to become pregnant (Ch. 2)

Information processing approaches The model that seeks to identify the ways individuals take in, use, and store information (Ch. 1, 5)

Information processing perspective A perspective that sees changes in cognitive abilities as gradual transformations in the capacity to take in, use, and store information (Ch. 11)

Initiative-versus-guilt stage According to Erikson, the period during which children aged 3 to 6 years experience conflict between independence of action and the sometimes negative results of that action (Ch. 8)

Institutionalism A psychological state in which people in nursing homes develop apathy, indifference, and a lack of caring about themselves (Ch. 18)

Intelligence The capacity to understand the world, think with rationality, and use resources effectively when faced with challenges (Ch. 9)

Intelligence quotient (or IQ score) A measure of intelligence that takes into account a student's mental *and* chronological age (Ch. 9)

Intimacy component The component of love that encompasses feelings of closeness, affection, and connectedness (Ch. 14)

Intimacy-versus-isolation stage According to Erikson, the period of postadolescence into the early 30s that focuses on developing close relationships with others (Ch. 14)

Intrinsic motivation Motivation that causes people to work for their own enjoyment, not for the rewards work may bring (Ch. 14)

Intuitive thought Thinking that reflects preschoolers' use of primitive reasoning and their avid acquisition of knowledge about the world (Ch. 7)

Klinefelter's syndrome A disorder resulting from the presence of an extra X chromosome that produces underdeveloped genitals, extreme height, and enlarged breasts (Ch. 2)

Kwashiorkor A disease in which a child's stomach, limbs, and face swell with water (Ch. 4)

Labeling theory of passionate love The theory that individuals experience romantic love when two events occur together: intense physiological arousal and situational cues suggesting that the arousal is due to love (Ch. 14)

Laboratory study A research investigation conducted in a controlled setting explicitly designed to hold events constant (Ch. 1)

Language The systematic, meaningful arrangement of symbols, which provides the basis for communication (Ch. 5)

Language-acquisition device (LAD) A neural system of the brain hypothesized to permit understanding of language (Ch. 5)

Lateralization The process in which certain cognitive functions are located more in one hemisphere of the brain than the other (Ch. 7)

Learning disabilities Difficulties in the acquisition and use of listening, speaking, reading, writing, reasoning, or mathematical abilities (Ch. 9)

Learning theory approach The theory that language acquisition follows the basic laws of reinforcement and conditioning (Ch. 5)

Least restrictive environment The setting that is most similar to that of children without special needs (Ch. 9)

Life events models The approach to personality development that is based on the timing of particular events in an adult's life, rather than on age per se (Ch. 16)

Life expectancy The average age of death for members of a population (Ch. 17)

Life review The point in life in which people examine and evaluate their lives (Ch. 18)

Lifespan development The field of study that examines patterns of growth, change, and stability in behavior that occur throughout the entire life span (Ch. 1)

Living wills Legal documents designating what medical treatments people want or do not want if they cannot express their wishes (Ch. 19)

Longitudinal research Research in which the behavior of one or more participants in a study is measured as they age (Ch. 1)

Mainstreaming An educational approach in which exceptional children are integrated to the extent possible into the traditional educational system and are provided with a broad range of educational alternatives (Ch. 9)

Male climacteric The period of physical and psychological change relating to the male reproductive system that occurs during late middle age (Ch. 15)

Marasmus A disease characterized by the cessation of growth (Ch. 4)

Marriage gradient The tendency for men to marry women who are slightly younger, smaller, and lower in status, and women to marry men who are slightly older, larger, and higher in status (Ch. 14)

Masturbation Sexual self-stimulation (Ch. 12)

Maturation The predetermined unfolding of genetic information (Ch. 1)

Memory The process by which information is initially recorded, stored, and retrieved (Ch. 5, 9)

Menarche The onset of menstruation (Ch. 11)

Menopause The cessation of menstruation (Ch. 15)

Mental age The typical intelligence level found for people at a given chronological age (Ch. 9)

Mental representation An internal image of a past event or object (Ch. 5)

Mental retardation A significantly subaverage level of intellectual functioning which occurs with related limitations in two or more skill areas (Ch. 9)

Metacognition The knowledge that people have about their own thinking processes, and their ability to monitor their cognition (Ch. 11)

Metalinguistic awareness An understanding of one's own use of language (Ch. 9)

Metamemory An understanding about the processes that underlie memory, which emerges and improves during middle childhood (Ch. 9)

Midlife crisis A stage of uncertainty and indecision brought about by the realization that life is finite (Ch. 16)

Mild retardation Retardation in which IQ scores fall in the range of 50 or 55 to 70 (Ch. 9)

Mnemonics Formal strategies for organizing material in ways that make it more likely to be remembered (Ch. 15)

Moderate retardation Retardation in which IQ scores range from around 35 or 40 to 50 or 55 (Ch. 9)

Monozygotic twins Twins who are genetically identical (Ch. 2)

Moral development The changes in people's sense of justice and of what is right and wrong, and in their behavior related to moral issues (Ch. 8)

Moratorium The status of adolescents who may have explored various identity alternatives to some degree, but have not yet committed themselves (Ch. 12)

Multicultural education A form of education in which the goal is to help minority students develop competence in the culture of the majority group while maintaining positive group identities that build on their original cultures (Ch. 9)

Multifactorial transmission The determination of traits by a combination of both genetic and environmental factors in which a genotype provides a range within which a phenotype may be expressed (Ch. 2)

Multimodal approach to perception The approach that considers how information that is collected by various individual sensory systems is integrated and coordinated (Ch. 4)

Mutual regulation model The model in which infants and parents learn to communicate emotional states to one another and to respond appropriately (Ch. 6)

Myelin A fatty substance that helps insulate neurons and speeds the transmission of nerve impulses (Ch. 4)

Nativist approach The theory that a genetically determined, innate mechanism directs language development (Ch. 5)

Naturalistic observation A type of correlational study in which some naturally occurring behavior is observed without intervention in the situation (Ch. 1)

Neglected adolescents Children who receive relatively little attention from their peers in the form of either positive or negative interactions (Ch. 12)

Neonate The term used for newborns (Ch. 3)

Neuron The basic nerve cell of the nervous system (Ch. 4)

Nonnormative life events Specific, atypical events that occur in a particular person's life at a time when they do not happen to most people (Ch. 1)

Nonorganic failure to thrive A disorder in which infants stop growing due to a lack of stimulation and attention as the result of inadequate parenting (Ch. 4)

Normative age-graded influences Biological and environmental influences that are similar for individuals in a particular age group, regardless of when or where they are raised (Ch. 1)

Normative history-graded influences Biological and environmental influences associated with a particular historical moment (Ch. 1)

Normative sociocultural-graded influences The impact of social and cultural factors present at a particular time for a particular individual, depending on such variables as ethnicity, social class, and subcultural membership (Ch. 1)

Normative-crisis models The approach to personality development that is based on fairly universal stages, tied to a sequence of age-related crises (Ch. 16)

Norms The average performance of a large sample of children of a given age (Ch. 4)

Obesity Body weight more than 20 percent higher than the average weight for a person of a given age and height (Ch. 7)

Object permanence The realization that people and objects exist even when they cannot be seen (Ch. 5)

Onlooker play Action in which children simply watch others at play, but do not actually participate themselves (Ch. 8)

Operant conditioning A form of learning in which a voluntary response is strengthened or weakened by its association with positive or negative consequences (Ch. 1, 3)

Operations Organized, formal, logical mental processes (Ch. 7)

Osteoporosis A condition in which the bones become brittle, fragile, and thin, often brought about by a lack of calcium in the diet (Ch. 15, 17)

Overextension The overly broad use of words, overgeneralizing their meaning (Ch. 5)

Parallel play Action in which children play with similar toys, in a similar manner, but do not interact with each other (Ch. 8)

Passion component The component of love that comprises the motivational drives relating to sex, physical closeness, and romance (Ch. 14)

Passionate (or romantic) love A state of powerful absorption in someone (Ch. 14)

Passive genotype–environment effects Situations in which parents' genes are associated with the environment in which children are raised (Ch. 2)

Peer pressure The influence of one's peers to conform to their behavior and attitudes (Ch. 12)

Perception The sorting out, interpretation, analysis, and integration of stimuli involving the sense organs and brain (Ch. 4)

Peripheral slowing hypothesis The theory that suggests that overall processing speed declines in the peripheral nervous system with increasing age (Ch. 17)

Permissive parents Parents who provide lax and inconsistent feedback and require little of their children (Ch. 8)

Personal fables The view held by some adolescents that what happens to them is unique, exceptional, and shared by no one else (Ch. 11)

Personality The sum total of the enduring characteristics that differentiate one individual from another (Ch. 6)

Personality development Development involving the ways that the enduring characteristics that differentiate one person from another change over the life span (Ch. 1)

Phenotype An observable trait; the trait that actually is seen (Ch. 2)

Physical development Development involving the body's physical makeup, including the brain, nervous system, muscles, and senses, and the need for food, drink, and sleep (Ch. 1)

Placenta A conduit between the mother and fetus, providing nourishment and oxygen via the umbilical cord (Ch. 2)

Plasticity The degree to which a developing structure or behavior is susceptible to experience (Ch. 4, 17)

Pluralistic society model The concept that American society is made up of diverse, coequal cultural groups that should preserve their individual cultural features (Ch. 9)

Polygenic inheritance Inheritance in which a combination of multiple gene pairs is responsible for the production of a particular trait (Ch. 2)

Postformal thought Thinking that acknowledges that adult predicaments must sometimes be solved in relativistic terms (Ch. 13)

Postmature infants Infants still unborn 2 weeks after the mother's due date (Ch. 3)

Practical intelligence According to Sternberg, intelligence that is learned primarily by observing others and modeling their behavior (Ch. 13)

Pragmatics The aspect of language that relates to communicating effectively and appropriately with others (Ch. 7)

Prelinguistic communication Communication through sounds, facial expressions, gestures, imitation, and other nonlinguistic means (Ch. 5)

Preoperational stage According to Piaget, the stage from approximately age 2 to age 7 in which children's use of symbolic thinking grows, mental reasoning emerges, and the use of concepts increases (Ch. 7)

Presbycusis Loss of the ability to hear sounds of high frequency (Ch. 15)

Presbyopia A nearly universal change in eyesight during middle adulthood that results in some loss of near vision (Ch. 15)

Preschools (or nursery schools) Child care facilities designed to provide intellectual and social experiences for children (Ch. 7)

Preterm infants Infants who are born prior to 38 weeks after conception (also known as premature infants) (Ch. 3)

Primary aging Aging that involves universal, and irreversable, changes that occur as people get older due to genetic preprogramming (Ch. 17)

Primary appraisal The assessment of an event to determine whether its implications are positive, negative, or neutral (Ch. 13)

Primary sex characteristics Characteristics associated with the development of the organs and structures of the body that directly relate to reproduction (Ch. 11)

Principle of hierarchical integration The principle that simple skills typically develop separately and independently but are later integrated into more complex skills (Ch. 4)

Principle of the independence of systems The principle that different body systems grow at different rates (Ch. 4)

Private speech Speech by children that is spoken and directed to themselves (Ch. 7)

Profound retardation Retardation in which IQ scores fall below 20 or 25 (Ch. 9)

Prosocial behavior Helping behavior that benefits others (Ch. 8)

Proximodistal principle The principle that development proceeds from the center of the body outward (Ch. 4)

Psychoanalytic theory The theory proposed by Freud that suggests that unconscious forces act to determine personality and behavior (Ch. 1)

Psychodynamic perspective The approach that states behavior is motivated by inner forces, memories, and conflicts that are generally beyond people's awareness and control (Ch. 1)

Psychological maltreatment Abuse that occurs when parents or other caregivers harm children's behavioral, cognitive, emotional, or physical functioning (Ch. 8)

Psychoneuroimmunology (PNI) The study of the relationship among the brain, the immune system, and psychological factors (Ch. 13)

Psychosexual development According to Freud, a series of stages that children pass through in which pleasure, or gratification, is focused on a particular biological function and body part (Ch. 1)

Psychosocial development The approach that encompasses changes in our interactions with and understandings of one another, as well as in our knowledge and understanding of ourselves as members of society (Ch. 1, 8)

Psychosomatic disorders   Medical problems caused by the interaction of psychological, emotional, and physical difficulties (Ch. 13)

Puberty   The period during which the sexual organs mature, beginning earlier for girls than for boys (Ch. 11)

Race dissonance   The phenomenon in which minority children indicate preferences for majority values or people (Ch. 8)

Rapid eye movement (REM) sleep   The period of sleep that is found in older children and adults and is associated with dreaming (Ch. 4)

Realistic period   The third stage of Ginzburg's theory, which occurs in early adulthood, when people begin to explore specific career options either through actual experience on the job or through training for a profession, and then narrow their choices and make a commitment (Ch. 14)

Recessive trait   A trait within an organism that is present, but is not expressed (Ch. 2)

Reciprocal socialization   A process in which infants' behaviors invite further responses from parents and other caregivers, which in turn bring about further responses from the infants (Ch. 6)

Redefinition of self versus preoccupation with work-role   The theory that those in old age must redefine themselves in ways that do not relate to their work-roles or occupations (Ch. 18)

Reference groups   Groups of people with whom one compares oneself (Ch. 12)

Referential style   A style of language use in which language is used primarily to label objects (Ch. 5)

Reflexes   Unlearned, organized involuntary responses that occur automatically in the presence of certain stimuli (Ch. 3, 4)

Reintegrative stage   The period of late adulthood during which the focus is on tasks that have personal meaning (Ch. 13)

Rejected adolescents   Children who are actively disliked and whose peers may react to them in an obviously negative manner (Ch. 12)

Resilience   The ability to overcome circumstances that place a child at high risk for psychological or physical damage (Ch. 8)

Responsible stage   The stage where the major concerns of middle-aged adults relate to their personal situations, including protecting and nourishing their spouses, families, and careers (Ch. 13)

Rhythms   Repetitive, cyclical patterns of behavior (Ch. 4)

Sandwich generation   Couples who in middle adulthood must fulfill the needs of both their children and their aging parents (Ch. 16)

Scaffolding   The support for learning and problem solving that encourages independence and growth (Ch. 7)

Schemas   Organized bodies of information stored in memory (Ch. 15)

Scheme   An organized pattern of sensorimotor functioning (Ch. 5)

School child care   Child-care facility provided by some local school systems in the United States (Ch. 7)

Scientific method   The process of posing and answering questions using careful, controlled techniques that include systematic, orderly observation and the collection of data (Ch. 1)

Scripts   Broad representations in memory of events and the order in which they occur (Ch. 7)

Secondary aging   Changes in physical and cognitive functioning that are due to illness, health habits, and other individual differences, but which are not due to increased age itself and are not inevitable (Ch. 17)

Secondary appraisal   The assessment of whether one's coping abilities and resources are adequate to overcome the harm, threat, or challenge posed by the potential stressor (Ch. 13)

Secondary sex characteristics   The visible signs of sexual maturity that do not directly involve the sex organs (Ch. 11)

Secular trend   A statistical tendency observed over several generations (Ch. 11)

Secure attachment pattern   A style of attachment in which children use the mother as a kind of home base and are at ease when she is present; when she leaves, they become upset and go to her as soon as she returns (Ch. 6)

Selective optimization   The process by which people concentrate on particular skill areas to compensate for losses in other areas (Ch. 15, 18)

Self-awareness   Knowledge of oneself (Ch. 6)

Self-care children   Children who let themselves into their homes after school and wait alone until their caretakers return from work; previously known as *latchkey children* (Ch. 10)

Self-concept   A person's identity, or set of beliefs about what one is like as an individual (Ch. 8)

Self-esteem   An individual's overall and specific positive and negative self-evaluation (Ch. 10)

Senescence   The natural physical decline brought about by aging (Ch. 13)

Sensation   The stimulation of the sense organs (Ch. 4)

Sensitive period   A point in development when organisms are particularly susceptible to certain kinds of stimuli in their environments, but the absence of those stimuli does not always produce irreversible consequences (Ch. 1, 4)

Sensorimotor stage (of cognitive development)   Piaget's initial major stage of cognitive development, which can be broken down into six substages (Ch. 5)

Separation anxiety   The distress displayed by infants when a customary care provider departs (Ch. 6)

Severe retardation   Retardation in which IQ scores range from around 20 or 25 to 35 or 40 (Ch. 9)

Sex cleavage   Sex segregation in which boys interact primarily with boys, and girls primarily with girls (Ch. 12)

Sexually transmitted disease (STD)   A disease that is spread through sexual contact (Ch. 11)

Sickle-cell anemia   A blood disorder that gets its name from the shape of the red blood cells in those who have it (Ch. 2)

Skilled-nursing facilities   A facility that provides full-time nursing care for people who have chronic illnesses or are recovering from a temporary medical condition (Ch. 18)

Slow-to-warm babies   Babies who are inactive, showing relatively calm reactions to their environment. Their moods are generally negative, and they withdraw from new situations, adapting slowly (Ch. 6)

Small-for-gestational-age infants   Infants who, because of delayed fetal growth, weigh 90 percent (or less) of the average weight of infants of the same gestational age (Ch. 3)

Social clock   The psychological timepiece that records the major milestones in people's lives (Ch. 14)

Social comparison   The desire to evaluate one's own behavior, abilities, expertise, and opinions by comparing them to those of others (Ch. 10)

Social competence   The collection of social skills that permit individuals to perform successfully in social settings (Ch. 10)

Social development   The way in which individuals' interactions with others and their social relationships grow, change, and remain stable over the course of life (Ch. 1)

Social problem-solving   The use of strategies for solving social conflicts in ways that are satisfactory both to oneself and to others (Ch. 10)

Social referencing   The intentional search for information about others' feelings to help explain the meaning of uncertain circumstances and events (Ch. 6)

Social smile   Smiling in response to other individuals (Ch. 6)

Social speech   Speech directed toward another person and meant to be understood by that person (Ch. 7)

Social support Assistance and comfort supplied by another person or a network of caring, interested people (Ch. 18)

Social-cognitive learning theory Learning by observing the behavior of another person, called a model (Ch. 1)

Socialized delinquents Adolescent delinquents who know and subscribe to the norms of society and who are fairly normal psychologically (Ch. 12)

Sociocultural theory The approach that emphasizes how cognitive development proceeds as a result of social interactions between members of a culture (Ch. 1)

Speech impairment Speech that deviates so much from the speech of others that it calls attention to itself, interferes with communication, or produces maladjustment in the speaker (Ch. 9)

Stanford-Binet Intelligence Scale A test that consists of a series of items that vary according to the age of the person being tested (Ch. 9)

State The degree of awareness an infant displays to both internal and external stimulation (Ch. 4)

States of arousal Different degrees of sleep and wakefulness through which newborns cycle, ranging from deep sleep to great agitation (Ch. 3)

Status The evaluation of a role or person by other relevant members of a group (Ch. 10, 14)

Stillbirth The delivery of a child who is not alive, occurring in less than 1 delivery in 100 (Ch. 3)

Stimulus-value-role (SVR) theory The theory that relationships proceed in a fixed order of three stages: stimulus, value, and role (Ch. 14)

Stranger anxiety The caution and wariness displayed by infants when encountering an unfamiliar person (Ch. 6)

Stress The response to events that threaten or challenge an individual (Ch. 13)

Stuttering Substantial disruption in the rhythm and fluency of speech; the most common speech impairment (Ch. 9)

Sudden infant death syndrome (SIDS) The unexplained death of a seemingly healthy baby (Ch. 4, 19)

Superego According to Freud, the aspect of personality that represents a person's conscience, incorporating distinctions between right and wrong (Ch. 1)

Surrogate mother A woman who agrees to carry a child to term in cases in which the mother who provides the donor eggs is unable to conceive (Ch. 2)

Survey research A type of study in which a group of people chosen to represent some larger population are asked questions about their attitudes, behavior, or thinking on a given topic (Ch. 1)

Syntax The way in which an individual combines words and phrases to form sentences (Ch. 7)

Tay-Sachs disease A disorder that produces blindness and muscle degeneration prior to death; there is no treatment (Ch. 2)

Teacher expectancy effect The cycle of behavior in which a teacher transmits an expectation about a child and thereby actually brings about the expected behavior (Ch. 10)

Telegraphic speech Speech in which words not critical to the message are left out (Ch. 5)

Temperament Patterns of arousal and emotionality that represent consistent and enduring characteristics in an individual (Ch. 2, 6)

Tentative period The second stage of Ginzberg's theory, which spans adolescence, when people begin to think in pragmatic terms about the requirements of various jobs and how their own abilities might fit with them (Ch. 14)

Teratogen A factor that produces a birth defect (Ch. 2)

Thanatologists People who study death and dying (Ch. 19)

Theoretical research Research designed specifically to test some developmental explanation and expand scientific knowledge (Ch. 1)

Theories Explanations and predictions concerning phenomena of interest, providing a framework for understanding the relationships among an organized set of facts or principles (Ch. 1)

Theory of mind Children's knowledge and beliefs about their mental world (Ch. 6)

Transformation The process in which one state is changed into another (Ch. 7)

Treatment A procedure applied by an investigator based on two different experiences devised for participants (See **Experiment**) (Ch. 1)

Treatment group The group in an experiment that receives the treatment (Ch. 1)

Triarchic theory of intelligence A model that states that intelligence consists of three aspects of information processing: the componential element, the experiential element, and the contextual element (Ch. 9, 13)

Trust-versus-mistrust stage According to Erikson, the period during which infants develop a sense of trust or mistrust, largely depending on how well their needs are met by their caregivers (Ch. 6)

Type A behavior pattern Behavior characterized by competitiveness, impatience, and a tendency toward frustration and hostility (Ch. 15)

Type B behavior pattern Behavior characterized by noncompetitiveness, patience, and a lack of aggression (Ch. 15)

Ultrasound sonography A process in which high-frequency sound waves scan the mother's womb to produce an image of the unborn baby, whose size and shape can then be assessed (Ch. 2)

Underextension The overly restrictive use of words, common among children just mastering spoken language (Ch. 5)

Undersocialized delinquents Adolescent delinquents who are raised with little discipline, or with harsh, uncaring parental supervision (Ch. 12)

Universal grammar Noam Chomsky's theory that all the world's languages share a similar underlying structure (Ch. 5)

Very-low-birthweight infants Infants who weigh less than 1250 grams (around 2.25 pounds) or, regardless of weight, have been in the womb less than 30 weeks (Ch. 3)

Visual impairment A difficulty in seeing that may include blindness or partial sightedness (Ch. 9)

Visual-recognition memory The memory and recognition of a stimulus that has been previously seen (Ch. 5)

Wear-and-tear theories The theory that the mechanical functions of the body simply wear out with age (Ch. 17)

Wechsler Adult Intelligence Scale-Revised (WAIS-III) A test for adults that provides separate measures of verbal and performance (or nonverbal) skills, as well as a total score (Ch. 9)

Wechsler Intelligence Scale for Children-Revised (WISC-III) A test for children that provides separate measures of verbal and performance (or nonverbal) skills, as well as a total score (Ch. 9)

Wisdom Expert knowledge in the practical aspects of life (Ch. 18)

X-linked genes Genes that are considered recessive and located only on the X chromosome (Ch. 2)

Zone of proximal development (ZPD) According to Vygotsky, the level at which a child can *almost*, but not fully, perform a task independently, but can do so with the assistance of someone more competent (Ch. 7)

Zygote The new cell formed by the process of fertilization (Ch. 2)

References

AAMR (American Association on Mental Retardation). (1992). *Mental retardation: Definition, classification, and systems of support.* Washington, DC: Author.

AAP/ACOG (American Academy of Pediatrics/ American College of Obstetricians and Gynecologists). (1992). *Guidelines for perinatal care.* Elk Grove, IN: Author.

AARP (American Association of Retired Persons). (1990). *A profile of older Americans.* Washington, DC: Author.

AAUW (American Association of University Women). (1992). *How schools shortchange women: The A.A.U.W. report.* Washington, DC: American Association of University Women Educational Foundation.

Abeles, R. P., Gift, H. C., & Ory, M. G. (Eds.). (1994). *Aging and quality of life.* New York: Springer.

Able, E. L., & Sokol, R. J. (1987). Incidence of fetal alcohol syndrome and economic impact of FAS-related anomalies. *Drug and Alcohol Dependence, 19,* 51–70.

Aboud, F. E., & Skerry, S. A. (1983). Self and ethnic concepts in relations to ethnic constancy. *Canadian Journal of Behavioral Science, 15,* 14–26.

Abu-Heija, A. T., Jallad, M. F., & Abukteish, F. (2000). Maternal and perinatal outcome of pregnancies after the age of 45. *Journal of Obstetrics & Gynaecology Research, 26,* 27–30.

Achenbach, T. A. (1992). Developmental psychopathology. In M. H. Bornstein & M. E. Lamb (Eds.), *Developmental psychology: An advanced textbook.* Hillsdale, NJ: Erlbaum.

ACOG (American College of Obstetricians and Gynecologists). (1994, February). Guidelines for exercise during pregnancy and the postpartum period. Washington, DC: Author.

Adams, C., & Labouvie-Vief, G. (1986, November 20). *Modes of knowing and language processing. Symposium on developmental dimensions of adult adaptations. Perspectives in mind, self, and emotion.* Paper presented at the meeting of the Gerontological Association of America. Chicago.

Adams, C. R., & Singh, K. (1998). Direct and indirect effects of school learning variables on the academic achievement of African American 10th graders. *Journal of Negro Education 67,* 48–66.

Adams, G. R., Montemayor, R., & Gullotta, T. P. (Eds.). (1996). *Psychosocial development during adolescence.* Thousand Oaks, CA: Sage Publications.

Adams, R. J., Mauer, D., & Davis, M. (1986). Newborns' discrimination of chromatic from achromatic stimuli. *Journal of Experimental Child Psychology, 41,* 267–281.

Adelmann, P. K., Antonucci, T. C., & Crohan, S. E. (1990). A causal analysis of employment and health in midlife women. *Women and Health, 16,* 5–20.

Adler, P. A., & Adler, P. (1994). Observational techniques. In N. K. Denzin & Y. S. Lincoln (Eds.), *Handbook of qualitative research.* Thousand Oaks, CA: Sage Publications.

Adler, P. A., Kless, S. J., & Adler, P. (1992). Socialization to gender roles: Popularity among elementary school boys and girls. *Sociology of Education, 65,* 169–187.

Adolph, K. E. (1997). Learning in the development of infant locomotion. With commentary by B. I. Bertenthal, S. M. Boker, E. C. Goldfield, & E. J. Gibson *Monographs of the Society for Research in Child Development, 62,* 238–251.

Adolph, K. E., Eppler, M. A., & Gibson, E. J. (1993). Crawling versus walking infants' perception of affordances for locomotion over sloping surfaces. *Child Development, 64,* 1158–1174.

Aiken, L. R. (2000). *Dying, death, and bereavement.* (4th ed.). Mahwah, NJ: Erlbaum.

Ainsworth, M. D. S. (1973). The development of infant-mother attachment. In B. M. Caldwell & H. N. Ricciuti (Eds.), *Review of child development research* (Vol. 3). Chicago: University of Chicago Press.

Ainsworth, M. D. S. (1993). Attachment as related to mother-infant interaction. *Advances in Infancy Research, 8,* 1–50.

Ainsworth, M. D. S., & Bowlby, J. (1991). An ethological approach to personality development. *American Psychologist, 46,* 333–341.

Ainsworth, M. D. S., Blehar, M. C., Waters, E., & Wall, S. (1978). *Patterns of attachment: A psychological study of the strange situation.* Hillsdale, NJ: Erlbaum.

Aitken, R. J. (1995, July 7). The complexities of conception. *Science, 269,* 39–40.

Akmajian, A., Demers, R. A., & Harnish, R. M. (1984). *Linguistics.* Cambridge, MA: MIT Press.

Akutsu, H. (1991). Psychophysics of reading—X. Effects of age-related changes in vision. *Journal of Gerontology: Psychological Sciences, 46,* 325–331.

Alan Guttmacher Institute. (1993a). *Report on viral sexual diseases.* Chicago: Author.

Alan Guttmacher Institute. (1993b). *Survey of male sexuality.* Chicago: Author.

Albers, L. L., & Krulewitch, C. J. (1993). Electronic fetal monitoring in the United States in the 1980s. *Obstetrics & Gynecology, 82,* 8–10.

Ales, K. L., Druzin, M. L., & Santini, D. L. (1990). Impact of advanced maternal age on the outcome of pregnancy. *Surgery, Gynecology & Obstetrics, 171,* 209–216.

Alessandri, S. M., Bendersky, M., & Lewis, M. (1998). Cognitive functioning in 8- to 18-month-old drug-exposed infants. *Developmental Psychology, 34,* 565–573.

Allan, P. (1990). Looking for work after forty: Job search experiences of older unemployed managers and professionals. *Journal of Employment Counseling, 27,* 113–121.

Allen, J. P., Philliber, S., Herrling, S., & Kuperminc, G. P. (1997). Preventing teen pregnancy and academic failure: Experimental evaluation of a developmentally based approach. *Child Development, 64,* 729–742.

Allison, A. C. (1954). Protection afforded by sickle cell trait against subtertian malarial infection. *British Medical Journal, 1,* 290–294.

Alloy, L. B., Acocella, J., & Bootzin, R. R. (1996). *Abnormal Psychology: Current perspectives.* New York: McGraw-Hill.

Altemus, M., Deuster, P. A., Galliven, E., Carter, C. S., & Gold, P. W. (1995). Suppression of hypothalamic pituitary adrenal axis responses to stress in lactating women. *Journal of Clinical Endocrinology and Metabolism, 80,* 2954–2959.

Ambuel, B. (1995). Adolescents, unintended pregnancy, and abortion: The struggle for a compassionate social policy. *Current Directions in Psychological Science, 4,* 1–5.

American Academy of Pediatrics Committee on Public Education. (1999, August). Media education (RE9911). *Pediatrics, 104,* 341–343.

American Academy of Pediatrics (Committee on Psychosocial Aspects of Child and Family Health). (1998, April). Guidance for effective discipline. *Pediatrics, 101,* 723–728.

American Academy of Pediatrics (Committee on Sports Medicine and Committee on School Health). (1989). Organized athletics for preadolescent children. *Pediatrics, 84(3),* 583–584.

American Academy of Pediatrics (Committee on Sports Medicine). (1988). Infant exercise programs. *Pediatrics, 82,* 800–825.

American Academy of Pediatrics. (1995). *Policy statement on length of hospital stay following birth.* Washington, DC: Author.

American Academy of Pediatrics. (1997, December). Breast-feeding and the use of human milk. *Pediatrics, 100,* 1035–1039.

American Academy of Pediatrics. (2000a). *Circumcision: Information for parents.* Washington, DC: American Academy of Pediatrics.

American College of Sports Medicine. (1997, November 3). *Consensus development conference statement on physical activity and cardiovascular health.* Available: http://www.acsm.org/nhlbi.htm.

American Council on Education. (1995). *The American freshman: National norms for fall 1994.* Los Angeles: University of California Los Angeles Higher Education Research Institute.

American Council on Education. (1995–1996). *Minorities in higher education.* Washington, DC: Office of Minority Concerns.

American Heart Association. (1988). *Heart facts.* Dallas, TX: Author.

American Psychiatric Association. (1994). *Diagnostic and statistical manual of mental disorders* (4th ed.). Washington, DC: Author.

American Psychological Association. (1992). *Ethical principles of psychologists and code of conduct.* Washington, DC: Author.

Ammerman, R. T., & Patz, R. J. (1996). Determinants of child abuse potential: Contribution of parent and child factors. *Journal of Clinical Child Psychology, 25,* 300–307.

Anand, K. J. S., & Hickey, P. R. (1987). Pain and its effect in the human neonate and fetus. *New England Journal of Medicine, 317(21),* 1321–1329.

Anand, K. J. S., & Hickey, P. R. (1992). Halothane-morphine compared with high-dose sufentanil for anesthesia and post-operative analgesia in neonatal cardiac surgery. *New England Journal of Medicine, 326(1),* 1–9.

Anders, T. F., & Taylor, T. (1994). Babies and their sleep environment. *Children's Environments, 11,* 123–134.

Andersen, B. L., Kiecolt-Glaser, J. K., & Glaser, R. (1994). A biobehavioral model of cancer stress and disease course. *American Psychologist, 49,* 389–404.

Anderson, R. N. (2001), *United States life tables, 1998. National vital statistics reports,* (Vol. 48, No. 18). Hyattsville, MD: National Center for Health Statistics.

Anderson, W. F. (1995, September). Gene therapy. *Scientific American,* 125–128.

Andersson, T., & Magnusson, D. (1990). Biological maturation in adolescence and the development of drinking habits and alcohol abuse among young males: A prospective longitudinal study. *Journal of Youth and Adolescence, 19,* 33–42.

Andrews, K., Francis, D. J., & Riese, M. L. (2000). Prenatal cocaine exposure and prematurity: Neurodevelopmental growth. *Journal of Developmental & Behavioral Pediatrics, 21,* 262–270.

Andrews, M. (1997). Life review in the context of social transition: The case of East Germany. *British Journal of Social Psychology, 36,* 273–290.

Angier, N. (2000, August 22). Do races differ? Not really, genes show. *New York Times,* pp. S1, S6.

Anisfeld, M. (1996). Only tongue protrusion modeling is matched by neonates. *Developmental Review, 16,* 149–161.

Ansberry, C. (1995, February 14). After seven decades, couple still finds romance in the 90s. *The Wall Street Journal,* pp. A1, A17.

Ansberry, C. (1997, November 14). Women of Troy: For ladies on a hill, friendships are a balm in the passages of life. *The Wall Street Journal,* pp. A1, A6.

Antonucci, T. C. (1990). Social supports and social relationships. In R. H. Binstock & L. K. George (Eds.), *Handbook of aging and the social sciences.* San Diego: Academic Press.

Antonucci, T. C., & Akiyama, H. (1991). Social relationships and aging well. *Generations, 15,* 39–44.

APA (American Psychological Association). (1996). *Violence and the family.* Washington, DC: Author.

Applebome, P. (1997, March 1). Dispute over Ebonics reflects a volatile mix that roils urban education. *The New York Times,* p. 8.

Apter, A., Galatzer, A., Beth-Halachmi, N., & Laron, Z. (1981). Self-image in adolescents with delayed puberty and growth retardation. *Journal of Youth and Adolescence, 10,* 501–505.

Archer, S. L., & Waterman, A. S. (1994). Adolescent identity development: Contextual perspectives. In C. B. Fisher & R. M. Lerner (Eds.), *Applied developmental psychology.* New York: McGraw-Hill.

Ardila, A., Rosselli, M. (1994). Development of language, memory, and visuospatial ability in 5- to 12-year-old children using a neuropsychological battery. *Developmental Neuropsychology, 10,* 97–120.

Aries, P. (1962). *Centuries of childhood.* New York: Knopf.

Arnett, J. J. (2000). Emerging adulthood: A theory of development from the late teens through the twenties. *American Psychologist, 55,* 469–480.

Aronson, E. (2000). *Nobody left to hate: Teaching compassion after Columbine.* New York: Freeman.

Artal, P., Ferro, M., Miranda, I., & Navarro, R. (1993). Effects of aging in retinal image quality. *Journal of the Optical Society of America, 10,* 1656–1662.

Asch, D. A. (1996, May 23). The role of critical care nurses in euthanasia and assisted suicide. *The New England Journal of Medicine, 334,* 1374–1379.

Aseltine, R. H., Gore, S., & Colten, M. E. (1994). Depression and the social developmental context of adolescence. *Journal of Personality and Social Psychology, 67,* 252–263.

Asendorpf, J. B., Warkentin, V., & Baudonniere, P. (1996). Self-awareness and other-awareness II: Mirror self-recognition, social contingency awareness, and synchronic imitation. *Developmental Psychology, 32,* 313–321.

Asher, S. R., & Parker, J. G. (1991). The significance of peer relationship problems in childhood. In B. H. Schneider, G. Attili, J. Nadel, & R. P. Weisberg (Eds.), *Social competence in developmental perspective.* Amsterdam: Kluwer.

Asher, S. R., & Rose, A. J. (1997). Promoting children's social-emotional adjustment with peers. In P. Salovey & D. J. Sluyter (Eds.), *Emotional development and emotional intelligence: Educational implications* (pp. 196–230). New York: Basic Books.

Asher, S. R., Singleton, L. C., & Taylor, A. R. (1982). *Acceptance vs. friendship.* Paper presented at the meeting of the American Research Association, New York.

Askham, J. (1994). Marriage relationships of older people. *Reviews in Clinical Gerontology, 4,* 261–268.

Aslin, R. N. (1987). Visual and auditory development in infancy. In J. D. Osofsky (Ed.), *Handbook of infant development (2nd ed.).* New York: Wiley.

Atchley, R. C. (1982). Retirement: Leaving the world of work. *Annals of the American Academy of Political and Social Science, 464,* 120–131.

Atchley, R. C. (1985). *Social forces and aging: An introduction to social gerontology.* Belmont, CA: Wadsworth.

Atchley, R. C. (2000). *Social forces and aging.* (9th ed.). Belmont, CA: Wadsworth Thomson Learning.

Atchley, R. C. (1989). A continuity theory of normal aging. *The Gerontologist, 29,* 183–190.

Atkins, C. J., Senn, K., Rupp, J., & Kaplan, R. M. (1990). Attendance at health promotion programs: Baseline predictors and program outcomes. *Health Education Quarterly, 17,* 417–428.

Attie, I., & Brooks-Gunn, J. (1989). The development of eating prblems in adolescent girls: A longitudinal study. *Developmental Psychology, 25,* 70–79.

Aved, B. M., Irwin, M. M., Cummings, L. S., & Findeisen, N. (1993). Barriers to prenatal care for low-income women. *Western Journal of Medicine, 158,* 493–498.

Avis, N. E., Stellato, R., Crawford, S., Bromberger, J., Ganz, P., Cain, V., & Kagawa-Singer, M. (2001). Is there a menopausal syndrome? Menopausal status and symptoms across racial/ethnic groups. *Social Science & Medicine, 52,* 345–356.

Axia, G., Bonichini, S., & Benini, F. (1995). Pain in infancy: Individual differences. *Perceptual and Motor Skills, 81,* 142.

Azar, B. (1995, January). "Gifted" label stretches, it's more than high IQ. *APA Monitor,* p. 25.

Azar, B. (2000, November). Hand-me-down skills. *Monitor on Psychology,* 64–66.

Azmitia, M. (1988). Peer interaction and problem solving: When are two heads better than one? *Child Development, 59,* 87–96.

Babad, E. (1992). Pygmalion—25 years after interpersonal expectations in the classroom. In P. D. Blanck (Ed.), *Interpersonal expectations: Theory, research and application.* Cambridge, England: Cambridge University Press.

Bader, A. P. (1995). Engrossment revisited: Fathers are still falling in love with their newborn babies. In J. L. Shapiro, M. J. Diamond, M. Grenberg (Eds.), *Becoming a father.* New York: Springer.

Bahrick, L. E., & Pickens, J. N. (1988). Classification of bimodal English and Spanish language passages by infants. *Infant Behavior and Development, 11,* 277–296.

Bailey, J. M., Kirk, K. M., Zhu, G., Dunne, M. P., & Martin, N. G. (2000). Do individual differences in sociosexuality represent genetic or environmentally contingent strategies? Evidence from the Australian twin registry. *Journal of Personality and Social Psychology, 78,* 537–545.

Bailey, W. T. (1994). A longitudinal study of fathers' involvement with young children, infancy to age 5 years. *Journal of Genetic Psychology, 155,* 331–339.

Baillargeon, R. (1987). Object permanence in 3 1/2- and 4 1/2-month-old infants. *Developmental Psychology, 23(5),* 655–670.

Baillargeon, R., & DeVos, J. (1991). Object permanence in young infants: Further evidence. *Child Development, 62,* 1227–1246.

Baines, C. J., Vidmar, M., McKeown-Eyssen, G., & Tibshirani, R. (1997, August, 15). Impact of menstrual phase on false-negative mammograms in the Canadian National Breast Screening Study. *Cancer, 80,* 720–724.

Baird, A., John, R., & Hayslip, Jr., B. (2000). Custodial grandparenting among African Americans: A focus group perspective. In B. Hayslip, Jr. & R. Goldberg-Glen, (Eds.) *Grandparents raising grandchildren: Theoretical, empirical, and clinical perspectives.* New York: Springer.

Baker, D. B. (1994). Parenting stress and ADHD: A comparison of mothers and fathers. *Journal of Emotional and Behavioral Disorders, 2,* 46–50.

Balaban, M. T., Snidman, N., & Kagan, J. (1997). Attention, emotion, and reactivity in infancy and early childhood. In P. J. Lang, R. F. Simons, & M. T. Balaban (Eds.), *Attention and orienting: Sensory and motivational processes* (pp. 369–391). Mahwah, NJ: Erlbaum.

Ball, J. A. (1987). *Reactions to motherhood.* New York: Cambridge University Press.

Ball, K., & Rebok, G. W. (1994). Evaluating the driving ability of older adults. Special Issue: Research translation in gerontology: A behavioral and social perspective. *Journal of Applied Gerontology, 13,* 20–38.

Baltes, M. M. (1995). Dependency in old age: Gains and losses. *Current Directions in Psychological Science, 4,* 14–19.

Baltes, M. M. (1996). *The many faces of dependency in old age.* New York: Cambridge University Press.

Baltes, P. B. (1987). Theoretical propositions of life-span developmental psychology: On the dynamics between growth and decline. *Developmental Psychology, 23*, 611–626.

Baltes, P. B. (1997). On the incomplete architecture of human ontogeny: Selection, optimization, and compensation as foundation of developmental theory. *American Psychologist, 52*, 366–380.

Baltes, P. B., & Baltes, M. M. (1990). Psychological perspectives on successful aging: The model of selective optimization with compensation. In P. B. Baltes & M. M. Baltes (Eds.), *Successful aging: Perspectives from the behavioral sciences.* Cambridge, England: Cambridge University Press.

Baltes, P. B., & Schaie, K. W. (1974, March). The myth of the twilight years. *Psychology Today,* 35–38.

Baltes, P. B., & Staudinger, U. M. (2000). Wisdom: A metaheuristic (pragmatic) to orchestrate mind and virtue toward excellence. *American Psychologist, 55*, 122–136.

Baltes, P. B., Staudinger, U. M., Maercker, A., & Smith, J. (1995). People nominated as wise: A comparative study of wisdom-related knowledge. *Psychology and Aging, 10*, 155–166.

Baltrusch, H. J., Stangel, W., & Tirze, I. (1991). Stress, cancer and immunity: New developments in biopsychosocial and psychoneuroimmunologic research. *Acta Neurologica, 13*, 315–327.

Bandura, A. (1977). *Social learning theory.* Englewood Cliffs, NJ: Prentice-Hall.

Bandura, A. (1978). Social learning theory of aggression. *Journal of Communication, 28*, 12–29.

Bandura, A. (1991). Social cognitive theory of moral thought and action. In W. M. Kurtines & J. L. Gewirtz (Eds.), *Handbook of moral behavior and development.* Hillsdale, NJ: Erlbaum.

Bandura, A. (1994). Social cognitive theory of mass communication. In J. Bryant & D. Zillmann (Eds.), *Media effects: Advances in theory and research. LEA's communication series.* Hillsdale, NJ: Erlbaum.

Bandura, A., Grusec, J. E., & Menlove, F. L. (1967). Vicarious extinction of avoidance behavior. *Journal of Personality and Social Psychology, 5*, 16–23.

Bandura, A., Ross, D., & Ross, S. (1963). Vicarious extinction of avoidance behavior. *Journal of Personality and Social Psychology, 67*, 601–607.

Bandura, A., Pastorelli, C., Barbaranelli, C., & Caprara, G. V. (1999). Self-efficacy pathways to childhood depression. *Journal of Personality and Social Psychology, 76*, 258–269.

Banich, M. T., & Nicholas, C. D. (1998). Integration of processing between the hemispheres in word recognition. In M. Beeman & C. Chiarello (Eds.), *Right hemisphere language comprehension: Perspectives from cognitive neuroscience* (pp. 349–371). Mahwah, NJ: Erlbaum.

Barer, B. M. (1994). Men and women aging differently. *International Journal of Aging and Human Development, 38*, 29–40.

Barinaga, M. (2000, June 23). A critical issue for the brain. *Science, 288*, 2116–2119.

Barkley, R. A. (1997a). *ADHD and the nature of self-control.* New York: Guilford Press.

Barkley, R. A. (1997b). Behavioral inhibition, sustained attention, and executive functions: Constructing a unifying theory of ADHD. *Psychological Bulletin, 121*, 65–94.

Barnett, R. C., & Rivers, C. (1992). The myth of the miserable working woman. *Working Woman, 2*, 62–65, 83–85.

Barnett, R. C., & Shen, Y-C. (1997). Gender, high-and low-schedule-control housework tasks, and psychological distress: A study of dual-earner couples. *Journal of Family Issues, 18*, 403–428.

Barnett, R. C., Raudenbush, S. W., Brennan, R. T., Pleck, J. H., & Marshall, N. L. (1995). Change in job and marital experiences and change in psychological distress: A longitudinal study of dual-earner couples. *Journal of Personality and Social Psychology, 69*, 839–850.

Barr, H. M., Streissguth, A. P., Darby, B. L., & Sampson, P. D. (1990). Prenatal exposure to alcohol, caffeine, tobacco, and aspirin: Effects on fine and gross motor performance in 4-year-old children. *Developmental Psychology, 26(3)*, 339–348.

Barr, R., & Hayne, H. (1999). Developmental changes in imitation from television during infancy. *Child Development, 70*, 1067–1081.

Barratt, M. S., Roach, M. A., Morgan, K. M., & Colbert, K. K. (1996). Adjustment to motherhood by single adolescents. *Family Relations, 45*, 209–215.

Barrett, D. E., & Frank, D. A. (1987). *The effects of undernutrition on children's behavior.* New York: Gordon & Breach.

Barrett, D. E., & Radke-Yarrow, M. R. (1985). Effects of nutritional supplementation on children's responses to novel, frustrating, and competitive situations. *American Journal of Clinical Nutrition, 42*, 102–120.

Bartecchi, C. E., MacKenzie, T. D., & Schrier, R. W. (1995, May). The global tobacco epidemic. *Scientific American,* 44–51.

Barton, L. J. (1997, July). A shoulder to lean on: Assisted living in the U.S. *American Demographics,* 45–51.

Bashore, T. R., Ridderinkhof, K. R., & van der Molen, M. W. (1998). The decline of cognitive processing speed in old age. *Current Directions in Psychological Science, 6*, 163–169.

Basseches, M. (1984). *Dialectical thinking and adult development.* Norwood, NJ: Ablex.

Bates, E., Bretherton, I., & Snyder, L. (1988). *From first words to grammar: Individual differences and dissociable mechanisms.* New York: Cambridge University Press.

Bates, J. E., Marvinney, D., Bennett, D. S., Dodge, K. A., Kelly, T., & Pettit, G. S. (1991). *Children's daycare history and kindergarten adjustment.* Paper presented at the biennial meeting of the Society for Research in Child Development, Seattle.

Bates, J. E., Marvinney, D., Kelly, T., Dodge, K. A., Bennett, D. S., & Pettit, G. S. (1994). Child-care history and kindergarten adjustment. *Developmental Psychology, 30*, 690–700.

Bauer, P. J. (1996). What do infants recall of their lives? Memory for specific events by 1- to 2-year-olds. *American Psychologist, 51*, 29–41.

Bauer, P. J., Wenner, J. A., Dropik, P. L., & Wewerka, S. S. (2000). Parameters of remembering and forgetting in the transition from infancy to early childhood. With commentary by Mark L. Howe. *Monographs of the Society for Research in Child Development, 65*, 4.

Baum, A. (1994). Behavioral, biological, and environmental interactions in disease processes. In S.

Blumenthal, K. Matthews, & S. Weiss (Eds.), *New research frontiers in behavioral medicine: Proceedings of the National Conference.* Washington, DC: NIH Publications.

Baumeister, R. F. (Ed.). (1993). *Self-esteem: The puzzle of low self-regard.* New York: Plenum.

Baumrind, D. (1971). Current patterns of parental authority. *Developmental Psychology Monographs, 4* (1, pt. 2).

Baumrind, D. (1980). New directions in socialization research. *Psychological Bulletin, 35*, 639–652.

Baydar, N., & Brooks-Gunn, J. (1998). Profiles of grandmothers who help care for their grandchildren in the United States. *Family Relations, 47*, 385–393.

Bayley, N. (1969). *Manual for the Bayley Scales of infant development.* New York: The Psychological Corporation.

Bayley, N., & Oden, M. (1955). The maintenance of intellectual ability in gifted adults. *Journal of Gerontology, 10*, 91–107.

Beal, C. R. (1994). *Boys and girls: The development of gender roles.* New York: McGraw-Hill.

Beal, C. R., & Belgrad, S. L. (1990). The development of message evaluation skills in young children. *Child Development, 61*, 705–712.

Bear, G. G., & Rys, G. S. (1994). Moral reasoning, classroom behavior, and sociometric status among elementary school children. *Developmental Psychology, 30*, 633–638.

Bearman, P. S, & Bruckner, H. (2001). Promising the future: Virginity pledges and first intercourse. *American Journal of Sociology, 106*, 859–912.

Becahy, R. (1992, August 3). AIDS epidemic. *Newsweek,* 49.

Beck, M. (1991, November 11). School days for seniors. *Newsweek,* 60–65.

Beck, M. (1992, May 25). Menopause. *Newsweek,* 71–79.

Beck, R. W., & Beck, S. W. (1989). The incidence of extended households among middle-aged black and white women. *Journal of Family Issues, 10*, 147–168.

Becvar, D. S. (2000). Euthanasia decisions. In F. W. Kaslow, et al. (Eds.), *Handbook of couple and family forensics: A sourcebook for mental health and legal professionals.* New York: Wiley.

Beehr, T. A., Glazer, S., Nielson, N. L., & Farmer, S. J. (2000). Work and nonwork predictors of employees' retirement ages. *Journal of Vocational Behavior, 57*, 206–225.

Begley, S. (1991, August 26). Choosing death. *Newsweek,* 43–46.

Begley, S. (1995, July 10). Deliver, then depart. *Newsweek,* 62.

Begley, S. (1998, December 28). Into the Gene Pool. (ethical aspects of genetic research) *Newsweek,* p68.

Begley, S. (1998a). Homework. In: *How to help your child succeed in school.* New York: *Newsweek* and Score. 48–52.

Begley, S. (1998b, March 30). Homework Doesn't Help. *Newsweek. 131*, 50–51.

Begley, S. (1999, March 15). Talking from hand to mouth. *Newsweek,* 56–58.

Begley, S. (2000). Wired for thought. *Newsweek Special Issue: Your Child,* 25–30.

Behrend, D. A. (1988). Overextensions in early language comprehension: Evidence from a signal detection approach. *Journal of Child Language, 15,* 63–75.

Beilin, H. (1996). Mind and meaning: Piaget and Vygotsky on causal explanation. *Human Development, 39,* 277–286.

Beilin, H., & Pufall, P. (Eds.). (1992). *Piaget's theory: Prospects and possibilities.* Hillsdale, NJ: Erlbaum.

Belkin, L. (1985, May 23). Parents weigh costs of children. *The New York Times,* p. A14.

Belkin, L. (1997, October 26). Pregnant with complications. *The New York Times Magazine,* pp. 54–68.

Belkin, L. (1999, July 25). Getting the girl. *The New York Times Magazine,* 26–35.

Bell, A., & Weinberg, M. S. (1978). *Homosexuality: A study of diversities among men and women.* New York: Simon & Schuster.

Bell, I. P. (1989). The double standard: Age. In J. Freeman (Ed.), *Women: A feminist perspective* (4th ed.). Mountain View, CA: Mayfield.

Bell, J. Z. (1978). Disengagement versus engagement—A need for greater expectation. *Journal of American Geriatric Sociology, 26,* 89–95.

Bell, S. M., & Ainsworth, M. D. S. (1972). Infant crying and maternal responsiveness. *Child Development, 43,* 1171–1190.

Belle, D. (1999). *The after-school lives of children: Alone and with others while parents work.* Mahwah, NJ: Erlbaum.

Bellezza, F. S., Six, L. S., & Phillips, D. S. (1992). A mnemonic for remembering long strings of digits. *Bulletin of the Psychonomic Society, 30,* 271–274.

Belluck, P. (2000, October 18). New advice for parents: Saying 'That's great!' may not be. *The New York Times,* p. A14.

Belmont, J. M. (1995). Discussion: A view from the empiricist's window. Special Issue: Lev S. Vygotsky and contemporary educational psychology. *Educational Psychologist, 30,* 99–102.

Belsky, J., & Rovine, M. (1988). Nonmaternal care in the first year of life and infant-parent attachment security. *Child Development, 59,* 157–167.

Belsky, J., Fish, M., & Isabella, R. (1991). Continuity and discontinuity in infant negative and positive emotionality: Family antecedents and attachment consequences. *Developmental Psychology, 27,* 421–431.

Belsky, J., Rovine, M., & Taylor, D. G. (1984). The Pennsylvania infant and family development project, III: The origins of individual differences in infant–mother attachment: Maternal and infant contributions. *Child Development, 55,* 718–728.

Belsky, J., Steinberg, L., & Walker, A. (1982). The ecology of day care: A critical review. *Child Development, 49,* 929–949.

Bem, S. (1987). Gender schema theory and its implications for child development: Raising gender-aschematic children in a gender-schematic society. In M. R. Walsh (Ed.), *The psychology of women: Ongoing debates.* New Haven, CT: Yale University Press.

Benbow, C. P., Lubinski, D., & Hyde, J. S. (1997). Mathematics: Is biology the cause of gender differences in performance? In M. R. Walsh (Ed.), *Women*

men & gender: Ongoing debates (pp. 271–287). New Haven, CT: Yale University Press.

Bendersky, M., & Lewis, M. (1998). Arousal modulation in cocaine-exposed infants. *Developmental Psychology, 34,* 555–564.

Benedict, H. (1979). Early lexical development: Comprehension and production. *Journal of Child Language, 6,* 183–200.

Benenson, J. F. (1994). Ages four to six years: Changes in the structures of play networks of boys and girls. *Merrill-Palmer Quarterly, 40,* 478–487.

Benenson, J. F., & Apostoleris, N. H. (1993, March). Gender differences in group interaction in early childhood. Paper presented at the biennial meeting of the Society for Research in Child Development, New Orleans.

Bengtson, V. L., & Schaie, K. W. (Eds.). (1999). *Handbook of theories of aging.* New York: Springer.

Bengston, V. L., Cutler, N. E., Mangen, D. J., & Marshall, V. W. (1985). Generations, cohorts, and relations between age groups. In R. H. Binstock & E. Shanas (Eds.), *Handbook of aging and the social sciences* (2nd ed.). New York: Van Nostrand Reinhold.

Bengston, V. L., Rosenthal, C., & Burton, L. (1990). Families and aging: Diversity and heterogeneity. In R. H. Binstock & L. K. George (Eds.), *Handbook of aging and the social sciences* (3rd ed.). San Diego, CA: Academic Press.

Bennett, A. (1992, October 14). Lori Schiller emerges from the torments of schizophrenia. *The Wall Street Journal,* pp. A1, A10.

Ben-Porath, Y. (1991). Economic implications of human lifespan extension. In F. C. Ludwig (Ed.), *Lifespan extension: Consequences and open questions.* New York: Springer

Benson, H. (1993). The relaxation response. In D. Goleman & J. Guerin (Eds.), *Mind-body medicine: How to use your mind for better health.* Yonkers, NY: Consumer Reports Publications.

Berenbaum, S. A., & Hines, M. (1992). Early androgens are related to sex-typed toy preferences. *Psychological Science, 3,* 202–206.

Berenbaum, S. A., & Snyder, E. (1995). Early hormonal influences on childhood sex-typed activity and playmate preferences: Implications for the development of sexual orientation. Special Issue: Sexual orientation and human development. *Developmental Psychology, 31,* 31–42.

Bergeman, C., Chipuer, H., Plomin, R., Pedersen, N., McClearn, G., Nesselroade, J., Costa, P., & McCrae, R. (1993). Genetic and environmental effects on openness to experience, agreeableness, and conscientiousness: An adoption/twin study. *Journal of Personality, 61,* 159–179.

Berger, L. (2000, April 11). What children do when home and alone. *New York Times,* F8.

Bergstrom, M. J., & Holmes, M. E. (2000). Lay theories of successful aging after the death of a spouse: A network text analysis of bereavement advice. *Health Communication, 12,* 377–406.

Berigan, T. R., & Deagle, E. A., III. (1999). Treatment of smokeless tobacco addiction with bupropion and behavior modification. *Jama: Journal of the American Medical Association, 281,* 233.

Berkowitz, L. (1993). *Aggression: Its causes, consequences, and control.* New York: McGraw-Hill.

Berman, A. L., & Jobes, D. A. (1991). *Adolescent suicide: Assessment and intervention.* Washington, DC: American Psychological Association.

Bernal, M. E. (1994, August). *Ethnic identity of Mexican-American children.* Address at the annual meeting of the American Psychological Association, Los Angeles, CA.

Bernard, J. (1982). *The future of marriage.* New Haven, CT: Yale University Press.

Berndt, T. J. (1999). Friends' influence on students' adjustment to school. *Educational Psychologist, 34,* 15–28.

Berry, J. W., Poortinga, Y. H., Segall, M. H., & Dasen, P. (1992). *Cross-cultural psychology: Research and application.* New York: Cambridge University Press.

Berscheid, E. (1985). Interpersonal attraction. In G. Lindzey & E. Aronson (Eds.), *Handbook of social psychology* (3rd ed.). New York: Random House.

Berscheid, E., & Walster, E. (1974). Physical attractiveness. In G. Lindzey & E. Aronson (Eds.), *Handbook of social psychology* (3rd ed.). New York: Random House.

Berscheid, E., & Walster, E. (1974b). Physical attractiveness. In L. Berkowitz (Ed.), *Advances in experimental social psychology* (Vol. 7, pp. 157–215). New York: Academic Press.

Berscheid, E., Walster, E., & Bohrnstedt, G. (1973). The happy American body: A survey report. *Psychology Today, 7(6),* 119–131.

Bersoff, D. M. N., & Ogden, D. W. (1991). APA Amicus Curiae briefs: Furthering lesbian and gay male civil rights. *American Psychologist, 46,* 950–956.

Berthier, N. E. (1996). Learning to reach: A mathematical model. *Developmental Psychology, 32,* 811–823.

Bertram, L., Blacker, D., Mullin, K., Keeney, D., Jones, J., Basu, S., Yhu, S., McInnis, M. G., Go, R. C. P., Vekrellis, K., Selkoe, D. J., Saunders, A. J., & Tanzi, R. E. (2000, December 23). Evidence for genetic linkage of Alzheimer's disease to chromosome 10q. *Science, 290,* 2302–2303.

Besseghini, V. H. (1997). Depression and suicide in children and adolescents. In G. Creastas, G. Mastorakos, & G. P. Choursos (Eds.), *Adolescent gynecology and endocrinology. Basic and clinical aspects* (pp. 94–98). New York: New York Academy of Sciences.

Best, C. T. (1994). The emergence of native-language phonological influences in infants: A perceptual assimilation model. In J. C. Goodman & H. C. Nusbaum (Eds.), *The development of speech perception: The transition from speech sounds to spoken words.* Cambridge, MA: MIT Press.

Betancourt, H., & Lopez, S. R. (1993). The study of culture, ethnicity, and race in American Psychology. *American Psychologist, 48,* 1586–1596.

Bianchi, S. M., & Casper, L. M. (2000). American Families. *Population Bulletin, 55,* No. 4.

Bianchi, S. M., & Spain, D. (1986). *American women in transition.* New York: Russell Sage Foundation.

Bickham, D. S., Wright, J. C., & Huston, A. C. (2000). Attention, comprehension and the educational influences of television. In D. G. Singer & J. L. Singer (Eds.). *Handbook of children and the media.* Thousand Oaks, CA: Sage.

Biedenharn, B. J., & Normoyle, J. B. (1991). Elderly community residents' reactions to the nursing home: An analysis of nursing home-related beliefs. *Gerontologist, 31,* 107–115.

Bierman, K. L., & Furman, W. (1984). The effects of social skills training and peer involvement on the social adjustment of preadolescents. *Child Development, 55,* 151–162.

Biernat, M., & Wortman, C. B. (1991). Sharing of home responsibilities between professionally employed women and their husbands. *Journal of Personality and Social Psychology, 60,* 844–860.

Bigler, R. S., Jones, L. C., & Lobliner, D. B. (1997). Social categorization and the formation of intergroup attitudes in children. *Child Development, 68,* 530–543.

Bijeljac-Babic, R., Bertoncini, J., & Mehler, J. (1993). How do 4-day-old infants categorize multisyllabic utterances? *Developmental Psychology, 29,* 711–721.

Bing, E. D. (1983). *Dear Elizabeth Bing: We've had our baby.* New York: Pocket Books.

Birch, E. E., Garfield, S., Hoffman, D. R., Uauy, R., & Birch, D. G. (2000). A randomized controlled trail of early dietary supply of long-chain polyunsaturated fatty acids and mental development in term infants. *Developmental Medicine and Child Neurology, 42,* 174–181.

Bird, G., & Melville, K. (1994). *Families and intimate relationships.* New York: McGraw-Hill.

Birren, J. E., Woods, A. M., & Williams, M. V. (1980). Behavioral slowing with age: Causes, organization and consequences. In L. W. Poon (Ed.), *Aging in the 1980s.* Washington, DC: American Psychological Association.

Birsner, P. (1991). *Mid-career job hunting.* New York: Simon & Schuster.

Bjorklund, D. F. (1997a). In search of a metatheory of cognitive development (or Piaget is dead and I don't feel so good myself). *Child Development, 68,* 144–148.

Bjorklund, D. F. (1997b). The role of immaturity in human development. *Psychological Bulletin, 122,* 153–169.

Bjorklund, D. F., & Pellegrini, A. D. (2000). Child development and evolutionary psychology. *Child Development, 71,* 1687–1708.

Bjorklund, D. F., Schneider, W., Cassel, W. S., & Ashley, E. (1994). Training and extension of a memory strategy: Evidence of utilization deficiencies in the acquisition of an organizational strategy in high- and low-IQ children. *Child Development, 65,* 951–965.

Black, J. E., & Greenough, W. T. (1986). Induction of pattern in neural structure by experience: Implication for cognitive development. In M. E. Lamb, A. L. Brown, & B. Rogoff (Eds.), *Advances in developmental psychology* (Vol. 4). Hillsdale, NJ: Erlbaum.

Black, M. M., & Matula, K. (1999). *Essentials of Bayley Scales of infant development II assessment.* New York: Wiley.

Blair, S. N., Kohl, H. W., Paffenberger, R. S., Clark, D. G., Cooper, K. H., & Gibbons, L. W. (1989). Physical fitness and all-cause mortality: A prospective study of healthy men and women. *Journal of the American Medical Association, 262,* 2395–2401.

Blake, J., & de Boysson-Bardies, B. (1992). Patterns in babbling: A cross-linguistic study. *Journal of Child Language, 19,* 51–74.

Blakeslee, S. (1995, August 29). In brain's early growth, timetable may be crucial. *The New York Times,* pp. C1, C3.

Blank, M., & White, S. J. (1999). Activating the zone of proximal development in school: Obstacles and solutions. In P. Llyod, & C. Fernyhough (Eds.), *Lev Vygotsky: Critical assessments: The zone of proximal development, Vol. III.* New York: Routledge.

Blasko, D. G., Kazmerski, V. A., Corty, E. W., & Kallgren, C. A. (1998). Courseware for observational research (COR): A new approach to teaching naturalistic observation. *Behavior Research Methods, Instruments, & Computers, 30,* 217–222.

Blascovich, J. J., & Katkin, E. S. (Eds.). (1993). *Cardiovascular reactivity to psychological stress and disease.* Washington, DC: American Psychological Association.

Blass, E. M., Ganchrow, J. R., & Steiner, J. E. (1984). Classical conditioning in newborn humans 2–48 hours of age. *Infant Behavior and Development, 7,* 223–235.

Blau, Z. S. (1973). *Old age in a changing society.* New York: New Viewpoints.

Blazer, D. (1991). Suicide risk factors in the elderly: An epidemiological study. *Journal of Geriatric Psychiatry, 24,* 175–190.

Bloch, H. (1989). On early coordinations of children and their future. In A. de Ribaupierre (Ed.), *Transition mechanisms in child development: The longitudinal perspective* (pp. 259–282). New York: Cambridge University Press.

Bloom, L. (1993). *The transition from infancy to language: Acquiring the power of expression.* New York: Cambridge University Press.

Blount, B. G. (1982). Culture and the language of socialization: Parental speech. In D. A. Wagner & H. W. Stevenson (Eds.), *Cultural perspectives on child development.* San Francisco: Freeman.

Bluebond-Langner, M. (1977). Meanings of death to children. In H. Feifel (Ed.), *New meanings of death.* New York: McGraw-Hill.

Blumberg, B. D., Lewis, M. J., & Susman, E. J. (1984). Adolescence: A time of transition. In M. G. Eisenberg, L. C. Sutkin, & M. A. Jansen (Eds.), *Chronic illness and disability through the life span: Effects on self and family.* New York: Springer.

Blumenfield, M., Levy, N. B., & Kaplan, D. (1979). The wish to be informed of a fatal illness. *Omega, 9,* 323–326.

Blumenthal, S. (2000). Developmental aspects of violence and the institutional response. *Criminal Behaviour & Mental Health, 10,* 185–198.

Blumstein, P., & Schwartz, P. (1989). *American couples: Money, work, sex.* New York: Morrow.

Blustein, D. L, & Palladino, D. E. (1991). Self and identity in late adolescence: A theoretical and empirical integration. *Journal of Adolescent Research, 6,* 437–453.

Boath, E. H., Pryce, A. J., & Cox, J. L. (1998). Postnatal depression: The impact on the family. *Journal of Reproductive & Infant Psychology, 16,* 199–203.

Bochner, S. (1996). The learning strategies of bilingual versus monolingual students. *British Journal of Educational Psychology, 66,* 83–93.

Bodnar, A. G., Ouellette, M., Frolkis, M., Holt, S. E., Chiu, C-P., Morin, G. B., Harley, C. B., Shay, J. W., Lichtsteiner, S., & Wright, W. E. (1998, January 16). Extension of life-span by introduction of telomerase into normal human cells. *Science, 279,* 349–352.

Bogatz, G. A., & Ball, S. (1972). *The second year of Sesame Street: A continuing evaluation.* Princeton, NJ: Educational Testing Service.

Bogenschneider, K., Wu, M-Y., Raffaelli, M., & Tsay, J. C. (1998). Parent influences on adolescent peer orientation and substance use: The interface of parenting practices and values. *Child Development, 69,* 1672–1688.

Boismier, J. D. (1977). Visual stimulation and wake-sleep behavior in human neonates. *Developmental Psychology, 10,* 219–227.

Bolger, N., Foster, M., Vinokur, A. D., & Ng, R. (1996). Close relationships and adjustments to a life crisis: The case of breast cancer. *Journal of Personality and Social Psychology, 70,* 283–294.

Bookheimer, S. Y., Strojwas, M. H., Cophen, M. S., Saunders, A. M., Pericak-Vance, M. A., Mazziotta, J. C., & Small, G. W. (2000, August 17). Patterns of brain activation in people at risk for Alzheimer's disease. *New England Journal of Medicine, 343,* 450–456.

Bookstein, F. L., Sampson, P. D., Streissguth, A. P., Barr, H. M. (1996). Exploiting redundant measurement of dose and developmental outcome: New methods from the behavioral teratology of alcohol. *Developmental Psychology, 32,* 404–415.

Booth, A., & Edwards, J. N. (1989). Transmission of marital and family quality over the generations: The effect of parental divorce and unhappiness. *Journal of Divorce, 13,* 41–58.

Booth, W. (1987, October 2). Big Brother is counting your keystrokes. *Science, 238,* 17.

Borden, M. E. (1998). *Smart start: The parents' complete guide to preschool education.* New York: Facts on File.

Borgatta, E. F. (1991). Age discrimination issues. *Research on Aging, 13,* 476–484.

Bornstein, M. H. (1989a). Sensitive periods in development: Structural characteristics and causal interpretations. *Psychological Bulletin, 105,* 179–197.

Bornstein, M. H., & Lamb, M. E. (1992a). *Development in infancy: An introduction.* New York: McGraw-Hill.

Bornstein, M. H., & Sigman, M. D. (1986). Continuity in mental development from infancy. *Child Development, 57,* 251–274.

Bornstein, M. H., & Tamis-LeMonda, C. S. (1989). Maternal responsiveness and cognitive development in children. In M. H. Bornstein (Ed.), *Maternal responsiveness: Characteristics and consequences* (pp. 49–61). San Francisco: Jossey-Bass.

Bornstein, M. H., Haynes, O. M., O'Reilly, A. W., & Painter, K. M. (1996). Solitary and collaborative pretense play in early childhood: Sources of individual variation in the development of representational competence. *Child Development, 67,* 2910–2929.

Boruch, R. F. (1998). Randomized controlled experiments for evaluation and planning. In L. Bickman & D. J. Rog (Eds.), *Handbook of applied social research methods* (pp. 161–191). Thousand Oaks, CA: Sage.

Bosworth, K., Espelage, D. L., & Simon, T. R. (1999). Factors associated with bullying behavior in middle school students. *Journal of Early Adolescence, 19,* 341–362.

Botvin, G. J., Epstein, J. A., Schinke, S. P., & Diaz, T. (1994). Predictors of cigarette smoking among inner-city minority youth. *Journal of Developmental and Behavioral Pediatrics, 15,* 67–73.

Bouchard, C., Tremblay, A. Despres, J. P., Nadeau, A., et al. (1990, May 24). The response to long-term overfeeding in identical twins. *New England Journal of Medicine, 322,* 1477–1482.

Bouchard, T. J., Jr. (1994, June 17). Genes, environment, and personality. *Science, 264,* 1700–1701.

Bouchard, T. J., Jr. (1997, September/October). Whenever the twain shall meet. *The Sciences,* pp. 52–57.

Bouchard, T. J., Jr., & Pedersen, N. (1999). Twins reared apart: Nature's double experiment. In M. C. LaBuda, E. L. Grigorenko, et al. (Eds.), *On the way to individuality: Current methodological issues in behavioral genetics.* Commack, NY: Nova.

Bouchard, T. J., Jr., Lykken, D. T., McGue, M., Segal, N. L., & Tellegen, A. (1990, October 12). Sources of human psychological differences: The Minnesota Study of twins reared apart. *Science, 250,* 223–228.

Boulton, M. J. (1999). Concurrent and longitudinal relations between children's playground behavior and social preference, victimization, and bullying. *Child Development, 70,* 944–954.

Boulton, M. J., & Smith, P. K. (1990). Affective bias in children's perceptions of dominance relationships. *Child Development, 61,* 221–229.

Bowen, D. J., Kahl, K., Mann, S. L., & Peterson, A. V. (1991). Descriptions of early triers. *Addictive Behaviors, 16,* 95–101.

Bowen, N. K., & Bowen, G. L. (1999). Effects of crime and violence in neighborhoods and schools on the school behavior and performance of adolescents. *Journal of Adolescent Research, 14,* 319–342.

Bower, B. (1985). The left hand of math and verbal talent. *Science News, 127,* 263.

Bower, T. G. R. (1977). *A primer of infant development.* San Francisco: Freeman.

Bowers, K. E., & Thomas, P. (1995, August). Handle with care. *Harvard Health Letter,* pp. 6–7.

Bowlby, J. (1951). Maternal care and mental health. *Bulletin of the World Health Organization, 3,* 355–534.

Boyd, G. M., Howard, J., & Zucker, R. A. (Eds.) (1995). *Alcohol problems among adolescents: Current directions in prevention research.* Hillsdale, NJ: Erlbaum.

Boylan, P. (1990). Induction of labor, complications of labor, and postmaturity. *Current Opinion in Obstetrics & Gynecology, 2,* 31–35.

Boysson-Bardies, B. de, & Vihman, M. M. (1991). Adaptation to language: Evidence from babbling and first words in four languages. *Language, 67,* 297–307.

Boysson-Bardies, B. de, Sagart, L., & Durand, C. (1984). Discernible differences in the babbling of infants according to target language. *Journal of Child Language, 11,* 1–15.

Brackbill, Y. (1979). Obstetrical medication and infant behavior. In J. D. Osofsky (Ed.), *Handbook of infant development.* New York: Wiley.

Braddock, O. (1993). Orientation- and motion-selective mechanisms in infants. In K. Simons (Ed.), *Early visual development: Normal and abnormal* (pp. 163–177). New York: Oxford University Press.

Bradley, C. L. (1997). Generativity-stagnation: Development of a status model. *Developmental Review, 17,* 262–290.

Bradley, R. H., & Caldwell, B. M. (1995). Caregiving and the regulation of child growth and development: Describing proximal aspects of caregiving systems. *Developmental Review, 15,* 38–85.

Bradley, R. H., Whiteside, L., Mundfrom, D. J., Casey, P. H., Kelleher, K. J., & Pope, S. K. (1994). Early indications of resilience and their relation to experiences in the home environments of low birthweight, premature children living in poverty. *Child Development, 65,* 346–360.

Brady, L. S. (1995, January 29). Asia Linn and Chris Applebaum. *The New York Times,* p. 47.

Brainerd, C. J., Reyna, V. F., & Brandse, E. (1995). Are children's false memories more persistent than their true memories? *Psychological Science, 6,* 359–364.

Braza, F., Braza, P., Carreras, M. R., & Muñoz, J. M. (1997). Development of sex differences in preschool children: Social behavior during an academic year. *Psychological Reports, 80,* 179–188.

Brazelton, T. B. (1969). *Infants and mothers: Differences in development.* (Rev. ed.) New York: Dell.

Brazelton, T. B. (1973). *The Neonatal Behavioral Assessment Scale.* Philadelphia: Lippincott.

Brazelton, T. B. (1983). *Infants and mothers: Differences in development* (Rev. ed.). New York: Dell.

Brazelton, T. B. (1990). Saving the bathwater. *Child Development, 61,* 1661–1671.

Brazelton, T. B. (1991). Discussion: Cultural attitudes and actions. In M. H. Bornstein (Ed.), *Cultural approaches to parenting.* Hillsdale, NJ: Erlbaum.

Brazelton, T. B., Christophersen, E. R., Frauman, A. C., Gorski, P. A., Poole, J. M., Stadtler, A. C. & Wright, C. L. (1999). Instruction, Timeliness, and Medical Influences Affecting Toilet Training. *Pediatrics, 103,* 1353–1358.

Brazelton, T. B., Nugent, J. K., & Lester, B. M. (1987). Neonatal Behavioral Assessment Scale. In J. D. Osofsky (Ed.), *Handbook of infant development* (2nd ed.) New York: Wiley.

Brecher, E. M., and the Editors of Consumer Reports Books. (1984). *Love, sex, and aging.* Mount Vernon, New York: Consumers Union.

Bredekamp, S. (Ed.). (1989). *Developmentally appropriate practice in early childhood programs serving children from birth through age 8.* Washington, DC: National Association for the Education of Young Children.

Brehm, S. S. (1992). *Intimate relationships* (2nd ed.). New York: McGraw-Hill.

Brennan, K. A., & Shaver, P. R. (1995). Dimensions of adult attachment, affect regulation, and romantic relationship functioning. *Personality and Social Psychology Bulletin, 21,* 267–283.

Brent, D. A., Perper, J. A., Moritz, G., & Liotus, L. (1994). Familial risk factors for adolescent suicide: A case-control study. *Acta Psychiatrica Scandinavica, 89,* 52–58.

Brescia, F. J., Sadof, M., & Barstow, J. (1984). Retrospective analysis of a home care hospice program. *Omega, 15,* 37–44.

Bridges, J. S. (1993). Pink or blue: Gender-stereotypic perceptions of infants as conveyed by birth congratulations cards. *Psychology of Women Quarterly, 17,* 193–205.

Briere, J. N., Berliner, L., Bulkley, J., Jenny, C., & Reid, T. (Eds.). (1996). *The APSAC handbook on child maltreatment.* Thousand Oaks, CA: Sage.

Brislin, R. (1993). *Understanding culture's influence on behavior.* Fort Worth, TX: Harcourt Brace Jovanovich.

Brock, A. M. (1991). Economics of aging. In E. M. Baines (Ed.), *Perspectives on gerontological nursing.* Newbury Park, CA: Sage.

Brockington, I. F. (1992). Disorders specific to the puerperium. *International Journal of Mental Health, 21,* 41–52.

Brody, J. (1994a, February 2). Fitness and the fetus: A turnabout in advice. *The New York Times,* p. C13.

Brody, J. E. (1994c, April 20). Making a strong case for antioxidants. *The New York Times,* p. B9.

Brody, J. E., & Benbow, C. P. (1987). Accelerative strategies: How effective are they for the gifted? *Gifted Child Quarterly, 3,* 105–110.

Brody, N. (1993). Intelligence and the behavioral genetics of personality. In R. Plomin & G. E. McClearn (Eds.), *Nature, nurture, and psychology.* Washington, DC: American Psychological Association.

Bromberger, J. T., & Matthews, K. A. (1994). Employment status and depressive symptoms in middle-aged women: A longitudinal investigation. *American Journal of Public Health, 84,* 202–206.

Bronfenbrenner, U. (1979). *The ecology of human development.* Cambridge, MA: Harvard University Press.

Bronfenbrenner, U. (1989). Ecological systems theory. In R. Vasta (Ed.), *Six theories of child development.* Greenwich, CT: JAI Press.

Brook, U., & Tepper, I. (1997). High school students' attitudes and knowledge of food consumption and body image: Implications for school-based education. *Patient Education & Counseling, 30,* 282–288.

Brooks, J., & Lewis, M. (1976). Infants' responses to strangers: Midget, adult, and child. *Child Development, 47,* 323–332.

Brooks-Gunn, J., & Matthews, W. S. (1979). *He and she: How children develop their sex role identity.* Englewood Cliffs, NJ: Prentice-Hall.

Brooks-Gunn, J., & Reiter, E. (1990). The role of pubertal processes. In S. Feldman & G. Elliott (Eds.), *At the threshold: The developing adolescent.* Cambridge, MA: Harvard University Press.

Brooks-Gunn, J., Klebanov, P. K., & Duncan, G. J. (1996). Ethnic differences in children's intelligence test scores: Role of economic deprivation, home environment, and maternal characteristics. *Child Development, 67,* 396–408.

Brooks-Gunn, J., Petersen, A. C., & Compas, B. E. (1994). What role does biology play in childhood and adolescent depression? In I. M. Goodyear (Ed.), *Mood disorders in childhood and adolescence.* New York: Cambridge University Press.

Brown, A. L., & Ferrara, R. A. (1999). Diagnosing zones of proximal development. In P. Llyod, & C. Fernyhough (Eds.), *Lev Vygotsky: Critical assessments: The zone of proximal development, Vol. III.* New York: Routledge.

Brown, B. (1990). Peer groups. In S. Feldman & G. Elliott (Eds.), *At the threshold: The developing adolescent.* Cambridge, MA: Harvard University Press.

Brown, J. D. (1991). Staying fit and staying well: Physical fitness as a moderator of life stress. *Journal of Personality and Social Psychology, 60,* 368–375.

Brown, J. D. (1998). *The self.* New York, McGraw-Hill.

Brown, J. D., & McGill, K. L. (1989). The cost of good fortune: When positive life events produce negative health consequences. *Journal of Personality and Social Psychology, 57,* 1103–1110.

Brown, J. L. (1987). Hunger in the U.S. *Scientific American, 256(2),* 37–41.

Brown, J. L., & Pollitt, E. (1996, February). Malnutrition, poverty and intellectual development. *Scientific American,* 38–43.

Brown, R. (1973). *A first language.* Cambridge, MA: Harvard University Press.

Brown v. Board of Education of Topeka (1954). U.S. Supreme Court. Washington, DC.

Browne, A. (1993). Violence against women by male partners: Prevalence, outcomes, and policy implications. *American Psychologist, 48,* 1077–1087.

Browne, B. A. (1998). Gender stereotypes in advertising on children's television in the 1990s: A cross-national analysis. *Journal of Advertising, 27,* 83–96.

Brownell, C. (1986). Convergent developments: Cognitive-developmental correlates of growth in infant/toddler peer skills. *Child Development, 57,* 275–286.

Brownell, K. D., & Rodin, J. (1994). The dieting maelstrom: Is it possible and advisable to lose weight? *American Psychologist, 49,* 781–791.

Brownlee, S., Cook, G. G., & Hardigg, V. (1994, August 22). Tinkering with destiny. *U.S. News and World Report, 117,* 58–65+.

Brubaker, T. (1991). Families in later life: A burgeoning research area. In A. Booth (Ed.), *Contemporary families.* Minneapolis, MN: National Council on Family Relations.

Bruce, M. L., & Hoff, R. A. (1994). Social and physical health risk factors for first-onset major depressive disorder in a community sample. *Social Psychiatry and Psychiatric Epidemiology, 29,* 165–171.

Bruck, M., & Ceci, S. J. (1999). The suggestibility of children's memory. *Annual Review of Psychology, 50,* 419–439.

Bruck, M., Ceci, S. J., & Francoeur, E. (2000). Children's use of anatomically detailed dolls to report genital touching in a medical examination: Developmental and gender comparisons. *Journal of Experimental Psychology: Applied, 6,* 74–83.

Bruck, M., Ceci, S. J., & Hembrooke, H. (1998). Reliability and credibility of young children's reports: From research to policy and practice. *American Psychologist, 53,* 136–151.

Bruck, M., Ceci, S. J., Francouer, E., & Renick, A. (1995). Anatomically detailed dolls do not facilitate preschoolers' reports of a pediatric examination involving genital touching. *Journal of Experimental Psychology: Applied, 1,* 95–109.

Buchanan, C. M., Eccles, J. S., & Becker, J. B. (1992). Are adolescents the victims of raging hormones? Evidence for activational effects of hormones on moods and behavior at adolescence. *Psychological Bulletin, 111,* 62–107.

Buchanan, C. M., Maccoby, E. E., & Dornbusch, S. M. (1996). *Adolescents after divorce.* Cambridge, MA: Harvard University Press.

Budd, K. (1999). The facts of life: everything you wanted to know about sex (after 50). *Modern Maturity, 42,* 78.

Budris, J. (1998, April 26). Raising their children's children. *Boston Globe 55–Plus,* pp. 8–9, 14–15.

Bukowski, W. M., Sippola, L. K., & Newcomb, A. F. (2000). Variations in patterns of attraction to same- and other-sex peers during early adolescence. *Developmental Psychology, 36,* 147–154.

Bullinger, A. (1997). Sensorimotor function and its evolution. In J. Guimon (Ed.), *The body in psychotherapy* (pp. 25–29). Basil, Switzerland: Karger.

Bullock, J. (1988). Altering aggression in young children. *Early Childhood Education, 15,* 24–27.

Bullock, M. (1995, July/August). What's so special about a longitudinal study? *Psychological Science Agenda,* 9–10.

Bumpass, L., Sweet, J., & Martin, T. (1990). Changing patterns of remarriage. *Journal of Marriage and the Family, 52,* 747–756.

Burbules, N. C., & Linn, M. C. (1988). Response to contradiction: Scientific reasoning during adolescence. *Journal of Educational Psychology, 80,* 67–75.

Burgess, R. L., & Huston, T. L. (Eds.). (1979). *Social exchanges in developing relationships.* New York: Academic Press.

Burkhauser, R. V., Holden, K. C., & Feaster, D. (1988). Incidence, timing, and events associated with poverty: A dynamic view of poverty in retirement. *Journal of Gerontology, 43(2),* S46–52.

Burnett, P. C. (1996). Gender and grade differences in elementary school children's descriptive and evaluative self-statements and self-esteem. *School Psychology International, 17,* 159–170.

Burns, D. M. (2000). Cigarette smoking among the elderly: Disease consequences and the benefits of cessation. *American Journal of Health Promotion, 14,* 357–361.

Burrus-Bammel, L. L., & Bammel, G. (1985). Leisure and recreation. In J. E. Birren & K. W. Schaie (Eds.), *Handbook of the psychology of aging.* New York: Van Nostrand Reinhold.

Burt, V. L., & Harris, T. (1994). The third National Health and Nutrition Examination Survey: Contributing data on aging and health. *Gerontologist, 34,* 486–490.

Bushman, B. J. (1993). Human aggression while under the influence of alcohol and other drugs: An integrative research review. *Current Directions in Psychological Science, 2,* 148–152.

Bushman, B. J., & Geen, R. G. (1990). Role of cognitive-emotional mediators and individual differences in the effects of media violence on aggression. *Journal of Personality and Social Psychology, 58,* 156–163.

Bushnell, I. W. R. (1998). The origins of face perception. In F. Simion & G. Butterworth (Eds.), *The development of sensory, motor and cognitive capacities in early infancy: From perception to cognition.* Hove, England: Psychology Press/Erlbaum (UK) Taylor & Francis.

Buss, A. H., & Plomin, R. (1984). *Temperament: Early developing personality traits.* Hillsdale, NJ: Erlbaum.

Buss, D. M., et al. (1990). International preferences in selecting mates: A study of 37 cultures. *Journal of Cross-Cultural Psychology, 21,* 5–47.

Bussey, K. (1992). Lying and truthfulness: Children's definition, standards, and evaluative reactions. *Child Development, 63,* 1236–1250.

Bussey, K., & Bandura, A. (1992). Self-regulatory mechanisms governing gender development. *Child Development, 63,* 1236–1250.

Butler, R. N. (1968). The life review: An interpretation of reminiscence in the aged. In B. Neugarten (Ed.), *Middle age and aging.* Chicago: University of Chicago Press.

Butler, R. N. (1990). The contributions of late-life creativity to society. *Gerontology and Geriatrics Education, 11,* 45–51.

Butler, R. N., & Lewis, M. I. (1981). *Aging and mental health.* St. Louis: Mosby.

Butterfield, E., & Siperstein, G. (1972). Influence of contingent auditory stimulation upon non-nutritional suckle. In J. Bosma (Ed.), *Oral sensation and perception: The mouth of the infant.* Springfield, IL: Charles C Thomas.

Butterworth, G. (1994). Infant intelligence. In J. Khalfa (Ed.), *What is intelligence? The Darwin College lecture series* (pp. 49–71). Cambridge, England: Cambridge University Press.

Button, E. (1993). *Eating disorders: Personal construct theory and change.* New York: Wiley.

Buunk, B. P., & Janssen, P. P. (1992). Relative deprivation, career issues, and mental health among men in midlife. *Journal of Vocational Behavior, 40,* 338–350.

Byard, R., & Krous, H. (1999). Suffocation, shaking or sudden infant death syndrome: can we tell the difference? *Journal of Paediatrics & Child Health, 35(5),* 432–433.

Byne, W., & Parsons, B. (1994, February). Biology and human sexual orientation. *Harvard Mental Health Letter, 10,* 5–7.

Byrd, R. S., Weitzman, M., & Auinger, P. (1997). Increased behavior problems associated with delayed school entry and delayed school progress. *Pediatrics, 100,* 654–661.

Byrne, B. (2000). Relationships between anxiety, fear, self-esteem, and coping strategies in adolescence. *Adolescence, 35,* 201–215.

Cadinu, M. R., & Kiesner, J. (2000). Children's development of a theory of mind. *European Journal of Psychology of Education, 15,* 93–111.

Cain, B. S. (1982, December 19). Plight of the gray divorcee. *The New York Times Magazine,* pp. 89–93.

Caldas, S. J., & Bankston, C. (1997). Effect of school population socioeconomic status on individual academic achievement. *Journal of Educational Research, 90,* 269–277.

Caldera, Y. M., & Sciaraffa, M. A. (1998). Parent-toddler play with feminine toys: Are all dolls the same? *Sex Roles, 39,* 657–668.

Campbell, F. A., Pungello, E. P., Miller-Johnson, S., Ramey, C. T., & Burchinal, M. (2001). The development of cognitive and academic abilities: Growth curves from an early childhood educational experiment. *Developmental Psychology, 37,* 231–242.

Campbell, J., Poland, M., Waller, J., & Ager, J. (1992). Correlates of battering during pregnancy. *Research in Nursing and Health, 15,* 219–226.

Campos, J. J., Langer, A., & Krowitz, A. (1970). Cardiac responses on the visual cliff in prelocomotor human infants. *Science, 170,* 196–197.

Camras, L. A., & Sachs, V. B. (1991). Social referencing and caretaker expressive behavior in a day care setting. *Infant Behavior and Development, 14,* 27–36.

Camras, L. A., Malatesta, C., & Izard, C. E. (1991). The development of facial expressions in infancy. In R. S. Feldman & B. Rime (Eds.), *Fundamentals of nonverbal behavior.* Cambridge, England: Cambridge University Press.

Canedy, D. (2001, March 3). Troubling label for Hispanics: 'Girls most likely to drop out'. *The New York Times,* p. A1.

Canfield, R. L., Smith, E. G., Breznyak, M. P., & Snow, K. L. (1997). Information processing through the first year of life: A longitudinal study using the visual expectation paradigm. With commentary by Richard N. Aslin, Marshall M. Hairth, Tara S. Wass, & Scott A. Adler. *Monographs of the Society for Research in Child Development, 62,* (2 Serial No. 250).

Caplan, L. J., & Barr, R. A. (1989). On the relationship between category intensions and extensions in children. *Journal of Experimental Child Psychology, 47,* 413–429.

Cappiello, L. A., & Troyer, R. E. (1979). A study of the role of health educators in teaching about death and dying. *Journal of School Health, 49,* 397–399.

Cardon, L. R., & Fulker, D. (1993). Genetics of specific cognitive abilities. In R. Plomin & G. McClearn (Eds.), *Nature, nurture, and psychology* (pp. 99–120). Washington, DC: American Psychological Association.

Carmody, D. (1990, March 7). College drinking: Changes in attitude and habit. *The New York Times.*

Carnegie Task Force on Meeting the Needs of Young Children. (1994). *Starting points: Meeting the needs of our youngest children.* New York: Carnegie Corporation.

Carpendale, J. I. M. (2000). Kohlberg and Piaget on stages and moral reasoning. *Developmental Review, 20,* 181–205.

Carpenter, S. (2000, October). Human genome project director says psychologists will play a critical role in the initiative's success. *Monitor on Psychology,* 14–15.

Carr, C. N., Kennedy, S. R., & Dimick, K. M. (1996). Alcohol use among high school athletes. *The Prevention Researcher, 3,* 1–3.

Carr, J. (1995). *Down syndrome.* Cambridge, England: Cambridge University Press.

Carrere, S., Buehlman, K. T., Gottman, J. M., Coan, J. A., & Ruckstuhl, L. (2000). Predicting marital stability and divorce in newlywed couples. *Journal of Family Psychology, 14,* 42–58.

Carroll, D. (1985). *Living with dying.* New York: McGraw-Hill.

Carroll, L. (2000, February 1). Is memory loss inevitable? Maybe not. *The New York Times,* pp. D1, D7.

Carstensen, L. L. (1995). Evidence for a life-span theory of socioemotional selectivity. *Current Directions in Psychological Science, 4,* 151–156.

Carstensen, L. L., & Charles, S. T. (1998). Emotion in the second half of life. *Current Directions in Psychological Science, 7,* 144–149.

Carstensen, L. L., Pasupathi, M., Mayr, U., Nesselroade, J. R. (2000). Emotional experience in everyday life across the adult life span. *Journal of Personality and Social Psychology, 79,* 644–655.

Carvajal, F., & Iglesias, J. (2000). Looking behavior and smiling in Down syndrome infants. *Journal of Nonverbal Behavior, 24,* 225–236.

Carver, C. S., & Scheier, M. F. (1993). On the power of positive thinking: The benefits of being optimistic. *Current Directions in Psychological Science, 2,* 26–30.

Case, R. (1991). Stages in the development of the young child's first sense of self. *Developmental Review, 11,* 210–230.

Case, R., & Okamoto, Y. (1996). The role of central conceptual structures in the development of children's thought. *Monographs of the Society for Research in Child Development, 61,* v–265.

Caspi, A. (2000). The child is father of the man: Personality continuities from childhood to adulthood. *Journal of Personality and Social Psychology, 78,* 158–172.

Caspi, A., & Moffitt, T. E. (1991). Individual differences are accentuated during periods of social change: The sample case of girls at puberty. *Journal of Personality and Social Psychology, 61,* 157–168.

Caspi, A., & Moffitt, T. E. (1993). *Continuity amidst change: A paradoxical theory of personality coherence.* Manuscript submitted for publication.

Cassel, W. S., Roebers, C. E. M., & Bjorklund, D. F. (1996). Developmental patterns of eyewitness responses to repeated and increasingly suggestive questions. *Journal of Experimental Child Psychology, 61,* 116–133.

Cassidy, J., & Berlin, L. J. (1994). The insecure/ambivalent pattern of attachment: Theory and research. *Child Development, 65,* 971–991.

Cassidy, K. W., Chu, J. Y., & Dahlsgaard, K. K. (1997). Preschoolers' ability to adopt justice and care orientations in moral dilemmas. *Early Education & Development, 8,* 419–434.

Catell, R. B. (1967). *The scientific analysis of personality.* Chicago: Aldine.

Catell, R. B. (1987). *Intelligence: Its structure, growth, and action.* Amsterdam: North-Holland.

Cauffman, E., & Steinberg, L. (1996). Interactive effects of menarcheal status and dating on dieting and disordered eating among adolescent girls. *Developmental Psychology, 32,* 631–635.

Ceci, S. J., & Bruck, M. (1993). The suggestibility of the child witness: A historical review and synthesis. *Psychological Bulletin, 113,* 403–439.

Ceci, S. J., & Bruck, M. (1995). *Jeopardy in the courtroom.* Washington, DC: American Psychological Association.

Ceci, S. J., & Hembrooke, H. (1993). The contextual nature of earliest memories. In J. M. Puckett & H. W. Reese (Eds.), *Mechanisms of everyday cognition* (pp. 117–136). Hillsdale, NJ: Erlbaum.

Ceci, S. J,. & Huffman, M. L. C. (1997). How suggestible are preschool children? Cognitive and social factors. *Journal of the American Academy of Child & Adolescent Psychiatry, 36,* 948–958.

Center for Communication & Social Policy, University of California. (1998). *National television violence study, Vol. 2.* Thousand Oaks, CA: Sage.

Center on Addiction and Substance Abuse. (1994). *Report on college drinking.* New York: Columbia University.

Centers for Disease Control. (1991). *Preventing lead poisoning in young children: A statement by the Centers for Disease Control.* Atlanta, GA: U.S. Department of Health and Human Services.

Centers for Disease Control and Prevention. (2000). *Obesity continues to climb in 1999 among American adults.* Division of Nutrition and Physical Activity, National Center for Chronic Disease Prevention and Health Promotions. Atlanta, GA: Centers for Disease Control and Prevention.

Cerella, J. (1990). Aging and information-processing rate. In J. E. Birren & K. W. Schaie (Eds.), *Handbook of the psychology of aging* (3rd ed.). San Diego, CA: Academic Press.

CFCEPLA (Commonwealth Fund Commission on Elderly People Living Alone). (1986). *Problems facing elderly Americans living alone.* New York: Louis Harris & Associates.

Chall, J. S. (1979). The great debate: Ten years later, with a modest proposal for reading stages. In L. B. Resnick & P. A. Weaver, (Eds.), *Theory and practice of early reading.* Hillsdale, NJ: Erlbaum.

Chan, C. G., & Elder, G. H. Jr., (2000). Matrilineal advantage in grandchild-grandparent relations. *Gerontologist, 40,* 179–190.

Chan, D. W. (1997). Self-concept and global self-worth among Chinese adolescents in Hong Kong. *Personality & Individual Differences, 22,* 511–520.

Chan, W. S., Chong, K. Y., Martinovich, C., Simerly, C., & Schatten, G. (2001, January 12). Transgenic monkeys produced by retroviral gene transfer into mature oocytes *Science, 291,* 309–312.

Chao, R. (1996). Chinese and European American mothers' beliefs about the role of parenting in children's school success. *Journal of Cross-Cultural Psychology, 27,* 403–423.

Chao, R. K. (1994). Beyond parental control and authoritarian parenting style: Understanding Chinese parenting through the cultural notion of training. *Child Development, 65,* 1111–1119.

Chappell, N. L. (1991). In-group differences among elders living with friends and family other than spouses. *Journal of Aging Studies, 5,* 61–76.

Charles, S. T., Reynolds, C. A., & Gatz, M. (2001). Age-related differences and change in positive and negative affect over 23 years. *Journal of Personality and Social Psychology, 80,* 136–151.

Chen, C., & Stevenson, H. W. (1995). Motivation and mathematics achievement: A comparative study of Asian-American, Caucasian-American, and East Asian high school students. *Child Development, 66,* 1215–1234.

Chen, X., Hastings, P. D., Rubin, K. H., Chen, H., Cen, G., Stewart, S. L. (1998). Child-rearing attitudes and behavioral inhibition in Chinese and Canadian toddlers: A cross-cultural study. *Developmental Psychology, 34,* 677–686.

Chen, Z., & Siegler, R. S. (2000). Across the Great Divide: Bridging the gap between understanding of toddlers' and older children's thinking. *Monographs of the Society for Research in Child Development, 65,* 2, Serial No. 261.

Cherlin, A. (1993). *Marriage, divorce, remarriage.* Cambridge, MA: Harvard University Press.

Cherlin, A., & Furstenberg, F. (1986). *The new American grandparent.* New York: Basic Books.

Cherry, K. E., & Park, D. C. (1993). Individual difference and contextual variables influence spatial memory in younger and older adults. *Psychology and Aging, 8,* 517–526.

Cheryan, S., & Bodenhausen, G. V. (2000). When positive stereotypes threaten intellectual performance: The psychological hazards of "model minority" status. *Psychological Science, 11,* 399–402.

ChildStats.gov. (2000). *America's children 2000.* Washington, DC: National Maternal and Child Health Clearinghouse.

Chin, J. (1994). The growing impact of the HIV\AIDS pandemic on children born to HIV infected women. *Clinical Perinatalogy, 21,* 1–14.

Chira, S. (1994, July 10). Teen-agers, in a poll, report worry and distrust of adults. *The New York Times,* pp. 1, 16.

Chiriboga, D. A. (1982). Adaptation to marital separation in later and earlier life. *Journal of Gerontology, 37,* 109–114.

Chiu, C., Dweck, C. S., Yuk-yue Tong, J., & Ho-yin Fu, J. (1997). Implicit theories and conceptions of morality. *Journal of Personality and Social Psychology, 73,* 923–940.

Choi, N. G., & Mayer, J. (2000). Elder abuse, neglect, and exploitation: Risk factors and prevention strategies. *Journal of Gerontological Social Work, 33,* 5–25.

Chomsky, N. (1968). *Language and mind.* New York: Harcourt Brace Jovanovich.

Chomsky, N. (1978). On the biological basis of language capacities. In G. A. Miller & E. Lennenberg (Eds.), *Psychology and biology of language and thought* (pp. 199–220). New York: Academic Press.

Chomsky, N. (1991). Linguistics and cognitive science: Problems and mysteries. In A. Kasher (Ed.), *The Chomskyan turn.* Cambridge, MA: Blackwell.

Chomsky, N. (1999). On the nature, use, and acquisition of language. In W. C. Ritchie, T. J. Bhatia (Eds.), *Handbook of child language acquisition.* San Diego: Academic Press.

Cicchetti, D. (1996). Child maltreatment: Implications for developmental theory and research. *Human Development, 39,* 18–39.

Cicchetti, D., & Beeghly, M. (Eds.). (1990). *Children with Down syndrome.* Cambridge: Cambridge University Press.

Cicchetti, D., & Toth, S. L. (1998). The development of depression in children and adolescents. *American Psychologist, 53,* 221–241.

CIRE (Cooperative Institutional Research Program of the American Council on Education). (1990). *The American freshman: National norms for fall 1990.* Los Angeles: American Council on Edcuation.

Ciricelli, V.G. (1995). *Sibling relationships across the life span.* NY: Plenum.

Clark, E. (1983). Meanings and concepts. In J. Flavell & E. Markham (Eds.), *Handbook of child psychology: Cognitive development* (Vol. 3). New York: Wiley.

Clark, J. E., & Humphrey, J. H. (Eds.). (1985). *Motor development: Current selected research.* Princeton, NJ: Princeton Book Company.

Clark, K. B., & Clark, M. P. (1947). Racial identification and preference in Negro children. In T. M. Newcomb & E. L. Hartley (Eds.), *Readings in social psychology.* New York: Holt, Rinehart & Winston.

Clark, M. S., Mills, J. R., & Corcoran, D. M. (1989). Keeping track of needs and inputs of friends and strangers. *Personality and Social Psychology Bulletin, 15,* 533–542.

Clark, M., & Mills, J. (1993). The difference between communal and exchange relationships: What it is and is not. *Personality and Social Psychology Bulletin, 19,* 684–691.

Clark, R. (1998). *Expertise.* Silver Spring, MD: International Society for Performance Improvement.

Clark, R., Hyde, J. S., Essex, M. J., & Klein, M. H. (1997). Length of maternity leave and quality of mother-infant interactions. *Child Development, 68,* 364–383.

Clarkberg, M., Stolzenberg, R. M., & Waite, L. J. (1995). Attitudes, values, and entrance into cohabitational versus marital unions. *Social Forces, 74,* 609–632.

Clarke-Stewart, A. (1993). *Daycare.* Cambridge, MA: Harvard University Press.

Clarke-Stewart, A., & Friedman, S. (1987). *Child development: Infancy through adolescence.* New York: Wiley.

Clarke-Stewart, K. A., & Bailey, B. (1990). Adjusting to divorce: Why do men have it easier? *Journal of Divorce, 13,* 75–94.

Clemetson, L. (2000, September 18). Love without borders. *Newsweek,* 62.

Cliff, D. (1991). Negotiating a livable retirement: Further paid work and the quality of life in early retirement. *Aging and Society, 11,* 319–340.

Clifton, R. (1992). The development of spatial hearing in human infants. In L. A. Werner & E. W. Rubel (Eds.), *Developmental psychoacoustics* (pp. 135–157). Washington, DC: American Psychological Association.

Clinton, J. F., & Kelber, S. T. (1993). Stress and coping in fathers of newborns: Comparisons of planned versus unplanned pregnancy. *International Journal of Nursing Studies, 30,* 437–443.

Cnattingius, S., Berendes, H., & Forman, M. (1993). Do delayed childbearers face increased risks of adverse pregnancy outcomes after the first birth? *Obstetrics and Gynecology, 81,* 512–516.

CNN/USA Today/Gallup Poll. (1997, February). How many children? *The Gallup Poll Monthly.*

Coats, E., & Feldman, R. S. (1995). The role of television in the socialization of nonverbal behavioral skills. *Basic and Applied Social Psychology, 17,* 327–341.

Cohan, C. L., & Bradbury, T. N. (1997). Negative life events, marital interaction, and the longitudinal course of newlywed marriage. *Journal of Personality and Social Psychology, 73,* 114–128.

Cohen, J. (1999, March 19). Nurture helps mold able minds. *Science, 283,* 1832–1833.

Cohen, P., Cohen, J., Kasen, S., Velez, C. N., Hartmark, C., Johnson, J., Rojas, M., Brook, J., & Streuning, E. L. (1993). An epidemiological study of disorders in late childhood and adolescence: I. Age- and gender-specfic prevalence. *Journal of Child Psychology and Psychiatry and Allied Disciplines, 34,* 851–867.

Cohen, S. E. (1995). Biosocial factors in early infancy as predictors of competence in adolescents who were born prematurely. *Journal of Developmental & Behavioral Pediatrics, 16,* 36–41.

Cohen, S., Tyrell, D. A., & Smith, A. P. (1993). Negative life events, perceived stress, negative affect, and susceptibility of the common cold. *Journal of Personality and Social Psychology, 64,* 131–140.

Cohen, S., Tyrell, D. A., & Smith, A. P. (1997). Psychological stress in humans and susceptibility to the common cold. In T. W. Miller (Ed.), *International Universities Press stress and health series, Monograph 7. Clinical disorders and stressful life events* (pp. 217–235). Madison, CT: International Universities Press.

Cohn, J. F., & Tronick, E. Z. (1989). Mother-infant face-to-face interaction: Influence is bidirectional and unrelated to periodic cycles in either partner's behavior. *Developmental Psychology, 24,* 386–392.

Cohn, R. M. (1982). Economic development and status change of the aged. *American Journal of Sociology, 87,* 1150–1161.

Colby, A., & Damon, W. (1987). Listening to a different voice: A review of Gilligan's in a different voice. In M. R. Walsh (Ed.), *The psychology of women.* New Haven, CT: Yale University Press.

Colby, A., & Kohlberg, L. (1987). *The measurement of moral adjudgment* (Vols. 1–2). New York: Cambridge Univesity Press.

Colditz, G. A., Hankinson, S. E., Hunter, D. J., Willett, W. C., Manson, J. E., Stampfer, M. J., Hennekens, C., Rosner, B., & Spetzer, F. E. (1995, June 15). The use of estrogens and progestins and the risk of breast cancer in postmenopausal women. *The New England Journal of Medicine, 332,* 1589–1593.

Cole, M. (1992). Culture in development. In M. H. Bornstein & M. E. Lamb (Eds.), *Developmental psychology: An advanced textbook* (3rd ed.). Hillsdale, NJ: Erlbaum.

Coleman, J. (1961). *The adolescent society.* Glencoe, IL: Free Press.

Coley, R. L., & Chase-Lansdale, P. L. (1998). Adolescent pregnancy and parenthood: Recent evidence and future directions. *American Psychologist, 53,* 152–166.

Collins, W. A., Gleason, T., & Sesma, A. (1997). Internalization, autonomy, and relationships: Development during adolescence. In J. E. Grusec & L. Kuczynski (Eds.), *Parenting and children's internalization of values: A handbook of contemporary theory* (pp. 78–99). New York: Wiley.

Collins, W. A., Maccoby, E. E., Steinberg, L., Hetherington, E. M., & Bornstein, M. H. (2000). Contemporary research on parenting: The case for nature and nurture. *American Psychologist, 55,* 218–232.

Colon, J. M. (1997). Assisted reproductive technologies. In M. L. Sipski & C. J. Alexander (Eds.), *Sexual function in people with disability and chronic illness: A health professional's guide* (pp. 557–575). Gaithersburg, MD: Aspen Publishers.

Coltrane, S., & Adams, M. (1997). Children and gender. In T. Arendell (Ed.), *Contemporary parenting: Challenges and issues. Understanding Families* (Vol. 9, pp. 219–253). Thousand Oaks, CA: Sage.

Committee on Children, Youth and Families. (1994). *When you need child day care.* Washington, DC: American Psychological Association.

Comstock, G., & Strasburger, V. C. (1990). Deceptive appearances: Television violence and aggressive behavior. Conference: Teens and television (1988, Los Angeles, California). *Journal of Adolescent Health Care, 11,* 31–44.

Condit, V. (1990). Anorexia nervosa: Levels of causation. *Human Nature, 1,* 391–413.

Condry, J. (1989). *The psychology of television.* Hillsdale, NJ: Erlbaum.

Condry, J., & Condry, S. (1976). Sex differences: A study of the eye of the beholder. *Child Development, 47,* 812–819.

Connor, R. (1992). *Cracking the over-50 job market.* New York: Penguin Books.

Cook, A. S., & Oltjenbruns, K. A. (1989). *Dying and grieving: Lifespan and family perspectives.* New York: Holt, Rinehart & Winston.

Coons, S., & Guilleminault, C. (1982). Developments of sleep-wake patterns and non-rapid-eye-movement sleep stages during the first six months of life in normal infants. *Pediatrics, 69(6),* 793–798.

Cooper, B. (2001). Nature, nurture and mental disorder: Old concepts in the new millennium. *British Journal of Psychiatry, 178,* (Suppl. 40), s91–s101.

Cooper, H. (1989). Synthesis of Research on Homework. *Educational Leadership, 47,* 85–91.

Cooper, N. R., Kalaria, R. N., McGeer, P. L., & Rogers, J. (2000). Key issues in Alzheimer's disease inflammation. *Neurobiology of Aging, 21,* 451–453.

Cooper, R. P., & Aslin, R. N. (1990). Preference for infant-directed speech in the first month after birth. *Child Development, 61,* 1584–1595.

Cooper, R. P., & Aslin, R. N. (1994). Developmental differences in infant attention to the spectral properties of infant-directed speech *Child Development, 65,* 1663–1677.

Cooperstock, M. S., Bakewell, J., Herman, A., & Schramm W. F. (1998). Effects of fetal sex and race on risk of very preterm birth in twins. *American Journal of Obstetrics & Gynecology, 179,* 762–765.

Corballis, M. C. (1999, March-April). The gestural origins of language. *American Scientist, 87,* 138–145.

Corballis, M. C. (2000). How laterality will survive the millennium bug. *Brain & Cognition, 42,* 160–162.

Coren, S., & Halpern, D. F. (1991). Left-handedness: A marker for decreased survival fitness. *Psychological Bulletin, 109(1),* 90–106.

Corliss, J. (1996, October 29). Alzheimer's in the news. *HealthNews,* pp. 1–2.

Cormier, K., Mauk, C., & Repp, A. (1998). Manual babbling in deaf and hearing infants: A longitudinal study. In E. V. Clark, (Ed.), *The proceedings of the twenty-ninth annual child language research forum.* Stanford, CA: Center for the Study of Language and Information.

Cornelius, M. D., Day, N. L., Richardson, G. A., & Taylor, P. M. (1999). Epidemiology of substance abuse during pregnancy. In P. J. Ott, R. E. Tarter, et al. (Eds.), *Sourcebook on substance abuse: Etiology, epidemiology, assessment, and treatment.* Boston: Allyn & Bacon.

Corno, L. (1996). Homework Is a Complicated Thing. Section 4: Grading the Policymakers' Solution. *Educational Researcher, 25,* 27–30.

Corr, C. (1991/1992). A task-based approach to coping with dying. *Omega, 24,* 81–94.

Costa, P. T., Busch, C. M., Zonderman, A. B., & McCrae, R. R. (1993). Correlations of MMPI factor scales with measures of the five factor model of personality. *Journal of Personality Assessment, 50,* 640–650.

Costa, P. T., & McCrae, R. R. (1997). Longitudinal stability of adult personality. In R. Hogan, J. A. Johnson, & S. R. Briggs (Eds.), *Handbook of personality psychology* (pp. 269–290). San Diego, CA: Academic Press.

Costa, P. T., Jr., & McCrae, R. R. (1988). Personality in adulthood: A six-year longitudinal study of self-report and spouse ratings on the NEO Personality Inventory. *Journal of Personality and Social Psychology, 54,* 853–863.

Costa, P. T., Jr., & McCrae, R. R. (1989). Personality continuity and the changes of adult life. In M. Storandt and G. R. VandenBos (Eds.), *The adult years: Continuity and change.* Washington, DC: American Psychological Association.

Cottreaux, J. (1993). Behavioral psychotherapy applications in the medically ill. *Psychotherapy and Psychosomatics, 60,* 116–128.

Cowan, C. P., & Cowan, P. A. (1992). *When partners become parents.* New York: Wiley.

Cowgill, D. O. (1968). The social life of the aging in Thailand. *Gerontologist, 8,* 159-163.

Cowley, G. (1997, June 30). How to live to 100. *Newsweek,* 58–67.

Cowley, G. (2000). For the love of language. *Newsweek Special Issue: Your Child,* 12–15.

Cowley, G. (2000, January 31). Alzheimer's : Unlocking the mystery. *Newsweek,* 46–51.

Cox, M. J., Owen, M. T., Henderson, V. K., & Margand, N. A. (1992). Prediction of infant–father and infant–mother attachment. *Developmental Psychology, 28,* 474–483.

Craik, F. I. M. (1984). Age differences in remembering. In L. R. Squire & N. Butters (Eds.), *Neuropsychology of memory.* New York: Guilford.

Craik, F. I. M. (1994). Memory changes in normal aging. *Current Directions in Psychological Science, 3,* 155–158.

Craik, F., & Salthouse, T. A. (Eds.). (1999). *The handbook of aging and cognition.* (2nd ed.). Mahwah, NJ: Erlbaum.

Cratty, B. (1979). *Perceptual and motor development in infants and children* (2nd ed.). Englewood Cliffs, NJ: Prentice-Hall.

Cratty, B. (1986). *Perceptual and motor development in infants and children* (3rd ed.). Englewood Cliffs, NJ: Prentice-Hall.

Crews, D. (1993). The organizational concept and vertebrates without sex chromosomes. *Brain, Behavior, and Evolution, 42,* 202–214.

Crockett, L. J., & Crouter, A. C. (Eds.). (1995). *Pathways through adolescence: Individual development in relation to social contexts.* Hillsdale, NJ: Erlbaum.

Cromwell, E. S. (1994). *Quality child care: A comprehensive guide for administrators and teachers.* Boston: Allyn & Bacon.

Crosby, W. (1991). Studies in fetal malnutrition. *American Journal of Diseases of Children, 145,* 871–876.

Crose, R., & Drake, L. K. (1993). Older women's sexuality. *Clinical Gerontologist, 12,* 51–56.

Cross, W. W., Jr. (1991). *Shades of black: Diversity in African-American identity.* Philadelphia: Temple University Press.

Crosscope-Happel, C., Hutchins, D. E., Getz, H. G., & Hayes, G. L. (2000). Male anorexia nervosa: A new focus. *Journal of Mental Health Counseling, 22,* 365–370.

Croyle, R. T., & Hunt, J. R. (1991). Coping with health threat: Social influence processes in reactions to medical test results. *Journal of Personality and Social Psychology, 60,* 382–389.

Csibra, G., Davis, G., Spratling, M. W., & Johnson, M. H. (2000, November 24). Gamma oscillations and object processing in the infant brain. *Science, 290,* 1582–1584.

Csikszentmihalyi, M., & Larson, R. (1984). *Being adolescent: Conflict and growth in the teenage years.* New York: Basic Books.

Culbertson, J. L, & Gyurke, J. (1990). Assessment of cognitive and motor development in infancy and childhood. In J. H. Johnson & J. Goldman (Eds.), *Developmental assessment in clinical child psychology: A handbook* (pp. 100–131). New York: Pergamon Press.

Culp, A. M., Clyman, M. M., & Culp, R. E. (1995). Adolescent depressed mood, reports of suicide attempts, and asking for help. *Adolescence, 30,* 827–837.

Cummings, E. M., Iannotti, R. J., & Zahn-Waxler, C. (1989). Aggression between peers in early childhood: Individual continuity and developmental change. *Child Development, 60,* 887–895.

Cummings, E., & Henry, W. E. (1961). *Growing old.* New York: Basic Books.

Cunningham, J. D., & Antill, J. K. (1994). Cohabitation and marriage: Retrospective and predictive comparisons. *Journal of Social and Personal Relationships, 11,* 77–93.

Cunningham, W. R., & Hamen, K. (1992). Intellectual functioning in relation to mental health. In J. E. Birren, R. B. Sloane, & G. D. Cohen (Eds.), *Handbook of mental health and aging.* San Diego, CA: Harcourt Brace.

Cutler, B. (1990). Rock-a-buy baby. *American Demographics, 12 (1),* 35–39.

Cutter, J. A. (1999, June 13). Coming to terms with grief after a longtime partner dies. *The New York Times,* p. WH10.

Cynader, M. (2000, March 17). Strengthening visual connections. *Science, 287,* 1943–1944.

Dahl, E., & Birkelund, E. (1997). Health inequalities in later life in a social democratic welfare state. *Social Science & Medicine, 44,* 871–881.

Dainton, M. (1993). The myths and misconceptions of the step-mother identity. *Family Relations, 42,* 93–98.

Daly, M., & Wilson, M. I. (1996). Violence against stepchildren. *Current Directions in Psychological Science, 5,* 77–81.

Daly, T., & Feldman, R. S. (1994). *Benefits of social integration for typical preschoolchildren.* Unpublished manuscript.

Damon, W. (1977). *The social world of the child.* San Francisco: Jossey-Bass.

Damon, W. (1983). *Social and personality development.* New York: Norton.

Damon, W. (1988). *The moral child.* New York: The Free Press.

Damon, W. (1995). *Greater expectations: Overcoming the culture of indulgence in America's homes and schools.* NY: Free Press.

Damon, W., & Hart, D. (1988). *Self-understanding in childhood and adolescence.* New York: Cambridge University Press.

Daniels, H. (Ed.). (1996). *An introduction to Vygotsky.* New York: Routledge.

Darnton, N. (1990, June 4). Mommy vs. Mommy. *Newsweek,* 64–67.

Darroch, J. E., & Singh, S. (1999). *Why is teenage pregnancy declining? The roles of abstinence, sexual activity and contraceptive use.* Occasional Report, No. 1. New York: The Alan Guttmacher Institute.

Dasen, P. (in press). Rapid social change and the turmoil of adolescence: A cross-cultural perspective. *World Psychology.*

Dasen, P., Inhelder, B., Lavallee, M., & Retschitzki, J. (1978). *Naissance de l'intelligence chez l'enfant Baoule de Cote d'Ivoire.* Berne: Hans Huber.

Dasen, P., Ngini, L., & Lavallee, M. (1979). Cross-cultural training studies of concrete operations. In L. H. Eckenberger, W. J. Lonner, & Y. H. Poortinga (Eds.), *Cross-cultural contributions to psychology.* Amsterdam: Swets & Zeilinger.

Davey, S. G., Frankel S., & Yarnell, J. (1997). Sex and death: are they related? Findings from the Caerphilly Cohort Study. *British Medical Journal, 315,* 1–4

Davidson, T. (1977). Wifebeating: A recurring phenomenon throughout history. In M. Roy (Ed.), *Battered women: A psychosociological study of domestic violence.* New York: Van Nostrand Reinhold.

Davies, M., Stankov, L., & Roberts, R. D. (1998). Emotional intelligence: In search of an elusive construct. *Journal of Personality & Social Psychology, 75,* 989–1015.

Davies, P. T., & Cummings, E. M. (1994). Marital conflict and child adjustment: An emotional security hypothesis. *Psychological Bulletin, 116,* 387–411.

Davis, C. G., Nolen-Hoeksema, S., & Larson, J. (1998). Making sense of loss and benefiting from the experience: Two construals of meaning. *Journal of Personality and Social Psychology, 75,* 561–574.

Davis, M., & Emory, E. (1995). Sex differences in neonatal stress reactivity. *Child Development, 66,* 14–27.

Davis-Floyd, R. E. (1994). The technocratic body: American childbirth as cultural expression. *Social Science & Medicine, 38,* 1125–1140.

de Anda, D., & Becerra, R. M. (2000). An overview of "Violence: Diverse populations and communities." *Journal of Multicultural Social Work, 8,* n1–2, p1–14.

De Gelder, B. (2000). Recognizing emotions by ear and by eye. In R. D. Lane & L. Nadel, (Eds.), et al., *Cognitive neuroscience of emotion. Series in affective science.* New York: Oxford University Press.

de Graaf, C., Polet, P., & van Staveren, W. A. (1994). Sensory perception and pleasantness of food flavors in elderly subjects. *Journals of Gerontology, 49,* P93–P99.

De Leo, D., Conforti, D., & Carollo, G. (1997). A century of suicide in Italy: A comparison between the old and the young. *Suicide & Life-Threatening Behavior, 27,* 239–249.

de Mooij, M. K. (1998). *Global marketing and advertising: Understanding cultural paradoxes.* Thousand Oaks, CA: Sage.

de Vries, B., Davis, C. G., Wortman, C. B., & Lehman, D. R. (1997). Long-term psychological and somatic consequences of later life parental bereavement. *Omega—Journal of Death & Dying, 35,* 97–117.

Dean, A., Kolody, B., Wood, P., & Ensel, W. (1989). Measuring the communication of social support from adult children. *Journal of Marriage and the Family, 44,* 71–79.

DeAngelis, T. (1994, December). What makes kids ready, set for school? *APA Monitor,* pp. 36–37.

Deaux, K., Reind, A., Mizrahi, K., & Ethier, K. A. (1995). Parameters of social identity. *Journal of Personality and Social Psychology, 68,* 280–291.

Decarrie, T. G. (1969). A study of the mental and emotional development of the thalidomide child. In B. M. Foss (Ed.), *Determinants of infant behavior* (Vol. 4). London: Methuen.

DeCasper, A. J., & Fifer, W. P. (1980). Of human bonding: Newborns prefer their mothers' voices. *Science, 208,* 1174–1176.

DeCasper, A. J., & Prescott, P. (1984). Human newborns' perception of male voices: Preference, discrimination, and reinforcing value. *Developmental Psychobiology, 17,* 481–491.

DeCasper, A. J., & Spence, M. J. (1986). Prenatal material speech influences newborns' perception of speech sounds. *Infant Behavior and Development, 9,* 133–150.

deChateau, P. (1980). Parent–neonate interaction and its long-term effects. In E. G. Simmel (Ed.), *Early experiences and early behavior.* New York: Academic Press.

DeClercq, E. R. (1992). The transformation of American midwifery: 1975 to 1988. *American Journal of Public Health, 82,* 680–684.

DeCristofaro, J. D., & LaGamma, E. F. (1995). Prenatal exposure to opiates. *Mental Retardation and Developmental Disabilities Research Reviews, 1,* 177–182.

DeFrain, J., Martens, L., Stork, J., & Stork, W. (1991). The psychological effects of a stillbirth on surviving family members. *Omega—Journal of Death and Dying, 22,* 81–108.

DeGenova, M. K. (1993). Reflections of the past: New variables affecting life satisfaction in later life. *Educational Gerontology, 19,* 191–201.

Dejin-Karlsson, E., Hanson, B. S., Oestergren, P. O., Sjoeberg, N.O., & Marsal, K. (1998). Does passive smoking in early pregnancy increase the risk of small-for-gestational age infants? *American Journal of Public Health, 88,* 1523–1527.

Delaney, C. H. (1995). Rites of passage in adolescence. *Adolescence, 30,* 891–897.

Dell, D. L., & Stewart, D. E. (2000). Menopause and mood. Is depression linked with hormone changes?. *Postgraduate Medicine, 108,* 34–36, 39–43.

DeMaris, A., & Rao, K. V. (1992). Premarital cohabitation and subsequent marital stability in the United States: A reassessment. *Journal of Marriage and the Family, 54,* 178–190.

Dembner, A. (1995, October 15). Marion Mealey: A determination to make it. *Boston Globe,* p. 22.

Demetriou, A., Shayer, M., & Efklides, A. (Eds.). (1993). *Neo-Piagetian theories of cognitive development: Implications and applications for education.* London: Routledge.

Demo, D. H., & Acock, A. (1991). The impact of divorce on children. In A. Booth (Ed.), *Contemporary families.* Minneapolis, MN: National Council on Family Relations.

Denham, S. (1998). *Emotional development in young children.* New York: Guilford Press.

Dennis, W. (1966a). Age and creative productivity. *Journal of Gerontology, 21,* 1–8.

Dennis, W. (1966b). Creative productivity between the ages of 20 and 80 years. *Journal of Gerontology, 11,* 331–337.

Dent, J. (1984, March). Laughter is the best medicine. *Reader's Digest, 124,* 38.

Dent-Read, C., & Zukow-Goldring, P. (Eds.). (1997). *Evolving explanations of development: Ecological approaches to organism-environment systems.* Washington, DC: American Psychological Association.

Desmarias, S., & Curtis, J. (1997). Gender and perceived pay entitlement: Testing for effects of experience with income. *Journal of Personality and Social Psychology, 72,* 141–150.

DeSpelder, L., & Strickland, A. L. (1992). *The last dance: Encountering death and dying* (3rd ed.). Palo Alto, CA: Mayfield.

Deutsch, M. (1967). *The disadvantaged child: Selected papers of Martin Deutsch and associates.* New York: Basic Books.

Deutsch, N. (2000, September 5). Menopause symptoms differ by race. Website: http://dailynews.yahoo.com/htx/nm/2000905/hl/monopause_1.html.

Deveny, K. (1994, December 5). Chart of kindergarten awards. *The Wall Street Journal,* p. B1.

deVilliers, P. A., & deVilliers, J. G. (1992). Language development. In M. H. Bornstein & M. E. Lamb (Eds.), *Developmental psychology: An advanced textbook.* Hillsdale, NJ: Erlbaum.

Devlin, B., Daniels, M., & Roeder, K. (1997). The heritability of IQ. *Nature, 388,* 468–471.

deVries, M. W. (1984). Temperament and infant mortality among the Masai of East Africa. *American Journal of Psychiatry, 141,* 1189–1194.

deVries, R. (1969). Constancy of generic identity in the years 3 to 6. *Monographs of the Society for Research in Child Development, 34,* (3, Serial No. 127).

DeWitt, P. M. (1992). The second time around. *American Demographics, 14,* 60–63.

DeWolff, M. S., & van Ijzendoorn, M. H. (1997). Sensitivity and attachment: A meta-analysis on parental antecedents of infant attachment. *Child Development, 68,* 571–591.

Dickenson, G. (1975). Dating behavior of black and white adolescents before and after desegregation. *Journal of Marriage and the Family, 37,* 602–608.

Dickson, K. L., Walker, H., & Fogel, A. (1997). The relationship between smile type and play type during parent–infant play. *Developmental Psychology, 33,* 925–933.

Diener, E. (2000). Subjective well-being: The science of happiness and a proposal for a national index. *American Psychologist, 55,* 34–43.

Diener, E., Suh, E. M., Lucas, R. E., & Smith, H. L. (1999). Subjective well-being: Three decades of progress. *Psychological Bulletin, 125*, 276–302.

DiFranza, J. R., & Lew, R. A. (1995, April). Effect of maternal cigarette smoking on pregnancy complications and sudden infant death syndrome. *The Journal of Family Practice, 40*, 385–394.

DiGiovanna, A. G. (1994). *Human aging: Biological perspectives.* New York: McGraw-Hill.

DiLalla, L. F., Thompson, L. A., Plomin, R., Phillips, K., Fagan, J. F., Haith, M. M., Cyphers, L. H., & Fulker, D. W. (1990). Infant predictors of preschool and adult IQ: A study of infant twins and their parents. *Developmental Psychology, 26*, 433–440.

Dildy, G. A. et al. (1996). Very advanced maternal age: Pregnancy after 45. *American Journal of Obstetrics and gynecology, 175*, 668–674.

DiMatteo, M. R., & Kahn, K. L. (1997). Psychosocial aspects of childbirth. In S. J. Gallant, G. P. Keita, & R. Royak-Schaler (Eds.), *Health care for women: Psychological, social, and behavioral influences.* Washington, DC: American Psychological Association.

Dion, K. L., & Dion, K. K. (1988). Romantic love: Individual and cultural perspectives. In R. J. Sternberg & M. L. Barnes (Eds.), *The psychology of love.* New Haven, CT: Yale University Press.

Division 44/Committee on Lesbian, Gay, and Bisexual Concerns Joint Task Force on Guidelines for Psychotherapy with Lesbian, Gay, and Bisexual Clients. (2000). Guidelines for psychotherapy with lesbian, gay, and bisexual clients. *American Psychologist, 55*, 1440–1451.

Dodge, K. A., & Coie, J. D. (1987). Social information-processing factors in reactive and proactive aggression in children's peer groups. *Journal of Personality and Social Psychology, 53*, 1146–1158.

Dodge, K. A., & Crick, N. R. (1990). Social information-processing bases of aggressive behavior in children. *Personality and Social Psychology Bulletin, 16*, 8–22.

Dodge, K. A., & Price, J. M. (1994). On the relation between social information processing and socially competent behavior in early school-aged children. *Child Development, 65*, 1385–1397.

Dodge, K. A., Bates, J. E., & Pettit, G. S. (1990, December 20). Mechanisms in the cycle of violence. *Science, 250*, 1678–1683.

Dodge, K. A., Pettit, G. S., McClasky, C. L., & Brown, M. M. (1986). Social competence in children. *Monographs of the Society for Research in Child Development, 51*, (2, Serial No. 213).

Doering, M., Rhodes, S. R., & Schuster, M. (1983). *The aging worker: Research and recommendations.* Beverly Hills, CA: Sage.

Doka, K. J., & Mertz, M. E. (1988). The meaning and significance of great-grandparenthood. *Gerontologist, 28*, 192–197.

Donlan, C. (1998). *The development of mathematical skills.* Philadelphia: Psychology Press.

Doress, P. B., Siegal, D. L., & The Midlife and Old Women Book Project. (1987). *Ourselves, growing older.* New York: Simon & Schuster.

Dornbusch, S. M., Ritter, P. L., & Steinberg, L. (1992). Differences between African Americans and non-Hispanic whites in the relation of family statuses to adolescent school performance. *American Journal of Education, 99*, 543–567.

Dornbusch, S., Carlsmith, J., Bushwall, S., Ritter, P., Leiderman, P., Hastorf, A., & Gross, R. (1985). Single parents, extended households, and the control of adolescents. *Child Development, 56*, 326–341.

Dortch, S. (1997, September). Hey guys: Hit the books. *American Demographics,* pp. 4–12.

Douglas, M. J. (1991). Potential complications of spinal and epidural anesthesia for obstetrics. *Seminars in Perinatology, 15*, 368–374.

Doussard-Roosevelt, J. A., Porges, S. W., Scanlon, J. W., Alemi, B., & Scanlon, K. B. (1997). Vagal regulation of heart rate in the prediction of developmental outcome for very low birth weight preterm infants. *Child Development, 68*, 173–186.

Douvan, E., & Adelson, J. (1966). *The adolescent experience.* New York: Wiley.

Downe-Wamboldt, B., & Tamlyn, D. (1997). An international survey of death education trends in faculties of nursing and medicine. *Death Studies. Vol. 21*, 177–188.

Downey, G., Silver, R. C., & Wortman, C. B. (1990). Reconsidering the attribution-adjustment relation following a major negative event: Coping with the loss of a child. *Journal of Personality and Social Psychology, 59*, 227–236.

Doyle, R. (2000, June). Asthma worldwide. *Scientific American, 28.*

Dreman, S. (Ed.). (1997). *The family on the threshold of the 21st century.* Mahwah, NJ: Erlbaum.

Drews, C. D., Murphy, C. C., Yeargin-Allsopp, M., & Decoufle, P. (1996). The relationship between idiopathic mental retardation and maternal smoking during pregnancy. *Pediatrics, 97*, 547–553.

Driedger, S. D. (1994, July 11). "Cancer made me stronger." *McCleans,* p. 46.

Dromi, E. (1987). Early lexical development. Cambridge, England: Cambridge University Press.

Dryfoos, J. G. (1990). *Adolescents at risk: Prevalence and prevention.* New York: Oxford University Press.

DuBois, D. L., & Hirsch, B. J. (1990). School and neighborhood friendship patterns of blacks and whites in early adolescence. *Child Development, 61*, 524–536.

DuBreuil, S. C., Garry, M., & Loftus, E. F. (1998). Tales from the crib: Age regression and the creation of unlikely memories. In S. J. Lynn, & K. M. McConkey (Eds.), *Truth in memory.* New York: The Guilford Press.

Duckitt, J. (1994). Conformity to social pressure and racial prejudice among white South Africans. *Genetic, Social, and General Psychology Monographs, 120*, 121–143.

Duke, M., & Nowicki, S., Jr. (1979). *Abnormal psychology: Perspectives on being different.* Monterey, CA: Brooks/Cole.

Dukes, R., & Martinez, R. (1994). The impact of gender on self-esteem among adolescents. *Adolescence, 29*, 105–115.

Duncan, G. J., & Brooks-Gunn, J. (2000). Family poverty, welfare reform, and child development. *Child Development, 71*, 188–196.

Duncan, G. J., & Smith, K. R. (1989). The rising affluence of the elderly: How far, how fair, and how frail. *Annual Review of Sociology.* Palo Alto, CA: Annual Reviews.

Duncan, P., Ritter, P., Dornbusch, S., Gross, R., & Carlsmith, J. (1985). The effects of pubertal timing on body image, school behavior, and deviance. *Journal of Youth and Adolescence, 14*, 227–236.

Dunham, R. M., Kidwell, J. S., & Wilson, S. M. (1986). Rites of passage at adolescence: A ritual process paradigm. *Journal of Adolescent Research, 1*, 139–153.

Dunn, A. L., & Blair, S. N. (1997). Exercise prescription. In W. P. Morgan (Ed.), *Series in health psychology and behavioral medicine. Physical activity and mental health* (pp. 49–62). Washington, DC: Taylor & Francis.

Dunn, L. M. (1968). Special education for the mildly retarded—Is much of it justifiable? *Exceptional Child, 35*, 5–22.

Dunphy, D. C. (1963). The social structure of urban adolescent peer groups. *Society, 26*, 230–246.

DuPlessis, H. M., Bell, R., & Richards, T. (1997). Adolescent pregnancy: Understanding the impact of age and race on outcomes. *Journal of Adolescent Health, 20*, 187–197.

Durant, J. E. (1999). Evaluating the success of Sweden's corporal punishment ban. *Child Abuse & Neglect, 23*, 435–448.

Durik, A. M., Hyde, J. S., & Clark, R. (2000). Sequelae of cesarean and vaginal deliveries: Psychosocial outcomes for mothers and infants. *Developmental Psychology, 36*, 251–260.

Durkin, K., & Nugent, B. (1998). Kindergarten children's gender-role expectations for television actors. *Sex Roles, 38*, 387–402.

Dutton, D. G. (1988). *The domestic assault of women: Psychological and criminal justice perspectives.* Boston, MA: Allyn & Bacon.

Dutton, D. G. (1994). *The domestic assault of women: Psychological and criminal justice perspectives* (2nd ed.). Vancouver, BC, Canada: University of British Columbia Press.

Dutton, M. A. (1992) *Empowering and healing the battered woman: A model of assessment and intervention.* New York: Springer.

Dweck, C. S. (1991). Self-theories and goals: Their role in motivation, personality and development. In R. Dienstbier (Ed.), *Nebraska symposium on motivation* (Vol. 36). Lincoln: University of Nebraska Press.

Dweck, C. S., & Bush, E. S. (1976). Sex differences in learned helplessness: I. Differential debilitation with peer and adult evaluators. *Developmental Psychology, 12*, 147–156.

Dyer, C. B., Pavlik, V. N., Murphy, K. P., & Hyman, D. J. (2000). The high prevalence of depression and dementia in elder abuse or neglect. *Journal of the American Geriatrics Society, 48*, 205–208.

Eacott, M. J. (1999). Memory of the events of early childhood. *Current Directions in Psychological Science, 8*, 46–49.

Eagly, A. H., & Steffen, V. J. (1984). Gender stereotypes stem from the distribution of women and men into social roles. *Journal of Personality and Social Psychology, 46*, 735–754.

Eagly, A. H., & Steffen, V. J. (1986). Gender and aggressive behavior: A meta-analytic review of the social psychological literature. *Psychological Bulletin, 100*, 309–330.

Eakins, P. S. (Ed.). (1986). *The American way of birth.* Philadelphia: Temple University Press.

Eaton, M. J. & Dembo, M. H. (1997). Differences in the motivational beliefs of Asian American and non-Asian students. *Journal of Educational Psychology, 89,* 433–440.

Eaton, W. O., & Enns, L. R. (1986). Sex differences in human motor activity level. *Psychological Bulletin, 100,* 19–28.

Eaton, W. O., & Yu, A. P. (1989). Are sex differences in child motor activity level a function of sex differences in maturational status? *Child Development, 60,* 1005–1011.

Eberstadt, N. (1994). Why babies die in D. C. *The Public Interest,* 3–16.

Ebstein, R. P., Novick, O., Umansky, R., Priel, B., Osher, Y., Blaine, D., Bennett, E. R., Nemanov, L., Katz, M., & Belmaker, R. H. (1996). Dopamine D4 receptor (1996) exon III polymorphism associated with the human personality trait of novelty seeking. *Nature and Genetics, 12,* 78–80.

Eccles, J. S., Wigfield, A., Flanagan, C., Miller, C., Reuman, D., & Yee, D. (1989). Self-concepts, domain values, and self-esteem: Relations and changes at early adolescence. *Journal of Personality and Social Psychology, 57,* 283–310.

Ecenbarger, W. (1993, April 1). America's new merchants of death. *The Reader's Digest,* 50.

Eckerman, C. O., & Oehler, J. M. (1992). Very-low-birthweight newborns and parents as early social partners. In S. L. Friedman & M. D. Sigman (Eds.), *The psychological development of low-birthweight children.* Norwood, NJ: Ablex.

Edelman, S., & Kidman, A. D. (1997). Mind and cancer: Is there a relationship? A review of evidence. *Australian Psychologist, 32,* 79–85.

Eden, D. (1990). Pygmalion without interpersonal contrast effects: Whole groups gain from raising manager expectations. *Journal of Applied Psychology, 75,* 394–398.

Edwards, C. P. (2000). Children's play in cross-cultural perspective: A new look at the Six Cultures study. *Cross-Cultural Research: The Journal of Comparative Social Science, 34,* 318–338.

Egan, M. C. (1994). Public health nutrition: A historical perspective. *Journal of the American Dietetic Association, 94,* 298–304.

Egan, S. K., & Perry, D. G. (1998). Does low self-regard invite victimization? *Developmental Psychology, 34,* 299–309.

Egeland, B., & Farber, E. A. (1984). Infant–mother attachment: Factors related to its development and changes over time. *Child Development, 55,* 753–771.

Egeland, B., & Hiester, M. (1995). The long-term consequences of infant day-care and mother-infant attachment. *Child Development, 66,* 474–485.

Egeland, B., Pianta, R., & O'Brien, M. A. (1993). Maternal intrusiveness in infancy and child maladaptation in early school years. *Development and Psychopathology, 5,* 359–370.

Eggebeen, D. J., & Hogan, D. P. (1990). Giving between generations in American families. *Human Nature, 1,* 211–232.

Ehlers, C. L., Frank, E., & Kupfer, D. J. (1988). Social zeitgebers and biological rhythms: A unified approach to understanding the etiology of depression. *Archives of General Psychiatry, 45,* 948–952.

Eimas, P. D., Sigueland, E. R., Jusczyk, P., & Vigorito, J. (1971). Speech perception in infants. *Science, 171,* 303–306.

Einbinder, S. D. (1992). *A statistical profile of children living in poverty: Children under three and children under six, 1990.* Unpublished document from the National Center for Children in Poverty. New York: Columbia University, School of Public Health.

Eisenberg, N., & Fabes, R. (1991). Prosocial behavior and empathy: A multimethod, developmental perspective. In. M. S. Clark (Ed.), *Review of personality and social psychology* (Vol. 12). Newbury Park, CA: Sage.

Eisenberg, N., & Zhou, Q. (2000). Regulation from a developmental perspective. *Psychological Inquiry, 11,* 166–172.

Eisenberg, N., Fabes, R. A., Guthrie, I. K., & Reiser, M. (2000). Dispositional emotionality and regulation: Their role in predicting quality of social functioning. *Journal of Personality and Social Psychology, 78,* 136–157.

Eisenberg, N., Futhrie, I. K., Fabes, R. A., Reiser, M., Murphy, B. C., Holgren, R., Maszk, P., & Losoya, S. (1997). The relations of regulations and emotionality to resiliency and competent social functioning in elementary school children. *Child Development, 68,* 295–311.

Eisenberg, N., Guthrie, I. K., Murphy, B. C., Shepard, S. A., Cumberland, A., & Carlo, G. (1999). Consistency and development of prosocial dispositions: A longitudinal study. *Child Development, 70,* 1360–1372.

Eisenberg, N., Wolchik, S. A., Hernandez, R., & Pasternack, J. F. (1985). Parental socialization of young children's play: A short-term longitudinal study. *Child Development, 56,* 1506–1513.

Ekman, P., & O'Sullivan, M. (1991). Facial expression: Methods, means, and moues. In R. S. Feldman & B. Rime (Eds.), *Fundamentals of nonverbal behavior.* Cambridge, England: Cambridge University Press.

Elkind, D. (1967). Egocentrism in adolescence. *Child Development, 38,* 1025–1034.

Elkind, D. (1984). *All grown up and no place to go.* Reading, MA: Addison-Wesley.

Elkind, D. (1985). Egocentrism redux. *Developmental Review, 5,* 218–226.

Elkind, D. (1988). *Miseducation.* New York: Knopf.

Elkind, D. (1996). Inhelder and Piaget on adolescence and adulthood: A postmodern appraisal. *Psychological Science, 7,* 216–220.

Ellis, L., & Engh, T. (2000). Handedness and age of death: New evidence on a puzzling relationship. *Journal of Health Psychology, 5,* 561–565.

Emery, R. E., & Laumann-Billings, L. (1998). An overview of the nature, causes, and consequences of abusive family relationships: Toward differentiating maltreatment and violence. *American Psychologist, 53,* 121–135.

Emslie, G. J., Rush, A. J., Weinberg, W. A., Kowatch, R. A., Hughes, C. W., Carmody, T., & Rintelmann, J. A. (1997). Double-blind, randomized, placebo-controlled trial of fluoxetine in children and adolescents with depression. *Archives of General Psychiatry, 54,* 1031–1037.

Endo, S. (1992). Infant–infant play from 7 to 12 months of age: An analysis of games in infant–peer triads. *Japanese Journal of Child and Adolescent Psychiatry, 33,* 145–162.

England, P., & McCreary, L. (1987). *Integrating sociology and economics to study gender and work.* Newbury Park, CA: Sage Publications.

Engle, P. L. & Breaux, C. (1998). Father's involvement with children: Perspectives from developing countries. *Social Policy Report, 12,* 1–21.

Engler, J., & Goleman, D. (1992). *The consumer's guide to psychotherapy.* New York: Simon & Schuster.

Englund, M. M., Levy, A. K., Hyson, D. M., & Sroufe, L. A. (2000). Adolescent social competence: Effectiveness in a group setting. *Child Development, 71,* 1049–1060.

Ennett, S. T., & Bauman, K. E. (1996). Adolescent social networks: School, demographic, and longitudinal considerations. *Journal of Adolescent Research, 11,* 194–215.

Epperson, S. E. (1988, September 16). Studies link subtle sex bias in schools with women's behavior in the workplace. *The Wall Street Journal,* p. 19.

Epstein, K. (1993). The interactions between breast-feeding mothers and their babies during the breast-feeding session. *Early Child Development and Care, 87,* 93–104.

Erber, J. T., Rothberg, S. T., & Szuchman, L. T. (1991). Appraisal of everyday memory failures by middle-aged adults. *Educational Gerontology, 17,* 63–72.

Erber, J. T., Szuchman, L. T., & Rothberg, S. T. (1990). Everyday memory failure: Age differences in appraisal and attribution. *Psychology and Aging, 5,* 236–241.

Erel, O., Oberman, Y., & Yirmiya, N. (2000). Maternal versus nonmaternal care and seven domains of children's develoment. *Psychological Bulletin, 126,* 727–747.

Erikson, E. H. (1963). *Childhood and society.* New York: Norton.

Erlandson, D. A., Harris, E. L., Skipper, B. L., & Allen, S. D. (1993). *Doing naturalistic inquiry: A guide to methods.* Newbury Park, CA: Sage.

Eron, L. D., & Huesmann, L. R. (1985). The control of aggressive behavior by changes in attitude, values, and the conditions of learning. In R. J. Blanchard and C. Blanchard (Eds.), *Advances in the study of aggression.* New York: Academic Press.

Erwin, P. (1993). *Friendship and peer relations in children.* Chichester, England: Wiley.

Espenschade, A. (1960). Motor development. In W. R. Johnson (Ed.), *Science and medicine of exercise and sports.* New York: Harper & Row.

Essex, M. J., & Nam, S. (1987). Marital status and loneliness among older women: The differential importance of close family and friends. *Journal of Marriage and the Family, 49,* 92–106.

Evans, G. W., Maxwell, L. E., & Hart, B. (1999). Parental language and verbal responsiveness to children in crowded homes. *Developmental Psychology, 35,* 1020–1023.

Eveleth, P., & Tanner, J. (1976). *Worldwide variation in human growth.* New York: Cambridge University Press.

Everett, S. A., Warren, C. W., Santelli, J. S., Kann, L., Collins, J. L., & Kolbe, L. J. (2000). Use of birth control pills, condoms, and withdrawal among U.S. high school students. *Journal of Adolescent Health, 27,* 112–118.

Everett, S. A., Malarcher, A. M., Sharp, D. J., Husten, C. G., Giovino, G. A. (2000). Relationship between cigarette, smokeless tobacco, and cigar use, and other health risk behaviors among U.S. high school students. *Journal of School Health, 70,* 234-40.

Evinger, S. (1996, May). How to record race. *American Demographics,* 36–41.

Ewbank, J. J., Barnes, T. M., Lakowski, B., Lussier, M., Bussey, H., & Hekimi, S. (1997, February 14). Structural and functional conservation of the caenorhabditis elegans timing gene clk-1. *Science, 275,* 980.

Eyer, D. (1992). The bonding hype. In M. E. Lamb & J. B. Lancaster (Eds.), *Birth management: Biosocial perspectives.* Hawthorne, New York: Aldine de Gruyter.

Eyer, D. E. (1994). Mother-infant bonding: A scientific fiction. *Human Nature, 5,* 69–94.

Fabsitz, R. R., Carmelli, D., & Hewitt, J. K. (1992). Evidence for independent genetic influences on obesity in middle age. *International Journal of Obesity and Related Metabolic Disorders, 16,* 657–666.

Fagot, B. I. (1978). The influence of sex of child on parental reactions to toddler children. *Child Development, 49,* 459–465.

Fagot, B. I. (1991). *Peer relations in boys and girls from two to seven.* Paper presented at the biennial meeting of the Society for Research in Child Development, Seattle, WA.

Fagot, B. I., & Hagan, R. (1991). Observation of parent reaction to sex-stereotyped behaviors: Age and sex effects. *Child Development, 62,* 617–628.

Fagot, B. I., & Leinbach, M. D. (1993). Gender-role development in young children: From discrimination to labeling. *Developmental Review, 13,* 205–224.

Faith, M. S., Johnson, S. L., & Allison, D. B. (1997). Putting the behavior into the behavior genetics of obesity. *Behavior Genetics, 27,* 423–439.

Falbo, T. (1992). Social norms and the one-child family: Clinical and policy implications. In F. Boer & J. Dunn (Eds.), *Children's sibling relationships.* Hillsdale, NJ: Erlbaum.

Falk, P. J. (1989). Lesbian mothers: Psychosocial assumptions in family law. *American Psychologist, 44,* 941–947.

Families and Work Institute. (1998). *Report on men spending more time with kids.* Washington, DC: Author.

Fangman, J. J., Mark, P. M., Pratt, L., Conway, K. K., Healey, M. L., Oswald, J. W., & Uden, D. L. (1994). *American Journal of Obstetrical Gynecology, 170,* 744–750.

Fanshel, D., Finch, S. J., & Grundy, J. F. (1990). *Foster children in a life course perspective.* New York: Columbia University Press.

Fanshel, D., Finch, S. J., & Grundy, J. F. (1992). *Serving the urban poor.* Westport, CT: Praeger.

Fantuzzo, J. W., & Mohr, W. K. (1999). Prevalence and effects of child exposure to domestic violence. *The Future of Children, 9,* 5.

Fantz, R. (1963). Pattern vision in newborn infants. *Science, 140,* 296–297.

Farel, A. M., Hooper, S. R., Teplin, S. W., Henry, M. M., & Kraybill, E. N. (1998). Very-low-birthweight infants at seven years: An assessment of the health and neurodevelopmental risk conveyed by chronic lung disease. *Journal of Learning Disabilities, 31,* 118–126.

Farhi, P. (1995, June 21). Turning the tables on TV violence. *The Washington Post,* pp. F1, F2.

Farrar, M. J., & Goodman, G. S. (1992). Developmental changes in event memory. *Child Development, 63,* 173–187.

Farver, J. M., & Frosch, D. L. (1996). L. A. stories: Aggression in preschoolers' spontaneous narratives after the riots of 1992. *Child Development, 67,* 19–32.

Farver, J. M., & Branstetter, W. H. (1994). Preschoolers' prosocial responses to their peers' distress. *Developmental Psychology, 30,* 334–341.

Farver, J. M., & Lee-Shin, Y. (2000). Acculturation and Korean-American children's social and play behavior. *Social Development, 9,* 316–336.

Farver, J. M., Kim, Y. K., & Lee-Shin, Y. (1995). Cultural differences in Korean- and Anglo-American preschoolers' social interaction and play behaviors. *Child Development, 66,* 1088–1099.

Farver, J. M., Welles-Nystrom, B., Frosch, D. L., & Wimbarti, S. (1997). Toy stories: Aggression in children's narratives in the United States, Sweden, Germany, and Indonesia. *Journal of Cross-Cultural Psychology, 28,* 393–420.

Fawzy, F. I. (1994). The benefits of a short-term group intervention for cancer patients. *Advances, 10,* 17–19.

Federal Interagency Forum on Age-Related Statistics. (2000). *Older Americans 2000: Key indicators of well-being.* Hyattsville, MD: Federal Interagency Forum on Age-Related Statistics.

Feeney, J., & Noller, P. (1996). *Adult attachment.* Thousand Oaks, CA: Sage.

Feifel, H. (1963). Relationship of physician to terminally ill patient. In N. L. Farberow (Ed.), *Taboo topics* (pp. 8–12). New York: Atherton.

Feinberg, A. W. (2000, October). Questions and answers. *HealthNews,* p. 10.

Feingold, A. (1992). Matching for attractiveness in romantic partners and same-sex friends: A meta-analysis and theoretical critique. *Psychological Bulletin, 111,* 304–341.

Feldman, R. S. (1982). *Development of nonverbal behavior in children.* New York: Springer-Verlag.

Feldman, R. S. (Ed.). (1992). *Applications of nonverbal behavioral theories and research.* Hillsdale, NJ: Erlbaum.

Feldman, R. S., & Prohaska, T. (1979). The student as Pygmalion: Effect of student expectation on the teacher. *Journal of Educational Psychology, 4,* 485–493.

Feldman, R. S., & Rimé, B. (Eds.). (1991). *Fundamentals of nonverbal behavior.* Cambridge, England: Cambridge University Press.

Feldman, R. S., & Theiss, A. J. (1982). The teacher and student as Pygmalions: The joint effects of teacher and student expectation. *Journal of Educational Psychology, 74,* 217–223.

Feldman, R. S., Philippot, P., & Custrini, R. J. (1991). Social competence and nonverbal behavior. In R. S. Feldman & B. Rime (Eds.), *Fundamentals of nonverbal behavior.* Cambridge, England: Cambridge University Press.

Feldman, R. S., Tomasian, J., & Coats, E. J. (1999) Adolescents' social competence and nonverbal deception abilities: Adolescents with higher social skills are better liars. *Journal of Nonverbal Behavior, 23,* 237–249.

Feldman, S. S., & Rosenthal, D. A. (1990). The acculturation of autonomy expectations in Chinese high schoolers residing in two Western nations. *International Journal of Psychology, 25,* 259–281.

Feldman, S. S., Biringen, Z. C., & Nash, S. C. (1981). Fluctuations of sex-related self-attributions as a function of stage of family life cycle. *Developmental Psychology, 17,* 24–35.

Feng, T. (1993). Substance abuse in pregnancy. *Current Opinion in Obstetrics & Gynecology, 5,* 16–23.

Fenson, L., Dale, P. S., Reznick, J. S., Bates, E., Thal, D. J., & Pethick, S. J. (1994). Variability in early communicative development. *Monographs of the Society for Research in Child Development, 59,* (5, Serial No. 242).

Fenwick, K., & Morrongiello, B. (1991). Development of frequency perception in infants and children. *Journal of Speech, Language Pathology, and Audiology, 15,* 7–22.

Fernald, A. (1984). The perceptual and affective salience of mothers' speech to infants. In L. Feagans, C. Garvey, & R. Golinkoff (Eds.), *The origins and growth of communication.* Norwood, NJ: Ablex.

Fernald, A. (1989). Intonation and communicative intent in mothers' speech to infants: Is the melody the message? *Child Development, 60,* 1497–1510.

Fernald, A., & Kuhl, P. (1987). Acoustic determinants of infant preference for motherese speech. *Infant Behavior and Development, 10,* 279–293.

Fernald, A., & Morikawa, H. (1993). Common themes and cultural variations in Japanese and American mothers' speech to infants. *Child Development, 64,* 637–656.

Fernald, A., Taeschner, T., Dunn, J., Papousek, M., Boysson-Bardies, B., & Fukui, I. (1989). A cross-language study of prosodic modifications in mothers' and fathers' speech to preverbal infants. *Journal of Child Language, 16,* 477–501.

Fernyhough, C. (1997). Vygotsky's sociocultural approach: Theoretical issues and implications for current research. In S. Hala (Ed.), *The development of social cognition.* (pp. 65–92). Hove, England: Psychology Press/Erlbaum, Taylor & Francis.

Feshbach, S. (1980). Child abuse and the dynamics of human aggression and violence. In J. Gerbner, C. J. Ross, & E. Zigler (Eds.), *Child abuse: An agenda for action.* New York: Oxford University Press.

Festinger, L. (1954). A theory of social comparison processes. *Human Relations, 7,* 117–140.

Fetterman, D. M. (1998). Ethnography. In L. Bickman & D. J. Rog (Eds.), *Handbook of applied social research methods* (pp. 473–504). Thousand Oaks, CA: Sage.

Fiatarone, M. S. A., & Garnett, L. R. (1997, March). Keep on keeping on. *Harvard Health Letter,* pp. 4–5.

Field, D., & Minkler, M. (1988). Continuity and change in social support between young-old and old-old or very-old age. *Journal of Gerontology, 43(4),* 100–106.

Field, T. (1990). *Infancy.* Cambridge, MA: Harvard University Press.

Field, T. (1999). Sucking and massage therapy reduce stress during infancy. In M. Lewis, & D. Ramsay (Eds.), *Soothing and stress.* Mahwah, NJ: Erlbaum.

Field, T. (2000). Infant massage therapy. In C. H. Zeanah, Jr. (Ed.), et al. *Handbook of infant mental health* (2nd ed.). New York: Guilford Press.

Field, T., & Roopnarine, J. L. (1982). Infant-peer interactions. In T. Field, A. Huston, H. Quay, & G. Finley (Eds.), *Review of human development.* New York: Wiley.

Field, T., & Walden, T. (1982). Perception and production of facial expression in infancy and early childhood. In H. Reese & L. Lipsitt (Eds.), *Advances in child development and behavior* (Vol. 16). New York: Academic Press.

Field, T., Greenberg, R., Woodson, R., Cohen, D., & Garcia, R. (1984). Facial expression during Brazelton neonatal assessments. *Infant Mental Health Journal, 5,* 61–71.

Field, T., Harding, J., Yando, R., Gonzalez, K., Lasko, D., Bendell, D., & Marks, C. (1998). Feelings and attitudes of gifted students. *Adolescence, 39,* 331–342.

Field, T. M. (1979). Games parents play with normal and high-risk infants. *Child Psychiatry and Human Development, 10,* 41–48.

Field, T. M. (1981). Infant gaze aversion and heart rate during face-to-face interactions. *Infant Behavior and Development, 4,* 307–313.

Field, T. M. (1982). Individual differences in the expressivity of neonates and young infants. In R. S. Feldman (Ed.), *Development of nonverbal behavior in children.* New York: Springer-Verlag.

Field, T. M. (1987). Interaction and attachment in normal and atypical infants. *Journal of Consulting and Clinical Psychology, 14,* 183–184.

Field, T. M. (1990). Alleviating stress in newborn infants in the intensive care unit. In B. M. Lester & E. Z. Tronick (Eds.), *Stimulation and the preterm infant: The limits of plasticity.* Philadelphia: Saunders.

Field, T. M. (1995a). Infant massage therapy. In T. M. Field (Ed.), *Touch in early development.* Hillsdale, NJ: Erlbaum.

Field, T. M. (1995b). Massage therapy for infants and children. *Journal of Developmental & Behavioral Pediatrics, 16,* 105–111.

Field, T. M. (Ed.). (1988). *Stress and coping across development.* Hillsdale, NJ: Erlbaum.

Field, T. M., & Millsap, R. E. (1991). Personality in advanced old age: Continuity or change? *Journal of Gerontology: Psychological Sciences, 46,* P299–P308.

Fields, J. & Casper, L.M. (2001). *America's Families and Living Arrangements: March 2000.* Current Population Reports P20–537. U.S Census Bureau Washington D.C.

Fields-Meyer, T. (1995, September 25). Having their say. *People,* pp. 50–60.

Fifer, W. (1987). Neonatal preference for mother's voice. In N. A. Kasnegor, E. M. Blass, & M. A. Hofer, (Eds.), *Perinatal development: A psychobiological perspective. Behavioral biology* (pp. 111–124). Orlando, FL: Academic Press.

Figley, C. R. (1973). Child density and the marital relationship. *Journal of Marriage and the Family, 35,* 272–282.

Finch, C. E. (1990). *Longevity, senescence, and the genome.* Chicago: University of Chicago Press.

Finch, C. E., & Tanzi, R. E. (1997, October 17). Genetics of aging. *Science, 278,* 407–410.

Fincham, F. D. (1998). Child development and marital relations. *Child Development, 69,* 543–574.

Fincham, F. D., Beach, S. R. H., Harold, G. T., & Osborne, L. N. (1997). Marital satisfaction and depression: Different causal relationships for men and women? *Psychological Science, 8,* 351–357.

Findlen, B. (1990). Culture: A refuge for murder. *Ms.,* pp. 1, 47.

Fingerhut, L. A., & Kleinman, J. C. (1990). International and interstate comparisons of homicide among young males. *Journal of the American Medical Association, 263,* 3292–3295.

Fingerhut, L. A., & MaKuc, D. M. (1992). Mortality among minority populations in the United States. *American Journal of Public Health, 82,* 1168–1170.

Finkbeiner, A. K. (1996). *After the death of a child: Living with loss through the years.* New York: The Free Press.

Finkelhor, D. (1997). The homicides of children and youth: A developmental perspective. In G. K. Kantor & J. L. Janinski (Ed.), *Out of the darkness: Contemporary perspectives on family violence* (pp. 17–34). Thousand Oaks, CA: Sage.

Finkelstein, D. L., Harper, D. A., & Rosenthal, G. E. (1998). Does length of hospital stay during labor and delivery influence patient satisfaction? Results from a regional study. *American Journal of Managed Care, 4,* 1701–1708.

Fiore, S. M., & Schooler, J. W. (1998). Right hemisphere contributions to creative problem solving: Converging evidence for divergent thinking. In M. Beeman & C. Chiarello (Eds.), *Right hemisphere language comprehension: Perspectives from cognitive neuroscience* (pp. 349–371). Mahwah, NJ: Erlbaum.

First, J. M., & Cardenas, J. (1986). A minority view on testing. *Educational Measurement Issues and Practice, 5,* 6–11.

Fischer, K. W., & Hencke, R. W. (1996). Infants' construction of actions in context: Piaget's contributions to research on early development. *Psychological Science, 7,* 204–210.

Fischer, K. W., & Rose, S. P. (1994). Dynamic development of coordination of components in brain and behavior: A framework for theory and research. In G. Dawson & K. W. Fischer (Eds.), *Human behavior and the developing brain.* New York: Guilford.

Fischer, K. W., & Rose, S. P. (1995). Concurrent cycles in the dynamic development of brain and behavior. *Newsletter of the Society for Research in Child Development,* p. 16.

Fish, J. M. (Ed.). (2001). *Race and intelligence: Separating science from myth.* Mahwah, NJ: Erlbaum.

Fishbein, H. D., & Imai, S. (1993). Preschoolers select playmates on the basis of gender and race. *Journal of Applied Developmental Psychology, 14,* 303–316.

Fishel, E. (1993, September). Starting kindergarten. *Parents,* pp. 165–169.

Fisher, C., & Tokura, H. (1996). Acoustic cues to grammatical structure in infant-directed speech: Cross-linguistic evidence. *Child Development, 67,* 3192–3218.

Fisher, J., Astbury, J., & Smith, A. (1997). Adverse psychological impact of obstetric interventions: A prospective longitudinal study. *Australian & New Zealand Journal of Psychiatry, 31,* 728–738.

Fishman, C. (1999, May). Watching the time go by. *American Demographics,* 56–57.

Fiske, S. T., & Taylor, S. E. (1991). *Social cognition* (2nd ed.). New York: McGraw-Hill.

Fivush, R. (Ed.). (1995). *Long-term retention of infant memories.* Hillsdale, NJ: Erlbaum.

Fivush, R., Kuebli, J., & Clubb, P.A. (1992). The structure of events and event representations: A developmental analysis. *Child Development, 63,* 188–201.

Flavell, J. H. (1985). *Cognitive development* (2nd ed.). Englewood Cliffs, NJ: Prentice-Hall.

Flavell, J. H. (1994). Cognitive development: Past, present, and future. In R. D. Parke, P. A. Ornstein, J. J. Rieser, & C. Zahn-Waxler (Eds.), *A century of developmental psychology.* Washington, DC: American Psychological Association.

Flavell, J. H. (1996). Piaget's legacy. *Psychological Science, 7,* 200–203.

Flavell, J. H., Green, F. L., & Flavell, E. R. (1995). The development of children's knowledge about attentional focus. *Developmental Psychology, 31,* 706–712.

Fleming, J. E., & Offord, D. R. (1990). Epidemiology of childhood depressive disorders: A critical review. *Journal of the American Academy of Child and Adolescent Psychiatry, 29,* 571–580.

Fletcher, A. C., Darling, N. E., Steinberg, L., & Dornbusch, S. M. (1995). The company they keep: Relation of adolescents' adjustment and behavior to their friends' perceptions of authoritative parenting in the social network. *Developmental Psychology, 31,* 300–310.

Flint, M. (1989). Cultural and subcultural meanings to the menopause. *Menopause Management, 2(3),* 11.

Florian, V., & Kravetz, S. (1985). Children's concepts of death: A cross-cultural comparison among Muslims, Druze, Christians, and Jews in Israel. *Journal of Cross-Cultural Psychology, 16,* 174–189.

Fogel, A. (1980). Peer vs. mother-directed behavior in one- to three-month-old infants. *Infant Behavior and Development, 2,* 215–226.

Fogel, A., Nelson-Goens, G. C., Hsu, H., & Shapiro, A. F. (2000). Do different infant smiles reflect different positive emotions? *Social Development, 9,* 497–520.

Folkman, S., & Lazarus, R. S. (1980). An analysis of coping in a middle-aged community sample. *Journal of Health and Social Behavior, 21,* 219–239.

Folkman, S., & Lazarus, R. S. (1988). Coping as a mediator of emotion. *Journal of Personality and Social Psychology, 54,* 466–475.

Forrest, R., & Forrest, M. B. (1991). *Retirement living: A guide to housing alternatives.* New York: Facts on File.

Fowers, B. J., & Richardson, F. C. (1996). Why is multiculturalism good? *American Psychologist, 51,* 609–621.

Fox, N., Kimmerly, N. L., & Schafer, W. D. (1991). Attachment to mother/attachment to father: A meta-analysis. *Child Development, 62,* 210–225.

Fox, N. F. (Ed.). (1994). *The development of emotion regulation: Biological and behavioral considerations.* (2–3, Serial No. 240).

Fozard, J. L., Vercruyssen, M., Reynolds, S. L., Hancock, P. A., et al. (1994). Age differences and changes in reaction time: The Baltimore Longitudinal Study of Aging. *Journal of Gerontology, 49,* 179–189.

Francasso, M. P., Lamb, M. E., Scholmerich, A., & Leyendecker, B. (1997). The ecology of mother–infant interaction in Euro-American and immigrant Central American families living in the United States. *International Journal of Behavioral Development, 20,* 207–217.

Franck, I., & Brownstone, D. (1991). *The parent's desk reference.* New York: Prentice-Hall.

Franzoi, S. L., Davis, M. H., & Vasquez-Suson, K. A. (1994). Two social worlds: Social correlates and stability of adolescent status groups. *Journal of Personality and Social Psychology, 67,* 462–473.

Freedman, D. G. (1979, January). Ethnic differences in babies. *Human Nature,* pp. 15–20.

Freedman, R., Adler, L. E., & Leonard, S. (1999). Alternative phenotypes for the complex genetics of schizophrenia. *Biological Psychiatry, 45,* 551–558.

Freiberg, P. (1998 February). We know how to stop the spread of AIDS: So why can't we? *APA Monitor, 32.*

Freiberg P. (1998, February). President's AIDS budget wins kudos. *Newsline/People with AIDS Coalition of New York,* 23-44.

French, S., & Swain, J. (1997). Young disabled people. In J. Roche & S. Tucker (Eds.), *Youth in society: Contemporary theory, policy and practice* (pp. 199–206). London, England: Sage.

Frenkel, L. D., & Gaur, S. (1994). Perinatal HIV infection and AIDS. *Clinics in Perinatology, 21,* 95–107.

Freud, S. (1920). *A general introduction to psychoanalysis.* New York: Boni & Liveright.

Freud, S. (1922/1959). *Group psychology and the analysis of the ego.* London: Hogarth.

Freudenberger, H. J., & Richelson, G. (1980). *Burnout: The high cost of high achievement.* New York: Bantam.

Fried, P. A., & Watkinson, B. (1990). 36- and 48-month neurobehavioral follow-up of children prenatally exposed to marijuana, cigarettes, and alcohol. *Developmental and Behavioral Pediatrics, 11,* 49–58.

Friedman, D., Berman, S., & Hamberger, M. (1993). Recognition memory and ERPs: Age-related changes in young, middle-aged, and elderly adults. *Journal of Psychophysiology, 7,* 181–201.

Friedman, H. S., Tucker, J. S., Schwartz, J. E., Martin, L. R., Tomlinson-Keasey, C., Wingard, D. L., & Criqui, M. H. (1995a). Childhood conscientiousness and longevity: Health behaviors and cause of death. *Journal of Personality and Social Psychology, 68,* 696–703.

Friedman, H. S., Tucker, J. S., Schwartz, J. E., Tomlinson-Keasey, C., Martin, L. R., Wingard, D. L., & Criqui, M. H. (1995b). Psychosocial and behavioral predictors of longevity: The aging and death of the "Termites." *American Psychologist, 50,* 69–78.

Friedman, W. J. (1993). Memory for the time of past events. *Psychological Bulletin, 113,* 44–66.

Friend, R. M., & Neale, J. M. (1972). Children's perceptions of success and failure: An attributional analysis of the effects of race and social class. *Developmental Psychology, 7,* 124–128.

Frishman, R. (1996, October). Hormone replacement therapy for men. *Harvard Health Letter,* pp. 6–8.

Frishman, R. G. (1997a). *The aging eye.* Cambridge, MA: Harvard Medical School Health Publications Group.

Fromholt, P., & Larsen, S. F. (1991). Autobiographical memory in normal, aging and primary degenerative dementia (dementia of the Alzheimer type). *Journal of Gerontology, 46,* 85–91.

Fry, C. L. (1985). Culture, behavior, and aging in the comparative perspective. In J. E. Birren & K. W. Schaie (Eds.), *Handbook of the psychology of aging.* New York: Van Nostrand Reinhold.

Fryer, D., & Payne, R. (1986). Being unemployed: A review of the literature on the psychological experience of unemployment. In C. L. Cooper and I. T. Robertson (Eds.), *International review of industrial and organizational psychology.* Chichester, England: Wiley.

Fu, W., Killen, M., Culmsee, C., Dhar, S., Pandita, T. K., & Mattson, M. P. (2000). The catalytic subunit of telomerase is expressed in developing brain neurons and serves a cell survival-promoting function. *Journal of Molecular Neuroscience, 14,* 3–15.

Fuchs, D., & Fuchs, L. S. (1994). Inclusive schools movement and the radicalization of special education reform. *Exceptional Children, 60,* 294–309.

Fugate, W. N., & Mitchell, E. S. (1997). Women's images of midlife: Observations from the Seattle Midlife Women's Health Study. *Health Care for Women International, 18,* 439–453.

Fuligni, A. J. (1997). The academic achievement of adolescents from immigrant families: The roles of family background, attitudes, and behavior. *Child Development, 68,* 351–368.

Fulgini, A. J. (1998). The adjustment of children from immigrant families. *Current Directions in Psychological Science, 7,* 99–103.

Fuligni, A. J., Tseng, V., & Lam, M. (1999). Attitudes toward family obligations among American adolescents with Asian, Latin American, and European backgrounds. *Child Development, 70,* 1030–1044.

Furman, W., & Buhrmester, D. (1992). Age and sex differences in perceptions of networks of personal relationships. *Child Development, 63,* 103–115.

Furnham, A., & Weir, C. (1996). Lay theories of child development. *Journal of Genetic Psychology, 157,* 211–226.

Furstenberg, Jr., F. F. (1996, June). The future of marriage. *American Demographics,* pp. 34–40.

Furstenberg, Jr., F. F., Brooks-Gunn, J., & Morgan, S. P. (1987). *Adolescent mothers in later life.* New York: Cambridge University Press.

Gable, S., & Lutz, S. (2000). Household, parent, and child contributions to childhood obesity. *Family Relations: Interdisciplinary Journal of Applied Family Studies, 49,* 293–300.

Gadow, K. D., & Sprafkin, J. (1993). Television "violence" and children with emotional and behavioral disorders. *Journal of Emotional and Behavioral Disorders, 1,* 54–63.

Gaertner, S. L., Mann, J. A., Dovidio, J. F., Murrell, A. J., & Pomare, M. (1990). How does cooperation reduce intergroup bias? *Journal of Personality and Social Psychology, 59,* 692–704.

Gagnon, S. G., & Nagle, R. J. (2000). Comparison of the revised and original versions of the Bayley Scales of Infant Development. *School Psychology International, 21,* 293–305.

Galambos, N. L., & Dixon, R. A. (1984). Toward understanding and caring for latchkey children. *Child Care Quarterly, 13,* 116–125.

Galbraith, K. M, & Dobson, K. S. (2000). The role of the psychologist in determining competence for assisted suicide/euthanasia in the terminally ill. *Canadian Psychology, 41,* 174–183.

Gallagher, J. J. (1994). Teaching and learning: New models. *Annual Review of Psychology, 45,* 171–195.

Gallup, G. G., Jr. (1977). Self-recognition in primates: A comparative approach to the bidirectional properties of consciousness. *American Psychologist, 32,* 329–337.

Gallup Poll (1998). Ideal number of children. Appeared in March 1998 *American Demographics,* p. 35.

Galper, A., Wigfield, A., & Seefeldt, C. (1997). Head Start parents' beliefs about their children's abilities, task values, and performances on different actives. *Child Development, 68,* 897–907.

Gans, J. (1990). *America's adolescents: How healthy are they?* Chicago: American Medical Association.

Garbaciak, J. A. (1990). Labor and delivery: Anesthesia, induction of labor, malpresentation, and operative delivery. *Current Opinion in Obstetrics and Gynecology, 2,* 773–779.

Garbarino, J., & Asp, C. (1981). *Successful schools and competent students.* Lexington, MA: Lexington Books.

Garber, M. (1981). Malnutrition during pregnancy and lactation. In G. H. Bourne (Ed.), *World review of nutrition and dietetics* (Vol. 36). Basel, Switzerland: Karger.

Gardner, H. (2000). *Intelligence reframed: Multiple intelligences for the 21st century.* New York: Basic Books.

Gardner, R. M., Stark, K., Friedman, B. N., & Jackson, N. A. (2000). Predictors of eating disorder scores in children ages 6 through 14: A longitudinal study. *Journal of Psychosomatic Research, 49,* 199–205.

Garnefski, N., & Arends, E. (1998). Sexual abuse and adolescent maladjustment: Differences between male and female victims. *Journal of Adolescence, 21,* 99–107.

Garnett, L. R. (1996, May). Keeping the brain in tip-top shape. *Harvard Health Letter,* pp. 3–4.

Garrity, C., Jens, K., & Porter, W. W. (1996, August). *Bully-victim problems in the school setting.* Paper presented at the annual meeting of the American Psychological Association. Toronto, Canada.

Gathercole, S. E. (1998). The development of memory. *Journal of Child Psychology & Psychiatry & Allied Disciplines, 39,* 3–27.

Gatz, M. (1997, August). *Variations of depression in later life.* Paper presented at the Annual Convention of the American Psychological Association, Chicago.

Gaulden, M. E. (1992). Maternal age effect: The enigma of Down syndrome and other trisomic conditions. *Mutation Research, 296,* 69–88.

Gauvain, M. (1998). Cognitive development in social and cultural context. *Current Directions in Psychological Science, 7,* 188-194.

Gavin, L. A., Furman, W. (1996). Adolescent girls' relationships with mothers and best friends. *Child Development, 67,* 375–386.

Gazzaniga, M. S. (1983). Right-hemisphere language following brain bisection: A twenty-year perspective. *American Psychologist, 38,* 525–537.

Geary, D. C. (1998). *Male, female: The evolution of human sex differences.* Washington, DC: APA Books.

Geary, D. C. (1996). International differences in mathematical achievement: Their nature, causes, and consequences. *Current Directions in Psychological Science, 5,* 133–137.

Geary, D. C., & Bjorklund, D. F. (2000). Evolutionary developmental psychology. *Child Development, 71,* 57–65.

Geddie, L., Dawson, B., & Weunsch, K. (1998). Socioeconomic status and ethnic differences in preschoolers' interactions with anatomically detailed dolls. *Child Maltreatment, 3,* 43–52.

Gelfand, M. M. (2000). Sexuality among older women. *Journal of Womens Health & Gender-Based Medicine, 9,* (Suppl 1), S-15-S-20.

Gelles, R. J. (1994). *Contemporary families.* Newbury Park, CA: Sage.

Gelman, D. (1994, April 18). The mystery of suicide. *Newsweek,* 44–49.

Gelman, R. (1972). Logical capacity of very young children: Number invariance rules. *Child Development, 43,* 75–90.

Gelman, R., & Baillargeon, R. (1983). A review of ome Piagetian concepts. In P. H. Mussen (Ed.), *Handbook of child psychology: Vol 3. Cognitive development* (4th ed., pp. 167–230). New York: Wiley.

Gelman, R., & Gallistel, C. R. (1978). *The child's understanding of number.* Cambridge, MA: Harvard University Press.

Gelman, S. A., & Kalish, C. W. (1993). Categories and causality. In R. Pasnak & M. L. Howe (Eds.), *Emerging themes in cognitive development. Vol. II: Competencies.* New York: Springer-Verlag.

General Social Survey. (1998). *National Opinion Research Center.* Chicago: University of Chicago.

Genesee, F. (1994). Bilingualism. In V. S. Ramachandran (Ed.), *Encyclopedia of human behavior.* San Diego: Academic Press.

George-Hyslop, P. H. S. (2000, December). Piecing together Alzheimer's. *Scientific American,* 76–83.

Gergen, M. M. (1990). Finished at 40: Women's development within the patriarchy. *Psychology of Women Quarterly, 14,* 471–493.

Gerrish, C. J., & Mennella, J. A. (2000). Short-term influence of breastfeeding on the infants' interaction with the environment. *Developmental Psychobiology, 36,* 40–48.

Gesell, A. L. (1946). The ontogenesis of infant behavior. In L. Carmichael (Ed.), *Manual of child psychology.* New York: Harper.

Gesser, G., Wong, P. T., & Reker, G. T. (1988). Death attitudes across the life span: The develop-ment and validation of the Death Attitude Profile (DAP). *Omega: Journal of Death and Dying, 18,* 113–128.

Gibson, E. J., & Walk, R. D. (1960). The "visual cliff." *Scientific American, 202,* 64–71.

Gibson, R. C. (1986). Older black Americans. *Generations, 10(4),* 35–39.

Gilbert, K. R. (1997). Couple coping with the death of a child. In C. R. Figley, B. E. Bride, & N. Mazza (Eds.), *The series in trauma and loss. Death and trauma: The traumatology of grieving* (pp. 101–121). Washington, DC: Taylor & Francis.

Gilbert, L. A. (1994). Current perspectives on dual-career families. *Current Directions in Psychological Science, 3,* 101–105.

Gilbert, S. (2000). *Counseling for eating disorders.* Thousand Oaks, CA: Sage.

Gilligan, C. (1982). *In a different voice: Psychological theory and women's development.* Cambridge, MA: Harvard University Press.

Gilligan, C. (1987). Adolescent development reconsidered. In C. E. Irwin (Ed.), *Adolescent social behavior and health.* San Francisco: Jossey-Bass.

Gilligan, C., Lyons, N. P., & Hammer, T. J. (Eds.). (1990). *Making connections.* Cambridge, MA: Harvard University Press.

Gilligan, C., Ward, J. V., & Taylor, J. M. (Eds.). (1988). *Mapping the moral domain: A contribution of women's thinking to psychological theory and education.* Cambridge, MA: Harvard University Press.

Ginzberg, E. (1972). Toward a theory of occupational choice: A restatement. *Vocational Guidance Quarterly, 12,* 10–14.

Gjerde, P., Block, J., & Block, J. (1988). Depressive symptoms and personality during late adolescence: Gender differences in the externalization-internalization of symptom expression. *Journal of Abnormal Psychology, 97,* 475–486.

Gladue, B. A. (1994). The biopsychology of sexual orientation. *Current Directions in Psychological Science, 3,* 150–154.

Glasgow, K. L., Dornbusch, S. M., Troyer, L., Steinberg, L., & Ritter, P. L. (1997). Parenting styles, adolescents' attributions, and educational outcomes in nine heterogeneous high schools. *Child Development, 68,* 507–529.

Gleason J. B. (1987). Sex differences in parent–child interaction. In S. U. Philips, S. Steele, & C. Tanz (Eds.), *Language, gender, and sex in comparative perspective.* New York: Cambridge University Press.

Gleason, J. B., Perlmann, R. U., Ely, R., & Evans, D. W. (1994). The babytalk register: Parents' use of diminutives. In J. L. Sokolov & C. E. Snow (Eds.), *Handbook of research in language development using CHILDES.* Mahwah, NJ: Erlbaum.

Gleason, J. B., Perlmann, R. U., Ely, R., & Evans, D. W. (1991). The babytalk register: Parents' use of diminutives. In J. L. Sokolov, & C. E. Snow (Eds.), *Handbook of research in language development using CHILDES.* Hillsdale, NJ: Erlbaum.

Gleick, E., Reed, S., & Schindehette, S. (1994, October 24). The baby trap. *People Weekly,* 38–56.

Gleitman, L., & Landau, B. (1994). *The acquisition of the lexicon.* Cambridge, MA: Bradford.

Glenn, N. D., & Weaver, C. N. (1977). The marital happiness of remarried divorced persons. *Journal of Marriage and the Family, 39,* 331–337.

Glenn, N. D., & Weaver, C. N. (1990). Quantitative research on marital quality in the 1980s: A critical review. *Journal of Marriage and the Family, 52,* 818–831.

Glick, P., Fiske, S. T., Mladinic, A., Saiz, J. L., et al. (2000). Beyond prejudice as simple antipathy: Hostile and benevolent sexism across cultures. *Journal of Personality and Social Psychology, 79,* 763–775.

Glick, P., Zion, C., & Nelson, C. (1988). What mediates sex discrimination in hiring decisions? *Journal of Personality and Social Psychology, 55,* 178–186.

Gluhoski, V., Leader, J., & Wortman, C. B. (1994). Grief and bereavement. In V. S. Ramachandran (Ed.), *Encyclopedia of human behavior.* San Diego: Academic Press.

Gogate, L. J., Bahrick, L. E., & Watson, J. D. (2000). A study of multimodal motherese: The role of temporal synchrony between verbal labels and gestures. *Child Development, 71,* 878–894.

Goldscheider, F. K. (1994). Divorce and remarriage: Effects on the elderly population. *Reviews in Clinical Gerontology, 4,* 253–259.

Goldsmith, H. H., & Harman, C. (1994). Temperament and attachment: Individuals and relationships. *Current Directions in Psychological Science, 3,* 53–57.

Goldsmith, L. T. (2000). Tracking trajectories of talent: Child prodigies growing up. In R. C. Friedman, & B. M. Shore, (Eds.), et al. *Talents unfolding: Cognition and development.* Washington, DC: American Psychological Association.

Goleman, D. (1985, February 5). Mourning: New studies affirm its benefits. *The New York Times,* pp. C1, C6.

Goleman, D. (1993, July 21). Baby sees, baby does, and classmates follow. *The New York Times,* p. C10.

Goleman, D. (1995). *Emotional intelligence.* New York: Bantam.

Golinkoff, R. M. (1993). When is communication a "meeting of minds"? *Journal of Child Language, 20,* 199–207.

Golombok, S., & Fivush, R. (1994). *Gender development.* Cambridge, England: Cambridge University Press.

Golombok, S., & Tasker, F. (1996). Do parents influence the sexual orientation of their children? Findings from a longitudinal study of lesbian families. *Developmental Psychology, 32,* 3–11.

Gomez, C. F. (1991). *Regulating death: Euthanasia and the case of the Netherlands.* New York: Free Press.

Gondolf, E. W. (1985). Fighting for control: A clinical assessment of men who batter. *Social Casework, 66,* 48–54.

Gongla, P., & Thompson, E. H. (1987). Single-parent families. In M. B. Sussman & S. K. Steinmetz (Eds.), *Handbook of marriage and the family.* New York: Plenum.

Goode, E. (1999, January 12). Clash over when, and how, to toilet-train. *The New York Times,* p. A1, A17.

Goodlin-Jones, B. L., Burnham, M. M., & Anders, T. F. (2000). Sleep and sleep disturbances: Regulatory processes in infancy. In A. J. Sameroff & M. Lewis, (Eds.), et al. *Handbook of developmental psychopathology* (2nd ed.). New York: Kluwer Academic/Plenum Publishers.

Goodman, G. S., & Reed, R. S. (1986). Age differences in eyewitness testimony. *Law and Human Behavior, 10,* 317–332.

Goodman, J. C., & Nusbaum, H. C. (Eds.). (1994). *The development of speech perception.* Cambridge, MA: Bradford.

Goodstein, R., & Ponterotto, J. G. (1997). Racial and ethnic identity: Their relationship and their contribution to self-esteem. *Journal of Black Psychology, 23,* 275–292.

Goodwin, M. H. (1980). Directive-response speech sequences in girls' and boys' task activities. In S. McConnell-Ginet, R. Borker, & N. Furman (Eds.), *Women and language in literature and society* (pp. 157–173). New York: Praeger.

Goodwin, M. H. (1990). Tactical uses of stories: Participation frameworks within girls' and boys' disputes. *Discourse Processes, 13,* 33–71.

Googans, B., & Burden, D. (1987). Vulnerability of working parents: Balancing work and home roles. *Social Work, 32,* 295–300.

Goold, S. D., Williams, B., & Arnold, R. M. (2000). Conflicts regarding decisions to limit treatment: a differential diagnosis. *Journal of the American Medical Association, 283,* 909–914.

Goossens, F. A., & Van Ijzendoorn, M. H. (1990). Quality of infants' attachments to professional caregivers: Relation to infant–parent attachment and day-care characteristics. *Child Development, 61,* 832–837.

Gordon, B. N., Baker-Ward, L., & Ornstein, P. A. (2001). Children's testimony: A review of research on memory for past experiences. *Clinical Child & Family Psychology Review, 4,* 157–181.

Gordon, J. W. (1999, March 26). Genetic enhancement in humans. *Science, 283,* 2023–2024.

Gorman, K. S., & Pollitt, E. (1992). Relationship between weight and body proportionality at birth, growth during the first year of life, and cognitive development at 36, 48, and 60 months. *Infant Behavior and Development, 15,* 279–296.

Gortmaker, S. L., Dietz, W. H., Sobol, A. M., & Welher, C. A. (1987). Increasing pediatric obesity in the United States. *American Journal of the Diseases of Children, 141,* 535–540.

Gortmaker, S. L., Must, A., Sobol, A. M., Peterson, K., Colditz, G. A., & Dietz, W. H. (1996). Television viewing as a cause of increasing obesity among children in the United States, 1896–1990. *Archives of Pediatrics & Adolescent Medicine, 150,* 356–362.

Goswami, U. (1998). *Cognition in children.* Philadelphia: Psychology Press.

Gottesman, I. I. (1991). *Schizophrenia genesis: The origins of madness.* New York: Freeman.

Gottesman, I. I. (1993). Origins of schizophrenia: Past as prologue. In R. Plomin & G. E. McClearn, (Eds.), *Nature, nurture, and psychology.* Washington, DC: American Psychological Association.

Gottfredson, G. D., & Holland, J. L. (1990). A longitudinal test of the influence of congruence: Job satisfaction, competency utilization, and counterproductive behavior. *Journal of Counseling Psychology, 37,* 389–398.

Gottfried, A. E., & Gottfried, A. W. (Eds.). (1994). *Redefining families.* New York: Plenum.

Gottfried, A. W., Gottfried, A. E., Bathurst, K., & Guerin, D. W. (1994). *Early developmental aspects:*

The Fullerton Longitudinal Study. New York: Plenum.

Gottlieb, G. (1991). Experimental canalization of behavioral development: Theory. *Developmental Psychology, 27,* 373–381.

Gottman, J. M. (1986). The world of coordinated play: Same- and cross-sex friendship in young children. In J. M. Gottman & J. G. Parker (Eds.), *Conversations of friends: Speculations on affective development* (pp. 139–191). Cambridge, England: Cambridge University Press.

Gottman, J. M. (1993). *What predicts divorce? The relationship between marital processes and marital outcomes.* Hillsdale, NJ: Erlbaum.

Gottman, J. M., & Katz, L. F. (1989). Effects of marital discord on young children's peer interaction and health. *Developmental Psychology, 25,* 373–381.

Gottman, J. M., Fainsilber-Katz, L., & Hooven, C. (1996). *Meta-emotion: How families communicate emotionally.* Mahwah, NJ: Erlbaum.

Gottschalk, E. C., Jr. (1983, February 21). Older Americans: The aging man gains in the 1970s, outpacing rest of the population. *The Wall Street Journal,* pp. 1, 20.

Gould, S. J. (1977). *Ontogeny and phylogeny.* Cambridge, MA: Harvard University Press.

Goyette-Ewing, M. (2000). Children's after school arrangements: A study of self-care and developmental outcomes. *Journal of Prevention & Intervention in the Community, 20,* 55–67.

Graber, J. A., Brooks-Gunn, J., & Warren, M. P. (1995). The antecedents of menarcheal age: Heredity, family environment, and stressful life events. *Child Development, 66,* 346–359.

Grady, C. L., McIntosh, A. R., Horwitz, B., Maison, J. M., Ungerleider, L. G., Mentis, M. J., Pietrini, P., Schapiro, M. B., & Haxby, J. V. (1995, July 14). Age-related reductions in human recognition memory due to impaired encoding. *Science, 269,* 218–221.

Graf, P. (1990). Life-span changes in implicit and explicit memory. *Bulletin of the Psychonomic Society, 28,* 353–358.

Graham, E. (1995, February 9). Leah: Life is all sweetness and insecurity. *The Wall Street Journal,* p. B1.

Graham, S. (1986). An attributional perspective on achievement motivation and black children. In R. S. Feldman, (Ed), *The social psychology of education: Current research and theory.* New York: Cambridge University Press.

Graham, S. (1990). Communicating low ability in the classroom: Bad things good teachers sometimes do. In S. Graham & V. S. Folkes (Eds.), *Attribution theory: Applications to achievement, mental health, and interpersonal conflict.* Hillsdale, NJ: Erlbaum.

Graham, S. (1992). "Most of the subjects were white and middle class": Trends in published research on African Americans in selected APA journals. *American Psychologist, 17,* 629–639.

Graham, S. (1994). Motivation in African Americans. *Review of Educational Research, 64,* 55–117.

Graham, S. (1997). Using attribution theory to understand social and academic motivation in African American youth. *Educational Psychologist, 32,* 21–34.

Graham, S., & Harris, K. R. (1997). Whole language and process writing: Does one approach fit all? In J. W. Lloyd, E. J. Kameenui, & D. Chard (Eds.), *Issues*

in educating students with disabilities. (pp. 239–258). Mahwah, NJ: Erlbaum.

Grambs, J. D. (1989). *Women over forty: Visions and realities.* New York: Springer.

Grant, V. J. (1994). Sex of infant differences in mother–infant interaction: A reinterpretation of past findings. *Developmental Review, 14,* 1–26.

Grantham-McGregor, S., Ani, C., & Fernald, L. (2001). The role of nutrition in intellectual development. In R. J. Sternberg & E. L. Grigorenko (Eds.), *Environmental effects on cognitive abilities.* Mahwah, NJ: Erlbaum.

Grantham-McGregor, S., Powell, C., Walker, S., Chang, S., & Fletcher, P. (1994). The long-term follow-up of severely malnourished children who participated in an intervention program. *Child Development, 65,* 428–439.

Gratch, G., & Schatz, J. A. (1987). Cognitive development: The relevance of Piaget's infancy books. In J. D. Osofsky (Ed.), *Handbook of infant development* (2nd ed.). New York: Wiley.

Grattan, M. P., DeVos, E. S., Levy, J., & McClintock, M. K. (1992). Asymmetric action in the human newborn: Sex differences in patterns of organization. *Child Development, 63,* 273–289.

Gray, L. C., Farish, S. J., & Dorevitch, M. (1992). A population-based study of assessed applicants to long-term nursing home care. *Journal of the American Geriatric Society, 40,* 596–600.

Gray-Little, B., & Hafdahl, A. R. (2000). Factors influencing racial comparisons of self-esteem: A quantitative review. *Psychological Bulletin, 126,* 26–54.

Green, C. P. (1991). Clinical considerations: Midlife daughters and their aging parents. *Journal of Gerontological Nursing, 17,* 6–12.

Greenberg, J., & Becker, M. (1988). Aging parents as family resources. *Gerontologist, 28,* 786–790.

Greene, K., Krcmar, M., Walters, L. H., Rubin, D. L., & Hale, J. L. (2000). Targeting adolescent risk-taking behaviors: The contribution of egocentrism and sensation-seeking. *Journal of Adolescence, 23,* 439–461.

Greenfield, P. (1995, Winter). Culture, ethnicity, race, and development: Implications for teaching theory and research. *SRCD Newsletter.* Chicago: Society for Research in Child Development.

Greenfield, P. M. (1976). Cross-cultural research and Piagetian theory: Paradox and progress. In K. F. Riegel & J. A. Meacham (Eds.), *The developing individual in a changing world: Vol. 1.* The Hague, The Netherlands: Mouton.

Greenfield, P. M. (1997). You can't take it with you. Why ability assessments don't cross cultures. *American Psychologist, 52,* 1115–1124.

Greenglass, E. R., & Burke, R. J. (1991). The relationship between stress and coping among Type A's. *Journal of Social Behavior and Personality, 6,* 361–373.

Greenhill, L. L., Halperin, J. M., & Abikoff, H. (1999). Stimulant medications. *Journal of the American Academy of Child and Adolescent Psychiatry, 38,* 503–512.

Gregory, S. (1856). *Facts for young women.* Boston.

Grey, W. H., (1999). Milken Institute, reported in Suro, R. (Nov. 1999). Mixed doubles. *American Demographics,* 57–62.

Grieser, T., & Kuhl, P. (1988). Maternal speech to infants in atonal language: Support for universal prosodic features in motherese. *Developmental Psychology, 24,* 14–20.

Griesler, P. C., & Kandel, D. B. (1998). Ethnic differences in correlates of adolescent cigarette smoking. *Journal of Adolescent Health, 23,* 167–180.

Griffith, D. R., Azuma, S. D., & Chasnoff, I. J. (1994). Three-year outcome of children exposed prenatally to drugs. *Journal of the American Academy of Child and Adolescent Psychiatry, 33,* 20–27.

Groome, L. J., Swiber, M. J., Atterbury, J. L., Bentz, L. S., & Holland, S. B. (1997). Similarities and differences in behavioral state organization during sleep periods in the perinatal infant before and after birth. *Child Development, 68,* 1–11.

Groome, L. J., Swiber, M. J., Bentz, L. S., Holland, S. B., & Atterbury, J. L. (1995). Maternal anxiety during pregnancy: Effect on fetal behavior at 38 to 40 weeks of gestation. *Developmental and Behavioral Pediatrics, 16,* 391–396.

Groopman, J. (1998 February 8). Decoding destiny. *The New Yorker,* p. 42–47.

Gross, J. (1991, June 16). More young single men hang on to apron strings. *The New York Times,* pp. A1, A18.

Gross, P. A. (1991). *Managing your health: Strategies for lifelong good health.* Yonkers, NY: Consumer Reports Books.

Gross, R. T., Spiker, D., & Haynes, C. W. (Eds.). (1997). *Helping low-birthweight, premature babies: The Infant Health and Development Program.* Stanford, CA: Stanford University Press.

Grossmann, K. E., Grossman, K., Huber, F., & Wartner, U. (1982). German children's behavior towards their mothers at 12 months and their fathers at 18 months in Ainsworth's strange situation. *International Journal of Behavioral Development, 4,* 157–181

Groves, B., Zuckerman, B., Marans, S., & Cohen, D. (1993). Silent victims: Children who witness violence. *Journal of the American Medical Association, 269,* 262–264.

Grusec, J. E. (1982). Socialization processes and the development of altruism. In J. P. Rushton & R. M. Sorrentino (Eds.), *Altruism and helping behavior.* Hillsdale, NJ: Erlbaum.

Grusec, J. E. (1991). The socialization of altruism. In M. S. Clark (Ed.), *Prosocial behavior.* Newbury Park, CA: Sage.

Grusec, J. E., & Goodnow, J. J. (1994a). Summing up and looking to the future. *Developmental Psychology, 30,* 29–31.

Grusec, J. E., & Kuczynski, L. E. (Eds.). (1997). *Parenting and children's internalization of values: A handbook of contemporary theory.* New York: Wiley.

Grych, J. H., & Clark, R. (1999). Maternal employment and development of the father–infant relationship in the first year. *Developmental Psychology, 35,* 893–903.

Gubrium, F. F. (1975). Being single in old age. *International Journal of Aging and Human Development, 6,* 29–41.

Gubrium, J. G. (1973). *The myth of the golden years: A socio-environmental theory of aging.* Springfield, IL: Thomas.

Guisinger, S., Cowan, P., & Schuldberg, D. (1989). Changing parent and spouse relations in the first

year of remarriage of divorced fathers. *Journal of Marriage and the Family, 51,* 445–456.

Gullotta, T. P., Adams, G. R., & Montemayor, R. (Eds.) (1995) *Substance misuse in adolescence.* Thousand Oaks, CA: Sage Publications.

Gump, L. S., Baker, R. C., & Roll, S. (2000). Cultural and gender differences in moral judgment: A study of Mexican Americans and Anglo-Americans. *Hispanic Journal of Behavioral Sciences, 22,* 78–93.

Gupta, U., & Singh, P. (1982). An exploratory study of love and liking and type of marriages. *Indian Journal of Applied Psychology, 19,* 92–97.

Gur, R. C., Gur, R. E., Obrist, W. D., Hungerbuhler, J. P., Younkin, D., Rosen, A. D., Skilnick, B. E., & Reivich, M. (1982). Sex and handedness differences in cerebral blood flow during rest and cognitive activity. *Science, 217,* 659–661.

Gur, R. E, & Chin, S. (1999). Laterality in functional brain imaging studies of schizophrenia. *Schizophrenia Bulletin, 25,* 141–156.

Guralnik, M. D., Ferrucci, L., Simonsick, E. M., Salive, M. E., & Wallace, R. B. (1995, March 2). Lower-extremity function in persons over the age of 70 years as a predictor of subsequent disability. *New England Journal of Medicine, 332,* 556–561.

Guthrie, G., & Lonner, W. (1986). Assessment of personality and psychopathology. In W. Lonner & J. Berry (Eds.), *Field methods in cross-cultural research.* Newbury Park, CA: Sage.

Guttentag, R. E. (1985). Memory and aging: Implications for theories of memory development during childhood. *Developmental Review, 5,* 56–82.

Guttman, M. (1997, May 16–18). Are you losing your mind? *USA Weekend,* pp. 4–5

Guyer, B. et al. (1995). Annual summary of vital statistics—1994. *Pediatrics, 96,* 1029–1039.

Haan, N. (1985). Processes of moral development: Cognitive or social disequilibrium? *Developmental Psychology, 21,* 996–1006.

Haan, N., Millsap, R., & Hartka, E. (1986). As time goes by: Change and stability in personality over fifty years. *Psychology and Aging, 1,* 220–232.

Hackel, L. S., & Ruble, D. N. (1992). Changes in the marital relationship after the first baby is born: Predicting the impact of expectancy disconfirmation. *Journal of Personality and Social Psychology, 62,* 944–957.

Haederle, M. (1999, January 18). Going too far? *People Weekly,* 101–103.

Hagestad, G. O., & Neugarten, B. L. (1985). Age and the life course. In R. H. Binstock & E. Shanas (Eds.), *Handbook of aging and the social sciences* (2nd ed.). New York: Van Nostrand Reinhold.

Haggerty, R., Garmezy, N., Rutter, M., & Sherrod, L. (Eds.). (1994). *Stress, risk, and resilience in childhood and adolescence.* New York: Cambridge University Press.

Hahn, C-S., & DiPietro, J. A. (2001). In vitro fertilization and the family: Quality of parenting, family functioning, and child psychosocial adjustment. *Developmental Psychology, 37,* 37–48.

Haight, B. K. (1991). Psychological illness in aging. In E. M. Baines (Ed.), *Perspectives on gerontological nursing.* Newbury Park, CA: Sage.

Haight, W. L., Wang, X., Fung, H. H., Williams, K., & Mintz, J. (1999). Universal developmental and variable aspects of young children's play: A cross-

cultural comparison of pretending at home. *Child Development, 70,* 1477–1488.

Haith, M. H. (1991, April). *Setting a path for the 90s: Some goals and challenges in infant sensory and perceptual development.* Paper presented at the biennial meeting of the Society for Research in Child Development, Seattle.

Haith, M. H. (1986). Sensory and perceptual processes in early infancy. *Journal of Pediatrics, 109(1),* 158–171.

Hakuta, K. U., & Garcia, E. E. (1989). Bilingualism and education. *American Psychologist, 44,* 374-379.

Hales, D. (1992). *An invitation to health: Taking charge of your life.* Menlo Park, CA: Benjamin/Cumings.

Hales, K. A., Morgan, M. A., & Thurnau, G. R. (1993). Influence of labor and route of delivery on the frequency of respiratory morbidity in term neonates. *International Journal of Gynecology & Obstetrics, 43,* 35–40.

Halford, G. S., Maybery, M. T., O'Hare, A. W., & Grant, P. (1994). The development of memory and processing capacity. *Child Development, 65,* 1338–1356.

Hall, E. G., & Lee, A. M. (1984). Sex differences in motor performance of young children: Fact or fiction? *Sex Roles, 10,* 217–230.

Hallberg, H. (1992). Life after divorce: A five-year follow-up study of divorced middle-aged men in Sweden. *Family Practice, 9,* 49–56.

Halliday, M. A. K. (1975). *Learning how to mean— Explorations in the development of language.* London: Edward Arnold.

Hallinan, M. T., & Williams, R. A. (1989). Interracial friendship choices in secondary schools. *American Sociological Review, 54,* 67–78.

Halpern, L. F., MacLean, W. E., & Baumeister, A. A. (1995). Infant sleep-wake characteristics: Relation to neurological status and the prediction of developmental outcome. *Developmental Review, 15,* 255–291.

Hamilton, C. (2000). Continuity and discontinuity of attachment from infancy through adolescence. *Child Development, 71,* 690–694.

Hamm, J. V. (2000). Do birds of a feather flock together? The variable bases for African American, Asian American, and European American adolescents' selection of similar friends. *Developmental Psychology, 36,* 209–219.

Hammer, R. P. (1984). The sexually dimorphic region of the preoptic area in rats contains denser opiate receptor binding sites in females. *Brain Researcher, 308,* 172–176.

Hammersley, R. (1992). Cue exposure and learning theory. *Addictive Behaviors, 17,* 297–300.

Hammond, W. A., & Romney, D. M. (1995). Cognitive factors contributing to adolescent depression. *Journal of Youth & Adolescence, 24,* 667–683.

Hamon, R. R., & Blieszner, R. (1990). Filial responsibility expectations among adult child–older parent pairs. *Journal of Gerontology, 45,* 110–112.

Hampson, J., & Nelson, K. (1993). The relation of maternal language to variation in rate and style of language acquisition. *Journal of Child Language, 20,* 313–342.

Hanna, E., & Meltzoff, A. N. (1993). Peer imitation by toddlers in laboratory, home, and day-care contexts: Implications for social learning and memory. *Developmental Psychology, 29,* 701–710.

Hansen, C. H. (1989). Priming sex-role stereotypic even schemas with rock music videos: Effects on impression favorability, trait inferences, and recall of subsequent male–female interaction. *Basic and Applied Social Psychology, 10,* 371–391.

Hansson, R. O., & Carpenter, B. N. (1994). *Relationship in old age: Coping with the challenge of transition.* New York: Guilford Press.

Happe, F. G. E., Winner, E., & Brownell, H. (1998). The getting of wisdom: Theory of mind in old age. *Developmental Psychology, 34,* 358–362.

Harkness, S., & Super, C. M. (1985). The cultural context of gender segregation in children's peer groups. *Child Development, 56,* 219–224.

Harlow, H. F., & Zimmerman, R. R. (1959). Affectional responses in the infant monkey. *Science, 130,* 421–432.

Harrell, J. S., Gansky, S. A., Bradley, C. B., & McMurray, R. G. (1997). Leisure time activities of elementary school children. *Nursing Research, 46,* 246–253.

Harrell, J. S., Bangdiwala, S. I., Deng, S., Webb, J. P., & Bradley, C. (1998). Smoking initiation in youth: The roles of gender, race, socioeconomics, and developmental status. *Journal of Adolescent Health, 23,* 271–279.

Harrell, S. (1981). Growing old in rural Taiwan. In P. T. Amoss & S. Harrell (Eds.), *Other ways of growing old.* Stanford, CA: Stanford University Press.

Harrell, J. S., Gansky, S. A., Bradley C. B., & McMurray, R. G. (1997). Leisure time activities of elementary school children. *Nursing Research, 46,* 246–253.

Harrington, R., Fudge, H., Rutter, M., Pickels, A., & Hill, J. (1990). Adult outcomes of childhood and adolescent depression. *Archives of General Psychiatry, 47,* 465–473.

Harris, J. R. (1998). *The nurture assumption: Why children turn out the way they do.* New York: Free Press.

Harris, J. R. (2000). Socialization, personality development, and the child's environments: Comment on Vandell. *Developmental Psychology, 36,* 711–723.

Harris, K.M. (in press). The health status and risk behavior of adolescents in immigrant families. In D.J. Hernandez (Ed.), *Children of immigrants: Health, adjustment, and public assistance.* Washington, DC: National Academy Press.

Harris, L. K., VanZandt, C. E., & Rees, T. H. (1997). Counseling needs of students who are deaf and hard of hearing. *School Counselor, 44,* 271–279.

Harris, M. B. (1994). Growing old gracefully: Age concealment and gender. *Journals of Gerontology, 49,* 149–158.

Harris, M. J., & Rosenthal, R. (1986). Four factors in the mediation of teacher expectancy effects. In R. S. Feldman (Ed.), *The social psychology of education.* Cambridge, MA: Cambridge University Press.

Harris, M. J., Milich, R., Corbitt, E. M., Hoover, D. W., et al. (1992). Self-fulfilling effects of stigmatizing information on children's social interactions. *Journal of Personality and Social Psychology, 63,* 41–50.

Harris, P. L. (1983). Infant cognition. In M. Haith & J. J. Campos (Eds.) & P. H. Mussen (Gen. Ed.), *Handbook of child psychology: Vol 2. Infancy and developmental psychobiology.* New York: Wiley.

Harris, P. L. (1987). The development of search. In P. Sallapatek & L. Cohen (Eds.), *Handbook of infant perception: From perception to cognition* (Vol. 2, pp. 155–207). Orlando, FL: Academic Press.

Hart, B., & Risley, T. R. (1995). *Meaningful differences in the everyday experience of young American children.* Baltimore, MD: Paul Brookes.

Hart, C. H., Yang, C., Nelson, D. A., Jin, S., Bazarskaya, N., & Nelson, L. (1998). Peer contact patterns, parenting practices, and preschoolers' social competence in China, Russia, and the United States. In P. Slee & K. Rigby (Eds.), *Peer relations amongst children: Current issues and future directions.* London: Routledge.

Hart, S. N., Brassard, M. R., & Karlson, H. (1996). Psychological maltreatment. In J. N. Briere, L. Berliner, J. Bulkley, C. Jenny, & T. Reid (Eds.). (1996). *The APSAC handbook on child maltreatment.* Thousand Oaks, CA: Sage.

Harter, S. (1990a). Identity and self-development. In S. Feldman & G. Elliott (Eds.), *At the threshold: The developing adolescent.* Cambridge, MA: Harvard University Press.

Harter, S. (1990b). Issues in the assessment of self-concept of children and adolescents. In A. LaGreca (Ed.), *Through the eyes of a child.* Boston: Allyn & Bacon.

Hartley, A. A. (1993). Evidence for selective preservation of spatial selective attention in old age. *Psychology and Aging, 8,* 371–379.

Hartshorne, T. S. (1994). Friendship. In V. S. Ramachandran (Ed.), *Encyclopedia of human behavior.* San Diego: Academic Press.

Hartup, W. W. (1983). Peer relations In P. H. Mussen (Ed.), *Handbook of child psychology* (Vol. 4, 4th ed.). New York: Wiley.

Hartup, W. W., & Stevens, N. (1997). Friendships and adaptation in the life course. *Psychological Bulletin, 121,* 355–370.

Hartup, W. W., & Stevens, N. (1999). Friendships and adaptation across the life span. *Current Directions in Psychological Science, 8,* 76–79.

Harvey, E. (1999). Short-term and long-term effects of early parental employment on children of the National Longitudinal Survey of Youth. *Developmental Psychology, 35,* 445–459.

Harvey, P. G., Hamlin, M. W., Kumar, R., & Delves, H. T. (1984). Blood lead, behavior, and intelligence test performance in preschool children. *Science of the Total Environment, 40,* 45–60.

Harway, M. (2000). Families experiencing violence. In W. C. Nichols & M. A. Pace-Nichols, (Eds.), et al. *Handbook of family development and intervention. Wiley series in couples and family dynamics and treatment.* New York: Wiley.

Harwood, R. L., Miller, J. G., & Irizarry, N. L. (1995). *Culture and attachment: Perceptions of the child in context.* New York: Guilford Press.

Harwood, R. L., Schoelmerich, A., Ventura-Cook, E., Schulze, P. A., & Wilson, S. P. (1996). Culture and class influences on Anglo and Puerto Rican mothers' beliefs regarding long-term socialization goals and child behavior. *Child Development, 67,* 2446–2461.

Hasher, L., & Zacks, R. T. (1984). Automatic processing of fundamental information: The case of frequency of occurrence. *American Psychologist, 39,* 1372–1388.

Haskins, R. (1989). Beyond metaphor: The efficacy of early childhood education. *American Psychologist, 44,* 274–282.

Hatfield, E. (1988). Passionate and companionate love. In R. J. Sternberg & M. L. Barnes (Eds.), *The psychology of love* (pp. 191–217). New Haven, CT: Yale University Press.

Hatfield, E., & Rapson, R. L. (1993). Historical and cross-cultural perspectives on passionate love and sexual desire. *Annual Review of Sex Research, 4,* 67–97.

Hatfield, E., & Sprecher, S. (1986). *Mirror, mirror . . . The importance of looks in everyday life.* Albany: State University of New York Press.

Hattery, A. (2000). *Women, work, and family: Balancing and weaving.* Thousand Oaks, CA: Sage.

Hauck, F. R. & Hunt, C. E. (2000). Sudden infant death syndrome in 2000. *Current Problems in Pediatrics, 30(8),* 237–261.

Haug, H. (1991). Aging of the brain. In F. C. Ludwig (Ed.), *Life-span extension: Consequences, intimacy, and close relationships.* New York: Springer.

Haugaard, J. J. (2000). The challenge of defining child sexual abuse. *American Psychologist, 55,* 1036–1039.

Havighurst, R. J. (1973). Social roles, work, leisure, and education. In C. Eisdorfer & M. P. Lawton (Eds.), *The psychology of adult development and aging.* Washington, DC: American Psychological Association.

Havighurst, R. J., Neugarten, B. L., & Tobin, S. S. (1968). Disengagement and patterns of aging. In B. L. Neugarten (Ed.), *Middle age and aging.* Chicago: University of Chicago Press.

Hawton, K. (1986). *Suicide and attempted suicide among children and adolescents.* Newbury Park, CA: Sage.

Hayden, T. (1998, September 21). The brave new world of sex selection. *Newsweek,* p. 93.

Hayflick, L. (1974). The strategy of senescence. *The Journal of Gerontology, 14,* 37–45.

Haymes, M., Green, L., & Quinto, R. (1984). Maslow's hierarchy, moral development, and prosocial behavioral skills within a child psychiatric population. *Motivation and Emotion, 8,* 23–31.

Hayne, H., & Rovee-Collier, C. (1995). The organization of reactivated memory in infancy. *Child Development, 66,* 893–906.

Haynie, D. L., Nansel, T., Eitel, P., Crump, A. D., Saylor, K., Yu, K., & Simons-Morton, B. (2001). Bullies, victims, and bully/victims: Distinct groups of at-risk youth. *Journal of Early Adolescence, 21,* 29–49.

Hayslip, B., Servaty, H. L., Christman, T., & Mumy, E. (1997). Levels of death anxiety in terminally ill persons: A cross validation and extension. *Omega—Journal of Death & Dying, 34,* 203–217.

Hayslip, B., Jr., Shore, R. J., & Henderson, C. E. (2000). Perceptions of grandparents' influence in the lives of their grandchildren. In B. Hayslip, Jr. & R. Goldberg, & G. Robin (Eds). *Grandparents raising grandchildren: Theoretical, empirical, and clinical perspectives.* New York: Springer.

Hayward, M., Crimmins, E., & Saito, Y. (1997). Cause of death and active life expectancy in the older population of the United States. *Journal of Aging and Health,* 122–131.

Hazell, P. (1993). Adolescent suicide clusters: Evidence, mechanisms and prevention. *Australian and New Zealand Journal of Psychiatry, 27,* 653– 665.

Hazan, C., & Shaver, P. (1987). Romantic love conceptualized as an attachment process. *Journal of Personality and Social Psychology, 52,* 511–524.

Healy, P. (2001, March 3). Data on suicides set off alarm. *Boston Globe,* p. B1.

Heatherton, T. F., Polivy, J., & Herman, C. P. (1991). Restraint, weight loss, and variability of body weight. *Journal of Abnormal Psychology, 100,* 78–83.

Hebert, T. P. (1998). Gifted Black males in an urban high school: Factors that influence achievement and underachievement. *Journal for the Education of the Gifted, 21,* 385–414.

Hecht, M. L., Marston, P. J., & Larkey, L. K. (1994). Love ways and relationship quality in heterosexual relationships. *Journal of Social and Personal Relationships, 11,* 25–43.

Heckhausen, J., Dixon, R. A., & Baltes, P. B. (1989). Gains and losses in development throughout adulthood as perceived by different adult age groups. *Developmental Psychology, 25,* 109–121.

Heinemann, G. D., & Evans, P. L. (1990). Widowhood: Loss, change, and adaptation. In T. H. Brubaker (Ed.), *Family relationships in later life.* Newbury Park, CA: Sage.

Hellman, P. (1987, November 23). Sesame street smart. *New York,* pp. 49–53.

Helson R., & Moane, G. (1987). Personality change in women from college to midlife. *Journal of Personality and Social Psychology, 53,* 176–186.

Helson, R., & Roberts, B. W. (1994). Ego development and personality change in adulthood. *Journal of Personality and Social Psychology, 66,* 911–920.

Helson, R., & Wink, P. (1992). Personality change in women from the early 40s to the early 50s. *Psychology and Aging, 7,* 46–55.

Helson, R., Stewart, A. J., & Ostrove, J. (1995). Identity in three cohorts of midlife women. *Journal of Personality and Social Psychology, 69,* 544–557.

Hendrick, C., & Hendrick S. (1989). Research on love: Does it measure up? *Journal of Personality and Social Psychology, 56,* 784–794.

Hendrie, H. C., Ogunniyi, A., Hall, K. S., Baiyewu, O., Unverzagt, F. W., Gureje, O., Gao, S., Evans, R. M., Ogunseyinde, A. O., Adeyinka, A. O., Musick, B., & Hui, S. L. (2001). Incidence of dementia and Alzheimer disease in 2 communities: Yoruba residing in Ibadan, Nigeria, and African Americans residing in Indianapolis, Indiana. *Journal of the American Medical Association, 285,* 739–747.

Henning-Stout, M. (1996). Gay and lesbian youths in schools. *Psychology Teacher Network, 6,* 2–4.

Henry, B., Caspi, A., Moffitt, T. E., & Silva, P. A. (1996). Temperamental and familial predictors of violent and nonviolent criminal convictions: Age 3 to 18. *Developmental Psychology, 32,* 614–623.

Henry, C. S., Sager, D. W., & Plunkett, S. W. (1996). Adolescents' perceptions of family system characteristics, parent-adolescent dyadic behaviors, adolescent qualities and adolescent empathy. *Family Relations: Journal of Applied Family & Child Studies, 45,* 283-292.

Henry, C. S., Stephenson, A. L., Hanson, M. F., & Hargett, W. (1993). Adolescent suicide and families: An ecological approach. *Adolescence, 28,* 291–308.

Hepper, P. G., Scott, D., & Shahidulla, S. (1993). Response to maternal voice. *Journal of Reproductive and Infant Psychology, 11,* 147–153.

Herbst, A. L. (1981). Diethylstilbestrol and other sex hormones during pregnancy. *Obstetrics and Gynecology, 58,* 355–405.

Herbst, A. L. (1994). The epidemiology of ovarian carcinoma and the current status of tumor markers to detect disease. *American Journal of Obstetrics and Gynecology, 170,* 1099–1105.

Herbst, J. H., McCrae, R. R., Costa, Jr., P. T., Feaganes, J. R., & Siegler, I. C. (2000). Self-perceptions of stability and change in personality at midlife. *The UNC Alumni Heart Study. Assessment, 7,* 379–388.

Herdt, G. H. (Ed.). (1998). *Rituals of manhood: Male initiation in Papua New Guinea.* Somerset, NJ: Transaction Books.

Herek, G. M. (1993). Sexual orientation and military service: A social science perspective. *American Psychologist, 48,* 538–549.

Hernandez-Reif, M., Field, T., Krasnegor, J., Martinez, E., Schwartzmann, M., & Mavunda, K. (1999). Children with cystic fibrosis benefit from massage therapy. *Journal of Pediatric Psychology, 24,* 175–181.

Herrnstein, R. J., & Murray, C. (1994). *The Bell Curve: Intelligence and class structure in American life.* New York: Free Press.

Hersch, P. (1999). A Tribe Apart. New York: Ballantine Books.

Hersen, M., & Van Hasselt, V. B. (Eds.). (1996). *Psychological treatment of older adults: An introductory text.* New York: Plenum.

Hess, J. L. (1990). The catastrophic health care fiasco. *The Nation, 250,* 193–203.

Hess-Biber, S. (1996). *Am I thin enough yet?* New York: Oxford University Press.

Hetherington, E. M. (Ed.) (1999). *Coping with divorce, single parenting, and remarriage: A risk and resiliency perspective.* Mahwah, NJ: Erlbaum.

Hetherington, E. M., & Blechman, E. A. (Eds.). (1996). *Stress, coping, and resiliency in children and families.* Hillsdale, NJ: Erlbaum.

Hetherington, E. M., & Clingempeel, W. (1992). Coping with marital transitions: A family systems perspective. *Monographs of the Society for Research in Child Development, 57,* (2–3, Serial No. 227).

Hetherington, E. M., Bridges, M., & Insabella, G. M. (1998). What matters? What does not? Five perspectives on the association between marital transitions and children's adjustment. *American Psychologist, 53,* 167–184.

Hetheringon, E. M., Stanley-Hagan, M., & Anderson, E. (1989). Marital transitions: A child's perspective. *American Psychologist, 44,* 303–312.

Hetherington, T. F., & Weinberger, J. (Eds.). (1993). *Can personality change?* Washington, DC: American Psychological Association.

Heubusch, K. (1997, September). A tough job gets tougher. *American Demographics,* p. 39.

Heward, W. L., & Orlansky, M. D. (1988, October). The epidemiology of AIDS in the U.S. *Scientific American,* 72–81.

Hewett, F. M., & Forness, S. R. (1974). *Education of exceptional learners.* Boston: Allyn & Bacon.

Hewitt, B. (1997, December 15). A day in the life. *People Magazine,* pp. 49–58.

HHL (Harvard Health Letter). (1997, May). *Turning up the volume,* p. 4.

HHS News. (2001, January 12). *Early Head Start shows significant results for low income children and parents.* Washington, DC: Health and Human Services.

Hill, R. D., Storandt, M., & Malley, M. (1993). The impact of long-term exercise training on psychological function in older adults. *Journal of Gerontology, 48,* P12–P17.

Hines, M., & Kaufman, F. R. (1994). Androgen and the development of human sex-typical behavior: Rough-and-tumble play and sex of preferred playmates in children with congenital adrenal hyperplasi (CAH). *Child Development, 65,* 1042–1053.

Hinshaw, S. P., Zupan, B. A., Simmel, C., Nigg, J. T., & Melnick, S. (1997). Peer status in boys with and without attention-deficit hyperactivity disorder: Predictions from overt and covert antisocial behavior, social isolation, and authoritative parenting beliefs. *Child Development, 68,* 880–896.

Hinton, J. M. (1967). *Dying.* Baltimore, MD: Penguin.

Hirsch, H. V., & Spinelli, D. N. (1970). Visual experience modifies distribution of horizontally and vertically oriented receptive fields in cats. *Science, 168,* 869–871.

Hirshberg, L. (1990). When infants look to their parents: II. Twelve-month-olds' response to conflicting parental emotional signals. *Child Development, 61,* 1187–1191.

Hirshberg, L., & Svejda, M. (1990). When infants look to their parents: I. Infants' social referencing of mothers compared to fathers. *Child Development, 61,* 1175–1186.

Hirsh-Pasek, K., & Michnick-Golinkoff, R. (1995). *The origins of grammar: Evidence from early language comprehension.* Cambridge, MA: MIT Press.

HMHL (Harvard Mental Health Letter). (1995, February). *Update on Alzheimer's disease—Part I.* Cambridge, MA: Harvard Medical School.

Hobart, C., & Grigel, F. (1992). Cohabitation among Canadian students at the end of the eighties. *Journal of Comparative Family Studies, 23,* 311–337.

Hocutt, A. M. (1996). Effectiveness of special education: Is placement the critical factor? *The Future of Children, 6,* 77–102.

Hofferth, S., & Sandberg, J. F. (2001). How American children spend their time. *Journal of Marriage and the Family, 63,* 295–308.

Hofferth, S. L., & Sandberg, J. (1998). *Changes in American children's time, 1981–1997.* Ann Arbor, MI: University of Michigan Institute for Social Research.

Hoffman, L. W. (1989). Effects of maternal employment in the two-parent family. *American Psychologist, 44,* 283–292.

Hoffman, L. W., McManus, K. A., & Brackbill, Y. (1987). The value of children to young and elderly parents. *International Journal of Aging and Human Development, 25,* 309–312.

Holahan, C. J., & Moos, R. H. (1987). Personal and contextual determinants of coping strategies. *Journal of Personality and Social Psychology, 52*, 946–955.

Holahan, C. J., & Moos, R. H. (1990). Life stressors, resistance factors, and improved psychological functioning: An extension of the stress resistance paradigm. *Journal of Personality and Social Psychology, 58*, 909–917.

Holden, C. (1987, October 9). Why do women live longer than men? *Science, 233*, 158–160.

Holden, G. W., & Miller, P. C. (1999). Enduring and different: A meta-analysis of the similarity in parents' child rearing. *Psychological Bulletin, 125*, 223–254.

Holland, J. C., & Lewis, S. (1993). Emotions and cancer: What do we really know? In D. Goleman & J. Gurin (Eds.), *Mind–body medicine*. Yonkers, NY: Consumer Reports Books.

Holland, J. L. (1973). *Making vocational choices: A theory of careers*. Englewood Cliffs, NJ: Prentice-Hall.

Holland, J. L. (1987). Current status of Holland's theory of careers: Another perspective. *Career Development Quarterly, 36*, 24–30.

Holland, N. (1994, August). *Race dissonance— Implications for African American children*. Paper presented at the annual meeting of the American Psychological Association, Los Angeles.

Hollenbeck, A. R., Gewirtz, J. L., Sebris, S. L., & Scanlon, J. W. (1984). Labor and delivery medication influences parent–infant interaction in the first post-partum month. *Infant Behavior and Development, 7*, 201–209.

Hollich, G. J., Hirsh-Pasek, K., Golinkoff, R. M., Brand, R. J., Brown, E. C., He, L., Hennon, E., & Rocrot, C. (2000). Breaking the language barrier: an emergentist coalition model of the origins of word learning. *Monographs of the Society for Research in Child Development, 65*, (3, Serial No. 262).

Holyrod, R., & Sheppard, A. (1997). Parental separation: Effects on children; implications for services. *Child: Care, Health & Development, 23*, 369–378.

Holzman, L. (1997). Schools for growth: Radical alternatives to current educational models. Mahwah, NJ: Erlbaum.

Hood, B. M., Willen, J. D., & Driver, J. (1998). Adult's eyes trigger shifts of visual attention in human infants. *Psychological Science, 9*, 131–139.

Hopkins, B., & Westra, T. (1989). Maternal expectations of their infants' development: Some cultural differences. *Developmental Medicine and Child Neurology, 31*, 384–390.

Hopkins, B., & Westra, T. (1990). Motor development, maternal expectation, and the role of handling. *Infant Behavior and Development, 13*, 117–122.

Horn, D. L., & Donaldson, G. (1980). Cognitive development II: Adulthood development of human abilities. In O. G. Brim & J. Kagan (Eds.), *Constancy and change in human development*. Cambridge, MA: Harvard University Press.

Hornik, R., & Gunnar, M. R. (1988). A descriptive analysis of infant social referencing. *Child Development, 59*, 626–634.

Horowitz, A. (1994). Vision impairment and functional disability among nursing home residents. *Gerontologist, 34*, 316–323.

Horwath, C. C. (1991). Nutrition goals for older adults: A review. *Gerontologist, 31*, 811–821.

Hoskins, I. (1992). Social security protection of women: Prospects for the 1990s. *Aging International, 19*, 27–32.

Houle, R., & Feldman, R. S. (1991). Emotional displays in children's television programming. *Journal of Nonverbal Behavior, 15*, 261–271.

Howard, A. (1992). Work and family crossroads spanning the career. In S. Zedeck (Ed.), *Work, families and organizations*. San Francisco: Jossey-Bass.

Howe, M. J. (1997). *IQ in question: The truth about intelligence*. London, England: Sage.

Howe, M. L., & O'Sullivan, J. T. (1990). The development of strategic memory: Coordinating knowledge, metamemory, and resources. In D. F. Bjorklund (Ed.), *Children's strategies: Contemporary view of cognitive development*. Hillsdale, NJ: Erlbaum.

Howes, C. (1987). Social competence with peers in young children: Developmental sequences. *Developmental Review, 7*, 252–272.

Howes, C., Galinsky, E., & Kontos, S. (1998). Child care caregiver sensitivity and attachment. *Social Development, 7*, 25–36.

Howes, C., Unger, O., & Seidner, L. B. (1989). Social pretend play in toddlers: Parallels with social play and with solitary pretend. *Child Development, 60*, 77–84.

Howie, L. (1993). Old women and widowhood: A dying status passage. *Omega, 26*, 223–233.

Howie, P. W. et al. (1990). Protective effect of breast feeding against infection. *British Journal of Medicine, 300*, 11.

Hsu, L. K. G. (1990). *Eating disorders*. New York: Guilford.

Hubel, D. H., & Wiesel, T. N. (1979). Brain mechanisms of vision. *Scientific American, 241*, 150–162.

Hudson, J. A., Sosa, B. B., & Shapiro, L. R. (1997). Scripts and plans: The development of preschool children's event knowledge and event planning. In S. L. Friedman & E. K. Scholnick (Eds.), *The developmental psychology of planning: Why, how and when do we plan* (pp. 77–102). Mahwah, NJ: Erlbaum.

Hudson, M. J. (1990). Hearing and vision loss in an aging population: Myths and realities. *Educational Gerontology, 16*, 87–96.

Huesmann, L. R. (1986). Psychological processes promoting the relations between exposure to media violence and aggressive behavior by the viewer. *Journal of Social Issues, 42*, 125–139.

Huesmann, L. R., Eron, L. D., Klein, R., Brice, P., & Fischer, P. (1983). Mitigating the imitation of aggressive behaviors by changing children's attitudes about media violence. *Journal of Personality and Social Psychology, 5*, 899–910.

Huesmann, L. R., Moise, J. F., & Podolski, C. (1997). The effects of media violence on the development of antisocial behavior. In D. M. Stoff, J. Breiling, & J. D. Maser (Eds.), *Handbook of antisocial behavior* (pp. 181–193). New York: Wiley.

Hughes, F. P. (1995). *Children, play, and development* (2nd ed.). Boston: Allyn & Bacon.

Hulanicka, B. (1999). Acceleration of menarcheal age of girls from dysfunctional families. *Journal of Reproductive & Infant Psychology, 17*, 119–132.

Humphrey, G. M., & Zimpfer, D. G. (1996). *Counseling for grief and bereavement*. New York: Wiley.

Hungerford, A., Brownell, C. A., & Campbell, S. B. (2000). Child care in infancy: A transactional perspective. In C. H. Zeanah, Jr. (Ed), et al. *Handbook of infant mental health* (2nd ed.). New York: Guilford Press.

Hunt, E., Streissguth, A. P., Kerr, B., & Olson, H. C. (1995). Mothers' alcohol consumption during pregnancy: Effects on spatial-visual reasoning in 14–year-old children. *Psychological Science, 6*, 339–342.

Hunt, J., & Hunt, L. (1975). Racial inequality and self-image: Identity maintenance as identity diffusion. *Sociology and Social Research, 61*, 539–559.

Hunt, M. (1974). *Sexual behaviors in the 1970s*. New York: Dell.

Hunt, M. (1993). *The story of psychology*. New York: Doubleday.

Hunter, J., & Mallon, G. P. (2000). Lesbian, gay, and bisexual adolescent development: Dancing with your feet tied together. In B. Greene & G. L. Croom, (Eds). *Education, research, and practice in lesbian, gay, bisexual, and transgendered psychology: A resource manual, Vol. 5.* Thousand Oaks, CA: Sage.

Huntsinger, C. S., Jose, P. E., Liaw, F., & Ching, W-D. (1997). Cultural differences in early mathematics learning: A comparison of Euro-American, Chinese-American, and Taiwan-Chinese families. *International Journal of Behavioral Development, 21*, 371–388.

Huppe, M., & Cyr, M. (1997). Division of household labor and marital satisfaction of dual income couples according to family life cycle. *Canadian Journal of Counseling, 31*, 145–162.

Huston, A. (Ed.). (1991). *Children in poverty: Child development and public policy*. Cambridge, England: Cambridge University Press.

Huston, T. L., Caughlin, J. P., Houts, R. M., & Smith, S. E. (2001). The connubial crucible: Newly-wed years as predictors of marital delight, distress, and divorce. *Journal of Personality and Social Psychology, 80*, 237–252.

Hwang, C. P., Lamb, M. E., & Sigel, I. E. (Eds.). (1996). *Images of childhood*. Mahwah, NJ: Erlbaum.

Hyde, J. S. (1994). *Understanding human sexuality* (5th ed.). New York: McGraw-Hill.

Hyde, J. S., Fennema, E., & Lamon, S. J. (1990). Gender differences in mathematics performance: A meta-analysis. Psychological Bulletin, 107, 139–155.

Hyde, J. S., Klein, M. H., Essex, M. J., & Clark, R. (1995). Maternity leave and women's mental health. *Psychology of Women Quarterly, 19*, 257–285.

Iacono, W. G., & Grove, W. M. (1993). Schizophrenia reviewed: Toward an integrative genetic model. *Psychological Science, 4*, 273–276.

Ikels, C. (1989). Becoming a human being in theory and practice: Chinese views of human development. In D. I. Kertzer & K. W. Schaie (Eds.), *Age structuring in comparative perspective*. Hillsdale, NJ: Erlbaum.

Illingworth, R. S. (1973). *Basic developmental screening: 0–2 years*. Oxford: Blackwell Scientific.

Ingersoll, E. W., & Thoman, E. B. (1999). Sleep/wake states of preterm infants: Stability, developmental change, diurnal variation, and relation with caregiving activity. *Child Development, 70*, 1–10.

Insel, P. M., & Roth, W. T. (1991). *Core concepts in health* (6th ed.). Mountain View, CA: Mayfield.

International Human Genome Sequencing Consortium (2001). Initial sequencing and analysis of the human genome. *Nature, 409,* 860–921.

International Literacy Institute. (2001). *Literacy overview.* Website: http://www.literacyonline.org/explorer/

Inzlicht, M., & Ben-Zeev, T. (2000). A threatening intellectual environment: Why females are susceptible to experiencing problem-solving deficits in the presence of males. *Psychological Science, 11,* 365–371.

Irani, K., Xia, Y., Zweier, J. L., Sollott, S. J., Der, C. J., Fearon, E. R., Sundaresan, M. Finkel, T., & Goldschmidt-Clermont, P. J. (1997). Mitogenic signaling mediated by oxidants in ras-transformed fibroblasts. *Science, 275,* 1649.

Irwin, E. G. (1993). A focused overview of anorexia nervosa and bulimia: I. Etiological issues. *Archives of Psychiatric Nursing, 7,* 342–346.

Isaksen, S. G., & Murdock, M. C. (1993). The emergence of a discipline: Issues and approaches to the study of creativity. In S. G. Isaksen, M. C. Murdock, R. L. Firestein, & D. J. Treffinger (Eds.), *The emergence of a discipline* (Vol. 1). Norwood, NJ: Ablex.

Isay, R. A. (1990). *Being homosexual: Gay men and their development.* New York: Avon.

Isingrini, M., & Vazou, F. (1997). Relations between fluid intelligence and frontal lobe functioning in older adults. *International Journal of Aging & Human Development, 45,* 99–109.

Izard, C., & Malatesta, C. (1987). Perspectives on emotional development I. Differential emotions theory of early emotional development. In J. D. Osofsky (Ed.), *Handbook of infant development.* New York: Wiley.

Izard, C. E., Frantauzzo, C. A., Castle, J. M., Haynes, O. M., Rayias, M. F., & Putnam, P. H. (1995). The ontogeny and significance of infants' facial expressions in the first 9 months of life. *Developmental Psychology, 31,* 997–1013.

Jackson, L. A., Gardner, P. D., & Sullivan, L. A. (1992). Explaining gender differences in self-pay expectations: Social comparison standards and perceptions of fair pay. *Journal of Applied Psychology, 77,* 651–663.

Jacobsen, L., & Edmondson, B. (1993, August). Father figures. *American Demographics,* pp. 22–27.

Jacobson, N., & Gottman, J. (1998). *When men batter women.* New York: Simon & Schuster.

Jacobson, N. S. (1987). Family type, visiting patterns, and children's behavior in the stepfamily: A linked family system. In K. Pasley & M. Ihinger-Tallman (Eds.), *Remarriage and stepparenting.* New York: Guilford.

Jacobson, S. W., Fein, G. G., Jacobson, J. L., Schwartz, P. M., & Dowler, J. K. (1985). The effect of intrauterine PCB exposure on visual recognition memory. *Child Development, 56,* 853–860.

Jacoby, L. L., & Kelley, C. M. (1992). A process-dissociation framework for investigating unconscious influences: Freudian slips, projective tests, subliminal perception, and signal detection theory. *Current Directions in Psychological Science, 1,* 174–179.

Jacoby, R., & Glauberman, N. (Eds.). (1995). *The Bell Curve debate.* New York: Times Books/Random House.

Jahoda, G. (1980). Theoretical and systematic approaches in mass-cultural psychology. In H. C. Triandis and W. W. Lambert (Eds.), *Handbook of cross-cultural psychology* (Vol. 1). Boston: Allyn & Bacon.

Jahoda, G. (1983). European "lag" in the development of an economic concept: A study in Zimbabwe. *British Journal of Developmental Psychology, 1,* 113–120.

Jahoda, G., & Lewis, I. M. (1988). *Acquiring culture: Cross-cultural studies in child development.* London: Croom Helm.

Jahoda, M. (1982). *Employment and unemployment.* Cambridge, England: Cambridge University Press.

James, W. (1890/1950). *The principles of psychology.* New York: Holt.

Jamieson, D. W., Lydon, J. E., Stewart, G., & Zanna, M. P. (1987). Pygmalion revisited: New evidence for student expectancy effects in the classroom. *Journal of Educational Psychology, 79,* 461–466.

Janda, L. H., & Klenke-Hamel, K. E. (1980). *Human sexuality.* New York: Van Nostrand.

Janssens, J. M. A. M., & Dekovic, M. (1997). Child rearing, prosocial moral reasoning, and prosocial behaviour. *International Journal of Behavioral Development, 20,* 509–527.

Jazwinski, S. M. (1996, July 5). Longevity, genes, and aging. *Science, 273,* 54–59.

Jenkins, J. E. (1996). The influence of peer affiliation and student activities on adolescent drug involvement. *Adolescence, 31,* 297–306.

Jenkins, J. M., & Astington, J. W. (1996). Cognitive factors and family structure associated with theory of mind development in young children. *Developmental Psychology, 32,* 70–78.

Jiang, W., Babyak, M., Krantz, D. S., Waugh, R. A., Coleman, R. E., Hanson, M. M., Frid, D. J., McNulty, S., Morris, J. J., O'Connor, C. M., & Blumenthal, J. A. (1996, June 5). Mental stress-induced myocardial ischemia and cardiac events. *Journal of the American Medical Association, 275,* 1651–1656.

Jiao, S., Ji, G., & Jing, Q. (1996). Cognitive development of chines urban only children and children with siblings. *Child Development, 67,* 387–395.

Johnson, A. M., Wadsworth, J., Wellings, K., & Bradshaw, S. (1992). Sexual lifestyles and HIV risk. *Nature, 360,* 410–412.

Johnson, C. H., Vicary, J. R., Heist, C. L., & Corneal, D. A. (2001). Moderate alcohol and tobacco use during pregnancy and child behavior outcomes. *Journal of Primary Prevention, 21,* 367–379.

Johnson, C. L., & Barer, B. M. (1992). Patterns of engagement and disengagement among the oldest old. *Journal of Aging Studies, 6,* 351–364.

Johnson, J. L., Primas, P. J., & Coe, M. K. (1994). Factors that prevent women of low socioeconomic status from seeking prenatal care. *Journal of the American Academy of Nurse Practitioners, 6,* 105–111.

Johnson, M. H. (1998). The neural basis of cognitive development. In D. Kuhn & R. S. Siegler (Eds.), *Handbook of child psychology: Vol. 2: Cognition, perception, and language* (5th ed., pp. 1–49). New York: Wiley.

Johnson, N. G., Roberts, M. C., & Worell, J. (Eds.). (1999). *Beyond appearance: A new look at adolescent girls.* Washington, DC: American Psychological Association.

Johnson, S. L., & Birch, L. L. (1994). Parents' and children's adiposity and eating style. *Pediatrics, 94,* 653–661.

Johnson, W., Emde, R. N., Pannabecker, B., Stenberg, C., & Davis, M. (1982). Maternal perception of infant emotion from birth through 18 months. *Infant Behavior and Development, 5,* 313–322.

Johnston, C. C. (1989). Pain assessment and management in infants. *Pediatrician, 16,* 16–23.

Johnston, L. D., Bachman, J. G., & O'Malley, P. M. (2000). *Monitoring the future study.* Lansing, MI: University of Michigan.

Jones, A., & Crandall, R. (Eds.). (1991). Handbook of self-actualization. *Journal of Social Behavior and Personality, 6,* 1–362.

Joseph, R. (1999). Environmental influences on neural plasticity, the limbic system, emotional development and attachment: A review. *Child Psychiatry & Human Development, 29,* 189–208.

Jost, H., & Songtag, L. (1944). The genetic factor in autonomic nervous system function. *Psychosomatic Medicine, 6,* 308–310.

Joy, M. (1997). Physician-assisted suicide: A brief historical and legal overview. *Journal of Long Term Home Health Care, 16,* 2–11.

Julian, T., McKenny, P. C., & McKelvey, M. W. (1992). Components of men's well-being at midlife. *Issues in Mental Health Nursing, 13,* 285–299.

Jusczyk, P. W., & Hohne, E. A. (1997, September 26). Infants' memory for spoken words. *Science, 277,* 1894–1896.

Juvenile Justice Clearinghouse. (1995). *Current statistics on World Wide Web page.* Washington, DC.

Kacapyr, E. (1997, October). Are we having fun yet? *American Demographics,* pp. 28–30.

Kagan, J. (1981). Universals in human development. In R. H. Munroe, R. L. Munroe, & B. B. Whiting (Eds.), *Handbook of crosscultural human development* (pp. 53–62). New York: Garland.

Kagan, J. (2000, October). Adult personality and early experience. *The Harvard Mental Health Letter,* 4–5.

Kagan, J., & Snidman, N. (1991). Infant predictors of inhibited and uninhibited profiles. *Psychological Science, 2,* 40–44.

Kagan, J., Arcus, D., & Snidman, N. (1993). The idea of temperament: Where do we go from here? In R. Plomin, & G. E. McClearn (Eds.), *Nature, nurture, and psychology.* Washington, DC: American Psychological Association.

Kagan, J., Arcus, D., Snidman, N., Feng, W. Y., Hendler, J., & Greene, S. (1994). Reactivity in infants: A cross-national comparison. *Developmental Psychology, 30,* 342–345.

Kagan, J., Kearsley, R., & Zelazo, P. R. (1978). *Infancy: Its place in human development.* Cambridge, MA: Harvard University Press.

Kahn, P. H., Jr. (1997). Children's moral and ecological reasoning about the Prince William Sound oil spill. *Developmental Psychology, 33,* 1091–1096.

Kahn, S., Zimmerman, G., Csikszentmihalyi, M., & Getzels, J. W. (1985). Relations between identity in young adulthood and intimacy at midlife. *Journal of Personality and Social Psychology, 49,* 1316–1322.

Kaitz, M., Meschulach-Sarfaty, O., Auerbach, J., & Eidelman, A. (1988). A re-examination of newborns' ability to imitate facial expressions. *Developmental Psychology, 24*, 3–7.

Kalb, C. (1997, Spring/Summer). The top 10 health worries. *Newsweek Special Issue*, 42–43.

Kalichman, S. C. (1998). *Understanding AIDS, second edition: Advances in research and treatment.* Washington, DC: APA Books.

Kalish, R. A., & Reynolds, D. K. (1976). *An overview of death and ethnicity.* Farmingdale, New York: Baywood.

Kalliopuska, M. (1994). Relations of retired people and their grandchildren. *Psychological Reports, 75*, 1083–1088.

Kaltiala-Heino, R., Rimpelae, M., Rantanen, P., & Rimpelae, A. (2000). Bullying at school—an indicator of adolescents at risk for mental disorders. *Journal of Adolescence, 23*, 661–674.

Kamhi, A. (1986). The elusive first word: The importance of the naming insight for the development of referential speech. *Journal of Child Language, 13*, 155–161.

Kane, R. A., Caplan, A. L., Urv-Wong, E. K., & Freeman, I. C. (1997). Everyday matters in the lives of nursing home residents: Wish for and perception of choice and control. *Journal of the American Geriatrics Society, 45*, 1086–1093.

Kane, R. I., Wales, J., Bernstein, L., Leibowitz, A., & Kaplan, S. (1985, April 21). A randomized controlled trial of hospice care. *The Lancet, 302*, 890–894.

Kaneda, H., Maeshima, K., Goto, N., Kobayakawa, T., Ayabe-Kanamura, S., & Saito, S. (2000). Decline in taste and odor discrimination abilities with age, and relationship between gustation and olfaction. *Chemical Senses, 25*, 331–337.

Kantrowitz, B., & Wingert, P. (1999, May 10). How well do you know your kid? (teenagers need adult attention). *Newsweek, 133(19)*, 36.

Kao, G. (in press). Psychological well-being and educational achievement among immigrant youth. In D. J. Hernandez (Ed.), *Children of immigrants: Health, adjustment, and public assistance.* Washington, D.C.: National Academy Press.

Kao, G., & Tienda, M. (1995). Optimism and achievement: the educational performance of immigrant youth. *Social Science Quarterly, 76*, 1–19.

Kaplan, H., & Dove, H. (1987). Infant development among the Ache of Eastern Paraguay. *Developmental Psychology, 23*, 190–198.

Kaplan, R. M., Sallis, J. F., Jr., & Patterson, T. L. (1993). *Health and human behavior.* P. 254. "Age specific breast cancer annual incidence." New York: McGraw-Hill.

Karmel, B. Z., Gardner, J. M., & Magnano, C. L. (1991). Attention and arousal in early infancy. In M. J. S. Weiss & P. R. Zelazo (Eds.), *Newborn attention: Biological constraints and the influence of experience* (pp. 339–376). Norwood, NJ: Ablex.

Karney, B. R., & Bradbury, T. N. (1995). The longitudinal course of marital quality and stability: A review of theory, method, and research. *Psychological Bulletin, 118*, 3–34.

Karoly, L. A., Greenwood, P. W., Everingham, S. S., Houbé, J., Kilburn, M. R., Rydell, C. P., Sanders, M., & Chiesa, J. (1998). *Investing in our children: What we know and don't know about the costs and benefits of early childhood interventions.* Santa Monica, CA: RAND.

Karpov, Y. V., & Haywood, H. C. (1998). Two ways to elaborate Vygotsky's concept of mediation: Implications for instruction. *American Psychologist, 53*, 27–36.

Kart, C. S. (1990). *The realities of aging* (3rd ed.). Boston: Allyn & Bacon.

Kartman, L. L. (1991). Life review: One aspect of making meaningful music for the elderly. *Activities, Adaptations, and Aging, 15*, 42–45.

Kaslow, F. W. (2001). Families and family psychology at the millennium: Intersecting crossroads. *American Psychologist, 56*, 37–44.

Kasser, T., & Sharma, Y. S. (1999). Reproductive freedom, educational equality, and females' preference for resource-acquisition characteristics in mates. *Psychological Science, 10*, 374–377.

Kastenbaum, R. (1985). Dying and death: A life-span approach. In J. E. Birren & K. W. Schaie (Eds.), *Handbook of the psychology of aging.* New York: Van Nostrand Reinhold.

Kastenbaum, R. (1999). Dying and bereavement. In J. C. Cavanaugh & S. K. Whitbourne (Eds.), *Gerontology: An interdisciplinary perspective.* NY: Oxford University Press.

Kastenbaum, R. (2000). *The psychology of death.* (3rd ed.). New York: Springer.

Kastenbaum, R. J. (1977). *Death, society and human experience.* St. Louis, MO: Mosby.

Kastenbaum, R. J. (1992). *The psychology of death.* New York: Springer-Verlag.

Katchadourian, H. A. (1987). *Biological aspects of human sexuality* (3rd ed.). New York: Holt, Rinehart & Winston.

Kate, N. T. (1998, March). How many children? *American Demographics,* p. 35.

Kates, N., Grieff, B., & Hagen, D. (1990). *The psychosocial impact of job loss.* Washington, DC: American Psychiatric Press.

Katrowitz, B., & Wingert, P. (1990, Winter/Spring). Step by step. *Newsweek Special Edition*, 24–34.

Katz, D. L. (2001). Behavior modification in primary care: The Pressure System Model. *Preventive Medicine: an International Devoted to Practice & Theory, 32*, 66–72.

Katz, L. G. (1989, December). Beginners' ethics. *Parents,* p. 213.

Katzell, R. A., & Guzzo, R. A. (1983). Psychological approaches to productivity improvement. *American Psychologist, 38*, 468–472.

Kaufmann, D., Gesten, E., Santa Lucia, R. C., Salcedo, O., Rendina-Gobioff, G., & Gadd, R. (2000). The relationship between parenting style and children's adjustment: The parents' perspective. *Journal of Child & Family Studies, 9*, 231–245.

Kauffman, J. M. (1993). How we might achieve the radical reform of special education. *Exceptional Children, 60*, 6–16.

Kaufman, J., & Zigler, E. (1987). Do abused children become abused parents? *American Journal of Orthopsychiatry, 57*, 186–192.

Kaufman, M. T. (1992, November 28). Teaching compassion in theater of death. *The New York Times,* p. B7.

Kavale, K. A., & Forness, S. R. (2000, Sep.–Oct.). History, rhetoric, and reality: Analysis of the inclusion debate. *Rase: Remedial & Special Education, 21*, Sep-Oct, 279–296.

Kazdin, A. E. (1990). Childhood depression. *Journal of Child Psychology and Psychiatry, 31*, 121–160.

Kazura, K. (2000). Fathers' qualitative and quantitative involvement: An investigation of attachment, play, and social interactions. *Journal of Men's Studies, 9*, 41–57.

Keating, D. (1980). Thinking processes in adolescence. In J. Adelson (Ed.), *Handbook of adolescent psychology.* New York: Wiley.

Keating, D. (1990). Adolescent thinking. In S. Feldman & G. Elliott (Eds.), *At the threshold: The developing adolescent.* Cambridge, MA: Harvard University Press.

Keating, D. P., & Clark, L. V. (1980). Development of physical and social reasoning in adolescence. *Developmental Psychology, 16*, 23–30.

Kecskes, I., & Papp, T. (2000). *Foreign language and mother tongue.* Mahwah, NJ: Erlbaum.

Keefer, B.L., Kraus, R.F., Parker, B.L., Elliotsl, R., et al. (1991). A state university collaboration program: Residents' prespectives. Annual Meeting of the American Psychiatric Association (1990, New York, New York). *Hospital and Community Psychiatry, 42* 62–66.

Keel, P. K., Leon, G. R., & Fulkerson, J. A. (2001). Vulnerability to eating disorders in childhood and adolescence. In R. E. Ingram & J. M. Price, (Eds). *Vulnerability to psychopathology: Risk across the lifespan.* New York, NY: Guilford Press.

Kellett, J. M. (1993). Sexuality in later life. *Reviews in Clinical Gerontology, 3*, 309–314.

Kellett, J. M. (2000). Older adult sexuality. In L. T. Szuchman, & F. Muscarella, (Eds), et al. *Psychological perspectives on human sexuality.* New York: Wiley.

Kelly, G. (2001). *Sexuality today: A human perspective.* (7th ed.) New York: McGraw-Hill.

Kemper, R. L., & Vernooy, A. R. (1994). Metalinguistic awareness in first graders: A qualitative perspective. *Journal of Psycholinguistic Research, 22*, 41–57.

Kenen, R., Smith, A. C. M., Watkins, C., & Zuber-Pittore, C. (2000). To use or not to use: The prenatal genetic technology/worry conundrum. *Journal of Genetic Counseling, 9*, 203–217.

Kennedy, G. E. (1990). College students' expectations of grandparent and grandchild role behavior. *Gerontologist, 30*, 43–48.

Kenrick, D. T., Keefe, R. C., Bryna, A., Barr, A., & Brown, S. (1995). Age preferences and mate choice among homosexuals and heterosexuals: A case for modular psychological mechanisms. *Journal of Personality and Social Psychology, 69*, 1166–1172.

Kerner, M., & Aboud, F. E. (1998). The importance of friendship qualities and reciprocity in a multi-racial school. *The Canadian Journal of Research in Early Childhood Education, 7*, 117–125.

Kessen, W. (1979). The American child and other cultural inventions. *American Psychologist, 34*, 815–820.

Kidwell, J. S., Dunyam, R. M., Bacho, R. A., Pastorino, E., & Portes, P. R. (1995). Adolescent identity exploration: A test of Erikson's theory of transitional crisis. *Adolescence, 30*, 785–793.

Kiecolt, K. J., & Fossett, M. A. (1997). The effects of mate availability on marriage among black Americans: A contextual analysis. In R. J. Taylor, J. S. Jackson, & L. M. Chatters (Eds.), *Family life in black America* (pp. 63–78). Thousand Oaks, CA: Sage.

Kiecolt-Glaser, J. K., & Glaser, R. (1986). Behavioral influences on immune function: Evidence for the interplay between stress and health. In T. Field, P. McCabe, & N. Schneiderman (Eds.), *Stress and coping* (Vol. 2). Hillsdale, NJ: Erlbaum.

Kiecolt-Glaser, J. K., & Kiecolt-Glaser, R. (1991). Psychosocial factors, stress, disease, and immunity. In R. Ader, D. L. Felten, & N. Cohen (Eds.), *Psychoneuroimmunology*. San Diego: Academic Press.

Kiecolt-Glaser, R., & Kiecolt-Glaser, J. K. (1993). Mind and immunity. In D. Goleman, & J. Gurin (Eds.), *Mind–body medicine*. Yonkers, NY: Consumer Reports Books.

Killen, M., & Hart, D. (Eds.). (1995). *Morality in everyday life: Developmental perspectives*. New York: Cambridge University Press.

Kim, J. (1995, January). "You cannot know how much freedom you have here." *Money*, p. 133.

Kim, K., Smith, P. K., & Palermiti, A. (1997). Conflict in childhood and reproductive development. *Evolution & Human Behavior, 18*, 109–142.

Kim, K., & Smith, P. K. (1999). Family relations in early childhood and reproductive development. *Journal of Reproductive & Infant Psychology, 17*, 133–148.

Kim, U., Triandis, H. C., Kagitçibais, Ç., Choi, S., & Yoon, G. (Eds.). (1994). *Individualism and collectivism: Theory, method, and applications*. Thousand Oaks, CA: Sage.

Kim, Y., & Stevens, J. H. (1987). The socialization of prosocial behavior in children. *Childhood Education, 63*, 200–206.

Kimball, J. W. (1983). Biology (5th ed.). Reading, MA: Addison-Wesley.

Kinsey, A. C., Pomeroy, W. B., & Martin, C. E. (1948). *Sexual behavior in the human male*. Philadelphia: Saunders.

Kitchener, R. F. (1996). The nature of the social for Piaget and Vygotsky. *Human Development, 39*, 243–249.

Kittell, L. A., & Mansfield, P. K. (2000). What perimenopausal women think about using hormones during menopause. *Women & Health, 30*, 77–91.

Kivett, V. R. (1991). Centrality of the grandfather role among older rural black and white men. *Journal of Gerontology: Social Sciences, 46*, S250–S258.

Klaczynski, P. A. (1997). Bias in adolescents' everyday reasoning and its relationship with intellectual ability, personal theories, and self-serving motivation. *Developmental Psychology, 33*, 273–283.

Klaus, H. M., & Kennell, J. H. (1976). *Maternal–infant bonding*. St. Louis, MO: Mosby.

Klein, M. C., Gauthier, R. J., Robbins, J. M., Kaczorowski, J., Jorgensen, S. H., Franco, E. D., Johnson, B., Waghorn, K., Gelfand, M. M., Guralnick, M. S., et al. (1994). Relationship of episiotomy to perineal trauma and morbidity, sexual dysfunction, and pelvic floor relaxation. *American Journal of Obstetrics and Gynecology, 171*, 591–598.

Kline, D. W., & Schieber, F. (1985). Vision and aging. In J. E. Birren & K. W. Schaie (Eds.), *Handbook of the psychology of aging* (2nd ed.). New York: Van Nostrand Reinhold.

Klinnert, M. (1984). The regulation of infant behavior by maternal facial expression. *Infant Behavior and Development, 7*, 447–465.

Klock, S. C., Greenfeld, D. A. (2000). Psychological status of in vitro fertilization patients during pregnancy: a longitudinal study. *Fertility & Sterility, 73*, 1159–1164.

Kmiec, E. B. (1999). Gene therapy. *American Scientist, 87*, 240–247.

Knaus, W. A., Conners, A. F., Dawson, N. V., Desbiens, N. A., Fulkerson, W. J., Jr., Goldman, L., Lynn, J., & Oye, R. K. (1995, November 22). A controlled trial to improve care for seriously ill hospitalized patients. The study to understand prognoses and preferences for outcomes and risks of treatments (SUPPORT). *Journal of the American Medical Association, 273*, 1591–1598.

Knecht, S., Deppe, M., Draeger, B., Bobe, L., Lohmann, H., Ringelstein, E. B., & Henningsen, H. (2000). Language lateralization in healthy right-handers. *Brain, 123*, 74–81.

Knight, K. (1994, March). Back to basics. *Essence*, pp. 122–138.

Knittle, J. L. (1975). Early influences on development of adipose tissue. In G. A. Bray (Ed.), *Obesity in perspective*. Washington, DC: U.S. Government Printing Office.

Knutson, J. F., & Lansing, C. R. (1990). The relationship between communication problems and psychological difficulties in persons with profound acquired hearing loss. *Journal of Speech and Hearing Disorders, 55*, 656–664.

Kocarnik, R. A., & Ponzetti, J. J., Jr. (1991). The advantages and challenges of intergenerational programs in long-term care facilities. *Journal of Gerontological Social Work, 16*, 97–107.

Kochanska, G. (1997). Mutually responsive orientation between mothers and their young children: Implications for early socialization. *Child Development, 68*, 94–112.

Kochanska, G. (1998). Mother-child relationship, child fearfulness, and emerging attachment: A short-term longitudinal study. *Developmental Psychology, 34*, 480–490.

Kohlberg, L. (1966). A cognitive-developmental anaylsis of children's sex-role concepts and attitudes. In E. E. Maccoby (Ed.), *The development of sex differences*. Stanford, CA: Stanford University Press.

Kohlberg, L. (1984). *The psychology of moral development: Essays on moral development* (Vol. 2). San Francisco: Harper & Row.

Kolata, G. (1994, August). Selling growth drug for children: The legal and ethical questions. *The New York Times*, pp. A1, A11.

Kolata, G. (1997, April 24). A record and big questions as woman gives birth at 63. *The New York Times*, pp. A1, A25.

Kolata, G. (1998). *Clone: The road to Dolly and the path ahead*. New York: William Morrow.

Kolb, B. (1989). Brain development, plasticity, and behavior. *American Psychologist, 44*(9), 1203–1212.

Kolb, B. (1995). *Brain plasticity and behavior*. Mahwah, NJ: Erlbaum.

Korkman, M., Autti-Raemoe, I., Koivulehto, H., & Granstroem, M. L. (1998). Neuropsychological effects at early school age of fetal alcohol exposure of varying duration. *Child Neuropsychology, 4*, 199–212.

Koski, L. R., & Shaver, P. R. (1997). Attachment and relationship satisfaction across the life span. In R. J. Sternberg & M. Hojjat (Eds.), *Satisfaction in close relationships* (pp. 26–55). New York: Guilford.

Koss, M. P., Goodman, L. A., Browne, A., Fitzgerald, L. F., Keita, G. P., & Russo, N. F. (1993). *No safe haven: Violence against women, at home, at work, and in the community*. Final report of the American Psychological Association Women's Programs Office Task Force on Violence Against Women. Washington, DC: American Psychological Association.

Kotre, J., & Hall, E. (1990). *Seasons of life*. Boston: Little, Brown.

Kraemer, H. C., Korner, A., Anders, T., Jacklin, C. N., & Dimiceli, S. (1985). Obstetric drugs and infant behavior: A re-evaluation. *Journal of Pediatric Psychology, 10*, 345–353.

Krause, N., & Borawski-Clark, E. (1994). Clarifying the functions of social support in later life. *Research on Aging, 16*, 251–279.

Kraybill, E. N. (1998). Ethical issues in the care of extremely low birth weight infants. *Seminars in Perinatology, 22*, 207–215.

Kreitlow, B., & Kreitlow, D. (1997). *Creative planning for the second half of life*. Duluth, MN: Whole Person Associates.

Kremar, M., & Greene, K. (2000). Connections between violent television exposure and adolescent risk taking. *Media Psychology, 2*, 195–217.

Kroger, J. (2000). *Identity development: Adolescence through adulthood*. Thousand Oaks, CA: Sage.

Krout, J. A. (1988). Rural versus urban differences in elderly parents' contact with their children. *Gerontologist, 28*, 198–203.

Krueger, J., & Heckhausen, J. (1993). Personality development across the adult life span: Subjective conceptions vs. cross-sectional contrasts. *Journals of Gerontology, 48*, 100–108.

Kryter, K. D. (1983). Presbycusis, sociocusis, and nosocusis. *Journal of the Acoustical Society of America, 73*, 1897–1917.

Kübler-Ross, E. (1969). *On death and dying*. New York: Macmillan.

Kübler-Ross, E. (1982). *Working it through*. New York: Macmillan.

Kübler-Ross, E. (Ed.). (1975). Death: *The final stage of growth*. Englewood Cliffs, NJ: Prentice-Hall.

Kuczynski, L., & Kochanska, G. (1990). Development of children's noncompliance strategies from toddlerhood to age 5. *Developmental Psychology, 26*, 398–408.

Kuhl, P. K., Andruski, J. E., Chistovich, I. A., Chistovich, L. A., Kozhevnikova, E. V., Ryskina, V. L., Stolyarova, E. I., Sundberg, U., & Lacerda, F. (1997, August 1). Cross-language analysis of phentic units in language addressed to infants. *Science, 277*, 684–686.

Kuhn, D. (2000). Metacognitive devleopment. *Current Directions in Psychological Science, 9*, 178–181.

Kuhn, D., Garcia-Mila, M., Zohar, A., & Andersen, C. (1995). Strategies of knowledge acquisition. With commentary by S. H. White, D. Klahr, & S. M.

Carver, and a reply by D. Kuhn. *Monographs of the Society for Research in Child Development, 60,* 122–137.

Kurdek, L. A. (1991). Correlates of relationship satisfaction in cohabiting gay and lesbian couples: Integration of contextual, investment, and problem-solving models. *Journal of Personality and Social Psychology, 61,* 910–922.

Kurdek, L. A. (1992). Relationship stability and relationship satisfaction in cohabiting gay and lesbian couples: A prospective longitudinal test of the contextual and interdependence models. *Journal of Social and Personal Relationships, 9,* 125–142.

Kurdek, L. A. (1993). The allocation of household labor in gay, lesbian, and heterosexual married children. *Journal of Social Issues, 49,* 127–139.

Kurdek, L.A. (1999). The nature and predictors of the trajectory of change in marital quality for husbands and wives over the first 10 years of marriage. *Developmental Psychology, 35,* 1283–1296.

Kurtines, W. M., & Gewirtz, J. I. (1987). *Moral development through social interaction.* New York: Wiley.

Labouvie-Vief, G. (1980). Beyond formal operations: Uses and limits of pure logic in life-span development. *Human Development, 23,* 141–161.

Labouvie-Vief, G. (1986). Modes of knowledge and the organization of development. In M. L. Commons, L. Kohlberg, F. Richards, & J. Sinnott (Eds.), *Beyond formal operations 3: Models and methods in the study of adult and adolescent thought.* New York: Praeger.

Labouvie-Vief, G. (1990). Modes of knowledge and the organization of development. In M. L. Commons, C. Armon, L. Kohlberg, F. A. Richards, T. A. Grotzer, & J. Sinnott (Eds.), *Adult development (Vol. 2). Models and methods in the study of adolescent thought.* New York: Praeger.

Ladd, G. W. (1983). Social networks of popular, average and rejected children in social settings. *Merrill-Palmer Quarterly, 29,* 282–307.

LaFromboise, T., Coleman, H. L., & Gerton, J. (1993). Psychological impact of biculturalism: Evidence and theory. *Psychological Bulletin, 114,* 395–412.

Lafuente, M. J., Grifol, R., Segarra, J., & Soriano, J. (1997). Effects of the Firstart method of prenatal stimulation on psychomotor development: The first six months. *Pre- & PeriNatal Psychology, 11,* 151–162.

Lakowski, B., & Hekimi, S. (1996, May 17). Determination of life-span in caenorhabditis elegans by four clock genes. *Science, 272,* 1010.

Lamaze, F. (1970). *Painless childbirth: The Lamaze method.* Chicago: Regnery.

Lamb, D. R. (1984). *Physiology of exercise: Response and adaptation* (2nd ed.). New York: Macmillan.

Lamb, M. (1994). Infant care practices and the application of knowledge. In C. B. Fisher & R. M. Lerner (Eds.), *Applied developmental psychology.* New York: McGraw-Hill.

Lamb, M. E. (1977). The development of mother–infant and father–infant attachments in the second year of life. *Developmental Psychology, 13,* 637–648.

Lamb, M. E. (1982a). The bonding phenomenon: Misinterpretations and their implications. *Journal of Pediatrics, 101,* 555–557.

Lamb, M. E. (1982b). Paternal influences on early socio-emotional development. *Journal of Child Psychology and Psychiatry and Allied Disciplines, 23,* 185–190.

Lamb, M. E. (1987). Predictive implications of individual differences in attachment. *Journal of Consulting and Clinical Psychology, 55,* 817–824.

Lamb, M. E. (Ed.). (1986). *The father's role: Applied perspectives.* New York: Wiley.

Lamb, M. E., Morrison, D. C., & Malkin, C. M. (1987). The development of infant social expectations in face-to-face interaction. *Merrill-Palmer Quarterly, 33,* 241–254.

Lamb, M. E., Sternberg, K. J., Hwang, C. P., & Broberg, A. G. (Eds.). (1992). *Child care in context: Cross-cultural perspectives.* Hillsdale, NJ: Erlbaum.

Lambert, P., Armstong, L., & Wagner, J. (1995, February 27). The vanishing. *People Weekly,* 32–42.

Lambert, W. E., & Peal, E. (1972). The relation of bilingualism to intelligence. In A. S. Dil (Ed.), *Language, psychology, and culture* (3rd ed.). New York: Wiley.

Lamberts, S. W. J., van den Beld, A. W., & van der Lely, A-J. (1997, October 17). The endocrinology of aging. *Science, 278,* 419–424.

Lamm, H., & Wiesmann, U. (1997). Subjective attributes of attraction: How people characterize their liking, their love, and their being in love. *Personal Relationships, 4,* 271–284.

Lamont, J. A. (1997). Sexuality. In D. E. Stewart & G. E. Robinson (Eds.), *A clinician's guide to menopause. Clinical practice* (pp. 63–75). Washington, DC: Health Press International.

Lamorey, S., Robinson, B. E., & Rowland, B. H. (1998). *Latchkey kids: Unlocking doors for children and their families.* Newbury Park, CA: Sage.

Lanctot, K. L., Herrmann, N., & Mazzotta, P. (2001). Role of serotonin in the behavioral and psychological symptoms of dementia. *Journal of Neuropsychiatry & Clinical Neurosciences, 13,* 5–21.

Lander, E. S., & Schork, N. J. (1994, September 30). Genetic dissection of complex traits. *Science, 265,* 2037–2048.

Landrine, H., & Klonoff, E. A. (1994). Cultural diversity in causal attributions for illness: The role of the supernatural. *Journal of Behavior Medicine, 17,* 181–193.

Landy, F. J. (1994, July/August). Mandatory retirement age: Serving the public welfare? *Psychological Science Agenda,* pp. 10–13.

Lane, W. K. (1976, November). *The relationship between personality and differential academic achievement within a group of highly gifted and high achieving children.* Dissertation Abstracts International., 37(5-A), 2746.

Lang, A. A. (1999, June 13). Doctors are second-guessing the "miracle" of multiple births. *The New York Times,* p. WH4.

Langer, E., & Janis, I. (1979). *The psychology of control.* Beverly Hills, CA: Sage.

Langford, P. E. (1995). *Approaches to the development of moral reasoning.* Hillsdale, NJ: Erlbaum.

Larsen-Freeman, D., & Long, M. H. (1991). *An introduction to second language acquisition research.* London: Longman.

Larson, R. W., Richards, M. H., Moneta, G., Holmbeck, G., & Duckett, E. (1996). Changes in adolescents' daily interactions with their families from ages 10 to 18: Disengagement and transformation. *Developmental Psychology, 32,* 744–754.

Larsson, B., & Melin, L. (1992). Prevalence and short-term stability of depressive symptoms in school children. *Acta Psychiatrica Scandinavica, 85,* 17–22.

Larwood, L., Szwajkowski, E., & Rose, S. (1988). Sex and race discrimination resulting from manager–client relationships: Applying the rational bias theory of managerial discrimination. *Sex Roles, 18,* 9–29.

Lassner, J. B., Matthews, K. A., & Stoney, C. M. (1994). Are cardiovascular reactors to asocial stress also reactors to social stress? *Journal of Personality and Social Psychology, 66,* 69–77.

Laszlo, J. (1986). Scripts for interpersonal situations. *Studia Psychologia, 28,* 125–135.

Lau, S., & Kwok, L. K. (2000). Relationship of family environment to adolescents' depression and self-concept. *Social Behavior & Personality, 28,* 41–50.

Lauer, J., & Lauer, R. (1985). Marriages made to last. *Psychology Today, 19(6),* 22–26.

Lauer, J. C., & Lauer, R. H. (1999). *How to survive and thrive in an empty nest.* Oakland, CA: New Harbinger Publications.

Laumann, E. O., Paik, A., & Rosen, R. C. (1999). Sexual dysfunction in the United States: Prevalence and predictors. *Journal of the American Medical Association, 281,* 537–544.

Laursen, B., Coy, K. C., & Collins, W. A. (1998). Reconsidering changes in parent-child conflict across adolescence: A meta-analysis. *Child Development, 69,* 817-832.

Laursen, B., Hartup, W. W., & Koplas, A. L. (1996). Towards understanding peer conflict. *Merrill-Palmer Quarterly, 42,* 76–102.

Lavanco, G. (1997). Burnout syndrome and Type A behavior in nurses and teachers in Sicily. *Psychological Reports, 81,* 523–528.

Lawton, M. P., Kleban, M. H., Moss, M., Rovine, M., & Glicksman, A. (1989). Measuring caregiving appraisal. *Journal of Gerontology: Psychological Sciences, 44,* 61–71.

Lazarus, R. S. (1968). Emotions and adaptations: Conceptual and empirical relations. In W. Arnold (Ed.), *Nebraska symposium on motivation.* Lincoln: University of Nebraska.

Lazarus, R. S. (1991). *Emotion and adaptation.* New York: Oxford University Press.

Lazarus, R. S., & Folkman, S. (1984). *Stress, appraisal, and coping.* New York: Springer.

Leaper, C., Anderson, K. J., & Sanders, P. (1998). Moderators of gender effects on parents' talk to their children: A meta-analysis. *Developmental Psychology, 34,* 3–27.

Leary, W.E. (1996, November 20). U.S. rate of sexual diseases highest in developed world. *The New York Times,* p. C1.

Leavitt, L. A., & Goldson, E. (1996). Introduction to special section: Biomedicine and developmental psychology: New areas of common ground. *Developmental Psychology, 32,* 387–389.

Leboyer, F. (1975). *Birth without violence.* New York: Knopf.

Lecanuet, J-P., Fifer, W. P., Krasnegor, N. A., & Smotherman, W. P. (Eds.). (1995). *Fetal develop-*

ment: A psychobiological perspective. Hillsdale, NJ: Erlbaum.

Lecanuet, J-P., Granier-Deferre, C., & Busnel, M-C. (1995). Human fetal auditory perception. In J-P. Lecanuet, W. P. Fifer, N. A. Krasnegor, & W. P. Smotherman (Eds.), *Fetal development: A psychobiological perspective.* Hillsdale, NJ: Erlbaum.

Lecours, A. R. (1982). Correlates of developmental behavior in brain maturation. In T. Bever (Ed.), *Regressions in mental development.* Hillsdale, NJ: Erlbaum.

Lee, C-K., Klopp, R. G., Weindruch, R., & Prolla, T. A. (1999, August 27). Gene expression profile of aging and its retardation by caloric restriction. *Science, 285,* 1390–1393.

Lee, J. (1997). Never innocent: Breasted experiences in women's bodily narratives of puberty. *Feminism & Psychology, 7,* 453–474.

Lefkowitz, E. S., Sigman, M., & Kit-fong Au, T. (2000). Helping mothers discuss sexuality and AIDS with adolescents. *Child Development, 71,* 1383–1394.

Legerstee, M., Anderson, D., & Schaffer, A. (1998). Five- and eight-month-old infants recognize their faces and voices as familiar and social stimuli. *Child Development, 69,* 37–50.

Leiblum, S. R. (1990). Sexuality and the midlife woman. Special Issue: Women at midlife and beyond. *Psychology of Women Quarterly, 14,* 495–508.

Leitenberg, H., Detzer, M. J., & Srebnik, D. (1993). Gender differences in masturbation and the relation of masturbation experience in preadolescence and/or early adolescence to sexual behavior and sexual adjustment in young adulthood. *Archives of Sexual Behavior, 22,* 87–98.

Leiter, J., & Johnsen, M. C. (1997). Child maltreatment and school performance declines: An event-history analysis. *American Educational Research Journal, 34,* 563–589.

Lelwica, M., & Haviland, J. (1983). *Ten-week-old infants' reactions to mothers' emotional expressions.* Paper presented at the biennial meeting of the Society for Research in Child Development.

Lemonick, M. D. (2000, October 30). Teens before their time. *Time, 67,* 68–74.

Lenssen, B. G. (1973). Infants' reactions to peer strangers. *Dissertation Abstracts International, 33,* 60–62.

Leonard, C. M., Lombardino, L. J., Mercado, L. R., Browd, S. R., Breier, J. I., & Agee, O. F. (1996). Cerebral asymmetry and cognitive development in children: A magnetic resonance imaging study. *Psychological Science, 7,* 89–95.

Leonard, L. B. (1998). *Children with specific language impairment.* Cambridge, MA: MIT Press.

Lepore, S. J., Palsane, M. N., & Evans, G. W. (1991). Daily hassles and chronic strains: A hierarchy of stressors? *Social Science and Medicine, 33,* 1029–1036.

Lerner, R. M., Fisher, C. B., & Weinberg, R. A. (2000). Toward a science for and of the people: Promoting civil society through the application of developmental science. *Child Development, 71,* 11–20.

Leslie, C, (1991, February 11). Classrooms of Babel. *Newsweek,* 56–57.

Lester, D. (1996). Psychological issues in euthanasia, suicide, and assisted suicide. *Journal of Social Issues, 52,* 51–62.

Levano, K. J., Cunningham, F. G., Nelson, S., Roark, M., Williams, M. L., Guzick, D., Dowling, S., Rosenfeld, C. R., & Buckley, A. (1986). A prospective comparison of selective and universal electronic fetal monitoring in 34,995 pregnancies. *New England Journal of Medicine, 315,* 615–619.

LeVay, S. (1993). *The sexual brain.* Cambridge, MA: MIT Press.

Levenson, R. W., Carstensen, L. L., & Gottman, J. M. (1993). Long-term marriage: Age, gender, and satisfaction. *Psychology and Aging, 8,* 301–313.

Levine, L. E., & Waite, B. M. (2000). Television viewing and attentional abilities in fourth and fifth grade children. *Journal of Applied Developmental Psychology, 21,* 667–679.

Levine, R. (1997a, November). The pace of life in 31 countries. *American Demographics,* pp. 20–29.

Levine, R. (1997b). *A geography of time: The temporal misadventures of a social psychologist, or how every culture keeps time just a little bit differently.* New York: HarperCollins.

Levine, R. V. (1993, February). Is love a luxury? *American Demographics,* pp. 29–37.

Levine, S. C., Huttenlocher, J., Taylor, A., & Langrock, A. (1999). Early sex differences in spatial skill. *Developmental Psychology, 35,* 940–949.

Levine, R. (1994). *Child care and culture.* Cambridge: Cambridge University Press.

Levinson, D. (1992). *The seasons of a woman's life.* New York: Knopf.

Levinson, D. J. (1986). A conception of adult development. *American Psychologist, 41,* 3–13.

Leviton, A., Bellinger, D., Allred, E. N., Rabinowitz, M., Needleman, H., & Schoenbaum, S. (1993). Pre- and postnatal low-level lead exposure and children's dysfunction in school. *Environmental Research, 60,* 30–43.

Levy, B. L., & Langer, E. (1994). Aging free from negative stereotypes: Successful memory in China and among the American deaf. *Journal of Personality and Social Psychology, 66,* 989–997.

Levy, D. H. (2000, August 20). Are you ready for the genome miracle? *Parade Magazine,* 8–10.

Lewin, T. (1995, May 11). Women are becoming equal providers: Half of working women bring home half the household income. *The New York Times,* p. A14.

Lewinsohn, P. M., Roberts, R. E., Seeley, J. R., & Rohde, P. (1994). Adolescent psychopathology: II. Psychosocial risk factors for depression. *Journal of Abnormal Psychology, 103,* 302–315.

Lewinsohn, P. M., Rohde, P., & Seeley, J. R. (1994). Psychosocial risk factors for future adolescent suicide attempts. *Journal of Consulting and Clinical Psychology, 62,* 297–305.

Lewis, C. S. (1958). The allegory of love: A study in medieval traditions. New York: Oxford University Press.

Lewis, C. S. (1985). A grief observed. In E. S. Shneidman (Ed.), Death: Current perspectives (3rd ed.). Palo Alto, CA: Mayfield.

Lewis, C., & Mitchell, P. (Eds.). (1994). Children's early understanding of mind: Origins and development. Hillsdale, NJ: Erlbaum.

Lewis, D. O., Yeager, C. A., Loveley, R., et al. (1994). A clinical follow-up of delinquent males: Ignored vulnerabilities, unmet needs, and the perpetuation of violence. Journal of the American Academy of Child and Adolescent Psychiatry, 33, 518–528.

Lewis, M., Feiring, C., & Rosenthal, S. (2000). Attachment over time. Child Development, 71, 707–720.

Lewis, R., Freneau, P., & Roberts, C. (1979). Fathers and the postparental transition. Family Coordinator, 28, 514–520.

Lewis, T. E., & Phillipsen, L. C. (1998). Interactions on an elementary school playground: Variations by age, gender, race, group size, and playground area. Child Study Journal, 28, 309-320.

Leyens, J. P., Camino, L., Parke, R. D., & Berkowitz, L. (1975). Effects of movie violence on aggression in a field setting as a function of group dominance and cohesion. Journal of Personality and Social Psychology, 32, 346–360.

Lickliter, R., & Bahrick, L. E. (2000). The development of infant intersensory perception: Advantages of a comparative convergent-operations approach. Psychological Bulletin, 126, 260–280.

Liebert, R. M., & Sprafkin, J. (1988). The early window: Effects of television on children and youth (3rd ed.). New York: Pergamon.

Life. (1999, May 1.) Johanna Hoagland & Erika Enslin-Franklin. p. 50.

Light, L. L. (1991). Memory and aging: Four hypotheses in search of data. Annual Review of Psychology, 42, 333–376.

Light, L. L. (2000). Memory changes in adulthood. In S. H. Qualls, & N. Abeles, (Eds), et al. Psychology and the aging revolution: How we adapt to longer life. (pp. 73–97). Washington, DC: American Psychological Association.

Lillard, A. (1998). Ethnopsychologies: Cultural variations in theories of mind. Psychological Bulletin, 123, 3–32.

Lillo-Martin, D. (1997). In support of the language acquisition device. In M. Marschark, & P. Siple (Eds.), Relations of language and thought: The view from sign language and deaf children. Counterpoints: Cognition, memory, and language. New York: Oxford University Press.

Lindholm, K. J. (1991). Two-way bilingual/immersion education: Theory, conceptual issues, and pedagogical implications. In R. V. Padilla & A. Benavides (Eds.), Critical perspectives on bilingual education research. Tempe, AZ: Bilingual Review Press.

Lindhout, D., Frets, P. G., & Niermeijer, M. F. (1991). Approaches to genetic counseling. Annals of the New York Academy of Sciences, 630, 223–229.

Linn, M. C. (1997, September 19). Finding patterns in international assessments. Science, 277, 1743.

Linz, D. G., Donnerstein, E., & Penrod, S. (1988). Effects of long-term exposure to violent and sexually degrading depictions of women. Journal of Personality and Social Psychology, 55, 758–768.

Lipman, J. (1992, March 10). Surgeon General says it's high time Joe Camel quit. The Wall Street Journal, pp. B1, B7.

Lippa, R. A., Martin, L. R., & Friedman, H. S. (2000). Gender-related individual differences and mortality in the Terman longitudinal study: Is masculinity hazardous to your health? *Personality & Social Psychology Bulletin, 26,* 1560–1570.

Lipsitt, L. P. (1986a). Toward understanding the hedonic nature of infancy. In L. P. Lipsitt & J. H. Cantor (Eds.), *Experimental child psychologist: Essays and experiments in honor of Charles C. Spiker* (pp. 97–109). Hillsdale, NJ: Erlbaum.

Liskin, L. (1985, Nov.–Dec.) Youth in the 1980s: Social and health concerns: 4. *Population Reports, 8,* No. 5.

Litovsky, R. Y., & Ashmead, D. H. (1997). Development of binaural and spatial hearing in infants and children. In R. H. Gilkey & T. R. Andersen (Eds.), *Binaural and spatial hearing in real and virtual environments* (pp. 571–592). Mahwah, NJ: Erlbaum.

Little, T. D., & Lopez, D. F., (1997). Regularities in the development of children's causality beliefs about school performance across six sociocultural contexts. *Developmental Psychology, 33,* 165–175.

Livson, N., & Peskin, H. (1980). Perspectives on adolescence from longitudinal research. In J. Adelson (Ed.), *Handbook of adolescent psychology.* New York: Wiley.

Llemery, K. S., Goldsmith, H. H., Klinnert, M. D., & Mrazek, D. A. (1999). Developmental models of infant and childhood temperament. *Developmental Psychology, 35,* 189-204.

Lloyd, B., & Duveen, G. (1991). Expressing social gender identities in the first year of school. *European Journal of Psychology of Education, 6,* 437–447.

Lobel, T. E., Bar-David, E., Gruber, R., Lau, S., & Bar-Tal, Y. (2000). Gender schema and social judgments: A developmental study of children from Hong Kong. *Sex Roles, 43,* 19–42.

Lock, R. D. (1992). *Taking charge of your career direction* (2nd ed.). Pacific Grove, CA: Brooks/Cole.

Locke, J. L. (1983). *Phonological acquisition and change.* New York: Academic Press.

Locke, J. L. (1994). Phases in the child's development of language. *American Scientist, 82,* 436–445.

Loehlin, J. C. (1992). *Genes and environment in personality development.* Newbury Park, CA: Sage.

Loftus, E. F. (1997, September). Creating false memories. *Scientific American,* 71–75.

Lonetto, R. (1980). *Children's conception of death.* New York: Springer.

Long, T., & Long, L. (1983). *Latchkey children.* New York: Penguin.

Lorenz, K. (1957). Companionship in bird life. In C. Scholler (Ed.), *Instinctive behavior.* New York: International Universities Press.

Lorenz, K. (1966). *On aggression.* New York: Harcourt Brace Jovanovich.

Lorenz, K. (1974). *Civilized man's eight deadly sins.* New York: Harcourt Brace Jovanovich.

Lorenz, K. Z. (1965). *Evolution and the modification of behavior.* Chicago: University of Chicago Press.

Lorion, R. P., Iscoe, I., DeLeon, P. H., VandenBos, G. R. (Eds.). (1996). *Psychology and public policy: Balancing public service and professional need.* Washington, DC: American Psychological Association.

Lourenco, O., & Machado, A. (1996). In defense of Piaget's theory: A reply to 10 common criticisms. *Psychological Review, 103,* 143–164.

Lowe, M. R. (1993). The effects of dieting on eating behavior: A three-factor model. *Psychological Bulletin, 114,* 100–121.

Lowrey, G. H. (1986). *Growth and development of children* (8th ed.). Chicago: Year Book Medical Publishers.

Lust, B., Suner, M., & Whitman, J. (Eds.). (1995). *Syntactic theory and first language acquisition.* Hillsdale, NJ: Erlbaum.

Luster, T., & McAdoo, H. P. (1994). Factors related to the achievement and adjustment of young African American children. *Child Development, 65,* 1080–1094.

Lykken, D., Bouchard, T., McGue, M., & Tellegen, A. (1993a). Heritability of interests: A twin study. *Journal of Applied Psychology, 78,* 649–661.

Lykken, D. T., McGue, M., Tellegen, A., & Bouchard, T. J., Jr. (1993b). Emergenesis: Genetic traits that may not run in families. *American Psychologist, 47,* 1565–1577.

Lyman, D. R., Milich, R., Zimmerman, R., Novak, S. P., Logan, T. K., Martin, C., Leudefeld, M. C., & Clayton, R. (1999). Project DARE: No effects at 10-year follow-up. *Journal of Consulting and Clinical Psychology, 67,* 590–593.

Lynam, D. R. (1996). Early identification of chronic offenders: Who is the fledgling psychopath? *Psychological Bulletin, 120,* 209–234.

Lyness, S. A. (1993). Predictors of differences between Type A and B individuals in heart rate and blood pressure reactivity. *Psychological Bulletin, 114,* 266–295.

Lyon, G. R. (1996). Learning disabilities. *The Future of children, 6,* 54–76.

Lynn J., Teno, J. M., Phillips, R. S., Wu, A. W., Desbiens, N., Harrold J., Claessens, M. T., Wenger, N., Kreling, B., & Connors, A. F., Jr. (1997). Perceptions by family members of the dying experience of older and seriously ill patients. SUPPORT Investigators. Study to Understand Prognoses and Preferences for Outcomes and Risks of Treatments [see comments] *Annals of Internal Medicine, 126,* 164–165.

Lyon, M. E., Benoit, M., O'Donnell, R. M., Getson, P. R., Silber, T., & Walsh, T. (2000). Assessing African American adolescents' risk for suicide attempts: Attachment theory. *Adolescence, 35,* 121–134.

Lynwander, L. (1995, February 5). Burying the poor. *The New York Times,* Sec. 13NJ, p. 1.

Lysynchuk, L. M., Pressley, M. & Vye, N. J. (1990). Reciprocal teaching improves standardized reading-comprehension performance in poor comprehenders. *Elementary School Journal, 90,* 469–484.

MacArthur Foundation Research Network on Successful Midlife Development. (1999). *What age do you feel most of the time?* Vero Beach, FL: MIDMAC.

Maccoby, E. B. (1999). *The two sexes : Growing up apart, coming together.* New York: Belknap.

Maccoby, E. E. (1980). *Social development: Psychological growth and the parent–child relationship.* New York: Harcourt, Brace, Jovanovich.

Macionis, J. J. (2001). *Sociology.* Upper Saddle River, NJ: Prentice Hall.

Mackenzie, K., & Peters, M. (2000). Handedness, hand roles, and hand injuries at work. *Journal of Safety Research, 31,* 221–227.

Mackey, M. C. (1990). Women's preparation for the childbirth experience. *Maternal-Child Nursing Journal, 19,* 143–173.

Mackey, M. C., White, U., & Day, R. (1992). Reasons American men become fathers: Men's divulgences, women's perceptions. *Journal of Genetic Psychology, 153,* 435–445.

MacPhee, D., Kreutzer, J. C., & Fritz, J. J. (1994). Infusing a diversity perspective into human development courses. *Child Development, 65,* 699–715.

MacWhinney, B. (1991). Connectionism as a framework for language acquisition. In J. Miller (Ed.), *Research on child language disorders.* Austin, TX: Pro-ed.

Maddox, G. L., & Campbell, R. T. (1985). Scope, concepts, and methods in the study of aging. In R. H. Binstock & E. Shanas (Eds.), *Handbook of aging and the social sciences* (2nd ed.). New York: Van Nostrand Reinhold.

Magai, C., & McFadden, S. H. (Eds.). (1996). *Handbook of emotion, adult development, and aging.* New York: Academic Press.

Mahoney, M. C., & James, D. M. (2000). Predictors of anticipated breastfeeding in an urban, low-income setting. *Journal of Family Practice, 49,* 529–533.

Maiden, A. H. (1997). Celebrating a return to earth: Birth in indigenous aboriginal, Tibetan, Balinese, Basque and Cherokee cultures. *Pre- & Peri-Natal Psychology Journal, 11,* 251–264.

Major, B., & Konar, E. (1984). An investigation of sex differences in pay expectations and their possible causes. *Academy of Management Journal, 27,* 777–792.

Malinowski, C. I., & Smith, C. P. (1985). Moral reasoning and moral conduct: An investigation prompted by Kohlberg's theory. *Journal of Personality and Social Psychology, 49,* 1016–1027.

Mancini, J. A., & Blieszner, R. (1991). Aging parents and adult children. In A. Booth (Ed.), *Contemporary families,* Minneapolis, MN: National Council on Family Relations.

Mandel, D. R., Jusczyk, P. W., & Pisoni, D. B. (1995). Infants' recognition of the sound patterns of their own names. *Psychological Science, 6,* 314–317.

Mandler, J. M. (1990). A new perspective on cognitive development in infancy. *American Scientist, 78,* 236–243.

Mandler, J. M., & McDonough, L. (1994). Long-term recall of event sequences in infancy. *Journal of Experimental Child Psychology, 59,* 457–474.

Mangan, P. A. (1997, November). *Time perception.* Paper presented at the annual meeting of the Society for Neuroscience, New Orleans.

Mangelsdorf, S., Gunnar, M., Kestenbaum, R., Lang, S., & Andreas, D. (1990). Infant proneness-to-distress temperament, maternal personality, and mother–infant attachment: Association and goodness of fit. *Child Development, 61,* 820–831.

Manson, A., & Shea, S. (1991). Malnutrition in elderly ambulatory medical patients. *American Journal of Public Health, 81,* 1195–1197.

Manstead, A. S. R. (1997). Situations, belongingness, attitudes, and culture: Four lessons learned from social psychology. In C. McGarty & S. A. Haslam (Eds.) et al., *The message of social psychology: Perspectives on mind in society.* Oxford, England: Blackwell Publishers, Inc.

Maratsos, M. P. (1983). Some current issues in the study of the acquisition of grammar. In P. H.

Mussen (Ed.), *Handbook of child psychology* (Vol. 3, 4th ed.). New York: Wiley.

Marcia, J. E. (1966). Development and validation of ego identity status. *Journal of Personality and Social Psychology, 3(5)*, 551–558.

Marcia, J. E. (1980). Identity in adolescence. In J. Adelson (Ed.), *Handbook of adolescent psychology*. New York: Wiley

Markus, H. R., & Kitayama, S. (1991). Culture and the self: Implications for cognition, emotion, and motivation. *Psychological Review, 98*, 224–253.

Marlier, L., Schaal, B., & Soussignan, R. (1998). Neonatal responsiveness to the odor of amniotic and lacteal fluids: A test of perinatal chemosensory continuity. *Child Development, 69*, 611–623.

Marsh, H. E., Craven, R., & Debus, R. (1998). Structure, stability, and development of young children's self-concepts: A multicohort-multioccasion study. *Child Development, 69*, 1030–1053.

Marsh, H. W. (1990). Influences of internal and external frames of reference on the formation of math and English self-concepts. *Journal of Educational Psychology, 82*, 107–116.

Marsh, H. W., & Holmes, I. W. M. (1990). Multidimensional self-concepts: Construct validation of responses by children. *American Educational Research Journal, 27*, 89–118.

Marsh, H. W., & Parker, J. W. (1984). Determinants of student self-concept: Is it better to be a relatively large fish in a small pond even if you don't learn to swim as well? *Journal of Personality and Social Psychology, 47*, 213–231.

Marsh, H. W., & Shavelson, R. (1985). Self-concept: Its multifaceted, hierarchical structure. *Educational Psychologist, 20*, 107–123.

Marshall, E. (2000, November 17). Planned Ritalin trial for tots heads into uncharted waters. *Science, 290*, 1280–1282.

Marshall, V. W. (Ed.). (1986). *Later life: The social psychology of aging*. Beverly Hills, CA: Sage.

Martikainen, P., & Valkonen, T. (1996). Mortality after the death of a spouse: Rates and causes of death in a large Finnish cohort. *American Journal of Public Health, 86*, 1087–1093.

Martin, B. A. (1989). Gender differences in salary expectations. *Psychology of Women Quarterly, 13*, 87–96.

Martin, C. L. (1993). New directions for investigating children's gender knowledge. *Developmental Review, 13*, 184–204.

Martin, C. L. (2000). Cognitive theories of gender development. In T. Eckes & H. M. Trautner, (Eds), et al. *The developmental social psychology of gender*. Mahwah, NJ: Erlbaum.

Martin, G. B., & Clark, R. D. (1982). Distress crying in neonates: Species and peer specificity. *Developmental Psychology, 18*, 3–9.

Martinez, R., & Dukes, R. L. (1991). Ethnic and gender differences in self-esteem. *Youth and Society, 22*, 318–338.

Masataka, N. (1996). Perception of motherese in a signed language by 6–month-old deaf infants. *Developmental Psychology, 32*, 874–879.

Maslach, C. (1982). *Burnout—The cost of caring*. Englewood Cliffs, NJ: Prentice-Hall.

Masling, J. M., & Bornstein, R. F. (Eds.). (1996). *Psychoanalytic perspectives on developmental psychol-ogy*. Washington, DC: American Psychological Association.

Maslow, A. H. (1970). *Motivation and personality* (2nd ed.). New York: Harper & Row.

Masten, A. S., & Coatsworth, J. D. (1998). The development of competence in favorable and unfavorable environments. *American Psychologist, 53*, 205–220.

Masters, W. H., Johnson, V., & Kolodny, R. C. (1982). *Human sexuality*. Boston: Little, Brown.

Mastropieri, M. A., & Scruggs, T. E. (1991). *Teaching students ways to remember: Strategies for learning mnemonically*. Cambridge, MA: Brookline Books.

Maternal and Child Health Bureau. (1994). *Child Health USA '93*. Washington, DC: U.S. Department of Health and Human Services.

Mathew, A., & Cook, M. L. (1990). The control of reaching movements by young infants. *Child Development, 61*, 1238–1257.

Mathews, J. J., & Zadak, K. (1991). The alternative birth movement in the United States: History and current status. *Women and Health, 17*, 39–56.

Matlin, M. M. (1987). *The psychology of women*. New York: Holt.

Matson, J. L., & Mulick, J. A. (Eds.). (1991). *Handbook of mental retardation* (2nd ed.). New York: Pergamon.

Matteson, M. A. (1988). Age-related changes in the integument. In M. A. Matteson & E. S. McConnell (Eds.), *Gerontological nursing: Concepts and practice*. Philadelphia: Saunders.

Matthews, K. A. (1982). Psychological perspectives on the Type A behavior pattern. *Psychological Bulletin, 91*, 293–323.

Matthews, K. A., Wing, R. R., Kuller, L. H., Meilahn, E. N., & Owens, J. F. (2000). Menopause as a turning point in midlife. In S. B Manuck, & R. Jennings, (Eds), et al. *Behavior, health, and aging*. Mahwah, NJ: Erlbaum.

Matusov, E., & Hayes, R. (2000). Sociocultural critique of Piaget and Vygotsky. *New Ideas in Psychology, 18*, 215–239.

Maxfield, M. G., & Widom, C. S. (1996). The cycle of violence. *Archives of Pediatrics & Adolescent Medicine, 150*, 390–395.

Mayberry, R. I., & Nicoladis, E. (2001). Gesture reflects language development: Evidence from bilingual children. *Current Directions in Psychological Science, 9*, 192–195.

Mayer, J. D. (2001). Emotion, intelligence, and emotional intelligence. In J. P. Forgas, (Ed). *Handbook of affect and social cognition*. Mahwah, NJ: Erlbaum.

Mayer, J. D., & Salovey, P. (1997). What is emotional intelligence? In P. Salovey & D. J. Sluyter (Eds.). *Emotional development and emotional intelligence*. New York: Basic Books.

Mayer, J. D., Salovey, P., & Caruso, D. R. (2000). Emotional intelligence as zeitgeist, as personality, and as a mental ability. In R. Bar-On, & J. D. A. Parker, James D. A. (Eds.), *The handbook of emotional intelligence: Theory, development, assessment, and application at home, school, and in the workplace*. San Francisco, CA: Jossey-Bass.

Mayo Clinic. (2000, March). Age-related macular degeneration: Who gets it and what you can do about it. *Women's Healthsource, 4*, 1–2.

Mayseless, O. (1996). Attachment patterns and their outcomes. *Human Development, 39*, 206–223.

McAdams, D. P., & de St. Aubin, E. (Eds.). (1998). *Generativity and adult development: How and why we care for the next generation*. Washington, DC: American Psychological Association.

McAdoo, H. P. (1988). *Black families*. Newbury Park, CA: Sage.

McAuliffe, S. P., & Knowlton, B. J. (2001). Hemispheric differences in object identification. *Brain & Cognition., 45*, 119–128.

McCabe, M. (1984). Toward a theory of adolescent dating. *Adolescence, 19*, 159–169.

McCarthy, M. J. (1994, November 8). Hunger among elderly surges: Meal programs just can't keep up. *The Wall Street Journal*, pp. A1, A11.

McCarty, M., & Ashmead, D. H. (1999). Visual control of reaching and grasping in infants. *Developmental Psychology, 35*, 620–631.

McCaul, K. D., Ployhart, R. E., Hinsz, V. B., & McCaul, H. S. (1995). Appraisals of a consistent versus a similar politician: Voter preferences and intuitive judgments. *Journal of Personality and Social Psychology, 68*, 292–299.

McClelland, D. C. (1993). Intelligence is not the best predictor of job performance. *Current Directions in Psychological Research, 2*, 5–8.

McCloskey, L. A., & Bailey, J. A. (2000). The intergenerational transmission of risk for child sexual abuse. *Journal of Interpersonal Violence, 15*, 1019–1035.

McCracken, A. L., & Gerdsen, L. (1991). Sharing the legacy: Hospice care principles for the terminally ill elders. *Journal of Gerontological Nursing, 17*, 4–8.

McCrae, R. R., & Costa, P. T., Jr. (1990). *Personality in adulthood*. New York: Guilford.

McCrae, R. R., Costa, P. T., Jr., Ostendorf, F., Angleitner, A., Hebíková, M., Avia, M. D., Sanz, J., Sánchez-Bernardos, M. L., Kusdil, M. E., Woodfield, R., Saunders, P. R., & Smith, P. B. (2000). Nature over nurture: Temperament, personality, and life span development. *Journal of Personality and Social Psychology, 78*, 173–186.

McDaniel, K. D. (1986). Pharmacologic treatment of psychiatric and neurodevelopmental disorders in children and adolescents: III. *Clinical Pediatrics, 25*, 198–204.

McDonald, M. A., Sigman, M., Espinosa, M. P., & Neumann, C. G. (1994). Impact of a temporary food shortage on children and their mothers. *Child Development, 65*, 404–415.

McDougall, G. J., Blixen, C. E., & Suen, L. (1997). The process and outcome of life review psychotherapy with depressed homebound older adults. *Nursing Research, 46*, 277–283.

McGreal, D., Evans, B. J., & Burrows, G. D. (1997). Gender differences in coping following loss of a child through miscarriage or stillbirth: A pilot study. *Stress Medicine, 13*, 159–165.

McGue, M., Bouchard, T., Iacono, W., & Lykken, D. (1993). Behavioral genetics of cognitive ability: A life-span perspective. In R. Plomin & G. McClearn (Eds.), *Nature, nurture and psychology* (pp. 59–76). Washington, DC: American Psychological Association.

McGuffin, P., Riley, B., & Plomin, R. (2001, February 16.) Toward behavioral genomics. *Science, 291,* 1232–1233.

McGuinness, D. (1972). Hearing: Individual differences in perceiving. *Perception, 1,* 465–473.

McKenna, J. J. (1983). Primate aggression and evolution: An overview of sociobiological and anthropological perspectives. *Bulletin of the American Academy of Psychiatry and the Law, 11,* 105–130.

McKenna, M. C., Kear, D. J., Ellsworth, R. A. (1995). Children's attitudes toward reading: A national survey. *Research Quarterly, 30,* 934–956.

McKenzie, R. B. (1997). Orphanage alumni: How they have done and how they evaluate their experience. *Child & Youth Care Forum, 26,* 87–111.

McKinlay, S. M., & Jefferys, M. (1974). The menopausal syndrome. *British Journal of Preventive & Social Medicine, 28,* 108–115.

McLoyd, V. C. (1998). Socioeconomic disadvantage and child development. *American Psychologist, 53,* 185–204.

McRae, S. (1997). Cohabitation: A trial run for marriage? *Sexual & Marital Therapy, 12,* 259–273.

McWhirter, D. P., Sanders, S., & Reinisch, J. M. (1990). *Homosexuality, heterosexuality: Concepts of sexual orientation.* New York: Oxford University Press.

McWhirter, L., Young, V., & Majury, Y. (1983). Belfast children's awareness of violent death. *British Journal of Psychology, 22,* 81–92.

Mead, M. (1942). *Environment and education,* a symposium held in connection with the fiftieth anniversary celebration of the Univeristy of Chicago. Chicago: University of Chicago.

Mealey, L. (2000). *Sex differences: Developmental and evolutionary strategies.* Orlando, FL: Academic Press.

Medina, J. J. (1996). *The clock of ages: Why we age— How we age—Winding back the clock.* New York: Cambridge University Press.

Mednick, S. A. (1963). Research creativity in psychology graduate students. *Journal of Consulting Psychology, 27,* 265–266.

Meece, J. L., & Kurtz-Costes, B. (2001). Introduction: The schooling of ethnic minority children and youth. *Educational Psychologist, 36,* 1–7.

Meeus, W. (1996). Studies on identity development in adolescence: An overview of research and some new data. *Journal of Youth & Adolescence, 25,* 569–598.

Mehler, J., & DuPoux, E. (1994). *What infants know: The new cognitive science of early development.* Cambridge, MA: Blackwell.

Mehran, K. (1997). Interferences in the move from adolescence to adulthood: The development of the male. In M. Laufer (Ed.), *Adolescent breakdown and beyond* (pp. 17–25). London, England: Karnac Books.

Meisels, S. J., & Plunkett, J. W. (1988). Developmental consequences of preterm birth: Are there long-term deficits? In P. B. Baltes, D. L. Featherman, & R. M. Lerner (Eds.), *Lifespan development and behavior* (Vol. 9). Hillsdale, NJ: Erlbaum.

Meiser, B., & Dunn, S. (2000). Psychological impact of genetic testing for Huntington's disease: An update of the literature. *Journal of Neurology, Neurosurgery & Psychiatry, 69,* 574–578.

Meltzoff, A. N. (1981). Imitation, intermodal coordination and representation in early infancy. In G. Butterworth (Ed.), *Infancy and epistemology.* Brighton: Harvester Press.

Meltzoff, A. N., & Moore, M. K. (1977). Imitation of facial and manual gestures by human neonates. *Science, 198,* 75–78.

Meltzoff, A. N., & Moore, M. K. (1989). Imitation in newborn infants: Exploring the range of gestures imitated and the underlying mechanisms. *Developmental Psychology, 25(6),* 954–962.

Meltzoff, A. N., & Moore, M. K. (1994). Imitation, memory, and the representation of persons. *Infant Behavior and Development, 17,* 83–99.

Meltzoff, A. N., & Moore, M. K. (1999). Persons and representation: Why infant imitation is important for theories of human development. In J. Nadel, & G. Butterworth, (Eds.), et al. *Imitation in infancy. Cambridge studies in cognitive perceptual development.* New York: Cambridge University Press.

Mendelowitz, D. (1998). Nicotine excites cardiac vagal neurons via three sites of action. *Clinical & Experimental Pharmacology & Physiology, 25,* 453–456.

Mendelson, B. K., White, D. R., & Mendelson, M. J. (1996). Self-esteem and body esteem: Effects of gender, age, and weight. *Journal of Applied Developmental Psychology, 17,* 321–346.

Menella, J. (2000, June). *The psychology of eating.* Paper presented at the annual meeting of the American Psychological Society, Miami.

Mercer, C. (1992). *Students with learning disabilities* (4th ed.). Columbus, OH: Merrill.

Mercer, J. R. (1973). *Labeling the mentally retarded.* Berkeley: University of California Press.

Meredith H. V. (1971). Growth in body size: a compendium of findings on contemporary children living in different parts of the world. *Child Development & Behavior, 6,* 153–238, 1971.

Merill, D. M. (1997). *Caring for elderly parents: Juggling work, family, and caregiving in middle and working class families.* Wesport, CT: Auburn House/Greenwood Publishing Group.

Meyer-Bahlburg, H. F. L., Ehrhardt, A. A., Rosen, L. R., Gruen, R. S., Veridiano, N. P., Vann, F. H., & Neuwalder, H. F. (1995). Prenatal estrogens and the development of homosexual orientation. *Developmental Psychology, 31,* 12–21.

Meyerhoff, M. K., & White, B. L. (1986, September). Making the grade as parents. *Psychology Today,* pp. 38–45.

Michael, R. T., Gagnon, J. H., Laumann, E. O., & Kolata, G. (1994). *Sex in America: A definitive survey.* Boston: Little, Brown.

Michel, G. L. (1981). Right-handedness: A consequence of infant supine head-orientation preference? *Science, 212,* 685–687.

Midlarsky, E., & Bryan, J. H. (1972). Affect expressions and children's imitative altruism. *Journal of Experimental Research in Personality, 6,* 195–203.

Mikhail, B. (2000). Prenatal care utilization among low-income African American women. *Journal of Community Health Nursing, 17,* 235–246.

Miller, A. B. (1991). Is routine mammography screening appropriate for women 40–49 years of age? *American Journal of Preventive Medicine, 7,* 55–62.

Miller, B. (1997b, March). The quest for lifelong learning. *American Demographics,* pp. 20–22.

Miller, C. A. (1987). A review of maternity care programs in western Europe. *Family Planning Perspectives, 19(5),* 207–211.

Miller, D. A., McCluskey-Fawcett, K., & Irving, L. (1993). Correlates of bulimia nervosa: Early family mealtime experiences. *Adolescence, 28,* 621–635.

Miller, J. L., & Eimas, P. D. (1995). Speech perception: From signal to word. *Annual Review of Psychology, 46,* 467–492.

Miller, K. J., & Mizes, J. S. (Eds.). (2000). *Comparative treatments for eating disorders.* New York: Springer.

Miller, N., & Brewer, M. (1984). *Groups in contact: The psychology of desegregation.* New York: Academic Press.

Miller, P. A., & Jansen op de Haar, M. A. (1997). Emotional, cognitive, behavioral, and temperament characteristics of high-empathy children. *Motivation and Emotion, 21,* 109–125.

Miller, P. H. & Seier, W. L. (1994). *Strategy utilization deficiencies in children: When, where, and why.* San Diego, CA: Academic Press.

Miller, P. H, Woody-Ramsey, J., & Aloise, P. A. (1991). The role of strategy effortfulness in strategy effectiveness. *Developmental Psychology, 27,* 738–745.

Miller, R. B., Hemesath, K., & Nelson, B. (1997). Marriage in middle and later life. In T. D. Hargrave & S. M. Hanna (Eds.), *The aging family: New visions in theory, practice, and reality* (pp. 178–198). New York: Brunner/Mazel.

Miller, S. A. (1998). *Developmental research methods.* (2nd ed.). Upper Saddle River, NJ: Prentice-Hall.

Miller, S. M., & Mangan, C. E. (1983). Interacting effects of information and coping style in adapting to gynecologic stress: Should the doctor tell all? *Journal of Personality and Social Psychology, 45,* 223–236.

Miller-Perrin, C. L., & Perrin, R. D. (1999). *Child maltreatment: An introduction.* Thousand Oaks, CA: Sage.

Mills, J. L. (1999). Cocaine, smoking, and spontaneous abortion. *New England Journal of Medicine, 340,* 380–381.

Milner, J. (1995, January). Paper presented at a conference, "Violence against children in the family and the community: a conference on causes, developmental consequences, interventions and prevention." Los Angeles: University of Southern California.

Minaker, K. L, & Frishman, R. (1995, October). Love gone wrong. *Harvard Health Letter,* pp. 9–12.

Minkowski, A. (1967). *Regional development of the brain in early life.* Oxford: Blackwell.

Minorities in Higher Education. (1990). *Report on minorities in higher education.* Washington, DC: Minorities in Higher Education.

Mishra, R. C. (1997). Cognition and cognitive development. In J. W. Berry, P. R. Dasen, & T. S. Saraswathi (Eds.), *Handbook of cross-cultural psychology, Vol. 2: Basic processes and human development* (2nd ed., pp. 143–175). Boston, MA: Allyn & Bacon.

Mistretta, C. M. (1990). Taste development. In J. R. Coleman (Ed.), *Development of sensory systems in mammals* (pp. 567–613). New York: Wiley.

Mittendorf, R., Williams, M. A., Berkey, C. S., & Cotter, R. F. (1990). The length of uncomplicated human gestation. *Obstetrics and Gynecology, 75,* 73–78.

Miyamoto, R. H., Hishinuma, E. S., Nishimura, S. T., Nahulu, L. B., Andrade, N. N., & Goebert, D. A. (2000). Variation in self-esteem among adolescents in an Asian/Pacific-Islander sample. *Personality & Individual Differences, 29,* 13–25.

Mizuta, I., Zahn-Waxler, C., Colre, P. M., & Hiruma, N. (1996). A cross-cultural study of preschoolers' attachment: Security and sensitivity in Japanese and U.S. dads. *International Journal of Behavioral Development, 19,* 141–159.

Mogelonsky, M. (1996, May). The rocky road to adulthood. *American Demographics,* pp. 26–35, 56.

Moldin, S. O., & Gottesman, I. I. (1997). Genes, experience, and chance in schizophrenia—Positioning for the 21st century. *Schizophrenia Bulletin, 23,* 547–561.

Mondloch, C. J., Lewis, T. L., Budreau, D. R., Maurer, D., Dannemiller, J. L., Stephens, B. R., & Kleiner-Gathercoal, K. A. (1999). Face perception during early infancy. *Psychological Science, 10,* 419–422.

Mones, P. (1995, July 28). Life and death and Susan Smith. *The New York Times,* p. A27.

Money, J., & Ehrhardt, A. A. (1972). *Man and woman, boy and girl: The differentiation and dimorphism of gender identity from conception to maturity.* Baltimore: Johns Hopkins University Press.

Montemayor, R., Adams, G. R., & Gulotta, T. P. (Eds.). (1994). *Personal relationships during adolescence.* Newbury Park, CA: Sage.

Moon, C., Cooper, R. P., & Fifer, W. (1993). Two-day-olds prefer their native language. *Infant Behavior and Development, 16,* 495–500.

Moore, C. (1996). Theories of mind in infancy. *British Journal of Developmental Psychology, 14,* 19–40.

Moore, K. L. (1974). *Before we are born: Basic embryology and birth defects.* Philadelphia: Saunders.

Moore, C., Pure, K., & Furrow, D. (1990). Children's understanding of the modal expression of certainty and uncertainty and its relation to the development of a representational theory of mind. *Child Development, 61,* 722–730.

Moos, R. H., & Lemke, S. (1985). Specialized living environments for older people. In J. E. Birren & K. W. Schaie (Eds.), *Handbook of the psychology of aging.* New York: Van Nostrand Reinhold.

Morelli, G. A., Rogoff, B., Oppenheim, D., & Goldsmith, D. (1992). Cultural variation in infants' sleeping arrangements: Questions of independence. Special section: Cross-cultural studies of development. *Developmental Psychology, 28,* 604–613.

Morgan, L. (1991). *After marriage ends.* Newbury Park, CA: Sage.

Morgane, P., Austin-LaFrance, R., Bronzino, J., Tonkiss, J., Diaz-Cintra, S., Cintra, L., Kemper, T., & Galler, J. (1993). Prenatal malnutrition and development of the brain. *Neuroscience and Biobehavioral Reviews, 17,* 91–128.

Morice, A. (1998, February 27–28). Future moms, please note: Benefits vary. *The Wall Street Journal,* p. 15.

Morita, Y., & Tilly, J. L. (2000). Sphingolipid regulation of female gonadal cell apoptosis. *Annals of the New York Academy of Sciences, 905,* 209–220.

Morrison, F. J. (1993). Phonological processes in reading acquisition: Toward a unified conceptualization. Special Issue: Phonological processes and learning disability. *Developmental Review, 13,* 279–285.

Morrison, J. H., & Hof, P. R. (1997, October 17). Life and death of neurons in the aging brain. *Science, 278,* 412–417.

Morrison, M. F., & Tweedy, K. (2000). Effects of estrogen on mood and cognition in aging women. *Psychiatric Annals, 30,* 113–119.

Morrongiello, B. A. (1997). Children's perspectives on injury and close call experiences: Sex differences in injury-outcome process. *Journal of Pediatric Psychology, 22,* 499–512.

Morse, R. M., & Flavin, D. K. (1992). The definition of alcoholism. *Journal of the American Medical Association, 268,* 1012–1014.

Moses, L. J., & Chandler, M. J. (1992). Traveler's guide to children's theories of mind. *Psychological Inquiry, 3,* 286–301.

Moshman, D., Glover, J. A., & Bruning, R. H. (1987). *Developmental psychology.* Boston: Little, Brown.

Moss, M. (1997, March 31). Golden years? For one 73-year-old, punching time clock isn't a labor of love. *The Wall Street Journal,* pp. A1, A8.

Mowry, B. J., Nancarrow, D. J., & Levinson, D. F. (1997). The molecular genetics of schizophrenia: An update. *Australian & New Zealand Journal of Psychiatry, 31,* 704–713.

Moyer, M. S. (1992). Sibling relationships among older adults. *Generations, 16,* 55–58.

Mroczek, D. K., & Kolarz, C. M. (1998). The effect of age on positive and negative affect: A developmental perspective on happiness. *Journal of Personality and Social Psychology, 75,* 1333–1349.

Mueller, E., & Vandell, D. (1979). Infant–infant interactions. In J. Osofsky (Ed.), *Handbook of infant development.* New York: Wiley.

Munakata, Y., McClelland, J. L., Johnson, M. H., & Siegler, R. S. (1997). Rethinking infant knowledge: Toward an adaptive process account of the successes and failures in object permanence tasks. *Psychological Review, 104,* 686–713.

Murguia, A., Peterson, R. A., & Zea, M. C. (1997, August). *Cultural health beliefs.* Paper presented at the annual meeting of the American Psychological Association, Toronto, Canada.

Murray, B. (1996, July). Getting children off the couch and onto the field. *APA Monitor,* pp. 42–43.

Murray, J. A., Terry, D. J., Vance, J. C., Battistutta, D., & Connolly, Y. (2000). Effects of a program of intervention on parental distress following infant death. *Death Studies, 4,* 275–305.

Murray, L., & Cooper, P. J. (Eds.). (1997). *Postpartum depression and child development.* New York: Guilford Press.

Murstein, B. I. (1976). *Who will marry whom? Theories and research in marital choice.* New York: Springer.

Murstein, B. I. (1986). *Paths to marriage.* Beverly Hills, CA: Sage.

Murstein, B. I. (1987). A clarification and extension of the SVR theory of dyadic pairing. *Journal of Marriage and the Family, 49,* 929–933.

Musick, J. (1993). *Young, poor, and pregnant: The psychology of teenage motherhood.* New Haven: Yale University Press.

Mussen, P. H. (1969). Early sex-role development. In D. A. Goslin (Eds.), *Handbook of socialization theory and research* (pp. 707–732). Chicago: Rand McNally.

Mussen, P. H., & Jones, M. C. (1957). Self-conceptions, motivations, and interpersonal attitudes of late- and early-maturing boys. *Child Development, 28,* 243–256.

Mutran, E. J., Reitzes, D. C., & Fernandez, M. E. (1997). Factors influencing attitudes toward retirement. *Research on Aging, 19,* 251–273.

Mutrie, N. (1997). The therapeutic effects of exercise on the self. In K. R. Fox (Ed.), *The physical self: From motivation to well being* (pp. 287–314). Champaign, IL: Human Kinetics.

Myers, M. G., Martin, R. A., Rohsenow, D. J., & Monti, P. M. (1996). The relapse situation appraisal questionnaire: Initial psychometric characteristics and validation. *Psychology of Addictive Behaviors, 10,* 237–247.

Myers, N. A., Clifton, R. K., & Clarkson, M. G. (1987). When they were very young: Almost-threes remember two years ago. *Infant Behavior and Development, 10,* 123–132.

Myklebust, B. M., & Gottlieb, G. L. (1993). Development of the stretch reflex in the newborn: Reciprocal excitation and reflex irradation. *Child Development, 64,* 1036–1045.

Myslinski, N. R. (1990). The effects of aging on the sensory systems of the nose and mouth. *Topics in Geriatric Rehabilitation, 5,* 21–30.

Nadeau, L., Boivin, M., Tessier, R., Lefebvre, F. & Robaey, P. (2001). Mediators of behavioral problems in 7-year-old children born after 24 to 28 weeks of gestation. *Journal of Developmental & Behavioral Pediatrics, 22,* 1–10.

Nagy, M. (1948). The child's theories concerning death. *Journal of Genetic Psychology, 73,* 3–27.

Nakagawa, M., Lamb, M. E., & Miyaki, K. (1992). Antecedents and correlates of the Strange Situation behavior of Japanese infants. *Journal of Cross-Cultural Psychology, 23,* 300–310.

Nangle, D. W., & Erdley, C. A. (Eds). (2001). *The role of friendship in psychological adjustment.* San Francisco: Jossey-Bass.

Nathanielsz, P. W. (1996). The timing of birth. *American Scientist, 84,* 562–569.

National Center for Education Statistics. (2000). *Dropout rates in the United States: 1999.* Washington, DC: National Center for Education Statistics.

National Center for Health Statistics. (1994). *Division of vital statistics.* Washington, DC: Public Health Service.

National Center for Health Statistics. (1996). *Percentage of births to single mothers.* Washington, DC: National Center for Health Statistics.

National Center for Health Statistics. (2000). *Health United States, 2000 with adolescent health chartbook.* Hyattsville, MD.

National Highway Traffic Safety Administration. (1994). *Age related incidence of traffic accidents.* Washington, DC: National Highway Traffic Safety Administration.

National Institute of Child Health and Human Development (NICHD). (1999). Child care and mother-child interaction in the first 3 years of life. *Developmental Psychology, 35,* 1399–1413.

National Research Council. (1991). *Caring for America's children.* Washington, DC: National Academy Press.

National Research Council. (1997). *Racial and ethnic differences in the health of older Americans.* New York: Author.

National Safety Council. (1989). *Accident facts: 1989 edition.* Chicago: National Safety Council.

NCES (National Center of Educational Statistics). (2000). *Digest of educational statistics.* Washington, DC: U.S. Department of Education, Office of Educational Research and Improvement.

Needleman, H. L., & Bellinger, D. (Eds.). (1994). *Prenatal exposure to toxicants: Developmental consequences.* Baltimore: Johns Hopkins University Press.

Needleman, H. L., Riess, J. A., Tobin, M. J., Biesecker, G. E., & Greenhouse, J. B. (1996, February 7). Bone lead levels and delinquent behavior. *Journal of the American Medical Association, 2755,* 363–369.

Neher, A. (1991). Maslow's theory of motivation: A critique. *Journal of Humanistic Psychology, 31,* 89–112.

Nelson, C. A. (1987). The recognition of facial expressions in the first two years of life: Mechanisms of development. *Child Development, 58,* 889–909.

Nelson, C. A. (1995). The ontogeny of human memory: A cognitive neuroscience perspective. *Developmental Psychology, 31,* 723–738.

Nelson, D.G.K., Jusczyk, P.W., Mandel, D.R., Myers, J. et al. (1995). *Infant Behavior & Development, 18,* 111–116.

Nelson, K. (1981). Individual differences in language development: Implications for development and language. *Developmental Psychology, 17(2),* 170–187.

Nelson, K. (1986). *Event knowledge: Structure and function in development.* Hillsdale, NJ: Erlbaum.

Nelson, K. (1989). Remembering: A functional developmental perspective. In P. R. Solomon, G. R. Goethels, C. M. Kelley, & B. R. Stephens (Eds.), *Memory: An interdisciplinary approach.* New York: Springer-Verlag.

Nelson, K. (1992). Emergence of autobiographical memory at age 4. *Human Development, 35,* 172–177.

Nelson, K. (1996). *Language in cognitive development: Emergence of the mediated mind.* NY: Cambridge University Press.

Nelson, L. J., & Cooper, J. (1997). Gender differences in children's reactions to success and failure with computers. *Computers in Human Behavior, 13,* 247–267.

Nelson, T. O. (1994). Metacognition. In V. S. Ramachandran (Ed.), *Encyclopedia of human behavior* (Vol. 3). San Diego: Academic Press.

Ness, R. B., Grisso, J. A., Hirschinger, N., Markovic, N., Shaw, L. M., Day, N. L., & Kline, J. (1999). Cocaine and tobacco use and the risk of spontaneous abortion. *New England Journal of Medicine, 340,* 333–339.

Nettelbeck, T., & Rabbitt, P. M. (1992). Aging, cognitive performance, and mental speed. *Intelligence, 16,* 189–205.

Nettles, S. M., & Pleck, J. H. (1990). Risk, resilience, and development: The multiple ecologies of black adolescents. In R. J. Haggerty, N. Garmezy, M. Rutter, & L. Sherrod (Eds.), *Risk and resilience in children: Developmental approaches.* New York: Cambridge University Press.

Neugarten, B. (1967). The awareness of middle age. In R. Owen (Ed.), *Middle age.* London: BBC.

Neugarten, B. L. (1972). Personality and the aging process. *The Gerontologist, 12,* 9–15.

Neugarten, B. L. (1977). Personality and aging. In J. E. Birren & K. W.Schaie (Eds.), *Handbook for the Psychology of aging.* New York: Van Nostrand Reinhold.

Neugarten, B. L. (1979). Time, age, and the life cycle. *American Journal of Psychiatry, 136,* 887–893.

Neugarten, B. L., & Neugarten, D. A. (1987). The changing meanings of age. *Psychology Today, 21,* 29–33.

Newcomb, A. F., & Bagwell, C. L. (1995). Children's friendship relations: A meta-analytic review. *Psychological Bulletin, 117,* 306–347.

Newcombe, N., Drummey, A. B., & Lie, E. (1995). Children's memory for early experience. *Journal of Experimental Child Psychology, 59,* 337–342.

Newston, R. L., & Keith, P. M. (1997). Single women later in life. In J. M. Coyle (Ed.), *Handbook on women and aging* (pp. 385–399). Westport, CT: Greenwood Press.

Ney, P. G., Fung, T., & Wickett, A. R. (1993). Child neglect: The precursor to child abuse. *Pre- and Peri-Natal Psychology Journal, 8,* 95–112.

Nguyen, L., & Frye, D. (1999). Children's theory of mind: Understanding of desire, belief and emotion with social referents. *Social Development, 8,* 70–92.

NIAAA (National Institute on Alcohol Abuse and Alcoholism). (1990). *Alcohol and health.* Washington, DC: U.S. Government Printing Office.

NICHD Early Child Care Research Network. (1997). The effects of infant child care on infant–mother attachment security: Results of the NICHD study of early child care. *Child Development, 68,* 860–879.

Nickman, S. L. (1996, January). Challenges of adoption. *The Harvard Mental Health Letter,* pp. 5–7.

Nihart, M. A. (1993). Growth and development of the brain. *Journal of Child and Adolescent Psychiatric and Mental Health Nursing, 6,* 39–40.

Nilsson, L. G., Bäckman, L., Erngrund, K., Nyberg, L. et al. (1997). The Betula prospective cohort study: Memory, health, and aging. *Aging Neuropsychology & Cognition, 4,* 1–32.

Nisbett, R. (1994, October 31). Blue genes. *New Republic, 211,* 15.

Nobuyuki, I. (1997). Simple reaction times and timing of serial reactions of middle-aged and old men. *Perceptual & Motor Skills, 84,* 219–225.

Nockels, R., & Oakeshott, P. (1999). Awareness among young women of sexually transmitted chlamydia infection. *Family Practice, 16,* 94.

Nolen-Hoeksema, S., & Girgus, J. S. (1994). The emergence of gender differences in depression during adolescence. *Psychological Bulletin, 115,* 424–443.

Nolen-Hoeksema, S., & Larson, J. (1999). *Coping with loss.* Mahwah, NJ: Erlbaum.

Nolen-Hoeksema, S., McBraide, A., & Larson, J. (1997). Rumination and psychological distress among bereaved partners. *Journal of Personality and Social Psychology, 72,* 855–862.

Noller, P., Feeney, J. A., & Ward, C. M. (1997). Determinants of marital quality: A partial test of Lewis and Spanier's model. *Journal of Family Studies, 3,* 226–251.

Norman, R. M. G., Malla, A. K. (2001). Family history of schizophrenia and the relationship of stress to symptoms: Preliminary findings. *Australian & New Zealand Journal of Psychiatry, 35,* 217–223.

Nossiter, A. (1995, September 5). Asthma common and on rise in the crowded South Bronx. *The New York Times,* pp. A1, B2.

Nowak, C. A. (1977). Does youthfulness equal attractiveness? In L. E. Troll, J. Israel, & K. Israel (Eds.), *Looking ahead.* Englewood, Cliffs, NJ: Prentice-Hall.

Nowak, M. A., Komarova, N. L., & Niyogi, P. (2001, January 5). Evolution of universal grammar. *Science, 291,* 114–116.

Nowak, R. (1994a, July 22). Genetic testing set for takeoff. *Science, 265,* 464–467.

Nowak, R. (1994b, March 18). Nicotine scrutinized as FDA seeks to regulate cigarettes. *Science, 263,* 1555–1556.

Nugent, J. K., Lester, B. M., & Brazelton, T. B. (Eds.). (1989). *The cultural context of infancy, Vol. 1: Biology, culture, and infant development.* Norwood, NJ: Ablex.

NPD Group. (1998). The reality of children's diet. Port Washington, NY: NPD Group.

Nyiti, R. M. (1982). The validity of "culture differences explanations" for cross-cultural variation in the rate of Piagetian cognitive development. In D. Wagner & H. Stevenson (Eds.), *Cultural perspectives on child development.* New York: Freeman.

O'Bryant, S. L., & Morgan, L. A. (1989). Financial experience and well-being among mature widowed women. *Gerontologist, 29,* 245–251.

O'Connor, M. J., Sigman, M., & Brill, N. (1987). Disorganization of attachment in relation to maternal alcohol consumption. *Journal of Consulting and Clinical Psychology, 55(6),* 831–836.

O'Connor, P. (1994). Very close parent/child relationships: The perspective of the elderly person. *Journal of Cross-Cultural Gerontology, 9,* 53–76.

O'Leary, S. G. (1995). Parental discipline mistakes. *Current Directions in Psychological Science, 4,* 11–13.

O'Neill, C. (1994, May 17). Exercise just for the fun of it. *The Washington Post,* p. WH18.

O'Toole, M. E. (2000). *The school shooter: A threat assessment perspective.* Washington, DC: Federal Bureau of Investigation.

OECD. (1998). Education at a glance: OECD indicators, 1998. Paris: Organization for Economic Cooperation and Development.

Ogbu, J. (1992). Understanding cultural diversity and learning. *Educational Researcher, 21,* 5–14.

Ogbu, J. U. (1988). Black education: A cultural eco logical perspective. In H. P. McAdoo (Ed.), *Black families.* Beverly Hills, CA: Sage.

O'Hare, W. (1997, September). *American Demographics,* pp. 50–56.

Oliver, M. B., & Hyde, J. S. (1993). Gender differences in sexuality: A meta-analysis. *Psychological Bulletin, 114,* 29–51.

Ollendick, T. H., Yang, B., King, N. J., Dong, Q., & Akande, A. (1996). Fears in American, Australian, Chinese, and Nigerian children and adolescents: A cross-cultural study. *Journal of Child Psychology and Psychiatry and Allied Disciplines, 37,* 213–220.

Oller, D. K., Eilers, R. E., Urbano, R., & Cobo-Lewis A. B. (1997). Development of precursors to speech in infants exposed to two languages. *Journal of Child Language, 24,* 407–425.

Olsho, L. W., Harkins, S. W., & Lenhardt, M. L. (1985). Aging and the auditory system. In J. E. Birren & K. W. Schaie (Eds.), *Handbook of the psychology of aging* (2nd ed.). New York: Van Nostrand Reinhold.

Olweus, D. (1995). Bullying or peer abuse at school: Facts and intervention. *Current Directions in Psychological Science, 4,* 196–200.

Ono, Y. (1995, October 15). Ads do push kids to smoke, study suggests. *The Wall Street Journal,* pp. B1–B2.

Onslow, M. (1992). Choosing a treatment program for early stuttering: Issues and future directions. *Journal of Speech and Hearing Research, 35,* 983–993.

Orbuch, T. L., House, J. S., Mero, R. P., & Webster, P. S . (1996). Marital quality over the life course. *Social Psychology Quarterly, 59,* 162–171.

Orr, A. L. (1991). The psychosocial aspects of aging and vision loss. *Journal of Gerontological Social Work, 17,* 1–14.

Osofsky, J. D. (1995a). Children who witness domestic violence: The invisible victims. *Social Policy Report, 9,* 1–16.

Osofsky, J. D. (1995b). The effects of exposure to violence on young children. *American Psychologist, 50,* 782–788.

Pachter, L. M., & Weller, S. C. (1993). Acculturation and compliance with medical therapy. *Journal of Development and Behavior Pediatrics, 14,* 163–168.

Paffenbarger, R. S., Kampert, J. B., Lee, I. M., Hyde, R. T., et al. (1994). Changes in physical activity and other lifeway patterns influencing longevity. *Medicine and Science in Sports and Exercise, 26,* 857–865.

Paikoff, R. L., & Brooks-Gunn, J. (1990). Physiological processes: What role do they play during the transition to adolescence? In R. Montemayor, G. R. Adams, & T. P. Gulotta (Eds.), *From childhood to adolescence: A transitional period?* Newbury Park, CA: Sage.

Painter, K. (1997, August 15–17). Doctors have prenatal tests for 450 genetic diseases. *USA Today,* p. 1–2.

Palincsar, A. S., & Klenk, L. (1992). Fostering literacy learning in supportive contexts. *Journal of Learning Disabilities, 25,* 211–225, 229.

Palmore, E. (1975). *The honorable elders: A cross-cultural analysis of aging in Japan.* Durham, NC: Duke University Press.

Palmore, E. (1979). Predictors of successful aging. *Gerontologist, 19,* 427–431.

Palmore, E. B. (1988). *The facts on aging quiz.* New York: Springer.

Palmore, E. B. (1992). Knowledge about aging: What we know and need to know. *Gerontologist, 32,* 149–150.

Paneth, N. S. (1995). The problem of low birth weight. *The Future of Children, 5,* 19–34.

Panneton, R. K. (1985). *Prenatal auditory experience with melodies: Effects on postnatal auditory preferences in human newborns.* Unpublished doctoral dissertation, University of North Carolina, Greensboro.

Papousek, H., & Bernstein, P. (1969). The functions of conditioning stimulation in human neonates and infants. In A. Ambrose (Ed.), *Stimulation in early infancy.* New York: Academic Press.

Papousek, H., & Papousek, M. (1991). Innate and cultural guidance of infants' integrative competencies: China, the United States, and Germany. In M. H. Borstein (Ed.), *Cultural approaches to parenting.* Hillsdale, NJ: Erlbaum.

Pappano, L. (1994, November 27). The new old generation. *The Boston Globe Magazine,* pp. 18–38.

Papps, F., Walker, M., Trimboli, A., & Trimboli, C. (1995). Parental discipline in Anglo, Greek, Lebanese, and Vietnamese cultures. *Journal of Cross-Cultural Psychology, 26,* 49–64.

Paris, J. (1999). *Nature and nurture in psychiatry: A predisposition--stress model of mental disorders.* Washington, DC: American Psychiatric Press.

Park, K. A., Lay, K., & Ramsay, L. (1993). Individual differences and developmental changes in preschoolers' friendships. *Developmental Psychology, 29,* 264–270.

Parke, R. D. (1989). Social development in infancy: A twenty-five year perspective. In D. Palermo (Ed.), *Advances in child development and behaviors.* New York: Academic Press.

Parke, R. D. (1990). In search of fathers: A narrative of an empirical journey. In I. Sigel & G. Brody (Eds.), *Methods of family research* (Vol. 1). Hillsdale, NJ: Erlbaum.

Parke, R. D. (1996). *New fatherhood.* Cambridge, MA: Harvard University Press.

Parke, R., Ornstein, P. A., Rieser, J. J., & Zahn-Waxler, C. (1994). The past as prologue: An overview of a century of developmental psychology. In R. D. Parke, P. A. Ornstein, J. J. Rieser, & C. Zahn-Waxler (Eds.), *A century of developmental psychology.* Washington, DC: American Psychological Association.

Parkes, C. M. (1997). Normal and abnormal responses to stress—A developmental approach. In D. Black, M. Newman, J. Harris-Hendricks, & G. Mezey (Eds.), *Psychological trauma: A developmental approach* (pp. 10–18). London, England: Gaskell/Royal College of Psychiatrists.

Parks, C. A. (1998). Lesbian parenthood: A review of the literature. *American Journal of Orthopsychiatry, 68,* 376–389.

Parlee, M. B. (1979, October). The friendship bond. *Psychology Today, 13,* 43–45.

Parmalee, A. H., Jr., & Sigman, M. D. (1983). Prenatal brain development and behavior. In P. H. Mussen (Ed.), *Handbook of child psychology* (Vol. 2, 4th ed.). New York: Wiley.

Parmalee, A. H., Wenner, W., & Schulz, H. (1964). Infant sleep patterns from birth to 16 weeks of age. *Journal of Pediatrics, 65,* 572–576.

Parnell, T. F., & Day, D. O. (Eds.). (1998). *Munchausen by proxy syndrome: Misunderstood child abuse.* Thousand Oaks, CA: Sage.

Parritz, R. H., Mangelsdorf, S., & Gunnar, M. R. (1992). Control, social referencing, and the infants' appraisal of threat. In S. Feinman (Ed.), *Social referencing and the social construction of reality in infancy.* New York: Plenum.

Parten, M. B. (1932). Social participation among preschool children. *Journal of Abnormal and Social Psychology, 27,* 243–269.

Pascoe, J. M. (1993). Social support during labor and duration of labor: A community-based study. *Public Health Nursing, 10,* 97–99.

Patterson, C. J. (1992). Children of lesbian and gay parents. *Child Development, 63,* 1025–1042.

Patterson, C. J. (1994). Lesbians and gay families. *Current Directions in Psychological Science, 3,* 62–64.

Patterson, C. J. (1995). Families of the baby boom: Parents' division of labor and children's adjustment. *Special Issue: Sexual orientation and human development. Developmental Psychology, 31,* 115–123.

Patterson, C. J., & Redding, R. E. (1996). Lesbian and gay families with children: Implications of social science research for policy. *Journal of Social Issues, 52,* 29–50.

Patterson, K., Dancer, J., & Clark, D. (1990). Myth perceptions of hearing loss, hearing aids, and aging. *Educational Gerontology, 16,* 289–296.

Pattison, E. M. (1977). *The experience of dying.* In E. M. Pattison (Ed.), *The experience of dying.* Englewood Cliffs, NJ: Prentice-Hall.

Pauker, S., & Arond, M. (1989). *The first year of marriage: What to expect, what to accept and what you can change.* New York: Warner Books.

Pavis, S., Cunningham-Burley, S., & Amos, A. (1997). Alcohol consumption and young people: Exploring meaning and social context. *Health Education Research, 12,* 311–322.

Pavlov, I. P. (1927). *Conditioned reflexes.* London: Oxford University Press.

Paxton, S. J., Schutz, H. K., Wertheim, E. H., & Muir, S. L. (1999). Friendship clique and peer influences on body image concerns, dietary restraint, extreme weight-loss behaviors, and binge eating in adolescent girls. *Journal of Abnormal Psychology, 108,* 255–266.

Payne, J. S., Kauffman, J. M., Brown, G. B., & DeMott, R. M. (1974). *Exceptional children in focus.* Columbus, OH: Merrill.

Pear, R. (2000, March 19). Proposal to curb the use of drugs to calm the young. *The New York Times,* p. 1.

Peck, R. C. (1968). Psychological developments in the second half of life. In B. L. Neugarten (Ed.), *Middle age and aging.* Chicago: University of Chicago Press.

Pedlow, R., Sanson, A., Prior, M., & Oberklaid, F. (1993). Stability of maternally reported temperament from infancy to 8 years. *Developmental Psychology, 29,* 998–1007.

Pelligrini, A. D., & Smith, P. K. (1998). Physical activity play: The nature and function of a neglected aspect of play. *Child Development, 69,* 577–598.

Peltonen, L., & McKusick, V. A. (2001, February 16). Dissecting the human disease in the postgenomic era. *Science, 291,* 1224–1229.

Pence, E., & Shepard, M. (1988). Integrating feminist theory and practice: The challenge of the battered women's movement. In K. Yllo & M. Bograd (Eds.), *Feminist perspectives on wife abuse.* Berkeley, CA: Sage.

Penninx, B., Guralnik, J. M., Ferrucci, L., Simonsick, E. M., Deeg, D., & Wallace, R. B. (1998). Depressive symptoms and physical decline in community-dwelling older persons. *Journal of the American Medical Association, 279,* 1720–1726.

Pennisi, E. (2000, May 19). And the gene number is...? *Science, 288,* 1146–1147.

Pennisi, E., & Vogel, G. (2000, June 9). Clones: A hard act to follow. *Science, 288,* 1722–1727.

People Weekly. (2000, May 8). Giant steps. p. 117.

Peplau, L. A., & Cochran, S. D. (1990). A relationship perspective on homosexuality. In D. P. McWhirter, S. A. Sanders, & J. M. Reinisch (Eds.), *Homosexuality/heterosexuality: The Kinsey scale and current research.* New York: Oxford University Press.

Peplau, L. A., Padesky, C., & Hamilton, M. (1982). Satisfaction in lesbian relationships. *Journal of Homosexuality, 8,* 23–25.

Pereira-Smith, O., Smith, J., et al. (1988, August). Paper presented at the annual meeting of the International Genetics Congress, Toronto.

Perez, C. M., & Widom, C. S. (1994). Childhood victimization and long-term intellectual and academic outcomes. *Child Abuse & Neglect, 18,* 617–633.

Perlmann, R. Y., & Gleason, J. B. (1990, July). *Patterns of prohibition in mothers' speech to children.* Paper presented at the Fifth International Congress for the Study of Child Language, Budapest, Hungary.

Perlmutter, M., & Hall, E. (1992). *Adult development and aging* (2nd ed.). New York: Wiley.

Perlmutter, M., Kaplan, M., & Nyquist, L. (1990). Development of adaptive competence in adulthood. *Human Development, 33,* 185–197.

Perozzi, J. A., & Sanchez, M. C. (1992). The effect of instruction in L1 on receptive acquisition of L2 for bilingual children with language delay. *Language, Speech, and Hearing Services in Schools, 23,* 348–352.

Perry, W. G. (1970). *Forms of intellectual and ethical development in the college years.* New York: Holt.

Petersen, A. (2000). A longitudinal investigation of adolescents' changing perceptions of pubertal timing. *Developmental Psychology 36,* 37–43.

Petersen, A. C., & Crockett, L. (1985). Pubertal timing and grade effects on adjustment. *Journal of Youth and Adolescence, 14,* 191–206.

Petersen, A. C., Sarigiani, P. A., & Kennedy, R. E. (1991). Adolescent depression: Why more girls? *Journal of Youth and Adolescence, 20,* 247–271.

Peterson, A. C. (1988, September). Those gangly years. *Psychology Today,* pp. 28–34.

Peterson, L. (1994). Child injury and abuse-neglect: Common etiologies, challenges, and courses toward prevention. *Current Directions in Psychological Science, 3,* 116–120.

Petitto, L. A., & Marentette, P. F. (1991, March 22). Babbling in the manual mode: Evidence for the ontogeny of language. *Science, 251,* 1493–1496.

Petraitis, J., Flay, B. R., & Miller, T. Q. (1995). Reviewing theories of adolescent substance use: Organizing pieces in the puzzle. *Psychological Bulletin, 117,* 67–86.

Pettingale, K. W., Morris, T., Greer, S., & Haybittle, J. L. (1985). Mental attitudes to cancer: An additional prognostic factor. *Lancet, 310,* 750.

Pettit, G. S., Bates, J. E., & Dodge, K. A. (1997). Supportive parenting, ecological context, and children's adjustment: A seven-year longitudinal study. *Child Development, 68,* 908–923.

Pettle, S. A., & Britten, C. M. (1995). Talking with children about death and dying. *Child: Care, Health & Development, 21,* 395–404.

Pfeiffer, S. I. (2001). Emotional intelligence: Popular but elusive construct. *Roeper Review, 23,* 138–142.

Pfeiffer, S. I., & Stocking, V. B. (2000). Vulnerabilities of academically gifted students. *Special Services in the Schools, 16,* 83–93.

Phelan, P., Yu, H. C., & Davidson, A. L. (1994). Navigating the psychosocial pressures of adolescence: The voices and experiences of high school youth. *American Educational Research Journal, 31,* 415–447.

Phillips, D. (1992, September). Death postponement and birthday celebrations. *Psychosomatic Medicine, 26,* 12–18.

Phillips, D. A., & Zimmerman, M. (1990). The developmental course of perceived competence and incompetence among competent children. In R. Sternberg & J. Kolligian (Eds.), *Competence considered.* New Haven, CT: Yale University Press.

Phillips, D. A., Voran, M., Kisker, E., Howes, C., & Whitebook, M. (1994). Child care for children in poverty: Opportunity or inequity? *Child Development, 65,* 472–492.

Phillips, D., & Smith, D. (1990, April 11). Postponement of death until symbolically meaningful occasions. *Journal of the American Medical Association, 269,* 27–38.

Phillips, R. D., Wagner, S. H., Fells, C. A., & Lynch, M. (1990). Do infants recognize emotion in facial expressions?: Categorical and "metaphorical" evidence. *Infant Behavior and Development, 13,* 71–84.

Phillips, S., King, S., & DuBois, L. (1978). Spontaneous activities of female versus male newborns. *Child Development, 49,* 590–597.

Phinney, J. S., & Alipuria, L. L. (1990). Ethnic identity in college students from four ethnic groups. *Journal of Adolescence, 13,* 171–183.

Phinney, J. S., Ferguson, D. L., & Tate, J. D. (1997). Intergroup attitudes among ethnic minority adolescents: A causal model. *Child Development, 68,* 955–969.

Phinney, J., Lochner, B., & Murphy, R. (1990). Ethnic identity development and psychological adjustment in adolescence. In A. Stiffman & L. Davis (Eds.), *Advances in adolescent mental health. Vol. 5. Ethnic issues.* Greenwich, CT: JAI Press.

Piaget, J. (1932). *The moral judgment of the child.* New York: Harcourt, Brace & World.

Piaget, J. (1952). *The origins of intelligence in children.* New York: International Universities Press.

Piaget, J. (1954). *The construction of reality in the child* (Margaret Cook, Trans.). New York: Basic Books.

Piaget, J. (1962). *Play, dreams and imitation in childhood.* New York: Norton.

Piaget, J. (1983). Piaget's theory. In W. Kessen (Ed.), P. H. Mussen (Series Ed.), *Handbook of child psychology: Vol 1. History, theory, and methods* (pp. 103–128). New York: Wiley.

Piaget, J., & Inhelder, B. (1958). *The growth of logical thinking from childhood to adolescence* (A. Parsons & S. Seagrin, Trans.). New York: Basic Books.

Piaget, J., Inhelder, B., & Szeminska, A. (1960). *The child's conception of geometry.* New York: Basic Books. (Original work published 1948)

Picard, E. M., Del Dotto, J. E., & Breslau, N. (2000). Prematurity and low birthweight. In K. O. Yeates & M. D. Ris, (Eds.), et al. *Pediatric neuropsychology: Research, theory, and practice. The science and practice of neuropsychology: A Guilford series.* New York: Guilford Press.

Pillay, A. L., & Wassenaar, D. R. (1997). Recent stressors and family satisfaction in suicidal adolescents in South Africa. *Journal of Adolescence, 20,* 155–162.

Pinker, S. (1994). *The language instinct.* New York: William Morrow.

Pipp, S., Easterbrooks, M., & Brown, S. R. (1993). Attachment status and complexity of infants' self- and other-knowledge when tested with mother and father. *Social Development, 2,* 1–14.

Pipp-Siegel, S., & Foltz, C. (1997). Toddlers' acquisition of self/other knowledge: Ecological and interpersonal aspects of self and other. *Child Development, 68,* 69–79.

Pitts, D. G. (1982). The effects of aging upon selected visual functions. In R. Sekuler, D. Kline, & K. Dismukes (Eds.), *Aging and human visual function.* New York: Alan R. Liss.

Plomin, R. (1994a). *Genetics and experience: The interplay between nature and nurture.* Newbury Park, CA: Sage.

Plomin, R. (1994b). Nature, nurture, and social development. *Social Development, 3,* 37–53.

Plomin, R. (1994c). The genetic basis of complex human behaviors. *Science, 264,* 1733–1739.

Plomin, R., & McClearn, G. E. (Eds.). (1993). *Nature, nurture, and psychology.* Washington, DC: American Psychological Association.

Plomin, R., & Rutter, M. (1998). Child development, molecular genetics, and what to do with genes once they are found. *Child Development, 69,* 1223–1242.

Poest, C. A., Williams, J. R., Witt, D. D., & Atwood, M. E. (1990). Challenge me to move: Large muscle development in young children. *Young Children, 45,* 4–10.

Polansky, E. (1976). Take him home, Mrs. Smith. *Healthright, 2(2).*

Polivy, J., & Herman, C. P. (1991). Good and bad dieters: Self-perception and reaction to a dietary challenge. *International Journal of Eating Disorders, 10,* 91–99.

Pollitt, E. (1994). Poverty and child development: Relevance of research in developing countries to the United States. *Child Development, 65,* 283–295.

Pollitt, E., Golub, M., Gorman, K., Grantham-McGregor, S., Levitsky, D., Schürch, B., Strupp, B., & Wachs, T. (1996). A reconceptualization of the effects of undernutrition on children's biological, psychosocial, and behavioral development. *Social Policy Report, 10,* 1–22.

Pollitt, E., Gorman, K. S., Engle, P. L., Martorell, R., & Rivera, J. (1993). Early supplementary feeding and cognition: Effects over two decades. *Monographs of the Society for Research in Child Development, 58,* v–99.

Pomerleau, O. F., & Pomerleau, C. S. (1989). A biobehavioral perspective on smoking. In T. Ney & A. Gale (Eds.), *Smoking and human behavior.* New York: Wiley.

Ponton, L. E. (1999, May 10). Their dark romance with risk. *Newsweek,* 55–58.

Ponza, M., & Wray, L. (1990). *Evaluation of the food assistance needs of the low-income elderly and their participation in USDA programs: Final results of the elderly programs study.* Princeton, NJ: Mathematical Policy Research.

Poole, D., & Lamb, M. (1998). *Investigative interviews of children: A guide for helping professionals.* Washington, DC: American Psychological Association.

Poon, L. W. (1985). Differences in human memory with aging: Nature, causes, and clinical implications. In J. E. Birren & K. W. Schaie (Eds.), *Handbook of the psychology of aging* (2nd ed.). New York: Van Nostrand Reinhold.

Pope, A. W. & Bierman, K. L. (1999). Predicting adolescent peer problems and antisocial activities: The relative roles of aggression and dysregulation. *Developmental Psychology, 35,* 335–346.

Popenoe, D. (1987). Beyond the nuclear family: A statistical portrait of the changing family in Sweden. *Journal of Marriage and the Family, 49,* 173–183.

Population Council Report. (1995, May 30). The decay of families is global, studies says. *The New York Times,* p. A5.

Porges, S. W., & Lipsitt, Lewis P. (1993). Neonatal responsivity to gustatory stimulation: The gustatory-vagal hypothesis. *Infant Behavior & Development, 16,* 487–494.

Porter, E. J. (1997). Parental actions to reduce children's exposure to lead: Some implications for primary and secondary prevention. *Family & Community Health, 20,* 24–37.

Porter, F. L., Porges, S. W., & Marshall, R. E. (1988). Newborn pain cries and vagal tone: Parallel changes in response to circumcision. *Child Development, 59,* 495–515.

Porter, R. H., Bologh, R. D., & Malkin, J. W. (1988). Olfactory influences on mother–infant interactions. In C. Rovee-Collier & L. Lipsitt (Eds.), *Advances in infancy research.* (Vol. 5). Norwood, NJ: Ablex.

Porzelius, L. K., Dinsmore, B. D., & Staffelbach, D. (2001). Eating disorders. In M. Hersen & V. B. Van Hasselt, (Eds). *Advanced abnormal psychology* (2nd ed.). New York: Kluwer Academic/Plenum Publishers.

Poulin-Dubois, D., Serbin, L. A., Kenyon, B., & Derbyshire, A. (1994). Infants' intermodal knowledge about gender. *Developmental Psychology, 30,* 436–442.

Power, T. G. (2000). *Play and exploration in children and animals.* Mahwah, NJ: Erlbaum.

Power, T. G., & Parke, R. D. (1982). Play as a context for early learning: Lab and home analyses. In L. M. Laosa & I. E. Sigal (Eds.), *The family as a learning environment.* New York: Plenum.

Pratt, M. W., Danso, H. A., Arnold, M. L., Norris, J. E., & Filyer, R. (2001). Adult generativity and the socialization of adolescents: Relations to mothers' and fathers' parenting beliefs, styles, and practices. *Journal of Personality, 69,* 89–120.

Pratt, W. F., Mosher, W. D., Bachrach, C., & Horn, M. (1984). *Understanding U.S. fertility: Findings from the National Survey of Family Growth.* Washington, DC: Population Reference Bureau.

Pratto, F., Stallworth, L. M., Sidanius, J., & Siers, B. (1997). The gender gap in occupational role attainment: A social dominance approach. *Journal of Personality and Social Psychology, 72,* 37–53.

Prechtl, H. F. R. (1982). Regressions and transformations during neurological development. In T. G. Bever (Ed.), *Regressions in mental development.* Hillsdale, NJ: Erlbaum.

Prentice, A. (1991). Can maternal dietary supplements help in preventing infant malnutrition? *Acta Paediatrica Scandinaica* (Supp. 374), 67–77.

Prescott, C., & Gottesman, I. (1993). Genetically mediated vulnerability to schizophrenia. *Psychiatric Clinics of North America, 16,* 245–267.

Press, I., & McKool, M., Jr. (1972). Social structure and status of the aged: Toward some valid cross-cultural generalizations. *Aging and Human Development, 3,* 297–306.

Pressley, M. (1987). Are keyword method effects limited to slow presentation rates? An empirically based reply to Hall and Fuson (1986). *Journal of Educational Psychology, 79,* 333–335.

Pressley, M. (1994). State-of-the-science primary-grades reading instruction or whole language? *Educational Psychologist, 29,* 211–215.

Pressley, M., & Levin, J. R. (1983). *Cognitive strategy research: Psychological foundations.* New York: Springer-Verlag.

Pressley, M. & Schneider, W. (1997). *Introduction to memory development during childhood and adolescence.* Mahwah, NJ: Lawrence Erlbaum.

Pressley, M., & VanMeter, P. (1993). Memory strategies: Natural development and use following instruction. In R. Pasnak & M. L. Howe (Eds.), *Emerging themes in cognitive development* (Vol. II). New York: Springer-Verlag.

Price, D. W., & Goodman, G. S. (1990). Visiting the wizard: Children's memory for a recurring event. *Child Development, 61,* 664–680.

Price, R., & Gottesman, I. (1991). Body fat in identical twins reared apart: Roles for genes and environment. *Behavior Genetics, 21,* 1–7.

Prigerson, H. G., Frank, E., Kasl, S. V., et al. (1995). Complicated grief and bereavement-related depression as distinct disorders: Preliminary empirical validation in elderly bereaved spouses. *American Journal of Psychiatry, 152,* 22–30.

PRIMEDIA/Roper (1998). *Adolescents' view of society's ills.* Storrs, CT: Roper Center for Public Opinion Research.

Prince, M. (2000, November 13). How technology has changed the way we have babies. *The Wall Street Journal,* pp. R4, R13.

Prince, R. L., Smith, M., Dick, I. M., Price, R. I., Webb, P. G., Henderson, N. K., & Harris, M. M. (1991). Prevention of postmenopausal osteoporosis. A comparative study of exercise, calcium supplementation, and hormone replacement therapy. *New England Journal of Medicine, 325,* 1189–1195.

Pugh, K. R., Mencl, W. E., Jenner, A. R., Katz, L., Frost, S. J., Lee, J. R., Shaywitz, S. E., & Shaywitz, B. A. (2000). Functional neuroimaging studies of reading and reading disability (developmental dyslexia). *Mental Retardation & Developmental Disabilities Research Reviews, 6,* 207–213.

Purdy, M. (1995, November 6). A kind of sexual revolution. *The New York Times,* pp. B1, B6.

Pyszczynski, T., Greenberg, J., & LaPrelle, J. (1985). Social comparison after success and failure: Biased search for information consistent with a self-servicing conclusion. *Journal of Experimental Social Psychology, 21,* 195–211.

Quade, R. (1994, July 10). Day care brightens young and old. *The New York Times,* p. B8.

Quinn, J. B. (1993, April 5). What's for dinner, Mom? *Newsweek,* 68.

Quinn, M. (1990, January 29). Don't aim that pack at us. *Time,* 60.

Quinn, P. C., & Eimas, P. D. (1996). *Perceptual organization and categorization in young infants.* Norwood, NJ: Ablex.

Quinnan, E. J. (1997). Connection and autonomy in the lives of elderly male celibates: Degrees of disengagement. *Journal of Aging Studies, 11,* 115–130.

Quintana, C. (1998, May 17.) Riding the rails. *The New York Times Magazine,* p. 66.

Rabain-Jamin, J., & Sabeau-Jouannet, E. (1997). Maternal speech to 4-month-old infants in two cultures: Wolof and French. *International Journal of Behavioral Development, 20,* 425–451.

Rabkin, J., Remien, R., & Wilson, C. (1994). *Good doctors, good patients: Partners in HIV treatment.* New York: NCM Publishers.

Radetsky, P. (1994, December 2). Stopping premature births before it's too late. *Science, 266,* 1486–1488.

Radke-Yarrow, M., Zahn-Waxler, C., & Chapman, M. (1983). Children's prosocial dispositions and behavior. In E. M. Hetherington (Ed.), *Handbook of child psychology: Vol. 4. Socialization, personality, and social development* (pp. 469–545). New York: Wiley.

Radziszewska, B. & Rogoff, B. (1988). Influence of adult and peer collaborators on children's planning skills. *Developmental Psychology, 24,* 840–848.

Raikkonen, K., Keskivaara, P., Keltikangas, J. L., & Butzow, E. (1995). Psychophysiological arousal related to Type A components in adolescent boys. *Scandinavian Journal of Psychology, 36,* 142–152.

Ramey, C. T., & Ramey, S. L. (1998). Early intervention and early experience. *American Psychologist, 53,* 109–120.

Ramsay, D. S. (1980). Onset of unimanual handedness in infants. *Infant Behavior and Development, 3,* 377–385.

Ramsey, P. G. (1995). Changing social dynamics in early childhood classrooms. *Child Development, 66,* 764–773.

Ranade, V. (1993). Nutritional recommendations for children and adolescents. *International Journal of Clinical Pharmacology, Therapy, and Toxicology, 31,* 285–290.

Randahl, G. J. (1991). A typological analysis of the relations between measured vocational interests and abilities. *Journal of Vocational Behavior, 38,* 333–350.

Rando, T. A. (1993). *Treatment of complicated mourning.* Champaign, IL: Research Press.

Rank, M. R., & Hirschl, T. A. (1999). Estimating the proportion of Americans ever experiencing poverty during their elderly years. *Journals of Gerontology Series B-Psychological Science and Social Sciences, 54,* S184-S193.

Ransom, R. L., Sutch, R., & Williamson, S. H. (1991). *Retirement: Past and present. In A. H. Munnell (Ed.), Retirement and public policy: Proceedings of the Second Conference of the National Academy of Social Insurance.* Washington, DC. Dubuque, IA: Kendall/Hunt.

Rao, V. (1997). Wife-beating in rural South India: A qualitative and econometric analysis. *Social Science & Medicine, 44*, 1169–1180.

Rapkin, B. D., & Fischer, K. (1992). Personal goals of older adults: Issues in assessment and prediction. *Psychology and Aging, 7*, 127–137.

Rauch-Elnekave, H. (1994). Teenage motherhood: Its relationship to undetected learning problems. *Adolescence, 29*, 91–103.

Raup, J., & Myers, J. (1989). The empty nest syndrome: Myth or reality? *Journal of Counseling and Development, 68*, 180–183.

Ravitch, D. (1985). *The troubled crusade: American education 1945–1980*. New York: Basic Books.

Raymond, J. (2000). The world of the senses. *Newsweek Special Issue: Your Child*, pp. 16–18.

Raynor, K., & Pollatsek, A. (Eds.). (1989). *The psychology of reading*. Englewood Cliffs, NJ: Prentice-Hall.

Reddy, L. A., & Pfeiffer, S. I. (1997). Effectiveness of treatment of foster care with children and adolescents: A review of outcome studies. *Journal of the American Academy of Child & Adolescent Psychiatry, 36*, 381–588.

Redshaw, M. E. (1997). Mothers of babies requiring special care: Attitudes and experiences. *Journal of Reproductive & Infant Psychology, 15*, 109–120.

Reese, E., & Cox, A. (1999). Quality of adult book reading affects children's emergent literacy. *Developmental Psychology, 35*, 20–28.

Reifman, A. (2000). *Revisiting The Bell Curve*. Psycoloquy, 11.

Reinis, S., & Goldman, J. M. (1980). *The development of the brain: Biological and functional perspectives*. Springfield, IL: Charles C Thomas.

Reis, H. T., Collins, W. A., & Berscheid, E. (2000). The relationship context of human behavior and development. *Psychological Bulletin, 126*, 844–872.

Reiss, I. L. (1960). *Premarital sexual standards in America*. New York: Free Press.

Reiss, M. J. (1984). Human sociobiology. *Zygon Journal of Religion and Science, 19*, 117–140.

Reissland, N. (1988). Neonatal imitation in the first hour of life: Observations in rural Nepal. *Developmental Psychology, 24*, 450–469.

Reitman, V. (1994, February 15). Tots do swimmingly in language-immersion programs. *The Wall Street Journal*, p. B1.

Remondet, J. H., & Hansson, R. O. (1991). Job-related threats to control among older employees. *Journal of Social Issues, 47*, 129–141.

Reschly, D. J. (1996). Identification and assessment of students with disabilities. The future of children, 6, 40–53.

Resnick, B. (2000). A seven step approach to starting an exercise program for older adults. *Patient Education & Counseling, 39*, 243–252.

Resnick, M. D., Bearman, P. S., Blum, R. W., Bauman, K. E., Harris, M. R., Jones, L., Tabor, J., Beuhring, T., Sieving, R., Shew, M., Ireland, M., Bearinger, L. H., & Udry, J. R. (1997). Protecting adolescents from harm: Findings from the National Longitudinal Study on Adolescent Health. *Journal of the American Medical Association, 278*, 823–832.

Reyna, V. F. (1997). Conceptions of memory development with implications for reasoning and decision making. In R. Vasta (Ed.), *Annals of child development: A research annual* (Vol. 12, pp. 87–118). London, England: Jessica Kingsley Publishers.

Ricciardelli, L. A. (1992). Bilingualism and cognitive development in relation to threshold theory. *Journal of Psycholinguistic Research, 21*, 301–316.

Ricciuti, H. N. (1993). Nutrition and mental development. *Current Directions in Psychological Science, 2*, 43–46.

Rice, F. P. (1999). *Intimate relationships, marriages, & families* (4th ed.). Mountain View, CA: Mayfield.

Rice, M. L., Huston, A. C., Truglio, R., & Wright, J. (1990). Words from "Sesame Street": Learning vocabulary while viewing. *Developmental Psychology, 26(3)*, 421–428.

Richards, H. D., Bear, G. G., Stewart, A. L., & Norman, A. D. (1992). Moral reasoning and classroom conduct: Evidence of a curvilinear relationship. *Merrill-Palmer Quarterly, 38*, 176–190.

Richards, M. H., & Duckett, E. (1991). Maternal employment and adolescents. In J. V. Lerner & N. Galambos (Eds.), *Employed mothers and their children*. New York: Garland.

Richards, M. H., & Duckett, E. (1994). The relationship of maternal employment to early adolescent daily experience with and without parents. *Child Development, 65*, 225–236.

Richards, M. P. M. (1996). The childhood environment and the development of sexuality. In C. J. K. Henry & S. J. Ulijaszek (Eds.), *Long-term consequences of early environment: Growth, development and the lifespan developmental perspective*. Cambridge, England: Cambridge University Press.

Richards, R., Kinney, D. K., Benet, M., & Merzel, A. P. C. (1990). Assessing everyday creativity: Characteristics of the lifetime creativity scales and validation with three large samples. *Journal of Personality and Social Psychology, 54*, 476–485.

Richardson, G. A., & Day, N. L. (1994). Detrimental effects of prenatal cocaine exposure: Illusion or reality? *Journal of the American Academy of Child & Adolescent Psychiatry, 33*, 28–34.

Richardson, V., & Champion, V. (1992). The relationship of attitudes, knowledge, and social support to breast-feeding. *Issues in Comprehensive Pediatric Nursing, 15*, 183–197.

Rimer, B. K., Meissner, H., Breen, N., Legler, J. & Coyne, C. A. (2001). Social and behavioral interventions to increase breast cancer screening. In N. Schneiderman & M. A. Speers, (Eds), et al. *Integrating behavioral and social sciences with public health*. Washington, DC: American Psychological Association.

Rimm, S. B., & Lovance, K. J. (1992). The use of subject and grade skipping for the prevention and reversal of underachievement. Special Issue: Challenging the gifted: Grouping and acceleration. *Gifted Child Quarterly, 36*, 100–105.

Ripple, C. H., Gilliam, W. S., Chanana, N., & Zigler, E. (1999). Will fifty cooks spoil the broth? The debate over entrusting Head Start to the states. *American Psychologist, 54*, 327–343.

Rizzo, T. A., Metzger, B. E., Dooley, S. L., & Cho, N. H. (1997). Early malnutrition and child neurobehavioral development: Insights from the study of children of diabetic mothers. *Child Development, 68*, 26–38.

Roberto, K. A. (1987). Exchange and equity in friendships. In R. G. Admas & R. Blieszner (Eds.), *Older adult friendships: Structure and process*. Newbury Park, CA: Sage.

Roberts, R. E., Phinney, J. S., Masse, L. C., Chen, Y. R., Roberts, C. R., & Romero, A. (1999). The structure of ethnic identity of young adolescents from diverse ethnocultural groups. *Journal of Early Adolescence, 19*, 301–322.

Robertson, S. S. (1982). Intrinsic temporal patterning in the spontaneous movement of awake neonates. *Child Development, 53*, 1016–1021.

Robinson, D. L. (1997). Age differences, cerebral arousability, and human intelligence. *Personality and Individual Differences, 23*, 601–618.

Robinson, J. P., & Bianchi, S. (1997, December). The children's hours. *American Demographics*, pp. 20–23.

Robinson, J. P., & Godbey, G. (1997). *Time for life: The surprising ways Americans use their time*. College Park: Pennsylvania State University Press.

Robinson, N. M., Zigler, E., & Gallagher, J. J. (2000). Two tails of the normal curve: Similarities and differences in the study of mental retardation and giftedness. *American Psychologist, 55*, 1413–1421.

Rochat, P., & Goubet, N. (1995). Development of sitting and reaching in 5- and 6-month-old infants. *Infant Behavior and Development, 18*, 53–68.

Roche, T. (2000, November 13). The crisis of foster care. *Time*, 74–82.

Rodkin, P. C., Farmer, T. W., Pearl, R., & Van Acker, R. (2000). Heterogeneity of popular boys: Antisocial and prosocial configurations. *Developmental Psychology, 36*, 14–24.

Roffwarg, H. P., Muzio, J. N., & Dement, W. C. (1966). Ontogenic development of the human sleep–dream cycle. *Science, 152*, 604–619.

Rogan, W. J., & Gladen, B. C. (1993). Breast-feeding and cognitive development. *Early Human Development, 31*, 181–193.

Rogers, A., & Hayden, T. (1997, June 30). Miracles that may keep you going. *Newsweek*, 59.

Rogers, C. R. (1971). A theory of personality in S. Maddi (Ed.), *Perspectives on personality*. Boston: Little Brown.

Rogoff, B. (1990). *Apprenticeship in thinking: Cognitive development in social context*. New York: Oxford University Press.

Rogoff, B. (1995). *Observing sociocultural activity on three planes: Participatory appropriation, guided participation, and apprenticeship*. New York: Cambridge University Press.

Rogoff, B., & Chavajay, P. (1995). What's become of research on the cultural basis of cognitive development? *American Psychologist, 50*, 859–877.

Rolls, E. (2000). Memory systems in the brain. *Annual Review of Psychology, 51*, 599–630.

Romaine, S. (1994). *Bilingualism* (2nd ed.). London: Blackwell.

Rönkä, A., & Pulkkinen, L. (1995). Accumulation of problems in social functioning in young adulthood: A developmental approach. *Journal of Personality and Social Psychology, 69*, 381–391.

Roodenrys, S., Hulme, C., & Brown, G. (1993). The development of short-term memory span: Separable effects of speech rate and long-term memory. *Journal of Experimental Child Psychology, 56*, 431–442.

Roopnarine, J. (1992). Father–child play in India. In K. MacDonald (Ed.), *Parent–child play*. Albany: State University of New York Press.

Roopnarine, J. L., Johnson, J. E., & Hooper, F. H. (Eds.). (1994). *Children's play in diverse cultures*. Albany: State University of New York Press.

Roper Starch Worldwide. (1997, August). Romantic resurgence. *American Demographics*, p. 35.

Rose, A. J., & Asher, S. R. (1999). Children's goals and strategies in response to conflicts within a friendship. *Developmental Psychology, 35*, 69–79.

Rose, M. R. (1999, December). Can human aging be postponed? *Scientific American*, 106–110.

Rose, S. A., & Feldman, J. F. (1995). Prediction of IQ and specific cognitive abilities at 11 years from infancy measures. *Developmental Psychology, 31*, 685–696.

Rose, S. A., & Feldman, J. F. (1997). Memory and speed: Their role in the relation of infant information processing to later IQ. *Child Development, 68*, 630–641.

Rose, S. A., & Ruff, H. A. (1987). Cross-modal abilities in human infants. In J. D. Osofsky (Ed.), *Handbook of infant development* (2nd ed.). New York: Wiley.

Rose, S. A., Feldman, J. F., Wallace, I. F., & McCarton, C. (1991). Information processing at 1 year: Relation to birth status and developmental outcome during the first 5 years. *Developmental Psychology, 27*, 723–737.

Rosen, D. (1997, March 25). The physician's perspective. *HealthNews*, 3.

Rosen, K. S., & Burke, P. B. (1999). Multiple attachment relationships within families: Mothers and fathers with two young children. *Developmental Psychology, 35*, 436–444.

Rosen, W. D., Adamson, L. B., & Bakeman, R. (1992). An experimental investigation of infant social referencing: Mothers' messages and gender differences. *Developmental Psychology, 28*, 1172–1178.

Rosenblatt, P. C. (1988). Grief: The social context of private feelings. *Journal of Social Issues, 44*, 67–78.

Rosenfeld, B., Krivo, S., Breitbart, W., & Chochinov, H. M. (2000). Suicide, assisted suicide, and euthanasia in the terminally ill. In H. M. Chochinov & W. Breitbart, (Eds.) *Handbook of psychiatry in palliative medicine*. New York: Oxford University Press.

Rosenfeld, M., & Owens, W. A., Jr. (1965, April). *The intrinsic–extrinsic aspects of work and their demographic correlates*. Paper presented at the Midwestern Psychological Association, Chicago.

Rosenman, R. H. (1990). Type A behavior pattern: A personal overview. *Journal of Social Behavior and Personality, 5*, 1–24.

Rosenman, R. H., Brand, R. J., Sholtz, R. I., & Friedman, M. (1976). Multivariate prediction of coronary heart disease during 8.5 year follow-up in the Western Collaborative Group Study. *American Journal of Cardiology, 37*, 903–910.

Rosenstein, D., & Oster, H. (1988). Differential facial responses to four basic tastes in newborns. *Child Development, 59*, 1555–1568.

Rosenthal, M. (1998). Women and infertility. *Psychopharmacology Bulletin, 34*, 307–308.

Rosenthal, R. (1987). Pygmalion effects: Existence, magnitude, and social importance. *Educational Researcher*, 37–40.

Rosenthal, R. (1994). Interpersonal expectancy effects: A 30–year perspective. *Current Directions in Psychological Science, 3*, 176–179.

Rosenthal, R., & Jacobson, L. (1968). *Pygmalion in the classroom: Teacher expectation and pupils' intellectual development*. New York: Holt, Rinehart & Winston.

Rosenzweig, M. R., & Bennett, E. L. (1976). Enriched environments: Facts, factors, and fantasies. In L. Petrinovich & J. L. McGaugh (Eds.), *Knowing, thinking, and believing*. New York: Plenum.

Ross Laboratories. (1993). *Ross Laboratories mothers' survey, 1992*. Division of Abbott Laboratories, USA, Columbus, OH. Unpublished data.

Ross, C. E., Microwsky, J., & Goldsteen, K. (1991). The impact of the family on health. In A. Booth (Ed.), *Contemporary families*. Minneapolis, MN: National Council on Family Relations.

Ross, R. K., & Yu, M. C. (1994, June 9). Breast feeding and breast cancer. *New England Journal of Medicine, 330*, 1683–1684.

Rosser, P. L., & Randolph, S. M. (1989). Black American infants: The Howard University normative study. In J. K. Neugent, B. M. Lester, & T. B. Brazelton (Eds.), *The cultural context of infancy: Vol. I. Biology, culture, and infant development*. Norwood, NJ: Ablex.

Rossman, I. (1977). Anatomic and body composition changes with aging. In C. E. Finch & L. Hayflick (Eds.), *Handbook of the biology of aging*. New York: Van Nostrand Reinhold.

Rotenberg, K. J., & Morrison, J. (1993). Loneliness and college achievement: Do loneliness scale scores predict college drop-out? *Psychological Reports, 73*, 1283–1288.

Roth, D., Slone, M., & Dar, R. (2000). Which way cognitive development? An evaluation of the Piagetian and the domain-specific research programs. *Theory & Psychology, 10*, 353–373.

Rothbart, M. K., Ahadi, S. A., & Evans, D. E. (2000). Temperament and personality: Origins and outcomes. *Journal of Personality and Social Psychology, 78*, 122–135.

Rothbart, M. K., Derryberry, D., & Hershey, K. (2000). Stability of temperament in childhood: Laboratory infant assessment to parent report at seven years. In V. J. Molfese & D. L. Molfese (Eds.), et al., *Temperament and personality development across the life span*. Mahwah, NJ: Erlbaum.

Rothbart, M. K., & Bates, J. E. (1998). Temperament. In N. Eisenberg (Ed.), *Handbook of child psychology: Vol. 3. Social, emotional, and personality development* (5th ed.) New York: Wiley.

Rothbaum, F., Weisz, J., Pott, M., Miyake, K., & Morelli, G. (2000). Attachment and culture: Security in the United States and Japan. *American Psychologist, 55*, 1093–1104.

Roush, W. (1995, March 31). Arguing over why Johnny can't read. *Science, 267*, 1896–1998.

Rovee-Collier, C. (1993). The capacity for long-term memory in infancy. *Current Directions in Psychological Science, 2*, 130–135.

Rovee-Collier, C. (1999). The development of infant memory. *Current Directions in Psychological Science, 8*, 80–85.

Rovee-Collier, C. K. (1987). Learning and memory in infancy. In J. D. Osofsky (Ed.), *Handbook of infant development* (2nd ed.). New York: Wiley.

Rovee-Collier, C. K., & Hayne, H. (1987). Reactivation and infant long-term memory. In H. W. Reese (Ed.), *Advances in child development and behavior* (Vol. 20). New York: Academic.

Rovee-Collier, C., & Gerhardstein, P. (1997). The development of infant memory. In N. Cowan (Ed.), *The development of memory in childhood* (pp. 5–39). Hove, England: Psychology Press/Erlbaum, Taylor, & Francis.

Rovner, B. W., & Katz, I. R. (1993). Psychiatric disorders in the nursing home: A selective review of studies related to clinical care. *International Journal of Geriatric Psychiatry, 8*, Special Issue, 75–87.

Rowe, D. C. (1994). *The effects of nurture on individual natures*. New York: Guilford Press.

Rowe, J. W., & Kahn, R. L. (1997). Successful aging. *Gerontologist, 37*, 433–440.

Rowe, J. W., & Kahn, R. L. (1998). *Successful aging*. New York: Pantheon.

Rubenstein, A. J., Kalakanis, L., & Langlois, J. H. (1999). Infant preferences for attractive faces: A cognitive explanation. *Developmental Psychology, 35*, 848–855.

Rubin, D. C. (1985, September). The subtle deceiver: Recalling our past. *Psychology Today*, pp. 39–46.

Rubin, D. C. (1986). *Autobiographical memory*. Cambridge, England: Cambridge University Press.

Rubin, D. C. (2000). Autobiographical memory and aging. In C. D. Park, & N. Schwarz, (Eds) et al. *Cognitive aging: A primer*. Philadelphia: Psychology Press/Taylor & Francis.

Rubin, D. C. (Ed.). (1996). *Remembering our past: Studies in autobiographical memory*. New York: Cambridge University Press.

Rubin, D. H., Krasilnikoff, P. A., Leventhal, J. M., Weile, B., & Berget, A. (1986, August 23). Effects of passive smoking on birthweight. *Lancet, 315*, 415–417.

Rubin, K. (1998). Social and emotional development from a cultural perspective. *Developmental Psychology, 34*, 611–615.

Rubin, K. H., Fein, G., & Vandenberg, B. (1983). In E. M. Hetherington (Ed.), *Handbook of child psychology. Vol. 4. Socialization, personality and social development* (pp. 693–774). New York: Wiley.

Ruble, D. (1983). The development of social comparison processes and their role in achievement-related self-actualization. In E. T. Higgins, D. N. Ruble, & W. W. Hartup (Eds.), *Social cognition and social development*. New York: Cambridge University Press.

Ruble, D. N., Boggiano, A. K., Feldman, N. S., & Loebl, J. H. (1989). Developmental analysis of the role of social comparison in self-evaluation. *Developmental Psychology, 16*, 105–115.

Ruble, D., & Brooks-Gunn, J. (1982). The experience of menarche. *Child Development, 53*, 1557–1566.

Ruda, M. A., Ling, Q-D., Hohmann, A. G., Peng, Y.B., & Tachibana, T. (2000, July 28). Altered nociceptive neuronal circuits after neonatal peripheral inflammation. *Science, 289*, 628–630.

Ruff, H. A. (1989). The infant's use of visual and haptic information in the perception and recognition of objects. *Canadian Journal of Psychology, 43,* 302–319.

Ruffman, T., Perner, J., Naito, M., Parkin, L., & Clements, W.A. (1998). Older (but not younger) siblings facilitate false belief understanding. *Developmental Psychology, 34,* 161–174.

Rule, B. G., & Ferguson, T. J. (1986). The effects of media violence on attitudes, emotions and cognitions. *Journal of Social Issues, 42,* 29–50.

Rumelhart, D. E. (1984). Schemata and the cognitive system. In R. S. Wyer, Jr., & T. K. Siull (Eds.), *Handbook of social cognition.* Hillsdale, NJ: Erlbaum.

Russell, G., & Radojevic, M. (1992). The changing role of fathers? Current understandings and future directions for research and practice. Special Section: Australian Regional Meeting: Attachment and the relationship the infant and caregivers. *Infant Mental Health Journal, 13,* 296–311.

Russo, R., & Parkin, A. J. (1993). Age differences in implicit memory: More apparent than real. *Memory and Cognition, 21,* 73–80.

Russon, A. E., & Waite, B. E. (1991). Patterns of dominance and imitation in an infant peer group. *Ethology & Sociobiology, 12,* 55–73.

Rust, J., Golombok, S., Hines, M., Johnston, K., & Golding, J.; ALSPAC Study Team. (2000). The role of brothers and sisters in the gender development of preschool children. *Journal of Experimental Child Psychology, 77,* 292–303.

Rusting, R. (1990, March). Safe passage? *Scientific American, 262,* 36.

Rutter M., & Garmezy, N. (1983). Developmental psychopathology. In E. M. Hetherington (Ed.), *Handbook of child psychology. Vol. IV. Socialization, personality, and social development.* New York: Wiley.

Rutter, M. (1987). Continuities and discontinuities from infancy. In J. D. Osofsky (Ed.), *Handbook of infant development* (2nd ed.). New York: Wiley.

Rutter, M., Bailey, A., Bolton, P., LeCouteur, A. (1993). Autism: Syndrome definition and possible genetic mechanisms. In R. Plomin & G. E. McClearn, (Eds.), *Nature, nurture, and psychology.* Washington, DC: American Psychological Association.

Rutter, M., Dunn, J., Plomin, R., & Simonoff, E. (1997). Integrating nature and nurture: Implications of person-environment correlations and interactions for developmental psychopathology. *Development and Psychopathology, 9,* 335–364.

Ryan, A. S. (1997). The resurgence of breastfeeding in the United States. *Pediatrics, 99,* e12.

Ryan, J. J., Sattler, J. M., & Lopez, S. J. (2000). Age effects on Wechsler Adult Intelligence Scale-III subtests. *Archives of Clinical Neuropsychology, 15,* 311–317.

Rycek, R. F., Stuhr, S. L., McDermott, J., Benker, J., & Swartz, M. D. (1998). Adolescent egocentrism and cognitive functioning during late adolescence. *Adolescence, 33,* 745–749.

Sack, K. (1999, March 21). Older students bring new life to campuses. *The New York Times,* p. WH8.

Sacks, M. H. (1993). Exercise for stress control. In D. Goleman & J. Gurin (Eds.), *Mind–body medicine.* Yonkers, NY: Consumer Reports Books.

Sadker, M., & Sadker, D. (1994). *Failing at fairness: How America's schools cheat girls.* New York: Scribner's.

Sagi, A. (1990). Attachment theory and research from a cross-cultural perspective. *Human Development, 33,* 10–22.

Sagi, A., Donnell, F., van Ijzendoorn, M. H., Mayseless, O., & Aviezer, O. (1994). Sleeping out of home in a kibbutz communal arrangement: It makes a difference for infant– mother attachment. *Child Development, 65,* 992–1004.

Sagi, A., van Ijzendoorn, M. H., & Koren-Karie, N. (1991). Primary appraisal of the Strange Situation: A cross-cultural analysis of preseparation episodes. *Developmental Psychology, 27,* 587–596.

Sagi, A., van Ijzendoorn, M. H., Aviezer, O., Donnell, F., Koren-Karie, N., Joels, T., & Harel, Y. (1995). Attachments in multiple-caregiver and multiple-infant environment: The case of the Israeli kibbutzim. *Monographs of the Society for Research in Child Development.*

Sagrestano, L. M., McCormick, S. H., Paikoff, R. L., & Holmbeck, G. N. (1999). Pubertal development and parent–child conflict in low-income, urban, African American adolescents. *Journal of Research on Adolescence, 9,* 85–107.

Salber, E. J., Freeman, H. E., & Abelin, T. (1968). Needed research on smoking: Lessons from the Newton study. In E. F. Borgatta & R. R. Evans (Eds.), *Smoking, health, and behavior.* Chicago: Aldine.

Sales, B. D., & Folkman, S. (Eds.) (2000). *Ethics in research with human participants.* Washington, DC: American Psychological Association.

Salmon, D. K. (1993, September). Getting through labor. *Parents,* pp. 62–66.

Salovey, P., & Sluyter, D. J. (Eds.). (1997). *Emotional development and emotional intelligence.* New York: Basic Books.

Salthouse, T. A. (1984). Effects of age and skill in typing. *Journal of Experimental Psychology: General, 113,* 345–371.

Salthouse, T. A. (1989). Age-related changes in basic cognitive processes. In APA Master Lectures, *The adult years: Continuity and change.* Washington, DC: American Psychological Association.

Salthouse, T. A. (1990). Cognitive competence and expertise in aging. In J. E. Birren, W. K. Schaie, & K. (Eds.) et al. *Handbook of the psychology of aging* (3rd ed.). San Diego, CA: Academic Press.

Salthouse, T. A. (1991). Mediation of adult age differences in cognition by reductions in working memory and speed of processing. *Psychological Science, 2,* 179–183.

Salthouse, T. A. (1993). Speed mediation of adult age differences in cognition. *Developmental Psychology, 29,* 722–738.

Salthouse, T. A. (1994a). Aging associations: Influence of speed on adult age differences in associative learning. *Journal of Experimental Psychology: Learning, Memory, and Cognition, 20,* 1486–1503.

Salthouse, T. A. (1994b). The aging of working memory. *Neuropsychology, 8,* 535–543.

Sanders, C. M. (1988). Risk factors in bereavement outcome. *Journal of Social Issues, 44,* 97–111.

Sanderson, C. A., & Cantor, N. (1995). Social dating goals in late adolescence: Implications for safer sexual activity. *Journal of Personality and Social Psychology, 68,* 1121–1134.

Sandis, E. (2000). The aging and their families: A cross-national review. In A. L. Comunian & U. P. Gielen (Eds.). *International perspectives on human development.* Lengerich, Germany: Pabst Science Publishers.

Sandler, B. (1994, January 31). First denial, then a near-suicidal plea: "Mom, I need your help." *People Weekly,* 56–58.

Sandoval, J., Frisby, Cl L., Geisinger, K. F., Scheuneman, J. D., & Grenier, J. R. (Eds.). (1998). *Test interpretation and diversity: Achieving equity in assessment.* Washington, DC: APA Books.

Sangree, W. H. (1989). Age and power: Life-course trajectories and age structuring of power relations in East and West Africa. In D. I. Kertzer & K. W. Schaie (Eds.), *Age structuring in comparative perspective.* Hillsdale, NJ: Erlbaum.

Sankar, A. (1981). The conquest of solitude: Singlehood and old age in traditional Chinese society. In C. L. Fry (Ed.), *Dimensions: Aging, culture and health.* New York: Praeger.

Sanoff, A. P., & Minerbrook, S. (1993, April 19). Race on campus. *U.S. News and World Report,* pp. 52–64.

Sanson, A., & diMuccio, C. (1993). The influence of aggressive and neutral cartoons and toys on the behavior of preschool children. *Australian Psychologist, 28,* 93–99.

Sarantakos, S. (1991). Cohabitation revisited: Paths of change among cohabiting and non-cohabiting couples. *Australian Journal of Marriage and the Family, 12,* 144–155.

Sarason, S., Johnson, J. H., & Siegel, J. M. (1978). Assessing the impact of life changes: Development of the Life Experiences Survey. *Journal of Consulting and Clinical Psychology, 46,* 932–946.

Sarrel, P. M. (2000). Effects of hormone replacement therapy on sexual psychophysiology and behavior in postmenopause. *Journal of Womens Health & Gender-Based Medicine, 9,* (Suppl. 1), S-25-3-32.

Sasser-Coen, J. R. (1993). Qualitative changes in creativity in the second half of life: A life-span developmental perspective. *Journal of Creative Behavior, 27,* 18–27.

Savage-Rumbaugh, E. S., Murphy, J., Sevcik, R. A., Brakke, K. E., Williams, S. L., & Rumbaugh, D. M. (1993). Language and comprehension in ape and child. *Monographs of the Society for Research in Child Development, 58,* (3–4, Serial No. 233).

Savin-Williams, R. C., & Berndt, T. J. (1990). Friendship and peer relations. In S. Feldman & G. Elliott (Eds.), *At the threshold: The developing adolescent.* Cambridge, MA: Harvard University Press.

Savin-Williams, R., & Demo, D. (1983). Situational and transituational determinants of adolescent self-feelings. *Journal of Personality and Social Psychology, 44,* 824–833.

Sax, L. J., Astin, A. W., Korn, W. S., & Mahoney, K. M. (2000). *The American freshman: National norms for Fall 2000.* Los Angeles: UCLA Higher Education Research Institute.

Saywitz, K. J., & Nathanson, R. (1993). Children's testimony and their perceptions of stress in and out of the courtroom. *Child Abuse & Neglect, 17,* 613–622.

Scanlon, J. W., & Hollenbeck, A. R. (1983). Neonatal behavioral effects of anesthetic exposure during pregnancy. In A. E. Friedman, A. Milusky, & A. Gluck (Eds.), *Advances in perinatal medicine*. New York: Plenum.

Scarr, S. (1992). Developmental theories for the 1990s: Development and individual differences. *Child Development, 63*, 1–19.

Scarr, S. (1993). Biological and cultural diversity: The legacy of Darwin for development. *Child Development, 64*, 1333–1353.

Scarr, S. (1996). Child care research, social values, and public policy. *The American Academy of Arts and Sciences Bulletin, 1*, 28–45.

Scarr, S. (1998). American child care today. *American Psychologist, 53*, 95–108.

Scarr, S., & Carter-Saltzman, L. (1982). Genetics and intelligence. In R. J. Sternberg (Ed.), *Handbook of human intelligence* (pp. 792–896). Cambridge, England: Cambridge University Press.

Scarr, S., Phillips, D., & McCartney, K. (1989). Working mothers and their families. *American Psychologist, 44*, 1402–1409.

Schaefer, R. T., & Lamm, R. P. (1992). *Sociology* (4th ed.). New York: McGraw-Hill.

Schaie, K. W. (1977–1978). Toward a stage of adult theory of adult cognitive development. *Journal of Aging and Human Development, 8*, 129–138.

Schaie, K. W. (1991). Developmental designs revisited. In S. H. Cohen & H. W. Reese (Eds.), *Life-span developmental psychology: Methodological innovations*. Hillsdale, NJ: Erlbaum.

Schaie, K. W. (1993). The Seattle longitudinal studies of adult intelligence. *Current Directions in Psychological Science, 2*, 171–175.

Schaie, K. W. (1994). The course of adult intellectual development. *American Psychologist, 49*, 304–313.

Schaie, K. W., & Willis, S. L. (1986). Can decline in adult intellectual functioning be reversed? *Developmental Psychology, 22*, 223–232.

Schaie, K. W., & Willis, S. L. (1993). Age difference patterns of psychometric intelligence in adulthood: Generalizability within and across ability domains. *Psychology and Aging, 8*, 44–55.

Schaie, K. W., Willis, S. L., Jay, G., & Chipuer, H. (1989). Structural invariance of cognitive abilities across the adult life span: A cross-sectional study. *Developmental Psychology, 25*, 652–662.

Schanberg, S., Field, T., Kuhn, C., & Bartolome, J. (1993). Touch: A biological regulator of growth and development in the neonate. *Verhaltenstherapie, 3(Suppl 1)*, 15.

Schatz, M. (1994). *A toddler's life*. New York: Oxford University Press.

Scheibel, A. B. (1992). Structural changes in the aging brain. In J. E. Birren, R. B. Sloane, & G. D. Cohen (Eds.), *Handbook of mental health and aging* (2nd ed.). San Diego: Harcourt Brace.

Scheiber, F. et al. (1992). Aging and the senses. In J. E. Birren, R. B. Sloane, & G. D. Cohen (Eds.), *Handbook of mental health and aging* (2nd ed.). San Diego: Harcourt Brace.

Schellenberg, E. G., & Trehub, S. E. (1996). Natural musical intervals: Evidence from infant listeners. *Psychological Science, 7*, 272–277.

Schiavi, R. C. (1990). Sexuality and aging in men. *Annual Review of Sex Research, 1*, 227–249.

Schkade, D. A., & Kahneman, D. (1998). Does living in California make people happy? A focusing illusion on judgments of life satisfaction. *Psychological Science, 9*, 340–346.

Schlegel, A., & Barry, H., III. (1991). *Adolescence: An anthropological inquiry*. New York: The Free Press.

Schmidt, P. J., & Rubinow, D. R. (1991). Menopause-related affective disorders: A justification for further study. *American Journal of Psychiatry, 148*, 844–852.

Schmitt, E. (2001, March 13). For 7 million people in census, one race category isn't enough. *The New York Times*, p. A1, A14.

Schneider, B. (1997). Psychoacoustics and aging: Implications for everyday listening. *Journal of Speech-Language Pathology & Audiology, 21*, 111–124.

Schneider, B. A., Bull, D., & Trehub, S. E. (1988). Binaural unmasking in infants. *Journals of the Acoustical Society of America, 83*, 1124–1132.

Schneider, B. A., Trehub, S. E., & Bull, D. (1980). High-frequency sensitivity in infants. *Science, 207*, 1003–1004.

Schneider, B. A., Atkinson, L., & Tardif, C. (2001). Child-parent attachment and children's peer relations: A quantitative review. *Developmental Psychology, 37*, 86–100.

Schneider, E. L. (1999, February 5). Aging in the third millennium. *Science, 283*, 796–797.

Schneider, W., & Pressley, M. (1989). *Memory between two and twenty*. New York: Springer-Verlag.

Schnur, E., & Belanger, S. (2000). What works in Head Start. In M. P. Kluger & G. Alexander, (Eds.) et al. *What works in child welfare*. Washington, DC: Child Welfare League of America.

Schofield, J. W., & Francis, W. D. (1982). An observational study of peer interaction in racially mixed "accelerated" classrooms. *Journal of Educational Psychology, 74*, 722–732.

Schreiber, G. B., Robins, M., Striegel-Moore, R., Obarzanek, M., Morrison, J. A., & Wright, D. J. (1996). Weight modification efforts reported by black and white preadolescent girls: National Heart, Lung, and Blood Institute Growth and Health Study. *Pediatrics, 98*, 63–70.

Schulenberg, J. E., Asp, C. E., & Peterson, A. C. (1984). School from the young adolescent's perspective. *Journal of Early Adolescence, 4*, 107–130.

Schulman, M. (1991). *The passionate mind: Bringing up an intelligent and creative child*. New York: Free Press.

Schulman, M., & Mekler, E. (1994). *Bringing up a moral child: A new approach for teaching your child to be kind, just, and responsible*. Reading, MA: Addison-Wesley.

Schulman, P., Keith, D., & Seligman, M. (1993). Is optimism heritable? A study of twins. *Behavior Research and Therapy, 31*, 569–574.

Schultz, A. H. (1969). *The life of primates*. New York: Universe.

Schultz, R., & Curnow, C. (1988). Peak performance and age among superathletes: Track and field, swimming, baseball, tennis, and golf. *Journal of Gerontology, 43*, P113–P120.

Schultz, R., & Heckhausen, J. (1996). A life span model of successful aging. *American Psychologist, 51*, 702–714.

Schulz, R. (Ed.). (2000). *Handbook on dementia caregiving: Evidence-based interventions for family caregivers*. New York: Springer Publishing.

Schulz, R., & Aderman, D. (1976). How medical staff copes with dying patients. *Omega, 7*, 11–21.

Schulz, R., & Ewen, R. B. (1988). *Adult development and aging: Myths and emerging realities*. New York: Macmillan.

Schuster, C. S., & Ashburn, S. S. (1986). *The process of human development* (2nd. ed.). Boston: Little, Brown.

Schutt, R. K., (2001). *Investigating the social world: The process and practice of research*. Thousand Oaks, CA: Sage.

Schwartz, D., Dodge, K. A., Pettit, G. S., & Bates, J. E. (1997). The early socialization of aggressive victims of bullying. *Child Development, 68*, 665–675.

Schwartz, I. M. (1999). Sexual activity prior to coital interaction: A comparison between males and females. *Archives of Sexual Behavior, 28*, 63–69.

Schwartz, J. E., Friedman, H. S., Tucker, J. S., Tomlinson-Keasey, C., Wingard, D. L., & Criqui, M. H. (in press). Childhood sociodemographic and psychosocial factors as predictors of longevity across the life-span. American Journal of Public Health.

Schwebel, M., Maher, C. A., & Fagley, N. S. (Eds.). (1990). *Promoting cognitive growth over the life span*. Hillsdale, NJ: Erlbaum.

Schweinhart, L. J., Barnes, H. V., & Weikart, D. P. (1993). *Significant benefits: The High/Scope Perry Preschool Study through age 27 (Monographs of the High/Scope Educational Research Foundation, No. 10)*. Ypsilanti, MI: High/Scope Press.

Scopesi, A., Zanobini, M., & Carossino, P. (1997). Childbirth in different cultures: Psychophysical reactions of women delivering in U.S., German, French, and Italian hospitals. *Journal of Reproductive & Infant Psychology, 15*, 9–30.

Scruggs, T. E., & Mastropieri, M. A. (1994). Successful mainstreaming in elementary science classes: A qualitative study of three reputational cases. *American Educational Research Journal, 31*, 785–811.

Sears, R. R. (1977). Sources of life satisfaction of the Terman gifted men. *American Psychologist, 32*, 119–129.

Secouler, L. M. (1992). Our elders: At high risk for humiliation. Special Issue: The humiliation dynamic: Viewing the task of prevention from a new perspective: II. *Journal of Primary Prevention, 12*, 195–208.

Segal, B. M., & Stewart, J. C. (1996). Substance use and abuse in adolescence: An overview. *Child Psychiatry & Human Development, 26*, 193–210.

Segal, J., & Segal, Z. (1992, September). No more couch potatoes. *Parents*, p. 235.

Segal, N. L. (1993). Twin, sibling, and adoption methods: Tests of evolutionary hypotheses. *American Psychologist, 48*, 943–956.

Segal, N. L. (2000). Virtual twins: New findings on within-family environmental influences on intelligence. *Journal of Educational Psychology, 92*, 188–194.

Segall, M. H., Dasen, P. R., Berry, J. W., & Poortinga, Y. H. (1990). *Human behavior in global perspective*. Boston: Allyn & Bacon.

Seidman, S. N., & Rieder, R. O. (1994). A review of sexual behavior in the United States. *American Journal of Psychiatry, 151,* 330–341.

Seifer, R., Schiller, M., & Sameroff, A. J. (1996). Attachment, maternal sensitivity, and infant temperament during the first year of life. *Developmental Psychology, 32,* 12–25.

Selig, S., Tomlinson, T., & Hickey, T. (1991). Ethical dimensions of intergenerational reciprocity: Implications for practice. *Gerontologist, 31,* 624–630.

Seligman, L. (1995). *Promoting a fighting spirit: Psychotherapy for cancer patients, survivors, and their families.* San Francisco: Jossey-Bass.

Seppa, N. (1996, December). Keeping schoolyards safe from bullies. *APA Monitor,* p. 41.

Seppa, N. (1997, February). Wisdom: A quality that may defy age. *APA Monitor,* pp. 1, 9.

Serbin, L. A., Poulin-Dubois, D., Colburne, K. A., Sen, M. G., & Eichstedt, J. A. (2001). Gender stereotyping in infancy: Visual preferences for and knowledge of gender-stereotyped toys in the second year. *International Journal of Behavioral Development, 25,* 7–15.

Serovich, J. M., & Greene, K. (1997). Predictors of adolescent risk taking behaviors which put them at risk for contracting HIV. *Journal of Youth & Adolescence, 26,* 429–444.

Serwint, J. R., Dias, M., & White, J. (2000). Effects of lead counseling for children with lead levels >=20 mug/dL: Impact on parental knowledge, attitudes, and behavior. *Clinical Pediatrics, 39,* 643–650.

Sesser, S. (1993, September 13). Opium war redux. *The New Yorker,* pp. 78–89.

Seymour, H. N., Abdulkarim, L., & Johnson, V. (1999). The Ebonics controversy: An educational and clinical dilemma. *Topics in Language Disorders, 19,* 66–77.

Shafer, R. G. (1990, March 12). An anguished father recounts the battle he lost—Trying to rescue a teenage son from drugs. *People Weekly,* 81–83.

Shantz, C. U., & Hartup, W. W. (Eds.). (1995). *Conflict in child and adolescent development.* New York: Cambridge University Press.

Shapiro, A. F., Gottman, J. M. & Carrère, S. (2000). The baby and the marriage: Identifying factors that buffer against decline in marital satisfaction after the first baby arrives. *Journal of Family Psychology, 14,* 124–130.

Shapiro, L. (1997, Spring/Summer). Beyond an apple a day. *Newsweek Special Issue,* 52–56.

Sharf, R. S. (1992). *Applying career development theory to counseling.* Pacific Grove, CA: Brooks/Cole.

Sharpe, R. (1994, July 18). Better babies: School gets kids to do feats at a tender age, but it's controversial. *The Wall Street Journal,* pp. A1, A6.

Shavelson, R., Hubner, J. J., & Stanton, J. C. (1976). Self-concept: Validation of construct interpretations. *Review of Educational Research, 46,* 407–441.

Shaver, P. (1994, August). *Attachment and care giving in adult romantic relationships.* Invited address presented at the annual meeting of the American Psychological Association, Los Angeles.

Shaver, P. R., Hazan, C., & Bradshaw, D. (1988). Love as attachment: The integration of three behavioral systems. In R. J. Sternberg & M. L. Barnes (Eds.), *The psychology of love* (pp. 68–99). New Haven, CT: Yale University Press.

Shaw, D. S., Winslow, E. B., & Flanagan, C. (1999). A prospective study of the effects of marital status and family relations on young children's adjustment among African American and European American families. *Child Development, 70,* 742–755.

Shaw, J. (1994). Aging and sexual potential. *Journal of Sex Education and Therapy, 20,* 134–139.

Shaywitz, S. E. (1996, November). Dyslexia. *Scientific American,* 98–104.

Shaywitz, S. E., Shaywitz, B. A., Pugh, K. R., Fulbright, R. K., Skudlarski, P., Mencl, W. E., Constable, R. T., Naftolin, F., Palter, S. F., Marchione, K. E., Katz, L., Shankweiler, D. P., Fletcher, J. M., Lacadie, C., Keltz, M., & Gore, J. C. (1999). Effect of estrogen on brain activation patterns in postmenopausal women during working memory tasks. *Journal of the American Medical Association, 281,* 1197–1202.

Shea, J. D. (1985). Studies of cognitive development in Papua, New Guinea. *International Journal of Psychology, 20,* 33–61.

Shea, K. M., Wilcox, A. J., & Little, R. E. (1998). Postterm delivery: a challenge for epidemiologic research. *Epidemiology, 9,* 199–204.

Shealy, C. N. (1995). From Boys Town to Oliver Twist: Separating fact from fiction in welfare reform and out-of-home placement of children and youth. *American Psychologist, 50,* 565–580.

Sheehy, G. (1976). *Passages.* New York: Dutton.

Sheets, R. H., & Hollins, E. R. (1999). *Racial and ethnic identity in school practices.* Mahwah, NJ: Lawrence Erlbaum.

Sheffield, J. V. (1997). General medicine update MIDDM, prevention of CAD, and risks and benefits of hormone replacement therapy. *Comprehensive Therapy, 23,* 303–309.

Sheingold, K., & Tenney, Y. J. (1982). Memory for a salient childhood event. In U. Neisser (Ed.), *Memory observed.* New York: Freeman.

Sheldon, K. M., Elliot, A. J., Kim, Y., & Kasser, T. (2001). What is satisfying about satisfying events? Testing 10 candidate psychological needs. *Journal of Personality and Social Psychology, 80,* 325–339.

Shepard, G. B. (1991). A glimpse of kindergarten—Chinese style. *Young Children, 47,* 11–15.

Sherman, E. (1991). *Reminiscence and the self in old age.* New York: Springer.

Sherry, B., Springer, D. A., Connell, F. A., & Garrett, S. M. (1992). Short, thin, or obese? Comparing growth indexes of children from high- and low-poverty areas. *Journal of the American Dietetic Association, 92,* 1092–1095.

Sherwin, B. B. (1991). The psychoendocrinology of aging and female sexuality. *Annual Review of Sex Research, 2,* 181–198.

Shevron, R. H., & Lumsden, D. B. (1985). *Introduction to educational gerontology* (2nd ed.). New York: Hemisphere.

Shiono, P. H., & Behrman, R. E. (1995). Low birth weight: Analysis and recommendations. *The Future of Children, 5,* 4–18.

Shneidman, E. S. (1983). *Deaths of man.* New York: Jason Aronson.

Shock, N. W. (1962). *The physiology of aging.* San Francisco: Freeman.

Shonk, S. M., & Cicchetti, D. (2001). Maltreatment, competency deficits, and risk for academic and behavioral maladjustment. *Developmental Psychology, 37,* 3–17.

Short, R. J., & Talley, R. C. (1997). Rethinking psychology and the schools: Implications of recent national policy. *American Psychologist, 52,* 234–240.

Shriver, M. D., & Piersel, W. (1994). The long-term effects of intrauterine drug exposure: Review of recent research and implications for early childhood special education. *Topics in Early Childhood Special Education, 14,* 161–183.

Shrum, W., Cheek, N., Jr., & Hunter, S. M. (1988). Friendship in school: Gender and racial homophily. *Sociology of Education, 61,* 227–239.

Shucard, J., Shucard, D., Cummins, K., & Campso, J. (1981). Auditory evoked potentials and sex-related differences in brain development. *Brain and Language, 13,* 91–102.

Shumaker, S. A., & Smith, T. R. (1994). The politics of women's health. *Journal of Social Issues, 50,* 189–202.

Shurkin, J. N. (1992). *Terman's kids: The groundbreaking study of how the gifted grow up.* Boston: Little, Brown.

Shute, N. (1997, November 10). No more hard labor. *U.S. News & World Report,* pp. 92–95.

Sieber, J. E. (1998). Planning ethically responsible research. In L. Bickman & D. J. Rog (Eds.), *Handbook of applied social research methods* (pp. 127–156). Thousand Oaks, CA: Sage.

Siegal, M. (1997). *Knowing children: Experiments in conversation and cognition.* (2nd ed.). Hove, England: Psychology Press/Erlbaum, Taylor & Francis.

Siegel, B. (1996). Is the emperor wearing clothes? Social policy and the empirical support for full inclusion of children with disabilities in the preschool and early elementary grades. *Social Policy Report, 10,* 2–17.

Siegel, L. S. (1989). A reconceptualization of prediction from infant test scores. In M. H. Bornstein & N. A. Krasnegor (Eds.), *Stability and continuity in mental development: Behavioral and biological perspectives.* Hillsdale, NJ: Erlbaum.

Siegler, I. C., & Costa, P. T. (1985). Health behavior relationships. In J. E. Birren & K. W. Schaie (Eds.), *Handbook of the psychology of aging* (2nd ed.). New York: Van Nostrand Reinhold.

Siegler, R. S. (1994). Cognitive variability: A key to understanding cognitive development. *Current Directions in Psychological Science, 3,* 1–5.

Siegler, R. S. (1995). How does change occur?: A microgentic study of number conservation. *Cognitive Psychology, 28,* 225–273.

Siegler, R. S. (1998). *Children's thinking.* (3rd ed.). Upper Saddle River, NJ: Prentice Hall.

Siegler, R. S., & Ellis, S. (1996). Piaget on childhood. *Psychological Science, 7,* 211–215.

Siegler, R. S., & Richards, D. (1982). The development of intelligence. In R. Sternberg (Ed.), *Handbook of human intelligence.* London: Cambridge University Press.

Sigman, M. (1995). Nutrition and child development: More food for thought. *Current Directions in Psychological Science, 4,* 52–55.

Sigman, M. D., Cohen, S. E., Beckwith, L., Asarnow, R., & Parmelee, A. H. (1992). The prediction of cognitive abilities at 8 and 12 years of age from neonatal assessments of preterm infants. In S. L. Friedman &

M. D. Sigman (Eds.), *The psychological development of low birthweight children*. Norwood, NJ: Ablex.

Sigman, M., Cohen, S. E., Beckwith, L., Asarnow, R., & Parmelee, A. H. (in press). Continuity in cognitive abilities from infancy to 12 years of age. *Cognitive Development.*

Sigman, M., Neumann, C., Jansen, A. A. J., & Bwibo, N. (1989). Cognitive abilities of Kenyan children in relation to nutrition, family characteristics, and education. *Child Development, 60,* 1463–1474.

Signorella, M. L., Bigler, R. S., & Liben, L. (1993). Development differences in children's gender schemata about others: A meta-analytic review. *Developmental Review, 13,* 106–126.

Silverstein, L. B., & Auerbach, C. F. (1999). Deconstructing the essential father. *American Psychologist, 54,* 397–407.

Simmons, R., & Blyth, D. (1987). *Moving into adolescence.* New York: Aldine de Gruyter.

Simons, K. (Ed.). (1993). *Early visual development: normal and abnormal.* New York: Oxford University Press.

Simons, M. (1995, September 11). Dutch doctors to tighten rules on mercy killings. *The New York Times,* p. A7.

Simonton, D. K. (1989). The swan-song phenomenon: Last-works effects for 172 classical composers. *Psychology and Aging, 4,* 42–47.

Simonton, D. K. (1997). Creative productivity: A predictive and explanatory model of career trajectories and landmarks. *Psychological Review, 104,* 66–89.

Simpson, J. A. (1990). Influence of attachment styles on romantic relationships. *Journal of Personality & Social Psychology, 59,* 971–980.

Singer, D. G., & Singer, J. L. (Eds.). (2000). *Handbook of children and the media.* Thousand Oaks, CA: Sage.

Singer, L. T., Arendt, R., Minnes, S., Farkas, K., & Salvator, A. (2000). Neurobehavioral outcomes of cocaine-exposed infants. *Neurotoxicology & Teratology, 22,* 653–666.

Singer, M. S., Stacey, B. G., & Lange, C. (1993). The relative utility of expectancy-value theory and social cognitive theory in predicting psychology student course goals and career aspirations. *Journal of Social Behavior and Personality, 8,* 703–714.

Singh, G. K., & Yu, S. M. (1995). Infant mortality in the United States: Trends, differentials, and projections 1950 through 2010. *The American Journal of Public Health, 85,* 957–964.

Singleton, L. C., & Asher, S. R. (1979). Racial integration and children's peer preferences. *Child Development, 50,* 936–941.

Sinnott, J. D. (1997). Developmental models of midlife and aging in women: Metaphors for transcendence and for individuality in community. In J. Coyle (Ed.), *Handbook on women and aging* (pp. 149–163). Westport, CT: Greenwood.

Sinnott, J. D. (1998). Career paths and creative lives: A theoretical perspective on late-life potential. In C. Adams-Price (Ed.), *Creativity and successful aging: Theoretical and empirical approaches.* New York: Springer.

Sinnott, J. D. (1998). *The development of logic in adulthood: Postformal thought and its applications.* New York: Plenum.

Skinner, B. F. (1957). *Verbal behavior.* New York: Appleton-Century-Crofts.

Skinner, B. F. (1975). The steep and thorny road to a science of behavior. *American Psychologist, 30,* 42–49.

Skipper, J. K., & Nass, G. (1966). Dating behavior: A framework of analysis and an illustration. *Journal of Marriage and the Family, 28,* 412–420.

Slater, A. (1995). Individual differences in infancy and later IQ. *Journal of Child Psychology and Psychiatry and Allied Disciplines, 36,* 69–112.

Slater, A., & Butterworth, G. (1997). Perception of social stimuli: Face perception and imitation. In G. Bremmer, A. Slater, & G. Butterworth (Eds.), *Infant development: Recent advances* (pp. 223–245). Hove, England: Psychology Press/Erlbaum, Taylor & Francis.

Slater, A., & Johnson, S. P. (1998). Visual sensory and perceptual abilities of the newborn: Beyond the blooming, buzzing confusion. In F. Simion, G. Butterworth, et al. (Eds.), *The development of sensory, motor and cognitive capacities in early infancy: From perception to cognition.* Hove, England: Psychology Press/Erlbaum (Uk) Taylor & Francis.

Slater, A., Mattock, A., & Brown, E. (1990). Size constancy at birth: Newborn infants' responses to retinal and real size. *Journal of Experimental Child Psychology, 49,* 314–322.

Slavin, R. E. (1995). Enhancing intergroup relations in schools: Cooperative learning and other strategies. In W. D. Hawley & A. W. Jackson (Eds.), *Toward a common destiny: Improving race and ethnic relations in America.* San Francisco: Jossey-Bass.

Sleek, S. (1997, June). Can "emotional intelligence" be taught in today's schools? *APA Monitor,* p. 25.

Slep, A. M., Smith, R., & O'Leary, S. G. (2001). Examining partner and child abuse: Are we ready for a more integrated approach to family violence? *Clinical Child & Family Psychology Review, 4,* 87–107.

Sliwinski, M., Buschke, H., Kuslansky, G., & Senior, G. (1994). Proportional slowing and addition speed in old and young adults. *Psychology and Aging, 9,* 72–80.

Slobin, D. (1970). Universals of grammatical development in children. In G. Flores D'Arcais & W. Levelt (Eds.), Advances in psycholinguistics. New York: American Elsevier.

Small, B. J., & Bäckman, L. (1999). Time to death and cognitive performance. *Current Directions in Psychological Science, 8,* 168–172.

Small, G. W. (1991). Recognition and treatment of depression in the elderly. The clinician's challenge: Strategies for treatment of depression in the 1990s, Phoenix, Arizona. *Journal of Clinical Psychiatry, 52* (Suppl.), 11–22.

Small, G. W., Mazziotta, J. C., Collins, M. T., et al. (1995). Apolipoprotein E. type 4 allele and cerebral glucose metabolism in relatives at risk for familial Alzheimer's disease. *Journal of the American Medical Association, 273,* 942–947.

Smedley, B. D. & Syme, S. L. (Eds.). (2000). *Promoting health: Intervention strategies from social and behavioral research.* Washington, DC: National Academy of Sciences.

Smetana, J. (1988). Concepts of self and social convention: Adolescents' and parents' reasoning about hypothetical and actual family conflicts. In M. Gunnar (Ed.), *21st Minnesota Symposium on Child Psychology.* Hillsdale, NJ: Erlbaum.

Smetana, J. (1989). Adolescents' and parents' reasoning about actual family conflict. *Child Development, 60,* 1052–1067.

Smetana, J., Yau, J., & Hanson, S. (1991). Conflict resolution in families with adolescents. *Journal of Research on Adolescence, 1,* 189–206.

Smith, J., & Baltes, P. B. (1997). Profiles of psychological functioning in the old and oldest old. *Psychology and Aging, 12,* 458–472.

Smith, M. (1990). Alternative techniques. *Nursing Times, 86,* 43–45.

Smith, P. K. (1978). A longitudinal study of social participation in preschool children: Solitary and parallel play re-examined. *Developmental Psychology, 12,* 517–523.

Smith, P. K. (1995). Grandparenthood. In M. H. Bornstein, *Handbook of parenting.* Hillsdale, NJ: Erlbaum.

Smith, R. (1999, March). The timing of birth. *Scientific American,* 68–75.

Smith, T. W. (1992). Hostility and health: Current status of a psychosomatic hypothesis. *Health Psychology, 11,* 139–150.

Smith, W., Mitchell, P., Webb, K., & Leeder, S. R. (1999). Dietary antioxidants and age-related maculopathy: The Blue Mountains Eye Study. *Opthalmology, 106,* 761–767.

Smotherman, W. P., & Robinson, S. R. (1996). The development of behavior before birth. *Developmental Psychology, 32,* 425–434.

Smuts, A. B., & Hagen, J. W. (1985). History of the family and of child development: Introduction to Part 1. *Monographs of the Society for Research in Child Development, 50* (4–5, Serial No. 211).

Snarey, J. R. (1985). Cross-cultural universality of social-moral development. A critical review of Kohlbergian research. *Psychological Bulletin, 97,* 202–232.

Snarey, J. R. (1995). In a communitarian voice: The sociological expansion of Kohlbergian theory, research, and practice. In W. M. Kurtines & J. L. Gerwirtz (Eds.), *Moral development: An introduction.* Boston: Allyn and Bacon.

Snow, R. (1969). Unfinished Pygmalion. *Contemporary Psychology, 14,* 197–199.

Snowdon, D. A., Kemper, S. J., Mortimer, J. A., Greiner, L. H., Wekstein, D. R., & Markesbery, W. R. (1996, February 21). Linguistic ability in early life and cognitive function and Alzheimer's disease in late life: Findings from the nun study. *Journal of the American Medical Association, 275,* 528–532.

Snowling, M. (2000). *Dyslexia: A cognitive developmental perspective.* (2nd ed.). New York: Blackwell Publishers.

Snyder, J., Horsch, E., & Childs, J. (1997). Peer relationships of young children: Affiliative choices and the shaping of behavior. *Journal of Clinical Child Psychology, 26,* 145–156.

Snyder, R. A., Verderber, K. S., Langmeyer, L., & Myers, M. (1992). A reconsideration of self- and organization-referent attitudes as "causes" of the glass ceiling effect. *Group and Organization Management, 17,* 260–278.

Socolar, R. R. S., & Stein, R. E. K. (1995, January 1). Spanking infants and toddlers: Maternal belief and practice. *Pediatrics, 95,* 105–111.

Socolar, R. R. S., & Stein, R. E. K. (1996). Maternal discipline of young children: Context, belief, and practice. *Developmental and Behavioral Pediatrics, 17,* 1–8.

Sohal, R. S., & Weindruch, R. (1996, July 5). Oxidative stress, caloric restriction, and aging. *Science, 273,* 59–63.

Soken, N. H., & Pick, A .D. (1999). Infants' perception of dynamic affective expressions: Do infants distinguish specific expressions? *Child Development, 70,* 1275–1282.

Solomon, A. (1995, May 22). A death of one's own. *New Yorker,* pp. 54–69.

Sondik, E. J. (1988). Progress in cancer prevention and control. *Transactions & Studies of the College of Physicians of Philadelphia, 10,* 111–131.

Sontag, S. (1979). The double standard of aging. In J. H. Williams (Ed.), *Psychology of women: Selected readings.* New York: Norton.

Sophian, C., Garyantes, D., & Chang, C. (1997). When three is less than two: Early developments in children's understanding of fractional quantities. *Developmental Psychology, 33,* 731–744.

Sorensen, K. (1992). Physical and mental development of adolescent males with Klinefelter syndrome. *Hormone Research, 37* (Suppl. 3), 55–61.

Sorensen, T., Nielsen, G., Andersen, P., & Teasdale, T. (1988). Genetic and environmental influences on premature death in adult adoptees. *New England Journal of Medicine, 318,* 727–732.

Sotos, J. F. (1997). Overgrowth: Section IV: Genetic disorders associated with overgrowth. *Clinical Pediatrics, 36,* 37–49.

Soussignan, R., Schaal, B., Marlier, L., & Jiang, T. (1997). Facial and autonomic responses to biological and artificial olfactory stimuli in human neonates: Re-examining early hedonic discrimination of odors. *Physiology and Behavior, 62,* 745–758.

Southern, W. T., Jones, E. D., & Stanley, J. C. (1993). Acceleration and enrichment: The context and development of program options. In K. A. Heller, F. J. Monks, & A. H. Passow (Eds.), *International handbook of research and development of giftedness and talent.* Oxford, England: Pergamon.

Spear, P. D. (1993). Neural bases of visual deficits during aging. *Vision Research, 33,* 2589–2609.

Spearman, C. (1927). *The abilities of man.* London: Macmillan.

Spelke, E. (1987). The development of intermodal perception. In P. Salapatek & L. Cohen (Eds.), *Handbook of infant perception* (Vol. 2). Orlando, FL: Academic Press.

Spelke, E. S. (1991). Physical knowledge in infancy: Reflections on Piaget's theory. In S. Carey & R. Gelman (Eds.), *The epigenesis of mind.* Hillsdale, NJ: Erlbaum.

Spence, S. H. (1997). Sex and relationships. In W. K. Halford & H. J. Markman (Eds.), *Clinical handbook of marriage and couples interventions* (pp. 73–105). Chichester, England: Wiley.

Spencer, J. (2001). How to battle school violence. http://www.msnbc.com/news/542211.asp?cp1=1#BODY.

Spencer, M. B. (1991). Identity, minority development of. In R. M. Lerner, A. C. Petersen, & J. Brooks-Gunn (Eds.), *Encyclopedia of adolescence* (Vol. 1). New York: Garland.

Spencer, M. B., & Dornbusch, S. M. (1990). Challenges in studying minority youth. In S. Feldman & G. Elliott (Eds.), *At the threshold: The developing adolescent.* Cambridge, MA: Harvard University Press.

Spencer, N. (2001). The social patterning of teenage pregnancy. *Journal of Epidemiology & Community Health, 55,* 5.

Spencer, S., Steele, C. M., & Quinn, D. (1997). *Under suspicion of inability: Stereotype threat and women's math performance.* Manuscript submitted for publication. Cited in Steele, 1997.

Spiegel, D. (1993). Social support: How friends, family, and groups can help. In D. Goleman & J. Gurin (Eds.), *Mind-body medicine.* Yonkers, NY: Consumer Reports Books.

Spiegel, D. (1996). Dissociative disorders. In R. E. Hales & S. C. Yudofsky, (Eds.), *The American Psychiatric Press synopsis of psychiatry.* Washington, DC: American Psychiatric Press.

Spiegel, D., Bloom, J. R., Kraemer, H. C., & Gottheil, E. (1989, October 14). Effect of psychosocial treatment on survival of patients with metastatic breast cancer. *Lancet, 2,* 888–891.

Spira, A., Bajos, N., Bejin, A., Beltzer, N. (1992). AIDS and sexual behavior in France. *Nature, 360,* 407–409.

Spitze, G., & Logan, J. (1990). More evidence on women (and men) in the middle. *Research on Aging, 12,* 182–198.

Sprecher, S., Sullivan, Q., & Hatfield, E. (1994). Mate selection preferences: Gender differences examined in a national sample. *Journal of Personality and Social Psychology, 66,* 1074–1080.

Springen, K. (2000). The circumcision decision. *Newsweek Special Issue: Your Child,* 50.

Springer, S. P., & Deutsch, G. (1989). *Left brain, right brain* (3rd ed.). New York: Freeman.

Squires, S. (1991, September 17). Lifelong fitness depends on teaching children to love exercise. *The Washington Post,* p. WH16.

Sroufe, L. A. (1994). Pathways to adaptation and maladaptation: Psychopathology as developmental deviation. In D. Cicchetti (Ed.), *Developmental psychopathology: Past, present, and future.* Hillsdale, NJ: Erlbaum.

Sroufe, L. A. (1996). *Emotional development: The organization of emotional life in the early years.* New York: Oxford University Press.

Stack, D., & Muir, D. (1992). Adult tactile stimulation during face-to-face interactions modulates five-month-olds' affect and attention. *Child Development, 63,* 1509–1525.

Stadtler, A. C., Gorski, P. A., & Brazelton, T. B. (1999). Toilet Training Methods, Clinical Interventions, and Recommendations. *Pediatrics, 103,* 1359–1361.

Stacy, A. W., Sussman, S., Dent, C. W., Burton, D., & et al. (1992). Moderators of peer social influence in adolescent smoking. *Personality & Social Psychology Bulletin, 18,* 163–172.

Stahl, S. M. (1997). Estrogen makes the brain a sex organ. *Journal of Clinical Psychiatry, 58,* 421–422.

Stanjek, K. (1978). Das Uberreichen von Gaben: Funktion und Entwicklung in den ersten Lebensjahren. *Zeitschrift fur Entwicklungpsychologie und Pedagogische Psychologie, 10,* 103–113

Stanley, J. C., & Benbow, C. P. (1983). SMPY's first decade: Ten years of posing problems and solving them. *Journal of Special Education, 17,* 11–25.

Starfield, B. (1991). Childhood morbidity: Comparisons, clusters, and trends. *Pediatrics, 88,* 519–526.

Staudinger, U. M., & Baltes, P. B. (1996). Interactive minds: A facilitative setting for wisdom-related performance? *Journal of Personality and Social Psychology, 71,* 746–762.

Staudinger, U. M., Fleeson, W., & Baltes, P. B. (1999). Predictors of subjective physical health and global well-being: Similarities and differences between the United States and German. *Journal of Personality and Social Psychology, 76,* 305–319.

Staudinger, U. M., Marsiske, M., & Baltes, P. B. (1993). Resilience and levels of reserve capacity in later adulthood: Perspectives from life-span theory. *Development and Psychopathology, 5,* 541–566.

Steele, C. M. (1997). A threat in the air: How stereotypes shape intellectual identity and performance. *American Psychologist, 52,* 613–629.

Steele, C. M., & Aronson, J. (1995). Stereotype threat and the intellectual test performance of African Americans. *Journal of Personality and Social Psychology, 69,* 797–811.

Steers, R. M., & Porter, L. W. (1991). *Motivation and work behavior.* (5th ed.). New York: McGraw-Hill.

Stein, J. A., Lu, M. C., & Gelberg, L. (2000). Severity of homelessness and adverse birth outcomes. *Health Psychology, 19,* 524–534.

Stein, J. H., & Reiser, L. W. (1994). A study of white middle-class adolescent boys' responses to "semenarche" (the first ejaculation). *Journal of Youth and Adolescence, 23,* 373–384.

Stein, Z., Susser, M., Saenger, G., & Marolla, F. (1975). *Famine and human development: The Dutch hunger winter of 1944–1945.* New York: Oxford University Press.

Steinberg, J. (1997, January 2). Turning words into meaning. *The New York Times,* pp. B1–B2.

Steinberg, J. (1998 March 19). Experts call for mix of two methods to teach reading. *The New York Times,* p. A1, A17.

Steinberg, K. K., Thacker, S. B., Smith, S. J., Stroup, D. F., Zack, M. M., Flanders, W. D., & Berkelman, R. L. (1991). A meta-analysis of the effect of estrogen replacement therapy on the risk of breast cancer. *Journal of the American Medical Association, 265,* 1985–1990.

Steinberg, L. (1990). Autonomy, conflict, and harmony in the family relationship. In S. Feldman & G. Elliott (Eds.), *At the threshold: The developing adolescent.* Cambridge, MA: Harvard University Press.

Steinberg, L. (1993). *Adolescence.* New York: McGraw-Hill.

Steinberg, L., & Silverberg, S. (1986). The vicissitudes of autonomy in early adolescence. *Child Development, 57,* 841–851.

Steinberg, L., Dornbusch, S., & Brown, B. B. (1992). Ethnic differences in adolescent achievement: An ecological perspective. *American Psychologist, 47,* 723–729.

Steiner, J. E. (1979). Human facial expressions in response to taste and smell stimulation. *Advances in Child Development and Behavior, 13,* 257.

Steinert, S., Shay, J. W., & Wright, W. E. (2000). Transient expression of human telomerase extends the life span of normal human fibroblasts. *Biochemical & Biophysical Research Communications, 273,* 1095–1098.

Steinhausen, H. C., & Spohr, H. L. (1998). Longterm outcome of children with fetal alcohol syndrome: Psychopathology, behavior, and intelligence. *Alcoholism, Clinical & Experimental Research, 22,* 334–338.

Steri, A. O. & Spelke, E. S. (1988). Haptic perception of objects in infancy. *Cognitive Psychology 20,* 1–23.

Stern, G. (1994, November, 30). Going back to college has special meaning for Mrs. McAlpin. *The Wall Street Journal,* p. A1.

Sternberg, R. J. (1982). Reasoning, problems solving, and intelligence. In R. J. Sternberg (Ed.), *Handbook of human intelligence* (pp. 225–307). Cambridge, England: Cambridge University Press.

Sternberg, R. J. (1985). *Beyond IQ: A triarchic theory of human intelligence.* New York: Cambridge University Press.

Sternberg, R. J. (1986). Triangular theory of love. *Psychological Review, 93,* 119–135.

Sternberg, R. J. (1987). Liking versus loving: A comparative evaluation of theories. *Psychological Bulletin, 102,* 331–345.

Sternberg, R. J. (1988). Triangulating love. In R. J. Sternberg & M. J. Barnes (Eds.), *The psychology of love.* New Haven, CT: Yale University Press.

Sternberg, R. J. (1990). *Metaphors of mind: Conceptions of the nature of intelligence.* Cambridge, England: Cambridge University Press.

Sternberg, R. J. (1991). Theory-based testing of intellectual abilities: Rationale for the Sternberg triarchic abilities test. In H. A. H. Rowe (Ed.), *Intelligence: Reconceptualization and measurement.* Hillsdale, NJ: Erlbaum.

Sternberg, R. J. (1995). For whom the Bell Curve tolls: A review of *The Bell Curve. Psychological Science, 6,* 257–261.

Sternberg, R. J. (1996). Educating intelligence: Infusing the triarchic theory into school instruction. In R. J. Sternberg & E. Grigorenko (Eds.), *Intelligence, heredity, and environment.* New York: Cambridge University Press.

Sternberg, R. J., & Grigorenko, E. (Eds.). (1996). *Intelligence, heredity, and environment.* New York: Cambridge University Press.

Sternberg, R. J., & Lubart, T. I. (1992). Buy low and sell high: An investment approach to creativity. *Current Directions in Psychological Science, 1,* 1–5.

Sternberg, R. J., & Wagner, R. K. (1993). The g-ocentric view of intelligence and job performance is wrong. *Current Directions in Psychological Science, 2,* 1–5.

Sternberg, R. J., & Wagner, R. K. (Eds.). (1986). *Practical intelligence: Nature and origins of competence in the everyday world.* New York: Cambridge University Press.

Sternberg, R. J., Conway, B. E., Ketron, J. L., & Bernstein, M. (1981). Peoples' conceptions of intelligence. *Journal of Personality and Social Psychology, 41,* 37–55.

Sternberg, R. J., Wagner, R. K., Williams, W. M., & Horvath, J. A. (1997). Testing common sense. In D. Russ-Eft, H. Preskill, & C. Sleezer (Eds.), *Human resource development review: Research and implications* (pp. 102–132). Thousand Oaks, CA: Sage.

Sterns, H. L., Barrett, G. V., & Alexander, R. A. (1985). Accidents and the aging individual. In J. E. Birren & K. W. Schaie (Eds.), *Handbook of the psychology of aging* (2nd ed.). New York: Van Nostrand Reinhold.

Stevens, J. C., Cain, W. S., Demarque, A., & Ruthruff, A. (1991). On the discrimination of missing ingredients: Aging and salt flavor. *Appetite, 16,* 129–140.

Stevenson, H. W., & Stigler, J. W. (1992). *The learning gap: Why our schools are failing and what we can learn from Japanese and Chinese education.* New York: Summit.

Stevenson, H. W., Chen, C., & Lee, S. Y. (1992). A comparison of the parent–child relationship in Japan and the United States. In L. L. Roopnarine & D. B. Carter (Eds.), Parent-child socialization in diverse cultures. Norwood, NJ: Ablex.

Stevens-Ratchford, R. G. (1993). The effect of life review reminiscence activities on depression and self-esteem in older adults. *American Journal of Occupational Therapy, 47,* 413–420.

Steward, E. P. (1995). *Beginning writers in the zone of proximal development.* Hillsdale, NJ: Erlbaum.

Stewart, A. J., & Ostrove, J. M. (1998). Women's personality in middle age: Gender, history, and midcourse corrections. *American Psychologist, 53,* 1185–1194.

Stewart, A. J., & Vandewater, E. A. (1999). "If I had it to do over again…": Midlife review, midcourse corrections, and women's well-being in midlife. *Journal of Personality and Social Psychology, 76,* 270–283.

Stewart, A. J., Copeland, A. P., Chester, N. L., Mallery, J. E., & Barenbaum, N. B. (1997). *Separating together: How divorce transforms families.* New York: Guilford Press.

Stipek, D. J., & Hoffman, J. (1980). Development of children's performance-related judgments. *Child Development, 51,* 912–914.

Stock, G., & Campbell, J. (2000). *Engineering the human germline: An exploration of the science and ethics of altering the genes we pass to our children.* New York: Oxford University Press.

Stohs, J. H. (1992). Intrinsic motivation and sustained art activity among male fine and applied artists. *Creativity Research Journal, 5,* 245–252.

Stolberg, S. G. (1998, April 3). Rise in smoking by young Blacks erodes a success story in health. *The New York Times,* p. A1.

Stolberg, S. G. (1999, August 8). Black mothers' mortality rate under scrutiny. *The New York Times,* pp. 1, 18.

Stolberg, S. G. (2001, August 15). Researchers discount a caution in debate over cloned humans. *The New York Times,* pA18.

Stone, R., Cafferata, G. L., & Sangl, J. (1987). Caregivers of the frail elderly: A national profile. *Gerontologist, 27,* 616–626.

Storfer, M. (1990). *Intelligence and giftedness: The contributions of heredity and early environment.* San Francisco: Jossey-Bass.

Strauch, B. (1997, August 10). Use of antidepression medicine for young patients has soared. *The New York Times,* pp. A1, A24.

Straus, M. A., & Gelles, R. J. (Eds.). (1990). *Physical violence in American families.* New Brunswick, NJ: Transaction.

Straus, M. A., & McCord, J. (1998). Do physically punished children become violent adults? In S. Nolen-Hoeksema (Ed.), *Clashing views on abnormal psychology: A Taking Sides custom reader* (pp. 130–155). Guilford, CT: Dushkin/McGraw-Hill.

Straus, M. A., & Yodanis, C. L. (1996). Corporal punishment in adolescence and physical assaults on spouses in later life: What accounts for the link? *Journal of Marriage and the Family, 58,* 825–841.

Straus, M. A., Sugarman, D. B., & Giles-Sims, J. (1997). Spanking by parents and subsequent antisocial behavior of children. *Archives of Pediatrics and Adolescent Medicine, 151,* 761–767.

Straus, M., Gelles, R., & Steinmetz, S. K. (1980). *Behind closed doors: Violence in the American family.* Garden City, NY: Anchor Press.

Streissguth, A. P., Randels, S. P., & Smith, D. F. (1991). A test-retest study of intelligence in patients with fetal alcohol syndrome: implications for care. *Journal of the American Academy of Child & Adolescent Psychiatry, 30,* 584–587.

Strelau, J. (1998). *Temperament: A psychological perspective.* New York: Plenum Publishers.

Striegel-Moore, R. H. (1997). Risk factors for eating disorders. In M. S. Jacobson, J. M. Rees, N. H. Golden, & C. E. Irwin (Eds.), *Annals of the New York Academy of Sciences: Vol. 817. Adolescent nutritional disorders: Prevention and treatment* (pp. 98–109). New York: New York Academy of Sciences.

Stroebe, M. S., Stroebe, W., & Hansson, R. O. (Eds.). (1993). *Handbook of bereavement: Theory, research, and intervention.* Cambridge, England: Cambridge University Press.

Stroebe, W., Stroebe, M., Abakoumkin, G., & Schut, H. (1996). The role of loneliness and social support in adjustment to loss: A test of attachment versus stress theory. *Journal of Personality and Social Psychology, 70,* 1241–1249.

Strube, M. (Ed.). (1990). Type A behavior. (Special Issue). *Journal of Social Behavior and Personality, 5.*

Suarez, E. C., & Williams, R. B., Jr. (1992). Interactive models of reactivity: The relationship between hostility and potentially pathogenic physiological responses to social stressors. In N. Schneiderman, P. McCabe, & A. Baum (Eds.), *Stress and disease processes.* Hillsdale, NJ: Erlbaum.

Sugarman, S. (1988). *Piaget's construction of the child's reality.* Cambridge, England: Cambridge University Press.

Sugden, J. (1995, January 23). Sanctuaries for broken children. *People Weekly,* 39.

Suinn, R. M. (2001). The terrible twos—Anger and anxiety: Hazardous to your health. *American Psychologist, 56,* 27–36.

Sullivan, M. W., Rovee-Collier, C. K., & Tynes, D. M. (1979). A conditioning analysis of infant long-term memory. *Child Development, 50,* 152–162.

Suls, J., & Wills, T. A. (Eds.). (1991). *Social comparison: Contemporary theory and research.* Hillsdale, NJ: Erlbaum.

Sulzer-Azaroff, B., & Mayer, R. (1991). *Behavior analysis and lasting change.* New York: Holt.

Sundin, O., Ohman, A., Palm, T., & Strom, G. (1995). Cardiovascular reactivity, Type A behavior, and coronary heart disease: Comparisons between myocardial infarction patients and controls during laboratory-induced stress. *Psychophysiology, 32,* 28–35.

Sung, B. L. (1985). Bicultural conflicts in Chinese immigrant children. *Journal of Comparative Family Studies, 16,* 255–270.

Super, C. M. (1976). Environmental effects on motor development: A case of African infant precocity. *Developmental Medicine and Child Neurology, 18,* 561–576.

Super, C. M., & Harkness, S. (1982). The infant's niche in rural Kenya and metropolitan America. In L. Adler (Ed.), *Issues in cross-cultural research.* New York: Academic Press.

Suro, R. (1999, November). Mixed doubles. *American Demographics,* pp. 57–62.

Suskind, R. (1994, September 24). Class struggle: Poor, black, and smart. *The New York Times,* p. A1.

Suskind, R. (1999). *A hope in the unseen : An american odyssey from the inner city to the ivy league.* New York: Broadway Books.

Susman-Stillman, A., Kalkose, M., Egeland, B., & Waldman, I. (1996). Infant temperament and maternal sensitivity as predictors of attachment security. *Infant Behavior & Development, 19,* 33–47.

Sussman, S. K., & Sussman, M. B. (Eds.). (1991). *Families: Intergenerational and generational connections.* Binghamton, NY: Haworth.

Suzuki, L. A., & Valencia, R. R. (1997). Race-ethnicity and measured intelligence. *American Psychologist, 52,* 1103–1114.

Swan, S. H. (1997). Hormone replacement therapy and the risk of reproductive cancers. *Journal of Psychosomatic Obstetrics and Gynaecology, 18,* 165–174.

Swanson, L. A., Leonard, L. B., & Gandour, J. (1992). Vowel duration in mothers' speech to young children. *Journal of Speech and Hearing Research, 35,* 617–625.

Swendsen, J. D., & Mazure, C. M. (2000). Life stress as a risk factor for postpartum depression: Current research and methodological issues. *Clinical Psychology-Science & Practice, 7,* 17–31.

Tajfel, H. (1982). *Social identity and intergroup relations.* London: Cambridge University Press.

Takahashi, K. (1986). Examining the Strange Situation procedure with Japanese mothers and 12-month-old infants. *Developmental Psychology, 22,* 265–270.

Takanishi, R., Hamburg, D. A., & Jacobs, K. (Eds.). (1997). *Preparing adolescents for the twenty-first century: Challenges facing Europe and the United States.* New York: Cambridge University Press.

Talkington-Boyer, S., & Snyder, D. K. (1994). Assessing impact on family caregivers to Alzheimer's disease patients. *American Journal of Family Therapy, 22,* 57–66.

Tamis-LeMonda, C. S., & Bornstein, M. H. (1993). Antecedents of exploratory competence at one year. *Infant Behavior and Development, 16,* 423–439.

Tamis-LeMonda, C. S., & Cabrera, N. (1999). Perspectives on father involvement: Research and policy. *Social Policy Report, 13,* 1–31.

Tannen, D. (1991). *You just don't understand.* New York: Ballantine.

Tanner, J. (1972). Sequence, tempo, and individual variation in growth and development of boys and girls aged twelve to sixteen. In J. Kagan & R. Coles (Eds.), *Twelve to sixteen: Early adolescence.* New York: Norton.

Tanner, J. M. (1978). *Education and physical growth* (2nd ed.). New York: International Universities Press.

Tappan, M. B. (1997). Language, culture and moral development: A Vygotskian perspective. *Developmental Review, 17,* 199–212.

Tardif, T. (1996). Nouns are not always learned before verbs: Evidence from Mandarin speakers' early vocabularies. *Developmental Psychology, 32,* 492–504.

Tasker, F. L., & Golombok, S. (1997). *Growing up in a lesbian family: Effects on child development.* New York: Guilford Press.

Tate, D. C., Reppucci, N. D., & Mulvey, E. P. (1995). Violent juvenile delinquents: Treatment effectiveness and implications for future action. *American Psychologist, 50,* 777–781.

Tatum, B. (1997). *"Why are all the black kids sitting together in the cafeteria?": And other conversations about race.* New York: Basic Books.

Taubes, G. (1997, February 21). The breast-screening brawl. *Science, 275,* 1056–1059.

Tavris, C., & Sadd, S. (1977). The *Redbook* report on female sexuality. New York: Delacorte.

Taylor, H. G., Klein, N., Minich, N. M., & Hack, M. (2000). Middle-school-age outcomes in children with very low birthweight. *Child Development, 71,* 1495–1511.

Taylor, R. J., Chatters, L. M., Tucker, M. B., & Lewis, E. (1991). Developments in research on black families. In A. Booth (Ed.), *Contemporary families.* Minneapolis, MN: National Council on Family Relations.

Taylor, S. E. (1991). *Health psychology* (2nd ed.). New York: McGraw-Hill.

Teerikangas, O. M., Aronen, E. T., Martin, R. P., & Huttunen, M. O. (1998). Effects of infant temperament and early intervention on the psychiatric symptoms of adolescents. *Journal of the American Academy of Child & Adolescent Psychiatry, 37,* 1070–1076.

Tegano, D. W., Lookabaugh, S., May, G. E., & Burdette, M. P. (1991). Constructive play and problem solving: The role of structure and time in the classroom. *Early Child Development and Care, 68,* 27–35.

Tellegen, A., Lykken, D. T., Bouchard, T. J., Jr., Wilcox, K. J., Segal, N. L., & Rich, S. (1988). Personality similarity in twins reared apart and together. *Journal of Personality and Social Psychology, 54,* 1031–1039.

Tenenbaum, H. R., & Leaper, C. (1998). Gender effects on Mexican-descent parents' questions and scaffolding during toy play: A sequential analysis. *First Language, 18,* 129–147.

Terman, D.L., Larner, M.B., Stevenson, C.S., & Behrman, R.E. (1996). Special education for students with disabilities: Analysis and recommendations. *The future of children, 6,* 4–24.

Terman, L. M., & Oden, M. H. (1959). *The gifted group at mid-life: Thirty-five years follow-up of the superior child.* Standord, CA: Standord University Press.

Termin, N. T., & Izard, C. E. (1988). Infants' responses to their mothers' expressions of joy and sadness. *Developmental Psychology, 24,* 223–229.

Terry, D. (2000, August, 11). U.S. child poverty rate fell as economy grew, but is above 1979 level. *The New York Times,* p. A10.

Tesman, J. R., & Hills, A. (1994). Developmental effects of lead exposure in children. *Social Policy Report, 8,* 1–17.

Tessor, A., Felson, R. B., & Suls, J. M. (Eds.). (2000). *Psychological perspectives on self and identity.* Washington, DC: American Psychological Association.

Tharp, R. G. (1989). Psychocultural variables and constants: Effects on teaching and learning in schools: Special issue: Children and their development: Knowledge base, research agenda, and social policy application. *American Psychologist, 44,* 349–359.

The Endocrine Society (2001, March 1). *The Endocrine Society and Lawson Wilkins Pediatric Endocrine Society call for further research to define precocious puberty.* Bethesda, Maryland: The Endocrine Society.

Thelen, E. (1979). Rhythmical stereotypes in normal human infants. *Animal Behavior, 27,* 699–715.

Thelen, E. (1994). Three-month-old infants can learn task-specific patterns of interlimb coordination. *Psychological Science, 5,* 280–285.

Thoman, E. B. (1990). Sleeping and waking states in infants: A functional perspective. *Neuroscience and Biobehavioral Review, 14,* 93–107.

Thoman, E. B., & Whitney, M. P. (1989). Sleep states of infants monitored in the home: Individual differences, developmental trends, and origins of diurnal cyclicity. *Infant Behavior and Development, 12,* 59–75.

Thoman, E. B., & Whitney, M. P. (1990). Behavioral states in infants: Individual differences and individual analyses. In J. Colombo & J. Fagen (Eds.), *Individual differences in infancy: Reliability, stability, prediction* (pp. 113–136). Hillsdale, NJ: Erlbaum.

Thomas, A., & Chess, S. (1977). *Temperament and development.* New York: Brunner-Mazel.

Thomas, A., & Chess, S. (1980). *The dynamics of psychological development.* New York: Brunner-Mazel.

Thomas, A., Chess, S., & Birch, H. G. (1968). *Temperament and behavior disorders in children.* New York: New York University Press.

Thomas, C. B., Duszynski, K. R., & Schaffer, J. W. (1979). Family attitudes reported in youth as potential predictors of cancer. *Psychosomatic Medicine, 4,* 287–302.

Thomas, J. (1986). Gender differences in satisfaction with grandparenting. *Psychology and Aging, 1,* 215–19.

Thomas, P. (1994, September 6). Washington's infant mortality rate, more than twice the U.S. average, reflects urban woes. *The Wall Street Journal,* p. A14.

Thomas, R. M. (2001). *Recent human development theories.* Thousand Oaks, CA: Sage.

Thompson, P. (1993). "I don't feel old": The significance of the search for meaning in later life. *International Journal of Geriatric Psychiatry, 8,* 685–692.

Thompson, R. A., & Limber, S. P. (1990). Social anxiety in infancy: Stranger and separation reactions. In H. Leitenberg (Ed.), *Handbook of social and evaluation anxiety.* New York: Plenum.

Thompson, R. A., & Nelson, C. A. (2001). Developmental science and the media. *American Psychologist, 56,* 5–15.

Thompson, W. C., Clarke-Stewart, K. A., & Lepore, S. J. (1997). What did the janitor do? Suggestive interviewing and the accuracy of children's accounts. *Law & Human Behavior, 21,* 405–426.

Thoresen, C. E., & Bracke, P. (1997). Reducing coronary recurrences and coronary-prone behavior: A structures group treatment approach. In J. L. Sira (Ed.), *Group therapy for medically ill patients* (pp. 92–129). New York: Guilford Press.

Thornberry, T. P., & Krohn, M. D. (1997). Peers, drug use, and delinquency. In D. M. Stoff, J. Breiling, & J. D. Maser (Eds.), *Handbook of antisocial behavior* (pp. 218–233). New York: Wiley.

Thornburg, K. R., Pearl, P., Crompton, D., & Ispa, J. M. (1990). Development of kindergarten children based on child care arrangements. *Early Childhood Research Quarterly, 5,* 27–42.

Thorne, B. (1986). Girls and boys together, but mostly apart. In W. W. Hartup & Z. Rubin (Eds.), *Relationships and development* (pp. 167–184). Hillsdale, NJ: Erlbaum.

Thorpe, J. A., Hu, D. H., Albin, R. M., McNitt, J., Meyer, B. A., Cohen, J. R., & Yeast, J. D. (1993). The effect of intrapartum epidural analgesia on nulliparous labor: A randomized, controlled prospective trial. *American Journal of Obstetrics and Gynecology, 169,* 851–858.

Thorsheim, H. I., & Roberts, B. B. (1990). *Reminiscing together: Ways to help us keep mentally fit as we grow older.* Minneapolis: CompCare Publishers.

Thorson, J. A., Powell, F., Abdel-Khalek, A. M., & Beshai, J. A. (1997). Constructions of religiosity and death anxiety in two cultures: The United States and Kuwait. *Journal of Psychology and Theology, 25,* 374–383.

Time (1980, September 8). People section.

Tincoff, R., & Jusczyk, P. W. (1999). Some beginnings of word comprehension in 6-month-olds. *Psychological Science, 10,* 172–175.

Ting, Y. (1997). Determinants of job satisfaction of federal government employees. *Public Personnel Management, 26,* 313–334.

Tobin, J. J., Wu, D. Y. H., & Davidson, D. H. (1989). *Preschool in three cultures: Japan, China, and the United States.* New Haven, CT: Yale University Press.

Toch, T. (1995, January 2). Kids and marijuana: The glamour is back. *U.S. News and World Report,* p. 12.

Toda, S., & Fogel, A. (1993). Infant response to the still-face situation at 3 and 6 months. *Developmental Psychology, 29,* 532–538.

Tomlinson-Keasey, C. (1985). *Child development: Psychological, sociological, and biological factors.* Homewood, IL: Dorsey.

Topolnicki, D. M. (1995, January). The real immigrant story: Making it big in America. *Money,* pp. 129–138.

Touwen, B. C. L. (1984). Primitive reflexes—Conceptual or semantic problem? In H. F. R. Prechtl (Ed.), *Continuity of neural functions from prenatal to postnatal life.* (Clinics in Developmental Medicine No. 94, pp. 115–125). Philadelphia: Lippincott.

Townsend, A., Noelker, L., Deimling, G., & Bass, D. (1989). Longitudinal impact of interhousehold caregiving on adult children's mental health. *Psychology and Aging, 4,* 393–401.

Trainor, L. J., Austin, C. M., & Desjardins, R. N. (2000). Is infant-directed speech prosody a result of the vocal expression of emotion? *Psychological Science, 11,* 188–195.

Treas, J., & Bengston, V. L. (1987). The family in later years. In M. B. Sussman & S. K. Steinmetz (Eds.), *Handbook of marriage and the family.* New York: Plenum.

Treasure, J., & Tiller, J. (1993). The aetiology of eating disorders: Its biological basis. *International Review of Psychiatry, 5,* 23–31.

Treffers, P. E., Eskes, M., Kleiverda, G., & van Alten, D. (1990). Home births and minimal medical interventions. *Journal of the American Medical Association, 2624(7),* 2203, 2207–2208.

Trehub, S. E., Schneider, B. A., Morrongiello, B. A., & Thorpe, L. A. (1988). Auditory sensitivity in school-age children. *Journal of Experimental Child Psychology, 46,* 272–285.

Trehub, S. E., Schneider, B. A., Morrongiello, B. A., & Thorpe, L. A. (1989). Developmental changes in high-frequency sensitivity. *Audiology, 28,* 241–249.

Trehub, S. E., Thorpe, L. A., & Morrongiello, B. A. (1985). Infants' perception of melodies: Changes in a single tone. *Infant Behavior and Development, 8,* 213–223.

Tremblay, R. E. (2001). The development of physical aggression during childhood and the prediction of later dangerousness. In G. F. Pinard & L. Pagani, (Eds.) *Clinical assessment of dangerousness: Empirical contributions.* New York: Cambridge University Press.

Triandis, H. C. (1994). *Culture and social behavior.* New York: McGraw-Hill.

Triandis, H. C. (1995). *Individualism and collectivism.* Boulder, CO: Westview Press.

Trippet, S. E. (1991). Being aware: The relationship between health and social support among older women. *Journal of Women and Aging, 3,* 69–80.

Troiano, R. P., Flegal, K. M., Kuczmarski, R. J., Campbell, S. M., & Johnson, C. L. (1995). Overweight prevalence and trends for children and adolescents. The National Health and Nutrition Examination Surveys, 1963–1992. *Archives of Pediatric and Adolescent Medicine, 10,* 1085–1091.

Troll, L. E. (1985). *Early and middle adulthood* (2nd ed.). Monterey, CA: Brooks/Cole.

Troll, L. E. (1986). Parents and children in later life. *Generations, 10,* 23–25.

Troll, L. E. (1989). Myths of midlife intergenerational relationships. In S. Hunter & M. Sundel (Eds.), *Midlife myths.* Newbury Park, CA: Sage.

Tronick, E. Z. (1995). Touch in mother–infant interactions. In T. M. Field (Ed.), *Touch in early development.* Hillsdale, NJ: Erlbaum.

Tucker, J. S., Friedman, H. S., Schwartz, J. E., Criqui, M. H., Tomlinson-Keasey, C., Wingard, D. L., & Martin, L. R. (1997). Parental divorce: Effects on individual behavior and longevity. *Journal of Personality and Social Psychology, 73,* 381–391.

Tucker, M. B., & Mitchell-Kernan, C. (Eds.). (1995). *The decline in marriage among African Americans: Causes, consequences , and policy implications.* New York: Russell Sage.

Tucker, P., & Aron, A. (1993). Passionate love and marital satisfaction at key transition points in the family life cycle. *Journal of Social and Clinical Psychology, 12,* 135–147.

Tulving, E., & Thompson, D. M. (1973). Encoding specificity and retrieval processes in episodic memory. *Psychological Review, 80,* 352–373.

Turner, J. C. & Onorato, R. S. (1999). Social identity, personality, and the self-concept: A self-categorizing perspective. In T. R. Tyler, & R. M. Kramer, (Eds); et al. *The psychology of the social self. Applied social research.* Mahwah, NJ: Lawrence Erlbaum Associates.

Turner, J. S., & Helms, D. B. (1994). *Contemporary adulthood* (5th ed.). Forth Worth, TX: Harcourt Brace.

Turner, P. H., Scadden, L., & Harris, M. B. (1990). Parenting in gay and lesbian families. *Journal of Gay and Lesbian Psychotherapy, 1,* 55–66.

Turner, P. J., Gervai, J., & Hinde, R. A. (1993). Gender-typing in young children: Preferences, behavior and cultural differences. *British Journal of Developmental Psychology, 11,* 323–342.

Turner-Bowker, D. M. (1996). Gender stereotyped descriptors in children's picture books: Does "Curious Jane" exist in the literature? *Sex Roles, 35,* 461–488.

U.S. Advisory Board on Child Abuse and Neglect. (1995). *A nation's shame: Fatal child abuse and neglect in the United States.* Washington, DC: Superintendent of Documents.

U.S. Bureau of Labor Statistics. (1995). *Workforce demographics and makeup.* Washington, DC: U.S. Department of Labor.

U.S. Bureau of Labor. Women's Bureau. (1998). *The median wages of women as a proportion of the wages that men receive.* Washington, DC: U.S. Bureau of Labor.

U.S. Bureau of the Census (2001). *Living arrangements of children.* Washington, DC: U.S. Bureau of the Census.

U.S. Bureau of the Census. (1990a). *Statistical abstract of the United States: 1990* (110th ed.). Washington, DC: U.S. Government Printing Office.

U.S. Bureau of the Census. (1990b). *Studies in marriage and the family: Single parents and their children.* (Current Population Reports, Series P-23, No. 167). Washington, DC: U.S. Government Printing Office.

U.S. Bureau of the Census. (1990c). *Current population reports* (pp. 25–917, 25–1095). Washington, DC: U.S. Government Printing Office.

U.S. Bureau of the Census. (1992). *Poverty in the United States: 1991.* (Current Population Reports, Series P-60, No. 181). Washington, D.C: U.S. Government Printing Office.

U.S. Bureau of the Census. (1993). *Child health USA.* Washington, DC: U.S. Government Printing Office.

U.S. Bureau of the Census. (1995). *Higher education statistics.* (Current Population Reports). Washington, DC: U.S. Government Printing Office.

U.S. Census Bureau. (1996). *Poverty by educational attainment.* Washington, DC: U.S. Census Bureau.

U.S.D.A. (1992). *Dietary guidelines.* Washington, DC: Author.

U.S. Department of Education, Office of Special Education and Rehabilitative Services. (1987). *Eighth Annual Report to Congress on the implementation of the education of the Handicapped Act, 1986.* Washington, DC: U.S. Government Printing Office.

U.S. National Center for Education Statistics. (1997). *Digest of education statistics 1997.* Washington, DC: U.S. Government Printing Office.

Ubell, E. (1996, September 15). Are you at risk? *Parade Magazine,* pp. 20–21.

Uhlenberg, P., Cooney, T., & Boyd, R. (1990). Divorce for women after midlife. *Journal of Gerontology, 45(1),* S3–S11.

UNESCO. (1990). *Compendium of statistics on illiteracy, No. 31.* Paris: Author.

Unger, R., & Crawford, M. (1992). *Women and gender: A feminist psychology* (2nd ed.). New York: McGraw-Hill.

Unger, R., & Crawford, M. (1996). *Women and gender: A feminist psychology* (3rd ed.). New York: McGraw-Hill.

Ungrady, D. (1992, October 19). Getting physical: Fitness experts are helping shape up young America. *The Washington Post,* p. B5.

United Nations. (1990). *Declaration of the world summit for children.* New York: Author.

Unruh, D. (1989). Toward a social psychology of reminiscence. In D. Unruh & G. S. Livings (Eds.), *Personal history through the life course.* Greenwich, CT: JAI Press.

Urberg, K. A. (1982). The development of the concepts of masculinity and femininity in young children. *Sex Roles, 8,* 659–668.

Urberg, K. A., Degirmencioglu, S. M., & Pilgrim, C. (1997). Close friend and group influence on adolescent cigarette smoking and alcohol use. *Developmental Psychology, 33,* 834–844.

Urquidi, V., Tarin, D., & Goodison, S. (2000). Role of telomerase in cell senescence and oncogenesis. *Annual Review of Medicine, 51,* 65–79.

USA Weekend, Aug. 22–24, 1997, p. 5.

Usdansky, M. L. (1992, July 17). Wedded to the single life: Attitudes, economy delaying marriages. *USA Today,* p. A8.

USDHHS (U.S. Department of Health and Human Services). (1990). *Health United States 1989* (DHHS Publication No. PHS 90–1232). Washington, DC: U.S. Government Printing Office.

Vaillant, G. E. (1977). *Adaptation to life.* Boston: Little, Brown.

Vaillant, G. E., & Vaillant, C. O. (1981). Natural history of male psychological health, X: Work as a predictor of positive mental health. *The American Journal of Psychiatry, 138,* 1433–1440.

Vaillant, G. E., & Vaillant, C. O. (1990). Natural history of male psychological health, XII: A 45-year study of predictors of successful aging. *American Journal of Psychiatry, 147(1),* 31–37.

Vajragupta, O., Monthakantirat, O., Wongkrajang, Y., Watanabe, H., & Peungvicha, P. (2000). Chroman amide 12P inhibition of lipid peroxidation and protection against learning and memory impairment. *Life Sciences, 67,* 1725–1734.

van Balen, F. (1998). Development of IVF children. *Developmental Review, 18,* 30–46.

van't Spijker, A., & ten Kroode, H. F. (1997). Psychological aspects of genetic counseling: A review of the experience with Huntington's disease. *Patient Education and Counseling, 32,* 33–40.

VandeBerg, L.R., & Streckfuss, D. (1992). Primetime televiosn's portrayal of women and the world of work: A demographic profile. *Journal of Broadcasting & Electronic Media, 36* 195–208.

van den Hoonaard, D. K. (1994). Paradise lost: Widowhood in a Florida retirement community. *Journal of Aging Studies, 8,* 121–132.

Van Der Veer, R., & Valsiner, J. (1993). *Understanding Vygotsky.* Oxford, England: Blackwell.

Van Der Veer, R., & Valsiner, J. (Eds.). (1994). *The Vygotsky reader.* Oxford, England: Blackwell.

VanEvra, J. (1990). *Television and child development.* Hillsdale, NJ: Erlbaum.

Van Manen, S., & Pietromonaco, P. (1993). Acquaintance and consistency influence memory from interpersonal information. Unpublished manuscript, University of Massachusetts, Amherst.

Van Riper, C. (1972). *Speech correction: Principles and methods.* Englewood Cliffs, NJ: Prentice-Hall.

Vance, B., Hankins, N., & Brown, W. (1988). Ethnic and sex differences on the Test of Nonverbal Intelligence, Quick Test of intelligence, and Wechsler Intelligence Scale for Children–Revised. *Journal of Clinical Psychology, 44,* 261–265.

Vandell, D. L. (2000). Parents, peer groups, and other socializing influences. *Developmental Psychology, 36,* 699–710.

Vaughn, V., McKay, R. J., & Behrman, R. (1979). *Nelson textbook of pediatrics* (11th ed.). Philadelphia: Saunders.

Veatch, R. M. (1984). Brain death. In E. S. Shneidman (Ed.), *Death: Current perspectives* (3rd ed.). Palo Alto, CA: Mayfield.

Vellutino, F. R. (1991). Introduction to three studies on reading acquisition: Convergent findings on theoretical foundations of code-oriented versus whole-language approaches to reading instruction. *Journal of Educational Psychology, 83,* 437–443.

Verbrugge, L. M. (1985). Gender and health: An update on hypotheses and evidence. *Journal of Health and Social Behavior, 26,* 156–182.

Vercellini, P., Zuliani, G., Rognoni, M., Trespidi, L., Oldani, S., & Cardinale, A. (1993). Pregnancy at forty and over: A case-control study. *European Journal of Obstetrics, Gynecology, & Reproductive Biology, 48,* 191–195.

Vereijken, C. M., Riksen-Walraven, J. M., & Kondo-Ikemura, K. (1997). Maternal sensitivity and infant attachment security in Japan: A longitudinal study. *International Journal of Behavioral Development, 21,* 35–49.

Vernon, J. A. (1990). Media stereotyping: A comparison of the way elderly women and men are portrayed on prime-time television. *Journal of Women and Aging, 2,* 55–68.

Vihman, M. M. (1991). Early syllables and the construction of phonology. In C. A. Ferguson, L. Menn, & C. Stoel-Gammon (Eds.), *Phonological development: Models, research, implications* (pp. 69–84). Hillsdale, NJ: Erlbaum.

Vincze, M. (1971). Examinations on the social contacts between infants and young children reared together. *Magyar Pszichologiai Szemle, 28,* 58–61.

Visscher, W. A., Bray, R. M., & Kroutil, L. A. (1999). Drug use and pregnancy. In R. M. Bray, M. E. Marsden, et al. (Eds.), *Drug use in metropolitan America.* Thousand Oaks, CA: Sage.

Vitaliano, P. P., Dougherty, C. M., & Siegler, I. C. (1994). Biopsychosocial risks for cardiovascular disease in spouse caregivers of persons with Alzheimer's disease. In R. P. Abeles, H. C. Gift, & M. G. Ory (Eds.), *Aging and quality of life.* New York: Springer.

Vitaro, F., & Pelletier, D. (1991). Assessment of children's social problem-solving skills in hypothetical and actual conflict situations. *Journal of Abnormal Child Psychology, 19,* 505–518.

Vizmanos, B. & Marti-Henneberg, C. (2000). Puberty begins with a characteristic subcutaneous body fat mass in each sex. *European Journal of Clinical Nutrition, 54,* 203–206.

Vogel, G. (1997, June 13). Why the rise in asthma cases? *Science, 276,* 1645.

Volkow, N. D., Wang, G. J., Fowler, J. S., Logan, J., Gerasimov, M., Maynard, I., Ding, Y. S., Gatley, S. J., Gifford, A., & Granceschi, D. (2001). Therapeutic doses of oral methylphenidate significantly increase extracellular dopamine in the human brain. *Journal of Neuroscience, 21,* 1–5.

Volling, B. L., & Belsky, J. (1992). The contribution of mother–child and father–child relationships to the quality of sibling interaction: A longitudinal study. *Child Development, 63,* 1209–1222.

Vondra, J. I., & Barnett, D. (1999). Atypical attachment in infancy and early childhood among children at developmental risk. *Monographs of the Society for Research in Child Development, 64,* (Serial No. 258).

Vygotsky, L. S. (1926/1997). *Educational psychology.* Delray Beach, FL: St. Lucie Press.

Vygotsky, L. S. (1979). *Mind in society: The development of higher mental processes.* Cambridge, MA: Harvard University Press. (Original works published 1930, 1933, and 1935.)

Wachs, T. D. (1992). *The nature of nurture.* Newbury Park, CA: Sage.

Wachs, T. D. (1993). The nature-nurture gap: What we have here is a failure to collaborate. In R. Plomin, & G. E. McClearn (Eds.), *Nature, nurture, and psychology.* Washington, DC: American Psychological Association.

Wachs, T. D. (1996). Known and potential processes underlying developmental trajectories in childhood and adolescence. *Developmental Psychology, 32,* 796–801.

Wagner, R. K., & Sternberg, R. J. (1985). Alternate conceptions of intelligence and their implications for education. *Review of Educational Research, 54,* 179–223.

Wagner, R. K., & Sternberg, R. J. (1991). *Tacit knowledge inventory.* San Antonio, TX: The Psychological Corporation.

Wagner, W.G., Smith, D., & Norris, W.R. (1988). The pschological adjustment of enuretic children: A comparison of two types. *Journal of Pediatric Psychology, 13,* 33–38.

Wahlsten, D., & Gottlieb, G. (1997). The invalid separation of effects of nature and nurture: Lessons from animal experimentation. In R. S. Sternberg & E. L. Grigorenko (Eds.), *Intelligence, heredity, and environment* (pp. 163–192). New York: Cambridge University Press.

Wakeley, A., Rivera, S., & Langer, J. (2000). Can young infants add and subtract? *Child Development, 71,* 1525–1534.

Walden, T. A., & Baxter, A. (1989). The effect of context and age on social referencing. *Child Development, 60,* 1230–1240.

Walden, T. A., & Ogan, T. A. (1988). The development of social referencing. *Child Development, 59,* 1240–1249.

Walker, A. J., & Pratt, C. C. (1991). Daughters' help to mothers: Intergenerational aid versus caregiving. *Journal of Marriage and the Family, 53,* 3–12.

Walker, A. J., Thompson, L., & Morgan, C. S. (1987). Two generations of mothers and daughters: Role position and interdependence. *Psychology of Women Quarterly, 11,* 195–208.

Walker, I., & Mann, L. (1987). Unemployment, relative deprivation, and social protest. *Personality and Social Psychology Bulletin, 13,* 275–283.

Walker, L. (1984). *The battered woman syndrome.* New York: Springer.

Walker, L. E. (1989). Psychology and violence against women. *American Psychologist, 44,* 695–702.

Walker, L. E. (1999). Psychology and domestic violence around the world. *American Psychologist, 54,* 21–29.

Walker, N. C., & O'Brien, B. (1999). The relationship between method of pain management during labor and birth outcomes. *Clinical Nursing Research, 8,* 119–134.

Walker-Andrews, A. S. (1997). Infants' perception of expressive behaviors: Differentiation of multimodal information. *Psychological Bulletin, 121,* 437–456.

Walker-Andrews, A. S., & Dickson, L. R. (1997). Infants' understanding of affect. In S. Hala (Ed.), *The development of social cognition: Studies in developmental psychology* (pp. 161–186). Hove, England: Psychology Press/Erlbaum.

Walker-Andrews, A. S., & Lennon, E. (1991). Infants' discrimination of vocal expressions: Contributions of auditory and visual information. *Infant Behavior and Development, 14,* 131–142.

Wallace, I. F., Rose, S. A., McCarton, C. M., Kurtzberg, D., & Vaughan, H. G., Jr. (1995). Relations between infant neurobehavioral performance and cognitive outcome in very low birthweight preterm infants. *Developmental and Behavioral Pediatrics, 16,* 309–317.

Wallerstein, J. S., & Blakeslee, S. (1989). *Second chances.* New York: Ticknor & Fields.

Wallerstein, J. S., Lewis, J. M., & Blakeslee, S. (2000). *The unexpected legacy of divorce.* New York: Hyperion.

Wallis, C. (1994, July 18). Life in overdrive. *Time,* pp. 42–50.

Walsh, B. T., & Devlin, M. J. (1998, May 29). Eating disorders: Progress and problems. *Science, 280,* 1387–1390.

Walster, H. E., & Walster, G. W. (1978). *Love.* Reading, MA: Addison-Wesley.

Walter, A. (1997). The evolutionary psychology of mate selection in Morocco: A multivariate analysis. *Human Nature, 8,* 113–137.

Walther, V. N. (1997). Postpartum depression: A review for perinatal social workers. *Social Work in Health Care, 24,* 99–111.

Wang, M. C., Peverly, S. T., & Catalano, R. (1987). Integrating special needs students in regular classes: Programming, implementation, and policy issues. *Advances in Special Education, 6,* 119–149.

Wang, M. C., Reynolds, M. C., & Walberg, H. J. (Eds.). (1996). *Handbook of special and remedial education: Research and practice* (2nd ed.). New York: Pergamon Press.

Wang, Z. W., Black, D., Andreasen, N. C., & Crowe, R. R. (1993). A linkage study of chromosome 11q in schizophrenia. *Archives of General Psychiatry, 50,* 212–216.

Wannamethee, S. G., Shaper, A. G., Walker, M., & Ebrahim, S. (1998). Lifestyle and 15-year survival free of heart attack, stroke, and diabetes in middle-aged British men. *Archives of Internal Medicine, 158,* 2433–2440.

Ward, R. A. (1984). *The aging experience: An introduction to social gerontology.* (2nd ed.). New York: Harper & Row.

Warin, J. (2000). The attainment of self-consistency through gender in young children. *Sex Roles, 42,* 209–231.

Warren, C. W., Kann, L., Small, M. L., & Santelli, J. S. (1997). Age of initiating selected health-risk behaviors among high school students in the United States. *Journal of Adolescent Health, 21,* 225–231.

Warrick, P. (1991, October 30). What the doctors have to say. *The Los Angeles Times,* p. E4.

Warshak, R. A. (2000). Remarriage as a trigger of parental alienation syndrome. *American Journal of Family Therapy, 28,* 229–241.

Waterman, A. (1982). Identity development from adolescence to adulthood: An extension of theory and a review of research. *Developmental Psychology, 18,* 341–358.

Waters, E., Merrick, S., Treboux, D., Crowell, J., & Albersheim, L. (2000). Attachment security in infancy and early adulthood: A twenty-year longitudinal study. *Child Development, 71,* 684–689.

Waters, E., Weinfield, N. S., & Hamilton, C. E. (2000). The stability of attachment security from infancy to adolescence and early adulthood: General discussion. *Child Development, 71,* 703–706.

Watkins, D., Dong, Q., & Xia, Y. (1997). Age and gender differences in the self-esteem of Chinese children. *Journal of Social Psychology, 137,* 374–379.

Watson, J. B. (1925). *Behaviorism.* New York: Norton.

Watson, J. K. (2000). Theory of mind and pretend play in family context. (False belief). *Dissertation Abstracts International: Section B: The Sciences & Engineering, 60,* 3599.

Waugh, E., & Bulik, C. M. (1999). Offspring of women with eating disorders. *International Journal of Eating Disorders, 25,* 123–133.

Weber, K. S., Frankenberger, W., & Heilman, K. (1992). The effects of Ritalin on the academic achievement of children diagnosed with attention-deficit hyperactivity disorder. *Developmental Disabilities Bulletin, 20,* 49–68.

Webster, R. A., Hunter, M., & Keats, J. A. (1994). Peer and parental influences on adolescents' substance use: A path analysis. *International Journal of the Addictions, 29,* 647–657.

Wechler, Issac, Grodstein, & Sellers (2000). *College binge drinking in the 1990s: a continuing problem: results of the Harvard School of Public Health 1999 College Health Alcohol Study.* Cambridge, MA: Harvard University.

Wechsler, D. (1975). Intelligence defined and undefined. *American Psychologist, 30,* 135–139.

Wechsler, H., Rohman, M., & Solomon, R. (1981). Emotional problems and concerns of New England college students. *American Journal of Orthopsychiatry, 51,* 719.

Weed, K., Ryan, E. B., & Day, J. (1990). Metamemory and attributions as mediators of strategy use and recall. *Journal of Educational Psychology, 82,* 849–855.

Wegman, M. E. (1993). Annual summary of vital statistics—1992. *Pediatrics, 92,* 743–754.

Weinberg, M. K., & Tronick, E. Z. (1996a). Beyond the face: An empirical study of infant affective configurations of facial, vocal, gestural, and regulatory behaviors. *Child Development, 67,* 905–914.

Weinberg, R. A. (1989). Intelligence and IQ: Landmark issues and great debates. *American Psychologist, 44(2),* 98–104.

Weinberger, D. R. (2001, March 10). A brain too young for good judgment. *The New York Times,* p. D1.

Weindruch, R. (1996, January). Caloric restriction and aging. *Scientific American,* 46–52.

Weiner, B. (1985). *Human motivation.* New York: Springer-Verlag.

Weiner, B. (1994). Integrating social and personal theories of achievement striving. *Review of Educational Research, 64,* 557–573.

Weinfield, N. S., Sroufe, L. A., & Egeland, B. (2000). Attachment from infancy to early adulthood in a high-risk sample: Continuity, discontinuity, and their correlates. *Child Development, 71,* 695–702.

Weisninger, H. (1998 March 14). Tutored by television. *TV Guide,* pp. 46, 48.

Weiss, A. S. (1991). The measurement of self-actualization: The quest for the test may be as challenging as the search for the self. *Journal of Social Behavior and Personality, 6,* 265–290.

Weiss, M. R., Ebbeck, V., & Horn. T. S. (1997). Children's self-perceptions and sources of physical competence information: A cluster analysis. *Journal of Sport & Exercise Psychology, 19,* 52–70.

Wellman, H. M., & Gelman, S. A. (1992). Cognitive development: Foundational theories of core domains. *Annual Review of Psychology, 43,* 337–375.

Wells, A. S., & Crain, R. L. (1994). Perpetuation theory and the long-term effects of school desegregation. *Review of Educational Research, 64,* 531–555.

Wells, K. B., Golding, J. M., & Hough, R. L. (1989). Acculturation and the probability of use of services by Mexican-Americans. *Health Services Research, 24,* 237–257.

Wenar, C. (1994). *Developmental psychopathology: From infancy through adolescence* (3rd ed.). New York: McGraw-Hill.

Wenner, M. V. (1994). Depression, anxiety, and negative affectivity in elementary-aged learning disabled children. *Dissertation Abstracts International: Section B: the Sciences & Engineering.* Vol 54(9–B), 4938.

Werner, E. E. (1972). Infants around the world: Cross-cultural studies of psychomotor development from birth to two years. *Journal of Cross-Cultural Psychology, 3,* 111–134.

Werner, E. E. (1993). Risk resilience, and recovery: Perspectives from the Kauai Longitudinal Study. *Development and Psychopathology, 5,* 503–515.

Werner, E. E. (1995). Resilience in development. *Current Directions in Psychological Science, 4,* 81–85.

Werner, E. E., & Smith, R. S. (1992). *Overcoming the odds: High risk children from birth to adulthood.* Ithaca, New York: Cornell University Press.

Werner, L. A., & Marean, G. C. (1996). *Human auditory development.* Boulder, CO: Westview Press.

Wertsch, J. V., & Tulviste, P. (1992). L. S. Vygotsky and contemporary developmental psychology. *Developmental Psychology, 28,* 548–557.

Westen, D. (1990). Psychoanalytic approaches to personality. In L. A. Previn (Ed.), *Handbook of personality: Theory and research.* New York: Guilford.

Wethington, E., Cooper, H., & Holmes, C. S. (1997). Turning points in midlife. In I. H. Gotlib & B. Wheaton (Eds.), *Stress and adversity over the life course: Trajectories and turning points* (pp. 215–231). New York: Cambridge University Press.

Whaley, B. B., Parker, R. G. (2000). Expressing the experience of communicative disability: Metaphors of persons who stutter. *Communication Reports, 13,* 115–125.

Wheeler, G. (1998, March 13). The wake-up call we dare not ignore. *Science, 279,* 1611.

Whitaker, R. C., Wright, J. A., Pepe, M. S., Seidel, K. D., & Dietz, W. H. (1997, September 25). Predicting obesity in young adulthood from childhood and parental obesity. *The New England Journal of Medicine, 337,* 869–873.

Whitbourne, S. K. (1986). *Adult development* (2nd ed.). New York: Praeger.

Whitbourne, S. K., & Wills, K. (1993). Psychological issues in institutional care of the aged. In S. B. Goldsmith (Ed.), *Long-term care.* Gaithersburg, MD: Aspen.

Whitbourne, S., Jacobo, M., & Munoz-Ruiz, M. (1996). Adversity in the elderly. In R. S. Feldman (Ed.), The psychology of adversity. Amherst: University of Massachusetts Press.

Whitbourne, S. K., Zuschlag, M. K., Elliot, L. B., & Waterman, A. S. (1992). Psychosocial development in adulthood: A 22-year sequential study. *Journal of Personality and Social Psychology, 63,* 260–271.

Whitbourne, S. K. (1996). The aging individual: Physical and psychological perspectives. New York: Springer.

Whitbourne, S. K. (2001). *Adult development and aging: Biopsychosocial perspectives.* New York: Wiley.

Whitehurst, G. J., & Fischel, J. E. (2000). Reading and language impairments in conditions of poverty. In D. V. M. Bishop, & L. B. Leonard (Eds.), *Speech and language impairments in children: Causes, characteristics, intervention and outcome.* Philadelphia: Psychology Press/Taylor & Francis.

Whitelson, S. (1989, March). *Sex differences.* Paper presented at the annual meeting of the New York Academy of Science, New York.

Whiteman, M. C., Deary, I. J., Fowkes, F., & Gerry R. (2000). Personality and health: Cardiovascular disease. In S. E. Hampson, (Ed.), et al., *Advances in personality psychology, Vol. 1.* Philadelphia, PA: Psychology Press/Taylor & Francis.

Whiting, B. B., & Edwards, C. P. (1988). *Children of different worlds: The formation of social behavior.* Cambridge, MA: Harvard University Press.

Wickelgren, I. (1996, March 1). Is hippocampal cell death a myth? *Science, 271,* 1229–1230.

Wickelgren, W. A. (1999). Webs, cell assemblies, and chunking in neural nets: Introduction. *Canadian Journal of Experimental Psychology, 53,* 118–131.

Wideman, M. V., & Singer, J. F. (1984). The role of psychological mechanisms in preparation for childbirth. *American Psychologist, 34,* 1357–1371.

Widom, C. S. (2000). Motivation and mechanisms in the "cycle of violence" In D. J. Hansen (Ed.), *Nebraska Symposium on Motivation Vol. 46, 1998: Motivation and child maltreatment* (Current theory and research in motivation series). Lincoln, NE: University of Nebraska Press.

Wierson, M., & Forehand, R. (1994). Parent behavioral training for child noncompliance: Rationale, concepts, and effectiveness. *Current Directions in Psychological Science, 3,* 146–150.

Wilcox, A., Skjaerven, R., Buekens, P., & Kiely, J. (1995, March 1). Birth weight and perinatal mortality: A comparison of the United States and Norway. *Journal of the American Medical Association, 273,* 709–711.

Wilcox, M. D. (1992). Boomerang kids. *Kiplinger's Personal Finance Magazine, 46,* 83–86.

Williams, D., & Griffen, L. (1991). Elder abuse in the black family. In R. Hampton (Ed.), *Black family violence: Current research and theory.* Lexington, MA: Lexington Books.

Williams, J. M., & Currie, C. (2000). Self esteem and physical development in early adolescence: Pubertal timing and body image. *Journal of Early Adolescence, 20,* 129–149.

Williamson, G. M., & Schulz, R. (1993). Coping with specific stressors in Alzheimer's disease caregiving. *Gerontologist, 33,* 747–755.

Willis, S. (1996). Everyday problem solving. In J. E. Birren, K. W. Schaic, R. P. Abeles, M.Gatz, & T. A. Salthouse (Eds.), *Handbook of the psychology of aging* (4th ed.). San Diego: Academic Press.

Willis, S. L. (1985). Educational psychology of the older adult learner. In J. E. Birren & K. W. Schaie (Eds.), *Handbook of the psychology of aging* (2nd ed.). New York: Van Nostrand Reinhold.

Willis, S. L., & Nesselroade, C. S. (1990). Long-term effects of fluid ability training in old-old age. *Developmental Psychology, 26,* 905–910.

Willis, S. L., Jay, G. M., Diehl, M., & Marsiske, M. (1992). Longitudinal change and prediction of everyday task competence in the elderly. *Research on Aging, 14,* 68–91.

Wilmoth, J. R., Deegan, L. J., Lundström, & Horiuchi, S. (2000, September 29). Increase of maximum lifespan in Sweden, 1861–1999. *Science, 289,* 2366–2368.

Wilmut, I. (1998). Cloning for medicine. *Scientific American, 279,* 58–63.

Wilson, M. N. (1989). Child development in the context of the black extended family. *American Psychologist, 44,* 380–385.

Wilson, R. S. (1983). The Louisville twin study: Developmental synchronies in behavior. *Child Development, 54,* 298–316.

Windle, M. (1994). A study of friendship characteristics and problem behaviors among middle adolescents. *Child Development, 65,* 1764–1777.

Wineburg, S. S. (1987). The self-fulfillment of the self-fulfilling prophecy. *Educational Researcher, 16,* 28–37.

Wingert, P., & Kantrowitz, B. (1997, October 27). Why Andy couldn't read (Bright children who are also learning disabled). *Newsweek, 130,* p56.

Winn, R. L., & Newton, N. (1982). Sexuality in aging: A study of 106 cultures. *Archives of Sexual Behavior, 11,* 283–298.

Winner, E. (1997). *Gifted children: Myths and realities.* New York: Basic Books.

Winsler, A., Diaz, R. M., & Montero, I. (1997). The role of private speech in the transition from collaborative to independent task performance in young children. *Early Childhood Research Quarterly, 12,* 59–79.

Wise, P. M., Krajnak, K. M., & Kashon, M. L. (1996, July 5). Menopause: The aging of multiple pacemakers. *Science, 273,* 67–70.

Wisnia, S. (1994, June 27). On the right track. *The Washington Post,* p. D5.

Witelson, S. (1989, March). *Sex differences.* Paper presented at the annual meeting of the New York Academy of Science, New York.

Witt, S. D. (1997). Parental influence on children's socialization to gender roles. *Adolescence, 32,* 253–259.

Wolf, A. M., Gortmaker, S. L., Cheung, L., & Gray, H. M. (1993). Activity, inactivity, and obesity: Racial, ethnic, and age differences among schoolgirls. *American Journal of Public Health, 83,* 1625–1627.

Wolff, P. H. (1963). Observations of the early development of smiling. In B. M. Foss (Ed.), *Determinants of infant behaviour* (Vol 4). London: Methuen.

Wolfner, G., Faust, D., & Dawes, R. M. (1993). The use of anatomically detailed dolls in sexual abuse evaluations: The state of the science. *Applied & Preventive Psychology, 2,* 1–11.

Wolfson, C., Handfield-Jones, R., Glass, K. C., McClaran, J., et al. (1993). Adult children's perceptions of their responsibility to provide care for dependent elderly parents. *Gerontologist, 33,* 315–323.

Wong, B. Y. L. (1996). *The ABCs of learning disabilities.* New York: Academic Press.

Wood, D., Bruner, J. S., & Ross, G. (1976). The role of tutoring in problem solving. *Journal of Child Psychology & Psychiatry & Allied Disciplines, 17,* 89–100.

Wood, J. (1989). Theory and research concerning social comparisons of personal attributes. *Psychological Bulletin, 106,* 231–248.

Wood, R. (1997). Trends in multiple births, 1938–1995. *Population Trends, 87,* 29–35.

Wood, W., Wong, F. Y., & Chachere, J. G. (1991). Effects of media violence on viewers' aggression in unconstrained social interaction. *Psychological Bulletin, 109,* 371–383.

Woolfolk, A. E. (1993). *Educational psychology* (5th ed.). Boston: Allyn & Bacon.

World Conference on Education for All. (1990, April). *World declaration on education for all and framework for action to meet basic learning needs,* Preamble, p. 1. New York: Author.

World Food Council. (1992). *The global state of hunger and malnutrition. 1992 report.* Table 2, p. 8. New York: Author.

World Health Organization. (1999). *Death rates from coronary heart disease.* Geneva: World Health Organization.

Worobey, J., & Bajda, V. M. (1989). Temperament ratings at 2 weeks, 2 months, and 1 year: Differential stability of activity and emotionality. *Developmental Psychology, 25,* 257–263.

Wortman, C. B., & Silver, R. C. (1990). Successful mastery of bereavement and widowhood: A life-course perspective. In P. B. Baltes & M. M. Baltes (Eds.), *Successful aging: Perspectives from the behavioral sciences.* Cambridge, England: Cambridge University Press.

Wortman, C., & Silver, R. C. (1989). The myths of coping with loss. *Journal of Consulting and Clinical Psychology, 57,* 349–357.

Wright, J. C., Huston, A. C., Reitz, A. L., & Piemyat, S. (1994). Young children's perceptions of television reality: Determinants and developmental differences. *Developmental Psychology, 30,* 229–239.

Wright, J. C., Huston, A. C., Truglio, R., Fitch, M., Smith, E., & Piemyat, S. (1995). Occupational portrayals on television: Children's role schemata, career aspirations, and perceptions of reality. *Child Development, 66,* 1706–1718.

Wright, R. (1995, March 13). The biology of violence. *New Yorker,* pp. 68–77.

Wright, S. C., Taylor, D. M. (1995). Identity and the language of the classroom: Investigation of the impact of heritage versus second language instruction on personal and collective self-esteem. *Journal of Educational Psychology, 87,* 241–252.

Wygant, S. A. (1997). Moral reasoning about real-life dilemmas: Paradox in research using the defining issues test. *Personality and Social Psychology Bulletin, 23,* 1022–1033.

Wynn, K. (1992, August 27). Addition and subtraction by human infants. *Nature, 358,* 749–750.

Wynn, K. (1995). Infants possess a system of numerical knowledge. *Current Directions in Psychological Science, 4,* 172–177.

Wynn, K. (2000). Findings of addition and subtraction in infants are robust and consistent: Reply to Wakeley, Rivera, and Langer. *Child Development, 71,* 1535–1536.

Xiaohe, X., & Whyte, M. K. (1990). Love matches and arranged marriages: A Chinese replication. *Journal of Marriage and the Family, 52,* 709–722.

Yankelovich, D. (1974, December). Turbulence in the working world: Angry workers, happy grads. *Psychology Today, 8,* 80–87.

Yardley, J. (2001, July 2). Child-death case in Texas raises penalty questions. *The New York Times,* p. A1.

Yarrow, L. (1990, September). Does my child have a problem? *Parents,* p. 72.

Yarrow, L. (1992, November). Giving birth: 72,000 moms tell all. *Parents,* pp. 148–159.

Yarrow, M. R., Scott, P. M., & Waxler, C. Z. (1973). Learning concern for others. *Developmental Psychology, 8,* 240–260.

Yee, M., & Brown, R. (1994). The development of gender differentiation in young children. *British Journal of Social Psychology, 33,* 183–196.

Yell, M. L. (1995). The least restrictive environment mandate and the courts: Judicial activism or judicial restraint? *Exceptional Children, 61,* 578–581.

Yelland, G. W., Pollard, J., & Mercuri, A. (1993). The metalinguistic benefits of limited contact with a second language. *Applied Psycholinguistics, 14,* 423–444.

Yerkes, R. M. (1923). *A point scale for measuring mental ability. A 1923 revision.* Baltimore, MD: Warwick & York.

Yllo, K. (1983). Using a feminist approach in quantitative research: A case study. In D. Finkelhor, R. J. Gelles, G. Hotaling, & M. A. Straus (Eds.), *The dark side of families.* Beverly Hills, CA: Sage.

Yllo, K., & Bograd, M. (Eds.). (1988). *Feminist perspectives on wife abuse.* Berekely, CA: Sage.

Young, H., & Ferguson, L. (1979). Developmental changes through adolescence in the spontaneous nomination of reference groups as a function of decision context. *Journal of Youth and Adolescence, 8,* 239–252.

Youniss, J. (1989). Parent–adolescent relationships. In W. Damon (Ed.), *Child development today and tomorrow.* San Francisco: Jossey-Bass.

Youniss, J., & Haynie, D. L. (1992). Friendship in adolescence. *Journal of Developmental and Behavioral Pediatrics, 13,* 59–66.

Yuill, N., & Perner, J. (1988). Intentionality and knowledge in children's judgments of actor's responsibility and recipient's emotional reaction. *Developmental Psychology, 24,* 358–365.

Zahn-Waxler, C., & Radke-Yarrow, M. (1990). The origins of empathic concern. *Motivation and Emotion, 14,* 107–130.

Zahn-Waxler, C., Robinson, J. L., & Emde, R. N. (1992). The development of empathy in twins. *Developmental Psychology, 28,* 1038–1047.

Zaidel, D. W. (1994). Worlds apart: Pictorial semantics in the left and right cerebral hemispheres. *Current Directions in Psychological Science, 3,* 5–8.

Zanjani, E. D., & Anderson, W. F. (1999, September 24). Prospects for in utero human gene therapy. *Science, 285,* 2084–2088.

Zarit, S. H., & Reid, J. D. (1994). Family caregiving and the older family. In C. B. Fisher & R. M. Lerner

(Eds.), *Applied developmental psychology.* New York: McGraw-Hill.

Zauszniewski, J. A., & Martin, M. H. (1999). Developmental task achievement and learned resourcefulness in healthy older adults. *Archives of Psychiatric Nursing, 13,* 41–47.

Zautra, A. J., Reich, J. W., & Guarnaccia, C. A. (1990). Some everyday life consequences of disability and bereavement for older adults. *Journal of Personality and Social Psychology, 59,* 550–561.

Zelazo, N., Zelazo, P. R., Cohen, K., & Zelazo, P. D. (1993). Specificity of practice effects on elementary neuromotor patterns. *Developmental Psychology, 29,* 686–691.

Zelazo, P. R. (1998). McGraw and the development of unaided walking. *Developmental Review, 18,* 449–471.

Zeskind, P. S., & Ramey, D. T. (1981). Preventing intellectual and interactional sequels of fetal malnutrition: A longitudinal, transactional, and synergistic approach to development. *Child Development, 52,* 213–218.

Zevon, M., & Corn, B. (1990). Paper presented at the annual meeting of the American Psychological Association, Boston.

Zigler, E., & Gilman, E. (1998). The legacy of Jean Piaget. In G. A. Kimble, M. Wertheimer, et al. (Eds.), *Portraits of pioneers in psychology, Vol. 3.* Mahwah, NJ: American Psychological Association.

Zigler, E. F., & Finn-Stevenson, M. (1995). The child care crisis: Implications for the growth and development of the nation's children. *Journal of Social Issues, 51,* 215–231.

Zigler, E., & Styfco, S. J. (1994). Head Start: Criticism in a constructive context. *American Psychologist, 49,* 127–132.

Zigler, E., Styfco, S. J., & Gilman, E. (1993). The national Head Start program for disadvantaged preschoolers. In E. Zigler & S. J. Styfco (Eds.), *Head Start and beyond: A national plan for extended childhood intervention* (pp. 1–41). New Haven, CT: Yale University Press.

Zillman, D. (1993). Mental control of angry aggression. In D. M. Wegner & J. W. Pennebaker (Eds.), *Handbook of mental control.* Englewood Cliffs, NJ: Prentice-Hall.

Zimmerman, M. A., & Arunkumar, R. (1994). Resiliency research: Implications for schools and policy. *Social Policy Report, 8,* 1–18.

Zito, J. M., Safer, D. J., dosReis, S., Gardner, J. F., Boles, M., & Lynch, F. (2000). Trends in prescribing of psychotropic medications to preschoolers. *Journal of the American Medical Association, 283,* 1025–1030.

Acknowledgments

Photographs

Chapter 1 Page 2 Ken Sherman, Phototake NYC; p. 3 Jose Cibelli (Courtesy of Dr. Cibelli of Advanced Cell Technology); p. 6 The Image Works; p. 9 Spencer Grant, PhotoEdit; p. 15 Lewis Hime, CORBIS; p. 16 CORBIS; p. 17 Jon Erikson, Courtesy of the Library of Congress; p. 19 Getty Images Inc.; p. 20 Everett Collection, Inc.; p. 23 Daniel Wray, The Image Works; p. 34 PhotoEdit; p. 25 Nina Leen, TimePix; p. 27 (top, left) Laura Dwight, Laura Dwight Photography; p. 27 (top, right) Sean Sprague; p. 27 (bottom, left) Laura Dwight, Laura Dwight Photography; p. 27 (bottom, right) Laura Dwight, Laura Dwight Photography; p. 30 Alexander Tsiaras, Stock Boston; p. 33 Courtesy of Donald J. Hernandez, Ph.D.; p. 37 George Shelley, Corbis/Stock Market

Chapter 2 Page 44 Stockphoto.com; page 45 Keri Pickett, People/InStyle Syndicaiton; page 47 (left) Don W. Fawcett, Photo Researchers, Inc.; p. 47 (middle) L. Willatt, E. Anglian Regional Genetics Srvc/Science Photo Library, Photo Researchers, Inc.; p. 47 (right) Peter Menzel, Stock Boston; p. 54 Bill Longcore, Photo Researchers, Inc.; p. 56 Jim Pickerell, The Image Works; p. 58 Jessica Wecker Photography © 1995 Jessica Boyatt; p. 60 The Cartoon Bank; p. 62 Aaron Haupt, Stock Boston; p. 65 B. Daemmrich, The Image Works; p. 67 The Cartoon Bank; p. 73 Dr. Yorgos Nikas, Photo Researchers, Inc.; p. 75 Bradley Smith; p. 76 Photo Researchers, Inc.; p. 78 John Chiasson, Getty Images, Inc.

Chapter 3 Page 84 David Muir, Masterfile Corporatin; p. 85 Vince Messina, MetroHealth Medical Center; p. 87 (left) Michael Newman, PhotoEdit; p. 87 (right) Owen Franken, CORBIS; p. 89 Michael Newman, PhotoEdit; p. 91 Peter Byron, Photo Researchers, Inc.; p. 92 Lawrence Migdale, Stock Boston; p. 94 Owen Franken, CORBIS; p. 97 Ansell Horn, Phototake NYC; p. 103 Michael Newman, PhotoEdit; p. 104 Michael Newman, PhotoEdit; p. 107 Myrleen Ferguson, PhotoEdit; p. 108 Laura Dwight, Laura Dwight Photography; p. 111 Laura Dwight, PictureQuest Vienna

Chapter 4 Page 116 Comstock Images; p. 117 Bob Daemmrich, The Image Works; p. 124 (left) Comstock Images; p. 124 (right) Comstock Images; p. 126 Ed Bock, Corbis/Stock Market; p. 129 (left) Laura Elliott, Comstock Images; p. 129 (middle) L. J. Weinstein, Woodfin Camp Associates; p. 129 (right) Laura Dwight Photography; p. 131 Laura Dwight, Laura Dwight Photography; p. 137 (top) Jose L. Pelaez, Corbis/Stock Market; p. 137 (bottom) Stuart Cohen, Comstock Images; p. 139 Bob Daemmrich, The Image Works; p. 139 The Cartoon Bank; p. 141 (top) Lawrence Migdale, Stock Boston; p. 141 (bottom) Mark Richards, PhotoEdit/Courtesy of Joe Campos & Rosanne Kermoian; p. 142 Michael Newman, PhotoEdit; p. 143 Owen Franken, CORBIS; p. 146 Laura Dwight, PhotoEdit

Chapter 5 Page 150 Camille Tokerud, Camille Tokerud Photography; p. 151 PictureQuest Vienna; p. 152 CORBIS; p. 156 Laura Dwight, PhotoEdit; p. 158 Owen Franken, Stock Boston; p. 161 Mark Richards, PhotoEdit; p. 162 David Sanders, The Arizona Daily Star; p. 163 Carolyn Rovee-Collier; p. 164 Alexander Alland, The Image Works; p. 165 Peter Brandt, PictureQuest Vienna; p. 169 Robert Brenner, PhotoEdit; p. 170 Helen I. Shwe; p. 173 The Image Works; p. 174 (top) Laura-Ann Petitto, McGill University; p. 174 (bottom) Custom Medical Stock Photo, Inc.; p. 176 Myrleen Ferguson Cate, PhotoEdit; p. 179 Laura Dwight Photography

Chapter 6 Page 184 Larry Williams, Masterfile Corporation; p. 185 Jan Mueller Photography; p. 187 (top, left) Courtesy Dr. Carroll Izard; p. 187 (bottom, left) Courtesy Dr. Carroll Izard; p. 187 (top, right) Courtesy Dr. Carroll Izard; p. 187 (bottom, right) Courtesy Dr. Carroll Izard; p. 189 Gary Conner, PictureQuest Vienna; p. 191 Laura Dwight Photography; p. 193 Fredrik D. Bodin; p. 194 Harlow Primate Laboratory; p. 195 Mary Ainsworth, University of Virginia; p. 196 (left) William Hamilton/Johns Hopkins University, Mary Ainsworth; p. 196 (middle) William Hamilton/Johns Hopkins University, Mary Ainsworth; p. 196 (right) William Hamilton/Johns Hopkins University, Mary Ainsworth; p. 197 Cleo Photography, PhotoEdit; p. 198 Keith Brofsky, PictureQuest Vienna; p. 200 Ken Straitor, Corbis/Stock Market; p. 203 Mark Andersen/RubberBall Productions, PictureQuest Vienna; p. 207 George Goodwin; p. 208 (top) Richard Lord, The Image Works; p. 208 (bottom) A. Ramey, PhotoEdit

Chapter 7 Page 214 Rommel; Masterfile Corporation; p. 215 Robert Harbison; p. 217 Laura Dwight Photography; p. 222 G. Degrazia, Custom Medical Stock Photo, Inc.; p. 223 Marcus E. Raichle, M.D.; p. 225 (left) Charles Gupton, Stock Boston; p. 225 (right) Skyold Photographs; p. 226 Ellen Senisi, The Image Works; p. 230 (left) Laura Dwight; Laura Dwight Photography; p. 230 (right) Laura Dwight, Laura Dwight Photograpy; p. 235 Steve Warmowski, The Image Works; p. 237 Mike Derer, AP/Wide World Photos; p. 240 PhotoEdit; p. 253 Robert Recio, Jr.

Chapter 8 Page 256 Rommel, Masterfile Corporation; p. 257 Myrleen Ferguson Cate, PhotoEdit; p. 259 Ursula Markus, Photo Researchers, Inc.; p. 262 (left) Laura Dwight, Laura Dwight Photography; 262 (right) The Image Works; p. 263 (top) Spencer Grant, Stock Boston; p. 263 (bottom) Myrleen Ferguson Cate, PhotoEdit; p. 267 J. Greenberg, The Image Works; p. 268 Jeff Greenberg, PhotoEdit; p. 269 Arlene Collins; p. 270 Nancy Richmond, The Image Works; p. 271 Frank Polich, AP/Wide World Photos; p. 274 Stephen Agricola, The Image Works; p. 279 Ellen Senisi, The Image Works; p. 280 Michelle Bridwell, PhotoEdit; p. 282 The Cartoon Bank; p. 283 Catherine Ursillo, Photo Researchers, Inc.; p. 284 Rick Kopstein; p. 285 Albert Bandura

Chapter 9 Page 292 Rommel, Masterfile Corporation; p. 293 Michelle Agins, New York Times Pictures; p. 295 Mary Kate Denny, PhotoEdit; p. 297 The Cartoon Bank; p. 299 Richard Hutchings, PhotoEdit; p. 301 Lester Sloan, Woodfin Camp & Associates; p. 304 Brent M. Jones, Stock Boston; p. 306 Jose Azel, Aurora & Quanta Productions; p. 309 Lawrence Migdale/Pix; p. 310 Penny Tweedie, Woodfin Camp & Associates; p. 313 Michael Newman, PhotoEdit; p. 316 B. Daemmrich, The Image Works; p. 318 US Department of Education; p. 322 Myrleen Ferguson, PhotoEdit; p. 327 B. Daemmrich, The Image Works; p. 331 Laura Dwight, PhotoEdit; p. 335 David Turnley, CORBIS; p. 339 Richard Hutchings, Photo Researchers, Inc.

Chapter 10 Page 344 Jim Craigmyle, Masterfile Corporation; p. 345 Cary Wolinsky, Stock Boston; p. 347 D. Young-Wolff, PhotoEdit; p. 349 Robert Houser, Comstock Images; p. 351 Lew Merrim, Photo Researcher, Inc.; p. 352 Richard Lord, The Image Works; p. 355 D. Young-Wolff, PhotoEdit; p. 357 Bob Daemmrich, The Image Works; p. 360 Bob Daemmrich, Stock Boston; p. 361 Richard Hutchings, PhotoEdit; p. 363 Jeff Greenberg, PhotoEdit; p. 368 McClynn, The Image Works; p. 370 (top) Phil Borden, PhotoEdit; p. 370 (bottom) Comstock Images; p. 371 (left) CORBIS; p. 371 (right) Melchior DiGiacomo; p. 373 Universal Press Syndicate; p. 374 B. Daemmrich The Image Works

Chapter 11 Page 383 The Terry Wild Studio, Inc.; p. 385 (top) Ellen Senisi, The Image Works; p. 385 (bottom) Ellen Senisi, The Image Works; p. 386 Ellen Senisi, The Image Works; p. 387 Tony Freeman, PhotoEdit; p. 390 (top) Express Newspapers, Getty Images Inc.; p. 390 (bottom) Bob Daemmrich, The Image Works; p. 392 The Image Works; p. 394 Bob Daemmrich, The Image Works; p. 395 Bob Daemmrich, The Image Works; p. 398 The Cartoon Bank; p. 401 Bob Daemmrich, The Image Works; p. 405 Arlene Collins, p. 406 Doreen Branch; p. 407 Jacques Chenet, Woodfin Camp & Associates; p. 409 Roger Mastroianni

Chapter 12 Page 414 Nancy Ney, Nancy Ney Studios, Inc.; p. 415 Dorothy Littell Greco, Stock Boston; p. 417 Jonathan Nourok, PhotoEdit; p. 419 Michael Newman, PhotoEdit; p. 419 Universal Press Syndicate; p. 420 D. Young Wolff, PhotoEdit; p. 423 Jonathan Nourok, PhotoEdit; p. 425 (top) G & M David de

Lossy, Getty Images Inc.; p. 425 (bottom) PhotoEdit; p. 427 Mary Kate Denny, PhotoEdit; p. 428 PhotoEdit; p. 429 R. Sidney, The Image Works; p. 431 Robert Brenner, PhotoEdit; p. 434 (top) Bob Daemmrich, Stock Boston; p. 434 (bottom) Ron Chapple, Getty Images, Inc.; p. 438 Michael Newman, PhotoEdit; p. 439 B. Daemmrich, The Image Works; p. 441 Paula Lerner, Woodfin Camp & Associates; p. 443 Evan Johnson

Chapter 13 Page 448 Nancy Battaglia, Nancie Battaglia Photography; p. 449 B. Daemmrich, The Image Works; p. 451 L. Kolvoord, The Image Works; p. 452 Adam Butler/Topham-PA, The Image Works; p. 454 Jeff Widener, Corbis/Sygma; p. 455 (top) Tony Freeman, PhotoEdit; p. 455 (bottom) B. Daemmrich, The Image Works; p. 456 David Pollack, Corbis/Stock Market; p. 458 Dr. Patricia Norris; p. 459 (left) Bob Daemmrich, The Image Works; p. 459 (right) John Eastcott/Yva Momatiuk, Woodfin Camp & Associates; p. 462 Drew Crawford, The Image Works; p. 464 Joseph Nettis, Stock Boston; p. 466 Bill Lai, The Image Works;p. 469 H. Dratch, The Image Works; p. 471 The Boston Globe; p. 472 Vicki Silbert, PhotoEdit; p. 474 PhotoEdit; p. 476 Jeff Greenberg, PhotoEdit

Chapter 14 Page 484 Comstock Images; p. 485 Anna Curtis; p. 488 Edward Keating, New York Times Pictures; p. 489 PhotoEdit; p. 490 Jeff Greenberg, The Image Works; p. 493 Haruki Sato/HAGA, The Image Works; p. 494 Journal–Courier/Joe Fasel, The Image Works; p. 498 Brian Yarvin, The Image Works; p. 499 Elena Rooraid, PhotoEdit; p. 500 B. Bachmann, The Image Works; p. 501 The Cartoon Bank; p. 503 Comstock Images; p. 506 David Young-Wolff, PhotoEdit; p. 507 Mark Richards, PhotoEdit; p. 508 The Cartoon Bank; p. 509 N. Richmond, The Image Works; p. 513 Rhoda Sidney, The Image Works

Chapter 15 Page 518 Dick Luria, Getty Images Inc.; p. 519 Brian Sipe; p. 522 Paul S. Conlkin, PhotoEdit; p. 524 Bonnie Ramin, PhotoEdit; p. 525 Getty Images, Inc.; p. 526 Doranne Jacobson, Doranne Jacobson/International Images; p. 528 Dana Fineman–Appel, Danna Fineman Appel; p. 530 Rhoda Sidney, PhotoEdit; p. 532 (left) Paul Barton, Corbis/Stock Market; p. 532 (right) George Goodwin; p. 535 Marc Romanelli, Getty Images Inc.; p. 536 Ebby May, Getty Images Inc.; p. 539 Amy C. Etra, PhotoEdit; p. 540 Robert Brenner, PhotoEdit; p. 541 Jack Vartoogian; p. 543 Rhoda Sidney, PhotoEdit; p. 544 Lawrence Migdale/Pix

Chapter 16 Page 550 Picture Perfect USA, Inc.; p. 551 Andrew Southam, aRT mIX (the agency); p. 552 D. Van Kirk, Getty Images Inc.; p. 556 Syracuse Newapapers/Al Campanie, The Image Works; p. 558 Michael J. Doolittle, The Image Works; p. 561 Paul W. Liebhart; p. 563 Flip Chalfant; Getty Images Inc.; p. 565 Ellen B. Senisi, The Image Works; p. 567 Richard Abamo, Corbis/Stock Market; p. 571 L. D. Gordon, Getty Images Inc.; p. 574 Cindy Marano; p. 575 Penny Wolin

Chapter 17 Page 582 Amwell, Getty Images Inc.; p. 583 Matt Klicker, The Image Works; p. 588 Joe Sohm, Corbis/Stock Market; p. 589 (left) Comstock Images; p. 589 (right) Benn Mitchell, Getty Images Inc.; p. 591 Dr. Douglas Rosene; p. 592 Paul Parker, Photo Researchers, Inc.; p. 595 Russ Kinee, Comstock Images; p. 596 Black Star; p. 597 The New England Journal of Medicine; p. 601 Peter Menzel, Stock Boston; p. 606 David Woods, Corbis/Stock Market; p. 609 Marcel Yva Malherbe, The Image Works

Chapter 18 Page 614 Comstock Images; p. 615 Hazel Hankin; p. 618 Roz Chast; p. 619 Cont/Reininger, Contact Press Images Inc.; p. 625 (left) Nathan Benn, Woodfin Camp & Associates; p. 625 (right) Lawrence Migdale, Lawrence Migdale/Pix; p. 628 E. Crews, The Image Works; p. 630 (left) Comstock Images; p. 630 (right) Comstock Images; p. 631 Mario Algaze, The Image Works; p. 634 Ted Kerasote, Photo Researchers, Inc.; p. 637 Rhoda Sidney; p. 639 The Image Works

Chapter 19 Page 646 Picture Perfect USA, Inc.; p. 647 Toni L. Sandys; p. Sean Cayton, The Image Works; p. 651 Paul Rezendes, Positive Images; p. 654 Arvind Garg, Photo Researchers, Inc.; p. 660 Herb Snitzer, Stock Boston; p. 663 A. Ramey, PhotoEdit; p. 664 Robert Picard; p. 666 David R. Frazier, David R. Frazier Photolibrary, Inc.; p. 667 Azerud, Corbis/Sygma

Frontmatter Page xxviii Robert S. Feldman

Figures and Tables

Chapter 1 Figure 1–1: From J. Kopp & J. B. Krakow, *Child development in the social context.* © 1982 by Addison Wesley Publishing Co., Inc. Reprinted by permission of Pearson Education, Inc.

Chapter 2 Figure 2–2: From Martin, J. A., & Park, M. M. (1999). Trends in twin and triplet births: 1980–1997. *National Vital Statistics Reports, 47,* 1–17; Figure 2–5: From J. W. Kimball, *Biology* (5th ed). Copyright © 1984. Reprinted by permission of the McGraw-Hill Companies; Figure 2–6: From Celera Genomics & International Humane Genome Sequencing Consortium, 2001; Figure 2–8: From T. J. Bouchard & M. McGue (1981). Familial studies of intelligence: A review. *Science, 264,* 1700–1701. Reprinted with permission of Dr. Matt McGue and Dr. Thomas Bouchard; Figure 2–9: From A. Tellegen et al. (1988). Personality similarity in twins reared apart and together. *Journal of Personality and Social Psychology, 54,* 1031–1039. Copyright © 1988 The American Psychological Association. Adapted with permission; Figure 2–10: From I. I. Gottesman, *Schizophrenia genesis: The origins of madness.* Copyright © 1991 by Irving I. Gottesman. Used with permission of W. H. Freeman and Co.; Figure 2–13: From K. L. Moore (1998). *Before we are born: Basic embryology and birth defects,* (5th ed.). Philadelphia: Saunders; Table 2–1: Reprinted with permission from McGuffin, P., Riley, B., & Plomin, R. (2001, Feb 16). Toward behavioral genomics. *Science, 291, 1232–1249.* Copyright 2001 American Association for the Advancement of Science; Table 2–3: From Kagan, J. Arcus, D., Snidman, N. (1993). The idea of temperament. Where do we go from here? In Plomin, R. & McCleary, G. E. (eds.) *Nature, nurture & psychology. Washington, DC: American Psychological Association.* Copyright © 1993 The American Psychological Association. Adapted with permission.

Chapter 3 Figure 3–2: Adapted from Finkelstein, D. L., Harper, D. A., & Rosenthal, G. E. (1998). Does length of hospital stay during labor and delivery influence patient satisfaction? Results from a regional study. *American Journal of Managed Care, 4,* 1701–1708; Figure 3–3: From National Center for Health Statistics (2001). *Health United States, 2000 with Adolescent Health Chartbook.* Hyattsville, MD: National Center for Health Statistics; Figure 3–4: From Infant and Child Health Studies Branch. (1997). *Survival rates of infants.* Washington, DC: National Center for Health Statistics; Figure 3–5: From F. C. Notzon (1990). International differences in the use of obstetric interventions. *Journal of the American Medical Assn., 263 (23).* 3286–3291; Figure 3–6: From National Center for Health Statistics (1997). *U.S. infant mortality rates by race of mother: 1975–1996.* Washington, DC; Public Health Service; Table 3–1: Adapted from Apgar, V. (1953). A proposal for a new method of evaluation in the newborn infant. *Current research in Anesthesia and Analgesia, 32, 260.* Used with permission of Lippincott, Wilkins & Williams; Table 3–2: Reprinted with permission from *Preventing low birthweight.* Copyright 1985 by the National Academy of Sciences. Courtesy of the National Academy Press, Washington, DC; Table 3–3: Adapted from International Labor Organiztion (1998). *Maternity leave policies.* Washington, DC: International Labor Organization; Table 3–6: From Eckerman, C. O., & Oehler, J. M. (1992). Very low birthweight newborns and parents as early social partners. In Friedman, S. L. & Sigman, M. B., *The psychological development of low birthweight children.* Norwood, NJ: Ablex.

Chapter 4 Figure 4–1: From Cratty, B. J. (1979). *Perceptual and motor development in infants and children.* All rights reserved. Reprinted by permission of Allyn & Bacon; Figure 4–3: From Bornstein, M. H., & Lamb, M. E. (eds.). (1992). Development psychology: An advanced textbook. p. 135. Hillsdale, NJ: Erlbaum; Figure 4–4: From *Human Anatomy, 5th edition,* by K. Van De Graaff, p. 339. Copyright© 2000 by The McGraw-Hill Companies, Inc.; Figure 4–5: Reprinted by permission of the publishers from *Postnatal development of the human cerebral cortex,* Vols I-VIII by J. L. Conel, Cambridge, Mass.: Harvard University Press, Copyright © 1939–1967 by the Presidents and Fellows of Harvard College; Figure 4–6: Reprinted from Roffwarg, H.P., Muzio, J. N., & Dement, W. C. (1966). Ontogenic development of the human sleep-dream cycle. *Science, 152,* 604–619. Copyright 1966 American Association for the Advancement of Science; Figure 4–7: From National Institute for Child Health & Human Development (1997). SIDS deaths and infant sleep position; Figure 4–9:

From World Food Council. (1992). *The global state of hunger and malnutrition. 1992 Report*. Table 2, p. 8. New York: World Food Council; Figure 4–10: From: Einbinder, S. D. *A statistical profile of children living in poverty: Children under three and children under six*. New York NY: National Center for Children in Poverty, Joseph L. Mailman School of Public Health, Columbia University; Figure 4–11: Reproduced with permission from Pediatrics, Vol 99, Page 6, 1997; Figure 4–13: Adaptation used with permission of Alexander Semenoick. Original appeared in Fantz, R. L. (May, 1961). The origin of form perception. *Scientific American*, p. 72; Figure 4–14: Reprinted with permission from Pediatrics, vol 77, Page 657, 1986; Table 4–2: Adapted from: Thoman, E. B., & Whitney, M.P. (1990). Behavioral states in infants: Individual differences and individual analyses. In J. Columbo, & J. Fagen (Eds), Individual differences in infancy: Reliability, stability, prediction. Hillsdale, NJ: Erlbaum; Table 4–4: Reproduced with permission from Pediatrics, Vol 89, Pages 91–97, 1992.

Chapter 5   Figure 5–6: Adapted from Bornstein, M.H. & Lamb, M.E. (1992). *Developmental psychology: An Advanced textbook*. Hillsdale, NJ: Erlbaum; Figure 5–8: From Gleason, J. B., Perlmann, R. Y., Ely, R., & Evans, D. W. (1991). The babytalk registry: Parents' use of diminutive. In J. L. Sokolov, & C. E. Snow (Eds), Handbook of Research in Language Development using CHILDES. Hillsdale, NJ: Erlbaum; Table 5–3: From the *Bayley Scales of Infant Development*. Copyright ©1993 by The Psychological Corporation. Reproduced by permission. All rights reserved. "Bayley Scales of Infant Development" is a registered trademark of the Psychological Corporation; Table 5–4: Adapted from Benedict, H. (1979). Early lexical development: Comprehension and production. Journal of Child Language, 6, 183–200. Copyright 1979. Reprinted by permission of Cambridge University Press; Table 5–5: From Brown, R., & Fraser, C. (1963). The acquisition of syntax. In C. N. Cofer and B. Musgrave (Eds.), *Verbal behavior and learning: Problems and processes*. NY: McGraw-Hill; Table 5–6: from B. G. Blount, B. G. (1982). Culture and the language of socialization: Parental speech. In D. A. Wagner & H. W. Stevenson(Eds.), *Cultural perspectives on child development*. San Francisco: Freeman. © by W. H. Freeman and Company. Used with permission.

Chapter 6   Figure 6–2: Adapted from Kagan, J., Kearsley, R. B., & Zelazo, P. R. (1978). *Intimacy, its place in Human Development*, p. 107. Cambridge, MA: Harvard University Press. Copyright © 1978 by the Presidents and Fellows of Harvard College; Figure 6–4: Adapted from Bell, S. M., & Ainsworth, M. D. (1972). Infant crying and maternal responsiveness. *Child Development*, 43, 1171–1190. © The Society for Research in Child Development, Inc.; Figure 6–4: Adapted from C. Tomlinson Keasey, (1985). *Child Development: Psychological, sociological, and biological factors*. Homewood, IL: Dorsey. Used with permission of Dr. Carol Tomlinson-Keasey; Figure 6–5: From U.S. Bureau of the Census (1997). Who's minding our preschoolers? Fall 1994 Update. *Current Population Reports, Household Economics Studies (Series P70–62)*. Washington, DC; U.S. Government Printing Office; Table 6–1: Adapted from Waters, E. (1978). The reliability and stability of individual differences in infant-mother attachment. *Child Development*, 49, 480–494. The Society for Research in Child Development, Inc. © The Society for Research in Child Development, Inc.; Table 6–2: Adapted from Thomas, A., Chess, S., & Birch, H. G. (1968). *Temperament and behavior disorders in children*. New York: New York University Press.

Chapter 7   Figure 7–1: From Lowrey, G. H. (1986). *Growth and development of children* (8th ed.). Chicago: Year Book Medical Publishers; Figure 7–2: From Zito, J. M., Safer, D. J., dosReis, S., Gardner, J. F., Boles, M., & Lynch, F. (2000). Trends in prescribing of psychotropic medications to preschoolers. *Journal of the American Medical Association*, 283, 1025–1030; Figure 7–3: From Needleman, H. L., Riess, J. A., Tobin, M. J., Biesecker, G. E., & Greenhouse, J. B. (1996, February 7). Bone lead levels and delinquent behavior. *Journal of the American Medical Association*, 275, 363–369; Figure 7–5: From Fischer, K. W., & Rose, S. P. (1995). Concurrent cycles in the dynamic development of brain and behavior. *Newsletter of the Society for Research in Child Development*, p. 16. The Society for Research in Child Development, Inc. © The Society for Research in Child Development, Inc.; Figure 7–11: Adapted from: Berko, J. (1958). The child's learning of English morphology. *Word*, 14, 150–177; Figure 7–12: From Hart, B., & Risley, R. T, (1995). *Meaningful differences in the everyday experience of young American children*. Paul H. Brookes Publishing, P.O. Box 10624, Baltimore, MD 21285–0624; Figure 7–13: From

Rideout, V. J., Foehr, U. G., Roberts, D. F., & Brodie, M. *(1999, November). Kids and media at the new millennium*. A Kaiser Family Foundation Report. Washington, DC: Henry J. Kaiser Family Foundation; Figure 7–14: (1997). U.S. Department of Education, National Center for Education Statistics. Children in various types of day care Washington, DC; Figure 7–15: Based on table 5–2, pg. 192 in Tobin J. J., Wu, D. Y. H., & Davidson, D. D. (1989). *Preschool in three cultures: Japan, China, and the United States*. New Haven, CT: Yale University Press. Reprinted with permission of Yale University Press; Table 7–1: From American Academy of Pediatrics. (2000). *Recommended childhood immunization schedule United States, January-December 2001*; Table 7–2: Adapted with permission from Charles C. Corbin, *A textbook of motor development*. Copyright © 1973 Times Mirror Higher Education Group, Inc., Dubuque, Iowa. All rights reserved. Used with permission of The McGraw-Hill Companies; Table 7–3: From Poole, D., & Lamb, M. (1998). Investigative interviews of children: A guide for helping professionals. Washington, DC: American Psychological Association. Copyright © 1998 by the American Psychological Association. Adapted with permission; Table 7–4: Reuse, Table of growing speech capabilities from *The Language Instinct*, by Steven Pinker. Copyright 1994 by Steven Pinker. Reprinted by permission of HarperCollins Publishers, Inc.

Chapter 8   Figure 8–1: Adapted from: Farver, J. M., Kim, Y. K., & Lee, Y. (1995). Cultural differences in Korean- and Anglo-American preschooler's interaction and play behaviors. *Child Development*, 66, 1088–1099. © The Society for Research in Child Development, Inc; Figure 8–2: From U.S. Department of Health and Human Services. (1997). Percentage of child abuse and neglect victims by type of maltreatment: 1996. Washington, DC: U. S. Dept. of Health and Human Services; Figure 8–4: Used with permission of the Center for Media and Public Affairs, Washington, DC; Table 8–3: From Baumrind, D. (1971). Current patterns of parental authority. *Developmental Psychology Monographs*, 4 (1, Pt. 2). Washington, DC: American Psychological Association Copyright © 1998 by the American Psychological Association. Adapted with permission.

Chapter 9   Figure 9–1: From Barrett, D. E., & Radke-Yarrow, M. (1985). Effects of nutritional supplementation on children's responses to novel, frustrating, and competitive situations. *American Journal of Clinical Nutrition*, 42, 102–120. © American Journal of Clinical Nutrition. American Society for Clinical Nutrition; Figure 9–3: From Cratty, B.J. (1979). *Perceptual and motor development in infants and children*. All rights reserved. Reprinted by permission of Allyn & Bacon; Figure 9–4: From National Center for Health Statistics. (1997). Asthma conditions of children under 18. Washington, DC: National Center for Health Statistics; Figure 9–5: From United Nations. (2000, August 4). Ritalin prescribed for children in countries around the world. Geneva: United Nations; Figure 9–7: From Dasen, P., Ngini, L., & Lavallee, M. (1979). Cross-cultural training studies of concrete operations. In L. H. Eckenberger, W. J. Lonner, & Y. H. Poortinga (Eds.), *Cross-cultural contributions to psychology*. Amsterdam: Swets & Zeilinger; Figure 9–8: From U.S. Bureau of the Census. (1993). Population Profile of the United States: 1991. *Current Population Reports*, Series P-23, No. 173. Washington, DC: U.S. Government Printing Office; Figure 9–9: From ©UNESCO 1990. Reproduced by permission of UNESCO; Figure 9–10: From U.S. Bureau of Census (1993). Current population projections. Washington, DC; Figure 9–11: Simulated items similar to those in the Wechsler Intelligence scale for Children: Third Edition. Copyright © 1990 by The Psychological Corporation. Reproduced by permission. All rights reserved. "Wechsler Intelligence Scale for Children" and "WISC-III" are registered trademarks of The Psychological Corporation; Table 9–1: Adapted from Chall, J. S. (1979). The great debate: Ten years later with a modest proposal for reading stages. In L. B. Resnick & P. A. Weaver, (Eds.). *Theory and practice of early reading*. Hillsdale, NJ: Lawrence Erlbaum Associates; Table 9–2: Reprinted with permission of the New Jersey Department of Education, Trenton, NJ; Table 9–3: From Walters, E., & Gardner, H. (1986). The theory of multiple intelligences: Some issues and answers. In R. J. Sternberg & R. K. Wagner (eds.), Practical Intelligence. Cambridge University Press. Copyright 1986. Reprinted with the permission of Cambridge University Press.

Chapter 10   Figure 10–1: From R. Shavelson, J. J. Hubner, & J. C. Stanton, (1976). Self-concept: Validation of construct interpretations. *Review of Educa-*

tional Research, 46, 407–441; Figure 10–3: Adapted from Dodge, K. A. (1985). A social information processing model of social competence in children. In M. Perlmutter (Ed.), Minnesota Symposia on Child Psychology (Vol 18), 77–126. Hillsdale, NJ: Erlbaum; Figure 10–4: From Hofferth, S., & Sandberg, J. F. (2001). How American children spend their time. *Journal of Marriage and the Family, 63,* 295–308; Figure 10–5: From National Center for Health Statistics. (1996). Percentage of births to single mothers. Washington, DC: National Center for Health Statistics; Figure 10–6: Adapted from Stevenson, H. W., & Lee, S. (1990). Contexts of achievement: A study of American, Chinese, and Japanese children. *Monographs of the Society for Research in Child Development. No. 221, 55,* Nos. 1–2. © The Society for Research in Child Development, Inc.; Table 10–1: Reprinted with permission of David A. Goslin, President, American Institute for Research, Washington, DC; Table 10–3: Adapted from Zarbatany, L., Haratmann, D. P., & Rankin, B. D. (1990). The psychological functions of preadolescent peer activities. *Child Development, 61,* 1067–1080. © The Society for Research in Child Development, Inc.; Table 10–4: From Shealy, C. N. (1995). From Boys Town to Oliver Twist: Separating fact from fiction in welfare reform and out-of-home placement of children and youth. *American Psychologist, 50,* 565–580. Copyright © 1995 by the American Psychological Association. Adapted with permission.

Chapter 11   Figure 11–1: From Cratty, B.J. *Perceptual and motor development in infants and children.* (2nd ed.). Copyright ©1986 by Allyn and Bacon. Reprinted/Adapted by permission; Figure 11–2: Adapted from Eveleth, P., & Tanner, J. (1976). Worldwide variation in human growth. New York: Cambridge University Press. Copyright 1976. Reprinted with the permission of Cambridge University Press; Figure 11–3: From Tanner, J. M. (1978). *Education and physical growth* (2nd ed.). New York: International Universities Press; Figure 11–4: Reprinted with permission of the Organization for Economic Cooperation and Development. Paris; Figure 11–5: From National Center for Education Statistics (2000). High school drop-out rates by race. Washington, DC: National Center for Education Statistics; Figure 11–6: From Johnson, Bachman, & O'Malley. (1999). Monitoring the future study. Ann Arbor, MI: University of Michigan Institute of Social Research. University of Michigan; Figure 11–7: Adapted from Wechsler, H., et al. (2000). College binge drinking in the 1990s: a continuing problem: results of the Harvard School of Public Health 1999 College Health Alcohol Study. Use with permission of Henry Wechsler, PhD; Figure 11–8: From UNAIDS. (1999). Cases of AIDS around the world. New York: United Nations; Figure 11–9: Reproduced with the permission of The Alan Guttmacher Institute, from The Alan Guttmacher Institute (AGI): *Sex and American's Teenagers,* New York, 1994; Table 11–1: From National Center for Education Statistics (1999, 2001). *National Assessment of Educational Progress (NAEP).* Washington, DC: National Center for Education Statistics.

Chapter 12   Figure 12–1: From U.S. Census Bureau. (2000). United States Census, 2000. Washington, DC: U.S. Census Bureau; Figure 12–2: From Boston Samaritans. (1991). Boston, MA; Figure 12–3: From Steinberg, L., & Silverberg, S. B. (1986). The vicissitudes of autonomy in early adolescence. *Child Development, 57,* 841–851. © The Society for Research in Child Development, Inc.; Figure 12–4: Adapted from Table 3, pg. 1035. Fulgini, A. J., Tseng, V., & Lam, M. (1999). Attitudes toward family obligations among American adolescents with Asian, Latin American, and European backgrounds. *Child Development, 70,* 1030–1044. © The Society for Research in Child Development, Inc.; Figure 12–5: Study completed by Roper Starch Worldwide; Figure 12–6: From Larson, R. W., Richards, M. H., Moneta, G., Holmbeck, G., & Duckett, E. (1996). Changes in adolescents' daily interactions with their families from ages 10 to 18: Disengagement and transformation. *Developmental Psychology, 32,* 744–754. Copyright © 1996 by the American Psychological Association. Adapted with permission; Figure 12–8: From *Newsweek,* Kantrowitz, B., & Wingert, P. (1999, May 10). How Well Do You Know Your Kid? (teenagers need adult attention) *Newsweek,* 36. © 1999 Newsweek, Inc. All rights reserved. Reprinted by permission; Figure 12–9; From National Center for Health Statistics. (1998). Teenage pregnancy rates. Washington, DC: National Center for Health Statistics; Table 2–1: From *Childhood and Society* by Erik H. Erikson. Copyright 1950. © 1963 by W. W. Norton & Company, Inc., renewed © 1978, 1991 by Erik H. Erikson. Reprinted by permission of W. W. Norton & Company, Inc.; Table 12–2:

Adapted from Marcia, J. E. (1990). Identity in adolescence. In J. Adelson (Ed.), *Handbook of adolescent psychology.* New York: Wiley. Copyright © 1990. Reprinted by permission of John Wiley & Sons, Inc.

Chapter 13   Figure 13–1: Adapted from S. N. Blair, H. W. Kohl, R. S. Paffenberger, D. G. Clark, K. H. Cooper, & L. W. Gibbons (1989). Physical fitness and all-cause mortality: A prospective study of healthy men and women. *Journal of the American Medical Association, 262,* 2395–2401. Copyright 1989, American Medical Association; Figure 13–2: From L. A. Fingerhut, & J. C. Kleinman, (1990). International and interstate comparisons of homicide among young males. Journal of the American Medical Association, 263, 3292–3295; Figure 13–3: From Centers for Disease Control and Prevention. (2000). *Obesity continues to climb in 1999 among American Adults;* Figure 13–4: Adapted from R. M. Kaplan, J. F. Sallis, Jr., & T. L. Patterson. (1993). *Health and human behavior.* New York: McGraw-Hill; Figure 13–5: Adapted from K. W. Schaie. (1977–1978). Toward a stage of adult theory of adult cognitive development. *International Journal of Aging and Human Development, 8,* 129–138. Copyright © 1978 Baywood Publishing Co.; Figure 13–6: Used with permission of Dr. Robert J. Sternberg; Figure 13–7: From R. J. Sternberg, & R. K. Wagner. (1993). The g-ocentric view of intelligence and job performance is wrong. *Current Directions in Psychological Science, 2,* 1–5; Figure 13–8: Based on W. Dennis (1966). Age and creative productivity. *Journal of Gerontology, 21,* 1–8; Figure 13–9: From National Center for Education. (2000). *The condition of Education 2000.* Web site: http://nces.ed.gov/pubs2000/coe2000/section1/s_table8_1.html; Figure 13–10: From U.S. Census Bureau. (1996). *Poverty by educational attainment.* Washington, DC: U.S. Census Bureau; Figure 13–11: From E. L. Dey, A. W. Astin, W. S. Korn, & E. R. Berz, (1990). *The American freshman: National norms for fall, 1990.* Los Angeles: Higher Education Research Institute, Graduate School of Education, UCLA; Figure 13–12 From C. M. Steele. (1997). A threat in the air: how stereotypes shape intellectual identity and performance. *American Psychologist, 52,* 613–629. © 1997 by The American Psychological Association; Table 13–1: From Cohen, S., Kamarck, T., & Mermelstein, R. (1983). A global measure of perceived stress. *Journal of Health and Social Behavior, 24,* 385–396; Table 13–2: Used with permission of Dr. Herbert Benson; Table 13–3: From H. Weschler, M. Rohman, & R. Solomon, R. (1981). Emotional problems and concerns of New England college students. *American Journal of Orthopsychiatry, 51,* 719. Reprinted with permission from the American Journal of Orthopsychiatry. Copyright 1981 by the American Orthopsychiatry Association; Table 13–4: Reprinted with permission of Scribner, a Division of Simon & Schuster from *Failing at Fairness: How American's Schools Cheat Girls,* by Myra & David Sadker. Copyright © 1994 by Myra & David Sadker.

Chapter 14   Figure 14–1: Adapted from National Opinion Research Center. (1998). Race and friends. Chicago, IL: General Social Survey. Used with permission of the National Opinion Research Center; Figure 14–2: Adapted from B. I. Murstein. (1987). FEEDBACK: A clarification and extension of the SVR theory of dyadic pairing. *Journal of Marriage and the Family, 49,* 929–933; Figure 14–3: Adapted from R. J. Sternberg (1986). Triangular theory of love. *Psychological Review, 93,* 119–135. © 1986 by the American Psychological Association. Adapted with permission; Figure 14–4: Adapted from L. H. Janda, & K. E. Klenke-Hamel. (1980). *Human sexuality.* New York: Van Nostrand; Figure 14–5: Based upon data from William H. Grey, Milken Institute, Santa Monica, California; Figure 14–6: From Fields, J., & Casper, L. M. (2001). *America's families and living arrangements: March 2000. Current Population Reports, pp.* 20–537. Washington, DC: U.S. Census Bureau; Figure 14–7: From U.S. Census Bureau. (2000). United States Census, 2000. Washington, DC: U.S. Census Bureau; Figure 14–8: From Adapted from statistics on divorce and out-of-wedlock births. (1995). New York: Population Council; Figure 14–9: From Kurdek, L.A. (1999). The nature and predictors of the trajectory of change in marital quality for husbands and wives over the first 10 years of marriage. *Developmental Psychology, 35,* 1283–1296. © 1999 by the American Psychological Association. Adapted with permission; Figure 14–10: From G. H. Gallup and F. Newport (1990). Virtually all adults want children, but many of the reasons are intangible. The Gallup Poll Monthly, Vol 297. Information collected by the Gallup Organization and published by the Gallup Poll (1998) on ideal number of children, *American Demographics, March, 1998, pg 35;* Figure 14–11: Adaptations of

Googans, B. & Burden, D. (1987). Vulnerability of working parents: Balancing work and home roles. *Social Work, 32,* 295–300; Figure 14–12: From U.S. Bureau of the Census. (2001). Employment and earnings January issues. *Current Population Reports, Series P-60.* Prepared by the Women's Bureau; Table 14–1: From C. A. Colarusso, R. A. & Nemiroff, (1981). *Adult development: A new dimension in psychodynamic theory and practice.* New York: Plenum; Table 14–2: Adapted from R. J. Sternberg (1986). Triangular theory of love. *Psychological Review, 93,* 119–135. © 1986 by the American Psychological Association. Adapted with permission; Table 14–3: From D. M. Buss, et al. (1990). International preferences in selecting mates: A study of 37 cultures. *Journal of Cross-Cultural Psychology, 21,* 5–47. Copyright © 1990 by Sage Publications. Reprinted by permission of Sage Publications; Table 14–4: From NORC (National Opinion Research Center). (1990). General social surveys 1972–1990: Cumulative codebook. Chicago: NORC. Used with permission of the National Opinion Research Center.

Chapter 15 Figure 15–1: Adaptation from D. G. Pitts. (1982). The effects of aging upon selected visual functions. In R. Sekuler, D. Kline, & K. Dismukes (Eds.), *Aging and human visual function.* New York: Alan R. Liss; Figure 15–2: From A. G. DiGiovanna. (1994). *Human aging: Biological perspectives.* New York: McGraw-Hill. Reproduced with the permission of the McGraw-Hill companies; Figure 15–3: Adapted from T. T. Michael, J. H. Gagnon, E. O. Laumann, & G. Kolata. (1994). *Sex in America: A definitive survey.* Boston: Little, Brown; Figure 15–4: From *USA Weekend* (1997, August 22–24). Fears among adults. Pg. 5 Copyright 1997 *USA Weekend;* Figure 15–7: From World Health Organization. (1999). Death rates from coronary heart disease. Geneva: World Health Organization; Figure 15–8: Adapted from R. M. Kaplan, J. F. Sallis, Jr., & T. L. Patterson. (1993). *Health and human behavior.* P. 254. "Age specific breast cancer annual incidence." New York: McGraw-Hill. Reproduced with the permission of the McGraw-Hill companies; Figure 15–9: Adapted from K. W. Pettingale, T. Morris, S. Greer, & J. Haybittle, J. L. (1985). Mental attitudes to cancer: An additional prognostic factor. *Lancet, 310,* 750. © by The Lancet Ltd. 1985; Figure 15–10: From W. Schaie. (1985). *Longitudinal studies of psychological development.* New York: Guilford Press Publications, Inc.; Table 15–1: Adapted from selected prevention and screening recommendations for older adults. *Journal of the American Geriatrics Society,* March 1997. Used with permission of Lippincott, Williams & Wilkins.

Chapter 16 Figure 16–1: Adapted from D. J. Levinson, with C. N. Darrow, E. M. H. Levinson, and B. Mckee (1986, 1992). *The seasons of a man's life.* p. 57. New York: Alfred A. Knopf. Copyright © 1978 by Daniel J. Levinson. Reprinted by permission of Alfred A. Knopf, Inc.; Figure 16–2: Adapted from John D. and Catherine T. MacArthur Foundation Research Network on Successful Midlife Development. (1999); Figure 16–3: Adaptations from P. T. Costa, C. M. Busch, A. B. Zonderman, & R. R. McCrae. (1993). Correlations of MMPI factor scales with measures of the five factor model of personality. *Journal of Personality Assessment, 50,* 640–650; Figure 16–4: Adapted from C. R. Figley. (1973). Child density and the marital relationship. *Journal of Marriage and the Family, 35,* 272–282. Copyrighted 1973 by the National Council on Family Relations, 3989 Central Ave. NE, Suite 550, Minneapolis, MN 55421. Reprinted by permission; Figure 16–5: From Walker, L. (1984). *The battered woman syndrome.* New York: Springer. Copyright © 1984. Used by permission of Springer Publishing Company, Inc., New York 10012; Table 16–1: Used with the permission of Roger L. Gould, M.D.; Table 16–3: From *A geography of time* by Robert Levine. Copyright © 1997 by Robert Levine. Reprinted by permission of Basic Books, a member of Perseus Books LLC.

Chapter 17 Figure 17–1: From U.S. Census Bureau. (2000). United States Census, 2000. Washington, DC: U.S. Census Bureau; Figure 17–3: Adapted from From Whitbourne, S. (2001). *Adult development and aging: biopsychosocial perspectives.* New York: Wiley. Copyright © 2001. Reprinted by permission of John Wiley & Sons, Inc.; Figure 17–5: From National Highway Traffic Safety Administration. (1994). Age related incidence of traffic accidents; Figure 17–6: From Bookheimer, S. Y., Strojwas, M. H., Cophen, M. S., Saunders, A. M., Pericak-Vance, M. A., Mazziotta, J. C., & Small, G. W. (2000, August 17). Patterns of brain activation in people at risk for Alzheimer's disease. *New England Journal of Medicine, 343,* 450–456. Copyright © 2000. Massachusetts Medical Society. All rights reserved; Figure 17–7: Adapted from Wannamethee, S. G., Shaper, A. G., Walker, M., & Ebrahim, S. (1998). Lifestyle and 15–year survival free of heart attack, stroke, and diabetes in middle-aged British men. *Archives of Internal Medicine, 158,* 2433–2440; Figure 17–8: From Budd, K. (1999). The facts of life: everything you wanted to know about sex (after 50). *Modern Maturity, 42,* 78; Figure 17–10: From Anderson, R. N. (2001), *United States life tables, 1998. National Vital Statistics Reports, vol. 48, no. 18.* Hyattsville, MD: National Center for Health Statistics; Figure 17–11: From K. W. Schaie. (1994). The course of adult intellectual development. P. 307 *American Psychologist, 49,* 304–313. Copyright © 1994 The American Psychological Association. Used with permission; Figure 17–12: From D. C. Rubin, S. E. Wetzler, & R. D. Nebes. (1986). Autobiographical memory across the lifespan. In D. C. Rubin (Ed.). *Autobiographical Memory.* Cambridge, England: Cambridge University Press. Copyright 1986. Reprinted with the permission of Cambridge University Press; Table 17–1: From E. B. Palmore. (1982). *The facts on aging quiz.* New York: Springer. © 1988 by Spring Publishing Company, Inc., New York, NY 10012. Used by Permission.

Chapter 18 Figure 18–1: From P. B. Baltes, & M. M. Baltes. (1990). Psychological perspectives on successful aging: The model of selective optimization with compensation. In P. B. Baltes & M. M. Baltes (Eds.), *Successful aging: Perspectives from the behavioral sciences.* Cambridge, England: Cambridge University Press. Copyright 1990. Reprinted with the permission of Cambridge University Press; Figure 18–2: From Federal Interagency Forum On Aging-Related Statistics. (2000). *Older Americans 2000: Key indicators of Well-Being (Older Americans).* Washington, DC: National Institute on Aging; Figure 18–3: Adapted from G. D. Heinemann, & P. L. Evans. (1990). Widowhood: Loss, change, and adaptation. In T. H. Brubaker (Ed.), *Family relationships in later life.* Newbury Park, CA: Sage. Copyright © 1990 by Sage Publications; Figure 18–4: From Federal Interagency Forum On Aging-Related Statistics. (2000). *Older Americans 2000: Key indicators of Well-Being (Older Americans).* Washington, DC: National Institute on Aging; Table 18–1: From R. C. Atchley. (1982). Retirement: Leaving the world of work. *Annals of the American Academy of Political and Social Science, 464,* 120–131. Copyright © 1982 by Sage Publications. Reprinted by permission of Sage Publications; Table 18–2: Reprinted with permission of the Gerontological Society of America, 1030 15th St., NW, Suite 250 Washington, DC 20005. From R. R. Hamon, & R. Blieszner, (1990). Filial responsibility expectations among adult child–older parent pairs. *Journal of Gerontology, 45,* 110–112. Reproduced by permission of the publisher via Copyright Clearance Center, Inc.

Chapter 19 Figure 19–1: From Hayward, M., Crimmins, E., & Saito, Y. (1997). Cause of death and active life expectancy in the older population of the United States. *Journal of Aging and Health,* 122–131. Copyright © 1997. Reprinted by permission of Sage Publications; Figure 19–2: From E. Kubler-Ross, (Ed.). *Death: The final stage of growth.* Englewood Cliffs, NJ: Prentice-Hall; Figure 19–4: From J. Lynn, J. M. Teno, R. S. Phillips, A. W. Wu, N. Desbiens, J. Harrold, M. T. Claessens, N. Wenger, B. Kreling, & A. F. Connors, Jr. (1997). Perceptions by family members of the dying experience of older and seriously ill patients. SUPPORT Investigators. Study to Understand Prognoses and Preferences for Outcomes and Risks of Treatments [see comments]. *Annals of Internal Medicine, 126,* 164–165; Table 19–1: From Knaus, W. A., Conners, A. F., Dawson, N. V., Desbiens, N. A., Fulkerson, W. J., Jr., Goldman, L., Lynn, J., & Oye, R. K. (1995, November 22). A controlled trial to improve care for seriously ill hospitalized patients. The study to understand prognoses and preferences for outcomes and risks of treatments (SUPPORT). *Journal of the American Medical Association, 273,* 1591–1598. Copyright 1995 American Medical Association.

Name Index

Subject Index

	ADOLESCENCE (12 to 20 years)	YOUNG ADULTHOOD (20 to 40 years)

PHYSICAL DEVELOPMENT

ADOLESCENCE (12 to 20 years)

- Girls begin the adolescent growth spurt around age 10, boys around age 12.
- Girls reach puberty around age 11 or 12, boys around age 13 or 14.
- Primary sexual characteristics develop (affecting the reproductive organs), as do secondary sexual characteristics (pubic and underarm hair in both sexes, breasts in girls, deep voices in boys).

YOUNG ADULTHOOD (20 to 40 years)

- Physical capabilities peak in 20's, including strength, senses, coordination, and reaction time.
- Growth is mostly complete, although some organs, including the brain, continue to grow.
- For many young adults, obesity becomes a threat for the first time, as body fat increases.
- Stress can become a significant health threat.
- In the mid-30's, disease replaces accidents as the leading cause of death.

COGNITIVE DEVELOPMENT

ADOLESCENCE

- Abstract thought prevails. Adolescents use formal logic to consider problems in the abstract.
- Relative, not absolute, thinking is typical.
- Verbal, mathematical, and spatial skills improve.
- Adolescents are able to think hypothetically, divide attention, and monitor thought through metacognition.
- Egocentrism develops, with a sense that one is always being observed. Self-consciousness and introspection are typical.
- A sense of invulnerability can lead adolescents to ignore danger.

YOUNG ADULTHOOD

- As world experience increases, thought becomes more flexible and subjective, geared to adept problem solving.
- Intelligence is applied to long-term goals involving career, family, and society.
- Significant life events of young adulthood may shape cognitive development.

SOCIAL/ PERSONALITY DEVELOPMENT

ADOLESCENCE

- Self-concept becomes organized and accurate and reflects others' perceptions. Self-esteem grows differentiated.
- Defining identity is a key task. Peer relationships provide social comparison and help define acceptable roles. Popularity issues become acute; peer pressure can enforce conformity.
- Adolescents' quest for autonomy can bring conflict with parents as family roles are renegotiated.
- Sexuality assumes importance in identity formation. Dating begins.

YOUNG ADULTHOOD

- Forming intimate relationships becomes highly important. Commitment may be partly determined by the attachment style developed in infancy.
- Marriage and children bring developmental changes, often stressful. Divorce may result, with new stresses.
- Identity is largely defined in terms of work, as young adults consolidate their careers.

THEORIES & THEORISTS

	ADOLESCENCE	YOUNG ADULTHOOD
Jean Piaget	Formal operations stage	
Erik Erikson	Identity-versus-confusion stage	Intimacy-versus-isolation stage
Sigmund Freud	Genital stage	
Lawrence Kohlberg	Postconventional morality level may be reached	